The Empire State

THE
EMPIRE

STATE

A History
of New York

Edited by Milton M. Klein

CORNELL UNIVERSITY PRESS

Ithaca and London

with the New York State Historical Association
Cooperstown, New York

Illustrations for *The Empire State* were selected by the New York State Historical
Association, in collaboration with Cornell University Press.

We acknowledge with gratitude a grant in support of this book's color illustrations
from Furthermore, the publication program of the J. M. Kaplan fund.
Inclusion of the color illustrations in the paperback edition is made possible by Francille
Firebaugh, Vice Provost for Land Grant Affairs, Cornell University.

First published 2001 by Cornell University Press
First printing, Cornell Paperbacks, 2005
Printed in the United States of America

Library of Congress Cataloging-in-Publication Data
The Empire State : a history of New York / edited by Milton M. Klein ;
with the New York State Historical Association, Cooperstown, New York.
    p. cm.
    Includes bibliographical references and index.
    ISBN-10 0-8014-3866-7 (cloth : alk. paper)
    ISBN-13 978-0-8014-3866-0 (cloth : alk. paper)
    ISBN-10 0-8014-8991-1 (pbk. : alk. paper)
    ISBN-13 978-0-8014-8991-4 (pbk. : alk. paper)
    1. New York (State)—History. I. Klein, Milton M. (Milton
Martin), 1917– . II. New York State Historical Association.
  F119 .E48 2001
  974.7—dc21   2001001669

Cornell University Press strives to use environmentally responsible suppliers and materials to
the fullest extent possible in the publishing of its books. Such materials include vegetable-
based, low-VOC inks and acid-free papers that are recycled, totally chlorine-free, or partly
composed of nonwood fibers. For further information, visit our website at
www.cornellpress.cornell.edu.

Cloth printing   10 9 8 7 6 5 4 3 2 1
Paperback printing   10 9 8 7 6 5 4 3 2 1

To Wendell Tripp
and to the memory of
David Maldwyn Ellis (1914–1999)

Contents

Foreword

"York State is a country." Carl Carmer, using an ancient contraction for the Empire State, thus suggested that New York is in many ways the equivalent of some of the world's nations. He compared it in particular to England, which is approximately the same size. The state's largest river, the Hudson, is for many miles a navigable tidal estuary that serves a major metropolis, New York City, just as the Thames estuary serves London. New York, like England, has a lake district, and it also has a northern highland as well as industrial centers in the central corridor from Albany to Buffalo, similar to the English Midlands. Carmer, the romantic, did not discuss population figures or gross domestic product. These are significantly less for New York than for England, although the land area and the diversity of its geography do place the state above many nations. But Carmer was right. In all the basic respects save the constitutional, New York State could be considered a country unto itself.

New York resembles a nation in one other respect. It has a long and complex history and an equally sophisticated historiography. And that is where *The Empire State: A History of New York* comes in. This is the third history of the state produced by the New York State Historical Association.

The first of these was the ten-volume *History of New York State*, edited by State Historian Alexander C. Flick with the unheralded assistance of Peter Nelson, Flick's indefatigable assistant in the state's Division of History and Archives. The project was stimulated in part by the New York State Historical Association's long-standing interest in, not to say envy of, the vigorous historiographical traditions of neighboring New England. The Association's trustees were still sufficiently touched by this spirit in 1929 to note with interest the publication of a five-volume history of Massachusetts, edited by Albert Bushnell Hart. In April 1930 Association president Dixon Ryan Fox declared, "The State of New York, having a great history, deserves a good *History*." Alluding to the Massachusetts history, he explained that the trustees had voted in January 1930 to commission a multivolume history of New York, with Flick as editor.

The first two volumes were published in 1933; the remaining eight volumes were in readers' hands by 1937. Published by Columbia University Press, it was a monumental work: ten volumes comprising ninety-nine chapters written by seventy authors. "If any local history society or village library does not have the work on its shelves," President Fox declared, "this is a scandalous condition which should be quickly rectified." It should, he added, also "have an honored place in the private library of every historically-minded person in the state." Whether this last hope was fulfilled or not, Flick's history soon became the standard work on the subject.

But histories, too, become history, and within ten years of its publication the trustees of the New York State Historical Association were considering another history of the state. This time, however, they had in mind a much more compact format. At their fall 1947 meeting they voted to support the publication of a single-volume history, and they commissioned David M. Ellis of Hamilton College and Neil A. McNall of Pennsylvania State College to write the volume with the collaboration of Association editor Mary Cunningham. At some point in the process, with Flick's ten-volume history in mind, the new work was given the title *A Short History of New York State*. A variety of obligations forced McNall to withdraw, and James Frost, professor of history and future dean of the State Teachers College at Oneonta replaced him, while Cunningham, originally an author, became editor and coordinator. Cornell University Press agreed to publish the book.

A Short History of New York State was off the press and officially launched in September 1957 at a presentation session with Governor Averill Harriman and at a special meeting of the New York State Historical Association at Hamilton College. The volume was exceedingly well received and was the recipient of an award from the American Association for State and Local History. The only notable criticism related to the title. To call a volume over 700 pages "a short history," Louis Jones observed, " brought a ten-year project to conclusion with a certain amount of laughter." By 1957 Alexander Flick's long history had obviously faded from casual memory.

The short history did not have time to fade. Widely circulated, it was also used as a ready reference and as a textbook in a number of college-level courses and was therefore subjected to constant scrutiny. Within ten years the Association's trustees agreed that, among other things, the appearance of a large number of monographs relating to the history of New York warranted a revision of the volume. At the same time, the misleading title would be changed to *A History of New York State*, with David Ellis assuming responsibility for the revision.

By the late 1980s the new edition was itself rather long in the tooth. The torrent of monographs relating to aspects of New York's history continued to increase, and the examination of neglected subjects and new perspectives became more intense. David Ellis suggested to the Association's trustees that a one-volume history was too small a canvas to contain a satisfactory landscape of New York's sophisticated history. He suggested a three-volume history of the state. The trustees decided, however, that it would be more practical to produce a completely new one-volume history in order to satisfy the growing demand from teachers and a new generation of students for a text at once authoritative and manageable. Milton M. Klein of the University of Tennessee agreed to edit this volume and six specialists in different eras of New York's past were commissioned to write the text. The full text was completed in 1999 and presented to Cornell University Press, which agreed to publish this volume, as it had its predecessor.

The result is before you—a completely new history of New York, which sweeps over several of its centuries and across its broad and variegated territory. A history that incorporates the monographic studies and new historical emphases of the past three decades, it is a volume that includes far more illustrations than the previous surveys, even including, thanks to the generosity of the Publication Program of the J. M. Kaplan Fund, a signature of color illustrations. It is a volume that the Association hopes will serve the needs of another generation of the "historically-minded," as it surely becomes another segment in the grand mosaic of New York State historiography. The words and work of those who crafted the volume join the words and work of those who created earlier studies of our history. They cannot all be mentioned, and it may be sufficient to note the comments of Dixon Ryan Fox in 1930 when he announced the conception of the first publication: "Supposing, for the moment, that there is no doubt that personality survives beyond the grave and takes continued interest in the affairs of men, there may be others who stand by with benevolent concern for this cooperative history. . . . [All] who have labored in this great domain between New England and the Lakes, and then passed on, must survey it with an earnest hope that they may find justice and appreciation within its pages."

GILBERT T. VINCENT
President, NYSHA

Preface

For over thirty years, the standard one-volume history of the Empire State has been *A History of New York State*, published by Cornell University Press for the New York State Historical Association. A cooperative effort by four authors, it appeared originally in 1957 as *A Short History of New York State*, but its 705 pages belied its title, and a revised edition was published ten years later with a title more appropriate to its 732 pages. It was, and is, a comprehensive narrative, covering political, economic, and cultural developments. Unfortunately, it has long been out of print. Two much shorter accounts appeared later, one by David Ellis (one of the authors of the larger work) titled *New York: State and City* (1979), and another by Bruce Bliven, *New York: A Bicentennial History* (1981), but neither was more than 250 pages in length, nor did they supersede the earlier *History*.

The present volume aims to once again offer students, scholars, and general readers a comprehensive, one-volume history of the state. It includes events of the last thirty years and also incorporates and emphasizes historiographical elements which today have been generally accepted as necessary for a comprehensive history: the role of women, African Americans, Native Americans, and aspects of social and intellectual history that were often neglected by historians in the past.

As with the earlier volumes, the present work is a cooperative effort—the work of six authors, each of whom is responsible for a chronological period in which he or she is a specialist. The editor has exercised general supervision of the project but has not attempted to direct the substantive efforts of the authors. Parts of the manuscript were read by Robert Wesser of the State University of New York at Albany and by James Crouthamel of Hobart and William Smith Colleges; the authors are grateful for their helpful suggestions. The entire manuscript was read by Grey Osterud of Acton, Massachusetts, and many of her suggestions have been incorporated into the manuscript. Tribute is paid here to Winifred Wandersee of Hartwick College, who originally undertook to write Part VI but whose untimely death precluded her participation. At the inception of the project, Stephen L. Schechter of Russell Sage College served as coeditor but was forced by other responsibilities to withdraw from that position. Grateful acknowledgment is made here for his valuable contributions. Kate Johnston, graduate assistant in the Department of History at the University of Tennessee, Knoxville, was especially helpful in revising Part II of the manuscript, and I am indebted to her for her assistance. At the New York State Historical Association, Kathy Stocking, Carole Mihalko, and Glenn Linsenbardt provided invaluable assistance, often at short notice. No historian can do research without the help of reference librarians. I am always amazed at the variety and wealth of sources with which they are familiar. I have consulted the reference librarians at the Hodges Library of the University of Tennessee, Knoxville, unashamedly, and I gratefully acknowledge their assistance.

The University of Tennessee, Knoxville, has been generous in providing space and facilities for the completion of this project. Particular thanks are extended to former officials of the university, Chancellor William Snyder, Provost John Peters, and Dean of Undergraduate Affairs Linda Maxson, as well as to current administrators Faye Julian and Nancy McGlasson, and to the latter's secretary, Lois Welch. I am also indebted to a host of undergraduate and graduate students associated with Ms. McGlasson's office who solved computer problems that the editor, an electronic novice, could not handle.

The book is dedicated to two individuals who worked indefatigably for many years to promote the study of New York State history and to bring it to a wider audience. David Ellis was not only a principal author of the earlier *Short History* but was also the initiator of the present project. His books and articles have been distinguished additions to our storehouse of knowledge about the state. Wendell Tripp served for thirty-five years as the editor of *New York History*, the scholarly journal published by the New York State Historical Association. His meticulous editorial skill, his broad acquaintance with the state's history, his abundant energy, and his unselfish devotion to his job have made that publication a major vehicle for transmitting knowledge of the state's history to a wide audience. It is hoped that the present volume will meet the high standards set by these two scholars and that it will be useful to all those who take pride in their association with the region that from early in our history as a nation has been called the Empire State.

MILTON M. KLEIN

Knoxville, Tennessee

Introduction

Milton M. Klein

New York has long held a position of prominence in the history of the United States. Almost from the founding of the British colonies in North America, British authorities took special interest in the New York province. The first governor of the colony, Richard Nicolls, reported to his superiors at home that New York City was "the best of all his Majestie's Townes in America." Several years later, one of the province's largest landowners and an ardent Anglican, Lewis Morris, urged the Church of England to establish a college in New York on the ground that the colony was "the centre of British America."

New York City, by the middle of the eighteenth century, was smaller in population than Philadelphia or Boston, but a visiting Englishman, Lord Adam Gordon, was surprised to find it so. New York, he observed, "had long been held" at home "the first in America." And in Scotland, an anonymous observer of American affairs recorded his belief that New York's location marked it as the "Capital of Engl[ish] Govern[men]t in America."

The city's shipping by the eighteenth century was well below that of other mainland ports, but a Swedish visitor, Peter Kalm, had been led to believe that New York City's commerce was more extensive than that of any other city in British North America. A French traveler in 1765 agreed: "The Situation of new york with regard to foreign markets Is to be prefered to any of the colonies," he remarked in his diary. New Yorkers themselves bluntly proclaimed that New York City was "the best Mart on the Continent."

The entire colony of New York seemed to represent the image of all the mainland British colonies in the diversity of its population. When that adopted American, Hector St. John de Crèvecoeur, raised the famous question of "What is an American?" the answer he gave—that the American was a "new man," "a strange mixture of blood, which you will find in no other country"—was based on what he saw while he was living in Orange County, New York. The heterogeneity of peoples he observed in New York was not so much atypical as a mirror of what the United States was to become. As the colony of New York welcomed immigrants from many European countries, so did a later United States, and the city became the gateway through which millions of migrants from the Old World passed the Statue of Liberty and entered a country where they hoped to find a better way of life.

The politics of colonial America were different from those of most of the other colonies. Here factions formed and primitive parties developed, utilizing practices that were to become the hallmark of American politics years later: a vigorous press, active electioneering, the formation of coalitions, and elections revolving around issues as much as personalities. Not surprisingly, when the historian Richard Hofstadter wrote about the emergence of a party system in the United States and the development of legitimate political opposition during the Jacksonian Era, he found in New York their most visible manifestation.

New York can boast of many firsts in the history of the British colonies in North America: the first chamber of commerce not organized under governmental auspices; the first play written and printed in the British North American provinces, in 1714; the first legislative proceedings to be printed in any of the colonies, in 1695; as well as the enrichment of American culture by such Dutch innovations as Santa Claus, bowling, crullers and cookies, bosses and boodle, and innumerable place names like Brooklyn, Harlem, Yonkers, and the Catskills.

When Herbert L. Osgood wrote his four-volume history of the American colonies in the eighteenth century between 1924 and 1928, he felt compelled to apologize for the extensive treatment given to New York. He explained that the four volumes dealt heavily with the French and Indian War, and "of course, in all military relations in which Canada was involved, New York was the strategic center of the colonial territory." Indeed, New York's strategic importance was recognized by the British government in a number of ways. It was the only colony in which regular troops were stationed throughout the colonial period. It was on the New York frontier that the rivalry between Britain and France was pursued during four international wars. It was in Albany that the most serious attempt was held to forge an intercolonial union before the Revolution. And it was in New York that the British Post Office in North America established its headquarters and to which it sent its first regular packet service from England to America, in 1755.

During the Revolution, British strategy focused on the conquest of New York as the best way to split the New England colonies from the South and thus end the war quickly. The colony's strategic importance had been foreseen almost a century earlier by one its governors, Lord Bellomont, who wrote to his superiors at home that New York, "being much in the center of the other colonies Challenge a preference to all the rest and ought to be looked upon as the capital Province or the Citadel to all the others; for secure this and you secure all the English colonies, not only against the French, but also against any insurrections or rebellions against the Crown of England."

New Yorkers did not lead the other colonies into revolution, but it was at Saratoga in 1777 that the most decisive battle between those of Lexington and Yorktown occurred. Properly called "the turning point of the Revolution," it brought France into the Anglo-American conflict and provided the fledgling United States with the arms and money that it required to win the war. And it was from New York City on November 25, 1783, that the British evacuated their last remaining troops from the new United States.

The building of the Erie Canal gave New York new importance. Even while the canal was being built, the London *Times* predicted that the completion of that waterway would make New York City the "London of the New World." And it was about this time that New York began to be called the "Empire State."

The origin of the term is shrouded in mystery. As early as April 10, 1785, George Washington, in a letter to New York City's Mayor James Duane referred to New York State as "the Seat of the Empire." Washington also appears to have applied the term "Pathway to Empire" to the state in a conversation with Governor George Clinton in the 1790s, but there is no documentary evidence of this. The authors of the concluding chapter of volume 6 of Alexander C. Flick's multivolume *History of New York State* (1933–37) entitled it "New York Becomes the Empire State" and observed that New York was being so called as early as 1819, because its population had exceeded Virginia's, but they provide no source for the statement, nor for another statement that by the time the Erie Canal was completed the name Empire State was universally acknowledged and accepted. The beginning of regular packet service from New York City to Liverpool by the Black Ball Line in 1818 may well have stimulated the use of the term "Empire State" because of the signal advantage the regularity of shipping gave to New York's merchants over those in other coastal cities. It does appear that by 1820, the phrase was being widely used. In 1849, a book written by one R. L. Christopher was titled the *Empire State Book of Practical Forms*, and, in 1871, a Mrs. S. S. Colt wrote a book titled *The Tourist's Guide through the Empire State*. Benson J. Lossing's 1888 history was entitled *The Empire State: A Compendious History of the Commonwealth of New York*.

It is doubtful that the origin of the term will ever be determined. When the WPA *Guide to the Empire State* was published in 1940, the distinguished New York State historian Dixon Ryan Fox confessed somewhat lamely in its early pages: "'The Empire State'—it would gratify the people of New York if they could discover who first dared that spacious adjective." Perhaps Paul Eldridge spoke the last word on the subject in his *Crown of Empire: The Story of New York State* (1957) when he raised the question humorously: "Who was the merry wag who crowned the State . . . [as the Empire State]? New York would certainly raise a monument to his memory, but he made his grandiose gesture and vanished forever."

In any case, the term took hold and has been memorialized in diverse ways, including the introduction of "The Empire State Express" by the New York Central in 1891 and the erection of the Empire State Building in 1931. Whatever its original meaning, some of its luster has dimmed as New York has been surpassed in population by California and then by Texas and has lost its primacy in the U.S. House of Representatives. But the state and its "Empire City" at the mouth of the Hudson still symbolize the "Golden Door" through which the "wretched refuse" of other countries, who, from 1990 to 1996, entered each year in about the same numbers as they did at the turn of the twentieth century, seek to improve their fortunes. Immigrants and visitors no longer come by ship, but the metropolitan airports of Kennedy, La Guardia, and Newark receive more international air travelers than any other passenger gateways in the United States. New York still has more Fortune 500 companies than any other state in the Union and more commercial bank deposits. The presence of the United Nations makes New York the international capital of the world, and the financial futures of countries everywhere still rest on what happens in Wall Street. Aspiring dramatists still set their eyes on making it on Broadway, and playing in Carnegie Hall or singing at the Met still mean something special to rising stars in the music world.

It is not merely local pride that impels the authors of this volume to trace the impressive history of New York State. The state has given much to the nation, and its place in the country's history merits the attention this book seeks to focus upon it.

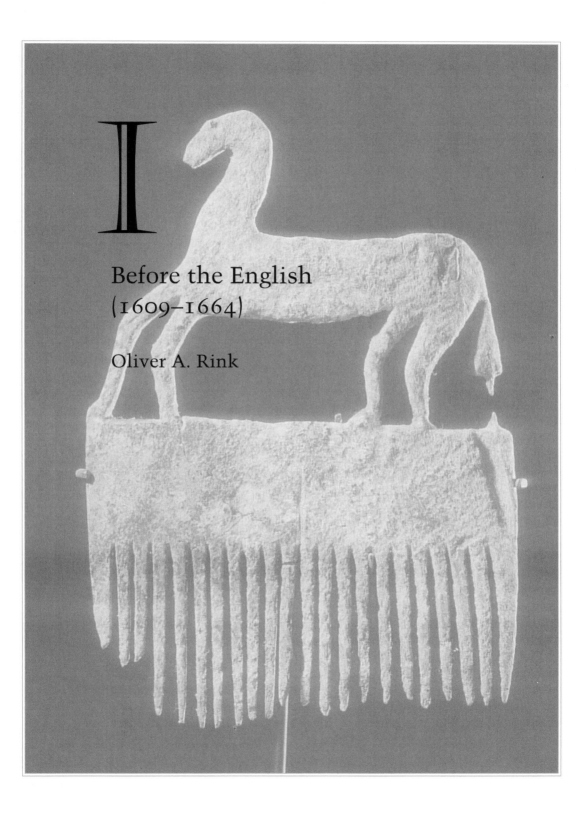

I

Before the English
(1609–1664)

Oliver A. Rink

Chapter 1

Native Americans before the Invasion

WHEN EUROPEANS ARRIVED IN THE REGION EVENTUALLY to be called New York, a complex and elaborate native economy that included hunting, gathering, manufacturing, and farming already existed there. The diversity of cultures that confronted the Europeans was in many ways a product of the diversity of the land. Thick woodlands traversed by rivers and streams, rolling hills and formidable mountains, alluvial valleys and narrow canyons, and a rich plant and animal population forced upon Native Americans a series of cultural adaptations that made of the area a complex and, at least to the minds of Europeans, daunting mosaic of Native American tribes, nations, languages, and political associations.

The region that fell under the political jurisdiction of the Dutch West India Company after 1621 comprised all or part of five present states—New York, New Jersey, Delaware, Pennsylvania, and Connecticut. Ethnographers refer to it as the Northeastern Cultural Area, which is usually divided into three sub-areas based on language and material culture: the Coastal Algonquian, Central-Northern Algonquian, and the Iroquoian.

Archaeologists and ethnographers, employing a variety of sophisticated scientific dating methods, have identified a Paleolithic culture in the region as late as 5000 B.C., followed by an early Archaic culture, itself replaced by at least two more Archaic cultures that existed as late as 1000 B.C. About the time of the fall of the Roman Empire in Europe, the first "Woodland Culture" appeared in the area, followed by a "Second Woodland" or "Owasco" culture that lasted to about 1100 A.D. or the time of the first Crusades. In the twelfth century, there emerged the distinct Iroquoian and Algonquian cultures that greeted the arrival of Europeans.

The Iroquois of the lower Great Lakes and Saint Lawrence Valley spoke a number of distinct and mutually unintelligible languages classified as Iroquoian. They were more formally structured, socially and politically, than the Algonquians. Skilled traders and ferocious warriors, they played a dominant role in the political history of New York throughout the colonial period.

The origins of the Iroquois go back before 2000 B.C., but it was during the mild climatic period about 1000 A.D. that the Iroquois colonized the Saint Lawrence Valley and cultivated maize. In these latitudes, maize had reached the extreme northern limit of its range, and probably the new food crop was initially only a supplement to hunting and gathering. By about 1300 A.D. some Iroquois villages had grown far beyond the limits of hunting and gathering settlements and may have already developed into dense habitations with the familiar "longhouses" surrounded by wooden palisades.

By the beginning of the fifteenth century, some of these villages may have numbered more than fifteen hundred inhabitants. Such dense populations placed great demands on resources, especially on the surrounding woods that were harvested for firewood and construction material. Villages had to be moved frequently so as not to deplete these resources.

During the fourteenth century, perhaps because of deteriorating climatic conditions resulting in cooler temperatures and a receding of the latitudinal limits of maize production, warfare among the Iroquois increased. Greater competition for good farmland and other strategic resources, such as game animals and firewood, may have played a decisive role in transforming the Iroquois into a warrior culture. War may have also provided a means for men to achieve status and power.

Population densities achieved by agriculture required a number of social adaptations. In the crowded living conditions of agricultural villages, political institutions were required for dealing with quarrels. Arguments left unchecked quickly raged out of control and threatened the security of the whole village. It was necessary to develop formal councils made up of representatives from each clan to adjudicate grievances and resolve differences.

Authority rested on reputation and personal relations rather than on jurisdictional units, such as townships, counties, and states, as in European society. Those who shared a common language felt a special affinity and generally regarded themselves as a single people, or tribe, but local political units tended to develop around the village or band council. The council was the governing body of the village, and its sachems constituted the political leadership. Below the level of politics the principal unit of social organization was the clan. Among the Iroquois, clans were generally exogamous; that is, marriages between men and women of the same clan were treated as incest and prohibited. Clans were generally matrilineal among the woodland cultures of New York; thus each individual belonged to the clan of his or her mother. Moreover, clan affiliation did not change with marriage. Exogamous marriage customs ensured that each village or band contained several clans. Hence, the key to political leadership on the village level was the ability to achieve consensus among the clans.

Clans drew their identity from the natural environment, taking the names of animals, or sometimes plants or natural phenomena. Members of a clan were part of an extended family and called one another brother and sister. In Iroquoia certain clans provided sachems, others were esteemed as shamans and healers, still others were noted for their religious leaders. Clans were expected to provide food and shelter for visiting members from other villages. Thus was created a web of kinship that bound several villages or bands together. Feuds between clans were discouraged, and customs arose to prevent individual incidents from escalating into open war. For example, when a clan member murdered someone from another clan, the clan of the murderer was expected to compensate the family of the victim at a rate determined by arbitrators or council sachems.

By the end of the sixteenth century, Iroquois tribes in what is now New York established confederacies to reduce internecine warfare. The confederacies were loosely knit associations more akin to a league of nations than a sovereign

An English map showing the land occupied by the Six Nations of the Iroquois by 1771. From *The Six Nations of New York* (Ithaca, N.Y.: Cornell University Press, 1995).

nation-state. A council composed of chiefs met regularly to resolve problems before they became blood feuds. The most famous of the confederacies was the Five Nations, or League of the Iroquois, which included the five great tribes or nations of New York and western Ontario: the Seneca, Cayuga, Onondaga, Oneida, and Mohawk. Later, during the European colonial period, the Tuscaroras were added.

According to Iroquois legend, the league was founded by Deganawidah, a mythic and sacred figure of mixed Huron-Mohawk blood. Hiawatha, a prophet, served as Deganawidah's earthly representative and traveled untiringly through the territory of the original Five Nations until he persuaded them to give up their intertribal warfare and blood feuds. Hiawatha conceived of an alliance to achieve permanent peace among old enemies and to provide mutual defense against outsiders.

The league was probably modeled after existing clan and community organizations. The Grand Council consisted of fifty life-appointed male sachems, or peace chiefs, each of whom was nominated by the headwoman of certain sachem-producing lineages in each clan. The Onondaga had fourteen sachems, the Cayuga ten, the Oneida and Mohawk nine each, and the Seneca eight. Consensus was required for most league actions, and tribal autonomy was usually left untouched. Council members possessed great prestige and were responsible for keeping the internal peace as well as representing the league and coordinating united warfare. An incompetent sachem could be removed, but the impeachment procedure required the approval of the headwoman in the sachem's own lineage.

Although the confederacy made the Iroquois the most formidable threat to European colonization, it also bred a strong sense of cultural superiority. The Iroquoian tribes to the west and south, especially the nonallied Huron, Erie, and Susquehannock eventually became the targets of the Five Nations' ambitions. Because the Iroquois considered themselves *Ongwi Honwi* (superior people), they never offered league membership to the non-Iroquoian-speaking peoples who came under their control. Instead, they provided membership in the "Covenant Chain," a term first suggested by the Dutch at a treaty signed with the Mohawk in 1618. The Covenant Chain, primarily a trade and military alliance, gave the Iroquois the authority to represent its members in negotiations with Europeans. However, Covenant Chain members were not allowed to vote or to have representation in the League council.

Their control of the fur trade and their initial distance from Europeans allowed the Iroquois to respond to the European invasion by political organization and shrewd negotiation. Moreover, their long history of resistance to other tribes and their fierce reputation as warriors ensured their cultural autonomy and survival throughout the period of European colonialism. The Algonquians, who inhabited the coastal plain and shallow river valleys, were not as lucky.

They were the first to experience the biological and cultural consequences of contact with Europeans and, in time, they faced the choice of destruction at European hands or assimilation and conquest by the confederacy.

The origin of the various Algonquian tribes of coastal North America is clouded in mystery. Some forms of the language have been traced to the Muskogean family of languages found in the Southeast. It is probable that the root language, which was shared by the prehistoric cultures of the eastern seaboard, dates to the years 4000–3000 B.C. The tribes of the coast spoke various dialects of Algonquian, and communication among tribes was fairly easy.

The tribes went by various names depending on those who designated them. Europeans, including the Dutch of New Netherland, assigned tribal names on the basis of the principal geographic feature of the surrounding area. Hence, the Raritan Indians were named after the Raritan River, the Delawares after the Delaware River, and so on. Occasionally Europeans would attempt to render the native tongue into phonetic Dutch or English, as in the case of the name for the Mohawks: to the Dutch the Iroquoian name for the tribe sounded like *Maquasen*; to the English it sounded more like *Mohowawogs*.

The woodland Algonquian tribes of New York had many common cultural practices. Most clans lived near rivers and streams or along the seacoast, where fish and mollusks could be easily harvested. Foraging for plant foods was also an important part of the seasonal cycle of food gathering shared by most of the woodland tribes of the region, including the Iroquois. The rivers and streams served as the best transportation links between widely scattered tribes, and the Native Americans of New York evolved a technology to exploit this feature of their geography.

Virtually all New York's Native Americans built and used canoes to trade and communicate across long distances. The design seems to have originated among the Algonquian tribes of the northeast seacoast, but the technology spread throughout Iroquoia as well. Thin sheets of birch or elm bark were stretched over a framework of saplings tied with ligatures made of root fibers. The exterior was sealed with pitch or tar, creating a nearly watertight hull. The canoes were elegant and swift vessels that could be paddled and maneuvered when heavily loaded because of the capacious design. At the same time, the boats were light for portage around waterfalls and rapids. Regional conditions were reflected in design modifications. For example, the Algonquian birchbark canoe of the Great Lakes had a deeper prow and more freeboard to handle the stormy lake waters. The combination of easily acquired materials for repair and light weight made these canoes the preferred means of river transportation throughout the colonial era.

Communication was also maintained by several well-worn trails that connected summer and winter lodgings and carried a trade in furs, pottery, baskets, and food among widely scattered villages. The trails were kept open by use and marked with symbols to assist the confused traveler. Moccasins, an invention of the woodland Indians, cushioned the feet in supple leather tied above the ankle and provided protection against the broken branches and thorns of the trail. Generations of European fur traders testified to their comfort and practicality by forsaking their poorly fitting European leather boots when trekking through the wilderness.

Native American weapons technology at the time of contact with Europeans consisted of bows and arrows, stone hatchets or tomahawks, and large war clubs generally hung from the arm with a leather strap. Warriors usually went into battle behind square shields made of cured leather stretched over a birch sapling frame. The shield covered the body from foot to shoulder but could be pierced by an arrow at close range. The arrival of Europeans with their metal technology and firearms transformed warfare among Native Americans. Within a generation after the arrival of the Dutch in the upper Hudson Valley, many Indians owned firearms and had learned to use them dexterously.

Native American languages in North America lacked an alphabet and thus a written form. Orality thus shaped political and social institutions and determined the direction of technological change. Religion and intellectual life evolved in an oral tradition, without scriptures or holy text. In oral cultures a myth not repeated or given expression in ritual quickly disappears. Much of what is known of Native American religious practices in the pre-contact period comes from European observers who often failed to see the diversity before their eyes. Nonetheless, it is possible to describe in general terms some of the common practices and beliefs of the indigenous peoples of New York.

Whether Algonquian or Iroquois, Native Americans employed the landscape as a mythopoeic ("myth-making") easel on which they painted word pictures that taught lessons about morality and the history of the clan. The stories were repeated by each generation until they become part of the clan's cultural heritage. Many of the stories were object lessons that revealed taboos and demonstrated the consequences of bad behavior. The landscape also served as the history text of the clan and community; its natural features were used as mnemonic symbols to recall the mythic migration routes used by ancestors, or as physical reminders of wars and great individual achievements.

For Native Americans, history was a tale constantly retold from the landscape. The mystical connection with the landscape produced a different conception of land ownership than that held by Europeans. Native Americans conceived of the land as a living entity, a network of spirits and souls to which they belonged. When a tribe or clan claimed a territory, they usually did so by reference to an oral history tradition that somehow connected them with a particular piece of geography. Ownership was tied to the use of resources in some tangible way. Thus, claim to a hunting ground, a piece of farmland, or a stretch of riverbank did not mean the same thing that it did to Europeans. As the Five

Nations would prove during the colonial period, claims could also be staked by warfare and intimidation.

Although each clan or community maintained a particular mythological relationship with its immediate environment, the woodland economy of mixed farming and hunting produced a number of similar beliefs. One of these involved the reciprocal relationship between hunter and prey. Hunting involved a religious connection between people and animals that took form in spatial terms. Hunting cultures believed in a mythic protector of animals, whose permission was required for a successful hunt. Hunters prepared for the hunt by spiritual communion with the game or the game's protector. Only when both hunter and prey had been made worthy through ritual could the hunt proceed. The hunt was, therefore, a mythic journey into a "hunting ground," where the hunter acted out a part in a cosmic play. The good hunter always remembered to give thanks to the animal master for the nourishment the sacrifice had provided. The coming of the European fur trade and the consequent expansion of the hunt to respond to market forces destroyed the delicate ecological relationship between Indian hunters and the game of the forest.

Agriculture also left its imprint on Native American culture. Most agricultural work was performed by women, who learned the skills from their mothers. The principal crop was maize, although Indian women were adept at raising a wide variety of beans, a few vegetable crops such as pumpkins and squash, and tobacco for personal use. Gathering was also a female task but not as exclusively as agriculture. Wild grapes, berries, and nuts were gathered by young girls and boys. With farming came a series of rituals that coincided with the agricultural calendar and celebrated the seasonal cycle of dearth and fecundity. The life rhythms of crops and wild plants were added to the mythic properties of the landscape.

Native American healing and curing techniques were based upon a conception of illness poorly understood by contemporary Europeans. The Indians of New York subscribed to two theories of disease. The first involved the theft of one's soul or life's vitality. The cure was fairly straightforward: determine the cause of the loss and the location where it occurred—someplace in the landscape; then, rescue the soul and return it to its owner. The techniques to effect the cure included trances, magical flight, and ritually dramatized rescue missions performed by a shaman. The second cause of illness involved some evil spirit penetrating the sufferer's body. The spirit was seen as the source of the pain, and the cure required its removal. Shamans employed several techniques. There was exorcism pure and simple, usually requiring chanting and ritualized behavior. More invasive techniques were also tried, including minor surgery.

The oral culture of Native Americans delineated the stages of life with ceremony and ritual. Deaths, marriages, and births marked the passage of time in the life of an individual and in the life of the clan. Native Americans seldom regarded death as natural unless it occurred peacefully in old age. An elaborate mythic system evolved to explain death and to provide comfort to the living. The Dutch lawyer, judge, and historian Adriaen Van der Donck, provided an early eyewitness account of how the *wilden* (Indians or savages, probably Mahican) around Fort Orange (present Albany) responded to death.

Whenever a soul has departed, the nearest relatives extend the limbs and close the eyes of the dead; and after the body has been watched and wept over several days and nights, they bring it to the grave, wherein they do not lay it down, but place it in a sitting posture upon a stone or a block of wood, as if the body were sitting upon a stool; then they place a pot, kettle, platter, spoon, with some provision and money, near the body in the grave; this they say is necessary for the journey to the other world. Then they place as much wood around the body as will keep the earth from it. Above the grave they place a large pile of wood, stone or earth, and around and above the same they place palisades resembling a small dwelling. All their burial places are secluded and preserved with religious veneration and care, and they consider it wicked and infamous to disturb or injure their burial places.[1]

Marriage and birth ceremonies were generally less elaborate than contemporary European customs. Most Algonquians practiced male polygamy in some form or another, while the Iroquois were largely monogamous but with relatively easy divorce that could be initiated by either partner. It was not at all uncommon for adult men and women to have several marriage partners in a lifetime. Some clans had proprietary rights to names that could be used only by offspring of the clan and given only in a naming ceremony shortly after birth. First marriages for young adults were usually occasions for the exchange of gifts between the two families, followed by a feast. Older couples were married with less ceremony.

Death, marriage, and birth were the peaks and valleys of life. They were ritualized and remembered, but for most Native Americans as for most Europeans, daily life was characterized by routine. From spring to early fall, the river Indians moved down to the estuaries and coastal regions where they lived off fish, mollusks, wild plants, and game. With the first frost, they retreated into the interior where they hunted forest game, partly for meat but also for furs and skins to make clothing and to keep out the frigid blasts of winter. They harvested the forest animals carefully, using virtually every bit of the carcass. After the taking of the fur or skin, they consumed the meat or dried it to make jerky. The bones and teeth they used for jewelry or tools, while the tendons were employed, along with root fibers, for bow strings.

1. Adriaen Van der Donck, *A Description of the New Netherlands*, ed. Thomas F. O'Donnell (Syracuse, 1968), 86–87.

On the eve of contact, political stability achieved through confederation, the spread of maize cultivation, and the introduction of new grain storage techniques permitted Native American population densities in the New York area to reach an all-time high. On the shoreline, in the verdant river valleys, and deep in the forest they lived oblivious to the coming invasion.

Chapter 2

The Dutch Stake Their Claim

THE FIRST EUROPEAN TO SIGHT THE EXQUISITE COASTLINE of the land that would one day be named New York was the Italian explorer Giovanni da Verrazano, whose ship, the *Dauphin*, sailed under the sponsorship of the king of France. In 1524 he entered lower New York Bay and dropped anchor off Staten Island near the entrance to the Narrows. His discovery was without consequence, for he did not linger long.

A Portuguese explorer, Estevar Gomes, sailed into the estuary a year after Verrazano's departure but once again left without naming or claiming the territory. French fur traders descended the Hudson River as early as 1540 seeking business with the Mahicans and Wappingers. Other Europeans may also have visited the area as traders or fishermen, but their discoveries remained unpublished and unmapped. Then in 1609 the famed Arctic explorer Henry Hudson sailed into New York Bay, penetrated the Narrows, and voyaged north to the shallows near present-day Albany. His published report and the testimony of members of his crew provided the first complete description of New York Bay, Staten Island, the great river that would bear his name, and the coast of North America from Delaware Bay to Cape Cod. The voyage also established a Dutch claim to the region.

The first concrete evidence of Henry Hudson, the explorer, appears in a journal of his first Arctic voyage. As master of a small vessel belonging to the Muscovy Company, he proposed "to goe to sea . . . for to discover a passage by the North Pole to Japan and China." It was not the famed northeast passage he sought but a direct route across the top of the world. This bold scheme was based on the belief that the continuous sunlight of the Arctic summer made the waters warmer near the pole and free of ice. If the timing was correct, Hudson theorized, an ice-free passage directly through the Arctic Sea over the North Pole would bring him to Asia. The theory was dashed when his ship was stopped by an ice barrier somewhere above 79 degrees north latitude. Hudson's second voyage of exploration was an attempt to find a northeast passage around Russia. On April 22, 1608, he set sail from England in a small ship with a crew of thirteen. This time the expedition reached the frozen island of Novaya Zemlya, in the Barents Sea, before progress was blocked by a wall of sea ice. Reluctantly he turned south and sailed back to England, arriving at Gravesend on August 26.

Hudson Sails for the Dutch

By the fall and winter of 1608–9, Hudson's quest for a northeast passage had become the talk of geographers and mariners alike. He accepted an invitation from the directors of the Dutch East India Company to come to Amsterdam and report on his explorations.

After much negotiation the company's governing board of directors, the Heeren XVII (literally "gentlemen seventeen") offered to sponsor a voyage of exploration in search of a northeast passage to Asia. Both sides agreed upon terms, and notaries prepared copies of a contract. With his friend, the well-known Dutch geographer Jodocus Hondius, serving as witness and interpreter, Henry Hudson signed the document on January 8, 1609, before a notary in Amsterdam.

Hudson was to sail on or about the first of April, "in order to search for a passage by the North, around by the North side of Nova Zembla [sic]." If he was successful in finding a northeast passage, he was to sail through it and then south to about 60 degrees latitude. The expedition was to be a reconnaissance, and Hudson was ordered to "obtain as much knowledge of the lands as can be done without any considerable loss of time, and if it is possible return immediately in order to make a faithful report and relation to the Directors."

For his efforts Hudson was to receive the sum of 800 guilders.[1] If by chance he did not return, the directors agreed to pay Katherine Hudson, his wife, 200 guilders in cash, in return for which the company could no longer be held liable by his heirs.

The contract specified that the directors would furnish Hudson with a small vessel or "yacht of about thirty lasts [sixty tons] burden, well provided with men, provisions and other necessaries." The vessel was built especially for the expedition in the shipyards of the East India Company in Amsterdam.

1. The guilder, also called the florin (fl.), was the basic silver coin of the Dutch economy and one of the most highly prized of all specie in the seventeenth century.

Christened the *Halve Maen* (Half Moon), she was a typical Dutch yacht with a rather flat keel that required eight feet of draft, ideal for the shallow rivers and canals of the Netherlands and excellent also for exploring rivers and streams along uncharted coasts. Her length was approximately sixty-five feet with a beam of about fifteen feet. Her cargo capacity was small, about eighty tons, but she was strong and seaworthy.

The *Half Moon* sailed from Amsterdam on April 4 and cleared the Texel, an island near the opening of the Zuider Zee, on the sixth. Sailing due north, she passed the North Cape on May 5 and pushed on into the Arctic Sea. Arriving on the coast of Novaya Zemlya, Hudson and his crew of twenty men found the sea ice impassable. Among the Dutch members of his crew there were some who had served in the East Indies. The Arctic conditions were especially hard on these men, and they complained about the cold. Hudson may have feared a mutiny.

At this juncture he decided to salvage the expedition by proposing a crossing of the North Atlantic to seek a northwest passage. Since the log book of this voyage has not survived, the only evidence of this decision is found in the contemporary account of the Dutch historian Emanuel Van Meteren. "Captain Hutson laid before them two propositions. The first of these was to go to the coast of America, to the latitude of 40 degrees, moved thereto mostly by letters and maps which a certain Captain Smith[2] had sent him from Virginia, and by which he indicated to him a sea leading into the western ocean, by the north of the southern English colony. . . . The other proposition was to direct their search through Davis's Straits. This meeting with general approval, they sailed thitherward on the 14th of May."[3]

The voyage was a harrowing feat in itself. In the Faroe Islands on May 31 the ship suffered damage to the foremast and had to limp across the Atlantic without it. On July 18, 1609, the *Half Moon* made landfall in North America, somewhere below 44 degrees north latitude.

Hudson took the first opportunity to replenish his stores. The crew fished in the teeming waters of the Grand Banks taking, according to one account, 118 cod in just five hours. While off the banks, the crew had their first encounter with Indians. Six natives in two canoes paddled out to greet the *Half Moon.* Some small gifts were exchanged, and crew and Indians shared a meal and drink. One of the Indians spoke some French, leading Robert Juet, an English officer who served with Hudson, to surmise that trade between the Indians and French fishermen who frequented these waters had become common. Juet also

2. Captain John Smith, founder of Jamestown and explorer of the North American coast.

3. J. Franklin Jameson, ed., *Narratives of New Netherland, 1609–1664* (New York, 1909), 6.

"La Pesche des Sauvages" (1678), drawn by a French explorer, Louis Nicholas, testifies to fishing's central place in the Iroquois economy. Thomas Gilcrease Institute of American History and Art, Tulsa, Oklahoma.

gleaned from the conversation that there were gold, silver, and copper mines nearby.

Sailing south, the *Half Moon* ran in toward the coast near the mouth of a river (perhaps the Penobscot). Hudson sent an expedition ashore to cut a new foremast and obtain fresh water. While the *Half Moon* lay at anchor two French boats arrived with Indians aboard. Hudson's crew immediately suspected treachery. Initially the encounter was friendly. According to Juet, some Indians came aboard with beaver pelts and "other fine furres, which they would have changed for redde gowns." Then inexplicably the crew of the *Half Moon* turned on the Indians with cannon and musket, perhaps a preemptive strike to stave off an expected attack.

Having murdered and robbed the Indians without provocation, the crew returned to work and weighed anchor. Hudson's role in this incident remains unknown, although one must assume he ordered his men to commit the plunder. In any case, Hudson had no intention of remaining in the area. Drawn perhaps by the speculations of his friend Captain John Smith, he set a course south.

The *Half Moon* reached Cape Cod by the first week of August. Having encountered nothing but fog and rocky shores for days, Hudson decided to take advantage of the relatively safe coastline to revictual. He sent five men ashore to obtain fresh water and anything else that could enliven the dreary fare of salted fish and hard biscuits. They returned some hours later reporting the discovery of wild grapes and "savages, which seemed very glad of our coming." The crew brought one Indian back with them, and Hudson entertained him lavishly with food and drink. Hudson personally offered him a gift of "foure glasse buttons" and ordered him returned to his people unharmed.

Skirting Nantucket and Martha's Vineyard, the *Half Moon* continued on southward. By the third week of August she had reached the Chesapeake Bay, but Hudson decided not to put in at Jamestown. Setting a course for the north, he continued his exploration of the coast, arriving at Delaware Bay on August 28. He declined to try entering the bay because of the dangerous shoals. Instead he continued northward, cruising the shore of New Jersey and approaching Sandy Hook on September 1.

Four days passed as Hudson coasted the Jersey shore, taking soundings and standing out to sea when onshore winds threaten to push the ship aground. On the morning of September 4, he brought the *Half Moon* into Sandy Hook harbor. Finding the waters safe and deep, he sent a boat ashore with a crew and net to fish. In the afternoon a delegation of Indians approached the ship with tobacco, seeking to trade for knives and beads. Robert Juet described them: "They goe in Deere skins loose, well dressed. They have yellow Copper. They desire Cloathes, and are very civill. They have great store of Maiz, or Indian Wheate, whereof they make good Bread."

That evening an onshore breeze arose suddenly and ran the ship aground, but, in the words of Robert Juet, she "tooke no hurt, thanked bee God, for the ground is soft sand and Oze." The next day Indians came aboard again with tobacco. For the first time the Indian party included women, who brought hemp to trade.

On the morning of September 6, Hudson dispatched a small boat with five men to explore the Narrows. They sounded the strait and reported later that the depth was between eighteen and twenty fathoms and offered a "very good riding for Ships." Continuing on, they discovered upper New York Bay, but when they were about to return to the *Half Moon* they were attacked by Indians in canoes. In the ensuing battle, the firearms of the Europeans proved worthless, as a rain squall wetted their matches. One man was killed, an Englishman named John Colman, shot through the neck with an arrow. The rest eventually rowed back to the *Half Moon*. The next day Colman's body was buried on Sandy Hook.

Hudson spent two more days in the lower bay conducting soundings and trading with the Indians. On September 9, shortly before the ship weighed anchor, several Indians came aboard. What transpired next did not bode well for future European-Indian relations. As Juet described it, "In the morning, two great Canoes came aboord full of men; the one with their Bowes and Arrowes, and the other in shew of buying of Knives to betray us; but we perceived their intent. Wee tooke two of them to have kept them, and put red Coates on them, and would not suffer the other to come neere us. So they went on Land, and two other came aboard in a Canoe: we tooke the one and let the other goe; but hee which wee had taken, got up and leapte over-boord." On September 11 the *Half Moon* departed New York Bay and rode the incoming tide up the river.

The Hudson, or North River as the Dutch called it, was an ancient river. Some ten million years ago, geographic theory suggests, a smaller river moved northward and joined the Hudson in the Highlands, forcing the Hudson to abandon its original easterly course and turn south toward the sea. During the Ice Age, when lower sea levels exposed the Continental Shelf, the Hudson flowed through it, gouging a trench that today extends far into the Atlantic as the Hudson Canyon. With the end of the Ice Age and the subsequent rise of the world's oceans, the Continental Shelf was once again submerged, leaving the Hudson channel well below sea level from north of Albany south to the edge of the Continental Shelf. The result is an estuary or tidal river whose flow is largely determined by the ocean tides.

The rhythm of the tides dictated the flow of maritime commerce and determined the pattern of settlement in the Hudson River Valley. In 1609 the tidal pattern offered Henry Hudson the hint of the northwest passage that he was seeking. Turning the *Half Moon* into the river he rode the tide into the heart of the continent.

When the wind and tide were favorable, the *Half Moon* made swift progress. "The fourteenth," Juet recorded, "in the morning being very faire weather, the wind South-east, we sayled up the River twelve leagues." By September 18, the *Half Moon* had reached a point just south of present-day Albany, where Hudson went ashore at the invitation of some Indians, probably Mahicans.

Johannes de Laet, a director of the Dutch West India Company and its historian, preserved Hudson's account of what followed. It is one of the few extant documents in which Hudson speaks in his own words.

I sailed to the shore in one of their canoes, with an old man, who was the chief of a tribe, consisting of forty men and seventeen women; these I saw there in a house well constructed of oak bark, and circular in shape, with the appearance of having a vaulted ceiling. It contained a great quantity of maize, and beans of the last year's growth, and there lay near the house for the purpose of drying enough to load three ships, besides what was growing in the fields. On our coming near the house, two mats were spread out to sit upon, and immediately some food was served in well made red wooden bowls; two men were also despatched at once with bows and arrows in quest of game, who soon after brought in a pair of pigeons which they had just shot. They likewise killed at once a fat dog, and skinned it in great haste, with shells which they get out of the water. They supposed that I would remain with them for the night, but I returned after a short time on board the ship. The land is the finest for cultivation that I ever in my life set foot upon, and it also abounds in trees of every description. The natives are a very good people; for, when they saw that I would not remain, they supposed that I was afraid of their bows, and taking the arrows, they broke them in pieces, and threw them into the fire.[4]

On September 19 Hudson dispatched a small boat upriver with several men to make soundings. The channel was becoming shallow, and Hudson may already have realized that his dream of discovering a northwest passage to the Pacific was lost. Within a few days the boat returned to confirm that the *Half Moon* had reached the end of the river's navigable channel. It must have been a crushing disappointment for Hudson. All that was left was the return voyage and the recriminations that awaited him.

On September 23 the *Half Moon* turned south with the ebbing tide. Swift progress was made as current, tide, and wind pushed the ship downstream. By the first of October the expedition was at Stony Point. As on the voyage upriver, Indians paddled out to meet the crew. But these were different Indians, "people of the Mountaynes," according to Robert Juet. At first they were fascinated with

4. Jameson, *Narratives of New Netherland, 1609–1664,* 49.

the ship and the weapons and offered furs for trade. Then one Indian climbed from his canoe up the rudder and into the cabin and stole Juet's pillow, two shirts, and two bandoliers. What followed was a running battle that resulted in several Indian deaths. News of the bloody encounter spread downriver, and Hudson and his crew found themselves under attack the next day. After killing seven Indians with musket fire and another three with cannon, the crew of the *Half Moon* bade farewell to the continent.

The return crossing was not without incident. The Dutch mate asked Hudson to winter in Newfoundland and explore Davis's Strait, between Greenland and Baffin Island (named for John Davis, who discovered it in 1585). Hudson may have considered this, but his English crew opposed another year in the northern latitudes. A compromise was reached to winter in Ireland, perhaps with the intent of exploring Davis's Strait in the spring. For reasons unknown, however, Hudson sailed to England, arriving in the first week of November.

Upon his arrival, Hudson sent letters to the Heeren XVII informing them of his discoveries in North America and his failure to find a northeast or northwest passage to Asia. In his report of the expedition, Hudson offered to take the *Half Moon* back across the Atlantic in search of the northwest passage, but this time in addition to his regular pay of 800 florins he demanded an extra 1,500 florins for expenses.

The Heeren XVII were not accustomed to such disobedience and ordered the ship and crew to return to Amsterdam as soon as possible. In the meantime, however, English authorities sequestered the ship and ordered Hudson and the other Englishmen to remain in England. After a series of negotiations involving the diplomatic corps of both nations, the English government agreed to release the *Half Moon*, and she sailed with her Dutch crew to Amsterdam in July 1610.

Although his third voyage had failed to find the fabled passage to Asia, Hudson's discoveries established the Dutch claim to what would soon become New Netherland. He made one final voyage in 1610–11. It ended tragically with a mutiny on June 22, 1611. In the frozen bay that would bear his name, Hudson, his son, and seven loyal crewmen were cast adrift, never to be heard from again.

With Hudson's death the first phase of Arctic exploration ended. The geographers and cartographers memorialized him with place names like Hudson's Bay, Hudson's Strait, and, perhaps most famous of all, the Hudson River, but his discoveries in America became the point of contention between the Netherlands and England for half a century.

When the news of Hudson's third voyage reached the ears of anxious investors and adventurers in Amsterdam on wings of rumor, however, the immediate official position of the East India Company was silence. The directors may have worried that a confrontation with the English over rights to

North America would jeopardize their operations elsewhere. In their continuing struggle against Spain and the forces of the Catholic Counter Reformation, the two Protestant sea powers needed each other. Moreover, the Heeren XVII simply did not see Hudson's discovery as significant. The East India Company's refusal to follow up on the discovery left the door open to the aggressive private merchants of Amsterdam.

Dutch Merchants Establish the Fur Trade

A sea captain named Hendrick Christiaensen, while returning from a voyage to the West Indies in late 1610 or early 1611, may have been the first Dutch sailor to visit the region after Hudson. His route ran via the Canary Islands and was determined by the trade winds and currents. It would become the usual route to New Netherland. Christiaensen's visit was most probably accidental, a result of his sailing north along the North American coast in search of the westerlies to return home. Christiaensen may not have even known of Hudson's earlier voyage and may thus have been unaware of his country's claim to the area.

From 1611 to 1614, Amsterdam merchants Arnout Vogels, Lambert Van Tweenhuysen, and Hans Hunger and furriers Leonard and Francoys Pelgrom financed several voyages to the Hudson River area to trade for furs. They competed frequently and sometimes violently with other merchants from the fishing ports of Hoorn and Monnikendam on the Zuider Zee, until the principal merchants in the trade decided to form a partnership under an exclusive charter offered by the States General in 1614.

On March 27, 1614, the States General issued a "resolution" or charter granting to "diverse merchants wishing to discover New Unknown Rivers, Countries, and Places" the exclusive right to make four voyages to the area. The resolution further stipulated that merchants taking advantage of such exclusive privileges must submit a detailed report including charts and maps within fourteen days after the return from any voyage of discovery.

Seven months after the passing of the resolution, the New Netherland Company was formed, including among its directors most of the merchants who had competed in the Hudson River fur trade between 1611 and 1614. The "Figurative Map" submitted by the company as proof of its rights was the first document to refer to the area as New Netherland. Its boundaries extended to the Connecticut River in the east and to the confluence of the Mohawk and "North River" (Hudson) in the north. Within these expansive limits the merchant investors of the New Netherland Company claimed exclusive trade rights for four voyages.

The New Netherland Company attempted somewhat later to acquire exclusive patent rights to the territory between the 38th and 40th parallels (Delaware Bay), but the States General refused to grant the company an exclusive patent to this area. In October 1618, the New Netherland Company asked for an extension of its patent to the area of Hudson's River, but that, too, was denied. By this time plans may already have been advanced for the West India Company to take over the area.

The New Netherland Company was a modest success in its three years of operation. By eliminating the competition among rival partnerships, the directors were able to organize the fur trade through annual spring voyages. In addition, the company constructed a trading post near present-day Albany and added greatly to the detailed geographical knowledge of the region.

The West India Company Takes Over

The founding of the West India Company in 1621 marked the formal end of private trading in the Western Hemisphere for citizens of the United Provinces.[5] Founded as a national monopoly with jurisdiction over all trade and colonies in the Western Hemisphere, the organization was an attempt by the Dutch government to reduce competition among its thousands of private merchants. Most important, the company provided the means to organize the formidable maritime resources of the United Provinces to attack Spanish holdings in the New World. The charter, approved by the States General in 1621, bore the marks of a decade of debate and compromise and displayed the peculiar features of Dutch politics.

Article One spelled out the national joint-stock company's monopoly. "For the period of twenty-four years no native or inhabitant of these provinces shall be permitted, to sail [to] or trade with the coasts and countries of Africa, to or with the countries of America or the West Indies nor to or with any islands situated on either side or between both, except in the name of this United Company."

The charter's bold language ignored the realities of politics, financial resources, and the company's byzantine corporate structure. The political obstacle came from foreign competition, especially that of the Hapsburgs, whose immense Spanish-Portuguese empire stretched across most of the company's domain. The areas untouched by the Catholic enemy were claimed and in some cases already settled by the United Provinces' erstwhile allies England and France. The most sought-after prizes were the mines and sugar plantations

5. The official title of the nation was the United Provinces of the Netherlands. Formed in the Treaty of Utrecht in 1579, the seven provinces fought an Eighty Years War against the Spanish Hapsburgs for their independence.

controlled by the Iberians. The struggling tobacco plantations of English Virginia and the fur trade of New France were only beginning to return profits. New Netherland's rich bounty of furs was a promising, but as yet unproven source of wealth. Thus, to the company's directors the best prospects appeared to be war against the Spanish and Portuguese.

Inadequate finances also dictated company policy. As late as 1623, the company had only twenty ships, far too few to undertake hemispheric-wide operations, and in the first five years it was dangerously dependent on government subsidies to maintain its operations. Although Article Thirty-Nine of the charter provided a government commitment of 1 million guilders, the initial capitalization was not reached until 1623. Hence, from 1621 until 1623 the company undertook no operations of its own, and the grand monopoly was thus forced to look to private merchants for support, either through the selling of shares or through loans. New Netherland was considered a good risk because it had attracted private capital and merchants before the establishment of the company. Brazil was the most promising of the other regions. It would become the center of company operations in the New World for twenty-five years, absorbing millions of guilders as thousands of lives were squandered in a failed attempt to carve a sugar empire out of the Amazon jungle. The company's preoccupation with Brazil and later with its sugar and slave trade in the West Indies left New Netherland in a vacuum of unconcern that ensured its continued exploitation by private merchants of Amsterdam.

The corporate structure of the West India Company provided yet another restraint upon the directors in their efforts to exploit the grandiose assertions of the charter of 1621. The administration was divided into five chambers, each representing not only a specified amount of the subscribed capital but also a distinct political and geographic constituency. The chambers met separately, maintained their own books and operations, and frequently competed with one another for trade. The most powerful chamber was the Amsterdam Chamber, whose share of the company's operations included New Netherland. Although the wealthiest and most influential of the chambers, it could not act without the consent of the others, which represented the Maas cities (Rotterdam, Delft, and Dordrecht), Middleburg, the Noorderkwartier (Northern Quarter or North Holland), and Groningen and Friesland.

The chamber system was a response to the provincial animosities that had long characterized Dutch political life. Modeled after the immensely profitable United East India Company, the chamber system of the West India Company was intended to inspire investor confidence by guaranteeing that local merchants exercised authority over the use of local capital. Yet the chambers remained branches of a single firm as seen in Article Eleven of the company charter, which fixed the amount of capital that each chamber might administer regardless of how much each chamber actually subscribed, and again in Article

Twenty-Eight, which specified that the directors would be paid on the basis of profits earned by the entire company rather than by the chambers they represented.

The principle of dispersed authority within a single commercial entity was further established by the creation of the Heeren XIX or "general assembly of directors." The Heeren XIX, or the Nineteen as they were usually called, was composed of representatives from the chambers, each chamber receiving two representatives for each one-ninth part of the capital it administered. The Nineteen's decisions were final and no chamber, regardless of its size or capital subscription, could refuse to carry out its orders.

Within the Nineteen, however, power followed capital. The Amsterdam Chamber elected eight directors, while Zeeland, the second most powerful, had only four representatives. Each of the remaining chambers was authorized two. The nineteenth director represented the States General. This complex and unwieldy corporate structure meant that decisions were seldom made quickly. With the attention of the directors focused on operations in Brazil and the West Indies, policy decisions for other areas, such as New Netherland, were left to the individual chambers.

The company that began as an instrument of war intended to carry the Protestant Reformation to the heart of the Spanish Main became, over time, a reluctant and sometimes befuddled government of thousands of European colonists in North America. In 1624 the company, or more correctly the Amsterdam Chamber of the company, financed a small-scale settlement of Europeans in New Netherland to protect and provision its fur trade operations. Once New Netherland became a home for Europeans, however, it could not be abandoned easily. Even the Nineteen had to respond to the determined pressure of the Amsterdam Chamber and commit the resources of the company to maintaining a Dutch colony on the Hudson.

The First Colonists

The first company voyage to New Netherland occurred in 1623 as part of a fifteen-ship expedition dispatched to various areas of the company's domain; the ship was a 60-ton yacht, the *Mackereel*. After an attempt to capture a Spanish prize off the coast of Africa, she made her way to New Netherland, arriving at the roadstead in Manhattan during the second week of December. She was anchored in the East River in the spring of 1624 when the 260–ton *Nieu Nederlandt* arrived with the first European colonists.

The arrival of the *Nieu Nederlandt* was the culmination of nearly two years of planning and countless negotiations between the directors of the Amsterdam Chamber and the heads of thirty Walloon families seeking livelihoods. The Walloons were French Protestants who had escaped persecution in France to settle in the southern Netherlands. During the Eighty Years War they became refugees once again, fleeing north to the United Provinces. As early as 1622 a delegation of family heads had petitioned the provincial States[6] of Holland and West Friesland "to be employed by the West India Company." The States carefully avoided taking a position on the petition and turned the matter over to the Amsterdam Chamber for consideration. The directors of the chamber favored the request and reported it to be "very serviceable to the company." A special commission in charge of New Netherland was established in the chamber, and the matter was turned over to it.

Although the identity of the petitioners has remained a mystery, it is highly likely they were the small group of Walloons Jesse de Forest had assembled in early 1621 for emigration to the New World. De Forest had initially sought permission of the English to go to Virginia, but because the Virginia Company was facing imminent bankruptcy at the time, permission was never granted. It seems probable, therefore, that he followed up his request to the English with a petition to the Dutch. De Forest had been an unsuccessful wool merchant and dyer. His finances were always precarious, and he had a large family to support. His leadership drew upon not only his membership in the clannish, French-speaking émigré culture but also upon his ambitions as an entrepreneur.

The Walloons were not particular where they were sent as long as they were employed. Although united by language and their immigrant status in the Netherlands, they were not an exclusively religious society on the model of the English Pilgrims, who were preparing to go to New Plymouth at about the same time. Many were in need of work, and even though the economy of the United Provinces was booming, the best jobs were not always available to immigrants. In July 1623, ten families departed for Guiana as part of the company's effort to establish a colony on the mainland of South America, but by January 1624, most of them were back in Amsterdam. De Forest and a few others stayed in South America, perhaps in the hope of making something out of the colony. Shortly afterward, however, de Forest died, and the Guiana colony was abandoned.

The Walloons were thus a hardy lot already tested in the dangerous occupation of overseas colonization when they sat down to negotiate terms with the New Netherland commissioners. On March 29, 1624, after weeks of discussions, thirty families heard a public reading of the "Provisional Orders" before they boarded the *Nieu Nederlandt* for the Atlantic crossing.

The Provisional Orders represent a curious mixture of incentives and

6. The provincial "States" were independent legislative bodies in the provinces. The States General was the national parliament.

responsibilities, intended both as a recruiting device and a set of regulations delineating company authority and the colonists' realm of personal freedom. The orders obligated the colonists "to obey and to carry out without any contradiction the orders of the company." Yet they were encouraged to seek out "mines of gold, silver, copper or any other metals, as well as of precious stones, such as diamonds, rubies and the like, together with pearl fisheries." To reward such effort, the company offered to pay the discoverer 10 percent of the net proceeds for a period of six years.

The Walloons received other incentives: free passage, free land, and even livestock at "reasonable prices." For those without ready cash, the company promised to provide credit toward purchases of livestock and other provisions without interest. The company commander was to allot land on the basis of family size but with an eye to the overall benefit of the colony. He could determine what crops were to be grown and the sites for settlement.

A mid-seventeenth-century Seneca comb embellished with the figure of a horse indicates the tribe's early contact with European colonists, who introduced domesticated animals to the region. Thaw Collection, Fenimore Art Museum, Cooperstown, N.Y. Photo by John Bigelow Taylor, New York City.

Special consideration was given to the fur trade, the expected source of the colony's wealth and the most likely means of recouping the expense of settling the Walloons. The colonists were expected to assist the other company employees in gathering furs, either as trappers or as traders. The company was to be the sole purchaser of the furs and the only agent allowed to ship them out of the colony. Prices were to be "reasonable," but they did not have to be competitive with those offered by the English. In this as in other matters, the Walloons were to serve as free colonists and company employees simultaneously, seeking their own fortunes while assisting the company in its quest for dividends.

In political and religious affairs, their sphere of freedom was more restricted. The company commander held most of the authority. Appointed by the company, he was nonetheless required to rule with a council drawn from among company employees and free colonists. His responsibilities were extensive, but his power to punish was somewhat limited by the requirement that all prosecutions for criminal offenses be conducted according to the laws of the United Provinces. A commander could enforce religious conformity, if he determined that public worship was not in accord with the severe Calvinist catechism adopted by the Synod of Dordrecht, but, in practice, most commanders remained indifferent to religious matters. Years passed before an ordained minister was dispatched to the colony and then only after a number of protests had been registered with the Classis of Amsterdam, the governing body of the Reformed Church for the city and the one charged with control of ecclesiastical matters in New Netherland. In the interim, the Walloons were largely left alone to worship as they wished. Even the commander's authority to punish "any one among them or within their jurisdiction [who] should wantonly revile or blaspheme the name of God or of our Savior Jesus Christ" was, given the age, hardly unusual.

The colonists were also bound to military service when called upon by the commander. In the first years of settlement, company officials were careful to appease the Indians of the region and generally avoid conflict. Hence this obligation did not weigh heavily on the Walloons in the 1620s.

Having agreed to the Provisional Orders, the thirty families set sail for New Netherland arriving after an uneventful crossing. The skipper of the *Nieu Nederlandt* was Cornelis Jacobsz May, a former employee of the New Netherland Company and an experienced explorer and sailor with a well-deserved reputation for courage and reliability. Anchoring off Manhattan Island in the late spring of 1624, May dispatched a sloop with two families and eight single men to the "South River" (Delaware) to set up a garrison. The intent of the directors was to make the Delaware garrison on High Island (present-day Burlington Island, near Burlington, New Jersey) the center of company operations. Other groups of families and single male company employees were sent to establish a trading post on the Connecticut River. Eight men were left on Noten (or Nut) Island (present-day Governor's Island) to commence fur trade operations there, and the remaining eighteen families were taken some 150 miles up the Hudson to a site that would eventually be named Fort Orange.

The site of Fort Orange was on the west bank of the Hudson River opposite Castle Island, the main base of operations for the old New Netherland Company. The island, now part of the modern port of Albany, had been the site of a small redoubt named Fort Nassau. In 1618 the diminutive fort, which measured just fifty-eight by fifty-eight feet, had been washed away by spring floods. When the West India Company decided to settle the Walloons in New Netherland, securing this area was a high priority. Its location just south of the confluence of the Mohawk and Hudson Rivers would become the center of the company's fur trade.

The dispersion of colonists was part of a plan to improve the fur trade by establishing agricultural support communities near the three major river systems of New Netherland. It was also a recognition that the entire area was under a jurisdictional cloud. The English government had already registered its objection to the Dutch settlements in a carefully worded letter from the English ambassador, Sir Dudley Carleton, to the States General in 1622. English settlements at New Plymouth and Jamestown had already established England's claim to a substantial portion of the North American seaboard. Thus, May's settlement of Walloons served two purposes: to provide a defense against a sea-launched attack from one of the English colonies and to stake out the most vital sites of the water-dependent fur trade. Under this plan Nut Island off the tip of Manhattan was to serve a role similar to that played by the island of Texel off the entrance to the Zuider Zee. Once or twice a year, shallow-bottomed coastal vessels would offload their furs onto ocean-going ships for transport to the fatherland.

In the meantime a massive expedition was being prepared in Amsterdam that would add many more settlers to New Netherland. The expedition, under the leadership of Willem Verhulst, was sponsored by the Amsterdam Chamber and represented the largest investment yet in the fledgling colony on the Hudson. Six ships in all, carrying hundreds of colonists, farm tools, seeds, provisions, and livestock, were outfitted for a mid-winter crossing in 1625. The 150–ton *Oranje Boom*, the lead vessel carrying most of the farming tools, seeds, and live plants, sailed alone from Amsterdam in January but nearly sank in a storm in the English Channel. Seeking shelter at Plymouth, the ship was seized by English customs agents when its cargo of tools, seeds, and plants was discovered. While it was in port, however, a plague (perhaps typhus) broke out and a few passengers died. Fearing the spread of the contagion, English authorities released the vessel. It made the crossing without further mishap and arrived in New Netherland after the rest of the fleet.

The detention of the *Oranje Boom* in England disrupted the carefully laid plans of the New Netherland commissioners. They had planned for the farming tools, seeds, and live plants to be waiting in New Netherland when the main body of the fleet arrived in spring. Instead, a four-ship squadron, under the command of Willem Verhulst, arrived in the early summer of 1625 before the *Oranje Boom*, and time was lost in establishing the colonists on their farms. A sixth ship, the *Ruijter*, failed to reach New Netherland because it was captured by Moorish pirates off the coast of Africa.

Willem Verhulst had only a brief tenure as commander of the colony, from 1625 to 1626. His orders were explicit, to transport to New Netherland "divers trees, vines, and all sorts of seeds" and to have them "planted and sown in their proper season" by the colonists. He was also ordered to strengthen the settlements established by May, especially the post on High Island in the Delaware. The directors may have been drawn to this site because they sought a post deep in Indian country that, unlike Fort Orange on the upper Hudson, was ice-free all year. They were clearly misinformed about the climate on the Delaware, however, because one winter it was reported that the river had frozen so solid that Indians from the west had been able to cross on foot to the Dutch trading post on the eastern bank.

Sometime during the performance of his duties, Verhulst was removed from office by his "council." This may be considered a mutiny since the council was composed of company employees. Verhulst may have angered some of the employees by his attempts to curb their participation in the fur trade. He is also reported to have berated many of the colonists for their failure to work the company farms. There is even some suggestion that Verhulst was the cause of some irregularities in the company books and may himself have profited from illegal trade in furs. His removal was the first of many untidy administrative changes in New Netherland. Verhulst's successor, Pieter Minuit, took over the duties of commander in the spring of 1626.

Minuit was well acquainted with the area and was an obvious choice for commander. He may have sailed to the colony on the *Oranje Boom* in 1625. Serving as consultant to a group of private investors, he had scouted the colony for precious metals and other marketable resources. When he arrived in New Netherland again in 1626, with his commission as company commander, he immediately saw the folly of trying to maintain three trading posts with a widely dispersed and vulnerable civilian population.

The first sign of trouble appeared in the spring of 1626 when an Indian war erupted at Fort Orange. The local garrison commander, Daniel Van Crieckenbeeck, had disobeyed explicit company orders and sided with the Mahicans in their war with the powerful Mohawks. While accompanying a Mahican war party in an attack on their enemies, he and three of his soldiers were killed in an ambush a short distance from the fort. The Mohawks were incensed that the Dutch had taken the side of their enemy, and they threatened to annihilate the Europeans at the fort and shut down the fur trade.

When news of the Mohawk war reached Minuit, he sailed immediately to Fort Orange. His solution was to appease the Mohawks by moving the families to Manhattan Island, which he had purchased from local sachems sometime between May 4 and June 26, 1626, for 60 guilders worth of trade goods. This satisfied the Mohawks, who allowed Minuit to leave behind at Fort Orange a handful of men to conduct the fur trade.

The colonists from Fort Orange were soon joined by the families evacuated from the trading posts on the Connecticut and Delaware Rivers. To maintain its presence on the Delaware, the company eventually built a new trading post on the eastern bank near present-day Gloucester, New Jersey, which it christened Fort Nassau. In the 1630s, the Dutch would return to Connecticut, establishing a trading post near present-day Hartford. In 1626, however, the expansive and vulnerable satellite trading system proved a failure. Henceforth, New Amsterdam, on the southern tip of Manhattan Island, would be the economic and administrative center of New Netherland. With its deep-water harbor free of ice year round, it proved to be the finest port in colonial America.

Chapter 3

Establishing a Colony

DURING PETER MINUIT'S ADMINISTRATION FROM 1626 TO 1631, the colony of New Netherland began to prosper within the narrow limits established by the policies of the New Netherland Commission. The fur trade increased in volume as thousands of skins passed through the warehouses of New Amsterdam bound for the fatherland. An official report stated that 63,000 pelts were purchased by the company between 1626 and 1632 worth approximately 454,000 guilders. For the farmers, who had staked their future on the colony, however, things had begun to turn sour.

Kiliaen Van Rensselaer, soon to become the principal spokesman for the patroon system, complained that the company had abandoned the farmers by refusing to invest adequately in agriculture. He chastised those he called "the contrary minded" for giving up too easily on farming. The "contrary minded" were the directors, who opposed further investment in New Netherland if it meant expanding the European population beyond the minimal needs of support for the trading posts. Their interests were in Brazil, where the initial success of conquering Bahia had been reversed by a Portuguese counterattack. In the war-weary atmosphere of the late 1620s, New Netherland simply did not rank high among the concerns of the Nineteen. As long as the furs continued to flow unabated, there was little enthusiasm for increasing expenditures on the colony on the Hudson.

Against this backdrop of miserly support, Peter Minuit worked tirelessly to improve the colony. His first order of business was to secure Manhattan Island with a fort. Plans for the fort had been sent out with the expedition of 1625 that had brought Verhulst and the rest of the Walloons to the colony. The engineer was Cryn Fredericksz, an experienced man in building fortifications. His "special instructions" outlined an impressive edifice with stone bastions and massive walls around which a moat was to be dug to provide protection against siege, but conditions in New Netherland forced a change of plans.

The relocation of families from the outlying trading posts created a housing crisis on Manhattan. With dozens of families facing a winter without shelter, Minuet had no choice but to enlist Fredericksz and his band of carpenters in constructing houses for the colonists. Some of the materials intended for the fort were diverted for the houses, forcing the engineer to build a smaller fort. The scaled-back structure was a simple blockhouse surrounded by palisades of red cedar and sod.

By September 1626, the southern tip of Manhattan Island was crowded with thirty log houses, a new fort, a countinghouse with walls of stone, and a mill with an upper loft so large that it could be used for church services. In Amsterdam, the chronicler Nicolaes Van Wassenaer enthusiastically recorded the arrival of a ship just returned from a voyage to New Netherland in November of that year. The cargo included 7,246 beaver pelts, 675 otter skins, 48 mink, and 36 wildcat hides. In terms his readers could appreciate, Van Wassenaer described New Netherland as a prosperous colony where every colonist could pursue his own fortune.

While this picture of prosperity must certainly have pleased the "contrary minded," the same year brought a more sobering description from the company secretary, Isaac de Rasiere. He reported that the colonists had become consumed with the fur trade to the point of neglecting their farming. The fur trade, indeed, dominated the economy of New Netherland as it transformed the ecology of the region. The demand for furs in the seventeenth century appeared insatiable. Every year the New Netherland peltry harvest expanded. In the late 1620s, the West India Company averaged just under 13,000 pelts per year from the Hudson; by the 1650s the annual take exceeded 45,000. The volume of trade goods shipped from Amsterdam increased every year beginning in the late 1620s, and archaeological excavations have found Dutch pottery, a principal commodity in the trade, as far west as Syracuse.

The most common Dutch trade goods, however, were metal objects, such as iron axes, hatchets, awls, needles, nails, fishhooks, knives, files, hoes, traps, and kettles. Cloth goods, such as blankets of various types and coarse hempen fabrics, were also in great demand. Liquor was part of virtually every transaction, either as a trade good or a gift to facilitate negotiation. Alcohol's deleterious effects on Native Americans are well documented. In the 1630s, the Dutch added muskets, powder, and shot to their trade and succeeded within a decade in arming the Iroquois to the teeth.

The fur trade created a consumer market for Dutch trade goods among Native Americans and helped speed the demise of Indian crafts. West India Company officials and private citizens took advantage of the market to acquire land. In the 1630s, the Dutch negotiated astounding deals, acquiring thousands of square miles of Indian territory for small quantities of metal products, cloth goods, liquor, and firearms.

The Patroonship System

The effects of the fur trade began to be seen only in the 1620s, when shareholders in the Amsterdam Chamber were presented with a new approach to colonization. The debate in the chamber between the faction led by Kiliaen Van Rensselaer and those he called the "contrary minded" revealed the paradoxical goals of the company's land policy in New Netherland.

Kiliaen Van Rensselaer. *Dictionary of American Portraits*, Dover, 1967. Courtesy of New-York Historical Society.

Van Rensselaer's initial investment in the West India Company was large, at least 6,000 fl., because he was designated a *hoofdparticipant* or principal shareholder. Only the principal shareholders could vote for chamber directors, and only principal shareholders were eligible to be directors. Although not part of the original directorate, he became a director when a vacancy occurred in 1625. As a director, he sat on the New Netherland Commission, where he soon made his presence felt.

For Van Rensselaer, a rich and influential Amsterdam jeweler, New Netherland was an obsession. From the moment of his arrival on the board of directors, he pressed for an agricultural colony on the Hudson. He had become convinced that the company's preoccupation with the fur trade kept the colony from prospering. His solution was a manorial system, and he eventually persuaded the company to adopt one.

The *patroonschappen*, or patroonships, were private fiefdoms owned and managed by the patroons for themselves and their investors. Tenants worked the land, ground the patroon's grain, and paid rent. They also had to obey his rules and appear in his court if accused of a crime. The first plan emerged from a subcommittee in 1628, but it was replaced by a more generous one on June 7, 1629.

The plan had the unwieldy name of "Freedoms and Exemptions for Patroons, Masters and Private Individuals, who will Settle any Colonies and Cattle in New Netherland." Put simply, the Freedoms and Exemptions offered land grants to patroons who, at their own expense, settled "within the space of four years, fifty souls, upwards of fifteen years old" on their estates. The company was particularly concerned that proper title was obtained from the Indians, whose good will was necessary to the fur trade.

Since water was the most efficient means of transportation and the key to the fur trade, the directors defined the size of the estates by river or coastal frontage. The patroonships were enormous, even by seventeenth-century standards; "four leagues [about twelve statute miles] along the coast or one side of a navigable river, or two leagues [six miles] along both sides of a river." From a river or coastline the patroon's domain was to extend "as far inland as the situation of the occupiers shall permit."

Patroons were given almost unlimited power over their tenants. The company farms and warehouses could not employ or give shelter to a patroon's tenant without written permission from the patroon. In matters of law the patroon's court had "high, middle, and low jurisdiction" and thus authority over capital crimes. These powers were somewhat restricted by the provision that allowed defendants in cases involving 50 fl. or more the right of appeal to the company commander at New Amsterdam. The Freedoms and Exemptions also gave the patroons the authority to appoint all magistrates within their domains and to confer titles upon their subjects.

The company subsidized the patroonships with low freight rates and credit. Cattle and farm implements were transported at company expense. The patroons complained later that this was an empty gesture, since company ships were in short supply and space aboard limited. The solution to the shipping shortage was in the clause that permitted the patroons to outfit their own ships, provided they took along a company supercargo. Kiliaen Van Rensselaer and the other patroons used this loophole to establish their own private trade network in the colony.

Patroons could also engage in the fur trade in areas where the company did not maintain a factor. This provision opened most of the colony to the patroons' agents and ships. The company required traders to take their furs first to Manhattan to be inventoried and assessed one guilder per pelt, but in cases of "contrary currents or otherwise," patroons were given permission to sail directly to the fatherland with their cargoes. Upon arrival in Holland the patroons were obligated to notify the company so that the cargo could be recorded and a 5 percent tax exacted. The "contrary minded" directors would later charge that the patroons used this clause to defraud the company of its revenue.

Patroons were also allowed to transport fish to "neutral lands." A company supercargo was supposed to be aboard all fishing vessels departing for the Mediterranean, but the sheer size of the potential trade defied regulation. Bribery and fraud were destined to make the fishing concession an open door for smuggling furs and tobacco to Europe. Patroons took advantage of this clause to earn profits even while their efforts to establish colonists on their patroonships languished.

The Freedoms and Exemptions also established rights and privileges for another class of landowner in New Netherland, the "private persons [who] on their own account, shall be inclined to go thither and settle." These individuals were to be allotted "as much land as they shall be able properly to improve." Possession of the land carried other rights, such as the right to hunt and fowl and to improve the land with the construction of fisheries or salt pans that would be the owner's as "absolute property, to the exclusion of all others." Private colonists, like the patroons, could also carry fish (presumably cod from the Grand Banks) to Italy and could collect prearranged finder's fees if they uncovered "any minerals, precious stones, crystals, marbles or such like, or any pearl fisheries." The source of this wealth, however, belonged to the patroon on whose land it was found.

The company promised to defend the colonists "against all foreign and domestic wars and violence" but placed responsibility for providing a minister and schoolmaster in the hands of the patroons. In the meantime so "that the service of God and zeal for religion may not be neglected among them," the patroons were ordered to provide a comforter of the sick (*ziekentrooster*).

The brief reference to religion and education marks a major shift in company policy. Religion and education were necessary elements in the establishment of a Dutch community in New Netherland. The penny-pinching "contrary minded" directors, who had wanted to keep New Netherland the site of a few trading posts with small agricultural support bases, had lost. Kiliaen Van Rensselaer and his soon-to-be fellow patroons Samuel Godijn and Samuel Blommaert envisaged a permanent colony inhabited by European women and children. They would not be employees of the company but tenant farmers and artisans, who worked the patroons' fields and granaries, and private merchants and traders, whose ownership of their own land made them independent.

The publication of the Freedoms and Exemptions set off a flurry of activity. Van Rensselaer, Godijn, and Blommaert had already staked out sites in New Netherland in January. Van Rensselaer's site was near Fort Orange on the Hudson; Godijn's proposed estate was on the banks of the Delaware River; Blommaert had his eye on the Connecticut Valley. Michael Pauw filed a claim for his patroonship of "Pavonia," centered at Ahisimus, near present-day Jersey City. Albert Burgh received a patroonship not far from Godijn's near the mouth of the Delaware River.

Of these only Rensselaerswyck, 150 miles distant from New Amsterdam near Fort Orange, succeeded in outliving the company that created it. Its success amid the failure of others is testimony to the indefatigable efforts of Kiliaen Van Rensselaer and his sons and nephew, who inherited the manor after the jeweler's death in 1643.

Rensselaerswyck was created in 1629, when Kiliaen Van Rensselaer's agent, Bastiaen Jansz Krol, purchased land from the Mahican tribes near Fort Orange. Within a year, stables were erected and a farm started; the patroon's cattle grazed in newly cleared meadows, and about twenty tenants lived in the patroon's houses. By 1632 the patroonship had three expansive farms and a large herd of cattle that kept the tannery busy and supplied the local inhabitants with hides for shoes, boots, and saddles. In the 1640s Van Rensselaer added a brewery and hired Evert Pels to operate it. Gristmills were functioning in the 1630s, and six sawmills produced finished lumber. In 1652 the village of Beverwyck was carved out of the patroonship to provide an independent municipal government for the people who lived on Rensselaerswyck land near the walls of Fort Orange. The patroonship's geographic extent was staggering, something over one million acres. It was probably the largest privately owned estate in North America in the seventeenth century.

Samuel Godijn's story is perhaps illustrative of the problems faced by the other patroons. Godijn and his partners, Van Rensselaer and Blommaert, selected the Delaware River area as the site for Swanendael. (The patroons needed partners to bear the initial cost of setting up their patroonships. Even Van Rensselaer was unable to lay his hands on enough cash and credit to equip a colony fully from his own resources. Godijn, Blommaert, Burgh, and Pauw were partners of Van Rensselaer, although his was the largest investment and the controlling capital in the partnership. Later when Rensselaerswyck began to prosper, the old partners demanded their rights, but for the most part Rensselaerswyck was Kiliaen's dream and his success.) Godijn eventually added several other partners to his patroonship, including the famed popularizer of Dutch overseas expansion and West India Company director Johannes de Laet and the explorer and ship's captain David de Vries.

Godijn's patroonship, Swanendael, was organized in 1630 as a whaling station and agricultural colony. The tract of land, running some twenty-four miles from the bay to Cape Henlopen, was purchased from three Indian sachems, representatives of the Lenape or Delaware Indians. Godijn was also involved in a scheme to colonize Tortuga Island in the West Indies. He and his partners prepared a dual purpose expedition to take sixty Huguenot peasants, all men, and their livestock to the Island of Tortuga, and, leaving there, sail to the Delaware with a handful of carpenters, artisans, and farmers to build a fort and begin planting crops.

Things went badly from the beginning. The ship carrying most of the employees destined for the Delaware was captured by pirates. The other ship, slower and heavily laden with huge granite blocks, heavy timbers, and forged iron braces for the fort at Swanendael, escaped capture, but when the men arrived at Tortuga, all that greeted them were the burned-out remains of the small settlement of Hollanders. A Spanish squadron had destroyed the colony some months earlier. The *Walvis*, under the command of Pieter Heyes, sailed to the Delaware.

Heyes put the Huguenot peasants ashore and offloaded the building materials. The Huguenots began clearing land for their crops, and the partnership's construction engineer, Gilles Honset, set about building the fort from plans he had drawn up in Amsterdam. The masonry redoubt was christened Fort Oplandt. All was in order when Captain Heyes set sail for the fatherland.

A few months later news reached Amsterdam that the settlement on the Delaware had been wiped out by local natives. The attack was a result of a misunderstanding between the settlers and the Indians. The colonists demanded justice for an Indian who had been accused of stealing a metal boundary marker. When the local sachem delivered the culprit's severed head to the compound, the settlers were shocked and accused the Indians of savagery. The reaction so surprised the sachem that he decided the Dutch could not be trusted. An attack in the spring of 1631 killed all thirty-two men who had been set ashore the previous year.

The news nearly shattered the partnership. After some wrangling over how to proceed, Godijn and his partners decided to send David de Vries, one of the patroons, to the Delaware to survey the loss. De Vries arrived in the first week of December 1631. His report described a grisly scene. The fort was burned out, and its roof sagged on one side. Dismembered human skeletons, ravaged by animal scavengers, littered the frozen fields. Around the perimeter of the compound lay the carcasses of the cattle, frozen stiff in bizarre positions. A few tobacco plants and the withered stalks of a once thriving corn field were all that remained of the hard work of the Huguenots.

The loss of the colony was one of many reverses suffered by Godijn and his partners in the 1630s. When the West India Company offered to buy back the patroonship for a small sum, the partners accepted. The other patroons suffered similar setbacks, and by 1636 all but Kiliaen Van Rensselaer had quit.

The failure of the patroon system as well as problems elsewhere in the West India Company's domain compelled the directors in 1640 to try once more to attract private investment in New Netherland. By giving up the fur trade monopoly and offering land on easy terms to small farmers and artisans, the revised Freedoms and Exemptions of 1640 completed the process that had started in 1628. The series of disasters and scandals in the 1630s forced the final concessions.

Foreign Threats and Indian Wars

The malaise that settled over New Netherland in the 1630s may be attributed not only to the failure of the patroonship system but also to the quality of leadership that prevailed in New Amsterdam. At the beginning of the decade, Kili-aen Van Rensselaer and his partners controlled the directorate of the Amster-dam Chamber. When Pieter Minuit quit in 1631 to pursue other adventures, Bastiaen Jansz Krol, Van Rensselaer's land agent, was appointed director of the colony. Thanks to Krol's effective negotiation with the Mahicans and Mohawks, Rensselaerswyck's boundaries expanded to cover both sides of the Hudson River with Fort Orange at its center on the western bank. In 1633, how-ever, Krol was replaced by Wouter Van Twiller, Van Rensselaer's incompetent and alcoholic nephew.

Van Twiller, a company clerk of limited experience, faced a difficult assign-ment. England was beginning to take notice of the colony on the Hudson, and English colonists were crowding Dutch fur traders in the Connecticut Valley. English vessels had penetrated the Hudson's "no trade zone," and the Dutch ship that returned Minuit to the Netherlands had even been detained at New Plymouth for illegally trading in "English America."

Such incidents were just the beginning of an Anglo-Dutch rivalry that brought the nations to war three times in the seventeenth century. These con-flicts were fought all over the world, from the Spice Islands of Indonesia to the English Channel and from the West Indies to the Hudson. In North America, the rivalry first flared in the Connecticut Valley, where a booming fur trade brought the Dutch and English into competition.

The Connecticut River Valley was a wilderness in the 1630s, inhabited by two bands of Algonquian-speaking Indians: the Mohegan of the lower valley and the Pequot, whose territory included northeastern Connecticut and Rhode Island. As early as 1624 the West India Company had attempted to lay claim to the fur trade of the area by settling a few Walloon families near the mouth of the river. Both tribes traded with itinerant Dutch traders after the evacuation of the satellite outpost on the Connecticut in 1626, but the annual peltry harvest reaching New Amsterdam from the valley was small.

Interest in the Connecticut Valley never waned among the patroons, but it may have been difficulties in the fur trade elsewhere in New Netherland that moved the directors to order Van Twiller to secure it with a fort. Everywhere in New Netherland, the Dutch were experiencing what appeared to be an ominous decline in the volume of pelts caused by competition and Indian rebellion. At Fort Orange, competition from the French caused a steep decrease in the peltry take. During this period the company changed its policy of strict neutrality in wars among Indians. In an effort to stem the loss of furs to the Saint Lawrence, the company moved to establish a firm alliance with the Mohawks.

With the Indians of the Connecticut Valley the Dutch took a number of approaches. During Van Twiller's administration, the company succeeded in acquiring title to the valley from the Pequots in 1633 in exchange for metal goods, liquor, and cloth, but the title was never recognized by the English.

When news reached Massachusetts Bay of the building of a Dutch fort named Good Hope, on the Connecticut River near present-day Hartford, Governor John Winthrop wrote a sternly worded letter to Director Van Twiller warning the Dutch governor not to erect any fortifications in the valley lest such a move be "misinterpreted."

Van Twiller tried to defend Dutch claims around Fort Good Hope with a show of force, but ultimately it was impossible to stem the tide of English immigrants. With the establishment of the English post at Fort Saybrook at the mouth of the Connecticut River, the Dutch were effectively cut off from their support base at New Amsterdam. English traders and increasingly English farmers clashed with the Dutch traders around Fort Good Hope. Although the company maintained its fort for years, the Pequot War of 1636–37 cleared the way for the English to settle the Connecticut Valley.

One year before the outbreak of that conflict, the company commander at Fort Orange, Marten Gerritsen, sent out an expedition into the Mohawk River Valley to secure a trading relationship with the Mohawks and their allies in the Iroquois league. It was headed by twenty-three-year-old Harmen Meyndertsz Van den Bogaert, the barber-surgeon at Fort Orange. His journal of the trek through the Mohawk Valley is the first European account of the northern Iroquoians.

Traveling by foot in the dead of winter, Van den Bogaert and his companions struggled through waist-high snow in the pine bush barrens west of Fort Orange. On the third day out of Fort Orange they came upon a village of "36 houses, row on row in the manner of streets." Its neat streets and well-constructed longhouses fascinated Van den Bogaert. He personally paced off the length of several of the structures and reported that some were greater than one hundred steps. He estimated their height to be about twenty-three feet. Their interior doors made of split planks with iron hinges impressed him, as did their storage areas bulging with maize. Most of the men were away on the hunt. Only one chief remained; he lived in a separate cabin at some distance from the village, because, in the words of Van den Bogaert, "many Indians here in the castle had died of smallpox."

The introduction of old world pathogens into immunologically vulnerable Indian populations is part of what historians have come to call the "Columbian Exchange," the interplay of culture, products, and disease between the European invaders and the native population of the Americas. The "virgin-soil epidemics," sparked by Old World germs, set in motion the greatest demographic decline in the history of the species. From Hudson Bay to Tierra del Fuego, wherever European or African germs found haven in the New World, there followed lethal epidemics.

The Mohawk may have acquired their smallpox in their dealings with the Dutch at Fort Orange or from the Algonquian tribes in New England, who had suffered earlier epidemics. The epidemics reaching the Iroquois in the 1630s had already rolled over the coastal Indians. Measles was probably one of the first gifts received by the native Americans who welcomed Hudson. Smallpox and other "poxes" as well as respiratory ailments became common among coastal bands of Algonquians after prolonged contact with Europeans.

In 1649, Adriaen Van der Donck expressed the belief that the Indians of New Netherland had been "ten times as numerous as they now are" before the coming of Europeans and "before the small pox broke out amongst them." The Indians he talked to affirmed that "their population had been melted down by this disease, whereof nine-tenths of them have died."

Such estimates were once dismissed as exaggerations, but the science of epidemiology suggests they may not be far off the mark. In virgin-soil epidemics the mortality rate is initially high, sometimes reaching 90 percent or more. Forty years after Hudson sailed into New York Bay the population of Indians who had been in almost constant contact with Europeans may have experienced mortality of this magnitude. Van den Bogaert's brief reference to smallpox among the Mohawk in the early 1630s indicates that the once isolated Iroquois were no longer safe from the ravages of the Columbian Exchange. The epidemiological frontier had moved into Iroquoia.

Nine days out of Fort Orange the travelers came to another Mohawk fortified village where their appearance caused quite a stir. The Indians of this region had had access to European products through Indian intermediaries, but they were clearly unfamiliar with Europeans. Van den Bogaert attempted to entice these Indians into the trading orbit of Fort Orange, aware that similar overtures were being made by the French. He returned to Fort Orange without an agreement, but he had traveled farther into Iroquoia than any other Dutch official to that time. His report was read by Marten Gerritsen and passed on to Van Twiller in New Amsterdam. In subsequent years company agents from Fort Orange would penetrate the Mohawk Valley and conclude an alliance with the powerful Mohawks.

The Dutch-Mohawk alliance set off a decade of violence known as the "beaver wars," which pitted the Mohawks and their allies against the Huron and other "French Indians" whose hunting grounds the Mohawks coveted. Driven by Europe's insatiable demand for furs and increasingly dependent on the Dutch for the trade goods they could no longer do without, the Mohawks struck out west and northwest to enlarge their hunting grounds. Thus, while the Dutch-Mohawk alliance meant peace to the Hudson Valley, it encouraged war almost everywhere else.

Meanwhile in New Amsterdam, Van Twiller's alcoholism caused several near disasters. On one occasion, while celebrating the gift of a bottle of claret, the director invited his staff to a drinking contest. At the end of the evening, long after the claret had been consumed, he opened a keg of cheap brandy. A fight erupted among his inebriated guests and to break it up, Van Twiller fired off a cannon in the middle of the compound. A spark from the powder ignited the roof of a nearby building, and the immobilized crowd watched the structure burn to the ground. The fort itself might have caught fire had not others responded to the alarm with a bucket brigade.

The directors of the Amsterdam Chamber were informed of such incidents by Van Twiller's many enemies. The director's close relationship with his uncle, Kiliaen Van Rensselaer, was a point of much grumbling in the colony. When the company's *schout-fiscaal* (a combination customs officer and chief accountant), Lubbertus Van Dinclage, complained that the director had illegally sold company cattle to Rensselaerswyck, Van Twiller threw him in jail. After bribing his jailer, Van Dinclage escaped to Virginia, where he caught a ship for Europe. When he finally arrived in Amsterdam, Van Rensselaer's opponents had him tell his story before a notary. They used the testimony and that of others to bring about Van Twiller's recall in late 1637. His replacement, Willem Kieft, arrived in the new year.

Kieft's appointment as director general of New Netherland marked the eclipse of the patroons in the Amsterdam Chamber. A former merchant, he was sent out to rescue the company's investment in the colony and to bring discipline back to company employees. He had barely settled at New Amsterdam when word arrived from Fort Nassau (on the east side of the Delaware River) that Pieter Minuit, former director general of New Netherland, had appeared in Delaware Bay at the head of a Swedish expedition.

Minuit, after assembling as many of the local sachems as he could, had negotiated and acquired two large tracts of land: one extending north from the Minquaes Kill to the Schuyl Kill (present-day Philadelphia); and one extending south to Bombay Hook. Construction of a fort on the west side of the river, christened Fort Christina after the Swedish queen, effectively screened the Dutch from the interior fur trade.

Kieft recognized at once the seriousness of the threat and penned an angry letter to Minuit, warning him that the colony would not be "suffered." The director general was not prepared, however, to support his words with military force. Moreover, since so much Dutch capital was tied up in the Swedish venture, there was little demand by the directors in Amsterdam to proceed quickly against New Sweden. In fact, the Swedish company was the brainchild of Willem Usselinx, an Antwerp merchant living in Amsterdam.

In 1623 Usselinx proposed a national trading company to Gustavus II Adolphus, king of Sweden. The king was impressed and commissioned Usselinx to form an international trading company chartered in Sweden. The Thirty Years War and the unexpected death of Gustavus II Adolphus held up the founding of the company for nearly ten years, but when circumstances once more permitted a reconsideration of the plan, there was little trouble in acquiring capital.

By secret partnership agreement, Samuel Blommaert, the wealthy merchant, sometime patroon, and director of the Amsterdam Chamber, agreed to form a syndicate of Dutch investors to subscribe half the capital. Blommaert may have been angry with the faction in the chamber that was opposed to the patroons. He was in an excellent position to know the state of affairs in New Netherland and the probability of success in the poorly defended Delaware Valley. Blommaert's investment in the New Sweden Company would raise questions about his patriotism, but no one questioned his business sense. The Delaware Valley provided access into the interior of America, a taproot of the fur trade that had yet to be seized effectively by a European power. Blommaert and his fellow Dutch merchants were only hedging their bets.

The presence of New Sweden embarrassed and frustrated two director generals of New Netherland. Blommaert and his fellow investors came under increasing pressure to dissolve their holdings in the Swedish company. The company did not go begging, however. The initial profits from the fur and tobacco trade drew many investors. By 1641 all the shares once held by Dutch investors had been bought back.

Kieft, of course, was not aware of the intimate ties between the directors of the Dutch West India Company and the New Sweden Company, but he could do little more than write angry letters, because New Netherland was soon to be engulfed in a protracted and bloody war with the Algonquian bands around Manhattan. New Sweden would have to wait until after the "pacification" of the coastal tribes.

New Netherland's Indian troubles began on September 15, 1639, when Kieft, under pressure from the directors in Amsterdam, decided to tax the Indians of the lower Hudson by exacting a tribute in pelts, maize, and wampum. Such measures were called for, according to Kieft, because the company had been "put to great expense both in building fortifications, supporting soldiers and sailors," and protecting the Indians "against their enemies."

The irony of taxing the Indians for the occupation of their land was missed by everyone but the Indians. Thirty years of contact with Europeans had taken its toll on the once numerous Algonquians of the lower Hudson estuary. Decimated by epidemics and crowded off their land, they found it increasingly difficult to escape contact with Europeans, especially after 1640 when new Freedoms and Exemptions were issued by the company to encourage European immigration to the underpopulated colony by opening up the fur trade and liberalizing the "patroonship" system to allow smaller and more restricted estates. Even more important, free land was offered to colonists who wished to settle permanently in the colony. As hundreds of new immigrants poured through New Amsterdam, towns sprang up on Long Island and across the Hudson.

To Europeans, Indian agriculture appeared inefficient and untidy. "They know nothing of ploughing, spading, and spitting up the soil, and are not neat and cleanly in their fields," observed one Dutchman. "They usually leave their fields and garden spots open, unenclosed, and unprotected by fencing, and take very little care of the same."

Native American farmers, without access to draught animals or plows, had evolved an agriculture that was intensive rather than extensive. Most commonly, several food plants were grown in the same plot of ground in mounds. For example, Indians often planted beans in the same mound with young maize and used the corn stalks as trellises. Later in the same season the mounds were replanted with pumpkins and squash.

The arrival of domestic animals from Europe transformed agriculture in New Netherland. Draught animals, harnessed to plows and wagons, enabled European farmers to vastly increase the acreage under cultivation. Livestock also set in motion a secondary economy based on processing domestic animals for food and hides. Cattle, oxen, horses, goats, sheep, and the ubiquitous hog accompanied Dutch farmers wherever they settled in New Netherland. And everywhere there were complaints from the Indians that their crops were being damaged. The destruction of Indian crops by semi-feral European livestock was a constant source of conflict by the 1630s.

In May 1640, Raritan Indians killed several hogs on Staten Island in retaliation for destruction done to their corn crop. Kieft and his council met to consider "serious complaints made by the Indians that their corn hills are trampled under foot and uprooted by hogs and other cattle." After some deliberation Kieft issued an ordinance to charge and command "all our inhabitants whose lands adjoin plantations of the savages to have their horses, cows, hogs, goats and sheep herded or else to prevent them by fences or otherwise from damaging the corn of the Indians." But for the Raritans it was too little and too late. In June the killing of European livestock increased, and in July Kieft declared war on the Raritans and embarked upon a campaign of genocide that threatened the coastal Algonquians with extermination.

The Dutch sent an expedition of fifty soldiers and twenty sailors in the summer of 1640 on a murdering and pillaging sweep through Raritan villages on Staten Island and elsewhere. Burning cornfields, sacking villages, and murdering women and children, the Dutch were able to drag a few sachems to the peace table. The Raritans were astounded to be asked to pay reparations.

The truce held until the following summer when a band of Raritans killed four tobacco farmers and burned a house and barn on Staten Island. Conceiving the incident as part of a general uprising, Kieft sought to draw the Indians of Long Island and the lower Hudson into an alliance that would protect New Amsterdam from attack. He persuaded the council to offer a bounty of "ten fathoms [sixty feet] of seawan [wampum]" for every head of a Raritan Indian delivered to him at Fort Amsterdam or twenty fathoms for the head of one of the warriors who had murdered the tobacco farmers.

Later that same year a wheelwright was murdered by an Indian who had come to his house to trade. When the director general demanded that the murderer be given up to Dutch authorities, a Raritan sachem replied "that he was sorry twenty Christians had not been murdered."

As alarm swept through the villages of New Amsterdam, Kieft decided to establish a council of "heads of families and householders" to advise him on the Indian rebellion. The Twelve Men, as they came to be called, recommended to Kieft that he lull the Indians into a sense of security by continuing to trade with them "until the opportunity presents itself and the will of God be made manifest." In the meantime two hundred coats of mail were requested from Fort Orange, and the director was advised to employ "as many Negroes from among the strongest and fleetest, and provide them each with a hatchet and a half-pike." The following year Kieft led a force of company soldiers and slaves, accompanied by local militias, on a rampage through Indian villages around New Amsterdam.

The last rebellion of Kieft's administration began in 1643, when a party of Mohawks traveled down the Hudson to exact tribute from a band of Wappingers. Most of the Wappingers fled to the old patroonship of Pavonia (near present-day Jersey City). Others made it to Fort Amsterdam, where they begged the protection of the Dutch. Kieft was not about to risk the lucrative alliance with the Mohawks to protect the Wappingers. Not only did he refuse protection, but he encouraged the Mohawks to take their revenge. After a Mohawk war party killed seventy Wappingers and took others as hostages, Kieft ordered the soldiers and militia to finish off the remaining refugees, including women and children. When dawn finally broke on the grisly scene all but thirty of the Wappingers were dead. The soldiers marched triumphantly back to Fort Amsterdam.

The slaughter at the "battle of Pavonia" enraged the coastal Indians. Farms were abandoned all over New Netherland, as outlying settlements came under attack. Boats crossing to Manhattan were filled with refugees. Indians even killed livestock on the farms north of the fort. To protect the livestock, Kieft issued a call for cattle owners to appear with tools on Monday, April 4, 1644, ready to build "a fence, palisade, or enclosure, beginning from the great bouwery to Emmanuel's plantation." The wall, as it came to be called, traversed a line roughly that of present-day Wall Street. It was intended to provide safe pasture for cattle.

The rebellion continued for months until a combined army of company soldiers and Dutch and English militia under the command of Captain John Underhill (a veteran of the Pequot War) set out on a relentless search-and-destroy campaign. The little army tracked down isolated bands of Indians and destroyed cornfields and villages. Three large Indian encampments were wiped out: two on Long Island and one in Connecticut. The tactics often involved striking a village while most of the men were away hunting. After surrounding the encampment and cutting off all avenues of retreat, the soldiers set the houses on fire. When the terrified Indians attempted to escape, they were usually slaughtered. After the killing, the village and cornfields were burned. A small number of prisoners were held to ransom Europeans at the conclusion of peace.

In 1645, exhausted, demoralized, and facing starvation the "River Indians" agreed to "a firm and inviolable peace." The treaty was signed in a formal ceremony before a Mohawk delegation at Fort Amsterdam on August 30. Representatives from at least ten tribes of the lower Hudson estuary appeared in New Amsterdam to conclude the peace. The next day Kieft proclaimed a day of thanksgiving throughout New Netherland and called on the colony's clergy to prepare special sermons for Wednesday, September 6.

The Indian wars devastated New Netherland. A letter penned by the leading citizens of New Amsterdam described the desperate scene on Manhattan Island. "Our fields lie fallow and waste; our dwellings and other buildings are burnt; not a handful can be either planted or sown this fall on the deserted places; the crops which God the Lord permitted to come forth during the past summer, remain on the field standing and rotting in divers places." Many colonists blamed the director general for the calamities that had befallen New Netherland. In fact, on the day the Indian rebellion ended, Kieft was trying to put down a political rebellion of his board of Eight Men.

The Eight Men had replaced the Twelve Men Kieft had assembled to advise him in his war against the river Indians in 1641. During the war, the Twelve Men asked for popular representation on the council. Kieft dissolved the group. When the Indian rebellions began anew in August 1643, he had no choice but to seek the assistance of the "leading families" once again. The Eight Men turned out, however, to be as difficult to lead as the Twelve, and by the end of the war Kieft had an angry falling out with them. The Eight Men wrote long letters to the directors in Amsterdam complaining of Kieft's conduct of the war and requesting a popular voice in the government. Their efforts eventually led to the company's decision to recall Kieft.

The Old World had arrived rather rudely in the Hudson estuary. New Netherland's polyglot population of northern Europeans, with their lethal germs and landscape-altering domestic animals, had pushed aside a once numerous people. Kieft's genocidal campaign not only hastened the decline of the coastal Algonquians but also opened up huge tracts of land for settlement. During the administration of Peter Stuyvesant, trade would boom, and thousands of new colonists would arrive, while the river Indians all but sank into oblivion.

4

Peter Stuyvesant and the New Immigrants

PETER STUYVESANT'S SEVENTEEN-YEAR ADMINISTRATION was the high-water mark of Dutch colonialism in North America. The end of the Indian uprising and a successful diplomatic effort to establish defensible boundaries with New England brought peace to New Netherland by 1650 and ushered in a period of growth and prosperity. For the first time in its history, New Netherland began to attract numbers of Europeans who wished to settle permanently. The surge in immigration stemmed partly from the West India Company's reevaluation of its North American colony in the light of dismal events in South America.

The Nineteen had sought a colony on the mainland of South America from the commencement of company operations in 1623. In 1624, while the modest plans to bring the Walloons to New Netherland were afoot, the company outfitted a fleet of twenty-three ships to attack Portuguese Brazil. The attack turned out to be an unmitigated disaster. The great fleet was decimated by a storm in mid-Atlantic, and the Portuguese defenders threw the Dutch soldiers back into the sea before they could consolidate their beachhead. Six years later the company returned with a still larger armada financed by Piet Heyn's capture of the Spanish silver fleet, but it would take seven years to pacify Pernambuco (N.E. Brazil). The directors, who had spent millions on the pacification, christened the colony "New Holland."

Governing New Holland's population of Portuguese Catholics proved to be beyond the skills of company officials. In June 1645 the Portuguese inhabitants of New Holland, who chafed under the rule of heretics, rose in rebellion. For the next nine years, the directors squandered most of the company's capital in an attempt to recapture Pernambuco and salvage the dream of a South American empire. Finally, in 1654, the Dutch were expelled from Brazil, and a stream of refugees left New Holland.

The prospects for a Dutch Protestant colony in North America were much better than they were in Brazil. By the late 1640s some directors certainly recognized that the opportunity for securing a foothold in North America was rapidly disappearing. Great Britain had emerged as the United Provinces' greatest rival for maritime trade, and the growth of the English colonies in New England and Virginia meant that New Netherland was surrounded by potential enemies. The appointment of the remarkable Peter Stuyvesant may have been part of the company's reassessment of New Netherland.

Stuyvesant was an experienced company employee who had served as the commissary of stores on the island of Curaçao and later military commander there. Driven by his devout Calvinist faith, Stuyvesant sought to carry the war to the Spanish. When the Spaniards briefly seized Bonaire, shortly after he became commander, he retaliated with an attack on Puerto Cabello on the coast of Venezuela. When his garrison faced starvation in the spring of 1644, he decided to seize the Spanish fort on the island of Saint Martin. The Spanish had just retaken the island from the Dutch and were dug in and well equipped. Disaster struck immediately when Stuyvesant's right leg was shattered by a Spanish cannon ball during the opening artillery exchange. The assault faltered when he was carried from the field near death. Shortly thereafter the expedition withdrew to Curaçao.

Peter Stuyvesant. Engraving by E. G. Williams. From D. H. Bruce, *The Empire State in Three Centuries* (New York, 1898).

The company surgeon on Curaçao performed a successful amputation of Stuyvesant's infected right leg. While he lay recovering, Portuguese rebels routed the Dutch at the battle of São Luis, in Dutch Maranhão, and 450 West India Company soldiers and dependents fled to Curaçao. With his garrison already on partial rations, Stuyvesant had to find a way to preserve the lives of hundreds of his countrymen. He solved the logistical problem by ordering some of the soldiers to New Netherland to assist Willem Kieft with the Indian uprising and dispatching an expedition to the island of Aruba to hunt sea turtles. He might have stayed on Curaçao but for the condition of his leg. After months in the tropical climate the stump had failed to heal properly. Fearing for the young commander's life, the surgeon ordered him home to the fatherland and probable retirement.

Stuyvesant might have retreated to a desk job at the West India House in Amsterdam, or he might have sought a pension and faded away in a country cottage. Perhaps he had something to prove, or perhaps he was simply unwilling to retire at thirty-four. In Amsterdam he lobbied for another post even as his recovery proved difficult and prolonged. Slowly the leg healed and the old vigor returned. In 1647, three years after leaving Curaçao, he stepped ashore in New Amsterdam, fit and anxious to begin work. He would sport a peg leg the rest of his life.

Stuyvesant lost no time in tackling the colony's problems. One of his first official acts was the issuance of an ordinance requiring drinking establishments to close at 9 P.M. daily and to remain closed on Sunday until 2 P.M. when no sermon was being given, or until 4 P.M. on sermon days. New Amsterdam was a hard-drinking town in the 1640s, with more barkeeps than bakers and a population, especially near the wharf, that was mostly male, itinerant, and young. At the end of a long and harrowing voyage, the bars of New Amsterdam proved irresistible to the rough and ready crews of company ships. Stuyvesant and his council recognized the lethal connection between drink and violence when they attached to the ordinance another law "to prevent the all too ready drawing of a knife, fighting, wounding and the mishaps resulting therefrom."

Stuyvesant targeted the town's illegal brewers with another ordinance that clamped down on the private brewing of beer. The ordinance was ignored for the most part, because two years later Stuyvesant was dismayed to find that so much grain was being diverted for beer production that the town faced a bread shortage. He ordered an immediate halt to the use of wheat in brewing.

The director general addressed the problem of taverns and public drunkenness no fewer than four times in his first three years in New Netherland. His frustration was best expressed in the preamble to a comprehensive tavern code in 1648. It stated "that our former orders issued against unreasonable and intemperate drinking at night and on the Sabbath of the Lord, to the shame and derision of ourselves and our nation, are not observed and obeyed." Even worse, the easy profits to be made in tavern keeping diverted the colonists from their first callings in trade and manufacturing. So greedy were the tapsters that "one full fourth of the City of New Amsterdam has been turned into taverns for the sale of brandy, tobacco and beer."

The selling of liquor to Indians was another problem that proved particularly vexing. In one of his first acts as director general, Stuyvesant outlawed liquor sales to Indians, but more than any of the other liquor regulations, this one proved to be a dead letter.

The political squabbles left over from the Kieft administration threatened Stuyvesant's sense of order and precipitated the first crisis of his administration.

The angry exchanges between Kieft and his Board of Twelve (later Eight) Men had paralyzed local administration. Board members charged Kieft with incompetence and their complaints had already reached the directors of the West India Company in Amsterdam. Kieft responded by accusing his critics of disloyalty and cowardice. By the time Stuyvesant arrived the situation had reached an impasse.

Stuyvesant attempted to ignore the simmering feud. His first order of business was to reorganize his council, the advisory committee that also sat with the director general as a court of justice. To the usual complement of company officials that included the commissary (combination company store and record keeper), the *schout* (prosecuting attorney and sheriff), and the *fiscal* (company secretary), Stuyvesant added a Board of Nine Men drawn from the leading citizens.

N. J. Visscher's map of New Netherland (ca. 1655). From I. N. Phelps Stokes, *The Iconography of Manhattan Island* (New York, 1915), vol. 1.

The Board of Nine had hardly had time to meet when two of its members approached Stuyvesant demanding a formal investigation of director general Kieft. To their dismay Stuyvesant exploded in a rage and charged the men with lese majesty. The controversy was referred to the company directors in the fatherland, but the ship transporting Kieft and his antagonists sank in a gale. Kieft drowned, but the two men survived to receive their hearing before the directors. By that time, however, the issue was moot.

European Immigrants

Stuyvesant's success in bringing stability to the colony's government, coupled with a well-orchestrated company campaign of pamphlets and broadsides, resulted in a surge of immigration in the late 1650s that more than doubled New Netherland's European population, which approached 9,000 by 1664. By the time of Stuyvesant's arrival in 1647 that population already was the most heterogeneous of any European colony in North America. Over the years the company had added to the clannish, French-speaking Walloons of the 1620s small numbers of farmers, soldiers, sailors, and traders drawn from the United Provinces and elsewhere in Europe. This vanguard of colonists consisted mostly of young men, who had come as employees of the company and later settled on farms on Manhattan Island or elsewhere. Others came as indentured servants, under contract for four to seven years, to work the farms of the company or to serve as tenants on one of the patroonships. Still others, lured by the romance of the fur trade, came looking for adventure. Of these, a few became *boslopers* (forest runners) and deserted "civilization" to live among the Indians. Most returned to the fatherland or moved on to another colony.

Those who stepped off ships at New Amsterdam in the 1650s, however, were a different lot, consisting largely of families. Their average size of 4.2 persons was significantly larger than the 3.72 average of Dutch families in the United Provinces. Nearly 70 percent of those arriving in New Amsterdam between 1657 and 1664 came as part of households headed by married couples; this included the great majority of those who arrived as indentures. Forty-three families in a sample of 176 households had four or more children, representing nearly a quarter of all families arriving in this period. In the fatherland, such large families constituted only 14 percent of all households. The lumping at the end of the family size scale suggests that immigrants to New Netherland in the late 1650s were, by and large, young and vigorous. Excluding the parents of the large families from the sample, over 61 percent appear to have been under twenty-five years of age.

The immigrants of the late 1650s included a surprisingly large number of "foreigners," about 25 percent in the sample. Foreign born (i.e., non-Dutch) comprised nearly half the European population of New Netherland at the time of the English conquest in 1664. Most of these colonists had sailed from Amsterdam, or occasionally Rotterdam, in company chartered ships. While the ships sat in port waiting for a full cargo or favorable wind, some of the immigrants appeared before Amsterdam notaries to have their promissory notes, wills, and other business papers notarized and made legal.

Whether the immigrants were Dutch or foreign, the notarial records reveal people who planned to stay permanently in America. Captains complained that their ships were overloaded with the colonists' worldly goods, and freightage contracts reveal that despite the high costs, most colonists struggled to pay the freight for their tools and cherished pieces of furniture. They appeared before the notaries to clear up old debts, collect money, and sever the legal ties that bound them to their old lives. The legalese of the notary can only hint at the deep emotional situations the records disclosed: a widowed father starting a new life by giving up his rights to a daughter in an orphanage; a son signing over to his brother a claim to a parent's estate; a pastor certifying the moral rectitude of a *ziekentrooster* (comforter of the sick), or a merchant dissolving a partnership with an old friend.

The voyage itself was ceaselessly unpleasant and frequently dangerous. The average crossing lasted seven weeks, and those making stops in Curaçao or elsewhere in the Caribbean could expect a three-month ordeal. Many died on the voyage; others had their health so broken that they failed to lift themselves above poverty in their new homes. Shipboard deaths fell heavily among the young, and many families arrived in New Amsterdam mourning the loss of a child. With all they owned and everything they could borrow, they came from the fatherland, the Germanies, France, England, Sweden, and Finland. It would be the largest European migration in the Dutch period.

One of the problems already facing Dutch authorities was the uneven distribution of European nationalities and ethnic groups in the colony. Eastern Long Island absorbed so many immigrants from New England in the 1640s that the region had become ethnically English. Knitting these Europeans into the Dutch fabric of New Netherland life was not easy. Stuyvesant undertook a personal embassy to Hartford in 1650 to conclude a treaty that conceded the eastern part of Long Island to the English, and he found it necessary to employ an English-speaking council member to communicate with the English towns on western Long Island. Of all the Europeans in New Netherland, the English were the most successful in resisting assimilation into the predominantly Dutch culture that came to bind together a wide variety of French, Germanic, and Scandinavian groups. The English villagers on Long Island remained loyal to their own institutional forms and grew to resent Stuyvesant for meddling in their affairs.

Other Europeans in New Netherland proved to be more tractable. Among the Swedes and Finns of the Delaware Valley, who were to fall to Dutch conquest in 1655, resistance was weak. The large number of ethnically Dutch colonists already living there and the similarities between the Dutch and Swedish languages in the seventeenth century may have assisted in the easy transition from Swedish to Dutch rule. Amsterdam's sponsorship of a large colonizing expedition in the years following the conquest also helped to swamp the Swedish and Finnish minorities in a flood tide of families from the fatherland.

In the 1650s yet another group of Europeans were added to New Netherland's ethnic mix. Dutch Jews, who had settled in Pernambuco in the 1640s, found themselves refugees after the collapse of Dutch Brazil in 1654. Destitute and homeless, twenty-three of them made their way to New Amsterdam only to be met with a wall of antisemitism from both the director general and the Reformed clergy. Their presence in the colony would bring about a crisis between church and state and help define a measure of toleration unique in colonial America (see Chapter 5).

Dutch Slavery and the Arrival of Africans

The next largest group of immigrants arriving in these years were Africans. The first Africans had arrived much earlier, perhaps as early as 1626. The exact date is uncertain, because the only reference to Africans being in New Netherland in that year comes from a document in 1644 which referred to slaves who had served in the colony "18 or 19 years." The most trustworthy evidence of Africans in the colony in the late 1620s comes from a letter of the Reverend Jonas Michaëlius, who confirmed the presence of African women slaves when he complained that he could not find women caretakers for his daughters because maid servants were not to be had and "the Angola slave women are thievish, lazy, and useless trash."

Most of these slaves were the booty of war, acquired by the West India Company in raids on Spanish and Portuguese colonies and ships and transported as cargo around the Americas until a buyer was found. Their enslavement had begun years before they arrived at New Amsterdam. Captured in war or kidnapped by their fellow Africans, they were sold to wholesalers who owned the barracoons that dotted the malarial coast of Guinea. After surviving the horrors of the middle passage, they were sold again in the Americas to Spanish or Portuguese masters. Some were "seasoned" on the sugar cane plantations of the West Indies. Others may have passed from hand to hand in a system that moved humans like cargo around the Spanish Main. They had been destined for short brutal lives under conditions that were the worst in the hemisphere. By the fortunes of war they found themselves in New Netherland.

The story of New Netherland's African Americans is frustratingly difficult to tell because of the sparse documentation. Their names appear fleetingly in the official records of the colony as litigants in court cases or parties to notarized agreements. In private records they occasionally appear as property in probate cases, or on bills of sale and manumission documents. Sometimes they were topics of concern for their masters and appear in private correspondence. A small percentage of Africans, both freedmen and slaves, had their marriages and baptisms recorded by Dutch ministers. The marriage and baptismal records chart the life cycle of the most acculturated of New Netherland's Africans, those who could function in Dutch and who were sufficiently familiar with Calvinist theology to be certified by the clergy. This admittedly sketchy evidence permits some generalizations.

The first blacks in New Netherland were company slaves, assigned to labor on the company's farms north of the fort. Most probably knew rudimentary Portuguese but could not understand Dutch, and they bore Portuguese names. By the 1630s enslaved Africans were a common sight on Manhattan, where a compound for them was built at company expense. This decade brought increasing numbers of "Spanish slaves" captured in raids along the Spanish Main. Their use of Spanish presented problems for both the company and private masters. The language of New Netherland's slaves by this date was most probably a patois of Spanish, Portuguese, and Dutch. Dutch eventually replaced Spanish and Portuguese as the language of Africans in New Netherland in the 1650s.

In the 1640s company slaves gained a special incentive for learning Dutch. The company began issuing a so-called half freedom release from slavery in return for an annual quitrent. The chances of qualifying for a half freedom were much improved if the slave was certified as Christian by a Dutch Reformed minister. Theoretically this required fluency in the Dutch language, but the first ministers, when confronted by contrite slaves seeking certification of their Christianity, were not always scrupulous in probing the penitents' understanding of theology or the Dutch language. In the last years of Dutch rule, the clergy tightened up the requirements, and the number of blacks baptized, both slave and free, fell off dramatically, from fifty-seven in the period 1639–55 to one in 1656–64. Dominie Henricus Selyns summed up the new attitude when he complained in 1664 that "we were sometimes asked by the negroes to baptize their children, but we refused, partly because of their lack of knowledge and faith, and partly because of the material and wrong aim on the part of the afore-mentioned negroes who sought nothing else by it than the freeing of their children from material slavery, without pursuing piety and Christian virtue."

Among some company slaves, Spanish was used into the 1660s and beyond. As late as 1662 a translator was needed in a court case involving a slave named Francisco, who had been seized from a Spaniard in 1652 and sold into slavery on Manhattan. After ten years in the colony, he still could not speak Dutch. In another case, "Domingo the Negro" was called to court to translate for another slave, Jan Angola. Jan's Dutch language skills were simply not up to the task of clearing his name in a complicated suit, even though he had lived among the Dutch for decades.

The demand for slaves was met with at least one direct shipment to New Amsterdam from the Guinea coast. The ship, the *White Horse*, sailed into New Amsterdam and dropped anchor in the roadstead on September 15, 1655. Her three hundred Africans, writhing in the late summer heat, comprised one of the most valuable cargoes ever shipped to the colony. At auction the slaves brought more than 1,200 fl. each. Such prices were more than competitive with those in the West Indies, where Spanish merchants in the late 1650s were willing to pay 150 pieces of eight for male field hands (370 fl.) and 200 pieces of eight (490 fl.) for childbearing couples consisting of a "merchantable Negro and Negress, one with another." The voyage of the *White Horse* must have earned a profit, but direct shipments of slaves from Africa to New Netherland were not common. Most of the slaves imported into New Netherland during the last years of Dutch rule came by way of Curaçao.

In the last half of the seventeenth century the Dutch island of Curaçao became one of the busiest ports of entry for slave ships in the Americas. Dutch participation in the Atlantic slave trade increased dramatically with the capture of the Portuguese slave factory of Elmina on the Guinea coast in 1638. Beginning in the late 1630s, the West India Company aggressively pursued profits in the trade. With the end of the Thirty Years War in 1648 and the expansion of company sugar operations in Brazil, the stage was set for a massive expansion of the Dutch slave trade. When New Holland collapsed, the company fortress on Curacao became the center of operations in the southern Caribbean. Situated just off the coast of Venezuela, the windblown island proved ideal as a distribution center for slaves throughout the Americas.

By the late 1650s the surge in European immigration set off an agricultural boom in New Netherland that extended through the English conquest. The expansion of European small grain agriculture followed the plow, and the plow required cleared land. Wheat farming in particular created seasonal labor demands, especially at harvest, making the colony's chronic labor shortage acute two months each year. Company slaves, who worked their own vegetable gardens and tended livestock the rest of the year, were sometimes hired out to farmers to help with the harvest. The relatively high wages paid to Europeans in New Netherland, itself a reflection of the labor shortage, made the use of rented slaves both logical and profitable. Stuyvesant, the largest slave owner in the colony with about forty slaves, hired his slaves out for all types of labor.

Unlike the experience of slaves in the plantation economies, the work performed by company slaves in New Netherland was not stigmatized as slave labor. Although most slaves worked in agriculture, some served as longshoremen in Manhattan, alongside white laborers. African women appear in the records as domestic servants, although they certainly were not exempt from field work when needed. Women slaves tended to live on more intimate terms with their masters, attending church with the family, caring for the children, and in general living in the embrace of Dutch culture, even as they formed their own families under the flexible provisions of Dutch slavery. In short, slaves in New Netherland had a range of privileges that scarcely seems possible in light of the institution's later history in New York and the rest of colonial America. They could marry and hire themselves out for wages with the permission of their owners. They could farm their own gardens and sell the produce on the open market. They could own livestock and graze their animals on company land. Occasionally they even sued whites in court.

The period of agricultural expansion that brought thousands of Europeans to New Netherland coincided with the beginning of the sugar boom in the West Indies and the spread of tobacco cultivation in the English Chesapeake. Consequently, slaves were in short supply, and prices rose steadily from the end of the Indian rebellions to the English conquest. In the twenty-eight years between 1636 and 1664, for example, the price of field hands in New Amsterdam increased by 600 percent.

Wages of free workers also increased in these years. A farm hand could earn 40 stivers (2 fl.) per day threshing grain in the patroonship of Rensselaerswyck

A vivid illustration of the colony's reliance on slave and free African American labor during this period appears in a cartouche from Matthew Seutter's 1673 map of New Netherland. From I. N. Phelps Stokes, *The Iconography of Manhattan Island* (New York, 1915), vol. 1.

in 1648, while workers in the wheat harvests of 1653 and 1656 could earn 50 stivers per day on the farms around Manhattan. By contrast, the prevailing wage for farm labor in the province of Holland at this time was only 15 to 20 stivers per day. With slaves so valuable, it is a wonder the Dutch freed so many.

On February 25, 1644, Director General Willem Kieft and his council manumitted Paulo Angolo, Big Manuel, Little Manuel, Manuel de Gerrit de Reus, Simon Congo, Antony Portuguese, Gracia, Pieter Santomee, Jan Francisco, Little Antony, and Jan of Fort Orange. In what appears to be an extraordinary act of generosity, the company also freed their wives and gave them land to farm. Some of these were older slaves, who had toiled for "18 or 19 years" in the service of the company. Unless released from that service, they could no longer "support their wives and children as they have been accustomed to in the past." The others were probably in their thirties or forties, recently married, and childless. Their emancipation was neither complete nor free. Each petitioner was obligated under the grant of freedom to "pay annually, 30 schepels [22.5 bushels] of maize, or wheat, pease, or beans, and one fat hog valued at 20 guilders."

The financial obligations were not overwhelming. Although the farms granted the freedmen and their wives were small, between three and six morgens (roughly six to twelve acres), they were large enough to support two people and to pay the quitrent on their freedom. Wheat yields of 81 to 108 schepels per morgen were common in the Hudson Valley, and the farms on Manhattan were the best developed in the colony. The annual payment of a hog did not represent a significant tax either, because hogs proliferated rapidly in New Netherland, and a single hog per year constituted less than 10 percent of the annual output of a good sow.

The last few lines of the 1644 "half freedom" would become the most controversial, although no one raised objections to it at the time. As the final condition of their emancipation the slaves had to give up their children "at present born or yet to be born to serve the honorable West India Company as slaves." Company directors were unprepared for the controversy that erupted some years later when the story of New Netherland's slave children reached the States General. In 1650 their High Mightinesses called in representatives of the West India Company and demanded an explanation of how "contrary to all public law" they had permitted "children of manumitted slaves" to be kept in slavery. The Nineteen passed the question to Stuyvesant, who, in turn, assigned the job of responding to Provincial Secretary Cornelis Van Tienhoven.

Van Tienhoven's carefully worded report was intended to assure his superiors that the children of the former slaves "are treated the same as Christians." Six years after the manumission of their parents only three children remained "in service." One served the company at its trading post on the Connecticut River; another worked for Stuyvesant on the company's farm; and the third worked with Martin Cregier, "who, as everyone knows, brought up the girl." In a first draft of his report Van Tienhoven wrote "[the slaves] were set free on condition that the children remain slaves." On second thought he changed it to read "on condition that their children serve the Company whenever it pleased." Van Tienhoven's report seems to have ended the matter. Further references to the slave children in the colony's records indicate that the company worked out agreements with the parents to release their children in return for cash payments and labor. Perhaps the success of such arrangements was the reason why the company never clarified its policy for dealing with the children of slaves given half freedom.

Scholars have debated the meaning of "half freedom" for years. To some, slavery in New Netherland was a uniquely enlightened form of human bondage that permitted more autonomy to slaves than any other system in the Western Hemisphere. Furthermore, half freedom has been seen as a particularly generous gesture on the part of the West India Company to reward long and faithful service, implicit in which was the idea that loyal service should be rewarded with freedom.

Others have argued that Dutch half freedom was not unique in the seventeenth century. The Portuguese had developed two classes of freedmen in the fifteenth century: the conditionally free or *forro*, who continued to pay a "quit" for their freedom even after manumission, and the *livre* or real freedmen. In the eighteenth century a similar system, perhaps derived from a Portuguese model in the Caribbean, developed in the low country of Georgia and South Carolina. Since both Portuguese and Dutch law were based upon Roman law, and since Rome had a complex system that recognized slaves, half-slaves, and freedmen, it may be that the impulse toward creating a category of half-free laborers was a product of the application of Roman-Dutch law.

In the seventeenth century, various forms of bondage existed side by side in colonial settings all over the Western Hemisphere. The iron cage of chattel slavery had not yet descended on Africans when the Dutch authorities at New Amsterdam grappled with definitions of freedom. Slavery in New Netherland evolved at a time when slave privileges and manumission practices were still in flux. Dutch half freedom may therefore be seen in the context of an evolving system of bound labor and not necessarily as evidence of a more benign and enlightened view of race.

Another consideration in the granting of half freedom may have been the cost of caring for slaves. Slave marriages were recognized by the company in 1644 as was the legitimacy of children born of those marriages. The half freedom, with its yearly quitrent, may be viewed as a pragmatic solution to the problem of an aging population of slaves with a growing number of dependents. By keeping the children of the slaves, the company stood to acquire "capital gains" in its labor force every time a child was born to a former slave. Seen in such light, the 1644 grant of half freedom to eleven company slaves and their wives was less an act of humanity than a wise business decision.

Although the slaves of 1644 comprised the largest group of company slaves on record as being manumitted, the practice of issuing half freedoms continued right up until the end of Dutch rule, albeit at a reduced pace. Records show, indeed, that several of the "half slaves" received complete emancipation in the 1650s.

Private citizens sometimes granted slaves half freedoms in return for a limited number of cash payments. In one case, Philip Jansz Ringo and his slave Manuel de Spanje appeared before secretary Cornelis Van Tienhoven, in February 1649, to place their signatures (a mark in the case of Manuel) on an agreement of emancipation. Manuel promised to pay his former master 100 fl. per year for three years. Payments could be made "in seawan [wampum], grain or such pay as is current here." Although the cost was high—farm laborers earned about 150 fl. per year—Manuel managed to complete the payments on his freedom. By 1651 he had acquired a patent to some farmland on Manhattan Island and was living as a freedman.

The experience of the most fortunate and humanely treated slaves was not, however, characteristic of all slaves in New Netherland. Dutch authorities permitted some of their slaves to marry, but such a privilege was the exception, not the norm. Moreover, the greatest obstacle to stable household formation for slaves was the persistent gender imbalance among Africans. With so few African women, most African men were unable to take advantage of the marriage privilege. Even among those who successfully formed families under slavery, the constant threat of being sold created difficulties that free families did not experience. For most blacks household formation came only after emancipation.

Yet while only a few free blacks had their wedding banns registered in the Dutch Reformed Church, the legitimacy of black marriages was not challenged in Dutch law. In matters ranging from probate to property sales, African American marriages were recognized by Dutch authorities and given the same legitimacy before the law as marriages among Dutch colonists. Free blacks generally adopted the Dutch practice of passing property from husband to wife and from parent to child with no special provisions based on gender. Dutch law expected parents to be responsible for their children, and parents were frequently called into court to answer for the behavior of their offspring. African Americans in New Netherland appear to have been treated no differently than Eurcpean Americans in such matters.

New Amsterdam's free blacks sought to provide for their children through apprenticeships in much the same way as working-class Hollanders. Susanna Anthony Robberts, "free Negress," when confronted with the problem of providing for her younger brother after the death of her parents concluded an apprenticeship arrangement with Wolphert Webber. She agreed to release her brother to three years of service "with express condition that the said Webber shall teach him, or cause him to be taught, reading and writing." When she was assured of the document's contents by the notary, she signed it with her mark.

New Amsterdam's free blacks grew by natural increase in the last years of the colony's existence, even as their percentage of the total black population declined. As more and more slaves were imported into the colony to meet the needs of agricultural expansion, the pace of manumissions slowed and the once flexible policy followed by the ministers to certify the Christianity of slaves was made more exacting and difficult.

In 1659 and again in 1660 Stuyvesant granted house and garden plots to a number of former slaves, including several who had received half freedom in 1644. The plots were located along the wagon road (present Fourth Avenue) near Stuyvesant's own bowery. Since they were at some distance from the farmland granted earlier, the grants may have been intended to establish a residential community for free blacks or represented an effort by Stuyvesant to rid New Amsterdam of free blacks by relegating them to a rural ghetto. A more likely explanation is that the free blacks sought these plots themselves to form a community, following a well-established custom among New Netherland's Europeans of living together along a road rather than in dispersed farmhouses that offered few opportunities for social interaction or mutual defense. Whatever the intent, the land grants of 1659 and 1660 established the first community of free blacks on Manhattan Island.

By the fall of 1660 the community of African Americans along the wagon road had grown to about forty people divided among fourteen families. Once a week they trekked with their children to Stuyvesant's adjacent farm for Sunday evening service, where they worshiped beside the director general and his family. Stuyvesant, who paid Dominie Henricus Selyns 250 fl. per year to conduct these services, required his own slaves to attend, making the reverend's congregation predominantly black.

The end of Dutch rule marked the beginning of the decline of the community of African Americans. Nine years after the English conquest, a census of the area revealed only twenty-four blacks still living between the fresh-water pond and Harlem. In 1679 Jasper Danckaerts described the community as lining both sides of the road and containing "many habitations of negroes, mulattoes and whites." Twenty years later, most of the free blacks along the wagon road had sold their land to white neighbors and moved to other communities in New Jersey, on Long Island, or in the Hudson Valley. Perhaps they were driven out by racism and wanted to escape the more restrictive racial policies of the English, or they may simply have left because their small farms could not sustain the next generation of children. They became part of the outmigration from Manhattan of Dutch-speaking people in the last decades of the seventeenth century.

Securing the Borders

A hundred and fifty miles up the Hudson River in the verdant heart of the fur trade area an ethnically diverse population of Europeans, Africans, and Native Americans congregated around Fort Orange. The land technically belonged to the million-acre patroonship of Rensselaerswyck which in 1648, under the directorship of Brant Van Schlichtenhorst, began to grant lots to the patroonship's nonagricultural artisans and craftsmen near the walls of the fort. When news reached Manhattan of Van Schlichtenhorst's actions, Stuyvesant proclaimed all land grants within 3,000 feet of the walls to be invalid. The 3,000-foot perimeter, the approximate length of a cannon shot, was needed to secure the fort. When Van Schlichtenhorst ignored the order and repeatedly violated company ordinances, Stuyvesant was faced with a matter that required the utmost delicacy.

Although Kiliaen Van Rensselaer had died in 1643, his heirs were powerfully connected to the government of the United Provinces and to the directorate of the West India Company. Stuyvesant wrote his superiors describing the activities of Van Schlichtenhorst and awaited their decision. In the meantime Stuyvesant had more pressing concerns. The growth of the English colonies to the north and the clamor arising from the English settlers on eastern Long Island forced the director general to move quickly to deal with the threat. To secure the colony's eastern flank he sought a treaty with the New England colonies. On the southern flank, the Swedish colony of New Sweden threatened to monopolize the entire fur trade of the Delaware Valley. The short-term solution was the construction of Fort Casimir on the Delaware to stave off the further expansion of New Sweden. Not until 1651 was Stuyvesant ready to return again to the problem at Fort Orange. By this time he had received permission from the company directors to proceed against Van Schlichtenhorst. Apparently Van Schlichtenhorst's confrontation with Stuyvesant had caused him to fall out of favor with the Van Rensselaer family, and the heirs of the patroon had agreed to replace him, in effect giving permission for the company to move against him.

Stuyvesant summoned Van Schlichtenhorst to New Amsterdam to answer charges of violating the chartered rights of the West India Company. When Van Schlichtenhorst arrived, Stuyvesant had him arrested. The plan was to ship him to Amsterdam on the first available vessel and let the directors and the Van Rensselaer family deal with him, but Van Schlichtenhorst escaped and made his way back to Rensselaerswyck. He continued to defy Stuyvesant by issuing land grants within the perimeter. When the spring thaw of 1652 allowed him to communicate with Johannes Dijckman, the commissary of Fort Orange, Stuyvesant set a new plan in motion. His first move was to have the council pass an ordinance proclaiming all the area within the 3,000-foot perimeter of the walls of

Fort Orange to be company land. Dijckman was then instructed to set boundary posts marking off the perimeter. Van Schlichtenhorst reacted predictably by pulling down the posts. Shortly thereafter Dijckman, acting on Stuyvesant's standing orders, arrived at Van Schlichtenhorst's house with eight soldiers. After arresting the director of Rensselaerswyck, the soldiers pulled down the patroon's flag and rang the fire bell to assemble the inhabitants of the community. Dijckman read an order proclaiming the establishment of the court of Fort Orange and village of Beverwijck. Inhabitants whose property fell within the perimeter were required to swear an oath of allegiance to the company. The incentives were attractive: by swearing allegiance to the company the inhabitants were freed from all their obligations to the patroonship. None refused.

In 1652 Beverwyck contained about 370 people living in 100 houses. By 1660 the population had grown to over 1,000 men, women, and children. The inhabitants were mostly Dutch and Scandinavian, although blacks appear among the first cases to be heard at the new inferior bench of justice in 1652.

By the last years of Dutch rule, New Netherland had become home to a wide variety of people. To the core population of Walloons and company employees had been added a virtual potpourri of European ethnic groups and Africans by the score, some free, others half free, but most still in chains. The colony that would become New York in 1664 had already been transformed by the new immigrants into the most multicultural enclave in North America.

Chapter *5*

Life in New Netherland

MOST OF THE NEW IMMIGRANTS CAME TO WORK THE land, and their labor transformed the economy of the colony in the 1650s and 1660s. The fur trade, although still earning profits for the company, no longer dominated life in New Netherland. Farming, on the other hand, which had initially been envisioned as a supplement to the fur trade, became by 1660 the principal means of livelihood for the vast majority of New Netherlanders.

Unlike New England farming, which was largely subsistence, the agricultural system that evolved in New Netherland was market-oriented and derived its distinct regional characteristics from Dutch tradition. Three settlement patterns emerged: the isolated farm, the patroonship, and the agricultural village. All three came from prototypes in different regions of the Netherlands.

Small, isolated farms were the tradition among the "reclaimers" who eked out a narrow existence in the wastelands of the Netherlands. In the colony on the Hudson, isolated farms were the norm in the earliest period of colonization and continued to be the preferred type of agricultural settlement pattern for many colonists. The isolated farm pattern dates from 1625, when the Provisional Orders instructed Commander Willem Verhulst to give families "as much land as they can properly cultivate." In the 1630s the company reached agreements with some farmers to work company farms for a specified number of years. After completing their contracts, most were given land of their own. By 1640 the colony contained two types of isolated agricultural units: boweries, which raised livestock and grew crops, and plantations, which only produced crops. A 1639 map of the lower Hudson estuary showed boweries and plantations on Manhattan Island, Governor's Island, and Long Island.

The patroonship, which made its appearance in the 1630s, was based on the medieval feudal estates along the Rhine River in the Netherlands, some of which dated back to the eighth century. Although the patroonship system met with only one success in New Netherland, Rensselaerswyck, with its manorial court, offered an alternative to company justice for its tenants. Moreover, Rensselaerswyck served as incentive for a much more successful English manorial system in the eighteenth century.

The third type of settlement pattern was the agricultural village or farming town that developed in the 1640s and expanded rapidly with the arrival of the new immigrants in the 1650s and 1660s. Under the expanded Freedoms and Exemptions of 1640, the company had no choice but to provide for a municipal government in the hopes of enticing the colonists to settle in villages that were more easily fortified against Indian attack. The English colonists on Long Island were the first to obtain town charters, beginning with Newtown in 1642.

The success of the Long Island English towns in acquiring self-government in New Netherland was, in part, the result of their homogeneity—cultural, religious, and linguistic. As "foreigners" in a Dutch colony, they persistently sought to maintain the familiar forms of English local government. Theirs was an English tradition of agricultural village settlement, more akin to New England than to the Dutch villages elsewhere in the colony.

By contrast, the first Dutch town to receive a municipal charter was Breuckelen (Brooklyn) in 1646, followed by Beverwyck (Albany) and Midwout (Flatbush) in 1652, New Amsterdam (New York City) in 1653, Amersfoort (Flatlands) in 1654, and New Utrecht, Boswyck (Bushwick), and Schenectady in 1661. The reluctance of Dutch New Netherlanders to settle in villages was a serious concern for the company. During the Indian rebellion of the 1640s, the directors ordered Kieft to gather the Dutch in villages, "as the English are in the habit of doing." Ten years later, in the midst of another Indian uprising, Stuyvesant ordered the inhabitants once again to abandon their isolated farmsteads, where "sad experiences have from time to time shown, that the separate dwellings of the country people, have led to many murders of people, the killing of cattle and burning of houses by the savage natives of this country."

Typical of a Dutch agricultural village was Harlem. House lots in the town were arranged along two parallel streets, with each household assigned a garden plot and four morgens (about eight acres) of farmland along the river flats. In addition, each farmer was given a small parcel of marsh to provide salt hay for cattle. The pattern in Schenectady was similar, with most inhabitants acquiring house lots along two sides of a street. Beyond Schenectady village in the arable lowlands near the banks of the Mohawk River, the properties were divided into long, thin bands comprising about fifty acres per parcel.

These villages were similar to the English open field system so prevalent in East Anglia and New England but were more likely modeled on the agricultural village tradition in the Netherlands, where open field villages were common, especially on the Drenthe plateau in the eastern part of the country. Such villages date to medieval times. The pattern of agricultural villages that emerged among the Dutch population of New Netherland probably borrowed forms that were the common tradition of many northern Europeans. These nucleated villages were also easier to defend and probably prevailed in the colony for both pragmatic and cultural reasons.

Crops and Farming Practices

Whether settled on isolated farms or in nucleated villages, the farmers of New Netherland pursued a typical northern European style of agriculture. Adriaen Van der Donck, in 1655, described farms in the colony as being particularly productive in the staples of the northern European diet. Chief among these were the small grains: wheat, rye, and barley, although the last was not grown in large quantities during the Dutch period. European fruit crops such as peaches, pears, and apples grew magnificently in New Netherland, and orchards were common on most farms. Dutch gardens provided an important element in the colonial diet, and here, too, the Dutch tended to follow their own traditions. Van der Donck described gardens in New Netherland as being essentially identical to those of the fatherland with the exception that all the vegetables grew better. During late summer and early fall New Netherlanders ate cabbages, parsnips, carrots, beets, endives, succory (chicory), dill, spinach, parsley, cresses, onions, leeks, and radishes. Dutch herb gardens flavored the cuisine with rosemary, lavender, hysop, thyme, sage, marjoram, balm, wormwood, chives, pimpernel, and tarragon.

The most significant difference between farming in New Netherland and the fatherland was the cultivation of New World crops borrowed from Native Americans. Chief among these was maize, called "turkey wheat" by the Dutch. In addition, New Netherlanders learned to grow tobacco, squash, pumpkins, watermelons, cucumbers, calabashes (gourds), and a wide variety of beans.

Livestock raising dated from the earliest years of colonization. In 1625 the company dispatched two ships with 103 horses and cattle and "all the hogs and sheep that they thought expedient." At first the livestock was confined to Governor's Island, but later the company, discovering that European quadrupeds bred prodigiously in the colony, transported the offspring of the original breeding stock all over New Netherland. As a general rule, Dutch farmers used both horses and oxen as draft animals, unlike New Englanders, who relied almost exclusively on oxen.

Hogs were the most common livestock in the colony, and like most European domestic animals they proliferated at an alarming rate, forcing farmers, both European and Indian, to fence their crops. By 1650 so many goats, sheep, and hogs were roaming the streets of New Amsterdam and climbing over the decayed walls of the fort that Stuyvesant and his council had to ban all animals between the fort and the company's bowery unless accompanied by a herder. The fines were heavy: 6 fl. "for each horse, cow, etc., found within the aforesaid limits on the public streets near the Fort." Second offenses were fined at twice the rate, and third offenses resulted in the confiscation of the animals.

The construction boom of the late 1650s created such a shortage of wood on Manhattan Island that unattended fences with usable scrap lumber became fair game for thieves. With the population of domestic animals rising, Stuyvesant had no choice but to issue another ordinance to protect the colony's food supply. In 1659, in response to "great complaints daily that the posts, rails, clapboards and other parts of the fences, put up around sown fields and gardens at great expense, trouble and labor for the protection of the crops, are stolen in the night as well during the day," the director general and his council passed an ordinance that provided severe penalties for those convicted of destroying fences on Manhattan Island. The law penalized first-time lumber thieves with whipping and branding. A second violation was punished "with the rope until death, without distinction of person."

The sheer numbers of animals made the task of assigning ownership and responsibility especially difficult. Livestock foraged in the common woods in the spring and summer, and in fall they were herded into shelters for the winter. Only then were the young horses, cattle, and swine branded or marked. Consequently herds of semi-feral livestock roamed at will in the colony, trampling and feeding on unfenced crops and causing headaches for their owners and the authorities. The inventory of Jonas Bronck (for whom the Bronx is named) is perhaps illustrative of the number of animals found on a medium-size farm in the lower Hudson estuary. At his death in 1643, the inventory listed four mares, one stallion, one colt, five milch cows, one young cow, two yoke of oxen, three yearling heifers, and one bull. The hogs were simply listed as "number unknown, running in the woods."

Art, Music, Architecture, and Tools

Dutch traditions prevailed in the cultural as well as the agricultural practices of the New Netherlanders. Dutch immigrants to New Netherland shared an artistic tradition that was the envy of Europe. This was, after all, the golden century of Pieter Bruegel, Frans Hals, Hendrick Terbrugghen, Jan Van Goyen, and Rembrandt Van Rijn. It is probable that some fine works of art made their way to the colony with the immigrants, although the evidence is sketchy at best. Inventories of the late seventeenth century hint at rich collections, at least in the estates of the wealthy. In New York City, for example, a 1685 inventory of Dr.

Jacob de Lange listed sixty-one paintings, consisting of landscapes, still lifes, genre, and Scripture paintings. Anne Grant in her *Memoirs of an American Lady*, described a visit to the Schuyler home in Albany in 1760: "the best bedroom was hung with family portraits, some of which were admirably executed; and in the eating room . . . were some fine scripture paintings."

The names of only a few painters of New Netherland have survived, and little is known of their works. The notable exception is Henri Coutourier (1592–1672) a Huguenot, whose portrait of Peter Stuyvesant, executed in the Dutch style, echoes the sophistication of the Dutch masters. In addition to Coutourier, at least a few other "limners" (from the Latin *luminare*, to illuminate or depict by drawing) plied their trade in New Netherland. Evert Duyckinck (1621–c. 1703), a glazier by occupation, who came to New Amsterdam before 1640, is recorded as a limner, although his only known works are some coats of arms enameled on the windows of the Reformed church at Beverwyck about 1656.

Choral music, primarily the unison singing of psalms was practiced by nearly all church-going inhabitants of the colony, and family and civic celebrations were almost always accompanied by some type of music played on a variety of instruments, including the fiddle, Jew's harp, drum, and tabor. In the more remote reaches of New Netherland, ethnic cultural traditions prevailed in music as they did in nearly everything else. Among the rural Dutch inhabitants a tradition of folk songs, lullabies, and nursery rhymes survived into the nineteenth century, but the introduction of "singing schools" by the English after the conquest, although intended to enhance the ritual of Protestant worship, brought an invasion of English forms into the predominantly Dutch culture of New York. By the first decades of the eighteenth century, choral music had been transformed, and Dutch musical practices faded rapidly thereafter.

The Dutch inhabitants of New Netherland drew from two traditions of architecture: one urban and one rural. Of the two, the rural tradition was to prove the more resistant to anglicization. As late as the third decade of the nineteenth century, Dutch features were still to be found in farmhouses and barns in New Jersey and upstate New York. By contrast, the urban tradition was shorter lived.

The first houses on Manhattan were very primitive one-room affairs made of bark and sod, but as the urgent necessity of clearing and cultivating passed, substantial homes of wood in a distinctive "Dutch-style" were built. In 1646 the Jesuit missionary Father Isaac Jogues observed at Albany houses made of milled lumber with thatched roofs but very little masonry except for the chimneys. Inside Fort Orange, however, larger houses already contained a remarkable number of civilized accoutrements, including leaded glass windows and green-glazed floor tiles.

The roofs of Dutch houses were usually steeper than English designs, a style more suitable to the Netherlands, where wind-driven rain could loosen the roof tiles. Although wooden shingles were substituted for the earthenware pantiles commonly used in the fatherland, the steep pitch of the roof was retained. Since land was expensive in the Netherlands, most homes were designed to make maximum use of it. Hence Dutch houses, even in land-rich New Netherland, were narrow at the base, frequently with overhanging second floors. The clearest image of such homes comes from Albany, the most Dutch-looking town in New Netherland. Its frontier location and its predominantly Dutch population made its architecture less susceptible to the wave of English designs that swept away many Dutch buildings in the eighteenth century. The old town, with its typical Dutch houses, built gable end to the street, appeared backward and alien to outsiders. A nineteenth-century traveler observed: "Every house, having any pretensions to dignity, was placed with its gable end to the street, and was ornamented with huge iron numericals, announcing the date of its erection; while from its eaves long wooden gutters, or spouts, projected in front from six or seven feet."

Dutch traditions also prevailed in rural architecture and material culture. One farm structure that gave to New Netherland a uniquely Dutch look was the hay rick or hay barracks. Hay ricks were everywhere in New Netherland from Rensselaerswyck to Long Island. A 1638 inventory of a Flatlands farm listed a hay rick forty feet tall. Used for drying and storing hay, they were essential to livestock raising in the damp climates of northern Germany and the Netherlands, where they have been traced by scholars to the Middle Ages. In New York they remained common on Dutch farms into the early twentieth century.

The Dutch barn with its large door on the gable end and its characteristic H-bent framing was an architectural tradition that originated in the eastern Netherlands and nearby regions of Germany. In its cavernous interior was room for most of the activities associated with small-grain farming and livestock raising. In the center was the threshing floor and immediately above it the garret, or loft, for storage of unthreshed grain or cured hay. Along one side were stalls for horses and along the other side a pen for cattle. In the poorer regions of the Netherlands it was not uncommon for a farming family to live in the barn with the livestock, usually in a walled-off area near the closed gabled end. In New Netherland, however, most Dutch barns were the exclusive domicile of livestock, feed, and tools.

Inventories of equipment and tools on Dutch farms reveal little that would not have been familiar to most Anglo-American farmers in the colonial era. Three items, however, seemed decidedly foreign to English colonists: the Dutch plow, the Flemish *sith* (scythe), and the Dutch wagon.

The Dutch plow commonly used in New Netherland originated in the province of Zeeland and the eastern and northern regions of Belgium. Sometimes called a "hog plow," it had as its most characteristic feature the pyramidal-shaped plowshare that dug a deep furrow. Most Dutch plows had only one handle, and a few were mounted on wooden wheels. A heavy plow designed for turning the wet loam of the Netherlands, it proved an excellent implement for plowing the root-bound soil commonly found after clearing old growth forests. The English two-handled "bull" plow, on the other hand, had a nearly horizontal plowshare and cut a much shallower furrow. It, too, had originated in the Netherlands, in areas where the soil was drier and a lighter plow was appropriate. It was first introduced in East Anglia in the sixteenth century. Like the Dutch plow of New Netherland, the English bull plow was carried to America by immigrants who came to work the land.

The Flemish *sith* had an L-shaped wooden handle and was used in conjunction with a *mathook*, which had a straight handle with a curved iron hook on the end. The *sith* was a more efficient tool than the sickle commonly used on English farms, because it did not require the worker to stoop low and grasp the stalks with the free hand. The technique, however, required a fluid motion and careful coordination of the worker's body and hands, for the user stood nearly upright grasping the stalks with the *mathook* in the left hand while cutting them with the *sith* in the right hand. Dutch farmers in New York and New Jersey continued to use the Flemish scythe until the end of the eighteenth century.

The Dutch wagon was an all-purpose farm vehicle, used for carrying manure, grain, and tools. On Sunday it became the family coach with a quick adjustment of the seats and the replacing of the rough-hewn sideboards with handsomely painted ones. On rainy days flat hoops were placed in the mortises along each side and cloth spread and tied over the whole, creating a dry and spacious interior beneath the canopy. With its distinctive deep front board, vertical side spindles, and large eight-spoke rear wheels, it was, in the words of Hector St. John de Crèvecoeur, who observed a Dutch wagon in Orange County, New York, in the 1760s, "extremely well-contrived and executed." Years later, large freight wagons very similar to the Dutch wagons of New Netherland would come to be associated in the public mind with the Conestoga region of Pennsylvania.

Family Life

In the seventeenth century, the Dutch family became increasingly child-centered, anticipating the modern family's devotion to nurturing the child and preparing the young for life as adults. No other Europeans celebrated the child in art and literature as much as the Dutch. Dutch parents were famous for indulging their children, and there is even evidence that a "youth culture" developed in the golden century. The popular moralist and poet Jacob Cats, called "Father Cats" by his adoring countrymen, believed children needed affection at least as much as discipline. In Dutch paintings children were depicted as children, not as miniature adults in grown-up clothing. They were also portrayed in everyday settings, at home and work, at play on the stoops and streets, having fun, and being bad. "Father Cats" called on all mothers, regardless of class and rank, to breastfeed their infants, and numerous eyewitness accounts testify that the practice was universal in the Netherlands. Dutch fathers were also instructed to take an active part in the raising of their children, and most Dutch families followed this advice, creating in the process nearly modern families with strong ties of love between parents and children and among siblings.

In New Netherland the development of families was slowed initially by the persistent gender imbalance. Not until the 1650s, when sufficient numbers of young women migrated to the colony, were Dutch family traditions woven into the fabric of colonial life. The number of children in the colony increased dramatically in the last years, prompting a series of laws to encourage schooling, formalize apprenticeship, and provide penalties for unacceptable behavior among the young. Stuyvesant, whose ideas of discipline derived from his strict Calvinism, believed the children of New Netherland to be spoiled and their parents overly indulgent. His solution was education, and to this end laws were passed establishing schoolmasters and schools in the towns and villages of the colony.

Formal education was emphasized less than apprenticeship, which by the late 1650s under Stuyvesant's direction became fairly regulated and uniform. Dutch apprenticeship arrangements, although similar to English practice, differed in one important aspect: Dutch parents were reluctant to board their children out of the home. Most of the apprenticeship contracts that have survived suggest that Dutch New Netherlanders preferred to keep their children at home even when they were apprenticed to a craftsman. When possible the parents placed their children with close relatives to learn a trade, or if that was not possible, with a neighbor. Such arrangements delayed the development of independence, but they may also have increased the bonds of affection between parents and their adolescent offspring.

In New Netherland, as in the fatherland, separate educational tracks existed for boys and girls. In this division, girls received considerably less attention than boys, although the ability to read and write was expected of all but the poorest. Women in New Netherland generally enjoyed a level of literacy similar to that attained by women in New England and much higher than that of females in the Chesapeake. While boys exercised some choice in the selection of apprenticeships, especially in the urban areas of New Netherland where a broader range of occupations existed, girls were expected to become wives and mothers. The responsibility for their training in household tasks fell to their mothers and older sisters, who taught them to prepare traditional Dutch dishes, to spin thread and make clothes, and to maintain the very high standard of cleanliness typical of Dutch households.

Regardless of gender, a child's education included moral and spiritual values, and Dutch children were expected to know the key elements of the Reformed faith. This was accomplished in the home by daily reading of the Bible. Children were required to read aloud from the *Statenvertaling*, the 1637 translation of the Bible authorized by the States General. Like the Geneva Bible of New England Puritans, the States Bible was the centerpiece of faith and the source of literacy for most people of Dutch heritage.

Sports and Recreation

Like other Europeans, the Dutch participated in various contests of skill and endurance, including horse racing, fowling, fencing, and sailboat racing, the last being a summer favorite. More than other Europeans, the Dutch found sports an appropriate subject for art, and consequently the artists of the Netherlands were the preeminent illustrators of recreations. Dutch artists in Europe and America frequently depicted people at play (including Native Americans), and much of what is known of sports in the early modern era comes from Dutch artists and woodcutters.

In the colonial period, the Dutch were the first Europeans to set aside separate space for sports activities. In New Amsterdam, a bowling green was established for a favorite Dutch variant of curling. Played on grass instead of ice, the game required the rolling of balls as near as possible to the "jack." Special ponds and fields were also reserved, depending on the season, for *kolven*, the pronunciation of which sounded much like "golfen" to the English ear. Using curved sticks, the participants hit balls across the ground or ice toward posts at either end of the playing field. *Kolven* was the American forerunner of golf, ice hockey, and field hockey, and its play spread throughout the middle colonies. In addition, the Dutch winter sports of ice-boating, sledding, sleigh riding, and ice-skating were common activities in New Netherland.

A few uniquely Dutch recreations did not survive long after the English conquest. One was a billiard-like game called "truck," usually played in taverns. Players used a cue to drive a ball through a wire wicket on a table, often wagering on the outcome. Other "games" involved what might be called "animal sports." Of these, the most common was *Papagaaischieten* ("shooting the parrot"), an annual marksmanship event following Pentecost, using live stationary targets. A particularly brutal animal sport was "cat clubbing," in which contestants took turns hurling a club at a suspended barrel containing a terror-stricken cat. The object was to shatter the barrel and release the cat, whereupon all the participants dashed after the crazed feline in an attempt to capture it.

The long winters in the Netherlands and in North America provided much time for indoor recreations such as card playing, dancing, and musical concerts. Although Dutch women seldom engaged in the "masculine" pastimes associated with firearms and "animal sports," they were welcomed to many of the indoor recreations. For middle- and lower-class women, however, recreation was often an extension of labor. Gardening, needlework, spinning matches, and quilting bees, for example, were important activities that helped cement the bonds of community among the women of colonial New Netherland.

Gender Rights and Family Law

Gender differences prevailed in Dutch culture, and, as in all western European societies in the seventeenth century, females were subordinated to men. However, in several important areas Dutch women in the fatherland and in New Netherland appear to have enjoyed more rights and privileges than they did under English law. Roman-Dutch law and age-old custom in the Netherlands provided a long tradition of equal property distribution among sons and daughters. Dutch respect for female property rights and the notion of community property within marriage produced in New Netherland a legal system that was considerably less restrictive for women than contemporary English practice.

Dutch law permitted single women of legal age to act independently in legal matters but severely restricted the independence of married women. Married women lost their independence with the exchange of marriage vows, and the husband took over the property of his wife and served as her guardian. In theory at least, wives were little more than servants to their husbands, but practical considerations modified legal definitions both in the fatherland and in New Netherland. Beginning in the late Middle Ages married women's legal status expanded as Dutch society underwent the commercial revolution that laid the groundwork for the golden century. Married women's economic roles grew as traders and merchants, who often acted independently while their husbands were out of the country. By the seventeenth century it was common practice for married women to enter binding contracts in numerous circumstances when trading with their husbands' permission. A married woman could engage in business under the protection of the law and without fear of having her contracts invalidated. With a properly notarized prenuptial agreement, she might even trade as an independent merchant in her own right.

Perhaps the most important difference between Dutch and English legal practice was the concept of community property in marriage. The custom of sharing all property equally between husband and wife dates back to the early Middle Ages in the Netherlands. It was brought over with the first Dutch colonists and remained an integral part of family law until the English con-

This painted "kast" (ca. 1630-1725) is an example of the large and elaborate cupboards that Dutch families in New York State gave to sons and daughters alike to hold valuable handmade textiles in preparation for marriage. The custom began in the seventeenth century but long outlived the Dutch colony, surviving into the nineteenth century.

quest. The law of community property ensured that should either spouse die intestate, the surviving partner would inherit one-half of all property owned jointly. The remaining half went to the couple's heirs. The dividing of property in this way established the principle that both parties had rights to an equal share of the common estate. In the early seventeenth century, the concept of community property was codified by the great Dutch jurist Hugo Grotius in his monumental *Jurisprudence of Holland* (1631), and it appears to have been followed consistently in New Netherland throughout the Dutch period. It was not an ironclad principle, for a couple could, by executing a prenuptial agreement, choose to maintain some property separately. Few couples chose to do so, however, and usually only when the relative wealth of bride and bridegroom was markedly unequal. For women, the law of community property meant that all their work in building up the estate of the family would not be lost through the appointment of an executor.

In New Netherland women often acted as plaintiffs or defendants in law suits for the recovery of debts. So common was this practice that Dutch officials only occasionally bothered to record the marital status of female litigants. Hence, it is difficult to determine how many women acted on behalf of themselves and their husbands or how many were in fact acting independently. Women usually appeared alone in court. There is only one case among hundreds in the records of the New Amsterdam court in which a male relative accompanied a woman to court. Furthermore, the success rate of women in legal suits was about the same as that of men.

Community property law created problems for widows when their husbands died owing money. Under such circumstances Dutch law was quite clear; the surviving spouse was responsible for all debts of the deceased partner. By placing her housekeys on the coffin and leaving the funeral chamber in borrowed clothing, a widow could protect her future earnings from her husband's creditors. In doing so, however, she renounced all potential benefits of the family estate. This custom was commonly invoked in the fatherland, in parts of Germany, and presumably in New Netherland. After her husband's burial, the only way a widow could escape paying her husband's debts was to petition the magistrates. Women who had assisted their husbands in buying or selling merchandise were not permitted to invoke the privilege, the assumption being that a wife's personal involvement in the family business necessarily determined her legal responsibilities.

Married women also exercised rights in determining who inherited the family estate. According to Dutch law either a husband or a wife could declare a will disposing of the half of the estate guaranteed each partner under the law of community property, or both partners could prepare a joint will that directed the line of inheritance should either spouse die. The joint declaration of inheritance was known as the mutual will. It was the most common type of will for Dutch married couples in New Netherland. Between 1638 and 1664, thirty-five wills appeared in the court records of New Amsterdam and Beverwyck. Of these, twenty-two were mutual wills prepared by married couples, eight were mutual wills prepared by betrothed couples, and only five were wills prepared by married men alone. Of these last, three were composed hastily by men facing imminent death after being wounded in war. Women were less inclined than men to declare wills in the absence of their spouse. Notaries were required to draft the mutual will in the presence and with the authorization of husband and wife. Both parties had to sign the finished testament to render it valid.

Dutch law provided for court-appointed guardians to look after the rights of minor children when one or both parents died. The guardians' sole responsibility was the protection of the financial interests of orphaned children until they reached the age of majority, which was twenty-five years under Dutch law. This legal practice reflected the belief that widowed parents should not be entrusted with sole control over their children's inheritance. Special courts known as Orphan Chambers were established in Dutch towns as early as the mid-fifteenth century to protect minors who had lost either parent. Magistrates usually appointed the widowed parent as guardian and at least two additional overseers from among the orphans' nearest and oldest male relatives. If no relatives were available, the court chose two respectable men from the community.

In the early years of New Netherland, the relatively small number of families precluded the need for a special court to handle the affairs of orphans, but by the mid-1650s that had changed. Concerned that minor children's rights were being abused by unscrupulous stepparents and relatives, the burgomasters and schepens of New Amsterdam established the colony's first separate Court of Orphan Masters in 1655. Two years later the burgomasters and schepens of Beverwyck appointed two Orphan Masters to serve the needs of children in that community. As in the fatherland, the court supervised the care of minor children by appointing guardians. Most often the court provided for orphaned children by arranging apprenticeships for them; in a few cases, it sent children back to Holland to be raised by relatives. The Orphan Masters usually consult surviving parent before deciding on the appointment of guardians, but u the courts in the fatherland they never formally appointed a widowed fathe mother as one of the children's overseers.

Orphan Masters ordered a settlement of the estate whenever the min needed special protection. Between 1655 and 1664, the New Amsterda Orphan Masters intervened in fifty-four cases in which children had lost only one of their parents. In thirty-two (or 59.3 percent) of these cases, the court ordered the orphans' guardians and widowed parent to pay the children their inheritance. More than two-thirds of these court rulings (twenty-two of thirty-two cases) were issued after a widowed parent had become engaged to remarry. This appeared to happen most frequently when the second marriage involved a partner with little or no property.

When the court ordered the settlement of an estate, the children's guardians frequently deposited the inheritance for investment with the Orphan Masters. The money was then lent out at interest in order to obtain funds for the minors' maintenance and education. The magistrates made loans to reliable borrowers such as the municipal government and the Reformed Church. In the 1660s these loans averaged an annual return of 10 percent. A surviving parent was permitted to use the interest toward the children's immediate support but could not touch the principal.

Dutch family law and customs did not apply to the English towns on Long Island, where the weakness of provincial government dictated a policy of non-intervention. There, as in the Chesapeake and New England colonies, English law and custom prevailed. Under English law, women possessed virtually no rights in matters of inheritance. Men could make wills without their wives' consent, and mothers could be excluded completely from guardianship over their children. English common law courts regarded minors as orphans only if the father died, since children inherited from him alone, and public officials were reluctant to intervene in such matters, unless forced to do so by obvious irregularities. The Dutch system of inheritance, on the other hand, was based upon a level of public intervention that seems almost modern in its concern for the rights of minors. The English conquest removed the legal safeguards for widows and married women. In the words of the historian David E. Narrett, "the institution of English law would lead eventually to a decline in the widow's authority over property, a greater emphasis on children's material advancement, and a weakening of public supervision of family relations."

Religious Life

Although support for the Reformed Church came rather late in the colony's history and then only after the West India Company had been forced to respond to the spiritual needs of its colonists, most Dutch-speaking families looked to the church for comfort and meaning in their lives. The Reformed Church emerged from the doctrinal squabbles of the early seventeenth century as the single most important institution in the lives of most New Netherlanders. Families attended church regularly, participated in its rituals, and sought solace from the dominies in times of sorrow and loss.

Church services were held twice each Sunday, in the morning and afternoon or early evening, and often during the week, when all were welcomed regardless of church membership. Although Calvinist doctrine eliminated most of the Catholic holidays, the Dutch continued to celebrate a number of special days with prayer and ritual. For example, holiday church service was held on the first and second Easter Day, Ascension Day, first and second Whitsuntide Day, first and second Christmas Day, and New Year's Day. Occasionally, upon decree of the director general, special services were held to give thanksgiving, as was the case following the treaty ceremony that ended the Indian rebellion during Kieft's administration. During times of trouble, the churches were often called upon to gather their congregations to pray for the deliverance of the colony from some impending calamity, such as a threatened war with England in the 1650s. Church services were well attended, although there was a falling off of attendance during harvest or hay-time.

Services lasted about ninety minutes and were preceded by the schoolmaster's ringing of the church bell. Schoolmasters carried out several functions, both secular and sacred. Besides teaching reading and catechism during the week, on Sunday they functioned as readers, singers, and sextons. Between the first and second ringing of the bell the schoolmaster read one or possibly two chapters from the Bible and after the third ringing the Ten Commandments and the Twelve Articles of the Confession of Faith. Schoolmasters were also responsible for leading, without musical accompaniment, the singing of psalms and hymns during the service. Prayers were an important part of the service and were said before and after the minister's sermon.

As in the Puritan churches of New England, the sermon was the core of the service and lasted a minimum of one hour. Dutch sermons were of two types: a morning sermon that emphasized the Gospels and an afternoon sermon that focused on a portion of the Heidelberg Catechism. For the most part, sermons contained optimistic messages of God's grace and forgiveness. They were more likely to put people to sleep than to make them aware of the precarious state of their souls.

Baptism was one of only two sacraments recognized by the Reformed Church, the other being communion. Baptisms were times of celebration, but in an age of high infant mortality there was also an element of urgency. Ideally the ceremony was conducted on the first Sunday following birth with only the father and witnesses in attendance, while the mother recuperated at home. After the baptism, close friends and relatives adjourned to the parents' home for a thanksgiving feast. In the case of sick babies, the ceremony might be moved to a weekday, if there appeared a chance that the child might die before Sunday service. Adult baptism was permitted only for those who had not previously been baptized. Adults were required to demonstrate a knowledge of Reformed theology in the presence of the minister.

Marriage, although not considered a sacrament, was performed in the church. Marriage banns were usually announced on three consecutive Sundays before a wedding ceremony could take place. Men younger than twenty-five and women younger than twenty could not marry without permission of their parents or guardians.

Only officially confirmed members of the church could partake of the sacrament of communion. Performed about four times a year around the holidays of Easter, Whitsuntide, and Christmas, it constituted the principal ritual of the church service. Lasting only a few minutes, communion was followed by the deacons' passing of the collection plate. Attendance generally peaked on communion Sundays as did collections.

The church did not recognize the ceremony of the last rites as a sacrament, but burial ceremonies were an integral part of church services. All of the deceased were buried, either in vaults beneath the church floor or, as was most common, in the adjacent graveyard. A solemn, prayer-filled ceremony sometimes preceded the actual interment of prominent church members, whereas simple graveside services, limited to a few remarks by the dominie, were common for indigent parishioners. Schoolmasters were required by their contracts to announce the death of church members in public and, at least in Flatbush, to dig the graves.

The Reformed Church employed comforters of the sick to visit and pray with the gravely ill, but death was faced communally in New Netherland. The dying man, woman, or child, when possible, passed on in the midst of a loving family, with friends and neighbors close at hand. Friends of the deceased assumed responsibility for laying out the corpse, preparing the house for the wake, and arranging the funeral procession and church services. A special official, known as the *aanspreecker* or funeral inviter, called upon friends and neighbors and formally invited them to the funeral. The funeral service was often preached at the home, where the corpse was laid out in a sturdy wood casket in the largest room of the house, called a dead room (*doedkamer*). Superstition required mirrors throughout the house to be covered or turned to the wall until the body was buried. Friends and relatives kept watch over the deceased all night and consumed large amounts of food and drink provided by the family of the deceased. The funeral service was followed by a procession to the graveyard, where a brief burial ceremony was attended mostly by men, except for the nearest female relatives of the deceased. The family gave mourners symbolic gifts including scarves, gloves, handkerchiefs, and monkey spoons. The monkey spoons, which were highly prized, were made of silver or pewter and so named for their figurine handles. After the burial, friends and relatives returned to the family home and continued drinking and eating long into the night, often becoming unruly.

The Reformed Church provided vital social services from education to poor relief, and at every important juncture in the life cycle it sanctified and preserved the fabric of Dutch culture. For most of the new immigrants it became the center of Dutch community life, a reminder of the fatherland, a link with all that had been left behind. In its struggle with the West India Company, moreover, the church helped define a church-state relationship unique in colonial North America.

Although the campaign for the West India Company in the early 1620s gave nearly equal weight to religion and commerce as corporate goals, the charter that finally emerged from the tangled committee structure of the States General contained no mention of religion. Company directors, for the most part, viewed New Netherland as an enterprise, one among many the company engaged in around the Western Hemisphere. For the Reformed clergy the colony provided an opportunity to carry on the Protestant Reformation beyond the line,[1] to wage

1. "Beyond the line" refers to a line of demarcation 370 leagues west of the Cape Verde Islands. The term is a convention used by colonial historians to refer to events in the Americas.

a cosmic struggle against papists and heretics, and to prove the mettle of the true Reformed Church.

Officially the company policy on religion followed the severe Calvinist theology adopted at the Synod of Dordrecht in 1618, but the reality of life in New Netherland made enforcing such a policy impossible. Whenever it was feasible the directors of the West India Company opted to do nothing about religion. When forced to confront the needs of their colonists for religious services, they did so grudgingly and turned to the Classis of Amsterdam for nominations of comforters of the sick and ordained ministers. In New Netherland the interests of the church clashed frequently with the interests of the company. The result was nearly constant friction between company officials and the provincial clergy. Many of these confrontations reached Amsterdam and became part of a larger argument over the role of the church in colonization. Four persistent issues came to define the church-state relationship in New Netherland: economic support for the colonial clergy, the role of the church among the Indians, the role of the clergy in colonial governance, and the enforcement of Calvinist orthodoxy among the colony's Europeans.

At the time of the English conquest, there were eleven Reformed churches in the colony. In all, thirteen ordained *predikanten* (preachers) served in New Netherland between 1628 and 1664, with perhaps twice that many *ziekentroosters* (comforters of the sick). Virtually every one of them complained of the failure of the company to provide adequate economic support for the church. In Amsterdam, too, the company directors and the leaders of the national church quarreled over the costs of maintaining clergy in the colony.

New Netherland's first ordained minister, the Reverend Jonas Michaëlius, experienced firsthand the indifference of the company toward the church. Having suffered the loss of his wife just seven weeks after his arrival in the colony and facing the daunting prospects of raising three small children in the wilderness of North America, he felt neglected and abandoned by the men who had hired him. Michaëlius's three years in New Netherland were miserable, although he seems not to have lost his desire to preach there. In 1637, some six years after his return from the colony, the Classis of Amsterdam recommended him once again for the post at New Amsterdam. The company directors vetoed his nomination and turned down at least two further pleas on his behalf. The reverend's reputation as a complainer with influential connections was more than enough to ensure his disqualification.

For a while, at least, one other source of support for a colonial church appeared promising, the patroons. In religious matters the Freedoms and Exemptions were more specific than the West India Company's charter. Article Twenty-Seven instructed the patroons "to find out ways and means whereby they may support a minister." They were further instructed to do this "in the speediest manner [so] that the service of God and zeal for religion may not be neglected." Kiliaen Van Rensselaer, the only successful patroon, however, responded as reluctantly as the company to the spiritual needs of his tenants. In 1642, a full decade after the settlement of his first tenants, Van Rensselaer hired the Reverend Johannes Megapolënsis to minister to the small congregation of Europeans on his estate. He also hired the good reverend to be his principal adviser in the colony, his eyes and ears, someone he could trust.

Megapolënsis held services for five years in the corner of the patroon's mill house on the east side of the river. In 1647 the company donated an old warehouse which was remodeled to hold a pulpit, nine benches for the congregation, and special benches for the elders and deacons. For nearly seven years, Megapolënsis and his successor, Gideon Schaats, held Sunday services in the warehouse, and every year the spring floods of the Hudson washed away more and more of the foundation until it had to be abandoned.

In 1656, Schaats became the first *predikant* at Fort Orange/Beverwyck to hold services in an edifice built expressly as a church. Yet even at this late date the company acted cautiously. After a meeting with the representatives of the patroonship, company officials decided to build a "blockhouse" church in the center of town to serve as both a house of worship and a refuge for the townspeople in case of Indian attack. On the ground floor were benches assigned to the women of the village. In the overhanging balcony the men sat "at the ready" to man cannon mounted behind portals on the north, west, and south sides of the building. The blockhouse church of Fort Orange may serve as a metaphor for the church-state struggle in New Netherland. Meant to serve the needs of both the church and the company, it defined the relative balance of power between church and state in the colony's northernmost settlement.

The congregation at New Amsterdam did not fare much better. The members constantly struggled to find space for services on the Sabbath. They were forced to endure a number of temporary housing arrangements until the company built a modest church in 1634. When the communicants outgrew this building in the 1640s, Director General Willem Kieft, after what one eyewitness called a drinking bout and what another described as an inebriated dare, pledged 100 guilders to start a building fund. He insisted, however, that the church be built inside the fort on land owned by the company. The only site inside the fort that was large enough to accommodate the church cut off the southeast wind for the gristmill, with the result that there were sometimes shortages of bread in the summer when the mill could not grind. Other problems arose when the congregation tried to hire a schoolmaster and maintain a poor fund. The company would not sanction or enforce tithing nor would it permit the church to acquire significant property.

Too close to the center of political authority to defy the director generals, the New Amsterdam church was in an especially vulnerable position. The deacons' poor fund may serve as an example. Both Willem Kieft and Peter

Stuyvesant borrowed heavily from the fund on behalf of the company, and not all the loans were paid back.

The company was even less enthusiastic in its support of the Reformed Church's mission among the Indians. The first church representatives to make contact with Native Americans in New Netherland were a comforter of the sick, Bastiaen Jansz Krol, and the Reverend Jonas Michaëlius. Krol served as both comforter of the sick and commissary at Fort Orange in the early years. It is doubtful that he could have persuaded the traders, Indian and white, to interrupt their alcoholic brawling and carousing to hold religious services. In any case, Krol's religious convictions were always subordinate to his economic sense.

Jonas Michaëlius was a different man altogether. He came to New Netherland a well-traveled and experienced preacher who had first served the company in Brazil, at Bahia. From Brazil he moved to a company factory on the West African coast. He considered himself an expert on savages because of his time on the slave coast. After four months in the colony he concluded that New Netherland's natives were uncivil, stupid, wicked, and devilish. His solution to the problem was to recommend that missionaries to the Indians learn their language, even though he considered the native tongues to be "childish." He also proposed that the parents be bribed to permit their children to be separated from them and taught Christianity and the Dutch language by "godly" schoolmasters.

Nothing ever came of Michaëlius's plan. He left New Netherland at the expiration of his three-year contract without a single Indian conversion, and it is doubtful that the West India Company would have supported such a scheme, in any case. In fact, one year later, as part of a new plan to stimulate settlement, the company shifted the costs of maintaining a ministry among the Indians to the patroons.

Johannes Megapolensis was the first Dutch Reformed minister to establish a religious beachhead among the Iroquois. Hired by the patroon to serve the tenants of Rensselaerswyck, he was also under obligation to spread the holy gospel among the Indians. The patroon had written once of his intention "to have the Christian Reformed Religion proclaimed there in order that the blind heathen might also be brought to the knowledge of our Savior, Jesus Christ," and he may have selected Megapolensis with this in mind.

Megapolensis began preaching to the Mohawks in 1643. His first task was to learn the Mohawk tongue. He turned to Bastiaen Krol for advice. Krol, who by this time had been among the Mohawk for two decades, told him that it was impossible for a Christian to learn the Mohawk language because they changed it every two or three years to confuse their enemies. Megapolensis thought Krol's theory ridiculous, pointing out that it would be impossible for a whole people to change their language.

He turned next to the traders around Fort Orange but found them of little help. The fur trade was conducted with a series of hand gestures and a rudimentary pidgin that contained Dutch, French, and Indian words. It was sufficient to carry on the fur trade, but it was wholly unsuited for preaching the gospel. The West India Company appeared perfectly satisfied with this level of communication and discouraged Megapolënsis's efforts.

Undaunted, the dominie set out to write a Mohawk-Dutch dictionary. The work, which proved to be tedious and difficult, caused him a great deal of anxiety, and he blamed the Mohawks, "as they are very stupid." But despite the difficulties, Megapolënsis persisted. The Mohawks who came to listen to the reverend were quick to point out the discrepancies between what was preached on Sunday and what went on the rest of the week. Megapolënsis reported that when the Mohawks witnessed him in prayer they laughed and asked what he was doing standing there alone and making so many words while everyone else remained silent. The good reverend, in a series of hand gestures and improperly pronounced Mohawk words, explained that he was admonishing the Christians not to steal, commit lewdness, get drunk, or commit murder. A Mohawk warrior listened intently and replied that it seemed a good idea to teach the Christians these things. He then asked the dominie, "Why do so many Christians do these things?"

His difficulties with the Mohawk language, notwithstanding, Megapolënsis's mission met with some success. Several of the Mohawks were baptized and admitted to the church, and their names stand today scattered among the Van Rensselaers, Van Schaicks, and Livingstons in the baptismal record book of the First Reformed Church of Albany. Yet the good reverend did not hold out much hope of success. Years later, in 1657, Megapolënsis and his colleague Samuel Drisius reported to the Classis of Amsterdam that the campaign to convert Native Americans had been a total failure. Furthermore, they despaired of ever achieving much "until they [the Indians] are subdued by the numbers and power of our people, and reduced to some sort of civilization." They told the story of what must have been considered a typical case of Indian conversion:

We have had an Indian here with us for about two years. He can read and write Dutch very well. We have instructed him in the fundamental principles of our religion, and he answers publicly in church, and can repeat the Commandments. We have given him a Bible, hoping he might do some good among the Indians, but it all resulted in nothing. He took to drinking brandy, he pawned the Bible, and turned into a regular beast, doing more harm than good among the Indians.[2]

2. J. Franklin Jameson, ed., *Narratives of New Netherland, 1609–1664* (New York, 1909), 399.

Megapolënsis spent seven years at Rensselaerswyck and Fort Orange before finally securing his release from the heirs of the patroon. In August 1649 he was in Manhattan, ready to return to the Netherlands, when he became part of the longest and most serious dispute between church and company in the colony's history.

It began when the Reverend Everardus Bogardus, who had some strongly held views about the proper roles of church and state in a Reformed society, fired off an angry letter to Director General Van Twiller condemning him for his drinking, calling him a "villain in his hide" and promising to "clamp him down so tight" in next Sunday's sermon that "his breastbone would crack." Van Twiller vowed to punish the dominie and in a drunken stupor even stalked the good reverend "with a drawn knife" in the streets of New Amsterdam. The director general's incompetence caught up with him, however, and he was replaced in 1638 by Willem Kieft.

After Kieft led the bloody and unprovoked attack on the Indians at Pavonia, a disgruntled settler named Maryn Adriaensen attacked the director general with a knife, intending to assassinate him. When the Reverend Bogardus stepped forward to defend Adriaensen, Kieft rebuffed the dominie and immediately sent the prisoner to the fatherland for trial. Bogardus saw this as an arbitrary exercise of power, and in the words of Kieft, he fulminated "wonderfully" from the pulpit for "nearly fourteen days." The relationship between Kieft and Bogardus deteriorated steadily. On Christmas Eve 1645, the reverend delivered a venomous sermon in which he stated "in Africa many animals interbreed because of the heat and in this manner many monsters are generated, but in this temperate climate I do not know where such monsters of men come from."

Kieft stopped attending Sunday service and even arranged to have the company soldiers drill just outside the church. While the congregation strained to listen to Bogardus, shouting himself hoarse in the pulpit, the director general marched his men to and fro, the roll of the drum echoing off the walls of the fort. Once he ordered a cannon discharged during the sermon. The dispute became a test of authority between the company and the church. In January 1646, Kieft and his council ordered Bogardus to appear before them to answer charges of stirring the people "to mutiny and rebellion" and making company officials "a scorn and laughing stock." Bogardus refused the summons and challenged the right of the West India Company to try him. When threatened with arrest as a "rebel contumacious toward justice" he penned a letter that in the words of Kieft was full of "needless subterfuge, calumny, injury, and profanation of God's Holy Word, as well as the contempt of justice and his lawful government."

Bogardus held the view that his ecclesiastical privileges protected him from prosecution for slander from the pulpit. It was a view not shared by the authoritarian Kieft, but the council offered a way out. The council proposed calling together an arbitration board composed of Reverend Johannes Megapolënsis, Reverend Francis Doughty, and "two or three impartial citizens of the provinces." Even Kieft appeared willing to let bygones be bygones provided the good reverend submitted to the arbitration. Bogardus refused the offer and informed the council that he preferred to have the accusations against him considered by Kieft's successor, Stuyvesant. The dispute was never resolved, because both Bogardus and Kieft lost their lives in a shipwreck on their way home to the Netherlands to defend themselves.

The series of disputes between the local ministers and the resident director generals left the political position of the Reformed Church in New Netherland largely undefined until the 1650s. The large increase in European immigration in these years brought a wide variety of people to New Netherland. The arrival of German Lutherans, Dutch Jews, English Quakers, and assorted dissenters was enough to send the local *predikanten* complaining to Director General Stuyvesant, whose own strongly held views on religion placed him squarely on the side of strict Calvinist orthodoxy. The issue of the enforcement of Calvinist doctrine brought the church and company into one final test of strength.

In October 1653, a group of Lutheran petitioners requested Stuyvesant to grant them permission to organize a congregation and conduct public services according to the Augsburg Confession. The Lutherans probably represented the largest non-Calvinist congregation in the colony. Stuyvesant could not categorically deny the petition without arousing the fears of every religious minority in New Netherland. But he also had to deal with the pastors of the New Amsterdam church, Johannes Megapolënsis and Samuel Drisius, who viewed the Lutherans as a threat, and, moreover, to grant the request would be a technical violation of his oath of office and an open invitation to other groups to seek similar concessions. In this matter, Stuyvesant acted with uncharacteristic restraint and reported the situation to his superiors in Amsterdam.

The company directors were unwilling to concede the request of the Lutherans, but they were upset at Stuyvesant for bringing the problem to them. Dutch officials could not hope to attract large numbers of Europeans to their colony if strict religious conformity were enforced. Hence, the directors instructed Stuyvesant "not to receive any similar petitions, but rather to turn them off in the most civil and least offensive way."

Nearly two years passed before the next challenge to Calvinist orthodoxy appeared. This time it involved Lutherans in the village of Middleburg on Long Island. When news reached the Reverends Megapolënsis and Drisius that a congregation of Lutherans were holding church services in Middleburg without a properly ordained minister, they reported the situation immediately to Stuyvesant and requested his assistance in putting a stop to this clear violation of the company's charter. This time the director general did not wait for authorization from the company directors. In February 1656, he issued an ordinance forbidding all religious conventicles not in conformity with the Synod of Dordrecht on the ground that "such gatherings lead to troubles, heresies and schisms." The council may have been somewhat less sure of its authority in this case, since it added an important qualifying statement that "the Director General and Council do not however hereby intend to force the consciences, to the prejudice of formerly given patents, or to forbid the preaching of Gods holy Word, the family prayers and divine service in the family."

When word of this ordinance reached Amsterdam, it set off a controversy that dragged on for years. The directors were particularly upset at Stuyvesant for what they perceived to be his obstinate refusal to heed their earlier advice. In an angry letter they ordered him "not [to] publish such or similar placats without our knowledge." The dispute with the Lutherans of Middleburg was finally settled some years afterward by a generous interpretation of the baptismal formula of the Reformed Church. The compromise angered Megapolensis and Drisius, but they were silenced when the directors threatened to replace them with two or three young ministers "not infected with scruples about unnecessary forms, which cause more division than edification."

The importance of economic considerations in defining the relationship between the company and the church in New Netherland is perhaps best illustrated by the dispute surrounding the arrival of twenty-three Jews from Brazil. The Jews were war refugees, forced to flee the colony of New Holland when it fell to the Portuguese. They came with little more than the clothes on their backs in the summer of 1654. Although their numbers hardly posed a threat to the Reformed Church, Reverend Megapolensis penned a long letter to the Classis of Amsterdam complaining that the arrival of the Jews "causes among the congregation here a great deal of complaint and murmuring."

The immediate concern was money for their support. Megapolensis reported that they came several times to his house, "weeping and bemoaning their misery." Only when the one Jewish merchant in town refused to "lend them a single stiver" did the reverend respond by tapping the Deacon's Fund for several hundred guilders. He warned the classis that "these people have no other God than the Mammon of unrighteousness, and no other aim than to get possession of Christian property, and to overcome all merchants by drawing all trade towards themselves." He ended his letter with the usual complaint about the number of schismatics, heretics, and unbelievers in the colony, and requested the pious fathers of Amsterdam to intercede with the directors of the company to prevent the still greater confusion that would arise, "if the obstinate and immovable Jews came to settle here."

Director General Stuyvesant, an antisemite of long standing, joined the reverend's campaign and requested permission from the directors of the company to ban Jews from New Netherland. He received their decision in April 1655. The Honorable Directors, having "weighed and considered" the problem, concluded that to ban these people, who had suffered so much loss in Brazil on behalf of the company, would be both "unreasonable and unfair." And more important, the Jews could not be banned "because of the large amount of capital they have invested in shares of this Company." Stuyvesant was told to act accordingly.

In 1656, in reply to a request from Stuyvesant concerning the rights of Jews to practice their religion, the directors recommended that they be segregated in their own community. The directors further instructed Stuyvesant to forbid the building of a synagogue, to bar Jews from public service, and to deny them the right to operate retail stores. Beyond such restrictions the directors were unwilling to go. The Jews of New Amsterdam were free to worship privately as long as such activities did not threaten the public peace. When the directors ordered Stuyvesant to turn a blind eye toward the practice of Judaism in New Amsterdam, they were only extending to the colony on the Hudson the same privileges permitted religious minorities in the fatherland.

Of all the religious minorities with which Stuyvesant had to contend, the humble members of the Society of Friends were the least tolerated. Quakers were the religious lepers of the seventeenth and early eighteenth centuries and were not welcomed anywhere in colonial America until the founding of Pennsylvania. Their appearance in New Netherland evoked a vile torrent of bigotry and persecution and threatened a political crisis as well.

The first Quakers arrived secretly in the colony in August 1657, when several came ashore from an English ship. The intruders might have gone unnoticed had they been content to bear their faith in silence, but such was not the temperament of Quakers. Two women from the landing party had the misfortune to be seized by the spirit shortly after disembarking, and they soon excited a large crowd of spectators. When news reached Stuyvesant that members of this reviled sect had the temerity to preach their heresy on the streets of New Amsterdam, he ordered them arrested. After a brief interview, he banished them from the colony. In the meantime, three Friends managed to cross the East River to Long Island. One of these, Robert Hodgson, took refuge in the English village of Hempstead.

Hempstead had been founded by English Calvinists some years earlier and was one of the more orthodox villages on the island. Thus when Hodgson attempted to preach in public, the selectmen promptly ordered his arrest. He was bound with rope and taken to New Amsterdam to be questioned personally by Stuyvesant. During the interview, Hodgson offended the director general by his refusal to remove his hat and his insistence on addressing Stuyvesant by the familiar pronoun. The director general, with the support of New Amsterdam's clergy, sentenced him to labor with the company slaves in the work gangs around the fort as punishment for his insolence. Hodgson, however, refused to work although he was repeatedly beaten and tortured. He was finally released and banished forever from the colony.

Hodgson's harsh treatment created sympathy among English villagers on Long Island, many of whom held antinomian beliefs that were compatible with the free will doctrine of the Quakers. In Gravesend, Flushing, and Jamaica, secret Quaker meetings were held, and the enthusiasm for the new religion spread. In the fall of 1657, at the urging of the Reverends Megapolënsis and Drisius, Stuyvesant issued a proclamation threatening any ship bringing Quakers to New Netherland with seizure. Colonists who entertained Quakers in their homes or attended Quaker meetings were subject to a fine of fifty Flemish pounds (300 fl.), with half the sum going to the informer.

The proclamation was received with some grumbling throughout New Netherland, but in the Long Island village of Flushing the response bordered on rebellion. Flushing's relationship with the Reformed Church was a troubled one that dated back several years. Founded in 1645 under a charter issued by Willem Kieft, the village had for some time refused the attempts of the Reformed clergy to provide a minister. Stuyvesant tried to resolve the dispute by forcing the services of the Reverend Francis Doughty on the village, only to discover that Doughty's Church of England theology was unacceptable to the independent-minded inhabitants. For months the villagers refused to attend his services or to pay his salary. Doughty finally gave up and took ship for Virginia in 1655, leaving Flushing without religious services until the arrival of the Quakers in 1657. In response to Stuyvesant's proclamation, the villagers, led by Sheriff Tobias Feake, directed the town clerk, Edward Hart, to draw up a remonstrance protesting the Dutch governor's high-handed tactics and articulating the principle of religious toleration. The document, known as the Flushing Remonstrance was signed on December 27, 1657, by thirty-one of the townspeople. It justified religious toleration and freedom of worship with elegant simplicity.

Right Honnorable.

You have been pleased to send up unto us a certaine Prohibition or Command that wee shoulde not receive or entertaine any of those people called *Quakers*, because they are supposed to bee by some seducers of the people for our parte wee cannot condem them in this case neither can wee stretch out our hands against them to punish bannish or persecute them for out of Christ God is a Consuming fire and it is a fearful [thing] to fall into the handes of the liveing God wee desire therefore in this case not to judge least wee be judged neither to Condem least wee bee Condemed but rather let every man stand and fall to his own Maister. . . .

The law of love, peace and libertie in the states extending to *Jewes Turkes* and *Egiptians* as they are Considered the sonnes of Adam, which is the glory of the outward State of Holland, . . . our desire is not to offend one of his little ones in what soever forme name or title hee appeares in whether presbyterian independant Baptist or Quaker but shall bee glad to see any thing of god in any of them: desireing to doe unto all men as wee desire all men should doe unto us which is the true law both of

Church and State. . . . Therefore if any of these said persons come in love unto us wee cannot in Conscience lay violent hands upon them but give them free Egresse and Regresse into our Towne and howses as god shall perswade our Consciences.[3]

Stuyvesant's reaction was swift and predictable. He arrested the selectmen who had signed the remonstrance along with Sheriff Feake. The defendants were charged with violating the director general's proclamation and the town's charter, which had outlawed all religious service except that offered or approved by the Dutch Reformed Church. Three of the defendants eventually recanted and were released, but Feake refused. Although Stuyvesant was willing to excuse him in return for a contrite request for a pardon, Feake would not budge. Finally, the director general ordered him removed from office, fined heavily, and banished from the colony.

The matter did not end there. Stuyvesant and the Reformed clergy spend the next four years trying to root out the remnants of Quakerism in the English towns on Long Island. Arrests were made, trials showcased, and colonists banished. By 1663 Stuyvesant's campaign of harassing Quakers came to the attention of the company directors. In a letter of reprimand, the directors admitted that "we heartily desire that these and other sectarians remained away from there, yet as they do not, we doubt very much, whether we can proceed against them rigorously without diminishing the population and stopping immigration, which must be favored at so tender a stage of the country's existence." They ended their letter by advising Stuyvesant to treat nonconformists lightly, or "at least not force people's consciences." Better to "allow every one to have his own belief, as long as he behaves quietly and legally, gives no offence to his neighbors and does not oppose the government," than to proceed too zealously in enforcing religious orthodoxy. Once again the company had stepped in to restrict the efforts of Stuyvesant and the clergy to enforce Calvinist orthodoxy.

In an age of religious intolerance, the profit-minded directors consistently pursued a secular fiscal strategy. The colony's Reformed clergy struggled mightily against this policy, but ultimately they failed to bar even the most despised religious sects from practicing their faith. Poorly funded, with virtually no support for its missionary activities, and constantly embroiled in controversy, the church was ill equipped to do battle with the company. For Stuyvesant such matters were important, for they spoke to the very heart of his own faith. Yet, after repeated rebukes from his superiors, he came to accept the unique Dutch compromise of outward adherence to an agreed-upon doctrine and practical indifference to its enforcement.

3. Edmund B. O'Callaghan and Berthold Fernow, eds. and trans., *Documents Relative to the Colonial History of the State of New York*, 15 vols. (New York, 1856–87), 14: 402–3.

Chapter 6

New Netherland's Last Years

AS THE TIDE OF NEW IMMIGRANTS SURGED AND THE MARI-time rivalry with Great Britain threatened to move from confrontation to war, Peter Stuyvesant turned his attention to diplomacy. With their teeming population and militant Puritanism, the New England colonies posed the greatest threat. The English government, moreover, had raised objections to Dutch settlements in North America for years. By the late 1640s the claims to New Netherland's lands were being made once again, and this time the English colonists had the numbers to support them.

New England's "great migration" had brought thousands of religious and economic refugees to the shores of North America in the 1630s and 1640s, and the quest for land had driven some across Long Island Sound to settle in territory claimed by the Dutch. Much of Long Island had become English, a fact conceded by Kieft when he issued charters to the English towns. Although soon to be embroiled in the Puritan Revolution and Cromwell Protectorate, the English government encouraged the encroachment of its subjects on Dutch territory by granting charters and patents to regions within the jurisdiction of New Netherland. Stuyvesant realized that little help would be forthcoming from the home countries, as the United Provinces and Great Britain braced for war.

From the moment of his commission in Amsterdam, Stuyvesant must have been aware that the future of New Netherland depended on his ability to compromise with the New England colonies about boundaries. Although generally known for his aggressive defense of Dutch rights whenever and wherever they were challenged, Stuyvesant proceeded cautiously. One of his first official acts was to send a letter of greeting to Governor John Winthrop of Massachusetts, in which he appealed to the common cause of Protestants against the hated papists, while reminding the New Englander that Holland had served as a refuge for many English dissenters during times of persecution. The director general made a point of asserting the "indubiate right" of the Dutch nation to all the land between the Connecticut and Delaware Rivers and offered to meet to resolve the boundary issues.

Governor Winthrop laid the letter before the commissioners of the United Colonies of New England, the mutual defense league that had been established after the disastrous Pequot War. Winthrop favored accepting the Dutch offer, but a majority of the commissioners advised a more cautious approach. Winthrop wrote Stuyvesant thanking him for his letter but left open the matter of a meeting, stating only that it might be possible "in proper time and place." Meanwhile, an incident involving a Dutch ship in New Haven created distrust on both sides.

Word reached New Amsterdam in August 1647 that the Dutch ship *St. Beninio* was trading with the English colonists at New Haven. The vessel, under command of Captain Cornelis Claesz Snoij from Edam, had been forced to seek refuge in the New England port after losing its water barrels in a storm. In compliance with West India Company regulations, Captain Snoij had sent word to Stuyvesant that he planned to make repairs in New Haven before continuing his chartered voyage to New Amsterdam. Stuyvesant was therefore furious to learn that Snoij was using the opportunity to trade with the English in clear violation of the company charter and that he planned an unauthorized voyage to English Virginia. As an example to others, Stuyvesant decided to seize the ship.

A Dutch ship, the *Swoll*, had recently been sold by Stuyvesant to the deputy governor of New Haven to raise revenue for the repair of the defenses on Manhattan Island. The vessel was to be delivered in New Haven in October, and Stuyvesant planned to use the occasion to seize the *St. Beninio*. On October 11, the *Swoll* sailed from the East River with seventy soldiers. When they arrived in New Haven harbor, the soldiers boarded the *St. Beninio*, cut it loose from its moorings, and sailed it away without incident. Upon its arrival in New Amsterdam, Stuyvesant confiscated the ship, its cargo, and rigging on behalf of the West India Company. The crew was held in custody only briefly, but Snoij was incarcerated for eight months in the stockade before being shipped in shackles to the fatherland.

The seizure of the *St. Beninio* and the receipt in New Haven a few days later of a letter from Stuyvesant citing Dutch claims to all the lands bordering Long Island Sound, prompted Governor Theophilius Eaton to send a blistering reply to New Amsterdam. Eaton accused Stuyvesant of making unsupportable claims to territory rightfully belonging to England and sending armed men to seize a ship without "so much as first acquainting any of the magistrates of this jurisdiction with the cause or ground thereof." The tone of Eaton's letter shocked Stuyvesant, and he attempted to soothe the governor's injured pride with a conciliatory letter that made no mention of the seizure of the *St. Beninio*. Matters might have settled themselves had not a new episode complicated Anglo-Dutch relations.

A few "miscontents" escaped the stockade at New Amsterdam and made their way to New Haven where they asked for asylum. Stuyvesant requested Eaton's assistance in extraditing the fugitives. Not only did the English governor refuse to return the men to Dutch custody, but Eaton lectured Stuyvesant on the need to adopt a more civil attitude toward English sovereignty. News of the dispute soon reached the commissioners of New England, and Winthrop persuaded them to intervene before the feud got out of hand. Winthrop drafted a letter to Stuyvesant promising to intercede on his behalf with Eaton to effect the extradition of the criminals. The letter was first sent to New Haven, where it was to serve as a warning to Eaton that the rest of the New England colonies disapproved of his militant posturing with the Dutch. The plan failed, however, because Eaton did not forward the letter to New Amsterdam, and he remained steadfast in his refusal to give up the fugitives.

Ignorant of Winthrop's attempts to resolve the controversy, Stuyvesant decided to retaliate by granting asylum to any fugitive from New Haven. The citizens of New Amsterdam complained that such a proclamation would be an open invitation to all the miscreants of New England and asked the director general to reconsider. Stuyvesant communicated secretly with the fugitives in New Haven, obtaining their return in response to a promise of amnesty. Shortly thereafter he rescinded the proclamation.

In 1649 a jurisdictional nightmare of competing colonial claims, patents, and charters pitted England, Holland, and Sweden in a struggle for control of the fur trade. On August 2, 1649, the commissioners of New England received a proposal from the Delaware Company of New Haven seeking official sanction for its fur trading colony on Delaware Bay. This was not the first time the Dutch had had to deal with English interlopers in the Delaware Valley. English colonists in 1641 had attempted to settle on the Schuyl Kill (present Philadelphia). Director General Kieft challenged the English claim to the area and was eventually able to persuade the other intruders in the Delaware, the Swedes, to cooperate with him in ousting the English from the valley.

The most formidable threat to Dutch rights, in fact, were the Swedes themselves, whose presence in the Delaware Valley had been a point of contention since the 1630s. New Netherland's director generals had been reluctant to move militarily against the Swedish settlements because of the international consequences that might result from an attack upon a friendly European power. By the late 1640s, however, New Sweden was growing with each arrival of new colonists. Moreover, the increased population had permitted the Swedes to expand their fur trade to the point that Dutch interests were seriously affected. In 1645, Andries Hudde became the new commander at Fort Nassau and instituted an aggressive policy of protecting Dutch trading interests in the valley. His counterpart, the governor of New Sweden, Johan Printz, was handicapped in his efforts to thwart the Dutch by an inconsistent supply of trade goods. Consequently, the better supplied Dutch traders were able to take advantage of the Swedes and entice the Indians to cross to the other side of the river. Printz retaliated by spreading rumors among the tribes of the region that the Dutch were planning to exterminate them. He also destroyed Dutch buildings on the west bank near the Schuyl Kill. For two years Stuyvesant played a waiting game with the Swedes, because he needed their cooperation in denying the valley to the interlopers from New Haven. Under his directions the Dutch attempted to cut off the supply of furs to Fort Christina by establishing a trading post on the Schuyl Kill called Beversreede. In the meantime, Stuyvesant pursued negotiations with New England to secure New Netherland's northern border.

The Protest of the Nine Men

Before negotiations could be worked out with the English, however, Stuyvesant had to face down a political rebellion on his Board of Nine Men. The crisis dated from December 1648 when Adriaen Van der Donck, former schout of Rensselaerswyck, was elected to the board. A lawyer from Breda and soon to be the proprietor of an estate near present-day Yonkers, Van der Donck became the leading voice of the new board and a constant source of opposition to Stuyvesant's authoritarian rule.[1]

Stuyvesant's aggressive policy of opposing the encroachments of New Netherland's English and Swedish neighbors and his efforts to curtail the ambitions of the patroon's officers at Rensselaerswyck placed the government of the colony in a constant state of crisis. Additionally, his suppression of illegal trading, especially the gun trade with the Indians, and his intrusive and moralistic regulations concerning taverns, beer brewing, and Sabbath keeping inevitably created animosity among the colonists. When he was forced to increase taxes for the support of his policies, the scene was set for a showdown between the director general and his Board of Nine Men.

Under Van der Donck's leadership, the board planned to send a delegation to the fatherland to demand political reforms. When Stuyvesant learned of this, he arrested Van der Donck, confiscated his papers, and expelled him from the board. Nevertheless, Van der Donck was able to prepare a long document in the

---

1. The name Yonkers is derived from his Dutch title of gentility, *Jonkheer* Van der Donck.

form of a report to the States General that was signed by him and the others on July 26, 1649, "in the name and on the behalf of the commonalty of New Netherland." The report, which constituted a scathing attack on the government of Stuyvesant and the West India Company, demanded more political freedom in the form of "suitable municipal government," greater economic freedom for the colony's inhabitants, a settlement of colonial boundary disputes with foreign governments, and an end to arbitrary rule.

The "Representation of New Netherland," as the document came to be called, minced no words when it came to assigning blame for the sorry state of the colony. The cause of the decay and "ruinous condition" of Netherland was best described as "bad government," most particularly the incompetent administration of Kieft. Although conceding that Director General Stuyvesant deserved some credit for attending to the most pressing problems with a vigor unknown in previous administrations, the remonstrants nonetheless blamed him for failing to repair the fort at New Amsterdam, which they described as "a molehill or a tottering wall, on which there is not one gun-carriage or one piece of cannon in a suitable frame or on a good platform." Furthermore, he had been "far more diligent and bitter in looking up causes of prosecution against his innocent opponents than his predecessor ever was." And finally, Director General Stuyvesant was a tyrant who baited his opponents constantly by asking their advice and then exploding "with ugly words which would better suit the fish-market than the council chamber." From such tyranny only their High Mightinesses the States General could deliver them by making an end of the "Honorable Company" and taking over the colony. Then New Netherland would prosper, and "every one would be allured hither by the pleasantness, situation, salubrity and fruitfulness of the country."

The "Representation" was taken to the Netherlands by a delegation of three emissaries selected by the disgruntled Board of Nine Men. There they presented the document to the States General and continued to denounce Stuyvesant and the West India Company. Stuyvesant countered by sending his colonial secretary, Cornelis Van Tienhoven, to the fatherland to defend his administration.

Van Tienhoven prepared his own report titled "Answer to the Representation of New Netherland" and skillfully maneuvered behind the scenes with the close cooperation of the Amsterdam Chamber of the company. He was successful in delaying action by the States General and in averting a take-over of the company's holdings in North America. His "Answer" was a clever defense of the company's policies and Stuyvesant's sometimes high-handed style of government. With the aid of influential members of the Amsterdam Chamber, Van Tienhoven blunted the thrust of criticism and returned to New Netherland in triumph.

Regardless of their united front in defense of Stuyvesant, however, the directors of the company were not pleased with events in the colony. They were most concerned that Stuyvesant's posturing with the New Haven colony might provoke a war, which in turn would lead to a take-over of the colony by the States General. They wrote Stuyvesant a letter that left little room for misunderstanding: "If we are compelled to a rupture with the English, we question not but the deputies of their High Mightinesses will take it amiss, especially as the delegates [of the Nine Men] have left nothing untried to persuade that college that you will be the cause of such a war." Stuyvesant was well aware of the consequences of war with the English colonies. Indeed, he had already adopted a less militant attitude toward his neighbors to the north. It turned out to be a wise policy, for less than a year later, the beheading of Charles I made the Cromwellian Rump Parliament an international pariah, forcing the Puritan oligarchy to offer an olive branch to its chief competitor and old Protestant ally.

The Hartford Treaty

England's Puritan Revolution placed the government of the Netherlands in a difficult situation. The execution of the English king inflamed Dutch public opinion and nearly threw the United Provinces into the arms of the absolutist governments of the Continent. England's Puritan leaders immediately recognized the danger and dispatched a delegation to The Hague seeking recognition and peace. At first Calvinist independents in the States General succeeded in gaining sympathy for the English regicides, and plans were even hatched for a Protestant alliance, but negotiations soon broke down over commercial matters. The brief thaw in Anglo-Dutch relations created a favorable atmosphere for a reconsideration of Stuyvesant's proposal for a colonial summit. The meeting was scheduled for Hartford, Connecticut, in September 1650.

Peter Stuyvesant arrived in Hartford on September 23 with Cornelis Van Tienhoven and a contingent of company soldiers. The commissioners of New England were already at work when the Dutch arrived, having spent much of their pre-summit schedule reviewing a list of grievances against the Dutch submitted by the delegates from New Haven. The grievances were presented to Stuyvesant later as proof of the injuries suffered by English colonists. The Dutch governor countered with his own carefully prepared list of complaints against English violations of Dutch sovereignty in the Connecticut and Delaware River Valleys. He tried to focus the discussions on boundary issues, which were in his view the heart of the problem. Numerous misunderstandings had arisen over the years, he noted, because the boundaries between English and Dutch colonial territory had never been formally established. He proposed, therefore, that the conference set aside the petty complaints about past incursions and injuries and concentrate instead on producing appropriate maps and other documents to submit to the respective home countries.

The boundary issues were referred to an arbitration board composed of Simon Bradstreet of Massachusetts, Thomas Prince and Thomas Willet, both of New Plymouth, and George Baxter of New Netherland. The last named was an English resident of Long Island, who served Stuyvesant as an assistant and interpreter during the conference. All the members of the board were English, and the discussions were conducted in English. After a long day of negotiations the men adjourned to prepare a document titled "Articles of Agreement," which was then signed by all participants.

The Articles of Agreement, known to posterity as the Hartford Treaty, set provisional boundaries between the Dutch and English colonies and left the evaluation of the legitimacy of respective claims to the diplomats of London and The Hague. The Dutch, however, paid a high price for peace with the English. Some of the more important concessions included giving up all claims to the Connecticut Valley, the reduction by almost two-thirds of Dutch territory on Long Island, the abandonment of all claims to the area around Hartford, and the reduction of Dutch territory on the eastern side of the Hudson Valley to a ten-mile corridor, six miles of which were to remain unsettled as a buffer zone. In what must be considered a singular victory for the Dutch, the New England commissioners agreed to withdraw their support of New Haven's claim to the Delaware, noting that any future attempt by New Haven to establish a colony there would not have their approval.

Although the Hartford Treaty was never to be approved by the English government, both sides found it convenient to honor the provisional boundaries until the early 1660s. Stuyvesant had little choice but to recognize the realities of demography. The English were already well established on the eastern end of Long Island, and the Connecticut Valley had ceased to be Dutch years before. In any case, the Hudson Valley was more prized as a highway for the fur trade than as a place for large-scale agricultural development, and the eastern corridor seemed more than adequate to protect Dutch interests. Having achieved what he could, Stuyvesant returned to New Amsterdam.

First Anglo-Dutch War Threatens New Netherland

The ink had hardly had time to dry on the Hartford Treaty before the First Anglo-Dutch War erupted in Europe. When the news of hostilities finally reached America in 1652, the war was already two months old. The immediate cause of the collapse of peace was the English Navigation Act of 1651. The act attempted to exclude all foreign ships from the English empire by prohibiting "the introduction into any territory of the Commonwealth of produce of any country in Asia, Africa, or America, except in vessels owned by Englishmen or by the inhabitants of English colonies, and manned by crews of which more than one half were of English nationality."

The Navigation Act was rightly viewed as a dagger pointed at the heart of Dutch commerce. Commercial competition between Holland and Great Britain had been keen for years, but the Navigation Act was something altogether new in the relationship between the two Protestant sea powers. For the Dutch, whose commitment to free trade was almost religious in its intensity, it was an act of war. Adding to the hysteria were a number of bloody confrontations "beyond the line" that had aroused nationalistic sentiment and given wing to rumors of atrocities. A jingoistic pamphlet war increased fears on both sides and contributed to a sense of impending crisis. Nowhere were the rumors more apocalyptic than in the North American colonies.

In New Netherland news of the war created panic among colonists in areas adjacent to English settlements. Stuyvesant had already commenced a review of the defenses of New Amsterdam months before his departure for Hartford in the hopes of preparing the colony for an expected naval and land assault from New England. He now turned the colony inside out trying to make it impregnable, but he also tried diplomacy.

Stuyvesant's first task was to quell rumors of a Dutch conspiracy to arm the Indians of the Connecticut Valley. Although Stuyvesant tried to reassure the English that such was not the case, the commissioners of New England took the rumors seriously and in April 1653 called a special meeting at Boston to investigate. The meeting produced a long document of accusations that alleged New Netherlanders were in "bloody colours" with the Indians of New England. Stuyvesant immediately penned a reply denying the charges and inviting a delegation from the commissioners to visit New Amsterdam under a flag of truce and see for themselves. The commissioners accepted the invitation and sent three men to Manhattan. At about the same time they also approved the recruitment of a five-hundred-man militia.

The English delegation arrived in New Amsterdam in the summer of 1653 determined to ferret out evidence of the Dutch contraband trade in firearms. When the English departed, they were firmly convinced of the conspiracy, although not one shred of evidence had been uncovered. At least one member of the delegation, John Leverett, had another purpose. Captain Leverett, who would command the militia force soon to be assembled in New England, used his time in New Amsterdam to reconnoiter the island's defenses, noting the most likely avenues of attack and calculating the strength of the Dutch defense forces.

No sooner had the delegation departed than Stuyvesant received news of ominous events on Long Island. The leaders of the New Haven colony had decided to contact English inhabitants on Long Island in an effort to drum up support for an invasion. The contact person was John Underhill, an Englishman living in New Netherland and the former commander of Kieft's militia during the Indian rebellions. When Stuyvesant heard that Underhill had been given the job of discovering the Dutch conspiracy to arm the Indians, he had him arrested, but, lacking evidence of treason, was forced to release him a short time later. Underhill returned to the English villages on Long Island and began to campaign openly against the Dutch. In one carefully staged provocation, he even went so far as to raise the flag of Parliament at Hempstead and to preach revolution against the Dutch. When Stuyvesant dispatched officers to rearrest him, he fled to Rhode Island, where he proceeded to stir up the colonists there.

The English towns on Long Island were a constant worry to Stuyvesant and the directors of the company. In the midst of the war, the directors urged Stuyvesant to keep a close eye on the English villages and to be more cautious in granting town charters to English inhabitants "that we may not nourish serpents in our bosom, who finally might devour our hearts." Stuyvesant found little use for such advice, since he knew all too well that any crackdown on the English of Long Island would provoke an attack from New England. He chose to ignore the growth of the fifth column on Long Island in favor of preparing the defenses of Manhattan Island.

Stuyvesant called an emergency meeting of the Council of New Netherland, together with the burgomasters and schepens of the newly chartered city of New Amsterdam, to consider measures for the defense of the colony. The council approved several resolutions at Stuyvesant's urging. One of these established a citizens' guard to police the town after dark. The fear of English saboteurs may have been the motive behind this action, because the guard was allowed to disband after the war. New Amsterdam would not have a permanent police force until 1658, when Stuyvesant established the Rattle Watch. Other resolutions pledged funds to repair the fort and raise taxes for the defense of the colony.

Meanwhile in New England, the meetings of the commissioners were becoming increasingly contentious as the colonies of New Haven and Connecticut pressed for an invasion of New Netherland, while Massachusetts and New Plymouth advised a more cautious approach. The New Haven men, who perhaps viewed the war as an opportunity to reassert their claims to the Delaware Valley, were so angered by the Bay Colony's reluctance to commit itself to offensive operations that they wrote directly to Oliver Cromwell and requested the sending of a fleet to invade the Dutch colony.

At about the same time the citizens of Rhode Island became aware that they had been left out of the war preparations of the other New England colonies. Rumors were rife that a combined force of Dutch and Indians were poised to attack Providence. The source of the rumors may have been John Underhill, whose presence in the colony no doubt contributed to anti-Dutch sentiment. Authorized by the Rhode Island government to strike a preemptive blow against the Dutch, Underhill moved his small expedition into the Connecticut Valley in July 1653 and forced the surrender of Fort Good Hope, the poorly defended Dutch outpost established by Van Twiller twenty years before. It was the last symbol of Dutch authority in the valley.

Stuyvesant was dismayed to learn of the surrender, but he could do nothing about it. The fall of Good Hope convinced him, however, that the next blow would fall on New Amsterdam. His first move was to secure his southern flank by sending two envoys to Virginia. The envoys were cordially received by Acting Governor Richard Bennett, but negotiations for a nonaggression pact failed. At the close of the year Stuyvesant sent Dominie Samuel Drisius to try again. Drisius succeeded in concluding a commercial treaty with the royalist government of Virginia without mention being made of the ongoing Anglo-Dutch War.

In February 1654 Oliver Cromwell sent four warships to New England for use in a planned invasion of New Netherland. The lord protector sought to respond to the urgent requests of his fellow Puritans while dealing a devastating blow to the United Provinces, but things went badly from the start. Owing to poor weather conditions in the English Channel the small fleet did not arrive in New England until June. Then troops had to be raised. Nearly five hundred militiamen in Massachusetts and virtually every able-bodied man in the New Haven colony volunteered for service in the expedition. By the end of June the ships had been revictualed and the troops readied for the assault.

In New Amsterdam Stuyvesant busied himself trying to prepare his subjects for the invasion only to discover that the English on Long Island were once again sowing discord. At Gravesend, his former assistant, George Baxter, had betrayed him by establishing communication with New England and attempting to organize a militia to assist in the invasion. At Middleburg, where Stuyvesant had attempted to force the Lutherans into the Calvinist fold, the inhabitants proposed to "open the ball." Stuyvesant issued a proclamation forbidding suspicious persons from moving their belongings to safer areas and imposed summary trials for those convicted of "stirring to mutiny" the citizens of the colony, but he was powerless to enforce it. Finally, on the eve of the fleet's departure, a merchant vessel arrived in New England bringing news of a truce. Celebrations erupted in the streets of New Amsterdam when Stuyvesant announced the peace.

Securing the Delaware Valley

The struggle for control of the Delaware Valley continued throughout the war with England. Shortly after the conclusion of the Treaty of Hartford, Stuyvesant had, without authorization from the West India Company, led a small army of one hundred men overland to the Delaware to link up with a squadron of eleven ships from New Amsterdam. The armada then sailed upriver to the old Dutch outpost of Fort Nassau on the east bank with drums beating in an impressive show of force. Although Stuyvesant could have driven the Swedes out of the valley, to have done so without written orders would have created an international incident the company could ill afford on the eve of a war with Great Britain. Instead, he opted to engage in intimidation. At Fort Nassau he disembarked his troops and proceeded to dismantle the fort. Everything movable was transported to another site on the west bank of the river known to the Dutch as Sant Hoeck (present-day Newcastle, Delaware). With its deep harbor and location south of the Swedish settlement at Fort Christina, the new site could command the river. Stuyvesant named the settlement Fort Casimir in honor of Ernst Casimir of the House of Orange-Nassau, a hero of the Eighty Years War from his own province of Friesland. The company directors were dismayed when they found out he had removed Fort Nassau without orders, and they warned him to take great care in protecting the new fort. They further admonished him to proceed cautiously with the Swedes, since the fatherland could not afford another enemy while at war with Great Britain.

In 1654 Stuyvesant was frantically preparing defenses on Manhattan for an anticipated invasion from New England when he learned that Fort Casimir had surrendered without firing a shot to a Swedish force led by Johan Rising, Printz's replacement as governor of New Sweden. The fall of Fort Casimir removed the only Dutch presence in the Delaware Valley, and the arrival, with Rising, of two hundred Swedish settlers threatened the loss of New Netherland's claim to the region. Peace with England allowed Stuyvesant the opportunity to deal decisively with New Sweden.

This time he had the full support of the company behind him. The directors ordered Stuyvesant to do his "utmost to revenge this misfortune not only by restoring matters to their former condition, but also by driving the Swedes at the same time from the river, as they did us."

Stuyvesant assembled five companies of soldiers on Manhattan, three hundred in all, and a fleet of seven ships. The fleet entered the river in late September 1655 and sailed without opposition past Fort Trinity, the Swedish name given to Fort Casimir after its surrender the year before. When Rising learned of this maneuver he realized the game was up. With Fort Christina cut off from the sea and Fort Trinity behind enemy lines, he sent his second-in-command, Hendrick von Elswick, downriver to negotiate terms with Stuyvesant. Von Elswick was surprised to learn that Stuyvesant would not negotiate any agreement except surrender. When confronted with the situation von Elswick remarked "Today me, tomorrow you." Rising surrendered Fort Christina on September 25.

Prosperity and the Merchant Class

Successful diplomatically, Stuyvesant faced serious internal problems, one of which arose paradoxically from the growing prosperity of the colony's merchant class. The development of an indigenous merchant community in New Netherland was delayed for years by the policies of the West India Company. Although a lively clandestine trade evolved between the settlers and the seamen who came ashore at Manhattan, the company monopoly served as too great a barrier to merchant enterprise in the early years of colonization.

The patroonship plan of the 1630s clearly favored Amsterdam merchants by granting to the wealthiest and most influential the right to exploit the colony as patroons. Of great concern to those who opposed the patroonship plan were the trade provisions that allowed patroons to outfit their own ships and conduct trade throughout the company's domain. These provisions spawned a lively trade between private agents of the patroons and the colonists of New Netherland, New England, and Virginia. In legalizing the intercolonial trade for the patroons and their agents, the company opened New Netherland to the Amsterdam merchants, who responded in the 1630s by building, chartering, and freighting dozens of ships for the North American trade.

The growth of New Netherland's merchant community accelerated after 1639, when the company abandoned the failed patroonship system. Under the so-called Articles and Conditions, colonists were free to trade in all colonial commodities, including furs. However, all furs had to be sold to the company. Private ships from the fatherland could sail freely to the colony and trade throughout the chartered territory provided a company supercargo was on board. The company retained the right to tax certain imports and exports and to levy a 10 percent "farm tax" based upon a farm's production in its fifth year of operation, but such restrictions were minor compared to the monopoly of the fur market claimed for the company.

The seeds of change were planted in 1640 when the company issued a new set of "Freedoms and Exemptions," which among other things provided two hundred acres of free land to each colonist who transported to the colony five family members or servants. Thereafter, the merchants of Amsterdam ensnared the transoceanic trade in their web of cartels, and the merchants of New Netherland exploited intercolonial trade, first as agents and partners of the Amsterdam merchants and eventually as competitors.

New Netherland's merchant community expanded rapidly in the late 1650s to become an important economic and political force in the colony. The role of Amsterdam merchants was crucial; they settled their agents in the colony and channeled credit into New Netherland through the use of bills of exchange drawn on the Exchange Bank of Amsterdam. Their credit agreements were guaranteed by formal written debt instruments negotiated by professional notaries in New Netherland. Written credit agreements in the form of notarized promissory notes were produced by New Amsterdam notaries as early as 1651. Debt disputes, moreover, were adjudicated by the director general and council.

The resolution of debt disputes brought the merchants into contact with the company as government, and the difficulties they encountered were partially responsible for the rebellion of the Board of Nine Men. The Nine Men had asked the States General in the "Representation of New Netherland" to create a municipal corporation for New Amsterdam. The merchants were particularly angered by Stuyvesant's perceived harassment of merchants who appeared before him to collect debts. His reluctance to repay company debts owed Manhattan merchants was another factor in the merchants' drive for municipal government.

After a three-year struggle and numerous petitions, the States General issued a charter for the city of New Amsterdam which took effect in February 1653. The charter established a new court of schout, burgomasters, and schepens. From 1653 until at least 1674, long after the colony had become New York and the titles of municipal officials had been changed to sheriff, mayor, and alderman, the court continued to adjudicate debts. The continuity of its procedures and the steady support it gave for debt collection enabled the merchants of New Netherland and New York to expand their operations, secure in the knowledge that contracts and notes were enforceable.

The expansion of colonial trade in the 1650s can be traced in various laws and ordinances approved by Stuyvesant and the council. To protect resident merchants from the competition of itinerant foreign traders, an ordinance of 1648 imposed a three-year residency requirement on all merchants in the colony. In 1649 Stuyvesant approved a law ordering "all wholesale and retail merchants, also bakers and others, who sell by the ell [about two feet English measurement], measure or weight not to use in delivering or receiving any other ell, weight or measure, than that of Amsterdam." Merchants discovered using nonstandard weights and measures were fined according to the customs of the fatherland. In 1658 the municipal government of New Amsterdam amended the law by requiring all measures and weights to be certified at the City Hall and a fee paid to the city treasury.

The director general and council even attempted to control the money supply by issuing ordinances regulating the quality and setting the price of wampum. In 1650 with an internal economy suffering from the depreciation of loose wampum, "among which is found much unpierced and only half finished [beads], made of stone, bone, glas, shells, horn, nay even of wood," the council declared that thereafter no loose wampum would be considered legal tender in New Netherland.

Indirect evidence of increased merchant activity is found in an ordinance of 1656 establishing Saturday as market day in the city. The market was to be held "on the Strand near the house of Master Hans Kierstede," and all who wished to sell farm products or anything else were directed to conduct their business there. Numerous contemporary accounts and observations by foreign visitors in later years testify to the vibrant role the market played in the city's commercial history. Many of New Netherland's most prominent merchants spent their apprenticeship in New Amsterdam's free market.

Similar developments in Albany point to the growth of indigenous merchant activity in the upper Hudson region during this period as well. The minutes of the Inferior Court of Justice for Fort Orange and Albany reveal that many of the cases adjudicated before this body involved suits for the payment of debts and requests for enforcement of commercial contracts. Out of approximately 1,586 entries for the years 1652–60, some 626 or about 40 percent are easily identified as creditor requests for payment of debts. In most of these cases, a written debt obligation virtually assured judgment for the plaintiff. The magistrates of Albany were as attentive to the needs of merchants as were the magistrates of New Amsterdam.

By the end of the Dutch period a merchant class had come to dominate the politics of the city of New Amsterdam, a trend that would continue after the English conquest. Prosperity was stimulated by the establishment of stable governmental institutions, and commercial opportunities grew as immigration brought thousands to the colony. As the newcomers fanned out over the landscape establishing farms, villages, and towns, they pressed hard against the Native Americans, who attempted to stem the tide of invasion.

Indian Rebellions

The first Indian rebellion of the Stuyvesant era erupted in 1655, while the director general was in the Delaware Valley dislodging the Swedes. The immediate cause of the hostilities was the murder of an Indian woman by a Dutch settler, who claimed he caught her stealing peaches from his orchard. The so-called Peach War, however, had deeper causes. Infuriated by Stuyvesant's failure to protect them from land speculators and squatters, not to mention unscrupulous traders who debauched their people with liquor while swindling them in deals for furs, the tribes of the lower Hudson, including Mahicans, Pachamis, Esopus, and Hackensack Indians, launched an assault on European settlements around New Amsterdam. Before a defense force could be assembled, many farms were burned and dozens of captives taken for ransom.

Facing what appeared to be an uprising of most of the Indians of the lower Hudson, Stuyvesant turned to New England for help. The English villages on Long Island were vulnerable to attack and implored Stuyvesant to protect them, but their fellow countrymen in New England refused to join with the Dutch in putting down the rebellion. After some brutal counterattacks on Indian villages, Stuyvesant seized the opportunity to negotiate a peace. Unable to consolidate their gains without risking annihilation, the Indians gave up their captives and ceased their attacks. The costs had been high for the European colonists of New Netherland: fifty settlers dead, five hundred cattle lost, and a season's corn burned to the stalks. Native American losses were calculated at sixty dead.

Caught in a web of shifting alliances and war, the Native Americans of New Netherland struggled to survive by trying to anticipate the winners in the conflicts among Europeans. In 1657 the Hackensack Indians and their neighbors concluded an alliance with New Netherland and resold Staten Island to the Dutch, who had abandoned it during the war. Gradually colonists returned to their farmsteads and an uneasy peace settled over the lower Hudson estuary.

The next uprising occurred on the west bank of the mid-Hudson Valley at Esopus (present Kingston), when Dutch settlers returned to lands they had abandoned during the Peach War. The Esopus Indians opposed the resettlement of Europeans on land they considered theirs. After a series of murders and other incidents involving the killing of livestock and burning of crops, the Dutch settlers called on Stuyvesant to put down the rebellion. Negotiations for a truce reached an impasse when Stuyvesant could not make good on a promise of payment for lands sold by the Indians to compensate for Dutch property losses.

On September 20, 1659, about a dozen colonists and company soldiers launched an unprovoked attack on a handful of Indians while they sat drinking liquor around a campfire. One warrior was killed and another captured and tortured. The following day, Esopus warriors attacked a party of men carrying dispatches to Stuyvesant. Within days, several hundred Esopus warriors attacked outlying farms and surrounded the colonists huddled in the fortified village. The siege lasted twenty-three days, until Stuyvesant, leading a force of 150 men, sailed upriver and relieved the embattled colonists. Stuyvesant's force, while large enough to lift the siege, could not pursue the Esopus warriors. Leaving a portion of his force behind to man the garrison, Stuyvesant returned to New Amsterdam and set about isolating the Esopus Indians by strengthening alliances with the Hackensacks and other tribes living near New Amsterdam. The treaties were the first formal negotiations with the Indians of the lower Hudson since the outbreak of the Peach War, and they succeeded in cutting off the Esopus Indians from their potential allies around Manhattan. In the meantime, the Dutch authorities at Fort Orange persuaded the Mohawks and Susquehannocks to pressure the Esopus into giving up their remaining lands near the Dutch village. The Esopus Indians signed a peace treaty with the Dutch on July 14, 1660, ceding most of the disputed land, but retaining farmland nearby.

The Second Esopus War broke out in the summer of 1663, when Dutch settlers, ignoring warnings from the Esopus Indians, persisted in building the settlement of Nieuwe Dorp (literally, "new village," near the present site of Hurley). Wiltwyck (the new name given Esopus in the town charter of 1661) was attacked, and Stuyvesant had to dispatch a force of 210 Europeans, African slaves, and Long Island Indians, led by Ensign Martin Cregier to the area. After relieving Wiltwyck, the small army went on a rampage of destruction, burning Esopus towns, destroying crops, and liberating European hostages. The indiscriminate killing of several Minisink and Wappinger Indians, as well as the slaughter of hundreds of Esopus men, women, and children, finally broke the will of the Native Americans of the mid-Hudson Valley. In a treaty signed in New Amsterdam on May 16, 1664, the Esopus gave up most of their best land and ceased to be a serious threat to European settlements of the region. Stuyvesant declared a day of thanksgiving to mark the end of the war.

The English Conquest

In the first months of 1664, King Charles II issued a patent to his brother, James, Duke of York and Albany. The grant encompassed an area of North America almost wholly occupied by the Dutch colony of New Netherland. While the patent was being prepared, an invasion plan was drawn up at the Council of Foreign Plantations by James himself and a few members of his household. The plan appeared to follow closely a scheme devised by Samuel Maverick of Massachusetts, who had petitioned the Council of Foreign Plantations as early as 1661 for an attack on the Dutch colony at Manhattan. It called for a naval force consisting of three frigates and several hundred soldiers, to be augmented by volunteers drawn from the New England colonies. The plan had been rejected in 1661 as premature and unjustified in view of the peace then prevailing between Great Britain and the Netherlands. By the spring of 1664, however, English-Dutch commercial competition along the African coast and the angry denunciations of the 1660 Navigation Act (a renewal of the act of 1651) coming from the Dutch ambassador at London presaged the resumption of war between the United Provinces and Great Britain. The duke of York authorized the outfitting of a fleet and the recruitment of an army of three hundred soldiers. Assembled in Portsmouth during the spring, the fleet departed England on May 15, 1664.

Stuyvesant had lived for years with rumors of rebellion among the English towns on Long Island, but in the 1660s the rumors became reality. In 1661 John Winthrop, Jr., son of the founder of Massachusetts Bay Colony, obtained a charter for Connecticut from the new king, Charles II, that not only permitted the annexation of the colony of New Haven but ignored the very existence of New Netherland. English jurisdiction was extended southward to encompass Long Island and west "to the South Sea [Pacific Ocean]." Connecticut authorities lost no time in declaring their sovereignty over Greenwich and West Chester on the mainland and Jamaica, Flushing, Gravesend, Hempstead, and Middleburg (now Newtown) on Long Island. Agents soon arrived in the villages of Long Island and proceeded "to stir up mutiny." The agents even circulated a petition for signatures that called on Connecticut to cast "the skirts of its government and protection" over the people.

Stuyvesant tried diplomacy again. In September 1663, he undertook a diplomatic junket to Boston, where he addressed, without success, the commissioners of the United Colonies, calling their attention to numerous violations of the Hartford Treaty.[2] In October 1663, he tried another approach by sending a delegation of three men to present Dutch grievances at the meeting of the Connecticut General Court (Assembly) in Hartford. The mission failed when the General Court refused to take up the Dutch complaints.

Four months later an Englishman named John Scott tried to persuade Stuyvesant to grant full independence to the English towns on Long Island, because Charles II had already granted his brother a patent for the land. Once again Stuyvesant sought the advice of the company directors, only to be told that the ships reported to be assembling at Portsmouth were intended for an invasion of New England, where, Dutch intelligence reported, the recalcitrant Puritans had still not made their peace with the Restoration. Consequently, Stuyvesant was completely unprepared for the arrival of the invasion fleet in the harbor before New Amsterdam on August 18, 1664.

The Dutch governor's first response was to send a message to Colonel Richard Nicolls, the fleet's commander, demanding to know his intent. At the same time he dispatched messages to Wiltwyck and Fort Orange warning of the arrival of the English and requesting aid immediately. He also sent a request for help to the Dutch towns on Long Island, but Nicolls did not give him time to mount a defense. While the population of New Amsterdam waited and Stuyvesant and his staff pondered the situation, Nicolls assembled his troops and the English militia from Long Island and moved from his base at Gravesend to Brooklyn. He then ordered two of his ships up the Hudson to prevent any aid from reaching the beleaguered city from the north. Panic swept the city as Dutch burghers pleaded with the director general to make a peace before the Long Island militia was turned loose on the city to plunder and pillage. At this juncture, Governor Winthrop of Connecticut offered himself as a mediator. Having received from Nicolls a guarantee that the Dutch could continue to trade and receive immigrants from the United Provinces, he came ashore under a flag of truce and entered the besieged city.

Stuyvesant was willing to fight; he had always been willing to fight, but the

---

2. The States General ratified the Hartford Treaty in 1656, but it was ignored by both the Puritan regicides and the Restoration Parliament. From the English point of view, there was no agreement on boundaries and hence no basis for compromise.

old soldier knew the situation was hopeless. With fewer than 150 professional soldiers at his command and a panic-stricken civilian population imploring him to surrender, he steeled himself against the humiliation and agreed to meet with Winthrop in a tavern along the Strand. There, in the shadow of the fort he had rebuilt, he began negotiations for the surrender of New Netherland.

Stuyvesant and the burgomasters who accompanied him listened politely as Winthrop outlined the terms. When he was finished Stuyvesant protested and asked for more time. Finally the discussions were broken off. Winthrop had brought with him a letter from Nicolls that put in writing his promise to respect Dutch property rights and to permit continued trade and immigration from the Netherlands. When Winthrop departed, the burgomasters asked Stuyvesant to read the letter to the magistrates and seek their opinion. In a fit of anger, he picked up the letter and ripped it to pieces before stomping out of the tavern. The burgomasters rushed to tell others of the contents of the letter, and within hours the entire town was abuzz. A crowd of citizens gathered before City Hall demanding to see the letter. Stuyvesant hurried to the scene and tried to calm the crowd by assuring them that they could defy the English, but it was no use. Rumors had spread that West India Company officials were smuggling their wives and children over to the English side, and even the company soldiers were showing signs of disloyalty. Finally, Stuyvesant ordered the letter pieced together and read to the people.

After the letter was made public, ninety-three of the wealthiest men in the city signed a petition beseeching Stuyvesant to agree to the terms of surrender. The remonstrance noted the poor condition of the city's defenses and the impossibility of holding off such a formidable armada. The petitioners feared the city would be sacked by the Long Island militia if a defense were attempted. The outcome would be "in a word, the absolute ruin and destruction of about fifteen hundred innocent souls." Stuyvesant could not argue with the logic of the petition, nor could he inspire the soldiers and citizens to fight an enemy who appeared exceedingly generous under the circumstances. Reluctantly, the old soldier agreed to surrender. On August 27, representatives of both sides met at Stuyvesant's farm and concluded an agreement of capitulation. Dutch soldiers were permitted to leave the fort with full military honors, and anyone who wished to return to the Netherlands was permitted to do so on the first available ship. Nicolls's terms were even more generous than those promised in the letter. Dutch cultural and commercial life was to remain untouched for the moment. All contracts, property, and inheritances were to remain legal and binding. The Reformed Church was left undisturbed, and direct trade with the fatherland was to continue for six months. For the time being, even the West India Company was allowed to continue using its property throughout the colony. And, finally, all local officials were to continue in office until the next election, at which time they were required to swear loyalty to England.

On August 29, 1664, with the beating of drums and the flag of the fatherland flying in a gentle breeze, Peter Stuyvesant, last governor of New Netherland, marched out of the fort at the head of his troops. Humiliated by the surrender, he refused to parade his soldiers before the English. Instead, he marched them directly to the wharf, where they boarded the *Gideon,* bound for Amsterdam. After a decent interval, Nicolls entered the fort with his men. The other Dutch garrisons at Fort Orange and on the Delaware surrendered within days. The history of New York had begun.

The Dutch Legacy

The fall of New Netherland did not signal the demise of Dutch culture. On the contrary, the English conquest and subsequent attempts to anglicize the colony may have helped to preserve it. With their language, laws, and religion threatened by a new dominant class of foreigners, the Dutch embraced even more tenaciously that which gave them their identity. The long history of "old Dutch ways" in New York and New Jersey bears testimony to the persistence of that culture.

In New York and New Jersey, where relatively large numbers of Dutch-speaking people continued to live under the shadow of English institutions, the language of the fatherland endured for many years. Dutch was abandoned most rapidly in New York City, where fluency in English early became advantageous and profitable, but even in the duke's own city, Dutch continued to be spoken into the mid-1700s by third-generation offspring of New Netherlanders. Outside Manhattan, enclaves of Dutch language survived even longer.

In the area around Albany, the European settlers were almost entirely ethnic Dutch, and here, in particular, the dominance of the Dutch language was indicative of the power of the Dutch ruling class. In 1749 the Swedish botanist Peter Kalm traveled through Albany and reported that its inhabitants were almost all Dutch. "They speak Dutch, have Dutch preachers and the divine service is performed in that language. Their manners are likewise quite Dutch."

The English cultural tide thus came later to the northern Hudson Valley than to Manhattan, but it came nonetheless. In 1755 the Albany area became the bivouac for the army preparing to invade Quebec. For years Albany bristled with British soldiers, many billeted in private homes because of a shortage of barracks. When Quebec fell to General James Wolfe in 1759, most of the soldiers left for Canada, but their contact with the Dutch citizens of the area had accelerated the process of anglicization and assimilation, especially for the younger generation.

In remote areas the Dutch language survived in a corrupted and archaic form known as *Laeg-Duits* or "Low Dutch." It was spoken in northern New Jer-

Detail of the Van Bergen overmantel (oil on wood, ca. 1733). Created to adorn the fireplace of a house built by Marten Van Bergen in Greene County in 1729, this painting offers a glimpse of Hudson Valley life in the late seventeenth century. Attributed to John Heaten. New York State Historical Association, Cooperstown, N.Y.

sey and in the small settlements west of Schenectady well into the nineteenth century. It differed from standard Dutch in its morphology, phonology, and syntax. Having evolved in isolation from the mother tongue, North American Low Dutch disintegrated into regional dialects. A nineteenth-century observer reported that "no Laag Duitser ever corrects any speaker no matter how gross his mistake. The reason seems to be that none of them, even the most fluent, is ever quite certain that he has the right of it."

One feature of Low Dutch, wherever it was spoken, was the presence of many words borrowed from English, although they were often inflected to transform them into "Dutch" words.[3] By the nineteenth century, spoken Amer-

3. The following example drawn from a writ filed in Albany in 1716 indicates just how creative this borrowing could be. Note the modifications in the English words "certify," "court," and "court house," and the verb "to try." "Deese sertifieseeren day wy geweest syn int coert huis der stat Albany sijnde in open coert waer een actie getryt wiert" ["By these it is certified that we have been in the court house of the City of Albany having seen a case tried in open court"]. Quoted in Charles T. Gehring, "Colonial Dutch," in *Encyclopedia of the North American Colonies* (New York, 1993), 3: 21.

ican Low Dutch had diverged so far from standard Dutch that visitors from the Netherlands had difficulty understanding it, and when Albany Dutch visited the Netherlands, they, too, were often surprised to find their language unintelligible to Hollanders. Cut off from the standardizing developments in Netherlands Dutch, American Low Dutch became a fossilized version of its seventeenth-century form and its speakers a relatively tiny ethnic group in the evolving mosaic of the New World.

The Dutch language and its dialects contributed many words to American English. Among the most common are boodle, boss, cole slaw, cookie, dingus, dope, dumb (stupid), logy, poppycock, Santa Claus, sawbuck (sawhorse), sleigh, snoop, spook, stoop (porch), and waffle. Even today some regions of New York display a number of unique Dutch words. In the Albany area, for example, farmers still describe a roofed structure for covering hay as a "hay barrack," a phonetic borrowing from the Dutch word *hooiberg*, and "olicook" is used for doughnut, a direct descendant from the Dutch *oliekoek*, literally oil cake.

The last stronghold of Low Dutch was the Reformed Church. Through its divine services, its schools, and its social institutions the Reformed Church preserved the language and maintained its use well into the nineteenth century. By the 1830s, however, few parishioners could understand the dialect, and many were moving to English churches. The ministers took to preaching in English, although "Dutch" services were held in some areas for members of the older generation. One speaker of Low Dutch recalled that when he was a boy in the 1830s there would occasionally be a Sunday service in Dutch, although he admitted that most of the congregation could not understand a word.

In the years following the conquest, the church stood as the most important Dutch institution. It survived and prospered, and for a time served as the principal barrier to the complete anglicization of the Dutch of New York. Among the inhabitants of New York City by the end of the seventeenth century, membership in the Reformed Church marked one as ethnically Dutch. The Reformed Church's preservation of the language in oral and spoken form and its continued association with the churches of the Netherlands provided the glue of Dutch culture. Its rituals and holidays reminded the people of their heritage. It also provided a social structure where young men and women could meet and marry.

The powerful tendency toward endogamous marriages for sons of Dutch parents accentuated Dutch ethnicity and helped Dutch merchants maintain their hold on a sizable portion of the city's trade. Until the middle of the eighteenth century, the Dutch of New York City formed a self-conscious ethnic group based on language and religion. It was not an exclusive group, for outsiders often entered through marriage to Dutch women, a trend that accelerated with the influx of English soldiers in the eighteenth century. Dutch women were at the core of ethnic identity in the Dutch community. Dutch parents may have been more tolerant of outsiders as sons-in-law because they relied on their daughters to preserve the culture at home. Under the generous inheritance customs of Dutch-Roman law and the mutual will, Dutch women were often prized catches for young English soldiers seeking to become established in New York. In such relationships, the wife's culture determined the religion and education of the children, making the family Dutch even though headed by an English father. The women made sure that their children spoke Dutch at home and attended the Dutch-language school run by the Reformed Church.

Although most vestigial Dutch folkways from the era of New Netherland disappeared by the first quarter of the nineteenth century, one particular celebration was kept alive by African Americans. The most boisterous holiday on the Dutch calendar was Whitsunday, or Pentecost, known as *Pinkster*. The religious purpose was to celebrate the appearance of the Holy Ghost to the disciples after the crucifixion of Christ, but it coincided with ancient folk rites of spring and carnival. In 1786 a Scottish physician, Alexander Coventry, who lived in Hudson, New York, reported that the holiday was celebrated by "the Dutch and the Negro." Several years later William Dunlap traveled through northern New Jersey during Pinkster and confirmed the biracial nature of the celebration: "The blacks as well as their masters were frolicking and the women [and] children looked pecularly neat and well dressed."

In the Albany area the celebrations became increasingly boisterous and ritualized in the eighteenth century. In the first years of the nineteenth century, blacks from the region came every year on the day following Pinkster to "Pinkster Hill." There they were commanded by a well-known slave known as "King Charles" who appeared dressed as a British soldier. He led the audience in dances accompanied by fiddle, flute, fife, Jew's harp, pipe, drum, banjo, and tabor. By 1811 it had become too much for the Albany Common Council, which banned the Pinkster celebration on the ground that it no longer reflected the beliefs of the Dutch Reformed Church. The discussions of the ban brought forth fears among whites that a holiday in which so many blacks acted so riotously was somehow dangerous to public safety.

Pinkster survived as a Creole celebration among African Americans far into the nineteenth century. By combining African customs and European traditions, black Americans achieved a level of public acceptance for the celebration of their African heritage not enjoyed otherwise. Indeed, Pinkster survived among African Americans longer than among Dutch Americans (at least to 1874 in parts of western Long Island), leading some scholars to suggest that nineteenth-century Pinkster celebrations were of African origin and not related except in nomenclature to the Dutch religious holiday. Perhaps, but the timing of the celebrations and their association with the era of Dutch rule make the old Dutch way of Pinkster a candidate for the longest surviving folkway of New Netherland.

The holiday most often associated with the Dutch of New Netherland is the festival of Saint Nicholas Day, celebrated in the Netherlands in the first week of December. Saint Nicholas, which sounds like Santa Claus to the English ear, was the patron saint of the city of Amsterdam. Every year he sailed into the city with his black servant, *Swaerte Piet* (Black Pete), and distributed small gifts to the well-behaved children of the city. Unfortunately, there are no records confirming the celebration of Saint Nicholas Day in New Netherland. The association of Santa Claus with Christmas is the product of the imaginations of the nineteenth-century writers Washington Irving and Clement Moore.

The final political postscript to the Dutch history of New York was written in the Third Anglo-Dutch War. In 1673 a Dutch fleet sailed into New York Bay and captured the city as easily as had Colonel Nicolls in 1664. The war did not go well for the English, and the Dutch were left holding New York for fifteen months until the colony was restored in November 1674 by the Second Treaty of Westminster. For a second time the Dutch had given up on North America. They would not have another chance. As the seventeenth century came to a close, New York was gradually but inexorably becoming English. However, the multiethnic and multiracial society left behind by the Dutch in 1664 would continue to characterize the population of New York for centuries.

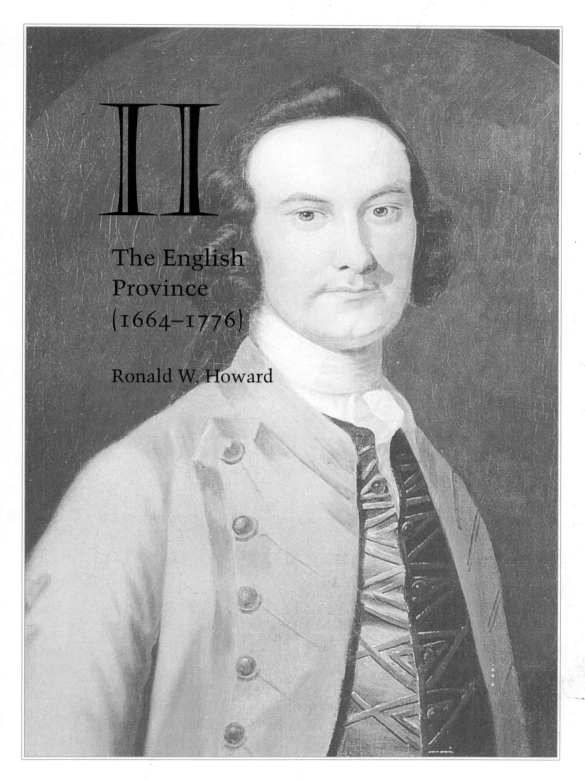

II

The English Province (1664–1776)

Ronald W. Howard

From Proprietary Colony to Royal Province

THE RESTORATION GOVERNMENT OF CHARLES II HAD many reasons for conquering New Netherland. The king's brother and heir apparent, James, Duke of York and Albany, could recite them all. Chief among them were Anglo-Dutch commercial rivalry, the growing economic importance of Britain's North American provinces, and the mercantile theory of empire. Of more immediate concern, Dutch merchants in New Amsterdam were violating the Navigation Acts of 1649, 1651, and 1660, which restricted trade with England and its colonies to English vessels manned by English crews. James also knew of another reason, one more personal than the general welfare and commercial prosperity of the British nation. Both James and his sovereign sibling needed money badly, and their advisers had convinced them that New Netherland was a rich prize that could be easily won. So King Charles made brother James the proprietor of the territory between the Connecticut River and Delaware Bay and provided him with four warships and three hundred soldiers to capture the fledgling colony.

New York thus began its existence as a conquered province, the proprietary holding of James, Duke of York and Albany. Its first two governors, Richard Nicolls (1664–67) and Francis Lovelace (1667–73), were both pragmatic executives who sought to reconcile erstwhile New Netherlanders to English rule. Their wise and tolerant leadership meant that the legacy of cultural diversity inherited from New Netherland not only survived but thrived in colonial New York. English immigration remained slight, mainly because James gave away the neighboring Jersies and acquiesced in William Penn's claim to the Delaware Valley, areas that proved more appealing than the Hudson Valley. Well into the eighteenth century, New York remained the least English of all Britain's American colonies, its society distinguished by firmly established pockets of ethnic and religious solidarity within a broader mosaic of ethnic and religious diversity. New York's odyssey from ducal domain to royal province would be accomplished in jolting fits and starts, complicated by unresolved political, economic, and cultural tensions, all of which became manifest in the popular uprising known as Leisler's Rebellion in 1689.

Imposing English Rule

Like all the other governors James would send to New York, Richard Nicolls was a staunch royalist, a professional soldier by education and training, and a long-time associate of the Stuart brothers, Charles and James. Nicolls proved himself an extraordinarily capable administrator, both as head of the royal commission sent out to capture New Netherland and as the first governor of James's sprawling American domain. "By his prudent management of affairs," wrote Samuel Maverick, a disgruntled New Englander who also served on the royal commission, "[Nicolls] kept persons of different judgments and of diverse nations in peace and quietness, during a time when a great part of the world was in warrs."

Like many of the people around the duke, Nicolls never quite trusted the Dutch, but he treated Dutch New Yorkers sensibly and humanely and recognized their importance to the duke's province. When the magistrates of New Amsterdam (now christened New York City) objected to swearing allegiance to King Charles, the politic Nicolls assured them that such an oath would not compromise their rights under the Articles of Capitulation or commit them to fight against their native country. Perhaps with the obstreperous New Englanders in mind, the governor wrote that Dutch settlers would likely "prove beter subjects than wee found in some of the other colonyes, and with a moderate permission both for time and trade, will support this government better than can be reasonably expected from newcomers of our own nation." Thanks largely to Nicolls's urging, leading Dutch and English New Yorkers began meeting weekly in the city and twice weekly on Long Island in an effort to promote social and political harmony.

Nicolls applauded Sir George Cartwright, the third member of the royal commission, for securing the surrender of the Hudson River settlements and Fort Orange without firing a shot. On the other hand, he was appalled that Sir Robert Carr, another member of the royal commission who was sent to capture the Dutch settlements on the Delaware, needlessly provoked bloodshed at New Amstel. "Lett not your eares bee abuzed with private Storyes of the Dutch being disaffected to the English," Nicolls cautioned Captain John Baker at Albany, as Beverwyck had been renamed, "for generally wee cannot expect they love us."

Dutch New Yorkers never loved Richard Nicolls, but they respected him, and it is easy to see why.

Following the instructions of the lord proprietor, Nicolls had the responsibility of establishing the duke's government throughout an impossibly far-flung colony. Moreover, its settlers were divided not only by ethnic and religious differences but by clashing political and economic interests. Territorially, the ducal proprietary included even more land than the Dutch had claimed for New Netherland. King Charles granted James not only the lands between the Connecticut River and Delaware Bay and western Long Island (basically New Netherland) but also eastern Long Island (previously affiliated with Connecticut), most of Maine, Nantucket Island, and Martha's Vineyard. Including parts of New England, the geographical configuration of the royal proprietary was deliberately designed to impress upon the independently minded Puritan colonies that the restored Stuart monarchy was not to be trifled with or taken lightly.

The duke's domain was inhabited not only by Dutch, English, and the assorted Europeans of New Netherland but also by New Englanders on eastern Long Island, the lands west of the Connecticut River, eastern Maine, Nantucket, and Martha's Vineyard, along with assorted Native American tribes. New Netherlanders, living in widely scattered and sparsely settled villages, had developed certain regional interests but virtually no sense of provincial identity. Early New Yorkers were much the same. Even larger and more scattered geographically than the Dutch colony it absorbed, the ducal proprietary was a hodgepodge of regions whose inhabitants had little in common and could not think in terms of the province as a whole.

The Duke's Laws of 1665

The government that Nicolls set up in New York was highly centralized in theory, but in practice it encouraged localism and regionalism and did little to integrate the settlers constitutionally, politically, or culturally. Under his charter from Charles II, James could govern as he pleased and make laws at will so long as they were consistent with the laws of England and did not obstruct judicial appeals to the king. Like other English proprietors, James appointed the governor and council, but he did not plan for an elected assembly, which was becoming a regular part of proprietary government elsewhere in British America. With New York's English population in a minority, it would hardly have been practical or politic to create a legislative assembly dominated by Dutchmen.

In February 1665, Nicolls convened thirty-four delegates from the towns on Long Island and the Bronx Peninsula (the only areas with English majorities) and had them ratify a frame of government and legal code known as the Duke's Laws. The Duke's Laws drew heavily on the laws and customs of other English colonies, particularly Massachusetts Bay and New Haven, as well as the ordinances and practices of New Netherland. The Duke's Laws called for the renewal of all land titles, religious toleration, and a structure of government that was much more English than Dutch. New Yorkers, whether of Dutch or English descent, were not altogether sure what to make of the legal code or the structure of government.

The Duke's Laws of 1665 created the County of Yorkshire, comprising of Staten Island, Long Island, and Westchester. No provision was made for an elected assembly or even town meetings, the most vital part of popular government in both New England and the English towns on eastern Long Island; nor did the laws provide for public schools as Massachusetts had. Initially the Duke's Laws applied only to the newly created county of Yorkshire; they did not apply to New York City and the Hudson Valley until 1674, or to the colony as a whole until 1676. In the end, because of a desire to placate erstwhile New Netherlanders, whether of Dutch or English descent, the Duke's Laws were broad regulations, leaving considerable room for discretion by local governments, church, and family. While clearly beginning the process of anglicizing both law and government in colonial New York, the laws more often than not deferred to community folkways and town and county governments.

The Duke's Laws defined the structure and practice of the courts and local government in Yorkshire itself. The county's three ridings each had its own court of sessions, composed of justices of the peace and undersheriffs. The latter heard appeals from the town courts, collected taxes, and entertained grievances from individuals and towns. The high sheriff of Yorkshire supervised all three courts of sessions, and he, like the justices and the undersheriffs, was appointed by the governor. At the lowest level of administration, the town, the Duke's Laws called for the freemen (landowners and taxpayers) to elect overseers and constables, who were to handle town business and resolve petty disputes.

Under the Duke's Laws, the governor and council met annually with the justices of the peace and the high sheriff as the court of assizes for Yorkshire, which served as the supreme court and where proposed legislation was discussed. The governor himself, assisted by his council, formulated provincial laws and used the occasion of the Yorkshire assizes to promulgate them. Outside of Yorkshire, Nicolls adjusted local government to the particular circumstances of the people involved. New York City was incorporated to include all of Manhattan Island, with its five aldermen, mayor, and sheriff replacing the four Dutch schepens, the burgomaster, and the schout of New Amsterdam. Records were kept in English as well as in Dutch, and English trial by jury began on a regular basis. Nicolls appointed both English and Dutch New Yorkers as aldermen, but only Englishmen served as mayor and sheriff. Unlike Nicolls, his successor, Colonel Francis Lovelace, on occasion even allowed the magistrates on the mayor's court to nominate their own successors, much as Peter Stuyvesant had done.

On the upper Hudson, where there were few English traders and farmers, Nicolls kept the government that had served Beverwyck and its environs—the five *commissaries* (magistrates) representing Albany, Schenectady, and Rensselaerswyck, and the schout—but required that the English commander of the garrison there should join the magistrates in making Indian policy. Rensselaerswyck Manor kept its own court and officials, while the Van Rensselaer family lobbied in England for confirmation of its million-acre patent. Elsewhere, Nicolls and Lovelace granted manorial rights to the owners of Fisher's Island and Shelter Island in Long Island Sound, Prudence Island in Narragansett Bay, Foxhall at the Esopus, and Pelham and Fordham in Westchester County. New Castle (formerly New Amstel) on the Delaware was initially neglected, except for its English garrison, whose commander sometimes acted as a magistrate. In 1669, inspired by rumors that a Swedish fleet was on its way to liberate them, the Swedes and Finns on the Delaware revolted against English rule. Lovelace easily put down the insurrection, and in 1672 he made New Castle the only officially designated bailiwick in New York, under a bailiff and six assistants, appointed by the governor.

Governors Nicolls and Lovelace imposed forms of local government where they were most needed and least likely to offend, but the provincial government resided completely with the governor and his council, both appointed by the duke. As Nicolls wrote in 1665 to Lord Clarendon, the chief minister of Charles II, "Our new Lawes are not contrived soe Democratically as the rest." In fact, the English towns on Long Island complained that they felt Nicolls had reneged on the promises he had made to them of freedoms as great as any in New England. They wanted a provincial assembly.

Previously only loosely attached to provincial governments at Hartford and New Haven, the towns on eastern Long Island—East Hampton, Southold, and Southampton—led the way in denouncing taxation without representation. However, all the English towns demonstrated various levels of resistance to renewing land patents and paying taxes. Despite the obvious dangers of pushing too hard too fast, Nicolls thought he understood the situation that confronted him on Long Island. "Democracy hath taken so deepe a Roote in these parts," he complained to Clarendon in 1666, "that the very name of a Justice of the Peace is an Abomination, whereof I have upon due Consideration of his [majesty's] interest layd the foundations of Kingly Government in these parts so farre as is possible which truely is grievous to some Republicans."

Despite the complaints from Long Island, the transition to English rule proceeded smoothly under Nicolls's diplomatic hands. While pressing the collection of taxes and fees for the renewal of land titles, Nicolls also made clear his commitment to protecting property rights, advancing trade, and encouraging agriculture and animal husbandry. (The yearly races at Hampstead Plains, which Nicolls inaugurated, were intended to improve the breeding stock of horses.) As the surrender terms stipulated, Nicolls kept the Amsterdam trade open for six months and occasionally granted exceptions thereafter. He even asked the Lords of Trade, the advisers to the crown on commercial regulations, to approve limited trade between New York and Amsterdam in order to reconcile the Dutch community to its new British masters, but he apparently received no reply.

On behalf of other Dutch New Yorkers, Peter Stuyvesant made much the same appeal again in 1667, explaining that without Dutch stroud (the heavy cloth used for blankets), the fur trade with the Indians might be lost to New York. The Lords of Trade agreed but then canceled this exception to the Navigation Acts the very next year. Despite the restrictions of English mercantile policy, however, commerce between Amsterdam and New York did continue, with Governor Lovelace and his brother Thomas becoming major participants, along with wealthy merchants like Cornelius Steenwyck, Eagidius Luyck, and Frederick Philipse.

Under Lovelace, too, Cornelius Steenwyck became the first Dutch mayor of New York City; Steenwyck and Cornelius Van Ruyven were also the first Dutch New Yorkers appointed to the governor's council. As for the Albany Dutch, the chief *handlaers*, or fur traders, who dominated both commerce and local government, were reasonably satisfied when Sir George Cartwright confirmed their monopoly of the fur trade and negotiated a treaty of commerce and defense with the Iroquois in September 1665. On western Long Island, the Dutch farmers adjusted well to English rule. Nonetheless, they generally settled disputes among themselves, either in the village court, or else informally, rather than resorting to the English-imposed court of sessions.

However self-serving his motives, Lovelace promoted cod fishing off Sandy Hook, whaling on Long Island, and shipbuilding on Manhattan. A report in 1669 noted nine ships in New York harbor loaded with Virginia tobacco, while ten thousand schepels of New York wheat were being shipped to Boston. To further expedite trade, Lovelace called in 1670 for an "exchange" or meeting of merchants every Friday from eleven to twelve at the corner of what became Bridge and Broad Streets. He also regularized communications and improved the post road from New York City to Boston.

The Andros Regime

After nine years under English rule, New York surrendered to a Dutch squadron in July 1673, just the first of several sudden political alterations that repeatedly modified the provincial government over the next eighteen years. In the Treaty of Westminster, signed in February 1674, however, the Dutch not only returned New Netherland to England but renounced all future claim to the province. In November, Edmund Andros (1674–82) arrived in America to head the restoration of the duke's government in New York. Like Nicolls and Lovelace before him, Andros was a professional soldier from an old family dedicated to the Stuart monarchy, but unlike his predecessors, he was both imperious and dogmatic. Accompanying the new governor were a hundred soldiers, along with trading goods sent by the duke, and several London merchants interested in commerce with the province. A new day was dawning for New York, one in which the English presence would be felt as never before.

The Duke's Laws were revived, and Dutch malcontents were urged to depart the province. Otherwise, the rights of all New Yorkers were confirmed, but only freedom of religion was explicitly included in the instructions Andros carried from the duke. Early in 1675, however, Andros announced that all residents should take an oath of fidelity and allegiance to the English government, much as the Dutch had done after the English surrender in 1673. A delegation of Dutch leaders—Cornelius Steenwyck, Johannes Van Brugh, Johannes DePeyster, Nicholas Bayard, Jacob Kip, Eagidius Luyck, William Beekman, and Anthony De Milt—asked for assurances that the oath of allegiance would not impair their "traditional rights." Angered by what he called Dutch impertinence, the governor placed the eight merchants under £200 bond and hauled them before the court of assizes.

One of the eight dissenters, Johannes DePeyster, wisely decided to take the loyalty oath. The other seven were tried by a jury of twelve Englishmen, found guilty of promoting rebellion and trading illegally (because they were considered aliens until they took the oath), and fined all their goods and chattels. The Dutch community was stunned and humiliated by such harsh treatment. Nicholas Bayard, nephew of the late Peter Stuyvesant, dared to speak out against the verdict and was placed in the "Hole" for two days. Andros denied their appeal to the king. Recognizing that it was futile to resist, the seven capitulated, took the oath of allegiance, and had their fines reduced to one-third of their estates.

In 1674, Andros extended the Duke's Laws to New York City and the Hudson Valley and in 1676 to the Delaware region. The official language of the courts became English, but in areas where the people mainly spoke Dutch, a second copy was kept in that tongue. The English system of jury trial, so foreign to Dutch-Roman law, was likewise imposed throughout the province. Andros also strengthened the British alliance with the Iroquois, proclaiming them subjects of the English king and under New York's jurisdiction. He aroused considerable controversy when he foisted an unorthodox dominie, the Reverend Nicholas Van Rensselaer, upon the Reformed Church at Albany and used the "English court system" to intimidate and punish merchant Jacob Leisler and his son-in-law, Jacob Milburne, both of whom denied the orthodoxy and legitimacy of Van Rensselaer's ministry.

On the other hand, Andros, ever the realist, suggested to James that an elected assembly might make it easier to raise much needed revenues. The duke, however, thought the disadvantages of popularly elected government far outweighed its advantages. "I cannot but suspect they would be of dangerous consequence," James replied, referring to elected representatives, "nothing being more knowne then the aptness of such bodyes to assume to themselves many privileges which prove destructive to, or very oft disturbe, the peace of ye governmt wherein they are allowed."

In any case, the governor and his council continued to make the laws and set provincial tax rates (assessed on both personal and real property) and customs duties, often following general guidelines from James. New Yorkers generally were taxed heavily, more than inhabitants of New England or New Jersey, in part because of the English troops the province maintained. Local taxes in Albany and New York City were higher because of special expenses. Albany handled negotiations with the Iroquois, and New York City had to maintain docks and wharves and pay a host of inspectors whose job it was to assure the quality of products produced in and commodities shipped from the port city. Andros took steps to secure Albany's monopoly of the fur trade from encroachment by traders in Schenectady, New York City, and the Connecticut River Valley. In return, Albany merchants were barred from trading directly with Europe. That privilege was reserved to New York City merchants, as was a monopoly of the bolting of flour and its export.

Andros recognized that the economy of provincial New York was changing. Even before 1664, shipments of animal pelts down the Hudson had begun to decline, caused by the depletion of nearby hunting grounds and rising competition from the French and their Indian allies. But if the fur trade was slackening, commerce in "land provisions of all sorts" was increasing remarkably. In 1678, Andros reported the annual export of some 50,000 bushels of wheat, along with "pease, beefe, pork, & some Refuse fish, Tobacco, beavers, peltry or furrs from the Indians, Deal & oake timber, plankes, pipestaues, lumber, horses, & pitch & tarr lately begunn to be made." Trade had been in the doldrums when Andros arrived in 1674. Four years later, he noted happily that from ten to fifteen ships of a hundred tons each were trading to New York yearly, as well as six smaller vessels belonging to New Yorkers, of which four had been constructed in the province.

The Dutch trade, especially with the islands of Curaçao and Saint Eustatius, remained more important to New York shippers than the British West Indies, where Boston merchants still dominated commerce. Little by little, however, Manhattan's merchants were creating an extraordinarily profitable commercial community that managed to secure control of the municipal government. This relatively small group of traders, numbering not more than one hundred in 1695 out of a city population of some thirteen hundred, secured charters for the city from both the Dutch and the English governors and filled municipal offices with their own numbers. By 1689, they constituted both the political and the economic elite of the island of Manhattan.

Economic regulations generated numerous complaints. London merchants trading to New York believed they were discriminated against. Long Islanders, especially those living on the "East End," resented having to import and export through New York City rather than Boston, which was nearer and handier. Andros and Receiver General William Dyre were said to favor, and indeed to be, trading partners of certain Dutch merchants, especially Frederick Philipse and Stephanus Van Cortlandt, the governor's closest advisers. In petitions to London, Andros was accused of persecuting Quakers (several of the British merchants belonged to the Society of Friends), stealing tax money intended for the Manhattan garrison, jailing his critics arbitrarily, and harassing selected merchants. In 1681, the duke felt compelled to recall Andros to London to answer his accusers, thereby pleasing many New Yorkers, who refused to pay either the custom duties or the property assessments the Andros regime had imposed.

Faced with the tax revolt in New York and popular suspicions in England that he was somehow involved in a Catholic plot to kill King Charles, the dispirited James approved a popularly elected assembly in his province; such a concession might placate New Yorkers and divert possible attacks in England against his proprietary charter and arbitrary government. At any rate, Colonel Thomas Dongan (1682–87), a Catholic and an Irish baronet, replaced the absent Andros as governor and brought with him instructions to call for assembly elections.

This first New York provincial chamber of deputies met for three weeks beginning October 17, 1683. It produced the remarkable Charter of Liberties and Privileges. While properly deferential, the document's language decidedly limited proprietary authority by emphasizing the rights of the people and their role in the provincial government. The supreme legislative authority, the charter stated, "shall forever be and reside in a Governour, Councell, and the people mett in General Assembly." Drawing from both the Magna Carta and the Petition of Right of 1628, the charter guaranteed legal rights and religious liberty. "Justice nor Right," proclaimed the charter, "shall be neither sold denyed or deferred to any man within this province."

The charter assembly of 1683, very likely at Dongan's behest, also reorganized New York's court system, providing for four levels of jurisdiction. The town courts were the first level, meeting monthly and limited to adjudicating minor disputes. Next came the courts of sessions, presided over by county justices of the peace, which met less frequently but exercised both original and appellate jurisdiction. The court of oyer and terminer and general jail delivery, which heard criminal cases, occupied the third judicial level. The latter replaced the court of assizes, which had met only once a year and after 1674 met only in New York City. The fourth level was the Supreme Court, consisting of the governor and council. After the duke became King James II in 1685, however, he dissolved the provincial assembly and rejected the charter of 1683. Dongan nonetheless kept the reorganized court system and the division of the province into ten counties, whose justices and sheriffs he appointed, thereby further expanding his patronage and influence over local government.

Roots of Cultural Diversity

The English conquest in 1664, the Dutch reconquest in 1673, and then the revival of English rule in 1674 all altered the governmental structure that had prevailed in New Netherland; but their impact upon the economic and cultural life of New York was less dramatic. Trade patterns began to shift, but only gradually, as New York merchants were attracted to London and the British West Indies; trade with Amsterdam and the Dutch islands continued, though at diminishing levels. Moreover, in many cases the changes in local government were more apparent than real, giving an English gloss to established Dutch procedures. Local folkways, especially in the countryside and small towns, still held sway, protected and perpetuated by community institutions, in particular the family, the church, and the school. This institutional triad continued to dominate cultural life.

The Duke's Laws recognized the importance of preachers and teachers for social stability and general improvement of manners and morals. Freedom of worship was granted to all Christians, and the Duke's Laws instructed every township in the county of Yorkshire to build a church capable of holding two hundred people. The overseers were also authorized to levy a tax for building and repairing the church, taking care of the poor, and maintaining the preacher. To promote social stability, the Duke's Laws regulated marriage, the treatment of children, servants, apprentices, and slaves, and the protection of orphans. To regulate the labor market, the laws prescribed that apprentices acquire the same relationship to their masters as children to fathers. Most children learned their trade or future occupation in the household, in the shop, or on the farm. Usually this occupational training took place at home, for both boys and girls, under the guidance of their parents and older siblings. In some instances apprenticeships were contractual or informally arranged outside the family homestead with kinfolk or friends.

One of the primary institutions of Dutch culture in New Netherland, the Dutch Reformed Church, was nonetheless compromised by English rule. Under Director General Stuyvesant, other religious groups, even Jews and Quakers, were tolerated, albeit reluctantly; but the Dutch Reformed Church was the state-supported, established faith. Nicolls gradually began to wean the Dutch clergy from their government subsidy in New York City. To collect their pay in 1668, the dominies were obliged to appeal to their congregants, going from house to house and asking for contributions. "You may imagine," moaned Dominie Samuel Megapolënsis, "the slights and murmuring occasioned thereby concerning the ministry and the ministers." Even in Albany, that bastion of Dutch political and economic influence, Dominie Gideon Schaats complained of being paid little and irregularly.

The Articles of Capitulation guaranteed the Dutch freedom of church discipline, and the duke of York, perhaps because of his Catholicism, was thoroughly devoted to religious toleration. His proclamation in 1668 granting Lutherans the privilege to worship publicly disturbed the Dutch Reformed ministers, who feared for the future of their faith in New York. "When we are dead," wrote the aged Dominie Johannes Megapolënsis, referring to Dominie Samuel Drisius and himself, "I fear there will be great confusion and scattering among our people at this place." His son, Samuel Megapolënsis, who had been educated for the ministry at Harvard, would shortly return to Holland.

The ministers reported that people filled the pews every Sunday and apparently liked what they heard; but they were not inclined to support the preachers. "They seem to desire," noted old Megapolënsis wryly, "that we should live upon air and not upon produce." The Dutch Reformed clerics received little sympathy from either Nicolls or Lovelace. At first, Lovelace's standard reply was, "If the Dutch will have divine service their own way, then let them also take care of and support their own preachers." But Lovelace relented in late 1669, following the death of Megapolënsis and, upon the request of the mayor and aldermen of New York City, allowed the latter to levy a tax toward the support of another dominie to be recruited from the Dutch republic. In the Dutch towns on Long Island, at Esopus, and at Albany, local governments likewise assisted in paying the Dutch clergy.

As was the case in New Netherland, cultural pluralism in early New York was sustained by the family. Mothers, fathers, and kinship networks usually introduced children to the religious and ethnic traditions that the congregation and schoolroom were expected to confirm. Because of the desire to placate erstwhile New Netherlanders, whether of Dutch or English descent, the provincial laws were applied only broadly, leaving ample room for discretion by both local governments and the family.

Prosperity and Problems

The fact that New York's population remained so sparse and so foreign worried Governor Dongan. He repeatedly urged that New Jersey should be returned to

New York and that Rhode Island and Connecticut should also be added to the province—all to enlarge New York's modest tax base. Another reason was to "balance the Interests of the French and Dutch Inhabitants of this Government" with those of English colonists. People were leaving New York for New Jersey and Pennsylvania, Dongan lamented, and although some of the Huguenots fleeing France following Louis XIV's revocation of the Edict of Nantes in 1685 were coming to New York, immigration remained very slight. By 1690, Philadelphia, founded but nine years earlier, numbered almost four thousand people, slightly larger than much older New York City.

New York's thin and scattered population (some 20,000 in 1688) made the friendship of the Indians imperative. The English continued the treaty relations begun by the Dutch with the Five Nations, and New York law required that purchase of Indian lands be subject to approval by the governor and that Indians have access to colonial local courts to settle disputes with colonists. Although Catholic himself, Dongan warned that French Jesuits living among the Iroquois were prying those Indians away from their alliance with the English. While urging London to send English Jesuits to counteract their French counterparts among the natives, the governor also encouraged the missionary work of Dominie Godfridius Dellius of Albany among the Mohawks. In 1687, French raids upon Iroquois villages led Dongan to mobilize the militia and raise property taxes. When militiamen went home without being paid, however, popular resentment toward Dongan's arbitrary rule intensified.

Despite rising political complaints, Dongan could boast that New York City was becoming a major American port. In 1687, thirty-three vessels traded from New York City. Nine or ten were ships of a hundred tons, and the other vessels ranged from forty to twenty tons. Although still in the shadow of Boston's mercantile community, especially with regard to trade with England, New York merchants were expanding their marketing network on their own. Aside from other North American ports, New York ships were trading to England, Holland, and the West Indies. New York carried "Beaver Peltry Oile and tobacco, when we can have it" to England. Furs and tobacco were also sent to Amsterdam, which remained a more important European entrepôt than London until after 1700.

Dongan, however, discreetly chose not to report on the Holland trade, perhaps because so much of it was illegal, that is, done without making the required stop in England to pay duties before landing the goods at a European port. Nor did he mention the developing trade between New York and Madagascar, whose location off the east African coast made it a thriving center for both the slave trade and piracy. "To the West Indies," he noted proudly, "we send Flower, Bread Pease Pork and sometimes horses; the returns from thence for the most part is rumm which pays the King a considerable excise and some molasses which serves the people to make drink and pays noe custome."

While praising improvements in commerce, the venal but astute Dongan knew that New York's prospects for both economic and political stability were still in jeopardy. Competition from enterprising traders and farmers in rapidly growing Pennsylvania threatened both the security and the prosperity of New York, taking population and trade from its older neighbor to the north. Most of the Delaware tobacco trade, which had formerly gone to New York City for reexport to England, was flowing through Philadelphia. Merchants in the Quaker colony were also cutting into the New York fur trade. Dongan himself undermined public confidence with his blatant Catholicism (he maintained his own chapel and priests), giving credence to the unfounded rumors that he was secretly a French agent. Most important, the governor and his inner circle of cronies shamelessly bullied Long Island towns into re-patenting their charters and land titles, always exacting new fees or grants of land or both from the towns. The governor even wangled a manor for himself on Staten Island.

Dongan's warnings of thinly populated New York's falling prey to the French and hostile Indians were taken seriously in London. However, instead of making another super colony with New York as its core, as Dongan had urged, the English government in 1688 annexed New York, along with New Jersey, to the Dominion of New England, presided over by none other than Sir Edmund Andros himself. Francis Nicholson, another military officer dedicated to the Stuart monarchy, became lieutenant governor of New York, while former governor Dongan settled into retirement on Staten Island. Nicholson and his provincial council were to enforce the laws made by Andros and the greater council for the Dominion of New England. The dominion did not possess an elected assembly. New York's land records were shipped to Boston, and the port of New York became more than ever a commercial satellite of Boston.

The crisis atmosphere in New York deepened with the onset of declining trade. Within the city itself, economic tensions were mounting. The richest 10 percent of the population in 1676 held over 50 percent of the wealth, a division much sharper than in either Boston or the Long Island towns. This top 10 percent was composed primarily of the merchant elite, which dominated the politics of both the city and the province. Through the mayor's court, the commercial aristocracy ran the city with an iron hand. In 1677 it brought the first criminal charges against strikers recorded in colonial America, firing twelve cartmen for refusing to follow instructions prescribed by the municipal government. In 1684 the mayor's court also fined the coopers for attempting to fix prices and prosecuted the cartmen again for resisting municipal regulations; in 1685 it dismissed all the porters for violating common council (the municipal legislature composed of the major and aldermen—and later assistants) rules for the cording of wood.

Under British rule, the ethnic makeup of the merchant elite changed considerably. Of the twenty-four richest men in New Amsterdam in 1664, only three were English. In 1676, of the forty-eight merchants judged substantial by Governor Andros, twenty-two were English. The richest merchants were still largely Dutch, but the English, with their superior commercial connections at home and elsewhere in the empire, were clearly moving up. Dutch New Yorkers filled the ranks of tradesmen, but their mobility was downward. Some of the leading Dutch merchants, especially Frederick Philipse, Stephanus Van Cortlandt, and later Nicholas Bayard, recognized the political and economic benefits of cooperating with the English conquerors. They remained in the Dutch Reformed Church but were tolerant and worldly enough not to be bothered by the Catholicism of Governor Dongan and his official circle.

Other Dutch New Yorkers were not so quick to embrace English rule. Some were ardent Calvinists who found Dongan's Catholicism particularly troubling. Rich merchants like Jacob Leisler, Abraham Gouverneur, and Peter Delanoy were among them, but the bulk of the Dutch dissidents were from the middling and working classes—artisans, shopkeepers, and farmers. Some were offended by the growing influence of the English and their culture. They shared the view of Dominie Caspar Van Zuuren, a Dutch Calvinist minister on Long Island, who wrote of a Flatbush justice of the peace in 1678, "He howls with the English and oppresses his own, the Dutch people, with unreasonable and unnatural zeal." Whether in the city, up the Hudson Valley, or on western Long Island, Dutch New Yorkers who disliked the English and felt threatened by the impact of English law and culture resented the anglicized Dutch, especially those wealthy merchants like Philipse and Van Cortlandt who profited so handsomely from their service to the English governors.

The English townsmen of Long Island also focused much of their hostility toward "the Dutch merchants" around Governors Lovelace, Andros, and Dongan. Their resentment over taxes, Dongan's graft, and New York City's monopolies had long been at the boiling point. Their militiamen, still angry because Dongan had not paid them for an earlier Albany expedition against the French, began the process in 1689 that brought down the dominion government in New York. Inspired by reports that William of Orange and Mary, his wife, had deposed James II, Bostonians pronounced the Dominion of New England dead on April 18, 1689, and jailed Andros. Wild rumors spread throughout New York, including one that Dongan (living on Staten Island) and his Catholic friends were plotting with the French who were expected to invade the province.

Leisler's Rebellion

Suffolk County "freeholders" launched the revolt, denouncing the "arbitrary power" they had long suffered under and expressing their intention of saving the province from "Popery and Slavery." They also sent their militia marching toward Manhattan. The New York City militia was also called out, ostensibly to maintain law and order, but also motivated by fears of a Catholic plot. On May 31, 1689, after Lieutenant Governor Nicholson quarreled with some of the militiamen and threatened them with his "papist" soldiers, various companies of the city militia took over the fort and announced that they would hold it until William and Mary sent someone of the Protestant religion to replace Nicholson. Nicholson fled Manhattan, and on June 8 the city militiamen elected one of their captains, Jacob Leisler, known for his wealth, Calvinism, and hatred of Catholicism, commander of the fort.

Born in Frankfurt, Germany, in 1640, the son of a Calvinist clergyman, Leisler had come to New Netherland in 1660 as a soldier for the West India Company. He traded modestly and then married Elsje Tymens, a wealthy widow with connections to some of the most prominent families in the province. Leisler turned out to be a shrewd businessman who soon made a fortune in trade, exporting furs, tobacco, whale oil, grain, and horses, and importing spices, slaves, finished cloth, and manufactured goods. He also accumulated extensive properties in New York City, Westchester County, and New Jersey, and on Long Island. By 1677, he was among the six wealthiest men in New York City; four years later, his wealth was exceeded by only one other in the city.

Leisler was a religious zealot. He had left the Reformed Church because he thought its minister, the Reverend Henricus Selyns, was not orthodox enough, and joined the French church whose minister, the Reverend Pierre Daille, was more to his conservative liking. The persecution of the Huguenots became an obsession with him, and he labored to settle French Protestants at New Rochelle. By 1689 he saw himself as a bulwark against unorthodox Anglican religious influence and as a defender of "the true Protestant faith" as he conceived it. Like many other inhabitants of New York, Leisler was motivated by a genuine fear of a Catholic plot and a sincere desire to support the Dutch prince, William of Orange, and his English consort, Queen Mary. King James's two Declarations of Indulgences, extending liberty of conscience to all Christians and suspending the penal laws against Catholics, seemed to Leisler and his followers merely a subterfuge aimed to remove the obstacles to popery and allow the extension of the Catholic religion in his dominions, at home and abroad.

Leisler's zeal led him to suspect that Van Cortlandt, Philipse, and Bayard were all in league with the Catholic plotters. Philipse and Van Cortlandt left the city, but Leisler arrested Bayard and kept him in prison for over a year. In December 1689, at the request of the militia-inspired committee of safety, Leisler accepted the commission of lieutenant governor, revived the 1683 Charter of Liberties as the legal code, and called for assembly elections. His authority for doing so was widely questioned, if cautiously approved by many.

In March 1690, following the February massacre by French and Indians of sixty-two people at Schenectady, the magistrates of Albany finally acknowledged Leisler's authority. Calling upon the New England colonies for assistance, Leisler took the lead in organizing an expedition against the French in Canada, which came to nothing. His regime in New York, meanwhile, became increasingly arbitrary and oppressive. Critics were imprisoned, including Dominie Rudolphus Varick on Long Island; the expulsion of others from the province, including Dominie Godfridius Dellius and Robert Livingston of Albany, lost Leisler the support of many in the merchant elite who had initially encouraged him. Of those from the upper classes who remained with Leisler, whether English or Dutch, most were related to him in some way. Interestingly, too, most of the Englishmen who supported him were married or had been married to Dutch women, which had led to a kind of cultural "batavianizing" parallel to the anglicizing of many of the Dutch.

Excepting East Hampton in Suffolk County, Leisler was recognized, albeit grudgingly, throughout the province as lieutenant governor. His control over eastern Long Island and Albany remained tenuous, but he appointed justices in all the counties and restored some semblance of order to the provincial government. His critics, however, had learned the importance of discrediting their political opponents in London. Former Lieutenant Governor Nicholson did much to turn the advisers of William and Mary against the mercurial Leisler, as did former Governor Andros. Nicholas Bayard, having been so mistreated by Leisler, led the chorus of accusations leveled against the "rebel," characterizing Leisler's followers as "Dutch rabble," who were an unworthy and seditious people. Reading his bitter commentary, one would hardly suspect that Bayard, though of Huguenot descent, had been raised in Holland and was a nephew of the late Peter Stuyvesant.

Leisler's tenure as lieutenant governor in New York lasted less than two years. King William appointed Henry Sloughter as governor (1691) to assume command of the colony and sent on Major Richard Ingoldsby as lieutenant governor in advance. When Ingoldsby arrived in New York City on January 30, 1691, Leisler refused to surrender the fort to him, provoking a battle that led to casualties on both sides. A few weeks later, Sloughter himself arrived, and Leisler turned over command to him; but by now there was sufficient evidence to charge Leisler and thirty-six of his followers with murder and treason. The trials were held in March. Only Leisler and his second-in-command, Jacob Milburne, were found guilty and sentenced to be hanged, drawn, and quartered. According to legend, a drunken Governor Sloughter signed their death warrants at the insistence of Nicholas Bayard and Leisler's other enemies. The sentences were carried out on May 16, 1691.

Leisler's Legacy

Three hundred years after the event, the meaning of Leisler's Rebellion is still unclear. Early historians portrayed the uprising as a popular movement of democracy against oligarchy, a kind of precursor of the American Revolution. There is scant evidence, however, that Leisler was interested in advancing democracy, and despite his revival of the assembly he did little else along these lines during the two years he controlled the province. Indeed, some of his critics charged that his rule was more arbitrary, ruthless, and dictatorial than any of his predecessors. Other historians viewed the Leislerian movement as simply one of rivals for power, prestige, and political office, Leisler and his followers having envied the success of English interlopers and Dutch collaborators. There is some evidence to support this view, since the major officeholders in Andros's administration were certainly not Leislerians. On the other hand, Leisler himself was not entirely a political outsider, having held a variety of government offices during the years before the rebellion.

A more recent interpretation argues that Leisler and others in the Dutch community were reacting against the increasing anglicization of the province. But while cultural antagonism was definitely a factor, there were influential Dutch and Dutch-related individuals among Leisler's harshest opponents. Other studies have recently emphasized the deep religiosity of Leisler and his followers. They were not only intensely anti-Catholic but represented a particularly orthodox brand of Calvinism which placed them at odds with others in the Reformed Church. These religious differences allegedly dated far back to the origins of the Reformed Church in Europe and continued in New York well after the Leislerian revolt. In leading the rebellion, then, Leisler's primary concern was—as he said—to protect and defend the "true Protestant" religion. Viewed in economic terms, however, the Leislerian revolt signified the protest of middling merchants, Dutch and others, against the economic domination of wealthy and privileged merchants, both Dutch and English. So goes the historiographical controversy, which shows no sign of abating after three hundred years.

Provoked by a welter of unresolved tensions, Leisler's Rebellion continued to influence the political history of the province of New York for years to come. In one sense, the movement was prompted by local influences and had local consequences. In broader perspective, the events in New York were part of the larger series of colonial protests that occurred in New England and Maryland, as well as New York, in the aftermath of the Glorious Revolution in England. The upheavals in the American provinces reflected the political instability of these colonies as they sought to define their constitutional relationship with their own governors and with imperial authorities in England. One thing was quite clear after 1689. The American colonies would continue to be dependencies of the Crown and Parliament, and it would take another century to work out an imperial relationship that would give these colonies greater autonomy and constitutional rights.

Chapter 8

Advancing English Culture

IN THE WAKE OF LEISLER'S REBELLION, WITH KING WILLIAM'S War (1689–97) apparently threatening the survival of the province, the ethnic and religious diversity of New Yorkers seemed almost subversive. "Our chiefest unhappiness here," wrote Charles Lodwick, militia colonel and merchant, expressing a common sentiment in 1692, "is too great a mixture of Nations, & English the least part." Cultural diversity was perceived as a problem that government policy should address. In both London and New York, therefore, plans were set in motion to make the former proprietary more like the other British colonies, beginning with Governor Sloughter's calling of a general assembly in 1691. Under Governor Benjamin Fletcher (1692–98), anglicizing efforts took a major turn, with the passage of the Ministry Act in 1693 and the chartering of Trinity Church in 1697.

Calling upon the resources of the Society for the Propagation of the Gospel in Foreign Parts, Governor Edward Hyde, Lord Cornbury (1702–8), attempted to bring the entire province into Anglican conformity. Cornbury's zeal on behalf of the English Church, however, worried New York's dissenters, both English and non-English. In fact, resistance to Anglican pretensions so strengthened the institutional support of ethnic and religious pluralism that many New Yorkers, including a few staunch Anglican politicos, renounced government intrusion in matters of faith and worship as counterproductive and disruptive of political and social harmony. Like Governor Robert Hunter (1710–19), they wanted to transcend the political and religious quarrels of the past two decades and sought reconciliation. Ironically perhaps, the pro-Anglican efforts of Fletcher and Cornbury almost certainly did less to anglicize New York's pluralistic society than the slow but steady expansion of British commerce and English common law accomplished.

War and Politics

Leisler's Rebellion and the Schenectady massacre of 1690 brought home the fact that New York was militarily unreliable, politically unstable, and the least English province in North America. The ongoing war against the French and Indians gave special urgency to the matter. So in 1691 the popularly elected general assembly became a permanent part of New York's government, as it was in other royal provinces. The assembly reenacted the Charter of Liberties of 1683 (rejected again in 1697 by the Privy Council) and passed the Judiciary Act of 1691. Modifying the old Judiciary Act of 1683, this latter measure did away with town courts and vested original jurisdiction over most criminal and civil matters in county justices, appointed by the governor. The Judiciary Act of 1691 hastened the triumph of English common law over Roman-Dutch law in New York.

Governor Fletcher succeeded the unfortunate Sloughter, who died just five months after arriving. Fletcher was a veteran soldier, hand-picked by William III to organize British America militarily against the French and their Indian allies. His commission made him governor of New York, New Jersey, and Pennsylvania, and commander of the militia of the Jersies, Connecticut, and Rhode Island as well as New York. His was not an easy task, particularly because New Yorkers were still divided into Leislerian and anti-Leislerian camps. Of New Yorkers, he reported in 1691, "A divided, contentious impoverished people I find them . . . neither Party will be satisfied with less than the necks of their Adversaries." The Leislerians were rightly suspicious of the new governor, who shortly disregarded his instructions to seek political reconciliation and allied himself with the anti-Leislerians in the assembly.

Even among the anti-Leislerians, Fletcher found little support in New York or elsewhere for an expedition against the French and Indians who were bludgeoning the Five Indian Nations, England's ally in King William's War. New England was pursuing its own military agenda, while Pennsylvania and the Jersies, shielded in part by New York's defense of the frontiers, were not inclined to contribute either troops or supplies to Fletcher's war effort, ostensibly because of Quaker influence in their respective governments. However, Fletcher did send out privateers to interrupt European trade with Canada and to seize enemy vessels. Privateers (privately owned ships temporarily commissioned by the colonial governor to conduct war against the enemy) brought profits to New York merchants who purchased shares in these marauding vessels.

Despite the boom in privateering, New Yorkers believed they were unfairly shouldering too much of the cost, both human and monetary, of frontier defenses during King William's War. In 1698 the province barely numbered 18,000 colonists, with 5,000 of them in New York City. Merchant Charles Lodwick reported that "most of the young men and those that can any way move,

New York City as it began to prosper in the early eighteenth century (1746). By Thomas Bakewell. From I. N. Phelps Stokes, *The Iconography of Manhattan Island* (New York, 1915), vol. 1.

depart this province . . . to the neighbouring Government where they are wholly free from Tax or any Contrybution toward the Common Security, to the great discouragement of this Province." In the name of colonial defense, both Fletcher and Lodwick recommended that Connecticut, New Jersey, and Pennsylvania be combined with the government of New York, "to strengthen that Province being the Frontier of all the North Parts of America against the French."

Left to his own devices by the British government, Fletcher, like other governors before and after him, cultivated allies within the province. He rewarded them with land grants and trading concessions, the first of which furthered the engrossment of the best territory in fewer hands. He also granted manorial status to the estates owned by Caleb Heathcote, Lewis Morris, Frederick Philipse, and Stephanus Van Cortlandt in Westchester County. Often receiving large fees for his trouble, the governor issued extravagant land patents. Dominie Godfridius Dellius, Peter Schuyler, and other friends of Fletcher patented 840 square miles northeast of Albany. Dellius and his associates also patented lands stretching fifty by two miles along the Mohawk River.

Little wonder that Richard Coote, Lord Bellomont (1698–1701), the governor who followed Fletcher, blamed these extravagant land grants for the slight population of the province. "What man will be such a fool," asked Bellomont, "as to become a base tenant to Mr. Dellius, Colonel Schuyler, Mr. Livingston . . .

when, for crossing the Hudson's River that man can for a song purchase a good freehold in the Jersies?" Bellomont, who owed his job to the Whig ministry that displaced Fletcher's Tory friends, also inveighed against his predecessor's trade policies. During King William's War, in 1698, Fletcher issued letters of marque and reprisal to New York sea captains, some of whom made their way to Madagascar and beyond, to the Indian Ocean, where privateering easily slipped into general piracy.

Several New York merchants, in particular Frederick Philipse and Stephen DeLancey, traded regularly with Madagascar, bringing back East Indian goods, gold coins, and slaves, all of which were readily available from the pirates based on that East African island. The pirates themselves were said to frequent New York City, reportedly encouraged to do so and protected by Fletcher himself. Lord Bellomont threw the pirates out of New York, or tried to, though he was greatly embarrassed by his own association with William Kidd, a well-respected New York sea captain. Having organized an expedition against piracy in the Red Sea and Indian Ocean, Kidd himself turned pirate before he was caught and executed in 1701.

Whatever the source of its prosperity, New York City bustled with commercial activity in the mid-1690s. In 1696 the common council reported sixty ships, forty boats, and sixty-two sloops trading to Manhattan. The next year Benjamin Bullivant, a Boston physician and former attorney general of

Massachusetts Bay, reported that Governor Fletcher was "pleased to walk the town with me and shew me the multitudes of greate & Costly buildings erected since his arrivall." Fletcher was particularly proud of handsome Trinity Church, built "of good brown square stone & brick exactly English fashion with a Large square steeple at the west end." As late as 1700, Fletcher's successor and harshest critic, Lord Bellomont, called New York City the "growingest town in America," with six ships above and eight under one hundred tons, two ketches, twenty-seven brigantines, and eighty-one sloops attached to the port. Still divided and contentious, New Yorkers were not quite as impoverished as when Fletcher found them.

Becoming More English

However disturbingly foreign its composition, New York's small population seemed to certain political leaders in both Britain and America to offer the opportunity for rapidly propagating English culture, both by immigration and other means. In the 1691 assembly, two bills, ostensibly addressed to the shortage of preachers and teachers in New York, were proposed, though not passed. One called for the maintenance of ministers in towns of forty or more families. The other provided for appointing schoolmasters "for the Educating and Instructing of Children and youth, to read and write English, in every Towne in the province." Neither bill came to a vote in an assembly composed almost exclusively of Dutch, English, and French dissenters.

Suspicions of cultural aggression, aroused by Sloughter's assembly proposals, were strengthened under Fletcher. In his first address to the assembly, while calling for efforts to revive trade and protect the province against the French, Fletcher also asked that "provision be made for the support and encouragement of an able ministry." What Fletcher wanted—and had been instructed to do by the Lords of Trade—was to strengthen the Church of England in New York. In 1693 the governor secured an ambiguous law that provided for the support of a "good and sufficient Protestant Minister" in six parishes, one in New York City, another on Staten Island, two in Queens County, and two in Westchester County. "I have gott them," Fletcher wrote the Lords of Trade, "to settle a fund for a Ministry in the City of New York and three more Countys which could never be obtained before, being a mixt People and of different Persuasions in Religion." Thereafter, Fletcher insisted that the Ministry Act established the Church of England in the four lower counties of New York. His interpretation pleased the Lords of Trade, especially one of them, Henry Compton, bishop of London, under whose ecclesiastical jurisdiction the American colonies fell.

The only Anglican preacher in New York, the Reverend John Miller, chaplain to the British garrison in Manhattan from 1692 to 1695, likewise looked to the "National Church" as an engine of cultural unity. Miller even proposed that an Anglican bishop should be designated for America and also made governor of New York and the surrounding colonies. Other dedicated Anglicans in New York included James Graham, merchant, lawyer, and speaker of the assembly; Caleb Heathcote, merchant, landlord, council member, and justice of the peace; and Lewis Morris, New Jersey landlord and politician, who had married Graham's daughter.

Although some were politically prominent, Anglicans were relatively scarce in colonial New York. In 1693 probably fewer than ninety Anglican families worshiped with Chaplain Miller and the soldiers, and his was the only Anglican congregation in the entire province. On the other hand, the Dutch Reformed Church had fifteen congregations, the Congregationalists and Presbyterians thirteen, the Huguenots four, the Lutherans two, and the Quakers perhaps three or four. But even as they were outnumbered by about forty to one, Heathcote and Morris nevertheless believed that Anglicans had a good chance of gaining religious hegemony, with the proper support of the provincial government and officials in England. Ministers were so few among English New Yorkers that Chaplain Miller thought dissenters would probably attend an Anglican service if one were available.

As for the Dutch Reformed, Leisler's Rebellion had badly divided their congregations. The dominies generally opposed Leisler and most of their congregants usually supported him. Dutch New Yorkers could be won over to the Church of England, Heathcote and Morris believed, if they were approached in a nonthreatening way. As for the Huguenots, French Protestants had every reason to look with favor upon the Anglican Church because it was sponsoring their removal to England and other parts of its empire. Fletcher subsidized several Huguenot clerics and Dominie Godfridius Dellius, whose ministry to the Native Americans was especially valued during King William's War.

A masterly if unscrupulous politician, Fletcher in 1696 incorporated the Dutch Reformed congregation in New York City, giving that church legal standing to sue, borrow money, and buy or sell property. The same year, a majority of Anglicans, for the first time, were elected to the New York City Vestry, the parish organization created by the Ministry Act, which called William Vesey, a Harvard graduate whose Anglican parents lived in Massachusetts, as their pastor. The tradeoff was obvious. In 1697, Heathcote and other New York Anglicans organized Trinity Church, and Fletcher issued a charter making Trinity the parish church for New York City under the Ministry Act, for all practical purposes establishing Anglicanism in New York County.

Out to undo Fletcher's land and trade polices, Lord Bellomont clashed with leading Anglicans, especially Pastor Vesey, and brought the anti-Leislerians back into leadership of the assembly. Bellomont persuaded the Board of Trade (the advisory body that replaced the Lords of Trade in 1696 and was particularly concerned with colonial commerce) to nullify several of Fletcher's land grants, including the patent for the valuable property known as the King's Farm, which had been bestowed upon Trinity Church. Under Bellomont, Anglican designs for New York were stymied, but with his sudden death in 1701, Anglican leaders expected more sympathetic treatment from the new governor, Lord Cornbury. Before Cornbury's arrival, however, Nicholas Bayard's Leislerian foes had him indicted, convicted, and sentenced to die for seditious libel against the provincial government. Although Bayard would appeal to England and be exonerated, anti-Leislerians were all the more embittered by the experience.

The Cornbury Administration

Cornbury, who immediately allied himself with the Anglicans and anti-Leislerians, believed that the time was ripe for advancing the Church of England in New York. Few of the Dutch churches had preachers, and, among English dissenters, only the Congregational churches had full-time ministers. Others usually did what the small Jewish congregation in New York City had done for decades: utilize lay readers, often the local schoolmasters. The Quakers meanwhile, who had no need for a professional clergy, were making inroads especially on Long Island and in Westchester County, outraging both Anglicans and more orthodox dissenters. Cornbury called upon the Society for the Propagation of the Gospel in Foreign Parts for assistance. Organized in 1701 under the leadership of Dr. Thomas Bray, the SPG, or the Venerable Society, as it was usually called, had as its purpose the propagation of Anglican Christianity in America, especially among the Native Americans and slaves but also among the colonists themselves, many of whom were reportedly lapsing into ignorance and infidelity, if not heathenism. Cornbury and New York Anglicans early on pointed out why the Venerable Society should give particular attention to New York: its proximity to the Five Indian Nations and Puritan New England, its religious diversity, and the paucity of preachers.

To make New York more of an English province, Cornbury moved on several fronts. Returning Anglican leaders and other anti-Leislerians to political power, the governor urged the assembly to erect "public schools in proper Places" throughout the province. The assemblymen would not go that far, but they voted to set up "a publick Free-School" in New York City to instruct "the youth and male children" of French and Dutch as well as English parents "in the languages or other learning usually taught in grammar school." Cornbury also subsidized the school conducted by William Huddlestone, clerk of Trinity Church, who taught his pupils the Anglican catechism and required them to attend Trinity Church services. The governor also encouraged SPG support of the catechetical school begun in 1704 by the pious Huguenot Elias Neau, who taught poor children, Native Americans, and slaves. Neau would shortly devote himself exclusively to teaching African Americans, slave and free.

To the joy of Rector Vesey, Cornbury restored to Trinity Church the lease to the valuable property on Manhattan known now as the "Queen's Farm," which Bellomont had previously annulled. Colonel Lewis Morris hoped that the property could be secured permanently in Anglican hands. "New York is the centre of English America," Morris wrote in 1704, "and an appropriate place for a College; and that farm in a little time would be of considerable value, and it is a pity such a thing should be lost for want of asking, which, at another time, won't be so easily obtained." The next year, Queen Anne bestowed the farm upon Trinity Church.

Cornbury induced the assembly to raise Reverend Vesey's salary and to issue another charter strengthening the relationship between Trinity Church and New York parish. Despite his best efforts, however, the assembly, composed overwhelmingly of dissenters, refused to change the Ministry Act of 1693 to read "an Anglican Minister" instead of "a good and sufficient Protestant Minister" or to expand its jurisdiction to Congregationalist Suffolk County. Thus rebuffed, Cornbury nevertheless insisted that his instructions from the Crown (which he refused to show) gave him full authority to determine who should preach and teach in New York. In Queens, Richmond, and Westchester Counties, where there was not a single Anglican congregation, Cornbury proceeded to appoint Anglican priests, most of them missionaries sent by the SPG. In Queens County, the governor removed recalcitrant justices of the peace and jailed or fined others for not enforcing the Ministry Act as he interpreted it.

Some New York Anglicans, including Caleb Heathcote and Lewis Morris, came to realize that Cornbury's zeal did more harm than good for their faith. In fact, the governor aroused English dissenters because of his roughshod imposition of Anglican priests at Jamaica and Hempstead on Long Island, his obvious desire to introduce Anglicanism into Suffolk County, his demand that all dissenting preachers appeal to him for a license, and rumors that an Anglican bishop would be located in New York. In 1706 the arrest and subsequent trial of the Reverend Francis Makemie, just recently elected moderator of the Philadelphia Presbytery, for preaching in a private home in New York City without Cornbury's license, became a cause célèbre for New York dissenters.

Dutch New Yorkers were likewise wary. Cornbury's policy of licensing dissenting preachers and teachers, they insisted, violated the Articles of Capitulation of 1664 protecting their religious freedom. The governor ignored their complaint. As long as Dutch New Yorkers had their own preachers and teachers, Cornbury confided to the missionary Thoroughgood Moore, they would never become good Englishmen. "And His Excellency was pleased to tell me last night," wrote Moore in 1705, "that without a Command, if the Queen would give leave, He would never suffer another Dutch Minister to come over." That same year, Cornbury explained himself more fully to the SPG: "I am of the Opinion that if as the Dutch Ministers die, their Churches were supplied with English Ministers that would with Schools be a means to make this colony an English Colony, which I am afraid will not easily be done without it, but that I submit to better Judgements." Better judgments would fortunately prevail, but Cornbury continued to license preachers and teachers, referring to his "Instructions from the Crown," whose specific provisions supposedly gave him that authority.

The governor was becoming a tremendous liability, threatening the credibility of both the Church of England and the royal government. His efforts to impose Anglican uniformity had backfired, steeling dissenters in their determination to perpetuate their respective ethnic and religious traditions. Word of his indebtedness and alleged peculation involving provincial finances and land grants was also reaching the public's ear, and was made all the more disturbing because of the continuing decline of the New York economy. The beginning of Queen Anne's War (1702–13) did nothing to revive commerce. By 1706, New York was exporting barely one-sixth of what it exported in 1700, and imports from England fell to 40 percent of their 1700 level. In 1708, Governor Cornbury complained that there were scarcely twenty-eight ships and sloops attached to New York. Between 1700 and 1710, the population of the colony increased only slightly, from nearly 20,000 to barely 22,000.

Cornbury and the assembly grew increasingly at odds just as the North American theater of Queen Anne's War was heating up. Cornbury even began to lose the support of at least some Anglican clergymen in New York and New Jersey, most of whom he had recruited. Rumors spread of his alleged fetish for wearing women's clothing. Even on Sundays, the governor reportedly would hurry from church, deck himself out in female garb, and parade around the balcony of the fort for all to see. Dressed in a gown, with light rouge and pearls, Cornbury was said to resemble closely his royal cousin, Queen Anne, though that likeness scarcely comforted scandalized Anglicans who had looked to him to remake colonial New York in England's image. Solid evidence of these charges is slim, limited to a few of Cornbury's political and religious critics, but belief in his transvestism was buttressed for years by a portrait of Cornbury in women's clothing that hung in the New-York Historical Society. Recent scholarship has argued persuasively that the portrait was not identified as Cornbury until 1867. There is little resemblance between the Cornbury in the portrait and other likenesses of the governor, so the incriminating painting seems to be a fabrication. His career after he left the colonies did not evidence the irresponsibility with which he was charged in New York. Nevertheless, stories of the governor's peculiar dressing habits and his extortions persisted for years thereafter, and, fabrication or not, they have become inextricably associated with Cornbury's controversial administration of New York.

Cultural Accommodation

Plans for a joint British-American invasion of Canada via the Saint Lawrence and Lake Champlain routes finally compelled the Godolphin-Marlborough ministry to recall Cornbury, even though he was a relative of the queen. John, Lord Lovelace (1708–9), replaced Cornbury as governor in late 1708, but he contracted an illness the winter of his arrival and died within the year. His successor as governor-general of New York and New Jersey was Colonel Robert Hunter (1710–19), a Scotsman and a friend of the popular literary figures Joseph Addison, Richard Steele, and Jonathan Swift. In order to reduce religious and ethnic antagonisms, Hunter made clear his reluctance to intervene in religious affairs, thereby incurring the displeasure of Rector Vesey and several SPG clerics. Nor did he invoke the gubernatorial prerogative of licensing teachers.

By bringing both Leislerians and anti-Leislerians into the provincial council, Hunter began to put to rest the bitter political legacy left by Leisler's Rebellion. Moreover, while Hunter was governor, the political-legal system inaugurated in 1691 also began to take root. Law, politics, and commerce were all channels through which English culture was dispersed throughout the province. Whether New Yorkers liked it or not, their society was becoming anglicized, more for some individuals than for others, in ways both subtle and overt. Of course, this process of anglicization had been going on since 1664, but by the time Hunter left New York to become governor of Jamaica in 1719, the impact of English law and custom had also become increasingly obvious, especially with regard to the status of women, children, Native Americans, and slaves.

English common law was transferred to New York by the Duke's Laws of 1665. It was extended to New York City and the Hudson Valley in 1674, strengthened by the Charter of Liberties of 1683 and the court system established along with it, and finally by the Judiciary Act of 1691. Under Roman-Dutch Law, women in New Netherland had a legal identity separate from their husbands. They possessed civil and property rights denied their gender under English common law. Women in the Dutch colony traded and ran shops, sued and were sued, inherited property equitably with their brothers, and willed their own property. Most important, married women enjoyed community property rights with their husbands. Under English common law, the married woman had no legal standing; her identity was completely submerged into her husband's under the legal principle called "feme covert." In both law and practice, daughters almost never inherited equitably with their brothers, and younger sons usually received less than the oldest brother, who might inherit almost everything under the custom of primogeniture.

After 1664, English common law and custom restricted the economic freedom and property rights of women in colonial New York. A few women, like Margaret Hardenbrock Philipse, continued trading in the name of her husband until her death, at which time she was the richest woman in New York, perhaps in all North America. Alida Schuyler Livingston and Maria Cortlandt Van Rensselaer in Albany County, Mary Spratt Alexander in New York City, and Martha Smith, wife of William "Tangier" Smith of Saint George's Manor on Long Island, were other upper-class women who continued as partners with their husbands or assumed control of the family businesses following the death of their spouses. However, according to the historian Linda Biemer's calculations, the number of female traders in Albany declined from forty-six in 1654–64 to six in 1685–1694. By 1700 there were none. In New Amsterdam (New York City), the corresponding numbers were 134 in 1653–63, and forty-three in 1664–73. There was a similar dramatic decline among female tapsters, brewers, launderers, and bakers. Because of their commercial activities, women had been quite active in New Netherlands courts, suing and being sued in civil cases. After 1664 fewer and fewer women were involved in disputes over contracts, although there was a remarkable increase in criminal cases involving women, suggesting that legitimate economic pursuits for women were severely limited by 1700.

Although their rights of inheritance were protected by the Articles of Capitulation, Dutch New Yorkers gradually abandoned the mutual or joint will and adopted English testamentary procedures. By 1700, Dutch New Yorkers on Manhattan had generally begun to write their wills in English rather than Dutch. Until the mid-1690s, not long after the passage of the important Judiciary Act of 1691, the provincial government continued to license notaries and court clerks especially to serve the Dutch-speaking public. Thereafter, local officials still accommodated the Dutch language, but the change in testamentary procedures came much earlier than the change in testamentary traditions. In fact, Dutch New Yorkers demonstrated considerable skills in writing wills designed to circumvent the English law of descent.

Until well after 1700, even in New York City, where anglicizing influences were strongest, husbands of Dutch background generally left possession of their estates to their wives. However, in his extensive study of colonial New York wills, the historian David Narrett did not find even one Dutch New Yorker after 1725 who allowed his wife to keep her half interest in his estate should she remarry. This significant shift marked the end of the community property tradition, based as it was on the wife being a co-owner of the family estate. After 1700, Dutch New Yorkers tended to bequeath their property and business interests to their sons, requiring the brothers to compensate their sisters.

The "Other" New Yorkers

The transition to English rule in New York also affected African Americans, slave and free, and Native Americans. In 1664, New York had about 700 blacks.

Some 375 lived in New York City, at least seventy-five of whom were free blacks, many of them possessing lands provided by the West India Company. A sizable black neighborhood emerged just north of New Amsterdam on the road to New Harlem. At least another dozen free blacks held land in the Dutch and English towns on Long Island. Most free blacks had begun life as slaves for the West India Company but by 1664 had achieved the status of "half-freedom," which permitted them to enjoy full personal liberty in return for a promise to work for the company when needed.

However burdensome their lot, slaves in New Netherland had fewer restrictions and more economic opportunity than they possessed in English New York. Fewer slaves were manumitted under the English, and the number of free black landholders declined, most free blacks becoming landless. As in New Netherland, slavery existed in early New York without legal sanction, but in 1682 the general court of assizes issued an ordinance prohibiting Negro or Indian slaves from leaving their masters' homes on Sundays or other prescribed days without the handwritten consent of their owners. Slaves caught without such a pass were subject to apprehension and whipping. In subsequent years other ordinances prohibited the assembly of four or more blacks (later reduced to three), barred them from carrying weapons, curtailed their right to trade, and limited their access to certain occupations.

In 1702 the provincial assembly passed the first comprehensive "Act for Regulating Slaves." The law incorporated the previous restrictions and added prohibitions on slave testimony in court except in cases of slave conspiracy, and then only against other slaves. A 1712 law barred slaves from owning property. Other regulations prevented slaves from purchasing strong drink without the consent of their masters. Ultimately, the racial uniqueness of blacks reduced them to the legal status of chattel, completely under the power of their owners.

One problem confronting New Yorkers, like their counterparts in other colonies, was how conversion to Christianity would affect the slave status of Africans. The Duke's Laws had prohibited the enslavement of Christians, raising the question of whether conversion of slaves would bring them freedom. Some slaves converted to the Dutch Reformed and Lutheran faiths because they believed such conversion would lead to emancipation. Fearful of the consequences of such slave actions, British authorities appealed to the spiritual head of the Anglican Church in America, the bishop of London, who ruled that conversion did not liberate slaves from their bondage. This position was enacted into law in New York in 1706. Despite such reassurance, New Yorkers continued to be reluctant to promote Christianity among their slaves.

In comparison to the French, the British did little to advance the Christian gospel among the Iroquois. English concern for the Native Americans was initially limited to maintaining the friendship the Dutch had enjoyed with the Iroquois. Governor Dongan recommended that English Jesuits be introduced among the natives, but nothing came of his suggestion. Both Dongan and Fletcher subsidized the missionary efforts of Dominie Godfridius Dellius among the Mohawks. In 1705, Governor Cornbury began paying Dominie John Lydius £50 a year to continue his mission to the Mohawk tribes, but the governor was otherwise singularly neglectful of the Iroquois, not holding regular councils with them or after 1702 providing them with the gifts they had come to expect from the English.

Inspired by the success of the French, Robert Livingston and Chaplain John Sharpe both called for SPG missionaries to be sent among the Indians, to learn their ways and their languages, much as the Jesuits had done so effectively, and to persuade them to trade with the English rather than the French. More informally, the Indian trade continued in New York, with Indians and Europeans interacting, sometimes forming lasting domestic relationships. Some of the interpreters hired by the Albany magistrates were men and women born of Indian and European unions. Most of the interpreters, however, were men, virtually all of them Dutch New Yorkers, captured in their youth by Native Americans. Several had even been adopted by Indian families, but they eventually returned to European society, where they were especially valuable as cultural mediators.

Those Iroquois tribes most closely allied with the English, especially the Mohawk Nation, suffered grievously during King William's War. Beginning with the Schenectady massacre of 1690, Count Frontenac brought fire and sword to Mohawk villages. As the French laid waste to crops and villages alike, the British failed to deliver on pledges of protection grandly proclaimed in the 1670s and 1680s when the Iroquois had the better of the "Beaver Wars" with the Susquehannock. While the Five Nations received the full fury of the French and their Indian allies, New York and neighboring British colonies equivocated over plans for invading Canada. Among the Iroquois, the credibility of the British was further compromised by land-grabbing schemes of Dominie Dellius and other friends of Governor Fletcher, and Anglophile Indians found their leadership seriously undermined by the negligence and greed of their British friends.

Condemning his predecessor's neglect of the Iroquois, Bellomont promised to build forts and station troops along the frontier. Nevertheless, the Iroquois in 1701 made treaties with both England and France, signaling their general desire to avoid future European struggles that might spill over into America. Trying to remain neutral while playing the British and French against each other became the central principle in Iroquoian diplomacy thereafter. It worked well for the Iroquois during Queen Anne's War, keeping the New York frontier relatively peaceful. The French and their Indian allies ravaged the New England borderlands, killing forty-two in their assault on Deerfield, Massachusetts, in 1704. Albany escaped participation entirely by negotiating an informal neutrality

Five Mohawk leaders visited England in 1710. At the request of Queen Anne, John Verelst painted portraits of four of them. Clockwise from top left: Tee Yee Neen Ho Ga Row, Ho Nee Yeath Taw No Row, Etow Oh Koam, Sa Ga Yeath Qua Pieth Tow.

agreement with the French in Montreal. Instead of the two cities competing for the furs, which were now obtained largely from Indians in the Great Lakes region, the Albanians would leave it to the Montrealers to acquire them, either from their own traders or from the Iroquois, and to exchange them with the Albanians for cheap, high-quality British-made goods.

In a calculated effort to generate support in Britain for an expedition against Canada, Peter Schuyler brought three Mohawk Anglophiles and a young Mahican to London, where they were presented as "kings" of the Five Nations. Schuyler's lobbying paid off. The SPG, much moved by the appeal of the four Indian sachems for Anglican missionaries, felt compelled in 1710 to begin its ministry to the Iroquois. The next year, Whitehall readied ships and troops for an assault upon Quebec; New York's assembly voted £10,000 to raise 600 troops, but the British force was diverted at the last minute to the Iberian Peninsula, and the colonial expedition against Canada fizzled.

New York escaped serious damage, as most of the fighting was done in the West Indies, the Carolinas, and the New England frontier. Moreover, some New York City merchants profited from a resumption of privateering. Eighteen vessels left Sandy Hook to search for enemy vessels, succeeding in destroying forty-four French and Spanish ships and bringing in about £60,000 in profits to investors. New York, in fact, captured more enemy prizes than any other British colony in North America, and privateering now became a way of life for many New York businessmen and sea captains. However, New York suffered rather than gained at the end of Queen Anne's War, as the French built a series of forts between Canada and New York, from which they could menace Albany and other outlying settlements.

By the end of the second decade of the eighteenth century, English law, commerce, and culture were all anglicizing the public life of the province in significant ways. The rights and opportunities of women, protected to a considerable degree by Roman-Dutch law and frontier conditions of New Netherland, were gradually but steadily eroded during the decades after the British conquest in 1664. Yet, at the same time, the failure of Cornbury's effort to bring New Yorkers into conformity with the Church of England underscored the fact that cultural pluralism remained deeply entrenched in the province. The family and the congregation were mutually supportive in ways that sustained rather distinctive Old World traditions and customs even as the progression of British culture in New York became more pronounced.

Chapter 9

A Mixed and Enterprising People

CONTRARY TO ENGLISH EXPECTATIONS, NEW YORK DID not undergo rapid settlement and commercial expansion after 1664. Trade and population stagnated initially and recovered only gradually and erratically. Not until the end of Queen Anne's War in 1713 did New York begin to experience its first extended period of sustained economic expansion, marked by a general upswing of trading activity and demographic growth, which lasted almost two decades. Thereafter, New Yorkers were increasingly drawn into the market economy that was beginning to emerge throughout British North America. Economic expansion in the province was advanced by legal developments, by the prevalence of generally weak and unobstructive local government, and by family and individual ambitions.

During the course of the eighteenth century, the steady improvement in road building and maintenance, the expansion of river, coastal, and overseas trade, and the availability of credit and consumer goods all brought the economies of the major trading centers, especially Albany and New York City, into closer integration with the countryside. Population growth, however modest, stimulated settlement and agricultural production and fostered commercial activity and manufacturing. Outside economic forces often held the key to boom or bust, but the provincial economy itself was becoming more complex, more diversified, and more specialized, not only in the urban centers but in rural areas as well.

Economic growth in New York contributed to a commercial ethos that became as characteristic of the province as its ethnic and religious diversity. This mercantile orientation, so striking in Albany and New York, seemed to be pervasive even in the bucolic villages of the Hudson Valley and on Long Island.

"The only principle of Life propagated among the young People," Cadwallader Colden lamented in 1748, speaking of New York generally, "is to get Money[,] and Men are only esteemed according to what they are worth, that is, the money they are possessed of." Commenting a decade later, Andrew Burnaby, a young Anglican preacher, found that New Yorkers were "almost all traders; therefore, habitually frugal, industrious, and parsimonious." Whether New Yorkers were more consumed with making money than New England merchants or Virginia planters is doubtful, but the commercial origins of New Netherland and the dominating influence of wealthy merchants and landlords in New York highlighted an aggressive materialism that encouraged white New Yorkers to accommodate their own ethnic and religious differences even as they enslaved Africans and dispossessed Native Americans.

An Emerging Market Economy

During the last years of Queen Anne's War, New York's economic fortunes began to turn favorable. The terrible epidemics of smallpox and yellow fever that had ravaged the lower Hudson Valley in the early 1700s began to subside, and between 1712 and 1720 the population of the province rose sharply from around 28,000 to almost 40,000. New York City also began to enjoy a revival of trade, thanks largely to the French and Indians concentrating their attacks on New England, leaving New York and the Iroquois pretty much alone. French privateers and naval vessels also focused on New England shipping, permitting New York merchants and privateers to make the most of their Yankee rivals' misfortunes.

Moreover, the political stability that accompanied Governor Hunter's enlightened leadership also contributed to New York's economic revival. In 1714, after four years of deadlock, Hunter struck a deal with the assembly to provide revenues for the next five years. To pay down the provincial debt accumulated during the Cornbury years, Hunter and the assembly agreed to issue £27,000 in bills of credit, redeemable from funds raised by the excise on retail liquor sales. An additional £22,000 in paper money was issued over the next few years, further easing the drag on trade caused by the chronic shortage of gold and silver coin in the American colonies. Landlord Lewis Morris, Hunter's leader in the assembly, made sure that revenues would be drawn largely from import and excise taxes, that is, from taxes on trade, rather than on the farms and great landed estates in New York. Local merchants were placated, however, by duties that favored New York shippers and vessels built in the province.

Trade statistics reflected the improvement. Between 1714 and 1717, New York cleared annually sixty-four ships totaling 4,330 tons, vastly more tonnage than in the depression years of the decade before. By 1721, 215 ships were clearing New York annually. New York imported from England goods worth several times what it exported to the mother country, and its enterprising merchants struggled to make up the imbalance by cultivating other markets in America and Europe.

Flour had become the colony's primary staple, supplemented by other "land provisions." New Yorkers sold flour and biscuits to planters in the southern colonies, but their best and largest market was the West Indies, especially Jamaica and the Dutch islands of Curaçao and Surinam, whence New York provisions were often smuggled to nearby French and Spanish colonies. "The Trade to the West Indies is wholly to the advantage of this Province," wrote Surveyor General Cadwallader Colden in 1723. In the two decades after 1710 the slave trade also reached its peak, as New Yorkers turned increasingly to enslaved Africans to meet their labor demands.

Changes in the fur trade troubled New York imperialists like Robert Livingston and William Burnet, Hunter's successor as governor (1720–28). Increasingly, Albany merchants secured furs by trading English and Dutch goods, cheaper in price and more highly prized by the Indians than French products, not to the Indians directly but to French traders in Montreal. The Albany-Montreal trade undermined French mercantilism, but it did nothing to weaken French influence among the western Indians. In 1720, Burnet persuaded the assembly to outlaw the lucrative fur trade between Montreal and Albany, in which New York City merchants like wealthy Stephen DeLancey were also involved.

Following the advice of Livingston and Colden, Burnet hoped to shift the provincial fur trade to Oswego, a trading post he built and fortified on the southern shore of Lake Ontario, thereby challenging French hegemony among the western Indians. In 1726, in the midst of the controversy, the Supreme Court of the province ruled against Albany's monopoly of the fur trade, effectively opening it to everyone. Three years later, however, the Board of Trade, influenced by the DeLancey mercantile interests, voided the statute banning the Montreal-Albany commerce. The end of the Albany monopoly and the legalizing of the Montreal-Albany trade further promoted economic development.

The emerging market economy was advanced also by the rise in the assembly of the so-called merchant faction, headed by Adolph Philipse and Stephen DeLancey, which had begun to undermine Morris and his "landed faction" in the late 1720s and continued to hold sway in the legislature until the late 1730s by making alliances with Governors John Montgomerie (1728–31) and William Cosby (1732–36). Increasingly at the mercy of international market forces, trade in New York was severely depressed through much of the 1730s. George Clarke (1736–43), who became governor after Cosby died in 1736, agreed in late 1737 to the issuing of £46,350 in bills of credit. Provincial loan offices were established in the various counties, where colonists could borrow paper currency secured by land and other collateral.

That infusion of currency coincided with another outburst of privateering associated with what became known in 1739 as the War of Jenkins' Ear against Spain in the Caribbean, giving yet a further boost to New York's economy. As the French joined the fray in what was called King George's War (1744–48), New York City became even more of a hive of privateers and center of commerce. Fifty-five privateers sailed from New York harbor between 1745 and 1748, taking almost 100 prizes between 1739 (when the war started in Europe) and 1748. One reason for New York's popularity with the sea raiders was the liberality of Judge Lewis Morris, Jr., the judge of the Vice-Admiralty Court sitting in New York. He generally favored the privateers and allowed their seizures to be condemned despite the protest of the owners, who were sometimes neutral Dutch rather than enemy French. On behalf of the privateers, it must be said that some of their work was not entirely selfish. They served as auxiliaries to the British Navy, transporting troops and supplies, serving as scouts, blockading enemy ports, and even engaging French warships in combat.

During the French and Indian War (1754–63), New York became the major theater of operations for the British army in North America. The colony issued bills of credit amounting to £535,000; much of it went to its own merchants who supplied soldiers recruited in New York. Provincial merchants were also heavily involved in the lucrative business of supplying the British army, whose expenses dwarfed those of provincial regiments. The farmers and craftsmen, as well as the merchants, profited. Despite the inevitable slump in commerce as the military operations in America ended after 1760, New Yorkers quickly positioned themselves to be the primary beneficiary of trade with Quebec, now in British hands. They thereby enlarged still further the province's immediate economic sphere, which already included New Jersey, Connecticut, and much of Rhode Island. The defeat of the French and their cession of disputed territory also brought an influx of land speculators and settlers to the New York frontier.

The colonial wars and the general mercantile expansion in the British Empire combined with agricultural settlement and commercial enterprise within the province itself to accelerate New York's economic growth in the eighteenth century. Its imports from Great Britain rose steadily, far outpacing its exports to the mother country (see Table 1).

The number of ships registered to the Port of New York also rose steadily. There were reportedly ninety-nine ships in 1746, increasing to 331 in 1749, 477 in 1762, and 709 in 1772. Rather than triangular trade, most New York shipping was bilateral, with almost half of it, before 1765, to and from the Caribbean, especially Jamaica, Curaçao, and the "logwood coast" of Honduras. After 1765, the North American coastal trade became the dominant focus of many New York merchants. Thanks to its diversified commercial network, its extensive

Table 1. Trade Between Great Britain and New York
(in thousands of British pounds sterling)

Year	New York Imports	New York Exports
1720	37.4	16.8
1730	64.4	8.7
1740	118.8	21.5
1750	267.1	35.6
1760	480.1	21.1
1770	476.0	69.9
1774	437.9	80.0

Source: From Cathy D. Matson, *Merchants & Empire: Trading in Colonial New York* (Baltimore: Johns Hopkins University Press, 1998), Appendix A, 320–21. Reproduced with permission of the author and Johns Hopkins University Press.

carrying trade to and from other ports, and its broad range of entrepôt and brokerage services, New York was the only northern colony that maintained a favorable balance of payments with Great Britain, despite the fact that it imported far more than it exported to the mother country.

The remarkable increase in trade, the issuance of paper money, and the importation of goods from England make it clear that New Yorkers were being drawn into a rapidly emerging credit-based, consumer-oriented market economy. They were not alone. Much the same was happening in New England and the colonial South. New York merchants lobbied heavily for provincial paper currency, made extensive use of bills of exchange and other types of promissory notes, and embraced creative methods of insuring their trade and commerce. Taking payment in produce as well as in cash, merchants also gave credit to town and country storekeepers, who in turn gave credit to their customers. As Deborah Rosen's impressive analysis of thousands of debt litigation cases and hundreds of probate inventories makes clear, New Yorkers in the countryside as well as in the town were increasingly purchasing consumer goods, borrowing money, going to court to enforce contracts and collect debts, and having their values and lifestyles shaped by the market economy.

Land Policy and Population Growth

Crucial to economic expansion in New York was population growth. In 1698, New Yorkers numbered approximately 18,000 people. By 1771 there were 168,000. This ninefold increase represented a relatively rapid growth rate of 3.1 percent annually (see Table 2). New York remained thinly populated, however,

Table 2. Population Charts

Counties	1698		1703	
	White	*Negro*	*White*	*Negro*
Albany	1453	23	2015	200
Ulster and Dutchess	1228	156	1481	145
Orange	200	19	230	33
New York	4237	700	3745	630
Richmond	654	73	407	97
Westchester	917	146	1709	198
Suffolk	2121	558	3158	188
Kings	1721	296	1569	343
Queens	3366	199	3968	424
Subtotal	15,897	2,170	18,282	2,258
Total:	18,067		20,540	

Counties	1723		1731	
	White	*Negro*	*White*	*Negro*
New York	5886	1362	7045	1577
Richmond	1251	255	1513	304
Kings	1774	444	1658	492
Queens	6068	1123	6731	1264
Suffolk	5266	975	7074	601
Westchester	3961	448	5341	692
Orange	1097	147	1785	184
Dutchess	1040	43	1612	112
Ulster	2357	566	2996	732
Albany	5693	808	7300	1273
Subtotal	34,393	6,171	43,055	7,231
Total:	40,564		50,286	

Counties	1737		1746	
	White	*Negro*	*White*	*Negro*
New York	8945	1719	9273	2444
Albany	9051	1630	**	**
Westchester	5894	851	8563	672
Orange	2547	293	2958	310
Ulster	3998	872	4154	1111
Dutchess	3156	262	8306	500
Richmond	1540	349	1691	382
Kings	1784	564	1686	645
Queens	7748	1311	7996	1644
Suffolk	6833	1090	7855	1399
Subtotal	51,496	8,941	52,482	9,107
Total:	60,437		61,589	

Table 2. Continued

Counties	1749 White	1749 Negro	1756 White	1756 Negro
New York	10926	2368	10768	2278
Kings	1500	783	1862	845
Albany	9154	1480	14805	2619
Queens	6617	1323	8617	2169
Dutchess	7491	421	13298	859
Suffolk	8098	1286	9245	1045
Richmond	1745	409	1667	465
Orange	3874	360	4456	430
Westchester	9547	1156	11919	1338
Ulster	3804	1006	6605	1500
Subtotal	62,756	10,592	83,242	13,548
Total:	73,348		96,790	

Counties	1771 Whites Males	Females	Negroes Males	Females
New York	9083	9643	1500	1637
Albany	20698	18131	2226	1651
Ulster	6120	5876	1091	863
Dutchess	10792	10252	750	610
Orange	5115	4315	368	294
Westchester	9566	8749	1777	1653
Kings	1268	1193	606	556
Queens	4286	4458	1156	1080
Suffolk	5912	5764	798	654
Richmond	1150	1103	351	243
Cumberland***	2132	1803	7	5
Gloucester***	371	344	6	1
Subtotal	76,493	71,631	10,636	9,247
Total:	148,124		19,883	

Source: Based on figures from Evarts B. Greene, and Virginia Harrington, *American Population before the Federal Census of 1790* (New York, 1932), 92–102.
** No figures are available for Albany County for 1746.
*** Cumberland Co. founded in 1770; Gloucester Co. founded in 1768.

largely because it had a relatively small population before 1700 and failed thereafter to attract large numbers of immigrants, as did its regional rivals, New Jersey and particularly Pennsylvania. Because so much of the most accessible territory in the province remained in the hands of manor lords and speculators, immigrants found it easier and cheaper to acquire their own farms in Pennsylvania or New Jersey rather than in New York.

Certainly this was the perception of many New Yorkers themselves, including that early crusader for land reform, Lord Bellomont. The Manor of Rensselaerswyck, for example, chartered in 1685 by Governor Dongan, covered a million acres, half of Albany County. The next year Dongan granted Robert Livingston a manorial patent for 160,000 acres, south of Rensselaerswyck and east of the Hudson River. Some of the nonmanorial patents Dongan issued were also quite large, like the Rumbout Patent, which engrossed 256 square miles of choice but unimproved land in Dutchess County.

Considerable fraud and outright bribery were involved in many of these grants. Technically, petitioners had to receive approval from the governor and council to buy the land in question from the Indians, have it surveyed, and finally have it patented, requirements that were seldom satisfied fully either before or after the patent was issued. Robert Livingston, for instance, purchased two widely separated blocks of land, amounting to a few thousand acres. However, the patent he acquired for Livingston Manor in 1686 neatly encompassed his original purchases together with all the land in between, which amounted to 160,000 acres; he did not bother to purchase the intervening property.

The huge land giveaways in New York finally alarmed the British government, which praised Bellomont's efforts to extinguish Fletcher's extravagant grants and made future grants contingent upon payment of the king's quitrent of £2.6d. per hundred acres and improvement of the land within three years. Bellomont's successor, Cornbury, however, outdid even Fletcher in approving large land patents, including one for 300,000 acres in the Mohawk Valley, the Kayaderosseras Patent (800,000 acres located west and largely north of where the Hudson and Mohawk Rivers meet), and the Hardenberg Patent (larger than the colony of Connecticut), located in Ulster and Orange counties.

The legitimacy of Cornbury's patents would be adjudicated for years, with mixed results, which hardly made the lands in question appealing to prospective settlers. After Cornbury, the Board of Trade instructed New York governors to limit grants to two thousand acres (reduced to one thousand acres in 1753) per patentee, to collect the king's quitrent, and to require that three acres out of every hundred so granted be improved within three years. Otherwise, the king could reclaim the land. These requirements were seldom enforced, and speculators still acquired large land grants by fraudulently inflating the number of patentees. Protesting Native Americans, even the loyal Mohawks who petitioned for decades against the Kayaderosseras grant, found that regardless of the fraud involved, once land was patented it generally passed from their hands forever. The white man's law favored the white man's property claims.

Although New York's appeal to potential settlers was diminished by such land grabbing, there are nonetheless many indications that lease arrangements became increasingly favorable to settlers in the eighteenth century. Even before 1700 most manors had lost their separate legal identities, though several retained assembly representation. Moreover, because lease arrangements often required the landlords to provide tools, housing, and livestock, more than a few settlers found tenantry more appealing than buying land. Pressures from the market economy as well as from the Crown encouraged landowners to recruit settlers. Finally, quite apart from the lands engrossed by manor lords and speculators, New York's relatively high taxes and proximity to the French and Indian frontier were reasons enough to repel many prospective settlers who chose, instead, to move to New Jersey or Pennsylvania.

Immigrants and Slaves

Various schemes were devised to populate New York. Because few immigrants were coming to the province, Bellomont encouraged the importation of slaves. He also lobbied the Board of Trade to support his plans for recruiting young men into the British army who would later settle in New York, manufacture naval stores, and eventually become landowners. This proposal came to nothing, but it was kept alive by Lord Cornbury and the resourceful Caleb Heathcote, mayor of New York City from 1711 to 1713. Heathcote's repeated petitions to the Board of Trade probably encouraged British officials to undertake a similar project with Palatine Germans fleeing the ravages of economic depression and French troops during Queen Anne's War.

Led by Joshua Kocherthal, a Lutheran minister, fifty or so Germans received money and land from the British Crown and settled at Newburgh in Orange County in 1709. Altogether, some three thousand Palatine Germans were transported to New York. About twenty-four hundred arrived in 1710 with the convoy that brought Governor Hunter to America; six hundred had died on the way. Palatine resentment grew after Hunter informed them that they were not to be given lands or allowed to become farmers, as they had expected. Instead, they were to establish a naval stores industry in New York. The Germans were shortly settled into seven hastily constructed villages—three on the west side of the Hudson and four on the east side (on lands purchased by Hunter from Robert Livingston)—in Ulster, Albany, and Dutchess Counties.

The experiment was a complete failure, producing little pitch and tar and making the Palatines miserable. In 1712, having gone £20,000 in debt to supply the poor Germans, Hunter announced he could no longer fund the enterprise.

The Germans were left on their own. A few remained in the camps, some became tenants of nearby landlords like Robert Livingston and Henry Beekman. Others moved to New York City or to northern New Jersey, while still others traveled to the Schoharie Valley, where they purchased land from the Mohawks—but then lost it because their deeds were not as secure as those of rival speculators. Frustrated yet again, many of the Germans left Schoharie, some going back to the Hudson Valley, though most moved to Pennsylvania and settled under more favorable circumstances.

Thanks in part to the Palatine Germans, New York's population rose from 20,540 in 1703 to 40,564 in 1723, an increase of almost 100 percent. Adding to this upward demographic trend was the increasing importation of African slaves. During that same twenty-year period, the African American population—whether slave or free, they were categorized in the census records as Negroes—rose from 2,258 to 6,171, representing 15 percent of the total population and sinking the roots of slavery more deeply in New York than in any other colony north of Maryland.

Frederick Philipse, the wealthiest man in the province, was one of the most successful New York slave merchants. After he died in 1703, his son, Adolphe Philipse, continued importing slaves as part of his general mercantile business. So did other leading merchants, including Gabriel Ludlow, Philip Livingston, and Nicholas De Ronde. Although the New York market for slaves was relatively small and rather selective, it was very lucrative and played an especially significant role in the economic development of both town and country.

The full extent of the slave trade in colonial New York is not known. From 1701 to 1774, custom records indicate that 4,398 slaves were legally imported. However, the high duty on slave imports encouraged smuggling, by which another two thousand or more bondsmen were probably brought into the province. At any rate, the census data reveal that the African American population increased as rapidly as that of the white colonists until near mid-century, still representing almost 15 percent of the total population in 1749. This occurred despite the fact that New Yorkers were known to import significantly more male than female slaves, because the latter were valued not for childbearing but for housework. The price of male slaves rose steadily: £16 in 1687, £40 in 1700, £60 in 1720, and £100 in 1760. Slave women sold for 20 to 40 percent less than males. Slave women were far fewer than their male counterparts until after 1750, when the sex ratio fell into balance and began to shift in favor of females.

Whether imported legally or illegally, New York's slaves came primarily from the West Indies until the Asiento ended in 1743, thereby terminating the privilege Britain had enjoyed since the Treaty of Utrecht in 1713 of selling five thousand slaves yearly in the Spanish colonies. Thereafter, African slaves were brought directly to New York, initially flooding the market and cutting their

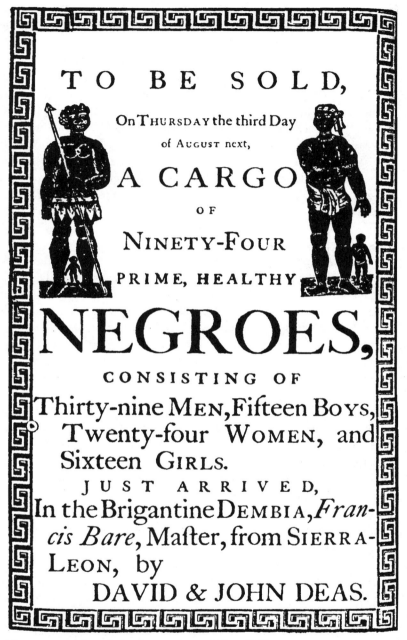

TO BE SOLD,

On THURSDAY the third Day
of AUGUST next,

A CARGO

OF

NINETY-FOUR

PRIME, HEALTHY

NEGROES,

CONSISTING OF

Thirty-nine MEN, Fifteen BOYS,
Twenty-four WOMEN, and
Sixteen GIRLS.

JUST ARRIVED,

In the Brigantine DEMBIA, *Francis Bare*, Master, from SIERRA-LEON, by

DAVID & JOHN DEAS.

Human cargo for sale in the province of New York. From *Dutchess County Historical Society Year Book* (1984).

price in half. After 1770, however, the supply of West African slaves became seriously depleted, and the price of slaves generally became higher than New Yorkers wanted to pay.

Of the 9,247 New York slaves counted in 1771, fully two-thirds lived in either New York City or Albany, where slave and free workers interacted closely and competed for both skilled and unskilled jobs. In 1691, after complaints from the licensed porters of New York City, the common council declared that "no slave be suffered to work . . . as a porter about any goods either imported or exported from or into this city"; but slaves continued to be employed by the market houses, much to the chagrin of the white porters. Similarly, in 1737, the coopers protested "the pernicious custom of breeding slaves to trades whereby the honest and industrious tradesmen are reduced to poverty for want of employ." Agreeing with the coopers, Lieutenant Governor George Clarke complained that slave competition had "forced many to leave us to seek their living in other countries."

The assembly, however, refused to restrict the use of slaves, whose labors were valuable to their owners and others. As newspaper advertisements make clear, slaves were regularly hired out, especially in the city and lesser towns but also in the countryside. In 1750 female domestics were hired for 2s. a day or 16s. a month. Depending upon their skills, male slaves were hired out for one year at £60 or more by 1760 and at £100 or more in the 1770s. In the 1760s, the services of one Albany slave were sold at the daily rate of 8s. for plowing, 5s. for mowing wheat, and 4s. for cutting wood. In New York City, a slave sailor received 2s.6d. daily, or 60s. a month.

Most New York slaves lived in their owner's household, which usually included the owner's wife and children and perhaps one or two other slaves. Such small-scale slaveholding made family life especially difficult for the bondsman, who, if he were to find a wife, would generally have to look outside his master's household. Slave mothers, fathers, and children were not likely to share the same household. Even in the southern counties of New York, where the proportion of African Americans was highest, slave women were in short supply until at least the 1750s, and even after the sex ratio came closer into balance, the physical separation of husband and wife, together with the fact that slave marriages were not legally recognized, placed severe strains on domestic relations among slaves. Given these obstacles to family life, it is not surprising that children were less common among the black population than white, or that black women tended to have fewer children than white women.

Slave craftsmen might buy their freedom and even purchase a wife and children from an obliging owner, but relatively few ever could. Most slaves had little chance of escaping bondage, though some ran away to Canada, joined the Indians, or formed outlaw bands. Enough slaves did one or the other to worry the provincial government. Of course, there were other ways slaves could express their resentment, ranging from doing work lackadaisically or feigning illness to destroying or stealing property. Rightly or wrongly, slaves were blamed for much of the petty crime, particularly in New York City, and laws were passed and periodically enforced prohibiting the sale of alcohol to or the purchase of property from slaves. Rumors circulated that certain white tavern keepers and prostitutes catered to blacks and instigated or abetted them in crime.

The Advance of Settlement

Like the population generally, slavery made its way up the Hudson, while becoming deeply entrenched in New York City and its immediate environs (see Table 2). By 1749, for example, blacks made up one-third of the population in Kings County, 20.9 percent in Ulster County, and 13.9 percent in Albany County. Thereafter, white settlers increased faster than the black population generally, especially in the upper Hudson Valley, with the proportion of African Americans falling to 9 percent in Albany County, 14 percent in Ulster, and 11.8 percent of the total provincial population by 1771. Although they were found throughout the province, the highest proportion of African Americans continued to be in the six lower counties: Kings (32 percent), Richmond (26 percent), Queens (20 percent), New York (14.4 percent), Westchester (13 percent), and Suffolk (11 percent).

As for European immigrants, except for a thousand or so Huguenots in the 1690s and the Palatine Germans early in the next century, European movement to New York remained modest until the 1760s. Following the Palatine debacle, German immigration slowed to a trickle. Scottish immigration increased modestly. Ulster Scots, better known as Scotch-Irish, also made their way to New York, many on board ships that had carried flaxseed to the Emerald Isle, but in smaller numbers than their Scottish cousins. After 1700 immigration significantly affected the small Jewish community in New York City, which probably never numbered more than seventy families before 1776, most of them involved in trade of one sort or another. The migrating Ashkenazi Jews, whose cultural roots were in eastern and southern Europe, became much more numerous than the Sephardim, whose traditions reflected the Jewish experience in Portugal and Spain.

Although immigration remained light, ships returning to New York from Britain and Europe almost always brought a few settlers from Germany, Scotland, Ulster, or England. Whether free or bound, immigrants tended to gravitate to areas where family or friends had settled previously. The French settlements at New Rochelle and New Paltz occasionally received new arrivals, though Huguenots were generally less likely to maintain their distinctive religion and folkways than other European immigrants. By 1720, Ulster Scots and Scotsmen had settlements at Goshen, Bethlehem, and Monroe in Orange County and at Wallkill in Ulster County, not to mention New York City, where a Presbyterian congregation was organized as early as 1716. German immigrants occasionally made their way to the earlier Palatine settlements in Dutchess and Ulster Counties and in the Mohawk and Schoharie Valleys. In short, immigrants from Britain and Europe, though less numerous or significant than in Pennsylvania, nevertheless contributed to the spread of settlements and reinforced cultural pluralism in colonial New York.

The pace of immigration picked up a bit in the late 1730s, promoted by Governor Cosby's proclamation of 1734 that 100,000 acres near Lake George would be made available to British Protestant families. A few years later, Captain Lachlan Campbell of Islay recruited to New York from his native Scotland some eighty-three Protestant families, estimated by some to number almost five hundred people. In 1741 a Scotch-Irishman, William Johnson, lately arrived in New York and shortly to become a leading fur trader and landowner, brought sixty fellow Ulster Scots to the Mohawk Valley estates he managed for his rich uncle, the naval commander and British politician Sir Peter Warren.

Johnson also recruited settlers from New England, which almost certainly provided more immigrants to New York than both England and Europe combined. New Englanders had been migrating to eastern Long Island and the region that became Westchester County since the 1640s; after 1700 they moved increasingly onto lands east of the Hudson which New York claimed but which Connecticut and Massachusetts still insisted belonged to them. The border dispute involved conflicting land claims among both New York and New England speculators, and New England squatters played a major role in the riots against New York landlords in the 1760s.

Whether from Britain, Europe, or New England, most immigrants to New York came in family groups. The majority were farmers, but some were artisans, merchants, doctors, preachers, and teachers. Among the most successful was Stephen DeLancey, a Huguenot refugee, who became a leading merchant, married Anne Van Cortlandt, and firmly established his family among the provincial elite. Cadwallader Colden and Archibald Kennedy, both Scots, settled in New York because they were promised positions in the provincial government, and they prospered as royal placemen. Far less privileged, another Scot, George Muirson, became a successful teacher and Anglican preacher. John Peter Zenger was one of the Palatine children apprenticed upon his arrival in America. He learned the printing trade in the shop of William Bradford, publisher of New York's first newspaper, the *New-York Gazette*. Hugh Gaine, an Ulster Scot, was a journeyman printer in the province before beginning his own business and publishing the *New-York Mercury*.

If the immigration rate was unimpressive, New York nevertheless enjoyed a fairly robust population growth due to natural increase which stimulated considerable outmigration from Albany in the north and especially from the more settled southern counties. Migration and trade through the province was facilitated by the Hudson-Esopus-Mohawk Rivers and by the developing road system. King William's War dramatized the poor condition of New York's roads.

"Plan of the City of New-York and Its Environs" (1766), by John Montresor. From I. N. Phelps Stokes, *The Iconography of Manhattan Island* (New York, 1915), vol. 1.

Accordingly, the New York assembly in 1703 ordered two roads built, both four rods wide. One followed a well-worn path from New York City through Westchester County into Connecticut and became known as the Boston Post Road. The other ran eastward across Long Island to East Hampton. Under Cornbury's regime, two additional roads were planned, running up either side of the Hudson Valley, through Westchester, Dutchess, and Albany Counties on the east and Orange, Ulster, and Albany Counties on the west. During the 1730s and 1740s these two roads, known as the King's Highway, emerged as significant thoroughfares. English common law followed the rivers and roads, guaranteeing contracts and facilitating the movement of people, goods, and money that an expanding market economy demanded.

Many of the migrants leaving the more heavily populated counties near New York City were of Dutch descent. Some moved northward, progressively populating the manor lands of Westchester County and settling on the huge estates in Dutchess and Albany Counties. Others crossed the Hudson and moved into Orange and Ulster Counties, where they were joined by Scottish and Scotch-Irish settlers. In Dutchess County, Henry Beekman proved remarkably adept at attracting Palatine and other German immigrants to the Beekman Patent.

Meanwhile, as grain became increasingly important as a commodity, Albany developed into a thriving regional distribution center, whose outmigrants moved westward to Schenectady and the Mohawk Valley, southward to Kinderhook, Coxsackie, and Catskill, and northward to Saratoga and Schaghticoke. The village of Kingston, located on the Esopus River about halfway up the Hudson to Albany, was another prime wheat farming area that attracted settlers from both Albany and the lower Hudson region. Until the late 1740s, Albany and the upper Hudson were populated largely by settlers of Dutch descent. However, King George's War brought several thousand British and provincial troops to northern New York, and the Yankee soldiers liked what they saw. By the 1750s, New Englanders were moving into the disputed lands of eastern Albany and Dutchess Counties and beyond into the Hudson and Mohawk Valleys.

Following the French and Indian War, the British Crown offered royal troops frontier land, much of it located in New York, on generous terms. Hundreds decided to become colonists, especially former regulars of the Scottish Highland regiments. Several of their officers, like Lieutenants Hugh Fraser and James Macdonald, obtained land grants and recruited settlers from the overpopulated Scottish Highlands. The surrender of Canada by the French set off a veritable frenzy of land speculation in western and northern New York, with speculators vying for settlers.

Some landlords tried to make their lands more attractive by building roads, laying out villages, constructing mills, and setting up schools. William Johnson, among other Mohawk Valley land magnates, not only brought over Scotch-Irish settlers but also recruited New Englanders, Englishmen, and Scots. German immigration to New York, especially to the Mohawk and Schoharie Valleys, also increased after the French and Indian War, thanks in part to Johnson's efforts. In northeastern New York, including the Green Mountain regions disputed with New Hampshire and Massachusetts, the Scotsman Philip Skene, the Irishman William Gilliland, and the German Charles Fredenburg all established wilderness settlements on their land grants. In the late 1760s the Beekman brothers acquired land at the upper end of the Champlain Valley and began developing what would become known as Beekmantown.

Between 1749 and 1771 immigration from New England, Britain, and Germany contributed significantly to the doubling of New York's population from 73,348 to 169,007. Over the entire eighteenth century, it was largely the internal migration resulting from natural increase that led to a much more equitable geographical distribution of settlements. In 1700, New York City and its environs contained more than half of all New Yorkers. By 1771 slightly more than 68 percent lived north of the city; Albany, Dutchess, and Ulster Counties, along with the disputed Vermont region, together contained almost 50 percent of the population. Until the 1750s more than half of New York's population was under sixteen years of age. By 1771, however, the increased immigration of adults after mid-century had reduced the proportion of young people to 46 percent.

Market Profits and Social Problems

The expanding market economy in New York provided male colonists with increasing opportunities for economic advancement, as even tenants were known to accumulate moderate personal wealth. Moreover, the growing availability of consumer goods—cloth, shoes, kitchen utensils, farm equipment, as well as clocks, watches, and furniture and china—raised the standard of living. Female colonists, however, found themselves increasingly marginalized by English rules of inheritance and the common law concept of coverture, even as the rigorous enforcement of contract law protected merchants, retailers, land speculators, and consumers—all of whom were agents of the market economy. Native Americans, male or female, and Africans, slave or free, found themselves exploited and victimized by impersonal market forces protected by an English legal system that accorded nonwhites few rights.

Even among white New Yorkers, the realization grew that economic and social change was a mixed blessing. As the market brought prosperity, it also brought depression; if some people were wealthier, growing numbers were poorer. Both the progress and the problems of the market economy were most visible in New York's two leading towns, Albany and especially New York City.

Each town grew and developed at different rates, but by 1750 both were significant urban centers, complete with specialized markets for a variety of produce and craft operations.

In 1697, Albany reported 175 households and 714 people. In 1756 it claimed 328 households and approximately thirteen hundred people. By 1779 the number of households had increased to 583 and people to approximately 2,332. Albany County, a huge geographical area later carved into a dozen counties and whose entire population the town of Albany served economically, grew by leaps and bounds. It totaled 1,476 colonists in 1698, 8,573 in 1731, 17,424 in 1756, and 42,706 in 1771. The city of New York also grew rapidly. It numbered almost 5,000 in 1698, 7,248 in 1723, 13,294 in 1749, and about 22,000 in 1771.

Manufacturing became increasingly important to both Albany and New York City. The iron industry attracted the attention of New York entrepreneurs including Philip Livingston, whose Ancram works sent pig and bar iron to both Albany and New York City. In 1728 the Walton family opened their shipyards on Manhattan; the Schermerhorns followed suit not long afterward, and both the Waltons and Schermerhorns purchased masts from the Van Schaacks in Albany. Shipbuilding stimulated the establishment of ropewalks to manufacture the rigging. In 1726 a chocolate factory was set up in Albany. In 1729 the Bayards launched their sugarhouse, and others would follow. Breweries and distilleries were built in both cities—twelve in New York City by 1767. Snuff making brought substantial amounts of tobacco from the Chesapeake to Manhattan. In both Albany and New York City, occupational categories increased and specialization became common after 1750. Among many of the merchants and some craftsmen, the living and work spaces became separate, as new homes were built away from their shops.

The pace of change picked up significantly in Albany during and after King George's War and accelerated even more during and after the French and Indian War. War brought money, merchants, and British soldiers and provincial troops from other colonies into this Dutch enclave. The newcomers to Albany and surrounding areas were led by several hundred New Englanders and lesser numbers of Scots, Germans, and Scotch-Irish, thereby hastening the process of anglicization. A Presbyterian church, for example, was erected to complement the already existing St. Peter's Church, where the Anglicans worshiped. The demographic change definitely threatened the dominance of the Albany Dutch.

In New York City, the rate of growth and change was nothing short of frenetic, bringing in its wake a plethora of trade disputes, the periodic ravages of epidemics, the need for better fire and police protection and sanitation facilities, and growing numbers of poor people. New York City freemen were united by their common devotion to material and economic well-being, but, compared to the citizens of Albany, who were beginning to experience some of the same problems, New Yorkers were much more divided ethnically, religiously, and racially. Moreover, merchants dominated the common council and imposed regulations upon craftsmen and workers that were self-serving and therefore deeply resented by others. Add to these stresses and strains the mounting unease among whites because of the growing presence of black slaves, and social tensions verged toward violence.

However frustrating their plight, few slaves dared to attack or kill their owners or other whites; and when such violence did occur, it was punished severely. After a slave revolt in April 1712, seventy Africans were arrested and jailed. Of the twenty-seven slaves who were tried for complicity in the plot, twenty-one were convicted and executed—either hanged, burned alive, racked and broken on the wheel, or gibbeted alive and in chains. As Governor Hunter reported to London, such brutal executions were designed to strike terror in the minds and hearts of the slaves. Slave controls were tightened, both in law and in practice, and the importation of slaves directly from Africa was curtailed. Further restrictions were placed on the manumission of slaves, and freed blacks, whose very existence was thought to undermine slave regulations, were prohibited from owning homes or any real property. Even the missionary efforts of Elias Neau, the SPG catechist to New York City's Negroes, came under suspicion because two of his former students were wrongly implicated in the plot.

Economic hard times and war with Spain and France exacerbated fears of slave conspiracy and revolt in the late 1730s. In 1738, for example, during a prolonged economic slump, an otherwise insignificant brawl among a few Kingston slaves prompted rumors that New York bondsmen were planning a general uprising. The onset of the War of Jenkins' Ear with Spain in 1739 and the likelihood of French intervention against Britain further intensified white anxiety and set the stage for the Great Negro Plot of 1741. Were the slaves planning to burn New York City and massacre the whites? Such were the claims made by Mary Burton, an indentured servant who became a celebrity testifying against her tavern-keeper master, John Hughson, his family, and his black and white friends and clients. Burton began by charging that Hughson, his wife and daughter, and a prostitute who lived at the tavern bought stolen property from slaves. Hughson may well have trafficked in stolen goods, but the culpability of his wife—and particularly his young daughter—is less likely. While this investigation was going on, New York City experienced a rash of fires and associated burglaries, and when a slave was caught looting a burning building in March, the growing insolence that whites perceived among the slaves took on a much more sinister meaning.

Convinced that a "villainous conspiracy" was afoot, the common council offered £100 to anyone who would expose it. Well aware of the reward, Mary Burton shifted her testimony from burglary to a diabolical plot allegedly hatched by the Hughsons, a whore named Peggy Kerry, and two slaves named Quack and Cuffee, who, she said, planned to set the city ablaze and kill the whites. Once the slaves were in control, John Hughson was to be proclaimed king and any surviving white women were to be divided among the slaves. In the frenzy that followed, some 160 blacks and twenty-one whites were arrested.

During the subsequent trials, not one New York attorney would defend the accused, and the attorney general, Richard Bradley, played fast and loose with the rules of criminal procedure to get Quack and Cuffee convicted. Faced with being burned at the stake, the two slaves, who had been promised clemency should they cooperate, only reluctantly as they approached the stake confessed and implicated John Hughson as "the first contriver of the plot." At the insistence of the crowd, Quack and Cuffee were burned anyway. Hughson, his wife, and Peggy Kerry were also found guilty and shortly hanged, though their bewildered and traumatized daughter Sarah was granted a reprieve for confirming the testimony of Burton, who implicated many others, including John Ury, a schoolmaster and former preacher whom Burton accused of being a Catholic priest. He, too, was executed, along with thirty-two slaves, some of whom were burned at the stake and others buried alive. More than seventy-two slaves were deported.

Justice Daniel Horsmanden of the New York Supreme Court wrote a pamphlet praising Attorney General Bradley and the New York City lawyers who assisted with the prosecution. However, no credible evidence exists that there ever was a conspiracy. To be sure, there was seething discontent among many slaves, as well as considerable slave involvement in crime, generally petty rather than grand theft. Yet there is nothing to suggest that Mary Burton's story of a slave plot to burn and kill was more than an elaborate lie that white New Yorkers wanted to believe. The question is why they wanted to believe it. Ury's shameful trial and execution reveal the Catholic as well as the racial prejudice behind this legalized massacre. New Yorkers' nervousness with an almost 20 percent slave population is also understandable. But their bloodlust in prosecuting the plot betrays a people deeply riven by social, economic, and ethnoreligious tensions and rivalry. However much they had learned to repress their distrust of one another in the name of economic progress and political stability, white New Yorkers could not deal with something as threatening as the possibility of a slave revolt without themselves lapsing into the same kind of barbarism they were purporting to prevent.

Chapter 10

Colonial Culture
The Sacred and the Secular

BETWEEN 1700 AND 1750, TWO OVERLAPPING, INTERACTING cultural patterns became firmly rooted in provincial New York. On the one hand, provincial politics and law and the lifestyles of the economic and social elite came progressively under the sway of English culture. The language of politics and government, of literary and polite discourse, and of the popular press was English, which advanced rapidly among the non-British upper classes. For many New Yorkers, however, not English but Dutch, German, or French continued to be the language of household conversation, daily life and labor, and particularly worship. In both domestic and religious life, ethnic folkways retained considerable potency, not only among the foreign born and their offspring but also among those of British descent such as the Scotch-Irish, Scots, and New Englanders.

This dynamic process yielded different results from place to place, but it accounts for the persistence of pluralism, even as culture became increasingly anglicized, which so fascinated and perplexed visitors to the province. Andrew Burnaby, a visiting Anglican priest, captured perfectly the evolving character of New York society at mid-century. "Being . . . of different nations, different languages, and different religions," wrote the young preacher, "it is almost impossible to give them any precise or determinate character." Burnaby identified only one characteristic shared by such variegated peoples: the importance they gave to trade and commerce and their common pursuit of economic gain. Yet by the time of Burnaby's travels, many New Yorkers were trying quite deliberately to define themselves and their province in terms that transcended both materialism and pluralism.

As early as the 1690s, Governor Fletcher and Anglican leaders looked to

English culture generally, and the Church of England particularly, as engines of social and cultural unity. Despite reversals resulting from Cornbury's zeal, New York Anglicans did not surrender their dream of provincial hegemony for the Church of England. Other New Yorkers, inspired by the religious revivals known as the Great Awakening, initially hoped that evangelical Christianity might cut across denominational differences and unite New Yorkers religiously. Still others, responding particularly to Enlightenment thought, found in rationalism, education, and English politics and law the mechanisms they thought necessary to forge common bonds among so disparate a people.

The Colonial Churches

Diversity in worship was lamented by many and celebrated by few New Yorkers. Even a tolerant cleric like the Reverend Gualterus Du Bois of the Dutch Reformed Church complained that New York's "perfect freedom of conscience for all except Papists" led only to "a spirit of confusion" and left many inhabitants "perplexed and misled." But to a rationalist like the attorney William Livingston, "the Variety of Sects . . . are a Guard against the Tyranny and Usurpation of one over another." Understanding provincial politics and enamored of Enlightenment ideas, Livingston in his exaltation of denominational diversity looked more to the secular future than to the religious past. Yet the eighteenth century was still very much an age of faith, even in commercially minded New York.

Religious rivalry significantly shaped New York's cultural pluralism. Trinity Church gave Anglicans an imposing presence in New York City, and Anglican insistence that the Ministry Act of 1693 established the Church of England in the four lower counties irritated dissenters until the American Revolution. Although wary of the English Church, Dutch Reformed pastors and lay leaders found it to their advantage to cooperate with Anglicans on occasion, as the chartering of the Dutch Church of New York City in 1696 made clear. Thereafter, only Anglicans and Dutch Reformed congregations were legally chartered, which allowed them to manage property and borrow money, a privilege denied other confessions. New York Anglicans did not exactly "lust for dominion," to use the young lawyer William Smith, Jr.'s colorful phrase, but they were not above discriminating against their rivals, especially Presbyterians.

After Cornbury's arrest and prosecution of Francis Makemie, organizer and moderator of the Philadelphia Presbytery, in 1707, Pennsylvanian Presbyterians and English Calvinists in New York developed closer working relations. In 1711, Congregationalists at Jamaica, Long Island, called George McNish, at the time moderator of the Presbytery of Philadelphia, who became known as the Father of American Presbyterianism. Challenging the Anglican claim of establishment in Queens County at every turn, McNish was instrumental in securing other Presbyterian ministers for Calvinist congregations on Long Island and in Westchester County. In 1716, McNish and fellow ministers Samuel Pumroy of Newtown and George Phillips of Setauket (Brookhaven) formed the Presbytery of Long Island, affiliated with the Synod of Philadelphia. The same year, the lay leaders Dr. John Nicoll and Gilbert Livingston formally organized a Presbyterian congregation in New York City.

Over the next decade, the leading Congregational churches on Long Island began joining the burgeoning presbytery. At the same time, Scottish and Scotch-Irish immigrants established their faith west of the Hudson, especially in Orange and Ulster Counties. East of the Hudson, migrants from western Connecticut embraced Presbyterianism, scattering congregations through Westchester and Dutchess Counties. In 1738 congregations in both New York and East Jersey were joined as the Presbytery of New York. Its most prominent preachers— Ebenezer Pemberton of New York City, Jonathan Dickinson of Elizabethtown, and Aaron Burr of Newark, New Jersey—were also leaders of the Philadelphia Synod. As fellow Calvinists, New Yorkers of Congregationalist background drifted easily into Presbyterianism. Most of them had some previous association with Connecticut, whose Saybrook Platform of 1708 was modeled after the Scottish Kirk. Between 1700 and 1750, Congregationalist churches declined in New York from nine to five but rebounded to twelve by 1775, owing mainly to the increased migration of New Englanders into the Hudson Valley (see Table 3).

Table 3. Protestant Congregations in New York in the Colonial Period

	1650	1700	1750	1775
Anglican	0	2	20	26
Baptist	0	0	4	10
Congregational	4	9	5	12
Dutch Reformed	2	19	48	76
French Protestant	0	4	4	4
German Reformed	0	0	7	10
Lutheran	2	2	26	26
Methodist	0	0	0	1
Moravian	0	0	1	2
Presbyterian	1	4	35	50
Quaker	0	8	14	22
Total	9	48	164	239

Source: From Richard W. Pointer, *Protestant Pluralism and the New York Experience: A Study of Eighteenth-Century Religious Diversity* (Bloomington: Indiana University Press, 1988), 4. Reproduced with permission of the author and the Indiana University Press.

Regarded as the bane of Protestantism by both Anglicans and orthodox Calvinists, Quakerism, whose presence in the region dated back to New Netherland, continued to claim the allegiance of some New York settlers. As Quakers migrated from western Long Island and New Jersey, they established congregations on Manhattan Island and up the Hudson in Orange County on the west and Westchester and Dutchess Counties on the east. Although by 1750 wealthy merchants and farmers belonged to the Society of Friends in New York, Quakerism was still strongly identified with the lower classes and had special appeal in frontier areas where squatters and tenants were at odds with landowners. Quaker congregations, though they increased from eight in 1700 to fourteen in 1750 and twenty-two in 1775, were generally quite small.

Huguenots maintained congregations in New York City and Westchester County but continually lost membership, particularly to Anglicanism. Anglicans also made inroads among the Palatine Germans, at least for a decade or so until the SPG stopped subsidizing their ministers, after which congregants generally reverted to Lutheran or German Reformed doctrine and liturgy. Thereafter, Lutheran clerics worried less about losing members to the Anglican than to the Dutch Reformed Church. The Classis of Amsterdam, which in the 1720s began supervising the German Reformed as well as the Dutch Reformed in America, could never supply enough preachers for either.

Not so much Anglicanism but "anglicization," that is, the spread of English language usage and English culture, threatened the vitality and integrity of the Dutch Reformed, French Reformed, Dutch and German Lutherans, and German Reformed, among whom national and religious identities became progressively fused. Continued immigration somewhat replenished ethnic and national identity, even among the small Jewish congregation in New York. Having organized their congregation, Shearith Israel, in 1709, New York Jews built their first synagogue in 1729; they secured their first native-born precentor, Gershom Mendes Seixas, in 1768, and maintained a school to perpetuate their folkways. Still, marriage outside the faith continuously eroded ethnoreligious particularism among Jews and other New Yorkers. The fundamental problem that each of the non-British religious groups faced was how to perpetuate their different traditions within a larger societal context that was increasingly English. Neither the Jews nor the French Reformed had a national religious authority to sustain them, but the other European groups did, as did the Anglicans, and they generally looked to ecclesiastical organizations across the Atlantic to send them ordained ministers.

Qualified preachers were always in short supply, and the lure of rival confessions meant that congregational membership could never be taken for granted. "Certain ones, apparently only for worldly reasons, have united with the Episcopalians," wrote Dominie Du Bois in 1741. Others had joined the Presbyterians. "Among them there is no confession demanded of one's faith," Du

Bois pointed out, "nor is there any discipline among them, as among us." In such an environment, "everyone does as he pleases," complained the Reverend Michael Christian Knoll in 1749, speaking of the Lutheran congregation in New York City. His members were lured from the faith of their fathers by reasons of "marriage, pride, and bread, so that one who is today a Lutheran, he or his child may tomorrow be a Reformed, a Moravian, or a Quaker, etc." Knoll's complaint was echoed by other religious leaders again and again.

The Great Awakening

Erupting from this maelstrom of competing Protestant confessions were the religious revivals known as the Great Awakening. The Awakening reached its peak between 1739 and 1745, but as early as 1728, Theodore Frelinghuysen, a Dutch Reformed preacher in the Raritan Valley of New Jersey, called for a conversion experience as evidence of salvation. Soon the Congregationalist Jonathan Edwards, the Presbyterian Gilbert Tennent, and the Anglican-Methodist George Whitefield made such an experience the hallmark of their revivalism. The impact of the Great Awakening in the middle colonies, particularly New York, was surely greater than historians have generally assumed. The conversion experience itself was faith-affirming, bringing solace to those whose beliefs may have been shaken by the multiplicity of creeds and unqualified clergymen.

While making thunderous appeals for Christian unity, the revivalists brought to a head mounting tensions between the traditionalists, who urged rather strict adherence to European standards, and the accommodationists, who sought to adjust to American conditions. When Whitefield arrived in New York City in November 1739, the Reverend William Vesey of Trinity Church, now designated by the Bishop of London as Commissary of Anglican affairs in New York, upbraided the youthful evangelist for "making a disturbance in Philadelphia, and sowing and causing divisions in other places" and refused him access to Trinity Church. Dominie Henricus Boel also refused Whitefield's request to preach in the Old Dutch Church. However, Boel's associate Dominie Du Bois, together with Dominie Frelinghuysen, Reverend Ebenezer Pemberton of the Presbyterian congregation, and the evangelist Gilbert Tennent and his brother William all joined Whitefield on the outskirts of town where the latter enthralled a crowd of two thousand people gathered in the fields.

Whitefield spoke the next evening to Ebenezer Pemberton's congregation and went on to preach in Westchester County, at Flatbush, in eastern Long Island, and on Staten Island. His sermons attracted people from every religious fellowship. While Christian unity was his message, Whitefield's appeal to the emotions and the criticism that he and associates like Gilbert Tennent addressed toward their fellow clergymen ultimately widened the cracks within the various confessions into substantial fissures. Anglican clerics generally deplored this "Spirit of Enthusiasm," as Isaac Brown, a Yale graduate and SPG missionary at Brookhaven, Long Island, wrote in 1740, "not so much that of Quakerism (which I fear'd Some time past) as a New Sect lately Spring [sic] up, who pretend to be followers of Mr. Whitefield, altho they Never Saw him, nor are Much acquainted with his Doctrine." Nonetheless, while the revivals disrupted dissenting congregations, Anglican clerics stepped up their proselytizing and gleefully noted the increase in their Sunday attendance.

Christian rationalists, like the young William Livingston, a Yale graduate and son of the second lord of Livingston Manor, found the emotionalism of the revivals both silly and repelling:

I can never persuade myself that Such Convulsions . . . Agitations, Swoons, fluctuations, trances, groanings, yellings, . . . howlings, cryings, Shreekings . . . down fallings, uprisings, tumblings, tossings, Shakings, quiverings, semi-quivers, . . . visions, succors, external notions of the Soul, and internal Hypocricy of the Same . . . are any sign that Christianity prevails among a people.

More orthodox critics of the Awakening, however, feared the excesses of the rationalists as much as the intemperance of the evangelists. Anglican ministers found they had much in common with conservative Presbyterians, Congregationalists, and Quakers, who also opposed the revivals. Similarly, evangelicals such as Reverend Henry Melchoir Muhlenberg of the Lutherans and Reverend Michael Schlatter of the German Reformed had much more in common with Ebenezer Pemberton, Gualterus Du Bois, and George Whitefield than with conservative clerics of their own faiths, who adhered strictly to European standards and denounced the Awakening for undermining orthodoxy. Schlatter organized a German Reformed Coetus in 1747, a local supervisory group of ministers, and as its superintendent he brought virtually all the congregations of German Calvinists in both New York and Pennsylvania under his benevolent leadership. Organizing the Pennsylvania Ministerium in 1748, Muhlenberg gradually brought Lutherans in New York into the religious association over which he presided.

Among the Dutch Reformed, too, by 1750, the evangelicals were dominant, and the Classis of Amsterdam finally gave its approval to establishing an American Coetus in 1754. The same year, William Livingston wrote that "the Dutch tongue, which, though once the common dialect of this province, is now scarcely understood, except by its more ancient inhabitants." In the next decade, preaching in English began at the New Dutch Church of New York City, which further prepared the way for the ultimate organization in America of a Dutch Reformed Classis under the leadership of the American-born Henry Livingston in the 1770s.

Among the English, the Congregationalists divided into the Old Lights who were against and the New Lights who were for the revivals; the Presbyterians similarly split into Old Side and New Side factions. In New York and New Jersey, where Presbyterianism was co-opting Congregational churches, Presbyterian clergy and congregants were overwhelmingly evangelical and generally of New England heritage. In 1738 they organized the Presbytery of New York and the Presbytery of New Brunswick. However, their intemperate attack upon preachers unwilling or unable to emulate the pulpit style of the evangelicals provoked the ire of the Synod of Pennsylvania, presided over by Scotch-Irish clerics, who expelled the New Brunswick preachers from the Synod in 1741.

After four years of close cooperation, the Presbytery of New York formally joined with the New Brunswick Presbytery to form the New York Synod, which remained independent of its Pennsylvanian counterpart until 1758, when the two synods merged voluntarily. By that time, the evangelical New Side Presbyterians had thoroughly routed their Old Side opponents, in Pennsylvania as well as in New York and New Jersey. The seventy-four preachers in the New York Synod outnumbered their Pennsylvania counterparts three to one, and by 1775 the number of Presbyterian congregations in New York numbered fifty, as opposed to twenty-six for their chief rivals, the Anglicans.

The Great Awakening began with the hope that Protestant diversity might be transformed into Christian unity. Broad coalitions and associations for and against the revivals did emerge, cutting across religious differences. Cooperation did not lead to Christian union, however, even among the evangelicals. In fact, the one Christian fellowship apparently dedicated to ecumenicalism, the Moravians, made little headway in New York. Their leader, the charismatic Count Zinzendorf, was suspected of harboring Catholic doctrines. Rather than fostering Protestant unity, the Great Awakening furthered the process already underway of transforming still inchoate European Christian confessions into self-reliant American religious denominations. Moreover, whatever brotherly love evangelical Protestants demonstrated toward one another in New York, it did not soften their anti-Catholicism, which was one of the sinister forces behind the brutal consequences of the so-called Slave Conspiracy of 1741. New York Catholics, few in number and served by priests from Philadelphia, knew better than to worship as openly as their Jewish neighbors.

In the aftermath of the Great Awakening, religious rivalry, especially between Anglicans and dissenters, increased markedly in New York. SPG preachers not only welcomed disgruntled dissenters into their fellowship but urged the Venerable Society to establish missions at Huntington in Suffolk County, Newburgh in Ulster County, and New Castle and New Salem in Westchester County. Anglicans also made advances among the Indians at Albany and on Long Island and stepped up the catechizing of slaves in New York City. In the Mohawk Valley, William Johnson initially supported both Anglican and Congregational missionary efforts, but by 1760 he withdrew his support of the New England preachers, suspecting they were trying to turn the Mohawks against Anglicans.

In 1741, under the spell of the Awakening, the leaders of the Presbytery of New York, acting as Correspondents for the Society in Scotland for Propagating Christian Knowledge, appointed Azariah Horton, a young Yale graduate and ordained minister, to preach to the four hundred or so remaining Montauk Indians on the southern shore of Long Island. Horton was succeeded by the Native American teacher and preacher Samson Occom. The ordination by the Presbytery of New York of Horton, Occom, and others born and educated in America made increasingly clear to Anglicans the disadvantage they labored under by having to send clerical prospects to England for ordination.

Education

Denominational rivalry took on an important educational dimension. During the 1740s, Anglican clerics in New York urged the SPG to expand its program of subsidizing schoolmasters who agreed to instruct their students in the prayers and catechisms of the Church of England. Nothing else was more important to advancing the English Church and its doctrines, insisted Thomas Colgan, SPG missionary to Jamaica, who in 1744 complained of dissenting teachers "whose daily business it is, to instill such notions & Principles in Young People as are destructive of good manners, and of all Religion and government." Similarly, William Vesey explained that over the years Trinity Church owed much of its growth to its charity school in New York City. Altogether, the SPG sent fifty-eight missionaries and subsidized dozens of schoolteachers before 1776. Their impact was perhaps less significant in terms of increasing Anglican adherents (who probably never numbered more than 10 percent of New Yorkers) than in "anglicizing" and advancing literacy among the inhabitants.

Dissenters, too, recognized the importance of schooling in the expansion of the faith, both for children and young adults. Increasingly, Anglicans lamented the presence of Presbyterian or Quaker schools. Among the Dutch Reformed, trustworthy schoolmasters were likewise highly prized for their teaching of the mother tongue as well as the catechism. Much the same attitude toward schoolmasters was displayed by Lutherans and German Reformed. The establishment by the Presbyterians of the College of New Jersey in 1746 made it abundantly clear which denomination was strategically placing itself to become the dominant faith of the middle colonies. The lesson was not lost on other dissenters or on Anglicans, whose pretensions were definitely being challenged by the educational efforts of dissenters.

The fact that schooling became so important in denominational rivalry reflected the importance of reading, writing, and arithmetic skills for trade and commerce and the expansion of literary culture in general. Schools and literacy training were part of an educational system that was largely structured according to class and gender. Children began their education in the household and usually continued it in the shop, in the classroom, on the farm, or in the countinghouse. Sons early on imitated and assisted their fathers and brothers and learned their trade while doing so. Daughters were similarly introduced to the details of housewifery by their mothers or sisters. In families where wives and husbands worked closely together, girls as well as boys might learn various aspects of the family business, but restrictions imposed upon women by English law and custom made this a diminishing phenomenon. In preparing the young for their life's work, New Yorkers, both rich and poor, drew upon the assistance of extended kinship structures and business relationships. Artisans sometimes agreed to train each others' children in complementary trades, but more often the father simply taught his son the craft he himself practiced.

Few children attended school for more than three months a year or for more than three years, the standard time allotted for schooling in many apprenticeship indentures. Boys were usually schooled longer than girls, though it was quite common, especially among Dutch New Yorkers, for girls as well as boys to have a little formal schooling. Estimates for the 1770s suggest that at any one time no more than one-quarter of the children of school age were actually in school in New York City, where at least fifty-five teachers taught between 1695 and 1775. Only children of the elite and occasionally poor boys with promise and community support received extensive schooling, including enough Latin and Greek to qualify them for admission to college.

If even New York parents with few skills and little money appreciated the importance of preparing their children for future employment, this was particularly true of the economic elite. "The Law or Commerce," wrote merchant John Watts in 1765, with regard to possible vocations for his sons, "seem to be the only alternative with us & such Numbers infest the first that the latter I think upon the whole is become full as Creditable." Watts might have mentioned medicine, another of the three aristocratic trades celebrated in England, but the enterprising businessman, reflecting the popular prejudices of the day, tended to view most lawyers as pocket-picking pettifoggers and most doctors as ignorant, murderous quacks. While formal apprenticeship declined among the crafts, it remained the primary path to becoming a merchant, lawyer, or doctor.

John Watts, for example, planned the education of his children well. His eldest son Robert learned commerce in the firm run by his father and his uncle Oliver DeLancey. His daughters were taught to be proper young ladies and married into families known for economic enterprise and social and political status. As for his two younger sons, John would study law in England, and Stephen, like Robert, would follow commerce. Years before, Robert Livingston and Stephen

DeLancey had adopted similar educational strategies for their progeny. So had Jeremias Van Rensselaer, Frederick Philipse, Stephanus Van Cortlandt, Lewis Morris, Gerardus Beekman, and Henry Lloyd. Philip Livingston, second lord of the manor, educated his eldest son Robert to manage his lands, while his younger sons were trained in the law and commerce to look after various other aspects of the vast Livingston family interests. At Albany, Leendert Gansevoort educated his oldest son to commerce, his second son to the family brewery business, and his third son to medicine.

Manners, Morals, and Cultural Refinement

The upper classes were the chief purveyors of British manners and morals in New York. It was relatively easy for the wealthy Jays and DeLanceys to move from the French Reformed Church to the Church of England. Economic and political success no doubt encouraged Dutch New Yorkers like the Philipses, Van Cortlandts, Bayards, and the Clermont branch of Livingstons to leave the Reformed Church and become Anglican. Yet it should be remembered that all four families continued to rely upon Dutch friends and kin to promote their commercial and political interests, even as they cultivated English connections in both the Old World and the New. Similarly, as provincial officials in the royal government, Scots such as Cadwallader Colden, Archibald Kennedy, and James Alexander, all of whom had been born and raised as Presbyterians, felt obliged to worship at Anglican Trinity Church.

Anglicanism was generally recognized as the religion of the elite. However, despite the expanding appeal of English culture and language and the allure of Anglican status, almost every other religious denomination had its wealthy adherents. Although extensively involved in British trade and politics, powerful Dutch New York families like the Van Rensselaers, Beekmans, Schuylers, and Van Dams remained in the Reformed Church. Similarly, Samuel and William Franklin, two of the wealthiest merchants in New York City, were Quakers. Moses Franks, another successful merchant, was Jewish, while the William Smiths, Senior and Junior, the leading lawyers in the province, were Presbyterian. Particularly among New Yorkers of Dutch, German, and Jewish background, upper-class families were links between the local culture of family and community and the provincial culture of politics, law, and commerce.

By the 1750s, New York's upper classes, like the elite elsewhere in British America, were concerned with refining provincial society according to the standards of English culture. Social and cultural reformers, like that trio of Yale-educated lawyers, William Livingston, William Smith, Jr., and John Morin Scott, certainly found much to criticize among materialistic, hard-drinking, fun-loving, and not especially learned or literate New Yorkers.

The upper classes, however, set the example for frivolity and conviviality, with one or another social club—that is, drinking club—meeting almost every evening. New York City had 166 taverns by 1744. In the 1750s, Albany had over a dozen taverns and inns, and country towns like Jamaica on Long Island usually had a tavern or two where the locals socialized and weary travelers found rest and refreshment. By mid-century the coffee house joined the tavern as another popular "public place" where self-selected groups of craftsmen and gentlemen regularly gathered to, in the words of Jonas Green, a Maryland printer and clubman, "converse, laugh, talk, smoke, drink, differ, agree, argue, philosophize, harangue, pun, sing, dance, and fiddle together."

Weekdays as well as Sundays, backgammon and card playing occupied the time of tavern patrons, sometimes in special rooms set aside specifically for that purpose. While men young and old fraternized in the taverns, women generally socialized and visited with one another at home. Various matriarchs like Mary Alexander and Mrs. Philip Schuyler were women of business, but they also presided over social circles that initiated younger women into the female world of quilting and sewing parties. Popular outdoor activities extending from Dutch days were fishing, hunting, skating, and sleighing, engaging both men and women. The English introduced cricket, golf, and tennis. Hunting was a popular male entertainment. Governor Cornbury and the Anglican minister John Sharpe were regulars at the hunt. Governor Cosby kept his own game preserve, and some of the rich gentry had their own deer parks. Young men and women joined together for picnics and other "frolics."

Tankard by Peter Van Dyke (1684–1751). Ownership of such objects was emblematic of the growing wealth of colonial New Yorkers. New York State Historical Association, Cooperstown, N.Y.

Like work itself, socializing was often segregated by race and class. Craftsmen patronized taverns that became identified with them, as did day laborers, free blacks, and slaves, whose haunts were often along the waterfront. Brothels were similarly segregated by the economic status of their respective neighborhoods. At the bottom of the socioeconomic ladder were New York's African Americans, numbering almost 20,000 by 1771. Blacks brought with them African and Caribbean customs of dancing, handicrafts, music, and storytelling. The laws that limited the gathering of slaves to three or four made sociability difficult, but not impossible.

The commercial ethos of the province seemed to some critics inimical to refinement and learning. "The City is so conveniently Situated for Trade," the Reverend John Sharpe had written of Manhattan in 1713, "and the Genius of the people so inclined to merchandise, that they generally seek no other Education for their children than writing and Arithmetick." By the 1740s, New York's lack of taste and learning became a recurring topic of both satire and serious prose in the popular press. "Our Youth here," wrote the pseudonymous *Americanus* in 1751, "it must be allowed, are endow'd with as good Natural Parts, as those of the other Provinces; and had they equal Advantages, are, no doubt, as Capable of Improvement: Ought not then a Reflection of this induce us to enter upon some Plan for the good of our Posterity, that be as advantageous to them?"

Certain plans were afoot, and had been for some time. As early as 1730, the Common Council of New York City set up a circulating library, which languished until joined with the New York Society Library in 1754. The latter was the brainchild of a group of young gentlemen—including Livingston, Smith, and Scott—who had earlier established a literary club called the "Society for the Promotion of Useful Knowledge," founded as an antidote to New York's more plentiful drinking clubs. In practice, booksellers and printers, some of whom ran their own circulating libraries, did more than the New York Society Library to make books available to the public.

Beginning with William Bradford in 1693, the number of printers—who were also booksellers—in New York City increased to three in 1742, four in 1750, six in 1762, and twelve by 1777. The number of imprints from the New York presses grew steadily: twenty per year in the 1730s, twenty-five in the 1740s, thirty-two in the 1750s, fifty-five in the 1760s, and 155 in 1774. They included not only government documents but increasing numbers of self-help books, almanacs, spelling books, some history, and poetry. In 1714, Bradford published the first drama known to have been composed in America, *Androboros: A Biographical Farce in Three Acts*, written by Governor Hunter (with the probable collusion of Lewis Morris) poking fun at Hunter's Anglican critics. Bradford also published Cadwallader Colden's *History of the Five Indian Nations Depending on the Province of New York in America* (1727). Of course, political pamphlets were staple fare for New York printers, but they also published a little verse, including William Livingston's pastoral poem *Philosophic Solitude, or The Choice of a Rural Life* (1747) and "An Evening Thought: Salvation by Christ, with Penetential Cries" (1761), by Jupiter Hammon, an African American poet living as a slave on Long Island.

In 1725, Bradford began publishing his *New-York Gazette,* and he continued until 1744. The second newspaper, begun by Bradford's apprentice John Peter Zenger, in 1733, was the *Weekly Journal,* which continued after Zenger's death in 1746 until 1752. Other newspapers followed, twenty-two before the American Revolution, most of short duration, all but one published in New York City.

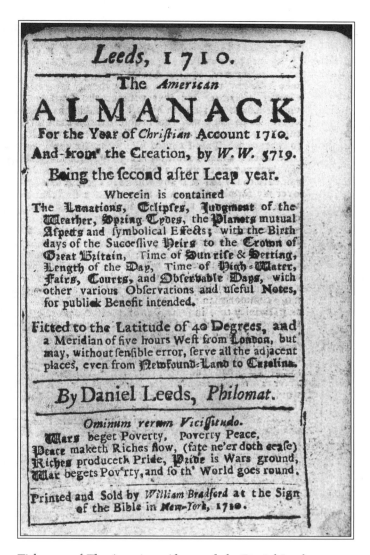

Leeds, 1710.

The *American*

ALMANACK

For the Year of *Christian* Account 1710.
And-from the Creation, by *W. W.* 5719.

Being the second after Leap year.

Wherein is contained
The Lunations, Eclipses, Judgment of the
Weather, Spring Tydes, the Planets mutual
Aspects and symbolical Effects; with the Birth
days of the Successive Heirs to the Crown of
Great Britain, Time of Sun rise & Setting,
Length of the Day, Time of High-Water,
Fairs, Courts, and Observable Days, with
other various Observations and useful Notes,
for publick Benefit intended.

Fitted to the Latitude of 40 Degrees, and
a Meridian of five hours West from London, but
may, without sensible error, serve all the adjacent
places, even from Newfound-Land to Carolina.

By Daniel Leeds, *Philomat.*

Ominum rerum Vicissitudo.
Wars beget Poverty, Poverty Peace,
Peace maketh Riches flow, (fate ne'er doth cease)
Riches produceth Pride, Pride is Wars ground,
War begets Pov'rty, and so th' World goes round.

Printed and Sold by *William Bradford* at the Sign
of the Bible in *New-York,* 1710.

Title page of *The American Almanack,* by Daniel Leeds,
printed in New York City in 1710. Collection of the New-York
Historical Society, negative number 55706.

In the early years newspapers primarily announced the arrival and departure of
ships, reprinted news from London papers, printed advertisements, and published government notices. Increasingly, though, they reprinted essays from the
literary magazines of London, like Joseph Addison's and Richard Steele's publications, the *Tatler* and the *Spectator,* which dealt with everything from
courtship and marriage through child rearing and schooling to death and taxes.

By the 1760s, fashionable New Yorkers were also patronizing portrait painters including John Wollaston, Lawrence Kilburn, Benjamin West, and John Singleton Copley. Copley stayed only five months in Manhattan but did thirty-seven paintings, clearing more than £300 sterling. In the 1740s, the New York Harmonic Society was established and began sponsoring regularly scheduled concerts and other musical entertainment. While the officers of such organizations were all males, the programs themselves usually included women performers. At about the same time, well-off young men and women, who regularly held formal and informal parties, formed New York City's Dancing Assembly and organized fortnightly balls during the fall and winter social season.

In imitation of London pleasure gardens, where the upper classes could stroll, eat and drink, and attend concerts and lectures, Samuel Fraunces opened Vauxhall Gardens in 1765 on a hill overlooking the Hudson. There the genteel classes might visit a fine wax museum, observe Italian fireworks, or partake of afternoon teas. Traveling troupes of actors began visiting New York in the 1730s; the first newspaper notice of a theatrical performance was on February 26, 1750, in the *New-York Weekly Post Boy*, announcing a company of actors from Philadelphia performing in a building on Nassau Street owned by the merchant Rip Van Dam. The first performance, on March 5, was of *Richard III*. The first American presentation of *Hamlet* occurred on December 17, 1751, in New York City, performed by the American Company, organized by an Englishman, David Douglass, and featuring the Hallam brothers, well-known thespians, in the new Chapel Street Theater.

Acting, however, did not satisfy the cultural yearnings of some New Yorkers. At the center of the small but growing circle of intellectuals in the province was the irascible Cadwallader Colden, provincial placeman and politician. Immensely learned, Colden cultivated interests in science, mathematics, medicine, and botany. He corresponded with Benjamin Franklin and other American scientists, various members of the Royal Society in England, and even Johannes Gronovius, the famed Leiden botanist and student of Linnaeus. Indeed, Franklin credited Colden with nurturing the idea of the American Philosophical Society, finally organized in 1743. New York had other less well-known intellectuals. Many of the preachers and teachers, some of the merchants, older lawyers like James Alexander, John Chambers, and William Smith, Sr., and the group of three young lawyers, Livingston, Smith, and Scott—some of whom intensely disliked the old savant personally and politically—shared Colden's desire to advance learning in New York.

King's College

New York's intellectual champions were organizers who sought to reform society in one way or another. They established not only libraries, debating clubs, and literary societies but also other voluntary organizations that proliferated in New York City after 1750, reflecting perhaps a desire for civic unity that transcended economic and religious differences. Even organizations that celebrated ethnic or religious distinctions, like the Saint Andrew's Society, founded by Scots in New York in 1756, performed the civil purpose of aiding the poor of that nationality. The Chamber of Commerce (1768), the Friendly Society of House Carpenters (1767), the Marine Society (1769), and the Society of the Hospital of the City of New York (1771) were all civic-minded organization that appealed to and advanced community interests.

The anxiety of New Yorkers about cultural diversity and popular rudeness invariably led to discussion of educational correctives. "Our schools are in the lowest order," bemoaned William Smith, Jr., in 1757, reflecting the common view; "our instructors want instruction, and through a long shameful neglect of all the arts and sciences, our common speech is extremely corrupt, and the evidences of a bad taste, both as to thought and language, are visible in all our proceedings, publick and private." For more than a decade, Smith and his upper-class friends had argued the need of a provincial college. No one provided a better rationale than William Livingston, certainly one of the most passionate advocates of the proposed institution. In 1749 he wrote:

The want of a liberal Education has long been our Reproach and Misfortune. Our Neighbours have told us in an insulting Tone, that the Art of getting Money, is the highest Improvement we can pretend to: That the wisest Man among us, without a Fortune, is neglected and despised; and the greatest Blockhead with one, caress'd and honour'd: That, for this Reason, a poor Man of the most shining accomplishments, can never emerge out of his Obscurity; while every wealthy Dunce is loaded with Honours.

In a newspaper essay published in 1751, *Aesculapius* looked to the proposed college to secure New York against such "Pests of Society" as "bad workmen in the Arts and Trades; poor Fools in the Pulpit; Mountebanks and Quacks in Physics, and Pettifoggers in our Court."

Some New Yorkers advocated the traditional college curriculum, the trivium and quadrivium, based on the classics and taught in Latin and Greek; others insisted upon a more utilitarian program of study, one emphasizing contemporary sciences, modern languages, and history. As it turned out, Dr. Samuel Johnson, the Anglican cleric who became the first president of King's College, as the proposed institution became known, tried both to keep the Latin and Greek emphasis and yet to bring in "the Arts of *Numbering*, and *Measuring*, of *Surveying* and *Navigation*, of *Geography* and *History*, of *Husbandry*, *Commerce*" and many other utilitarian subjects.

Trinity Church offered land for the college and financial assistance for its prospective president, Samuel Johnson. In return, New York Anglicans expected the College of New York to reflect their faith. William Livingston, William Smith, Jr., and John Morin Scott strongly objected. In November 1752, this triumvirate established the *Independent Reflector*, New York's first magazine, with Livingston doing most of the writing. This eloquent and witty little periodical drew its inspiration from both the literary magazines of Addison and Steele and the polemical *Independent Whig*, the crusading political journal of radical Whig ideologues John Trenchard and Thomas Gordon.

"The true Use of Education," wrote Livingston in early 1753, "is to qualify Men for the different Employments of Life, to which it may please God to call them." The graduates of the College of New York, Livingston argued, would—and should—eventually come to occupy every office of importance in the province. "They will appear on the Bench, at the Bar, in the Pulpit, and in the Senate, and unavoidably affect our civil and religious Principles." In short, the college was expected to transform New York society into its own refined image.

Given New York's religious pluralism, the triumvirate insisted that the college should not favor one Christian confession over another. "Let not the Seat of Literature, the Abode of the Muses, and the Nurse of Science," Livingston warned, "be transform'd into a Cloister of Bigots, an Habitation of Superstition, a Nursery of ghostly Tyranny, a School of rabbinical Jargon." Anglicans responded in kind, labeling Livingston, Smith, and Scott the "Presbyterian Triumvirate." Samuel Johnson and other Anglican apologists portrayed Livingston and his friends as either godless freethinkers or unprincipled Presbyterians. The verbal battle was harsh. Calling for a nondenominational Christian college, Livingston wrote a nonsectarian "Protestant Prayer" which he proposed as representative of the kind of religious doctrine he thought best for the proposed institution. Enraged Anglicans pointed out that the prayer reflected more the influence of the Enlightenment than traditional Christianity.

The triumvirate distributed their views widely in broadsides and pamphlets published in Dutch, German, and French, as well as English. They even published a few issues of yet another journal, the *Occasional Reverberator*, and ran a year-long series known as the "Watch-Tower" in the *New-York Mercury* in 1754–55. Petitions against "Trinity Church College" were circulated among New York's non-Anglican religious groups, British and non-British. The result was that the provincial assembly, reflecting the fears of New York's cultural minorities, refused to charter the college or release the college lottery funds previously raised by the assembly. Lieutenant Governor James DeLancey, however, decided to break the impasse. In October 1754 he issued a charter, incorporating King's College. It called for the president and a majority of the trustees always to be Anglican and for the Book of Common Prayer to be used in daily chapel services. Dissenting students, however, were allowed to attend non-Anglican Sunday services.

In the end, the college did get half of the £3,443 of lottery money. The other half went to the city of New York to erect a new jail and to refurbish the house of detention where quarantined sailors were isolated from the public. William Smith, Sr., quipped that the compromise divided the money "between the two pest houses." Between 1758 and 1776 the college awarded 167 degrees, including a good many that were honorary. Of the latter, fifty-nine went to ordained or prospective Anglican clerics, thus reinforcing the dissenter charge that the college was an instrument of the Church of England. Johnson was replaced in 1763 by Myles Cooper, a more uncompromising Anglican priest. A vigorous fund-raising campaign, at home and abroad, brought in some £14,000 sterling and gave the college's friends hope that it was on the way to a flourishing future. But as Cooper conceded in 1779, dissenters still held the college in contempt as a "bigoted" institution and preferred to send their sons to Yale or the College of New Jersey. As the controversy over King's College made clear, fear of cultural aggression remained an issue of considerable political potency.

Chapter 11

Provincial and Imperial Politics

NINETY YEARS AGO CARL BECKER MADE THE CLASSIC argument that the American Revolution in New York was a struggle not only over home rule but over who should rule at home. According to Becker, the rich and well born, who had hitherto monopolized government and politics and kept the franchise very restricted in New York, as they confronted the formidable challenge of parliamentary taxation, deliberately sought the support and involvement of the common sort. Between 1760 and 1776, New York aristocrats unwittingly democratized politics and undermined their own political hegemony in the newborn state.

Particularly since World War II, the Becker thesis has undergone considerable revision. Becker's assumption that the New York economic elite dominated politics has stood the test of recent scholarship. No amount of revision can remove the manor lords from the Hudson Valley or their wealthy relatives who dominated commerce and the law from New York City and Albany. Historians have found, however, that there was significantly more movement in and out of the upper classes than Becker apparently thought. Moreover, recent scholarship has undermined, if not completely discredited, Becker's contentions that before the revolutionary era few adult white males could vote, that politics whirled around personalities and self-seeking factions rather than popular issues or principles, and that in the aristocratic world of provincial politics little accountability existed between politicians and the relatively few people who could vote.

The primary difference between Becker and his recent critics is that Becker dramatized the democratizing impact of the American Revolution. In fact, rather than looking back to the Middle Ages of powerless peasants and ruthless nobles, as Becker suggested, politics in provincial New York was, in many ways, remarkably modern even before the Revolution. According to Milton M. Klein, "The extraordinary diversity of the colony's citizenry compelled its political leadership to build coalitions, court other interest groups, balance tickets, awaken political consciousness, and enlist the support of large numbers of voters."

Here was a society that manifested many of the signs of an emerging liberalism—individualism, acquisitiveness, commercialism, cultural diversity, religious accommodation (if not tolerance), and voluntarism. Political participation in early New York was wonderfully integrative and provided for a remarkably successful (given the level of diversity) means of conflict resolution. "Representatives of diverse cultural groups," claims historian Alan Tully, with regard to both eighteenth-century New York and Pennsylvania, "found that they could retain their distinctiveness and still interact as members of one provincial society finding accommodations, and on what many might perceive as rational, pragmatic grounds, around belief in the importance of such notions as individual property rights." Native Americans, African Americans, and even white women found themselves marginalized—or worse—but white adult males participated in an increasingly inclusive, responsive political system, which was not always fair or just but generally strengthened their rights and freedoms.

As the eighteenth century wore on, the politics of diversity in New York developed certain regular features. First in importance was the rise of the assembly, the popularly elected branch of provincial government. The lower house—as the assembly was called—regulated county government and continuously sapped authority from the governor and council in the name of popular rights and the public welfare. A second feature of New York politics was its fairly inclusive suffrage with regard to adult white males, of whom between 50 percent and 80 percent met the property qualifications to vote in local and provincial elections; in some communities, the number may have approached 100 percent. After 1750 elections regularly turned out over 50 percent of the eligible voters, and the landed magnates, merchants, and lawyers, who generally sought and dominated provincial office, knew they could hardly take the ordinary voter for granted.

A third feature of provincial politics was its contentiousness. Arising naturally out of the struggle of so many competing cultural and economic interests, political strife became commonplace and was increasingly perceived as necessary to achieve that balance between liberty and authority so essential to good government. The concept of a loyal opposition, which Georgian England had so much trouble acknowledging as legitimate, found acceptance in both theory and practice in eighteenth-century New York. Fourth, as literacy increased so did popular interest and participation in political affairs. The more divisive the issue, the more likely the battling elites would make special appeals to "the people." Popular participation in provincial politics—and in a host of local government positions ranging from fence viewer to constable and justice of the peace—made the concepts of representative government and popular rights all the more fundamental to the thinking of ordinary New Yorkers.

Fifth, besides the local and the provincial, there was a third dimension to politics in colonial New York: the imperial. Between 1689 and 1763, Britain and France engaged in four wars that significantly involved the North American colonies. New York played a central role in all these conflicts, Albany and New York City being especially prominent. The colony itself occupied a strategic position in the rivalry between France and Britain. In each war, the British planned to invade Canada, and New York was the logical route. Conversely, the French in Canada sought to conquer New York so as to secure an ice-free port at New York City, to gain influence over the Iroquois, who were traditionally allied to the British, and to secure control of the fur trade, which Montrealers shared with the inhabitants of Albany. Albany was the principal staging area of any expedition against Canada, with troops being assembled, quartered and supplied there. New York City, as we have seen, became pivotal in the sea war against France. In short, imperial policy, especially the colonial wars themselves, not only shaped economic developments in the province but also impacted provincial politics in ways great and small.

The Rise of the Assembly

The early years of the New York assembly, established on a permanent basis in 1691, were not particularly auspicious. Leisler's Rebellion, and the trial and execution of Leisler and Milburne which followed, poisoned politics for the next twenty years, as the vengeful treason trial of the anti-Leislerian Nicholas Bayard in 1701 so plainly demonstrated. Governors Fletcher, Bellomont, and Cornbury, however, all did their part to convince feuding New Yorkers that they had much more to fear from the royal governor than they did from each other. The peculations attributed to the Fletcher regime, the income-threatening reforms of Bellomont, and the alleged excesses of Cornbury led the assembly to assert its authority in the name of popular rights and authority. Cornbury disputed the assembly's pretensions, insisting that the lower legislative chamber had no rights, save "as the Queen is pleased to allow you." More than once, the irate governor warned the assembly "you can in no wise meddle with the money." But concern for "the money" always animated New York politicians.

The assembly was grappling with a fundamental, and obvious, problem of provincial government. "If a governor were not a man of honour and probity," Robert Livingston observed, "he could oppress the people when he pleased. He had but to strike in with one party, and they assisted him to destroy the other."

If the problem was obvious, so was its solution. New York's factions, the Leislerians and anti-Leislerians, should stop trying to punish each other, join together through the assembly, and use the assembly's power to limit the Crown prerogative. That was the lesson that Fletcher, Bellomont, and particularly Cornbury taught New York's elite. Internecine struggles continued, of course, but general agreement was reached on basic principles: keeping taxes low, salaries of royal officials relatively modest, and the Crown from threatening land and liberty.

Upon the arrival of Governor Hunter in 1710, the assembly insisted on a yearly revenue bill; Hunter, following his instructions, wanted the revenue settled for at least five years. After four years of deadlock, he complained to Whitehall that "ye Assembly . . . claim . . . all ye privileges of a House of Commons and stretch . . . themselves beyond what they were ever imagined to be . . . [in Britain]. . . . They will be a Parliament." Hunter's legislative manager, Lewis Morris, warned that the assembly, in reaction to Cornbury, had gone too far in eroding the Crown's authority. Resorting to satire, the aristocratic Morris wrote, "The Clods [assemblymen] like a Vicious horse that had throwne his rider and run away with the reins on his neck Seem'd to despise all manner of restraint and was for taking into their hands the Exercise of all the powers of the Steward [governor] and Lord [monarch] of the mannour [New York] too."

Yet the "clods" won out, because the assembly had the power of the purse and was intent upon using it. In 1714, Hunter struck a deal with the New York assembly that secured his reputation as perhaps the best governor the province ever had. He secured agreement to a five-year revenue bill and, in return, approved a naturalization bill conferring citizenship upon foreign-born New Yorkers, a vital measure because the Navigation Acts forbade noncitizens from trading in the colonies. During Hunter's regime (1710–19), the assembly-appointed provincial treasurer emerged as more important than the Crown-appointed receiver general over the allocation of provincial funds.

In the lower house, Morris marshaled support for Hunter, assisted by the able Robert Livingston, whose political ascension Hunter himself advanced by approving an assembly seat for Livingston Manor in 1716. From 1718 to 1725, Livingston served as speaker of the assembly. He and the redoubtable Morris led a majority coalition in the assembly drawing support from Hudson River landlords and farmers and New York City artisans. Morris was the governor's primary adviser and received the chief justiceship of the province as his reward in 1715; he also remained in the assembly.

William Burnet, Hunter's friend and successor as governor (1720–28), was drawn into an ambitious program of westward expansion. Speaker Robert Livingston, who also served as Indian commissioner and secretary of Indian Affairs at Albany, had long advocated challenging the French in the west. He and Morris, joined by Cadwallader Colden, pressed for a ban on the Albany-Montreal trade. As a result, much of the mercantile community fought back against the "Landed party," as they labeled Burnet and his supporters, challenging the Morris-Livingston coalition (which Burnet protected by not calling general elections) in special by-elections called upon the death or resignation of assembly members. In 1722, Adolphe Philipse won election from Westchester County, Morris's home base, campaigning against import duties and in favor of the Montreal trade. In 1724, denouncing Burnet's trade policy, Myndert Schuyler won an assembly seat from Albany in another by-election.

Popular opinion was turning against the Morris-Livingston coalition because of its obvious reluctance to hold general assembly elections, its cozy relationship with Governor Burnet, and its controversial trade policy. By-election losses continued to weaken the Landed party. By 1725, the year Stephen DeLancey was reelected to the assembly from New York City, the balance of power had shifted enough for Adolphe Philipse to be elected speaker, following the retirement of the ill Robert Livingston. In a clumsy effort to thwart his rivals, Governor Burnet challenged Stephen DeLancey's election, claiming the wealthy Huguenot merchant was not a citizen, despite the naturalization law of 1714. The assembly, asserting its right to judge its own members, unanimously accepted DeLancey. Later, in 1726, Burnet agreed to call a general election for the assembly, the first since 1716. Adolphe Philipse, running from New York City and winning, was again elected speaker. Morris remained in the assembly, representing the Borough of Westchester, but the Landed party was in decline, hastened perhaps by the transfer of Governor Burnet to Massachusetts in late 1728.

Provincial merchants did not neglect the third dimension of New York politics, the imperial. They complained to British officials and to their business associates in London about Burnet and his trade policy. The Board of Trade decision in 1729 approving the Albany-Montreal trade was due at least in part to such lobbying.

The Philipse-DeLancey coalition, or Merchant party, as it was sometimes called, enhanced its influence under the administration of General John Montgomerie (1728–31). Although the coalition moderated trade duties, the assembly did not raise land taxes or pursue the Board of Trade's recommendation that royal quitrents be more rigorously collected. In fact, many of the merchant princes, including Philipse, DeLancey, and Peter Schuyler, were major land speculators. Dominating the assembly for most of the next twenty years, the Philipse-DeLancey coalition protected mercantile interests while generally satisfying other elements of the community on both the provincial and the local level. By 1732, because Philipse-DeLancey leaders enjoyed good relations with Governors Montgomerie and Cosby, the assemblymen identified with them became known as the Court party and their Morrisite opponents as the Country party.

The Zenger Affair and Its Aftermath

Chief Justice Lewis Morris was down but not out. Adding insult to injury, Governor Montgomerie dismissed Lewis Morris, Jr., from the council after the son burst into a blustering tirade characteristic of his volatile father. As early as 1728 the Morrisites were enlivening campaign rhetoric with a series of newspaper articles titled "Letters to Ape," accusing Adolphe Philipse and his lieutenants of sacrificing the liberties and welfare of the people. Morris and his friends drew heavily from the opposition political theory and rhetoric of the so-called Country party in England that denounced corruption and injustice under the Whig ministry of Sir Robert Walpole. In 1732, with the arrival of the avaricious William Cosby as governor, the stage was set for a confrontation between a provincial executive and his aggressive critics.

The Morris-Cosby affair is more than a thrice-told tale. Personality shaped the controversy, but so did principle. Central to the story is the famous John Peter Zenger trial and its implications for freedom of the press. William Cosby, a none-too-successful admiral in the British navy, owed his appointment as governor of New York to relatives in the Walpole ministry. Thomas Pelham, Duke of Newcastle, was his first cousin, and the earl of Halifax was his brother-in-law. Cosby came to New York because of its lucrative governorship, and he intended to make the most of it. His "influence at home," he thought, was powerful enough to overcome any provincial opposition to his self-serving ambitions. More than any governor since Cornbury, Cosby asserted gubernatorial authority in ways that eroded the Philipse-DeLancey coalition's assembly majority by the late 1730s.

Shortly after arriving, Cosby demanded that Rip Van Dam, president of the council, pay him half the salary Van Dam had earned as acting governor during the eleven months between Cosby's appointment and his arrival in New York. Supported by a majority of the council, Van Dam, a respected merchant, refused. Rather than risk a jury trial, Cosby sought an equity court settlement. But since the governor presided over the court of chancery, the only equity court in existence in the province at the time, Cosby felt compelled to create another, a court of exchequer, presided over by the three Supreme Court justices. Adding more drama to the case was the fact that Morris, chief justice of New York, was also the president of the New Jersey Council and had served as acting governor of that province between Montgomerie's death and Cosby's arrival, just as Van Dam had in New York. Should New York's court of exchequer find for Cosby, would not the grasping governor come after Morris next?

This depiction of the New Dutch Church, built at Liberty and Nassau Streets in 1731, was dedicated to Rip Van Dam, president of New York's Royal Council. Museum of the City of New York.

As the Cosby-Van Dam hearing began, Morris raised doubts about the legality of a gubernatorial-established equity court. Van Dam's counsels, James Alexander and William Smith, Sr., having been forewarned by Morris, argued that only the legislature could sanction equity courts. Morris thereupon pronounced the proceedings against Van Dam out of order. When James DeLancey, the Cambridge-educated son of wealthy Stephen DeLancey, and Frederick Philipse, the nephew of Adolphe Philipse, the second and third justices of the Supreme Court, refused to go along with him, Morris upbraided his junior colleagues and stormed out of the courtroom.

Morris had thrown down the gauntlet, and Cosby responded by removing him from the chief justiceship. He bestowed that honor upon the young James DeLancey, the first New Yorker to be trained at the Inns of Court. Cosby also made it clear he intended to punish land speculators associated with the emerging Morris-Alexander assembly coalition who were vying for the Oblong or Equivalent Patent stretching along the border with Connecticut. As the dispute headed toward chancery, where the governor made no secret of how he intended to rule, Adolphe Philipse intervened. The speaker made it clear that the legislative majority would not tolerate a "Court of Chancery . . . under the Exercise of a Governor, without consent in General Assembly" because it would be "contrary to Law . . . and of dangerous Consequences to the Liberties and Properties of the people."

In October 1733, Morris, a vain and arrogant man who was aristocratic to the core, presented himself as the people's champion in the assembly by-election in Westchester County and won handily, even though the county sheriff disqualified some thirty Quaker votes that would have gone to Morris. Inside the assembly the Morrises (his son had been elected from the Borough of Westchester in 1732) began pulling together a minority coalition based on dissatisfaction with Cosby and the Philipse-DeLancey leadership in the lower house. By November the Morris-Alexander-Smith junto had emerged, even establishing a rival newspaper to Bradford's *New-York Gazette*. Called the *New-York Weekly Journal*, it was printed in the shop of young John Peter Zenger, a Palatine immigrant who had learned his trade as an apprentice of William Bradford, the government printer. In their first issue (November 5, 1733), Alexander and Smith, its primary editors, announced they would apply "the Lash of Satyr . . . to wicked Ministers."

The *Weekly Journal* was filled with biting commentary, virulent in its denunciation of Cosby, Ape (as Adolphe Philipse was labeled), and others associated with the impolitic governor. The *Weekly Journal* also reprinted essays from England, ranging from the whimsical and didactic pieces of Joseph Addison and Richard Steele to the dark and brooding political jeremiads of John Trenchard, Thomas Gordon, and other so-called Commonwealth Men, who saw in the rise of the Walpole ministry the utter decay of English freedom. In true

Country party fashion, the Morrisites excoriated Cosby for cronyism, for abusing his patronage authority, for establishing illegal courts, and for extorting money from people seeking land patents and other government services.

Angered beyond words by the acerbic *Weekly Journal*, Cosby sought assembly action to censor the newspaper; but he was rebuffed. Nor would the New York grand jury indict the printer, despite vigorous complaints that his paper was libeling the government. Finally, flying in the face of popular opinion, Cosby acted with only the endorsement of the council. The governor had copies of the *Weekly Journal* publicly burned; Zenger was arrested in 1734 and put on trial the next year for seditious libel.

Zenger's lawyers, the Morrisite leaders James Alexander and William Smith, challenged the legality of DeLancey's commission as chief justice and made clear their intent to turn the proceedings into an extended indictment of Governor Cosby. In retaliation, DeLancey suspended the two senior lawyers from further practice before the Supreme Court. However, by August 4, 1735, the day the trial began, Smith and Alexander had secured the services of Andrew Hamilton of Philadelphia, generally regarded as the very best lawyer in British America.

The Zenger trial became a public relations disaster for Cosby and the Philipse-DeLancey assembly coalition. Cosby's determination to shut down the opposition press only lent credence to charges of "tyranny, arrogance, and corruption" leveled against the money-hungry governor. The unreasonable bond of £400 set by Chief Justice DeLancey aroused considerable public sympathy for the unfortunate Zenger. Yet Hamilton had his work cut out for him. Under the law of seditious libel, the jury was to consider only whether the defendant published the offensive words, which he never denied, not to judge whether the words actually constituted a libel. That important determination was supposedly made through the indictment process, either under the direction of a grand jury or by the attorney general filing an information with the concurrence of an obliging judge. The latter method of indictment had been used against Zenger.

Contrary to the law and established practice, Hamilton argued, truth should be a justifiable defense in a libel trial. Despite being ruled out of order, the seasoned lawyer returned to that argument at every opportunity throughout the day-long proceedings. "I know . . . [the jury has] the right beyond all dispute to determine both the law and the fact," he insisted, "and whence they do not doubt of the law, they ought to do so," thus leaving it to the judgment of the jurors themselves whether the words were libelous or not.

Insisting that the English law of libel was not applicable in the colonies, Hamilton drew a sharp distinction between the king's government in England and government in the name of the king in America. In the latter, he argued, free speech was more fundamental to good government and just as important in preserving political freedom as the principle of popular representation. After briefly deliberating, and despite Chief Justice DeLancey's instructions to the jury to consider only whether Zenger published the offensive newspaper, the foreman announced "Not Guilty," to the delight of Hamilton and the boisterous crowd in the courtroom.

As Cosby became increasingly disliked, the Philipse-DeLancey coalition retained its hold in the assembly only because the governor refused to call general elections. The Morrisites, captivated by their own rhetoric, pushed the limits of traditional political thought and practice. They proposed an agenda of reform that was as radical as it was appealing to the public. It included annual or triennial assembly elections; the sitting of the council separately from the governor; the creation of courts only upon assembly approval; the appointment of judges on good behavior; new rules for gubernatorial appointment of councillors and sheriffs and coroners (even suggesting the popular election of the latter two county officials); the better regulation of land patents to prevent "exorbitant fees"; and the regular apportionment of assembly seats according to population.

Scholars have rightly questioned the lasting impact of the Zenger decision, because it did not markedly change the law of seditious libel. Yet it surely focused attention upon both freedom of speech and the legitimacy of political opposition. In New York the law of seditious libel would be invoked again but by the assembly against impertinent critics, never again by regular common law courts. Moreover, the larger dispute between Morris and Cosby energized New York politics as never before. While Lewis Morris appealed his removal as chief justice to the Board of Trade, his friends in New York circulated petitions throughout the counties, acquiring hundreds of signatures condemning Cosby as the lord of misrule. New Yorkers were receiving a lesson in practical politics, whether they wanted it or not.

However justified in his own mind, Morris's accusations against a sitting colonial governor were not welcomed by imperial officials. Convinced of his own importance, Morris suffered immensely from being ignored. "Would to God we were with you and free from Cosbys Rule in any Station of life not Slaves," he moaned in letters from London. "Oh happy Americans too happy to know your blest state." Although the Privy Council did agree that Cosby had given insufficient reasons for dismissing Morris as chief justice, the lords did not restore the belligerent manor lord to that important office; nor would they remove his nemesis as governor.

Cosby, however, was in failing health and died in March 1736. His demise immediately provoked another dispute, this time between George Clarke, longtime councillor and provincial secretary, and Rip Van Dam, the senior councillor. Before his death, Cosby had suspended Van Dam from the council so that Clarke would have senior status. Van Dam protested the suspension and claimed his right to serve as acting governor, having the support of the Morris-

Alexander assembly faction. Returning from England, Morris was hailed by Van Dam and others as the leader of the people's interests, the spokesman for colonial political reform, who would right this wrong. Political emotions were running so high that Cadwallader Colden believed the province was on the verge of civil war. However, the arrival of royal instructions in the fall naming Clarke lieutenant governor settled the matter, and Clarke defused Morrisite opposition by calling for assembly elections for the spring of 1737.

Vindication for Lewis Morris came at the polls, the first general assembly election since 1728. Both Adolphe Philipse and Stephen DeLancey lost in New York City; Lewis Morris, Sr., and Jr., won in Westchester County, and Lewis Morris, Jr., became speaker of the lower house. The intensity of the contest is revealed in the resort to antisemitic demagoguery by William Smith, Sr. Assured that the Jewish vote, though quite small, was going to DeLancey and Philipse, Smith insisted that Jews did not have the franchise and had their ballots thrown out; for more than a decade afterward, Jews were effectively disfranchised.

Both sides were, however, quite willing to compromise. Clarke, who had served as provincial secretary and councillor for thirty years, offered concessions to the Morrisites. He approved a triennial election bill, though it was disallowed in London in 1738. In 1739, as the War of Jenkins' Ear began, Clarke also felt compelled to accept a one-year revenue bill, the first New York governor to concede that to the assembly. Moreover, the younger Lewis Morris and Clarke developed a good working relationship, while the elder Lewis Morris left New York in 1738 to assume the governorship of New Jersey, where this spokesman for popular rights became a stalwart defender of Crown prerogative.

Once allied with Governor Clarke, the Morris-Alexander coalition also made the transition from "country" to "court" party without any apology or explanation, much to the chagrin of former supporters in New York City. The death of Garret Van Horne, elected the previous May, forced a by-election in New York County in September 1737. The winner was none other than Adolphe Philipse, defeated just three months before, whose victory margin was only fifteen votes in what Cadwallader Colden described as "such a struggle I never saw," as the sick, lame, and blind were taken to the polls.

Philipse's political resilience may well have quickened the extreme opportunistic impulses of the Morrises, Junior and Senior, and their political associates. While his father assumed the royal governorship of New Jersey, Lewis, Jr., the speaker, fully exploited his relationship with Governor Clarke, replacing virtually all the judicial and militia officers of Westchester County with his own friends and clients. There was considerable truth in Philip Livingston's comment, made after the 1737 elections, that New Yorkers "Change Sides as Serves our Interest best not the Countries." Yet important political principles were also involved; the people had spoken out against one political coalition identified with the governor and in favor of another identified with popular rights, and George Clarke had made further gubernatorial concessions to the assembly.

The Ascendance of James DeLancey

In 1743, Governor Clarke and the assembly were working so well together that the Board of Trade approved a bill calling for assembly elections every seven years. The upper-class leadership had good reason to pull together rather than apart during these troubling years. In 1741, New York City was apparently threatened from below, first by an abortive bakers' strike over the rising price of wheat and the fixed price of bread. Far more menacing, of course, was the so-called Slave Conspiracy of 1741, with all its public hysteria, vicious racial and religious prejudices, and judicially sanctioned torture and murder. In 1739, Adolphe Philipse succeeded Lewis Morris, Jr., as speaker, but the détente between the lower house and Governor Clarke continued smoothly enough.

Meanwhile, the old political coalitions—Philipse-DeLancey versus Morris-Alexander—lost much of their coherence. Certain regional political figures, however, continued to solidify their influence, thanks to their effectiveness in getting the provincial legislature to respond to local needs and the judicious use of local patronage. Lewis Morris, Jr., for the time being, was dominant in Westchester, though the Philipses and DeLanceys were always watching and waiting in the wings. In Dutchess County, Henry Beekman dominated local politics. He had married into the powerful Livingston clan and was widely respected as one of the largest landowners in the province. His influence even spilled over into Ulster County as well. In Queens County, the Jones and Hicks families often supplied the assemblymen; the Nicoll family still held sway in Suffolk County.

Young James DeLancey, the chief justice, was emerging as the quintessential Anglo-American political leader. The eldest son of the fabulously wealthy Stephen DeLancey, James was related to much of the New York upper class through his mother, Anne Van Cortlandt. Born in 1703, he was sent to England in 1721, where he entered Corpus Christi College, Cambridge, and later studied law at Lincoln's Inn in London. Returning to New York in 1725, he was shortly admitted to the bar and began practicing law. In 1728, he married Anne Heathcote, the only child of the late Caleb Heathcote, master of Scarsdale Manor and enterprising merchant. The next year, when James was twenty-nine, Governor Montgomerie, a good friend of his father, appointed him to the provincial council. Two years later, Montgomerie obligingly made him the second justice of the Supreme Court. James was only thirty-one years old.

Named chief justice by the controversial Governor Cosby, DeLancey had his political mettle tempered by the struggles of the Cosby years. The Zenger case taught DeLancey lessons in both legal procedure and popular politics that he never forgot. While Clarke was governor, DeLancey set about mending political fences. Affable, generous, witty in conversation, and known for his quick intelligence, the urbane DeLancey made friends easily and was a genius at political coalition building. He inherited many of his father's political friends in the assembly and elsewhere, and his rowdy younger brother Oliver excelled at rallying supporters, whether in New York City or in the river towns along the Hudson. Another brother, Peter, married one of Cadwallader Colden's daughters and became an influential landlord and political ally in Westchester County.

As chief justice, DeLancey was in a superb position to build political support. His influence within the expanding legal community was obvious. Moreover, judges of the Supreme Court rode the circuit annually through the counties, one judge sitting with two or more county justices of the peace in quarterly sessions. Perambulating about the province, accompanied by a bevy of lawyers and local justices, DeLancey cultivated friends and clients in every town and county in the province. As even his harshest critics admitted, no manor lord, farmer, tradesman, or day laborer could resist the gregarious chief justice's charms. Meeting four times a year in New York City, the Supreme Court enjoyed almost unlimited power to hear cases on appeal, either commercial or land cases, making every Supreme Court justice, and in particular the chief justice, a man whose good opinion other men sought to claim. DeLancey also sat on the provincial council, where all requests for land patents were considered, and it was under his leadership in the 1740s that the council emerged as less an advisory body to the governor and more a legislative body in its own right.

Without strong support in England, however, DeLancey would never have reached the level of political hegemony he later achieved in New York. To begin with, his wife's relatives, the Heathcotes, were well established politically and financially in the mother country. One of his wife's cousins, Sir John Heathcote, sat in Parliament and served as Prime Minister Robert Walpole's political manager for Rutland County. As fate would have it, DeLancey's tutor at Cambridge, Thomas Herring, rose from obscurity to become the archbishop of Canterbury in 1747. James's father Stephen had long done business with the London firm of Baker and Company, whose principals, William and Samuel Baker, were frequently consulted by the Board of Trade about American affairs. The Bakers would prove valuable political lobbyists for DeLancey.

So would his brother-in-law, Commodore Peter Warren, who captained a ship patrolling North America and the West Indies. In 1745, during the War of the Austrian Succession, Warren commanded the British squadron that secured the surrender of Fortress Louisbourg on Cape Breton Island, New France, taking prizes that made him immensely wealthy and touted as a national hero. At the battle off Cape Finisterre in 1747, he won further acclaim for his seamanship.

As his reward, Warren was made Knight of the Bath, promoted from rear admiral to vice admiral, and made a member of Parliament from Westminster. Rich and famous, Warren was of inestimable assistance to James DeLancey's leadership of New York politics.

By the time George Clinton replaced George Clarke as governor in 1743, DeLancey was eclipsing the aging Adolphe Philipse, still speaker of the assembly, as a political leader. Clinton made the chief justice his primary adviser, recognizing the latter's extensive influence over both the council and the assembly. On DeLancey's advice, Clinton conceded to the lower house not only an annual provincial revenue bill but also considerable oversight of specific appropriations. In 1744 the governor rewarded DeLancey by changing his commission as chief justice from tenure "at pleasure" to "good behavior," which meant that the governor could not dismiss the chief justice without good cause, as Cosby had done to Lewis Morris in 1733. The cordial relationship between the chief justice and the governor began, however, to break down in 1746, apparently because of differences over the prosecution of King George's War.

After the assembly elections of 1745, DeLancey completed his political alliance with David Jones, chosen speaker to succeed Adolphe Philipse, whose defeat was due in part to the machinations of the chief justice. Succeeding to what remained of the old Philipse-DeLancey coalition, DeLancey had key support in New York City, Westchester, Albany, Schenectady, and Rensselaerswyck. Jones, an Anglican lawyer from Queens, brought support from Suffolk, Kings, Ulster, and Orange Counties. Together with Jones, DeLancey, clearly the senior partner in their joint leadership, forged a coalition that had little interest in the War of Jenkins' Ear, begun against Spain in 1739, or its expansion into King George's War as France and its Indian allies joined the fray in 1744.

DeLancey's attitude toward King George's War angered Clinton, who apparently harbored visions of leading a colonial expedition against the French. The New York governor watched jealously as New Englanders took the offensive and played the leading role in the conquest of Fortress Louisbourg. Although the war was concentrated along the New England frontier, French and Indian raiding parties made forays into New York, the worst being against Saratoga in 1745, which practically wiped out the village. Under Clinton's prodding, the Assembly voted funds for raising New York militia and ordered them to Albany to guard against an attack from the French. Clinton never got to lead a military force into New France, but his appointment of William Johnson as Indian agent played a role in the Iroquois launching some raids against French settlements in Canada.

Blaming DeLancey for not mobilizing the Assembly fully in support of war, Clinton found himself another chief adviser, Cadwallader Colden, councillor, surveyor general, and the most disliked public official in the province. Over the years Colden had not endeared himself to the New York elite with his criticism of provincial land policy and his defense of the royal prerogative. Clinton thought his own considerable "interest" in England would be enough to show DeLancey who was boss. The youngest son of the seventh earl of Lincoln, Clinton had married the sister of Thomas Pelham-Holles, Duke of Newcastle, and his brother Henry Pelham. The Pelhams were mainstays in the Walpole ministry; the duke of Newcastle, as southern secretary from 1724 to 1748, had oversight of the American colonies. Convinced he had bountiful support in Whitehall, Clinton, though angered by DeLancey's defection, assured Councillor Colden that "I don't doubt but carry my point [in London] even to turn out the C. J. tho' he fancy himself so great a Man."

Once King George's War ended in 1748, Clinton went on the offensive against DeLancey and refused to accept an annual salary bill from the assembly. He removed DeLancey's associates from the council and replaced them with opponents of the chief justice like James Alexander, William Smith, and William Johnson; Clinton also placed Johnson completely in charge of Indian affairs, bypassing the Albany commissioners. Using his appointive powers, the governor began building local political support, county by county. Alexander and Smith in New York City, William Johnson in Albany County, Colden in Ulster County, and Robert Hunter Morris in Westchester County, acting as Clinton's agents, made changes in sheriffs, justices of the peace, and other local officials to make sure that the DeLancey-Jones forces could not take their election for granted.

Although faced with a considerable challenge, the DeLancey-Jones coalition—assisted by Frederick Philipse, the wealthy merchant, Supreme Court judge, and Dutchess County landlord; Oliver and Peter DeLancey, the chief justice's brothers; Henry Beekman in Dutchess County; and Philip Livingston in Albany County—emerged from assembly elections in 1748 stronger than ever. What Clinton could not overcome in the minds of ordinary New Yorkers was the obvious threat he posed as governor to the dominance of the assembly in the provincial government.

The combating elites worked hard at coalition building, cultivating county politicians and making calculated appeals to the voters. All this electioneering educated New Yorkers to both political practice and ideas. Although Clinton was unsuccessful in his bid to overthrow DeLancey and Jones from their dominance in the assembly, his efforts made it clear yet again that an aggressive royal governor, however much the office had been limited heretofore, might mobilize one part of the ruling elite against the others, might revive the volatile issue of land titles, and might threaten the rights and freedom of the people generally by diminishing the authority and integrity of the representative assembly. Given the impasse, Clinton agreed in 1751, again, to accept a one-year salary in return for the assembly's pledge to pay the salary arrears of other officials and to begin to pay down the war debt.

Then, heartened by what he believed was Privy Council support, Clinton broke the truce with DeLancey and Jones, dissolved the assembly in November 1751, and called for new elections. Once again, just three years after the last, New Yorkers experienced a vigorous political campaign, made all the more aggressive because Clinton, expecting to return to England at any time, knew it would be his last chance to defeat the DeLancey-Jones coalition. Clinton took some comfort from the election results; Philip Schuyler and Hans Hansen, two of his critics, lost in Albany, thanks to William Johnson's electioneering. But otherwise the Clinton candidates fared badly. In New York City, DeLancey influence was so strong that it was commonly said the swaggering Oliver DeLancey could have nominated his "Four Coach Horses," and they would have won. Despite his own considerable intrusion into local affairs, Clinton simply could not compete with DeLancey and Jones when it came to cultivating county magnates and succeeding in the assembly on the local issues—ranging from the maintenance of roads and the eradication of wolves and blackbirds, to grain inspection and county taxes—so popular with their constituents.

DeLancey Hegemony and the French and Indian War

Following the 1751 elections, James DeLancey was at the penultimate stage of his career. The ultimate came two years later when an embittered George Clinton returned to England, surrendering the lieutenant governor's commission to his archrival. In the end, DeLancey's influence at Whitehall was greater than Clinton's. Although somewhat sympathetic to Clinton's plight, Lord Halifax had decided that the dispirited governor was not the man to revive the royal prerogative in New York. Halifax definitely expected Clinton's successor, Sir Danvers Osborne, to undo the damage that had been done to Crown authority because of the compromises Clinton and his predecessors had made with the assembly. Indeed, detailed instructions accompanied Osborne to New York, and the lofty expectation they imposed on the new governor may well have added to the mental instability he had suffered since the death of his young wife some years before. At any rate, a few days after arriving in early October 1753, Osborne hanged himself.

As lieutenant governor, James DeLancey succeeded the unfortunate Osborne as chief executive, and except for the months when Governor Charles Hardy (1755–57) was actually in the province, he headed the government until his own death in 1760. His cooperation with Governor Hardy further convinced the Board of Trade that DeLancey was restoring the prerogative of the Crown and yet keeping the goodwill of the assembly. In reality, the assembly conceded little, but its trust in DeLancey brought a stability to the provincial government that New York had seldom known. Recognizing the improvement in royal government in New York, Whitehall relented in 1756, allowing New York governors to accept one-year revenue bills. DeLancey also won kudos from landowners as well as the merchant community with whom his family had been so closely identified. In the early 1750s, when New England settlers, some egged on by the Massachusetts assembly, called into question the legitimacy of Livingston, Van Rensselaer, and Beekman land titles, DeLancey fully supported the landlords.

Ever the charmer, DeLancey shored up strained relations with former political foes, including William Johnson, his relative through Admiral Warren and one of Clinton's most stalwart supporters. In 1754, Johnson was at DeLancey's side during the Albany Congress, where neither representatives of the colonies nor the Indians showed little desire to unite and resist French encroachment on western lands. In 1755, as the French and Indian War began in earnest, DeLancey gloried in Johnson's victory at Lake George, which earned the Mohawk Valley landlord a knighthood and £5,000 from King George II. Both Johnson and DeLancey disliked Governor William Shirley of Massachusetts, who had succeeded to command of British forces following General Edward Braddock's defeat and death trying to take Fort Duquesne. Once Shirley fell from favor in 1756, DeLancey threw his political influence fully behind the war effort, raising both taxes and provincial troops in record numbers. His critics during King George's War, expansionists like William Livingston, Archibald Kennedy, and Cadwallader Colden, found themselves acting in concert with the lieutenant governor. DeLancey even cajoled Colden to support legislation allowing the permanent division of land patents, something the old Surveyor General had vigorously opposed before and would oppose again, claiming it legitimatized fraudulent land claims and made impossible the collection of the royal quitrents.

DeLancey's enthusiasm for the French and Indian War, in contrast to his lethargic support of King George's War, is easily explained. Circumstances were much different. This fourth and last colonial war between the French and the British, having begun not in Europe but in America over Ohio Valley lands, posed a major threat to New York and her frontier settlers. Now as opposed to then, DeLancey was the acting governor, not just the leader of a self-interested assembly coalition. Moreover, the Montreal–Albany trade, long a staple component of Delanceyite commercial policy, was less important than it had been a decade earlier. Thanks to the British settlement at Oswego and William Johnson's trading network in the Mohawk Valley, furs were now flowing directly into English hands rather than via Montreal. Uncharitable critics also liked to point out that DeLancey's younger brother, Oliver, and other political associates benefited immensely from lucrative wartime contracts for supplies. Truth to tell, many New Yorkers profited handsomely as their province became the principal theater of the war. Albany served as the primary staging areas as British troops and supplies were assembled for campaigns against New France, and New York City once again emerged as the capital of privateering. Seventy-five sea-raiders sailing from the city between 1754 and 1763 captured almost 400 prizes and enriched captain, crews, and investors with almost £1,500,000 in profit.

If the war brought prosperity for many, it also brought death and destruction for others and the real threat that the French just might defeat the British. Except for the Battle of Lake George, New Yorkers fared badly during the early years of the war. In 1756, Fort Bull fell to the French and opened the way for the Marquis de Montcalm's destruction of Oswego. In 1757, along the eastern frontier, Montcalm's combined French and Indian forces took Fort William Henry (built two years earlier by William Johnson on the south shore of Lake George), after which some 200 of the surrendering English troops were massacred by the Indians. As French and Indians raided the Palatine villages in the Mohawk Valley, most settlers abandoned central New York. In July 1758, although outnumbered five to one, Montcalm successfully defended Fort Carillon (later called Ticonderoga) against ferocious frontal assaults ordered by General James Abercrombie in command of fifteen thousand British soldiers.

Montcalm and the French looked unbeatable after Abercrombie's failure at Fort Carillon. The tide of battle, however, was already turning in favor of the British, thanks largely to the tireless efforts of William Pitt, the man who became prime minister in late 1756 and made clear his determination to drive the French from North America. The resourceful Pitt won over American politicians like James DeLancey by promising to reimburse colonial governments for recruiting, outfitting, and supplying ever larger numbers of colonial troops. Whereas the New York Assembly spent about £72,000 during King George's War, its indebtedness from the French and Indian War amounted to £291,000. Moreover, Pitt changed commanders in America until he found a winning general, Jeffrey Amherst, who took the French fortress of Louisbourg in the summer of 1758. In August, Colonel James Bradstreet took Fort Frontenac on the northeast shore of Lake Ontario and prepared the way for British victories on the Great Lakes. With the fall of Fort Frontenac, the western Indians began to drift away from their alliance with the French. In 1759, Amherst's second in command at Louisbourg, James Wolfe, captured Quebec in the celebrated campaign that took both his life and Montcalm's. The next year, Amherst, moving up the Lake George and Lake Champlain route, took Montreal, largely bringing military operations to an end on the North American continent. Victory was at hand, and Lieutenant Governor James DeLancey's astute handling of governmental affairs had contributed in crucial ways to military success.

Political Alignments in Provincial New York

The DeLancey-Jones coalition, like the Philipse-DeLancey coalition that preceded it, succeeded admirably because it thoroughly identified itself with popular rights and freedoms, embodied in the representative assembly, and because its members, though almost always of the elite, were very responsive to the local needs of their constituents. Their common focus upon limiting the governor's prerogative and preserving and expanding assembly authority has led scholars to call these two political coalitions, which dominated the assembly between 1725 and 1760, the popular Whigs. They were more in alignment with traditional Lockean political theory, conventional wisdom about the British mixed constitution, and grassroots political organizing than their critics generally were.

Their critics—the Morris-Alexander faction that opposed Adolphe Philipse and Stephen DeLancey in the late 1720s and 1730s, and the Livingston-Alexander faction that emerged in the 1750s to oppose James DeLancey and David Jones—have been labeled the provincial Whigs. Less concerned with governing than with criticizing their popular Whig rivals, the provincial Whigs were inclined to utilize the extremist rhetoric of the Radical Whig–Country party opponents of the Walpole ministry in Britain. Like the so-called Country politicians in England, the provincial Whigs accused the assembly leadership of bribery, financial malfeasance, threats to private property, election illegalities, and undermining basic freedoms. Freedom of the press was the most sensational issue that Lewis Morris used to bludgeon Governor Cosby and Philipse-DeLancey representatives in the 1730s, as he and James Alexander broke their hold on the assembly in the 1737 election. But the provincial Whig leaders were so very opportunistic that they lost their ideological edge once they gained the upper hand in the provincial government, principle giving way to self-aggrandizement. Moreover, the provincial Whigs, unlike the popular Whigs, never demonstrated much of the "common touch" when it came to currying popular support and keeping it.

The resurgence of another provincial Whig coalition in the 1750s began with an unlikely issue—that of Anglican preference in the administration and chapel services of the proposed College of New York. The exaggerated warnings of Livingston, Smith, and Scott, the provincial Whig triumvirate—that the college, if given an Anglican disposition, would represent the first steps in the forced conformity of New Yorkers to the Church of England—resonated among many New York dissenters. Both DeLancey and Jones were Anglicans, but they had prevailed politically because they had gained the trust and approval of dissenters, who made up the vast majority of their supporters. Anxious to dispose of the issue, Lieutenant Governor DeLancey issued a charter for King's College, with its Anglican preference, in 1754. By the time of the next general election, held in accordance with the septennial act in 1759, the King's College controversy had faded significantly; it did, however, apparently influence some dissenters in voting against Speaker Jones, who lost his seat from Queens County.

There were other signs that the DeLancey-Jones coalition was weakening. Rival merchants accused the DeLanceyites of securing the most lucrative supply contracts during the French and Indian War. Moreover, the rise of the DeLancey-Jones coalition had signaled the political dominance of New York City in particular and the seaboard communities generally over the upper Hudson Valley, where resentment was building against regulatory agencies on Manhattan that exercised oversight of flour, beef, pork, fish, wood, and leather products produced upriver. Four members of the Livingston family won election to the assembly in 1758, most of whom were known for their antagonism toward the lieutenant governor. Had he lived, the astute James DeLancey might well have reconstituted his popular Whig coalition, but he died of heart failure in 1760. Without him, his popular Whig faction lost discipline, drive, and most of its coherence and identity. Politics in the 1760s would become quite fluid, shaped by British imperial politics quite as much as by provincial issues.

12

The Coming of the Revolution

IN THE DECADE BEFORE THE AMERICAN REVOLUTION, THE basic problem for New Yorkers was that they, like other American colonials, had no direct influence over Parliament, whose policy seemed inimical to American rights and liberties. The French and Indian War exacerbated differences between Great Britain and its American colonies. Many New Yorkers profited immensely from this Great War for Empire. The British army established its North American headquarters in New York City, and Albany served as the primary staging area for British and provincial troops planning the invasion of Canada. Manhattan also emerged as a major center of privateering. But as military operations in North America wound down with the fall of Montreal in 1760, New York merchants suddenly lost lucrative military contracts, and the provincial economy plunged into a lingering postwar depression.

Economic hard times made New Yorkers all the more resentful of changing imperial regulations. Because of its huge war debt and expanded administrative duties with the annexation of New France, Whitehall decided to abandon its relaxed policy toward British North America which historians have named "salutary neglect." First came the Proclamation Line of 1763, which flew in the face of colonial expectations of unimpeded westward expansion. Next came plans for the British to garrison 10,000 regular troops in Canada, Florida, and along the western frontiers, which was followed in turn by the American Revenue (Sugar) Act of 1764 and the Stamp Act of 1765, both of which were designed to raise money in the colonies to defray imperial expenses. Parliament, under the leadership of George Grenville (1763–65), felt compelled to tax the Americans because Britain's £147 million debt threatened the fiscal integrity of the nation. Startled by the dramatic shift in imperial policy, New

Yorkers, like other colonists, protested first through their provincial assembly, and, when assembly petitions seemed to do little good, they increasingly resorted to extralegal committees.

The End of Salutary Neglect

The election of four Livingston family members to the provincial assembly that opened in 1759, together with the defeat of Speaker David Jones, and James DeLancey's death in 1760 signaled that New York politics were in flux once again. The new speaker, William Nicoll of Suffolk County, a well-known DeLanceyite, was unwilling or unable to perpetuate the DeLancey-Jones coalition under his leadership. Partisan affiliations became further blurred as the provincial economy weakened and as tensions mounted with the mother country. In New York the protest against parliamentary supremacy was nurtured by economic depression and growing frustration with royal government, the latter personified by Lieutenant Governor Cadwallader Colden. As the senior councillor, Colden became chief executive upon the death of DeLancey in 1760. Having reached an accommodation with the lieutenant governor in the late 1750s, Colden now made clear his determination to restore the Crown's authority eroded over the years by the New York assembly.

The first battle came over the issue of judicial tenure. Colden was convinced that James DeLancey's formidable political machine rested upon his commission as chief justice during good behavior, instead of at pleasure, the former amounting to life tenure. Colden announced that henceforth judicial tenure would be at the pleasure of the Crown. The assembly disagreed but had to give way when Whitehall issued orders prohibiting colonial governors from granting judicial tenure on good behavior.

Colden disliked lawyers, and during the dispute over judicial tenure his harshest critics were the three Presbyterian lawyers William Livingston, William Smith, Jr., and John Morin Scott, his adversaries from the King's College controversy. Expecting little good from the gentlemen of the bar, Colden warned London that the triumvirate's aim was to "propagate their principles both in Religious and Civil matters and for that end make use of every artifice they can invent to calumniate the administration in every Exercise of the Prerogative." Another confrontation with the lawyers shortly followed. It involved the sanctity of jury trials.

In the summer of 1763, Waddel Cunningham, a merchant, was accused of savagely beating and stabbing Thomas Forsey, who owed Cunningham money, leaving Forsey incapacitated for more than eighty days. In the criminal proceeding, Cunningham was fined £30. In the civil case, heard before the Supreme Court, Forsey was awarded damages of more than £1,500. Public sympathy definitely favored Forsey, but Cunningham asked the Supreme Court to permit an appeal to the governor and council. According to traditional procedures, appeals from common law courts could be made to the governor and council only by writs of error or by a bill of exceptions filed in the case by reason of irregular court proceedings.

Cunningham's appeal was based on the jury's decision and the facts, which the Supreme Court unanimously rejected as a basis for appeal. The attorney general agreed, and so did the governor's council; but Colden argued that his commission as lieutenant governor allowed the appeal. While a chorus of critics accused him of subverting "the ancient and wholesome Laws of the land," Colden acidly remarked that justice had prevailed for centuries in his native Scotland without jury trials. Taking the offensive, Colden further charged the lawyers, judges, and councillors with "Indecency, Want of Respect to the King's Authority, and . . . unwarrantable Freedoms." Coming as it did a year after the Proclamation Line of 1763 and the very same year as the Sugar Act and the announcement of plans for the Stamp Act, the controversy over the sanctity of trial by jury highlighted changes in imperial policy that New Yorkers absolutely deplored.

Unlike technical arguments over judicial tenure, Colden's critics, in arguing against royal interference with the privilege of jury trials, had an issue that appealed mightily to New Yorkers. The more Colden ranted and raved, the more he encouraged the assembly and legal community to make common cause against him. "The Old Body was allways dislik'd enough," wrote Robert R. Livingston, "but now they would preferr Beelzebub himself to him." The press was filled with the dispute, and the triumvirate—Livingston, Smith, and Scott—led the way in castigating Colden as that "evil Genius," "old mischief Maker," and "Petty T[yran]t." In fact, Colden was so universally despised by 1765 that New York's violent reaction to the Stamp Act was almost as much a protest against this crotchety personification of British authority as it was against the dreaded internal tax imposed by Parliament. Not until 1768 would the Privy Council decide that Colden was wrong and his critics right about the restrictions under which decisions in jury trials could be appealed to the governor and council.

While the *Forsey v. Cunningham* case agitated the public, New Yorkers encountered in rapid succession the Proclamation Line of 1763, the Sugar Act (officially called the American Revenue Act) and the Currency Act in 1764, and both the Stamp Act and a Quartering Act in 1765. The temporary ban on western settlement, so strongly recommended by Indian Commissioner Sir William Johnson in the wake of the bloody uprising of 1763 known as Pontiac's Rebellion, worried more than a few New Yorkers, farmers as well as land speculators. Of more immediate concern was the American Revenue Act. This measure actually reduced the duty of 1733 on foreign-produced molasses imported into the American colonies; but it raised the rate on foreign sugar products and a variety of other foreign goods. Moreover, for once, the British government seemed intent upon collecting the tax. Enforcement incentives were beefed up; another vice admiralty court was established in North America, at Halifax. Most disturbing, this tax was—as the title of the law makes clear—not so much a trade regulation as a revenue measure meant to defray the expense of governing and protecting Britain's newly enlarged North American empire.

Reaction to Parliamentary Taxation

Protesting both the Revenue Act and the proposed stamp tax, the New York assembly sent petitions to the king, lords, and commons, prepared respectively by John Morin Scott, William Livingston, and William Smith, Jr. New York City merchants, still in the throes of economic depression, warned that the Sugar Act would be ruinous for both England and its American colonies. If the tax on foreign molasses and other commodities were enforced, New Yorkers could not make enough money to continue importing £600,000 sterling worth of British goods annually. More than money, though, was involved here. Political principles nurtured by generations of governmental practice made colonial Americans uneasy with so-called imperial reforms. "It is a standing Maxim of *English Liberty*," William Livingston had written in 1752, "that no Man shall be taxed, but with his own Consent." His cousin Judge Robert R. Livingston was appalled by the Revenue Act of 1764 and wondered if after the rumored stamp tax Parliament might not even tax land in the colonies. Taxes imposed by London undermined the entire edifice of English rights and liberty, making Americans little more than slaves, complained William Smith, Jr.

Other New Yorkers doubted that petitions alone would influence Parliament. Among the skeptics were merchants Isaac Sears, John Lamb, and Alexander McDougall, popular leaders with close ties to the lesser tradesmen, artisans, and laborers in New York City. Sears and McDougall had made modest fortunes as privateers in the French and Indian War; Lamb, formerly a maker of mathematical instruments, had lately become an importer of wines. As leaders of the Sons of Liberty, organized during the fall of 1765, all three were identified with antimercantile thinking common among lesser merchants and retailers, who felt especially burdened by imperial trade regulations. A native of Connecticut, Sears was a self-made man whose radicalism made him suspect among the more established political leadership. McDougall, a native of Ireland, had married a wealthy woman, opened a popular tavern, and moved easily among the political elite. Less economically secure than either McDougall or Sears, Lamb, a native of New York City, spoke Dutch, German, and French as well as English; he was invaluable in organizing support for the Sons of Liberty in the heterogeneous city.

If they resented the American Revenue Act of 1764, the Sons of Liberty were inflamed by the Stamp Act. Scheduled to go into effect on November 1, 1765, it required the use of special stamped paper for newspapers and most legal and commercial documents. The taxing measures were all the more onerous because of continuing economic recession, brought home by rising numbers of business failures, bankruptcies, and poor families crowding into the municipal almshouse. The Livingstons, who had gained the upper hand in the assembly, were prominent in the proceedings of the Stamp Act Congress, which Massachusetts called and which met in New York from October 7 to 25, 1765.

Attended by delegates from nine colonies, the congress issued a declaration that condemned in no uncertain terms taxation without representation. Representing New York, Robert R. Livingston and Philip Livingston served on different committees, which wrote petitions to George III and the House of Lords, respectively. Both petitions denounced the Stamp Act, deplored the imposition of taxes without the consent of the colonial assemblies, and protested the expanded jurisdiction of vice admiralty courts.

In August, James McEvers, the designated stamp agent for New York, resigned his position, his friends having warned him that "a Storm was Rising." In September, John Holt, Livingstonite printer and publisher of the *New-York Gazette, or, The Weekly Post Boy*, invited citizens to attend the funeral of "Lady N—th Am—can Liberty," scheduled for November 1, promptly at 7 o'clock in the evening. Street dramas were being planned, but patrician leaders, both Livingstons and DeLanceys, counseled peaceful protest. "Whenever the stamp-paper arrives," urged a letter to the *Post Boy*, "let us not sully our character by any violent measures; let them lie disregarded." What the patrician politicians had in mind was an economic boycott.

On October 31, the day before the Stamp Act was to go into effect, New York City merchants were the first Americans to agree formally to stop importing British goods until the act was repealed. Later that same day Manhattan shopkeepers and retailers also subscribed to the boycott. Merchants and shopkeepers in other cities followed suit. In the countryside ordinary citizens were urged to produce more homespun cloth. Westchester County farmers, for instance, cooperated by sowing more flaxseed and raising more sheep. Household spinning wheels and looms worked overtime making clothes so that English cloth would not be needed. Simplicity was urged even at funerals, as mourners were told to abandon the extravagant ritual of distributing mourning scarves, gloves, and spoons, all of which were usually imported from abroad.

The public demonstrations began on schedule. As night fell on November 1, two crowds formed, both of which proclaimed their loyalty to George III and his government. One crowd assembled on the Commons, and the other gathered downtown. Numbering in the hundreds, each carried an effigy of the despised Colden; one had him hanging from a movable gallows. The downtown crowd approached Fort George, broke open the governor's coach house, put its effigy of Colden inside the coach, and pulled it to the coffeehouse, where a throng of gentlemen cheered them on.

The two crowds shortly came together, numbering over two thousand, and confronted Fort George. They hurled insults as well as brickbats at the soldiers, who nevertheless held their fire. At length, the rioters appeased themselves by burning Colden's fine coach and sleigh on the Bowling Green and breaking streetlamps and windows about the town. They totally destroyed the beautiful mansion of Major Thomas James, commander of British troops at Fort George, whose infamous words that he would cram the Stamp Act down the throats of New Yorkers had to be avenged. Adding insult to injury, the rioters even drank all of Major James's wine and rum.

The Stamp Act riots, together with the boycott of British goods launched by merchants and retailers, thrust New York into the forefront of American resistance to parliamentary supremacy. At this juncture, however, the Livingston coalition in the assembly moved to restore calm. Colden contributed to the truce by announcing he would not distribute the noxious stamps, leaving their disposition to Sir Henry Moore, the newly appointed governor who was expected shortly in New York. Defusing the situation further, the common council offered to remove the stamps from the fort and store them. Arriving in New York on November 13, Governor Moore also decided against distributing the stamps, more of which he brought with him, and to open Fort George, which had been closed and prepared for battle, to the public again. The siege mentality in New York City was broken at last. The boycott continued, and the stamps remained guarded and stored at the City Hall, but peace generally prevailed. "I am obliged to suspend a Power which I am not able to exert," Moore explained to Whitehall.

Virtually all trade had been suspended because Captain Archibald Kennedy, the naval officer for the Port of New York, would not clear vessels without stamped documents. "King Sears," as his upper-class critics called him, and his Liberty Boys wanted to force the issue. If, as Americans claimed, the Stamp Act was unconstitutional, merchants and lawyers should ignore the stamp requirements and continue their respective businesses. The Livingstons, however, were unwilling to defy Parliament so openly. Angered by what they perceived as Livingston perfidy, the Sons of Liberty urged city lawyers to resume the practice of law without stamps. Again, the Livingstons, who dominated the legal profession in the city, refused to cooperate. However, young James DeLancey, Jr., son of the deceased chief justice, educated at Eton, Cambridge, and Lincoln's Inn and formerly a captain in the British army, agreed with the Liberty Boys, beginning an association that contributed to the restoration of DeLancey leadership in the assembly after the elections of 1768 and 1769.

Outside of New York City, reaction to the Stamp Act was much more restrained. Various towns and villages organized their own chapters of the Sons of Liberty. On Long Island, Oyster Bay's Sons met on February 22, 1765, and protested the Stamp Act as an "arbitrary and unconstitutional" act. Huntington's Sons met in March, and, up the Hudson, Fishkill's Sons organized in April. In Albany, forty-eight merchants signed a protest against the stamp tax but then paid little attention to it. The Albany Liberty Boys, however, sought assurances from local officials that none would apply for the position of stamp collector. When Postmaster Henry Van Schaack hesitated, the Sons mobbed his home, seized his sleigh, set it afire, and then dragged it triumphantly through the streets. The next day, Van Schaack appeared before the Sons, appropriately contrite, and renounced any desire to seek or accept the position of stamp collector, whereupon he was cheered and "genteely conducted to his Lodging."

Patrician leaders, regardless of their political affiliation, recognized that the violence of November 1 had gotten out of hand. In January 1766, Oliver DeLancey, James's uncle, worried aloud about "civil war" and what would happen to their family "in such a Scene of Confusion and Distress." The situation remained volatile, with renewed rioting a distinct possibility, reason enough perhaps to counsel moderation. The Livingstonites especially did not want to embarrass Governor Moore, who favored them and upriver political interests, as against the seaboard political interests so thoroughly identified with the old DeLancey coalition. Events in England were also encouraging. The Grenville government fell in July 1765, even before the Stamp Act riots; and its successor, the Rockingham ministry, opposed both the American Revenue Act of 1764 and the Stamp Act of 1765. Moreover, British merchants, whose economic plight was made worse by the American boycott, were lobbying Parliament for relief.

The spread of tenant unrest on the Hudson Valley estates further hastened the provincial elite's decision to embrace moderation. Generally hard economic times—exacerbated by drought in 1763 and again in 1764, by continuing border disputes with Massachusetts primarily and Connecticut to a lesser degree, and by migrating New Englanders attracted to the underpopulated land east of the Hudson River—contributed to the rural uprisings. They began in the fall of 1765 in Dutchess County on the Highland Patent of Philip Philipse, Beverly Robinson, and Roger Morris and spread in the spring of 1766 southward to Cortlandt Manor in Westchester County and northward to Livingston and Van Rensselaer Manors in Albany County. Some of the Highland Patent protesters (more than a few from Connecticut) held title from the Wappinger Indians, who insisted that the Highland Patent issued years before to Adolphe Philipse did not extinguish the Wappinger tribe's claim to ancestral lands. In 1765, however, the New York Supreme Court rejected the appeal of Chief Daniel Ninham on behalf of his tribesmen.

To the north, speculators holding title from Massachusetts had for years sold or leased to settlers lands claimed by the Livingstons and Van Rensselaers.

Albany County saw the worst of the violence, in which at least four people were killed. In Dutchess County roving bands of disgruntled tenants broke open the jail at Poughkeepsie and made plans to march on New York City but were disappointed when the Sons of Liberty refused to join their movement against the landlords. In June 1766, Governor Moore dispatched British regulars to the Highland Patent, where several skirmishes were fought before the ringleaders were captured. One of them, William Pendergast, was indicted for "High Treason" and sentenced to death, but he was ultimately pardoned by George III. The Livingstonites, including William Livingston together with William Smith, Jr., and John Morin Scott, played prominent roles in prosecuting the protesters. If the New York elite required an object lesson in the benefits of imperial government, either to settle "jarring" boundary disputes with neighboring colonies or to put down disgruntled squatters and lease-holders, the so-called tenant uprisings of 1765 and 1766 provided it.

Pressure from British merchants and weariness on the part of Parliament paid off. In March 1766 the Stamp Act was repealed, and New Yorkers, like other Americans, were too busy celebrating to pay much attention to the Declaratory Act proclaiming parliamentary supremacy over the colonies. However, the audacity of the Liberty Boys, who burned nine boxes of stamps in January and turned out 5,000 hostile males to intimidate New York City customs officials in February, convinced General Thomas Gage, commander of British troops in America, that more soldiers should be concentrated in New York City and other American port towns. The Rockingham ministry resisted Gage's troop buildup, even as it liberalized the Sugar Act of 1764, reducing the tax on molasses from 3d. to 1d. per gallon. Plans were also afoot to moderate the Currency Act of 1764, but Rockingham fell from power in late 1766. His currency reform was forgotten, whereas Gage's plan for concentrating troops in American cities was adopted by the new ministry organized by William Pitt, Lord Chatham, whose ill health shortly made Charles Townshend, chancellor of the exchequer, the de facto prime minister.

Following the repeal of the Stamp Act, New Yorkers generally believed that Britain had conceded and that their relationship with the mother country was improving. "A New Constitution will be form'd in time between the Mother Country and the Colonys," wrote the councillor and merchant John Watts. Inspired by the pleasant turn of events, William Smith, Jr., another councillor and as much of a Livingston as Watts was a DeLancey, believed that the time had come for America to redefine its place within the British Empire. "The Constitution . . . ought to bend, and *sooner or later* will bend," wrote Smith; "unless it is the Design of Heaven to infatuate and destroy us as a Nation."

Charles Townshend thought otherwise. In sympathy with Gage's earlier plans, Townshend announced that Americans would have to pay "external taxes" on glass, lead, paint, paper, and tea—to help pay the estimated £40,000 required for the civil establishment in America. If New Yorkers needed another reason to resent General Gage and his "Lobsterbacks," as British regulars were called, the Townshend duties were it. The assembly's power of the purse was now in jeopardy.

Along with the Townshend duties, several companion measures were passed by Parliament in early 1767. One set up an American Board of Customs, strengthened the very next year by the establishment of four vice admiralty courts in North America. A third statute, called the New York Restraining Act, specifically required the suspension of the New York assembly should it fail to comply with the Quartering Act of 1765.

Although landed magnates found soldiers useful against rioting tenants, many New Yorkers resented the troops. They were known for drinking and carousing, assaulting civilians, and cutting down every Liberty Pole New Yorkers erected. Soldiers also frequently worked as day laborers, competing with civilian workers. American colonists viewed the Quartering Act as nothing more than an additional tax, requiring them to supply, feed, and house British troops. While not officially acknowledging the Quartering Act, the Livingston-led assembly kept the Restraining Act at bay simply by allocating several thousand pounds for Gage's use. The general found it convenient not to oppose—or expose—the charade, which gave the Livingstons some political cover and provided his troops with what they needed.

The DeLanceys Take Charge

If New Yorkers were reluctant to confront the Quartering Act, their response to the Townshend duties was even more ambivalent. Having led the way in opposing the Stamp Act, New Yorkers hung back, preferring to wait on what Boston and Philadelphia might do. Meanwhile, Governor Moore, according to the terms of the New York Septennial Act, was compelled to call for assembly elections in early 1768. Having gained the endorsement of Sears and the Liberty Boys back in 1765, James DeLancey, Jr., gave the Livingstonites a run for their money in the city. Joining Captain DeLancey as candidates were the wealthy merchants Jacob Walton and James Jauncey. The DeLanceyites did not run a fourth candidate, deciding to concede the city seat held by Philip Livingston, a popular merchant. Instead, they focused their attacks upon the other Livingstonite candidate, the lawyer John Morin Scott.

The DeLanceyites went after both lawyers and Livingston politicians for not opposing the Stamp Act more aggressively. Scott was said to have spoken against the famous Virginia Resolves of 1765; he was also accused of urging lawyers to use the stamps and saying the public be damned. In short, the Livingstonites' moderate stand during the Stamp Act Crisis was deplored as nothing less than opportunistic political trimming, something the DeLancey-ites were equally adept at. Perhaps with the Livingston trio in mind, the DeLanceyites portrayed New York City lawyers as the servants of oppressive Hudson River manor lords.

The Livingstonites found it difficult to garner much public sympathy by defending lawyers, and when William Livingston, their chief propagandist, tried to revive religious antagonisms by presenting the DeLanceyites as advocates of Anglican religious aggression and the Livingstonites as the defenders of dissent, the appeal to denominational prejudice probably hurt the Livingstons more than it helped them. In the election, Philip Livingston came in first, but James DeLancey was a close second, while both Walton and Jauncey ran well ahead of Scott. Robert R. Livingston was also defeated in Dutchess County, but the Livingston faction was still influential enough to elect Philip Livingston speaker.

With the political momentum beginning to tilt in their favor, the DeLanceys urged the assembly not to vote funds for the army (in defiance of the Restraining Act) and to endorse the Massachusetts Circular Letter of 1768, which denounced the Townshend Acts. To do the former would trigger the suspension of the assembly, and to do the latter would dissolve it, as ordered by Lord Halifax, the first secretary of the newly created American Department of State. Deciding to risk dissolution, the Livingstons brought the Massachusetts Circular Letter before the assembly, which approved the provocative measure, forcing Governor Moore to call another general election in 1769.

Once again the Livingstonites played the religious card. They tried to connect the DeLanceyites with Anglican efforts to secure an American bishop, blamed the DeLanceyites for the council's denial of charter privileges to Presbyterian congregations, and generally presented themselves as champions of religious freedom and Protestant dissenters. On the other hand, the DeLanceyites minimized their own Anglicanism, played upon the distrust that other dissenters had toward Presbyterians, and continued to emphasize that businessmen rather than lawyers should represent New York City. Throughout the province the DeLanceyites once again portrayed the Livingstonites as fainthearted during the Stamp Act Crisis, and they won support from rich and poor alike as they spoke of revitalizing the New York economy.

James DeLancey became the hero of the hour when, in the midst of the 1769 campaign, he turned down appointment to the provincial council, saying he would rather be an elected representative of the people. Supported by the Sons of Liberty, the DeLanceyites scored a resounding victory in New York City. Even the heretofore popular Philip Livingston went down to defeat, falling before the former mayor and wealthy merchant John Cruger. DeLanceyites did well throughout the province and were back in charge of the New York assembly.

Having painted the Livingston party in general, and the city's lawyers in particular, as soft on American rights, the DeLanceys ran the risk of having the tables turned against them. The Sons of Liberty, to whom the DeLanceys owed so much in the city elections, expected them to take a hard line against both the Townshend duties and the Quartering Act. The DeLanceys, on the other hand, were particularly concerned about reviving the economy. The lack of specie and the need for paper money, so highly restricted by the Currency Act of 1764, remained vexing problems that troubled the commercially minded DeLanceys. Not until the fall of 1768 did New York City merchants, pressured by the Sons of Liberty, join Boston merchants in boycotting British imports.

The Livingstonites continued to play upon the religious fears of the dissenters, even organizing a Society of Dissenters to combat Anglican pretensions and "for the Preservation of their common and respective civil and religious *Rights* and *Privileges."* More provocative than that, Livingston spokesmen like Philip Schuyler and George Clinton hammered away at the Quartering Act, knowing full well that New York's noncompliance would activate the Restraining Act and bring indefinite suspension of the assembly. The DeLanceyites responded in kind, expelling from the assembly two Livingston representatives for not living in the district that elected them, a law seldom enforced before.

The sudden death of Governor Moore in September 1769 meant that the Livingston party had lost a valued ally. Acting Governor Colden, though heartily disliked by all sides, wasted no time in reconciling with the majority DeLancey coalition. With Colden on their side, the DeLanceyites, like the Livingstonites before them, sought to finesse their way around the Quartering Act. They voted £2,000 for the British army on condition that half of that sum be raised from the interest on £120,000 worth of bills of credit to be issued by the province. The additional currency was deemed crucial to improving the provincial economy, and old Colden had to defy his instructions as governor and sign the measure in contravention of the Currency Act of 1764. The Privy Council later approved this exceptional measure but not before the compromise on the Quartering Act had created a firestorm of protest that led the Sons of Liberty to break with the DeLanceyites.

The DeLanceyites were hoisted by their own petard. The man who sprang the trap was Alexander McDougall, the leader of the Liberty Boys most closely associated with the Livingstonites. On December 16, 1769, the day after the army revenue bill passed the assembly, McDougall published pseudonymously a broadside titled *To the Betrayed Inhabitants of the City and Colony of New York.* He berated the nefarious Colden and heaped scorn upon the scheming DeLanceys for bowing before the Quartering Act. Another broadside by McDougall two days later lamented "the late base inglorious Conduct of our General Assembly, who have in opposition to the loud and general Voice of their Constituents; the Dictates of sound Policy, and the ties of Gratitude, and the glorious Struggle we have engaged in for our invaluable Birth Rights, dared to vote supplies to the Troops without the least Shadow of a pretext for their pernicious Grant." The Livingstonites joined the attack with glee.

The DeLanceyites were not amused. Both council and assembly proclaimed the broadsides libelous, and Colden offered a £100 reward toward the discovery of the author. Under pressure, James Parker, the printer, admitted that McDougall was the author, which led to his arrest and imprisonment. Playing his role to the limit, McDougall gained fame and notoriety as the "Wilkes of America," remaining in jail "for the liberty of his country," as the famed English radical John Wilkes had done, though the wealthy McDougall easily could have made bail. Sears and Lamb came to McDougall's defense, deserting their alliance with the DeLanceys. Not since 1765 had the leaders of the Liberty Boys been so united. Only Joseph Allicocke, a lesser leader and Lamb's brother-in-law, kept his allegiance to the DeLanceys.

As McDougall's broadsides were agitating the public, the tensions between British soldiers and civilians reached a new high in New York City. In January 1770 soldiers chopped down the Liberty Tree on the town commons and unceremoniously cut it to pieces, enraging the Liberty Boys. The next day, three thousand New Yorkers gathered to protest the provocative deed, and only the timely intervention of city magistrates kept the crowd from taking their fury out on nearby soldiers. On January 19, 1770, a group of civilians, many of them Sons of Liberty, mixed it up with the redcoats in what was called the "Battle of Golden Hill," during which several soldiers and citizens were bloodied. Stories of this skirmish were circulated and perhaps contributed to the popular climate that led to the more famous Boston Massacre six weeks later.

Generally appalled by the outbreaks of violence, New Yorkers were delighted by word in early 1770 that the Townshend duties had been repealed, all except the one on tea. The merchant community believed the boycott on British goods had done its work again and should be abandoned (save for British tea) at once. So did most DeLancey leaders, but the Sons of Liberty objected, drawing support from Livingston assemblymen and from town meetings in Boston and Philadelphia. Evidence was mounting, however, that Boston merchants, despite their repeated denials, were cheating on the boycott and smuggling in British goods. Moreover, in New York City, artisans as well as merchants were suffering economically and wanted to resume trade with Britain. In July, after considerable wrangling back and forth, New York's Committee of Inspection, the extralegal organization enforcing the boycott, agreed to a city-wide poll which ended the nonimportation movement. Despite the criticism they received from both the Sons of Liberty and the Livingston coalition, the DeLanceys remained popular enough to win heavily in the New York City Common Council elections in October. "Last Saturday," exulted the future loyalist printer James Rivington, "a Struggle was made by the McDougall party to

Advertisement.
To the Publick.

A RETURN having been made to the Committee of Inspection, of the Sense of the Inhabitants of this City, whether to import every Thing except T E A, or any other Article subject to Duty, or to abide by the present Non-Importation Agreement.---It appears there is a great Majority in Favour of Importation, and the Inhabitants will govern themselves accordingly ;---but that it is expected —— they give strict Orders to their different Correspondents, Masters of Vessels and others, not to ship or take on board any Tea, or any other Article whatsoever, which now is, or may hereafter be subject to Duty for the Purpose of raising a Revenue in America, on Pain of incurring their highest Displeasure.

By Order of the Committee,
ISAAC LOW, *Chairman.*
New-York, July 9, 1770.

A 1770 advertisement admonishes against importing tea or other items subject to Townshend duties into New York. New York State Historical Association, Cooperstown, N.Y.

get the better in City Elections, of the Royalists, but the latter prevailed and Established an Everlasting and invincible Superiority."

To be called "royalists" did not bode well for the DeLanceyites. Perhaps it was inevitable, though, given their domination of the assembly, efforts to advance both liberty and commerce, and working relationship with Lieutenant Governor Colden (who had to give way in October 1770 to the new governor, John Murray, Earl of Dunmore). The Livingston minority did all it could to portray their rivals as sacrificing American liberty to commercial gain. The Livingstons also maneuvered the DeLanceys into opening assembly sessions to the public, knowing that in Philip Schuyler and George Clinton they had by far the most eloquent speakers in the lower house. Schuyler embarrassed his rivals by pushing bills for secret-ballot voting and exempting non-Anglicans from the church tax in the four lower counties where Anglicans claimed establishment.

The Drift to Revolution

Following the repeal of the Townshend duties and the end of the boycott, the imperial crisis waned in New York. Whitehall's approval of currency issues lessened public antagonism toward Britain. However, with the Tea Act in May 1773, giving the financially troubled British East India Company a monopoly of tea sales in America, the North ministry inadvertently made the remaining Townshend duty on tea a popular issue. Smugglers particularly resented the Tea Act because, with its monopoly, the British East India Company could sell the commodity more cheaply than anyone else. Americans of all stripes, honest and dishonest, could unite against the Tea Act. As William Smith, Jr., noted on October 13, 1773, "Vertue and Vice being thus united, . . . we shall repeat all the Confusions of 1765 and 1766." Smith proved much more of a prophet than he could have known. "—Time will shew the Event," he continued. "Our Domestic Parties will probably die, and be swallowed up in the general Opposition to the Parliamentary Project of raising the Arm of Government by Revenue Laws." That is exactly what happened, but even the prescient Smith could not have known that this third crisis would provoke the breakup of the Anglo-American empire.

After a decade of protesting and cooperation with like-minded fellows in other colonial ports, the Sons of Liberty were ready to spring into action against the Tea Act. They and their Livingston allies encouraged the formation of patriotic committees throughout the province to meet this latest crisis. Calling for yet another boycott, the Liberty Boys said no East India tea would be landed in New York, upon pain of death. William Tryon, governor of New York since July 1771, faced a serious dilemma. As chief executive, he was obliged to enforce the law. Yet, should he land the tea, rioting and violence would surely result. General Gage expected a fight, but Tryon worked out a compromise whereby New York's East Indian tea agents agreed to send ships laden with tea back to Britain. Some months after the Boston Tea Party, New York had a tea party of its own. The captain of the *London* lied about having taxed tea aboard his ship. When the townspeople learned the truth, they boarded his vessel on the evening of April 22, 1774, and threw eighteen chests of tea overboard.

The revival of the imperial quarrel weakened the credibility of the DeLanceyites, who, while very much opposed to parliamentary taxation, were determined not to be co-opted by Isaac Sears and John Lamb or even Livingston rivals like Philip Schuyler and George Clinton. British reaction to the Boston Tea Party worked against the DeLanceys. In retaliation for the Boston Tea Party, Massachusetts was punished by a series of parliamentary measures the Americans dubbed the Intolerable Acts. In the battle for the minds and hearts of the people, the Intolerable Acts (the British called them the Coercive Acts) designed to punish Massachusetts did more than Isaac Sears or John Lamb could ever have done to convince New Yorkers that Parliament intended to crush American liberties. Also emerging from Parliament in 1774, a stricter Quartering Act and the Quebec Act legalizing the Catholic Church and setting up an arbitrary provincial government for Canada, both reinforced the worst fears of parliamentary supremacy that Americans had.

William Smith, Jr., was shocked and appalled by the Intolerable Acts. "We shall lose all that Attachmt we once had to so great a Degree for the Parent Country," he lamented on May 18, 1774. Oliver DeLancey exclaimed that he would gladly give up his fortune to prevent the closure of the Port of Boston, and Peter Van Schaack, a young DeLanceyite lawyer, felt this assertion of parliamentary supremacy left America little choice. "An appeal to the sword," concluded Van Schaack, "I am afraid is inevitable." Rhetorical flourishes aside, New Yorkers were remarkably united against the Intolerable Acts; yet they were such a diverse people, riven by so many economic and social tensions, that they were finding it difficult to agree on how they should resist parliamentary abuse.

The Liberty Boys urged another boycott of all British goods, one approved by an all-colony congress with reliable mechanisms of enforcement. Their Livingston allies generally endorsed the idea. DeLancey leaders, many of whom were merchants, were repelled by thoughts of banning commerce and wanted to delay any action; some even urged Massachusetts to pay for the tea destroyed at Boston. After considerable maneuvering and compromise, the inhabitants of New York City selected a Committee of Fifty-one, the mother of revolutionary committees in the province. Of that number, more than two-thirds were known DeLanceyites.

To the chagrin of Sears and McDougall, the delegates recommended by the Committee of Fifty-one to attend the First Continental Congress—Philip Livingston, Isaac Low, James Duane, John Jay, and John Alsop—were all patrician politicians, and except Livingston all were thoroughly identified with the DeLancey coalition. Many New Yorkers, especially merchants associated with the DeLanceys, expected the Continental Congress to be firm with Parliament and yet heal the breach between the mother country and its American colonies. Consequently, they were taken aback when the Congress agreed to the Continental Association, which called for a progressively stricter program of economic coercion: first a boycott of all British and Irish imports, starting on

December 1, 1774; next, nonconsumption of British and particular foreign goods, beginning on March 1, 1775; finally, if Britain remained unresponsive, an American embargo on all exports to Britain, Ireland, and the West Indies, beginning September 10, 1775.

Moreover, the Continental Congress called upon every community to set up committees to enforce the Association, which, in retrospect, marked the beginnings of the transition from provincial status to statehood and independence. Such was the view of the loyalist historian Thomas Jones, and certainly of Prime Minister North, George III, and Colonial Secretary Lord Dartmouth, who, egged on by General Gage, were ready to use military force. In New York City, the Committee of Fifty-one was replaced by the Committee of Sixty, whose task it was to enforce the Continental Association. Radical influence on this committee was more pronounced; moderate New Yorkers were not quite sure what to do, recognizing that relations with the mother country were deteriorating rapidly.

Much to the disappointment of General Gage and other British officials, New York merchants, despite their misgivings, upheld the Continental Association. Besides merchants, there were others whose attachment to the British Empire made them especially wary of American resistance: Crown officials like Cadwallader Colden and the customs collector Andrew Elliot; Anglicans like President Myles Cooper of King's College, Samuel Seabury, Thomas Bradbury Chandler, and Charles Inglis, all Episcopal priests; Quakers, fearful of the radical drift toward war; even a Whig ideologue such as William Smith, Jr., whose land speculations and legal training probably led him to continue seeking compromise. New immigrants, especially recent arrivals from continental Europe as well as Britain, were generally more supportive of the mother country.

Certain Anglican clergymen in New York saw the Continental Congress as tyrannical. The most prolific was Samuel Seabury, the SPG missionary in Westchester, who wrote and published anonymously no fewer than four pamphlets in 1774 and 1775. Seabury made it clear that radical leaders were taking the American colonies into civil war and rebellion. "If I must be enslaved," Seabury declared, "let it be by a King at least, and not by a parcel of upstart, lawless committee-men." Among patrician New Yorkers, there was growing sentiment that the "lesser sort" were exercising too much political influence. English officials definitely played upon those fears. Rumor had it that the North ministry was "buying" support in the New York assembly. In fact, Lieutenant Governor Colden and, after 1771, Governor William Tryon were especially generous with land grants during this time, the lion's share going to men who would become loyalists. Anxious to pick up support wherever he could, Lord Dartmouth even told Tryon that the Presbyterian congregation in New York City should apply again for incorporation.

Women and Minorities on the Eve of the Revolution

After Lexington and Concord, New Yorkers were generally swept along in the flow of events. They knew that if war continued, it would surely reach them. Their province was too strategic militarily, located in the center of the North American colonies, with a magnificent harbor and rivers running deep into the continental interior. The sobering possibility of military struggle in their province gave New Yorkers food for thought. New York City continued to lead provincial resistance to Parliament, that much is clear. But even on Manhattan—and more so elsewhere in the province—it is difficult to gauge the depth of popular commitment because the resistance movement was led by adult white males. The extent to which women, African Americans, and Indians participated or were affected by the agitation and ideas associated with the coming of the American Revolution is problematic in New York, as it is in the other colonies; our knowledge is limited by the paucity of source materials and by generations of neglect by historians. More is known about the proliferation of extralegal committees in the countryside, but the sources there are frequently few and sketchy.

In the popular agitation against the Sugar Act, Stamp Act, Townshend duties, and finally the Coercive Acts in 1774, New York women took part insofar as their roles allowed. In the wake of news of Lexington and Concord, New York City was furiously aroused. "Men, women, children, all ranks and professions," remarked a visitor to Manhattan in May 1775, are "mad with Politics." That observation might have been exaggerated, but from the start many women enthusiastically embraced the American cause and made their sentiments public. When the Stamp Act provided that marriage licenses carry the hated stamps, one writer, supposedly a woman, boldly proclaimed in the *New-York Gazette* on December 6, 1765, that "the young Ladies of this Place are determined to join Hands with none but such as will to the utmost endeavor to abolish the Custom of marrying with License."

"Daughters of Liberty" joined hands with the Sons of Liberty in organizing boycotts of British goods and advised New York women to use "your own country linen" instead of imported British cloth. Groups of women organized spinning clubs to produce American-made cloth so that they could "vie with the men, in contributing to the Preservation and prosperity of their Country, and equally share the Honour of it." After Lexington and Concord, the militant women of Kinderhook tarred and feathered a suspected Tory. Women in New York joined their compatriots in other colonies in boycotting British tea in response to the Tea Act and substituted coffee or other liquids made from strawberries, raspberries, currants, and sassafras.

African Americans, whether male or female, had less impact on the imperial quarrel. Nonetheless, the rhetoric of the Sons of Liberty trickled down to

New York's slaves and free blacks. Certainly, Whig talk of liberty encouraged some New Yorkers to call for emancipation of the colony's slaves. John Jay, one of the staunchest of New York's antislavery advocates, declared that unless the colony was prepared to free the slaves, "her own prayers to Heaven for liberty will be impious." The enslaved themselves became somewhat more demanding as they heard Whig denunciations of British "slavery" over the colonies and American assertions of natural rights. A few slaveholders, especially Quakers, responded to the antislavery appeals appearing in newspapers and elsewhere by manumitting their own bondsmen.

Some slaves took advantage of the general unrest by trying to escape. In Ulster County, in 1775, about twenty slaves were arrested for allegedly plotting a rebellion. In New York City, two so-called tory Negroes were hanged for "engaging to murder their masters who were supporters of liberty." In August 1776 the fear of slave revolts led the New York Provincial Congress to pass a Militia Act providing for a detachment of troops especially assigned "to guard against the insurrection of slaves." Both the Albany and Schenectady Committees of Safety deported unruly slaves to New England, where they were presumably less of a threat.

Sir William Johnson. By John Wollaston (painted ca. 1749–67). Albany Institute of History and Art.

For most African Americans, generally without property themselves and nontaxpayers, the calls for defense of American property and freedom from parliamentary taxation aroused little sympathy. Among free blacks, there were exceptions, such as Sam Fraunces, a West Indian of mixed French and African descent, whose tavern on the corner of Broad and Pearl Streets became a center of revolutionary agitation for New York's radicals. It was in Fraunces Tavern that the Stamp Act was discussed and attacked, and there also in 1774 that the Sons of Liberty planned New York's own Tea Party on April 22. But Fraunces, like perhaps Joseph Allicocke, who some have said was a mulatto, was the exception to the rule, even among free blacks. As the historian Graham Hodges has observed, "blacks watched the unfolding conflict carefully, choosing sides according to their best interests, and were less pro-British than pro-black."

Like African Americans, New York's Indians took little interest in the early stages of the Anglo-American controversy. Their traditional loyalty was to the Crown, nurtured by years of good relations between the Iroquois Confederacy and Sir William Johnson, who, in addition to being superintendent of Indian Affairs for the Northern District, was also "Colonel of the Six Nations." The boycotts occasioned first by the Stamp Act and later the Townshend duties did halt the flow of gifts to the Six Nations, thereby undermining Johnson's task of keeping the Indians pacified. Johnson's death in July 1774 left the Iroquois Confederacy in confusion. In the words of one observer, the Iroquois were now "scattered like a flock of sheep." Guy Johnson, William's nephew and successor as Indian commissioner, urged the Iroquois to maintain neutrality, a position also advocated by the Indian commissioners sent by the Continental Congress.

As Whigs and loyalists in Albany and Tryon Counties began fighting with each other, however, it became difficult for Native Americans to remain neutral. Guy Johnson soon joined the British forces, and he took the Mohawks with him. The Oneidas, under the influence of Presbyterian missionary Reverend William Strickland, first remained neutral and then took up the patriot cause, along with the Tuscaroras. The other tribes of the Iroquois Confederacy sided with the British. Soon Indians were fighting Indians and burning each other's villages in a war that ultimately proved harmful to both those who were pro-British and those who were pro-American. The statement of Seneca Chief Kayashuta in 1775 proved to be prophetic: "We must be Fools indeed to imagine that they regard us or our Interests who want to bring us into an unnecessary War." For Native Americans as well as African Americans, the coming of the American Revolution meant little. In the end, it turned out to be a white man's conflict, with a peace that would bring no lasting benefits to either minority.

Loyalists and Patriots

Following the passage of the Intolerable Acts, most New Yorkers outside of Manhattan moved cautiously toward rebellion. Between 1774 and 1776 it became increasingly evident that Suffolk, Orange, and Ulster Counties were strongly in the patriot camp; Kings County was more patriot than loyalist, though some interpreted the stolid temper of the Dutch farmers as loyalism. Richmond (Staten Island) remained staunchly royalist, while Queens appeared to be pro-British but was more accurately neutral, certainly not pro-American. Although the other counties were divided internally, their inhabitants were always more pro-American than pro-British.

The city of Albany, for example, remained in Whig (patriotic) hands, and so did Schenectady. The Albany Sons of Liberty, though quite active in 1765 and 1766, ignored the boycott adopted by New York City against the Townshend duties in 1769. But in May 1775 a heretofore secret Albany Committee of Correspondence went public, electing Abraham Yates as its chairman. Loyalism was most pronounced among some Anglicans, disgruntled tenants of patriotic

Van Rensselaer and Livingston landlords, and some Dutch who resented New England immigrants. Similarly, in Tryon County, established from western Albany County in 1771, loyalism owed much to Anglican ministers and the Johnson family. The Johnsons were good landlords, and their tenants and many neighboring landowners followed their lead. Nevertheless, Whig sentiment was alive in Tryon County, particularly in the Palatine District, where Nicholas Herkimer and others established a patriotic committee. Just as Yates and his Albany committee ran their county, Herkimer and his friends took over in Tryon when Guy Johnson and his "Scotch gang" fled to Canada in May 1776.

In the three recently created northeastern counties—Cumberland, Gloucester, and Charlotte—Vermont separatists were predominant. As early as 1773, Ethan Allen and his Green Mountain Boys had been opposing the territorial claims of both New Hampshire and New York. After rioting occurred in Cumberland County in 1774, Allen and his cohort Seth Warner were condemned to death in the Riot Act passed by the New York Assembly. Allen, however, became a patriotic celebrity after he took Fort Ticonderoga in May 1775, and for the next year his militia cooperated with those of New York. Tensions remained, however, between Yorkers and Vermont committeemen in Charlotte County. Not loyalism but disputes over rival land claims disrupted these sparsely settled frontier counties as rebellion against Britain loomed. In July 1776, Allen and his supporters began the process of proclaiming Vermont independent of both New York and New Hampshire, adding yet another intriguing subplot to the American Revolution.

Farther down the east bank of the Hudson from Albany County, the inhabitants of Dutchess County were divided. The number of outright loyalists there has probably been exaggerated, but the settlers were generally reluctant to make common cause with Boston; some were Anglicans, other were tenants reacting against patriotic Beekman and Livingston landlords, and still others were inspired by the same anti–New England sentiment common in the northern counties. News of Lexington and Concord, however, led a county convention to draw up a "Revolutionary pledge," which a thousand freeholders signed; significantly, nine hundred others refused to do so, but militant loyalism was not strong enough to do more than irritate the patriotic committeemen who governed the county. Westchester County was more bitterly divided, the influence of the loyalist Frederick Philipse and DeLancey families counterbalanced somewhat by the patriotic Morrises and Van Cortlandts. A respected landlord, Philipse carried many of his tenants with him into loyalism.

On the other side of the Hudson, Orange and Ulster Counties drifted into the patriot camp by early 1775 and remained there. In neither county were there great differences in wealth as most of the inhabitants were freeholders or tenants of small landholders. The politics of both counties had been fairly stable, although the election controversy in 1769 apparently contributed to some loyalist activity in southern Orange County. In Ulster, near the end of 1774, Kingston elected a committee to enforce the Continental Association, and New Windsor set up a "Committee of Observation" in March 1775. Over the winter of 1774–75 various towns in Ulster reportedly held meetings to burn copies of Reverend Samuel Seabury's *Letters of a Westchester Farmer*, an attack on the Continental Congress and the local committees enforcing the Association.

Regarding Long Island, recent studies have shown that the bitter divisions in Queens County reflected less opposing views on imperial matters than enmities related to local religious (Anglican versus Presbyterian) and political feuds among families. The Coldens and Anglican preachers fostered loyalism. In any case, the Continental Congress ordered the New Jersey militia and several companies of regular troops to enter Queens in January 1776 and begin disarming suspected loyalists. Ultimately, Congress published a "Black List" of the disaffected and ordered nineteen of them transported to Philadelphia.

Suffolk County had a few prominent Anglican families who opposed the "deluded abbetors of the rebellious Saints in Boston." Among these were Benjamin Floyd and the Anglican pastor James Lyon. They both figured prominently in a royalist statement signed by residents of Brookhaven in March 1775. Most Suffolk County residents, however, were Congregationalists, settlers from New England, or Presbyterians, and they vastly outnumbered the loyalist Anglicans. Although less active than their New England neighbors in Suffolk County, the sturdy Dutch farmers of Kings County showed their mettle well enough when General William Howe's soldiers landed on Long Island on August 22. Although outnumbered and outclassed in armament, militia from both Suffolk and Kings Counties assembled and fought the British invaders.

On Staten Island (Richmond County), Reverend Richard Charlton and his large Anglican congregation stood by the king. The Anglicans voted down "a few Republican malevolent Spirits" who proposed to send delegates to the New York Provincial Congress. Knowing well they would be welcome there, Major General James Robertson, formerly barracks master of British forces in America, persuaded Howe to begin his invasion of New York by occupying Staten Island on July 2, 1776.

Statehood and Independence

Altogether, New York patriots fashioned a system of more than 150 local extralegal political action committees. From New York City, and later Albany, the committees spread to outlying areas, up and down the Hudson and Mohawk Valleys and across Long Island. After Lexington and Concord, the committees, many of them enforcing the Continental Association and reorganizing county militia, became much more formalized, generally larger in terms of membership, and aggressive in seeking out pockets of loyalism. As governmental power flowed from established local and county governments into the hands of the extralegal committees, the provincial assembly became less important. Dedicated to both liberty and empire, the DeLancey majority would neither oppose nor support the Continental Association. Nor did it interfere with the Committee of Sixty's enforcement of nonimportation.

In fact, the assembly tried to find a middle ground. While ignoring the Continental Congress, the lower house passed a "State of Grievance" denouncing taxation without representation, admiralty courts, and parliamentary legislation from the Currency Act of 1764 to the Coercive Acts of 1774. Petitions were also readied for the king, lords, and commons making the same points. Colden and General Gage both interpreted the assembly's actions as setting itself against the rebellious Continental Congress. Viewing the assembly as obstructive, Isaac Sears and Alexander McDougall decided that a provincial congress should be called to represent the entire colony in the selection of delegates to the Second Continental Congress. A struggle ensued within the Committee of Sixty, but the DeLanceys, who found themselves being pushed toward loyalism despite their fundamental opposition to parliamentary supremacy, could not stop the committee from nominating—and the city from voting overwhelmingly to send—eleven delegates to a provincial convention set for April 20, 1775, on Manhattan.

The Battles of Lexington and Concord on April 19, 1775, meant that America and Great Britain were at war. The reaction in New York City was one of solidarity with suffering Massachusetts. Cargos headed for the British army in Boston were seized and destroyed, and the Sons of Liberty formed themselves into a battalion of over eight hundred men, many of them well armed. The Committee of Sixty was shortly replaced by a Committee of One Hundred, and a Second Provincial Congress was called for May 22, 1775. The Committee of One Hundred contained even fewer DeLancey supporters than the Committee of Sixty; the Livingston–Liberty Boys partnership held sway. A crestfallen James DeLancey took ship for London in May. He would never return.

The militancy of the Liberty Boys led the British troops to leave their barracks in the city and go aboard the *Asia*, the sixty-four-gun warship that sat menacingly in the harbor. But the alliance between the Livingstons and the Sons of Liberty was coming undone. Even as the Liberty Boys took heart because DeLanceyites like John Jay and James Duane had embraced the Continental Association, Sears and Lamb worried that most patrician leaders, whether Livingstons or DeLanceys, were too much bent on reconciliation to stay the course. Robert R. Livingston manifested this mind-set in May 1775: "Every good man wishes that America may remain free: in this I join heartily; at the same time, I do not desire, she should be wholly independent of the mother country." William Smith's prophecy had come true. Although not radical enough for Sears or Lamb, a Whig coalition was emerging in the province, moving reluctantly but steadily toward rebellion. Its core was made up mostly of Livingstons but also drew significantly from moderate Liberty Boys and De-Lancey leaders.

The revolutionary Whigs dominated both the Committee of One Hundred and the Committee of Safety, which served as an executive body while the provincial congress was not in session. Sears recognized, with some disgust, what was happening; he left the province in October, returning only to wreck James Rivington's openly loyalist press the following month. In December, Lamb, who had joined the American expedition against Quebec, was wounded and captured by the British. Even New York City was no longer in the hands of firebrands like Sears and Lamb, but of reluctant revolutionaries and patriotic Whigs, keenly aware of their precarious position.

New York was considered by many contemporaries, and by many historians since, to be a stronghold of Toryism; but the generalization is clearly unfounded. There were centers of royalism in the rural counties, where loyalist leaders drew up declarations of allegiance to the king, but they attracted minimal attention even in supposed Tory strongholds like Westchester and Dutchess Counties. On Long Island, thanks to the efforts of the Coldens, Queens County was said to be belligerently loyalist, though indifferent or neutral perhaps better describes its inhabitants. In October 1775, fearing capture by the rebels, Governor Tryon fled to the *Asia*, from where he tried unsuccessfully to rally the loyalists. In February 1776, Tryon dissolved the assembly and called for elections. Twenty-nine representatives were elected, and only four of them would become loyalists. Thirteen of the Whigs elected would also serve in the Third Provincial Congress, which convened in May. By that time, Tryon had dissolved the assembly one last time.

New York's more radical neighbors regarded the province as pro-British or at least duplicitous. When the Third Provincial Congress, elected in April 1776, hesitated to discuss independence, Connecticut patriots warned New York not "to dally, or be merely neutral." And a Connecticut general remarked on "the suspicious light in which the New York Congress are viewed by the rest of the Continent." In June 1776 an exasperated John Adams wrote, "What is the Reason, that New York is still asleep or dead, in Politics and War? . . . Have they no sense, no Feeling? No sentiment? No Passions? While every other Colony is rapidly advancing, their Motions seem to be rather retrograde."

It should be remembered, however, that by June 1776 New York was facing imminent warfare. The largest flotilla of warships ever seen in America, with more than 30,000 soldiers aboard, anchored threateningly off Sandy Hook. At this supreme moment of crisis, the politics of diversity made it impossible for New Yorkers to reach broad agreement on what should be done. Consensus was more easily achieved in homogenous colonies like Connecticut and Virginia.

But New Yorkers were against parliamentary supremacy, and they were moving toward statehood, thanks to progressively more sophisticated extralegal committee structures. On July 2, 1776, Howe began landing 10,000 troops on Staten Island. The hour of decision was at hand. New Yorkers who would not proclaim their loyalty to the king faced the prospect of losing everything, including their lives.

Republicanism, so distasteful to patricians like Robert Livingston, John Jay, and James Duane, was the only alternative to subservience to the Crown. Hope for compromise was not completely dead, but the tremendous presence of the British army and navy made it much less likely than before. In June 1776 delegates were elected throughout the colony to the Fourth Provincial Congress, which convened at White Plains on July 9. That very same day, the delegates endorsed independence from Britain and proclaimed themselves the Convention of the Representatives of the State of New York. The future of New York—and the American republic—was now in the hands of the gods of war.

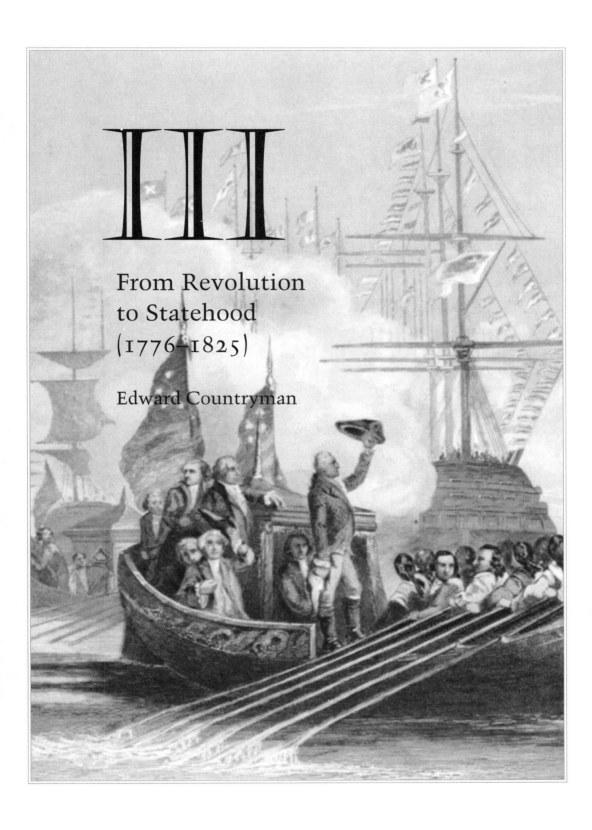

III

From Revolution to Statehood (1776–1825)

Edward Countryman

Chapter 13

"Never a More Total Revolution"

"ELECTED DELEGATES," BEGAN THE "RESPECTFUL ADDRESS" that the "Mechanicks in Union, for the City and County of New York" sent to the Third Provincial Congress. It was May 1776. Colonial institutions had collapsed. Popular committees and the congress itself held power. New York needed a new constitution, and the congress was calling a special election to give its successor the authority to write one. But it had said nothing about how the constitution would take effect. Now the mechanics asserted New Yorkers' "right which God has given them, in common with all men, to . . . accept or reject" any constitution and make it "truly binding." This was no "humble petition," such as they might have presented only a few years in the past. They were making demands, not requests.

These butchers, bakers, and saddle makers, these millers, brewers, and coopers, these carpenters, these shipwrights, and these bricklayers were wrestling with the central political problem of the American Revolution: how a people can be their own sovereigns. A new congress was elected not long afterward. At independence it renamed itself the "Convention of the People." But popular ratification never happened. The congress/convention first met in New York City. During the summer of 1776 everyone there watched helplessly as the British sailed into the harbor, under the joint command of the Howe brothers, Admiral Lord Richard and General Sir William. Staten Island fell, then Long Island, followed by the city itself, upper Manhattan, and lower Westchester County. All would remain in British control until 1783. But though the enemy was overwhelming, George Washington saved the American army by a series of superb retreats. Meanwhile the convention drew ever back. It finally stopped in Kingston, where in April 1777 it simply proclaimed that a new constitution was in effect.

Ending one order and beginning another; political outsiders demanding a say in how their world would be run; invasion, destruction, flight, confusion: these are among the core themes of New York's American Revolution. As early as May 1775, one correspondent wrote to England that there was "never a more total revolution" than in New York. When the convention finished its work, New York was broken. The Southern District was in British hands. For the prosperous loyalist farmers of Richmond, Kings, Queens, and Nassau Counties, that posed no problem. In the patriot zone loyalists did not flee, not, at least, at first. They stayed and resisted, plaguing Westchester, Dutchess, and Albany Counties with draft refusal, militia unreliability, harboring of spies, and banditry. In the Mohawk Valley civil war swirled both Iroquois and white people into a vortex of violence and destruction. In the far northeast the counties called Cumberland and Gloucester turned themselves into the state of Vermont.

Nobody found it easy. Robert R. Livingston, Jr., became "sick of politics and power" and would not "give one scene of Shakespeare for a 1000 Harringtons, Lockes, Sidneys, and Adams to boot." About the same time, very ordinary farmers in western Albany County retreated to the Helderbergh escarpment to work out their own course. One, John Commons, put the question, telling Congress's supporters to leave the meeting and the king's to stay. But he himself "did not know who was right."

To unravel this tangle we must follow three separate threads. One traces different sorts of people through the Revolutionary crisis. The second leads through the war's course. The third shows certain notable white men trying to organize political power in the new republican order. One way or another the Revolution affected everyone in New York, and everyone in New York affected it. But those ways differed enormously.

A Revolution for All New Yorkers

The mechanics' "respectful address" to the Third Provincial Congress grew out of years of revolutionary politics in which their own interests as well as the Grand Cause were at stake. As early as December 1767, "a Tradesman" was asking the *New-York Journal* why coverage of "our distressed situation" had fallen off: "Is Money grown more plentiful? Have our Tradesmen full employment? Are we more frugal? Is Grain cheaper? Are our Importations Less?" Three years later "Brutus" addressed the issue of imports again, as Parliament was repealing all but one of its Townshend duties on imported goods. Colonials had responded to the taxes with nonimportation from Britain. Now merchants wanted to resume trade, maintaining that the decision was theirs to make. But Americans who produced competing goods had benefited rather than suffered from the boycott.

Brutus, who probably was the skilled toolmaker John Lamb, one of the leaders of the Sons of Liberty, thought nothing was "more flagrantly wrong than the assertion . . . that the Mechanics have no right to give their Sentiments." By 1773 Lamb and his fellow artisans were meeting "at Beer Houses . . . to concert measures." Then they bought a meeting place of their own, naming it Mechanics' Hall. In 1774 the aristocratic Gouverneur Morris watched such men elect the city's first revolutionary committee: "The mob begin to think and to reason," he wrote to a friend. "Poor Reptiles! With them it is a vernal morning [but] 'ere noon they will bite." Morris got it wrong. The artisans—independent craftsmen who owned their own shops together with journeymen and apprentices—had been thinking and reasoning throughout the crisis. Now they knew who they were in the Revolution. They knew what they wanted from it too.

The story is different for farmers. As already noted, many prosperous freeholders in the southernmost counties were indifferent to the Revolution. The anguished Helderbergh debaters were not prosperous or freeholders; they were hill-farming tenants on the great manor called Rensselaerswyck. There is a generalization that tenants chose the side their landlord opposed. The generalization has its truth, as patriot landlords like the Van Rensselaers and Livingstons and loyalists like Beverly Robinson learned. But Frederick Philipse, third lord of the Westchester manor of Philipsburgh, had protected his tenants and respected their customs. So had Sir William Johnson at "Kingsborough," in the Mohawk Valley. Both Philipse and Johnson tenants joined their landlords, on the Crown's side. In the west-bank Hudson Valley counties of Orange and Ulster there were no great estates. Popular loyalism appeared there, but only in pockets.

The people who created Vermont were New Englanders, coming mostly from Connecticut, like their leader and self-appointed spokesman Ethan Allen. Their legal titles to the land they claimed were weak, derived from grants that New Hampshire had made prior to 1764, when the Privy Council in London decided the Green Mountains belonged to New York. Doubtful titles or not, they wanted nothing to do with either New York's politics or its great estates and tenantry. Vermont's separate revolution saw little overt loyalism, and its people contributed mightily to the American cause. But a point did come when its leaders flirted with the British authorities in Montreal, despairing of American recognition for what New York insisted was only a "pretended state."

By 1775 the six Iroquois nations were at the center of a huge web of diplomacy, war, and trade. "Iroquoia"—their "ambiguous empire"—stretched from the upper Mohawk Valley, across the Finger Lakes, the Lake Ontario Plain, and the central Southern Tier, to the lands of the Seneca west of the Genesee River. Its capital was Onondaga (now Syracuse), where the Iroquois League's council fire burned. Iroquois and other Indians dealt with European power most often at Johnson Hall, Sir William Johnson's mansion on his Kingsborough estate. Johnson had won both his baronetcy and his fortune by serving Britain as Indian

"Johnson Hall" (oil on canvas, 1903). By Edward Lamson Henry. Albany Institute of History and Art.

superintendent for the northern colonies. He meant Kingsborough to be a quasi-feudal buffer between Iroquois and whites. His vision fitted both Iroquois needs and Britain's policy of keeping Indians and settlers apart, as set forth in the Proclamation Line of 1763. When Sir William died in 1774, his son Sir John Johnson succeeded him as baronet and his nephew Colonel Guy Johnson as superintendent. Together they expected to keep Sir William's vision alive. They did not expect either colonial independence, or the destruction of their world.

The Iroquois had large grievances. In 1714 war had forced the Tuscaroras out of their Carolina home to a New York refuge as the sixth nation. The Mohawks—"keepers of the eastern gate"—remembered losing the 800,000-acre Kayaderosseras Patent. In 1763 the Senecas—"keepers of the western gate"—had joined the multitribe anti-English war called the Conspiracy of Pontiac. In 1774 their chief Serihowane complained to Sir William about violations of the Proclamation line: "Brother . . . your people are ungovernable, . . . more so than ours. . . . Brother . . . your People entirely disregard, and despise the settlement agreed upon by their Superiors and us. . . . But we hope . . . that you will restrain your people . . . and make them lay aside their ill designs, and encroachments." As Serihowane spoke, Virginia and Pennsylvania were encroaching on the upper Ohio Valley and challenging Iroquois dominion over client Delawares, Mingos, and Shawnees. Whoever won, there would be land-grabbing investment companies, and the Iroquois knew it. Finally, Indians had their own stance toward the Quebec Act of 1774. Whites in the thirteen colonies regarded the Quebec Act as a major grievance, not only for its recognition of the Catholic faith of the conquered *habitants*, but also because it gave control of western lands to the former French province. To Indians, however, the act would be a safeguard to their control of their own land.

When the Revolution broke, black people formed a fifth of New Yorkers. Virtually all were slaves. They labored for artisans, lawyers, clergymen, and merchants in the towns. They worked for great landlords and for middling farmers on Long Island, in the Hudson Valley, and along the Mohawk River all the way to Johnson Hall. They did a major part of New York City's and Albany's dirtiest work. They remembered that in 1712 and again in 1741 whites had hanged and burned alive slaves who dared to rebel.

Even in 1776 most white New Yorkers did not see that the slavery all around them mocked their own claims to liberty. When Revolutionary leaders wanted to disavow a riot, they attributed it to "Negroes and boys." As the old order crumbled in 1775 and 1776, Revolutionary committees ordered corporal punishment for slaves found outside at night. The Revolution was to be a white person's struggle. Nonetheless, the Revolution made a difference to New York's black people, and they made a difference to it. Ultimately it ended slavery itself and gave them the chance to form a distinctive free community. But the difference came slowly and with great difficulty. Many black New Yorkers did rally to the British, who offered the king's freedom to slaves who would take up arms against rebel masters. Others gained American freedom by serving in the rebel army. But not until 1799 did New York begin to demolish the institution of slavery.

Among artisans and merchants, landlords and farmers, loyalists and patriots, Indians and slaves, Dutch and English, half the population was female. Unlike urban workers, many tenant farmers, Indians, and slaves, women did not form a distinct, self-conscious group on the Revolution's eve. The lines of class, race, ethnicity, and region cut too deep and the loyalties those lines circumscribed were too strong. During the crisis between the colonies and Britain, American women did gather as "Daughters of Liberty," but they did so mostly under male sponsorship. With independence, patriot women began going further. Some "commenced perfect statesmen" and began to "feel nationly." But male patriots used the image of the self-centered foolish girl to condemn anyone who put personal comfort ahead of patriotic sacrifice.

At the war's end a would-be wit wrote in the *New-York Gazetteer* of an imagined "female legislature" whose members debated "bewitching kisses . . . pouting lips . . . and . . . the Currency of Rapture." He revealed more about his own anxieties than about what New York women were thinking. But the Revolution did mark a major break in the ways the two sexes related to each other. Before it, male and female were simply "the distinctions of nature" that were not to be challenged. By the Revolution's end, what we now call gender was a

subject that women and men alike discussed seriously, and women were starting to act in society on their own.

War in the South, the North, and the West

No state experienced the Revolutionary War with greater ferocity or over a
longer period than New York. The first armed conflict came on May 10, 1775,
when Green Mountain Boys under Ethan Allen and Benedict Arnold took Fort
Ticonderoga. Allen had been condemned to death by name in colonial New
York's "Bloody Act" of 1774 for his leadership of the Vermont insurgency. Now
he accepted a commission from the provincial congress. The Green Mountain
Boys joined the Revolutionary militia. During 1776 and 1777 New York provided the stage for two of the war's main military dramas. The first was the
conquest of the Southern District. The second was the march of one army into
it from the north while another invaded from the west.

When the British withdrew from besieged Boston to Halifax in March 1776,
New York City was their next objective. By June they were ready to move, and
32,000 fresh, well-equipped, and well-trained soldiers, including hired German
"Hessians," embarked by sea to capture the city. As their vessels entered the
Narrows early in July, they began to land on Staten Island. Clearly, they would
not remain there. To face them George Washington had roughly 28,000 troops.
They were ill trained and ill equipped, and only 19,000 were fit for duty. As the
British fleet and forces grew, 12,000 Americans placed themselves along what is
now Brooklyn Heights, Park Slope, and Bay Ridge. The British crossed the Narrows to Brooklyn on August 26, quickly realized that the inexperienced Americans had not protected their left flank near the site of Prospect Park, rounded it
capturing thousands of rebel troops, and penned seven thousand more into
Brooklyn Heights. Had they moved even part of their fleet into the East River to
complete the encirclement, the whole American army would have been lost.
Quite possibly the Revolution would have been defeated.

But the British fleet held back and, with a foggy night to conceal them and
a fleet of New England fishing boats to carry them, the remaining Americans
escaped across the East River to Manhattan. It was one of George Washington's
finest moments in command. Instead of pressing their advantage, the British
proposed a peace conference, which duly was held on Staten Island and which
duly failed. Not until September 15 did they move again. Washington did not
try to defend the city, and as the Americans retreated a fire consumed about
one-sixth of its buildings. The retreating Revolutionaries may or may not have
set the blaze.

American victory in a skirmish on Harlem Heights on September 16
boosted morale, but Manhattan Island could not be held. The retreat continued

into Westchester as far as White Plains, where the two main armies finally met on October 28. The British won the day. But they took heavy losses, and the Americans successfully crossed the Hudson into New Jersey. Almost three thousand Americans were left marooned at an upper Manhattan fort named in Washington's honor. They surrendered on November 16.

New York City became British headquarters. With the Royal Navy controlling the harbor, there could be no attempt at recapture. The city offered a refuge for loyalists and a base for privateering. Its only drawback was that its British-controlled hinterland of Staten Island, Long Island, northern Manhattan, and lower Westchester was too small to provide it with enough food or firewood. Supplies had to cross the American lines illegally or come with difficulty and expense by sea. By the war's end every tree on Manhattan had been cut for fuel. Until the end, skirmishers and guerrillas ("cowboys" and "skinners") raided back and forth across Long Island Sound and along the front that bisected Westchester County.

Revolutionaries sensationalized the death of Jane McCrea in 1777 to rally resistance against General Burgoyne's army, though McCrea herself was a loyalist. Copy after John Vanderlyn (ca. 1835). New York State Historical Association, Cooperstown, N.Y.

The second great drama was the Saratoga crisis, in the late summer and autumn of 1777. The British plan was simple. Sir William Howe would send one column up the Hudson from New York City. General John Burgoyne would lead another south from Montreal through the Champlain Valley. Colonel Barry St. Leger would descend the Mohawk with a third, from Oswego. The three would converge at Albany.

The plan's execution was abysmal. Howe simply did not do his part, striking instead at Philadelphia with a sea-borne expedition through Chesapeake Bay. Perhaps he was jealous that the plan was Burgoyne's idea. Perhaps, as some historians have speculated, he did not really want to win. Sir Henry Clinton did lead a small force upriver to Kingston in October. The expedition burned the town and then turned back.

Burgoyne started southward in mid-June. Perhaps he did not want to win either. As a member of Parliament he did take the American side during the lat-

This modern photograph shows Fort Ticonderoga's strategic position on the portage between Lake Champlain and Lake George. New York State Department of Economic Development.

ter years of the war. Whatever his inner feelings, his British and German regulars and Indian and Canadian allies took Fort Ticonderoga on July 5 without a fight, after they placed a few cannon above it on undefended Mount Defiance. Burdened both by heavy baggage and by their own inertia, however, they failed to capture the fleeing American garrison, which destroyed crops, scattered cattle, and blocked the road that led southward with fallen trees. The British and their allies took nearly a month to get from Ticonderoga on lower Lake Champlain to Fort Edward on the upper reaches of the Hudson River. The distance is not vast.

When Burgoyne's troops reached Fort Edward they were hungry. Vermont and New Hampshire militia defeated a force of Hessians that Burgoyne sent to capture supplies at Bennington. The main force continued south, reaching old Saratoga (Schuylerville) in mid-September. There they encountered a rapidly swelling American army of regular troops and militiamen. It was led by Major General Horatio Gates, who had replaced Albany's Philip Schuyler as the American commander. Gates was a former British officer who had begun his career in the very same regiment as Burgoyne, at almost the same time. The Americans pinned the British down, and Burgoyne surrendered to his former comrade on October 17. Gates was delighted that they had met again. Burgoyne was not, even though he may have sympathized with the American cause.

Even before Saratoga, St. Leger's expedition from Oswego had foundered. It drew heavily on Americans for membership, including loyalists under Sir John Johnson and Indians behind the Mohawk Thayendanagea (Joseph Brant). The total force numbered around 1,700. They besieged Fort Stanwix (Rome), which was held by a much smaller group of Americans. On August 6 they fought American militia under Nicholas Herkimer at Oriskany in a terrible battle of neighbors. Herkimer was among the many killed. Technically the British won, since they held the field. But St. Leger gave the whole venture up when Benedict Arnold came west with a relief force detached from the main army that was waiting for Burgoyne. With the western threat ended, Arnold hurried east again.

After 1777 eastern New York saw only two significant military developments. On July 16, 1779, an American force led by Anthony Wayne captured a strong British emplacement at Stony Point, on the lower Hudson. Strategically it meant little, but it did boost morale. In September 1780 a frustrated and self-pitying Benedict Arnold tried to hand West Point over to the British. At the same time, redcoats moved into Fort Ticonderoga, which had stood vacant since Burgoyne's defeat. Arnold's treason and the reoccupation may have been linked, setting up another campaign along the Hudson-Champlain corridor. But by this time the main theater had shifted to the Carolinas. When Arnold's plot failed, Britain gained a talented general who was also a deeply flawed man. Their liaison officer, Major John André, was captured, tried for spying, and executed. That balanced the execution in 1776 of Washington's spy Nathan Hale, in New York City. Each man's brave death turned him into a figure of legend.

Though pressure eased in eastern New York after 1777, it remained high in the west, where the Revolution became a drawn-out civil war. The issues included both the Iroquois nations' future on their own lands and the social order among whites.

During the winter of 1774–75 a few Mohawk Valley settlers began gathering secretly as a committee of correspondence. They came into the open after Lexington and Concord in April 1775. The committeemen were patriots and opponents of the Johnsons; they were also hungry for Johnson and Iroquois land. Sir William's heirs understood the challenge. In May, Johnson "dependents" invaded a Revolutionary meeting and "their Number being so Large, and the people unarmed, struck Terror into most of them." In June, Sir John himself horsewhipped a candidate for a patriot militia captaincy who argued back after a rebuke.

The following month the county sheriff arrested a rebel named John Fonda. Fonda's friends surrounded Johnson Hall, which was fortified with light artillery, and Johnson supporters defended it. The patriots sent to Albany for heavier weapons than their own muskets. The committee there arranged a truce instead. In the autumn Sir John and his followers fled west, establishing a base at Niagara. Many, though not all, of the Iroquois rallied to them.

St. Leger's expedition in 1777 provided the first test for the Iroquois/loyalist forces. The following year Iroquois and loyalist raiders destroyed Cobleskill, Andrustown, German Flats, Unadilla, and Cherry Valley. What they did was not mindless savagery. The Indians were defending their way of life. The loyalists were defending their vision of white and perhaps Indian society. In the summer of 1779 Generals John Sullivan and James Clinton led a major American expedition westward. Meeting almost no resistance, they ruined Iroquois towns and crops as far as the Genesee River. Worse for the Indians, the soldiers saw the richness of the Iroquois domain. Raiding continued both ways until the war ended. By one estimate two thousand women were widowed, seven hundred buildings burned, twelve thousand farms abandoned, and hundreds of thousands of bushels of grain destroyed. The Johnsons and their most prominent supporters were exiled. The Iroquois confederacy fell apart, and the six separate nations nearly perished as well. Saving themselves from what the Revolution inflicted upon them proved immensely difficult.

The Free State of New York

When they sent their "Respectful Address" to the provincial congress in May 1776, New York City artisans believed that a referendum could decide the new distribution of power. When the state constitution was proclaimed eleven months later, a referendum was impossible. The Southern District was controlled by the British. The patriot zone was torn asunder. Vermont was independent. There was great danger that the remaining rebel area might fall as well. The street-leader-turned-general Alexander McDougall worried that in an open vote the Revolution's enemies might "get a representation of the majority of the State and make a surrender of our rights."

War, destruction, dislocation, exile, enmity, flight, danger, and fear: these formed New York's matrix as it became a republic. Debate covered the whole range of Revolutionary political thought. "Spartanus" wanted to form "our government . . . as if we had never had any form of government before," with a single-house legislature, annual elections, and a weak "president" to administer the state's business. That was roughly what Pennsylvania did adopt. An "Independent Whig" thought the old structure good enough. Another writer wanted to borrow the existing charter of Connecticut. One proposal sought a £10,000 qualification and life membership for the upper house and a governorship with all the powers of its colonial predecessors, including an absolute legislative veto.

The real business of drafting did not get underway until late in 1776. By then public debate was a luxury and most of the work was done by John Jay, with the cooperation and support of Robert R. Livingston, Gouverneur Morris, and James Duane. Livingston expressed their strategy. They would swim "with a stream which it is impossible to stem" and yield "to the torrent" in order "to direct its course."

These men abhorred Pennsylvania's extreme democracy. Instead of a weak president, their state would have a governor, popularly elected for a three-year term by property holders worth at least £100. The same electorate would choose a state Senate whose members would serve overlapping four-year terms. Adult male freeholders worth at least £20, rentholders who paid 40s., and "freemen" of New York City and Albany would choose a whole new Assembly every year. Sitting as a "Council of Revision," the governor, the chancellor, and the supreme court justices could veto proposed laws, though the legislature could override them by a two-thirds vote. The governor would share patronage with four senators in a "Council of Appointment."

The new constitution was not democratic. But neither was it reactionary, like the "fortress" of high property requirements for voting and office and of infrequent elections that Maryland's frightened elite built around itself at the same time. Jay and the rest of the "council of conspiracy" (as their associate William Duer called them) realized their limits. "Another turn of the winch," wrote Jay, "would have cracked the cord." The constitution of 1777 proved popular, and it did not become a subject for debate until decades later. The men who wrote it were sure that their own sort would run the state. Jay did become chief justice and Livingston chancellor. Philip Schuyler, a major general, a Van Rensselaer in-law, and an Albany County landlord, was their man for governor, and Jay looked forward to calling him "your excellency." Schuyler himself expected that "chuse who they will," he would "command them all."

But Philip Schuyler never governed New York. Instead the office went to George Clinton of Ulster County, who held it continuously until Jay succeeded him in 1795. Clinton was no upstart. A former student in the prestigious law office of William Smith, Jr., he had served in the colonial assembly and won brigadier general's rank in the Continental Army. But now Smith laughed at the very idea of his one-time clerk becoming "George the Governor." To Schuyler, Clinton's "family and connections" did "not entitle him to so distinguished a predominance." Revolutionary New York's democratization did not come with institutional change, as happened in Pennsylvania. Nor, when he took office, did Clinton intend to overthrow the old elite. But a permanent change was underway, and Clinton did emerge as both its leader and its symbol.

Chapter 14

"The Rights of Mankind"

BETWEEN GEORGE CLINTON'S ELECTION AS GOVERNOR OF New York in 1777 and Thomas Jefferson's as president of the United States in 1800, New York's public life changed dramatically. A partisan culture took shape, replacing the family politics of the colonial epoch with a strange new hybrid. In one sense the new politics meant a direct, responsive relationship between rulers and the people they governed. This manifested itself most visibly between the late 1770s and the mid-1780s, as "the people" (meaning, of course, the male electorate) and the legislature sought to define what New York's revolution would mean. In another sense, it was about high principle and the nation's future, most discernibly during the struggle over the federal Constitution. The new politics meant "the Art of Hook and Snivey," or trickery and deceit, as political leaders "made interest" with one another in order to win office. The role that Aaron Burr and Alexander Hamilton took during the messy election of 1800 presented that "art" in its most developed form. At its vague borders, state politics also meant the possibility that people who had been excluded from public life might find their own voices and win a share of power.

George Clinton was a plain man and a natural republican. In the colonial assembly he once responded to an outrageous claim of power by saying that the public would "judge of the justice of it." His core voters in 1777 were plain soldiers, who knew both his style as a general and Schuyler's, and preferred his. By the mid-1780s his support among urban workingmen, independent farmers from counties like his own Ulster, and tenants on the great estates had grown so strong that he faced little challenge for reelection. But his coalition was not stable. Those groups did not blindly adhere to a single "Clintonian" perspective. Each had its own problems and its own interests.

Many men like George Clinton began to come to power, especially in the state legislature. Some were New York City dwellers who had gone into exile rather than submit to the British conquest. They were appointed to their seats in the Assembly and the Senate rather than elected, until the British withdrew in 1783. Then they threw themselves into urban politics. Among them were merchants, like the old street radicals Isaac Sears and Alexander McDougall, and artisans like John Lamb and the candle maker Isaac Stoutenburgh. There were self-taught lawyers like Albany's Abraham Yates, and farmers from the valleys of the Hudson and the Mohawk. Almost all these men had served political apprenticeships in local and county office and on the popular committees of the independence crisis. But in colonial New York none of them could have reached the level they now occupied.

One reason for their emergence was simply that the new institutions were larger than the old. The provincial council of twelve appointed members gave way to a state Senate of twenty-four, elected for four-year terms. The Assembly expanded from twenty-seven seats to seventy. Before independence many years could elapse between assembly elections. After it they became annual. The old order's patchwork of seats for counties, for some manors, and for some towns gave way to rough proportional representation for counties alone, with regular censuses to change the distribution as population shifted. Competition ran high. There were elections during the 1780s when a county did not carry a single assembly member over from one session to the next.

When the new legislature gathered for the first time at Kingston on September 10, 1777, its members had no immediate program beyond the survival of the state and of themselves. Within a month, Sir Henry Clinton's feint up the river scattered them. They did not meet again until 1778. At the local and county levels committees continued to hold power, despite the state constitution's dismissal of these bodies as "temporary expedients, to exist no longer than the grievances of the people should remain without redress." Those committees did not actually dissolve until 1778, and they formed again in 1779 as a crisis seemed about to overwhelm the constitutional government. Achieving stability took time.

The War and the People

At the state's beginning, there was the war. Through the late 1770s and the early 1780s war issues determined the public agenda. The new government needed to raise supplies for its own troops and the Continental line, deal with loyalism, and cope with the enormous economic disruption that the war brought.

Loyalists presented more serious problems in New York than in any other state. Even before independence the Third Provincial Congress named a committee on "intestine enemies." In February 1778 the newly convened legislature created "Commissioners for Detecting and Defeating Conspiracies." At first the official emphasis was on converting loyalists if possible and controlling them when necessary, though already really active Tories found themselves harassed, imprisoned, and exiled. When the "Hickey Plot" to kidnap Washington was discovered in July 1776, its participants were arrested at midnight. "Young Mr. Livingston" persuaded one to talk by advising him to prepare to die. Early in 1779 the Council of Revision successfully vetoed a Confiscation Act.

But almost from the start the economy was out of control. Supplies ran out because of the war's demands, hoarding, and absolute shortages. Like continental dollars, the state's paper money inflated until by 1779 it was almost worthless. As with loyalism, the legislature tried at first only to keep matters in hand. To men at the center there seemed only one solution. Gouverneur Morris put it to Clinton in February 1779: "For God's sake tax."

To "the subjects of this state" (as official proclamations called them) neither controlling the loyalists nor taxing the economy into a state of soundness seemed enough. Sporadic uprisings in 1777 and 1778 tried to deal with both problems directly. Some were led by women. In 1779 new popular committees appeared, part of a larger revival that began in Philadelphia and swept through all the northern states. Crowds and committeemen harassed both loyalists and "hoarders" who concealed needed supplies. They sought out and distributed those supplies, and they set "just" prices for work and for goods.

It was a familiar pattern that was known all over America and over England and continental Europe as well. In time of trouble small communities could close out the world and protect themselves. Historians have tried to describe the pattern with such terms as "moral economy of the crowd" (to suggest that uprisings were not mindless rebellions of the belly) and "corporatism" (to indicate a vision of the good of the whole). But this crisis was different. It marked the birth pangs of an American national economy. The Revolution was at stake, for if every small community closed off its commerce and served only its own needs the army would starve and collapse. Larger issues than local supplies were at stake, and larger measures than price controls and embargoes were needed.

At first Clinton shared the position of men like Jay and Morris. In 1778 he sought "the approbation of the Senate" for a strong tax bill. But, he told Morris, "this I despair of." He voted in the Council of Revision to veto the first confiscation bill. As late as 1782 Alexander Hamilton gave him credit for "the vigorous execution of some necessary laws that bore hard upon the people."

But when a new session of the legislature convened in the autumn of 1779, the governor realized that its members would ignore the "sense that your constituents loudly express" at both their own and the government's peril. The leg-

When British troops withdrew from New York on November 25, 1783, they nailed the Union Jack to a flagpole at the Battery and greased the pole. Young John Van Arsdale became a hero when he climbed the pole and replaced the British flag with the Stars and Stripes. This poster marked New York's celebration of the centennial of Evacuation Day.

New York State Historical Association, Cooperstown, N.Y.

islators did listen and they responded. They adopted an ungainly mode of taxing according to "circumstances and abilities . . . collectively considered" which allowed popularly elected assessors to charge what they believed a person could pay. They changed the state's loyalist policy from control to punishment, beginning with another confiscation bill which won Clinton's support and became law. The legislature passed enough Tory laws to fill a good-sized volume, some of them enacted after the treaty of peace supposedly put an end to persecution. In 1784 a British critic of the now-successful Revolution published just such a volume in London with the goal of demonstrating that New York was defying the treaty.

Among the laws that the book included was the "Citation Act" of 1782, which protected patriot debtors against loyalist and British creditors. The Trespass Act of 1783 allowed patriots who fled the Southern District to bring damage suits against persons who used their property during the occupation. Loyalists were declared "outside the protection of the laws." The legislature could do little about inflation and supplies: that was a national problem. But popular uprisings gradually ceased. The revived committees dissolved by the end of 1779. In the legislature, partisanship began to appear around these two issues, the loyalists and the economy, as legislators who voted together on the one subject found themselves voting together on the other as well.

"The Rulers of This State"

Between 1779 and the mid-1780s men like Clinton—the artisans' and farmers' representatives who found their own political careers in the Revolution—took control of the state. Within the legislature they moved ever closer to one another, until a member's vote on one issue was likely to predict both who was voting with him and how he would vote on many others. Twice, in 1784 and 1786, these men rejected attempts to give the Confederation Congress a taxing power on imports. To one of them, the former shoemaker-turned-lawyer Abraham Yates of Albany, yielding the power to tax would have cost the state its "precious jewel, sovereignty."

Following Clinton's advice, state legislators proved responsive to what constituents said. Though Hamilton once called the legislators "the rulers of this state," their own self-image was closer to "elected delegates." The very word "subject" disappeared in official parlance. The legislators were unremittingly hostile to loyalists, even after the peace treaty required the states to end all persecution. Their sense of economics was summed up in the way they continued to tax by "circumstances and abilities." They wanted the state, not Congress, to control relations with Indians, and they did not mean the Indians well.

Strictly speaking, these men did not become a "party." Modern historians have called them "Clintonians," but until the great debate of 1787–88 about the federal Constitution they avoided public labels. Clinton did not offer "programs" to the legislature, as a modern governor might. Voting in the seventh session of the legislature in 1784, the first in which the downstate members were actually elected, showed downstate assemblymen with an artisan electorate taking a different stance on many issues from upstaters who had been elected by farmers. Each group was thinking for itself. Nonetheless, people were thinking politically, in terms of the social and regional groups to which they belonged. They were learning to forge public alliances. A partisan culture that accepted the fact of political division was emerging.

This emerging partisan stance proved popular with voters. It ensured Clinton's unopposed reelection in 1780 and 1786 and his victory in contested elections in 1783, 1789, and 1792. But it did not please the Philip Schuylers, John Jays, James Duanes, and Robert R. Livingstons of New York State. These men, and the social type they represented, lost their state-level power by the early 1780s. Schuyler retreated into petulant anger. Jay went first to Congress, where he presided for a time, and then to Spain as American minister. Livingston became Congress's secretary for foreign relations. Among them Duane found himself most able to take a stand, when the Council of Appointment made him mayor of New York City upon the British departure. Presiding in the mayor's court, Duane heard the important lawsuit that the patriot widow Elizabeth Rutgers brought in 1784 against the loyalist Joshua Waddington under the Trespass Act. Waddington had occupied and used her property under the authority of the British commander in chief for one period and the authority of a civilian commissary general for another. The mayor's decision denied Rutgers's claim for the period when Waddington had acted under military authority but allowed it for the time under the

Alexander Hamilton (1804). By William Rollinson, after a painting by Archibald Robertson. New York State Historical Association, Cooperstown, N.Y.

commissary. By also finding that the legislature did not intend to abrogate the peace treaty, the mayor brought an effective end to patriot use of the Trespass Act.

It fell to Alexander Hamilton, West Indies migrant, Washington's wartime aide-de-camp, lawyer, and Schuyler's son-in-law, to work out an alternative to Clinton's popular party and to begin mobilizing people around what he stood for. Hamilton was a man of both intelligence and practicality. Privately he thought in terms of class and economics. The taxation system was "evil" and "radically vicious." The "safety of all those who have anything to lose" required the "principal people" to unite. At the war's end the most he could say for Clinton was that he was a "man of integrity." One legislator tried "to do well whenever he can hit upon what is right"; most of the rest were crude demagogues. The public Hamilton was more circumspect. In his 1784 "Letters from Phocion" he argued for the rights of former loyalists under the terms of the Treaty of Paris, taking the moral high ground of national honor and the meaning of American liberty.

The eighth legislative session, in 1784 and 1785, marked the high point of postwar political disputes. By this time, Hamilton's project of uniting men of property was beginning to work, particularly in Albany County. Its state senator, Abraham Yates, deserved "to be pensioned by the British" for his foolish ideas. Assemblymen Matthew Adgate and Jacob Ford were "New England adventurers . . . who made tools of the Yates and their Associates." Hamilton wrote to landlords like the Livingstons and Van Rensselaers about the "truly alarming" quality of the legislature. They responded so effectively that all ten Albany County assemblymen were replaced in the election of 1785, between the eighth session and the ninth.

By the mid-1780s only one great issue did not fit within the new politics: slavery. Virtually unquestioned by whites in the colonial period, the institution now was under attack from many quarters, including slaves themselves. At the end of 1783 many sailed to freedom with the departing British fleet. They found it in Canada, the West Indies, Britain, and Sierra Leone. Others ended their slavery by fighting on the American side. All around New York slavery was starting to break up. Vermont abolished it entirely when it declared its independence in 1777, making itself the first place in the western world where being black meant automatically that a person was free. Gradual abolition began in Pennsylvania in 1780. Slavery ended entirely in Massachusetts by 1783. White New Yorkers formed a manumission society in 1784, and friends of the society brought a bill to end slavery to the highly partisan eighth legislative session.

The way that people lined up on slavery cut across all other issues. Alexander Hamilton thought slavery was unqualifiedly evil, freed his own slaves, and joined the manumission society. Governor Clinton joined it too. John Jay became the society's president. Writing in 1785, an artisan-politician named Hugh Hughes called slavery "cruelty in the extreme" and the country's "severest reproach." But most of the people who owned the state's 19,000 slaves wanted to keep them. Some were rich landlords; some were townspeople; many were small farmers, especially in George Clinton's home base of Orange and Ulster Counties. Though the governor joined the manumission society, it was only a gesture. He did little more.

Manumission was the one major issue in the eighth Assembly whose pattern of votes did not fit with the large alignment that was polarizing around Clinton and Hamilton. The bill passed after a fierce and prolonged debate, with vote after vote in both the Assembly and the Senate. Under its terms slavery slowly would end, but the freed people would not gain legal or political equality with whites. They would be denied the rights to vote, to hold public office, and to be legal witnesses. Interracial marriage would be illegal. The Council of Revision vetoed the bill, saying that it did so because of the disabilities that the bill imposed on the people it would free. Not until 1799 did New York actually pass its law for gradual emancipation, and not until 1827 would its last slaves be freed.

Conservative New York Nationalism

By 1785 Hamilton and men like him had a larger change in mind. They won the Assembly election that year in crucial Albany County. But George Clinton was still governor. In 1783 he defeated both Philip Schuyler and Dutchess County politician Ephraim Paine, which, one wit wrote, "is no small matter, when you consider that two to one is odds, even at football." In 1786 no one dared to run against him. From the conservatives' perspective, there needed to be a permanent solution, and national politics offered the route to it. All over the country, people were coming to regard what was happening in the states as disastrous. Looking at Virginia, Thomas Jefferson and James Madison thought so just as strongly as Hamilton did when he looked at New York. It was not just that there were too many men with gnarled hands and muddy boots and unlettered minds in the legislatures. It was also what they did. States did not pay their bills and debts. They passed laws to protect debtors. New York, especially, flouted the peace treaty by its continued persecution of loyalists. To John Jay it went against its own best interests too: "What does it signify where . . . these People are buried? I would rather see the Sweat of their Brows fertilize our Fields than those of our Neighbours." Twice New York blocked Congress's attempt to gain an independent revenue. On the second occasion Governor Clinton did not think the issue important enough to call a special legislative session.

Hamilton was one of the driving forces behind the movement that led to the Philadelphia Convention of 1787, called to propose amendments to the moribund Articles of Confederation. Recognizing both the role he had played thus far and his own talents, the legislature chose him as one of New York's delegates. But it also sent Albany County's Robert Yates and John Lansing. Neither had much in common with Hamilton.

New York's constitution of 1777, with its strong governorship and Senate, provided something of a model for the United States Constitution, with its presidency and strong Senate. But within the convention, the state had little impact. Gouverneur Morris did play a major role as chairman of the Committee of Detail, which produced the final draft of the Constitution. But he was representing Pennsylvania rather than his native state. Yates and Lansing did little more than observe, and both left early. Hamilton made one major speech, astonishing the delegates with his own plan for a government modeled on Britain's parliamentary monarchy, including a life presidency that would amount to an elective kingship. Then he left too, returning only at the very end after Washington himself pleaded that he come back. But New York became one of the most crucial states in the campaign for ratification.

The state's importance was several-fold. One reason is that the Constitution would create an American common market that would transcend local interests for the sake of a national economy. New York harbor was the best port in the country, and it would be crucial to that market's success. Then, too, many of the Constitution's supporters thought that New York was the home of some of the most pernicious Confederation-era politics. More than any other except Rhode Island's, they thought, its legislature had to be stopped. A third reason was that in New York the Constitution's opponents found one of their own best chances to thwart the whole process of ratification.

Governor Clinton and the legislature were slow to call a ratifying convention, thinking, perhaps, that enough other states would reject the Constitution to render one unnecessary. The convention did not assemble until June 1788. That long delay gave Hamilton, Jay, and James Madison the chance to write their eighty-five *Federalist* essays. Hastily produced and addressed only to New York's "considerate People," these rank among the great pieces of republican political analysis and theory. New Yorkers who opposed the Constitution were also at work, both with their pens, producing some of the most important Antifederalist writing, and in day-to-day, face-to-face politics.

The United States Constitution was ratified by New York State on July 16, 1788, at the Dutchess County courthouse, shown here as it appears on an 1804 Dutchess County map. From *150th Anniversary of the Founding of the Government of New York State* (Poughkeepsie, 1938).

Voting for delegates to the ratifying convention at Poughkeepsie was open to all free adult males. Federalists and Antifederalists were in open, organized opposition. Turnout was much heavier than at a normal poll. The Constitution's opponents won in Suffolk, Queens, and every county north of Westchester, though Federalists had strong minorities in the counties of Columbia, Albany, and Montgomery, which then included the whole Mohawk Valley and western frontier. When the convention began its business in Poughkeepsie on June 17, 1788, it looked set to reject the Constitution by forty-six votes to nineteen. But in the end it accepted the document, thirty to twenty-seven.

The reason was largely timing. By the time the convention met, eight states of the necessary nine had accepted the Constitution; North Carolina and Rhode Island had rejected it. If the convention had said no immediately, New Hampshire and Virginia both might have followed; Antifederalism was strong in both. But the delegates decided to debate the Constitution clause by clause. Hamilton and Robert R. Livingston were foremost among the Federalists, and Melancton Smith (who came from New York City but sat for Dutchess County) among the Antifederalists. Governor Clinton presided, and nobody pretended that he was neutral. He thought that the Antifederalists were "friends of the Rights of Mankind." Hamilton attacked him in print; rumor had it that he wrote the powerful essays signed "Cato." The whole issue changed on June 21, when New Hampshire ratified. The required total of nine states had been reached, and the Constitution would take effect whatever New York did. The only question was whether New York would belong to the re-formed United States.

Talk about separating the largely Federalist Southern District from the rest of the state may have aided ratification. Federalists also helped their cause by conceding at the right moments on the right issues, particularly the question of amendments. No Federalist wanted amendments that would force the Philadelphia Convention to reassemble. None wanted amendments as an absolute condition of ratification. But Queens County's Samuel Jones, once a loyalist and now an associate of Governor Clinton, offered the formula of ratifying "in full confidence" of future changes, particularly the addition of a bill of rights. When the final vote came on July 26 a few Antifederalists switched sides. Others abstained, and the Federalist cause triumphed. New York City became the first seat of the new government. Washington assumed the presidency there on April 30, 1789. Chancellor Robert R. Livingston administered the oath, shouting "long live George Washington, President of the United States," when the ceremony was done.

One group that had been central to the politics of revolution also proved central to the politics of federal union: the artisans of New York City. During the war years they scattered in exile and military service. When they returned in 1783 they renewed their prewar alliance with small-merchant street leaders like Isaac Sears, John Lamb, and Alexander McDougall. Five artisans were elected to the Assembly in the city's first postwar election, as were Sears and Lamb. McDougall won a seat in the Senate. Reporting to John Jay in Spain, Robert R. Livingston called the winners "violent Whigs, who are for expelling

President George Washington's reception in New York City on April 23, 1789. Engraved by J. Rogers after a painting by J. McNevin. New York State Historical Association, Cooperstown, N.Y.

all Tories." Hamilton had such men in mind as much as upstaters when he opened his campaign to reshape the state's politics.

Nonetheless, artisans were moving toward Hamilton's understanding of the country's ills and how to cure them. Peace brought a short burst of spending and then a deep trading depression. The state government could do little about it. A strong national government promised more. In 1788 the artisans and Hamilton stood together. When the state ratified the Constitution, the city mounted an enormous parade. A float bearing a model of a "Federal Ship" named *Hamilton* took pride of place, manned by real seafarers. Some five to six thousand artisans marched by craft groups, each with its own banner. The skinners, breeches makers, and glovers put the central case: "Americans, encourage your own manufacturing." About the same time, a crowd menaced the business places of Antifederal leader John Lamb and Antifederal printer Thomas Greenleaf. No mechanic sat in New York City's delegation to Poughkeepsie. But their demand of 1776 that a new constitution be made "truly binding" by giving "all men" the chance to "accept or reject" it finally had been satisfied.

In 1789 Governor Clinton faced election again, and for the first time he stood a real chance of losing. His opponent was Robert Yates of Albany, an Antifederalist justice of the state Supreme Court. Yates had been one of the watchdogs sent to the Philadelphia Convention to keep Hamilton under control. Now Hamilton presided at the meeting that nominated him for governor, while Schuyler tried to dissuade other candidates from entering. Yates's "family and connections" were no better than Clinton's, but that counted much less in 1789 than it had in 1777. Winning the office was what mattered, not the social background of whoever won.

Clinton beat Yates, but by only 3.5 percent of the total ballots cast. He won again against Jay in 1792, in an election marked by bitter scandal, particularly in William Cooper's Otsego County. This time his margin was less than one percent. Three years later the governor finally stood down and Jay succeeded him. Clinton's career was not over. But it was the end of his great era in state politics. He returned to the governorship in 1801, and in 1805 he became Jefferson's vice president. When Jefferson left the presidency some, including Clinton himself, thought it was Clinton's turn. But James Madison became president, and Clinton continued as vice president instead until his death in 1812. He is buried not in New York State, but rather in the Congressional Cemetery in Washington.

The Elements of Partisanship

Two major patterns developed within the state's public life during the 1790s, one in New York City and to some extent in Albany, and the other in the rural counties. The urban development was "artisan republicanism." The rural development was a political culture in which great men continued to dominate lesser ones, though by different means from those Hudson Valley landlords had used in the colonial era.

Urban craftsmen supported the Constitution in 1788 for complex reasons. Its promise of prosperity was central. The old social model of small, cohesive communities that could close out the world was almost dead. That model had been a driving force as New Yorkers responded to the crises of the empire and the wartime economy. But the war itself marked the beginning of a national American economy in which townspeople necessarily had to participate. New York City was sending its ships and its goods all over the world. Albany was the only major town that was Antifederalist, but "the rude hand of innovation" was transforming it from a Dutch outpost and frontier headquarters into a way station for New Englanders pouring west and a manufacturing center. Images of happy isolation would not do, as the Federalists understood. They realized that they had to address the interests of specific groups: merchants, mechanics, farmers, landholders, public creditors, soldiers, lawyers, judges, and clergymen.

In New York City they ran their message in both the *Daily Advertiser*, a merchants' paper, and the *Journal*, which many artisans read.

Federalists drew all these themes together in a powerful set of arguments about the nature of American liberty. Their imagery combined the memory of the Revolution, the powerful figure of George Washington, national strength, economic well-being, and political involvement. Working townsmen accepted these points in 1788. This was what they thought the Revolution came to. The fusion was genuine. But during the 1790s their political union with the likes of Hamilton and Jay frayed and came apart

The breakup took time. Jay could not have sought the governorship in 1792 or won it in 1795 without artisan support. Part of his winning appeal in 1795 was that he had just negotiated a treaty with Britain. It promised to resolve both the old issues left over from the peace of 1783 and the new ones raised by the war between Britain and revolutionary France. During the campaign for the governorship the terms of the treaty remained unknown, while the United States Senate debated it within a closed chamber. The treaty was published on July 4, 1795, three days after Jay took office.

Jay's treaty opened the West Indies to American vessels, resuming a commerce that the Revolution had disrupted. It also promised that by 1796 British troops would evacuate the American forts they continued to hold on the northern frontier, including five within New York itself. Beyond that, however, the treaty brought little except uproar.

The reasons ran deep. Since the outbreak of the French Revolution, New Yorkers had divided about it and its British enemy. To men of cautious mind the revolution quickly became dangerous. But to many of New York City's workingmen its appeal was strong. Part of the reason was gratitude for French aid in America's own revolution. Part was a sense that the French were continuing what Americans had started. The French Revolution's greatest English-language defender was Thomas Paine, the author of *Common Sense*. He had returned to England and then gone on to France, where he became a deputy in the National Assembly. In *The Rights of Man* he defended the French Revolution's politics. In *The Age of Reason* he defended its rejection of Christianity. New Yorkers read both. They joined Democratic-Republican societies that imitated French revolutionary clubs like the Girondins and the Jacobins. They wore the cap of liberty. They addressed one another in the French style as Citizen and Citizeness. Edmond Genet, the French minister who offended Washington by attempting to appeal directly to the American people, married George Clinton's daughter.

The people who read Paine, wore the cap of liberty, and called one another "Citizen" were the same people who had honored Alexander Hamilton when they paraded to celebrate the Constitution in 1788. When things looked worst between the United States and Britain, in the summer of 1794, they paraded once again, carrying their tools behind the banners of their different trades. But this time it was "to work a day gratis" building fortifications on Governor's Island, in case war came. War did not come. The Democratic-Republican societies dissolved and caps of liberty went out of fashion, but the terms of the city's popular politics for the next quarter-century had been set. On each of the two emerging sides, Federalist and Democratic-Republican, those terms combined a vision of the American Revolution's meaning, an attitude toward the larger world, a sense of how and for whom prosperity might best be reached, and an underlying dimension of social class. In New York City especially, class would set many of the terms of public debate for the next half-century, until it flowered into an openly political workingmen's movement at the end of the 1820s.

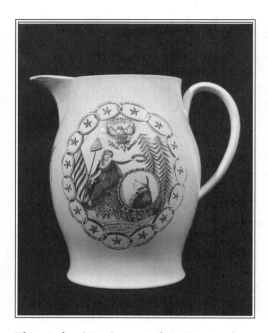

This pitcher (1804) was made in Liverpool, England, for overseas trade with the new nation. It is decorated with patriotic figures, including a chain of the states, an American eagle, and Liberty crowning George Washington with a laurel wreath. New York State Historical Association, Cooperstown, N.Y.

In the countryside landlords had long been used to dominating their tenants. Colonial-era open-air voting made it easy, and when secret ballots began to be used after 1787 landlords simply handed out prepared ballot papers and watched the voters deposit them. By the mid-1790s the western counties were filling up and there the problem was not so simple, as the experience of William Cooper in Otsego County shows. Like most western landholders, Cooper had abandoned the idea of a tenanted estate. He wanted to sell his land, at the best possible price. But he still fancied himself a squire, able to run the lives of the villagers and farmers who surrounded him.

Cooper understood the psychology of control. He and his sort developed elaborate political devices to make their "interest" seem unbeatable. A candidate himself had to remain in the background, not visibly pushing his cause. But friends could do it for him, with public meetings, newspaper announcements, and public bets about who would win. Behind these lurked the knowledge that the candidate usually was a man of great power. Such a man could evict a tenant and withhold credit and business from a freeholder or an artisan. He could arrange for his friends to give or refuse their business too.

In the gubernatorial election of 1792, Cooper's electoral methods led to statewide dispute. Otsego County gave a heavy majority to Jay over Clinton.

Construction on Government House began in 1790 at the foot of Broadway in New York City for President George Washington, but the United States capital was moved, and the house instead became the residence of Governors George Clinton and John Jay. From I. N. Phelps Stokes, *The Iconography of Manhattan Island* (New York, 1915), vol. 1.

Jay's votes there and in other disputed counties seemed enough to give him the governorship. But the *New-York Journal*, the Clinton party's main paper, printed affidavit upon affidavit alleging that the voters had been intimidated. The dispute went to the legislature, which decided that Clinton had won. Which side actually used more trickery that year remains an open question. Clinton did not contest the election of 1795.

The high principles and the low scheming of New York politics were never more tangled than in the presidential election of 1800. The Federalists were in trouble nationally, and their man Jay was governor of New York. But Jefferson's Democratic-Republicans won the new legislature, which would pick the state's electors. With Clinton in semi-retirement, Jefferson's backers were led by Aaron Burr, who became the vice presidential candidate. Alexander Hamilton proposed to Jay that he call a special session of the old legislature to choose the electors, instead of leaving it for the newly elected members. That would give New York's vital electoral votes to the Federalists. Jay disdainfully and honorably refused and the Jefferson-Burr ticket won, with an equal number of electoral votes for both men. It was an accident, caused by the original language of the Constitution and made impossible thereafter by the Twelfth Amendment, which separates electoral college voting for president and vice president. Burr seized upon the accident to try to become president himself. The same Alexander Hamilton who had tried earlier to manipulate the election stopped him. Hamilton regarded Jefferson as dangerous, but Burr as a scoundrel. Hamilton paid for his opinion with his life when he and the vice president crossed the Hudson to duel at Weehawken, New Jersey, in 1804. Hamilton fired first that day, intending to miss. Burr shot to kill.

New York politics in the 1780s and 1790s were a matter for white men, as politics in the colonial era had been. White women, Native Americans, and African Americans were simply excluded from elections and officeholding. But men of humble origins were close to power now, and they dealt with the states' citizens differently from the way colonial rulers had dealt with their "subjects."

This new political life was not necessarily pretty, but it was not necessarily ugly and corrupt either. At its worst, it meant the "private Irish ways" that Clinton knew how to use, the "hook and snivey" of Cooper or Burr, and Hamilton's scheming in 1800. At its best it meant broad public discussion of what New York, the United States, and even the world should be. Thanks to Federalism, New York entered the national union, even though it did so on terms that many of its people did not actually want. Thanks to new men like Clinton, to Antifederalism, and to Democratic-Republicanism, the state became a place where great families did not necessarily rule. At the same time, New York was beginning a surge of expansive, creative social energy that was all its own.

15

A New Empire

AT THE MOMENT OF INDEPENDENCE IN JULY 1776, NEW York consisted of three long, thin strips of territory. Those strips covered Long Island, the Hudson Valley as far north as Fort Edward, and the Mohawk Valley to Johnson Hall. New York City and Albany each marked a point where two of the strips converged. To the west lay Iroquoia, linked to New York politically by the Covenant Chain (the diplomatic agreements that implied dependence to New York and alliance to the Six Nations), and economically by the remnants of the fur trade.

Fifty years later New York had established and filled in its familiar modern boundaries. How its northern and western land was laid out, who owned that land, and how it would be used were all understood in new terms. The old links between the Iroquois and Britain were gone; in their place was the state's assertion of sovereignty over the whole territory within its boundaries, qualified by the federal government's role in all Indian relations. Iroquois law was gone too. Any murder would be tried in a court of law, rather than "covered" by adoption or payment, or revenged by the victim's family. The fur trade continued, but the pelts that were making John Jacob Astor a rich man came from the Rocky Mountains and the Pacific Northwest. When the Erie Canal opened in 1825, New York possessed a far more powerful means than trading in skins to ensure its economic dominance over its western neighbors. As the great change began, observers coined the enduring nickname of Empire State. The apt phrase bespoke New York's future as well as its breadth and its beauty.

The foundation of this new empire would be commerce. Amid all the disruption that it brought, the American Revolution in New York proved immensely stimulating to entrepreneurs. The destruction of the loyalists, who had formed a sizable proportion of the colonial elite, opened a wide gap at the top, among the great merchants and the holders of vast tracts of land. The war created large demands for munitions and supplies, opening possibilities both for producers and for traders. Established trading links across the ocean and with the West Indies were broken by both war and exile, and when peace returned, new links had to be forged. The Bank of New York's founding in 1784 marked a new era, in terms of how capital would be raised and employed. Colonial New York City had an insurance industry, a network of large-scale debts and mutual obligations, a Chamber of Commerce, and a formal Merchants' Exchange. But its financial life was organized around the fortunes of separate individuals. The Bank of New York began to turn the city into a money market, where securities could be exchanged and capital raised through impersonal institutions.

People began to see new opportunities, whether it was in overseas trade, on land that had been the Indians', or in enterprises in which New Yorkers could organize their own production and exchange. All of these changes were part of the American Revolution, and they set the direction for the state's development during the nineteenth century, in city and countryside alike. None of these changes occurred without very high cost to individuals and to whole groups. The result, nevertheless, was an economy in the young state that was both markedly more vibrant and decidedly more risky than the economy of the old colony.

Changes on the Land

"Utica, a village in the State of New York, thirty years since a wilderness," proclaimed a piece of chinaware that was made there in 1824, which meant that it was wilderness in 1794. Only twenty-two "years since," in 1802, the Reverend John Taylor had not seen wilderness when he passed through. He counted eighty-two dwellings arranged around a crossroads, all of which he drew neatly upon a map. In 1792 another visitor had not seen wilderness either. Instead, he described an "enchanted ground" with "an extensive well built town, surrounded by highly cultivated fields." But the image of a wilderness that had existed sometime in the past could not be erased. A decade earlier than his own visit, that 1792 visitor reported, the place had been the "haunt of tribes" and the "hiding place of wolves."

The china-maker, the missionary, and the passer-through did have their point. During the five decades after independence, western New York changed enormously. Understanding the condition it left behind as a baseline wilderness helped to make sense of what had followed. Unwittingly Utica's witnesses were making another point as well, as they pushed the wilderness ever deeper into a past that none of them had actually seen. The land the whites visited, observed, and made their own was not in the least the product of undirected nature. For at

least two centuries it had belonged to the Six Nations of the Iroquois Confederacy. The newcomers built their Empire State on the ruins of the Iroquois
empire.

The land was not "New York" at all while the Iroquois possessed it. The
colonial government tried to dominate the Six Nations, but to them the whites
were allies, or perhaps enemies, not suzerains. In 1753 Chief Hendrick of the
Mohawks declared his people's absolute independence to colonial Governor
George Clinton (a distant relative of the Revolutionary chief executive):
"Brother when we came here to relate our Grievances about our lands, we
expected to have something done [and] we have told you that the Covenant
Chain of our Forefathers was like to be broken. . . . [nothing has been done and]
So Brother you are not to expect to hear of me any more, and Brother we desire
to hear no more of you."

After independence whites unquestionably were in charge. Aside from wel-
coming them into Canada, the British abandoned their Indian allies. New York's
position was that Indians who had joined the British had forfeited all their
rights. The state asserted an absolute right to deal with friendly or neutral Indians, as well, with the same goal of acquiring their land. For the most part, the
plan succeeded. There were still Iroquois in New York in 1800, but they were
"poor enervate creatures," in the words of one unsympathetic white, "con-
temptible compared with their former greatness!" They faced a different task
from the triumphant whites. It was somehow to survive defeat and degradation.
They achieved it, holding onto some of their land and all of their identity.

When the Revolution ignited into war, both British and colonials urged the
Iroquois to stay out of the conflict. It was a "quarrel among brothers." But the
Six Nations could not avoid the war, any more than they could have stayed out
of the earlier imperial wars between France and Britain. The Mohawks, particularly, recognized that a British defeat would leave them defenseless against
white land-seekers. Most joined the British side, and their leader Thayendanagea (Joseph Brant) became a frontier commander of note. Thayendanagea
knew white culture well. Sir William Johnson married his sister, and he had
studied in Connecticut with the Reverend Eleazar Wheelock. He visited Britain
more than once, consorted with royalty, and had his portrait painted by both
George Romney and Gilbert Stuart.

For the other five nations, the Onondagas, Oneidas, Cayugas, Tuscaroras,
and Senecas, the issue seemed more complex. Some tried to stay neutral, and
the Oneidas and Tuscaroras joined the American side. But the Sullivan-Clinton
expedition of 1779 made little distinction between Iroquois who fought against
the Americans, Iroquois who kept their own counsel, and Iroquois who chose
the American side. What the soldiers saw was the immense richness of the Finger Lakes and Genesee region. Iroquois women already farmed it. Now white
men wanted it, so they could farm it themselves.

Red Jacket, prominent Seneca moral and political leader, wearing a peace medal given to him in 1792 by President Washington. Lithograph of a painting by Charles Bird King. New York State Historical Association, Cooperstown, N.Y.

After the Revolution many people interested themselves in New York's western lands. Massachusetts had a claim under its old royal charter. Officers and soldiers of the Revolutionary army were promised land in return for their service. Speculators and boosters like William Cooper and Pennsylvania's Robert Morris sought land. So did European capitalists and aristocrats.

When the war ended the state government forced a series of treaties upon the Iroquois, stripping them of their holdings except for scattered reservations. In the far west of the state were Allegany, Cattaraugus, Buffalo Creek, and Tonawanda; in the central part there were reservations bordering Cayuga Lake, Oneida Lake, and Onondaga Lake. None of these was small, but they were not large enough to support the old frontier exchange economy of female agriculture, male hunting, and the fur trade. Nor could they support the complex culture and way of life that the old economy had underpinned. With the disappearance of their economy, the Iroquois lost the respect of other Indians. Before the Revolutionary War, Mingos and Shawnees farther west had deferred to the Six Nations. After it they treated visiting Senecas as beggars. Understanding their own plight, many Iroquois became "miserable beings" surrounded by "cellars of rum and whiskey." Their reservations declined into rural slums.

Whites of ill will or indifference expected the Indians to "quit all this part of the country." Whites of relatively good will, like Presidents George Washington and Thomas Jefferson, wanted to see them become small farmers, taking on European ways along with the means of European agriculture. To become a wholly farming people meant a major change in what it meant to be a man or woman, since women had done the field work in the old Iroquois order. Horticulture had always been a necessity of Iroquois life; what changed was that Iroquois men learned to do it.

In the midst of their defeat, the great Iroquois achievement was to form a new view of their place in the world and a new way of life, upon terms that remained their own. A Seneca named Ganeodiyo, which translates into English as Handsome Lake, sank for a time beneath drink and despair. But in the Indian tradition of prophetic dreams, visions came to him. They inspired him to create a new religion, suited to the conditions within which Senecas now had to live, if they were to live at all. His Gaiwiio, or Good Word, borrowed from Christian ritual, included the Catholic practice of confession. It also borrowed from Christian morality, sanctifying permanent marriage rather than the easily broken unions that the old economy and clan structure had allowed. Most important, Ganeodiyo persuaded his people to give up alcohol, the symbol of their despair.

His project benefited from favorable circumstances. The mountainous Allegany Reservation where he lived was the most remote in the state, and when its peoples' own situation was at its worst, white expansion was still well to the east. The rebirth benefited as well from the support of Quaker missionaries, who became the chosen agents of federal and state policy under Jefferson. The achievement was the Indians' own. Against almost impossible odds, they survived both as individuals and as a distinctive people. A map of western New York in 1809 did not even show their reservations, but they did not lose what remained to them and they never surrendered their identity. New York surrounded them, but it did not engulf them. Realistically, they knew that their empire was gone, a "lost land." Most eastern tribes, including some Iroquois, were driven beyond the Mississippi River during the 1830s' era of "Indian Removal." But many Iroquois either stayed in New York or returned.

Land Jobbers and Developers

Unlike the Iroquois, colonial New York's greatest loyalists did not survive. In 1779 the state legislature passed a Confiscation Act that named seventy-nine of them directly. It attainted these for life, exiling them, seizing their real and personal property, and threatening them with death should they return. It was easy to bring legal proceedings against others who were not named in the act itself. The immediate effect was to seize property in the patriot zone, including the Mohawk Valley estates of the Johnson family, sizable holdings in Dutchess and Westchester Counties belonging to families like the Philipses, and the upstate speculations of such land operators as Oliver DeLancey. When the war ended, downstate holdings were seized as well, including the extensive New York City town lands that the DeLancey family had owned.

Patriot tenants of loyalist landlords enjoyed first option at purchasing the confiscated land. Some great colonial estates, such as the Westchester County holdings of the Philipse family, did fall largely into former tenants' hands. Much of the New York City property, however, ended up belonging to speculators. The total sum that was seized was very large. A mere dozen of the greatest loyalist exiles sought compensation from the British government that totaled £729,868, New York currency. Unquestionably the claimants inflated their losses, but the figure does give an order of magnitude. Whether the property ended up with former tenants or with speculators, the Confiscation Act redistributed a very sizable proportion of what had been colonial New York.

The seizure and purchase of Iroquois land redistributed far more, both in extent and in potential wealth. Much of the land was claimed by the governments of both New York and Massachusetts. Each had claims under the patchwork of British Crown grants, but they resolved the issue in 1786 at a conference in Hartford. East of Seneca Lake, New York would have both political jurisdiction and actual ownership, save for the "Boston Ten Townships" near Binghamton. There, and west of Seneca Lake, New York would have governmental jurisdiction only. About six million acres would belong to Massachusetts as a corporate landlord under New York law, until they were sold.

The policy of Massachusetts was to sell quickly and pocket the results. The first offer to purchase came from Oliver Phelps and Nathaniel Gorham who, together with other partners, bid about $1 million for the entire tract. Indian title had to be cleared, and in 1788 at Buffalo Creek the Iroquois surrendered ownership of more than a third of the whole tract, receiving a bare $5,000 and annual payments of $500. It was an amazing bargain, but Phelps and Gorham could not keep up their payments to Massachusetts. In 1790 they found themselves compelled to return two-thirds of what they had tried to take.

Robert Morris tried next. In 1790 he purchased over a million acres of what Phelps and Gorham still had and another four million acres direct from Massachusetts. He, in turn, sold large tracts to the English investor Sir William Pulteney and to Dutch bankers organized as the Holland Land Company. The Dutch syndicate's purchase from him was 3.3 million acres, and it acquired another 100,000 from New York State near modern Cazenovia, which it named for its New York agent, Theophilus Cazenove. Ultimately, Morris's venture contributed to his spectacular bankruptcy. Most of the other speculators in the Massachusetts land titles gained little. The Holland Land Company had four decades of trouble with its tract and finally sold out its interest in 1835.

New York's own record is more complicated. At first its methods represented an improvement over earlier practice, if the measure of improvement be taken as citizens' open access to the land. Colonial grants often had been secret, but the state's basic land law required that the official maps be accessible and that land be sold at open vendue. In the colonial period officials had gotten rich on land fees. The Beekman family had to pay £745 when they received their grant on Lake Champlain in 1768, including £375 to the governor, who received £12.10s. per thousand acres granted. Another £370 went to four other officials. A purchaser would also owe a permanent annual quitrent of 2s.6d. per hundred acres. A state law of 1785 limited fees to £3 for the governor and £5 for the sur-

The Holland Land Company's sale of real estate, including large tracts of land seized by the state in the 1779 Confiscation Act, contributed to the settlement of much of western New York. The office is now a museum; it is shown here in a 1905 photograph.
Courtesy of the Holland Land Office Museum, Batavia, N.Y.

veyor. Rather than allow haphazard "locations," the state began surveying public land into townships six miles on a side. In 1786 it specified that every fourth township be sold in 640-acre lots.

In 1782 the state established a "Military Tract" sprawling eastward from Seneca Lake. Former soldiers could acquire land there by warrants, with a basic grant for privates of six hundred acres. The plan reflected the absence of anything else with which to pay the soldiers. It also reflected a vision of post-Revolutionary politics in which citizen-soldiers would indeed turn their swords into plowshares. But it did not work out. Indian title was not wholly cleared from the Military Tract until 1789. By then many warrants for land in the tract belonged to speculators who had bought them up cheaply. Speculators acquired more when the state finally began distributing the land directly. They, not former soldiers, presented as many as half of the claims in the first batch that was processed. By this point squatters were on the land in sizable numbers, seeking to use actual possession to bargain with the holders of legal titles. The confusion persisted for ten years.

Large-scale speculators did acquire land from New York during the 1780s, but it was by the thousands of acres, not the millions that Massachusetts distributed. The largest purchase was the 500,000 acres that Alexander Macomb bought along the Saint Lawrence River between 1787 and 1791. In 1789 the state still owned seven million acres of "waste and unappropriated land." In 1791, however, it empowered its commissioners to sell land "on such terms and in such manner as they shall judge most conducive to the interests of the state." Farms for citizen-soldiers and small tracts bought directly from the state now disappeared as goals of policy. The whole purpose became simply to get the land into private hands, and, in the words of historian Alfred Young, the commissioners "proceeded to dispose of land on a scale that might have made the most generous royal governor . . . blush." By the end of the summer of 1791 more than 5.5 million acres had been handed out in a mere thirty-five grants. Alexander Macomb alone acquired 3,635,200 acres.

The land commissioners included Governor Clinton, the attorney general, the secretary of state, the state treasurer, and the state auditor. All of these, including Clinton, gained handsomely. So did most of the politicians who had taken the governor's side in the disputes of the 1780s and over the federal Constitution. Melancton Smith and Marinus Willett of New York City purchased 6,000 acres on the Chenango River for £1,125. The Washington County legislators Alexander Webster, Edward Savage, and John Williams bought a whole township for £4,062. Albany County's Matthew Adgate acquired 86,400 acres for an investment of £10,782. Federalists were among the purchasers too, most notably Alexander Macomb.

Clinton himself liked to draw a distinction between "land jobbers," who held land empty while they waited for the market to rise, and "the land promoter, who sold land quickly and invested in developing his area." That may have been like the classic definition of perversion or superstition: whatever another person happens to practice. Ethan Allen excoriated land jobbers furiously in the pamphlets that he wrote during the Green Mountain insurgency against New York. But he speculated happily in Green Mountain land himself. What the actual beneficiaries of the great post-Revolution handout did with their land does not seem to have varied much from relatively minor grantees to operators on a huge scale. All of them wanted land values to rise. All appreciated that land standing entirely empty would not gain value. Virtually all presented easy terms to early purchasers whose "improvements" would start the market on an upward course. Most came to understand that it could even make sense to negotiate with squatters for the sake of long-term market value.

A Capitalist Countryside

The new owners wanted the land put into use. Fields, fences, roads, houses, orchards, and barns were what made the difference, and landowners could not provide these on their own. Colonial-era landlords often had given new tenants strong inducements to settle, especially when an estate was young. Free or reduced rent for a while, gifts of farm animals, and aid in constructing buildings all were possible, but the long-range goal had been to build great estates that the landowning family would always possess. It did not happen to every grant; Cortlandt Manor ended up as parcels in separate hands. But Philipsburgh, Livingston Manor, Rensselaerswyck, and the Beekman holdings in Dutchess County all testified to the power of the great-estate model. As late as 1769 Sir William Johnson was seeking formal manorial status for Kingsborough.

The great difference after the Revolution was that large operators acquired western land not to hold it but rather to sell it. Truly great speculators like Robert Morris and Alexander Macomb, middling ones like William Cooper, James Duane, and Matthew Adgate, relatively small ones like Governor Clinton and his brother James all had roughly the same idea in mind. The law expressed the new reality when it put a formal end to feudal tenure in 1786.

Some of the old ways survived. The Van Rensselaers held onto Rensselaerswyck, where Stephen Van Rensselaer III retained the "quarter sale," giving the landlord both first refusal when tenants sold their "improvements" and a proportion of those improvements' value even if somebody else bought the lease. In practice Van Rensselaer rarely enforced those clauses and left rents uncollected. Philip Schuyler's post-Revolutionary leases for his own Albany County holdings were written in different terms. As a colonial landlord, he had rented his land the old way, granting leases that would last three lives or longer and that imposed obligations of road service, barn building, and orchard planting. He enforced the quarter-sale clause. After the war Schuyler began giving those privileges up in return for higher rent. He also started leasing his land for much shorter terms. He began insisting on retaining the right to flood a tenant's fields if he decided to build a dam for a mill. He would sell the freehold itself for the right price. Neofeudalism was giving way to rural capitalism. Schuyler the developer, not Van Rensselaer the good patroon, understood where the future lay.

Farther north and west the vestiges of the old order were weaker. In 1768 the Beekman family received 30,000 acres from the royal governor. Before independence they made gestures toward settling it with tenants from Scotland, part of the great wave of north British migrants who were becoming American frontierspeople. In their plan the migrants would become subtenants, dealing with the Beekmans through a fellow Scot named Daniel Macleod. He would pay the Beekmans a fixed rent and would get whatever he could from the actual settlers. It was a familiar arrangement both to New York landowners and to Scots.

After independence the Beekmans found that tenancy would not work. In 1785 they had the grant surveyed into separate tracts, a sign of their "reluctant decision . . . to prepare for the disposition of their property . . . to individual settlers." They continued trying to issue leases, complete with requirements that the tenant "build a frame house, clear a reasonable number of acres, plant an orchard, and cut no timber on land not leased." But by 1789 they had learned that very few would rent from them, even with easy terms at the lease's start. The time had come to sell.

In the west as well, the gentlemanly vision persisted for a while. A promotional tract written for European readers in 1792 sketched a scheme for large communities in which ten gentlemen each possessing 5,000 acres would lord it over smaller farmers who leased their land. As late as 1802 the touring Yankee missionary John Taylor commented that "the same evil operates here . . . as in many parts of this country—the lands are most of them leased. This must necessarily operate to debase the minds and destroy the enterprise of the settlers. . . . If men do not possess the . . . soil, they never will . . . feel independent. And . . . they will always be under the influence of their landlords."

Taylor's fellow New Englanders Nathaniel Gorham and Oliver Phelps never felt the lure of owning a great estate; their vast holding was to be sold. They knew that the Yankees to whom they had to appeal simply did not want leaseholds. They also knew that their prospective purchasers were commercially minded, with no desire to retreat into rustic self-sufficiency. In the Massachusetts and Connecticut towns that the migrants were leaving, the aftermath of the Revolution had brought the possibility of refinement and gentility to people who had money to spend. Migrant New Englanders wanted gentility too, and they wanted the means to afford it. That meant selling what they produced in urban markets, not growing as much as they could of what their families needed and trading with neighbors for the rest.

But the markets of Albany and New York City were hundreds of miles to their east. So Phelps and Gorham set out to create instant "city-towns" with the amenities that a New England market town enjoyed. As in Worcester or Springfield, so too in Canandaigua. Settlement there began in 1789. Five years later the town had a central square, a courthouse, a main street, and forty houses "attractively painted, and many surrounded by neat gardens and lawns." By the turn of the nineteenth century the town had increased to seventy households, with a steepled church and more than forty businesses. The picture-book prettiness of towns throughout the Finger Lakes and the Lake Ontario plain, like Chittenango, Skaneateles, Dryden, Auburn, Geneva, and Seneca Falls, grew from the same desire.

New Englanders founded most such places. After the Revolution they began moving into New York State by the tens of thousands, and they put their own permanent imprint upon it, north, that is, of a line that roughly separates their zone of expansion from another zone whose architecture, field patterns, and townscapes owe more to Pennsylvania. The Yankees brought their own sense of how women and men should live, and they expected their old ways to continue on this new ground. In 1784 Hugh White traveled from Middletown,

Connecticut, to found Whitestown, in what became Oneida County. He did not set out to be a gentleman on his 1,500 acres, but he did establish himself as a patriarch. His ancestors, who had included five successive men also named Hugh White, had a long tradition of coalescing around a patriarch's control of the family land. Members of the rising generation might remain under such a man's authority well into their adult lives. White's early actions after the move suggest that he saw no reason why this should change.

But it did change rapidly. This Hugh White became a businessman. He built sawmills on Sauquoit Creek. He fertilized his fields according to the best knowledge of the time. He and his neighbors understood that in day-to-day terms they would deal with one another within an economy of barter and borrow, perhaps among siblings, in-laws, and cousins. But Whitestown never developed the dense connections between families and across generations that had kept Middletown people in their places. White intended that some of the lumber emerging from his sawmills and some of the grain that grew in his fields would be sold in distant markets, for cash profit. The city of Utica began to take form, offering possibilities for individualism and mobility that no colonial New England town had presented. White's Connecticut ancestors had been involved in commerce too. But this Hugh White's world was far more open than theirs.

Commerce required transport, and the initial answer was to build roads. A map drawn in 1809 showed turnpikes spanning the state. There were two separate routes all the way to Lake Erie and another "now making." Feeder routes linked such communities as Owego, Bath, Ithaca, Auburn, Mexico, and Salina. By 1822 western New York had four thousand miles of highway. The Great Western Turnpike, which had begun as an Iroquois trading path and now is U.S. Route 5, provided the central spine. But the turnpikes remained narrow. In times of rain or the great spring thaw they became impossibly muddy. Sleighs offered a great improvement over wagons in speed and efficiency, but they could operate only in the winter. Two decades into the nineteenth century the largest among the towns that the turnpikes joined contained barely 6,000 people. In 1810 only 23,000 were living along the whole length of the Genesee River.

Nonetheless, virtually all the land was in private hands, and women and men were settling upon it. Most of it was still forest. Forest is not necessarily wilderness; the Iroquois had managed the forest and traded the furs it produced for their own gain. For carrying furs to market it was enough to use canoes, small boats, and the backs of people and beasts. The settlers, however, set out to clear the forests. If they could, they sold the timber they felled. If they could not, they burned it and sold the ashes. Once their fields were cleared they traded the products of their farms. These were bulky and expensive to transport. Canoes, pack animals, and human back muscles would not do.

In 1814 it cost $2.00 to send a barrel of flour 130 miles across western New York on a wagon or a sled. It cost only $0.25 to ship the same barrel 150 miles from Albany to New York City on a river sloop. As early as 1724 Cadwallader Colden had proposed that a canal be built through the great opening that the Mohawk River and Wood Creek cut in the Appalachian chain. Then, it was just a vision. By the eighteenth century's end the building of a canal was becoming a pressing need. When western New York's turnpikes were mapped in 1809, the cartographer also showed a "proposed canal" between the Tonawanda River near Buffalo and the valley of the Genesee, a distance of roughly 80 miles. Within another decade and a half, a real canal 363 miles long would link Lake Erie to the Hudson.

"A View of New Amsterdam" (1648). The earliest known image of New Amsterdam. Residents of the colony are believed to have presented the drawing to The Hague as part of a grievance against the Dutch West Indian Company: the first such protest by any group of colonial Americans. *Austrian National Library, Vienna.*

Window (1656). Attributed to Evert Duyckinck. A window displaying the Van Rensselaer coat-of-arms, one of several heraldic windows made for the Reformed Protestant Dutch Church in Albany. Painted glass. *Metropolitan Museum of Art (Photograph © 1998), bequest of Mrs. J. Insley Blair, 1951. (52.77.46)*

Van Bergen Overmantel (ca. 1733). Attributed to John Heaten. This decorative wooden panel from the fireplace of a house built by Marten Van Bergen in Greene County in 1729 provides a rare contemporary

Chippendale-Style Corner Chair (ca. 1760). For his leadership in the Battle of Lake George in 1755, Sir William Johnson (1715–1774) was awarded a baronetcy and thereafter served as England's Superintendent of Indian Affairs for North America. His home, now a state historic site in Johnstown (Johnson Hall), was elegantly furnished in English fashion; this chair was made in New York City for Johnson. *Photograph by Richard Walker. Fenimore Art Museum, Cooperstown, N.Y.*

representation of everyday life among the Dutch community of eighteenth-century New York State. *Photograph by Richard Walker. Fenimore Art Museum, Cooperstown, N.Y.*

"Joseph Brant" (1786). By Gilbert Stuart. Thayendanegea, or Joseph Brant, a member of the Mohawk nation, became well-versed in English culture under the patronage of Sir William Johnson. Brant rose to authority in the Iroquois confederacy, eventually leading the Iroquois in support of the British during the American Revolution. Oil on canvas. *Photograph by Richard Walker. Fenimore Art Museum, Cooperstown, N.Y.*

"Robert Fulton" (1806). By Benjamin West. Robert Fulton is best known today for inventing the steamboat. The background of this likeness features another of Fulton's innovations: the torpedo. Oil on canvas. *Photograph by Richard Walker. Fenimore Art Museum, Cooperstown, N.Y.*

"Battle of Lake Erie" (ca. 1825–1850). Anonymous (after Thomas Birch). The sea battle of September 10, 1813, was nearly lost when Commander Oliver Hazard Perry left his shattered flagship to continue the fight in another vessel. Perry's legendary victory proved key to the United States' defeat of Great Britain in the War of 1812. Oil on canvas. *Photograph by Richard Walker. Fenimore Art Museum, Cooperstown, N.Y.*

"Landscape Scene from *Last of the Mohicans*" (1827). By Thomas Cole. Cora of James Fenimore Cooper's *Last of the Mohicans* kneels at the feet of Tamenund to beg her freedom from Magua. Drawing on his friend Cooper's literary imagery and sketches of the New York and New Hampshire wilderness, Cole, founder of the Hudson River school of scenic painters, created a soaring landscape. Oil on canvas. *Photograph by Richard Walker. Fenimore Art Museum, Cooperstown, N.Y.*

Whig Political Banner (ca. 1840). By Terrence J. Kennedy. A large Whig campaign banner, most likely carried in parades and displayed at political gatherings in the early 1840s, promoting the Whig position against international trade and in favor of the development of domestic industries and coastal and internal transportation. Oil on canvas. *Photograph by Richard Walker. Fenimore Art Museum, Cooperstown, N.Y.*

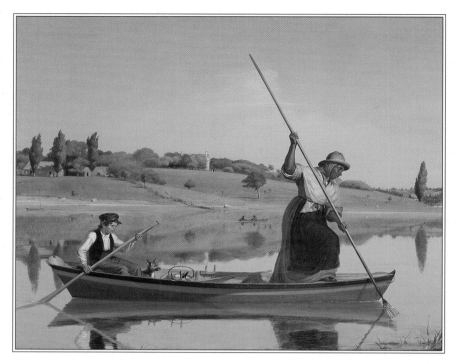

"Eel Spearing at Setauket" (1845). By William Sidney Mount. This acclaimed American genre painting was commissioned by George W. Strong, whose Long Island boyhood resembled the artist's in that African Americans taught both to fish. Oil on canvas. *Photograph by Richard Walker. Fenimore Art Museum, Cooperstown, N.Y.*

"A Ride for Liberty: The Fugitive Slaves" (ca. 1862). By Eastman Johnson. African Americans frequently "stole" themselves from slavery and fled to the north. New York's abolitionists, both black and white, aided the fugitives, defying laws they believed to be immoral. Some acted as "conductors" on the Underground Railroad, an informal, clandestine passage of safe houses and routes. Oil on board. *Brooklyn Museum of Art, gift of Gwendolyn O. L. Conkling. 40.59.A.*

Album Quilt (1857). By Anna Putney Farrington. Album quilts are divided into blocks, each depicting a different symbol or sentiment. The quilts are usually associated with Baltimore, but this example from Yorktown, New York, demonstrates a flamboyance of color and scale that distinguishes New York quilts. *Photograph by Richard Walker. Fenimore Art Museum, Cooperstown, N.Y.*

"Poestenkill" (1862). By Joseph H. Hidley. During the second half of the nineteenth century, hundreds of towns promoted themselves with printed bird's-eye prospects emphasizing pleasant residential areas and expanding business opportunities. Hidley, a house and sign painter by trade, painted promotional views of Poestenkill and surrounding towns in Rensselaer County, near Albany. Oil on wood panel. *Photograph by Richard Walker. Fenimore Art Museum, Cooperstown, N.Y.*

"Niagara" (1857). By Frederic E. Church. The scale and majesty of New York's Niagara Falls inspired American artists throughout the nineteenth and twentieth centuries. Oil on canvas. *Corcoran Gallery of Art, Washington, D.C., Museum Purchase, Gallery Fund. 76.15.*

"Zouaves at the Astor House" (ca. 1860). Anonymous. The Zouave movement—borrowing its name, drills, and colorful uniforms from the French Army—reawakened a martial spirit among volunteer companies just before the Civil War. Here a company marches down Park Place in New York City past the Astor House, one of the nation's finest hotels. Oil on canvas. *Photograph by Richard Walker. Fenimore Art Museum, Cooperstown, N.Y.*

"Mink Trapping in Northern New York" (1862). By Arthur Fitzwilliam Tait. Adirondack trappers sold their pelts to fur traders in communities along the Mohawk River. The lithographic firm of Currier and Ives published large reproductions of a dozen of Tait's popular Adirondack hunting and fishing scenes. Oil on canvas. *Munson-Williams-Proctor Arts Institute, Museum of Art, Utica, N.Y. 67.92.*

Cradleboard (ca. 1870). Mohawk. When the Mohawk were moved from the Mohawk Valley to reservations on the New York–Canada border after the Revolution, they maintained many of their customs, including the use of traditional cradles. *Photograph by Richard Walker. Fenimore Art Museum, Cooperstown, N.Y.*

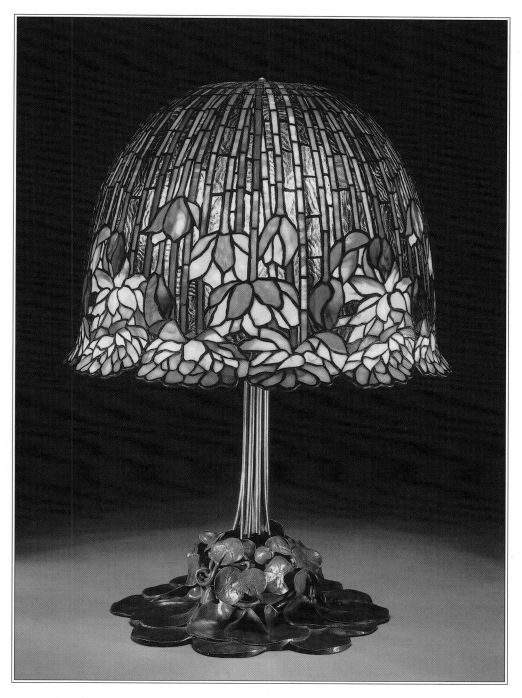

Water-Lily Table Lamp (ca. 1904–1915). Designed by Louis Comfort Tiffany. An early electric lamp, a masterwork of American art-nouveau design. New York City, home of the Tiffany Studios, was the center for design and production of high-quality luxury goods at the turn of the twentieth century. *Metropolitan Museum of Art (Photograph © 1998), gift of Hugh J. Grant, 1974. (1974.214.15ab)*

Postcard (ca. 1910). Business continues as usual in downtown Oswego, despite heavy snow. Oswego is located in the heart of New York's notorious "lake effect" snowbelt and often receives over 150 inches of snow in the course of a winter. Paper postcard, postmarked 1911.

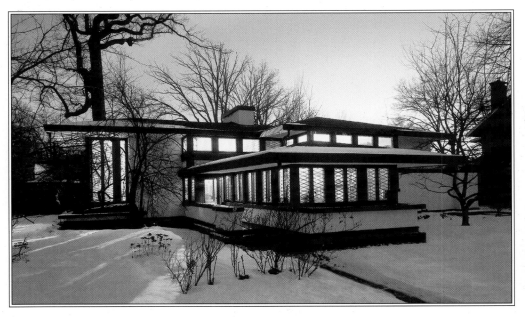

Davidson House (ca. 1903–1905). Designed by Frank Lloyd Wright. The Davidson House in the Darwin D. Martin House complex in Buffalo. With several structures and a designed landscape, the complex is by many accounts Wright's most extensive Prairie Style composition. *Photograph by Biff Henrich/Keystone Film Productions, Inc.*

"Childhood's Garden" (1917). By Charles Burchfield. American modernist painters aspired to represent diverse sensory experiences in a visual medium. Burchfield distorted space, color, and proportion to depict the remembered emotion of a New York garden, rather than its physical realities. Watercolor on paper. *Munson-Williams-Proctor Arts Institute, Museum of Art, Utica, N.Y. 57.90.*

New York Central Railroad Poster (1938). By Leslie Ragan. A streamlined art-deco advertisement for the New York Central Railroad's Twentieth Century Limited, one of the great institutions of passenger rail travel. The all-Pullman luxury train guaranteed a 16-hour trip between New York and Chicago, passing through the Hudson and Mohawk valleys. © *2001 Poster Plus, Chicago, Ill.*

"Lower Manhattan" (1930). By Reginald Marsh. Marsh painted New York City's theaters, breadlines, shop windows, and dance marathons in an animated and colorful style. This view of lower Manhattan's skyline captures the city's vitality even as the nation entered the Depression. Egg tempera on linen on masonite. *Munson-Williams-Proctor Arts Institute, Museum of Art, Utica, N.Y. 57.195.*

"Sugaring Off" (1945). By Anna Mary Robertson [Grandma] Moses. An annual winter ritual—the processing of sap into maple syrup. "Grandma" Moses, who began painting late in life, drew on her experience of rural life in upstate New York to imagine an earlier and presumably less complex time in the state's history. Oil on canvas. © 1949 and 1976, Grandma Moses Properties Co., New York. *Photograph by Richard Walker. Fenimore Art Museum, Cooperstown, N.Y.*

"Dress Shop" (1972). By Ralph Fasanella. This depiction of a garment factory in New York City's Chatham Square is dedicated to the workers killed in the 1911 fire in the Triangle Shirtwaist factory. The artist was born to Italian immigrants and spent his youth working alongside his mother and siblings in the New York City garment industry. Oil on canvas. *Photograph by Richard Walker. Fenimore Art Museum, Cooperstown, N.Y.*

"Number 2, 1949" (1949). By Jackson Pollock. Jackson Pollock spread his canvases on the floor, and dripped, poured, and spattered pigments onto them. His innovative technique earned him widespread critical acclaim in the 1950s, as well as a leading place among the New York school of Abstract Expressionists. Oil, enamel, and aluminum paint on dyed fabric. *Munson-Williams-Proctor Arts Institute, Museum of Art, Utica, N.Y. 54.38.*

Rose Center for Earth and Space (2000). Designed by James Stewart Polshek. Perhaps New York City's most dramatic piece of recent architecture, this addition to the American Museum of Natural History serves as a museum of technology and planetarium, replacing its predecessor, the much-loved Hayden Planetarium. *Transparency K18941, photograph by AMNH. Courtesy Department of Library Services, American Museum of Natural History.*

"Andy Warhol" (1970). By Alice Neel. Andy Warhol was one of the most prominent artistic personalities of the 1960s and 1970s. Neel shows him pale and weakened after a shooting attempt on his life. Oil on canvas. *Photograph copyright © 2001: Whitney Museum of American Art, New York. Whitney Museum of American Art, gift of Timothy Collins.*

16

"A Large and Valuable Canal"

ON A MAP, THE ROUTE FOR A CANAL ACROSS NEW YORK seems obvious. The valley of the Mohawk leads from where the river joins the Hudson at Waterford to Wood Creek. The creek flows west into Oneida Lake. Low hills and flat, sometimes wet country spread beyond, separating Lake Ontario to the north and the Finger Lakes to the south. The north-flowing Seneca and Genesee Rivers cross the route, as does a ridge of dense, hard rock not far east of Lake Erie. Piercing that ridge, crossing the Genesee and Irondequoit Creek, building through the Montezuma marshes north of Cayuga Lake, and descending the sixteen miles east of Schenectady where the Mohawk River drops fast to sea level present the main difficulties. As obstacles, these do not compare with the mountain ranges that cross western Pennsylvania, Maryland, Virginia, and the Carolinas. The difference in altitude between Lake Erie and the Hudson is only 565 feet. The height of the westernmost "mountain ridge" is only 76 feet. "It appears," wrote canal enthusiast Jesse Hawley, "as if the Author of nature . . . had in prospect a large and valuable canal."

Nonetheless, the Erie Canal that New York built between 1817 and 1825 was one of the great public works of the nineteenth century. By then England had a large canal system, but in the United States the longest artificial waterway ran for only twenty-seven miles. To construct the canal the state had to overcome both the political problem of generating public support and the financial problem of raising very large sums for long-term investment. Despite the route's advantages, the canal presented severe engineering difficulties, and the state had only amateur civil engineers to meet them. The canal—Clinton's Ditch—is firmly and rightly associated with the imagination and drive of De Witt Clinton, nephew of the Revolutionary governor, but it sprang from the enterprise and energy of an entire free people. Its construction marked as momentous a change in New York's material, economic, and social life as the Revolution had marked in its political life half a century earlier.

"Little Short of Madness"

New York enjoys two natural breaks in the Appalachian mountain chain. The picturesque gap where the Hudson River bursts through the Bear Mountain and West Point highlands provides the only sea-level access between the Great Valley of the Appalachians and salt water. South of the highlands, the Hudson flows home to the sea, but the Great Valley shears away from the coast and runs west of the fall line to Georgia. To the highlands' north, the valley continues in a virtually straight line to where the Hudson emerges from the Adirondack Mountains. From there northward the valley holds Lake Champlain. The Hudson is at sea level from its mouth almost to its confluence with the Mohawk, allowing ocean-going vessels to reach Albany. Even above its first rapids it presents few problems for sizable boats. Only a few miles separate boatable river water at Fort Edward from Whitehall at Lake Champlain's southern end. To connect the two presented no technical difficulty.

Despite how it looks on a map, the wide opening between the Catskills and the Adirondacks was another matter. The first obstacle was the thunderous Cohoes Falls, immediately above the Mohawk River's mouth. From there to Schenectady the river was unnavigable, requiring a long, expensive portage from Albany. In 1792 Philip Schuyler and his associates Goldsbrow Banyar and Elkanah Watson surveyed the Mohawk from Schenectady to Wood Creek. They found the whole riverbed strewn with stones, gravel banks, and large rocks. In 121 miles, the surveyors counted twenty-four rapids. Some could be traversed easily; at others the water ran so swiftly "as to render the ascent for large batteaux very difficult." In many places the channel was only a foot or two deep. In some it was so shallow that even "an empty batteau must be drawn up." The thirty-nine-foot drop at Little Falls required a three-quarter-mile portage over ground that was "stony, rocky, and rough."

The surveyors were working for Schuyler's Western Inland Lock Navigation Company, which proposed to open the Mohawk. The final drop to the Hudson presented too difficult an obstacle, but the company did clear many rapids above Schenectady. It built locks around Little Falls, and it dug a short canal across the two-mile portage between the Mohawk and Wood Creek. The company was a private venture with public backing. As Schuyler put it, "the Interest of the W. Canal company and that of the Community . . . are mutual." That amounted to the whole theory of private corporations in his time, but he still overstated. The company's interest was to make a profit, and the community's was to acquire cheap, reliable transportation. The company made a profit only twice, in 1798 and 1813. It did improve transport. Thanks to its work, boats as large as sixteen tons burden began traveling between Oneida Lake and Schenectady. The cost of shipping grain, lumber, and ashes eastward and manufactured goods west dropped considerably. But the portage to Albany remained, and west of Oneida Lake there remained only roads.

Schuyler's vision was of improvements along the Mohawk. In 1807 and 1808 the Geneva flour dealer Jesse Hawley wrote a series of essays that suggested a mainline canal right across the state, with others feeding into it. Hawley wanted not to improve upon nature but to conquer it. The rivers of central and western New York point in many directions, and down the Mohawk toward Albany is only one. The Delaware leads to Philadelphia, the Susquehanna to Baltimore, and the Allegheny to Pittsburgh and eventually New Orleans. The Niagara, Genesee, Oswego, and Black Rivers flow into Lake Ontario. That lake and the Richelieu River that drains Lake Champlain empty into the Saint Lawrence. Hawley's project was to overcome all these and create one large commercial web that would be anchored at New York City.

Achieving that goal would be beyond any private resources. Since the whole north-central United States would benefit, Hawley proposed that it be a national project, funded from Washington. Until 1816 New York's plans for a canal rested on the hope that the United States would pay for it. In February 1808, Assemblymen Joshua Forman and Benjamin Wright introduced a canal resolution based on federal finance. They expected to take advantage of a plan that President Thomas Jefferson had announced to use surplus revenue for internal improvements. Jefferson himself was taken aback by New York's boldness. He told Forman that George Washington's old proposal for a short canal around the falls of the Potomac was still languishing for lack of finance and "making a canal 350 miles through the wilderness . . . is little short of madness . . . at this day."

War with Britain, Again

Deteriorating relations with Britain that led to the War of 1812 put a halt to further proposals. The war itself demonstrated a canal's value. The initial American strategy aimed at a conquest of Canada. Two of the three projected expeditions would set out from New York, one under Stephen Van Rensselaer crossing the Niagara River and the other under Henry Dearborn starting for Montreal from Plattsburgh. Both the Van Rensselaer and Dearborn expeditions failed when militiamen refused to leave state soil. In the Niagara case the refusal meant that troops who actually had crossed and who seemed about to secure a victory were forced to surrender.

This view of the Battle of Plattsburgh, taken from an old print, shows British forces crossing the Saranac River and the courthouse burning. From Benson J. Lossing, *The Pictorial Field-Book of the War of 1812* (New York, 1868). New York State Historical Association, Cooperstown, N.Y.

Lake Erie, the Niagara River, Lake Ontario, the upper Saint Lawrence Valley, and Lake Champlain formed the major theater for most of the action that followed. In 1812 the British attacked Ogdensburg and Sackets Harbor but were repulsed each time. An ice-borne expedition early in 1813 attacked Ogdensburg again. In April of that year Americans crossed Lake Ontario to York (Toronto), where they burned public buildings. Then they moved on to the mouth of the Niagara. The British returned to Sackets Harbor late in May, again without success, tried to cross the Niagara River, succeeded in burning Black Rock and Buffalo, and won control of Lake Champlain. At the year's end the American forces that had taken Fort George, on the Canadian side of the Niagara's mouth, had been forced back across the river. The Americans' brightest spot came when Oliver Hazard Perry won permanent control of Lake Erie, on September 10, 1813.

Fighting continued along the Niagara frontier in 1814, with engagements on the Canadian side at Chippewa and Lundy's Lane. The major conflict, however, came on Lake Champlain, which was still under British control. Plans were underway for an army of 11,000 men to start southward, though it seems doubtful that anybody in London really expected to avenge Burgoyne's defeat. To meet the invasion there was only an American force of 4,700, many not able to fight. The British plan stalled when Captain Thomas Macdonough regained control of the lake on September 11, defeating a larger British fleet. With that, New York's War of 1812 ended. Fears of a British attack on New York City never became reality.

For New Yorkers as much as anyone else, the War of 1812 was fundamentally inconclusive. Many people opposed it, though opposition was not as general as in New England. The continued fighting along New York's frontier did demonstrate how expensive and difficult it was to convey supplies and heavy weapons overland to lake vessels and to border forts. When the war ended, the state made another attempt at securing federal financing for its canal project, citing the possibility of further wartime necessity. President James Madison seemed sympathetic. In 1811 he had expressed constitutional doubts about internal improvements, but after the war he accepted federal sponsorship for the Second Bank of the United States and for the Cumberland Road across Virginia and Kentucky. But when in 1816 a major improvements bill that included funding for a New York canal did pass Congress, Madison vetoed it, and Congress did not override the veto. If New York wanted a canal, it would have to finance and build one on its own.

A Free People's Enterprise

Perhaps anticipating that it would do the job itself, New York appointed its canal commissioners in 1810. Their task was to choose between the "interior route" direct to Lake Erie and a shorter alternative to Lake Ontario with another canal around the Niagara barrier. They opted for the Erie route, on the ground that most traffic entering Lake Ontario would continue down the Saint Lawrence to Montreal. They were optimistic about canal use, projecting an annual eastward flow of 250,000 tons, and revenues large enough to cover an investment of $10 million. By 1814 the state was receiving large donations of land to help finance a canal, including 100,000 acres from the Holland Land Company, which expected its western holdings to rise enormously in value should one be built. What it gave, however, proved to be "virtually unsaleable land . . . in the mountains of southwestern New York."

The canal's proponents argued that it would benefit the whole, whether of the United States or just New York. In large terms this was true: without the canal Montreal rather than any United States city might have become the Midwest's great trading port. But Philadelphia, Baltimore, Alexandria, and New Orleans can be forgiven for not wanting to see New York City gain the advantage that a canal would present, and for not wanting to help pay for it. There were also New Yorkers who doubted the motives of the canal's supporters or the likely results. Surveyor General Simeon De Witt declared in 1808 for the Ontario route, specifically so that the Holland Land Company would not benefit. In his words, New York City "tradesmen, mechanics, and laborers" were "fearful of taxation, suspicious of the interests of a landed or moneyed aristocracy, and contemptuous of the canal as a 'visionary project.'" In 1817 editor Mordecai Manassas Noah of New York City called the proposal a "Budget of Blunders" and predicted that the canal would be "a monument of weakness and folly." Hudson Valley farmers feared competition from the owners of better land to the west, once that area's products acquired easier access to markets. Other farmers in the Southern Tier, who would not benefit from the canal, begrudged the easy access to markets it would offer to people along its route. Samuel Beach of Jefferson County wanted the canal to terminate at the Seneca River, so that it would not benefit "the shores of Lakes Erie, Huron, and Michigan."

There was no simple breakdown of opinion. Despite Hudson Valley opposition, Assemblyman George Tibbitts of Rensselaer County became one of the canal's strongest proponents. Enlightened owners of western lands understood that opposition would be lessened if they accepted a special tax upon themselves. Mordecai Noah's hostility was balanced by Assemblyman Elisha Williams's projection of the canal's benefits: "If the canal is to be a shower of gold, it will fall upon New-York; if a river of gold, it will flow into her lap."

De Witt Clinton's own role illustrates the complexity of canal politics. He began public life firmly identified with the Democratic Republicanism of his uncle, George Clinton. From its beginning, however, the canal project was associated with George Clinton's opponents, starting with Philip Schuyler and continuing with the equally visionary Gouverneur Morris. Like Schuyler and Morris, Assemblymen Forman, Wright, and Tibbitts were all Federalists. De Witt Clinton was recruited in 1810 to be a Democratic-Republican sponsor in the legislature, making the project bipartisan. From then until his death in 1827, the canal was his project. He pushed it as canal commissioner (1816–24), as mayor of New York City (1803–7, 1808–10, 1811–15), and as governor (1817–23, 1825–27). He joined the other commissioners in declaring for the interior route to Erie rather than the shorter route to Ontario. He lobbied for federal aid. In 1816 he was the main author of an influential petition from New York City for "an interior canal to Lake Erie . . . 'through the most fertile country in the universe.'" He had a hand in abandoning the original impractical idea of a single long inclined plane, substituting locks between level stretches. In 1817 he saw the bill authorizing finance and initial construction through the legislature. By then, Clinton was in open rivalry with Martin Van Buren, though both supposedly were in the same Democratic-Republican party. Nonetheless, when Van Buren finally gave the canal his support, Clinton crossed the floor of the state Senate to thank him and shake his hand. It was on a canal platform that Clinton became governor later that same year.

The act of 1817 created a canal fund under state control. The fund became one of the central elements in how the state financed not just the canal but much of the rest of its development over the next quarter-century. The fund was to be supported by canal tolls, which would be used to repay private investment in long-term bonds. The amount that needed to be raised was daunting: the final surveyors' report projected construction costs of $7,000,000 at a time when the total amount of banking and insurance capital in the state was less than $21,000,000. Initial expectation of the canal commissioners had been that the capital would come from foreign sources. Two London insurance companies did invest heavily in the first loan, in 1817, but it became clear that neither other foreign investors nor large American sources were interested. During the first three years of construction most of the money came from New Yorkers themselves, individuals of substantial, but not great savings, whose investments were made in relatively small amounts. Of the sixty-nine subscribers to a loan in 1818, fifty-one invested $2,000 or less, and twenty-seven less than $1,000.

After 1820 the pattern changed. By then construction was well advanced, the canal was open across the central part of the state, and revenues were beginning to flow. Bigger American investors began to buy canal bonds, in sums above $10,000. This may have been despite the Panic of 1819; it may also have been that the Canal Fund offered safety and good returns in the midst of the financial turbulence that the panic caused.

Many of the new investors were based in New York City, and the sums individuals were willing to put in rose sharply. In 1822 John Jacob Astor bought $213,000 of canal stock. Non–New Yorkers also started to see the canal positively. The Second Bank of the United States bought $45,000 worth of stock, and the English money market got involved. Canals in England were a huge success, and New York's venture attracted favorable coverage in the British press. English investors began to acquire the bulk of new canal loans and even to buy up shares in older loans. By 1824, Baring Brothers had $322,923, and New York canal certificates were trading actively in Britain. Investment came from other countries as well, including one source in China. New York's canal had won world fame, and its canal certificates had earned world respect.

The small sums that New Yorkers themselves invested in the early loans represented both the achievements of their existing commercial economy and their belief in a much more prosperous future. The large sums that began to come from London represented the much greater complexity and power of the British economy. By the early 1820s that economy's industrialization was well advanced, and the owners of British capital faced the problem of investing a surplus that was becoming too large for Britain to absorb. During the nineteenth century British capital flowed to much of the rest of the world. In many places that received it, the effect was to turn the recipient economy into a satellite, controlled not locally but rather from London and serving British needs.

Against this background, New York's financial achievement is striking twice over. The state raised significant venture capital from its own resources. Then it attracted large-scale foreign investment without becoming subordinate to foreign direction. Only $800,000 was put into the canal during the period of small-scale local investment between 1817 and 1819. But this is what built the canal's middle section. It showed the technical competence of surveyors, engineers, and contractors and helped to banish the fears of those who felt that the technological problems involved were insuperable. When foreigners entered, it was to take part in a successful going concern, not to establish a venture on their own.

As late as 1824 Americans still held most of the canal bonds and by then the canal was almost built. Thereafter the American share did dwindle, until by 1836 "$2,896,000 was held by foreigners while only $548,000 remained in the possession of Americans." The canal commissioners were absolutely scrupulous about paying off capital when certificates became due. In 1822 the *Times* of London "informed its readers that the canals would make New York City the 'London of the New World.'" That New York City did become a world financial capital owes something to the heavy British investment that the *Times* was encouraging, but the investment was on New Yorkers' terms, in a project that New York never ceased to control.

Building Clinton's Ditch

Construction began near Rome on July 4, 1817, as dignitaries watched the first contractor plant his spade. The central section between Utica and the Montezuma marshes was built first. It offered the fewest engineering difficulties, tapped a richly productive hinterland, and required the lowest cost. The first water entered the canal the year after construction began, and the middle section was completed by 1819. From the central section, contractors built both eastward and westward. The canal reached Little Falls in 1821, and by 1822 it was open between Schenectady and Rochester. The junction with the Hudson was made by the end of 1823. By then construction to the west extended as far as Brockport. In 1824 the canal arrived at the instant town of Lockport, on the ridge just east of Lake Erie. The next year it was completed all the way to Buffalo, after a strenuous political tussle between Buffalo and Black Rock to win the western terminus.

New Yorkers celebrated at every stage of construction. The boat *Chief Engineer* bore the commissioners from Utica to Rome in 1819 to mark the completion of the first section. The same boat opened the section to Little Falls in 1821; it was steered briefly by a waterman who once had conveyed George Washington during the Revolution. De Witt Clinton himself planned the jubilee when the canal reached the Hudson. The marquis de Lafayette traveled ceremonially along most of the canal's route in June 1825 in what amounted to a rehearsal for the grand official opening. The celebration of actual completion that autumn was enormous. On October 26, cannon boomed one by one the whole distance from Buffalo to New York City and back, while a procession of boats started east from Buffalo. It was led by the *Seneca Chief*, which was carrying Clinton and the other members of an official party. Two real Seneca Indians followed as passengers on the *Noah's Ark*. Balls, illuminations, salutes, speeches, and processions met the flotilla as it proceeded east, except at Schenectady, which was losing its portage business. From Albany, the canal boats were towed down the Hudson by steam power. In a final grandiose ceremony at Sandy Hook on November 4, Clinton poured Erie water into the sea.

The joy was unfeigned, and it was not restricted to the canal main line and the Hudson Valley. The Champlain Canal was completed in 1823, breaking Montreal's control of the northern New York economy. Jesse Hawley's vision of a system that would serve the whole state, rather than a single canal, was beginning to take shape, and by mid-century that system was fully in place. So heavy was the mainline canal's use that enlargement of it began as early as 1836.

Small contractors organized most of the actual construction, sometimes working on sections as short as a quarter mile. The one exception to private contracts comprised the difficult ascent of the westernmost ridge and a seven-mile cut through the ridge itself, including two miles that had to be blasted through solid rock. This was beyond any single individual's or company's means, so the state took over actual construction. The engineers who designed the canal taught themselves as they went, and they helped to create the American civil engineering profession. One, John B. Jervis, rose from chopping wood to working on the Delaware and Hudson Canal, the Croton Aqueduct, and New York's early railroads. Another, Canvass White, solved the problem of building through wet land by discovering a cement that grows harder under water.

Learning as they went, the canal builders attempted to build a wooden aqueduct across Irondequoit Creek and then constructed an embankment of earth and stone that stood 70 feet high and covered a 245-foot culvert that carried the creek itself. They built an aqueduct 802 feet long across the Genesee. Conquering the white water below Schenectady required crossing the Mohawk River twice and building twenty-seven locks. The aqueducts were 748 feet and 1,188 feet long, respectively. The Aztecs of pre-Columbian Mexico had accomplished engineering feats on such a scale, but nothing like the Erie Canal's works had been achieved by anyone in the British colonies or in the young United States.

The canal grew from a spirit of change, and where it went it brought more change. In the far north, the Champlain Canal outstripped the Richelieu River in carrying forest products. The difference was more than simple board feet. Wood went down the Richelieu to Canada as roughly squared timber. It went along the canal to the New York market as finished lumber, and that meant adding considerable value to it. It also meant making life more complex and potentially richer in the forest communities of the Adirondacks and the Champlain Valley. The canal stimulated northern agriculture as well. During the ten years after the system was opened, the Clinton County community of Beekmantown increased the actual usage of its arable land from 29 percent to 50 percent.

The effect was even more striking along the main line. In 1823, 1,329 boats arrived at Albany. The canal fleet totaled 2,000 boats by the time of Lafayette's triumphal progress. In 1826, the first year of full operation, Albany saw almost 7,000 arrivals. In 1812 the commissioners had projected eastbound traffic of 250,000 tons annually. The actual total in 1826 was 302,170 tons, and 32,435 tons were shipped west. The canal turned western New York into a major grain region, creating a wheat-growing belt 150 miles long and 40 miles wide across the western part of the state. New York City was the premier American flour port as early as 1827, and Rochester emerged as the first western milling center. The population of the counties along the canal's route tripled during the quarter-century after 1810.

Inventing the Future

The Erie Canal was both a material achievement for New Yorkers' own good and a cultural statement that New Yorkers made about themselves to the world. It was a stunning innovation in its own right, but also part of a larger process that affected education, religion, the press, literature, and the arts. Like most of their fellows, colonial New Yorkers had valued continuity and tradition. As late as 1786, "A Citizen" of Albany had protested against a rise in local mill tolls. He cited "immemorial custom . . . a law not written, established by long usage and consent," and expected that to end the matter. Now New Yorkers were coming to value innovation instead, in practically every imaginable field.

New York State granted its first individual patent in 1780, "for making a certain species of blubber and oyl proper for currying and dressing of leather." The same year that "A Citizen" wrote his protest against innovation, the state provided its first statutory protection to innovators by adopting a copyright law. In 1789 the legislature resolved an extended debate about steam navigation by granting a short-term monopoly to John Fitch, who claimed that he worked out a practical system for applying steam power to river craft. This growing willingness to give legal protection to change rather than to tradition was part of a larger transformation in the practice of American law. That change, from protection for what already was to protection for what might be, would underpin the nineteenth century's enormous changes in how Americans understood and used and developed their private property.

Robert Fulton's success in actually operating the steamboat *Clermont* in 1807 realized what Fitch had promised, and provided remarkable parallels to the Erie Canal itself. Both the canal and the boat had a sponsor who in his own life bridged the gap between the old ways of the colonial aristocracy and the new ways of emergent capitalism. The canal's was Philip Schuyler; the boat's was Robert R. Livingston, for whose Hudson Valley estate the historic vessel eventually was named. The involvement in the canal of Stephen Van Rensselaer, who was both the patroon of Rensselaerswyck and the founder of Rensselaer Polytechnic Institute, the nation's first engineering school, demonstrates the same transformation in the conduct of New York's grandees. But the sponsorship that De Witt Clinton gave to the canal project after 1810 and the way he was joined by Martin Van Buren in 1817 suggest that the canal also was the product of the popular republican politics that the Revolution had created in New York. The way that middling New Yorkers provided the all-important initial financing was a powerful sign that this was a popular as well as an elite venture.

Patents, copyrights, canal fever, and the founding of the Rensselaer Institute all suggest that New Yorkers were starting to attach new value to creative knowledge. In 1784, the first year of full independence, the legislature amended the charter of King's College, renaming it Columbia, separating it from the Episcopal Church, and establishing it as the nucleus of the University of the State of New York. Three years later the college and the university were legally separated, the latter taking on the supervisory function over all education in the state that it still exercises. The legislature began receiving petitions for charters to establish academies and colleges elsewhere. Union College in Schenectady, the state's first successful new institution of higher learning, was chartered in 1795. Hamilton (1812) and Hobart (chartered as Geneva College in 1825) followed.

The state was slower to spend money on common schooling. As early as 1782 Governor Clinton called the legislature's attention to a "chasm in education," but thirteen years later he was complaining that the chance for learning was still "confined to the children of the opulent." A law passed that year established a fund of $50,000 annually for common schooling, on the basis that the state's contribution would be matched with local money. More than 1,300 grammar schools were in operation by 1799, but their effects are hard to measure. The state's funding law was allowed to expire in 1800 in order to reduce taxes. Charity education, usually under church auspices, rather than public education remained the most likely way for a child whose parents were not well off to learn. After 1805 the New York [City] Free School Society attempted under Quaker sponsorship to provide "for the children of the churchless poor on a large scale." An African Free School was founded in 1820 under the auspices of the largely white New York Manumission Society. Like colleges, a comprehensive school system grew fitfully, but it was getting under way, and the legislature passed a law mandating local schools in 1812. More than 440,000 New York children were actually in school by 1828. During the nineteenth century's second quarter, the organization, methods, and contents of education all became major items on the public agenda.

The emergence of what became a lively press, usually linked to political parties, may have aided the cause of literacy as much as actual schooling. New York City had offered exciting journalism even in the colonial era, and the newspapers of the 1780s present a rich picture of newly independent America's social, economic, and political life. The first paper to publish every weekday, the *Daily Advertiser*, was appearing by the end of the Confederation period. It took a staunchly Federalist position in the debate on the Constitution. In the 1790s Federalist papers were appearing upstate, and in 1801 Alexander Hamilton personally founded the *New York Evening Post* to aid the Federalist party's cause. A Jeffersonian press also appeared. Like formal schooling, journalism spread unevenly at first, with papers appearing and then foundering, but by 1825 there were presses in most towns of any size. Many of them were turning out books as well as newspapers, magazines, and job printing.

Young women as well as young men felt the stirrings of personal liberation and the sense of unprecedented possibilities that the new era offered. Elizabeth Cady of Johnstown was the granddaughter of a minor Revolutionary leader. She came of age along the Erie Canal's route, on land that the Johnsons had dominated in their semifeudal style half a century earlier. She yearned for the kind of higher education that her brother acquired at Union College, and even for a career of her own. Cady did acquire the best education available to a young woman of her time at Emma Willard's Troy Female Seminary, which opened in 1821 on the site now occupied by Russell Sage College. That was as far as she could go. Prior to the founding of Cornell University in 1868, no New York college would grant a woman a degree.

Other western New York women were less forward than the young Elizabeth Cady, but the period between 1800 and 1825 saw them responding to a growing sense that patriarchal families had reached the end of their historical time. The clearest sign was the emergence of voluntary associations, such as the Female Charitable Society of Utica. These women did not intend to challenge the existing order; on the contrary, they wanted to move an unformed society toward "traditional religious values." Those values had rested on the old New England ideal of the covenanted community, whose members were unequal but who acted as a whole, under the direction of the fathers of the town and church. But the women of the Female Charitable Society were speaking and acting on their own. Their group was as "self-created," as self-determining, and in practice as antipatriarchal as the male Democratic-Republican societies of the mid-1790s had been.

Groups like the Female Charitable Society were linked to Protestant churches, and they were part of a transformation of Christianity during the state's first fifty years. The Anglican Church, which had been formally established and supported by tax money in some counties during the colonial era, was made independent of the state. Its richest single institution, Trinity Church in New York City, retained its large holdings of Manhattan land despite a legislative challenge in 1785. Free of both the state tie and their historical link to the diocese of London, Anglicans became Protestant Episcopalians and were able to have bishops of their own, the Reverend Samuel Provoost being the first to hold that office. Catholicism slowly became legal. It received what amounted to toleration at the time of independence. A clause in the state constitution which required that citizens forswear all foreign rulers, including the pope, fell into disuse after 1790. In 1800, however, there were still only two Catholic churches. Catholics won full political citizenship in 1806, including the right to vote and hold office, and New York City's first Catholic bishop (John Connolly) took up his office in 1814. The Jewish population, mostly Sephardic, remained small, reaching only five hundred people in 1812, with no hint of the role that Jews would come to play in New York life.

The greatest religious innovation in the late eighteenth and early nineteenth centuries came among the more evangelical churches, including Presbyterians, Methodists, and Baptists. These were part of what historian Nathan Hatch calls a general "democratization of American religion." Methodists enjoyed considerable success in New York City, with fifteen churches by 1825. They were working to appeal to black New Yorkers as well as to white ones. As early as 1790 the area around the John Street Methodist Church included a community of free black households. In 1796 a separate black-led Methodist church opened, and another followed in 1800. Yet despite their considerable success among both the urban poor of both races, neither the Methodists nor any other denomination proved capable of organizing the city's burgeoning chaos.

Evangelicals did achieve very great success among the New Englanders who were spreading west along the Mohawk Valley and the Lake Ontario plain. There were frontier revivals in 1799–1800, 1807–8, and 1815, all part of the "Second Great Awakening." Western New York was on its way to becoming the "Burned-Over District," famed in the nineteenth century for its fervent revivalism and for its people's determination that what was wrong in the world should be made right. Mormonism, utopian socialism, prison reform, temperance, antislavery, and ultimately the nineteenth-century woman's movement that is so firmly associated with Elizabeth Cady Stanton's name all emerged from the same matrix as that small group of women who formed the Female Charitable Society of infant Utica. All betrayed an anxiety that the world's problems were mounting. All bespoke confidence that Christian people of good will could resolve those problems by voluntary action.

In the midst of this cultural swirl the early republican state also produced two writers of the first rank, Washington Irving and James Fenimore Cooper, as well as one of real merit in James Kirke Paulding. Neither Irving nor Cooper confined his attention exclusively to New York subjects, but both drew extensively upon New York history for their material. Irving poked fun at the state with tales like "Rip Van Winkle" and "The Legend of Sleepy Hollow" and with his *Knickerbocker's History of New York*. Cooper considered the state's history and problems in novels as diverse as *The Spy, Satanstoe, The Chainbearer*, and *The Pioneers*. Paulding's novels, several of which were set in New York during the colonial and Revolutionary periods, reflected the author's fears that the simple American republic was being corrupted by aggressive commercialism and industrialism. Folk art likewise proliferated, but not until Thomas Cole, Frederic Church, and other members of the mid-century Hudson River School would the state produce a major group of painters.

The Erie Canal was much more than just a long, thin strip of water. It represented the pooling of enormous creative energy, and its completion marked the end of New York's frontier stage. The same bustling energy that produced the canal spilled over into virtually every aspect of the young state's public life. The canal system provided the most visible sign of the state's mastery over the land and resources that it now called its own. The landscape that was organized around it could not have been more foreign, more strange, to an Indian who had survived from the days of Iroquois control, as the two Senecas aboard the canal boat *Noah's Ark* must have felt during the great triumphal procession from Buffalo to Sandy Hook. The people who now filled that landscape were for the most part countrymen and countrywomen. One reason for the early nineteenth century's waves of religious enthusiasm was the countryside's sense that the life of towns was to be feared.

Nonetheless, in their growing commerce with the world's goods, in the knowledge that they acquired from their schools and newspapers, in the possibilities that were opening for their children, in the faith many of them expressed during the great revivals, in the novels about their own situation that were becoming available to read, and in their discontents with the world as it was, these rural New Yorkers were becoming part of a very large web of economics and culture. The towns that began to flourish in the Hudson Valley, along the routes of the Erie and Champlain Canals, in the rich country of the Finger Lakes and the Genesee, and even on the northern frontier were places where many strands of that web crossed, creating the possibility of a more complex way of life than any farm could offer. New York City was where the web found its center and where life became the most complex of all.

17

New York City, New York's Cities

IN THE YEAR 1790 PRESIDENT GEORGE WASHINGTON WAS among New York City's residents, dwelling first on Franklin Square and later in the McComb Mansion on Broadway, near Trinity Church. Congress was meeting in Federal Hall, on Wall Street. Graceful federal architecture was replacing the burned-out, dilapidated half-ruin that the British had evacuated at the end of 1783. Both the children of wealth and poorer youth who imitated their bored, disdainful ways were displaying early versions of New York style. Nonetheless, the New York of 1790 was a recognizable development of the New York of 1740 or even 1690. The city still stood alone in a landscape of farming country and villages. It was still a secondary commercial center that a pedestrian could cross in a good hour's walk. Most of its 33,000 people lived south of where City Hall now stands.

Fifty years later the outline of Manhattan Island, the layout of downtown streets, and the view to Staten Island were all still much the same. But there would have been no recognizing the New York City where President Washington had lived. The population was ten times as large. In two more decades it would reach 800,000 on Manhattan Island and one million if Brooklyn was counted. To house and employ these people the city was growing rapidly northward along Manhattan's length. In the poorer parts, such as Five Points on the East Side, people were piled so densely upon one another that privacy did not exist. In 1840 as in 1790 a sizable minority of New Yorkers were black. In 1826, one year before New York slavery's final demise, an upstate newspaper called the city "that paradise of Negroes." In fact, it was no heaven. Most black New Yorkers lived in deep poverty and with diminished rights. The state constitution of 1822 imposed a $250 requirement for black males to vote while reducing the property requirement drastically for whites. But black men and women had created their own distinctive community, and they were forging their own urban freedom.

No longer did New York City stand alone; instead, it tied together an urban network that covered New York State, much of New Jersey and Connecticut, the Great Lakes country, the upper Mississippi Valley, and the Cotton Kingdom. Even by 1825, when the Erie Canal was completed, the city had acquired its enduring position as the American metropolis.

Becoming the American Metropolis

The transformation of New York from provincial port to national metropolis had many causes. In the long term, the building of the state's canal system was central, by giving New York command of a hinterland that no other American city could match. But in terms of interior commerce the canal was no more than a beginning. Cornelius Vanderbilt's shift from water-borne transport to rail and the building of the lines that became the New York Central and the Erie Railroad came next. Connection upon connection to the rest of the world would follow. The canal was only one innovation in a long sequence of changes.

New York's emergence as the premier American city and eventually a world metropolis began well before the canal. In 1790 it had 11,000 fewer people than its rival Philadelphia. During the decade that followed, both cities grew by 27,000 people, but New York was growing faster. By 1810 it was in the lead, 96,000 to 91,000. In 1820, with the canal still five years from completion, New York had 123,000 people to Philadelphia's 112,000. A decade later New York's lead was 40,000 people, and by 1840 it rose to 92,000.

Major changes in the city's economy accompanied this demographic surge. Sail started to give way to steam. Irregular, unpredictable voyages began to be replaced by scheduled services. Against all apparent geographical logic, the city captured much of the commerce of the cotton South, including its transatlantic trade in both directions. But New York became more than a carrier of other places' goods. What its rich people did with their money changed. For the most part very rich colonials had put their fortunes safely into land or loans that were secured by land. In effect, their fortunes "went to sleep." Now moneyed individuals found ever-widening investment possibilities. Banks, canal bonds, rural land purchased for speculation rather than for safety, urban real estate in a rapidly rising market, textile factories, iron foundries, shipyards, engineering works—all these beckoned. The city became the informal capital of a complex region. That region included other towns that also traded and manufactured and a highly productive and increasingly capitalist countryside. Within it an advanced system of transport and communications bound together its people and their polities and businesses.

New York's great era of building sail-driven clipper ships still lay in the future. But rivermen on the Hudson grasped quickly what was coming. They showed their own feelings by trying to ram the *Clermont*'s paddle wheels. Initially, steam travel was only for well-off passengers, with sailing vessels continuing to carry freight and the poor. But steam power spread to harbor ferries, other rivers, and coasting voyages. In 1819 the *Savannah* made the first steam-driven voyage across the Atlantic. Its namesake city in Georgia was its home port, but it was built in Fitchett and Crockett's New York yard.

The early nineteenth century saw the emergence of New York harbor as a major center for mechanical engineering, with only Glasgow's River Clyde to rival it in producing "new devices for propelling steamships." Robert Fulton and Robert R. Livingston themselves began the industry, building an engine plant in Jersey City. When Fulton died in 1815 the premier engine builder James Allaire took over their business and moved it to Corlear's Hook, near the East River shipyards, using iron that was smelted in his New Jersey furnaces. New York's shipyards and engine works built and repaired steam vessels for the Hudson River, for coasting and long-haul ocean trade, and for many other ports. Thanks to its steam-engine shops the city was acquiring a community of mechanical innovators who framed their thought in terms of heavy machinery, much as the state's civil engineers were thinking in terms of earth, rock, cement, and the flow of water. Heavy capitalization; technological change; the beginning of mechanical engineering; new advantages for New York's sea-borne trade: all these came together in Allaire's yard and the competitors that followed.

Changes in maritime technology led to changes in the law of commerce. Initially, the state legislature gave a monopoly of steam navigation on New York waters to Robert Fulton and his Livingston backers. Not only did they have the exclusive right to traffic within the state, but out-of-state steamboats were forbidden to enter. But steam technology was too simple to be monopolized and too effective to be ignored. Connecticut responded to New York's exclusion of out-of-state boats by banning New York vessels from its own ports. The young Cornelius Vanderbilt of Staten Island made his name and began to build his fortune by operating federally licensed ferries across New York harbor in violation of the state monopoly. The ultimate result was the United States Supreme Court decision in *Gibbons v. Ogden* (1824) that Congress had the paramount power to regulate interstate commerce. With that, the state monopoly was dead.

Precisely at 10:00 A.M. on January 5, 1818, the Black Ball line's sailing vessel *James Monroe* cast loose from a pier on the East River for Liverpool, despite a snowstorm. The ship carried only "seven passengers . . . a cargo of small value . . . and the letter bag brought down from the coffee house at the last minute." Until then transatlantic and coastal commerce meant whatever vessel could be had, with no fixed schedules and frequently no fixed route, except for the monthly mail brigs that the British government had been operating since the colonial period. The *James Monroe* belonged to a fleet of four vessels which Black Ball promised would sail on fixed dates, "full or not full," whatever the weather. In strict terms the promise could not be kept, because no vessel under sail could guarantee how long its voyage would take. Genuinely regular departures and predictable arrivals had to wait until the Cunard Line transferred its steam-powered service from Boston to New York in mid-century. Nonetheless, the on-time departure of the *James Monroe* marked the beginning of New York's permanent transatlantic primacy in scheduled services.

During the first decades of the new century, New York merchants gained control of much of the trade of the booming cotton South. The South had always depended on others for its carrying trade, and the entry of New York ships into its cotton trade is not surprising. But New York did more than carry cotton direct to the mills of England and, to a much smaller extent, to the American Northeast. It managed to divert much of the eastbound English trade to its own piers for transshipment and to carry the manufactured goods white southerners wanted, wherever they had been made. The earlier tobacco South had been forced by British legislation to ship its product to mainland Europe via British ports, with no gain to itself. Now, without legislation, much of the new southern staple was benefiting New York City the same way, though most of it was on its way to Britain's factories.

A Web of Cities

As New York City seized national predominance, towns all over the state began to pass the "urban threshold." Legally, Albany had been a city since colonial days, but until the Revolution it remained a self-enclosed, mostly Dutch community that served the British military in wartime and traded furs. Like New York City, it owed its post-Revolutionary development to the west. Like New York's, that development began well before the Erie Canal.

Some of the Yankees who crossed the Berkshire Mountains after independence found Albany a good place to stay. By 1820 the city had 12,000 people. Its Dutch were now a small minority, though their language and their customs would endure for decades to come. Yankees controlled Albany's commerce and manufacturing. Even before the canal the port could handle up to two hundred river vessels at once. The year that canal construction began, the city built a four-thousand-foot pier to accommodate up to a thousand canal boats at a time. In that year almost half the city's adult males were involved in manufacturing, working in fifty-eight separate establishments. In 1820 the city's largest enterprises included "three tanneries, four breweries, four distilleries, four air furnaces, a prospering tobacco factory, a thriving hatmaking business, and brick-yards." With the canal's completion came iron manufacturing, a wholesale lumber trade, and a large-scale printing business.

In 1695 the seventeen blocks within Albany's walls were dominated by a fort, roughly where the state capitol building now stands. A crude map drawn in 1770 still shows the fort, now looming over some forty built-up blocks that spread down Capitol Hill to the flats along the Hudson. When Surveyor General Simeon De Witt drew another map in 1794 the fort was gone, though the city still had a barracks. De Witt added out-of-town mansions belonging to the Schuyler and Yates families. His map showed six separate churches and their equally separate burial grounds, as well as a market, a courthouse, a prison, and a ferry house on the riverbank. The Albany that De Witt saw still displayed much the same outline and occupied much the same space, with some fifty irregularly shaped blocks of buildings.

Its public life, however, was changing. Colonial Albany had been a "city state," ruled by its largely Dutch town fathers and under the strong influence of nearby great landlords such as the Livingstons, the Van Rensselaers, and the Johnsons. Now it had had a revolution. For a time its most powerful man was Abraham Yates, self-taught lawyer and one-time cobbler. Practically alone

Church and Market Streets, Albany (1805). The image shows both Dutch and newer English architectural styles. By James Eights. New York State Historical Association, Cooperstown, N.Y.

among major towns, it was in 1788 Antifederalist in its politics. Perhaps that measured the influence of the deeply Antifederal Yates and his mistrust of "high flyers." Yates lost on the question of the Constitution, but he remained a diehard Antifederalist. In 1790 Governor Clinton and the Council of Appointment made him Albany's mayor.

Five years after the Erie Canal was opened another map showed a wholly different Albany. The old city remained visible in outline, but it had become the core of a much larger place, with roughly one hundred new blocks. Now the city was differentiated by function and by class. Clustered around the intersection of State and Pearl Streets were twenty-one blocks that formed a central business district. Eighteen consisted of businesses only; three blocks continued the older pattern of mixing business and residence, with work and family life going on in much the same space. Sixteen more blocks close to the business zone comprised middle-class housing exclusively. Twenty-eight blocks held mixed middle-class and working class-residences. All the rest was working-class housing, surrounding the whole city with "a miserable collection of hovels" inhabited by "mostly mechanics." Working people dwelt in a thin belt that faced the canal basin and the river, in another belt that was farthest up the hill, and in densely packed districts in both the north and south ends of the city. Many of them were young single males, occupying Albany's many boarding houses.

Albany was undergoing a smaller-scale version of what historian Sean Wilentz calls the "metropolitan industrialization" that was underway in New York City. This sort of industrialization did not lead straight to enormous factories, like the textile mills being built in Lowell, Massachusetts, or that would appear in Rensselaer and Cohoes. Small shops persisted, but their proprietors stood an ever-smaller chance of reaching the point where they could run their businesses on their own terms. Contract work bound them to conditions that somebody else decided. Central shops turned them from masters of their businesses and their crafts into workers for wages. "Putting-out" broke production into distinct stages and separated people who had different skills, often by the sex of the worker. Clothing, shoes, and furniture were becoming "sweated trades." Subcontracting was having much the same effect on construction work. The goal of rising from apprenticeship in a craft to a point where one truly controlled one's skills and one's business was giving way to the reality that some people would work all their lives for others.

While New York exploded and Albany grew, other towns were changing. In 1820 Kingston occupied seventeen blocks. It was still a village, less advanced than Albany, and its people had not yet segregated themselves by function or social class. Twenty-nine of its fifty business places had the owner's residence on the same site. But Kingston already had twenty-one sites that were used exclusively for business. Just after the Erie Canal main line came into full use, Kingston became the Hudson River terminus of the Delaware and Hudson

Canal, reaching southwest to Port Jervis. That canal's sole purpose was to carry Pennsylvania anthracite coal to the Hudson for shipment south to New York. The canal transformed Kingston from a Dutch community that served the marketing needs of small Ulster County farmers into a secondary city that not only shipped coal but also made heavy goods, including cement, machinery, and iron castings. Together with Newburgh, Poughkeepsie, Hudson, Troy, West Troy (Watervliet), and Cohoes, it was becoming part of the Hudson Valley's nineteenth-century urban industrial network.

Westward, the process of urbanization followed the progress of the Erie Canal. When the Reverend John Taylor made his missionary tour of the Mohawk and Black River country in 1802, he drew maps of the major places he passed through. Little Falls already enjoyed the benefit of the Western Inland Lock Navigation Company's short canal, but it contained only a few houses, a

As transportation improved in the early nineteenth century, even people in remote areas craved luxury goods and cultural "refinement." "The Itinerant Artist" (oil on canvas, ca. 1830). By Charles Bird King. New York State Historical Association, Cooperstown, N.Y.

mill on the Mohawk, and an octagonal church. Whitestown had forty-four houses and three churches, stretched out over "nearly one mile." Utica had eighty-two buildings and Rome had fifty-five, dominated by the bulk of Fort Stanwix. These were the only places that Taylor thought significant enough to draw.

Someone making the same expedition with the same intent a quarter-century later would have filled page after page with sketches. By 1820 Syracuse had 1,814 people, Rochester had 1,502, and Buffalo had 2,095. In 1825 Lockport had 3,007 people. Rochester was taking the first steps toward the domination of flour milling that it would enjoy for decades to come. Utica had become a commercial center of considerable note, and local leaders initiated a stock offering to finance a steam-driven textile mill. The Utica Cotton Works that resulted was soon followed by three additional factories, with a total investment of $500,000 and 1,200 employees. Western New York's industrial development was beginning, even as the frontier closed. The full effects of that development were still to be felt. But the main lines it would take were now clear. The old New York in which city and countryside were radically separated was disappearing. In its place was emerging a complex economic region, with a great metropolis, important second-level centers, a web of smaller places that were becoming cities rather than mere market towns, and a rich agricultural zone as commercial as New York City itself, all bound together by the best transport the age had to offer.

Slavery Dies

The young nineteenth century offered new possibilities and new challenges to all New Yorkers, but most especially to the people of the cities. In New York City, in Albany, and in the smaller places of the Hudson Valley and the canal main line, townspeople struggled to understand the possibilities and to meet the challenges. What these were and how people met them depended on the race, gender, and class of the people concerned.

It was a writer in the *Ulster Sentinel* of Kingston who called New York City a "paradise of Negroes." Ulster County was a place where slavery died hard, and the full context showed the writer's own stance. As slavery broke up and its victims began leaving the scenes of their torment, the *Sentinel* opined: "A few of this ill-fated race, more wise and faithful than the rest, still remain in their own chimney corners to spend their days in comfort; [while] the wicked ones, the thieves, the drunkards, and the bullies, are all gone to that paradise of negroes, the City of New York! There let them stay, a curse or blessing to those who made themselves so busy in their behalf." The following year "a coloured boy" of Kingston received a life sentence on a charge of burglary while a white man was sentenced to only "three years for assault and battery with intent to kill." The black people of Ulster County had good reason to think that its chimney corners offered no refuge and that their best chances lay in New York City, "paradise" or no.

New York adopted gradual emancipation in 1799, but the law took until July 4, 1827, to reach its full effect. During that quarter-century the black communities of New York City and Albany defined themselves on terms at least partly their own. Even under slavery, the cities offered possibilities that the countryside did not. Urban slaves could escape their masters' and mistresses' eyes to meet, commiserate, celebrate, plot, mourn, and love in a world of taverns and dance halls that whites rarely saw. Newly free black New Yorkers had to face poverty and violence, and for some of them petty crime and prostitution seemed the only way to survive. But in the early nineteenth century New York City did offer black males a fair chance of finding work at a skilled trade. It was during New York slavery's long, slow breakup that the black community began to develop the churches, benevolent societies, and small businesses that became its own sinews.

One result was the festival called "Pinkster," celebrated each spring in both New York City and Albany. The name derives from Pentecost, the Christian festival forty days after Easter. A black king presided at Pinkster in each city, and for the festival's duration what seemed to be African music, dancing, stories, and food filled the streets. But Pinkster also was in the European tradition of carnival, the annual festival of misrule when stifling social roles could be reversed, unspeakable truths could be uttered, and the tensions of an unequal society briefly could find release. White plebeians' resistance against British policy in the 1760s had drawn on the same carnival tradition of an open-air theater that could easily turn into political protest. For the whites the carnival tradition had taken the form of "Pope's Day" each November 5, celebrating the English heritage of Protestant liberty. For the blacks it became Pinkster, and it was genuinely both African and American. Pinkster demonstrated how "black and white lived in one another's pockets," mixing together African traditions that had survived enslavement with customs of protest acquired from the ruling race's culture. African Americans elsewhere developed similar festivals; the New England equivalent was the annual "negro election." But Pinkster itself was unique to New York.

Middle-Class Women Organize

White women also found new possibilities in the cities. A married women's property law granting effective economic independence from husbands was still in the future in the early nineteenth century; its absence was one of the major items on the bill of indictment against men that the Seneca Falls women's rights convention issued in 1848. So was protest concerning the difficulty of securing divorces. In New York, the Revolution had not changed the ancient doctrine of coverture, which subordinated women to their husbands in matters of property, contracts, wills, and lawsuits. A 1787 statute gave the courts the power to grant absolute divorces in cases of adultery, but otherwise women had to resort to the legislature for a private act that would permit separation, not divorce. So prominent a woman as Nancy Shippen, daughter of a major Philadelphia family, found it virtually impossible to divorce her disreputable but apparently faithful husband Henry Beekman Livingston in 1789. The possibility of securing a private act in the legislature was beyond even her powers of wealth and family distinction.

Nonetheless, by the early nineteenth century New York women were beginning to act independently in the public arena. They sought formal legal incorporation in groups like New York City's Society for the Relief of Poor Widows with Small Children (1802) and its Association for the Relief of Respectable, Aged, Indigent Females (1815), Whitestown's Female Charitable Society (1810), and Albany's Society for the Relief of Distressed Women and Children (1804). Such groups marked the beginnings of a distinctive "women's sphere," radically separate from the world of men. At its worst this meant choking middle-class domesticity; at its most liberating, it meant the possibility of genuinely independent thought, activity, and sisterhood.

Gender, Class, and Community

The workingwomen of Albany's north and south ends faced different problems. So, in much larger numbers, did the women who found in New York City "a way station of . . . misery, an asylum for all kinds of survivors looking for another chance." These women had to work to survive, whether at needle trades, as servants, in provisioning and peddling, at traditional work like spinning, or, at worst, in prostitution. They enjoyed little protection from men, which was demonstrated graphically in 1793. A young New York City seamstress named Lanah Sawyer brought a charge of rape against Harry Bedlow. Bedlow was a gentleman, and his successful defense was that a woman like Sawyer could expect a man like him to try to have his way with her in return for an evening's entertainment. Bedlow had not committed rape, his lawyer argued, but simply seduction, an "art" of which he was an "accomplished practitioner."

Like black New Yorkers, the white working poor developed a world of which middle-class whites knew little. For workingwomen, the open neighborhood, rather than the closed household, became the focus of daily life and the means of survival. An economy of borrowing and pawning permitted families to

get through difficult times. Middle-class children were becoming economic lia-
bilities, and the rate of pregnancies per middle-class marriage was starting to
fall. Whether that was due to contraception or to abstinence is not as important
as the growing awareness of the women and men involved that fertility could be
controlled. But the children of the poor had to contribute whatever they could
gain, even if it was by begging and scavenging. "Of the children brought before
me for pilfering, nine out of ten are those whose fathers are dead and who live
with their mothers, and are employed this way," wrote a magistrate in 1830. A
set of unwritten customs took shape to govern how neighbors and strangers
dealt with one another. New York's streets were noted for their violence in the
early nineteenth century, and genteel observers looked at it all in horror. But
beneath the turmoil, the workingwomen of the city were living within patterns
that made sense to themselves and to the people around them.

The middle-class abolitionist and feminist Lydia Maria Child once observed
an incident that summed up the gender-, class-, and group-bound street culture
of New York City in the early nineteenth century. "A gentleman in a downtown
crowd ordered an old, unnamed Irish woman to move out of his way. 'And
indade I won't get out of your way; I'll get right in your way,'" the woman
replied. She was claiming the city's sidewalks as her own, within the American
tradition of equal rights. The formal politics of the young state addressed the
problem of equal voices for equal citizens, too. But during the nineteenth century's first quarter it did so in a way that spoke only to the needs and interests
of white men.

18

The Empire State and the Albany Regency

A BEGUILING SET OF MEN ACTED THE MAIN ROLES ON New York's political stage during the early nineteenth century. The Revolutionary generation was passing. John Jay went into a long retirement when he left the governorship in 1801. George Clinton was a spent force, though he served as governor again from 1801 to 1804 and as vice president until his death in 1812. Alexander Hamilton left public life, at least officially, and practiced law in New York City until Aaron Burr shot him in 1804. By killing Hamilton and then by scheming to detach the Mississippi Valley from the United States, Burr ruined his own political future. Philip Schuyler was in decline, though he remained interested in the western canal project.

Not all of them went quickly. Rufus King migrated from Massachusetts, joined Philip Schuyler as one of New York's first two United States senators in 1789, went on to diplomacy, and returned to start two more terms in the Senate in 1813, still a Federalist. Robert R. Livingston remained an aristocrat in his personal ways. But he abandoned Federalist politics after he failed to win public office under President Washington. He made common cause with Governor George Clinton, became a diplomat for Thomas Jefferson, purchased Louisiana for the United States, sponsored the *Clermont*, and joined the canal commission in 1811. Stephen Van Rensselaer kept alive all that Philip Schuyler stood for, as Federalist politician, military man, patroon, and canal commissioner. New figures began to appear: George Tibbits of Rensselaer County, Elisha Williams of Columbia, James Kent, chancellor of the court of chancery. All these, including King, Schuyler, and Livingston, were part of what historian David Hackett Fischer calls "the revolution of American conservatism," as men of caution and property learned to manipulate what they no longer could dominate. That phrase provides a better way of understanding their position and their tactics than the older idea of aristocracy's absolute decline.

These figures had to cope with a new situation that was not of their making: the surge of "lesser" men into the political arena that the Revolution made possible. In 1788 the great majority of those "lesser" men in New York were Antifederalists. Once the federal Constitution took effect, those new men who had taken control of the state had to cope in their own turn with a situation they had not made or desired: the existence of the United States in its modern political form.

George Clinton (oil on canvas, ca. 1812). By Ezra Ames. New York State Historical Association, Cooperstown, N.Y.

Some simply withdrew from the larger stage, like Abraham Yates, the former congressman and state senator, settling into parochial security as mayor of Albany. Most former Antifederalists coped better, as the careers of the uncle and nephew George and De Witt Clinton show. The older Clinton was perhaps the Constitution's most formidable single opponent, yet he ended his political career as vice president of the United States. For a time he entertained presidential ambitions of his own. The younger Clinton became his uncle's secretary in 1793. His own career took him to a short term in the United States Senate, and he too dreamed of the presidency, seeking it in 1812. But New York was his arena, and he stood in that arena's center until his sudden death in 1827. Like George Clinton before him, Daniel Tompkins advanced from the governorship (1807–17) to the vice presidency under James Monroe. Like both Clintons and Aaron Burr, he was a president who might-have-been.

William L. Marcy, Samuel A. Talcott, Benjamin Butler, Silas Wright, Edwin Croswell, Azariah Flagg, and Churchill C. Cambreleng coalesced as a distinct political leadership during the late 1810s. They became one of the centers of the emergent Democratic party. So strong was their rule for a time that their opponents christened them the Albany Regency, in a negative-campaigning effort to brand them as quasi-monarchists. The name stuck, although it exaggerated the power that they actually held. Marcy, Wright, and Flagg were New England born, and Cambreleng came from North Carolina. Their New York involvement was a sign of how attractive the state was becoming to people from elsewhere. But at the Regency's center was Martin Van Buren, whose Dutch family had the deepest possible New York roots in Kinderhook, Columbia County. In 1836 Van Buren would be the first New Yorker to win the presidency of the United States.

"I don't pretend to comprehend their politics," observed Oliver Wolcott, another migrant. "It is a labyrinth of wheels within wheels, and it is understood only by the managers." But those "managers" formed a generation of genuine achievement. They dealt with the War of 1812. They oversaw the building of the Erie Canal. They invented and worked out the implications of modern American party politics, and on this count the credit is largely Van Buren's. They came to grips with the limits and the inadequacies of the political settlement that the state had made in 1777, and in 1821 they produced a new state constitution. Through it all they maneuvered, fought, forgave, coalesced, and split with one another in a political ballet that expressed their personal ambitions as much as any larger issues. By 1826 New York had adopted the principle that any white adult male could vote and hold public office. It also had adopted the understanding that public life required organization—outright partisanship—as much as it required patriotism and public spirit. These were among the prime tenets of the "democracy in America" that the French commentator Alexis de Tocqueville astutely observed not long afterward.

The Chief Engineer and the Little Magician

After Jefferson's election to the presidency in 1800, Federalism was dead as a national political force. The continuing careers of King, Kent, Tibbits, and their like demonstrate that it was not at all dead in New York. But the main debates and struggles took place among the political heirs of George Clinton rather than between them and the heirs of Alexander Hamilton. The complex relationship of alliance and rivalry between De Witt Clinton and Martin Van Buren shows the limits of early Democratic-Republican politics.

The younger Clinton was the son of the Revolutionary general James Clinton, who co-led the expedition of 1779 against the Iroquois. James Clinton became a minor beneficiary of the great sell-off of state land in 1791, acquiring a thousand acres on the Chenango River for £200. This may have sparked his son's enduring western interest and led to his involvement with Philip Schuyler's Western Inland Lock Navigation Company. No more a friend to Schuyler than were his father and uncle, the son publicly accused the general of using the company for his own purposes. By the beginning of the new century De Witt Clinton was a state senator, and he moved briefly to the United States Senate before becoming mayor of New York City in 1803. We already have seen his role in advocating, financing, and building the Erie Canal.

No friend to Governor Morgan Lewis (1804–7) either, Clinton attempted in 1806 to engineer a reconciliation between his own family's wing of the Democratic-Republican party and the followers of Aaron Burr. The attempt failed, and a bewildering dance of political factions ensued. Burrites who rejected Clinton's overtures became "Martling Men" (for the proprietor of a tavern where they met). They took control of New York City's Tammany Society, which had been a friendly association and now began its long career as a formidable political force. In 1807 De Witt Clinton lost the mayoralty, thanks to opposition from Tammany, from old Federalists who still regarded his family as the political enemy, and from supporters of Governor Lewis, who were calling themselves Quids. The word is Latin, and the reference was to their claim to represent the essence ("quiddity") of republicanism. Clinton himself supported Daniel Tompkins for the governorship but broke with him quickly after Tompkins won.

The next year Clinton supported his uncle George rather than James Madison for the presidency. His reasoning was that Virginians had held the office long enough and that since two previous vice presidents, Jefferson and John Adams, had moved up when the time came, it was his uncle's turn. That won him no friendship from Madison (who did not like George Clinton either). In 1810 Clinton sought the vacant lieutenant governorship in a special election. A massive Tammany meeting launched a campaign against him with support from Madison, Tompkins, and the remaining Federalists. Nonetheless, Clinton won, and he used the victory as the basis for his own presidential bid two years later, challenging Madison with the official endorsement of the Democratic-Republicans of New York. He ran an astute campaign. Federalists were sure that like them he opposed the War of 1812. Others believed that he would prosecute the war more effectively than Madison. He carried much of the Northeast. But Madison was reelected on the strength of western and southern votes.

The Clintons had become a political family of note and weight, and a connection with them was highly desirable. That is one reason why Federalists supported De Witt Clinton's presidential bid. Another reason is that his own policies were on a course which approached theirs. Both the canal and the war provide evidence. In 1812 Clinton also had the support of his fellow Democratic-Republican Martin Van Buren, who managed his campaign in the state. But that campaign marked the beginning of their permanent political estrangement. It also started Van Buren down the intellectual path that led him to work out the enduring principles of American partisanship. If the Erie Canal formed De Witt Clinton's legacy to his state, parties in their modern form were what Martin Van Buren bequeathed to the country.

Van Buren was the son of a tavern keeper, which meant that he genuinely was without "family" in the sense of the term that Philip Schuyler had used to disparage George Clinton in 1777. Van Buren's people were plebeian patriots, the sort who supported George Clinton and Thomas Jefferson. His native

Columbia County was Federalist country, and early in his life he associated with Columbia County's premier Federalist family, the Silvesters. He resisted invitations to join them politically, however, linking instead with Kinderhook's Republican gentry, the Van Nesses. All his life Van Buren had a complex relationship with grandees. As a rising figure in Washington during the early 1820s, he shared lodgings with Rufus King, and the Federalist King eventually became Van Buren's Democratic ally. When Van Buren was American minister to England in 1831–32, he consorted happily with royalty and titled aristocrats. After his presidency he purchased the Van Ness home, named it Lindenwald, and made it into a stately dwelling in ostentatious Victorian style. Touring Europe in 1853, he took pleasure in meeting the king of Belgium and Pope Pius IX. But always Van Buren valued what he regarded as the Revolution's fruits of republicanism, liberty, and equality. For most of his life he equated fidelity to the Revolution itself with party regularity as a Democrat.

Van Buren supported De Witt Clinton in 1812 because the New York Democratic-Republican party did. Clinton's defeat presented Van Buren with a dilemma. He was no Federalist, and he ardently supported the War of 1812. To him, "WAR ALONE" formed "our only refuge from national degradation." He maneuvered successfully to reestablish himself in the favor of Governor Tompkins, who also supported the war, and of President Madison. Tompkins had the difficult task of mobilizing New Yorkers to support a war that was fought largely on their own borders. The opposition came not only from Anglophile Federalists but from militiamen who did not want to serve and from citizens who did not want to be taxed. When General Stephen Van Rensselaer led an expedition to the Niagara frontier in 1812, he had to watch helplessly as his New York militia refused to cross the river into Canada and rescue a trapped American force. Though a Federalist, he resigned his command in disgust. The land war went ill all along the Saint Lawrence, Ontario, and Niagara frontier, and both Buffalo and Black Rock were burned by the British in 1813. Van Buren served Tompkins and Madison well in the state legislature and on the hustings, taking a major hand in keeping New York from joining the New England states in outright opposition at the Hartford Convention of 1814.

The war's seemingly successful end gave Van Buren the advantage of having been on the winning and patriotic side. But he had to deal with the way that Clinton was using the canal issue to make his own political comeback, particularly after it became clear in 1816 that New York would build a canal either on its own or not at all. Van Buren's own natural constituency, Hudson Valley farmers, had their doubts about the canal, and in 1816 he voted in the state Senate against beginning construction. But he had long since graduated from county to state-level politics, and his ambitions ran still higher. He knew that in most of the state canal enthusiasm was high. He covered himself when he voted against construction by calling for another survey along the projected route. His goal became not to stop the canal but to win some of the credit for himself and his own faction. He did so by making a powerful speech in favor of the canal on the state Senate floor in 1817, citing the desire of "the People" and predicting that the canal would "raise the state to the highest possible pitch of fame and grandeur."

Though Clinton publicly thanked Van Buren, the rivalry between the two was in no sense ended. By 1819 Van Buren was disparaging Clinton as the "Magnus Apollo," and Clinton was responding that Van Buren was an "arch-scoundrel" and a "confirmed knave." Better than Clinton at understanding popular politics, Van Buren began organizing his "Bucktail" faction (so called from the decorations members wore on their hats) to get permanent control of the state. This was the core of what became the Albany Regency and eventually the Democratic party.

Van Buren finally succeeded because, as the astute if partisan observer Thurlow Weed noted, "opposition to the Erie and Champlain canals . . . ceased." This had been Clinton's issue and when it became a matter of general agreement it no longer could win office for Clinton or his followers. Clinton's enemies took control of the state legislature as early as 1820, and by 1823 he was no longer governor. Now they set out to remove him even from the canal commission. They succeeded in doing so in March 1824 by legislative resolution, but his supporters fought back with massive protest meetings and returned Clinton to the governorship later that year. A chastened Van Buren realized his party's mistake, telling his lieutenant Roger Skinner, who had organized the removal, "that there is such a thing in politics as killing a man too dead!" Clinton remained a political force until his actual death three years later, but by this time Van Buren had shifted his own arena and his ambitions to the national level. A new cast of characters would control New York during the century's second quarter.

Factions Become Parties

The tangled narrative of New York politics after 1800, with its Quids, Martling Men, Tammanys, Clintonians, Bucktails, Albany Regency, and old Federalists suggests the dimensions of the problem that the Little Magician of Kinderhook faced. Without coherence there could be no political direction. Clinton had vision and energy. What he lacked was the talent to keep his supporters together once he had them mobilized. Much more the opportunist, Van Buren understood how to create a disciplined political organization.

Van Buren's great insight was the necessity of political parties in an open society. New Yorkers had been "factious" since colonial days; they had turned their Revolutionary coalition into a "partisan culture" during the 1780s; they had outright parties by the 1790s. But like the rest of the young republic's people they were suspicious of the very idea of internal division. James Madison's famous discussion of how to control self-interested "faction" in *The Federalist*, No. 10, struck a resonance in New York public culture. What Madison wrote sprang from the classically republican belief that citizens of good will could arrive at an understanding of their large, shared public interest. Madison himself retreated from this, suggesting that the causes of faction were inherent in liberty and that its ill effects would best be controlled by allowing conflicting interests to cancel one another out. But he did hope that a republican elite would be able to act in a genuinely public-spirited and "disinterested" manner. Madison's insight was brilliant and his presentation was superb, which is why that essay ranks among the classics of political theory. The shifting quicksand of New York politics after 1800 demonstrated where Madison's prescription actually led.

A practical man who never had a higher education, Van Buren cut through the intellectual remnants of classical republicanism. Addressing the state constitutional convention of 1821, he defended partisan political competition. The issue was public appointments, and Van Buren's proposal was to put them into the hands of the governor. The old Council of Appointment had long since become a forum for partisan self-seeking, particularly if the state senators who made up the council and the governor who chaired it were of different parties. To Van Buren the issue was twofold. In practical terms public appointments were necessary to build party support. Getting control of justiceships of the peace was the issue in 1821; getting control of the jobs the canal system offered was one reason why the Regency evicted Clinton from the commission three years later. But Van Buren also understood "the partiality and attachment, which men of the same political sentiments have for each other." If the power of appointment was "put in the hands of the executive" it would be "not for himself, but to secure to the majority of the people that control and influence . . . to which they are justly entitled." Should a new majority replace one party with another, the new rulers would still be the people's agents. Those agents would have as much right as their predecessors to hire and fire public servants in the people's name. In Van Buren's treatment, political spoilsmanship became a branch of democratic theory.

In practice, the Albany Regency insisted on a discipline among its followers that was as strict as any American political machine ever has exacted. When Van Buren went to Washington as United States senator in 1821 the Regency became his means for keeping control of the state. Foreshadowing party leaders like William Marcy "Boss" Tweed and George Washington Plunkitt of nineteenth-century Tammany Hall and Albany's twentieth-century Daniel O'Connell, Van Buren and his associates decided among themselves what public policy would be. Then they used the press and a network of officeholders to see that what they had decided was implemented. The *Albany Argus* was central to how they worked. Its printer, Moses Cantine, was the official state publisher, and the paper was read statewide. In Van Buren's own words, "without a paper thus edited at Albany, we may hang our harps on the willows. With it the party can survive a thousand . . . convulsions." In this manner was decreed "the will of Pope Martin the First," as one hostile observer called him.

The Regency was a machine, however, not a dictatorship. Van Buren and his associates took every possible step to consolidate their control, and they justified what they were doing in the name of "the people," as many an actual dictator has done. But they understood the idea of a "public trust" which they could lose. They realized that if they lost it they would have to retire. Nor, for all its contribution to American political practice, was the Regency the sole creator of democracy in New York. Van Buren always imagined himself an enemy of aristocracy, and he was the chief architect of what became the state's Democratic party. But he could not claim a copyright on populist rhetoric.

The effective phrase "Albany Regency," with its overtones of royalty, was coined by Van Buren's enemies, who began calling themselves "the People's party" in 1823. The actual people, meaning the voting male electorate, drove the point home forcefully when the machine killed De Witt Clinton "too dead" in 1824. The defeat of the Regency after its vindictive removal of Clinton from the canal commission was in the name of "CLINTON and LIBERTY." That, rather than anything Van Buren did, has been called "the acme in the battle for democracy in New York."

Democracy and Race

By the standards of the early nineteenth century, democracy arrived in New York between 1821 and 1826. In the former year a constitutional convention met at Albany and drastically revised the constitution of 1777. It was an assembly of many talents. Among its members were Federalists James Kent, Peter Augustus Jay, and Stephen Van Rensselaer and Republicans Daniel D. Tompkins, Erastus Root, and Martin Van Buren. Van Buren's group had 110 of 126 seats.

The actual spark that caused the convention to be called was the fact that the Council of Revision had vetoed an attempt to call one the previous year. The council itself was a casualty; the new constitution abolished it and gave a qualified veto on laws to the governor alone. The convention also abolished the unwieldy Council of Appointment. It made such high offices as secretary of state and comptroller elective by the legislature, and following Van Buren's lead it put the office of justice of the peace in the governor's gift. There were more than 2,500 justiceships and that enormous number presented massive possibilities for patronage. The term of the governor who would appoint the justices was reduced from three years to two, and the higher courts were reorganized and enlarged.

The convention changed specific property requirements for voting into a requirement of paying taxes, working on the roads, or serving in the militia. The change raised the total number of people who could vote, since the new minimum requirement was considerably easier to meet than the old had been. The new constitution also ended the distinction between people who could vote for only assemblymen and people who could vote for senators and the governor as well. Any person who met the new requirement could vote in any election. Abolishing the old property requirements provoked strong rhetorical opposition, put most effectively by Chancellor Kent, who predicted "corruption, injustice, violence, and tyranny" from widened suffrage. But during the debate Van Buren disavowed the idea of absolute democracy. He and his followers were no "Jacobins of France," he said. They would not "undervalue this precious privilege, so far as to confer it . . . upon everyone, black or white, who would be kind enough to condescend to accept it." It was not until five years later that New York completely abolished all property requirements for its white male voters.

As with the attempted abolition of slavery in 1785, the one issue that cut across the predictable lines of division turned on race. By 1821 the state had roughly six thousand black male voters. They came close to losing the vote altogether when a drafting committee called "for something close to white manhood suffrage." Many of Van Buren's supporters who wanted manhood suffrage were also perfectly happy with complete black exclusion. One of them declared in the convention that black peoples' "minds . . . were not competent to vote." It was the Federalists, the upholders of an older social vision and a more limited view of the polity, who supported black suffrage.

Van Buren himself did not go as far as his more racist supporters. He agreed in principle with the Federalist position, and he voted against the proposal to exclude black people from elections entirely. Free black people paid taxes, he reasoned, and he was too much a son of the Revolution to accept the idea of taxation without any possibility of political representation. But Van Buren also knew how most of his constituents felt, and he knew that most black voters would support his political enemies, not his friends. The principle of black voting survived, but he accepted a later proposal that a $250 freehold be required. The new requirement drastically reduced the number of black men eligible to vote. Given the realities of poverty and urban residence in the lives of most former New York slaves, it might as well have been an absolute exclusion.

The convention finished its work in November 1821, and the new constitution went into effect the next year. Its makers cannot be criticized for not being ahead of their time. But it seems a fair judgment that they resolved the issues of the early nineteenth century rather than prepared for the issues that New York and the United States were about to face. If "the people" meant the white male electorate, New York did approach democracy during De Witt Clinton's and Martin Van Buren's political heyday. The debate between the Hamiltonian view of active government for the sake of the few and the Jeffersonian view of limited government in the name of the whole people was over. Both sides had won. New York's government would be active, and it would be for the sake of what the era conceived to be the whole. Partisanship was a fact of life, and implicitly the constitution recognized it. Representing a New York that Yankees now dominated, the convention could not have foreseen the tensions that massive Irish and German Catholic immigration would bring in the next two decades. It did not even foresee the convulsive opposition to Freemasonry that was about to burst upon the western part of the state.

The issue which the convention saw but ducked was race. The members of the convention showed that they understood its importance by debating it at length. But they resolved their debate in favor of black inequality, as did the rest of their white America. Van Buren's own ambivalent stance foreshadowed his personal and political future. As an architect of the national Democratic party and a major supporter of Andrew Jackson, he would be central to the deliberate exclusion of the slavery question from national political debate during the 1830s and early 1840s. As the Free Soil party's presidential candidate in 1848, he would have a large hand in the disruption of the cross-section, pro-slavery, racist democracy that he himself had helped to put into institutional form. But even he could not have foreseen that within his own lifetime the enslavement and degradation that most white Americans still justified by race and the legal inequities and political exclusion that seemed to be the natural, God-given lot for people who were female would become public political issues of the first import. New Yorkers of the generation that followed Van Buren's own would raise that new agenda forcefully.

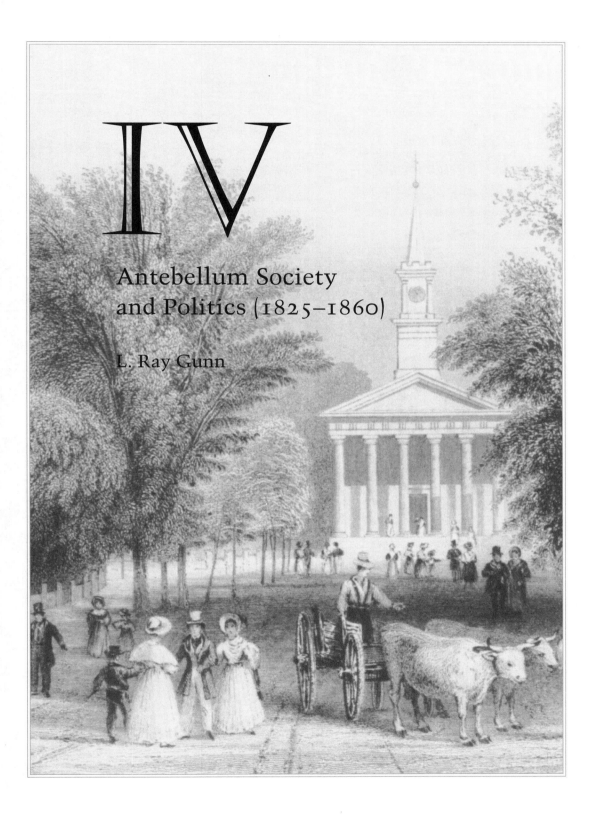

IV

Antebellum Society and Politics (1825–1860)

L. Ray Gunn

19

New York Modernizes
Economic Growth and Transformation

ON THE MORNING OF NOVEMBER 4, 1825, THE *SENECA CHIEF* and a flotilla of canal barges, escorted by Hudson River steamboats, entered New York harbor on the final leg of a historic journey. The *Seneca Chief*'s arrival at the great harbor, nine days and 425 miles after its departure from Buffalo, marked the completion of the first through passage from Lake Erie to New York City via the Erie Canal and the Hudson River. A ceremonial "Wedding of the Waters" of Lake Erie and the Atlantic Ocean off Sandy Hook officially concluded more than a week of pageantry as New Yorkers from Buffalo to the Battery joined in exuberant celebration. After eight years of effort and at a cost of more than $7 million, the dream of a canal linking the Great Lakes and the city on the Hudson had been realized.

The completion of the Erie Canal capped more than three decades of growth and development. By the 1820s, New York ranked first in the nation in population; led in the production of wheat; dominated the import and export trade; was poised to overtake Pennsylvania and Massachusetts in manufacturing output; and boasted the nation's most populous city. With its superb natural harbor and its strategic location at the mouth of one of the greatest navigable rivers on the continent, New York City surpassed all rivals for commercial supremacy after 1815, becoming the principal entrepôt for British goods entering the country, the American terminus for the first Atlantic packet line providing scheduled service to and from England, and the axis of the southern cotton trade with Europe. The opening of the Erie Canal was the final link in the city's ascendancy, allowing it to garner the trade of western New York beyond the Mohawk River and, ultimately, of the new states of the Ohio Valley.

"Lockport on the Erie Canal" (watercolor, 1832). By Mary Keys. Munson-Williams-Proctor Arts Institute, Museum of Art, Utica, N.Y. 55.45.

As remarkable as these achievements were, however, the next four decades witnessed even more extraordinary developments. Between 1825 and 1860, the Empire State emerged at the forefront of the movement toward modernization transforming American society, politics, and the economy. During these years, the state experienced spectacular population growth, urbanization, and immigration. Through a combination of public financing and entrepreneurial initiative, New Yorkers built a network of canals and railroads that was the envy of the world. Agriculture became increasingly commercialized and diversified and, in the process, reached new heights of productivity. The volume of commerce flowing into and out of the state through the Port of New York continued to expand at the same time that modern forms of business enterprise grew up to restructure the state's economy. Perhaps most striking of all, during the quarter-century following the opening of the Erie Canal, New York became the leading industrial state in the nation.

If the state spearheaded the process of national growth, it was also among the first to experience the wrenching consequences of social and economic change. Rapid population growth and urbanization, both fueled by massive immigration, generated new social problems and cultural tensions. While the "transportation revolution" penetrated the most remote corners of the state and integrated them into a market economy, it also produced new fault lines in New York society and politics—between those who supported and those who opposed state support for economic development and between those who embraced and those who resisted the growth of the market economy. The decline of household and handicraft production and the growth of manufacturing catapulted New York to the forefront of the world's most dynamic economies, but the changing relations of production undermined the status of skilled craftsmen and artisans, forced many of them into the ranks of an emerging industrial labor force, and produced a self-conscious working class. Simultaneously, the forces of industrialization and the growing market mentality combined to forge a new, modern, bourgeois sensibility among the middle class. Finally, although economic growth enhanced the quality of life and broadened the social and economic horizons of many New Yorkers, for countless others it brought new uncertainties, new inequalities of wealth, a loss of opportunity and status, and a hardening of class lines.

Population Growth and Urbanization

Demographic changes were among the most striking developments transforming New York in the decades preceding the Civil War. By 1820 the state's inhabitants numbered 1,372,812, a fourfold increase over 1790. Although the rate of growth was slower than in the earlier period, the state nevertheless grew an average of 29 percent each decade between 1820 and 1860, reaching a total of nearly four million people on the eve of the Civil War. New York City, which had replaced Philadelphia as the nation's largest urban center by 1810, more than kept pace with the state's population growth, reaching 348,943 by 1840. Two decades later, in 1860, it became the first American city to reach the one million mark. By that year, nearly one in four New Yorkers resided in the great seaport at the mouth of the Hudson.

The growth of New York City, while especially dramatic, was part of a much broader process of urbanization that was rapidly transforming the very character of the state's population. Albany, the state capital and the commercial center of upstate New York, had also grown rapidly in the late eighteenth and early nineteenth centuries, reaching a population of 12,630 by 1820. In the next decade it doubled in size and, in spite of a declining rate of growth, could boast more than 57,000 inhabitants by 1855. The process of urbanization was further fueled by the growth of the state's smaller towns and cities and by the appear-

Poughkeepsie, like other Hudson River ports, experienced rapid growth in the early years of the new republic. It had become an important urban center by the time J. M. Evans completed this painting (ca. 1840). New York State Historical Association, Cooperstown, N.Y.

ance of entirely new communities. Older Hudson River communities like Catskill and Poughkeepsie had grown rapidly in the years after the Revolution and were soon joined by new towns like Hudson and Troy. As the population shifted westward after 1800, the towns and villages along the Mohawk swelled. Later the extension of the Erie Canal into the westernmost counties of the state unleashed the most spectacular urban growth yet. Indeed, in the two decades between 1820 and 1840, western New York experienced the highest rate of urbanization of any region in the country. Utica grew by 330 percent; Rochester by 1,244 percent; and Buffalo by 769 percent. In combination with the rapid expansion of New York City, such growth rates dramatically changed the urban-rural balance in the state. By 1860, 39.3 percent of the population were city dwellers, up from 11.7 percent in 1820.

Although a high birth rate accounted for much of this growth (despite national fertility rates that were declining), foreign immigration contributed as well. Some 5.5 million immigrants entered the United States between 1815 and

1860; most disembarked at the Port of New York. Annual arrivals increased from fewer than 8,000 in 1817 to 30,000 in 1830 and continued to rise. Some 327,000 German, Irish, English, Scottish, and Welsh immigrants landed in New York City in 1854 alone. Thousands simply passed through and made their way to western New York and beyond, via the Hudson River and the Erie Canal, further swelling the ranks of the foreign born in places like Buffalo and Rochester. Many others, particularly the Irish, settled permanently in New York City, despite low-paying jobs and wretched living conditions. According to the state census of 1855, the foreign born constituted some 26 percent of the state's population. In 1860 immigrants, including some 200,000 Irish, accounted for 48 percent of the population of New York City.

A Revolution in Transportation

No other event was more emblematic of New York's growth and development after 1825 than the successful completion of the Erie Canal. The state had begun to confront the problem of transportation in the late eighteenth and early nineteenth centuries, chartering private companies to build turnpikes linking the principal towns along the Hudson and Mohawk with their agricultural hinterlands. By 1821, 278 companies had been incorporated, while some 4,000 miles of turnpike connected the various regions of the state and provided links with Massachusetts and Connecticut to the east and Vermont to the north. Even as private entrepreneurs built an extensive network of roads, however, some New Yorkers envisioned cheaper and more efficient modes of transportation. By 1815, James Geddes, a western New York surveyor, De Witt Clinton, the mayor of New York City and the future governor of the state, and others were pushing for a canal linking the Hudson River and Lake Erie. Efforts to enlist private capital for the project were unsuccessful; so too was a request for federal assistance. Finally, in 1817, the legislature authorized the building of a canal at public expense. Construction began between Rome and Utica in July 1817. By 1823 the canal between the Genesee and the Hudson was in operation, and the final section was completed in late October 1825.

The success of the Erie was apparent even before the official opening. Traffic on the finished sections generated some $300,000 in tolls in 1824, and knowledgeable observers predicted revenues would reach $1 million by 1826. The actual amount collected in that year was somewhat less ($687,976), but optimistic canal boosters were not disappointed. Between 1826 and 1835 annual revenues doubled to $1,375,673 and then more than doubled again in the next twelve years, reaching a pre–Civil War peak of $3,333,347 in 1847. The rising volume of commerce traversing the state via the canal is an even more important measure of its success. A total of 218,000 tons of freight was transported on the canal in 1825. The tonnage increased dramatically each year thereafter, reaching 4,650,000 in 1860, more than twenty times the amount carried in the year of the Erie's completion.

Anxious to share in the prosperity generated by improved transportation, sections of the state not affected by the Erie demanded comparable public works. Northern New York benefited from the Champlain Canal, linking Lake Champlain with the Hudson, which had been authorized at the same time as the Erie and was completed in 1822. In 1825 the state legislature approved surveys for a possible seventeen additional canals. Nine major projects subsequently were funded and built, including the Oswego, the Cayuga, the Seneca, the Chemung, the Chenango, the Genesee Valley, and the Black River Canals. By 1841 more than six hundred miles of canals were in operation, another three hundred miles were under construction, and the state had embarked on a massive enlargement of the original Erie.

As important as they were to the state's growth in the second quarter of the nineteenth century, canals would eventually be superseded by the establishment of a modern rail system. At first, however, railroads were conceived primarily as supplements to the canal system; they were prohibited from carrying freight in competition with the state-owned canals until 1851. The state legislature incorporated the first railroad company in 1826, only one year after the completion of the Erie Canal. Opened in 1831, the Mohawk and Hudson connected Albany and Schenectady along sixteen miles of track. A frenzy of railroad building followed, as entrepreneurs and communities eager to promote economic development lobbied the legislature for corporate charters. In 1832 the Saratoga and Schenectady Railroad extended the Hudson and Mohawk northward. Simultaneously, promoters began to establish rail service into western New York. Between 1832 and 1842, separately chartered companies built the Utica and Schenectady, the Tonawanda, the Syracuse and Utica, the Auburn and Syracuse, the Auburn and Rochester, and the Attica and Buffalo Railroads. With the opening of the last in November 1842, through rail service between Albany and Buffalo was established. A decade later, in 1853, Erastus Corning consolidated the various companies along the route to form the New York Central Railroad. Two years before, the Erie Railroad had been completed, linking the Hudson River and Lake Erie by a direct route through the southern tier of the state. Other roads pushed northward along the Hudson to Albany, and the Northern Railroad, connecting Ogdensburg and Lake Champlain, opened in 1850. By mid-century some thirty railroads served the state, with 1,649 miles of track, and another 1,000 miles under construction.

This "transportation revolution" transformed society and the economy wherever its influence was felt. The construction of canals and, later, railroads lowered the cost of transportation and opened new areas of the state to com-

A handbill distributed in 1838 by the Ithaca and Owego Railroad. From LeRoy W. Kingman, *Early Owego* (Owego, 1907).

mercial farming. Customary modes of production declined and were replaced by production for the market. Regions newly opened to the market experienced unprecedented urbanization and dramatic increases in nonagricultural employment. In short, the extension of the transportation network played a critical role in the creation of a modern, diversified, market-oriented economy.

The most immediate and direct consequence of improved transportation facilities was the commercialization of agriculture. The expansion of the cash market was, of course, an uneven process that was under way in some parts of the state long before the Erie Canal was completed. Indeed, relatively few farmers were completely isolated or engaged exclusively in subsistence agriculture even in the late eighteenth century. For those who were, life was difficult and harsh. The scarcity of money necessitated a barter economy in which farm products, livestock, or the farmer's labor was traded with neighbors or at a country store. The standard of living on such farms was low. But only those in the most remote regions, well in advance of the line of settlement and some distance from rivers and streams, experienced such circumstances.

Even at an early date, most farmers were better situated in relation to the Hudson and the Mohawk and were well within the hinterlands of New York City, Albany, or smaller river towns such as Catskill. By the turn of the century, for example, eastern New York farmers were already producing wheat, potash, corn, or lumber for the New York City and, ultimately, national and international markets. Farmers in the northern and western regions of the state were not as fortunate but still managed to get surplus agricultural products to market in sufficient quantities to generate a welcome infusion of cash into the largely self-sufficient local economy. Wheat farmers one hundred miles up the Mohawk River were exporting surpluses as early as 1800. Some frontier farmers found markets for surplus beef, flour, or potash in Quebec, via Lake Ontario and the Saint Lawrence River. Still others traded down the Susquehanna to Baltimore. Thus, many farmers participated in local, regional, and even limited national and international markets in the early nineteenth century, but the high cost of transportation severely limited the volume of interregional trade until the canal era.

Declining freight rates made possible the extension of the market into all regions of the state in the half-century before the Civil War. The result, to quote David M. Ellis, the leading historian of New York agriculture in this period, was that "farming as a way of life was yielding place to the concept of farming as a means of profit." The adjustment was by no means easy. While access to broader markets meant the possibility of greater profits to successful farmers in newly opened areas, it also meant new, stiffer competition for older, more mature agricultural regions. Commercialization necessitated a new appreciation of the impersonality and interdependence of the market and price system. In some areas the result of commercialization was rural decline and the outmigration of population, as many farmers left in search of better and cheaper lands or migrated into the newly burgeoning cities appearing throughout the state. In the Hudson River Valley and along the Mohawk River, commercialization contributed to the emergence of an antirent movement as tenants revolted against the leasehold system of land tenure.

Viewed broadly, however, the response to commercialization involved countless individual choices as farmers sought to adjust to rapidly shifting market patterns. Eastern New York farmers, for example, lost their preeminence in the production of wheat in the 1820s and 1830s because of a combination of soil exhaustion and increasing competition from the western part of the state. By 1840 the center of wheat culture had moved westward to the Genesee country. Forced to seek alternative sources of income, farmers along the Hudson and Mohawk Rivers resorted to cattle and sheep grazing and dairy production. When western competition began to threaten wool producers, the region turned increasingly to cattle grazing and dairying. The state ranked first in the nation in beef production in the 1840s, but fell to third place by 1860 as a result of competition from cattle raised in the Midwest and brought to the East by rail. By this time, however, New York had become the leading dairy state in the country. It also led in the production of potatoes, hops, flax, and lumber and remained one of the principal suppliers of cattle, wool, wheat, and other grains.

The significance of transportation developments went well beyond their direct effect on agriculture and commerce. In the western counties, for example, construction of the Erie Canal contributed to economic diversification by providing a source of nonagricultural employment, stimulating new extractive industries such as lumbering and quarrying, attracting outside entrepreneurs to the region, and increasing local bank reserves as construction funds were transferred into the area. The operation of the canal led to further diversification as transshipment, warehousing, financial, and distribution facilities were built. Similarly, land values in the counties traversed by the canal grew by 91 percent between 1820 and 1846, an increase substantially greater than that for the state as a whole. Population growth, as we have already seen, skyrocketed in the region. The household production of textiles declined sharply between 1820 and 1845 as families and communities along the route of the Erie gained access to distant markets. At the same time, manufacturing and commercial employment grew, while the proportion of workers engaged in agriculture remained stable.

There were, of course, many variations of this transformation, depending upon local circumstances and the nature of a region's prior relationship to the market. In Onondaga County, for example, the completion of the Erie and Oswego Canals fundamentally altered established trade patterns that had been centered on the Seneca and other turnpikes running through its borders, and generated a wholesale shift of social, economic, and political activities to areas serviced by the new canals. Turnpike settlements declined as the canals garnered more and more of the interregional trade, as entrepreneurial talent and development capital migrated out of the older settlements to the flourishing villages and towns on the canals, and as population shifted northward toward the new transportation facilities. Initially, declining transport costs and increased accessibility to national markets stimulated agriculture in the county, produc-

316   ANTEBELLUM SOCIETY AND POLITICS

ing higher profits and growth in the amount of land under cultivation, but the new trade patterns were also destabilizing. Onondaga farmers began to experience direct competition from wheat and wool producers farther west, even as intraregional trade became more costly owing to the deterioration of local transportation facilities. Simultaneously, rural processing industries declined as industrial activity became increasingly concentrated at key locations along the canal. A principal beneficiary of this economic reorientation was the village of Syracuse. Strategically located at the junction of the Erie and Oswego Canals, the city rose to regional dominance as population, business, and capital migrated out of declining turnpike villages. Rapid population growth (900 percent in the 1820s), the concentration of commercial and industrial activity in the city, and its designation in 1829 as county seat established Syracuse as the economic and political center of Onondaga County.

Farther west, the completion of the Erie Canal led to the emergence of Rochester and Buffalo as regional economic centers. Rochester, located in the wheat-producing Genesee country, dominated the grain trade and quickly became the nation's leading producer of flour and a major manufacturing center. Buffalo's rise to prominence as a commercial center was equally dramatic. As the western terminus of the Erie Canal, the city served as the transshipment point for agricultural goods from northern Ohio sent eastward via Lake Erie and the canal. Both cities experienced spectacular population growth, reaching 20,000 inhabitants by 1840.

Although it would remain the most underdeveloped region in the state in this period, northern New York also felt the impact of transportation improvements. The completion of the Champlain Canal in 1822 opened an all-water route from Lake Champlain to Albany and New York City and reduced the region's dependence upon Quebec as a market for its agricultural and forest products. With the decline of transport costs, goods that had previously gone northward to Canada began to be diverted downstate to New York City, while more and cheaper imports flowed into the region. The north country, in short, was increasingly integrated into a statewide marketing system dominated by the Port of New York.

The social and economic consequences of transportation improvements were not limited to the least developed regions of the state. Older and more mature communities felt their effects as well. Kingston, situated on the west bank of the Hudson River between New York City and Albany, is a case in point. A stable agricultural community of about 3,000 in 1820, Kingston was transformed into a booming commercial city by the construction of the Delaware and Hudson Canal linking it to the Pennsylvania anthracite coalfields. Its population soared to 16,000 by 1860, while the city's economy grew and became more modern and diversified.

The Road to Industrial and Commercial Supremacy

Inextricably entwined with these changes, and ultimately overshadowing them, was the dramatic growth of manufacturing in the state. Even before 1825 New York had been one of the leading manufacturing states in the country. By 1814 it ranked second to Pennsylvania in the value of manufacturing output. It led in the household production of textiles and in the number of manufacturing corporations, and only Massachusetts had more capital invested in industry. Although much of this activity grew out of developments already under way in the late eighteenth century or can be traced to the growth of extractive industries in rural, frontier areas, the Embargo and Non-Intercourse Acts and the War of 1812 also stimulated the manufacturing sector of the state's economy. The disruption of trade with Great Britain forced New Yorkers to produce for themselves goods that could no longer be imported, while commercial capital was diverted to new manufacturing ventures. The state also actively encouraged industry by providing premiums and bounties for the production of some items.

Despite these early beginnings, however, the most important period of manufacturing development came in the second quarter of the century. It was a complicated and uneven process involving the new market forces unleashed by transportation improvements, the transformation of existing crafts in the city of New York, and the appearance of the factory system of production in some industries. The opening up of the West after 1825 created new markets for manufacturers, and the commercialization of agriculture generated profits sufficient to enable farmers to purchase eastern manufactured goods. The growth of regionally based processing industries in the areas serviced by newly built canals and railroads also contributed to the boom in manufacturing. Simultaneously, in New York City, manufacturing output rose as a result of the restructuring of established handicraft industries. As Sean Wilentz explains this process of "metropolitan industrialization," many of the city's manufacturers cut costs and increased output without resorting to mechanization and factory organization by subdividing their work and contracting it out to low-paid laborers, thereby accelerating the decline of the craft system of production already under way. This "bastard artisan system," according to Wilentz, would continue to characterize New York manufacturing processes in industries like the consumer finishing trades into the twentieth century.

The rise of the factory system of production also contributed to the growth of manufacturing. The factory did not become the dominant mode of production until after the Civil War, but it had come to play an increasingly significant role in some sectors of the economy by the 1840s. The textile industry is illustrative. As new regions of the state were absorbed into the market, the household manufacture of textile goods declined—from an estimated 16.5 million yards in 1825 to less than one million in 1855. During these same years, the factory transformed cotton and woolen production. By 1823 the state had incorporated some 36 companies devoted to cotton manufactures. Less than a decade later, in 1831, 112 mills employing more than 5,500 workers and capitalized at $3.6 million were operating in New York. At mid-century the total was 86 such establishments capitalized at $4.1 million. A similar trend was evident in the woolen industry. By 1850 the number of woolen mills in the state had grown to 249, with an aggregate capitalization of $4.4 million. Indeed, by this time, factories had begun to appear in virtually every field of industrial activity.

The general dimensions of industrial growth during this period are revealed in federal and state census data on manufacturing output and capitalization. In 1835, for example, there were some 13,667 manufacturing establishments in New York with a combined output of $59 million, a 58 percent increase in the value of manufacturing since 1814. Half a decade later, in 1840, the state had $55 million invested in manufacturing enterprises and produced goods valued at $96 million. By mid-century New York was indisputably the leading industrial state in the nation, with capital investments of nearly $100 million and an annual industrial output of more than $237 million. It was first in iron casting; second in the production of woolen goods and wrought iron, and in distilleries and breweries; fifth in cotton textiles; and seventh in the production of pig iron. The state also dominated regional and national markets in metal goods, wood products, flour, and leather goods. At the center of this burgeoning industrial economy was New York City which, by 1860, was the principal manufacturing center in the country.

Although the growth of manufacturing was statistically the most dramatic economic development in this era, the state's share of the nation's commerce continued to expand as well. Overall, foreign trade declined as a proportion of the U.S. economy, but imports and exports grew substantially in the pre–Civil War years, and New York was the direct beneficiary of this expansion. The phenomenal growth of internal trade unleashed by the "transportation revolution" and the opening of the West combined with its locational advantages enabled New York City not only to maintain but also to solidify its commercial supremacy. The adoption of the auction system in 1817, which required that all goods offered at auction had to be sold regardless of potential losses, ensured its early dominance of the import trade. The city thus became the linchpin in a commercial network that extended from the manufactories of Europe and New England to the farmers and country storekeepers of the interior and the cotton producers of the South. New York City's merchants served as intermediaries, distributing imported manufactured goods into the newly opened markets of the interior and collecting and transporting farm products destined ultimately for foreign markets. By 1860, two-thirds of the nation's imports and one-third of its exports passed through the Port of New York. Textiles, principally from

England, dominated imports until passage of the tariffs of 1816 and 1832 strengthened the competitiveness of domestic producers. Iron, steel, sugar, and coffee also figured prominently in the import trade as did the products of the intercoastal trade and the developing commerce with the Far East and Latin America.

Cotton, more than any other single product, was responsible for New York City's preeminence in foreign commerce. For most of the period from 1820 to 1860, southern cotton accounted for more than 50 percent of total U.S. exports. By the early 1820s the city's merchants had succeeded in capturing the bulk of this traffic through an elaborate triangular trade linking the southern cotton ports, European ports like Liverpool and Havre, and New York. Ships engaged in the cotton trade typically followed one of two routes to the markets of Europe: directly from Charleston, Savannah, Mobile, or New Orleans to Europe, back to New York, and then completing the triangle by returning to the southern ports; or directly to New York where the cargoes were reexported to Europe. Either way, the merchants of New York City benefited. In the first instance, ships returned from Europe laden with immigrants and freight and then ran down the coast with cargoes destined for the southern ports or in ballast. Profits were even greater, however, when the cotton flowed first to New York, where it was unloaded, reloaded, and then shipped to England or to the Continent. Not only did this provide profitable cargoes for eastbound packets returning to Europe, it also ensured that an even greater proportion of European imports reached the South by way of the city on the Hudson. This diversion of the cotton trade through New York allowed the city's commission merchants, cotton brokers, insurance brokers, bankers, and shippers to dominate southern commercial activity down to the Civil War.

As the variety of business concerns involved in the cotton trade suggests, the growth of commerce and manufacturing, the transportation revolution, and the appearance of more rapid and efficient communications wrought dramatic changes in the marketing and distribution of goods and generally transformed the way in which business was conducted. The general or all-purpose merchants who typically owned their own ships and combined the functions of importer and exporter, wholesaler and retailer, banker and insurer, shipper and forwarder gave way increasingly to more specialized enterprises concentrating on a particular product or function. Specialization was a direct response to the rising volume of trade, an explosion in the number of commercial transactions, and the increasing impersonality of the expanding market economy. New economic institutions and a new type of businessman emerged to negotiate this new, fast-paced, and sometimes bewildering environment.

Chief among the business innovations of this period was the rapid proliferation of the private business corporation. From a device used principally for public purposes, the corporation had been transformed by the 1830s into a modern, private instrument of economic organization that enjoyed the advantages of unlimited life and limited liability. New York entrepreneurs quickly realized the advantages of the corporate form, not least its utility in pooling large sums of investment capital, and adopted it with increasing frequency in the early nineteenth century. From a mere 28 corporations for the entire period before 1800, the number of incorporations in the state grew to more than 1,300 by 1840. Equally important, the use of corporate charters spread to mining, manufacturing, banking, insurance, and other forms of enterprise that were less clearly associated with public purposes, further fueling the trend toward differentiation and specialization of economic functions.

The expansion of the banking system aptly illustrates these tendencies. In 1800, exclusive of the Bank of the United States, four banks, with a total capitalization of $3,370,000, operated in the state: the Bank of New York (established in 1784), the Bank of Albany (1792), the Bank of Columbia (1793), and the Manhattan Bank (1799). After the turn of the century, however, the number of banks grew rapidly. Six were incorporated between 1801 and 1810, while another twenty-three received corporate charters in the next decade. By 1835, eighty-six banks were spread across the state, with a total capitalization nearly ten times that of 1800. A decade later, in 1846, there were 152 banks in New York, capitalized at nearly $43 million.

Banks played a critical role in the state's extraordinary economic growth during this period. They were the principal mechanisms for pooling capital for investment in transportation, commerce, and manufacturing. They issued bank notes that circulated as currency and helped to monetize economic relationships in the emerging market economy. They also contributed to the development of a cash-based credit system by extending credit and rationally managing the flow of money. It was precisely because banks performed these critical functions in the modernizing economy of the period that the state sought ways to regulate and rationalize their activities. The first sustained effort at regulation came in 1829 with the creation of the Safety Fund Banking System, which established a fund to ensure the redemption of bills issued by insolvent banks and set up a banking commission to supervise the operation of Safety Fund banks in the state.

An even more significant development in banking policy occurred in 1838, when the state legislature, responding to widespread demands that corporate bank charters be made more available, passed the Free Banking Act. Under the terms of this law any number of persons could establish a banking association, with a minimum of $100,000 capitalization, simply by filing a certificate with the secretary of state specifying its name, location, amount of capital stock, names of shareholders, and the date it would begin operation. To ensure financial responsibility, the Free Banking Act required that banks participate in a security-deposit system, report semiannually to the state comptroller, and maintain a minimum specie reserve of not less than 12.5 percent of the amount of bills or notes in circulation. The result was to throw open the banking industry to virtually all comers, provided they could meet these minimum conditions. In 1851 the state further consolidated the supervision and regulation of banks by creating a Bank Department.

The insurance industry experienced a similar pattern of growth and diffusion. From modest beginnings in the eighteenth century when individual underwriters provided such insurance as was available, the industry grew and became more specialized in the first half of the nineteenth century. As with banking, it was the emergence of the corporation that brought about this transformation. Between 1800 and 1835, ninety-four companies were incorporated by the state legislature, principally to provide fire and marine insurance, although life insurance companies had also begun to appear. An additional thirty had been formed by 1845. The state's response to this growth was to pass general incorporation laws for insurance companies in 1849 and 1853 and, as was the case with banking, to develop regulatory mechanisms for supervision of the industry. This culminated with the creation of an independent Insurance Department in 1859.

Banking and insurance were in some respects unique enterprises in that they were both the consequences of, and catalysts for, modernization. But what was happening in these industries was replicated throughout the New York business world. Specialized firms appeared in commerce, manufacturing, finance, transportation, and retailing. Although most apparent in the great emporium of New York City, modern forms of economic organization transformed business and commerce throughout the state.

New York City's prominence in commerce and manufacturing was matched by its growing dominance of the state and national capital market. After the demise of the Second Bank of the United States in 1836, the city began to replace Philadelphia and Boston as the leading money market in the country. Its central role in foreign commerce and in the emerging national communications network positioned the city strategically at the nexus of the national and international credit system. Its bankers and merchants provided financial services and extended credit to southern planters, western farmers, country storekeepers, and merchants in the smaller cities and towns throughout the state and the country. They, in turn, relied upon such commercial banking houses as Prime, Ward and King in New York and the Baring Brothers of London for access to the international money market. The result was a network of credit extending from London to New York and to the farthest reaches of the national market economy.

The railroad construction boom of the 1840s and 1850s clinched New York's financial ascendancy. By mid-century railroad entrepreneurs turned increasingly to the city as a source of cheap and plentiful capital for new projects. Trading in the growing number of railroad securities elevated the New York Stock Exchange, relatively insignificant since its founding in 1817, to the pinnacle of the nation's financial system. In the 1850s, hundreds of thousands of shares in railroads, banks, insurance companies, public bonds and securities, and other business enterprises were traded weekly. By the end of the decade, New York City had established undisputed hegemony over a highly centralized national capital market and credit system.

From the perspective of 1860, New Yorkers could look back on a period of unprecedented growth and development. Rapid population growth, urbanization, massive immigration, the completion of the transportation network, the expansion of the market, the commercialization of agriculture, and the growth of manufacturing had fundamentally transformed the state's economy. The economic potential so enthusiastically proclaimed during the canal celebrations of 1825 had been more than fulfilled. More important, three and one-half decades after the completion of the Erie, the "Empire State" exhibited most of the characteristics of a modern, diversified, interdependent economy and was poised for still further development under the impact of industrialization later in the century.

Chapter 20

Society, Religion, and Reform

FUNDAMENTAL SOCIAL AND CULTURAL CHANGES ACCOM-
panied the transformation of New York's economy after 1825. The market revolution broke down traditional relationships and generated new social, cultural, and political conflicts. Rural New Yorkers were absorbed into regional,
national, and international markets. The growth of manufacturing and the
emergence of new methods of production transformed the world of the artisan
and precipitated the formation of a working class. Other New Yorkers—small
producers, employers, nonmanual workers, and the traditional "middling
sort"—began to coalesce into a coherent, self-conscious middle class.

Throughout the state, but especially in the western counties traversed by
the Erie Canal, economic change converged with and fed the religious enthusiasm of the Second Great Awakening. Evangelical Protestantism spread rapidly
in the first third of the century, transforming religious practice and spawning
numerous efforts to reform or purify society by ridding it of alcohol, slavery,
and other perceived social ills. Other religious movements arose to advocate
even more radical solutions to society's problems or to urge withdrawal from it
altogether. Economic forces also transformed the family and redefined the role
of women. Middle-class women assumed a larger role in religious activities,
swelled the ranks of reform organizations, and eventually challenged their own
inferior status.

Massive immigration produced an increasingly heterogeneous society, generating in the process new ethnic, religious, and racial divisions. Native-born
Protestant New Yorkers, anxious to preserve their social and cultural dominance, responded to the foreign "threat" with virulent nativism and anti-
Catholicism. Simultaneously, fears of social instability combined with genuine

323

humanitarian impulses to produce a new awareness of poverty, crime, disease, insanity, and other forms of dependency in society. By mid-century, the state had constructed an elaborate system of prisons, asylums, poorhouses, houses of refuge, and other institutions in response.

Working-Class Formation and Labor Protest

Among the many consequences of economic development and commercialization, none affected the public and private lives of New Yorkers more profoundly than the emergence of classes. By the 1850s, clearly identifiable working and middle classes had appeared in New York, the result of economic growth and industrialization, cultural factors such as religion and ethnicity, political ideology, and the symbiotic relationship between the classes themselves.

The process and timing of working-class formation varied according to industry and locality. An enlarged wage-earning class was an inevitable consequence wherever the growth of manufacturing occurred, as the transformation of Buffalo, Rochester, Troy, and other towns and cities demonstrated. In New York City, the appearance of a working class was directly related to the reorga-

"Troy, New York" (1838). By W. J. Bennett. Print Collection, New York State Historical Association, Cooperstown, N.Y.

nization of the crafts to meet the increased demand for manufactured goods. The traditional artisan regime, in which masters, journeymen, and apprentices worked in close proximity to produce shoes, clothes, and similar items, began to give way to what the historian Sean Wilentz has called a "bastard system" in many of the traditional trades. Eager to take advantage of an expanded market, master craftsmen and entrepreneurs cut costs and increased output by subdividing the process of production and relying upon low-paid, semiskilled or unskilled workers (women, children, and immigrants) to perform most of the labor. This division of labor and the practice of contracting out the simpler tasks drove down the price of the finished product and undermined the competitive position of craftsmen. Those unable to adapt to the new system fell into the ranks of wageworkers, while others moved in the opposite direction, joining the ranks of the managers or the manufacturing elite. In the new regime, workers were paid piece rates or daily wages, more of the work was contracted to "outworkers," labor was more closely supervised, and the pace of work was intensified.

But the process was by no means universal. The experience of workers was as varied as the diverse and complex paths to industrialization in New York City. The bastard system was most typically found in the consumer finishing trades such as clothing and shoes, which relied on labor-intensive responses (sweating) to the onset of industrialization. The printing industry, in contrast, was transformed by both a growing division of labor and mechanization, while the metal trades, responding to the increased demand for steam engines, resorted to capital-intensive factory production. Some trades, moreover, like shipbuilding and food preparation (especially butchering) grew but retained the traditional artisan system virtually intact.

Artisans drew upon the language of republicanism to fashion an ideology of resistance to the economic debasement of the crafts. The market revolution, the fragmentation of production, and the growth of wage labor, they argued, threatened such key republican ideals as independence and equality. In effect, workers sought to preserve the traditional artisanal order and stem the erosion of their position in society by identifying their interests with those of the republic at large. Internal divisions among artisans diluted the effectiveness of this strategy in the 1820s and 1830s, but artisan republicanism remained a powerful influence in the struggle to forge a distinctive working-class critique of industrial capitalism into the 1850s.

Although important beyond their numbers, artisans did not represent the entirety of the wage-earning working class in New York City. The ranks of traditional unskilled labor—dockworkers, construction workers, cartmen, and day laborers—grew as the population expanded and the pace of commerce quickened. In 1855 there were some 20,000 unskilled laborers, mostly Irish, in the city. Even more numerous were those engaged in domestic service. An esti-

The economic and social decay attending the Panic of 1837 are dramatized in "The Times," a cartoon by Edward W. Clay. New York State Historical Association, Cooperstown, N.Y.

mated 32,000 Irish women and blacks worked as servants in upper- and middle-class homes. Thus, the influx of immigrants in the 1840s and 1850s had as profound an impact on the formation of a working class as the reorganization of the crafts earlier. By the 1850s, four out of five manual workers were foreign born. Unskilled and semiskilled immigrant labor had effectively replaced artisans as the core of the emerging working class.

Labor's response to worsening conditions was to organize, strike, and, on occasion, enter politics directly. In the spring of 1829, a radical Working Men's movement sprang up in New York City and successfully prevented employers' efforts to lengthen the workday. The organization went on to nominate candidates in the autumn legislative elections and to adopt a Working Men's platform calling for such reforms as the abolition of private banks and chartered monopolies, the end of imprisonment for debt, the passage of a mechanic's lien law, and changes in the electoral system. The Working Men received a third of the votes in 1829 and sent one of their candidates to the state Senate. But within a year the movement had succumbed to internal divisions between radicals and more moderate members and to cooptation by the established political parties.

In the early 1830s labor protest shifted from politics to union organizing.

Journeyman printers in New York City formed the Typographical Association in 1831, and in 1833 the city's carpenters and tailors went out on strike demanding higher wages. That same year, nine organized trades came together to form the General Trades' Union of the City of New York. Under its direction, craft unions grew rapidly. Fifty new unions appeared between 1833 and 1836, a period that also witnessed some forty strikes by wage-earning journeymen. By 1836, the peak of unionism among craft workers, upwards of two-thirds of wage earners were organized, mostly in the bastardized trades. With the Panic of 1837, during which as many as one-third of workers lost their jobs, the union movement lost momentum. Over the next two decades, periods of prosperity brought renewed union activity, but economic downturns, such as those in 1854–55 and 1857, inevitably undermined such efforts. Irish and German immigration in the 1840s increased the supply of cheap labor and allowed manufacturers to continue the practice of subdividing and contracting. Ethnic, religious, and racial tensions further fragmented the labor movement. Finally, relatively high wages and a standard of living that compared favorably with workers in other industrializing countries slowed the growth of a full-blown working-class consciousness prior to the Civil War.

Even so, a working-class culture appeared in New York City by the middle of the nineteenth century. Predominantly working-class neighborhoods took shape as workplaces and living spaces became differentiated and as better-off New Yorkers moved out of the lower wards into their own distinctive areas. Families crowded into the rapidly proliferating tenements, while the boarding-house became the principal source of housing for the flood of single male immigrant workers entering the city in the 1840s and 1850s. The social and cultural life of workers—particularly male workers—revolved around the boarding-house, saloon, and fire company. The theater, black minstrels, and prizefighting emerged as distinctive forms of working-class entertainment. So, too, a brawling, personalistic style of politics became characteristic of working-class neighborhoods. The culture of New York's workers was never monolithic, of course, criss-crossed as it was by ethnic, religious, occupational, and gender differences, but the lives of workers at mid-century were clearly distinguishable both from their artisan predecessors and from their middle- and upper-class contemporaries.

The Emergence of a Middle Class

The same social and economic revolution that defined a new wage-earning class also gave rise to a distinctive middle class. In eighteenth-century society, the "middling rank" had been dominated by handworking artisans, enjoyed only modest economic circumstances, and was poorly differentiated from the bottom ranks of the social structure. By the mid-nineteenth century, according to Stuart Blumin, a revolution in the relationship between manual and nonmanual labor had produced a "white-collar, suburbanizing middle class" with its own lifestyle and unique outlook. Increasingly, nonmanual work was aligned with entrepreneurship and salaried employment. Just as many artisans had become wage earners as a result of the reorganization of production, a smaller number became manufacturers, contractors, supervisors, and retailers who no longer participated in the productive process directly. Ownership became separated from manual labor. The increasing scale and complexity of business generated new positions for clerks, bookkeepers, managers, and others who worked with their heads. By the 1850s, nonmanual businessmen and employees accounted for 40 percent of the total workforce in urban centers like New York City.

The specialization of firms within the nonmanual sector of the economy also shaped the developing middle class. Enterprises concentrating on a particular product or function replaced the general wholesale merchant. Retailing emerged as a distinct economic activity and became increasingly specialized.

By 1850, a new middle class enjoyed the consumer goods and leisure pursuits—including extended vacations—once reserved for those with inherited wealth. Shown here as it was sketched in 1838 by W. H. Bartlett, Ballston Springs was a popular New York State resort. From Nathaniel P. Willis, *American Scenery* (1840).

Notable examples of the "retail merchant," a term invented in the antebellum period, included New York City's A. T. Stewart and, later, Lord and Taylor and Brooks Brothers, but countless smaller businessmen also shaped an increasingly important retail sector. Manual and nonmanual workplaces became more differentiated. Whether production and retailing continued on the same premises or were physically separated from each other, the work environment of managers, clerks, financiers, and others who labored with their heads increasingly diverged architecturally and stylistically from those engaged in manual labor.

Economic circumstance, patterns of consumption, and lifestyle further distinguished nonmanual workers and proprietors from wage earners. Members of the new middle class earned significantly more than skilled workers, who typically struggled just to meet minimal family expenses. As measured by income, wealth, or opportunity for mobility, class boundaries hardened during the antebellum years. More disposable income, furthermore, allowed nonmanual workers to take advantage of newly available consumer goods. Finer clothing, larger and more elaborately furnished houses, distinctive residential areas away from the workplace, and new forms of leisure and entertainment defined a middle-class standard and style of living markedly different from that of the working class.

In addition to the transformation of the workplace and residential segregation, the emergence of the middle class in New York was intimately bound up with changes in the family, in gender roles, and in religious sentiment. In her study of Utica, for example, Mary Ryan locates the core of middle-class self-definition in the "ideal of domesticity." The economic revolution of the early nineteenth century separated the home from the workplace and gave birth to the concept of separate female and male spheres of activity. Women came to be identified uniquely with the home and domesticity, men with work outside the home and with the public sphere generally. In the process of constructing and internalizing a distinctive identity, the middle class sanctified the home, motherhood, and domestic values. Women, perceived as morally and spiritually superior to men, assumed the principal role in child rearing. A new conception of family appeared as men and women who aspired to the social respectability associated with middle-class status devised conscious strategies to ensure that they attained and perpetuated it. Increasingly, native-born, middle-class families limited the number of their children, kept them at home longer to ensure their moral instruction in middle-class values, provided them with as much formal education as possible to ensure their success in entering the ranks of nonmanual workers, and encouraged sons to delay marriage until they had established themselves firmly in the middle class.

Religion, too, played a critical role in middle-class formation. In Utica and elsewhere, evangelical Protestantism was the principal source of middle-class women's moral authority and the impetus for women's growing involvement in a host of reform movements. Similarly, in Rochester and other cities experiencing the growth of manufacturing in these years, entrepreneurs turned to evangelicalism in their efforts to reassert their moral authority as traditional relationships between employees and employers broke down. Precisely how all this occurred is intimately bound up with the larger story of the rise of evangelical Protestantism in New York.

Charles Grandison Finney and the Second Great Awakening

Successive waves of religious revivalism rocked the United States between 1795 and 1837. Arising on the Kentucky and Tennessee frontier and spreading through New England, this Second Great Awakening peaked in western New York in the decade after 1825. Alienated from orthodox Calvinism, revivalist ministers preached an optimistic message of personal autonomy and human potential for salvation. An emotional style of preaching and other "new measures" instilled in sinners a desire to accept God and be saved. Thousands caught the revival spirit and converted, dramatically swelling church rolls. Evangelicalism had its greatest impact in New York during the ten years between 1825 and 1835. In the western region along the line of the Erie Canal, the frequency and intensity of revivals produced what contemporaries called the "Burned-Over District." The region was fertile ground for awakening. Its largely Yankee population had already been exposed to revivals in their native New England in the 1790s. The market revolution, furthermore, was in full swing in towns and rural communities along the canal route, creating unusually favorable conditions for the spread of evangelical Protestantism.

Charles Grandison Finney was the leading figure in the revivals. Born in Connecticut, Finney grew up in Oneida County and on the shore of Lake Ontario. In 1818, at the age of twenty-six, he began to study law in the town of Adams. Three years later, following a dramatic conversion to Christianity, Finney embarked on a career in the ministry. After several years of study and preaching in the communities around Adams, he became a fully ordained Presbyterian minister on July 1, 1824. Already well known in the small towns of northern New York, Finney gained wider fame as a result of his successful revival in the town of Western in September 1825. Western was followed by revivals in Rome, Utica, Auburn, Troy, Little Falls, Philadelphia, New York City, and, most important, Rochester, where for six months in the winter of 1830–31 he conducted one of the most important revivals in American history. In 1832, Finney accepted the invitation of Arthur and Lewis Tappan to become pastor of the Second Free Presbyterian Church in New York City. Three years later, he moved to Ohio to become professor of theology and eventually president of Oberlin College.

Finney's theology began with the concept of individual free will, the belief that salvation resulted from a conscious choice between good and evil rather than a preordained and immutable act of God. Emotion rather than rigid doctrine was the way to truth. Through such "new measures" as public prayer, protracted meetings, the "anxious bench," door-to-door visitation, and emotionally charged extemporaneous preaching, Finney exhorted sinners to accept God's grace and acknowledge Christ as their savior. But the individual's responsibility did not end with conversion. Two additional principles ensured that evangelicalism would have a profound impact on society. The doctrine of millennialism held that there would be a thousand years of peace and harmony on earth before the Second Coming of Christ, while perfectionism held that human beings were capable of ridding themselves of sin and attaining a Godlike perfection. Thus, once saved, converts were energized to seek the salvation of others and to reform society, thereby hastening the arrival of the Kingdom of God on earth.

The roots of revivalism were diverse and complex. The evangelical spirit grew initially out of a profound spiritual crisis, was nurtured and strengthened by the democratic and egalitarian impulses unleashed by the Revolution, and provided social stability and a sense of community for converts in the sparsely populated areas of the frontier. By the 1820s and 1830s, however, evangelical Protestantism grew most rapidly in the towns and cities of the state and appears to have received sustenance from the profound social and economic changes wrought by the market revolution. Finneyite revivals were most successful in newly emerging manufacturing towns and in areas just entering the market economy. Converts came disproportionately from among businessmen, especially manufacturers, their families, and those they employed. In Rochester, some historians have argued, evangelicalism was the mechanism by which the business elite reasserted the control it had lost over workers in the early stages of industrialization. Confronted by an increasingly fragmented community, the widening social gulf between masters and workers, and all the social ills accompanying rapid economic growth, business leaders and their wives embraced Finney's evangelical message. Here and elsewhere, the rising middle class internalized such evangelical values as industry, discipline, sobriety, and self-reliance and promoted those same values among their employees as a means of imposing order and ensuring a reliable, disciplined workforce. In the process, as Paul E. Johnson puts it, they forged "the moral imperative around which the northern middle class became a class."

Women, particularly, found the evangelical message appealing. The majority of converts at revivals were women, usually the wives and daughters of middle-class businessmen, or men who were brought to the church by female members of their family. Indeed, it was the convergence of evangelical sentiment with the economic changes of the early nineteenth century which produced the concept of separate male and female spheres and gave birth to the ideal of domesticity. Ironically, the same ideology that restricted women to the home and to domestic activities because of their moral and religious superiority over men became the basis for an enlarged role for women in the churches and in the proliferating reform movements of the era.

Evangelicalism and Reform

Evangelical Protestants were in the vanguard of a broad movement to eradicate sin and reform American society in this period. A host of benevolent associations grew up to spread the gospel and ameliorate social ills. Bible and tract societies distributed religious literature. Missionary societies sought new converts in the West, in Asia, and in the nation's cities. Sunday school unions carried the evangelical message to children, particularly those of the poor. Moral reform societies addressed the problem of prostitution. Other voluntary associations worked to preserve the sabbath, spread temperance ideals, and end slavery. New York was at the center of this "benevolent empire." Much of the reform effort grew directly out of the social and religious ferment of the Burned-Over District. Many national reform organizations were headquartered in New York. The leaders of reform—men and women like Finney, Theodore Dwight Weld, Elizabeth Cady Stanton, Gerrit Smith, and Arthur and Lewis Tappan—came disproportionately from New York. The Tappan brothers were particularly important. Successful New York City merchants and the founders of the Mercantile Agency, the forerunner of Dun and Bradstreet, Arthur and Lewis Tappan were ubiquitous in reform circles, organizing, leading, and financing reform activities.

A striking example of the nature of benevolent reform is sabbatarianism. Although laws against sabbath breaking had been standard in the colonial period, the growth of religious pluralism and new constitutional guarantees of religious freedom had eroded such penalties by the beginning of the nineteenth century. Market expansion accelerated that process and magnified fears that religion was on the decline and traditional communal rituals threatened. For many, sabbath breaking symbolized, in Robert Abzug's words, "the corrosive effect of the marketplace." In Rochester in 1828, concerned businessmen turned to sabbatarianism in an attempt to regain their lost authority over workers and to stem the tide of social disorder. The city's elite petitioned the legislature to close the canal locks on the sabbath and organized boycotts of those who conducted business on Sunday. Josiah Bissell organized his own stage and boat company, the Pioneer Line, to be operated only six days a week. The Tappans, who ran their own businesses on Christian principles, lent moral and financial support to sabbatarians like Bissell and led efforts to force the observance of the sabbath in New York City. In 1828 they joined Lyman Beecher of Massachusetts and others to form the "General Union for Promoting the Observance of the Christian Sabbath in the United States," a national organization devoted to preserving the sabbath, principally by lobbying Congress to halt Sunday mail deliveries. In the end, the sabbatarian crusaders failed. Congress ignored their petitions. The general public was alienated by their coercive tactics. The Pioneer Line went out of business. And in cities like Rochester sabbatarianism split the elite and forced them to seek other solutions to the enigma of class relations in an industrializing society.

Another important reform movement that drew strength from both evangelicalism and the early nineteenth-century economic transformation was the crusade against alcohol. The consumption of alcoholic beverages had long been an accepted part of the preindustrial work regime, leisure activities, and social practices ranging from weddings to elections to funerals. With no moral stigma attached to drinking and with the supply of inexpensive spirits rising rapidly, Americans drank with abandon. By 1830 Americans aged fourteen and above consumed the equivalent of 7.1 gallons of absolute alcohol annually, the highest level in American history. Concern over intemperance had been expressed sporadically in the late eighteenth century, most notably by the Philadelphia physician Benjamin Rush, but organized opposition to alcohol was slow to develop. The first organization in the country devoted specifically to the cause of temperance appeared in Saratoga County, New York, in 1808. Members pledged to abstain from distilled spirits, limit the use of wine to religious ceremonies, and subject themselves to fines and penalties for violations of the pledge. But such efforts remained local and of little consequence. Early temperance societies were elite dominated, pursued limited goals, stressed moderation rather than abstinence, and ultimately failed.

By the mid-1820s conditions were ripe for a resurgence of temperance agitation and for a fundamental reorientation of its goals and methods. Perceptions of liquor as a social problem grew along with rising consumption. Evangelicalism infused the movement with a moral fervor and millennial vision lacking in earlier efforts and provided leaders skilled in revivalistic methods of persuasion. The "benevolent empire," furthermore, supplied a proven network for the dissemination of temperance materials. Finally, commercialization and the growth of industry created an audience receptive to the temperance message, either as a solution for perceived social disorder or as a mechanism for personal self-improvement. Lyman Beecher set the movement on a new course in late 1825 with a series of sermons calling for total abstinence from hard liquor, and in February 1826 the American Society for the Promotion of Temperance was founded in Boston.

New York figured prominently in the movement from the beginning. By 1829, the year the New York State Temperance Society was founded, some seventy-eight local branches were in existence. Four years later an estimated

250,000 New Yorkers had taken the pledge. The state organization coordinated the distribution of temperance tracts, sent out lecturers to denounce the evils of alcohol, and lobbied for restrictions on the sale of liquor. On the national level, the American Tract Society of New York, generously funded by Arthur Tappan, became the leading publisher and distributor of temperance literature. Gerrit Smith played a major role in the 1833 Philadelphia convention which restructured the national organization into what became the American Temperance Union. Stephen Van Rensselaer was chosen president of the new organization. E. C. Delavan, a wealthy Albany merchant and secretary of the New York State Temperance Society, subsidized the publication of the *Albany Temperance Recorder*, which became the leading journal of the national movement. These and other leaders of the New York society were also involved when the American Temperance Union, meeting in Saratoga Springs in 1836, adopted a pledge of total abstinence. Some two thousand local societies, however, repudiated the new "teetotal" pledge, and membership in the state declined from an estimated 229,000 in 1836 to 131,000 in 1839. By 1840 the temperance movement was virtually moribund.

The formation that same year of the Washington Temperance Society in Baltimore revitalized and transformed the movement, however. Led by ex-drunkards of the working class and eschewing religion, the Washingtonians targeted the hardcore drinker rather than the moderate user of alcohol and provided him with a support group of reformed drunkards. Combining traditional temperance techniques, the emotionalism of revival meetings, and the parades and rituals of the new politics, the movement spread quickly. The first Washington Temperance Society in New York City was established in 1841. By 1843 the city led the nation, with 60,000 members, while additional branches appeared across the state. Artisans dominated the movement, and women played a prominent role through parallel Martha Washington societies. By 1842, New York City boasted forty women's societies with 6,000 members drawn largely from the lower-middle and working classes. Women spoke at temperance rallies, organized benevolent activities, and worked tirelessly to reform intemperate men. Despite its early and spectacular success, however, the Washingtonian movement began to fragment by the middle of the 1840s, a victim of internal conflicts over leadership and goals, competition with older temperance societies, and an inability to control its local branches.

Other temperance organizations appeared, but the most important development in the late 1840s was the turn to political action. Convinced that moral persuasion had failed and concerned that their authority was threatened by the Washingtonians, many traditional temperance advocates adopted more coercive goals: the strict regulation of the sale of liquor or its prohibition altogether. In 1846, New York voters approved a local option law in a statewide referendum. Although New York City was exempted, more than 80 percent of the state's towns subsequently chose not to issue licenses for the sale of liquor. But the victory was short-lived. Under pressure from liquor interests and others opposed to prohibition, the legislature repealed the law in 1847. A statewide prohibition law would be passed in 1854, but by that time the temperance cause was inextricably entwined with electoral politics and the party realignment of the mid-1850s.

The most important movement to emerge from the evangelical reform milieu of the 1830s was abolitionism. New York had taken the first step toward emancipation in 1799, when the state adopted a law providing for the eventual emancipation of all slaves born after July 4 of that year. Other measures improving the condition of slaves followed, and in 1817 the legislature declared that all slaves born before 1799 would be freed in 1827. The gradual emancipation of slaves over some four decades was due in part to organized antislavery agitation. The first state abolition society appeared in New York City in 1785. In 1808 a state manumission society was incorporated. And when the American Colonization Society was organized in 1816, many New Yorkers found the idea of removing freed slaves to Africa appealing. Arthur Tappan and Gerrit Smith, among other prominent New Yorkers, were early supporters of colonization. By the early 1830s, however, some New Yorkers had become dissatisfied with colonization and sought alternative strategies to end slavery. The emergence of evangelical revivalism heightened awareness of the immorality and sinfulness of slavery. Equally important, on January 1, 1831, William Lloyd Garrison of Boston published the first issue of the *Liberator*, a newspaper committed to immediate, unconditional abolition. Abandoning colonization for the Garrisonian view, Arthur Tappan and other antislavery men established the New York City Abolition Society in 1833. Later that year, the Tappan brothers and Theodore Dwight Weld joined Garrison, James G. Birney of Kentucky, and other abolitionists to form the American Anti-Slavery Society.

Headquartered in New York and largely run by Lewis Tappan and his associates, the society condemned colonization and demanded the immediate abolition of slavery. It spread the abolitionist message by establishing local auxiliaries, distributing abolitionist periodicals, sending out antislavery agents, and petitioning Congress to end slavery. By 1834 there were more than two hundred local societies in New York state alone. As the movement grew, however, it inevitably aroused opposition. Moderates found the demand for immediate abolition shockingly radical. Many politicians, anxious to avoid the issue, joined in suppressing the distribution of abolitionist literature through the mail. In 1836 southern and anti-abolitionist congressmen imposed a "gag rule" in the House of Representatives, prohibiting the consideration of any petitions dealing with slavery. And across the North, state legislatures and constitutional conventions imposed new restrictions on the civil and political rights of free blacks, at the polls, in the schools, and in the courts. Mobs disrupted meetings, assaulted speakers, and rioted against abolitionism. In 1834 rioters attacked and virtually destroyed Lewis Tappan's home in New York City. In October 1835 delegates to a convention in Utica were met by a mob, forcing the removal of the meeting to the town of Peterboro. Despite such opposition, the delegates went on to organize the New York State Anti-Slavery Society. After the incident, Gerrit Smith committed himself and his considerable resources to the abolitionist cause.

By the mid-1830s internal divisions over ideology and tactics posed as serious a threat to the movement as opposition from without. The antislavery forces were increasingly divided between advocates of moral suasion and those who urged direct political action. The former believed that the path to emancipation lay in convincing slaveholders and other Americans of the evil and sinfulness of slavery. The latter emphasized petitions to Congress, pressure on the major political parties, and third-party action. Garrison's personality and his increasingly radical positions only exacerbated the divisions. When he and others defended the role of women in the movement and announced their support for women's rights, the stage was set for a formal split in the ranks of abolitionism. The occasion was the annual meeting of the society in New York in 1840. When a woman, Abby Kelley, was elected to an important committee, delegates opposed to Garrison and to the participation of women walked out. Garrison and his followers retained control of the American Anti-Slavery Society, while the Tappans and James G. Birney organized the American and Foreign Anti-Slavery Society and became committed to political action through the newly formed Liberty party. Birney went on to run for the presidency in 1840 and 1844, but gained few votes. Abolitionism became even more fragmented during the 1840s but managed to keep the issue of slavery in the public eye until it could no longer be avoided.

The controversy over the role of women in the abolitionist movement dramatized the inferior status of women in American society. Religion and reform were among the few legitimate outlets for middle-class women who felt confined by the ideal of domesticity. They had played crucial roles in the Bible, tract, and missionary societies of the 1820s and in almost all the important reforms of the era, but it was their involvement in abolitionism that politicized women reformers and produced a women's rights movement. Identifying with the plight of slaves, many came to see themselves as victims of social injustice and male tyranny. In New York, and throughout the United States, women could not vote, hold political office, or participate in public affairs. They were denied entry into most professions and opportunities for higher education. Married women were subject to the will of their husbands in most matters, including control over their property and earnings, and were disadvantaged in divorce and child custody proceedings. In short, women were considered inferior to men and effectively without rights.

Although a few women successfully challenged the barriers of discrimina-

Elizabeth Cady Stanton and Susan B. Anthony (ca. 1870). National Museum of American History, Smithsonian Institution, Washington, D.C.

tion earlier, it was not until the 1840s that the first organized women's rights movement appeared. As early as 1840, Lucretia Mott and Elizabeth Cady Stanton, furious at their exclusion from the World Anti-Slavery Convention in London, discussed the possibility of holding a convention to promote the rights of women. Their idea came to fruition in July 1848, when the first convention devoted to women's rights was held in Seneca Falls, New York. Mott and Stanton organized the meeting and drafted the Declaration of Sentiments setting forth women's grievances. Modeled after the Declaration of Independence, the Seneca Falls Declaration proclaimed the equality of men and women and indicted "man" for his systematic oppression of women. The convention adopted resolutions calling for legal equality, educational and professional opportunities for women, the right to control their own property, and, most controversial, the right to vote. In demanding full citizenship for women—indeed, by holding a public meeting on the issue at all—they repudiated the ideal of domesticity and its notion of separate spheres for men and women.

Despite widespread opposition, advocates of women's rights went on to organize additional local and national meetings and to lobby for changes in the legal status of women. A second women's rights convention was held in Rochester a month after Seneca Falls. Such meetings became common in the 1850s, as Mott, Stanton, Susan B. Anthony, Ernestine Rose, Amelia Bloomer, and others became more vocal and more effective in the assertion of women's rights. Bloomer edited the *Lily*, a temperance and women's rights newspaper, and gained lasting fame for her support of dress reform, lending her name to the Turkish-style pantaloon women's rights advocates wore to protest the restrictive female garb of the day. Stanton, Anthony, and Rose organized petition campaigns for legislative action on women's rights, and in 1854 Elizabeth Cady Stanton became the first woman to address the New York state legislature.

The greatest advances came in the area of women's property rights. In 1848, after a decade of lobbying and debate, the legislature passed the Married Women's Property Act, which gave women control over any property that they brought to the marriage or that they inherited or otherwise received while married. After another dozen years of agitation, the legislature passed the Earnings Act in 1860. Married women gained control over their own earnings, the right to sue and be sued, joint guardianship over their children, and the right to one-third of the real estate of husbands who died intestate. The ultimate goal of the movement, however, continued to elude women. Another sixty years of political activity would be required for women to attain the right to vote. The decade of the 1850s laid the foundations for the subsequent women's rights movement and elevated Susan B. Anthony and others to national leadership of that movement.

Religious Ferment in the Burned-Over District

Evangelical Protestantism was not the only religious development in this period with important social consequences. The Burned-Over District also spawned religious enthusiasms on the fringes or outside of the evangelical tradition and, in some cases, in opposition to it. These movements were typically more plebeian in origin, appealed to those bypassed or victimized by the market revolution, were unsympathetic to reform, and sought to preserve the traditional patriarchal family. One such group were the followers of William Miller. A Washington County farmer who had joined the Baptist Church in 1816, Miller systematically studied the Bible and concluded that the Second Coming of Christ was imminent. This premillennial vision obviated efforts at reform, since society would inevitably grow worse until the Second Coming. As his following grew and as anticipation of Christ's physical reappearance mounted,

Miller became increasingly specific, finally predicting that the momentous event would occur on March 21, 1843. Thousands of believers waited anxiously for the expected millennium. When March 21 passed uneventfully, Miller recalculated the date to October 22, 1844, but was again disappointed. Many of his followers thereupon returned to their traditional religious moorings; others persisted in their adventist beliefs, but the movement was fragmented. Miller died in 1848 without seeing the Second Coming, but one of his legacies was the emergence of the Seventh-Day Adventist Church, a direct descendant of the Millerites which persists to this day.

Even further removed from mainstream evangelical Protestantism, but more enduring, was the Church of Jesus Christ of Latter-Day Saints (Mormons) founded by Joseph Smith. Smith was the son of poor but religious parents who moved from New England to Palmyra, New York, in 1816, in search of a new

This contemporary cartoon spoofs William Miller's prediction that the world would end in 1843. New York State Historical Association, Cooperstown, N.Y.

start. In 1820, at age fifteen, he reported a remarkable conversion experience in which the Savior and God the Father appeared to him and warned him against the false beliefs of existing religions. Later, he claimed that the Angel Moroni had appeared to him in Palmyra and directed him to golden tablets on which was inscribed a new biblical dispensation. Translating the inscriptions with the aid of magical stones, Smith dictated an account of God's dealings with the inhabitants of the New World. It was a story replete with tales of lost tribes of Israel, bloody strife among the peoples of ancient America, the appearance of Christ in the Western Hemisphere, and prophecies of a new, purer church arising in the New World. Publication of the Book of Mormon in 1830 was met with disbelief and controversy. The Church of Jesus Christ, formally established in April 1830, attracted few believers at first, but many ordinary people, victimized by the market revolution and buffeted by social disorder and religious uncertainty, found Joseph Smith's vision of restored primitive Christianity, communalism, and patriarchy appealing. In 1831 Smith and his followers moved from New York to Kirtland, Ohio, where the church grew steadily, despite hostility and persecution. Later migrations took the Mormons to Missouri, to Illinois, where Smith would be murdered by a mob, and ultimately, under the leadership of Brigham Young, to Salt Lake City, Utah.

Alternatives to mainstream Protestantism came in many forms during this time of religious ferment. Whereas adventists eagerly awaited the establishment of the Kingdom of Heaven, utopian communitarians sought to establish a perfect society on earth. In New York, communitarianism is most clearly associated with John Humphrey Noyes. Born in Vermont and educated at Dartmouth, Andover Theological Seminary, and Yale, Noyes was the guiding spirit of one of the most successful communitarian experiments in American history. Converted by Charles Finney in 1831, he became committed to perfectionism, the belief that salvation brought perfection and the ability to live in the world without sin. In subsequent years he embraced communal ownership of property and "complex marriage," wherein those who had achieved perfection shared spouses as well as material possessions. After a six-year sojourn in Putney, Vermont, where his unorthodox views on marriage and sexuality became increasingly controversial, Noyes and a small band of followers established the Oneida Community in western New York in 1848. For three decades the community lived according to perfectionist and communal principles, practiced "complex marriage" (though sexuality and reproduction were strictly regulated), and adopted such other unpopular ideas as communal child rearing and female equality. Oneida also prospered economically, until a combination of secularization from within and criticism from without transformed the community. In 1879, yielding to outside pressure, Noyes recommended a return to individual marriage. Private property was also reinstituted, and two years later, in 1881, Oneida was reorganized as a joint-stock corporation.

One of the strangest manifestations of the religious ferment that burned over western New York in this period was the rise of spiritualism. Thousands of men and women in New York and the eastern United States became fascinated in the mid-nineteenth century with the spirit world. Emanuel Swedenborg, an eighteenth-century Swedish philosopher and mystic, had taught that the spirit world was a tangible place where imperfect souls would continue to progress toward perfection after death and that it was possible to converse with the spirits of the dead. Swedenborgian beliefs found a receptive audience in liberal Protestant circles, particularly among Universalists and Quakers, where orthodox Christianity was losing ground. The lectures and writings of Andrew Jackson Davis, the "Poughkeepsie Seer," also contributed to the spread of spiritualism, but it did not take hold among the general public until the spring of 1848, when word spread of strange occurrences in a small village in western New York.

Kate and Margaret Fox were the teenage daughters of a poor farmer who had recently moved to the town of Hydesville, near Rochester. In March, the sisters began to report unusual rapping noises that they claimed emanated from the spirit of a peddler who had been murdered and buried under the house some years before. Soon the sisters announced that they could communicate with the spirit. When an older sister living in Rochester organized public demonstrations of their talent, Kate and Margaret Fox became instant sensations. Four decades later, the sisters admitted that they had made the rapping noises by manipulating the joints of their toes, but the immediate impact of the Foxes' "spirit rappings" was a surge of popular interest in spiritualism. Throughout the country, mediums appeared who claimed to be able to communicate with the spirit world through seances. While spiritualism was especially prevalent among the poor and less educated, such highly educated and prominent men as Horace Greeley, William Cullen Bryant, and Robert Dale Owen also expressed at least some affinity for it. Worldwide, spiritualists claimed a million adherents by the mid-1850s, with one-third of these concentrated in New York. Although it never achieved the status of a fully organized church or reform movement, spiritualism grew out of the same social and religious ferment that had produced adventism, revivalism, perfectionism, and all the other "enthusiasms" of the Burned-Over District. Indeed, as Whitney Cross has written, it was "the last great excitement in the region."

Catholicism and Its Opponents

The rapidly growing Roman Catholic Church was of greater concern to evangelical Protestants than the new sects appearing in the Burned-Over District. Fueled by Irish and German immigration, the number of Catholics in the state rose from about 13,000 in 1815 to almost 250,000 by 1855. Catholicism was the single largest religious denomination in the state and nation in 1860, and New York City was its capital. More important, during these years the Catholic Church was transformed from a relatively insignificant institution dominated by Anglo-Americans to an urban and immigrant community of great diversity and influence.

The expansion of the church and the growth of immigration unleashed an unprecedented wave of anti-Catholicism and nativism. Anti-Catholic sentiments deeply rooted in the Anglo-American Protestant tradition reemerged in the 1830s. Simultaneously, native-born Protestant workers felt increasingly threatened by competition from cheap immigrant labor. The growing involvement of Catholic immigrants in politics only added to the fear of foreign influence. Such resentments erupted in 1834. In August, a mob attacked and burned the Ursuline convent in Charlestown, Massachusetts. Later that fall, Samuel F. B. Morse, the New York City artist and inventor, published a series of letters charging that the pope was conspiring with certain European powers to subvert American democracy by encouraging immigration. Morse set the tone for the future course of nativism in New York by linking traditional anti-Catholicism with new concerns over immigration.

By 1835 nativists in New York City had turned to politics to counter the immigrant and Catholic "threat." After an unsuccessful foray in the spring elections, the Native American Democratic Association was formed in June. The NADA platform opposed foreigners in office, pauper and criminal immigration, and Catholic influence in American institutions. Capitalizing on the lack of Whig candidates in the race, the NADA won 39 percent of the vote in the November city elections. Anticipating even greater gains, nativists nominated Morse for mayor the following spring, but with the Whigs contesting the election, he attracted only 6 percent of the vote. In 1837, in the midst of the financial panic and with Whig support, nativists elected a mayor and common council, but as immigration became a national issue in the late 1830s, the influence of the NADA waned.

A dispute over the New York City schools rekindled nativist agitation in the early 1840s. The Public School Society, a private association that received a share of the state's common school fund, had long controlled the city's school system. Decidedly Protestant, the schools relied upon the King James Bible and used blatantly anti-Catholic textbooks. Unwilling to send their children to Protestant schools, Catholics organized an alternative system and sought a share of the public funds, but to no avail. The issue exploded onto the political scene in 1840, when William H. Seward, the recently elected Whig governor, proposed that a portion of the public funds be used for "the establishment of schools in which they [immigrant children] may be instructed by teachers speaking the same language with themselves and professing the same faith."

Despite vigorous efforts by Bishop John Hughes, the common council rejected Catholic claims. Kept alive by Hughes and Seward, the issue dominated the 1841 legislative elections in the city. Catholics supported a proposal to do away with the Public School Society in favor of an elected commissioner in each ward, while Protestants favored the existing arrangement. Fearful of Democratic defections on the issue and frustrated by the lack of Whig support, Hughes organized an independent Catholic ticket but was unable to prevent a Whig victory. The Democrat-controlled 1842 legislature pushed through a law extending the state public education system to New York City, mandating elective commissioners from each ward to supervise public education, and barring state funds to any school teaching religious doctrine, but it was a partial victory. Nativists quickly engineered the election of Protestant commissioners who continued many of the previous practices.

The assertiveness of the Catholic leadership in the school controversy contributed to the emergence of the American Republican party in June 1843. Advocating a longer naturalization period, repeal of the school law, use of the King James Bible in the schools, and the exclusion of foreigners from public offices, the party received nearly a quarter of the vote in the 1843 elections and swept businessman and publisher James Harper into the mayor's office in the spring of 1844. But its victories were fleeting. Fallout from a series of bloody riots in Philadelphia in 1844 undermined the nativist movement, while Whig and Democratic defectors to nativism returned to traditional partisan allegiances. Many nativists eschewed political action altogether, turning instead to such semisecret fraternal societies as the Order of United Americans, a workingmen's organization founded in New York City in December 1844, and the United Sons of America and the Order of United American Mechanics, two Philadelphia groups formed in 1845. All three urged limits on the immigration of foreign workers. Political nativism would remain submerged until a massive surge of immigration in the late 1840s and a political crisis in the early 1850s unleashed a new wave of anti-immigrant and anti-Catholic sentiment.

The Institutional Response to Social Disorder

Nativism was symptomatic of deeper concerns about the health and well-being of society. New Yorkers joined other Americans in the antebellum period in associating rapid economic development, population growth, and immigration with social disorder and instability. Particularly troublesome was the perceived increase in crime, poverty, delinquency, insanity, and other forms of dependency and the inadequacy of prevailing methods for dealing with such problems. Traditionally, deviant and dependent members of society had been the responsibility of the family and the local community. The poor, for example, were typically cared for by family members or by neighbors in their homes. Almshouses were rarely used except for the most seriously ill and for strangers with no community ties. Similarly, punishment for criminal behavior was based on a system of fines, whipping, confinement to the stocks, and, in extreme cases, hanging. Jails held criminals until sentence could be carried out but were not part of the punishment itself. The same informal, family- and community-based approach applied to care for the insane and for orphans and delinquent children.

The early nineteenth century witnessed a profound change in social practice. In their efforts to combat disorder and to preserve a stable society, New Yorkers turned to specialized institutions as the preferred solution to the problems of deviancy and dependency. Fear of crime, concern over the appalling conditions in local jails, and the belief that criminal behavior was rooted in environmental causes led to the establishment of penitentiaries designed to reform criminals by insulating them from the social factors that bred crime. New York had experimented with incarceration as punishment at Newgate prison established in 1796, but it was Auburn prison, which opened in Cayuga County in 1817, that catapulted the state into the front ranks of penal reform. The Auburn or congregate system of prison management, which was subsequently extended to the new Sing Sing prison at Mount Pleasant near Sing Sing village in 1825, entailed separating prisoners into individual cells at night but allowing them to work together during the day. Strict silence enforced by harsh discipline was the rule. The internal workings of the prison were carefully regimented in the belief that a properly constructed and moral environment would contribute to the rehabilitation of the criminal. Pennsylvania invented an alternative system of total isolation, but it was New York's congregate system that most states copied as the penitentiary movement spread in the 1830s and 1840s.

Institutionalization also became the preferred method of treatment for the insane. As with crime, reformers and medical observers concluded that insanity had its roots in social conditions. Dorothea Dix, Samuel Gridley Howe, and other reformers exposed the horrible conditions in which many of the insane were kept and joined with psychiatrists to urge the construction of specially designed asylums for the care of the mentally ill. Although preceded by such private institutions as Bloomingdale Asylum in New York City, the first fully public institution was established by the state legislature in 1836 and opened its doors seven years later. The State Lunatic Asylum at Utica was designed and administered with a view to curing mental illness by removing patients from their harmful environment, treating them with kindness, limiting punishment, and providing a carefully regimented moral atmosphere for their rehabilitation.

The response to poverty followed the same pattern. Believing that pauperism was on the rise and that it threatened social stability, private philanthropists and public officials systematically studied the causes of poverty and offered alternatives to outdoor relief. An 1819 report of the Society for the Prevention of Pauperism in New York City attributed poverty to intemperance and urged the establishment of almshouses and workhouses. The Yates Report, a systematic survey of poor relief conducted by Secretary of State John Yates in 1824, condemned the existing system and recommended that the state adopt indoor relief in the form of county poorhouses as the principal mechanism for dealing with poverty. A decade later, poorhouses had appeared in fifty-one of the fifty-five counties in the state. Although outdoor relief (support of paupers in community households) was not entirely eliminated, some 10,000 New Yorkers received indoor relief at mid-century. Despite such growth, however, the gap between the promise and the performance of almshouses was so great that in 1857 a legislative committee could describe them as the "most disgraceful memorials of the public charity."

Children were also the objects of the movement to institutionalize dependent groups in antebellum New York society. Private groups led the way, establishing asylums for the care of orphaned and abandoned children. Between 1830 and 1850 some twenty-seven orphan asylums appeared in the state, often with public financial support. At the same time, houses of refuge for juvenile delinquents—reformatories—became the preferred method for dealing with juvenile offenders, underage vagrants, and disobedient children. In the 1840s, state-supported houses of refuge were built in New York City and Rochester. By the 1850s, however, reformers such as Charles Loring Brace had become disenchanted with the prisonlike character of such institutions and began to advocate alternatives to incarceration, such as boarding out juvenile offenders with families.

In almost every instance, the utopian promise of institutionalization had proved illusory by mid-century. The goal of establishing well-ordered environments to reshape the poor into responsible citizens, to cure the insane, and to rehabilitate the criminal was undermined by overcrowding, poor management, public indifference, considerations of economy, and the changing character of deviant and dependent groups. The institutions would remain in place, but the hopes and expectations of early nineteenth-century reformers would fade as asylums became little more than places to house society's outcasts. In a larger sense, however, the ambiguous record of the state's response to the problems of crime, poverty, and insanity is emblematic of New Yorkers' struggle to negotiate the social and cultural conflicts of the increasingly modern and pluralistic society that emerged in the three decades before the Civil War.

New York at the Crossroads of Culture

NEW YORK'S COMMERCIAL PREEMINENCE AND THE CEN-trality of New York City in the emerging national and international communications network ensured that the city and state would play a leading role in the cultural and intellectual developments of pre–Civil War America. By the 1820s a distinctively American culture had begun to appear, the product of post-Revolutionary democratization, nationalistic demands for literary and artistic independence from Great Britain and Europe, increased literacy and the rapid spread of print culture, advances in education, and the emergence of a commercialized popular culture in the nation's towns and cities. In the second quarter of the nineteenth century, New York was both a beneficiary of these trends and a catalyst in the broader cultural transformation of which they were a part.

Newspapers and the Dissemination of Information

The growth of New York as a cultural center was bound up with its dominance of the nation's commerce and the flow of news and information. New York City had surpassed Philadelphia, Boston, and all other contenders for commercial supremacy in the three decades after 1815. By 1860, two-thirds of all goods imported into the United States and one-third of all exports passed through the port at the mouth of the Hudson River. Apart from its obvious economic significance, this pattern of trade established New York as the nexus for the dissemination of foreign and domestic news and information. Ships arriving at New York harbor brought newspapers, pamphlets, mail, and other printed material from Great Britain and the European Continent. The city's editors vied with one another to be the first to publish the latest European news, which they typically printed verbatim. From New York, information spread to the other major cities along the Atlantic seaboard, where newspapers simply plagiarized stories from the New York press, then into the immediate hinterland, and ultimately as far west and south as existing trade routes allowed. As early as 1817 New York had established an informational hegemony over its competitors, and it solidified that dominance in the coming decades with the establishment of packet services connecting New York with Liverpool, Le Havre, and London; the completion of the Erie Canal route into the interior; and the appearance of transatlantic steamships, which cut the time between European ports and New York City by almost half.

Newspapers were the principal disseminators of public information before the invention of the telegraph, and their proliferation was one of the most important cultural developments of the early nineteenth century. As the population grew and spread westward and as new towns and cities were established, the number of newspapers exploded, increasing from 66 in 1810, to more than 200 by 1840, and 671 in 1855. Before the 1830s most were small, limited in content to commercial and political subjects, and expensive, and appeared weekly. They typically served a rather limited, local readership. Beginning in the 1830s, however, newspapers began to take on more modern characteristics. Technological innovations in printing and improved transportation combined to produce dramatic increases in circulation. At the same time, more and more specialized newspapers and periodicals began to appear. By 1855 there were papers devoted exclusively to commercial, religious, agricultural, scientific, and literary and artistic affairs. Similarly, foreign-language newspapers served the growing immigrant population, and many reform and professional associations had their own periodicals.

Not surprisingly, the spread of newspapers followed the migration of population across the state. Newspapers appeared early in such western settlements as Schenectady, Utica, Rochester, and Buffalo, and gained in importance as those towns grew and prospered in the 1820s and 1830s. The first newspaper in Buffalo, the weekly *Gazette*, appeared in 1811, while the *Rochester Gazette* became that city's first paper in 1816. The *Utica Observer*, which grew into one of the most important Democratic papers in the region, began publication in 1817. A decade later, in 1827, the *Rochester Advertiser* became the first daily published west of Albany. By 1860 every major city in the state had at least one daily newspaper.

Among upstate journals in this period, the most important were the *Albany Argus* and the *Albany Evening Journal*. The *Argus* was founded in 1813 and first achieved state and national prominence in the 1820s when Edwin Croswell assumed its editorship and the paper fell under the control of the state Democratic party. When slavery, internal improvements, and other issues split the

Democratic party in the 1840s, the *Albany Atlas* was established by the radical or "Barnburner" wing of the party but was reunited with the *Argus* in 1858. In 1830, Thurlow Weed began publishing the *Albany Evening Journal*. Initially an antimasonic paper, the *Evening Journal* quickly emerged as the leading Whig party newspaper in the state and the foundation for Weed's political power.

The center of newspaper publishing, not only for the state but for the nation as well, was unquestionably New York City. As the historian Edward K. Spann has put it, referring to the post-1840 period, "New York was a newspaper town in a newspaper-reading age." It had not always been so. Although the city had led the state in the creation of newspapers in the late eighteenth and early nineteenth centuries, most had been short-lived, and even the successful ones, such as the *Evening Post, Commercial Advertiser*, and *Mercantile Advertiser*, had appealed primarily to political and commercial elites and enjoyed limited circulation.

The first signs of change came in the decade of the 1820s. In 1826, William Cullen Bryant joined the *Evening Post*, succeeding William Coleman as editor three years later. During a remarkable career spanning half a century, Bryant was one of the dominant voices in American journalism. Under his leadership the *Evening Post* became a strong advocate of Democratic party principles during the 1830s and 1840s and an equally strong supporter of antislavery and the Republican party thereafter. Two other important papers appeared in 1827: the *Morning Courier*, which became the *Courier and Enquirer* in 1829 and which was edited by the volatile James Watson Webb for the next three decades, and the *Journal of Commerce*, established by the wealthy merchant and reformer Arthur Tappan. These developments enlivened New York City journalism as the major papers engaged in intense competition for news and readers. But the new papers were very much in the traditional mold, appealing primarily to commercial and political elites able to pay the $8–$10 annual subscription. Although single issues could be purchased at the printer's office for six cents, the price was beyond the reach of the city's masses, most of whom in any event had little interest in the advertising and shipping news printed in the papers.

It was the rise of the "penny" press in the 1830s that decisively transformed newspaper publishing and journalism and, in the process, helped revolutionize American popular culture. The introduction of steam-driven cylinder presses and improvements in the manufacture of paper brought about vast changes in the printing process and made larger circulations possible. Publishers could now offer daily editions for as little as one or two cents. In addition to lower prices, the penny papers employed street vending rather than subscription sales, adopted a more open and market-oriented advertising policy, were politically independent, and emphasized news that appealed to the urban working and middle classes rather than information primarily of interest to the elite. They were, in short, mass-oriented, democratic, and sensational, filling their pages with police reports, lurid accounts of murders and sexual crimes, exotica of all kinds, and even elaborate hoaxes. Skyrocketing circulation attested to their success in appealing to the urban mass audience.

The first successful penny newspaper was the *Sun*, established in New York City by Benjamin Day in 1833. When its circulation increased from 300 to 19,000 in two years, imitators soon followed. In 1835, James Gordon Bennett began publishing the *Morning Herald*, which quickly became the trend setter for the new journalism. Bennett had a particular knack for discerning public taste in news. Moreover, he was a genuine innovator, introducing a daily financial column, emphasizing comprehensive and timely news coverage, and using regular correspondents both in the United States and in Europe. Although frequently criticized for his flamboyance and sensationalism, over the next three decades Bennett built the *Herald* into the largest and most influential paper in the United States.

By mid-century two other important papers appeared to challenge Bennett and the *Herald*. In 1841 Horace Greeley established the *Tribune*, thus beginning one of the most distinguished careers in American journalism. A Vermont printer, Greeley came to New York City in the early 1830s and initially edited a weekly journal called the *New Yorker*. He became increasingly involved in Whig politics and attracted the attention of party leaders William H. Seward and Thurlow Weed. Within less than a decade of its founding, the *Tribune* achieved national prominence and an extensive circulation through-

A cheap pamphlet—close cousin to the penny newspapers—describing in lurid detail the 1836 murder of Helen (Ellen) Jewett, a New York City prostitute, by one of her clients. New York State Historical Association, Cooperstown, N.Y.

out the northern states. Although a penny paper, the *Tribune* eschewed sensationalism and acquired a reputation for morality, comprehensive news coverage, and powerful editorials on the issues of the day. It was also known for its high-quality staff, which included at various times Margaret Fuller, George

Ripley, Bayard Taylor, and Charles A. Dana. Greeley himself emerged as one of the most influential voices in state and national Whig and, later, Republican party councils and as an eloquent and enthusiastic advocate of such diverse reforms as temperance, abolitionism, women's rights, public education, free homesteads, Fourierism, and vegetarianism.

Less passionate and reform-oriented but equally important in the history of journalism was the *New York Times*, established by Henry J. Raymond in September 1851. Raymond consciously sought to avoid what he regarded as Greeley's faddishness and Bennett's sensationalism and to create a more moderate and dignified newspaper in the mold of the London *Times*. The *New York Times* not only provided comprehensive coverage of the news, foreign as well as domestic, but also included features on literature and the arts and general stories that appealed to the entire family. By 1861 the *Times* surpassed both the *Tribune* and the *Herald* within New York City, although it never achieved the national circulation of the *Tribune* in the pre–Civil War years.

New York City was also home to several significant African American newspapers during this period. *Freedom's Journal*, the first black newspaper published in the United States, appeared in March 1827, just four months before the final abolition of slavery in the state. Edited by Samuel E. Cornish and John Russworm, the paper proclaimed its determination "to plead our own cause" and to advance the goals of black freedom and citizenship. It suspended publication, however, in March 1829, after only two years. It was succeeded briefly by *Rights of All*, a monthly edited by Cornish, but that too collapsed by October 1829. After a seven-year hiatus, during which no black papers were published, the *Weekly Advocate* appeared in January 1837. Two months later, it became the *Colored American*, the most enduring black newspaper of the era. Under the leadership of Samuel Cornish and, later, Charles B. Ray, the *Colored American* became an important link among black communities in the north and a national voice on behalf of black rights. Other black publications appeared sporadically during this period—such as David Ruggles's *Mirror of Liberty*, the *Colored Man's Journal*, and the *Anglo-African Magazine*—but all were short-lived. Outside New York City the most important black paper in the state was Frederick Douglass's *North Star*, which first appeared in Rochester in 1847.

The growth of the European immigrant population in New York City was (not surprisingly) accompanied by the establishment of foreign-language newspapers. Six German papers, three French, and one Italian appeared before the Civil War. Most were short-lived, but *Le Courrier des Etats-Unis* (established in 1828) and *New Yorker Staats-Zeitung* (1834) continued publication well into the twentieth century.

Although the great daily newspapers were the most visible evidence of New York City's journalistic dominance, they were but the tip of the iceberg. By 1857 the city was home to some 104 newspapers, mostly weeklies, with a diverse readership and an annual circulation of 78 million. Noteworthy examples were the popular and influential *Harper's Weekly* and the *New York Ledger*. Among the numerous specialized journals published in the city, some achieved national significance. The *Scientific American* disseminated much-needed technical information, while the *American Railroad Journal*, edited by Henry Varnum Poor, became the leading periodical devoted to the railroad industry. Since New York City was the center of the ladies' garment and fashion industry, a magazine catering to that commercial sector appeared as well; Frank Leslie's *Ladies Gazette of Fashion and Fancy Needlework* was published in the city from 1854 to 1857.

Frederick Douglass. From Douglass, *My Bondage and my Freedom* (1855).

During the 1840s and 1850s, New York also led the nation in the publication of influential monthly magazines. These ranged from the faddish *Phrenological Journal* to important farm periodicals such as the *American Agriculturist* and Freeman Hunt's widely read *Merchant's Magazine*. One of the most significant of such publications, from both a political and an intellectual standpoint, was the *United States Magazine and Democratic Review*. Established in Washington in 1837 by John L. O'Sullivan, the *Democratic Review* moved to New York City in 1840 and quickly became the most influential voice of the Van Buren or radical wing of the Democratic party. But it was also much more than that. O'Sullivan envisioned a journal that would combine politics with literary and cultural criticism of the highest order. For a few brief years, from 1840 to 1846, when he was forced to sell the magazine, the dream was realized. In addition to the political commentary of leading reform Democrats, the *Democratic Review* published essays, stories, and criticism by Nathaniel Hawthorne, Horatio Greenough, Orestes Brownson, John Greenleaf Whittier, Parke Godwin, and other intellectuals of the day. One measure of its influence was the establishment, in 1845, of a Whig rival: the *American Review: A Whig Journal of Politics, Literature, Art and Science.*

The most highly regarded literary and cultural journal of the era was *Putnam's Monthly*. Conceived in 1852 by Charles Francis Briggs, George William Curtis, and George P. Putnam as an independent magazine devoted to publishing original works by American writers, *Putnam's* gave voice to the vibrant cultural and intellectual life of New York City in the mid-1850s. Through the political writings of contributors such as Parke Godwin, furthermore, *Putnam's* played a major role in national politics, helping to prepare northern public opinion for the antislavery ideology of the emerging Republican party. For all of its brilliance, however, *Putnam's* dominated the New York City literary scene for a mere five years, succumbing to financial difficulties during the depression of 1857.

The same locational advantages and technological developments that made New York the newspaper capital of the nation ensured its preeminence in book publishing as well. The Harper & Brothers publishing company had been established in 1817, the same year that work on the Erie Canal began, and quickly took advantage of the lower transport costs made possible by the canal to undersell local and regional publishers and capture the religious and school book trade. By the 1850s, Harper & Brothers was indisputably the greatest publishing house in the country. But the city was also home to its principal competitors, D. Appleton & Company, John Wiley, Charles Scribner, and G. P. Putnam, to name only the most enduring and familiar. Indeed, by 1860, printing and publishing was the leading industry in the city. New York publishers led the early nineteenth-century revolution in print culture, printing inexpensive editions of foreign novels (usually pirated), mass-distributing and marketing the sentimental literature so popular among the middle class, and printing the cheap and often lurid fiction that attracted urban working-class readers. With publishing so heavily concentrated in New York, it was inevitable that the city would also become a mecca for writers with more serious aspirations.

Literary Developments from Irving to Melville

New York was already clearly demarcated on the national literary map by 1825. Washington Irving, William Cullen Bryant, and James Fenimore Cooper were among the first generation of American writers to blend nationalistic strivings for literary independence with the new romantic sensibilities to produce a distinctively American literary voice. Irving's short stories and essays in *Salmagundi* (1807), his satirical *Knickerbocker's History of New York* (1809), and his *Sketch Book* (1819), which included "Rip van Winkle" and "The Legend of Sleepy Hollow," established him as the first American writer to achieve international recognition. Although his later writings, which included *A Chronicle of the Conquest of Granada*, *The Alhambra*, and a five-volume biography of Washington, were not as distinguished and he spent seventeen years in exile in Europe, Irving remained the most famous writer in America until his death in 1859.

What Irving did for the American short story and essay, William Cullen

Bryant did for American poetry. Born in western Massachusetts, where he practiced law for ten years in his youth, Bryant moved to New York City in 1825 and, as we have already seen, joined the staff of the *Evening Post* the following year. He was already regarded as the nation's most distinguished poet and critic. Influenced by the English romantic poets and by his own upbringing in the Berkshires of Massachusetts, Bryant's poetry celebrated nature. His most important poem, "Thanatopsis," a meditation on death, was first drafted when he was only seventeen years old and was published in 1817. In it Bryant fused religion and nature in a distinctively American idiom and earned for himself a national and international reputation. The theme of "religion as nature" appears even more prominently in such later works as "To a Waterfowl" (1818) and "A Forest Hymn" (1825). After 1825, Bryant's attention turned increasingly to his duties as editor of the *Evening Post* and his passionate advocacy of liberal reform. Although he continued to write verse until his death in 1878, his later poems fell far short of his earlier work. He was, nevertheless, a significant voice in the development of a distinctive national literature.

James Fenimore Cooper played an even more crucial role in the production of a national literature and was, arguably, the most famous American novelist in the second quarter of the nineteenth century. Born and raised in Cooperstown, the Otsego County community that his father, Judge William Cooper, had carved out of the wilderness in the late eighteenth century, Cooper attended Yale, married into the influential DeLancey family, and, after a stint in the U.S. Navy and the merchant marine, settled down in Westchester County. In 1820, he published *Precaution*, an eminently forgettable novel in the British style. One year later, however, he found his subject matter and his distinctive American voice in *The Spy*, a highly successful romantic adventure set in Westchester County during the British occupation at the time of the Revolution. In a remarkable burst of creativity, five more novels appeared over the next six years: *The Pioneers* (1823), *The Pilot* (1823), *Lionel Lincoln* (1825), *The Last of the Mohicans* (1826), and *The Prairie* (1827). Although he continued to write during the 1830s and 1840s, producing, among other works, *The Pathfinder* in 1840 and the *Deerslayer* in 1841, the mid-1820s was the period of his greatest creativity and originality.

Cooper's contribution to the early American literary tradition rests on his success in exploiting indigenous ideas and themes. Building upon his own recollections of the frontier in upstate New York, his novels, particularly the Leatherstocking Tales, explored the conflict between wilderness and civilization. In *The Pioneers*, he introduced one of the most popular and memorable figures in American literature, Natty Bumppo. Through four subsequent novels, Cooper developed the character of the legendary frontier scout—variously known as Leatherstocking, Hawkeye, or Deerslayer—portraying him as the living symbol of natural nobility, innocence, and self-reliance standing against the encroachments of law and culture. Cooper's vivid descriptions of the New York landscape combined with the power of his storytelling ensured him a wide audience both in America and Europe.

Although a vigorous defender of American democracy in his early work, in his later years Cooper became an equally vocal critic of American civilization. After a seven-year sojourn in Europe (1826–33), he returned to the United States disillusioned and fearful that the America he had so highly praised in Europe was disappearing. In works of social criticism like *A Letter to His Countrymen* (1834) and *The American Democrat* (1838) and in novels such as *Homeward Bound* (1838) and *Home as Found* (1838), Cooper criticized his native land for its vices, materialism, and provincialism. By the 1840s he could even be found defending the rights of property and of the landed aristocracy against the threat of rebelling tenants in the antirent wars of that decade.

Natty Bumppo, beloved character from the novels of James Fenimore Cooper, appears as the successful hunter in "The Turkey Shoot" (oil on canvas, 1857). By Tompkins H. Matteson. New York State Historical Association, Cooperstown, N.Y.

Although Cooper, Bryant, and Irving dominated the literary scene in the second quarter of the century, New York produced writers of more enduring significance in these years as well. While not a native New Yorker, Edgar Allan Poe came to the city in 1844 and quickly published "The Raven," perhaps his most famous poem. In 1845 he published *Tales* and *The Raven and Other Poems* and began editing the *Broadway Journal*, a literary review founded by Charles F. Briggs, who would go on to edit the more famous *Putnam's Monthly* in the 1850s.

Walt Whitman, in contrast, was in every respect a New Yorker. Born in Huntington, Long Island, in 1819, and raised in Brooklyn, Whitman took up the printing trade at an early age and apprenticed or worked at several newspapers during his teens and twenties. In 1846 he began a two-year stint as editor of the *Brooklyn Eagle*, and, after a brief visit to New Orleans, he wrote for the *Freeman*, a daily newspaper of Free Soil principles. During these years he taught school, became a carpenter, and published a temperance novel. More important, he absorbed the sights, sounds, and emotions of the lively and diverse urban environment of New York City in all its exuberance. It was here that he developed his abiding faith in democracy, individualism, and the common man. It was here, too, that he internalized the language and rhythms of popular speech that so clearly marked his poetry. It all came together in 1855 with the publication of the first edition of *Leaves of Grass*, a book of poems that broke all the existing rules of poetry by using free verse and blunt, common language and exploring themes previously deemed inappropriate by "respectable" audiences. Although a popular failure when it first appeared, *Leaves of Grass*, which subsequently went through twelve revisions, is unquestionably one of the greatest accomplishments of the "American Renaissance" of the 1850s and of American literature generally. Indeed, Walt Whitman has appropriately been called the bard of American democracy.

Whitman's poetry expressed an almost mystical faith in individualism and democracy. Herman Melville, his contemporary, explored the darker side of individualism and questioned the optimistic moral assumptions of American society. Born in New York City in 1819, Melville was the product of prominent families in both Massachusetts (the Melvilles) and New York (the Gansevoorts). He grew up and attended school in Albany, where his mother moved after the death of his father. After working at various jobs—clerk, farmhand, and schoolteacher—he sailed with a merchant ship on the New York-to-Liverpool run at age eighteen. Four years later, in one of the most formative experiences of his life, he joined the crew of the whaling vessel *Acushnet*. When the ship reached the Marquesas Islands a year and a half later, he deserted, lived with the native people in the remote valley of Typee, and ultimately made his way to Tahiti. He eventually enlisted on the U.S. Navy frigate *United States* and returned home in 1844.

Melville's years at sea and his adventure in the South Pacific provided the subject matter for his most important novels. Within two years of returning, he published *Typee* (1846), a fictionalized account of his time in the Marquesas, and followed that a year later with *Omoo* (1847), based on his stay in Tahiti. Both were essentially romantic adventure tales, overlaid with the author's moralizing about the innocence of the islanders and the corrupting influence of the more "civilized" sailors and missionaries. Both were also immediately successful and established Melville's fame. Over the next four years, he published four more novels in quick succession: *Mardi* (1849), *Redburn* (1849), *White-Jacket* (1850), and *Moby-Dick* (1851). Still other novels would come later, most notably *Pierre* (1852), *The Confidence Man* (1857), and *Billy Budd*, which was published posthumously in 1924, but Melville's greatest achievement was *Moby-Dick*. In his powerful tale of Captain Ahab's obsessive pursuit of a great white whale, Melville probed such universal questions as the nature of good and evil, free will versus fate, and the destructive potential of unfettered individualism. Unappreciated and largely unread in Melville's lifetime, *Moby-Dick* has since come to be regarded as possibly the greatest novel in all of American literature.

The Hudson River School of Painting

Artistic developments in the second quarter of the century closely paralleled those in literature. Just as Irving, Cooper, and Bryant had given birth to a national literary tradition by infusing their work with indigenous themes narrated in a distinctively American voice, so, too, artists began to strive for the creation of a distinctively American art free from Old World influences. Before the 1820s, American painting was firmly rooted in the European, and especially British, tradition. Portraiture and history were the principal subjects of late eighteenth- and early nineteenth-century artists, most of whom studied in Europe. Particularly influential was Benjamin West, a native Pennsylvanian who resided in England and was so well regarded there that he succeeded Sir Joshua Reynolds as head of the Royal Academy in 1792. West's American students included John Trumbull, Gilbert Stuart, Charles Willson Peale, Thomas Sully, and Samuel F. B. Morse, among others, all of whom achieved a measure of distinction in the traditional style of painting.

The first truly American school of painting appeared in the 1820s and was uniquely associated with New York. Although founded by Thomas Doughty, the Hudson River School of landscape painting is most famously associated with Thomas Cole. A transplanted Englishman, Cole began his career as a portrait painter but quickly turned his palette and brush to the magnificent vistas of the Hudson River and the Catskill Mountains. Cole's powerful, realistic and evocative paintings of the New York landscape inspired awe and wonder in the viewer. Like William Cullen Bryant's poetry, his depictions of the physical grandeur of America seemed infused with religious import. Yet, at the same time, a central theme of many of his paintings was the ambiguous relationship between nature and man, wilderness and civilization. Other representatives of the Hudson River School included Asher Durand, already famed as an engraver before he turned to landscapes; John F. Kensett, perhaps the most popular of the group; and Frederic E. Church, whose search for ever more spectacular subjects for his paintings took him farther and farther from New York.

Another New Yorker, William Sidney Mount, achieved fame as a genre painter, meticulously and lovingly depicting commonplace scenes of everyday life on Long Island. After 1857, Nathaniel Currier and James Merritt Ives took the popularization of art one step further. Capitalizing on the new technology of color lithography, Currier and Ives began mass-producing and distributing the color prints illustrating everyday life in America that would become so common in middle-class homes.

Education

The cultural and intellectual landscape of pre–Civil War New York was also transformed by significant developments in education and the general diffusion of knowledge. At the close of the Revolution, New York's political leaders had envisioned a comprehensive system of state supervision of schools and colleges. To implement that vision, in 1784 the legislature created the University of the State of New York to be governed by a Board of Regents. Over the course of the next quarter-century, however, the Board of Regents' role was reduced to providing oversight of the state's colleges and academies, while the legislature, local communities, and various private associations took the first steps toward the establishment of a common school system in New York.

Although laws to encourage the establishment of schools had been passed as early as 1795 and 1805, the basic framework for the state's common school system in the first half of the nineteenth century was created between 1812 and 1814. Briefly, the proceeds from a permanent school fund were to be distributed to towns on the basis of population, and the towns would be expected to match the state grant with new taxes. In addition, localities were authorized to cover any deficits in school operations by taxing the parents of students. The poor were exempt from paying this "rate bill," provided they were willing to sign an oath claiming poverty. New York City was a special case. An 1813 law authorized the common council to distribute the city's share of state funds to various private and religious societies that were operating charity schools. Under this system, the Public School Society, a private association, controlled the city's public schools until Catholic resentment at Protestant control exploded in the early 1840s and led to the creation of a public board of education.

After 1812 the number of district schools increased rapidly, providing thousands of New York children with at least a rudimentary education. Of course, the quality of instruction varied from community to community. Instruction rarely went beyond the three R's, and teacher training was minimal. Not all New Yorkers, furthermore, chose or were able to take advantage of the common schools. Attendance was not compulsory in this period, and many families could not afford the loss of income they would have incurred by sending their children to school. Often those who could not pay the rate bill kept their children out of school rather than publicly admit their indigence. According to a state report, an estimated 46,000 eligible children were not attending school in 1846. Adding to these problems, some New Yorkers resisted efforts to expand and improve the public school system. The fear of higher taxes, Catholic demands for public funding of their own schools, and opposition from existing private schools were formidable obstacles to the cause of educational reform.

Despite such resistance, demands for an entirely free public elementary school system rose steadily in the second quarter of the century, and the legislature was ultimately compelled to respond. An 1849 law, which was overwhelmingly approved in a public referendum, abolished the rate system and established a statewide system of free schools. Citing the additional tax burden, opponents demanded its repeal, but the law was reaffirmed in a second referendum. Finally in 1851 the legislature reimposed the rate bill but appropriated sufficient funds for the support of schools that most rural districts were not required to collect the odious rate bills. Free schools did not become a complete reality until the final abolition of the rate system in 1867. In the meantime, in 1854, the state established the Office of State Superintendent of Public Instruction to oversee New York's public school system.

Publicly funded secondary education progressed much more slowly. In the first half of the nineteenth century, few New Yorkers attended school beyond the elementary level. Those who did, especially young men bound for college or for a teaching career, attended private academies. From the beginning the Board of Regents had been empowered to charter such academies, and it did so with increasing frequency after the War of 1812. Some academies were chartered directly by the legislature, which at various times also set aside small sums of money to encourage the creation of such institutions. Still other private schools operated without charters. However they were established, the number of private academies increased steadily in the decades before the Civil War, fueled by the rapid growth of towns and villages across the state. By 1855 an estimated 36,000 New Yorkers of high school age were enrolled in private academies. The overwhelming majority, of course, were boys, either preparing for college or taking advantage of a growing emphasis on bookkeeping, teacher preparation, and other practical subjects.

Free public high schools were largely a phenomenon of the post–Civil War decades. As early as the 1850s, however, so-called free academies had begun to appear in some cities and towns in the state in response to the demands of local communities. New York City was among the first to establish such institutions, but some upstate towns like Rochester had a high school by the end of the decade. Altogether, New York could boast some twenty-two public high schools by 1860, and the number would expand rapidly after the 1867 law requiring that all public education be tax supported.

Although some private academies admitted both boys and girls and there had been female academies since the Revolution, in general educational opportunities for young women beyond the elementary level were few. It was precisely to remedy this situation that a female seminary movement grew up in the early nineteenth century. Many of the early seminaries focused on preparing young girls for the genteel life they were expected to live in this age of "separate spheres." One of the pioneers of the movement, however, and of female education generally, was Emma Hart Willard, who had other ideas. By the time she moved from Middlebury, Vermont, where she had been teaching in a female academy, to New York in 1819, she was already a vocal advocate of greater educational opportunities for women. Willard argued not only that properly educated mothers were essential for a virtuous citizenry in a republic, but also that women needed to be trained to become teachers and in subjects comparable to those offered in men's colleges. In 1819 she petitioned the governor and legislature of New York to establish a system of state-funded schools for young women. Although unsuccessful in that endeavor, two years later she accepted the invitation of the Troy Common Council to establish a female seminary there. The Troy Female Seminary, where Willard applied her vision of women's education, rapidly became one of the most important and influential such institutions in the country. More than 12,000 women attended the seminary between 1821 and 1872, many of whom went on to establish their own academies based on the educational principles introduced by Emma Willard.

Educational opportunities for black New Yorkers were of course more limited than those for whites. Most black families could not afford to take advantage of the private schools that appeared from time to time, while the system of gradual emancipation meant that before 1827 many black children literally did not have the freedom to pursue an education. Still, as early as 1787, the New York Manumission Society had established an African Free School specifically for black children. Despite initial opposition from the white community, enrollments gradually increased over the years, particularly after the formal end of slavery. By 1834 there were seven African Free Schools in New York City, with an enrollment of 1,400. By that time, however, support for the schools had become too burdensome for the Manumission Society, and the schools were transferred to the control of the Public School Society of New York. Two decades later, in 1853, the black schools, along with the society's white schools, were absorbed into the public system administered by the New York City Board of Education. Throughout the antebellum decades, black leaders and organizations as well as white charitable societies attempted to establish black schools in various towns and cities across the state, but most were short-lived. By the 1830s black children had also begun to attend public schools. Despite rulings by the state superintendent in 1841 and 1847 that the public schools were open to "all" children, black students frequently experienced hostility and humiliation in racially mixed schools. Increasingly, local communities resorted to separate public schools for blacks, although the state never required separate facilities.

Although very few New Yorkers attended college or professional schools in the early nineteenth century, and many of those who did went out of state, the period is notable for the establishment of important institutions of higher learning that have endured. The half-century after the end of the Revolution witnessed the chartering of Columbia College (previously King's College) in 1784, Union College in 1795, Hamilton in 1812, and Hobart in 1825. In addition, the United States Military Academy at West Point was established in 1802 and quickly became famous not only for its military training, but also as the source of most of the formally educated engineers in pre–Civil War America. The next three decades were an even more extraordinary period in the history of higher education in New York. Religious and denominational impulses produced new institutions, including St. Johns (Roman Catholic, 1840); Madison, which later became Colgate (Baptist), and Rochester (Baptist) both 1846; St. Lawrence (Universalist, 1856); Alfred (Seventh-Day Adventists, 1857); Genesee College, which became Syracuse University after the Civil War (Methodist Episcopal, 1851); and St. Stephens, the forerunner of Bard College (Protestant Episcopal, 1860). In 1831, New York City civic leaders established the University of the City of New York (which later became New York University) as a nondenominational and more open alternative to Columbia. The Free Academy, which was the forerunner of the College of the City of New York, opened its doors in 1847. And finally, in 1855, the Elmira Female College became the first institution of higher education for women established in the state.

Although for most New Yorkers professional training still consisted of an apprenticeship with an established practitioner, opportunities for a formal education in the various professions had also expanded by the middle of the century. The Rensselaer Institute, which was chartered in 1826, became a national leader in civil engineering. Law schools were established at New York University (1835), Albany (1851), and Columbia (1858), and other institutions began to incorporate the study of law into the curriculum. Similarly, those who aspired to become doctors could choose between learning the profession at the feet of an established physician and a more formal education at one of the new medical colleges established at New York University (1837), Albany Medical College (1839), and the University of Buffalo (1846).

New York also led in the popular dissemination of knowledge and practical information through lyceums, mechanics' institutes, and public and private libraries. The lyceum, whose roots lay in the British adult education movement and in the American tradition of voluntary association, swept the country in the late 1820s and the 1830s. Essentially local associations established to spread scientific and practical knowledge and to provide a venue for the discussion of contemporary cultural and intellectual trends, lyceums sponsored lectures, collected books, and provided meeting places for debates, concerts, and the like. Amos Eaton appears to have established the first lyceum in the state at Troy in 1818. But their numbers grew rapidly over the next decade, and in 1831 the New York State Lyceum was created, the first state lyceum in the country. New Yorkers like Stephen Van Rensselaer also played a prominent role in the National Lyceum, which was founded in 1831. Closely related to the lyceum was the mechanics institute, typically an association of men in a particular occupation devoted to intellectual improvement. Prominent examples included the General Society of Mechanics and Tradesmen, which established a program of adult education in 1836; the Mechanics Institute of New York City, begun in 1831; Rochester's Mechanics Institute, established in 1826; and the Albany Institute, which became famous for its extensive library.

The proliferation of lyceum and mechanics institute libraries was part of a much broader growth in the number of libraries in the state during the first half of the century. The State Library was established in Albany in 1818 and, with support from the legislature, developed extensive legal and documentary collections. The state also provided support for academy libraries. In 1836, furthermore, the legislature approved an annual appropriation of $55,000 to promote the establishment of small libraries in each of the state's common school districts. Although the success of the program was uneven, especially in some rural districts, there were an estimated 1.6 million volumes in such libraries by 1853. Perhaps the most enduring achievement of the era was John Jacob Astor's bequest of $400,000 in 1848 to establish a public library in New York City. The Astor Library, which opened in 1854, became the preeminent reference library in the country and later provided the foundation for the incomparable New York Public Library.

Scientific Achievements

New Yorkers made significant contributions to the growth of scientific knowledge in this period as well. Although New York City remained in the shadow of

Boston and Philadelphia in the pre–Civil War decades, harbingers of its future status in the scientific community were clearly apparent. Because of its population, commercial base, and dominance of the publishing industry, the city was rapidly becoming the center for the publication of scientific journals. By mid-century it had caught up with Boston in the number of such publications each originated, and three decades later, as more and more scientific societies and periodicals located their headquarters in the metropolis, it was outpublishing Boston by a margin of seven to one. New York University, furthermore, gained prominence in the scientific community as a result of the work of John W. Draper and Elias Loomis. Draper, a professor of chemistry, made his mark in the study of the chemistry of radiant energy and light and his pioneering work in the scientific applications of photography, including astronomical photography. Loomis enjoyed a distinguished career in astronomy and meteorology, first at New York University and later at Yale. New York City was also the home of Samuel F. B. Morse, whose magnetic telegraph, patented in 1844, revolutionized mid-nineteenth-century communications.

Albany, with its complex of schools, libraries, and institutes, and Troy, the home of Rensselaer Institute, were also centers of American science in the second quarter of the century. Amos Eaton, senior professor at Rensselaer Institute after 1824, was one of the era's leaders in the field of natural history and science. Eaton's articles on geology, chemistry, mineralogy, and surveying, as well as his textbooks such as *Manual of Botany*, were among the best and most influential of the period. Even more influential was one of his students at Rensselaer, James Hall. In 1836, Hall was appointed to the New York State Geological Survey, with primary responsibility for the westernmost area of the state. His 1843 report on the geology of the region became a classic in the field. It also set him on course to becoming the acknowledged leader in invertebrate paleontology. Commissioned by the state in 1843 to prepare a one-volume report on New York's paleontology, Hall began a half-century investigation of the subject, which culminated with the publication of the thirteenth volume in 1894. The magnificent result has been described as "the most ambitious single scientific enterprise undertaken by a state government in its time."

The most famous scientific name associated with New York during this period was unquestionably Joseph Henry. Born in Albany in 1797 and raised in poverty, Henry developed an interest in science at an early age. He attended Albany Academy where, in 1826, he became professor of mathematics and natural philosophy. During his years at the academy, Henry conducted numerous experiments in electromagnetism. Among his many achievements was the discovery in 1830 of electromagnetic induction, which he arrived at independently of Michael Faraday, and which made possible the invention of Morse's telegraph and its subsequent commercial development. In 1832, Henry was appointed professor of natural philosophy at Princeton, where he continued his research in electricity, demonstrating many of the principles that underlay future developments in telegraphic communications, the telephone, radio, and the electrical industry generally. In 1846 he became the first secretary and director of the newly established Smithsonian Institution, whose power and influence in the emerging American scientific community would be due largely to Henry's vision and stewardship over the next three decades.

Popular Culture

Developments in the fine arts, "serious" literature, education, science, and publishing were but components of a much broader cultural transformation in the first half of the nineteenth century. The period also witnessed the emergence of a lively, commercialized popular culture. For all of their later fame and significance, Whitman and Melville, for example, were not as widely read in their own time as other, more popular, novelists. The revolution in print technology and lowered transportation costs made novels more affordable than ever before. Foreign novels by authors like Charles Dickens were reproduced cheaply and distributed to a mass audience. Middle-class New Yorkers, like other Americans of the time, were voracious consumers of sentimental novels. Written by women and for women, sentimental novels stressed middle-class domesticity, the sanctity of the home, and the indomitable character and morality of women in contrast to the greed and immoral behavior of men. They employed melodramatic stories to juxtapose female virtue and Christian spirituality with the corrupting influence of politics and the market. Sentimental novels such as Susan Warner's *Wide, Wide World* (1850) and Harriet Beecher's Stowe's *Uncle Tom's Cabin* (1852) were enormously popular, outselling all other categories of fiction when they appeared.

The urban working class, furthermore, was a ready audience for the new, more democratic forms of entertainment and amusement that arose in the second quarter of the century. Cheap fiction and dime novels appeared in profusion from the 1830s to the 1850s, and workers, already the principal audience for the penny papers, consumed such popular literature as avidly as the middle class read sentimental novels. Sensational, melodramatic, violent, and sexually explicit, adventure fiction and exposé novels of the sort churned out by George Thompson, Ned Buntline, and others accounted for three-fifths of all fiction published in America in the three decades before the Civil War.

Popular working-class culture was distinct from genteel culture in other ways as well. In the newly emerging working-class neighborhoods, as noted earlier, social and cultural life—particularly for single male workers—revolved around the boardinghouse, saloon, and fire company. Often such meeting places, especially fire companies, formed the basis for rival clubs that were more likely to engage one another in urban combat than to protect the neighborhood from the scourge of fire. Frequently they were also the locus for a brawling, personalistic style of working-class politics. In addition to fighting, drinking, and bragging, New York City's male workers engaged in a variety of so-called blood sports. Cockfighting and dogfighting were particularly popular and were often sponsored by neighborhood saloons. Prizefighting grew in popularity as the immigrant population increased, and ring opponents often reflected the ethnic and occupational divisions within working-class neighborhoods.

The theater was another popular form of urban entertainment, one that brought all classes into uneasy and sometimes tumultuous contact. One of the first signs of cultural development in the burgeoning towns and cities across the state was the staging of theatrical performances and the construction of playhouses. Albany, Syracuse, Buffalo, Troy, and Brooklyn, among others, had established theaters and begun booking dramatic performances as early as the 1820s. None, however, could compete with New York City. In the four decades from 1820 to 1860, the number of major theaters in the metropolis rose from one to fourteen, with the Park, the Bowery, the Chatham, and the Astor Place Opera House being the most famous. Touring companies of actors from England and Europe invariably included the city on their itinerary, often choosing it for their American debut, and New York City quickly came to dominate the American theatrical scene, a position it has held ever since.

As with literature and art, drama in the early nineteenth century was heavily British in content. Shakespeare, whose works had not yet taken on the aura of "highbrow" culture, was enormously popular among all classes of theatergoers. His plays, especially the tragedies, were the most commonly performed of any dramatist, although they were often very loosely adapted to appeal to popular tastes. So, too, the seventeenth- and eighteenth-century British dramatists' works were regularly performed. Other theater fare included melodramas and, increasingly, plays with specifically American themes written by native playwrights. Examples of the latter included James Nelson Barker's *The Indian Princess*, Samuel Woodworth's *The Forest Rose*, John Augustus Stone's *Metamora*, Robert M. Bird's *The Gladiator*, and George L. Aiken's adaptation of *Uncle Tom's Cabin*. Characters drawn directly from the streets of New York, like Mose the Bowery B'hoy, also became common on the city's stages, especially in working-class theaters.

The performers were as important during this period as the plays themselves, and here, too, British influence was strong. The great British actors Edmund Kean, William Macready, and Junius Brutus Booth all had their debuts in New York City in the 1820s and continued to influence the American stage in the succeeding decades. Indeed, Booth remained in America and established one of the premier families in the history of American theater. His son, Edwin Booth, who first appeared on stage in New York in 1850, went on to become the leading American actor in the Civil War era. Another British transplant was Fanny Kemble. The daughter of Charles Kemble, one of Great Britain's most renowned actors, Fanny charmed New York audiences in the 1830s. Prominent American actors, some of whom were already breaking away from the British tradition to create a uniquely American style, included James Henry Hackett; Thomas Hamblin, manager of the Bowery Theater; Charlotte Cushman; and, most important, Edwin Forrest, whose expressive, muscular style was especially popular with American theatergoers. Forrest was unquestionably America's first great native-born actor. Significantly, he also personified the growing tension between American and British performers and the cultural nationalism of the day.

Theater has been called the most democratic of all the art forms in the early nineteenth century. The social and economic changes that swept over the state and nation after 1815 broadened the potential audience for theatrical performances, while the economics of theater—the need to fill up the hall night after night—ensured that popular tastes and desires were taken into account in scheduling productions. As a result, the audiences were remarkably diverse, although carefully segregated (by price) in the actual seating. Typically, the more genteel theatergoers occupied boxes near the stage, while a much broader spectrum of "middling class" patrons were to be found in the pit. The cheaper seats in the gallery or balcony were the territory of the working classes, except for the upper gallery, which was reserved for blacks and prostitutes.

Theater performances in the early nineteenth century were anything but the decorous events they have since become. Audiences, particularly those relegated to the gallery, were noisy, boisterous, and ever ready to express their opinions of the actors, either verbally or by hurling food and other debris at the stage. Genteel theatergoers, of course, found such behavior scandalous. For their part, working-class patrons grew increasingly critical of the elevated tone and speech and undemocratic demeanor of English actors, a style and manner they also resented in the city's elites. By the 1830s, this undercurrent of class tension had become so pervasive that theaters began to be differentiated by class and type of performance. The upper classes patronized the Park Theater, the middle class was increasingly associated with the Bowery, and the Chatham was frequented by working-class men and women.

The raucous behavior of theater audiences often spilled out into the streets, as class resentments, tensions between supporters of rival actors, and national and ethnic pride periodically erupted into violence. Although theater riots had occurred earlier, the most famous such incident was the Astor Place riot of 1849. The immediate cause was a long-standing rivalry between the American-born Edwin Forrest and the popular English actor William Macready. Forrest's broad and melodramatic interpretations of Shakespeare made him a particular favorite among the working class. Macready was a traditional Shakespearean actor, whose style was more restrained and true to the text, and who appealed to genteel, educated theatergoers. To Forrest's partisans, especially Irish workers, Macready symbolized British aristocracy and everything inimicable to American democracy. The feud between the two actors and their supporters came to a head on May 9 when a working-class mob rioted outside the Astor Place Opera House where Macready was performing. When the militia intervened and fired on the crowd, twenty rioters were killed and more than 150 injured. In the wake of the Astor Place riot, theaters became even more differentiated along class lines.

For a time, in the 1820s, black New Yorkers had their own theater. In 1821, Allen Royce, a black businessman, opened the African Grove at the corner of Mercer and Bleeker Streets. The first black theater in America, the African Grove became the focal point for cultural events aimed at the city's African American population. In addition to opera, ballet, and other musical fare, the theater produced dramatic performances by Henry Brown's African Company and other black actors. Several performers, most notably James Hewlett and the renowned Ira Aldridge, launched major national and international stage careers at the African Grove. Citing the rising incidence of racially motivated violence against blacks and black cultural institutions, city authorities closed the theater in 1829.

"Serious" music played a somewhat less prominent role in New York's cultural life in this period than theater, but it was by no means absent. Opera gained in popularity before the Civil War, and touring opera companies regularly visited the city. The New York Philharmonic Society was established in 1842 and gave its first concert on December 7 of that year. The Academy of Music was established in 1854. In addition, international artists almost invariably included New York City and other major towns and cities in the state on their American itineraries. Jenny Lind, the internationally renowned singer, for example, began her 1850 tour of the United States in New York at the Castle Garden.

By the early 1840s a new form of entertainment was appearing in New York and other cities across the north: the blackface minstrel show. Born a decade earlier when an actor named Thomas D. Rice began to perform imitations of African American dances while made up in blackface, the minstrel show spread rapidly, appealing especially to urban working-class males. Minstrel shows incorporated songs, dances, and short, humorous skits performed by white actors (faces blackened with burnt cork) affecting black dialect and mannerisms. Highly formulaic, minstrel shows typically revolved around humorous give-and-take between characters named "Tambo" and "Bones" or "Uncle Ned" and "Zip Coon." While audiences were exposed to white interpretations of some aspects of African American culture and to social and political barbs aimed at the elite, minstrel shows were ultimately deeply racist and perpetu-

An African Grove theater playbill advertising an evening's entertainment, to include an opera and a performance of Shakespeare's "Richard III." From Eileen Southern, *The Music of Black Americans: A History* (New York: Norton, 1971).

ated the grossest stereotypes of blacks. Their immense popularity among New York's white workingmen reflects the pervasiveness and depth of racial prejudice in American society and culture in the decades before the Civil War.

If it were possible to distill the essence of the new, commercialized popular culture of the mid-nineteenth century into a single individual, that person would have to be Phineas Taylor Barnum. P. T. Barnum was both creator and purveyor of the new democratic entertainment so eagerly consumed in these years, and his American Museum helped make New York City the entertainment capital of pre–Civil War America. A native of Connecticut and already a failure in several business enterprises, Barnum first moved to New York in 1834. For the better part of a decade he tried his hand at various entertainment ventures, including a scheme to exhibit an elderly black woman named Joyce Heth to a gullible public as the 169-year-old nurse of George Washington. Against all logic, the public came—and they paid. After several more years of financial ups and downs, in 1841 Barnum bought Scudder's American Museum in New York City and quickly converted it to his own purposes. Through shrewd marketing and publicity, dramatic presentations, and an emphasis on novel and exotic attractions designed to appeal to the public's curiosity, he built the American Museum into the best known such enterprise in America. Among his most famous "curiosities" were General Tom Thumb (a two-foot-tall midget from Connecticut named Charles Stratton) and the "Feejee Mermaid." Although a public relations genius (he was truly America's greatest showman), Barnum was ultimately successful because he was able to capitalize on the mass demand for amusement and entertainment unleashed by a revolution in popular culture.

Chapter 22

From Factions to Parties
The Emergence of the Second Party System

IN 1825 NEW YORKERS INHABITED A POLITICAL WORLD IN transition. The political culture that emerged from the Revolution had been the product of classical republican theory, a tradition of elite rule, and one of the most conservative state constitutions of the era. Habits of deference, a restricted suffrage, and a highly centralized system of patronage combined to give New York a distinctive political style. Even at the height of Federalist and Republican competition, politics typically took the form of intense and bewildering factionalism revolving around prominent families and individual notables and their allies. Although these patterns were modified somewhat after 1800, attitudes and practices formed in the preindustrial, deferential world of the late eighteenth century continued to shape New York politics into the 1820s.

Embedded among these remnants of traditional practices, however, were the seeds of a new politics that would, over the course of the next quarter-century, fundamentally transform the political culture of the state. The emergence of an increasingly pluralistic and market-oriented society gave birth to and nurtured new democratic expectations. Barriers to popular participation came down, ushering in an era of universal white male suffrage. Hundreds of previously appointive offices became the objects of electoral competition. New political fault lines appeared, and new issues became salient in response to the market revolution, the onset of industrialization, and dramatic demographic changes. Most striking, by 1838 a modern, competitive, mass-based system of politics appeared. Crystallizing in the middle of the 1830s, Democratic and Whig party competition dominated New York politics until the 1850s, when nativism, sectionalism, and slavery destroyed the second party system in the state and the nation.

The Albany Regency in Ascendance

Political and constitutional developments in the early 1820s provide the first hints of these momentous events. By 1820 factional divisions within the dominant Republican party had hardened into two de facto parties under the leadership of De Witt Clinton and Martin Van Buren. Although coalitional in nature and somewhat transient, these alignments persisted through the middle of the decade, with neither group achieving a decisive advantage. Van Buren and the Bucktails (so called because of the deer tails on the hats worn by Tammany Hall opponents of Clinton) dominated the legislature for most of the period, while the Clintonians controlled the governorship for all but two years between 1817 and 1828. Clinton's followers also delivered most of the state's electoral votes to John Quincy Adams in the 1824 presidential election. The future of New York politics, however, lay not with Clinton but with his opponents. Already the more united and disciplined of the two alliances, the Bucktails, through their control of the constitutional convention of 1821, helped to initiate sweeping changes in the environment of politics. Capitalizing on those changes, they then fashioned a modern, disciplined political organization that dominated the state for the next two decades.

Demands for constitutional change arose out of widespread dissatisfaction with the undemocratic and conservative features of the constitution of 1777. Particularly objectionable were highly restrictive property qualifications for voting, the Council of Revision, which was empowered to veto legislation, and the Council of Appointment, which was charged with filling a vast array of public offices from the state to the local level of government. Although they had not initiated the calls for constitutional reform, Van Buren and the Bucktails saw in a convention the opportunity to advance their political fortunes in the state. In the spring of 1821, against Clintonian opposition, the legislature submitted the question of holding a convention to the people. New York voters overwhelmingly approved the measure, and delegates were subsequently chosen. On August 28, 1821, 126 delegates convened in Albany. With more than three-fourths of the delegates, the Bucktails dominated the convention, selecting the presiding officer, Daniel D. Tompkins, and appointing fellow Bucktails to chair the standing committees. Key Bucktail delegates included Samuel Young, Erastus Root, Peter R. Livingston, and Van Buren himself. In opposition was a small but formidable band of Old Federalists led by Chancellor James Kent and including Abraham Van Vechten, Stephen Van Rensselaer, Elisha Williams, and Peter Augustus Jay.

Despite a determined defense of the status quo by conservatives, the convention dramatically revised the fundamental law of the state. The suffrage was extended to every adult white male twenty-one years of age who had been a resident of the state for one year and the county or town for six months and who paid state or county taxes, served in the militia, or worked on public highways. Moderate delegates fought off an attempt to exclude all blacks from voting and granted the suffrage to those who had resided in the state for three years and possessed a freehold worth $250. Universal white male suffrage would not be achieved until 1826 with the removal of the tax or militia requirement for voting, but the new constitution increased the number of eligible voters in the state to more than four-fifths of the adult white male population.

The convention also abolished the Councils of Appointment and Revision. The appointing power was dispersed to different political subdivisions or, in some cases, to the people themselves. The principal state officers were to be elected by the legislature and, with the exception of the treasurer, who would be chosen annually, would serve three-year terms. Sheriffs, county clerks, and coroners were to be elective; mayors (with the exception of New York City) were to be appointed annually by common councils; and justices of the peace were to be selected by county boards of supervisors and judges of county courts. Members of the militia would elect all but the highest-ranking officers. The governor would appoint all other officers, military and civil, including judges, with the advice and consent of the Senate. The convention vested the veto power in the executive, subject to a two-thirds legislative override, and reduced the governor's term of office from three to two years. The number of senatorial districts was expanded from four to eight, and a new Supreme Court and a system of circuit courts were created, thereby paving the way for the end of Federalist domination of the judiciary.

The new constitution that took effect in December 1822 fundamentally reshaped the government and politics of New York. Some historians, emphasizing the reform of the suffrage and elimination of the archaic Councils of Appointment and Revision, have viewed it as a milestone in the advance of democracy. Others, focusing on the shortcomings of the suffrage provisions, have characterized it as a holding action by conservative opponents of universal suffrage. The practical political effect of constitutional reform, however, is clear; it virtually assured the ascendancy of the Bucktails over their opponents. In almost every instance, the new mechanisms for dispensing patronage favored the Bucktails. The new constitution enlarged the power of the Senate, normally dominated by the Bucktails, while diminishing that of the Assembly, a Clintonian stronghold. The governor was given a role in major appointments, but his shortened term of office increased his dependence upon the political process. In this and in appointments made at the local level, particularly of justices of the peace, the superior organization of the Bucktails gave them a decided advantage.

Between 1822 and 1825, Van Buren and the Bucktails solidified their control of the state. After Clinton chose not to seek reelection, Joseph Yates recaptured the governorship for the Bucktails in 1822, giving them command of both the legislative and executive branches. Exploiting their control of the state patronage, Bucktail leaders filled the newly created judicial positions with friends, appointed Bucktails to state offices, and staffed thousands of local offices with loyal supporters. By the end of 1823 a formidable political organization, directed by a coterie of leaders dubbed by their opponents the "Albany Regency," was in place at all levels of state government.

Regency efforts to influence national presidential politics were not so successful. Van Buren, who had been elected to the United States Senate in 1821, was anxious to strengthen the political ties between Albany and Washington and to use the Regency's domination of New York as a power base from which to control the selection of the next president. In 1823 the Regency determined to support William H. Crawford of Georgia in the following year's election. The Clintonians, who supported Andrew Jackson, and other anti-Crawford men seized the occasion to demand that the selection of presidential electors be removed from the legislature and given to the people directly. The Regency, which controlled the legislature, refused to relinquish this advantage, whereupon their opponents formed a new "People's party" to pursue the change and to nominate candidates for the 1824 election. When the People's party convention met in September 1824, Clinton, whom the Bucktails had injudiciously removed from the state canal board earlier, emerged as the leading candidate for the gubernatorial nomination. His political fortunes thus revived, Clinton was nominated and in the ensuing election defeated the Bucktail candidate, Samuel Young. To add insult to injury, the Clintonians, through the clever maneuvering of Thurlow Weed, orchestrated a stunning upset in the legislature which delivered twenty-six of the state's thirty-six electoral votes to John Quincy Adams for the presidency. In the subsequent balloting in the United States House of Representatives, New York's congressional delegation cast the decisive vote in Adams's favor.

Despite a disastrous year and notwithstanding the fact that De Witt Clinton would be reelected to the governorship in 1826, the Bucktails had forged a political machine of unprecedented power and efficiency. Combining modern forms of organization and intense partisan loyalty, the Albany Regency dominated the state through the decade of the 1830s and, in the process, revolutionized the practice of politics itself. The Regency consisted of a remarkable group of men united by their common middle-class backgrounds, mutual trust, and a radically new vision of party. The undisputed leader was Martin Van Buren who, from a succession of state and national offices, directed the political activities of the Regency. After Van Buren, prominent members included William L. Marcy, Samuel A. Talcott, Roger Skinner, Benjamin Knower, Benjamin Butler, Silas Wright, Edwin Croswell, Azariah C. Flagg, John A. Dix, and Churchill C. Cambreleng. Together these men formulated party policy, influenced the legislative caucus, dispensed patronage, enforced party discipline, and disseminated Regency positions on the issues of the day through the *Albany Argus* and other party organs around the state. Although not all members of the Regency held public office, most did, and some for long periods of time. Indeed, Regency men frequently traded state or national offices among themselves, as the politics of the moment dictated.

Regency control was never absolute. Legislators regularly took their cues from party leaders on matters that were clearly partisan in nature, but party loyalty sometimes took second place when purely local or regional issues were involved. Caucus members frequently wrangled among themselves over appointments. Occasionally an unusually independent caucus rejected Regency nominations, and the wishes of local party organizations were customarily considered when making appointments at the local level. Still, party unity and loyalty were the glue that held the organization together, and nothing so distinguished the Regency from its opponents in the 1820s and 1830s as its insistence upon party discipline.

It was precisely its celebration of partisanship that gave the Regency its modern cast and ushered in a radically new type of politics. Conditioned by classical republicanism to believe that parties, or factions, were by definition representative of something less than the public good and therefore subversive of republican government, Americans had traditionally looked upon any manifestation of "party spirit" or "partisanship" with dread. At best, parties were perceived as a necessary evil; at worst, they were symptomatic of fundamental weaknesses in the republic. By the end of the 1820s, however, Martin Van Buren and the Regency had fashioned a new view of parties. Rejecting the traditional presumption of societal harmony, Van Buren argued that in a free, pluralistic society, conflict and parties were inevitable. Far from threatening society, democratically organized parties were the agencies through which the people could participate in government and, by subordinating individual desires to broader party purposes, effectively check potential abuses of power. Parties also served to unite a diversity of local and regional interests, thereby containing potentially divisive forces and strengthening the Union. Here was a totally new conception of political parties that asserted the positive benefits of partisan competition in a free society and that legitimized the activities of organizations like the Albany Regency.

The Regency's electoral successes after 1825 amply demonstrate the efficacy of its vision of politics. Clinton continued as governor until his death in February 1828, but he was followed by a succession of prominent Regency men. Van Buren himself was nominated and elected in 1828 but resigned the following year to become secretary of state in President Jackson's cabinet. Lieutenant Governor Enos Throop succeeded him and was elected in his own right in 1830. Following Throop, William L. Marcy served three consecutive terms as governor until William H. Seward and the rising Whig party finally broke the Regency's lock on the executive in 1838. The Bucktails similarly controlled both branches of the legislature until the Whigs captured the Assembly in 1837. Regency success at the polls, furthermore, assured its control of the principal state offices. Such Regency stalwarts as Marcy, Azariah Flagg, and Abraham Keyser held the key administrative posts of comptroller, secretary of state, and treasurer for most of the period from the mid-1820s to the 1840s.

While political skill and acumen played their role, the intricacies of presidential politics and the disorganization of the opposition contributed to the Regency's domination of state politics. Having failed in his efforts to orchestrate Crawford's election to the presidency, Van Buren embarked in 1826 on a plan to unite supporters of Crawford and John C. Calhoun into a new national coalition against John Quincy Adams and on behalf of Andrew Jackson. Months of delicate maneuvering ensued, capped by an unlikely alliance with Van Buren's old nemesis, De Witt Clinton, a longtime Jackson supporter. In September 1827 the Regency publicly proclaimed its support for Jackson. The following January, the legislative caucus formally nominated him for the presidency. The opposition, meanwhile, was in disarray due to the awkwardness of Clinton's pro-Jackson stance. Clinton's death in February removed this barrier to unity, but by then the pro-Adams forces were confronted by an even more serious challenge: the growth of Antimasonic agitation among their supporters in the western regions of the state.

Antimasonry burst onto the political scene with the mysterious disappearance of William Morgan of Genesee County on September 14, 1826. Morgan, a Batavia stonemason and member of the Masonic Order, had published an exposé of the secrets and rituals of Freemasonry. Outraged at this betrayal of the sacred oaths of the order, local Masons retaliated by setting fire to the publisher's shop and having Morgan and his collaborator, David Miller, arrested on trumped-up charges. Both were subsequently released from jail, but Morgan was kidnapped off the street and spirited away by his captors, most likely to the abandoned Fort Niagara. He was never seen again. After months of protest and speculation, he was presumed dead, murdered by Freemasons to protect their order, the crime covered up by complicitous public officials sympathetic to Masonry.

Morgan's disappearance ignited a firestorm of popular protest and launched what the historian Paul Goodman has called "the first mass movement in American history." Fueled by the tensions and anxieties accompanying commercialization and dedicated to the preservation of republican equality through the destruction of the Masonic Order, Antimasonry expanded rapidly across western New York, moved southward into Pennsylvania, and eventually infected all the states of New England. As it spread and as the difficulty of ridding the republic of Masonry through persuasion alone became apparent, what had begun as a social movement began to assume a political character. Eventually, Antimasonic parties would emerge throughout the Northeast, becoming dominant in a few states, holding the balance of power in others, and influencing the formation of the second party system wherever they appeared.

In New York, Antimasonry further complicated the political landscape on the eve of the 1828 election. Its egalitarian message combined with Jackson's membership in the Masonic Order threatened Regency power in the western counties. To ensure maximum electoral support, Van Buren himself accepted the Bucktail nomination for governor, with the understanding that he would resign if Jackson were elected president and he were offered a cabinet post. Enos Throop, a westerner viewed favorably by Antimasons, was the Regency's choice for lieutenant governor. Meanwhile, the Antimasons, while opposed to Jackson and the Regency, were reluctant to unite with the Adams people behind a common slate of candidates for state offices. In the end, despite efforts by Rochester editor Thurlow Weed to forge an alliance against the Regency, the Adams forces nominated Smith Thompson for governor and Francis Granger for lieutenant governor. The Antimasons selected Solomon Southwick as their gubernatorial candidate and officially announced their neutrality in the presidential contest, although most supported Adams over Jackson.

With three separate slates of candidates for state offices and with New Yorkers voting simultaneously for president and governor for the first time in the state's history, the November election was both confusing and lively. Van Buren and Jackson emerged victorious, but neither won impressively. Van Buren was elected governor with three thousand fewer votes than the combined totals of his two opponents. Jackson polled just under 51 percent of the popular vote and won twenty of the state's thirty-six electoral votes. The Bucktails retained control of the state and delivered a narrow victory in the presidential race, but the results could not have been reassuring. They had failed to carry the northern and western counties and, most troubling of all, had ultimately won the day only because the opposition had been unable to unite behind a single ticket.

The Opposition Takes Shape

The 1828 election was a milestone in the transformation of New York politics. In the three years after 1825, Van Buren and other national leaders had forged a new, national Democratic party linking the North and the South for the first time since Jefferson. At the same time, Van Buren revived the fortunes of the Regency in state politics. More important, by 1828 significant changes in the underlying basis of politics were beginning to appear. Constitutional provisions eliminating property qualifications for voting, providing for the popular election of presidential electors (adopted in 1826), and mandating the election of literally thousands of local offices gave an unprecedented popular dimension to

New York politics. These changes, in combination with new, more popularly based organizational structures and closely contested elections, dramatically increased voter participation. Seventy percent of adult white males voted in 1828, as compared with 56 percent four years earlier. The election also marked the beginnings of partisan stability in the state's electorate. Before 1827, change and volatility rather than stability appear to have characterized voter alignments. With the election of 1828, however, a long period of partisan stability began, as first the Democratic party and subsequently its opponents became firmly established among the New York electorate.

The immediate consequence of the election was the collapse of the Adams organization and the emergence of the Antimasons in the forefront of the opposition to the Regency. A talented younger generation of leaders—men like Thurlow Weed, Francis Granger, William Henry Seward, and Millard Fillmore—whose initiation into state politics had come largely through Antimasonry, set out in 1829 to forge a new political coalition to challenge the Democrats. Their initial efforts centered on strengthening the Antimason party in New York and building an organization to carry the Antimasonic crusade to the nation at large. Over the course of the next five years, Antimasonry turned into an almost exclusively political enterprise, as professional politicians came increasingly to dominate the movement. By the end of the period, however, Antimasonry disappeared as an independent political force. In its place the far more formidable Whig party arose to challenge the Democrats on their own terms.

Both state and national politics shaped the process by which the Whig party appeared in New York between 1829 and 1834. After the 1828 defeat, Weed vigorously pursued his efforts to unite the anti-Regency and anti-Jackson forces but with only limited success at first. In February 1829 the Antimasons reasserted their independence of any other parties in future elections and called for a national Antimasonic convention. By the summer of 1830, with the Adams party no longer a factor, the Antimasons were, effectively, the only organized opposition in the state. In its August convention the party nominated Francis Granger for governor and called upon all anti-Regency New Yorkers to join in support of the Antimasonic ticket. Enos Throop, who had succeeded Van Buren when he resigned the governorship in 1829, was the Regency nominee. Throop and the Regency carried the November election, but Granger polled a very promising 47.9 percent of the vote.

At this point, presidential politics once more entered into the calculations of New York's political leaders and further complicated efforts to create a unified party in opposition to the Democrats. At the national level, in anticipation of the 1832 election, Jackson's opponents were beginning to coalesce into the National Republican party with Henry Clay of Kentucky as its standard-bearer. In New York, Clay supporters had begun to organize as early as December 1830, and in June 1831 convened in Albany to select delegates to the National Republican convention. Three months later, the Antimasonic national convention, with Thurlow Weed, William H. Seward, and other New Yorkers participating, nominated William Wirt for the presidency. In December the National Republican convention met and formally nominated Henry Clay. Thus, two anti-Jackson coalitions, each vying for permanency, were in place by the end of 1831. The following May the Democratic national convention nominated Jackson for a second term and selected Van Buren as his vice presidential running mate.

Intent upon electing an anti-Regency slate of state officers and preventing a Jackson victory in New York, National Republican and Antimasonic leaders maneuvered desperately to bring the two groups together behind a common ticket. Clay's vocal defense of his connections to the Masonic Order, however, kept them apart. In the end, the intrusion into New York politics of the bank issue—specifically, Jackson's July 10, 1832, veto of the bill rechartering the Second Bank of the United States—enabled leaders to forge an uneasy alliance against what was perceived as a common enemy. In June 1832 the Antimasons again nominated Francis Granger for governor and approved a slate of presidential electors carefully crafted to include supporters of both Wirt and Clay. The National Republicans convened in July and endorsed the Antimasonic ticket, although they appear to have done so more out of expediency than out of any genuine sense of unity. Meeting in Herkimer in September, state Democrats nominated a slate of candidates headed up by William L. Marcy for governor. Early indications suggested that the Democrats might be in trouble, but they ultimately carried the state for Jackson and Marcy by appealing to Masons (even those formerly anti-Regency), by drawing some votes away from the Antimasons, and by capitalizing on Jackson's personal appeal.

Despite their defeat, an anti-Regency opposition had clearly begun to crystallize by 1832. Granger's 48.8 percent of the vote was nearly one percentage point better than his 1830 showing, while the Democrats' presidential ticket, even with Van Buren in the second spot, improved only slightly over the 1828 results. Still lacking, however, was a unified leadership and organization. That would be achieved over the course of the next two years as Antimasonry waned and new allegiances were forged. With the formal dissolution of the party in early 1834, Antimasonic leaders joined with the National Republicans to create a new anti-Jacksonian party. Using the name Whig for the first time in the New York City municipal elections of 1834, the anti-Regency forces captured control of that city's common council and initiated plans for a state convention to be held in September. The Utica convention formally adopted the name Whig and nominated William H. Seward as its candidate for governor. In the hotly contested election that ensued, the Regency retained control of the state, returning Marcy to the governorship and a Democratic majority to the legislature. Although the Regency's opponents were at last coming together behind a unified leadership, Whig organization and electoral support were still no match for the Democrats. Two years later, the Whig party suffered another stinging defeat. With Van Buren heading the national Democratic ticket and Marcy, a two-term incumbent governor, seeking reelection, the Regency slate of candidates swept the state in 1836 with more than 54 percent of the vote.

With huge majorities in both houses of the legislature, Marcy reelected to a third term as governor, and Van Buren in the White House, the Regency was at the pinnacle of its power. Democratic control of the state, and of the patronage that went with that control, appeared secure. At the local level, to quote the always astute political observer and contemporary historian of New York politics Jabez D. Hammond, "the democratic party was perfect in its organization and discipline." Indeed, according to Hammond, "never did a political party, whose ascendency depended on the voice of a free and intelligent people, seem more firmly and permanently established, than the democratic party in the state of New York, in the winter of 1837."

Nevertheless, the Regency's power proved illusory. Its electoral success concealed deepening divisions within the party over banking policy. So long as attention focused on the battle between Jackson and the Bank of the United States, party leaders managed to smooth over fundamental differences within the party between those who opposed all banks on hard money grounds and those whose hostility extended only to the national bank. To the horror of hard money Democrats, the destruction of the national bank and the transfer of federal deposits to state banks unleashed new demands for state bank charters, a demand readily met by the Democratic-controlled state legislatures of 1834 and 1835. Responding to the proliferation of new banks and to the disclosure of political favoritism in the distribution of bank stocks, hard money Democrats raised the charge of monopoly and special privilege and challenged conservative Democrats for control of the party.

The most dramatic manifestation of these differences occurred in New York City. In 1835 hard money Democrats openly challenged conservative, pro-bank Tammany Hall. Following months of maneuvering and escalating antimonopoly rhetoric, the two factions collided head-on in October. When the Democratic party convened at Tammany Hall on the 29th to nominate candidates for the upcoming election, the pro-bank forces, which controlled the podium, pushed through their slate of candidates without regard to the opposition. When the insurgents protested, the Tammany regulars left the hall, extinguishing the gas lights on their way out to stymie any further deliberations. Familiar with such tactics in the past, the dissidents had come prepared with the new friction matches, called loco-focos, which they now used to light candles, allowing them to proceed with the nomination of their own slate of anti-bank candidates. The Loco-Foco or Equal Rights party, as New York's hard money, anti-bank Democrats came to be called, advocated equality of rights and an end to all forms of government monopoly. Unsuccessful in New York City elections, the

Loco-Focos nevertheless influenced the subsequent direction of state politics. In 1836 they formed a coalition with New York City Whigs and cooperated with Whigs in the state legislature to block the incorporation of any additional banks. More important, in 1837 Van Buren and the Democratic party effectively adopted the Loco-Foco program.

Already buffeted by internal divisions over banking, the Democrats suffered an even more devastating blow from an unanticipated source. The speculative boom that had fueled the American economy in the mid-1830s suddenly burst in the spring of 1837, triggering an unprecedented financial panic and sending the economy plummeting. The Panic of 1837 and the ensuing depression were brought on by a constriction of credit by the Bank of England and a simultaneous decline in the British demand for American cotton, but many New Yorkers blamed the economic downturn on the Democrats' banking and credit policies. In this atmosphere of popular discontent, Whigs seized the opportunity to challenge Democratic preeminence in state and national politics.

The first signs of trouble appeared in New York City in the spring of 1837. With the financial panic in full swing and with the Democratic legislature refusing to suspend an 1835 law prohibiting the circulation of small bills, the Whigs captured the mayor's office and a large majority of the common council. Van Buren's announcement of his plan to divorce the banks from the federal government and establish an independent treasury system further exacerbated the Democrats' problems. Democratic banking interests, opposed to the removal of federal deposits from state banks, began moving to the Whigs. The impact of the panic and the erosion of support in the banking community produced stunning losses in the November elections. "A perfect tornado," in Jabez Hammond's words, "swept through nearly every county in the state." Whigs captured 101 of 128 state Assembly seats and made huge gains in local elections in what some Democrats called the Regency's worst defeat since 1824.

The disaster of 1837 was but a prelude to even more serious political losses the following year. With economic conditions worsening, the Whigs already in control of the Assembly, and the governorship itself up for grabs in the upcoming elections, the Regency was at its most vulnerable. Meeting in Utica on September 12, 1838, the Whig party nominated William H. Seward and Luther Bradish for governor and lieutenant governor. On the very same day, the Democrats nominated Marcy and Albert H. Tracy for reelection. Unable to heal the deep divisions within the party or to deflect Whig charges of Democratic radicalism and hostility toward banks, the Regency went down to defeat. Seward and Bradish carried the state by a margin of 10,000 votes, while the Whigs retained a two-to-one margin in the Assembly. With the exception of the Senate, which would be added the following year, Whig control of the state was complete.

Whig electoral success in 1838 ended nearly two decades of Bucktail-Democratic dominance of state politics and marked the emergence of a united, well-organized opposition as skillful in the ways of politics as the Regency itself. Under the shrewd leadership of Thurlow Weed, William H. Seward, Francis Granger, Millard Fillmore, and others, a Whig party machine took shape that rivaled that of the Democrats in structure and organization, in the effective use of the patronage, in maintaining party discipline and unity, and in formulating party policy. Whereas Van Buren directed the Regency while holding various public offices, Weed exercised similar control over the affairs of the Whig party as editor of the *Albany Evening Journal* and state printer, with the vast patronage that position brought. Like the Democrats, the Whigs developed a statewide network of party newspapers to disseminate party propaganda, with the *Evening Journal* and Horace Greeley's *Jeffersonian* and, later, *New York Tribune*, taking the lead. And finally, adopting the position New York Democrats had pioneered, Whigs grudgingly acknowledged the validity and value of partisanship as the operative norm in politics.

Whigs and Democrats

The process by which modern, mass-based political parties grew up in New York was neither as "clean" nor as straightforward as this statewide perspective suggests. Such a view obscures the local and regional variations in the dynamics of party formation and understates the social and economic basis of political developments. The precise mechanisms by which the Bucktail Democrats sustained themselves through more than two decades of political turbulence and by which diverse opponents of the Democrats coalesced under the Whig party label varied from one locality to the next and from election to election. Professional politicians like Van Buren and Weed built coalitions, consolidated like-minded interests into durable political organizations, and provided the linkage with national party structures. But social, economic, and cultural forces at the local level—particularly the market revolution, the onset of industrialization, ethnocultural conflict, and the cleavages they produced—determined the shape of the coalitions out of which statewide party edifices were constructed. The exact mix of those forces, their impact, and the local response were as varied as the different social worlds of New York City, the towns and villages of the Burned-Over District, and the Hudson River counties.

Acknowledging these complications, one can nevertheless make some generalizations about party development and partisan behavior in this period. First, the second party system grew out of the Bucktail-Clintonian rivalries of the 1820s, and political allegiances forged in that earlier period continued to exert a powerful influence on leaders, voters, and entire communities as the new Democratic and Whig parties took shape in the 1830s. Second, while socioeconomic issues ranging from Jackson's war on the Bank of the United States to differences over the proper response to the market revolution influenced new partisan choices and reinforced old ones, this did not translate into a crude division along class lines. Not surprisingly, both parties drew their leaders from the upper ranks of the social strata—although the very wealthy in New York City and other urban centers appear to have been disproportionately Whig—and neither party enjoyed overwhelming support from any particular socioeconomic group in the electorate. Third, while ethnocultural and religious conflict was very real and, in some places and at certain times, intense, ethnoreligious and socioeconomic identifications interacted in complex ways and were often mutually reinforcing, making it difficult for the modern historian to assign primacy to one or the other. Fourth, the two parties shared, at least at their centers, large areas of agreement. For Democrats and Whigs alike, political analysis began with republicanism and the centuries-old struggle between power and liberty that republican theory postulated. Neither party, moreover, posed a fundamental challenge to the basic premises of free enterprise and private property. Fifth, and finally, both parties were more coalitional than monolithic, embracing a spectrum of views and tolerating a range of commitments that extended from the ideologically pure to the pragmatically political.

In short, tendencies rather than sharp ideological dividing lines differentiated the two parties from each other. The most important such tendency relates to their contrasting responses to the transformation of social relations that accompanied the market revolution. In general, those New Yorkers who were most intimately tied in to the market economy, those most sympathetic to the direction of economic change, and those who benefited the most from commercialization became Whigs. Democrats, in contrast, appear to have been drawn disproportionately from among those least affected by commercialization, those who most feared its consequences, and from those, such as urban workers, whose status was directly undermined by the new market forces.

Different assessments of the costs and benefits of economic change produced competing visions of the role of government in promoting economic development. Democrats, fearful that capitalist expansion would erode the economic status and political independence of the "producing classes" and certain that an activist government would inevitably benefit special interests at the expense of the majority, sought to limit government to the protection of equal rights for all and to the establishment of general rules that would allow the free play of natural economic forces. On the national level, this meant that Democrats opposed close ties between government and banks, high tariffs, and public support for internal improvements. New York Democrats similarly espoused the principles of limited government and lamented the huge debt incurred in promoting internal improvements in the state, but in practice they were often compelled to support such improvement projects by the exigencies of local and regional politics.

Whigs began with a different set of assumptions about the nature of government and articulated a more positive role for government. In contrast to the Democrats' belief in an inherent conflict between "producers" and "nonproducers," Whigs stressed the harmony of interests in a diverse society and the mutually beneficial consequences of economic development. Far from viewing the market revolution with fear and apprehension, Whigs embraced it as the fulfillment of the promise of America and sought to direct its progress. An activist government, encouraging and protecting manufacturing interests, subsidizing internal improvements, and regulating the currency and credit system, was essential to the Whig vision of economic progress and development.

The Whigs' predilection for government activism and paternalism extended beyond the economic realm. Just as they sought to rationalize and direct the forces of market change, Whigs advocated the use of government to instill the values of evangelical Protestantism and middle-class respectability in an increasingly diverse society. In the name of social order, cultural uniformity, and moral progress, Whigs embraced a reform agenda that included support for temperance legislation, sabbatarianism, and, for some at least, nativism. Democrats, in contrast, rejected the use of government to impose one group's moral vision on society, placed greater value on liberty, equality (for whites), and personal autonomy, and celebrated cultural diversity. The Whig message, and the distinctive value system it reflected, appealed to native-born evangelical Protestants, while Democratic support came principally from nonevangelical Protestants, immigrants generally, and Roman Catholic Irish immigrants in particular. Thus, ethnocultural and religious issues and identifications further distinguished the two parties. Whether cultural or socioeconomic conflict took precedence, however, or whether they were mutually reinforcing as some have suggested remains a point of contention among historians.

The Whigs' rise to power and the overthrow of the Regency were part of a broad and fundamental reconfiguration of the political landscape. As noted earlier, the first decades of the nineteenth century were a period of transition from a political culture founded on classical republicanism, limited political participation, deference to elites, factionalism, and antipartyism. By the time of Seward's election, all the ingredients of a new, more modern system of politics had appeared: a mass electorate, competitive political parties led by professional politicians, acceptance of the legitimacy of parties, and a pervasive ideology of political equality. Indeed, political developments in New York were the cutting edge of a massive transformation of politics heralding the creation of what the historian Joel Silbey has called "the American political nation."

Chapter 23

Politics and Policy

THE ELECTION OF 1838 INAUGURATED A NEW ERA IN NEW York politics. For the next decade, until new forces and issues began to challenge the second party system, Democratic and Whig electoral competition structured the political life of the state. For most of the period, continuity and stability in voting behavior and partisan identification were the norm. Intensely competitive elections, in which the two parties battled ferociously for the narrow spectrum of the electorate that spelled victory or defeat, was one consequence of this pattern. Another was unprecedented levels of voter participation as New Yorkers flocked to the polls in local, state, and presidential elections. It was thus within a framework of sustained partisan competition that the state confronted the social and economic challenges accompanying modernization and began a reevaluation of politics and governance that would produce a new constitution in 1846.

Fiscal Crisis and Retrenchment

Economic issues and the role of government in promoting internal improvements dominated state politics in the years following Seward's 1838 election to the governorship. At issue was whether to continue to expand the state's transportation network by borrowing against anticipated future revenues. Bowing to the demands of unimproved regions of the state, a succession of legislatures in the 1830s authorized new canals and voted generous subsidies for the construction of railroads. By 1836 the pleas for sectional parity had become so irresistible that the Democrat-controlled legislature approved a massive enlargement of the original Erie Canal and the construction of the Black River and Genesee Valley Canals. Borrowing to finance these improvements, the state became hostage to continuing economic prosperity and steadily rising receipts from state-owned canals. Governor William L. Marcy and Comptroller Azariah C. Flagg repeatedly warned that overconstruction and shortfalls in projected revenues were rapidly depleting the General Fund, but enthusiasm for state-funded internal improvements continued unabated. With the Panic of 1837, the state's credit, already fragile, suffered a devastating blow. The general decline of economic activity exacerbated the existing revenue shortfalls, adding to the rapidly accumulating state debt. Public faith in the state's ability to honor its financial obligations plummeted. By 1838, New York 6 percent stocks sold below par, and they declined to 20 percent below their face value over the next three years.

Despite such strains on the treasury, Whigs remained enthusiastic about the long-term economic benefits of state-funded internal improvements. In 1838 Governor Seward and a Whig-controlled legislature authorized a $4 million loan to complete the Erie Canal enlargement project. A year later, the governor recommended an additional $12 million for the Genesee Valley and Black River Canals, thus initiating a deliberate policy of deficit spending. It was a bold move but one supported by optimistic estimates of future canal revenues. Samuel Ruggles, chairman of the ways and means committee of the Assembly, confidently reported in 1838 that the state could safely borrow and repay up to $40 million without resorting to additional taxation. Such policies flowed logically from the Whig vision of an interdependent, industrializing society and of the shared benefits of positive government action that would bring that society into being. Seward, according to modern historians, was the archetypal "modernizing" Whig who embraced the market revolution and sought to harness an activist government to the service of economic development. The immediate result of Whig policy, however, was a $16 million increase in the state debt and heightened awareness of the precariousness of the state's finances. By 1840 the debt had risen to $20 million, and it reached $27 million in 1842.

The state's financial woes might well have spelled an early reversal of Whig political fortunes, but in 1840 the political tide ran strongly against Van Buren and the Democrats and in favor of the Whigs. At the national level, depressed economic conditions, discontent with Van Buren's Independent Treasury plan among bankers, Democratic party factionalism, the emergence of a unified national Whig party, and an unprecedented surge of voters to the polls swept William Henry Harrison into the White House and produced Whig majorities in both houses of Congress. At the state level, Democrats hoped to capitalize on Seward's vulnerability by nominating Silas Wright, United States senator and their strongest candidate, for governor. When Wright refused, they settled upon

William C. Bouck, a former member of the canal commission from Schoharie County, to lead the state ticket. In the fall, Seward won reelection with a 5,000-vote margin over Bouck, while Harrison outpolled Van Buren in his home state by some 13,000 votes.

With the election over, development policy and the debt crisis returned to center stage. As stocks continued to fall in value and some states defaulted on their debts, the need to restore public faith in New York's credit became critical. The Democratic party was deeply divided on the issue. Conservatives such as Edwin Croswell, editor of the *Albany Argus*, Daniel Dickinson, William C. Bouck, Henry Foster, and Horatio Seymour favored the continuation of the improvement program but at a slower pace than the Whigs proposed, in order to minimize its impact on the state's credit. Radicals, led by Azariah C. Flagg, Michael Hoffman, Samuel Young, Arphaxed Loomis, and Silas Wright, opposed any increase of the state debt for internal improvements, favored a general retrenchment in expenditures, and sought to limit the legislature's power to contract debts in the future. In February 1841, Arphaxed Loomis of Herkimer County introduced a series of constitutional amendments requiring that laws authorizing the creation of a debt be submitted directly to the people for prior approval. The "People's Resolutions," as they were called, were defeated, resubmitted in the 1842 legislature, and defeated again, but the debt-restriction principle reappeared later in the movement for constitutional revision.

Radical Democrats regained control of the legislature in the 1841 elections and initiated a new approach to development policy. They now proposed to suspend work on improvement projects and to stabilize the state's finances by levying a one-mill tax to be allocated equally to the General Fund and to canal work. This "Stop and Tax" law passed in the Assembly on March 19, 1842, with most of the negative votes coming from Whigs. Despite the spirited opposition of Conservative Democrats and Whigs, it also passed the Senate nine days later. For the remainder of 1842, debate over the "Stop and Tax" policy dominated state politics. Most Democrats supported the tax bill, as did New Yorkers living in the vicinity of completed canals. It was also received favorably in New York City, particularly among bankers, who had helped conceive the plan. Opposition centered among Whigs and in communities along the line of uncompleted canals. Governor Seward tried to reverse the policy in a special legislative session in August but was unable to convince the Democratic majority. By that time the value of state stocks had begun to recover, and confidence in the state's credit was restored. New York would eventually resume construction on the canals, but the "Stop and Tax" policy anticipated a much broader retreat from state economic activity and the establishment of a modern, rational financial system based on taxation.

Slavery, Antirentism, and Constitutional Reform

Seward had decided as early as the spring of 1841 not to seek reelection for a third term as governor. His refusal to cooperate with Virginia in that state's efforts to recapture fugitive slaves harbored in New York alienated many of his supporters. His proposal for the establishment of special schools for immigrant children similarly hurt him with Protestant voters. These setbacks, combined with his inability to restore work on the canals and a general economic recovery likely to benefit the Democrats, spelled electoral embarrassment in 1842. With Seward out of the picture, the Whigs chose his lieutenant governor, Luther Bradish, as their candidate for governor. In September, Democrats nominated William C. Bouck and Daniel Dickinson, both conservatives, for governor and lieutenant governor and accepted a Radical demand that the party endorse the "Stop and Tax" policy. As Seward had anticipated, the Democrats easily won the ensuing election.

The Democratic party, however, remained bitterly divided between the Conservatives, or Hunkers, as they were now being called, and the Radicals, or Barnburners. Radicals feared that Bouck would abandon the suspension policy—and with good reason. In his 1843 legislative address, the governor proposed continuation of the Erie Canal enlargement and further work on the Black River and Genesee Valley Canals. Then, in the spring of 1844, Horatio Seymour, a young Conservative Democrat in his second term as assemblyman, introduced a bill allowing the use of a portion of any surplus canal revenues for the completion of these projects. Whigs joined with the Conservative Democrats to enact the new policy into law. After this defeat, Radicals became convinced that only a constitutional provision could ensure the continuation of the suspension policy.

As the election of 1844 approached, other issues and concerns temporarily overshadowed the debate over canal policy. Nationally, southern Democrats, suspicious of Van Buren's ambiguous stand on the annexation of Texas, denied him the party's nomination for the presidency and orchestrated the selection of James K. Polk of Tennessee instead. The Whigs, meanwhile, nominated Henry Clay of Kentucky. With banks, tariffs, the annexation of Texas and Oregon, and the expansion of slavery the central issues of the campaign, New York became a crucial battleground. Democrats were fearful that with Van Buren out of the picture and with the pro-annexation Polk leading the national ticket, Clay would not only carry the state, but the Whig candidates for state office would also be swept to victory. Emboldened by this political assessment, Radical Democrats pressed for a stronger gubernatorial candidate to strengthen the Democratic ticket in the state. The obvious choice was Silas Wright, who was highly popular among New York Democrats, nationally visible as a United States senator, and untainted by the internecine squabbling over canal policy. A

Wright candidacy promised to unite the Radicals and Conservatives behind the ticket, while deflecting Conservative criticism of Radical opposition to Bouck. Wright reluctantly accepted the nomination after a lengthy period of soul-searching and direct appeals to his party loyalty by Van Buren. Shortly thereafter, the Whigs nominated Millard Fillmore of Buffalo as their standard-bearer.

Although slavery played a major role in the 1844 campaign, it was the presidential candidates' positions that were at issue, since both Fillmore and Wright were opposed to slavery's extension. Complicating the situation, however, was the role of the Liberty party. By the late 1830s, some abolitionists had become convinced that political action would be required to rid the country of slavery. In 1840 these political abolitionists formed an independent party and nominated James G. Birney, a former Kentucky slaveholder and now a New York antislavery newspaper editor, for the presidency. Although the Liberty party received fewer than one percent of the national vote, its leaders continued to organize and agitate. In 1844, hoping to provide the balance of power in a close election, the party again nominated James G. Birney for the presidency and Alvan Stewart, a Utica lawyer, for governor. The Democratic and Whig parties were thus faced with the challenge of holding on to their core constituencies while losing as little as possible to the Liberty party on the slavery issue.

The emergence of political nativism added to the complexity of the election. As noted earlier, the American Republican party was formed in the summer of 1843, following a decade of increasing resentment toward immigrants and Catholics. The nativists scored a stunning victory in the New York City elections of 1844, winning the mayoralty and a majority in the common council, but chose not to field an independent state ticket, preferring to ally themselves with the Whigs in the city and selected counties. American Republicans supported the Whig gubernatorial and presidential candidates in return for Whig endorsement of nativist congressional and local candidates.

Democratic and Whig strategists also had to contend with antirentism in 1844. The leasehold system of land tenure had survived from the colonial period into the nineteenth century in several counties in the Hudson River Valley. Large tracts of land in Columbia, Rensselaer, Delaware, and Albany Counties remained in the hands of a small number of landlords who, just as their fathers and grandfathers had done, rented the land to tenant farmers. Tenants, many of whom had occupied the same land for generations, resented the semifeudal rent payments to landlords and demanded the right to purchase their property outright. Indeed, some regarded their long-term occupancy of the land as in itself qualifying them as freeholders. Resistance to the leasehold system had appeared sporadically for almost a century, but with the death of Stephen Van Rensselaer in 1839, and subsequent attempts by his heirs to collect back rents, tenant resentment flared into full-scale revolt and spread throughout eastern New York. Disguised as Indians and resorting to violence, groups of farmers intimi-

The *Microscope*, a satirical Albany newspaper, made outrageous fun of New York State forces they organized for a military campaign to quell antirent disturbances in 1840. New York State Hicial Association, Cooperstown, N.Y.

dated sheriffs and landlord representatives sent to dispossess the tenants. This "Helderberg War" (named for the Helderberg Hills of the Catskill Mountains where Rensselaer tenants first met to demand rent reform) ended when Governor Seward dispatched troops to restore order. But the issue would not go away, and when their pleas to the legislature were rebuffed, tenants turned to politics, organizing, endorsing legislative candidates, and pressuring the two major parties to support their cause.

The 1844 campaign was one of the most exciting and hotly contested in New York history. More than 92 percent of the electorate went to the polls, the highest turnout between 1826 and 1865. Influenced by both national and state issues, New Yorkers gave Polk a 5,000-vote plurality over Clay in the presidential race, while Wright defeated Fillmore for the governorship by a 10,000-vote margin. The Liberty party received slightly more than 15,000 votes, leading some historians to assert that had these votes gone to the Whigs, Clay would have captured the state's thirty-six electoral votes and thus the presidency.

With the election over, Democratic party unity once more began to unravel. The Barnburner and Hunker factions, temporarily submerged during the camts of the Day—Helderberg Campaign Eclipsed !

paign, reappeared as the focus shifted back to local and partisan issues. Conservatives elected Horatio Seymour as speaker of the Assembly and gained control of one of the United States Senate seats. The state officers were split in roughly equal proportions between the two factions. The Hunkers' greatest gains, however, came in the area of national political patronage. Polk appointed William L. Marcy secretary of war, thereby undercutting the Radicals, and gave the Hunkers control of important patronage in the state. With this setback, and with the two factions closely balanced in strength, Governor Wright found it increasingly difficult to maintain party discipline, a situation that the Whigs were quick to exploit in the legislature.

Two issues dominated Silas Wright's term as governor: the resurgence of the antirent agitation and the continuing problem of state finances and, by extension, constitutional revision. During the campaign, Wright had struggled to develop a politically safe position on the antirent question. Expressing some sympathy for the tenants' plight, he nevertheless concluded that no remedy was possible until the tenants ceased their violent activities. Faced with the immediate prospect of losing their homes, the tenants were not persuaded, and the disturbances continued. Indeed, when the new governor endorsed a law outlawing the wearing of disguises and signaled his determination to enforce existing laws, tenant resistance stiffened and the situation deteriorated, especially in

Schoharie and Delaware Counties. Finally, in August 1845, when antirenters killed a deputy sheriff in Delaware County, Wright declared martial law, dispatched troops to the area, and offered a reward for the capture of the guilty parties. Once order was restored and the ringleaders arrested and tried, Wright proposed a three-part program to address the tenants' grievances. Most of the plan was enacted into law, but it fell short of satisfying the antirenters, who went on to seek their revenge against Wright in the November 1846 elections.

By 1845 the issue of state finances was inextricably entwined with the question of constitutional revision. Leading Radicals had become convinced that the public works suspension policy could be secured against future legislative repeal only through a constitutional provision. In 1843 Herkimer County Democrats had proposed a debt restriction amendment similar to the earlier People's Resolutions, but the legislature refused to take action. Meanwhile, the movement to call a constitutional convention to consider a wide range of proposed reforms gained momentum. In an attempt to deflect that momentum, Conservative Democrats in 1844 proposed a series of constitutional amendments to limit the legislature's power to create debts, to abolish property qualifications for holding office, and to reform the judiciary. Approval required passage by two successive legislatures and acceptance by the people in a general election.

The 1844 legislature approved the amendments, and, with Governor Wright's support, it appeared they would pass the second hurdle in 1845. However, advocates of a convention kept up their pressure, aided by antirent demands for a convention to abolish the leasehold system and by Whigs, who held the balance of power in the legislature. Thus, when the amendments came before the Assembly for the required second passage, they were defeated by a coalition of Whigs and Barnburners, who then passed a bill calling for a convention. Voters overwhelmingly approved of the convention in a November referendum, whereupon 128 delegates were chosen at a special election in April 1846, with Democrats in a clear majority. On June 1 the delegates convened in Albany to begin their work. Four months later, on October 9, the convention adopted a new constitution with only six dissenting votes. Less than a month later, New Yorkers approved the new document by more than a two-to-one margin.

Constitutional Revision and the Birth of the Liberal State

Although the fiscal crisis and partisan considerations shaped the decision to call a convention, constitutional revision sprang from deeper roots. In the broadest sense, it marked the culmination of a decades-long debate over political economy and the proper role of government in society. For more than half a century, New Yorkers had accepted state intervention to stimulate and direct the course of economic development. Applying mercantilist principles, the state had subsidized agriculture, manufacturing, and transportation-related activities, invested directly in private enterprise, loaned money to farmers and other businessmen, and used the public credit to facilitate the construction of railroads. It had also granted tax exemptions to favored enterprises and dispensed special privileges or legal advantages to the legions of entrepreneurs who besieged the legislature for corporate charters. In more dramatic moves, the state had built and directly operated the Erie Canal and the vast system of feeder and lateral canals it spawned. As the economy expanded and grew in complexity, the state took the first tentative steps toward the regulation of business, writing restrictive clauses into special corporate charters and establishing a permanent commission to oversee banking operations. Finally, government stimulated development by creating and maintaining a legal order and institutional environment conducive to economic growth and private enterprise. The state, in short, played a pivotal role in the transformation of New York's economy in the early nineteenth century.

By the 1840s, however, New Yorkers of diverse political persuasions had begun to question many of the underlying assumptions of the state's political economy and the governmental system that had produced it. Some, imbued with Jeffersonian Republican ideals, had never really accepted the goal of rapid economic development and now lamented the disruptive social consequences of market expansion. Many Democrats, deeply suspicious of government activism, concluded that public economic policies had benefited a few special interests at the expense of the many, as they had long predicted. Still others objected to the unplanned, ad hoc, particularistic nature of public policy and the financial disarray it had produced. Democratic impulses and demands for greater popular involvement also shaped the growing debate over the nature of governance. And New Yorkers attuned to the social and economic realities of the market and the liberal ideology it spawned pressed for the adoption of laissez-faire principles.

Radical Democrats like Michael Hoffman, who had led the "Stop and Tax" movement, concerned about the rising state debt, demanded constitutional limitations on the state's power to borrow, but the Radicals' demands went beyond financial retrenchment. They also advocated a general curtailment of legislative authority, judicial reorganization, and election of state officers. The demands of other New Yorkers converged with and, on some points, overlapped those of the Radicals. Antirenters continued to press for land reform. Prominent Whigs such as Horace Greeley, while unsympathetic to the goal of financial retrenchment, supported judicial reform, restraints on legislative power, the election of executive officers, and, parting company with the Radicals, unlimited black suffrage. Many in the newly emerging legal profession demanded sweeping changes in the court system and in legal practices. Out of this diverse reform agenda, the convention fashioned a new constitution that fundamentally transformed the nature of governance in the state.

The constitution of 1846 curtailed the legislature's power to distribute pub-

lic largess to special interests, imposed tighter standards of legislative procedure, and strengthened the mechanisms of popular control. The convention
dealt with the immediate financial crisis by mandating that a sinking fund be
established out of canal revenues for the retirement of the debt. For the longer
term, it prohibited the legislature from lending the state's credit to individuals
or corporations and limited total state indebtedness to $1 million. Any new
obligation in excess of that amount would require popular approval and new
taxes dedicated to its repayment. Convention delegates addressed the charges of
"special privilege" in the granting of corporate charters as well, requiring that
most corporations be created by general law and prohibiting the legislature from
granting any special charter for banking purposes. And, last, the old mercantilist laws mandating state inspection of export commodities were formally
abolished and the elaborate system of inspectors dismantled. Taken together,
such constitutional provisions signaled a radically diminished role for government in economic affairs.

In addition to restricting the scope of government, the new constitution
expanded the opportunities for popular participation. It reduced senatorial
terms from four to two years and created single-member districts for senators
and assemblymen. The convention also stripped the legislature of its appointive
power, mandating the popular election of the principal state officers (secretary
of state, comptroller, treasurer, attorney general, and state engineer), and
reduced the terms of those officers from three to two years. Similarly, local
administrative officials previously appointed by the governor and the Senate
were now to be elected by the people, as were all state and local judicial officers.

The popular election of judges, one of the most important innovations, was
part of a much broader reorganization of the state's judicial system. The new
constitution abolished the Court for the Trial of Impeachments and for Correction of Errors, the court of last resort under the state's first constitution, and
created in its place a Court of Appeals, with final appellate jurisdiction, to be
made up of eight judges. It also established a new Supreme Court with general
jurisdiction in law and equity, to be composed of thirty-two justices elected
from eight judicial districts, and a system of county courts, with civil jurisdiction. Moreover, the convention instructed the legislature to appoint commissioners to revise and simplify the rules and practice of the New York courts.

Some issues that had figured prominently in the constitutional reform
movement were left unresolved. The convention sidestepped the explosive
issue of granting unlimited suffrage to blacks, providing that the question be
submitted directly to the people in a referendum. In November, New Yorkers
voted overwhelmingly in favor of retaining the $250 freehold qualification.
Despite decades of political agitation and popular referenda in 1860 and 1869,
unlimited black male suffrage would be achieved in New York only with the
ratification of the Fifteenth Amendment to the federal Constitution in 1870.

Similarly, in the case of the antirent controversy, the convention prohibited feudal tenures and limited future leases of agricultural lands to no more than twelve years, but this did nothing to provide relief to existing tenants, and many antirenters later took out their anger and frustration on Governor Wright in the November 1846 election.

Still, the delegates had wrought a constitutional revolution. They had imposed stringent limitations on the state's ability to incur debts and lend its credit, dismantled the remnants of the mercantilist policy system, proscribed government's direct involvement in economic development, broadened the basis for participation in the political system, and transferred important political authority to the people directly. As the historian James A. Henretta has noted, "the era of the expansive republican 'commonwealth' had given way to that of the limited classical liberal state."

The Second Party System in Crisis

A more immediate consequence of constitutional reform was that it neutralized many of the issues that had distinguished Democrats and Whigs. Economic questions in general, and the proper role of government in the economy in particular, had been at the core of the two parties' definitions of themselves and their opponents. The new restrictions on the state's economic role, rigid limitations on the public debt, constitutionally mandated general incorporation laws, and the prohibition against special bank charters effectively removed issues that had dominated partisan discourse for two decades or more. Of course, economic issues did not suddenly disappear from the political arena. Successive legislatures after 1846 debated the privileges and restrictions to be included in the general incorporation laws mandated by the constitution. Similarly, between 1846 and 1860, the state fashioned rudimentary mechanisms to regulate the banking, insurance, and railroad industries. The canal expansion issue even reappeared in the early 1850s, when Thurlow Weed orchestrated the passage of new legislation to enlarge the Erie Canal. Still, as the two parties' positions on economic questions converged, or as such issues were depoliticized altogether, an important focal point of partisan competition, and thus loyalty and cohesion, disappeared. The result was a gradual erosion of the partisan alignments that had characterized the second party system.

Intraparty squabbling and the emergence of new, noneconomic issues hastened this process. Democratic party unity, already severely strained, was the first casualty. Meeting in Syracuse on October 1, 1846, the state convention, dominated by Radical delegates, nominated Silas Wright for a second term as governor. Conservatives, still bitter over Wright's veto of a canal bill in 1845 and his support for constitutional reform, abandoned the governor in the fall election. President Polk, whose patronage policies had previously favored the Conservatives, made a belated effort to bolster Wright's candidacy, but it came too late to have any effect. Adding to these difficulties was Wright's unpopularity among antirenters and the resentment of many western New Yorkers over his veto of the canal bill.

Taking advantage of Democratic disarray, the Whigs nominated John Young for governor and Hamilton Fish for lieutenant governor. Young had been instrumental in fashioning the coalition of Radical Democrats, antirenters, and Whigs that in 1845 had pushed through legislation calling for a constitutional convention. He was also well regarded by antirenters, who promptly accepted Young as their gubernatorial candidate. On election day the Whigs swept the state, capturing the executive, both houses of the legislature, and a majority of the state's representatives to Congress. Only Fish, among major Whig candidates, failed to win election. He lost to incumbent Democrat Addison Gardiner. Opposition in the canal counties and among antirenters contributed to Wright's defeat, but the decisive factor was the defection of Conservative Democrats. The election left the Whigs in control of state government and the Democratic party in shambles.

The intrusion of the slavery issue exacerbated existing divisions within the Democratic party. Radicals, at both the state and national levels, had opposed the annexation of Texas in 1845 because it would add another slave state to the Union. When war broke out between the United States and Mexico in 1846, Congressman David Wilmot of Pennsylvania introduced an amendment to an appropriations bill to prohibit slavery in any territory acquired from Mexico. Preston King, a Radical congressman from New York, proposed that slavery be excluded from *any* territory acquired in the future. Neither of these resolutions passed in the House of Representatives, but the Wilmot Proviso and the question of slavery in the territories came to dominate national political debate and fatally intensified the factionalism within the Democratic party in New York.

By 1847 Radicals and Conservatives were struggling for control of the state party and for the soul of the national Democratic organization. Anti-Polk Democrats pinned their hopes for regaining control of the party on Silas Wright, whom they wanted to nominate for the presidency in 1848, but the former governor died suddenly on August 27, the victim of a heart attack. Wright's death deprived northern antislavery Democrats of their strongest candidate to challenge the Polk forces on the national level and threw the state party into turmoil. When the state convention met in Syracuse two weeks later, all hope for reconciliation vanished. The Hunker-dominated convention nominated a slate of candidates for state offices. When they went on to vote down a resolution in support of the Wilmot Proviso, the Barnburners walked out. In late October, John Van Buren, the former president's son, and other younger Democrats organized a mass protest meeting of Barnburners in Herkimer. The assembly of four thousand resolved not to nominate a separate slate of candidates, although

Van Buren and others disavowed the Hunker slate and pledged to oppose any Democratic presidential candidate in 1848 who favored the extension of slavery. Profoundly divided, the Democrats were overwhelmed by the Whigs in the November 1847 elections.

As attention focused on the upcoming presidential election in 1848, the Barnburners were more determined than ever to regain control of the state Democratic organization and to press their antiextension views on the national party. Meeting in Utica in February, they repudiated the Hunker slate of delegates to the national convention and selected their own. They also reaffirmed their commitment to the Wilmot Proviso, though moderating their earlier pledge to oppose any presidential candidate who favored the extension of slavery. When the Democratic convention met in Baltimore in May, it was thus confronted with two competing delegations from New York, each professing to be the legitimate representatives of the state party.

Many antiextension Democrats saw Martin Van Buren as the logical successor to Silas Wright as their standard-bearer, but the ex-president was evasive and noncommittal. While appearing to support the Wilmot Proviso, he was principally concerned with control of the party. He flatly rejected his son's proposal that his name be placed in nomination at the convention but provided detailed political advice to the Barnburners. The convention, anxious to avoid an outright schism among the New York delegates, adopted a compromise that would allow the two delegations to share the state's votes equally. But it was not enough, and when the convention nominated Lewis Cass of Michigan for the presidency, the Barnburner delegates walked out.

Having bolted the national party, Barnburner leaders such as John Van Buren and Samuel J. Tilden laid plans to hold their own convention to nominate a separate slate of candidates. The difficulty was in finding someone willing to lead a third-party campaign for the presidency. When Thomas Hart Benton and John A. Dix both declined, attention focused on Martin Van Buren. The ex-president refused to allow his name to be placed in nomination but prepared a lengthy letter that made clear his commitment to "free soil" and his approval of a third-party movement. When the delegates gathered in Utica on June 22, they once again endorsed the Wilmot Proviso and, ignoring Van Buren's wishes, nominated him for president. Henry Dodge of Wisconsin was nominated for vice president (although he declined to run) and Senator John Dix for governor.

Van Buren ultimately accepted the nomination and determined to build a national coalition of Barnburners, Liberty men, and Conscience Whigs to challenge the two major parties. Despite some misgivings, the leaders of the other antislavery factions concluded that Van Buren offered the best chance to break the slave power. Some 20,000 delegates met in Buffalo on August 9 to form a new national party committed to "free soil" in the western territories. The motives of the assembled delegates ranged from principled opposition to the extension of slavery to purely pragmatic intraparty politics. Eventually the convention adopted a platform that included something for all factions but unequivocally opposed the extension of slavery into the territories. Van Buren was then nominated for president over John Parker Hale, the Liberty candidate, and Charles Francis Adams was selected for vice president.

As the election of 1848 approached, all the ingredients seemed to be in place for the final disruption of the second party system. A third party committed to challenging the two major parties on the slavery issue was in the field, appealing to Wilmot Proviso Democrats, Conscience Whigs, and the remnants of the Liberty party. The Democratic party, furthermore, was deeply divided, especially in New York. The Whig party was also divided, but Thurlow Weed devised a political strategy that simultaneously minimized the disruptive effect of the slavery issue and exploited the schism among Democrats. Passing over Henry Clay, the party nominated Zachary Taylor for president and Millard Fillmore for vice president. Hamilton Fish was the Whig candidate for governor. The Democratic party, whose support of Cass for the presidency had provoked the Barnburner defection, nominated Reuben H. Walworth for governor.

In the end, the Free Soil campaign failed to produce the massive defections from the major parties needed for victory. Taylor defeated Cass for the presidency, while Van Buren received only 10 percent of the vote nationally and carried no states. The Free Soil party siphoned votes disproportionately from the Democrats, but Taylor would have won even if there had been no third-party movement. In New York, Van Buren received more votes than Cass and clearly contributed to Taylor's victory. More significantly, the Whigs routed the Democrats in the state contests, electing Fish to the governorship, thirty-two of the state's thirty-four congressmen, 108 of the 128 members of the Assembly, and a majority of the state Senate. Whig domination of the legislature, moreover, made possible the election of Seward to replace Dix in the United States Senate.

Despite some weakening of party loyalty in response to the slavery issue and the lopsided Whig victory, the 1848 election did not mark the demise of the second party system in the state. The vast majority of Free Soil voters came from the ranks of the Democratic party, while the Whig electorate remained constant in comparison with the 1844 vote. Even the prominent role the Barnburners played in the national Free Soil movement and the bitter split in the Democratic party must be balanced against the fact that Barnburners and Hunkers would soon make common cause again. Still, it was hardly politics as usual. The electoral stability and party cohesion that had been the norm for most of the previous decade could no longer be taken for granted. Partisan identification was weakening; the issue of slavery was becoming increasingly unmanageable; and explosive new issues such as temperance and nativism were just over the horizon.

Chapter 24

Politics Transformed
Slavery, Nativism, and the Rise of the Republican Party

THE DECADE OF THE 1850s WAS ONE OF THE MOST TUR-
bulent in the political history of New York. Already weakened by internal divisions over state issues and the emergence of the Free Soil movement, the Democratic and Whig parties confronted new challenges at mid-century that would fundamentally transform politics in the state. Following the lead of Maine, the opponents of alcohol renewed their campaign for a statewide prohibition law. Political nativism, dormant for almost a decade, reawakened in the early 1850s to challenge the dominant political parties. And overshadowing everything was the seemingly insoluble problem of slavery. The convergence of these issues disrupted traditional partisan identifications and ultimately destroyed the second party system. When the dust finally settled, the Democratic party had been transformed, the Whig party had ceased to exist, and a new Republican party had emerged on the scene.

Factionalism Rampant: Hards, Softs, and Silver Grays

Reeling from their disastrous loss in the election of 1848, Democratic party leaders moved quickly to heal the schism between the Barnburner and Hunker factions. Electoral success and control of the spoils of office, they realized, depended upon party unity. Achieving that unity, however, was no simple matter. The Barnburners insisted on adherence to the Wilmot Proviso, while the Hunkers refused to repudiate the national Democratic party platform and worried that their influence would be diminished in a reunited party. In August 1849 joint conventions were held in Rome to select a common slate of candidates for state offices. No progress toward reconciliation was made, but more and more Democrats came to realize that compromise was inevitable. Indeed, the Hunkers themselves were split on the issue. Those who opposed reconciliation and adhered strictly to the national party platform on the question of slavery in the territories were now called "Hards." William L. Marcy and other Hunkers who acknowledged congressional authority over slavery in the territories and sought reunion with the Barnburners were referred to as "Softs."

In September the Hunkers and Barnburners worked out what amounted to a union ticket, with each group nominating four candidates for the eight state offices up for election. It was further agreed that opinions on the issue of slavery should not be a test of allegiance to the Democratic party. The union ticket was formalized in a joint convention that met in Syracuse on September 14. The convention also adopted a face-saving resolution on the slavery issue, reaffirming the Barnburner contention that Congress possessed the power to prohibit slavery in the territories but acknowledging the differences of opinion on the subject within the Democratic party. This became the basis for a shaky reunion of the New York Democratic party. The political advantages of unity were amply demonstrated in the 1849 election. Democrats outpolled Whigs by a small margin statewide, were victorious in four of the eight state races, and made dramatic gains in the legislative contests. Whigs maintained a tenuous control over the legislature but could no longer count on a divided Democratic party for Whig victories.

In choosing party unity and the promise of offices over principle, the Barnburners had taken the first steps toward the final abandonment of the Free Soil party. National political events accelerated that tendency. Out of power at the federal level because of the Whig victory in the 1848 presidential election, Democrats were no longer constrained by the dictates of national policy positions with which they disagreed. For a brief moment, the reconstitution of the party on antiextension grounds seemed possible. Such hopes were dashed, however, by events in Washington. In January 1850 Henry Clay introduced a series of resolutions in Congress designed to resolve all outstanding sectional issues and settle the question of the status of slavery in the newly acquired territories. As subsequently modified and passed, this Compromise of 1850 provided for the admission of California as a free state, the abolition of the slave trade (but not slavery itself) in the District of Columbia, the passage of a more effective fugitive slave law, and the creation of the territories of Utah and New Mexico without reference to slavery. This last provision, by incorporating the principle of popular sovereignty, was the death knell of the Wilmot Proviso.

During the debate over the compromise, leading New York Democrats conceded as much. Anxious to solidify the party unity achieved in 1849, John Van Buren and others intensified their efforts to heal the breach with the Hunkers and rationalized their abandonment of Free Soil principles by proclaiming that the compromise had made antiextension agitation unnecessary. At the state convention in September the two factions joined together to nominate Horatio Seymour for governor, endorse the Compromise of 1850, and purge the party platform of references to the Wilmot Proviso.

Whereas the compromise had contributed to Democratic unity, it precipitated a near-fatal split in the Whig party. New York's Whigs were already divided between the radical supporters of William H. Seward and Thurlow Weed on the one hand, and the conservative supporters of Millard Fillmore and Francis Granger on the other. Seward's vocal opposition to the compromise in the Senate deepened that division. When it became clear that Fillmore, who assumed the presidency after Zachary Taylor's death in July, supported the compromise, the battle for control of the state party heated up. At issue was the party's position on slavery and the distribution of national patronage in New York. At the state convention in Utica on September 26, Weed and Seward delegates passed resolutions supporting Seward's actions and affirming the principles of the Wilmot Proviso. Infuriated, Granger and the Fillmore delegates walked out. Granger's silver-gray hair became the basis for the designation of this faction as the "Silver Grays." In the end, both factions nominated Washington Hunt for governor, and he went on to defeat Seymour in November by the narrow margin of 262 votes. The Whigs lost all the remaining state offices and split the congressional delegation evenly with the Democrats, but they retained control of the legislature, which enabled them to elect Hamilton Fish to the Senate in early 1851.

Thus, by the end of 1850, both major parties in New York were wracked by internal divisions over the issue of slavery, but, in the interest of winning state elections, they had managed to fashion shaky truces among their contending factions. Barnburner Democrats, second-guessing their earlier endorsement of the Compromise of 1850, now attacked the fugitive slave law in the hope of using the issue to regain control of the party from the Hunkers and to help stem the defection of antiextension voters to the Whig party. But they stopped short of advocating a repeat of 1848. The Whig party, despite its partial victory in 1850, was in an even more precarious position, held together only by the herculean efforts of Thurlow Weed to accommodate the Fillmore faction and New York City Whigs involved in the southern cotton trade.

At this juncture, Weed determined to defuse the slavery issue by diverting attention from the Compromise of 1850 to a traditional state issue on which Whigs of all factions could agree: canal policy. In the spring of 1851 Governor Washington Hunt proposed a $9 million bond issue to enlarge the Erie Canal network. When the bill passed the Assembly, thirteen Democrats resigned their Senate seats to prevent its passage in that body. Governor Hunt thereupon called for special elections to fill the vacant seats, and in a special session of the legislature which met in June and July the $9 million enlargement was passed.

The law was declared unconstitutional in 1852 and would not be implemented until 1854, after the passage of a constitutional amendment authorizing the enlargement. In the meantime, Weed's strategy had shifted the basis of state politics away from slavery and temporarily forestalled the disintegration of the Whig party; but it was not enough to ensure Whig victory in the fall elections. Democrats achieved a two-vote majority in the Assembly, tied the Whigs in the Senate, and captured all but two of the state offices, including control of the influential canal board.

The canal issue would continue to play a role in New York campaigns through 1852 and 1853, but with a presidential contest looming, slavery could not be relegated to the back burner indefinitely. The Barnburners, committed now to remaining within the Democratic party, hoped to identify a presidential candidate in 1852 who would be broadly acceptable to northerners, while maintaining their opposition to the Compromise of 1850. They ultimately endorsed William L. Marcy, leader of the Hunker faction, but Marcy was not to be the nominee. After forty-nine ballots, the Democratic national convention selected a dark horse candidate, Franklin Pierce of New Hampshire. To the disappointment of the Barnburners, the convention also reaffirmed the party's support for the compromise, including the fugitive slave act. In September the state convention nominated Horatio Seymour for governor and Sanford B. Church for lieutenant governor and endorsed the national Democratic platform.

Whig party unity on state issues did not extend to the national arena. When the national party convened in Baltimore on June 16, the Silver Grays and Sewardites continued their maneuvering for control. Seward and Weed supported General Winfield Scott for the nomination over their fellow New Yorker and the incumbent president, Millard Fillmore. After fifty-three ballots, Scott was nominated, but to Seward's dismay the convention then proceeded to adopt a platform that endorsed the Compromise of 1850. The New York Whigs subsequently renominated Washington Hunt for governor and acquiesced in the national party's position on the extension of slavery.

The ensuing election was a disaster for the Whigs. Nationally, Scott won only four states. In the South, where the Whig candidate was perceived to be controlled by Seward and the antislavery faction, former Whig voters flocked to temporary "Union" parties or stayed at home in droves. In the North, internal divisions, huge increases in the largely Democratic immigrant vote, the resurgence of nativism, and the emergence of the temperance issue combined to overwhelm Whig candidates. In New York, Seymour polled 22,000 more votes than Hunt and captured forty-three of the fifty-nine counties, while Democrats maintained control of the Assembly by a two-to-one margin.

Despite having elected their first governor since Silas Wright's defeat in 1846, the Democratic party had by no means put an end to factionalism. Old wounds were inflamed in 1853 as the legislature debated plans to complete the enlargement of the Erie Canal. Disputes over federal patronage, particularly President Pierce's appointment of William L. Marcy as secretary of state, deepened the divisions. By the time the state convention met in September, the party had clearly divided into Barnburners, led by John Van Buren and John A. Dix; moderate Hunkers, or Softshells, such as Seymour and Marcy; and conservative Hunkers, or Hardshells, led by Daniel S. Dickinson. When the party convened in Syracuse, a dispute over the seating of delegates provoked the Hardshells to bolt the convention. In the end, two separate slates of candidates for state offices were nominated. The result was predictable: the Whig party won majorities in both houses of the legislature and captured control of the canal board. After the election, the divisions within the Democratic party only deepened.

The Whig party was not much better off. To be sure, they won the election in 1853, which enabled them, in alliance with moderate and conservative Hunker Democrats, to push through a constitutional amendment in 1854 providing, finally, for the canal enlargement. But the Whig victory was a result largely of their ability to exploit a divided Democratic party. Electoral success concealed deep-seated threats to the continued existence of the party. Indeed, by 1854 the second party system itself stood on the brink of disintegration.

Slavery, Temperance, and Nativism

The convergence of three issues—slavery, temperance, and nativism—precipitated the final collapse of the existing two-party system and the realignment of state politics. Of the three, slavery was unquestionably the most important. In January 1854 Congress began consideration of what would become the Kansas-Nebraska Act. Introduced by Senator Stephen A. Douglas of Illinois, the bill provided for the organization of the territories of Kansas and Nebraska and stipulated that any states formed out of those territories could enter the Union with or without slavery, "as their constitution may prescribe at the time of their admission." In the meantime, the inhabitants themselves could determine the status of slavery in the newly created territories. The effect of the bill would be to repeal the Missouri Compromise of 1820, which had excluded slavery north of 36° 30' in the Louisiana Purchase, and shatter the tenuous sectional peace established by the Compromise of 1850.

The bill sent shock waves throughout the North. Anti-Nebraska protest meetings sprang up by the hundreds, bringing together those opposed to the extension of slavery without regard to existing party affiliations. At a mass meeting in New York City on January 30, even conservative merchants with close economic ties to the South joined Silver Gray and Seward Whigs, Barnburner Democrats, and Free Soilers in denouncing Douglas and urging the defeat of the Nebraska bill. In the coming weeks, similar meetings were held in communities across the state. Most striking was the ferocity of anti-Nebraska sentiment and the pervasiveness of the indignation. Everywhere, it seemed, strictly partisan considerations were put aside in order to advance the larger antislavery objective. Only Hardshell Democrats, a few newspapers such as the *Journal of Commerce*, and the Irish resisted the tide.

Despite the popular outrage in the North, the Kansas-Nebraska bill was destined to become law. William H. Seward led the antislavery forces in the Senate, arguing powerfully for the doctrine of a "higher law" that superseded the acts of Congress and the Constitution, but he could not prevent passage of the bill on March 4, 1854. Opponents were more hopeful in the House, but after several months of acrimonious debate, the Pierce administration succeeded in convincing enough northern Democrats to support the bill to ensure its passage on May 22.

The Kansas-Nebraska Act shook the very foundations of politics in New York and the nation. At first the magnitude of the anti-Nebraska protest suggested the feasibility of a new, unified antislavery party in the North. By the summer of 1854 efforts to create such a party were already underway in Maine, Vermont, Wisconsin, Indiana, Ohio, and Michigan, while the name "Republican" was increasingly being applied to the movement. The process was much more convoluted in New York, and a new antislavery party did not appear in the state for another year. In the short term the effect of the law in New York was to intensify existing divisions within the two parties. Hard and Soft Democrats split down the middle on the issue of repealing the Missouri Compromise, while Barnburners disagreed among themselves over whether to join a new antislavery party or remain within the Democratic fold. The two factions within the Whig party enjoyed a momentary unity in their common opposition to the Nebraska bill but could not agree on a course of action once the bill became law. Seward and the radicals demanded retaliation against the South, while conservatives like Hamilton Fish, Millard Fillmore, and Francis Granger sought sectional peace rather than confrontation. The eventual breakup of the Whig party seemed inevitable, and some, like Horace Greeley, urged the formation of a new Republican party, but Seward and Weed were not prepared to abandon the Whig party just yet, at least not until Seward's reelection to the United States Senate in 1855 was assured. In any event, slavery was but one of the issues disrupting New York politics in 1854, and it was by no means certain that antislavery would be the basis for any new political party that might be created.

One of the issues competing with antislavery for the attention of voters and political leaders was temperance. By the mid-1840s, New York temperance advocates had abandoned the tactic of moral persuasion in favor of direct political action to achieve their objectives. Voters approved a local option law in

1846, only to see it repealed by the state legislature the following year. There matters stood until 1851 when temperance forces in Maine, led by Neal Dow, won passage of a law prohibiting the manufacture and sale of all intoxicating liquors. This "Maine Law" became the model for prohibitionist activities across the country. In New York temperance forces, led by Myron H. Clark of Canandaigua, came within two votes of passing a prohibition law in the 1853 legislature. Determined to build upon their strength, temperance reformers endorsed legislative candidates from the two major parties in the fall election and succeeded in electing an anti-liquor majority. The 1854 legislature subsequently passed a prohibition law by a large margin, but Governor Seymour vetoed the bill on constitutional grounds, thereby ensuring that temperance would be an issue in the gubernatorial election in 1854.

Even more disruptive of traditional political affiliations than temperance was the reappearance of political nativism. For most of the previous decade, nativism and anti-Catholicism had remained submerged just beneath the surface of politics and public life. New Yorkers harboring anti-immigrant sentiments or fearful of the Catholic Church's growing power joined the Order of United Americans, the United Sons of America, or other semisecret fraternal organizations but had relatively little direct political impact. By 1854 that had dramatically changed. The emergence of the Know Nothing party gave new life and political expression to the nativist resentments of many New Yorkers and posed still another threat to the electoral viability of the traditional parties.

The American or Know Nothing movement grew out of the Order of the Star Spangled Banner, a fraternal society founded in New York City in 1849. Characterized by strict secrecy, elaborate rituals, and a hierarchical structure, the society sought to eliminate Catholic and immigrant influence in politics by supporting only native-born Protestants for office. By the fall of 1853 their secretive efforts to influence Whig and Democratic party nominations in New York City and state elections began to draw public attention. When suspected members were asked about their activities, they responded simply, "I know nothing," thus giving the movement its name. Under the leadership of James W. Barker, a New York City merchant and former Whig activist, Know Nothingism spread rapidly in early 1854, moving outward from its base in New York City to infect towns and communities all across the state. In June a National Grand Council, with Barker as its president, was created to direct Know Nothing activities in the national political arena. Over the next six months, Know Nothing membership nationwide grew from about fifty thousand to more than one million.

The phenomenal growth of Know Nothingism in 1854 was due to the unprecedented levels of immigration over the previous decade—some three million immigrants arrived in the United States between 1845 and 1854—and to the fact that the overwhelming majority of newcomers were Catholic. The rising tide of immigration rekindled long-standing religious animosities and intensified native-born Protestant fears that Catholic and foreign influence in the political process threatened to corrupt and pervert republican institutions. Hardly new, such fears were given new power and plausibility by renewed Catholic demands for public financing of parochial schools and the continuing controversy over the use of the Bible in public schools. A dispute over the ownership of church property added fuel to the fire. When Catholic bishops, anxious to defuse congregational disputes between lay boards of trustees and the clergy, began to demand laws giving control of all church property to the bishops, Protestants responded with outrage. The Vatican's decision to send a papal nuncio, Gaetano Bedini, to the United States to resolve the property disputes only exacerbated the situation, provoking widespread controversy and protest and feeding Protestant suspicions that the pope had sinister designs on America.

Although Know Nothingism exploited the deeply rooted anti-Catholicism in American society, its appeal was also profoundly political. It was the growing role of Catholics and immigrants in the political process, not just their religion, that concerned Know Nothings. The association of immigrants with voter fraud and corruption; the growing importance of the immigrant vote in the Democratic party; President Pierce's appointment of a Catholic, James Campbell, as postmaster general; and the courting of immigrant voters by political leaders such as Seward, Weed, and Seymour were all evidence of an imminent threat to the republic. Such charges met with widespread acceptance precisely because they reinforced New Yorkers' dissatisfaction and frustration with existing parties and politicians. The Know Nothings were thus able to present themselves as the party of reform, the best hope for breaking the Catholic immigrant grip on politics, restoring political power to the people (i.e., native-born Protestants), and preserving the purity of republican institutions. The fact that its message overlapped with that of the temperance and antislavery movements strengthened the extraordinary appeal of Know Nothingism, particularly in upstate and western New York, where relatively few Catholics and immigrants were to be found.

The Emergence of the Republican Party

By July 1854 the old political order in New York was in complete disarray. Traditional party loyalties could no longer be taken for granted in a political environment in which temperance, nativism, and antislavery vied with one another and with more conventional issues for the attention and support of voters. Democratic and Whig leaders, accustomed to managing highly structured parties built on intense and enduring partisan identifications, were ill prepared for the political sea change they now confronted. It only remained to determine whether a new alignment of politics would come about on the basis of antislavery, nativism, or, perhaps, temperance.

The Democrats approached the 1854 elections no more unified than they had been the previous year. Meeting in their state convention on July 12, the Hards adopted resolutions endorsing the Nebraska Act, affirming the principle of congressional nonintervention in territorial affairs, and explicitly criticizing President Franklin Pierce for his interference in local politics. Adding insult to injury, the convention then nominated Greene C. Bronson, whom Pierce had removed as collector of customs the previous year, for governor. The Soft Democrats, meeting on September 6, were themselves divided between Pierce supporters like Horatio Seymour and William L. Marcy, who sought to fashion a compromise on the Nebraska question, and Barnburners like Preston King, who were adamant in their opposition to the extension of slavery. When the Seymour forces proposed resolutions declaring the repeal of the Missouri Compromise "inexpedient and unnecessary," but discouraging any resistance or opposition to it, Preston King and one hundred Barnburner delegates left the convention in protest. The remaining delegates nominated Seymour for a second term as governor and endorsed his antiprohibition stance in the hope that liquor, not slavery, would be the issue in the fall elections. The Democratic party, however, was now more deeply divided than ever, with one faction, the Barnburners, actively looking for an alternative.

The Whig party was equally at risk in the political uncertainty of 1854. Already weakened by extensive voter defections and vulnerable to further inroads by the supporters of temperance and nativism, the party now confronted growing pressure for the fusion of antislavery Whigs and Democrats into a new organization. By summer a new Republican party had emerged in Michigan and Wisconsin, and efforts at fusion were under way in a number of other New England and midwestern states. Pro-fusion sentiment, led by Horace Greeley, was strong in New York, but there were equally powerful forces intent upon preserving the organizational integrity of the Whig party, at least for the present. Weed and Seward, while strongly opposed to the Kansas-Nebraska Act, were fearful that if antislavery Whigs defected to a new party, the Know Nothings and their Silver Gray allies would seize control of the Whig organization. They were also convinced that Seward's reelection to the United States Senate in 1855 depended upon the preservation of a united Whig party.

The first challenge came in mid-August, when anti-Nebraska delegates from across the state met in convention at Saratoga. Many believed that the meeting was the first step toward forming a new party, but Weed successfully blocked such efforts by orchestrating the selection of "safe" or pro-Seward delegates wherever possible and persuading Horace Greeley to oppose any plan to nominate a separate slate of antislavery candidates for the fall elections. These actions, along with the skillful parliamentary maneuvering of Henry J. Raymond, editor of the *New York Times* and a Weed ally, ensured that no new party would emerge from the Saratoga meeting. Instead, the convention passed resolutions strongly condemning the extension of slavery and agreed to reconvene at Auburn on September 26, after the Whig convention, to consider possible further action.

When the Whigs met in Syracuse on September 19, Weed confronted a new challenge. Delegates elected with temperance or Know Nothing support expected the Whig platform and nominee to reflect their concerns. Temperance advocates, furious at Seymour's veto of the prohibition bill, threatened to name a separate slate of candidates. The Know Nothings and conservative Silver Grays hoped to nominate one of their own for governor and seize control of the party from Weed; and there was still the possibility that the anti-Nebraska forces might yet choose to name separate candidates if the Whig nominees were unacceptable on the slavery issue. Unable to secure the nomination of his own candidate, George W. Patterson, Weed reluctantly agreed to the nomination of Myron H. Clark for governor. Clark was the favorite of the temperance people and had the additional advantage of being associated with a Know Nothing lodge. Raymond was nominated for lieutenant governor. A cautiously worded platform condemned the Nebraska Act but staked out no new or dramatic ground on the issue. With Clark at the head of the ticket, it was not deemed necessary even to mention the Maine Law.

Vindication of Weed's strategy to preserve the Whig party came in late September. The anti-Nebraska convention met in Auburn as planned on September 26. Simultaneously the state temperance convention and that of the Free Democrats, the radical remnant of the Free Soil party, convened in that same city to consider nominating separate tickets. In the end, all three endorsed the Whig party ticket, although none was enthusiastic about the candidacy of Raymond for lieutenant governor. Both the anti-Nebraska and Free Democratic conventions adopted the name "Republican" and established a state Republican committee, but the gesture meant little. Weed had successfully prevented fusion in New York. He was less successful in containing the threat posed by the Know Nothings and Silver Gray Whigs who, meeting in October, nominated a separate ticket headed up by Daniel Ullmann, a conservative Whig from New York City. Although the Know Nothings refused to adopt a platform, Ullmann's opposition to the Nebraska Act was widely known, and his supporters reassured doubters that, if elected, he would sign a prohibition law.

With Hard Democrat, Soft Democrat, Whig, and Know Nothing tickets in the field, the 1854 election can only be described as chaotic. In the confusion of issues and candidates, even shrewd politicians like Weed found it impossible to predict the outcome. Voter turnout was light, and those who did vote appear to have been moved more by nativism and temperance than by opposition to the extension of slavery. Ullmann received an astonishing 122,000 votes, carrying much of western New York and even doing well in lower Hudson Valley counties, but it was not enough for victory. In an extremely close race, Clark defeated Seymour by a mere 309 votes. The Whigs won strong majorities in both houses of the legislature, while Seward Whigs and Barnburners won twenty-seven of the state's thirty-three congressional seats. Thus, New York's delegation would be overwhelmingly anti-Nebraska.

The Whigs paid a heavy price for their victory in 1854. Know Nothing success in traditional Whig strongholds in central and western New York cast doubt on the party's ability to hold onto its electoral base. Equally disturbing, Horace Greeley, angry that Weed had successfully defeated fusion and resentful that he had been passed over for lieutenant governor, announced that he would no longer follow the political guidance of Weed and Seward. The Democrats' political future was also uncertain. The Hards lost significant ground because of their unbending endorsement of the Nebraska Act and defections to the Know Nothings. The Softs' equivocation on the slavery issue produced disastrous results in the congressional elections, but their strong showing in state contests provided some grounds for optimism. In the end, however, neither party could avoid the political upheaval under way in 1854. The election was the prelude to a fundamental realignment of partisan loyalties and the emergence of a new antislavery party.

The reelection of William H. Seward to the United States Senate was the first order of business for those desirous of creating such a party in New York. The Whigs had a clear majority in both houses of the 1855 legislature, but the conflicting loyalties of assemblymen elected in 1854 made it extremely difficult to predict Know Nothing strength. Seward supporters feared that an alliance of Know Nothings and Hard Democrats could block his return to the Senate. In the end, the skillful maneuvering of Weed, combined with Seward's great popularity and the fact that many Know Nothing legislators represented antislavery districts, ensured Seward's reelection with comfortable margins in both the Senate and the Assembly.

The spring of 1855 brought renewed efforts to "fuse" antislavery Whigs and Democrats into a new Republican party. Events in Kansas—the election of a pro-slavery legislature through fraud and intimidation and the spread of violence and political disorder—inflamed northern public opinion and pushed the slavery issue once more to center stage. Equally important, Thurlow Weed had now concluded that the time had come to abandon the Whig party. Quiet negotiations between Weed and antislavery Democrats such as Preston King and Reuben E. Fenton began in May. Over the next two months the leaders of the fusion movement worked out the complicated details that would bring the former political enemies together. On July 20, 1855, the call went out for Whig and Republican state conventions to meet simultaneously in Syracuse on September 26. Although the call for delegates did not explicitly mention fusion, there was little doubt that the creation of a new Republican party was the objective.

Initially the two conventions met separately, allowing Weed, King, and other leaders to orchestrate the final merger. Nominations for state offices were carefully apportioned among Whig and Democratic candidates. A joint resolutions committee fashioned a platform demanding that slavery be excluded from the territories; condemning President Pierce's actions in Kansas; and denouncing the Know Nothings for their secrecy and their antirepublican principles. The Whig convention then adjourned, and its delegates marched en masse to the Republican meeting hall where they were met with resounding cheers. Adopting the name "Republican," the combined delegates appointed a state committee composed of equal numbers of former Democrats and Whigs, thereby formally giving birth to the New York Republican party.

Republican prospects for the fall elections looked promising. A remnant of conservative Whigs, led by Washington Hunt and Hamilton Fish, held a separate convention, but no one took this attempt to salvage the Whig party very seriously. The Democrats remained divided, with the Hards firm in their support of the Kansas-Nebraska Act and the Pierce administration, while the Softs papered over their internal differences concerning slavery by equivocating on the territorial issue. The Know Nothings had their own problems. Many rank-and-file members, particularly rural supporters from the Burned-Over District, refused to endorse the national party's pro-southern stance on the extension of slavery and forced the inclusion of a plank in the state party platform condemning the Kansas-Nebraska Act.

The Republicans failed to capitalize on the seeming disarray of their opponents. Hampered by inadequate organization (the Whig party apparatus had essentially disintegrated), their inability to define themselves as the clear choice for anti-Nebraska voters, and the superior organization and continuing appeal of the Know Nothings, the new party's candidates received some 10,000 fewer votes than Know Nothing candidates in the November election. The Soft Democrats came in third, while the Hards were a distant fourth. Forty-four Republican assemblymen were elected, while the Know Nothings won thirty-nine seats and the Softs and Hards combined won forty-five. Although they had lost to the Know Nothings, Republican leaders took heart from the fact that the party had done so well in its first campaign, finishing ahead of both the Hard and Soft Democrats, and anticipated even greater success in 1856.

Republican optimism proved to be warranted. The party steadily gained strength in the winter and spring of 1856 as antislavery men in the other major parties increasingly defected to its ranks. The Soft Democrats capitulated to the demands of the national party and adopted a pro-southern stance on Kansas and slavery, thus leaving Free Soil Democrats little choice but to move toward the Republicans. Millard Fillmore's nomination for the presidency by the American (Know Nothing) party in February had a similar effect on antislavery Know Nothings and some conservative Whigs who had been reluctant to accept the fact that the Whig party was dead. By late spring, these events, together with a concerted effort to build a statewide Republican organization, had significantly broadened the electoral base of the party.

Dramatic events in Washington and Kansas at the end of May further bolstered Republican prospects. New Yorkers across the political spectrum were shocked by news of the brutal assault on Massachusetts Senator Charles Sumner on May 22 at the hands of Preston S. Brooks, a congressman from South Carolina. Offended by personal remarks that Sumner made in a speech against a Brooks relative, Senator Andrew P. Butler, Brooks attacked Sumner in the Senate chamber, beating him senseless. In Republican minds, Brooks's actions only reinforced the perception of southern aggressiveness in defending the institution of slavery. Further evidence of southern intentions came from Kansas. On May 21, pro-slavery forces attacked the free-state town of Lawrence, killing one person and burning the hotel, newspaper offices, and a number of homes. The Brooks-Sumner affair and the escalation of violence in Kansas inflamed public opinion in New York and persuaded many undecided voters and politicians to join the Republican fold.

Presidential politics also worked to the advantage of New York's Republicans. Meeting in Cincinnati on June 2, the Democrats nominated the pro-southern James Buchanan of Pennsylvania for president and forced the Softs to accept the national party position that slavery could not be excluded from any territory in the United States. The American party convention, under the control of southern delegates, had already nominated Fillmore. As the June 17 date for the first national Republican convention approached, state leaders knew that the party's success in New York depended upon the selection of a presidential candidate who would not alienate groups the party was trying to attract. That meant someone acceptable to antislavery Know Nothings and someone moderate enough on the slavery issue to satisfy conservative Whigs. Seward failed on both counts and was also seen as too radical to win critical swing states. In addition to such considerations, Weed calculated that Seward's chances for gaining the presidency would be greater in 1860. Thus, the nomination went to John C. Frémont, a popular hero with little or no political record that could be held against him.

With the national conventions out of the way, the leaders of New York's parties turned their attention to their respective state tickets. The Hard and Soft Democrats met in a joint convention on July 30 and nominated Amasa J. Parker, an appeals court judge, for governor. A confident Republican party met in Syracuse six weeks later and nominated John A. King for governor and Henry

R. Seldon for lieutenant governor. Already weakened by internal division and by the growing salience of the slavery issue, the Americans chose Erastus Brooks as their state standard-bearer.

In the ensuing election James Buchanan won the presidency, but the new Republican party achieved a resounding victory in New York. Frémont out-polled Buchanan in the state by 80,000 votes. King became the first Republican governor in New York history, with a 65,000-vote margin over Parker, and the Republicans captured eighty-two Assembly seats, nearly twice as many as the Democrats and Know Nothings combined. Heavy Republican majorities in upstate and western New York overwhelmed the Know Nothings in their base and more than counterbalanced the strong Democratic showing in and around New York City. In fact, the Democratic party sustained a major defeat in 1856 and was relegated to minority status for the next six years. The election accelerated the decline of the Know Nothings and ensured that they would never again enjoy the strength and appeal they had had at their peak in 1855.

New York and the Crisis of the Union

The election of 1856 was the final act in the formation of the Republican party in New York. It also signaled the end of the confusion that had characterized the disintegration of the second party system and the beginning of a new political era. From the mid-1850s to the present, New York politics has been dominated by electoral competition between Republicans and Democrats. More immediately, however, the emergence of the Republican party was symptomatic of a fundamental realignment of politics at the national level. That realignment, in turn, was part of a much larger and more significant drama: the increasingly strident debate over slavery and the growing crisis of the Union. Between 1856 and 1861, New York Republicans struggled simultaneously to solidify the new party's position in the state and to shape events that would determine the destiny of the nation.

Despite Republican electoral success in 1856, party unity was anything but assured. Ex-Democrats chafed under Weed's control, a fact that became evident in 1857 during the contest to choose a new United States senator to succeed Hamilton Fish. Weed's candidate was Preston King, a former Democrat who had played an important role in the formation of the party. He was challenged by Ward Hunt, James S. Wadsworth, and David Dudley Field. King ultimately prevailed, but not without leaving a residue of anti-Weed resentment in some quarters within the party.

External events also dampened Republican political prospects in 1857. The Kansas issue had temporarily subsided. Not even the Supreme Court's Dred

Scott decision upholding the constitutionality of slavery could rekindle the emotional antislavery fervor of the previous year. On top of that, a financial panic struck in August 1857, elevating economic issues to the forefront of the political agenda and tainting the party in power in Albany. Capitalizing on all this, the Democrats were victorious in the state elections in the fall.

Republican political fortunes revived in 1858, as the slavery issue once more captured national attention. In the waning months of 1857, pro-slavery forces in Kansas had pushed through the Lecompton Constitution guaranteeing to Kansans the right to own slaves. When President Buchanan accepted it as legitimate and urged the admission of Kansas as a state, Republicans and many northern Democrats denounced the president's capitulation to southern demands. Stephen Douglas of Illinois called the Lecompton Constitution a fraud and a clear violation of the principle of popular sovereignty. After months of contention, another referendum was held in Kansas in August 1858, and the Lecompton Constitution was rejected by a huge margin. Kansas would thus remain a territory for the time being, but the Lecompton affair drove a wedge through the ranks of the national Democratic party and solidified Douglas's position as undisputed leader of the northern Democrats.

Two other events ensured that slavery would play a prominent role in the 1858 elections. In Illinois the Republican party nominated Abraham Lincoln to contest Stephen A. Douglas's seat in the United States Senate. In perhaps the most famous such confrontation in American political history, Lincoln and Douglas debated the slavery issue in a series of seven face-to-face meetings. The Illinois legislature ultimately reelected Douglas to the Senate, but the debates helped to differentiate the Republican and northern Democratic positions on slavery and elevated Lincoln to national prominence. Shortly after the last of the Lincoln-Douglas debates, William H. Seward reasserted his own claim to leadership of the antislavery forces. In a speech delivered at Rochester on October 25, he characterized the conflict between North and South in the most radical terms yet: "It is an irrepressible conflict between opposing and enduring forces, and it means that the United States must and will, sooner or later, become either entirely a slave-holding nation, or entirely a free labour nation."

With the national debate over slavery as backdrop, New York's parties turned their attention to the state elections. The Republicans met at Syracuse on September 8. Anti-Weed forces put forth their own candidate, Timothy Jenkins, for governor, but in the end Weed successfully orchestrated the nomination of Edwin D. Morgan, former chairman of the Republican state committee and of the Republican national convention. Their efforts to fuse with the Republicans rebuffed, the American party nominated their own candidate for governor, Lorenzo Burrows. After a tumultuous battle over whether to seat the New York City delegation representing Tammany Hall or the followers of the erratic ex-

Tammany Hall headquarters during the presidential campaign of 1856. From *Frank Leslie's Illustrated Newspaper*, November 8, 1856.

mayor Fernando Wood, the Democratic state convention once again nominated Amasa J. Parker for governor and proclaimed its satisfaction with the Buchanan administration's handling of the Kansas issue. Although the margin of victory was less than in 1856, Morgan handily defeated Parker for the governorship, while Republican and anti-Lecompton candidates overwhelmingly dominated the legislative and congressional elections.

By 1859 national events and the upcoming presidential election increasingly overshadowed state politics. When the party conventions met in September, the selection of delegates to the national Democratic and Republican conventions in 1860 was as important as selecting candidates for the fall elections, if not more so. Democrats remained divided between Hards and Softs, with the further complication of a bitter contest in New York City between Tammany

Hall and Fernando Wood's Mozart Hall. Wood attempted to force his delegation on the convention, but in the end the Softs controlled the proceedings and selected mostly pro-Douglas delegates to the Democratic national convention. The majority of the Republican convention delegates favored Seward's candidacy for the presidential nomination, although some prominent New York politicians would actively work on behalf of Abraham Lincoln. In the fall elections, Republicans scored another victory, capturing six of the nine contested state offices and solidifying their position as *the* antislavery party in New York. The American party suffered a devastating defeat and would never again field candidates in the state. Also of note, Fernando Wood was resoundingly reelected as mayor of New York City.

The sense of crisis over slavery and the Union was heightened during the campaign by news from northern Virginia. On October 17, 1859, John Brown and a group of eighteen followers attacked and captured the federal armory at Harpers Ferry. Brown was already notorious for his violent antislavery activities in Kansas, particularly the attack on pro-slavery settlers at Pottawatomie Creek. With the financial and moral support of northern abolitionists such as Gerrit Smith of New York, Brown hoped now to foment an insurrection among Virginia's slaves, but the anticipated uprising did not occur. Federal forces under the command of Colonel Robert E. Lee quickly captured or killed all the participants in the plot. Brown himself was subsequently tried, convicted, and hanged. Although unsuccessful in its immediate objective, John Brown's raid inflamed passions on both sides of the slavery issue, reinforced the radical image of the Republican party, and fed southern fears of a northern plot against the institution of slavery.

Seward, Lincoln, and other Republican leaders denounced Brown's actions and offered reassurances of the party's moderation, but the apprehensions created by the events at Harpers Ferry had by no means dissipated when the Democratic and Republican national conventions met in the spring of 1860 to nominate candidates for the presidency. The Democrats met first, on April 23, in Charleston, South Carolina, but were unable to agree on a platform or a candidate. After anti-Douglas southern delegates withdrew, the convention adjourned, with plans to meet again in six weeks in Baltimore. In the end, the sectional divisions within the party proved irrevocable. Meeting in two separate conventions, northern Democrats nominated Stephen A. Douglas for the presidency, while southern Democrats chose John C. Breckinridge of Kentucky.

Earlier, on May 9, a group of conservative ex-Whigs and Americans, anxious to prevent a breakup of the Union, established the Constitutional Union party and nominated John Bell of Tennessee for president. When the Republicans met in Chicago a week later, William H. Seward was the leading candidate for the presidential nomination. Despite a formidable New York delegation, the support of Governor Morgan, who was the chairman of the Republican national committee, and the behind-the-scenes maneuvering of Thurlow Weed, that support had substantially eroded by the third day of the convention. The opposition of many former Know Nothings, his reputation as a radical on the slavery issue, his association with Weed, and, not least, the skill of Abraham Lincoln's convention managers doomed Seward's candidacy. On the third ballot, after having led for the first two, he watched helplessly as anti-Seward delegates coalesced around the candidacy of Abraham Lincoln and won him the nomination. Seward and Weed were thus denied the prize for which they had struggled so diligently for a decade.

The presidential election of 1860 was the most momentous in American history, and New York played a critical role in it. The state's thirty-five electoral votes were deemed crucial to Lincoln's chances by supporters and opponents alike. In an effort to prevent a Republican victory in the state, Democrats engineered a fusion of the Douglas, Bell, and, ultimately, Breckinridge tickets. But in the end even this combined opposition could not stop Lincoln. The Republican candidate carried New York (by a 50,000-vote margin) along with every other free state and was elected president. Edwin D. Morgan was reelected governor, while the Republicans captured both houses of the legislature and won twenty-three out of thirty-three congressional seats.

Lincoln's election was the spark that ignited the long simmering tensions between North and South. Many southerners refused to accept the election of a Republican president committed to halting the further spread of slavery. Thus, by early February 1861, the seven Deep South states from South Carolina to Texas had seceded from the Union and established the Confederate States of America. Initially New York's political leaders were divided in their reaction to southern secession. Many New Yorkers had little sympathy for the Republican party's position on slavery or for demands for greater black equality. Others, particularly New York City merchants with strong ties to the South, worried about the adverse effects of disunion or civil war on the state's economy and their own commercial interests. At one point, in early January 1861, Mayor Fernando Wood went so far as to propose that New York City secede from the Union, thereby preserving its commercial relations with southern cotton producers; and some Democratic party leaders like Horatio Seymour argued that the southern states should be allowed to leave the Union peacefully.

Despite such sentiments, the majority of New Yorkers concluded with Lincoln that secession was illegal under the Constitution and that preservation of the Union was paramount. In Washington, Seward, who was to be Lincoln's secretary of state, worked tirelessly toward that end in the months preceding the new president's inauguration. Nor would most New Yorkers tolerate such ill-conceived schemes as that of Fernando Wood. Horace Greeley labeled the New York City mayor a traitor and a blackguard. John A. Dix, then President Buchanan's secretary of the treasury, responded to Wood by ordering that "if anyone attempts to haul down the American flag, shoot him on the spot." Efforts would continue throughout the early months of 1861 to find a peaceful solution to the growing crisis, but when southern forces fired on Fort Sumter on April 12 and four more states quickly left the Union, there was no doubt as to where New York stood. The state was among the first to respond to President Lincoln's call for militia to suppress the southern rebellion. Over the next four years, nearly 465,000 New Yorkers would take up arms, while the accumulated wealth of more than a quarter-century of unprecedented economic growth would be committed to the preservation of the Union.

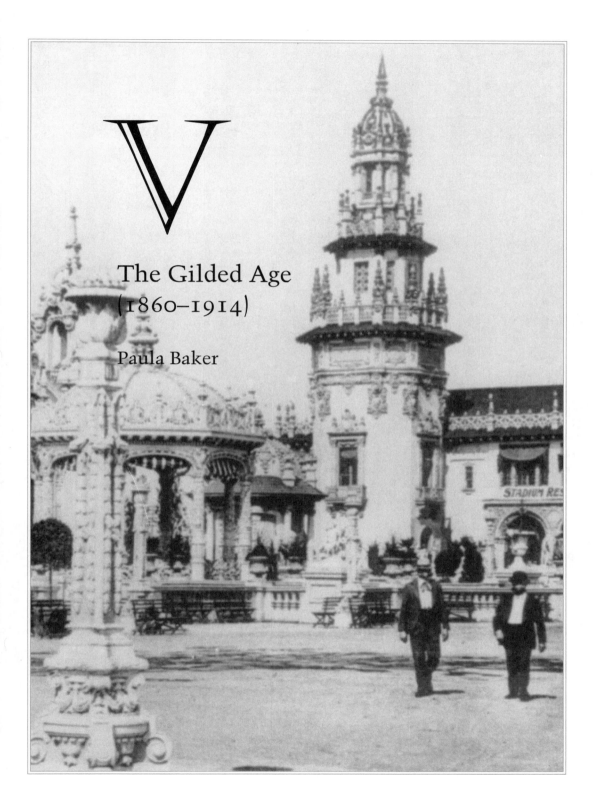

V

The Gilded Age
(1860–1914)

Paula Baker

25

New York during the Civil War and Reconstruction

A CROWD NUMBERING PERHAPS A QUARTER MILLION PEOPLE gathered in Union Square on April 20, 1861, to proclaim their support for the Union. William Evarts, a New York City Republican and lawyer, had considered organizing a mass meeting immediately after the firing upon Fort Sumter eight days earlier had made war certain between North and South. Evarts had feared an embarrassingly sparse turnout, but in a week's time the city was swept up in pro-Union feeling. Marchers representing the trades and voluntary organizations paraded to the square. In between selections of martial tunes performed by numerous brass bands, twenty speakers condemned the lawless acts of southern secessionists to the cheers of the crowd. The audience saved their wildest approval for Major Robert Anderson and his men, just back from Fort Sumter, who brought with them symbols of southern treachery: the Sumter flag and shattered flagstaff. Surveying the scene from a balcony, Jane Woolsey, a young upper-class New Yorker, commented, "Now we don't feel that the social fabric is falling to pieces at all, but that it is getting gloriously mended."

New Yorkers—and people throughout the North—had reason to be concerned about the "social fabric" of the state, especially of New York City. Myriad divisions set New Yorkers against one another and seemed to be heightened in the tense months between the election of Abraham Lincoln in 1860 and the fall of Fort Sumter. Class conflicts commonly figured in the political and economic life of the state's large cities. Compounding tensions among classes were divisions within them: the state's economic elite, for example, was hardly of a single mind on the war, party and policy, and how best to defuse conflicts with the working classes. Class tensions overlapped with ethnic and religious strife, as Protestants and mostly poor and working-class Catholics clashed politically and culturally, and natives remained wary of immigrants. Racial distinctions also divided New Yorkers, although the state was overwhelmingly white. The long-standing mutual suspicions of urban and rural residents also impeded unity. Sometimes containing and channeling, and sometimes whipping up these divisions, were the political parties, themselves often factionalized. Yet for a few days at least, all these fissures seemed to dissolve. The often warring political and economic elite—even those like New York City Mayor Fernando Wood, who had only recently proposed that the city withdraw from the Union to become a "free city"—pulled together in order to raise volunteers and funds for the cause.

Unity, however, did not last long. In New York, as in the rest of the Union, public feeling about the war followed the fortunes of the Union army. With every defeat, support for President Lincoln and sometimes for the war itself fell. State Republican politicians divided on Lincoln's policies and virtues as a leader, and Democrats differed about whether the war should be continued. Some poor and working-class Irish, feeling themselves to be victims of a fight to free the slaves, opposed the war and participated in the draft riots of 1863. The war made some New Yorkers rich, but inflation and increased taxes added economic hardship to the terror, or the pain, of losing a brother, husband, or father. Union victory in 1865 did not soothe the conflicts exacerbated by the war. Instead, it added new issues and raised new questions. If the federal government could exercise relatively sweeping powers during the war and Reconstruction, what else might government accomplish? Workers looked to the state for laws limiting the working day; various reformers saw the opportunity to enlarge state power in education, public health and welfare, and other areas; middle- and upper-class women's participation in the war encouraged them to expand their roles in public life. Not surprisingly, national issues commanded an unusual amount of attention during the Civil War and Reconstruction years, and national issues had state and local ramifications. The period's unsettled politics would carry through the rest of the nineteenth century.

New York in 1860

Even as national issues and decisions affected New York, New York events affected the nation, if only because it was the most populous and richest state in the Union. Census takers counted 3,880,735 people in New York in 1860, nearly 800,000 more than in 1850 and almost one million ahead of the next most populated state, Pennsylvania. Although the Panic of 1857 slowed immigration, as would the Civil War, immigrants accounted for much of the population gain. About one-quarter of the state's population was foreign born in 1860.

The proportion was higher in some cities: in 1870, nearly 45 percent of New York City's and 37 percent of Brooklyn's population were foreign born. Ireland sent the largest number; the migration of Irish men and, increasingly, women to the United States, Canada, Australia, and elsewhere would continue through the early twentieth century. The German states accounted for the next largest group. Only in Chautauqua County did groups other than the Irish or Germans—Swedes and Norwegians—constitute a substantial proportion of the population. Among the native born, African Americans formed roughly 2 percent of the total population, while slightly more than five thousand Native Americans lived in New York, mostly in the western and northern parts of the state.

Both the foreign and native born swelled the population of the state's cities. Between 1850 and 1860, Brooklyn grew by 64 percent, Buffalo by 48 percent, and New York City by 37 percent. Troy, Oswego, Newburgh, and Rochester all increased their population by more than one-quarter. In the 1860s the state incorporated new cities, including Cohoes, Binghamton, Lockport, Newburgh, Ogdensburg, and Watertown. These newly minted cities excited the ambitions of boosters elsewhere who dreamed of the industry, railroad, or state institution that would push their villages into larger and more splendid places. Although the 1860s and early 1870s were some of the best years economically on New York's farms, the population of many rural counties was stagnant or even declining between 1850 and 1860. By 1870, more rural counties had lost population, as some residents moved to cities or farther west. Immigrants did not replace the departing native born: in the most extreme case, in 1860 less than 3 percent of the residents of rural Schoharie County had been born outside of the United States, and that proportion dropped by 1870.

Although it was the pride of boosters, urban expansion in the 1850s and 1860s made for crowded and unhealthy conditions. Numerous families jammed into apartments in airless tenements that lacked all sanitary facilities. Those who lived in basement apartments not only lacked adequate air and light but also risked diseases borne by waste when outdoor privies backed up. New York and other cities grew without a plan: builders erected houses beyond the points where city services like streets existed; slaughterhouses operated next door to residential buildings. People tolerated such urban squalor because cities offered more work and, for some, fabulous opportunities.

The value of New York's manufactured goods was the highest in the nation, and the state was second to Pennsylvania in the number of its manufacturing establishments. In value, the products of its flour mills, most prominent in Rochester but also located in Albany and Buffalo, led the list of the state's manufactures. Drawing on midwestern wheat through the Great Lakes and Erie Canal and to a lesser extent from western New York farms, New York processed more flour than any other state. The textile industry was important throughout the Mohawk Valley: in Utica, Amsterdam, Mohawk, and Johnstown, workers

An 1880s trade card for Warner's Safe Yeast, which was manufactured in Rochester. New York State Historical Association, Cooperstown, N.Y.

made carpets, gloves, and woolen and cotton cloth. Furniture makers located in Chautauqua County villages such as Jamestown; leather, paper, packaging, lumber, and lumber products sustained villages in northern New York and towns elsewhere.

New York City still maintained some major manufacturing establishments, especially shipbuilders, and remained the nation's leading manufacturing center, but as the cost of land increased, manufacturing shifted to smaller, more labor-intensive businesses like the garment industry. As a premier port city and important financial center, New York also was home to insurance companies, importers, and banks and brokerage houses that were the cornerstone of the nation's financial system. Printing and publishing were other major industries. Providing services to residents and visitors created jobs in bakeries, butcher shops, and small stores. In retail there were also grand dry-goods stores like A. T. Stewart's and Macy's. At least five hundred brothels catered to all classes; their profits exceeded those of any industry except the garment trade in the 1860s. Linked in various ways to prostitution were other amusements: fine hotels, theaters, minstrel shows, working-class theaters, numerous saloons and beer gardens, and the streets.

New York had suffered through the Panic of 1857 but had largely recovered by 1860. The prosperity of New York City and other areas in the state stemmed, in part, from the southern trade. Banks lent money to cotton growers; New York shippers carried goods between the North and South and also to Europe and Great Britain; manufacturers of inexpensive textiles and clothing (as well as luxury items) sold to southern markets. But the state's and city's financial future was based as much on the western United States and overseas trade as it was on the South. Making the most of natural and man-made transportation advantages—rail, canal, and deep water port—New York was a wealthy state.

How rich is hard to calculate exactly. According to the census, the state's real and personal property was worth around $1.4 billion, or 12 percent of the national total. But the census provided another statistic—the "true" value of New Yorkers' property, and that was over $1.8 billion. Even the "true" figure was vastly understated, and in that there is an often overlooked but important story. Like other states, New York relied on property taxes to fund local governments and, through much of the late nineteenth century, the state government as well. Personal as well as real property was supposed to be taxed, but personal property tended to be hidden from assessors; wealthy (and not so wealthy) people paid a fraction of what their personal property was worth, if they paid at all. Meanwhile, the state and local governments still needed to spend money to meet the demands of a growing population for streets, police, schools, public sanitation, and other services. Most of the tax burden fell on the increasingly unhappy owners of real property. The tax base, in short, was inadequate for the services that had to be provided. It was also inadequate for the needs of the leaders of the major parties, who looked to private sources—candidates, wealthy individuals, people holding public jobs, and businesses—to fund everything from campaigns and elections to the jobs that rewarded the faithful. Fiscal issues hardly gripped New Yorkers' attention as did slavery and the prospect of disunion, but financial questions figured into many of the social and political conflicts of the late nineteenth century.

New York's politics were muddled enough without nagging fiscal problems. The Democratic party produced much of the confusion. New York City could roll up large Democratic majorities, but no Democratic faction could fully control the party. Various "Democracies"—McKeon Democrats (named after their leader, John McKeon), Mozart Hall Democrats and Tammany Democrats (named after their meeting places), and Young Democrats (so named to signify their emphasis on new issues)—appeared and disappeared and divided the city's Democratic vote. These factions sometimes arose because of disagreements about policy: the "Young Democracy," for one, sought to move away from Tammany's reliance on race and toward economic issues. More often factionalism arose from personal and patronage disagreements. Republican leaders also had to balance factions: chiefly the more radical group—former Free Soil Democrats led by Horace Greeley—and the more moderate wing—former Whigs headed by

William H. Seward and, with diminishing force, Thurlow Weed. To run a successful campaign, party leaders had to devise ways to "harmonize" the various factions.

Yet beyond the sight of the state's politicians, voters had settled into a reasonably stable pattern of allegiances to the Republicans and Democrats by 1860. The pattern was not tidy, as it reflected the many divisions in a diverse state. It was, in part, an upstate and downstate split. Although there were reliable Democratic cities and counties upstate (mostly along the Hudson River Valley), the Republican party counted on upstate votes, together with Democratic disunity, to offset Democratic strength in New York City and Brooklyn. For some groups, ethnic and religious loyalties translated into party loyalties. Irish Catholics were reliably Democratic, as were descendants of "old Dutch" families; New England migrants and their sons were attracted to the Republican party. Both parties won their share of German voters, though Germans also showed an independent streak in New York City politics. The major parties created coalitions of working-class, middle-class, and wealthy voters, so no simple class division aligned voters between the parties. But this did not mean that class was absent from politics: ethnicity, religion, and class were interwoven, for example, in tensions between working-class Irish Catholic Democrats and middle- and upper-middle-class Protestant Republicans. And while earlier labor parties had faded by 1860, new parties that emphasized class issues would emerge later. Finally, purely local patterns of settlement and animosity shaped the loyalties of other voters. Yet, despite its complexity, a relatively stable partisan alignment of voters had replaced the chaos in the electorate of the 1850s.

A little instability went a long way, however. Under normal circumstances, the margin between regular Democratic and Republican strength was slight, which made for extremely hard-fought campaigns. At times, party workers turned to straightforwardly corrupt tactics: intimidating voters, buying votes, and stuffing ballot boxes. But 1860 was not a normal year. The outcome in New York mattered even more than usual, since the Republicans could not win the presidency without the state. Most New York Republicans had hoped to nominate Seward, but they swallowed their disappointment and supported Lincoln. Democrats came into the election more divided than usual. In addition to the standard differences over patronage and local matters, the national division between northerners who endorsed Stephen A. Douglas as a pro-Union moderate and southerners who supported John C. Breckinridge as a states' rights nominee entered into state politics. Worse, a coalition led chiefly by former Know Nothing politicians drew up a slate of Constitutional Unionist electors for John Bell. Some New York Democrats, led by Mayor Fernando Wood and including some of the poorest Irish Catholic immigrants and wealthiest merchants, sought to tie the state to Breckinridge. Wood himself engaged in a series of bewildering maneuvers attempting to gain control of the state party and to throw the election into the United States House of Representatives. The various anti-Lincoln factions did not combine until October, and then only partially. They drew up a slate of presidential electors divided among Douglas, Breckinridge, and Bell, and different factions offered their own candidates for lesser offices. The election was a Republican triumph, with Lincoln losing New York City but winning the state with 53.7 percent of the vote. Republican Edwin D. Morgan won another term as governor. Even at the city level, Tammany managed to elect only one candidate.

These returns seemed to reflect a united Republican party and divided Democrats, but one ballot question demonstrated the opposite. In 1860, as in 1846, New York voters were asked to decide whether to amend the state's constitution and lift the property restriction on suffrage that applied only to African American men. The ballot question was hardly the only issue important to voters in 1860, but African Americans worked hard for the amendment: they held a free suffrage convention, organized speakers, and formed suffrage clubs, including forty-eight in New York City alone. But as Frederick Douglass sadly remarked, Republicans and even some abolitionists ignored the amendment. Republican newspapers typically claimed that black suffrage was not a party issue. Other Republican editors assured their readers that their party did not favor "social equality." If Republican spokesmen ducked the question to preserve their chances at the polls, Democratic partisans, for neither the first nor the last time, used the race card to build unity and support. Democrats, they said, "demand emancipation for the white man of the State" while Republicans "in every speech dwell upon the eternal negro." Without Democratic intercession, some party leaders warned, blacks would take jobs and political power away from deserving whites. From there, in keeping with the racist stereotype, a newspaper claimed "The negroes of Five Points . . . will be privileged to take on their arms the palefaced beauties of the Caucasian race in the city of New York." Almost all Democrats were among the 63.3 percent of New York voters who turned down the amendment. Yet the clear majority could not have been won without Republican votes. Republican divisions on questions about the fate of slavery and African Americans and Democratic unanimity on white rights would be important in many political struggles through the Civil War and Reconstruction years.

Preparations and War

Uncertainty and a desperate search for alternatives to war marked the months between Lincoln's election and the attack on Fort Sumter. Governor Morgan called upon the North as well as the South to exercise moderation; in a letter to President-Elect Lincoln in December he even suggested that the United States buy Cuba, which might satisfy southern expansionist ambitions. In his annual address Morgan argued that states did not have the right to secede, but he still pursued compromises, such as asking the state legislature to repeal the state's personal liberty law. Horace Greeley, the mercurial editor of the influential *New York Tribune*, proposed that the South be allowed to secede in order to avoid war—one point on his erratic path of positions on northern policy. New York merchants, concerned about the nation's economic future as well as their own, urged sectional reconciliation at a mass meeting; Thurlow Weed imagined that a people's convention might succeed in averting a crisis where politicians had failed.

Even more than Republicans, Democrats looked for some compromise that could avert war. New York City Democrats held a mass meeting which urged Lincoln to ignore the abolitionists (identified as the source of the trouble) and not antagonize the South. The Democratic *Albany Argus*, in a variation on Wood's idea of a free city, recommended that New York claim independence and form a new federation that included the West and Midwest. But Fort Sumter settled matters. President Lincoln called upon the loyal states for 75,000 troops, asking for seventeen regiments and 13,180 men from New York. Lincoln's preparations for war brought an enthusiastic response in New York, just as it did across the North. The New York legislature authorized the organization of forty regiments, 30,000 men to fill them, and $3 million (to be paid back by the federal government) for the men and their supplies. The number of volunteers surpassed the apparent military need. Private citizens contributed another $35 million in the form of loans to the federal government. In the wake of the Union Square meeting, organizers raised an additional $15 million in the city.

There were men and money but also confusion. No mechanism existed to organize the crush of volunteers and resources. Some men signed three-month enlistments; others signed on for two or three years, or the duration of the war. And while the federal government called for troops, early on it could not provide them with arms and other supplies. The state, meanwhile, only had 8,000 weapons (many of them useless) for the first 20,000 volunteers. The sudden demand launched a bidding war for arms among the states which spanned both domestic and European manufacturers. The process of raising regiments was also tangled. The state raised regiments, but so did individuals and groups. The rival Tammany Hall and Mozart Hall Democratic clubs showed their loyalty through their individual regiments; other regiments drew together German, Polish, and French New Yorkers, while the Garibaldi Guard incorporated Italians, Croats, Hungarians, French, and Spaniards. Individuals with a taste for adventure and publicity—among them Democratic Congressman Daniel Sickles and former Lincoln law clerk Elmer Ellsworth—also received approval for their regiments. At this point, however, the federal government rejected efforts to raise African American regiments.

At the Battle of Cross Keys in western Virginia in June 1862, this artillery battery was composed entirely of Buffalo residents of German descent. Lithograph by R. Buerger. Buffalo and Erie County Historical Society.

The confusion resulting from the mix of state, federal, local, and individual control was only gradually, unevenly, and partially resolved in favor of federal leadership. Authority was divided even within New York, as final control was not lodged in any part of state government. Conflicts over authority showed in the sometimes rocky relationships between voluntary organizations—among them the United States Sanitary Commission, the Union League, and the Women's Central Association of Relief, all led by wealthy New Yorkers with Republican ties—and the state and, at times, the federal government.

Despite the logistical problems, however, New York would provide the largest number of men for the Union armies. Money was perhaps as important as men, and New York City banks, as the nation's financial center, had to be rallied behind the war effort. If volunteers rushed forward at first, the bankers were more circumspect. United States Secretary of the Treasury Salmon P. Chase sent representatives to meet with the city's leading bankers early in the war to reassure them about the Union's management of the war and to discuss terms for loans. The bankers agreed that a consortium of New York, Boston, and Philadelphia banks would loan $50 million to the federal government (with New York picking up $35 million of that) at 7.3 percent interest (when other plausible investments returned around 5 percent). The federal government could, if necessary, borrow another $100 million under the same terms.

It was not simply putting profits above patriotism that held back the bankers. Some bankers opposed any deal, since the federal government had no plans for taxes to defray the costs of the war, which meant that inflation would surely devour any investment in federal notes. The onset of the war produced a business and banking panic. Banks could not collect debts owed by southerners, and uncertainty produced a run on gold, with $3.5 million withdrawn from the banks in ten days. Serious questions about the northern economy—especially in importing, but also in firms that relied on southern trade—shut down businesses. From there, dockworkers were thrown out of work, and women in the garment trades lost jobs. Unemployment remained high through the summer of 1861, and the Workingmen's Union of New York City called for public works spending to put men back to work. The families of volunteers also experienced hardship. Wives of new soldiers marched on City Hall in New York City to highlight their difficulties; unless granted relief they threatened to urge men to stay out of the Union army. New York City installed a relief program, as did the private Union Defense Committee: wives received $3 per week, as well as $1 for a first child and 50 cents for additional children.

The initial economic shock, however, lifted by the fall of 1861, and the wartime recovery was on. Demand for the produce of New York farms expanded. Towns like Ilion (home of the largest Remington rifle plant) grew with the demand for guns. Soon textile mills upstate and the garment industry in New York City had as much work as they could handle. Indeed, for both the corrupt and the merely opportunistic, the war presented once-in-a-lifetime opportunities. J. Pierpont Morgan and his associates turned healthy profits reselling previously rejected arms to the federal government. Others profited more honestly if just as handsomely from government contracts. The war expanded New York's industries and confirmed its leading place in the national economy.

Support and Dissent

The first battle of the Civil War doused the initial euphoria that greeted the call to arms. Some enthusiastic northerners, including Horace Greeley, could scarcely wait for the engagement which would be, no doubt, the first step on the triumphal march to Richmond, the Confederate capital. Indeed, the early reports in New York about the first battle of Bull Run (Manassas) on July 21, 1861, hailed a great Union victory. The late newspaper editions reversed the score, to the dismay of many New Yorkers: Bull Run turned out to be an embarrassing, disorganized northern retreat. Adding further insult to the defeat, one unit consisting of men from New York who had enlisted for three months refused to fight as they were near the end of their service. Bull Run inspired a rush of selling on Wall Street. It also sent some Unionists into despair. Greeley moaned in a letter to President Lincoln that "we are utterly disgracefully routed, beaten, whipped," and wondered whether the Union should sue for peace. Others were exasperated with Lincoln, his administration, and the Union generals. But to calmer assessors, Bull Run indicated that the war would not be short or painless. Lincoln ordered the induction of more three-year men and sought to raise more funds.

The pattern of elation and despair evidenced by northern reaction to Bull Run would be repeated throughout the war. New Yorkers, like other northerners, rode the tremendous highs and lows, as civilians followed news of the war closely in daily and extra editions of city newspapers. Yet if many New Yorkers hung on the news, they did so for different reasons and remained divided over the wisdom and meaning of the Union cause. New Yorkers' views of the war shaped the state's politics and social relations. They also mattered nationally, especially because of New York's reputation as a state given to lukewarm support for the war, if not outright southern sympathies. National events influenced everything from the moods of individuals to party fortunes, just as some developments in New York had national consequences.

On an individual level, George Templeton Strong's reactions to events illustrate the ebb and flow of confidence in the Union and its leaders. Strong, a wealthy New York City attorney and a member of numerous elite groups that supported the war, is perhaps the northern equivalent of South Carolina's Mary Chesnut: quotable, opinionated, and a careful follower of events. He never trusted Lincoln's competence, and he lost patience as his doubts deepened in 1862 after the second battle of Bull Run: Lincoln did not measure up to the job, and his only notable trait in Strong's view was his "fertility of smutty stories." By Gettysburg, Strong had become more hopeful about the Union effort. "The result of this victory is priceless," he wrote. "The Army of the Potomac has at last found a general that can handle it, and has stood nobly up to its terrible work in spite of his long disheartening list of hard fought failures." Hope had not dulled Strong's critical sense, however. When Confederate forces under Jubal Early threatened Washington in July 1864 while the Union siege of Petersburg dragged on, Strong commented that "I see no bright spot anywhere, only humiliation and disaster." Only the capture of Atlanta in September 1864, "the greatest event of the war," calmed his fears of a Union defeat.

National politics and the course of the war—themselves connected— moved many New Yorkers besides Strong and from there affected state politics. Successful party leaders in Civil War–era New York had to maneuver quickly: wartime events and their impact on public sentiment demanded frequent reassessment of political strategies. With the rush of patriotism at the beginning of the war, most leaders of both parties believed wisdom lay in minimizing both intraparty squabbling and interparty competition. Thus in 1861 most Republican activists and Democrats in favor of vigorous prosecution of the war united behind a "People's Union" ticket for the minor offices that were at stake. It easily defeated a separate Democratic slate constructed by those who believed that democracy required party competition even in wartime and had misgivings about the war.

Such nonpartisan cooperation could not last, because party men differed about the purpose, wisdom, and conduct of the war and also maneuvered to advance their factions. The Democratic party typically took a complicated position: it supported the war and opposed the illegal act of secession but hoped for a political settlement and denounced the Lincoln administration for its unconstitutional grab for expanded executive power. But even a position that complex could not cover all the factions at all times. The timeworn division between upstate (or Regency) and downstate Democrats (divided largely between the Tammany Hall and Mozart Hall organizations) persisted through the war, and the factionalism itself grew worse. Most pro-administration Democrats—the War Democrats like John Dix and the merchant A. T. Stewart—sometimes joined forces with Republican factions in state elections, while the downstate Mozart faction's criticism of Lincoln was boundless and vituperative. Other Democrats, usually Tammanyites and much of the Albany Regency leadership, tried to balance maintaining a distinctive Democratic party and patriotic support for the Union. They often focused on legalities, such as the questionable extension of national power, rather than racism or the evils of the war.

Republican leaders split largely into two groups, with the status of African Americans as the main line of division. "Conservatives," identified with Thurlow Weed, worried about the political effects of emancipation and sometimes allied with War Democrats. Horace Greeley and other abolitionists comprised the "radical" faction. They sought to further federal power and called for abolition early and often. The party as a whole hedged its bets. James S. Wadsworth, a Union general, former Free Soil Democrat, and Republican candidate for governor in 1862, assured voters that they should not fear a slave rebellion and crowds of freedmen coming north to compete with white workers for jobs, as they preferred the South with its "congenial climate and vast tracts of land."

These factions emerged, disappeared, and reconstituted themselves under the tug of events. The election of 1862 mostly went the Democrats' way. A string of military failures deepened doubts about ultimate Union victory. President Lincoln's suspension of the writ of habeas corpus and his threat to institute a draft if enough volunteers did not appear confirmed the fears of those concerned with runaway federal power. The preliminary Emancipation Proclamation issued in September 1862 signaled that now the war had a new purpose—ending slavery, not merely restoring the Union—which disturbed conservatives. In 1862 efforts to put together a bipartisan ticket failed, and the Republican gubernatorial convention nominated Geneseo's James Wadsworth while the Democrats turned to Horatio Seymour, a former governor satisfactory to most factions. Democratic campaigners hammered on the themes of the federal threat to traditional liberties and the folly of emancipation. Sensing the Lincoln administration's unpopularity, Republicans sought to distance their party from it and instead charged the Democrats with disloyalty that deepened the war. Cassius M. Clay, the Kentucky abolitionist, proclaimed that "the hanging of such men as Seymour and Wood would have saved thousands of lives." Seymour defeated Wadsworth in the governor's race, and Democrats took half of the state Assembly seats. Seventeen Democrats won congressional seats; the winners included men accused of copperhead sympathies such as Fernando Wood, Benjamin Wood, and James Brooks. Only fourteen Republicans emerged with victories.

National events shaped this election. Although some Republicans blamed their party's defeat on the disfranchisement of Union soldiers, the outcome would have been the same even if all soldiers had voted Republican. Swings that followed the fate of Union forces more than party loyalties mattered to enough voters to give the Democrats the victory. As the *Tribune* editorialized, "general dissatisfaction with the slow or no progress of our Armies, a wide-spread feeling that, through the incapacity of our military leaders, the blood and treasure of the loyal millions are being sacrificed" had soured the electorate on the Republican party.

In turn, New York's election results had national implications. Leaders of both parties understood the results in New York to be a measure of public confidence in the war and Lincoln's policies. The news was not good for Republicans: Democratic gains in New York, along with similar returns in other northern states, seemed to indicate that time was running out on the Lincoln administration. The new Democrats in New York's congressional delegation and the possibility that the state might also send a Democratic senator to Washington only made matters worse.

Yet voting was not the only way New Yorkers demonstrated their attitudes toward the war, nor was it the only measure of the impact of war on the state. Other forms of participation were arguably more important than elections. Participation took many forms, from the organization of voluntary groups to riots, and mobilized citizens other than the white males who constituted almost the entire electorate.

The support of African Americans for the war never wavered with the news from the battlefields. An example of this commitment was the protracted struggle to organize black regiments in New York State. From the firing on Fort Sumter, many African Americans wanted a part in what they saw as a war against slavery. In 1861 the local *Anglo-African Magazine* called for black men to organize and arm, as the "South must be subjugated or [free blacks] shall be enslaved." Frederick Douglass urged that "THE SLAVES AND FREE COLORED PEOPLE BE CALLED INTO SERVICE AND FORMED INTO A LIBERATING ARMY." Lincoln, Secretary of War Simon Cameron, and Governor Morgan received assurances that "colored regiments, armed and equipped, [are] ready for immediate service" and could be maintained "at private expense." Yet early in the war no northern states organized African American units, and Lincoln and Cameron, concerned about reactions in loyal border states, approved this choice. Lincoln reconsidered his position as the war went on, and by the time of the Emancipation Proclamation in 1863, he was ready to use black troops if only for the psychological effect they might have on the South. By then, however, New York had a Democratic governor, and Seymour refused the offers of African Americans to fight, even as the state failed to meet its troop quota and as black men signed up to serve in neighboring states.

Political calculations—holding the fragile Democratic coalition together—figured into his decision, but so did racism. Arming African Americans, Seymour said in the 1862 campaign, would bring "butchery of women and children, . . . scenes of lust and rapine, of arson and murder unparalleled in the history of the world." Late in 1863, however, African Americans secured federal permission to organize a regiment, and then two more. In less than sixty days, 2,300 African Americans volunteered; by the end of the war a total of 4,125 men enlisted out of a total eligible population of roughly 9,000. Fourteen percent died in the war.

White women were not struggling against the bonds of slavery (although some were fond of such rhetoric), but some saw unparalleled opportunities in the war for advancing their causes and political influence. For Josephine Shaw Lowell, and no doubt other young, middle-class women with abolitionist ties, the early 1860s were "extraordinary times and splendid to live in." Such women seized the opportunity to press forward their political ideas. For the most radical—largely woman suffragists and abolitionists—there was the National Women's Loyal League, founded in New York City in May 1863. Members ran petition drives aimed at pushing Lincoln further along an antislavery direction. Some of these women went on to work for the political rights and the improved material conditions of freedmen and women, especially through education. "A new field has opened to us," claimed the Rochester Ladies' Anti-Slavery Society in 1863, as its members looked forward to "comforting, cheering, advising, educating the *freed* men, women and children of the race upon whom . . . the chains seemed so securely fastened." Others took part in the war by serving as nurses, which left them proud of their hard work and efforts to bring order out of chaos but uneasy with the sentimental "mother" or "angel" image that their role as female nurses reinforced.

Politically well connected and less radical women engaged in even more visible brands of activism in support of the war. A case in point was the Woman's Central Association of Relief, organized in New York City. Its initial call early in 1861 was signed by women with such familiar surnames as Raymond, Astor, Roosevelt, Cooper, Bellows, and Fish, while younger, equally well-placed women such as Josephine Shaw Lowell, Louisa Lee Schuyler, and

Affluent society women of New York City met at the Cooper Institute in April 1861 to organize the Woman's Central Association of Relief. From *Frank Leslie's Illustrated Newspaper*, May 4, 1861.

Georgeanna Woolsey did most of the day-to-day work. The association's members provided supplies to the army, trained and sent nurses and agents to battlefield hospitals, and established chapters to help systematize the flow of aid. They attracted most attention through their spectacular fundraising fairs. One, held in Long Island and Brooklyn, raised $400,000; the largest of all, in New York City, featured imported luxury items and brought in $2 million from wealthy donors. More important in the long run, however, was the ideology the association attached to its work. These women vigorously rejected older ideas about benevolence that emphasized sentiment, religiosity, and female self-sacrifice. Expert guidance, science, and system had to replace well-intentioned giving. "Numerous societies, working without concert, organization, or head . . . are likely to waste their enthusiasm in disproportionate efforts," argued one of their early publications. These women stressed the superiority of their business methods and centralized organization. Not all of this went down easily among women attached to the older ethic of benevolence: upstate chapters sometimes rebelled, preferring to give directly to "their" regiments and to retain local autonomy. But the new scientific ideal presaged a lasting change in charitable work.

The new commitment to science in charitable work was shared by some elite men who supported the war but were frustrated by what they saw as incompetence in the state and federal governments. Henry Bellows, pastor of New York City's First Unitarian Church, and other elite Republicans were unimpressed with the ability of the army's Medical Service to prevent needless loss of life through proper sanitary conditions and medical care. Bellows's first step was to support the Woman's Central Association of Relief. Going further, in May 1861, he and a group of New York City doctors went to Washington to propose that the army work with the Sanitary Commission—a private organization that would furnish medical supplies, inspect camps, advise military doctors, and organize nurses. Its services would be free to the government, since its officers would be paid by private contributions. Both sides were distrustful—the army of civilian meddlers and Bellows and his group of the army's competence—but the Sanitary Commission functioned throughout the war as a quasi-governmental agency that exemplified the mix of public and private and state and local authority during the period. The commission also advanced the same ideals of tough-minded action and science and system that benevolent women promoted. Members of the Sanitary Commission feared that both well-meaning civilians and even the army, riven as it was by politics, lacked the necessary system and discipline. They would try to infuse the same ideology into postwar public life.

An even purer articulation of this dual attitude of distrust for partisan politics and faith in centralized power was furnished by the Union League. Some 350 men, appalled by the election of Seymour and moved by a strong belief in the war, formed the club early in 1863. Their ambitions went well beyond a single election and even the war. Their concern was to promote nationalism over what they saw as narrow sectionalism and blind partisanship. The league, according to Frederick Law Olmsted—the landscape architect and former head of the United States Sanitary Commission—was a "true American aristocracy" that could lead in building new institutions to bind a society divided by class, ethnicity, and race and create a powerful, centralized, Christian state. The members' nationalism shaded into nativism. Publicly and privately, some of them complained about the number and quality of immigrants entering the country, especially the Irish. They sought a paternalistic relationship with the working classes, in which honest, native-born laborers would sensibly follow elite guidance.

One of the Union League's most notable projects during the war was the assistance it provided blacks in raising an African American regiment. As a contrast to the immigrant working class, some Union League members acclaimed African Americans as models of patriotism and hard work. Inevitably, the league's championing of African Americans further aroused the suspicions of much of the white working classes toward the organization and its agenda.

Here was an explosive combination: a pro-war Republican elite, male and female, with an aggressive social agenda; a Democratic political elite troubled by both the war and the broader changes sought by Republicans; restive working classes, many hostile to Republican paternalism if not the war—all in the context of racial tension. The eruption came in July 1863. The occasion was the federal government's decision to institute a draft. For some time, there had been few true volunteers, and cities and states offered bounties to meet their quotas of men. As the war dragged on and the demand for men grew, the draft seemed to be the only answer. The federal government conducted a census to determine the number of eligible men and to identify the places where enlistments fell below the quotas. Federal officials then drew names in each congressional district at random. There were loopholes, however. Men engaged in certain essential lines of work gained exemptions, and, most controversial, a man could buy a substitute for $300.

Republicans in New York cheered the draft as a step demanded by military necessity. Moreover, many of them suspected that Democrats, especially in New York City, had avoided service up until then. Democrats instantly fought the introduction of the draft. Supporters of the war like Samuel Tilden and Governor Seymour hunted for legal means to block the draft. These "loyal" Democrats believed it was unconstitutional; they also argued that the procedure was flawed. The census was inaccurate, since it overcounted in New York City because of the large transient population. New York City was not given credit for many of its men who had enlisted, since some had been lured upstate or to other states that offered more generous bounties. Peace Democrats, associated with Mozart Hall, immediately denounced the draft as unfair: it was a scheme to sacrifice poor white men and Democrats. Racism was never far absent from these arguments. According to Benjamin Wood, brother of Fernando and editor of the Democratic *Daily News*, the draft "would compel the white laborer to leave his family destitute and unprotected while he goes forth to free the negro, who, being free, will compete with him in labor."

Such rhetoric—and even the division among elites—hardly helped matters, but working-class New Yorkers did not need the guidance of Democratic politicians. Some were already plainly unhappy with the financial costs of the war. Wages had not come close to meeting inflation. By mid-1863, prices had gone up 43 percent since 1860 according to one estimate, while wages had risen only 12 percent. Although many working-class men saw themselves just as patriotic as any member of the Union League, others distrusted the war and the Republicans who sought to represent it as a crusade against slavery or for the primacy of national over state power. Then there were existing racial hatreds, now bound up with the war, the Union League, and its agenda. Some white waterfront workers early in 1863 had attacked and nearly lynched two African Americans who lived near the docks. African American men seemed not only competitors for jobs but threats to a way of life.

On Saturday, July 11, names were drawn without incident, but that Monday those employed at many of the city's factories, shops, and construction sites failed to show up for work. Instead they marched to the Ninth District Provost Marshal's office on Third Avenue, urging other workers to join them on their way. They also cut telegraph poles, pulled up railway tracks, and beat policemen. Later that morning, members of Black Joke Engine Company No. 33, angered that firemen did not receive draft exemptions, entered the provost marshal's office, broke the selection wheel, set fire to the building, and pummeled a deputy provost marshal who tried to get the firemen to fight the fire. One hour later, federal officials suspended the draft in New York City.

With this incident, a week of rioting began. On July 13, the rioters were a diverse lot, including skilled and unskilled workers, men and women, and people of different nationalities. Their targets usually bore a relationship to the draft: the site where its names were to be drawn, the elite Republicans who supported conscription, and public officials who enforced it. Some of the early participants were satisfied with this display and the temporary suspension of the draft, but events soon moved beyond their control. The riots became more the work of unskilled workers and the Irish and were less strictly focused on the draft. Male and female rioters set fire to houses where police were rumored to be hiding, attacked police, and ransacked the houses of prominent Republicans. Along with those symbols of authority, African Americans continued to be a main target. Groups of men and boys burned the Colored Orphan Asylum on Fifth Avenue and tenements where blacks lived. Wild gangs, with the approval of large crowds, beat, mutilated, lynched, burned, and drowned African American men. The connections between the rioters' targets and the draft and the war grew more vague as the riot went on: they attacked brothels and German, Jewish, and Chinese persons and their property. By the end of the week, the battle had shifted to the defense of neighborhoods against the police and military forces brought in to quell the riot. In the end perhaps as many as 119 people were dead, including 82 rioters; 178 soldiers and 128 civilians were injured; and $1.5 million worth of property had been lost. Later 450 men and women were arrested; 81 were tried, and 67 were convicted.

If the riot revealed massive conflicts among New Yorkers, so did efforts to deal with its consequences. Some of the early rioters, including the firemen, joined efforts to restore order as soon as Monday evening. Working-class Germans, too, participated in block watches to protect property. Divisions among elite New Yorkers also reemerged. Some Union League members hoped to see martial law declared, the rioters punished severely, and the city brought under military control—with luck under Benjamin Butler, a New England abolitionist and general famous for his ironfisted control of Union-occupied New Orleans. In the meantime Union Leaguers became the core of the Committee of Merchants for the Relief of Colored People Suffering from the Late Riot, which made a substantial amount of money available to African Americans to rebuild

A mob destroys the Provost Marshal's office in Manhattan during the draft riots of July 1863. From *Frank Leslie's Illustrated Newspaper*, July 25, 1863.

their lives in the city. Tammany politicians, as well as members of the Catholic hierarchy, hoped that their personal presence in troubled parts of the city would be enough to calm the revolt, and they believed that stopping the draft would end the disturbance. Lincoln rejected the pleas of Seymour and others to suspend the draft permanently—and also the pleas of those who urged military rule. The draft resumed, without violence, with a reduced number of men drawn from New York City. Despite Republican opposition, Tammany politicians on the New York City Board of Supervisors created a fund that gave men the money to buy substitutes and offered $300 bounties to those who signed in their places.

In the somewhat longer run, the riot left Tammany in control of the Democratic party in New York City. Peace Democrats still had an audience, but it was shrinking rapidly because they seemed associated with violence and treason. Tammany's gains did not translate into statewide power, however. Memories of the insurrection in New York City (and a smaller one in Troy), together with the war's turn in the Union's favor gave Republicans victories in the off-year elections of 1863. And things went nearly as well for the GOP in 1864. Military successes had done wonders for Lincoln's prospects for reelection, and even the normally fractious New York Republicans fell easily behind his candidacy. They also nominated former Free Soil Democrat Reuben E. Fenton of Chautauqua County for governor. On the Democratic side Seymour had once seemed a probable presidential nominee, but he withdrew his name from consideration. The New York delegation supported the eventual winner, General George McClellan. Despite his protests, Seymour received the Democratic gubernatorial nomination. The 1864 election campaign featured Democratic claims that another large draft was in the works, charges of corrupt electoral practices, and even a rumor about a pending rebel raid from Canada on Buffalo and Oswego. Lincoln and Fenton nonetheless carried the state, although not by much, and Fenton would enjoy substantial Republican majorities in the New York State Senate and Assembly. As testament to the fallout from the draft riot and the political independence of German voters, C. Godfrey Gunther, a previous Tammany nominee, defeated both a Republican and a combined Tammany-Mozart ticket in the mayor's race in New York City, running as the candidate of an independent Democratic faction.

One month after Lincoln took the oath of office for his second term, the war finally came to an end. People across New York State greeted the news with great celebrations, which were followed days later by public demonstrations of mourning after Lincoln's assassination. But the issues and conflicts within New York that the war highlighted persisted well after Appomattox. Class divisions—conflicts within and between classes—continued through the 1870s. Working-class organization and activism increased, while the state's political and economic elites renewed efforts, at times at cross-purposes, to maintain control. Women's organizations consolidated their wartime gains. A final consequence of the war for New York was financial. Coupled with spending on roads, bridges, public buildings, and other improvements, the payment of bounties doubled the state debt immediately after the war. Cities, towns, and counties more than matched the state's spending. Debt and the taxes to pay it formed the context for some of the subsequent conflicts among New Yorkers.

Reconstruction and the Uses of the State

One lesson Reconstruction taught Americans was the potential power of government. Yet ambitions to use the resources of government in New York collided with both political opposition and limits set by the state's economic circumstances. The state's economy had not only grown but had changed substantially during the first two-thirds of the nineteenth century. Agriculture was still important to it in the 1860s and 1870s, but industry, commerce, finance, and services now produced great fortunes as well as working- and middle-class jobs. Wealth also appeared in new forms. According to the historian Alfred Chandler, New York City by the 1850s had become "one of the largest and most sophisticated capital markets in the world," chiefly through innovations in marketing railroad securities. Railroad building demanded much more capital than earlier enterprises required, and Wall Street bond traders connected the railroads with both American and European investors. The expansion of the bond market was one sign of this complex economy, led by large financial institutions and corporations, unbounded by city or even state lines, and geared to services as much as or more than goods.

The tax system, however, was stuck in the early nineteenth century. More than three-quarters of the state's taxes came from real property. While the tax code also targeted personal property, as a state commission looking into the matter in 1870 put it, "the valuation of personal property for purpose of taxation generally, and in New York especially, is a mere semblance and a libel upon the intelligence and honesty of both those who enact and those who administer the laws." Personal property slipped by assessors and the state government was equally lax in catching new forms of wealth and profit, especially corporate profits. Years of practice, meanwhile, had failed to make assessments of real property anything but erratic. The value of the railroads' holdings varied from place to place from almost nothing to one-third of a town's total tax income, and individual assessments were just as bad. "In short," summarized the 1870 tax commission, "there cannot be found in a single instance in the whole state . . . where the law as respects valuation of real estate is fully complied with and where the oaths of assessors are not wholly inconsistent with the exact truth."

Uneven assessments and the narrow tax base might not have mattered but for the expansion of state and local spending. State debt, which hovered in the $25 million range in the 1840s and 1850s, shot up to more than $50 million in the mid-1860s. The bounty debt alone ran more than $20 million from 1865 to 1873. Cities and towns spent even more heavily for similar purposes: they contracted their own debts to cover the additional bounties they offered, the bridges, roads, and public buildings they constructed, and the subsidies they offered railroads as an inducement to pass through their boundaries. By 1867 local debts added up to more than twice the state debt. Since both the state and local governments taxed the same things, they placed a huge burden on real estate. This concerned some in state government—hence the investigation by the state tax commission in 1870; but their recommended reforms produced nothing, and the state simply raised tax rates. Cities and towns, meanwhile, forestalled taxpayer anger by following the railroads into the bond market. New York City sold millions of dollars worth of bonds in Europe and America for bounties and public improvements. This was a boon for city politicians, as bonded debt allowed them to spend where restive real property owners would have cramped their style. As an added bonus, bond funding extended city patronage to small, often Irish, contractors: firms could receive payment immediately instead of having to wait for tax collections, which only the largest could do. Bonded debt was a short-term solution, but for a time it offered benefits to investors, Tammany politicians, ethnic contractors, and owners of real property.

The mismatch between plans for government and the resources to accomplish them remained a nagging political problem through the rest of the century. It came to the surface in Democratic complaints about Republican spending and Republican charges about Democratic incompetence and urban corruption. It also appeared in farmers' petitions demanding a "fairer" system of taxation and in revolts by urban middle-class voters. Fiscal problems also loomed in the background of two major political conflicts in New York during Reconstruction: Republicans' attempts to expand state power, and the rise and fall of William Marcy Tweed's Tammany Hall. They would likewise figure in the efforts of organized farmers and workers to harness the power of the state in their interests.

As the historian James C. Mohr has put it, New York State Republicans saw New York City during the years immediately after the Civil War as a "surrogate South." If Radical Republicans in Congress gained control over federal policy toward the South, their counterparts in Albany largely marginalized the Weed faction and laid plans to reform New York City government using the state's power. It was a matter of both political arithmetic and ideological commitment. New York Republicans believed the party needed compelling state issues if it was to survive: running against the slave power forever would mean following the way of the Whigs. Republicans also hoped to break the lock the Democrats had over New York City. Finally, Radicals sought to apply some of the lessons of the war—especially how centralized power could achieve rationality, order, and efficiency—to the state.

The most successful Republican programs melded ideology and practical politics. In the 1865 legislative session, for example, Republicans proposed the reform of New York City's fire department. The volunteer force had been discredited by the draft riots and was believed to be inefficient. The Republican plan aimed to replace volunteers with a paid force, which would be supervised by a committee appointed by the governor. There was something here for nearly everyone: reduced risks for insurance companies; centralized, expert control for Radical Republicans and members of elite urban reform associations like the Citizens' Association founded at the end of the war; and a swipe at the fire companies that politically minded Republicans saw as adjuncts to Tammany Hall. It was an unbeatable combination, and after squabbling over the makeup of the commission, the state legislature passed the measure.

Republicans had similar success with the Metropolitan Board of Health, also aimed at New York City. This state-appointed board was to monitor public sanitation, with emergency powers, if need be, to enforce its rules. Legislation creating it passed in 1866, just in time for another appearance of cholera. The previous two epidemics had taken thousands of lives. This time an accurate understanding of the disease's cause, together with the board's energy in attacking the sources of its spread, minimized the death toll. Republicans then expanded the power of state government by enacting tenement inspection legislation in 1867. The law mandated standards covering ventilation, fire escapes, and drainage and sewer hookups for new construction; banned farm animals from the city, including the foraging pigs that had fascinated European visitors; and set fines for landlords who violated the new standards. The Republican legislature also expanded state support for education, which included giving the state's share of federal land-grant money to Cornell University. Republicans intended all this legislation both to do good and to attract new voters, especially working-class Democrats.

The Republican plan appeared to work during the years following the war. In the state Senate, usually Republican because of the overrepresentation of rural districts, the party held a 27–5 advantage in 1865; even in the Assembly it had a decisive 89–39 margin. That advantage widened in the election of 1866. Some Weed Republicans had joined the Democrats that year, and their defection gave the Radicals firmer control over the party. But Republican gains had more to do with national events than with any success the party had achieved in permanently winning new adherents on the basis of state policies. Andrew Johnson's unpopular conciliatory policies toward the South, the return of secessionists to public office, and the excesses of the "black codes" they enacted in the former Confederate states strengthened the position of Radical Republicans in Congress and throughout the North. Pushing momentary advantage, Republican leaders in New York tried to solidify their gains by drafting a new constitution. This marked the peak of Republican power in the state.

Since the delegates to the constitutional convention of 1867 were overwhelmingly Republican (61 percent) and Radical at that, it appeared that Republicans would have no trouble producing the document they wanted. All the Democrats could do was drag their feet—stalling by arguing about the number of delegates and meeting places and times and denying quorums by their absence. Convention delegates discussed revamping the state judiciary system and changing the tax structure. They spent much of their time on suffrage rules, including extending the residency requirement from ten to thirty days, granting the vote to women, and removing the property restriction on African American men. The residency requirement was a Republican slap at Tammany; despite petitions from woman suffragists across the state, their cause had little support among politicians of either party.

African American suffrage proved most controversial. For some Republicans, political calculation recommended changing the rule: the addition of black voters, especially since they were concentrated downstate, might improve the party's fortunes. For others, lifting the property restriction was a matter of principle. Republicans risked looking foolish, since they supported African American suffrage in the South; it was also a matter of simple fairness. The delegates received numerous petitions from African Americans and carried on a debate that had scarcely changed since 1860 or even earlier in the nineteenth century. They argued about natural versus political rights and about differences between social and political equality. With a firm Republican majority, this time the property restriction seemed certain to be removed from the constitution.

Changing national events and the question of African American suffrage, however, divided Republicans and sank the convention. Wide support for congressional Radicals—and even the backing of moderate Republicans—lasted as long as white southerners acted as if the South had not suffered defeat. By 1867, Republicans and northern voters began shying away from much federal intervention in changing the political and economic balance of power between the races in the South. In New York, Democrats saw issues—black suffrage and the excesses of spending and state power—that might reverse their slide. Attacking the Republicans' alleged fondness for political and social equality between blacks and whites and their morbid commitment to the dead Civil War past, Democrats won all state offices in 1867, regained control of the Assembly, and nearly amassed a majority in the Senate. Their victories mirrored those in Connecticut and Ohio and near wins in Republican strongholds like Maine, Vermont, and California.

Democrats credited the African American suffrage issue with their success. Many Republicans were inclined to agree. By September 1867, Democrats pressed for submitting the convention's document in its entirety to the voters, while a significant number of Republicans sought to split off the African American suffrage question for a separate vote. Members of both parties surmised that African American suffrage would bring on the defeat of the new constitution. In the end, dispirited Republicans delayed the vote on the constitution until after the November election and arranged for it to be submitted to voters in pieces: New Yorkers cast ballots on separate taxation, suffrage, and judiciary articles, as well as on the body of the document. The judiciary article, which streamlined the structure of the Court of Appeals, expanded the terms of Supreme Court justices, and gave the legislature the power to appoint those judges, alone passed in 1869. Only the adoption of the Fifteenth Amendment in 1870 removed the suffrage restriction on black men.

Once in power, Democrats set to work dismantling some of the Republican legislative handiwork. Just as Democrats in Washington sought to lift federal power from the South, New York Democrats aimed to limit the power of the state government over New York City. The so-called Tweed Charter of 1870 returned the administration of the fire department, the board of health, and tenement inspection to New York City officials. The new charter had not only Tammany's blessing (hence the name) but also that of "good government" advocates. It promised accountability, since it created a strong mayor with the power to appoint heads of important departments. It also promised fiscal controls: a new board of supervisors that included the mayor and comptroller approved funds, and a board of audit reviewed expenditures. Reformers saw in the new charter a blueprint for responsible government that was locally controlled, beyond the whims of state politicians. The benefits to Tammany were also clear, since its leader, William Marcy Tweed, extended his reach to all of the city's resources.

Home rule was part of the ideology many Democratic leaders hoped would get them beyond Civil War issues and reliance on blatant racism. It fitted not only with the party's position on the South but also with the neo-Jacksonian package Democrats offered as their vision for post-Reconstruction America: limited state intervention, free trade, decentralization, hard currency, and frugal government. While searching for a new footing for the party, Democrats also understood the need for organization. For a few years, Tammany provided both. It supported home rule for New York City and the South and President Ulysses S. Grant's handling of Reconstruction; in New York City it skillfully yoked together hostile groups and minimized social tensions. Through municipal contracts, low taxes, and leadership in championing the city's interests against the state, Tammany benefited urban elites and the middle classes. Democratic supporters also appreciated Tammany's ability to temper class conflict. Expanded city services, political recognition of ethnic groups, and jobs seemed to satisfy the working and laboring classes. Tammany funded its work in two ways. For party work, it drew upon corporate sponsorship (especially its ties with the Erie Railroad) and kickbacks from city contractors and those who received offices and jobs. Bondholders supported city building programs. This financial support, tight political organization, and policy positions that seemed to put the war to rest, together with skilled use of patronage and bribes, allowed the Hall to control the city, the county, and the state.

But not for long. In 1871, revolts from both above and below shook Tammany's power and its commanding place in the Democratic party. First came the revolt of the bondholders. By the spring of 1871, holders of city securities had already grown dubious about the size of the city's debt and lack of assurances about how the money was spent. Their fears were confirmed in July 1871, when James O'Brien, an ex-sheriff, made city and county accounts available to the hostile *New York Times*, confirming the worst suspicions about Tammany's operation. Wall Street bankers and European and American bondholders responded by severing credit to the city.

The *New York Times* demanded, "Who stole the people's money?" This well-known cartoon by Thomas Nast, "'Twas him," suggests the Tweed Ring's response as news of the corruption scandal broke. From *Harper's Weekly*, August 19, 1871.

With its lifeblood cut off, Tammany found it difficult to combat the corruption scandal that soon engulfed it: taxpayers as well as creditors had reasons to back away from Tammany Hall. Without evidence, the *New York Times* had hammered at the corruption of the "Tweed Ring." Apparently with evidence (although without attribution), the newspaper printed article after article in the summer of 1871 detailing padded contracts and kickbacks that netted the "ring" perhaps as much as $54 million. Thomas Nast, a cartoonist for *Harper's Weekly*, gave the story powerful visual punch. Nast had a talent for creating images (he originated the Tammany Tiger, the Democratic donkey, and the Republican elephant and elaborated the image of the simian-featured Irishman and the part-insect Chinese). Through his pen, readers across the country became familiar with the corpulent Tweed, the "Elegant" dandy Mayor A. Oakey Hall, Peter "Brains" Sweeny, and Comptroller Richard "Slippery Dick" Connolly, the last two rendered as stereotypical Irishmen. A rumor (never authenticated) that Tweed attempted to bribe both the *Times* and Nast added to their self-righteous luster.

Tammany's inability to hold together its ethnic and class coalition compounded its problems. Irish Protestants celebrated July 12, the anniversary of the Battle of the Boyne, with parades that sometimes turned rough: the 1870 march had inspired a violent confrontation with Irish Catholics. In 1871, city police acting for Mayor Hall turned down the Orangemen's request for a parade permit, which Protestant businessmen and merchants saw as a craven concession to Irish Catholics. Democratic Governor John T. Hoffman, with his presidential dreams and need to distance himself from Tammany Hall in mind, revoked the police order. Flanked by police and a military escort, the Orangemen paraded; Irish Catholic men, women, and children, blocked their path and confronted the marchers. The troops fired, killing thirty-seven and wounding sixty-seven, most of them Irish. Tammany had managed to alienate both Irish Catholics and the Protestant elite and middle classes, while kindling recollections of the draft riots.

In the wake of Tammany's failure to provide services and maintain peace, the corruption charges stuck. Tammany to this point had been able to tamp down challenges to its power from upstate Democrats, from rival factions in New York City, and from the inevitable disgruntled former followers. Now all scrambled to wrest away control of the Democratic party. A coalition of Republicans, independent Germans, and Democrats formed the Committee of Seventy to investigate charges that the "Tweed Ring" padded payrolls and contracts, took kickbacks, and offered and received bribes.

Samuel Tilden, then a politically ambitious Democratic politician, waited for evidence to pile up and then led the attempt to reform the party from within. For some urban elites, however, the problem was systemic, not the fault of bad men. E. L. Godkin, the crusading, elitist editor of the *Nation*, and other Union Leaguers saw newspaper exposés of ring rule as evidence that mass parties inevitably disintegrated into bossism; only nonpartisanship and an electorate limited to the propertied classes could deliver honest and efficient government. Nothing that drastic occurred. Tweed, after one mistrial, was tried in November 1873, found guilty of 204 offenses, and sentenced to twelve years in prison (reduced to one on appeal) together with a fine of $12,750 (reduced to $250). The Committee of Seventy brought a civil suit against him after he served his criminal sentence, but he escaped from jail while awaiting trial. Caught in Spain and returned to New York ill and poor, Tweed died on April 12, 1878. Connolly and Sweeny left the country before they could be prosecuted, although Sweeny eventually paid a fine and returned. Others paid fines far less than the amounts they allegedly stole, while still others turned state's evidence and went unpunished.

Governor Samuel Tilden, both reviled for his sanctimoniousness, vanity, and caution and celebrated for his honesty and tact, led the purge of the "Tweed Ring" from the Democratic party. Born in New Lebanon in 1814, he traced his political career back to the days of Martin Van Buren. His direct link to the party's golden age—together with the ties he made with upstate Democrats and

New York City elites as a result of his work as a corporate attorney—put him in a good position to remake the party. He supported the reformed Tammany organization, under "Honest John" Kelly, to head the Democratic party in New York City against various contending factions. Tilden's quick work in removing "ring" Democrats and overseeing their prosecution prevented the Republican party from taking full advantage of the Tweed scandal. Moreover, Republicans had troubles of their own. The Crédit Mobilier scandal of 1872, involving bribes by a railroad company to leading Republicans in Congress, was only the most spectacular revelation of corruption to surface during the Grant administration, while fraud connected to canal contracts tainted Republicans from districts along the Erie Canal.

Both parties claimed that their misdeeds ought not be held against them: they blamed the alleged decline in public morals on the general deterioration of civic virtue in the wake of the war. Perhaps voters believed this or something like it; in any event, neither party suffered irreparable harm. "Liberal Republicans"—a faction that drew together some abolitionists, "good government" reformers, and Union League Republicans—bolted the GOP out of disgust with Grant and state-level corruption. They imagined they could affect a realignment—the principled against the venal—which would draw honest men from both sides of the partisan divide into a new party. While their approach to politics, which stressed a rational, educated, nonpartisan electorate, became important in the early twentieth century, their movement failed to budge the two main parties. Meanwhile, the Republicans gained some ground in New York. John Dix, a former War Democrat, won the 1872 governor's race, and Republicans regained Assembly and Senate seats.

But an event beyond the control of state (or other) politicians returned the Democrats to power. In 1873, Jay Cooke, a New York banker famous for his efforts to raise money during the Civil War, planned to underwrite the purchase of the projected transcontinental Northern Pacific Railroad. At this point $15 million had been sunk into the road although only five hundred miles were in operation, but Cooke tried to salvage the investment by floating a $100 million bond issue. There was already a great deal of instability in the industry, and Cooke had trouble finding buyers. On September 17 he announced that his bank, Jay Cooke and Company, could not pay depositors, and the next day it closed its doors. Other banks panicked and called in loans. The stock market reeled, businesses shut down, workers lost their jobs, and the Panic of 1873 was on. Although manufacturing picked up by 1875 and railroads, construction, and mining improved by 1877, wages and prices continued to drop. The depression, precipitated by the banking crisis, lasted more than five years, and was obviously not the fault of one man's overreaching. Larger economic forces, including world industrial expansion and overcapacity in many sectors that affected

Europe as well as America, had much more to do with the long-term slide of wages and prices.

The New York State Democratic party benefited from the depression of 1873, more because Republicans had been in office than because of anything the Democrats promised to do about economic conditions. In office, Governor Dix had concentrated on pushing through reforms that were part of the defeated state constitution: removing the property qualification for African American voters, revamping the state contracting system, arming the governor with a line-item veto and a three-year term, and allowing the state to sell canals other than the Erie. Samuel Tilden followed Dix as governor and, while in keeping with his neo-Jacksonian beliefs (and the already shrinking bounty debt) his administration cut state taxes, he continued the focus on rooting out official corruption. His term opened with continued efforts to punish the "Tweed Ring" and closed with action against the "Canal Ring." The depression changed the political party in power but not state policies.

Farmers and Workers and Discontent

The years around the Civil War were prosperous ones for many New York farmers. Urban expansion made even more valuable their major advantage: proximity to the nation's largest markets. According to the standard study of index prices of agricultural products, prices for New York products peaked in 1868. Land values rose with prices. In 1871 the Central New York Farmers' Club estimated that an acre of good dairy land in their region went for $150. Yet even in the golden years, there were signs of trouble ahead for New York agriculture.

High prices encouraged some farmers to plant the state's abundant marginal land and to expand their holdings, taking on debt they would find difficult to cover. Many farmers used inefficient methods. More important were the advantages midwestern farmers enjoyed over those in New York State. While many New York farmers, with poor or exhausted soil, had to buy feed for cattle or dairy herds, midwestern farmers tended to avoid this cost. Inventors of better plows and other implements had the flat midwestern terrain in mind, not the hilly Northeast, where some of the tools could not be put to good use. Finally, transportation costs increasingly hurt the state's farmers. Already the Erie Canal had helped drive wheat growing and cattle raising out of the state by dramatically lowering the cost of shipping these products from the Midwest, although the war provided a reprieve. Railroads added to New Yorkers' troubles, as they charged more for hauling shipments within the state than for trips halfway across the country. Even without the depression, New York farmers were in for a painful readjustment.

Most New York farmers practiced diversified agriculture rather than intensive cultivation of a staple crop. Their access to transportation and therefore markets varied. Soil quality differed even within single towns. What farmers typically produced for market also varied across the state. Dairy farming was important in most parts of New York (the state was still the nation's top producer), although, depending on transportation and other factors, processed products like cheese and condensed milk were more commonly sold than perishable butter or fluid milk. Given variations in climate, soil types, and markets, farmers in different parts of the state focused on vegetables, meat, hops, grain, or fruit. Despite the variety, however, the boom was over by 1873–74.

The lack of common experiences, difficulties in communication, and diversified agriculture made concerted action among farmers difficult. Not only did farmers on Long Island not have a great deal in common with those in Saint Lawrence County, but what they did have in common—diversification—worked against organization by encouraging the idea that harder work and better management were the keys to successful farming. According to one member of the Cortland County Farmers' Club, hard times were retribution for moral lapses: farmers "had things their own way during the war; grew restless and lived beyond their income, and should put up with the hard times and do the best that circumstances would allow." Nonetheless, New York farmers did begin to organize. The nation's first Grange (Patrons of Husbandry) appeared in Fredonia, Chautauqua County, and the Order was organized statewide in 1873. Oliver Hudson Kelley, a clerk in the federal Department of Agriculture, is usually credited with conceiving the idea for the organization after his trip to the South in 1866. The Grange adapted Masonry—the rituals, secrecy, and ceremonial offices—to country life in the effort to relieve rural isolation, celebrate the farm family (including women), and promote fellowship.

Under the pressure of the depression, the Grange quickly became a political and economic as well as social organization. It grew especially strong in the Midwest, where Grangers supported railroad regulation and cooperative purchasing. The Grange did not catch on in New York to the same extent as in the Midwest, but it did establish 362 chapters (subordinate Granges) and attract about 17,000 members (most reasonably well off) by January 1876. New York Grangers sought to avoid entanglement in party politics and narrow partisanship, but this did not rule out advocacy of government policies. Grangers sought state regulation of the railroads so that charges would be pro-rated, removing the long-haul advantage. They wanted pressure on property taxes relieved by the assiduous collection of taxes on personal property, which they suspected to be underestimated in New York City in large amounts. Reflecting the interests of some of the female leadership, the Grange also supported the prohibition of alcohol and woman suffrage. To reduce the farmers' traditional problem of buying at retail and selling at wholesale, the Grange organized cooperatives for purchasing supplies and providing inexpensive fire insurance.

The political and economic efforts of New York Grangers were not a large success. There was corruption in the Manhattan Grange, where the Worthy Master in charge of cooperative purchasing made off with the Patron's money. The fire insurance plan failed, too. Both programs of economic self-help also faced the hostility of merchants and insurance companies. Meanwhile the Grange's political projects stalled. Effective railroad regulation waited until the 1880s, when a coalition of agricultural organizations and New York City merchants overcame the close ties between many state politicians and the railroads. No one ever figured out how to systematically tax personal property. With these setbacks, membership plummeted—down to 9,500 in 1877. Nonetheless, given the difficulties in organizing farmers, it is a measure of the discontent in the countryside that the Grange accomplished anything. The Grange's demands on government persisted as the organization recovered later in the nineteenth century.

Industrial workers in New York did not conspicuously share farmers' concern with taxes. Nor was what they shared with one another immediately clear. Ethnicity, race, age, skill, and sex divided New York's industrial workforce. The state's cities drew immigrants in large numbers, which sometimes alarmed native-born workers; new technologies allowed for further subdivisions of production and narrowing of skills; and the importance of services and of light manufacturing (as in the garment industry) in New York City created more demand for women in that city's industrial workforce than in many others. Yet New York had a strong tradition of organized labor, nurtured by immigrants experienced in European trade unionism.

With established city and statewide organizations, some New York workers sought to apply the Reconstruction example of government activism to labor and translate their most important demand—the eight-hour day—into state law. For labor organizations, the eight-hour-day movement was about the dignity of workers amid the degradation of skills brought by industrialization—about workers' capacity and need for leisure, self-improvement, and citizenship. Some Radical Republicans echoed workers' claims, as they fitted with both Republican free labor ideals and practical hopes that respectable tradesmen—especially Germans—could be moved away from the Democratic party. Yet many Republicans saw the idea of a legislated working day as a violation of higher economic law. In 1866 workers' organizations from Rochester, Utica, and Oswego, as well as New York City and Brooklyn, sent petitions carrying 27,000 signatures in favor of an eight-hour law to the state legislature. The law failed to pass: Republicans divided on the bill, although a majority of Democrats supported it, despite the opposition of the party press. The New York State

Workingmen's Assembly tried again in 1867. The bill that came to a vote, however, was a disappointment: it covered all except farm workers, but the mechanism for enforcement was not clear, and the bill guaranteed freedom of contract, which made the eight-hour provision meaningless. This bill, too, seemed headed for failure. A strike of construction workers in New York City, however, helped its passage. So the eight-hour principle was enshrined in a law, albeit an unenforceable one.

That eight-hour legislation proved to be only symbolic did not discourage labor organizations from further political activity. During the depression of the 1870s, workers in many cities favored government action to ease unemployment through public works programs. In New York City, some labor activists believed that machine politics had contributed to the depression and politicians had an obligation to relieve it. Efforts to secure relief lasted longer in New York City than in many other cities and culminated in a different sort of intervention than workers had in mind.

Several thousand workers met in New York City in December 1873 and created a Committee of Public Safety, consisting of trade union representatives, Socialists, and antimonopoly activists. The committee asked the city to appropriate $100,000 to a Labor Relief Bureau, staffed by their members and some aldermen. When city officials refused to meet with them, the committee planned a parade to be held a few weeks later in which marchers would proceed to City Hall to demand public works spending, aid to the unemployed, and an end to evictions during the winter months. The police approved a meeting in Tompkins Square but limited the parade route and prohibited a stop at City Hall. Governor Dix refused to reverse the police order. The night before the meeting, the police revoked even the meeting permit. Nonetheless, perhaps seven thousand people gathered at Tompkins Square on January 13, 1874, in freezing weather as the meeting was about to begin. The police commissioner and mounted patrolmen also arrived and ordered the crowd to disperse. Before anyone could move, the patrolmen waded into the crowd swinging their sticks. Some German workers fought back and hundreds were injured, but soon the square was cleared. Even then the police moved to the surrounding streets, beating bystanders and arresting people who appeared to be assembling in groups. With this, the relief movement collapsed, amid charges that workers' actions signaled the appearance of European communism in America. Despite the fears of working-class insurrection aroused by the Tompkins' Square "riot" and efforts to constrain the use of public areas, labor organizations continued both political and economic action. The riot, however, persuaded one onlooker, Samuel Gompers, that radicalism could not secure workers' demands.

Neither major party had much interest in pressing the causes of farmers' and workers' organizations. These issues tended to split the parties, and party leaders had trouble enough holding together their jittery factions. With neither party able to gain more than a weak hold on power, with extremely competitive and volatile elections, with continued fiscal problems, and with the parties dependent on private capital to finance their operations, it is not surprising that the Democrats and Republicans did not leap at the chance to strike out in new regulatory or spending directions. Social, cultural, and economic change, however, often translated into conflicting demands upon the state and pushed party government to the edge during the closing decades of the nineteenth century.

Chapter 26

Making Sense of Mass Society

IN THE TRADITIONAL VIEW, THE GILDED AGE WAS NOTHING but decades of unrelieved corruption and bad taste between the years of righteous struggle during the Civil War and the redemption of the Progressive Era. There was plenty of political corruption—the purchase of individual voters and entire legislatures, kickbacks, bribes, and the theft of elections. Politics, at times, turned on the morally if not financially paltry stakes of patronage. And if bad taste is measured by the extent of excess consumption, then the Gilded Age was aptly named. From the grandiose "cottages" that industrial magnates built at Newport, Rhode Island, to the sumptuous mansions of New York City's Fifth Avenue and the gingerbread houses of the middle and upper-middle classes, ostentation was the fashion. According to Henry George, critic, reformer, and New York City mayoral candidate in 1886, this was the motto and moral spirit of the period: "Get money—honestly if you can, but at any rate get money!"

But it was not all greed, corruption, and conspicuous displays of wealth in the Gilded Age. At different times and for different reasons, workers' and farmers' organizations fought the growing centralization of business (and therefore of economic and political power) and what they saw as the predominant ethic of greed. Laborers also struggled for shorter hours and higher wages, while farmers sought lower taxes and limits on government. Many groups and individuals offered critiques of Gilded Age politics, society, and culture. Some blamed drink, others prostitution for the spiritual bankruptcy they saw around them. Their conflicts with those they sought to reform through the agency of the state added to political tensions. Mass culture emerged as an important industry, with New York City as its center, further frightening those who

Wealth and leisure on display in an afternoon promenade in front of Saratoga Springs' elegant Grand Union Hotel. From *Frank Leslie's Illustrated Newspaper*, August 21, 1875.

feared the loss of a moral and cultural core. Despite the reputation of the Gilded Age as the heyday of laissez faire, state governments, including New York's, expanded their regulatory powers and control over local affairs. Limits on the revenue that could be wrung out of the tax system, however, continued to serve as a brake on the use of state power. Rather than bleak and morally lifeless, the Gilded Age might better be seen as a period of creativity, as New Yorkers, like others across the nation, tried to define a new mass society before its main lines were set.

Workers, Farmers, and Politics

Railroad workers were among those hurt in the depression of the 1870s. They had endured pay cuts, irregular hours, and the loss of some privileges—free passes for travel and the permission to live rent free in shacks along the tracks. When the Baltimore and Ohio announced a 10 percent wage cut in July 1877, workers in Martinsburg, West Virginia, struck. The governor called out the local militia, but the troops would not get traffic moving: they and many townspeople sided with the striking workers. The Martinsburg strike eventually was put down by federal troops, but not before it had spread. Railroad workers in Pennsylvania, Maryland, and New York also went out, and soon the confrontations extended as far south as Texas and west to Illinois. This was the first widespread, almost nationwide industrial dispute.

In New York State the strike affected cities and towns served by the Erie Railroad. (Cornelius Vanderbilt ignored the strike and spent $100,000 to keep New York Central workers on the job.) In these places the Martinsburg pattern was repeated. Striking workers and a sympathetic crowd in Buffalo stoned the militia brought in to run the trains, forced men who had not joined them to stop work, and seized the Erie roundhouse and barricaded it. No freight trains left Buffalo. The strike expanded beyond the railyards to include work stoppages at planing mills, car works, a bolt and nut factory, hog yards, coal yards, tanneries, and other businesses. In the village of Hornellsville, Erie workers also struck. Here, too, the six hundred troops sent to get the trains running failed, as they, along with much of the community, tended to support the strikers rather than the Erie. The local middle class as well as the working class often saw their communities at stake, under the attack of outside power, but broad sympathy for the strikes did not last. Through the summer and early fall, fears of a general worker insurrection and of communism (especially since a workers' group briefly seized political control of Saint Louis) accompanied the strikes. Everywhere the workers lost and public support evaporated when violence occurred.

The strikes and the conditions that gave rise to them affected New York State politics, first through the Greenback party. As its name suggests, the party's main issue was currency: Greenbackers blamed the depression on the contraction of the money supply after the Civil War. During the war, the Union government announced that its currency was no longer redeemable in metal but instead was backed by federal bonds. When the federal government resumed specie payment at the face value of the paper, the amount of greenbacks in circulation declined, pleasing creditors, bondholders, and those convinced that money must have an "absolute" value to inspire confidence at home and abroad. According to Greenbackers, resumption drove down wages and prices and especially hurt debtors, who faced the unhappy prospect of having to pay back their loans in deflated—that is, more expensive—currency.

The currency issue dominated Greenback campaigns in the West and Midwest, where the party attracted farmers taken with the "cheap money" idea. Yet the party platform also included a moral critique of the power of capital and positions on a wide range of issues. In New York, the Greenbackers were more a labor than a farmer party, formed in the teeth of the depression and in the wake of the strikes. New York Greenbackers articulated a scathing critique of monopolies and the dominance of capital over labor and politics and argued for an eight-hour workday, the end of convict labor and the importation of Chinese workers, and public control of railroads. In the off-year election of 1877, the party began to attract support in New York, especially in the Southern Tier, where workers formed political organizations in Painted Post, Corning, and

Elmira. The Greenback party reached its peak in 1878. The Democratic party all but disappeared in Steuben and Chemung Counties, where Greenbackers replaced Democrats on the county boards of supervisors. Voters in 17 assembly districts covering parts of Chemung, Cortland, and Oswego Counties, and New York City sent Greenbackers to the state capitol. The party won 14 percent of the vote statewide, but gained more than 25 percent in Cattaraugus, Chemung, Chenango, Oswego, and Sullivan Counties, while Albany, Cortland, Steuben, Tioga, and Warren Counties posted Greenback returns above the state total.

The party continued to field candidates into the 1880s, but its support declined after 1878. It did not help that the depression began to lift. Greenbackers also suffered from the typical pains of new parties. Internal dissension—upstaters pitted against downstaters, currency reformers against labor reformers—made settling on platforms and candidates difficult. The party never built an effective statewide organization, since Greenbackers, like members of many nineteenth-century third parties, believed their party was above politics, the trimming of principles, patronage, and petty organizational concerns. Greenbackers who had the necessary political skills to build an organization seemed suspiciously like the despised politicians. The party's voters drifted back to their major party moorings—for most, the Democratic party—or attached themselves to new third parties that soon formed.

In New York State, as in the rest of the nation, those who sought to build new parties had to contend most of all with the intense partisanship inspired among voters by the Democrats and Republicans. Most men stuck by the major parties, even when they were dissatisfied with their party's performance. The major parties held men's imaginations. The party press recalled the great deeds of the party's recent past—in prosecuting the Civil War or in protecting liberties amid the conflict—as well as, for Democrats, the shining and more distant past of Jefferson and Jackson. Party affiliation connected men with a tradition, made them not cogs in a machine but personifications of the attributes of manhood: loyalty, steadfastness, and the ability to work for the good of an organization bigger than any individual. The parties also insisted that the fate of the nation hung on their election: high tariffs, for example, would bring ruin or real prosperity. The pageantry of political campaigns reinforced partisanship. October brought torchlight processions of uniformed members of local political clubs and large rallies with speakers and bands. November brought the efforts of neighbors to get out the vote and the rituals of election days: taking off a few hours or the entire day to go to the polls, casting ballots that those crowding around could see, eating and drinking, returning or staying to see the returns as they came in, and perhaps joining a victory celebration.

The major parties did not maintain voters' loyalties with rhetoric and ritual alone. Ethnic and religious ties reinforced party loyalties, especially for Irish Catholic Democrats and evangelical Protestant Republicans. Keen competition between the parties in New York State also made every vote seem important. Only once during the 1880s—in the 1882 election—did more than 3 percent of the statewide vote separate the winning and losing party. Finally, organization and patronage got voters to the polls and enhanced party loyalty. Both the Democrats and Republicans built elaborate structures that extended from the state level to city precincts and the smallest rural towns. The men who made up this vast workforce kept party leaders in touch with local conditions—what issues might help, what faction might bolt, what it would take to get out the vote. Party workers also were points on a network that distributed favors such as jobs for themselves and their friends and printing contracts for newspapers. Other favors came more cheaply—helping a son out of trouble with the police, sending a copy of a state publication like *The Birds of New York* or a free pass on a railroad, or giving advice or a loan. All of this effort produced high voter turnout (in the 80 to 90 percent range, even in off-year elections) and relatively stable party loyalties.

The resources, rhetoric, and traditions of the major parties were obstacles for farmers' and workers' organizations. Yet political conditions in New York State also presented some advantages. While the state's close elections provided a potent argument against casting a ballot for a party that would surely lose, tight competition was also a boon to third parties, since any one that could get 2 or 3 percent of the vote statewide held the balance of power. Strong party ties made involvement in politics divisive for farmers' and workers' organizations, but they could swear off party politics and work as a lobbying group. Labor organizations tried the third-party course and farmers the path of nonpartisanship.

Annual meetings of the New York State Grange routinely featured pleas for nonpartisanship and farmer unity on the grounds that party politics distracted farmers from serious issues and denied them their rightful place in government. Local farmers' groups concurred. According to a speaker at the Central New York Farmers' Club in December 1896, if farmers did not learn "that in union there is strength, and act upon it, they need expect little consideration or have much influence in public affairs." The state Grange had a positive political agenda that its leaders hoped unity would put into law. It passed resolutions and sent petitions to Albany on such topics as taxation (collecting taxes on personal as well as real property), the Erie Canal (which should be funded by the nation or by its users, not by New York taxpayers), and support for agricultural education, temperance legislation, and woman suffrage. Local subordinate Granges sometimes featured talks about breaking the expansive power of monopolies, but they constructed a mostly negative political agenda—reducing taxes, spending at both the state and local levels, and the salaries of public officials. Speakers blamed the very existence of politicians for many of their problems. "We have too many laws and Lawyers, too many offices and office-seekers," declared one farmer.

The success of either the negative or positive legislative program is hard to gauge. Farmers hardly needed the Grange to point out that they did not like a tax system that hit real property but left personal property, including bank accounts and stock portfolios, untouched. In rural towns and counties, raising money for new projects—roads, bridges, or waterworks—tended to be a struggle that involved repeated elections and hard-fought campaigns. Conservative government was the rule where the Grange was weak in the 1880s: the poorest farming areas had the least energetic governments and also the lowest Grange membership. With or without Grange inspiration, local governments in rural areas remained inexpensive and provided few services.

The state Grange always stood ready to take credit for laws that had some connection with agriculture or rural communities. It claimed a major role, for example, in railroad regulation. The state Grange passed numerous resolutions urging the legislature to eliminate the price advantage enjoyed by western farmers who shipped their products over long distances. The New York legislature's Hepburn Committee investigated differential rates, stock-watering, and special deals granted certain shippers in 1879. This effort, however, was as much a response to the demands of New York City merchants, who sought to regain traffic lost to other east coast cities, as it was to Grange agitation.

Overall, nonpartisanship was more a wish than a practice in state and national elections. As one female member of a Grange in Scriba, Oswego County, remarked in 1882, "they could express themselves here as being independent but when they come to vote it would be the *same old Ticket*." Agricultural organizations admonished farmers to vote for farmers or, recognizing that voters usually stuck with their traditional parties, for candidates who promised to attend to agricultural interests. Third parties devoted to agricultural concerns had even sparser results than nonpartisanship. The Populist party in New York, for example, enjoyed its best year in 1893, when it gained 1.7 percent of the votes statewide and carried only one town (tiny Ward in Allegany County) in the entire state. While some planks in the Populist platform, especially railroad regulation, action against monopolies, and lightening the tax burden on real property, appealed to New York farmers, rural voters operated in an economy too diversified to let them make common cause with staple-crop farmers of the South and Midwest.

Labor organizations at times enjoyed better results in organizing third parties in late nineteenth-century New York. A spectacular case was the United Labor party (ULP) and the 1886 campaign of its candidate for mayor of New York City, Henry George. The Central Labor Union sponsored the ULP, whose candidates in previous elections garnered roughly 1 percent of the vote—a typical total for a labor ticket in the city. But a pattern of police brutality against strikers (Samuel Gompers claimed that in the spring of 1886, it was "so flagrant that labor's patience reached the breaking point") and an especially egregious case of the court's ties with capital (a grand jury claimed that a settlement reached between unionized musicians, waiters, and bartenders and the owner of a music hall constituted extortion, while a Tammany-nominated judge oversaw the conviction of five union negotiators) united labor organizations. Workers proclaimed their goals on placards they carried in a parade for George's candidacy: "Down With Bribable Judges, Corrupt Legislators, and Vile Police Despotism!" "Boycott the Enemies of Labor!" and "No Charity: We Want Fair and Square Justice."

George appealed not only to union members but also to Socialists, middle-class reformers, Irish nationalists, and his own personal following built on his famous plan for the single tax. A single high tax on land promised to improve housing (no taxes would be levied on buildings or improvements, and land would be too expensive to hold for speculative purposes) and encourage free trade (the single tax would replace the tariff). George also supported workers' right to organize and the end of police harassment of labor. He received 31 percent of the vote, which put him ahead of the Republican candidate, Theodore Roosevelt, but behind Abram S. Hewitt, a reform-minded Democrat who had amassed his fortune in manufacturing iron and steel products. The ULP coalition disbanded after George's defeat: George focused his efforts on free trade, the Socialists on their own party, and ethnic groups on their own organizations. But from that point on, labor and ethnic groups became forces to be reckoned with in city politics, especially by Tammany.

One important labor organization that supported the George campaign was the Knights of Labor. Beginning as a minor secret society founded in Pennsylvania in 1869, the Knights expanded rapidly in the 1880s. By 1886, it claimed 750,000 members and a chapter in virtually every county in the nation. The Knights combined the appeals of unionism with fraternalism. At a time when fraternal orders were extremely popular, the Knights featured the rituals, fellowship, and sickness and death benefits common to such organizations. Terence V. Powderly, a former railroad worker who became Grand Master Workman in 1879, believed that conflict between labor and capital was not inevitable ("I curse the word class," he once said) and that arbitration could settle disputes more effectively than strikes. Nonetheless, the Knights' expansion owed much to a successful strike in 1885 against Jay Gould's Missouri Pacific Railroad in the Southwest. Local assemblies sponsored a large number of strikes in 1886 and 1887, years when the number of strikes nationwide more than doubled over the totals of the first five years of the decade. The Knights supported such staple demands of labor as the eight-hour day, an end to convict and contract labor, and the creation of a bureau of labor statistics, but like many organizations and third parties in the late nineteenth century, the Knights also offered a broad critique of Gilded Age society. Their platforms as well as songs and banners decried the values of money, competition, and greed that had come to dominate society and touted the superiority of the producer classes over the parasitic politicians, lawyers, and speculators. With this wider analysis in mind, the Knights were willing to organize the unskilled as well as the skilled, blacks as well as whites, immigrants and the native born, women along with men, and even shopkeepers and businessmen as well as wageworkers and their spouses (usually wives), so long as they subscribed to the organization's principles.

The Knights of Labor did not form a workers' party and did not usually search for alliances with third parties until the 1890s, when the Order was weak, but it was active in local politics at times. The 415 local assemblies and some of the estimated 68,000 members in New York City in 1886 participated in the George campaign. The Knights' assemblies turned to local politics in villages as well as in large cities. In 1885, for example, workers in Homer, Cortland County, established an assembly, which drew especially heavily from the village's wagon and carriage shops. Rumors that the Knights planned to strike Homer's largest carriage maker caused its owner to lock out the workers. Powderly himself came to Homer to try to mediate the dispute; this effort failed, as did a workers' cooperative carriage shop and a boycott of conveyances made in Homer. A full slate of Knights' candidates for Homer village offices polled 40 percent of the vote in the March 1886 elections, but fell short of gaining control. With neither politics nor economic pressure able to break the deadlock, some workers went back to the shops having pledged to abandon the Knights. Others moved out of town.

The Grange continued to recover in the 1880s and 1890s by stressing fraternalism. As a fraternal organization, it reached its peak after World War II, but then returned to the numbers it had in the mid-1870s. The Knights of Labor, however, went into rapid decline after 1886. After the Haymarket massacre in Chicago in May, in which violence broke out at an eight-hour rally and city officials blamed anarchists and the Knights, the Order lost public support and the internal fault lines of the group over strike policy, the place of craft unions, and the role of politics opened wider. But the efforts of farmers and workers to shape economic relations and their critiques of the values of industrial society and politics demonstrate the effects of economic change and faith in politics during the late nineteenth century. The expanded scale of industrial enterprise and the finer divisions of labor pushed more people into wage work and further diminished the skills required for many jobs. Rapid transportation, the centralization of industries, and the growing importance of financial houses in underwriting the transportation and industrial systems transformed relationships between workers and their communities and the wider economy. For many working-class families, maintaining stable lives was difficult. Workers could expect frequent bouts of unemployment, since much production was seasonal, and there was a good chance of being injured in many lines of work. Even without such disasters, supporting a family on a single income was often impossible.

Beyond precarious material circumstances, organized workers lamented the loss of dignity attached to work: the extent to which money measured value and diminished skills made workers a mere factor of production. Grangers, too, deplored what seemed to be the wider culture's devaluation of farm labor, which they regarded as the basis of civilization. Farmers and workers looked for personal solutions to their problems: moving, working harder, supplementing family income with the labor of the entire family, changing jobs, or varying the crop mix. They also formed organizations that sought collective economic solutions through strikes or cooperative buying and selling. Some farmers and workers searched for political solutions by organizing new parties, supporting particular pieces of legislation, and trying to curb the role of the courts and police in labor disputes. In this way they were critics of the Gilded Age party system, of patronage-driven politicians and their connections with capital, but also part of it. The political efforts of farmers and workers were testimony to the importance of politics to Gilded Age culture.

Late Nineteenth-Century Cultural Conflict

Farmers and workers were hardly alone in criticizing Gilded Age society or in searching for political solutions. A series of cultural issues concerning how people ought to organize their lives and what habits and values they ought to follow sparked controversy in late nineteenth-century New York. Groups of middle-class white reformers who identified various social evils and set to work to correct them occupied one side. Those who were the targets of reform, chiefly immigrants and the poor, had their own aspirations, which sometimes coincided with the reformers' but often did not. The political parties, state and local government, and an expanding mass commercial culture became sites and symbols of cultural conflict. For some the parties appeared to be supporting vice, and for others they were protecting personal freedoms; for those given to blaming the parties, expanded state authority seemed to be a good way to restore social harmony. The competing values of personal freedom, cultural autonomy, and social order emerged in conflicts over everything from the uses of the street to the uses of the state. A few examples can illustrate the scope of the struggles: immigration and immigrant life, charity, temperance, prostitution and sexuality, education, the lives of Native Americans, and efforts to construct high culture.

The state's population continued to expand in the late nineteenth century with the help of immigration. Still the nation's most populous state, New York grew by 40 percent between 1870 and 1900, to over 7.2 million people. The movement to the cities continued, so that by 1900, 56 percent of the state's residents lived in cities of over 100,000 (New York City, including Brooklyn, Buffalo, Rochester, and Syracuse). Only 27 percent of New Yorkers lived in rural areas, which were losing population in absolute terms by 1880. In the state as a whole, the percentage of foreign born still hovered in the one-quarter range, as it had since mid-century, but most of the fastest-growing cities, including New York, Yonkers, and Buffalo, were homes to a larger proportion of immigrants than the state average. While Ireland and Germany were still the birthplaces of most of the foreign born, southern and eastern Europe began to outstrip the northwestern region as the main source of immigrants between 1890 and 1900. Italians, Russians, Poles, and people from the Austro-Hungarian Empire formed the largest part of the so-called new immigration, which would accelerate until World War I. The newcomers brought to New York what seemed to some of the native born large numbers of people with such strange languages, religions, and customs that their assimilation into American life might be impossible.

The new immigrants came to the United States for reasons that varied from individual to individual, but deteriorating conditions in their home countries spurred people to consider the massive project of moving thousands of miles to a country with unfamiliar customs, language, and physical features. In southern Italy—the source of most Italian migrants—families had made ends meet through a combination of tenancy, sharecropping, ownership of small plots of land, and day labor. Their economic strategies fell apart by the 1880s. High taxes that came with the unification of Italy in 1870, crop failures in the Mediterranean region, widespread availability of inexpensive mass-produced products that curtailed the demand for artisan-made goods, and competition in agricultural products from the United States and elsewhere unraveled the peasant economy. The southern peasants were left with the prospect of staying and suffering the consequences, moving to cities, or leaving for America, in many cases with the hope of returning with sufficient money to buy enough land to make a living.

Industrialization and the expansion of markets also caused economic dislocations in eastern Europe, but for Jews in the Russian empire (in which one-half of the world's Jewish population lived) matters were even worse. Jews were confined to a Pale of Settlement, the twenty-five northern and western regions of the empire. After the pogroms of 1880–81, Czar Alexander I restricted land ownership to Christians. Jewish men and women worked as artisans and peddlers, but even that became difficult as factory-made goods reduced the demand for artisanal skills. Suffering the consequences of overcrowding, industrialization, and antisemitism, many migrated; between 1881 and 1914, one-third of all Jews left the Russian empire. Few planned to return.

These two large groups of immigrants, along with Catholics and Orthodox

Christians from Poland, Russia, and other areas of eastern Europe and the Mediterranean, changed the life and culture of New York's cities, as urban life changed the immigrants. In the near term, immigrants provided a labor force for expanding industries. On the basis of skills and customs acquired in the Old World, personal preference, available opportunities, prejudice, and links with kin and friends, different immigrant groups filtered into certain industries. Italian men in Buffalo found work in the booming construction trades, mostly as laborers. Such work fitted their requirements. Many Italian immigrants were young single men, and they preferred outdoor to factory work and jobs that did not tie them down but provided enough money for a profitable return to Italy. Italian women, especially married ones, tended not to work for wages—industrial Buffalo provided few opportunities for women, and Italian culture dictated that women run the home. Yet many took in boarders and worked the harvests in the lake shore orchards and vineyards of western New York. Many Poles, meanwhile, had had some industrial experience in Europe and took factory jobs, especially in the expanding steel industry outside Buffalo. In New York City, Jewish men and women, along with many Italians, dominated the skilled and unskilled workforce in the men's and women's clothing industry.

New York City had a larger percentage of female workers than most of the upstate industrial cities. Women, most single but some married, worked either in factories or in their cramped tenement apartments making boxes, artificial flowers, and clothing. The greater tendency of Jewish women to work for wages (and to join labor organizations) reflected experiences in east European shtetls, where many women had performed wage work and some had had contact with socialist ideas.

Also in the near term, urban life required the immigrants to make major adjustments from traditional patterns. In an older telling of the immigrant saga, historians overstated the disintegration of extended families and immigrant cultures. Since the 1970s, some historians have corrected this interpretation by stressing how immigrants bent their energies toward retaining familiar customs and ethnic identities. The most reasonable interpretations recognize both disintegration and resourceful struggles in the New World. Most immigrants took the only available choice: they mixed the old and the new in order to build better lives. Sometimes they created an ethnic identity (or had one created for them) where none had existed. "Us Slovaks didn't know we were Slovaks until we came to America and they told us!" recalled one immigrant to Brooklyn in the early twentieth century. Most lived in nuclear family households but relied on relatives for passage money, a place to live for short stretches, help in sickness and hard times, and assistance in finding work.

Numerous obstacles stood in the way of better lives: dangerous and poorly paying jobs, irregular employment, and language barriers. Housing was another. In New York City, Jewish and Italian immigrants tended to live on the Lower

East Side, Jewish in the formerly German neighborhoods west of the Bowery, Italians in the old Irish settlements east of the Bowery. The tenements that the immigrants could afford, especially in the old Irish section, were notoriously bad: extremely overcrowded, airless, lightless, and lacking in all facilities. By the 1880s, facilities in the new apartments on the old German East Side were modern but still cramped: apartments meant to shelter one or two families might hold six instead. Housing in Buffalo, New York's second largest city after New York's five boroughs had been consolidated, was not quite as tight, and residents had options other than tenements. But there, too, three-to-five-story buildings housed twelve to thirty-five families. With rents high, with large families (Italian women in Buffalo averaged 4.5 children and Polish women 7.8 at the turn of the century), with evictions common, and with dense concentrations of population, immigrant housing was depressing and conducive to high rates of illness and infant mortality. The novelist Anzia Yezierska wrote, "To the greenhorns it seemed as if the sunlight had faded from their lives and buildings like mountains took its place."

What city apartments failed to offer, the streets sometimes did. Important parts of everyday life took place on the streets: the play, socializing, gossip, and commerce that maintained social networks and relieved the grimness of urban

An ethnic, working-class neighborhood on the Lower East Side of Manhattan (ca. 1900).
New York State Historical Association, Cooperstown, N.Y.

life. Shops and street vendors offered fruits and vegetables immigrants had never seen and canned food that seemed luxurious. The streets advertised fashion and American style and opened the allurements of city life, especially for the young and single. Young women were anxious to replace shapeless clothes from the old country that marked them as greenhorns and poor, with cheap but fashionable shirtwaists and hats. Outside tenements and factories there were ice cream parlors, nickel theaters, and other commercial establishments that promised a break from the claims of work and family. Immigrant mothers expected their children, especially their daughters, to hand over their pay to help support the household, but the daughters sometimes found ways to keep a bit for small treats. Through their contact with street life as well as the school system, the children of immigrants helped socialize their parents and acted as guides to what America had to offer.

Both the grim and the more exciting sides of immigrant life bothered some members of the native-born middle and upper classes. They blamed immigrants for the conditions in which they lived: the newcomers preferred cramped housing and never developed habits of cleanliness. Clannishness, evidenced by crowding and patronizing of ethnic merchants, as well as strange languages, customs, and religions, made these immigrants poor material for American citizenship. The size of immigrant families raised fears about race suicide: Anglo-Saxons, who reproduced at not nearly the prolific rate of the new immigrants, would soon become a marginal minority in a country they thought was rightly theirs. Even some long-settled German Jews were alarmed by the influx of east European Jews and feared that their presence would ignite antisemitism. The stylish dress of young immigrant men and women was seen as a sign not of assimilation but of bad character: wasting money on finery showed spendthrift ways when immigrants ought to scrimp and struggle. In rural areas, too, immigrants came in for bad press. Newspapers near Howes Cave, Schoharie County, warned readers about the hot-tempered Italians who lived in boardinghouses near the limestone quarry and their fondness for fighting and knives. Even though immigrants made the comforts of middle- and upper-class life possible through their work as servants and producers of consumer goods, some of the beneficiaries of their labors were far more impressed with the threats these newcomers seemed to pose.

Rather than merely complain, some middle- and upper-class New Yorkers thought they must act. They joined with members of groups like the American Protective Association in a nationwide campaign for immigration restriction that, with the exception of excluding the Chinese in 1882, did not succeed until the 1920s. In the meantime, efforts to combat poverty often but not always targeted immigrants. In rural areas throughout the state, poverty was no stranger—farm laborers lived in dilapidated shacks with facilities below the less-than-lavish rural standards, and even some owners of farms fared little better. Women members of some village Protestant churches formed groups that provided relief to the poor, but they often focused on members of their own churches who had been hit with a bad stretch of luck, such as illness or a fire. Otherwise these women sent contributions to the faraway poor—African American children in southern schools or Indians on western reservations. The local poor made do as they could or fell under the care of county supervisors of the poor, who were under steady pressure to keep expenditures down.

Some urban poverty reformers were disappointed with the disbursement of even such small amounts of aid. It lacked system, and there was nothing as important as system to those who made up the Charity Organization movement in the late nineteenth century. The first city-wide Charity Organization Society (COS) was formed in Buffalo in 1877 by middle- and upper-class residents distressed by the unrest of the depression years and the political pressures on city government to provide relief to the unemployed. Women, especially those who had been involved in the Sanitary Commission during the Civil War, dominated the membership of the COS, and they tried to apply the lessons learned in the war and the example of poverty reform in England to American cities.

COS branches did not dispense aid. When asked what portion of donations to the New York City branch went to the poor, Josephine Shaw Lowell, a Sanitary Commission veteran and COS board member, happily said "Not one cent." Instead they provided what they saw as the necessary coordination of the work of many voluntary organizations that allocated relief. They sent volunteers (later paid workers) to the homes of the poor to identify the worthy and determine what sort of aid they needed. Some merely needed the example of thrift and character the visitor provided by her presence; others who needed loans or some other assistance in the estimation of the visitor would be directed to the relevant agency. COS workers aimed to make sure that the unworthy—drinkers or those suspected of malingering—did not receive aid and that the worthy were given the right kind, since even they could be lulled into dependency. As a test of a willingness to work, the New York branch asked men to chop wood. The COS also sought accountability in poor relief. The head of the Buffalo COS even had his widowed mother itemize how she spent the weekly check he sent to her for her support.

The COS concern with efficiency and system in charity washed over other agencies that dealt with the poor. The New York State Board of Charities, created in the 1860s to oversee the state's poorhouses, reflected some of the COS ideas about poverty. Josephine Shaw Lowell joined the board in 1876. Some private citizens were not convinced that the Board of Charities fully complied with its mission to oversee the state's almshouses. In 1872 they formed the State Charities Aid Association, a voluntary association that did its own inspections of poorhouses. Everywhere charity workers worried that indiscriminate

Photographer Jacob A. Riis recorded heartbreaking images of urban poverty in turn-of-the-century New York. "Street Arabs in the Area of Mulberry Street." The Jacob A. Riis Collection, Museum of the City of New York.

aid would perpetuate bad traits and that without the COS's rational, nonpolitical administration, politicians and soft-hearted donors would create additional poverty.

It is not surprising that immigrants and poor people in general avoided the ministrations of the COS and other agencies. Upon an encounter with a friendly visitor, one immigrant woman in New York City remarked, "By pictures and lectures she show us poor people how we should live without meat, without milk, without butter, and without eggs. Always it's on the tip of my tongue to ask her, can't you learn us how to live without eating?" Aside from hostility toward the impractical (and condescending) advice that friendly visitors seemed to offer, immigrant families had other reasons to avoid them and other manifestations of relief. Many immigrants and other poor people were embarrassed to accept relief. To go on the public dole reflected badly not only on the individual but also on that person's family and community, which were supposed to take care of their own. COS visitors also seemed to intrude upon matters poor families considered private: inquiring about whether a husband had deserted his family and should be charged with nonsupport, for example. Those in need looked first to family and to neighbors, who sometimes took up collections to prevent a family from being evicted. Working-class families also purchased insurance as a hedge against a disaster that could lead to poverty. They bought policies that covered burial expenses and provided death benefits for children as well as parents. They also joined lodges and mutual benefit societies, often with ethnic ties, that supplied assistance in the case of illness. Churches also offered help to needy members.

Cultural Conflict and the Uses of Government

Like poverty, the temperance issue was not directly connected to immigration but involved conflict with some immigrant groups. Campaigns to persuade individuals to give up drink went back to the 1820s; there had also been a failed effort to use state power to severely limit alcohol sales in 1855. The issue then faded until the 1870s, when groups of women, especially in the Finger Lakes region and western Southern Tier of New York (and parts of the Midwest) revived the battle against drink. In villages such as Watkins (now Watkins Glen) and Penn Yan, evangelical women not only engaged in the usual fasts and prayers that drinkers might repent, but took their meetings to places where liquor was sold, such as hotels and saloons. These "praying bands" also participated in village elections. Since 1870, local towns had been electing excise commissioners who determined whether applications for licenses should be approved, and collected the fees. Although they could not vote, temperance women supported candidates who promised to grant no new licenses, and they worked the polls on election days. They had some successes, but usually the "woman's crusade" for temperance did not create lasting "dry" policies.

For these women—mostly evangelical Protestants of the middle class— liquor was a social and moral evil that especially harmed their sex. Married men drank away their paychecks and left their wives and children destitute. Liquor made men mean and violent. Temperance advocates disagreed about whether drink caused poverty or was a symptom of the degradation poverty induced, but they agreed that, as moral agents and victims, women had the right to speak out on this issue even if it involved them in politics.

The Woman's Christian Temperance Union (WCTU) picked up where the "woman's crusade" left off. Formed in 1874 at a Sunday school teachers' convention in Chautauqua County, it soon became the single largest women's group in the nation under the leadership of the beloved Frances Willard. Willard's talent was in allowing chapters to maintain as broad or as narrow a focus as they wished, all under the banner of temperance and female morality. Some New York locals concentrated on drink alone—license questions and temperance education. Others expanded the moral mandate into wider areas. Large locals operated missions for homeless women and employment offices; the state WCTU ran a home for unwed mothers. Willard also supported woman suffrage—the "Home Protection Ballot"—as a way to achieve both temperance and morality in public life. With this packaging, many WCTU locals went along, despite some of the state leadership's fear that having the vote would diminish women's moral influence on politics in the early 1880s. Temperance women became a new constituency in the woman suffrage movement.

Although temperance appeared to be a "female" issue, far from all women supported the WCTU's aims, and some men joined the cause. The Prohibition party stood not only against alcohol but also against monopolies and partisan corruption and in favor of woman suffrage and reform in policies toward Indians. In New York, the party received most of its support from the Republican bastions in the western Southern Tier and in a few northern counties. Although in its best years (the middle 1880s) it garnered only 4 percent of the statewide vote, it sometimes handed the Republican party defeats in state elections from the early 1880s through the early 1890s. In 1888, when the Republicans offered a "dry" candidate for governor and the Prohibitionists won only 2 percent of the vote, even that margin was enough to elect a Democrat. Tight party competition gave temperance voters power far beyond their numbers.

Republican managers had to do something to eliminate the Prohibition vote. They found the solution in the Raines Liquor Tax Law passed in 1896. Among other things, the law abolished local licensing boards, created a State Department of Excise charged with enforcing the act, and taxed saloons on a sliding scale based on population. Towns could make the law tougher by voting themselves dry, but no municipality could ease it by voting to permit Sunday sales. This was enough to satisfy all but the most extreme dry. The Raines Law also generated revenue—$11 million in 1896 alone, most of which came from New York City and Brooklyn. One-third of this windfall went to the state, with the rest going to cities and towns. Thus the law opened a new source of tax dollars (good news for both parties), while also solving once and for all the political challenge of the Prohibition party.

Liquor policy generated so much political controversy in the Gilded Age because it touched deeply held cultural values as well as economic and political concerns. While a good number of upstate Protestant Republicans would have been happy to abolish saloons or to eliminate the sale of alcohol, other groups, especially both "old" and "new" immigrants, just as badly wanted to keep institutions that were important in their communities. In New York's cities and large villages, saloons were community centers for men as well as places to get a drink: they were places where regulars picked up their mail, found jobs, secured loans, and received cheap or free meals. They were places to go for political talk, union meetings, gossip, or simply relief from crowded dwellings.

Different saloons catered to different clienteles and tastes—from the family-oriented German beer gardens to rough haunts where one could find prostitutes and gambling. Some New York City saloons were sites of a developing gay male subculture, where "fairies" (men who had a culturally feminine demeanor) mixed openly and freely with "straight" men. For "dry" Republicans, temperance symbolized moral purity, responsible family life, and Americanism. For its opponents, temperance was an attack on personal liberty, a social world, and legitimate cultural norms. Republicans who catered to Prohibitionists might win back their votes, but they risked losing support on the other side of the temperance divide. In 1895, Republicans alienated German voters by strictly enforcing Sunday closing laws in New York City, which was enough to cost the Republican and anti-Tammany Democrat coalition that year's municipal election. Practical politicians counted votes and tax and fee revenues and found the Raines Law the most suitable compromise.

Mass commercial entertainment vied with liquor as a target for reformers. The expansion of commercial recreation blurred the division between the respectable and the dissolute formed in large part by family life and gender. Both working- and middle-class urban families spent some of their leisure time together. Working-class families in the late nineteenth century enjoyed the free or cheap entertainment in the cities—talk on the streets, music from street musicians, shows from roaming acrobats, and snacks from street vendors selling hot corn and baked potatoes. Families threw house parties, and ethnic lodges organized dances. For both the middle and working classes, picnics and excursions to parks brought families together.

Yet men and women of both classes spent much of their leisure time apart. Men had a variety of options: lodges, poolrooms, baseball teams, and street corners for working-class men, clubs and halls for the middle class, and saloons for both. Women had fewer choices—visits at home or on stoops; or the clubs and church groups that brought in mostly middle-class women. Large department stores also made the necessary chore of shopping into leisure by opening lounges and tea rooms for their female customers. A woman who intruded on male spaces such as saloons or who loitered on street corners would be taken to be a prostitute.

By the late nineteenth century, however, new commercial establishments brought men and women together. Nickel theaters, dance halls, and inexpensive excursions to amusement parks and picnic groves attracted young working-class people, eager for places where they could meet away from the gaze of parents. Coney Island, part of which was a middle-class resort in the 1880s, also became a destination for working-class young people. They were drawn to the beach, variety shows, saloons, penny arcades, bands for dancing, and shooting galleries. The midway rides of Sea Lion Park and Steeplechase Park added to Coney Island's appeal in the late 1890s. By 1900, 300,000–500,000 people turned out on pleasant weekends. Saloons did not lack for attendance, and a subculture of single men still thrived in the largest cities, but mixed-sex commercial leisure proved extremely popular.

This was fun that had not yet spread to rural areas. Noncommercial recreation, often mixed with work or moral and intellectual uplift, held on in villages and on farms. Grangers delivered talks on matters like "contentment," combating noxious weeds, and Grange fellowship. They debated the qualities of good husbands and wives and enjoyed snacks such as popcorn or, to bring out a crowd, a meal such as an oyster supper. There were church suppers, fairs, sleigh and wagon rides, card games, and parties that followed hard chores demanding extra labor. Visits from friends and family were frequent. Occasionally itinerant acrobats or animal trainers passed though villages. None of this turned much of a profit, and most of it brought together both sexes and all ages. Men and boys on farms enjoyed many more trips to town (and perhaps stops at saloons) than their wives or daughters did, and some women belonged to women's church groups or the WCTU. But neither the commercialism nor the sex segregation common in cities and large villages characterized rural leisure.

Leisure also remained racially segregated for the most part. In New York City's black neighborhoods, clubs, saloons, and cafés ranged from dives (according to the writer Paul Laurence Dunbar, one was "a social cesspool, generating a poisonous miasma and reeking with the stench of decayed and rotten moralities") to Cooper and Ransom's wine and billiard saloon, with rooms, as a *New York Globe* article described them, "elegantly frescoed and richly papered, the floors being covered with rich Brussels." Such clubs offered music (including New York City's first exposure to ragtime), dancing, and, in some cases, gambling and prostitution. While both black and white ministers denounced the cafés and saloons, black churches, schools, and clubs presented discussions that drew men and women of all ages. Even in a village such as Geneva, a men's debating club discussed propositions like "the condition of the colored man is not better than it was previous to the war," before African American audiences in the 1870s.

How young urban men and women spent their free time was first a matter of conflict between generations, as parents tried to shelter their children (especially their daughters) from city temptations. It became a political issue as well in the twentieth century, as reformers sought to protect the morals of young women. In the meantime, commercial entertainment—and the vice industry—had a different sort of connection with politics. It was a stock Republican charge: Tammany politicians, as well as the police officers they appointed, fed their own pockets and that of the machine with profits from gambling, prostitution, and illegal liquor sales. The charge was not a fabrication. Police routinely ignored saloons open on Sundays; some received kickbacks from prostitutes in exchange for their lax prosecution of the laws, while others thought it pointless to prosecute prostitutes. Some ward politicians, such as Timothy D. ("Big Tim") Sullivan, an assemblyman from New York City's fourth ward (the Five Points slum) in the late 1880s and a powerful Tammany ward leader, owned saloons and invested in gambling operations. To the extent that anti-vice reformers and politicians suggested that vice existed because of political support, they exaggerated the special role played by Tammany in the vice industry. Neither Democratic nor Republican politicians had much incentive to shut down popular Sunday sales unless a saloon's patrons caused a disturbance. Neither prostitution nor gambling needed the help of politicians to flourish, although some ward captains offered protection to these enterprises and received financial support in return. The fees ran as high as a $500 initiation fee with a $40 per month additional charge in some New York City neighborhoods.

The sensational charges missed one connection between politicians and commercial entertainment. Ward politicians like Sullivan understood changing leisure patterns in the city and moved profitably with them. Sullivan himself mixed forms of commercial entertainment with politicking. The "chowders" he organized were all-day affairs, beginning with parades that he led through his ward to waiting ferries, followed by a picnic in the countryside, where his constituents of all ages and sexes enjoyed food, beer, music, dancing, games, and gambling, and ending with another parade and fireworks in the evening. If Sullivan's "chowders" featured some of the elements of popular commercial leisure, along with an appreciation of the tastes of the ethnic groups in his district, Sullivan also understood that commercial entertainment had a better future than vice. He moved his investments to music halls, vaudeville theaters, burlesque houses, and eventually, movie theaters. Sullivan understood the connections between the emerging mass culture and politics better than his accusers and some historians who have seen mass culture as something that diminished political participation.

Nonetheless, anti-vice reformers campaigned to rid New York's cities of prostitution and amusements that they believed led women into temptation and to cut links between vice and politics. During the late nineteenth century, a series of private organizations—the Society for the Prevention of Cruelty to Children (1874), the Society for the Suppression of Vice (1873), the Society for the Prevention of Crime (1878), and the City Vigilance League (1892)—were founded in New York City and spread to cities across the state and nation. Dominated by white Protestant Republican middle-class men, these organizations nonetheless were nonpartisan and nonsectarian. Their members believed there were plenty of laws on the books to combat the evils they identified; the problem was with enforcement. Thus members of these groups used public power to advance their campaigns. In 1876 the state attorney general gave the Society for the Prevention of Cruelty to Children the power to represent the state in child abuse cases. That group, along with the Society for the Prevention of Crime, investigated and helped close concert saloons (the precursor of cabarets) where prostitutes worked. SPC members advised New York City mayors William R. Grace and Abram S. Hewitt and helped organize police raids and revoke the licenses of nine hundred concert saloons.

These raids forced prostitution out of some urban venues, but prostitutes simply moved to tenements and hotels. One of the Raines Law's provisions also served to change the geography of prostitution. Only saloons attached to hotels were permitted to remain open on Sundays, the saloon owners' banner business day. To stay open, more than one thousand saloons in New York City alone suddenly gained ten "rooms" (often merely partitions), which allowed them to legally qualify as hotels. As devoted to efficiency as any COS agent, many saloon keepers sought to make the new rooms pay by renting the spaces to several customers a night—unmarried couples looking for privacy, or prostitutes and their customers. Soon prostitutes waited for assignments in the back rooms of "Raines Law hotels." Because of the Raines Law, prostitutes could be found everywhere from dives to the elegant Luchow's restaurant in New York City.

As campaigns against mass culture, vice, poverty and alcohol indicate, using the state to attack social problems in the late nineteenth century was both tempting and frustrating. The state's potential power was too great to pass up, but members of organizations dedicated to battling these evils believed they could not rely upon the state to enforce the laws. One source of frustration was party politics, which was inseparable from government: partisan calculations shaped policies, and the pervasiveness of politics led many New Yorkers to be suspicious of expanded state power. Another frustration was the state's limited financial resources and bureaucratic expertise. Members of charity, anti-vice, and anti-liquor organizations tried to use state power through their private organizations, and sometimes succeeded.

Education, however, was an exception to the rule of partisan government and weak administration. Through the 1850s and 1860s, state officials carried on what they saw as the battle against parochialism and lax and variable standards by increasing the state's control over district schools, while also increasing the money the state spent on education. In the 1850s the state instituted a .75 mil tax on real property, which greatly enhanced revenue and made school commissioners subject to election in assembly districts rather than being appointed by county supervisors, which was supposed to reduce the influence of local politicians. The School Law of 1864 increased state power over teacher training and school commissioners. Through the 1880s and 1890s, the state assumed responsibility for certifying teachers and tried to put teeth into the compulsory education law by giving commissioners the power to monitor school attendance. The state made the 160-day school year mandatory and required those between the ages of eight and sixteen to be in school. Districts followed the rules or lost state money. Public schools were hardly unsullied by

By the 1890s, school attendance was mandatory for all New Yorkers between the ages of eight and sixteen. "Kept In," by Edward Lamson Henry, shows a public school near Kingston, New York (oil on canvas, 1888). New York State Historical Association, Cooperstown, N.Y.

politics, but no one argued that partisan politics belonged in the system, which smoothed the way for enlarged state power over education.

The conviction that schools ought to remain beyond politics gave New York women interested in woman suffrage or education an opening. In 1880 the legislature extended the right to vote for school district officials and to hold offices on local school boards to women who raised children or paid taxes. The law covered all but the largest cities. In 1892 women gained the right to vote for county school commissioners and to run for that post. School suffrage was one of the few shreds of progress woman suffragists could boast of in the late nineteenth century. Susan B. Anthony's claim that women already had the vote, courtesy of the Fourteenth Amendment, lost in the courts when she was tried for attempting to vote illegally in 1872. Suffragists failed to get the word "male" removed from the state's electoral laws in the constitutional convention of 1894. Legislators were amenable to school suffrage, however: education fitted with women's supposed expertise in family matters. And if education was supposed to be beyond politics, then who better to both run for and perhaps even hold office than otherwise disfranchised women? The idea that women voters and officials would "largely increase the efficiency of the school management," as Governor Alonzo B. Cornell put it in 1880, persuaded legislators in most northern states to grant women this partial suffrage.

But though woman suffrage in school district elections illustrated ideas about education and politics, it did little for the suffrage movement. Partial suffrage did not have a trickle-up effect. Only a mass movement pushed woman suffrage forward in the early twentieth century, and many suffragists were unimpressed with partial suffrage. The Albany Woman Suffrage Society sarcastically urged its members to vote to show "they appreciate the crumbs of justice doled out by the ruling powers."

After a surge of interest in the early 1880s, when suffragists, teachers, and some prominent women ran for the offices and won posts in Saratoga Springs, Woodhaven, Queensbury, Middletown, New Hudson, Wellsville, Fayetteville, and numerous other places, district elections returned to normal. Some women continued to run for office. School meetings usually passed with little fanfare or popular interest, although occasionally spending, taxation, religious issues, or merger propositions ignited heated, even violent, confrontations. The 1892 law quickly wound up in the courts, and in 1894 the Court of Appeals decided that women could hold these offices but could not vote for their occupants. Thousands of women nevertheless voted in the 1893 elections, and women ran for county school commissionerships in almost every assembly district in the state, usually as third-party candidates. Four women won, joining two women who were elected in 1890. Women's votes were helpful to the winning women candidates, but with men's votes alone, more women—often teachers or former teachers—ran for and won offices after 1894. In 1900, nine school commissioners were women. Women's successes in school elections indicate that expertise and nonpartisanship were important to many New York voters, at least in education.

The extent to which education was out of the considerable reach of partisan politics allowed for the expansion of state control, but education's cultural and economic importance made some reforms difficult to achieve or implement even if passed. Efforts to have decisions about merging tiny rural school districts moved to the state level failed in the state legislature until the 1930s. Small as many of them were, these schools were important local institutions, and rural residents believed that the decision to eliminate them belonged in the districts themselves. Rural voters may have believed that experts rather than party hacks ought to be responsible for education, but they also believed that a crucial element in running schools was knowledge of local values and conditions.

A combination of political and cultural forces, however, brought centralized school administration to New York City. A monopoly of sorts—a "School Ring"—had been running the city system according to reformers. The most important ordinary decisions in the largest school system in the nation had been made at the ward level. Ward trustees, five per ward, selected locations for new buildings, arranged contracts for buildings, repairs, and supplies, picked teachers from a list prepared by the city superintendent, and passed out teaching assignments and promotions. For reformers this system was chaotic, wasteful, and produced no end of problems: overcrowded schools, politicized appointments, a demoralized staff, and out-of-date instructional ideas.

The reformers were a diverse lot, including charity reformers, people concerned with inculcating Protestant and "American" values among recent immigrants, municipal reformers, and a women's organization, the Public Education Association. They differed about the substance of what the schools ought to promote—everything from "Americanism" to the value of cultural diversity and vocational training and lessons on the evils of tobacco and alcohol. They agreed, however, that a centralized system, a single board of education, with a board of superintendents dominated by professional educators, was the answer. Reformers exaggerated the problems in the school system, especially overcrowding, and the extent of politicization, but after years of work, they won passage of a bill reorganizing the city educational system in 1896. Their achievement, ironically enough, had to do with politics. They persuaded Republicans that the bill would help them with voters—that the aura of statesmanship would fall upon candidates damaged by association with the Republican statewide machine.

The campaign to reorganize the New York City system was not a battle of the poor against the rich. Most of the vocal opponents belonged to respectable middle- and working-class organizations: teachers' and administrators' groups, ethnic and Catholic organizations, labor unions, and regular Republicans and Democrats. Poor people were not consulted by either side. Nor was centralization a struggle of cosmopolitanism against localism—each side had its measure of both these traits. Like the state's attempt to centralize rural school districts, the New York City case came down to differing understandings of the kind of knowledge that was important in running the schools properly. The new system did not end overcrowding or the other ills, which had more to do with the money the city was willing to spend than with the administrative system. But those who worked in the New York City schools learned to look to the administrators as their most important constituency, not to the people in the wards.

Centralized control, in this case from the state, also seemed to be the answer for whites concerned about the lives of Indians in New York. The proposed 1868 state constitution placed land held by Indian nations under the control of the state, but that plan went down with the rest of the constitution. Events both in New York and at the national level brought renewed attention to the New York tribes in the 1870s and 1880s. When the Erie Railroad built a line from New York City to Dunkirk and the Great Western laid track from Salamanca to Cincinnati, Ohio, they passed through the Seneca Nation in Allegany and Cattaraugus Counties. The Senecas leased the right of way to the railroads, as well as land for workers' housing. The leases raised questions about the competence of the Seneca Nation to lease the land and the jurisdiction of the state and federal governments over the Senecas. New York State invalidated the leases in 1875; but the federal Congress reauthorized them later that year. In 1890, the Senecas extended the leases to ninety-nine years. The federal government, meanwhile, also moved against the sovereignty of Indian nations and the lands that defined them. The Dawes Act in 1887 ended federal recognition of tribal governments, put land in the hands of individuals rather than tribes as a whole, and gave the federal government the power to sell "surplus" land. Tribal government seemed the cause of backwardness among Indians according to those who criticized the reservation system. Allotting land to individuals would open up a great deal of territory to white settlers, a consideration reformers did not miss.

White reformers and some state legislators in New York also linked disposition of land to the moral state of the New York Indian nations. The legislature charged a committee in 1888 to survey "the social, moral and industrial condition" of New York tribes—and, not incidentally, to determine land under cultivation, how the land was allocated, and the state of treaties governing Indian land. Investigators spotted moral degradation on their visits to reservations: "pagan" factions were in control of the Onondaga and Seneca Nations, which slowed the spread of Christianity's "civilizing" influence. Since the nations had not fully adopted New York's court system, there was, according to the investigators, no justice. The school system had not done enough for the Senecas or Mohawks, since the students' parents had not let go of their native languages. The Indians were "wholly without ambition to work" and locked in "chronic barbarism." Some who testified before the committee did not find moral standards among Indians remarkably lower than those of the white population. Still, the report echoed the ideas of charity reformers: "The aid from the State and nation and from public charity is not enough to support the Indians in comfort and decency and health, but is just enough to discourage and often destroy effort on his [sic] part to assist himself."

Legislators hoped the committee report would point a way toward applying the principles of the Dawes Act to New York tribes. As things stood, the preemptive rights to the small amount of land left to Senecas in the Ogden Company purchase in 1842 were retained by the Ogden Land Company, a firm that had purchased Seneca lands with the hope of profitably selling tracts to white settlers. Reformers proposed state control of Indian land, allotting land to individual Indians, and American citizenship, rather than tribal membership. Citizenship and especially individual ownership of land would not only establish prudence and thrift but also resolve questions about tribal leases and free up land. Members of New York tribes were not of a single mind on how to respond,

The Frank Logan house on the Onondaga Nation reservation near Syracuse (ca. 1905).
Photo by Fred R. Wolcott. Courtesy of Onondaga County Parks, Office of Museums and Historical Sites.

but few took up the offer of citizenship. Most Senecas rejected the federal government's offer in 1895 to straighten out land claims, since they feared that tribal government would be lost. The reservation system—and conflicts over land claims—remained.

The Gilded Age secured that label not because of the attempts of the Senecas to retain tribal status or the efforts of vice reformers or the criticisms of agricultural and labor organizations but because of the displays of opulence among the rich. Here, as in the production and extension of forms of mass culture, New York was the national center. Each of the state's cities had local elites, but New York City was home to the state's—and the nation's—elite. Because it was the headquarters of communications, commerce, and finance, men who made fortunes elsewhere, such as Collis Huntington of the Union Pacific Railroad and the steel magnate Henry Clay Frick wound up in New York City. They joined wealthy New Yorkers in building sumptuous (or garish, depending on one's tastes) homes: millionaires' row along Fifth Avenue featured William Vanderbilt's block-long mansion. The owners filled their homes with their European finds, including not only paintings, sculpture, and tapestries but also dismantled and rebuilt stairways and ceilings. Newspaper columns chronicled the social lives of the "Four Hundred" wealthiest and most prominent families, the names on Mrs. William Astor's guest list, and extravagant parties. The newspapers also reported the charitable activities of the elite—gifts to a fund for newsboys, J. Pierpont Morgan's contribution that built the Cathedral of St. John the Divine, support for the Young Men's Christian Association and the East Side Boy's Club, donations to universities such as Syracuse, Rochester, Cornell, Buffalo, and Columbia that allowed the schools to keep pace with rapidly changing universities nationally, and contributions to cultural institutions such as the symphony and opera. Yet New York's elite was not of a piece. It was divided by politics, religion, economic interests, and ethnicity. As was the case earlier in the nineteenth century, these divisions helped diffuse the influence of the upper class in New York society and politics.

Some observers saw the cultural life of the rich in the late nineteenth century as an obscene exercise of excess. A larger number of critics in the twentieth century agreed. In the early decades of the twentieth century, New Yorkers tried to trim some of the excesses, especially the gap between the rich and poor, and to resolve some of the conflicts of the Gilded Age. Progressive Era efforts, however, were somewhat less directed toward overturning dominant social values than were the reform movements of the Gilded Age. Gone, too, by the twentieth century was the ambivalence about state power. Reformers—whether women's groups, labor organizations, or middle- and upper-middle-class crusaders—would seek to use state power directly rather than obliquely. First, however, came an attack on the political parties that were so much a part of Gilded Age culture and politics and so much an obstacle to a larger role for the state in society.

Chapter 27

"Progress" and Politics

IN 1900, PLANS MOVED FORWARD FOR THE PAN-AMERICAN Exposition to be held in Buffalo the following year. Like Chicago's Columbian Exposition of 1893 and Atlanta's Cotton States and International Exposition of 1895, this one would celebrate technological progress. The Electric Tower, a structure illuminated by the marvel of tens of thousands of incandescent light bulbs, stood at the center of the fairground. Surrounding it were buildings devoted to the subjects of "Manufacturers," "Liberal Arts," "Machines," "Transportation," "Agriculture," and "Electricity," also traced in light. Planners hoped the exposition's midway would edify as well as entertain, so along with rides and an animal show starring Jumbo, a nine-ton elephant, a portion of the Buffalo grounds featured "The Old Plantation," with, according to the *Buffalo Evening News*, "genuine southern darkies, two hundred of them." As the opening date approached, New York politicians received letters from constituents angling for patronage jobs at the fair. Buffalo's boosters had grander hopes than these supplicants. Their attractions celebrated the passage of slavery from the cause of America's bloodiest war to nostalgic, quaint entertainment, the pace of technological progress, and the arrival of a unified America to preeminence in the world. And no doubt they hoped to show that Buffalo, now much more than just an old canal city, was a leader in manufacturing, transportation, and service industries in the United States.

Those interested in charting progress could (and did) cite statistics that pointed upward. Workers' standard of living in New York State was improving. The state still led the nation in manufacturing—in the amount of capital devoted to industry, the number of wage earners, the amount of wages paid, and the value of products. New York State was important in some heavy industries

A view of the Pan-American Exposition in Buffalo, New York. From *Pan-American Exposition* (Buffalo, 1901), a book sold as a souvenir.

such as steel, which was concentrated around Buffalo; it was also dominant in some areas of light manufacturing. Much of the nation's women's and men's clothing and a good deal of its jewelry and silverware were made in New York City. Men and women in Troy produced more than 85 percent of the collars and cuffs in the nation, and those in Gloversville and Johnstown manufactured close to two-thirds of the country's leather gloves. Possessing forests, cheap access to the upper Midwest, and a large publishing industry, New York State was the source of 21 percent of the country's wood pulp and paper. The state led in dairy production and in the value of buckwheat, hay, hops, potatoes, onions, beans, apples, and small fruit sold; it was second to California in grapes. Farmers also benefited from better prices than they had seen in the late nineteenth century. And though the tabulators of progress were not likely to count such achievements, New York City remained an innovator in forms of mass commercial entertainment. Vaudeville houses, penny arcades, and nickelodeons vied for customers by the first decade of the twentieth century, while young men and women created new dances—"pivoting" and "spieling," in which rap-

Workers at the International Cheese Plant in Cooperstown in 1912. Smith-Telfer Collection, New York State Historical Association, Cooperstown, N.Y.

idly spinning dancers touched—in the city's dance halls. Soon, New York City would also be the home of the nascent movie industry.

Others were not so certain that "progress" described what was happening to their world. Grangers mused about change; one in Manchester wondered whether life had become "too complicated now-a-days for real enjoyment." Anti-vice reformers were certain things had become worse. Members of the Committee of Fifteen, formed in New York City in 1900, patrolled dance halls in an effort to curb the prostitution that the police could not control and in fact abetted. The immigrants who continued to find their way to New York State in larger numbers than ever hoped for progress, but some of the native born did not take their presence to be a sign of it. Socialists hardly opposed expanded industrial production, but they did object to the gap between the rich and poor and to the highly uneven sharing of the fruits of progress. There was a less focused but no less important sense among a broad swath of New Yorkers that socially, morally, and politically, things were slightly—or terribly—wrong. Perhaps Buffalo's boosters also came to question progress. The exposition never made back the money invested in it; even Jumbo turned on his captors and, then becoming a victim of the available wiring, was put to death by electrocution. The exposition became famous as the place where Leon Czolgosz assassinated President William McKinley on September 6, 1901. Some eighty years later, with many more reasons to doubt the reality of progress, T-shirts proclaimed Buffalo "The City of No Illusions."

Uneasiness about the direction of change in the early twentieth century translated into efforts to remake New York society and politics. Historians once called this reform campaign at the local, state, and national levels the "Progressive Movement" and debated its origins, timing, goals, and larger meaning. That debate has trickled away leaving no firm conclusions except that there was no unified progressive movement. A welter of groups with contradictory or conflicting goals attempted to change society and politics, and no straight line connected what reformers wanted and what happened as a result of their work. If complexity is now the standard interpretation of progressivism nationally, there was plenty of it in New York State. A dizzying number of groups with plans for change maneuvered for influence. Almost everything seemed in need of reform—food, housing, work, religious practices, education, health, leisure, the family, child rearing, and much more. Those who were targets of other people's crusades often had reform agendas of their own. Many reformers came armed with scientific methods and ideals: they hoped the precise gathering of facts would yield solutions to problems that served the interests of the whole public, rather than just small segments of it. Others followed what they saw as a religious mandate for reform; still others mixed the two. Whatever the target of reform and the assumptions that underpinned action, reformers found that the force of government was necessary to achieve their objectives. A state actively engaged in improving social conditions became the focus of their plans. First, however, reformers would have to remake politics if government was to serve the public interest.

How Late Nineteenth-Century Politics Worked—and Failed

The political parties, not permanent bureaus, agencies, or commissions, conducted most of the work of politics and government in the late nineteenth century. They staged elections with little state support or interference. In a hierarchical series of conventions (not primaries), the parties nominated candidates. The parties, not candidates, planned and conducted the campaigns, arranging for speakers, rallies, and literature. The parties laid out the appeals, campaign events, and materials. Newspapers, most of which were affiliated with one of the parties, repeated their party's claims. Party organizations canvassed voters to discover strengths and weaknesses in their campaigns and the things that needed to be done before election day. The parties printed the ballots. In New York, each cluster of offices (presidential, state, judicial, local) required a separate ticket, and Democrats and Republicans used different colors or sizes to identify themselves. On election day, party workers "bunched" the tickets, and ticket peddlers pushed them on voters at the polling places, which included saloons, barber shops, firehouses, and country stores. Party workers helped voters get to the polls and paid those who needed encouragement. After the election, party leaders distributed the favors available from the pot of state, local, and national offices.

Elections in New York took on special importance since it was one of the small band of states in which the parties were of roughly equal strength and which thus possessed the swing electoral votes that dictated the outcomes of national elections. New York governors and other prominent officials therefore automatically became prospects for the presidency and important cabinet posts. New York also contained the nation's premier patronage job: Collector of the Port of New York, the holder of which oversaw the flow of much of the nation's imported goods and appointed hundreds of employees. The collectorship was as important to many businessmen as it was to politicians, since honest and efficient collection made their work predictable. The stakes of politics in New York were high.

With all that was on the line, party leaders struggled to perfect their organizations and mute factional quarrels. A string of state "bosses" directed the Republican organization. Utican Roscoe Conkling, the handsome (he was reputed to have the finest torso in the nation), eloquent, and flamboyant (he carried on a public affair with a married woman in Washington, D.C.) United States senator, controlled the party in the 1870s through his ruthless elimination of enemies, mastery of conventions, and lock on the disposition of federal patronage in New York. His faction, the Stalwarts, however, battled the Half-Breeds—a rival wing of the party—at both the state and national levels over support for President Grant and patronage. Conkling fell from power spectacularly in 1880. President James A. Garfield, a Half-Breed, named a Conkling enemy, William H. Robertson, to be Collector of the Port. Astonishing the Senate, the party, and the nation, both Conkling and New York's junior senator, Thomas Collier Platt, resigned their seats in May 1881. With federal patronage in the hands of the Half-Breeds, the state legislature replaced them with Warner Miller and Elbridge C. Lapham.

The "Senatorial Suicide" made Platt the object of ridicule, but with patient work he came back to lead the state party by 1888 and held on until 1901. Born in Owego in 1833, Platt studied at a local academy and briefly at Yale but returned to the central Southern Tier and "drifted into politics," as he put it in his autobiography. Platt attended the layers of conventions, learned their rules, and rose through the ranks from Tioga county clerk to United States senator. Party loyalty and regularity were his most important political commitments. His experience with Conkling taught Platt about the dangers of overreaching and the art of leading where followers were willing to go. To that, and to his deft handling of patronage, the "Easy Boss" owed his success.

The Democrats typically did not recognize a state "boss," but for a few years in the late 1880s and early 1890s, David Bennett Hill came close. Hill began his political career as a ward leader in Elmira at the age of twenty-one, and, like Platt, he worked his way through the panoply of offices and conventions. Serving as governor from 1884 to 1891 and then as United States senator, Hill adeptly used patronage to maintain a working alliance among the party's major local powers: Hugh McLaughlin of the Brooklyn Democracy, Richard Croker of Tammany Hall, William F. Sheehan of Buffalo, and Edward Murphy of Troy. Like Platt, Hill believed most of all in his party's success; he summarized his approach to politics in the slogan "I am a Democrat." His control of the party slipped in 1892 because of a series of small scandals: the seizure of mail that contained election returns certifying a Republican victory in Dutchess County in 1892; the calling of a "snap caucus" that excluded Hill's adversaries to select national convention delegates in 1892; and the passage of "ripper bills" that revised Buffalo's city charter to give greater control to Sheehan. Hill served in the United States Senate until 1897, but his days as the central figure in the state party were over.

As an organization, the Democrats grappled with two major problems. On one side, a "reform" wing of the state party found both Hill and the city machines repulsive. This faction, identified with Grover Cleveland, rejected party regularity as the measure of political virtue and promoted civil service reform—making what were patronage jobs permanent and subject to appointment through competitive examinations. Reform Democrats could appeal to dissatisfied Republicans and independents, homeless in a partisan polity, as well as Democrats. Cleveland himself demonstrated that. His victory in the 1881 mayoral election in Buffalo was by the largest majority recorded up to that time. His reputation for fiscal and political probity won him the governor's race in 1882, and despite Republican charges that he had fathered an illegitimate child, he easily carried New York in the 1884 presidential election.

The other problem involved maintaining unity in the Democratic urban base, especially in New York City and Brooklyn, the source of most Democratic votes. The tough-minded and shrewd Richard Croker took control of Tammany after the death of "Honest John" Kelly in 1886 and maintained it until his resignation in 1902. During his tenure, Tammany won five of six mayoral elections, in part because Croker kept intact Tammany's alliance with the corporate attorneys, bankers, and businessmen that Kelly had forged after the fall of "Boss" Tweed. Like Kelly, Croker limited increases in debt and taxes, as those city elites wished, but also recognized the working class through stable patronage and services and funds for district outings or "chowders." Croker also stabilized the growth of the city's electorate—Tammany no longer naturalized and registered as many immigrants as possible—which slowed the demand for patronage. Still, factional struggles and problems with urban reformers continued in New York's large cities. In Brooklyn, Seth Low, an independent Republican, deposed the Brooklyn Democratic machine in 1881, although Hugh McLaughlin's organization soon reasserted control. In New York City, Henry George's labor-sponsored challenge in 1886 nearly brought down Tammany, while state and national Democratic leaders occasionally defied Tammany by recognizing rival organizations like Irving Hall and the County Democracy. Local conditions and state and national political skirmishes made machine control something achieved rather than assured.

Other chronic problems also served to make "boss" rule tenuous. Local party workers had considerable power, which they understood and used. Among other things, they bundled and peddled the tickets, arranged for rallies, canvassed and rounded up voters, and distributed favors. They provided state leaders with "intelligence" about local conditions. Local workers could—and did—"knife" candidates (replace one person's name with another on a ticket) who displeased them. They also assembled irregular bundles of tickets, which forced newspapers to repeatedly print regular tickets and warn voters to watch out for odd bunches. "Cut out the Electors ticket found in our columns today," advised a Batavia newspaper. "Attempts to cheat you will be plenty. Be careful." Sometimes knifings served the purposes of a statewide faction. Cleveland supporters blamed his defeat in the presidential election of 1888 on Hill, who won reelection as governor while Cleveland lost. They returned the favor against regular Democrats by knifing those candidates in 1893. But more often voters knifed a nominee in order to honor or punish a local candidate. Party workers got out the vote, but the extent of their responsibilities gave them the power to overturn party decisions.

Raising money also was a persistent problem. The parties required substantial amounts of cash for workers, rallies, favors like the fabled turkeys and buckets of coal, district outings, and the votes of individuals or sometimes assemblymen and senators. Tax dollars were insufficient for some of these tasks and unavailable for purely partisan functions. So the parties developed their own alternative tax system. They assessed candidates (rich men were always a welcomed addition to a ticket) for the privilege of running; they also assessed holders of political jobs. The vice economy too enriched the Democrats in particular, as owners of brothels and gambling establishments and illegal liquor dealers paid police and politicians for protection from harassment.

Corporations also paid into the alternative tax system, although politicians differed over how to tap them. Some, such as Conkling, wanted corporate money but also independence from specific corporations. They preferred picking up contributions in a haphazard way that some businessmen thought flirted with extortion. They threatened to pass regulations that affected a corporation or industry (a "strike bill") and got paid for their inaction. By the 1890s, politicians like Platt (and many businesses) favored stable relationships with corporations: regular contributions came with regular support. This was especially important when civil service rules began to cut into the number of political appointees who could be assessed. Platt established solid connections with transportation, utility, construction, and insurance firms, which paid for party operations, reduced buccaneering by individual legislators, and actually saved money for the corporations. Important politicians of both parties increasingly made tidy side incomes by serving as corporate officers. The parties needed to fund their large organizations but dreaded the controversy that the vice economy, assessments, and business connections sometimes inspired.

The policies that parties produced reflected their structural strengths and weaknesses. Democratic and Republican legislators concentrated on measures that passed out favors with little controversy, which suited the purposes of decentralized organizations that could afford few defections. Like those in the rest of the nation, the New York State legislature kept busy primarily with local bills—revised charters and the like that rarely caused conflict or debate. State economic policies also normally aroused little conflict: they consisted largely of measures that distributed favors and promoted what politicians believed would advance economic development. Legislators wrote generous corporate charters, fostered improvements in transportation (even well past its prime the Erie Canal was repeatedly upgraded, and it was made largely toll-free by 1882), tried to maintain low taxes, and aided agriculture through support of agricultural societies, research, and education. The parties' corporate sponsors had their interests protected. Bills dealing with liquor, electoral rules, and, sometimes, the large cities, caused a good deal more controversy, since they, unlike economic legislation, tended to affect partisan fortunes directly.

The parties could also generate innovative laws at times. Conservation is one example. The Adirondack "wilderness" attracted little notice until the mid-nineteenth century—speculators tried to turn over parcels of land, but territory so wild, isolated, and ill suited to farming attracted few takers. In the second half of the century, however, tourists and adventurers drawn by the scenery, sportsmen enticed by the abundant fish and game, and miners and lumbermen lured by iron ore and stands of spruce and white pine discovered the Adirondacks. Sportsmen and tourists, mostly well-off residents of New York City, together with the New York Board of Trade and Transportation, sought legislation that would protect the region from further development. They succeeded in 1883. The legislature passed a law that withdrew state land in ten forest counties from sale. This was followed by an 1885 law that created a forest preserve in the Adirondacks and a commission—the second in the country after California's—to manage it. The statute declared that "lands now or hereafter

A turn-of-the-century canoeing camp on Lake George in the Adirondacks. American Canoe Association Collection, New York State Historical Association, Cooperstown, N.Y.

constituting the Forest Preserve shall be kept forever as wild forest lands." They were not to be sold or leased or "taken by any person or corporation, public or private." The creation of the Adirondack Park in 1892 preceded federal law creating national forests by six years. A state constitutional amendment in 1894 incorporated the language of the 1885 statute and further protected the unique park—in which year-round residents lived on private property in the midst of a state forest. In 1904 similar action led to the creation of the Catskill Park.

Innovation of a different sort led to the creation of Greater New York in 1898. The successful effort led by Andrew H. Green to combine New York City, Brooklyn, Staten Island, the Bronx, and Queens into one consolidated city began in 1888. New York City's mercantile elite hoped for a more orderly, rational, and functional city with a unified transportation system and tax policy. Opposed by some Brooklyn residents, who feared that Tammany corruption would overrun the "City of Churches," by some Manhattanites, who wondered about footing the tax bill for the extension of city services to Staten Island, Queens, and what would become the Bronx, and by some upstate legislators, who feared the creation of an even larger alien city, the plan was nevertheless approved by Platt. While it was by no means clear that a unified New York would strengthen the Republican party downstate, Platt hoped that a new city charter would open the way for greater state control over city government. Legislation that created a commission to produce a plan for a consolidated government passed in 1896; a charter for Greater New York, opposed by most Democratic legislators, was signed into law by Republican Governor Frank S. Black in 1897.

Most voters, it seems, were not intensely dissatisfied with how the parties governed them. As individuals many of them requested the favors politicians dispensed—free passes for train trips, jobs, introductions, and the like. In asking for favors they pointed with pride to their partisanship, and they felt they had earned tokens of recognition in return for regular support. The parties' principles—the Democrats' defense of free trade, limited government, and personal choice and the Republicans' advocacy of vigorous economic development and attacks on vice—apparently satisfied most voters, since most supported the same party's candidates year after year, from the top of the ticket to the bottom.

Still, there were signs of discontent. Many voters believed that in their own communities there were issues too important to be left to the parties. Services like gas, electricity, and public transportation upon which urban residents depended should not, many thought, be handed to the parties to be the objects of deals with private contractors. In 1891, for example, citizens of Jamestown decided to construct their own municipal electrical power plant, removing politics, they hoped, from the power supply. Other cities did not go that far in the late nineteenth century, but municipal utilities remained a source of controversy. In villages and rural towns many local elections were conducted without party labels, and voters made it clear that crucial matters like tax assessments should be free of politics. Partisan hoopla was fine for state or presidential elections, but many voters felt it had no place in questions of immediate and direct importance.

Some citizens, especially those in the upper-middle class, went further. They were appalled by both parties and longed for a system in which the best men—themselves, for instance—would run government for the good of all. The partisan system was inefficient, corrupt, and allowed ignorant ethnic voters to promote shrewd but greedy professional politicians to positions of authority. Ridiculed as "mugwumps" by partisans, they supported civil service reform and the creation of nonpartisan, professional, and businesslike government, especially at the municipal level. Tied to neither party, they supported men like Grover Cleveland in state and national elections and Seth Low in Brooklyn through urban good government clubs. Charles C. P. Clark, an Oswego physician, even constructed an antipartisan plan of government for his city that the legislature twice approved but Governor Roswell P. Flower twice vetoed in the late nineteenth century. The "mugwumps" lacked popular appeal; their elitism and nativism were hardly platforms for building mass support. It would take a serious depression to spur change in the partisan balance and party rule.

Politics and the Depression of the 1890s

Grover Cleveland was not a lucky man. Elected to the presidency in 1884 and defeated in 1888, he won a second term in 1892, seeming vindication for his vision of the Democratic party and public policy: distance from urban machines, propriety in politics, hard money, and low tariffs. He did not have much time to savor his victory, however. A major industrial depression hit in the spring of 1893 and dragged on until 1897. The first signs of it in the United States concerned the railroads, specifically the Philadelphia and Reading Railroad's declaration of bankruptcy; in May, the New York stock market crashed after some weeks of wild fluctuation. Panic spread to the banks (128 closed across the country in June alone); and factory closings, layoffs, and cutbacks followed bank failures. European investors dumped American securities, and the supply of gold in the United States Treasury hit a dangerously low level. Like the depression of the 1870s, this one had roots in a long-term glut in worldwide productive capacity and flat wages in the United States and Europe, not in specific policies that American politicians advanced. But it would become Cleveland's and the Democrats' depression.

Cleveland, like the Democrats in power in New York State, hoped to ride out a brief panic, but public officials acted when the panic lengthened into a major depression. Federal relief was not a consideration, as Cleveland affirmed that the government had no business directly supporting citizens. But he believed that the panic began because of a mistaken policy, the Sherman Silver Purchase Act of 1890, which provided for the coinage of silver as well as gold. Cleveland resolved he would return the nation to "sane" currency, "hard money"—the gold standard. Using all of his political capital and alienating western and midwestern Democrats, he won repeal, though not the end of the depression. In New York, Governor Roswell P. Flower, a wealthy Watertown banker and the choice of both Hill and Croker, echoed Cleveland's belief in the moral duty of government to reject the "paternalism" of direct relief. He did, however, quickly let out canal construction contracts and continued work on the state capitol. In New York City, rallies of socialists and anarchists on the Lower East Side inspired the *New York Times* to call for suspending immigration for the rest of the year. In part in response to the demands of the unemployed, New York City organized relief efforts, to which Tammany was a main contributor.

The state election of 1893, however, had more to do with squabbles among Democrats than the depression. A major rift between Cleveland and Hill over the Democratic ticket and purges and counterpurges of supporters of the two from federal and state patronage rolls left Democrats demoralized. The state ticket headed by a Hill candidate lost. In municipal elections in Albany, Troy, and New York City, Democratic "machine" candidates came away with victories, but blatant violence and intimidation in Troy in particular inspired citizens to form good government groups and plan revenge. The results pleased Cleveland and his faction, as they hoped the losses would break Hill's power but leave their forces in better shape for election days to come.

In 1894 the lengthening depression mattered to voters, and Republicans achieved one of the largest midterm election landslides up to that time. The Republicans argued that low tariffs had caused the depression and high tariffs would end it. Leaving no advantage unexploited, the party also highlighted Democratic corruption. A legislative committee headed by State Senator Clarence Lexow of Rockland County opened hearings in the spring that documented the lurid specifics of the vice industry and the connections of the police to it. In cities where the 1893 election had been marred by fraud, electoral corruption was also an issue that worked against the Democrats. The Democratic ticket, headed by Senator Hill as candidate for governor, campaigned on ethnic and religious issues, charging that the Republicans were anti-Catholic and anti-immigrant bigots, but the Republicans gained fifteen congressional seats, 105 of 128 Assembly seats, and the state Senate. Levi P. Morton, a banker and former vice president, won the gubernatorial race. While some Cleveland supporters continued to believe that the election was nothing more than a setback for the machines and Hill, it was in fact part of a major realignment that made the Republicans the stronger party in the state until the 1920s.

There was another bonus for the Republicans. With the state apparently in their grasp in 1892, the Democratic legislature approved holding a constitutional convention. Voters selected delegates in 1894, and the Republican landslide resulted in the GOP's securing all of the 15 at-large seats and 83 of the 160 district representatives. The party took advantage of the edge. The constitution proposed an apportionment scheme that reinforced the Republican rural base. The size of the Senate and the Assembly increased from 32 to 50 and 128 to 150, respectively, which added urban seats but maintained rural strength. The new constitution required voters in cities with more than five thousand people to register in person (an antifraud and antimachine rule), and the separation of national and state from local elections in cities of more than fifty thousand (to reduce the impact of Tammany on national and state elections and to boost the chances of reform candidates). The terms of the office of the governor and other elected state officials, which had been three years since 1876, returned to two years.

Otherwise, the convention trimmed the demands of some groups. Anti-Catholic organizations wanted to bar public assistance to sectarian institutions; Catholic leaders initially sought aid for both schools and churches. The constitution allowed public aid to sectarian charities but not to schools. The Grange still called for prorated railroad rates, equal taxation of personal and real property, and federal control of the Erie Canal. The constitution gave the legislature the power to approve canal improvements and use taxes or bonds to fund them. Labor organizations had an ambitious agenda: a strengthened eight-hour provision, employer liability for industrial accidents, urban home rule, restrictions on industrial work done in tenements and occupations that women and children could perform, an exemption of labor from anticonspiracy laws, and more. The constitution outlawed only commercial convict labor. Urban good government groups also sought municipal home rule and separate local elections, but secured only the latter. The state woman suffrage organization and local Political Equality clubs devoted their efforts to gathering petitions and preparing for the convention, but the delegates rejected woman suffrage. Voters ratified the new constitution in 1894.

The Republican party cemented its gains in the next two elections. Democrats regained some ground in the off-year elections of 1895, when conflicts over strict enforcement of Sunday closing laws moved German voters back to the Democratic side, although the Republicans still controlled the state. In 1896, William McKinley of Ohio, known for his championing of high tariffs, secured the Republican presidential nomination after pledging fealty to hard money, as eastern Republicans wished. The Platt machine put forward for governor Frank S. Black, a lawyer and former congressman known statewide for his prosecution of the Troy electoral frauds. The Democrats were badly split at both the national and state levels. Southern and western delegates to the national convention battled easterners over the currency issue; the New York delegation, split between Cleveland and Hill forces, united to back hard money. They failed. The convention nominated silverite William Jennings Bryan of Nebraska and wrote a platform that criticized the Cleveland administration's hard money policy and its use of federal troops to put down the Pullman strike in Chicago. New York Democrats, unhappy about both the candidate and platform, went home and promptly divided. Some Cleveland backers threw their support to a third party made up of hard money Democrats. After searching for some other way out, Hill and Tammany wound up weakly supporting both the ticket and the platform. In the disarray, they even had trouble lining up someone to run for governor. For New York Democrats the Bryan candidacy was a disaster. Platt's man, Frank Black, was elected governor.

The 1896 election wiped out the Democrats' small gains of 1895. Republicans successfully reached farmers and urban workers (failing only with Irish Catholics) and picked up the support (financial and electoral) of the New York City upper class that had backed Tammany. Adding patriotism and evocations of the Civil War to their appeals, the GOP achieved the most decisive presidential victory in twenty-four years. In New York State, no Democratic presidential candidate had lost either New York City or Brooklyn since 1848; Bryan lost both. The party that won 49 percent of the vote in the 1892 election (versus 45.6

percent for the Republicans) received only 38.7 percent. In all of New York and New England, Schoharie County alone gave Bryan a majority. A major partisan realignment had taken place over four elections, which left the Democracy the minority party in New York State and the downstate counties the leadership of the party. The partisan stalemate that had held in New York State politics since the 1870s was over.

Politicians and Reformers Revamp the Political System

The Republican party began a long period of dominance in New York State politics, yet it would both participate in and react to the waning of party government. The party had to accommodate a variety of groups that demanded changes in state and municipal policies. Dissatisfaction with urban politics, which had been confined largely to upper-middle-class mugwumps, attracted a larger base. Some New Yorkers were alarmed by the connections between large corporations and politicians, the connections between money and politics. Others wanted a less partisan and more professional state government involved in regulating areas of the economy. By the first decade of the twentieth century the functions of state government, the methods of party finance, and the place of parties in the political system would be substantially different from what they were in the nineteenth century. An expanded tax base helped make some of these changes possible. And voters changed along with government: the committed partisanship and avid participation characteristic of the nineteenth century began to fade. These changes were not a matter of major party politicians being blindsided by reformers. Politicians wrote the laws that solidified the major parties' place in politics even as partisanship weakened. In piecemeal fashion, politicians, citizens' groups, and business organizations created a substantially different political system in the early twentieth century.

Signs of trouble ahead for Republican leadership appeared as early as 1897, when many voters registered discontent not just with the Democrats or Republicans but with party government. Republicans lost the highest state office contested that year and also all the state's largest cities. Independent voters and organizations produced these defeats, as candidates sponsored by citizens' groups in New York City, Rochester, and Syracuse came in second to Democrats while regular Republican nominees held down third place. Republican legislators responded to the independents' strength by giving them some of what they wanted. A new primary election law in 1898 pleased independents, since it might make independent nominations easier to secure. Still, many voters suspected that the Republican machine abused power. An investigation provided proof, revealing $1 million in overcharges on a canal improvement project, the reclassification of political appointees to the civil service list (preventing their removal), and Governor Black's "starchless" civil service law that gave Republican politicians wide discretion in hiring.

Platt and the Republican organization believed that only a candidate who appealed to independents, who seemed free from the direction of the Platt machine, could possibly win the gubernatorial election in 1898. Platt's lieutenants turned to Theodore Roosevelt. A former assemblyman and New York City police commissioner, and a newly proclaimed hero of the Spanish-American war, Roosevelt had long kept his distance from the regular party organization. Like many other members of New York's upper class, he criticized machine rule, but he also respected professional politicians. And he believed independents to be at best impractical and, at worst, "quite as potent forces for evil as the most corrupt politician." Roosevelt accepted the party nomination with the agreement that he would consult with Platt but also with others. Weaving between independent organizations and the regular organization and highlighting his martial achievements in a vigorous campaign, Roosevelt came away with a close victory.

Roosevelt's talent for attracting publicity kept him in the news, while party regulars continued to fear the Rough Rider. Yet his was a mostly uneventful term as governor. Meeting regularly with Senator Platt, Roosevelt followed some of the Easy Boss's advice, trimmed other suggestions, and in a few cases rejected his directions. Independents received some attention in the form of a more effective civil service law, revised city charters, and a few appointments, but in keeping with Platt's wishes, Roosevelt left untouched many of the most divisive issues, such as the growing problem of corporate trusts and the close connections between some businesses and politicians. His attempt at tax reform—signing into law a tax on public service franchises—was tied up in the courts for twelve years.

Roosevelt went on to the vice presidency in 1900 and, with McKinley's assassination, to the presidency in 1901. Republican Benjamin B. Odell, Jr., Platt's second in command, former congressman, and Newburgh businessman, replaced Roosevelt as governor. Odell's first term was a pleasant surprise to many independents, since he not only crossed Platt and replaced him as party leader but amassed a record of achievement in office that substantially surpassed Roosevelt's. Yet especially in his second term, Odell encountered a good deal more difficulty satisfying the many groups that wanted something from the state. In addition to interests that traditionally asked for and received state support—the transportation, utilities, construction, and insurance industries—other groups pursued their ends more aggressively. The Workingmen's Federation, a lobbying group representing the growing number of unionized workers, succeeded in getting a stronger (but still mainly ineffective) law making employers liable for industrial accidents. With other groups it lobbied for a child labor law (passed, but stripped of serious enforcement provisions in 1903). Merchant and manufacturing groups that had normally focused their attention on federal tariff schedules also made demands on the state, if only to guard their interests against other lobbies. In addition to this stepped-up interest group activity, Odell and the legislature also had to field criticisms about politicians' corrupt ties with companies that did business with the state.

Increased demands on government made it more difficult for politicians to govern in the usual way, passing out favors and supporting economic growth. What helped labor organizations hurt manufacturers; railroad regulations favored by merchants cut into railroad profits. Any way that politicians looked they faced unpopular choices that distributing favors did not present. This was enough of a challenge to party government, but investigations of connections between business and government cut to the core of party finance as well as to established patterns of policy-making. In 1905 and 1906 the legislature investigated the gas, electrical, and life insurance industries and their political dealings. The investigations, pursued by the inquiry committee's council, Charles Evans Hughes, uncovered corrupt business practices of long standing (fraudulent bookkeeping, prohibited investments, and the like) and the purchase of political influence through contributions to the Democratic and Republican parties and individual politicians. The life insurance investigation hurt Republicans: New York Senator Chauncey Depew regularly received a $20,000 retainer from Equitable; Odell had suspicious connections with the industry; and Platt funneled tens of thousands of insurance company dollars into party coffers. The two investigations demonstrated systematic patterns of political corruption that tainted both parties. Many voters, and even the partisan press, called for an end to these abuses of power.

The revelations brought some immediate results and eventually helped change state policy-making. New legislation banned corporate contributions to the parties and regulated lobbying. The investigations sent both parties scrambling for respectability: in the off-year elections of 1905, candidates trumpeted their distance from party machines. The probes also launched Hughes's political career. He went on to win the Republican gubernatorial nomination and the election in 1906.

The Hughes administration consolidated and advanced political reform, including the use of expert commissions to regulate industries and separate politics from economic policy. Public service commissions in transportation and utilities were supposed to use analytical methods with the trappings of science to arrive at rates and regulations that served the public, not the interests. New York's 1906 law (passed under Governor Frank Higgins's administration) governing the insurance industry that regulated insurance companies' organization and investments and prescribed regular audits became a model for legislation in other states. Under the 1907 Moreland Act, the governor could open an investigation into the conduct of any state department, commission, or bureau. A workmen's compensation bill—the nation's first—was passed and signed in 1910, although it was declared unconstitutional in 1911. There was no end to special bills and incentives to economic growth, the staples of party government, but now the state government regulated industries as well as promoted them.

New laws also sought to break the connection between money and politics and to change how the parties operated. Legislation passed almost unanimously in 1906 outlawed corporate contributions to the parties, defined what constituted permissible campaign expenditures, and required the parties to give a precise accounting of campaign contributions and spending. Claiming that "all that is worst in our public life finds its readiest means of access to power through the control of the nominating machinery of parties," Governor Hughes worked for a new system of direct nominations in 1909. The opposition of party leaders, however, blocked passage of direct primary legislation until 1913.

These were important innovations in government. Regulation extended the government's responsibility in the economy and moved the locus of power. Those interested in the gas industry were just as—or more—likely to deal with the Public Utilities Commission as with the legislature. As significant as the expansion of the state's regulatory power was, however, its impact can be overstated. In practice, regulation often worked like distribution by other means. Corporations used regulation as an alternative form of state support against potential competitors. Although affected industries tended to oppose regulations initially, they learned how to make the new rules work in their favor and often gained direct representation on regulatory boards. The public interest was still elusive, even for the supposedly nonpolitical, disinterested experts in the agencies.

Without the fanfare of investigations, the creation of a new state tax system settled an old problem and opened numerous political possibilities. The state's reliance on real property taxes had been a constraint on spending, a constant irritant to the Republicans' rural base as well as to middle-class urban residents, and an incentive for politicians to rely upon their own assessment system for party funds. The 1896 Raines Liquor Tax Law provided welcome revenues to both the state and local governments. New taxes on inheritances and corporations pushed forward by Governor Odell further reduced the state's need for property taxes. By 1905, 80 percent of state revenue came from these new sources, and Odell was close to his goal of abolishing the property tax for state purposes. Although corporations might have balked at having the state tax burden shift in their direction—bitter fights broke out in other states over this issue—there was little complaint in New York. Odell's campaign to cut state spending through reorganization and staff cuts helped calm corporations. A dream of tax reformers—separate sources of funds for different levels of government—was close to reality.

The breakthrough in tax policy raised new prospects for groups with plans to use governmental power. Except in campaign rhetoric, the ideal of economical government fell before mounting spending on traditionally popular items: transportation, prisons, asylums, and education. State support of such programs allowed representatives to return tax money to their districts; in some parts of New York attracting a state institution such as a school, prison, or hospital amounted to the main strategy for economic survival. More innovative were efforts to improve the lives and employment conditions of working-class New Yorkers, which brought together the unusual combination of Tammany Hall politicians and elite women's organizations. This alliance neatly served the needs of both groups and created a new phase of progressive reform, one less concerned with good government and institutional change than with using state power to "improve" the lives of citizens.

The Democratic party had not fully recovered from the disasters of the 1890s by the early twentieth century. Despite its big-city base, it retained its traditional ideology of small government, personal liberty, and home rule, which fitted poorly with the realities of an urban, industrial society. The party's few electoral victories had more to do with independent candidates who siphoned off Republican votes than with Democratic strength. Independents and an outmoded ideology were not the Democrats' only problems. The Socialist party, once limited to a small number of German immigrants, threatened Tammany in working-class wards by the 1910s. More than the Democrats, the Socialists spoke directly to the immediate problems of working-class New Yorkers and moved beyond internal quarrels and the party's base in German neighborhoods to attract east European Jews and native-born voters. Finally, money to support Tammany's operations became scarce. Tammany (like the Republican party) no longer had the wide stream of political jobs and corporate contributions to fund its operations. Tammany needed a new direction.

Elite women interested in public service had their own problems. Those who felt confined by their class and gender traditionally had carved out places for themselves in charitable work. By the early twentieth century new approaches to charity that stressed environmental causes of poverty (and the need for professionals to root them out) increasingly shut out elite women from work with the poor. The Charity Organization Society ideology struck the new reformers—middle to upper-middle class, often with a college education—as needlessly cruel and, worse, unscientific and unprofessional. As elite women lost their claim to the poor, ideas about "authenticity" and work made working-class life seem romantic. Working-class women led real lives, in contrast to the genteel, stilted, and emotionally parched comforts of the upper class. "We all lived in dolls' houses and I for one wanted to get out onto the world of real things," wrote Rheta Childe Dorr, a reformer and journalist recalling her impatience with the life of an upper-middle-class matron. Elite women imagined that working-class women had the independence they craved: "Our sisters of the poorer class have the most fundamental right for which we are struggling—the right for economic independence, the right to continue their chosen work after marriage," wrote one.

Yet, while heavily romanticizing working-class life, elite women nonetheless believed workingwomen's long hours, dangerous conditions, and low wages cried out for remedy. They were ready to supply it. One organizational outlet was the Consumers' League. Founded in 1890, the Consumers' League soon had branches in New York's larger cities. Barring both employers (except of servants) and employees from membership, the league at first aimed to use women's power as consumers to change the conditions of working-class women. The group published "white lists" of stores that treated their salesclerks reasonably well, and urged women to shop at the approved stores and to shop early, so that clerks' hours might be shortened. When this approach changed neither consumers' behavior nor storeowners' practices, the Consumers' League moved in new directions. In 1899, Florence Kelley, an alumna of Chicago's Hull House settlement, took over leadership of the organization. Uninterested in building a mass membership, the Consumers' League looked to scientific investigations of working conditions, publicity of those findings, and legislation to fix substandard conditions.

A more direct way to reach working-class women was through the Women's Trade Union League (WTUL), formed in 1903. Upper-class women (known as "allies") joined workingwomen in WTUL branches, though relations between them were often tense. Workers and "allies" differed over the purpose of the organization. Was it to promote unionism, as most of the working-class members wanted? Was it to work for legislation that protected women workers? To lift up working-class women culturally, as some "allies" believed? To agitate for such feminist causes as woman suffrage? Despite such conflicts, the WTUL helped to form International Ladies' Garment Workers' Union (ILGWU) locals. In New York City, the number of unionized women rose from 8,000 in 1900 to 71,000 by 1913. The WTUL also helped women who struck Troy's collar factories. The 1909 shirtwaist strike in New York City was perhaps the high point of cross-class cooperation in support of unionization.

Through the fall of 1909, employees (mostly women) struck three shirtwaist factories. WTUL members joined picket lines to witness the harassment and beatings of strikers. When police mistakenly arrested WTUL member Mary Dreier, a socialite, the cause gained a great deal of publicity. The ILGWU called a meeting at Cooper Union on November 22. After two hours of boring speeches, Ukranian immigrant Clara Lemlich, an organizer of one of the ongoing strikes, stood and asked the audience of shirtwaist makers to take an old Jewish oath: "If I turn traitor to the cause I now pledge, may this hand wither from the arm I now raise." The thousands assembled agreed to a general strike against shirtwaist factories in the city.

Estimates varied, but perhaps as many as 30,000 workers, three-quarters of the workforce, did not report to work the next day. Conditions that inspired Lemlich to strike were not limited to three factories, since the ruthlessly competitive garment industry encouraged all employers to exploit labor. In the busy season workers put in up to seventy-hour weeks, but they had no work during slack times. Wages varied with skill, but competitive pressure (and the fact that women could be paid far less than men) kept them low. Many workers even paid for the electricity to run their machines and for their needles and thread. Few garment workers belonged to unions: teenaged girls, whom established unions considered poor material for organization, dominated the workforce. Ethnic divisions did not help: 55 percent of the shirtwaist workers were Russian Jews, 35 percent were Italian, and 7 percent were native born, including a small number of African American women who broke through the discriminatory practices of both factories and the union. Only 3 percent of the strikers were Italians, while African Americans debated taking jobs as strikebreakers, since the unions rejected them anyway.

The strikers' demands included a requirement that employers pay for materials, a fifty-three-hour week and limits on overtime, and most important of all, recognition of the union. The strikers received broad public support: New York City's elite (most conspicuously Alva Belmont, the former Mrs. William K. Vanderbilt, and Anne Morgan, niece of financier J. P. Morgan) joined with Lower East Side socialists in endorsing the strikers' demands. The small firms settled with their workers quickly, and by November 27, one-third of the shirtwaist workers were back on the job. A group of larger companies offered to meet most of the demands except the union shop. Many supporters of the strikers (including the AFL, but not the WTUL) urged them to take the deal. The shirtwaist workers trickled back to their jobs, most with this agreement, but some with none at all.

Two years later a tragedy reminded New Yorkers of the harsh conditions that remained for women workers. Before closing time on March 25, 1911, fire broke out at New York City's Triangle Shirtwaist factory (located in the Asch Building on Washington and Greene Streets), where some five hundred women, mostly young Jewish immigrants, worked. Although a modern "fireproof" building, it was a firetrap like most garment factories, with bundles of cloth strewn around, lint thick in the air, and no sprinkler system. Fire blocked one exit; the owner locked the other to prevent workers from sneaking out or stealing. As the fire spread, women leapt from the building, some onto a spiked iron fence directly below the fire escape. "Jumping from ten stories up! They are going through the air like bundles of clothes and the firemen can't stop them

A firefighter looks on as a victim is lowered from the upper floors of the Triangle Shirtwaist factory after the tragic fire of March 1911. From *Harper's Weekly*, April 1, 1911.

and the policemen can't stop them and nobody can help at all," exclaimed one observer. Out of the five hundred employees, 146 died—in less than fifteen minutes—and many more were hurt. The factory owners were tried for but not convicted of negligence. In 1914 a judge ordered them to pay $75 in damages to each of the twenty-three families who had sued.

The Triangle fire proved to the "allies" in the WTUL (as well as to some women workers) that unionization only partially addressed the problems of women in industry. Male-led AFL unions showed little interest in organizing women. The WTUL's success was limited to a few industries. Government regulation improved on unionization by covering all female and child workers immediately. It also offered benefits to a number of groups. The AFL opposed regulating the wages, hours, and working conditions of adult men, since they should rely on unions, not government. But government could help female and child workers, since AFL leaders believed they were impossible to organize and regulating their labor could remove them as potential competitors in some lines of work. For elite women, state regulation provided a chance to do good, to exercise political influence, and to gain direct access to public policy by serving in the regulatory agencies.

For a new generation of Tammany leaders—men like Assemblyman Alfred E. Smith, State Senator Robert F. Wagner, and ward leader, Assemblyman, and Congressman Timothy D. ("Big Tim") Sullivan—labor law was part of a new direction for Tammany. Reform Republicans had paid attention to the demands of organized labor and labor reformers—during the Hughes administration, the legislature passed fifty-six laws dealing with labor in some form. But the new fiscal order freed up state funds and made it possible for Tammany to reformulate Democratic party politics. Tammany moved away from the personal, individual favors characteristic of the old machine toward providing benefits through state legislation to entire groups. These changes pointed toward the direction that the Democratic party would follow through the 1920s and 1930s.

In the early twentieth century, new regulations concerning working-class life and labor became law through the efforts of a coalition of organized labor, reform organizations (especially those staffed by women), reform Republicans, and Tammany politicians. Following the Triangle fire, Smith and Wagner led the Factory Investigating Commission in 1911, which conducted hearings about conditions in New York State's canneries, textile plants, garment shops, and other industries. They discovered long hours and unsafe working conditions which, they said, jeopardized women's health and therefore the well-being of future generations. With intensive lobbying by reform groups and the help of the AFL, the legislature in 1912 limited to fifty-four the hours women could work in factories. Bowing to the wishes of upstate legislators, the law excluded canneries (which required concentrated seasonal work), but they were brought under the law in 1913. The state government also stepped up the regulation of tenements, likewise in the interest of public health. In 1901, building codes that required getting light into windowless tenement rooms, adding fireproof fire escapes, and removing backyard privies passed into law. A protracted struggle involving reform groups, organized labor, insurance companies, Tammany politicians, and employers produced a new workmen's compensation act to cover victims of industrial accidents. These interests had argued for over a decade about how workers would be compensated; they emerged with a bill in 1913. In contrast to nineteenth-century reformers, progressive-era groups did not overlook enforcement and administration of the new laws. They tried to make certain that an adequate number of inspectors enforced the laws and that these new employees were experts covered by civil service rules.

An even longer list of initiatives did not make it through the legislature, stymied by the opposition of various interests, existing law, or disagreements among reformers. In 1913, a Consumers' League investigation of women's wages found that most women did not earn nearly enough to maintain an adequate standard of living. Women worked to support themselves, their dependents, and their families; few took jobs for "pin money." The Consumers' League believed a minimum wage for women was the solution. The Factory Investigating Committee confirmed the Consumers' League's findings in 1914, but the league's voluntary minimum wage plan failed to pass the legislature. The Consumers' League and other reform groups also sought to abolish industrial homework (regulated since 1899) in 1909. But the Court of Appeals decision in *In re Jacobs* (1885), which held that banning homework violated the individual right to earn a livelihood, blocked action. Reform groups also called for publicly owned housing, but this, too, met opposition, especially from real estate and construction interests.

Whether legislation regulating women's employment improved conditions for women workers is an open question. For some women, maximum-hours legislation meant lost wages and an additional barrier to the kinds of work women could do, which further limited women's opportunities in an already highly segregated workforce. Enshrined in these laws was the idea that women, like children, needed the special help of the state. Similar legislation covering men waited until the 1930s, as the Supreme Court's 1905 decision in *Lochner v. New York* invalidated a New York law limiting the hours of bakers—men, the court reasoned, could take care of themselves. But whatever such laws meant for individual women, by the beginning of World War I the government (especially the state government) was involved directly in the lives of citizens, and an increasing number of groups looked to government for solutions to economic and social problems.

Yet while government was doing more, fewer voters took the time to participate in politics. Those who did were less likely to demonstrate the rabid partisanship characteristic of the nineteenth century, although partisanship had hardly disappeared. How the paradox of government activism and declining participation developed has been the subject of debate among historians for decades. What is clear is that three groups, reformers, voters, and politicians, each contributed to transforming the state's political culture.

Reformers wanted an electoral system that reflected the judgment of "intelligent" voters, those who examined the candidates and their positions without regard to party. To get there they believed they needed to curb the power of bosses over the electoral process. They proposed replacing privately printed tickets with state-printed ballots. Party tickets, reformers believed, gave the machines too much control over elections, allowed for "trading" between the parties that, for example, brought the defeat of Cleveland in 1888, and put independent tickets at a disadvantage, since they lacked the workforce that parties could mobilize. Reformers touted the Australian ballot, one that listed all candidates and offices, printed by the state and available only at polling places, as the ideal system. To eliminate what they believed was rampant vote-buying and intimidation, they also sought secrecy in voting, and they believed voting booths, where voters could discharge their duty in private, could achieve this.

In 1890, the reformers' wishes appeared to be granted. New laws mandated state-printed tickets and the use of voting booths. To minimize the chaos around polling places and possible scrutiny of voters, barriers prevented observers from milling around ballot boxes. Under the new system, voters could pick up ballots only at polling places, although they could obtain "pasters" to replace the name of one candidate with another, from any source. If not the Australian ballot, the new procedures seemed to be a real reform achievement.

But reformers soon noticed that these rules strengthened the major parties. The "party column" ballot instituted in 1890 diminished competition from independents and renegade partisans. Separate ballots for the two major parties made it harder to vote a split ticket or to support an independent candidate, since voters had to use pasters. Split-ticket voting actually declined in the 1890s. The rules also dampened competition from third parties. The state printed ballots only for parties that had gathered enough signatures (as many as six thousand for state offices by 1896) or gained a high enough percentage of the vote in past elections. These electoral reforms also saved the parties some of the expenses of elections, as they passed the costs to the state government. Most important, state party leaders gained further command of the conduct of elections. State control of ballots and polling places greatly reduced the power and importance of local party workers and eliminated both revolts from below and significant expenses. Gone were the ticket peddlers and district leaders who demanded payment from candidates for including their names in bundles of tickets and who knifed unsatisfactory candidates. Major party leaders no longer relied so heavily on their unofficial tax system to fund their operations and gained greater regularity in and control over elections.

But they also lost some voters along the way. By the first decade of the twentieth century, voters split their tickets at higher rates than ever. While in the late nineteenth century voters departed from straight party tickets when they considered local offices, in the twentieth century they split their tickets for the top offices, where strong personalities or programs attracted or repelled voters. Voter turnout also began a long slide. The presidential election years of 1896 and 1900 drew just under 85 percent of New York voters; by 1908 turnout had fallen to just under 80 percent, and by 1910 it had dropped below 70 percent. The new electoral rules accounted for some of the rise in split-ticket voting and decrease in turnout: registration requirements eliminated some voters, and Australian ballots, introduced in 1895, worked as informal literacy tests (voters had to be able to read the ballots) and made casting split tickets easier. The reduced number and importance of party workers no doubt also contributed to falling turnout, as fewer partisans urged their neighbors out to the polls. The parties also cut back on elaborate campaign rallies and counted on advertising and campaign literature instead of spectacles to move voters. The young, poor, recent immigrants, and marginally literate disproportionately dropped out of (or failed to join) the electorate. The parties no longer socialized them into electoral politics as they once had, and the new rules discouraged their participation.

The rules alone, however, cannot explain the behavior of voters. Many chose to select candidates without the same regard for party that held in the nineteenth century. Many demanded more from government than favors and hoopla. Their new demands surfaced first in local politics, as citizens sought less partisan and more efficient city and village services. As the state government picked up more and more tasks (in addition to education) that immediately affected the lives of citizens, voters began to apply the same standards to the state that they had applied to local governments and educational policy. With more at stake than patronage and favors, many voters sought government that represented their interests more directly, and saw the partisan favors and jobs as corrupt, not normal. Pressure put on legislators by various groups increased state government activism; in turn, government activism changed the expectations for politics and government of the broader citizenry.

Revised expectations for government and decreasing partisanship created an opening for the woman suffrage movement: women were just as affected by state policy as men (more so, according to some suffragists). Women were at least as concerned about "good," nonpartisan government as men were, as demonstrated by participation of some mostly upper-class women in municipal reform campaigns. New women's organizations—the Woman's Municipal League, the Women's Henry George Society, and the Independence League, for example—expressed women's diverse political views.

A new generation of woman suffrage leaders took advantage of the opportunity the changed political climate presented, while also building on existing efforts to bring women together across the class divide. Harriot Stanton Blatch, daughter of Elizabeth Cady Stanton, returned to New York from England in 1902. Although of the upper class herself (she had married into a rich British family), she believed that work, education, and professional achievement, not wealth, fitted women for leadership. Such professional women needed to recognize their dependence on the labor of other women—"a Bridget to do the home-building for her"—and the extent to which a poor or working-class man or woman "needs the suffrage more" than the wealthy did. In 1907, Blatch formed the Equality League of Self-Supporting Women, which brought together profes-

Some 500,000 New Yorkers looked on as supporters of women's suffrage marched shoulder-to-shoulder through the streets and through Central Park in May 1912. Many of the marchers carried soapboxes for impromptu speeches along the parade route. From *Harper's Weekly*, May 11, 1912.

sional and trade union women interested in woman suffrage. The group used tactics—the first all-woman parade in New York City in 1907 and outdoor rallies in New York City, Syracuse, Troy, Albany, and Poughkeepsie in 1908—designed to gain publicity that suffragists had shunned in the past as "unwomanly." These militant techniques drew from the example of British suffragists and also from American unions and the Socialist party.

New demands on government helped change the constituency of the suffrage movement. While middle-class women and active Grange members still formed the movement's core in rural areas and small towns, in the cities working-class and immigrant—especially Jewish—women were becoming an increasingly prominent presence in the campaign. If rural and small town suffragists, many of them also members of the Woman's Christian Temperance Union, saw the vote as a means to the goal of prohibition, urban working-class suffragists believed that the ballot in their hands could inspire better laws concerning employment conditions, housing, and public health. African American woman suffragists, barred from participation in the white women's organizations, established their own groups.

The task of orchestrating the efforts of suffragists with widely different goals fell to the capable Carrie Chapman Catt. Born in rural Wisconsin and a graduate of Iowa State College, Catt had worked as a schoolteacher, administrator, and journalist before turning to full-time suffrage work in the 1890s. Demonstrating her talents for organization, tracking details, and encouraging new leadership learned in numerous campaigns in the West and Midwest, Catt in 1907 formed the Interurban Council, which brought together most suffrage groups in New York City. This group was the basis for the Woman Suffrage Party, begun in 1909, which organized suffragists in the city along the lines of the political parties down to the assembly-district level. Described by a colleague as being "like the brains of the body, sending her instructions out to the tiniest nerves," Catt coordinated the efforts of a large and diverse movement. Her Woman Suffrage Party would become the basis for the Empire State Campaign Committee, which launched an unsuccessful campaign for a state constitutional amendment in 1915.

Reforming the Cities

More than changing the laws or electoral rules, reform, for some New Yorkers, required direct involvement in the lives of the poor. Inspired by the example of London's Toynbee Hall and New York City's short-lived Neighborhood Guilds in the mid-1880s, reformers organized settlement houses, renovated buildings where they would live alongside the urban poor. These reformers were young (most were in their twenties), college educated (at a time when few Americans attended college), unmarried, and from middle- or upper-middle-class families. Settlements attracted more women than men, and women tended to stay in the settlements longer. Some residents, like New York City's Lillian Wald and Chicago's Jane Addams, became national leaders. The settlement movement expanded rapidly. New York City's first settlement was formed in 1889, and soon there were many others in New York City's poor and working-class neighborhoods and in the state's other large cities.

The settlement idea spread so quickly because it blended idealism, practical reform, and personal satisfaction for the settlement residents. At their most idealistic, settlement workers sought through personal contact to minimize the chasms that seemed to separate the working classes and the immigrants from the native born. They hoped as well that a settlement house might be the catalyst for the regeneration of an entire neighborhood. To foster both mutual understanding and improved conditions, settlement workers organized a great variety of programs: art exhibitions and homemaking classes to inculcate middle-class aspirations; nurseries, kindergartens, and vocational classes to improve children's chances of rising in America; English-language and citizenship classes to help adults. Many offered handicraft classes and traditional dances to remind immigrants of the beauty of their ethnic traditions. Living in poor city neighborhoods and trying to improve them allowed settlement workers to believe they had joined real life; they experienced the vitality they imagined the poor alone enjoyed. They felt they gained at least as much as the poor from their efforts. Settlement women, also, found useful employment in a society that allowed few lines of work for college-educated females.

Settlement residents soon discovered that their efforts in local reform fell far short of solving the problems of urban neighborhoods. They enlisted city governments to expand their projects, as Lillian Wald's work at New York City's Henry Street Settlement demonstrates. Wald proposed an experiment in 1901: the settlement would send out nurses to city schools to prove that attention to children's health would prevent high absenteeism and drop-out rates. The experiment worked, and Wald persuaded the city government to pick up the cost of the nurses. The Henry Street Settlement did the same with hot lunches for schoolchildren. In the settlement workers' view, it was not only inadequate but wrong for the Salvation Army (as a religious organization) to provide this service, and Wald convinced the city to replace the voluntary program. Settlement teachers demonstrated that mentally and physically handicapped children could learn, and in 1908 city schools began offering programs for these children. The costs of settlement parks and playgrounds also were transferred to the city in the first decade of the twentieth century.

Yet even the best city programs, settlement leaders determined, still left untouched what they saw as the root causes of poverty and social chaos. Wald and other settlement residents turned to the state government to repair what they regarded as the structural underpinnings of society. The movement's leaders tried to shape public opinion through often highly emotional and sentimental exposés of social problems, with the hope that an aroused public would demand legislative change. New York City settlement residents assisted in the passage of the 1901 tenement regulations by publicizing the miserable conditions in which too many poor and immigrant families lived and by lobbying for the law. The Tenement House Law of 1901 required buildings constructed after that date to meet new standards concerning light, space, and ventilation. With less success, the reformers sought to impress the public with the dangers of overcrowding for both those packed into crowded tenements and the middle-class public, since consumers bought goods made in crowded tenements friendly to the spread of contagious diseases. They displayed their exhibit dramatizing overcrowding and its consequences at the Museum of Natural History and elsewhere, but without a concrete plan of action the issue faded. Settlement residents also worked with—and often joined—reform groups like the Consumers' League, WTUL, and others interested in labor, immigration, and urban conditions. By working to "prevent" rather than merely ameliorate social problems, members of all these groups helped expand the role of government in everyday life.

In communicating with the poor rather than with government officials, they had more difficulty. Some settlement women came to envy the easy familiarity of machine politicians with immigrant New Yorkers but never managed to emulate the politicians' success. Some European immigrants, especially women and children, made use of settlement facilities. Most, however, never darkened the door of a settlement. As a 1913 report of the National Federation of Settlements pointed out, the settlements had a great deal of trouble attracting men and boys in particular to their services. Boys used settlement facilities to hone their boxing skills but little else. Some immigrant men even objected to their wives and children visiting the settlements: they feared disruption of their traditional authority within their families, according to settlement leaders.

All but those settlement workers most attentive to and skilled at cultural translation had difficulties bridging class and ethnic differences. Some workers hardly tried; their efforts to communicate stopped at campaigns to "Americanize" immigrants. In Buffalo, for example, Mary Remington's Welcome Hall offered the usual settlement staples—nurseries, kindergartens, vocational education, housekeeping classes, and the like—to its Italian neighbors. Embedded in these services was the conviction that the inhabitants of Buffalo's Little Italy needed to be lifted out of their backwardness and that the surest sign of progress was their acceptance of "American" middle-class values, habits, culture, and patterns of family organization. Since children might be more easily changed than adults, Welcome Hall organized them into groups like the "Try to do

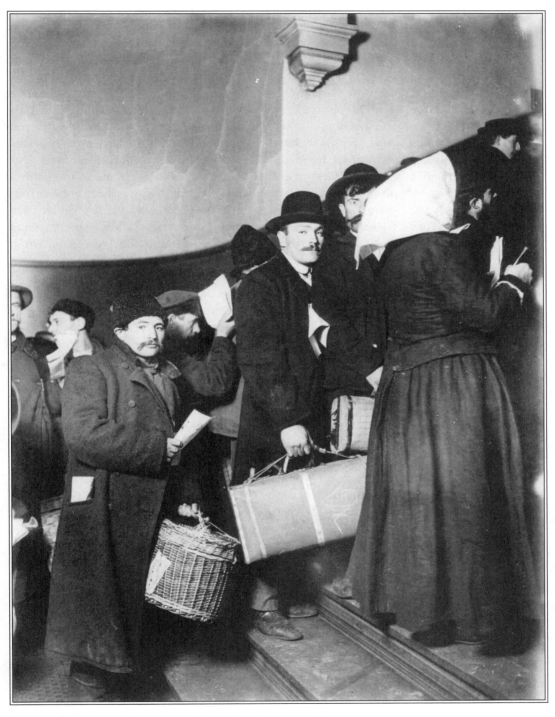

Immigrants waiting to be processed at Ellis Island (ca. 1910). New York State Historical Association, Coopers-town, N.Y.

Right" club. For Remington, the goal was to assimilate immigrants as fast as possible, and assimilation meant abandoning native cultures.

For other settlement leaders, the problem was not a refusal to embrace American ways but adopting the wrong ones too well. Settlements had trouble attracting young women to their activities, as the women preferred commercial entertainments. This alarmed settlement workers, since these women and girls, they feared, posed easy marks for disreputable men, even those who would trap the women into "white slavery." Commercial leisure activities themselves, according to reformers, lured women into vice: by dancing suggestively with men and accepting "treats" in exchange for sexual favors, young women moved step by step into prostitution. Nonetheless, reformers subscribed to the current theory that leisure and play were essential to a well-adjusted life. So by 1910, New York City settlements ran one hundred and sixty clubs for young women and girls, with the hope that the availability of wholesome recreation would diminish the popularity of dance halls, movie theaters, and excursions. They also provided folk dances and chaperoned dances as an alternative to commercial offerings. Employing sticks as well as carrots, settlement leaders worked with anti-vice reformers to regulate commercial entertainment by outlawing the sale of liquor in dance halls, requiring female chaperons at dances, and prescribing how men and women danced. In the end, neither the reformers' alternatives nor their attempts to control young people's entertainment choices could overcome the attraction of the mass culture that entrepreneurs supplied.

Although many settlement workers struggled to reach immigrants, few even tried to help African Americans. Some blamed European immigrants: if settlement activities attempted to include both blacks and whites, whites would stay away. Some subscribed to the virulent racism of their time. Assimilating the "races" of southern and eastern Europe would be hard enough; bringing in African Americans would be just short of impossible. But most settlement leaders were early-twentieth-century racial liberals. They recognized the extreme discrimination of whites against African Americans, deplored the South's Jim Crow system, were sympathetic toward the plight of African Americans, but believed they could do nothing. Unlike European immigrants, they concluded, African Americans had no culture to change or encourage. The tragedy and cruelty of slavery had destroyed culture, family ideals, and proper gender roles among African Americans. Time might change things, but for now, most settlement leaders sadly concluded, work among African Americans was pointless.

Yet the rapidly growing African American population in New York State needed assistance. Relatively small numbers of blacks had moved from the South to the North and West just after the Civil War, but during the 1890s the migration increased dramatically. New York also attracted migrants from the Caribbean islands, although the great majority came from southern states.

The black population of New York doubled; most migrants (about two-thirds) settled in Manhattan. They were typically young—the first generation born in freedom—and women outnumbered men. This was the beginning of the Great Migration of African Americans to the North from the South that would transform both regions.

Southern blacks made their way North for many reasons—to escape the tightening system of segregation in southern states, to discover whether stories about economic opportunities in the North were true, to find out if there was something more that life could offer than the pinched chances open to the poor and black in the rural South. Some found success. T. Thomas Fortune, founder and editor of the *New York Age*, Madame C. J. Walker, purveyor of cosmetics and hair treatments, and P. B. S. Pinchback, Reconstruction governor of Louisiana, were among the most prominent southern migrants to New York City. A small African American middle class, including ministers, doctors, teachers, lawyers, business people, and real estate entrepreneurs provided services to the growing black population. These men and women supported the churches, political clubs, small businesses, hotels, mutual benefit and insurance societies, and institutions like Young Men's Christian Associations that anchored African American social and intellectual life in New York's cities. By the first decade of the twentieth century, signs of the cultural movement that would become famous as the Harlem Renaissance were already visible in the musical and literary achievements of African Americans in New York.

Most migrants came north with little in the way of education, skills, or resources. In the early twentieth century 90 percent of African Americans worked as laborers, especially in menial service jobs. Employment agencies took advantage of their poverty and limited opportunities by locking them into jobs no one else would take in exchange for room and board under miserable conditions; the agencies even trapped some women into prostitution. Housing conditions grew worse as the migration widened. Residential segregation had been patchy during the Gilded Age: the state's biggest cities did not have largely black neighborhoods, although African Americans made up most of the residents of particular blocks or buildings. By the first decades of the twentieth century, however, the development of African American ghettos was under way. Increasingly African Americans could find housing only in black neighborhoods, where landlords took advantage of high demand and low supply by charging excessive rents. Under such circumstances, building and sanitation conditions deteriorated rapidly, which contributed to a substantially higher child mortality rate in black neighborhoods.

For a time, nonetheless, it seemed that rampant discrimination and segregation would not be the future of New York's African American residents. Although economic discrimination clearly existed, some political barriers fell in the late nineteenth century. New York State abolished segregation in public accommodations (transportation, theaters, and restaurants), repealed a law against miscegenation, and replaced the last separate black schools with ward-based schools. These were not the first steps toward integration but instead the last for decades. That progress in race relations stalled or even reversed was the fault, according to some established African Americans in New York, of the migrants. Lacking not only skills but also a sense of how to live in a city, they reinforced stereotypes which long-standing residents had fought hard to overcome.

Others, using settlement houses and clubs, tried both to combat racism and to improve migrants' chances in urban New York State. Victoria Matthews, for example, founded the White Rose Mission in New York City in 1897. Matthews herself moved from the South to New York City in 1873 and was a domestic before acquiring an education and securing work as a writer. Her settlement house concentrated on helping female migrants adjust to the city, find decent housing, and avoid employment agents. To accomplish these things it supplied short-term housing and organized classes in housekeeping, nutrition, and vocational subjects. It also offered cultural uplift in the form of readings by the poet Paul Laurence Dunbar and talks by Booker T. Washington. The Lincoln Settlement in Brooklyn, led by Dr. Vernia Morton Jones, aimed its activities at the young, offering a nursery and kindergarten. In Buffalo, African American women's clubs sought to encourage both self-help and racial uplift. The Phillis Wheatley Club, with a largely but not entirely middle-class membership, focused on health and education for African Americans by running well-baby clinics and classes on hygiene and nutrition. It also sought to combat stereotypes of African Americans as morally lax. Because of that stereotype, Buffalo police ignored prostitution and gambling in black neighborhoods. The club pressured the city to crack down on these activities.

A few settlements attempted to promote racial integration while also providing services to poor neighborhoods. A branch of Lillian Wald's Henry Street Settlement, for example, ran integrated classes, although some activities separated African American and Jewish residents as they requested. A few individuals also worked to bring together black and white New Yorkers. Mary White Ovington, a white woman whose abolitionist parents left her with a strong commitment to racial justice, dedicated herself to work with African Americans after spending time as a settlement resident in an immigrant neighborhood. She wrote *Half a Man* (1911), a sociological account of African American life, and was among the founders of the National Association for the Advancement of Colored People in 1909. The NAACP itself, under the leadership of the scholar and civil rights activist W. E. B. DuBois, fought discrimination, segregation, and racial prejudice. Race riots in northern cities in the early twentieth century made clear that racism was an American, not a southern, problem, but the work of the NAACP aside, improved race relations were not among the achievements of progressive reform.

Reforming the Countryside

Although farms and small towns had once been assumed to nurture virtue and good values in contrast to urban evil, reformers in the early twentieth century spotted rot even in the countryside. Decay took many forms: run-down farms and houses that showed a lack of pride, overly ornate and expensive homes that flaunted city values inappropriate to country life, too many churches that reflected intellectual narrowness, and needlessly grueling work and too little play, which created psychological lethargy. If cities suffered from overcrowding, the countryside, reformers believed, was emptying out as those with the most initiative and imagination fled, and the old and dull clung to dying village communities. While their needs were not as pressing as those urban conditions created, rural society and its economy needed help, which reformers sought to supply.

What was missing in rural areas was "intelligence" as reformers understood it, a willingness to recognize the limits of one's knowledge, to call upon expert advice, to experiment with new ideas and technologies. Traits such as independence and hard work, once widely admired, now struck reformers as backward in an interdependent society newly appreciative of the value of leisure. Those involved in agricultural education especially noticed this lack of intelligence in farming practices, as New York farmers seemed to stick stubbornly with outmoded methods in producing and marketing their crops. After the United States Congress provided funding for agricultural education in 1862, New York State funneled its share to the new Cornell University's College of Agriculture; the state also supported an agricultural experiment station in Geneva. Both institutions struggled, but in the 1890s enhanced state funding allowed them to expand their efforts to reach farmers with news of improved scientific methods. Among their offerings were articles on various farming problems and their solutions, "short courses" for farmers during the winter months, and reading lists for farm families. With the state Department of Public Instruction, they prepared courses for teachers in rural districts and helped make agriculture part of the rural school curriculum. Agricultural reformers hoped that better methods would make New York farmers more productive and, more grandly, that contact with scientific methods would encourage bright young men to stay on the farms and help the less talented shake off their mental torpor. These measures did not reach farmers' wives, so the Cornell College of Agriculture created an extension program for them. This included organizing local study clubs, producing a monthly bulletin, and suggesting appropriate readings. These efforts led ultimately to the creation of a Department of Home Economics at the college.

Rural culture and society needed as much repair as the rural economy, according to reformers. One expression of the "country life movement" was President Theodore Roosevelt's 1906 Country Life Commission, whose investigators found substandard roads, schools, houses, churches, and social opportunities. The commission recommended increased government involvement, especially in education, but Congress failed to act. With support from private foundations and universities, however, social scientists picked up where the politicians left off. They surveyed country schools and recommended consolidated township schools that could offer the range of courses, especially in agricultural and home economics, that district schools did not. Children, perhaps, might prove more malleable than their elders. Churches, too, ought to be consolidated: rural people continued the wasteful support of too many churches, and their narrow sectarianism prevented any engagement with social issues. Churches, like schools, ought to bring communities together and introduce rural residents to new values.

E. Z. Smith, a tractor dealer in Hallsville, New York, demonstrates an International Harvester engine and plow in 1913. New York State Historical Association, Cooperstown, N.Y.

Most farmers were unimpressed with the pressure toward science and social reform. New York State farmers already produced more than enough, they believed, and scientific agriculture did not address what they saw as their core problems: expensive and scarce farm labor, low prices, and high taxes. While the New York State Grange invariably sent petitions supporting state aid for agricultural education, few local Granges did so or subscribed to the reading lists. The state's farmers appreciated the commission's work and its attention to their favorite problems, but they also resented the reformers' intrusive style and focus on issues other than labor, taxes, and prices. The commission, according to a Rensselaer County farmer, proposed "something in line of settlement work in our large cities and [farmers] rather object to their being investigated, as they feel amply able to take care of themselves."

Change was coming in both farming practices and the political and social ideas of rural New Yorkers, but it had more to do with developments in the economics of agriculture and the expansion of government power. While the typical New York State farm was still diversified, specialization was becoming more common. Tasks formerly performed on farms (often by women) increasingly became major businesses. Butter and cheese production was shifting from farm homes to factories; the branded and uniform factory products commanded higher prices than homemade versions. The production of chickens and eggs, too, was becoming less a sideline and more a distinct business. Dairy farmers looked carefully at replacing their "general purpose" cows with purebreds or grades suited to their market: Holsteins for fluid milk and Guernseys for cheese and butter, for example. The growing dominance of a few large creameries that processed and sold farmers' produce encouraged such concentration and close attention to detail. While prices were relatively strong, the changing economics of agriculture showed in the decreasing number of farms and amount of acreage under cultivation. The trend pointed toward fewer, more efficient farmers who let marginal land slip into forest.

The state government indirectly both encouraged these changes and transformed rural men's ideas about what government could do for them. Government action encouraged new political organization. In 1907, New York City's Health Department wrote regulations covering not only creameries but also farmers: scientists had determined that the milk of diseased cows carried bacteria that caused tuberculosis and other illnesses. In response to regulations that required the inspection of dairies as well as to the power of the creameries in setting prices, farmers in Orange County formed the Dairymen's League in 1907. Unlike the Grange, the Dairymen's League did not promote fraternity among rural people. It focused on political issues connected with dairy farming and marketing plans to benefit farmers. The organization grew slowly at first, but by 1916 a successful strike against the creameries made the Dairymen's League one of the most powerful farmers' organizations in New York State.

Other new groups, with the support of government, organized farmers' interests while spreading the gospel of science in the farm and home. The first Farm Bureau appeared in Broome County in 1910 under the auspices of the Binghamton Chamber of Commerce and the Delaware, Lackawanna, and Western Railroad. Designed to improve farmers' access to new methods that might boost profits, the Farm Bureau drew on the expertise of the United States Department of Agriculture (USDA) and the New York State College of Agriculture. The college supplied county agents in 1912 to those counties that supported Farm Bureaus. Most agricultural counties began to provide support after 1914, when the United States Congress passed the Smith-Lever Act, which funded agricultural extension services. The Farm Bureau and county agents linked agricultural schools, experiment stations, and the USDA. In New York, county agents tried to interest farmers in joining the Farm Bureau and also promoted the value of labor-saving methods for the farm and home. The new agricultural organizations concentrated on making farming more profitable through politics and science; they left moral issues such as the evil of drink to women's organizations and the Grange.

These new groups lobbied for causes that farmers had once largely ignored. Good roads—graded, paved, built, and maintained by experts rather than by gangs of local men, and connected to a reasonable system—had been a cause of bicycle enthusiasts during the late nineteenth century. Most farmers had regarded good roads as an expensive frill and usually opposed public spending for road improvement, but farmers' organizations in the twentieth century successfully lobbied for aid that channeled state support to rural areas. A 1905 constitutional amendment allowed the state to float bonds for improved roads; a 1908 law set up a system of state, county, and town roads with the costs divided among them, and in 1912 most of the costs were moved to the state. Agricultural organizations made sure that rural areas received more than their share of the state's bounty.

Tales of political corruption and squalid urban conditions in New York's cities did not move the state's rural residents to change their political and social behavior and expectations. Such stories were consoling, not alarming, as they repeated truths rural New Yorkers already believed. Progressive ideas and patterns of behavior instead came through political and economic change. Rural citizens still complained about taxes and spending, but they benefited more than any Tammany politician from the increased state expenditures made possible by the new tax system. With government providing new services, rural New Yorkers came to expect them as a matter of right. Government action had changed rural New Yorkers' political ideas and social organization.

Historians rightly have explored the complexities and contradictions of progressivism—the tendencies toward both democracy and bureaucratic elitism, the drive toward social justice coupled with an equal desire to control a potentially disruptive lower class, the stress on cultural pluralism that excluded African Americans from full participation in American life. It is no surprise that a package of political, intellectual, and social changes appearing in countries from the United States to New Zealand in various ways does not fit into tidy categories or resists depiction as a simple moral drama that pitted good against evil. In New York State, progressivism brought a significant restructuring of public finance, the role of government in everyday life, and the places of the parties and citizens in politics. Reform mobilized groups—women, labor, members of growing educational and social welfare bureaucracies—that became important political actors. Progressive reform had its ironies. Though one goal of reformers was to weaken the political parties, political reform actually allowed the parties to gain a stronger hold on elections, even as they lost strong popular followings. Progressivism had its weaknesses, especially in race relations, but the progressive conviction that problems existed and that they could be solved changed the political and social order in New York State.

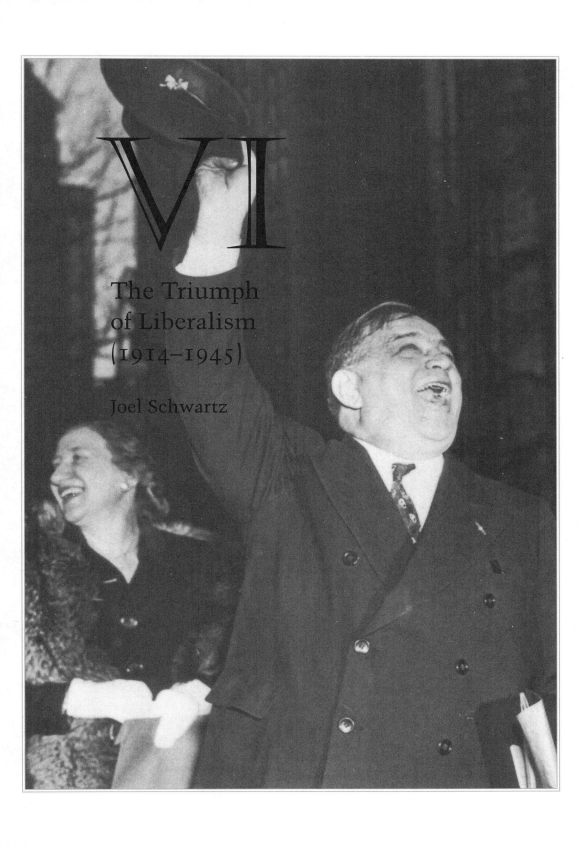

VII

The Triumph
of Liberalism
(1914–1945)

Joel Schwartz

Chapter 28

Progress under Siege

THE EVENTS OF SUMMER 1914 IN EUROPE THAT LED TO World War I staggered New York State. On Friday, July 31, the war scare froze brokers' loans on Wall Street and forced the stock exchange to suspend trades. As London and Paris hoarded gold, the value of New York City municipal bonds, which paid interest in dollars, plummeted on the Paris Bourse. Squeezed by their European counterparts, New York commercial banks recalled loans, which closed shoe, glove, and textile factories across the Mohawk Valley. With the outbreak of war, German markets were shut to Monroe County apple growers, who saw $3 per barrel prices fall to $1.17 by autumn. Turmoil brought recession across the state. In January 1915, New York City had 300,000 jobless, 16.2 percent, a figure matched in many cities by the spring.

New York responded with a mix of voluntary efforts and government activism that were the chief instruments of progressive reform. Manhattan bankers organized a gold pool to guarantee municipal finances in Europe. Cities like Rochester opened municipal employment exchanges, and in New York City industrial leaders raised funds to put the jobless to work. The war crisis posed an unprecedented challenge to progressive reformers. But they were able nonetheless to intensify the government intervention and private-sector initiatives that made New York the leader of the states in social betterment.

The Progressive Legacy

By 1914, the citizens' movement known as progressivism had had a profound impact on state politics. The Republican party had been torn by Theodore

519

THE LATEST ARRIVAL AT THE POLITICAL ZOO

Bull Moose presidential candidate Theodore Roosevelt was
chided for a change of heart regarding corporate campaign contributions. By E. W. Kemble. From *Harper's Weekly,* July 20, 1912.

Roosevelt's strenuous citizenship and by Charles Evans Hughes's boast that as
governor he was "retained [only] by the people." One-fourth of Republican state
assemblymen had become insurgents, who bridled at the orders of party bosses
like George W. Aldridge of Rochester and William Barnes, Jr., of Albany; or, like
Bainbridge Colby of Rensselaer County and Chauncey J. Hamlin of Erie, who
bolted the GOP altogether to join the upstart Progressive party. Many of the latter had been carried along by Roosevelt's Progressive presidential campaign in
1912, the same election in which the Progressive candidate for governor, Oscar
S. Straus, garnered 25 percent of the vote.

But whether these mavericks stayed within the Republican party or challenged it from without, they united on the essentials. They agreed upon the necessity for strong regulation of public utilities and, where necessary, even municipal ownership of gas and electric plants. They favored limits on the factory labor of women and children, and were appalled by the Social Darwinist tone of the Court of Appeals decision *Ives v. South Buffalo Railway Co.* (1911), which nullified the Workmen's Compensation Law of 1910. Most took the desirability of the direct primary as gospel, and a good many championed woman suffrage. Bosses bent to progressive tides and supported good government stars including John Lord O'Brian of Buffalo and Charles S. Whitman, New York County district attorney, who was elected governor in 1914.

For Democrats, the citizens' revolt brought nothing less than a change in political culture. Charles F. Murphy, the dignified leader of Tammany Hall, could prevail over such bosses as Brooklyn's Patrick H. McCarren and Norman E. Mack of Buffalo but also faced mavericks like Thomas Mott Osborne, mayor of Auburn, and the New York City newspaper mogul William Randolph Hearst, whose Independence League was a perennial headache. An even more potent challenge came from Jewish Socialists, who vied with Tammany for working-class votes on the Lower East Side. Murphy shrewdly ran reform gubernatorial candidates, like Glens Falls banker John A. Dix in 1910 and Manhattan Congressman William Sulzer in 1912. When Sulzer's landslide (during the GOP split that year) carried the legislature, Murphy advanced the political fortunes of State Senator Robert F. Wagner and Assemblyman Alfred E. Smith, who had led investigations into the 1911 Triangle fire. Murphy made Wagner Senate majority leader and Smith Assembly speaker, the first Tammany lawmaker so honored.

Murphy walked a fine line between Tammany discipline and citizens' demands. He supported Governor Dix's progressive ideas—for example, state water power development and a state Industrial Commission to correct workplace abuses. But when Sulzer refused to give Tammany adequate patronage, Murphy arranged the "ingrate's" impeachment on charges that he had made false statements on campaign spending. After the Triangle fire and the agitation by reformers like Rose Schneiderman of the Women's Trade Union League, Murphy maneuvered Democrats behind laws to limit child and women's labor and the 1913 constitutional amendment to override the *Ives* decision. Swallowing hard, Murphy accepted the Primary Law of 1914, which allowed parties to "designate" favored candidates and came to see how Tammany might benefit from woman suffrage by "guiding" new voters. The woman suffrage amendment lost badly in 1915 but passed in 1917, largely because of Tammany's work on the Lower East Side. With the legislature's overrepresentation of upstate, rural districts—its "Constitutional Republicanism"—Murphy's cadre of big-city Democrats totaled perhaps twenty senators and one-third of the Assembly. But his grasp of social issues gave Democrats near-parity in statewide contests.

The New York media debated the women's suffrage amendment, which failed to win widespread popular support until 1917. He: Woman Suffrage will kill Chivalry! She: Is that a threat—or a promise? From *Harper's Weekly*, October 9, 1915.

In the state's municipalities, angry citizens rose against corrupt public services. In the 1913 New York City mayoral race, the "Fusion" of Hearst Independents and Republicans elected reform Democrat John Purroy Mitchel. Mitchel not only accepted fiscal austerity—to meet bankers' demands for an emergency $100 million loan; he seemed to revel in cold parsimony. He applied the Bureau of Municipal Research's audits to the "outputs" of street sweepers and civil service workers, and he sent his charities commissioner, John A. Kingsbury, on a campaign against wasteful "outdoor" relief. Mitchel's crusades pleased taxpayers, but working-class parents resented application of the Gary (Indiana) school plan, which regimented children into all-day schools, and Catholics were stung when Kingsbury's investigators called their orphanages a "public scandal."

The good government movement became entrenched in upstate cities. Buffalo, in 1914, was the largest American city to adopt government by commissioners elected at-large on nonpartisan ballots. This civic spirit, Mayor Louis P.

Fuhrmann said, turned City Hall into a Friday night "town meeting." On the advice of Buffalo's Charity Organization Society, municipal relief was handed out according to a strict "means" test, which, the society claimed, turned recipients into responsible citizens. In Rochester, citizens led by industrialist George Eastman and *Evening Times* publisher Frank Gannett forced Boss Aldridge to support Mayor Hiram H. Edgerton, a GOP reformer who imposed cost-cutting recommended by the local Bureau of Municipal Research. Efficiency and order were the watchwords at the Rochester Board of Education, which enlarged kindergartens and intermediate schools, hired psychologists to place "mentally defective" students in special classes, and ran adult evening schools to prepare immigrants for citizenship.

The revolt against waste and corruption left an insurgent mood in normally Republican territory. In Schenectady, the Protestant minister and Socialist George R. Lunn was elected mayor in 1911 on promises of efficient public services, including a municipally owned electric plant. Taxpayers elected maverick Republicans mayors in Jamestown and Watertown on platforms that pledged municipal ownership of utilities run as conservative business propositions. In Westchester County, the Civic League's attack on "the high cost of pauperism" elected V. Everit Macy, who ran as a combined Democrat-Progressive, county superintendent of the poor. Going with the trend, GOP boss William L. Ward pulled strings in Albany for the Westchester County Welfare Law of 1916, which established a county department of public welfare with far-reaching power. In their attacks against corruption, disgruntled Republicans and independent Democrats had recast the scope of local government.

Progressives hoped to write the era's reforms into the state constitution at the 1915 convention. Advocates of executive power including Republican delegates Elihu Root, George W. Wickersham, and Henry L. Stimson wanted to provide the governor with a cabinet and an executive budget (gubernatorial, rather than legislative initiative, in drawing up spending proposals) to end administration that Root called "loose, confused and ill-regulated." Welfare leaders sought to overturn *In re Jacobs*, the 1885 Court of Appeals decision that struck down legislation to regulate cigar making in tenements. When standpat Republicans like William Barnes, Jr., pushed an amendment barring special privileges "to any class of individuals," Wickersham and Stimson joined Democrats State Senator James A. Foley and Assemblyman Al Smith to adopt provisions for juvenile courts and workmen's compensation and against manufacturing in tenements. But the attempt to "centralize" the governor's powers was anathema to legislative Republicans, and Democrats resented yet another denial of what Al Smith said was his city's "proper share" of seats in the Assembly. With thumbs-down from Tammany and the Republican Old Guard, voters overwhelmingly rejected the amendments.

Just the same, the momentum remained with the progressive tradition. In 1914 Acting Governor Martin H. Glynn, a reform Democrat, was challenged by Charles S. Whitman, New York County district attorney, who had made head-lines pursuing police implicated in the murder of the gambler Herman Rosen-thal. Whitman ignored Glynn, vilified Tammany, and won easily. He proved a "lawyerly governor," who focused on government reorganization and deferred to Republican conservatives in the legislature when they trimmed the power of the Industrial Commission. In the 1916 election, both gubernatorial rivals claimed the progressive mantle. Samuel Seabury, associate judge of the Court of Appeals, had eked out a victory in the Democratic primary. A patrician reformer, Seabury favored municipal ownership of transit lines, broader cover-age of workmen's compensation, and limits on court-ordered injunctions against strikes. He was popular on the Lower East Side, but Tammany was wary of his independent ways and sat on its hands. Governor Whitman had the Republican, Progressive, and Hearst endorsements, and coasted to reelection.

The real verdict, however, ran with the tide of public authority. Govern-ment had appropriated private property in the Forest Preserve and at Niagara Falls and Saratoga Springs, while the New York City Board of Water Supply took thousands of acres for the Ashokan Reservoir system and subjected thousands more to the city's eminent domain in the watershed. The state's "police power" was extended by the Industrial Commission, the New York City Tenement House Department, and municipal health departments to factories, sanitary facilities, and housing. Albany undertook giant works like the $200 million State Barge Canal, which made a channel of the Mohawk River and dammed East and West Canada Creeks—a construction project half the volume of the Panama Canal. Governor John Dix cited the Barge Canal's hydroelectric poten-tial to justify demands for a state power authority.

With increasing confidence, Albany supervised and superseded local social welfare. State aid extended to county tuberculosis hospitals, health programs, and district schools. Money went into the improvement of child welfare, prison reform, and the attack on delinquency. Proclaiming that "public health is pur-chasable," State Health Commissioner Dr. Hermann M. Biggs advocated aid for community dispensaries in rural areas. The Central Rural School Law of 1914 increased money for localities that accepted state coordination of local schools. Sophie I. Loeb and Hannah Einstein, aided by Assemblyman Smith, helped enact the Mothers' Pension Law of 1915, which authorized county boards to disburse home relief to widows with children.

The state undertook a sweeping transformation in the handling of the retarded and felons. Charles Bensten, superintendent of the State School for Mental Defectives at Rome, advocated small farm "colonies" that allowed greater training for the "unteachable feeble-minded." A leader in prison reform, Thomas Mott Osborne of Auburn, argued for indeterminate sentences, earned privileges, and parole. As warden of Auburn and Sing Sing prisons, Osborne applied his ideas for inmate self-government, what he called "mutual welfare leagues." Attacking incarceration in grim, walled institutions, reformers anticipated opening places of hope and individual striving. What all these progressives really created, however, was a web of administrative rules over parents, children, and dependent citizens that was the bedrock of the welfare state.

The administrative realm was ratified by the Court of Appeals after jurists, shaken by the outcry against *Ives*, quietly bowed to state authority. Chief Judge Willard Bartlett, a conservative Brooklyn Democrat, cited "industrial conditions" to uphold the One Day of Rest in Seven Law of 1913, and a solid majority in *People v. Charles Schweinler Press* (1915) supported the legislature's limit on night work for women. After his appointment in 1914, Judge Benjamin N. Cardozo's oracular opinions brought new stature to the tribunal. In *MacPherson v. Buick Motor Co.* (1916), Cardozo applied the common law concept of "privity" in product liability beyond the immediate vendor, proclaiming that the manufacturer, no less than the car dealer, was responsible for a defect in the automobile and could be sued by the consumer. While Cardozo was refashioning the common law of contracts and torts for modern needs, under his influence the court sanctioned a crucial enlargement of public authority.

Progressives called upon trained experts to handle modern social problems. Their activist state was buttressed by institutions like the New York School of Philanthropy in Manhattan, which educated social workers in the scientific analysis of poverty and corrections, and the Bureau of Municipal Research in New York City, which also offered programs in public administration at Syracuse University. Social research was sponsored by the Russell Sage and Rockefeller Foundations, while corporate ventures in applied social science included studies in workmen's compensation pursued by the Metropolitan Life Insurance Co. Private social research remained ambivalent toward government effort. Met Life became a pillar of corporate initiatives in health care and the prevention of industrial accidents. The first claim on New York School of Philanthropy graduates was the Charity Organization Society, and the St. Vincent de Paul Society turned to Fordham University's School of Social Service for trained workers in the Catholic tradition. Still, government took over an increasing number of programs in "categorical" aid, like home relief and widows' pensions, whose effectiveness had been demonstrated by private agencies.

The need for social welfare experts turned colleges into secular universities committed to public service. Under Reverend Boothe C. Davis, Alfred University, a Seventh-Day Baptist institution, enlarged to include the State College of Ceramics and the State School of Agriculture. Fordham University, a small campus at Rose Hill in the Bronx, added schools of pharmacy and social work and opened a school of business in downtown Manhattan. Troy's Russell Sage College, under President Eliza Kellas, emphasized home economics and nursing

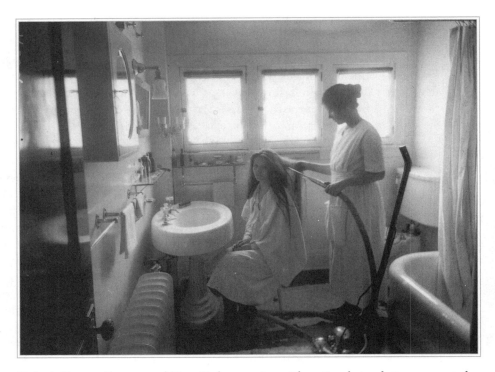

Today's Housewife, a central New York magazine with national circulation, promoted a "hygienic" model bathroom. The seated woman's hair is being styled with a modern contraption still unfamiliar to most readers in 1921: a hairdryer. New York State Historical Association, Cooperstown, N.Y.

to provide women "a liberal education and a wide choice in life work." The most telling changes occurred in the eleven state normal schools, which became four-year colleges. The largest, Buffalo State Normal, developed home economics and vocational education, while Albany State College for Teachers ran extension courses in Troy and Schenectady.

Public attention focused on the making of the modern research university. Chancellor James R. Day remade Syracuse University with a college of business administration, a library school, and the country's largest school of forestry. Led by President Jacob Gould Schurman, Cornell University added a quadrangle for the arts and sciences and increased spending in basic research at the State College of Agriculture, where Dean Liberty Hyde Bailey preached the merits of "rural civilization." Under President Nicholas Murray Butler, Columbia University absorbed independent schools of philanthropy, journalism, and business to become a multiversity on Morningside Heights. A haughty conservative (and the Republican vice presidential candidate in 1912), Butler nonetheless supported the graduate research faculties that made the reputations of the historian James Harvey Robinson and the anthropologist Franz Boas.

Benefactor George Eastman and President Rush Rhees enlarged the University of Rochester's "restricted reputation" by founding the University Medical School, affiliated with Strong Memorial Hospital. The University of Buffalo, then a small medical school, established an undergraduate college in 1914, although the university remained a group of "practically autonomous schools." Albany Medical College was revived by Dean Thomas Ordway, who built a relationship with Union College, upgraded laboratories, and raised funds from the Rockefellers, Willis R. Whitney of General Electric, and Lucius N. Littauer of Gloversville.

The Empire of Business

In 1914 the state led the United States in manufacturing, with New York City alone accounting for one-tenth of the nation's output. Manufacturing moved away from "outwork" in sweatshops and reduced child labor to one percent of the workforce. Entrepreneurs lauded examples of industrial progress, like Henry D. Perky's air-conditioned factory at Niagara Falls, which baked "shredded wheat" breakfast cereal, and Olympian Knit Goods in New Hartford, whose electrical machinery evoked comments that "the sweat shop method has passed away." But one-fifth of the state's 1.3 million factory workers still labored in New York City garment lofts and in canneries near Auburn, where during the seasonal rush women and children shelled peas for $12 per week.

The epitome of modern industrialism was Rochester-based Eastman Kodak, which controlled 90 percent of the U.S. camera market. The vertically integrated firm produced its own raw materials, subcontracted lenses from suppliers such as Bausch & Lomb, and sold heavily advertised brands, "Kodak" and "Brownie," through exclusive dealerships in major cities. Disciplined manufacturing and aggressive marketing had become the keys to business success. At Endicott, Computing-Tabulating-Recording (CTR) president Thomas J. Watson centralized the mass production of Hollerith machines, devices that processed data on punched cards. CTR's assets were the Hollerith brand and Watson, an inspired salesman, whose obsession with service won clients like Met Life and the New York Central Railroad. Nabisco, which operated the world's largest bakery on Manhattan's West Side, dueled for market share with Loose-Wilson (Sunshine Biscuits). Nabisco stayed ahead with massive advertising of biscuits with household names including "Uneeda" and "Lorna Doone." In progressive New York, quality assembly and reliable brands ensured consumer confidence.

Manufacturers also had to behave with prudence in the face of the Sherman Antitrust Act. At CTR that meant a subtle game of infringement suits and patent licenses (to office equipment competitors like Remington Typewriter) to fend off federal antitrust inquiries. Owen D. Young, counsel to General Electric, reviewed patent and license agreements with an eye toward "fair play," but worried about GE's holding company, Electric Bond & Share, whose equipment and capital-investment services controlled scores of public utilities. Increasingly, CEOs pursued industrial research to protect corporate patents and reputations as providers of advanced products. At the GE Research Laboratory in Schenectady, Willis R. Whitney's staff developed the tungsten filament that captured 71 percent of the U.S. lamp market and the audion tube that gave GE its patent stake in radio. AT&T's Western Electric Research Branch in Manhattan was firmly supported by AT&T president Theodore N. Vail. The research branch would bolster the telephone monopoly's pool of patents and deliver the social performance that the public demanded. Vail's mantra for AT&T—"One System, One Policy, Universal Service"—could well have described market ambitions at CTR, Eastman Kodak, and GE.

Semimonopoly control of markets helped corporations absorb the cost of welfare capitalism. Shoe manufacturer Endicott Johnson ran dining halls, dispensed aid in a Workers Medical Service and Relief Department, and built housing in a planned town, West Endicott. Doting on this welfare realm, CEO George F. Johnson liked to think of his shoeworkers as "family." Profit-sharing, pioneered by Solvay Process of Syracuse, was adopted by firms such as Dutchess Bleachery in Wappingers Falls and F. C. Huyck & Co. of Rensselaerville, which, Edmund N. Huyck confidently explained, joined workers' "personal interest . . . in the success of the business." Several plans became industry bywords, notably Eastman Kodak's "wage dividend" and GE's welfare plan, which included preferred stock purchases. GE also experimented with production schedules to steady seasonal swings in employment. The efforts made Owen D. Young and Vice President Gerard Swope widely known as progressive capitalists.

Outside the large industrial corporation, working-class living standards usually depended on union-scale wages or family earnings. While the state counted nearly 600,000 union members, the great majority were in nonfactory work, like New York City's AFL building trades, and railroad engineers, shopmen, and pockets of skilled tradesmen such as carpenters in Dolgeville and trolleymen in Lansingburgh. Seasonal layoffs depressed earnings in the building trades, among Buffalo dock and marine workers, and in New York City's garment, confectionery, and paper box industries. Women's work made the difference in family earnings, particularly in New York City and Rochester, where the needle trades employed Jewish and Italian seamstresses. Families also got by on handouts. In New York City, some 10,000 resorted to the Charity Organization Society, and thousands more sought help from the St. Vincent de Paul

Society, United Hebrew Charities, and others. In Buffalo 800 families regularly applied for relief, a figure that reached 2,300 when stevedore and construction jobs halted in the winter.

New York City banks' enormous resources kept Manhattan the national finance center, despite federal reserve legislation designed to decentralize the money supply. In August 1914, Benjamin Strong, the newly appointed governor of the Federal Reserve Bank of New York, refused advice to suspend gold redemption and goaded member banks to contribute a bullion fund to keep the U.S. dollar "on gold" and make New York the wartime mecca for foreign deposits. Under Strong's bulldog leadership, the New York Reserve District became first among equals in matters of open-market operations and rediscount rates, an authority that overshadowed Washington's.

Established merchant and commercial banks like J. P. Morgan & Co., National City Bank, and Chemical National Bank offered absolute liquidity and financial services to blue-chip clients. A virtual private banker to corporate heads, J. Pierpont Morgan, Sr., upheld the "Gentleman Banker's Code," which eschewed speculation or violations of fiduciary trust. His bank sold standard railroad bonds (particularly equipment trust certificates) collateralized on loco-motives and other rolling stock, but remained the ultimate lender for quality industrials and a leader in bankruptcy reorganization. Morgan's death in 1913, along with the arrival of midwesterners like the Chicago utility financier Samuel Insull and the Cleveland investors, the Van Sweringen brothers, upset establishment ways. Some Wall Streeters sensed the new market opportunities. At National City Bank, President Frank A. Vanderlip exploited federal reserve legislation to compete for commercial paper in other reserve districts. The first major bank to open a foreign office (Buenos Aires), National City in 1915 also acquired a British subsidiary for a European presence that soon reached Moscow.

The New York Stock Exchange largely traded railroad shares, although new industrials, like American Locomotive and General Motors, were soon listed. The Curb Exchange, an outdoor market literally on Broad Street, traded lower-priced issues and over-the-counter stocks. But the exchanges remained in the bankers' shadow. Most prestige corporations raised capital from commercial banks or the investment-house sale of corporate debt, not sales of common stock. (This practice would soon change in the wake of wartime Liberty Loan drives, which involved 22 million Americans and created a new investor consciousness.) Integral to Wall Street finance were corporate law firms like Sullivan & Cromwell and Cravath, Swayne & Moore, which handled railroad bonds and corporate reor-ganizations, mainly railroad bankruptcies. The progressive environment ushered in the "big case," complex antitrust and rate litigations that could entail what a Sullivan & Cromwell partner called "the economics of an entire industry."

Manhattan's retail establishment, which traditionally serviced the wealthy "carriage trade," was transformed by the practices of mass merchandizers. While B. Altman's and Lord & Taylor still provided personal services, such as ladies' lounges, writing rooms, and restaurants to upscale clientele, other retailers were increasingly turning to high-pressure sales gimmicks and advertising. In 1912 John Hartford and George Hartford, Jr., ended premiums, free delivery, and charge accounts at the Atlantic & Pacific Tea Company and substituted spartan "cash-and-carry" stores that were standard in appearance and prices. By 1915 the Hartfords had converted or opened 7,500 "economy" A & P stores. Watertown merchant Frank Woolworth built a chain of variety stores headquartered in the Woolworth Building, the 792-foot "Cathedral of Commerce," which opened on April 24, 1913. The world's tallest building controlled an empire that grew to 1,081 five-and-ten-cent stores by 1919. Opening the "world's largest store" on Herald Square, R. H. Macy's adopted a policy of fixed prices, cash sales, and heavy advertising. It was soon joined across the street by a Philadelphia rival, Gimbel's, in the battle for customers who poured out from the subways.

Industrial corporations and retailers alike spent millions on advertising to create brands like Kodak and Lorna Doone. J. Walter Thompson's agency emerged as the country's foremost wholesaler of print space, mainly in magazines, leading the transformation toward the "creative" agency that offered corporate clients a full range of services. By 1916 Thompson employed 117 people in five offices, handling some 300 clients. Retiring that year, he sold the company to an employee group headed by Stanley B. Resor and his wife, Helen Landsdowne, who became the most important woman in American advertising. Resor was president from 1916 to 1955; Landsdowne was a vice president of the firm and introduced the idea of celebrity endorsement of products, like Pond's soaps.

Vibrant Cities

Immigration and prosperity gave prominence to cities; the 1915 state census listed three-fourths of New York's 9.7 million people as "city" dwellers, with 52 percent in the great metropolis on the Hudson. Between 1910 and 1920 every major city except Troy increased in population. Buffalo, Rochester, and Syracuse grew between 20 and 36 percent. New skylines and civic plazas handled the crush of business. Albany used municipal condemnation to build the Hudson Bridge, remove piers, and break ground for the Delaware & Hudson Building and trolley plaza. Even downtown Troy saw shade trees and sidewalk awnings give way before advancing commercial activity.

Municipal construction and land use controls changed the social geography of New York City. Subway hubs at 34th Street and Times Square, along with the

1913 ordinance that required height limits and "setbacks" on skyscrapers, spread the Wall Street office district into midtown. Rising rents displaced factories and tenement dwellers from lower Manhattan at the same time that the $200 million Dual Subway contracts (to the Interborough Rapid Transit and Brooklyn-Manhattan Transit Companies) extended transit routes into Brooklyn and Queens. Comprehensive zoning in 1916—the first for an American city—guided the land rush in the outer boroughs. Real estate syndicators like Henry Morgenthau, Sr., followed the 1901 Tenement House Law's specifications for larger rooms and courtyards to build stylish apartment houses near subway stops in Washington Heights in Manhattan, the Grand Concourse in the Bronx, and Coney Island Avenue in Brooklyn. Between 1908 and 1918, 540,000 "Old Law" tenement units in Manhattan and Brooklyn were supplemented by 372,000 "New Law flats" in subway neighborhoods. One million people were living in steam-heated apartments in the outer boroughs.

The cities were notable for immigrant "colonies," like the 30,000 residents of Buffalo's "Polonia," and the half million Jews from Poland and Rumania on Manhattan's Lower East Side. It was calculated that 43 percent of Rochester's Italians came from 12 Sicilian communes, and 17 percent came from 427 others, a myriad of family "chains." These colonies were centers of the "tramp" for work. From Utica's Fifth Ward, Italian men trudged for day labor on the barge canal and the New York Central Railroad. Buffalo's West Side docks and rail yards were the hub of another Italian tramp, which stretched from the rail yards of Dunkirk to Chautauqua's vineyards along Lake Erie. An estimated 545,000 Italians near Mulberry Bend and Greenwich Village in New York City worked on docks and construction sites, then in candy and paper box factories during the winter months. In 1916, some 350,000 Jews in New York City did manual work, mostly in the city's garment lofts; but another third were in "business"—mostly peddlers with pushcarts.

Immigrant families benefited from female and adolescent labor when local opportunity and ethnic tradition permitted. Few women found employment in Rome and Schenectady, where industry was dominated by copper and locomotive works. By contrast, they made up 40 percent of the workforce in Gloversville and Johnson City, where glove and shoe factories gave jobs to thousands of female cutters and stitchers. In Buffalo, only 5 percent of married Italian women worked outside the home, probably because of the city's heavy industry and male dominance of the Italian household. While Jewish women were the mainstay of New York City's needle trades, only 13 percent of the city's Italian women worked outside the home. Immigrant ways also retarded upward mobility. Buffalo's Poles distrusted white-collar advancement. In 1916 Polonia accounted for one-fifth of Buffalo's population but only 1.6 percent of high school enrollment. In Jamestown, where Swedish furniture makers dominated the economy, 43 percent of Swedish men were skilled manual workers as late as 1920. For Jamestown's Swedes, the path to success was through craft work and vocational high schools, not college.

Forces within and without buffeted the immigrant colonies in the name of progress. In Buffalo, Polonia was dominated by Saint Stanislaus, the "mother church," where priests blessed *swiecone*, the Easter food. There were also secular influences like the Adam Mickiewicz Library, whose meeting rooms celebrated the Polish poet and free thinker. Rochester's Italians drew the attention of Americanizers as diverse as Republican leader Clement Lanni and Catholic Bishop Bernard McQuaid, who set his Irish hierarchy on that mission. On the Lower East Side, progressive efforts included the Hebrew Educational Alliance, which offered a range of courses for young people and adults, and the *kehillah*, a Jewish community council led by Reform Jews, who sought a governing framework for their brethren. Ardent Americanizers like Julia Richman focused on the public schools, Richman herself becoming the first Jew to be appointed a district superintendent in the city school system.

Mass transit, together with the cutoff of immigrants after 1914, transformed the immigrant colonies, and family earnings and ambitions hastened the move of immigrants into Americanizing neighborhoods. Buffalo's trolley system began to spread Polonia into Kensington-Bailey and South Buffalo. In New York City, the Mulberry Street colony dispersed into Italian neighborhoods in East Harlem and the South Bronx. Jewish garment workers took the subway into Brownsville and Crown Heights in Brooklyn and to Pelham Parkway in the Bronx. Some 275,000 Jewish children attended New York City public schools in 1918, but only 65,000 (24 percent) received any religious instruction, and in Brooklyn and Queens the figure was 12 percent. In the face of this crisis of Americanization, Rabbi Mordecai M. Kaplan proposed to "reconstruct" Judaism as part of a progressive America that anticipated the neighborhood coziness of the "Jewish center." Rabbi Bernard Revel took the opposite tack in 1915 by creating Yeshiva University as a center of Orthodox learning that included secular studies.

For urban blacks, Jim Crow patterns hardened in employment and housing. While nearly 700 blacks were in the Buffalo workforce in 1910, 85 percent were in service jobs, including 326 waiters. Construction of New York City's Pennsylvania Station, completed in 1911, displaced African Americans from Manhattan's West Side into Harlem, where African American realtors such as Philip Payton rented large New Law apartments that had been built for German Jews. While white landlords adopted Jim Crow "gentlemen's agreements" to enclose Harlem within firm boundaries, its sheer numbers supported local entrepreneurs who sold "race" products; cabarets, dance halls, and theaters; and black nationalists like Marcus Garvey.

Ethnic neighborhoods lent a scrappy, pickup quality to sports that had not yet become fully professionalized. Basketball was a loosely organized system of barnstorming teams like the Buffalo Germans and Troy Trojans of the New

York Club League and the largely Jewish Original Celtics, whose stars, Nat Holman and Joe Lapchick, played in local armories and, Lapchick remarked, "bargained with managers for every game." Professional football existed on a leaner scale. In 1921 trucker Tim Mara bought the New York Giants franchise for $2,500. The International League baseball clubs included Binghamton, Buffalo, Syracuse, and the superb Rochester Hustlers, whose fans saw star players sent up to the majors. Big league baseball in New York City meant the Giants, led by manager John J. McGraw and pitcher Christy Mathewson, who dominated the National League from their turf at the Polo Grounds. The American League franchise, the lowly Highlanders, were Polo Grounds tenants until the brewer Jacob Ruppert bought the team for $460,000 and went on a hiring spree for his newly named Yankees, drawing away Boston's general manager, Ed Barrow, and a pitcher-outfielder named George Herman Ruth.

Between 1910 and 1915 suburbs around Buffalo, Rochester, Syracuse, Albany, Utica, and Schenectady grew faster than their central cities, as automobiles compounded the impact of the streetcar. Modern, one-story, electrified factories required suburban space, accentuating the growth of Buffalo's industrial suburbs including the Tonawandas, Depew-Lancaster, and Lackawanna, and those around Syracuse in East Syracuse, Split Rock, and Geddes. Greater Utica was pushed by real estate developers like Hugh R. Jones, who subdivided the Yahnundasis Golf Club and the residential section along Proctor Boulevard. Commuter railroads opened up Westchester County, and Nassau County commuters on the Long Island Railroad tripled between 1910 and 1920, to more than 31,000. So many motorcars wheeled through Nassau and Queens in 1915 that the Long Island Railroad showed lantern slides in theaters to warn drivers not to race trains at grade crossings.

The arrival of growing numbers of Irish, Italians, and Jews unnerved such Westchester communities as New Rochelle, where residents deplored Main Street's "ramshackle" buildings, and Park Hill, Yonkers, which realtors restricted against saloons, trolleys, and the "foreign element." Reformers hit upon a systemic solution in 1914—the fifteen-mile Bronx River Parkway, which controlled the "contagion" of crowding by limiting commercial land use. Suburban defenses included anti-saloon laws enacted by local option in Scarsdale, Yorktown, and White Plains and, on Long Island, dry suburbs. Suburbanites used progressive regulations to contain the ethnic invasion from downtown.

Progressive Culture

In 1914 New York City was America's capital of modern culture. Its writers and artists, primed by European examples, had rediscovered what the critic Van

Wyck Brooks called the "great organic personalities," Walt Whitman and Herman Melville, and shook off Victorian euphemism for sordid fact. They had flocked to the 1913 Armory Show's display of Paris modernists such as Picasso and Matisse, and of American "Ashcan" painters like Robert Henri. The city mixed the ideas of the European avant-garde with its own commercialism and street-wise vernacular, producing an amalgam marketed to the rest of the country.

The cultural revolt was centered in Greenwich Village. Its brownstones hosted intellectual salons, like those of heiress Mabel Dodge Luhan, where labor radicals, outrageous French Dadaists, and liberated women sneered at capitalist money-grubbing and the confinements of bourgeois marriage. The Village inspired the communal arts—actors' companies like the Provincetown Players and art colonies like Woodstock. It had little galleries like Alfred Stieglitz's Photo-Secession at 291 Fifth Avenue, which hung the latest French cubists, and "little magazines" like the *Masses*, edited by Marxists John Reed and Max Eastman, and the *Dial*, edited by Gilbert Seldes, which intermixed French symbolist poetry with stories of downtrodden workers. For all their disaffection from mainstream America, Greenwich Villagers were strident literary nationalists. They believed that their art, which rejected middle-class convention and embraced the vulgar but vibrant immigrant world below 14th Street, would redeem America's soul.

The ferment reached midtown media firms, searching for novelties for the American market. New York City's daily newspapers ran the gamut from the *New York Times* and Joseph Pulitzer's revered *New York World* to the *Sun* and *Morning Telegraph*, which competed with columns on horse racing, vaudeville, and sports. While some mass-circulation magazines, including *Harper's* and the *World's Work*, had withdrawn from muckraking sensationalism to publish mainstream reportage and sentimental literature, others positioned themselves for the new, progressive woman. In 1914, Condé Nast, who had earlier acquired *Vogue*, edited by Edna Woolman Chase, "the technical advisor . . . to the woman of fashion," added *Vanity Fair*, under editor Frank Crowninshield, whose taste for high-gloss journalism made "appeals to their intellect." *Smart Set*, edited by essayist H. L. Mencken and theater critic George Jean Nathan, moved from coverage of high society to serious literature for a "civilized minority."

The staid and genteel book trade was unsettled by the new culture. Frank N. Doubleday saw publishing as more than "a dignified literary avocation," while newcomers such as Alfred A. Knopf and Boni & Liveright avidly printed the European moderns. Doubleday opened stores in midtown and pushed mail orders to seize the retail mark-up. Albert Boni sold "Little Leather Library" books in Woolworths, while his partner, Horace Liveright, launched the Modern Library, 60-cent reprints of Nietzsche, Ibsen, and Wells. Nevertheless, trade publishing remained solidly middlebrow. Best-selling authors like Booth Tarkington and Gene Stratton Porter paid the bills at Doubleday and Page, and another house, Harper, stayed profitable with Zane Grey's westerns.

Despite the Armory Show, the National Academy of Design and the Metropolitan Museum of Art closed ranks against cubism and other modern movements. The French avant-garde remained almost a private obsession for wealthy collectors like the attorney John Quinn, and for Alfred Stieglitz, whose Photo-Secession Gallery and magazine, *Camera Work*, showcased Picasso, Braque, and his American favorites, Arthur B. Davies, John Marin, and Georgia O'Keeffe (whom Stieglitz would marry in 1924). An important alternative to European abstraction developed around Gertrude Vanderbilt Whitney, heiress and sculptor, who admired the representational works of Robert Henri. Guided by her friend Juliana Force, she started the Whitney Studio Club in 1918 to support representational painters, mostly Henri students, against the National Academy's indifference. Whitney also supported Woodstock, the Art Students League summer school, which became a painters' colony known for a lyrical realism called the "American scene."

With the shift to midtown, Broadway came of age as America's center for mass-produced theater. Its nerve center was the syndicates controlled by brothers from Syracuse, Lee and J. J. Shubert, and the United Booking Office, headed by Benjamin F. Keith and Edward F. Albee, who packaged vaudeville "headliners" for a national circuit of four thousand theaters. Vaudeville had matured into elaborate "revues," a melange of acts like mimic Elsie Janis, singer Al Jolson, whose "boundless" force, marveled the critic Gilbert Seldes, embodied New York, and parades of showgirls, especially Florenz Ziegfeld's "Follies." Some revues featured African Americans, like the singer-comedian Bert Williams and James Reese Europe's Clef Club Orchestra. The toast of white society, Jim Europe played elegant ragtime (named for its ragged, syncopated rhythm) and wrote uptempo music for the white dance team Vernon and Irene Castle, who made the fox-trot a national sensation.

Serious drama remained Broadway's pathetic invalid because theatergoers in jewels and tuxedos paid to see melodrama and posturing stars. Producer David Belasco's scenic realism was legendary, but his plays, the critic George Jean Nathan sniffed, were "show-shop piffle." Impresario Charles Frohman, on the other hand, was respected for his productions of Shakespeare, Shaw, and the American immortals Clyde Fitch and Edward Shelton. However, the Theatre Guild had defied "commercially minded" Broadway with productions of Ibsen and Shaw, and, in the Village, the Provincetown Players put on new drama, controversial plays on feminist themes by Susan Glaspell and one-act experiments by Eugene O'Neill about lower-class roughnecks and African Americans. In 1920 the Provincetown Playhouse staged O'Neill's *Emperor Jones*, his study of "Negro" primitivism set to a 78-beats-per-minute "tom-tom-tom," and also *Beyond the Horizon*, which won the Pulitzer Prize. There remained a certain romanticism to O'Neill's observations: "Oh—those cursed hills," intoned a *Beyond the Horizon* hero; "how I've grown to hate the sight of them."

Classical music meant social evenings for New York's upper crust at the New York Symphony and rival Philharmonic Society. New York Symphony director Walter Damrosch had been at the helm since the 1880s, conducting rigid performances of the European romantics. The classical repertoire did not include the contemporary Europeans who had shaken the musical scene, let alone New Yorker Charles Ives, who composed dissonant assemblies of American folk tunes and ragtime. Damrosch could not stand Ives and dismissed ragtime as "a low form of art." The Metropolitan Opera's first undisputed star, the Italian tenor Enrico Caruso, not only saved the opera; his recordings brought the first boom to New York City's record industry. There were also efforts, said a patron of the Century Opera Society, to bring music "into the lives of families." On 62nd Street, the society programmed Sunday matinees with 25-cent seats, and at City College's Lewisohn Stadium outdoor summer concerts were staged for the masses. In this vein, David Sarnoff, a young assistant at the Marconi Wireless Company (and later head of the National Broadcasting Company), envisioned, in 1915, the radio receiver as a "household utility" to bring music into homes.

New York City's output of vernacular culture strengthened its hold on American popular music. West 28th Street music publishers—"Tin Pan Alley"—scoured the Lower East Side for ethnic tunes, then sent song "pluggers" into saloons and theaters across New York and other cities to generate demand for sheet music and piano rolls. The publishers wanted a modern version of "Negro" ragtime and found Irving Berlin, a Jewish singing waiter in a Chinatown dive, whose nifty "Alexander's Ragtime Band" proved a sensation. In 1914, Berlin wrote eighteen songs for *Watch Your Step*, a revue that showcased the Berlin style—tunes easy to remember and easy to sing. George Gershwin, a song plugger for publisher T. B. Harms, took New York pop music much further. Gershwin had formal training at the piano and a percussive style learned from cutting piano rolls and listening to Harlem ragtime. In 1918 he wrote "Swanee," which Al Jolson sang and T. B. Harms turned into a hit. Gershwin was soon contributing songs to Broadway revues that combined African American rhythms with sophisticated lyrics (increasingly written by his brother Ira). The Alley's confections were quintessential New York. They blended wise guy, immigrant sentiments and African American syncopation into songs the country would pay to hear.

Rural Enclosure

In 1915 rural New York, 1.6 million in the countryside, 860,000 in hamlets, and 4,800 Indians on eight reservations felt the long arm of metropolitan wealth. On the tip of Long Island, the Montauk Association, a private club favored by Standard Oil partners, bought salt meadows for grouse hunting and posted no-trespass signs. Vast enclosures covered the Adirondacks after Alfred G. Vanderbilt and his friends built the Raquette Lake Railway and acquired private "camps" like William C. Whitney's 97,000 acres around Long Lake and William Rockefeller's 50,000 acres in southern Franklin County. The state legislature in 1892 had authorized creation of private parks to protect fish and game. Rockefeller imported English deer, hired seventy-five gamekeepers, and removed squatters who lived off trout and venison.

Large portions of the Adirondacks were also put to the use of progressive citizenship. The Lake Placid Education Foundation was developed by Columbia University librarian Melville L. Dewey to help restore the "efficiency" of college teachers and librarians (except those who were Jews, blacks, or tuberculosis patients). After Dr. Edward L. Trudeau succeeded in treating tuberculosis at the Adirondack Cottage Sanitarium on Saranac Lake, some 1,500 "health seekers" settled into nearby hotels and boardinghouses. Saratoga's State Senator Edgar T. Brackett attacked what he regarded as the scandal of high-stakes poker at local casinos, and spa waters that were wasted to supply fizz for soda pop. Brackett backed the legislation that created the Saratoga Springs State Reservation Commission, which purchased 122 springs, developed the spa as a tourist mecca, and sold "Saratoga Soft Sweet Spring Water." While the wealthy were refashioning the Adirondacks, the Catskills were claimed by the democratic motorcar and New York City Jews, who arrived in 1908 at Tannersville and in 1917 at the Hotel Kaaterskill, formerly "restricted" to Christians. Soon more Jews were spending summer escapes in Catskills hotels and bungalows, creating the basis for the "Borscht circuit" of summertime vaudevillians, mostly Jewish singers and comedians.

Metropolitan demand for newsprint ended nomadic lumbering and booms (log rafts) on Adirondack rivers. Increasingly, spring booms were replaced by steady train shipments. Railroads also moved hardwoods—birch, maple, and beech—that were impractical for the booms, while pulpwood mills, which used sulfates to reduce fiber content, encouraged clear-cutting. It brought "the slashing of everything in sight," wrote the historian Alfred Donaldson, a "ruthless, reckless warfare" against the Adirondacks.

Developers and conservationists haggled over hydroelectric sites, particularly after completion of the Hudson River Water Power Co.'s dam at Spiers Falls in 1903 (at the time, the fourth-largest hydro facility in the world). Proponents of "giant power" eyed the Sacandaga River north of Albany and the Moose and Black Rivers in the Adirondacks, whose reservoirs would drown parts of the Forest Preserve. The struggle for the Black River pitted Watertown businessmen against the Association for the Protection of the Adirondacks. Developers pushed through the 1913 Burd Amendment, which allowed flooding of portions of the Forest Preserve for river "regulation," and the Machold Law of 1915, which authorized public water districts. Conservationists won a state bond issue in 1916 to fund enlargements of Adirondack and Palisades Interstate Parks. Trying to meet both interests, Conservation Commissioner George D. Pratt expanded park land with the bond issue but also backed the 1919 engineer survey which proposed reservoirs on the Black and Moose Rivers. While wilderness advocates prevented clear-cutting in places like the Saddlebrook Range near Lake Placid, they lost ground to advocates of timber harvests and power development.

Rural New Yorkers had their lives transformed by giant utilities. After Public Service Commission (PSC) approval in 1909, telephone switchboards were acquired by regional companies like Syracuse-based Central New York Telephone and Telegraph, which operated across eleven counties. With the PSC's nod in 1915, the Watertown entrepreneur John Byron Taylor built his gas and electric company into Northern New York Utilities, whose grid stretched from

Cooperstown's first multi-operator telephone switchboard opened in 1920. New York State Historical Association, Cooperstown, N.Y.

the Saint Lawrence to Port Leyden on the Black River. Towns as far away as Auburn were connected by Syracuse-based "interurbans" (long-range trolleys). These, in turn, were absorbed by William K. Vanderbilt's New York State Railways, which owned systems in Oneida and Utica. Smaller trolley hubs like Herkimer and Ilion served as centers of regional employment for workers in Little Falls, Mohawk, and Frankfort.

Although New York led the nation in apples, vegetables, and hay and forage for dairying, the number of farms declined from 215,597 in 1910 to 193,195 in 1920. While spreading suburbs chewed up acreage, another factor was competition from midwestern and southern producers of canned fruits and vegetables. The decline was severe in the hill country between Albany and Utica, and also in Tompkins County, where abandonment alarmed rural spokesmen like Cornell's agricultural dean, Liberty Hyde Bailey. Many farmers switched to specialized crops. Those around Speonk, Remsenburg, and the Moriches in Suffolk County raised six million bushels of potatoes, while Dix Hills and Babylon farms centered on laying hens. Some 25,000 acres of vineyards around Keuka Lake made Hammondsport the state's focus for wine production. The ten-mile belt of tableland along Lake Ontario from Niagara Falls to Oswego produced the country's largest crop of barreled apples for cider and confectionary use, half the state's peaches, and Niagara grapes, quinces, and cherries.

Concrete roads and motor vehicles completed the transformation of farm life. Driving west from Elmira in 1916, Theodore Dreiser saw roads crowded with Ford Model Ts used "as a family carryall." Truck transport quadrupled market range, encouraging the shift to high-profit perishables like fruits, vegetables, and milk, but also increased competition from out of state. Squeezed between the cost of barns, greenhouses, and pure-bred Holsteins, farmers looked to the Farm Institute, which sponsored lectures on agricultural improvement, and the New York State Horticultural Society. Thousands flocked to Farm Bureaus, a service agency often founded by local businessmen. The Broome County Farm Bureau, the nation's first, was a virtual chamber of commerce for local agriculture and sponsored everything from the Cow Testing Association to the Tri-County Seed Growers' Association. By 1914, New York had twenty-five county bureaus, with particularly active ones in Jefferson and Chemung Counties.

The Dairymen's League Cooperative Association owed much to socialist Jewish dairymen in Sullivan and Orange counties, who believed cooperative purchases and sales were the first step toward building the rural commonwealth. By 1916 the league had a membership of 16,000 farmers, who saw it as a "regulator" of prices offered by wholesalers like Borden's and Nestlé's. In October, the league staged a two-week withholding of milk for higher prices which forced dealers to cave in. During 1917 membership soared to 100,000, while wartime demand nearly doubled milk prices. In 1918 the league opened

Members of the home bureau of the Onondaga Nation reservation meet in 1918 to can vegetables. New York State College of Home Economics Records, Division of Rare and Manuscript Collections, Cornell University Library.

a wholesale distribution system and worked with the New York State Grange Exchange and the State Federation of Farm Bureaus to improve the cooperative buying of feed, fuel, and implements. At Syracuse, in June 1920, the Grange Exchange reorganized into the Cooperative Grange League Federation Exchange, Inc., better known as "GLF," which provided farmers one-stop marketing and purchasing services.

War and Reconstruction

New Yorkers had an enormous stake in the outcome of the European war. During 1915 and 1916, J. P. Morgan & Co. floated Wall Street's largest syndications, $2 billion loans to the British and French governments, spread among sixty-one U.S. banks and trust companies. Morgan's Export Department, headed by Edward R. Stettinius, Sr., parceled British and French orders for munitions among U.S. manufacturers (which ultimately totaled $3 billion or nearly half of Allied purchases). By spring 1915, the surge in orders ended the recession and brought an export boom to the Port of New York. In the meantime, well-off New Yorkers convinced the U.S. Army to open the Military Instruction Camp for Business and Professional Men near Lake Champlain—what became popularly known as the Plattsburgh movement. The first contingent included New York City Mayor John Purroy Mitchel, Henry Stimson, and Theodore Roosevelt's two sons, all of whom paid for their officer training. During the summer of 1916, "preparedness" rallies, like Buffalo's mammoth parade on June 24, occurred in major cities. But many New Yorkers deplored the martial fervor. Some progressives, led by the Manhattan settlement leader Lillian D. Wald, formed the American Union Against Militarism (AUAM), to avoid tragedy and "reaction at home."

On April 6, 1917, the United States declared war against the Central Powers. Within days, Governor Charles S. Whitman named county home defense committees, which organized neighbors to take a military census of eligibles for the draft, cultivate patriot farms, and volunteer for the American Red Cross. The U.S. marshal for Western New York, Rochester attorney John D. Lynn, "quietly" surveyed 15,000 German and Austro-Hungarian aliens in his seventeen-county district. Although President Woodrow Wilson ordered "enemy aliens" cleared from proximity to army camps, shipyards, and ordnance plants, Marshal Lynn arranged permits for 1,116 who lived and worked in "forbidden zones." "No settled resident of Rochester was sent to an internment camp," Lynn asserted, although his office scrutinized the loyalty of thousands.

The war split New Yorkers with honest doubts about its purpose. Led by AFL president Samuel Gompers, organized labor pledged to uphold war production and avoid strikes, and President Wilson reciprocated by addressing the AFL convention in Buffalo, the first president to do so. But the Amalgamated Clothing Workers branded the war an imperialist conflict, an argument that the New York City Socialist party used to attack the draft. When super-patriots hounded dissenters and conscientious objectors, Socialist Roger N. Baldwin founded the AUAM's Civil Liberties Bureau (forerunner of the American Civil Liberties Union) to defend dissidents and was soon imprisoned himself for refusal to register for the draft.

Municipal politics reflected the dissent, as in Schenectady, where Socialist metalworkers at GE formed a local AUAM, and in Buffalo, where the Socialist mayoral candidate won 14,000 votes on a peace platform in 1917. That year, as well, in New York City, the flag-waving Mayor Mitchel was challenged by Socialist lawyer Morris Hillquit, who said draftees were being sacrificed "on the altar of capitalist greed." Boss Murphy countered with Brooklyn magistrate John F. Hylan (called "Red Mike" for his nasty temper). With Hearst newspaper support, Hylan sneered at British imperialism and promised city-owned transit,

A World War I recruiting poster. From *Mid-Week Pictorial* of the *New York Times*, June 1917.

which Tammany called the "practical part of the Socialist program." Hylan won an easy victory, but Hillquit finished just behind Mitchel and helped elect ten Socialist assemblymen.

New York State sent 367,864 men to the colors, or 9.8 percent of all American soldiers, sailors, and marines. Plattsburgh alumni goaded the army to build camps of instruction at Sackets Harbor and at Madison Barracks, southwest of Utica, which trained 27,000 officers. Draftees from New York City and

Long Island went into the U.S. Army 77th Division, bivouacked at Camp Upton on Long Island, while those from western New York went into the 78th Division, mustered at Fort Dix, New Jersey. The 47th "Rainbow" Division, National Guard, at Camp Mills, Mineola, Long Island, included the "Fighting 69th" Infantry Regiment, commanded by Lieutenant Colonel William J. Donovan and chaplained by Father Francis P. Duffy. Harlem's "Hellfighters," the 15th Regiment, trained at Camp Whitman upstate before shipping out as the 369th Regiment. In October 1918, the 77th Division's 308th Regiment stood fast at the Argonne and became the legendary "Lost Battalion." The division's casualties included 1,990 dead and nearly 10,000 wounded. Nine New Yorkers won the Congressional Medal of Honor, including "Wild Bill" Donovan, one of the most decorated officers in U.S. history.

New York's corporate and social welfare leaders helped run the war on the home front. Edward Stettinius left Morgan's purchasing operation to become the army's supply czar. Colonel Donovan's Buffalo law partner, John Lord O'Brian, former U.S. attorney for the Western District, went to the U.S. Justice Department to develop the government's system of alien internment and passport control. Social work administrator Mary Van Kleeck headed the Women's Branch of the Army Ordnance Department, which coordinated female employment in war plants, and Raymond B. Fosdick of the Rockefeller Foundation directed the Commission on Training Camp Activities, which organized wholesome recreation to keep draftees "healthy mentally and spiritually."

Allied victory depended on New York's credit markets and factories—the corporate bigness that progressives had guarded against. Member banks of the New York Federal Reserve absorbed the bulk of U.S. Treasury bond sales, a deflator countered by the arrival of British and French gold for munitions purchases. The Morgan contracts provided for the purchase of hundreds of thousands of Lee-Metford rifles from Remington Arms at Ilion and Lewis machine guns from Savage Arms in Utica, where 1918 output of Lewis guns was two-thirds that of Britain and Canada combined. AT&T's long-distance employees were drafted en masse into the U.S. Army Signal Corps, and, by 1918, Computing-Tabulating-Recording's Washington, D.C., facility was churning out 80 million Hollerith cards a month for the government's statistics.

Government pressure, along with welfare capitalism, brought an enlargement of corporate welfare plans and talk of "industrial democracy." Eastman Kodak, producing photographic equipment for the Army Signal Corps, developed a health and welfare department and built company housing, Kodak-Vista, in the suburbs north of Rochester. In 1918, War Department advisers averted a clash between Rochester manufacturers and the Amalgamated Clothing Workers. Patriotic appeals by the union president, Sidney Hillman, moved holdout businessman Jeremiah Hickey (of Hickey-Freeman Clothiers) to agree to the forty-four-hour week and collective bargaining in exchange for a production flexibility that an executive deemed "the introduction of scientific management." The Rochester accord, modeled on the 1910 "protocol" in the New York City garment trades, called for "joint control" of labor issues by a board of impartial mediators.

The push for all-out production, however, sidetracked many progressive goals. At Buffalo and Hammondsport (hometown of the aviator Glenn H. Curtiss), the Curtiss Aëroplane Company manufactured 11,000 JN4D ("Jenny") trainers and was exempted from the One Day of Rest in Seven Law. The War Department's demand for explosives and the electric power to process them encouraged Allied Chemical's takeover of German chemical patents and Buffalo investor Jacob F. Schoellkopf, Jr.'s merger of smaller utilities into the Niagara Falls Power Co. At the end of the war, the U.S. Navy midwived the formation of the "radio trust," as the GE subsidiary, Radio Corporation of America, was known, and the U.S. Justice Department ended litigation against the Eastman Kodak "camera trust."

Wartime fervor also allowed conservatives to pursue 100 percent Americanism at the expense of dissidents. Rochester's Americanization campaign was spearheaded by the chamber of commerce, which organized factory committees for a census of foreign-born employees and their loyalties, climaxing in a July 4, 1917, rally at Exposition Park. With the slogan "PAY UNTIL IT HURTS," Rome's War Chest Association distributed pledge cards among factory workers and secured 96 percent compliance. Buffalo's Fourth Liberty Loan Campaign, which operated out of police precincts, canvassed house to house and raised $66 million. Too often, civic solidarity could turn ugly. At the Justice Department, John Lord O'Brian sanctioned the efforts of the private, super-patriotic American Protective League, whose 1918 "slacker raids" in New York City netted 50,000 draft dodgers. Anti-Germanism also put the national prohibition amendment at the center of Governor Whitman's agenda.

Public opinion was further soured in Buffalo, Rochester, and Syracuse when wartime shortages and congestion spiraled rents and squeezed public utilities, particularly, transportation services (dependent on 5–cent fares). The crush of war workers on Buffalo-Lackawanna's grain docks and in the steel mills and rail yards brought "utter breakdown" to the International Railway's trolley service. Mayor Mitchel's clamp-down on spending for street improvements worsened traffic along the New York City waterfront, and rents later soared around the Brooklyn Navy Yard, prompting Mayor John F. Hylan to attack landlord "profiteers." The federal government tried to ease congestion with housing projects like the 115-unit Lansingdorp Village at Watertown for workers at New York Air Brake Co. When housing shortages affected production at Newburgh Shipyards, President Thomas C. Desmond got a citizens' subscription—and federal loans—to build Colonial Terrace. But political rhetoric and private efforts could not alleviate fundamental distortions in the economy.

Wartime trauma worsened with the Spanish influenza, which reached the New York Port of Embarkation in September 1918 and then spread into a global pandemic. It felled men in the Brooklyn Navy Yard, overwhelmed the Henry Street Visiting Nurse Service, and panicked Bellevue Hospital laundresses, who "abandoned" their washtubs. By late October, the city had 3,000 cases per day, with 10 percent mortality. The flu sickened half the population of Watkins Glen and forced Rochester to shut schools, theaters, and saloons. In Utica the death toll obliged public works employees to help cemetery workers dig graves; and in Buffalo the health commissioner commandeered casket firms to ensure coffins sold "at cost." During the last week of October, 231 died around Albany, with the Watervliet Arsenal particularly hard hit. By early November, New York City was averaging 5,500 cases per day and nearly 800 deaths when a cold snap ended the scourge. Across the state, the virus caused one-half million cases and 45,000 deaths.

In mid-epidemic—and the first state election in which women could vote—Democrat Alfred E. Smith challenged the Republican incumbent, Charles Whitman. Governor Whitman had trounced Judge Seabury in 1916, but Smith was another matter. A quick-witted son of Irish-Catholic immigrants, who left public school to work at the Fulton Fish Market, Smith was spotted by Tammany and in 1904 sent to the state Assembly, where he spent ten years mastering legislative procedure and paying his dues. On the Factory Investigating Commission (after the Triangle fire), he saw women and children toil under conditions that made him mutter, "It's uncivilized," and join social reformers to enact state regulations on safety and hours. In 1918, Smith headed a formidable coalition of Tammany Irish and Jewish voters, including a notable group of reformers like Rose Schneiderman and Abram Elkus. While Whitman wanted "prohibition in state and nation," Smith spoke for a people's referendum, appealing to Yorker pride and Irish votes. He bucked the Republican tide in 1918 to win by 15,000 votes.

Governor Al Smith had a card-file brain for facts and a mind that sniffed out "the baloney." His knowledge of legislative practice was unmatched, and he made sure his staff closely tracked pending bills. He asked Conservation Commissioner George Pratt to stay on and made superb new appointments like U.S. Army Colonel Frederick Stuart Greene as commissioner of public highways, the social worker Frances Perkins to the Industrial Commission, and the prison reformer Lewis E. Lawes as warden of Sing Sing. Smith's program included a state referendum on prohibition, state-owned hydroelectric power, a strict forty-eight-hour limit on women's work in factories, and a state commission to determine a "living wage." He sent Perkins on a mission to modernize the Industrial Commission's inspection of factories, and he supported proposals by State Health Commissioner Dr. Hermann M. Biggs for a comprehensive system of rural health.

The centerpiece of Governor Smith's 1919 agenda was the brainchild of Belle Moskowitz, an influential progressive who advised Smith behind the scenes. Moskowitz suggested what became the New York State Commission on Reconstruction, a blue-ribbon panel, headed by reformers Abram Elkus and Robert Moses, to study the social "inefficiencies" exposed by the war. Its reports proposed a regional agency for the Port of New York, coordination of public and private construction projects into an employment "reserve" for hard times, and a state planning agency and mortgage bank for low-rent housing. Its most important element was gubernatorial reorganization to "leave the Governor," Smith said, "to direct his attention to the great, big problems." The governor would have a four-year term, a formal cabinet, and an executive budget.

Smith's program was soon caught in the turmoil that came with canceled war orders and cuts in factory overtime and wages. In November 1918, some 16,000 stevedores struck the docks of New York City, and the Amalgamated Clothing Workers strung pickets outside the factories housing the men's suit industry. A month later trolleymen walked off the International Railway, stranding Buffalo for twenty-four days. That December, 14,000 machinists and metalworkers struck GE's Schenectady plants, proclaiming the "fight for

Within months of the end of World War I in November 1918, a commandeered German troopship brought 10,000 soldiers of the U.S. Army's 27th Division home to New York. From *Mid-Week Pictorial* of the *New York Times*, March 1919.

Democracy here, as well as 'over there.'" The upheaval grew worse during 1919. In September, Buffalo workers at Lackawanna Steel, Rogers, Brown, and Donner joined the national steel strike. Strikers attacked scabs at Lackawanna Steel, trolleymen mobbed attempts to move the cars at Olean, and 4,000 copper workers menaced company officers at Rome.

Trying to control the political fallout, Governor Smith appointed a Reconstruction Labor Board to mediate strikes, and he sent Frances Perkins to Rome to lead Industrial Commission hearings into the copper workers' walkout. But public opinion had turned against labor agitators. On May 1 a crowd of soldiers stormed the office of the *Call*, New York City's Socialist paper, and beat up staffers. In mid-November, U.S. Attorney General A. Mitchell Palmer ordered the arrest of alleged Bolsheviks in New York City, the earliest of his raids on radicals. A month later, Palmer staged more roundups in Buffalo, Rochester, and Utica. In Albany, Republicans organized the Joint Committee of the Legislature Investigating Seditious Activities, chaired by State Senator Clayton R. Lusk of Cortland. The committee proposed bills to prosecute "criminal anarchy" and require the Board of Regents to close schools whose curricula were "detrimental to the public interest." On January 7, 1920, Assembly Speaker Thaddeus C. Sweet refused to seat five New York City Socialists whom the Assembly Judiciary Committee branded as "perpetual traitors."

Governor Smith berated the Assembly and vetoed the Lusk bills, but his agenda was gone. In 1919, the legislature rebuffed the referendum on going "dry" and ratified the Eighteenth (Prohibition) Amendment. For good measure, it enacted the Mullan-Gage Law to require enforcement by local attorneys and police. Speaker Sweet attacked gubernatorial reorganization and throttled Smith's bills for the "living wage" commission and the forty-eight-hour factory law. The legislature ignored Commissioner Biggs's rural health package and Smith's proposal for state-owned hydroelectric power. Meanwhile the Joint Legislative (Lockwood) Committee sidestepped Smith's calls for a comprehensive approach to city planning and housing and instead forwarded what became the Emergency Rent Laws of 1920, which barred "unjust" rent increases, and also state tax cuts on real estate and mortgages to stimulate private builders of homes and apartments. The sole reconstruction measure that passed established the Port Authority of New York and New Jersey in 1921 to improve freight transport for the bi-state region.

The public mood grew even uglier with hard times. Alarmed by inflation, Benjamin Strong, the Federal Reserve governor, ordered a sharp increase in the rediscount rate during the spring of 1920. The credit squeeze, along with canceled war contracts, brought a vicious deflation that reached bottom in the summer of 1921, when factory payrolls had shrunk by one-fourth. The recession staggered Utica's knitting mills and brought renewed strikes of trolleymen in Cooperstown, Troy, and Albany, and mob attacks on scabs in Watervliet.

Rochester building trades workers struck unsuccessfully against wage cuts, while a strike by the United Shoe Workers ended up with the Rochester union broken. After the October 1920 collapse in milk prices, Borden's, Nestlé, and other major milk buyers ended their contracts with the Dairymen's League.

Caught in the downdraft, the 1920 Democratic ticket led by Governor Smith and George Lunn, the Schenectady Socialist turned Democrat who won the U.S. Senate primary, never had a chance. Although an estimated half-million Republicans crossed party lines to vote for Smith, Republican presidential candidate Warren Harding swept New York City and helped elect the sardonic, conservative, former Court of Appeals judge, Nathan L. Miller of Syracuse, as governor. Republicans chose as Senate majority leader Clayton R. Lusk, who revived his education bills, which Governor Miller promptly signed. Miller dismantled the Industrial Commission, and, backed by State Senator Mortimer Y. Ferris and Black River businessmen, pushed through the Waterpower Law of 1921, which created a State Water Power Commission to license sites for development by private utilities. Republican lawmakers sponsored the State Judiciary Constitutional Convention of 1921, which urged judges to rein in administrative bodies like the Public Service Commission. "Everywhere," wrote a labor partisan, "idealism seemed shattered beyond revival."

Nevertheless, New York had made extraordinary progress in the World War I era. Infant mortality and tuberculosis rates had declined, while child labor had nearly disappeared. The 1,700 deaths on the highways in 1922 were more than those from typhoid, scarlet fever, whooping cough, and polio combined. Conservatives attacked government encroachment, but Court of Appeals Judge Cuthbert W. Pound declared that "nothing is more elementary" than the power of administrative boards for "order-making," and even Senator Lusk accepted state responsibility to act "in times of industrial depression." The debate, in fact, had shifted to Al Smith's unfinished agenda—state-owned hydroelectric power, the "living wage," and strong, executive government—and the mix of government intervention, scientific philanthropy, and corporate welfare needed to achieve it.

Chapter 29

The Electric Age

IN THE 1920s, NEW YORK STATE WAS DOMINATED BY BIG-city life, particularly the electric culture that pulsed from Manhattan. The U.S. Census considered the state 84 percent urban in 1930, while New York City comprised 55 percent of the state population of 12.6 million. Regional centers like Buffalo, Rochester, and Syracuse grew beyond their municipal boundaries, turning their hinterlands into tributaries to metropolitan needs. But more than anything else, "metropolitan" meant Manhattan—Wall Street legal services and high finance, Madison Avenue publishing and advertising, Harlem sheen and Times Square lingo. The city's media broadcast an urban experience that was exciting, frantic, and sometimes destructive. In F. Scott Fitzgerald's *Great Gatsby* (1925), his celebrated novel of the Roaring Twenties, Gatsby's sedan mowed down a villager near Queensboro's "valley of ashes." The novel caught the metropolis's dangerous grip on the countryside.

Metropolitan Worlds

Changes accelerated within metropolitan regions, as cities replaced nineteenth-century buildings and remade streets with improvements suited to the automobile. With construction of the State Barge Canal, the abandoned Erie Canal bed provided "Erie Boulevards" for Syracuse, Schenectady, Utica, and Rochester, where the city built a subway trolley. Municipalities also beautified uptown subdivisions. Buffalo spent $1.5 million for the State Teachers College on Scajaquada Creek, part of a cultural center that included the Albright Art Gallery and the Buffalo Historical Society. The city's North Park, North Main, and

Kensington sections expanded by 143 percent; suburbs such as Tonawanda grew by 354 percent, and Kenmore Village boomed from 3,160 to 16,482.

In New York City, old districts including the Lower East Side and the Brooklyn Navy Yard lost population, while outlying areas surged. Mayor John F. Hylan's administration (1918–25) built schools, hospitals, and boulevards across the outer boroughs and completed $148 million in subway construction. During the 1920s Manhattan went from one-quarter million more people than Brooklyn to 700,000 fewer, while Queens, the fastest growing county in the state, had more than one million residents in 1930. The tide spread into Westchester and Nassau Counties (which grew 65 percent between 1920 and 1925), whose combined population of 819,000 reached 6.5 percent of the state's.

Solid wages, sharp declines in European immigration, and the aspirations of the second generation completed the change of colonies into ethnic neighborhoods. In 1927, Buffalo's Little Italy had an estimated 20,000 savings accounts, which provided down payments for better housing along Busti Avenue and Seneca east of Main Street. To meet the demand, Buffalo builders completed 28,000 homes, most with individual garages. A mid-1920s survey of Polonia families found that although half the babies were still delivered by midwives, nearly half the families had cars and two-thirds owned their own homes. Saint Stanislaus spun off uptown parishes that were reached by "Father Justin's Rosary Hour," radio broadcasts of Catholic inspiration in English. The writer Jerre Mangione remembered that his Italian relatives left Mount Allegro, an inner-city neighborhood near Eastman Kodak, for Rochester's outskirts, "where they could enjoy the luxury of a vegetable garden."

Immigrant New York City accelerated its dispersal along subway routes. Subsidized by state and local tax relief, builders completed 420,734 apartments by 1929, nearly one-third of the city's multiple dwellings; and 218,000 one- and two-family homes, mostly in Queens. Irish and Italians were drawn to single- and two-family dwellings in East Flatbush, Brooklyn, and Ridgewood, Queens. Before the war, half the Italians in Greenwich Village belonged to immigrant aid societies, compared to only 10 percent by 1930. "The peers, kin and non-kin, scattered," wrote the historian Donna R. Gabaccia; "their contact became visits rather than everyday interaction." Jews left the Lower East Side for working-class neighborhoods like Hunts Point in the Bronx, and Brownsville, Brooklyn, which was 95 percent Jewish by 1930. Middle-class Jews settled along Jerome Avenue and East Fordham Road, where neighbors strolled on the sabbath and gossiped in front of their apartments.

The 1920s saw the emergence of a sizable urban black population as the Great Migration mounted from the southern states. The number of African Americans nearly doubled to 413,000 or 3.3 percent of the state in 1930, but 341,000 lived in New York City, and nearly half of them in Harlem, the country's largest black community. Jim Crow constrained Harlem's boundaries, forcing high population density, exorbitant rents, and spillover into other ghettos near the Brooklyn Navy Yard and in the Morrisania section of the South Bronx. During the decade, the Puerto Rican population grew sevenfold to 45,000, increasingly funneled into East Harlem. Buffalo's black community, which tripled to 13,500 by 1930, moved into the Broadway-Michigan area. Even in Oswego, the heart of abolitionist territory, the rise in black migrants hardened the racial job ceiling. No blacks worked at American Can and U.S. Radiator except as janitors and common laborers.

While metropolitan areas expanded, their central cities remained within frozen municipal boundaries. Buffalo's population growth spread into Williamsville and Tonawanda, but the city remained a scant forty-two square miles. Rochester stretched along Monroe Avenue and into Meadowbrook, near Twelve Corners, a subdivision favored by Kodak executives. But after Rochester annexed parts of Brighton and Irondequoit and took five thousand acres in the "big steal" from Greece, suburban voters ended the possibility of further annexation in 1922, the same year that five towns in Rensselaer County defeated a "Greater Troy" movement. With minor exceptions like Utica's extension to Sauquoit Creek, the era of municipal expansion ended—with immediate repercussions. In 1927, Buffalo voters adopted fiscal retrenchment, promised by a strong mayor and city council. In 1928, the Schenectady Bureau of Municipal Research warned that the move of taxable property "beyond our present city lines" would force the city to cut capital outlays. Even New York City heard an advisory commission claim that debt for subways and other improvements had overloaded fiscal capacity.

Political—and fiscal—power increasingly went to suburban Republicans like Thomas E. Broderick, the Irondequoit reformer, who became party leader of Monroe County. Westchester GOP boss William L. Ward, credited with making Westchester "the cleanest county in the state," oversaw the Westchester County Park Commission's $80 million system of recreation grounds and parkways, including Saw Mill River and Sprain Brook. The Niagara Frontier Planning Board, chaired by Chauncey J. Hamlin of Buffalo, coordinated the work of the Erie County Park Commission, which laid out Chestnut Ridge and Ellicott Creek, and the "Greater Motorways System" around Buffalo. A major exception to quality suburban government was G. Wilbur Doughty's brazen Nassau County machine, which protected gamblers and prohibition violators. Nassau's corruption touched off a citizens' charter revolt and Ku Klux Klan rallies in Port Washington and Bayshore. Klansmen threatened not only Jews and Italians, but politicians in cahoots with bootleggers. In 1925 Doughty's machine defeated a movement for county charter reform.

New York City benefited from advanced planning initiatives, thanks to the Port of New York Authority, the bi-state regional compact created in 1921, and the privately sponsored Regional Plan of New York (RPNY). The Port Authority laid out blueprints for freight dispersal to New Jersey, Brooklyn, and Queens, served by railroads and truck highways across the region's outer counties. Launched by the Russell Sage Foundation as a planners' think tank, RPNY supported dispersal of industry and workers into "satellite communities." The idea was dismissed by critics like Lewis Mumford and Clarence Stein, who dreamed of fully planned towns in forested "greenbelts." Their celebrated prototypes were seventy-acre Sunnyside, an English garden village located near the Long Island Railroad's Sunnyside Yards in Queens—hardly a greenbelt!—and the planned suburb of Radburn in northern New Jersey.

Professional sports operated within a regional urban system, anchored in New York City. At Madison Square Garden on July 2, 1921, promoter Tex Rickard staged a bout between Jack Dempsey, the American heavyweight champion, and Georges Carpentier of France that had a million-dollar gate and a radio audience of 300,000. The New York Celtics were a mainstay of the American Basketball League, along with the Brooklyn Arcadians, Rochester Centrals, and Syracuse Stars. Big-city powers dominated professional baseball: John McGraw's New York Giants, lords of the Polo Grounds, the upstart New York Yankees, and even the Brooklyn Dodgers, perennial losers in the National League. Minor league teams like the Binghamton Triplets drew fans who drove or took the trolley from Endicott and Johnson City. Syracuse was a "colonial outpost" of the St. Louis Cardinals, until St. Louis executive Branch Rickey moved the team to Rochester's modern ballpark and renamed it the Red Wings. Under managers Warren Giles and Billy Southworth, the Red Wings dominated the International League and won the 1928 pennant over the Buffalo Bisons, but Rochester fans knew that their beloved Wings belonged to St. Louis, which could move the team at any time.

Impulse Manhattan

In the 1920s, midtown Manhattan was the heart of the culture that pulsed with electric energy. Greenwich Village may have been the outpost of the European avant-garde, the place where Americans glimpsed T. S. Eliot's "Waste Land" or French surrealism, but modern culture had been absorbed by a midtown "smart set," who drank in Times Square speakeasies, talked about Freud and Picasso, and visited Harlem for "hot jazz." They staffed the *New York World*'s newsroom, the Associated Press wire service, and the National Broadcasting Company studio that sent America the latest word on what New Yorkers were up to. At the Algonquin Hotel "Round Table" luncheon, journalists and theater people like Alexander Woollcott, Dorothy Parker, and George S. Kaufman exchanged flip repartee in time to make the newspapers' evening deadlines. As

One of the first issues of *The New Yorker*, March 7, 1925. In 1925, editor Harold Ross was managing the fledgling *New Yorker* with a tiny staff in an office with one typewriter. Bumping into Dorothy Parker, an advisory editor, Ross grumbled, "I thought you were coming into the office to write a piece last week. What happened?" Parker replied, "Somebody was using the pencil." Division of Rare and Manuscript Collections, Cornell University Library.

the literary historian Ann Douglas pointed out, "New York's essential product" in the 1920s had become "attention itself."

Manhattan was a place of preternatural crowds—what the poet Hart Crane called "Multitudes bent toward some flashing scene." Hundreds of thousands poured from subways and railroad terminals into nearby commercial towers. Their demand for office space prompted real estate speculations, such as the Chanin and Chrysler Buildings, and when the Empire State Building was completed in 1931, New York boasted ninety-three skyscrapers over thirty stories. They were vertical cities designed for controlled congestion, like the forty-story Equitable, whose elevators moved 96,000 people a day. Lunch crowds jammed fast-food outlets like Horn & Hardart "automats," where food was dispensed from windowed lockers opened by the correct number of nickels. Crowds gave New York world renown, particularly after the start of ticker-tape parades, invented by city greeters in 1919 to welcome Edward, the Prince of Wales. Crowds had become a New York art form as well as its economic necessity.

In skyscraper offices, financial, publishing, and media partners handled industrial capitalists and literary prima donnas. Sullivan & Cromwell epitomized the "metropolitan" law firm, which specialized in corporate practice, particularly mortgages and reorganizations. Sullivan formed the giant utilities holding company Niagara Mohawk Power Corporation and arranged patent assignments for office equipment firms that merged into Remington Rand. Another influential firm, Milbank, Tweed, counseled the Interborough Rapid Transit Co.'s fight against the 5-cent subway fare, while attorneys at Shearman & Sterling won the 1922 *Kings County Lighting Co.*

v. Newton case, which declared the Public Service Commission's mandated rate of 80 cents per thousand cubic feet of gas confiscatory. The most powerful Wall Street firms were almost shadow governments, making policy on antitrust and public utility regulation.

In the 1920s, Madison Avenue solidified its grip on American advertising. Between 1915 and 1929, advertising "billings" grew five- and tenfold in autos, food and beverages, drugs and toiletries. The Batten Agency had 126 employees in 1916 but 272 in 1928, when it merged with Barton, Durstine and Osborn. At another agency, J. Walter Thompson, Stanley Resor fashioned a complex, full-service advertising firm by adding statistical and investigative departments and subjecting trainees to a two-year course. His wife Helen Lansdowne Resor shaped the agency's creative touch and landed clients such as General Motors, whose billings paid for J. Walter Thompson's expansion to Europe and Latin America. The Resors also pioneered radio spots. By 1930, J. Walter Thompson was packaging twenty-three hours per week, and matching sponsors with stars and big draws like Bing Crosby and the "Kraft Music Hall."

The mass media gave journalism a tawdry, neon excitement, particularly in editorial offices near Times Square. In 1919, Joseph M. Patterson launched the *Illustrated Daily News*, the country's first tabloid, whose front page "pix" made easy reading in crowded subways. William Randolph Hearst's *Daily Mirror* and Bernarr MacFadden's *Evening Graphic* countered with their own mix of sports, gangland rubouts, and Broadway gossip. All three were brilliantly combined in Walter Winchell's *Graphic* column, which doted on "palookas" and "thigh grinders," his neologisms for prizefighters and striptease artists. Adolph S. Ochs's *New York Times* stayed above the tabloid fray and survived, but the *Herald* buckled and was purchased by *New York Tribune* owner Ogden Reid and his wife, Helen Rogers Reid, whose wealth and moderate politics made the *Herald-Tribune* the country's most important Republican paper. Joseph Pulitzer's *New York World* was carried on by editor Frank Cobb and feature writer Heywood Broun, the legendary denizen of Broadway, Times Square, and uptown literary salons.

Wire-service journalism inspired the compressed feature magazine. In 1922 DeWitt Wallace and his wife Lila Acheson Wallace began the *Reader's Digest*, which offered articles in "compact form" as a "service to readers." A year later, Yale graduates Henry R. Luce and Briton Hadden founded *Time* magazine, a package of the week's news in short, breezy prose. Luce poured *Time*'s profits into *Fortune* in 1930 and into a dramatized version of radio news, "The March of Time," in 1931. Media competition forced out general magazines like the *Century* and *Scribner's*. The survivors were "slick-paper" names, like *Ladies' Home Journal*, *Collier's*, and *Liberty*, which alternated sentimental short stories and back-slapper politics. The Butterick Company published the *Delineator*, aimed at suburban women, and pulp magazines like *Adventure*, known for its tales of exotic travel. A chief rival, Street and Smith, published *Black Mask Magazine*, which showcased mystery writer Dashiell Hammett, and juvenile magazines, like *Bill Barnes' Air Trails*.

With the move of the book trade to midtown, family firms like Harper & Brothers became corporations with marketing divisions and specialty departments. After Doubleday exploited mail orders (and radio tie-ins), Harry Scherman started the Book-of-the-Month Club, while Harold Guinzburg countered with the Literary Guild, both of which marketed brand-name authors. Newer firms like Knopf, Simon and Schuster, and Boni & Liveright competed to bring fresh literary voices to what Harper's editor Cass Canfield called an "alert" Jewish audience. Horace Liveright chased authors with outlandish royalties, hired Ezra Pound to scout Europe for talent, and, when he published Sigmund Freud's *General Introduction to Psychoanalysis* (1922), persuaded Freud's nephew, public relations manager Edward L. Bernays, to ballyhoo its appearance. Liveright also tilted with the Society for the Suppression of Vice and the Catholic archdiocese's Clean Books League. For all the innovation, however, Boni & Liveright's only best seller was Anita Loos's novel *Gentlemen Prefer Blondes* (1926), and Simon & Schuster's nonfiction winner was *The Cross Word Puzzle Book* (1924), a perennial moneymaker.

Increasingly, midtown's search for novelty led to Harlem, particularly after white intellectuals like Carl Van Vechten glamorized African American "primitivism," and black showmen Noble Sissle and Eubie Blake kindled an appetite for black revues with their *Shuffle Along* (1921). Whites trooped uptown to see black chorus girls on the Cotton Club's jungle stage and to hear James P. Johnson and Willie "the Lion" Smith play jazz at Small's Paradise. Harlem's nightlife contributed energy to its literary "Renaissance," which produced work including James Weldon Johnson's *God's Trombones* (1927), a collection of folk music and Negro spirituals, Langston Hughes's anthems like "The Negro Speaks of Rivers" (1921), and the rich evocation of black dialect in Zora Neale Hurston's short stories. Alain Locke compiled examples of this artistic achievement in *The New Negro* (1925), a volume that proclaimed Harlem's metropolitan sophistication and pride in things African. While Jim Crow kept blacks from midtown restaurants and theaters (not to mention the segregated Cotton Club), Harlem's energy had enormous impact on Manhattan's media.

With seventy-six theaters and 95,000 seats to fill, Broadway impresarios were as frantic as their productions. Producers invoked contract "stop clauses" to yank shows that lost money and free stages for new productions. With ruthless determination they were able to open 264 revues, musicals, and dramas during the 1927–28 season. The revue was dominated by Irving Berlin, Jerome Kern, and George Gershwin, but *Shuffle Along* made reputations for composer Eubie Blake and singer Florence Mills and opened doors for other black performers. Increasingly, revues added story lines: George and Ira Gershwin's *Lady,*

Be Good! (1924) starred dancers Fred and Adele Astaire; and Jerome Kern and Oscar Hammerstein II's *Show Boat* (1927), written for the African American baritone Paul Robeson, pointed toward the serious "book" musical to come.

Broadway's dramatic tastes were touched by experimental companies like Eva Le Gallienne's Civic Repertory Theatre, an actors' cooperative that staged classics and charged $1.50 a seat. The Theatre Guild produced Elmer Rice's *Adding Machine* (1923), a montage of office-speak done in the style of German expressionism, and Eugene O'Neill's *Desire under the Elms* (1924) and *Strange Interlude* (1928), powerful plays of misfits pursued by relentless fate. But for most Broadway audiences, drama meant the doughboy language of *What Price Glory?* (1924), and "genius" the rumpled, manic director Jed Harris, whose hits included Ben Hecht and Charles MacArthur's *Front Page* (1928).

New Orleans jazz (first played in Manhattan by white bands during 1917) drifted into Harlem's cheap dance halls, where it stimulated the "Harlem stride," a lurching piano style popularized by James P. Johnson and Thomas W. "Fats" Waller, and Southern Delta blues, black women's laments about men who ran off. Harlem companies like Pace-Handy sold "race" music, organized jazz orchestras, and recorded Gertrude "Ma" Rainey and Bessie Smith, singers who ignited a craze for the blues. More important, in Harlem's cabarets New Orleans syncopation turned into "bucking" contests between cornets and saxophones, the call-and-response at the heart of jazz. The most successful of the new jazzmen, Fletcher Henderson, took his band to midtown, the whites-only Roseland Ballroom, in 1924. The Henderson band became famous for the call-and-response of the brass section and the improvised solos of trumpet player Louis Armstrong and Coleman Hawkins on the tenor sax.

The arrival of Harlem sound brought upheaval to Manhattan's music establishment. After the success of *Shuffle Along*, Tin Pan Alley scrambled to sign and record composers like James P. Johnson and Eubie Blake. George Gershwin wrote near-jazz tunes for his Broadway revues, and white band leaders like Paul Whiteman and Vincent Lopez turned out elegant "cover" versions. In 1924 Whiteman commissioned Gershwin, Kern, and Berlin (but no African Americans) to write pieces for a concert that would show, Whiteman said, how far modern music had come from "discordant jazz." (The otherwise forgettable program included the premier of Gershwin's *Rhapsody in Blue*.) Whiteman's orchestrations, which blended strings and saxophones, became the New York standard heard on the radio. They even affected band leader Duke Ellington, the Cotton Club's new star in the late 1920s, who wove the minor scale and unorthodox tonalities into a textured, layered sound. Ellington became the master of New York concertized jazz and was one of the few African Americans with a radio hookup from Harlem.

Classical composers including Virgil Thomson and Aaron Copland were drawn to New York, the center of symphonic tradition, on their way to study modern composition in Paris. Their European jaunts not only brought them an acquaintance with Erik Satie's tonal structures and Igor Stravinsky's astringent classicism, but also sparked the avid French interest in jazz. Copland returned to New York and, with Thomson, founded the League of Composers to encourage Paris-trained classicists to write an American music. With a league commission, Copland wrote *Music for the Theatre* (1925), a dissonant piece with a jangled version of "East Side, West Side" and burlesque bump-and-grind. The critics were uncomfortable with it, and so was the New York Symphony director Walter Damrosch, who preferred more traditional compositions by Charles Martin Loeffler and Deems Taylor.

In general, the New York musical establishment kept the modernists at a distance. Damrosch overcame his skepticism about jazz, became an admirer of Gershwin, and commissioned his bluesy *Piano Concerto in F* (1925) and the exuberant *An American in Paris* (1928). Damrosch also did his duty with a 1926 concert, "Modern Music—Pleasant and Unpleasant," which included Copland and another American modernist, Bernard Rogers. More experimental composers like Henry Cowell were another matter altogether, however. Cowell explored "tone clusters" and American folk music, and even dabbled in an electronic "synchronous" noise. With the French modernist Edgar Varèse, Cowell organized the New York–based New Music Society to pursue these eclectic sources. But new music's limited exposure became narrower still when the Philharmonic Society absorbed the New York Symphony in 1928 and gave the baton to Arturo Toscanini, who devoted his total energies to nineteenth-century European romantics.

Faced by continued snubs from New York's art establishment, modernist painters depended on private patrons, like Alfred Stieglitz and Gertrude Vanderbilt Whitney. The Stieglitz circle of abstractionists, notably John Marin and Georgia O'Keeffe, increasingly lost ground in the 1920s to the Whitney Studio Club, a far more eclectic group of stylistic experimenters. Its painters included Nyack-born Edward Hopper, who captured the haunting loneliness of the modern city in canvases such as *Manhattan Bridge Loop* (1928), and Stuart Davis, a "precisionist" whose *Eggbeater* series was a landmark in New York–style modernism, which applied European abstraction to Manhattan's machine and skyscraper look. Another force altogether was a group of wealthy collectors such as John Quinn, Abby Aldrich Rockefeller, and Lizzie Bliss, buyers of the latest cubist, fauvist, and surrealist works from private galleries in New York and Paris.

In the late 1920s, private ambitions were finally realized in solid institutions. The stimulus came with the death of John Quinn, the owner of America's largest private modern art collection, mostly cubism and surrealism, and yet another rebuff to Mrs. Whitney's aesthetic tastes from the lofty Metropolitan Museum. In 1929, one of Quinn's acquaintances, Mary Quinn Sullivan, joined

Abby Aldrich Rockefeller and Lizzie Bliss in donating cubist treasures to found the Museum of Modern Art, by which they meant contemporary European art. A year later, Mrs. Whitney endowed the Whitney Museum of American Art to display her American scene painters.

Manhattan embraced modern radio, when General Electric allowed RCA executive David Sarnoff to venture beyond radiotelephony. In 1926, Sarnoff organized the National Broadcasting Company to send subscription broadcasts of New York City talent to stations in the NBC Red and Blue networks (linked by AT&T land lines). Sarnoff hired New York Philharmonic impresario Arthur Judson to sign performers, but when the deal collapsed Judson set up the United Independent Broadcasters. Poorly financed, United was absorbed by Philadelphia's Columbia Phonograph, then by Philadelphia cigar manufacturer William S. Paley, who thought radio could sell La Palina Cigars. Taking charge of the Columbia Broadcasting System in 1928, Paley offered affiliates "sustaining programs" at $5,000 per evening hour. In 1929, when CBS had sixty affiliates, Paley leased headquarters on Madison Avenue and wondered how to take on NBC, which had developed shows like *Amos 'n' Andy* that had changed America's evening habits.

New York's most important stimulus to modern culture was the stainless-steel look of Manhattan itself. It inspired the vogue in streamline design championed by Norman Bel Geddes, the Broadway scenic designer who turned his skills to industrial products, and Walter Dorwin Teague, another Broadway alumnus, who opened a New York office in 1927 devoted to the airstream restyling of consumer products. A Bel Geddes apprentice, Henry Dreyfuss, gave a radiator-grill sleekness to everything from GE toasters to the American Locomotive Company's Hudson J-3a, which pulled the 20th Century Limited from New York City to Chicago. The midtown skyline gained icons of modernism like the Chrysler Building (1930) and Raymond Hood's McGraw-Hill Building (1931). Sleek ocean liners moored at West Side piers disgorged European intellectuals, who came to see modernism at work.

The Economic Establishment

During the 1921 recession, New York State manufacturing crossed an economic divide. Its durable goods economy centered on Schenectady manufacturers like General Electric and American Locomotive. The New York Central Railroad hauled one-seventh of U.S. freight in a 12,000-mile empire of track that included freight yards in West Albany, Selkirk, and Utica. But the core of the factory sector was 7,200 clothing firms concentrated in New York City and Rochester, which employed an average of nineteen workers but produced 80 percent of U.S. women's apparel and 43 percent of men's clothing. While the recession humbled heavy equipment makers, it also warned producers of mass-market "commodity" goods that New York's highly stylized consumer economy was vulnerable to newer industries, capitalized on a larger and more productive scale.

In 1919 New York State had nearly 1.5 million employees in manufacturing, but by 1929 that force declined 9.3 percent. Old industries such as textiles, carpets, and woolens slashed payrolls. The list of closed factories included Wolcott & Campbell Spinning in Utica, John K. Stewart textiles in Amsterdam, and even the electrified wonder, Olympian Knit Goods of New Hartford. Businessmen blamed low-wage southern competitors—and Albany legislators, "forever tinkering with the laws that govern labor." Salamanca furniture firms like Fancher, tanneries in Olean and Randolph, and the world's largest glue works, Gaensslen, Fisher & Co. in Gowanda, felt competition from the Carolinas. In contrast, manufacturers of business machines, industrial chemicals, and photographic equipment steadily added workers. Among the high fliers were Eastman Kodak and Bausch & Lomb, which tripled their workforces between 1919 and 1925. In 1927, New York factory hands earned an average of $1,497 per year, almost $200 (13 percent) above the U.S. average. A Cornell University economist estimated that the purchasing power of New York factory workers had risen nearly one-fifth between 1920 and 1928.

The 1921 recession brought hard lessons about corporate structure, product diversification, and marketing. GE president Gerard Swope consolidated scattered lamp works, mass-produced the sealed-motor refrigerator, and poured money into the Schenectady Research Laboratory. Swope engaged the advertiser Barton, Durstine and Osborn to develop GE's image among consumers for "everything electrical going into the American home." In the mid-1920s, Thomas J. Watson changed CTR to International Business Machines, consolidated customer services at IBM's Manhattan headquarters, and began to plan with a "Future Demands Department." His rival, James H. Rand, Jr., brought under single management Remington Typewriter, American Kardex, and other subsidiaries, while focusing on the New York City market with product demonstrations at "The Remington Rand Business Show." Cluett, Peabody, located in Troy, expanded from starched collars to underwear, handkerchiefs, and "Sanforized" (preshrunk) Arrow shirts, whose collars and cuffs were stiffened by a patented chemical process.

Inevitably, corporate reorganizations shifted control of business to larger regional cities. After Lackawanna Steel was taken over by Bethlehem in 1922, nearly every other major Buffalo steelmaker was absorbed by giants based elsewhere. The city's flour mills came under the ownership of holding companies in Minneapolis and New York City, and local bakeries, along with facilities in Albany and Syracuse, became part of Nabisco, which also took over Niagara Falls's Shredded Wheat Company. Syracuse lost control of Smith-Premier, a typewriter maker, to Remington; Semet-Solvay, the country's leading manufacturer of soda ash, was absorbed by New York–based Allied Chemical; and in 1922 General Motors took over auto-parts maker Brown-Lipe-Chapin Co.

Unions faded in open-shop cities, where businessmen followed the "American Plan," a sophisticated combination of union-busting tactics and programs to win the organizational loyalty of workers. Rochester's Industrial Management Council, whose members included Eastman Kodak, Bausch & Lomb, and General Railway Signal, shied away from strong-arm tactics, like forcing workers to sign "yellow-dog" contracts. They preferred to follow Kodak executive Marion B. Folsom's emphases on company social insurance and employment stabilization schemes. In Troy, Cluett, Peabody remained "open" with standard wages, internal promotion, and retention of older employees as "privileged workers." General Electric's welfare plan carried out Owen D. Young's notion of a "cultural wage." The company allowed employees with one year's service to buy discounted bonds of GE Employees Securities Corp., and 30,000 took advantage of the plan by 1925. Gerard Swope installed a "plan of representation" for workers at GE Schenectady and promised "businesslike" dialogue with the AFL.

Unions across New York City lost ground during the 1920s. The women's garment trades were battered by the 1921 recession, when manufacturers sent work to nonunion, "outside" shops that did low-wage piecework. Cost-cutting during a 1926 slowdown let Communists gain control of key union locals. They squared off against International Ladies' Garment Workers' Union moderates like Benjamin Schlesinger and David Dubinsky, who preached cooperation with management and pension-fund welfare. Dubinsky managed to oust the Communists, but they regrouped as the Needle Trades Workers Industrial Union and in 1928 called a strike against the ladies' garment shops that shattered the ILGWU. Unions hung on in specialized trades and in businesses that faced ruin from work stoppages. In New York City, seasonal work had been unionized by the American Federation of Musicians, the International Longshoremen's Association, and the building trades. Strike threats persuaded some businessmen, particularly in the garment and produce industries, to deal with racketeers, who sold them "protection" from union intimidation. Some of New York's worst gangsters "broke legs" for Amalgamated Clothing Workers business agents, Sam Kaplan's Motion Picture Operators Union, and Joe Ryan's International Longshoremen.

What remained of the radical left withered under Coolidge prosperity. Socialists withdrew into the Jewish Forward Association and the Workmen's Circle, a Yiddish fraternal order. Others kept the faith at Manhattan's Rand School and Brookwood Labor College, organized in 1921 at Katonah, Westchester County, to "arouse" class consciousness. Communists were torn by factions loyal to Soviet leader Joseph Stalin and his exiled rival, Leon Trotsky. Driven from the Communist party, Trotskyists carried on a bitter anti-Stalinist crusade.

The Professionalization of Reform

Progressive reform became institutionalized in bureaucratic ministries staffed by trained professionals. The Henry Street Settlement in New York City, for example, ran the Visiting Nurse Service, and the United Neighborhood Houses campaigned for housing improvement, mother's pensions, and related social betterment. They were joined by administrators of public schools like Leonard Covello of Benjamin Franklin High School in East Harlem and Julia Richman of Seward Park on the Lower East Side, who tried to influence the work of social agencies in their neighborhoods. Increasingly, social welfare meant "social case work," a kind of psychological counseling among the poor to prevent the "antisocial behavior of later years." In most cities, private charities distributed the bulk of relief and even laid claim to disburse public relief to prevent its falling into the hands of machine politicians.

By the late 1920s, half of America's largest foundations were headquartered in New York City, for example, Russell Sage, Rockefeller, and Milbank Memorial. They supported epidemiological studies of TB, delinquency, and poverty. Their findings provided models for categorical aid and case work that were adopted by philanthropic agencies and state and local governments. In 1922, Milbank spent $2 million in Cattaraugus County setting up a model organization for rural health care, including a county health officer, a laboratory, and school nurses. More important, Milbank spurred the participation of private efforts like the local Red Cross, the Portville and Gowanda Nursing committees, and the Olean Anti-Tuberculosis Association. The New York State Tuberculosis Association, administered by social worker Harry L. Hopkins, offered demonstration projects in TB prevention. By 1923 the impact of private philanthropy and public funds had created 10,000 TB beds in hospitals across the state, one-sixth of the national supply.

The 1920s saw the completion of state authority to classify and handle dependents. Responsible for care of the insane and feeble-minded, New York counted 40,000 "mental defectives," including 10,000 requiring institutionalization. The state embarked on construction of an additional hospital for the insane in 1923, operated Letchworth Village in Rockland County with 1,400 beds for "mental defectives," and opened institutes for defective delinquents at Napanoch (male) and Bedford Hills (female). Professional reform focused on youth lured into delinquency by the modern city. The Rochester Department of Charities, the Child Welfare League, and the Society to Protect Children joined forces in a Comprehensive Child Welfare Council. All the state's counties had children's courts by 1929, and Dutchess, Suffolk, and Cayuga had county boards of child welfare. While only Westchester had a county department of public welfare, the State Charities Aid Association lobbied to apply Westchester's Poor Law reform to the rest of the state. New York's experience in handling delinquents and felons also contributed to the movement to regulate parole and to infuse corrections departments with social work principles.

By 1928, nearly 2.8 million New Yorkers went to school, including 2 million in public schools from kindergarten to twelfth grade, 168,000 working youths in "continuation schools" (which offered after-hours classes in high school subjects), and 225,000 adults in evening schools. High school enrollment soared from 87,000 in 1905 to over 400,000 in 1929, with nearly a sixfold increase in continuation schools between 1920 and 1927. Buffalo typified the investment in public education. It added twelve "intermediate" schools during 1920 and expanded adult education, which enrolled 17,000, or roughly one of fifteen residents, by 1923.

Higher education swung between experimental trends and brazen marketing. The war encouraged curriculum reform, ushering in courses like Columbia University's "Contemporary Civilization," whose texts in European history influenced general education across the country; and area studies, the particular interest of Cornell president Jacob Gould Schurman. The new seriousness was behind the vow of Fordham's president, Father Edward P. Trunan, to end football recruiting and to purge "the commercial element from Collegiate athletics." In response to wartime repression, outspoken academics such as Columbia University historians Charles A. Beard and James Harvey Robinson in 1919 helped launch the New School for Social Research, an independent faculty of social scientists dedicated to citizen education. The experimental ethos permeated Sarah Lawrence College in Bronxville, founded in 1928 to educate women with self-directed studies in the humanities and social sciences.

The decade saw expansion of private universities offering higher education to the masses. By 1929, under President Nicholas Murray Butler, Columbia University had nearly 49,000 students, including 16,000 in summer school and 19,500 taking home extension courses. The Columbia empire also included Seth Low Junior College in Brooklyn and Saint Stephens College (later Bard) in upstate New York. In 1925 New York University enrollment totaled 20,000, including 5,400 in the School of Commerce, whose Wall Street division had 1,900; and the University Heights Campus in the Bronx. Under President Rush Rhees, the University of Rochester opened the Eastman School of Music and began a $10 million drive to develop the River Campus. Led by Chancellor Samuel P. Capen II, who turned "autonomous schools" into a real campus, the University of Buffalo expanded to a 150-acre site on the city line. Syracuse University opened the School of Citizenship and Public Affairs, which trained a generation of city managers and municipal researchers.

Government developed imposing public education systems. The New York State College for Teachers at Albany headed a network of ten state normal schools, including Buffalo, Cortland, Oswego, and Plattsburgh. The push for subject matter in teacher training transformed the New York State College for Teachers at Buffalo, which expanded its pedagogical program and offered the four-year B.A. degree. The State Normal School at Oswego developed a three-year curriculum and an industrial arts specialty. In 1926, the state legislature reorganized City College and its women's campus, Hunter College, into a municipal system administered by a Board of Higher Education. A branch in the Bronx was opened (later Lehman College) and a two-year extension in Brooklyn, which became a full-fledged college in 1930. Hunter's summer and extension sessions made it the largest college for women in the nation.

Older colleges viewed mass enrollments of new ethnics, particularly Jews, as a mixed opportunity. At City College, the student body rapidly changed from middle-class Protestants and German Jews to working-class Jews from the Lower East Side. The prospect of losing Jewish students to secular City College prompted Bernard Revel to found Yeshiva University in Washington Heights to combine Jewish studies with "a full education in modern thought and culture." That same prospect gave Nicholas Murray Butler the rationale to impose severe quotas on Jewish applicants to Columbia College. After Jews surged into the NYU Heights Campus, the university forced down the figure to 30 percent by 1922 (although fiscal pressures brought the ethnic group back to 54 percent by 1929). Even Fordham felt the tide and considered offers from Jewish philanthropists to build a medical college. But Father Trunan chose to develop schools of law, social work, and accounting, fields popular among Fordham's largely Irish student body.

Sweeping institutional gains came in social medicine. Abraham T. Flexner of the Rockefeller Institute and adviser to the (Rockefeller) General Education Board had tried to force adoption of the "full-time" principle among medical faculties at Columbia and Cornell and found himself rebuffed by professors with lucrative private practices. Flexner turned to Rochester, where President Rhees had compatible interests. A General Education Board grant and $5 million from George Eastman created the University of Rochester Medical School. Dean George Whipple (who shared the 1934 Nobel Prize in medicine) created a research-oriented school integrated with the university and hospital. Another triumph for Flexner, Albany Medical College affiliated with Albany Hospital and embarked on extension work in northeast New York. A Rockefeller Foundation grant established a "cooperative effort through the whole region radiating from the medical school and teaching hospitals."

Toward Urban Liberalism

Al Smith came into his own during the 1922 campaign against Republican Governor Nathan L. Miller. The gubernatorial nomination was Smith's for the asking, but he refused to run with publisher William Randolph Hearst, the favorite for the U.S. Senate nomination. Smith forced Charles F. Murphy and Brooklyn boss John H. McCooey to back Dr. Royal S. Copeland, New York City health commissioner. A prominent Methodist and "dry," Copeland defused the prohibition issue and freed Smith to take the offensive against Governor Miller. Smith claimed that Miller used the Mullan-Gage Law for police-state enforcement of prohibition and made the State Water Power Commission a tool of the power companies. He won with a record margin of 387,000 votes. The tide elected Copeland and brought the Democrats control of the state Senate by one seat. Smith called his campaign "a promissory note" to the people of New York.

Al Smith served four two-year terms as governor of New York. Museum of the City of New York.

Governor Smith gave the citizens superb government as a matter of practical Tammany politics. Charles Murphy wanted Tammany credited for modern improvements and was proud that his protégé was being touted for president. Senate Majority Leader James J. Walker, an amiable but shrewd tactician, parlayed the one-vote majority into an effective system. In the 1923 session, Governor Smith gained repeal of the anti-Bolshevik Lusk-Fearon Laws, approval of a $300 million state bond issue to eliminate railroad grade crossings, and enactment of a program for county health facilities. He brought back Frances Perkins to the Industrial Board, where she expanded coverage of workmen's compensation to a host of "hazardous" occupations. Warning the State Water Power Commission to reject applications for private power sites on the Saint Lawrence River, Smith proclaimed hydroelectricity the "property of all the people" and called for a state development agency modeled on the Port Authority. In 1924, Smith gained legislation for the State Council on Parks, which, under Robert Moses, coordinated the work of twelve regional commissions.

In the 1924 gubernatorial contest, Smith's record forced Republican leaders to back the popular insurgent, Assemblyman Theodore Roosevelt, Jr. Tammany boss Charles Murphy had died in April, which left Smith leader of the state Democratic party and chief strategist of the campaign. He made the most of the opportunity, going on the stump and the radio, proclaiming his progressive record. Young TR attacked the Ku Klux Klan and promised "constructive liber-alism" on labor legislation, but he was no match for Smith on water power, parks, and welfare. While President Calvin Coolidge took New York in a land-slide, Governor Smith beat Roosevelt by nearly 100,000 votes.

Governor Smith brought the transformation of state finance for public schools to its culmination. Two years of hearings by the legislature's Commit-tee of 21 on Rural Schools, largely supported by the Agricultural Conference Board, produced the (Cole-Rice) Central School Law of 1925, which offered $9 million in state aid for construction and bus transport to districts that closed one- and two-room schools. The law also mandated equal effort in school sup-port, requiring local property taxes with state supplements to pay teachers a $1,500 minimum salary. In 1925, Smith named Reconstruction Commission alumnus Michael Friedsam to head a commission on school finance. The Fried-sam report (1926) advocated a $16.5 million increase in state school aid focused on larger cities and designed to relieve local tax burdens. Smith got the Fried-sam recommendations through the legislature, although many communities refused to surrender control over education. Nevertheless, Governor Smith's state aid package, which was only $9 million in 1919, reached $82 million by fiscal 1926.

In 1925 Governor Smith, demonstrating his skills in citizens' politics, ful-filled the Reconstruction Commission goal of government reorganization. Smith proposed constitutional amendments to reduce the number of statewide elective offices, consolidate gubernatorial agencies under cabinet control, and create an executive budget. He won avid support from good government Repub-licans, like Richard S. Child of the New York State Association, and, after vot-ers approved in 1925, he appointed a commission headed by Republicans Charles Evans Hughes and John Lord O'Brian to advise on implementation. After the executive budget amendment was adopted in 1928, Smith appointed Republican Joseph C. Wilson, a Rochester businessman, to carry it out. Smith wanted a four-year term for governor (along with the lieutenant governor, comptroller, and attorney general), but not timed to coincide with the Republi-cans' quadrennial presidential romps, and persuaded voters to defeat the mea-sure. (The four-year term with elections in nonpresidential years was approved by the voters in 1937.)

Governor Smith appointed the New York State Commission on Housing and Planning, chaired by Clarence Stein, and gained passage of the State Hous-ing Law of 1926, establishing a State Board of Housing to grant tax exemptions for low-rent, "limited-dividend" projects. The board launched fourteen projects, including the Amalgamated Dwellings on New York City's Lower East Side, for a total of 11,000 units. In June 1926, Smith supported Robert Moses's struggle for Long Island park land against obstruction by wealthy property owners, telling a radio audience: "I cast my lot with the many." Running for reelection in 1926 against Manhattan Congressman Ogden L. Mills, Governor Smith stumped the state and won by a landslide. His coattails brought an upset victory for State Supreme Court Judge Robert F. Wagner over U.S. Senator James W. Wadsworth, Jr.

Smith attacked the attempt by the lame duck, GOP-controlled State Water Power Commission to approve power-site license applications in December 1926 for the Frontier Corporation (GE, Alcoa, and Du Pont) and American Super Power Corporation. Proposing a state power authority, Smith declared that the Saint Lawrence, Niagara, and other rivers could generate eight times the electricity that the Edison Co. provided Manhattan. In May 1927, GOP business leaders met at Watertown to counter the public relations impact of Smith's water power bill. Supreme downstate, Smith now threatened Republican interests on their own ground.

Al Smith had transformed New York government and politics. He regularly met with editors from metropolitan dailies to confer on major issues like housing, the executive budget, and water power. Millions grew familiar with his raspy voice on the radio, although nothing compared to Smith on the stump, sarcastic and finger-jabbing, playing to the galleries like the actor he wanted to be. He convinced voters to approve a staggering $465 million in construction bonds for railroad grade crossings, parks, and hospitals. When Republicans objected that his bond issues hid operating expenses within the capital budget, Smith took to the radio, carrying the voters with him. Through adept use of prison reformers and the Moreland Act (which allowed the governor to investigate the conduct of state departments), Smith created the Department of Corrections and changed the law to regularize parole grants and institute indeterminate sentences (range of years rather than fixed terms). The state park system alone was a colossal achievement. Driven by Robert Moses's ambition and Smith's fervent support, it included half the acreage of state parks and forests in America.

By 1928 Governor Smith, having doubled state employees and annual spending, had revolutionized the scale of government. He goaded the legislature into enacting a personal income tax and an inheritance tax. In 1913 state and local tax collections were $28.65 per capita (in constant 1930 dollars), second to Massachusetts and California among urban states. By 1930 the figure had soared to $90.64, 12 percent more than the no. 2 figure, New Jersey's. That year New York collected $148.7 million in state income, inheritance, and corporate taxes—13 percent of all state and local taxes. The figure amounted to one-fourth of all state inheritance taxes and three-fifths of all state income taxes. Smith pushed combined state and local expenditures on education (which jumped 230 percent between 1918 and 1929) and hospitals and public health (340 percent), although the largest increase went for debt payment, which climbed to 10 percent of all local expenditures in 1930.

Critics derided Smith as a Tammany wire-puller, with a weakness for piece-meal, categorical reforms—activism without a plan. Yet Smith's programs had visionary reach and foresaw a web of metropolitan progress, of roads and parks and rural assistance. His emphasis was ironic given his working-class Irish-Catholic suspicion of Protestant high-hats. But no politician subscribed more to the promises of professionals, the efficiency-minded centralizers and manage-rial experts, the administrators of child care, corrections, and services for the mentally ill, the professional pedagogues, highway engineers, and city planners. By some exotic transmutation, the kid who swam off the East River docks became the architect of modern New York.

Smith also completed Boss Murphy's transformation of the Democratic party. If Murphy won Tammany its initial influence among Jewish voters, Smith brought about a firm ethnic allegiance. Jews helped Smith pile up huge pluralities in New York City and diminish the GOP presence from thirty-three assemblymen in 1920 to seven by 1925, from eleven senators in 1920 to just one in 1930. After Murphy's death in 1924, Tammany was headed by Judge George W. Olvaney, who never had the old man's authority, and Bronx leadership passed to the brainy lawyer Edward J. Flynn. Smith soon bypassed Olvaney, becoming de facto boss of the state and city organizations. Fed up with Mayor Hylan's loud-mouth ways, Smith in 1925 forced the bosses to come up with another mayoral candidate, Senate Majority Leader James J. Walker. A Tin Pan Alley songster and skirt chaser, Jimmy Walker had a "When are you going to get wise?" attitude toward public office. But he remained popular as long as the city economy hummed. He ran again in 1929, beating GOP Congressman Fiorello H. La Guardia, although Socialist Norman Thomas did well amid a flurry of unemployment.

Partly because of Smith's battering, other cities underwent political change. In Albany, war veteran Edward J. O'Connell and his brothers took over Boss Barnes's bailiwick with the election of Democratic Mayor William Hackett in 1921. Rochester witnessed a similar dissolution of the Old Guard after Boss Aldridge died in 1922. His GOP successors, James L. Hotchkiss and Harry J. Bareham, Sr., refused to join the 1924 campaign for the creation of a city man-ager position, which was backed by George Eastman's money, Frank Gannett's editorials, and door-to-door volunteers from the Women's City Club. The char-ter election, which installed reform Mayor Joseph C. Wilson and City Manager Stephen B. Story, split the GOP apart. In Utica, Al Smith's impact forwarded the mayoral career of Democrat Charles S. Donnelley, with his organization sup-porters William Bray and Charles S. McKernan. Rufus P. Elefante started out a Republican, then joined Smith's 1928 presidential campaign and brought Utica's Italians into the fold. Smith's welfare and public works also challenged Republican fiefdoms on the metropolitan fringe. Westchester County GOP boss William Ward responded with suburban public services and an "urban" county charter. Nassau GOP boss G. Wilbur Doughty was more hidebound, but his nephew and successor, J. Russel Sprague, accommodated demands for activist government.

Smith broadened a Democratic party still beholden to corporate interests and Tammany. The party's titular leader was the 1924 presidential nominee, John W. Davis, a Wall Street lawyer, whose "fine list of clients" included J. P. Morgan & Co., and whose conservatism garnered just 29 percent of the New York vote. Franklin D. Roosevelt, the coddled son of Dutchess County gentry, was appointed assistant navy secretary in the Wilson administration and became the Democratic vice presidential nominee in 1920. Stricken by polio in 1921, he was sustained by family wealth, a modest law practice, and a sunny Episcopalian faith. Wheelchair bound, Roosevelt kept contact with his party, largely through his wife, Eleanor, who joined the New York Consumers' League and organized the state Democratic Women's Committee. Smith's entente with Jewish liberals was epitomized by banker Herbert H. Lehman, a bluff extrovert whose social conscience was molded in the ethical Judaism of New York City's Temple Emanu-El. Tapped by Governor Smith for a needle trades arbitration board, Lehman became a patron of David Dubinsky's practical unionism and chief fund-raiser for Smith's 1928 campaign.

Throughout the 1920s, the Court of Appeals tilted left under Chief Judge Frank H. Hiscock, Benjamin N. Cardozo, who succeeded him in 1927, and associates including Republican Cuthbert W. Pound and Democrat Irving Lehman, the banker's studious brother. By all accounts, Cardozo, with his self-effacing demeanor and dense, almost gnomic arguments lofted the institution into the nation's leading court of common law. His decisions clarified the meaning of "consideration" in contract law, and his *Palsgraf* opinion (1928) drastically limited the "proximate cause" doctrine in liability law, freeing a railroad from liability for an accident not directly caused by the railroad's negligence.

Cardozo was also impatient with common law that was "inconsistent with the sense of justice or with the social welfare." In *Adler v. Deegan* (1929), he refused to question the state's police power to regulate tenements: "If the moral and physical fiber of its manhood and its womanhood is not a State concern, the question is, what is?" A guarded civil libertarian, he attacked the police "third degree," but he begged to differ, in *People v. Defore* (1926), with the U.S. Supreme Court's "exclusionary rule" on tainted evidence: Must the criminal go free, he asked, "because the constable has blundered?" And he led the court toward a recognition of organized labor. In *Interborough Rapid Transit Co. v. Lavin* (1927), the court adopted Robert F. Wagner's brief that the Railway Workers Union, despite yellow-dog contracts, had a "right to win converts" among subway employees.

In 1928, Governor Smith, worried about holding New York in the presiden-

tial election, arm-twisted Franklin Roosevelt into running for governor, jocu-
larly suggesting that Herbert Lehman, the candidate for lieutenant governor,
could handle the more onerous duties. Roosevelt faced a formidable opponent,
State Attorney General Albert Ottinger, the first Jew nominated for governor by
a major party. Roosevelt campaigned, a reporter noted, with crutch and cane,
"leaning forward on these supports so that he could draw his feet after him in a
sliding gait." Calling himself "an upstate farmer," he toured the Mohawk Valley by canal boat, promising farm relief and state water power. In Buffalo he
pledged a minimum wage for women and children and a commission to study
old-age pensions. Republican Herbert Hoover beat Smith in New York by nearly
100,000 votes, but Roosevelt squeezed past Ottinger by 26,000.

In Albany, Governor Roosevelt did more than preside. He replaced Smith's
entourage with a kitchen cabinet headed by Albany newsman Louis M. Howe,
party stalwart James Farley, and speechwriter Judge Samuel Rosenman. In a
showdown over the executive budget with GOP Senate Leader John Knight,
who forwarded bills to initiate budgeting by legislative committee, Roosevelt
vetoed Knight's gambit and won his case in the Court of Appeals. Announcing
that "new social conditions bring new ideas of social responsibility," Roosevelt
proposed a forty-eight-hour workweek for women and children and sweeping
social welfare reform. Although the hours bill failed in the legislature, the Public Welfare Law of 1929 established Albany's responsibility for "state poor"
(unsettled paupers) and county welfare districts to administer "adequate" home
relief. The legislature's Commission on Old Age Security refused Roosevelt's
ideas for a system of contributory insurance and instead authorized state aid to
county relief for the aged. Though it was hardly the social insurance Roosevelt
wanted, he signed it as half a loaf. The following year, Roosevelt and the vigorous lobby of the New York Consumers' League gained passage of the Forty-
Eight-Hour Law.

Roosevelt had more success putting his stamp on public power. As chairman
of the Public Service Commission he appointed the utilities expert Milo R. Malt-
bie, who replaced tedious rate investigations with private conferences with executives to talk down power rates. The legislature defeated Roosevelt's first demand
for publicly owned power but enacted in April 1931 a law creating a five-man
State Power Authority. Roosevelt promptly appointed noted public power advocates, attorney Frank P. Walsh (as chairman) and long-time progressive Morris
Llewellyn Cooke. Favoring electric rates based on "prudent investment value,"
Roosevelt popularized the notion of public power as a "birchrod" to drive down
private rates. The utilities hamstrung the Power Authority in litigation, but New
York provided a blueprint for the New Deal's Tennessee Valley Authority.

Roosevelt's greatest challenge came from an unexpected quarter—corrections
and prison reform. Changes in the law that regularized parole, and the Baumes
Law of 1927, which mandated life imprisonment after a fourth felony conviction,

fomented unrest in upstate prisons. In December 1928 rioters at Auburn took the warden hostage and killed eight convicts and a guard. July 1929 riots at Clinton and Auburn resulted in five killed and several score injured. Governor Roosevelt appointed a committee headed by the penologist Sam A. Lewisohn to investigate prison grievances, resulting in widespread reorganization. The legislature reconstructed Auburn and shifted its female population to an enlarged facility at Bedford Hills. Meanwhile the Lewisohn Committee drafted the State Parole Law of 1930, which required the board to review the moral progress of inmates who served minimum sentences, thereby applying social work to corrections. Roosevelt appointed Walter N. Thayer, Jr. as commissioner of correction to reform prisons, while Lewisohn headed a Temporary State Commission that proposed medium-security facilities and systematic time off for good behavior.

As a consequence of parole reform, the Columbia law professor Raymond Moley entered Roosevelt's inner circle. Moley brought other experts on economics and social science to Albany like Rexford G. Tugwell and Adolf A. Berle, forming a group of advisers that would later be called the "brains trust." Roosevelt fortified his law-and-order image (hurt by the emerging Tammany scandal involving the police, city magistrates, and Mayor Walker) when Republicans challenged him in the 1930 gubernatorial elections by nominating Manhattan federal prosecutor Charles H. Tuttle. He trounced Tuttle by 725,000 votes. For the first time, a Democrat had won a majority—168,000 votes—upstate, a feat not even managed by Al Smith.

The Neotechnic Countryside

During the 1920s, twenty-five upstate counties lost population while eleven others stagnated. The decline stretched across agricultural districts and even affected Hudson Valley counties like Putnam and Columbia. It shrank places like Saranac Lake, which lost tuberculosis clients to the Veterans' Administration hospital at Tupper Lake. Extractive industries dwindled with competition from more productive fields. Adirondack lumbering never recovered from the 1913 tariff reductions on Canadian pulpwood, and, by 1929, Allegany "rock oil" producers kept small refineries open only around Olean. The social critic Lewis Mumford claimed that rural New York was ready for the "neotechnic" phase of human history, when electricity and automobiles would make possible new forms of human habitation in balance with the environment.

State and county spending doubled the mileage of surfaced roads by the late 1920s. State Highway Commissioner Frederick Greene pushed major improvements like State Route 17, the Mohawk Turnpike, and Route 20, which connected Albany and Auburn. Modern concrete had a drastic effect on transit service. Route 17 forced sharp curtailments of trolley schedules on the Olean, Bradford and Salamanca Railway, routes that were taken over by Greyhound, West Ridge, and other bus companies. In 1928, the Delaware & Hudson Railroad began running buses between Glens Falls, Saratoga Springs, and Ballston Spa. When the Delaware & Hudson sought permits from the Public Service Commission to cut steam passenger service in 1928, the Cooperstown Chamber of Commerce trooped to Albany to protest, in vain, the loss of trains to Albany and Binghamton.

Power grids and automobiles bolstered regional centers at the expense of rural villages. Northern New York Utilities joined with businesses in Watertown and the Black River Regulating District to complete Stillwater Dam, while Glens Falls businessmen created the Hudson River Regulating District to control the Sacandaga River. The automobile allowed farm families to bypass villages on their way to regional centers. The effect, commented Hartford town historian Isabella Brayton in 1929, "has materially lessened the volume of local trade . . . while resuscitating the outlying farming country." Street fairs, farmers' markets, and business blocks closed, as farmers flocked to regional five-and-dimes that stayed open on Saturday nights, and to chain theaters like Schine Enterprises of Gloversville, which took over seventy-eight theaters across the state. Another consolidating force was the Central School Law of 1925, which subsidized construction of regional high schools and modernized the curriculum with courses in business and home economics. By 1930 state grants were funding half the school costs in rural villages.

Many localities fought their shrinking status with 1920s boosterism. Merchants in regional centers like Binghamton proclaimed all-day Saturday sales. For its part, the Utica *Observer-Dispatch* urged merchants to make rural villagers "feel that they are part of the Utica community." Several hamlets organized the Mohawk Valley Towns Association to promote tourism and the Battle of Oriskany Day, celebrating the local militia's heroism in the American Revolution. In 1925 Saratoga County leaders gained legislative enactment of the Saratoga Battlefield Commission, which sponsored the Schuylerville Pageant to commemorate the defeat of British General John Burgoyne in 1777.

Agriculture retreated at an accelerated pace in the 1920s. The state had 193,195 farms in 1920 but only 159,806 in 1930, while acreage dropped from 20.6 million to 17.9 million during the same period. In the first half of the decade, abandonment and suburban home construction chewed up farmland at the rate of 270,000 acres per year, particularly on the outskirts of the big cities. During the 1920s, suburban Westchester County lost 72 percent of its farms and 58 percent of its farm acreage. Even Chautauqua County saw the farm count decline from 7,100 in 1920 to 6,411 in 1930, while the average farm grew slightly in acreage and added 6 percent to the value of its land and buildings. On the outskirts of cities, skyrocketing land values forced the change from general farming to specialized, "kitchen" crops, dairying, and poultry.

Agricultural cooperatives, which allowed farmers to realize savings from group buying and marketing, matured during the 1920s. Successful marketers included the Producers' Co-operative Commission Association of East Buffalo, small co-ops like the Hartford Dairymen's League at Fort Edward, and the Dairymen's League Cooperative Association, which signed up 60 percent of the state's 85,000 dairy farmers and ran more than one hundred plants to make butter, ice cream, and condensed milk. But truck transport and improved roads, which widened the individual farmer's access to city markets, frustrated co-op control of milk shipments. While the Dairymen's League boasted "absolute farmer control" of milk marketing—and 51,493 dairymen contracts in 1922— another 10,000 refused to renew. Some were non-poolers by conviction or simply free riders on the league's price schedules. By the late 1920s, nearly half of all dairymen, mostly smaller operators with under fifty-five acres, remained outside the three major co-ops. Forced to ally with the producers' cartels, the league in 1925 sold a portion of its by-product business to the Borden Company.

With good reason, farm organizations turned to politics. The State Grange mobilized lodges to enable the farmer to "defend his interests"; and the New York Agricultural Conference Board organized a common lobby for the Grange, county Farm Bureaus, the Dairymen's League, the Horticultural Society, and local cooperatives. Trying to unburden agriculture, they favored the elimination of state taxes on fuel, state takeover of county road repair, and increased subsidies to remove railroad grade crossings. They championed state support for cooperative marketing and for advice on scientific husbandry from the state agricultural colleges.

Persuaded by Mumford's "neotechnic" ideas, New York City reformers argued that upstate deserved scientific management. Their concern grew when electric companies sought new hydroelectric sites and U.S. Secretary of Commerce Herbert Hoover talked about "giant power highways" to transmit generating capacity throughout the Northeast. In 1926, the (Stein) Commission on Housing and Planning reported that urban populations in the "Great Valley L" (Hudson and Mohawk) were fast spreading into rural districts with the adoption of modern conveniences like the automobile, electric power, and the telephone. Fearing loss of the rural way of life, the commission proposed to contain settlement within the "natural contours" of the landscape. Through planning, land use limits, and zoning it would have the fringes of the Mohawk and Hudson Valleys "intelligently controlled."

Wall Street

World War I fastened Wall Street on America and on the world. J. P. Morgan & Co., thanks to Allied purchasing and Federal Reserve Governor Benjamin Strong's buildup of gold reserves, became the center of an intricate system of intra-Allied credit which underwrote German reparations. Loans arranged by Morgan-led syndicates in New York kept Weimar Germany solvent and enabled the Bank of England to back sterling with gold in 1925. Foreign debt financed during the war also created a Wall Street market in European and Latin American securities, which doubled during the mid-1920s, while the market in foreign bills of exchange grew tenfold later in the decade. The New York market's sheer size and ability to capitalize deals stymied Wilsonian attempts to decentralize credit resources. In 1929, New York City, with less than 0.5 percent of the nation's banks, had 23 percent of bank assets and eight of its twelve largest banks, including Chase National, the world's biggest.

The war and the increase in corporate profits and financial operations transformed commercial banks and "democratized credit." While private, gentlemen's bankers, led by J. P. Morgan & Co., still molded Wall Street's image, business increasingly sought adventurous deal makers. In the early 1920s, National City Bank pioneered branch banking and, in 1928, became the first commercial bank to offer consumer loans and expanded checking accounts. In 1930, National City had eighty-three foreign branches and did enough business in China to provide nearly one-third of its profits. Firms like GE were powerful enough to arrange stock and bond flotations, which lessened their dependence on commercial bank loans and led bankers to worry about "the disappearing large borrower." Loan broker S. W. Straus & Co. opened its headquarters in Manhattan in 1921, pushing new investment opportunities. Straus pioneered first-mortgage real estate bonds, which included the financing of the Chanin and Chrysler Buildings.

The New York Stock Exchange had a weakness for glamour stocks, particularly companies that capitalized on the wonders of electricity. One attraction was utilities, whose financing allowed highly leveraged ownership of operating companies, like GE's Ebasco. Investors suspended judgment when a darling like Radio Corporation of America skipped quarterly reports and its stock rose thirtyfold between 1923 and 1929. Wright Aëronautical, worth $16 per share in 1925, soared to $220 in May 1927, after Charles A. Lindbergh flew from Long Island to Paris. With the spreading euphoria, demand for "call money," short-term brokers' loans, which used purchased stock as collateral, created its own supply of credit—brokers' loans that rose to $2.6 billion in December 1926. In July 1927, European central bankers met with New York Reserve Governor Strong, who agreed to a lower rediscount rate to prop up the British pound. The move eased credit and furthered the boom atmosphere on Wall Street.

The Great Bull Market saw the Dow Jones Industrial Average (an index of the total prices of selected stocks, including Alco, AT&T, and GE) jump from 159 in 1925 to 300 in December 1928, then soar to 382.01 on September 5, 1929. The flow of call money grew fivefold between 1926 and 1929, as industrial corporations added their own idle cash. The stock frenzy drew in National City

Bank, whose retail arm, the National City Company, became the largest securities dealer in the country. Albert Wiggin, head of the Chase National Bank and "the most popular banker on Wall Street," set up a securities affiliate, whose speculations included his bank's own stock. As the equities affiliates of commercial banks and investment trusts mushroomed, the small circle of investment bankers who traditionally filled a "watchdog" role was overwhelmed. The bull market rose despite the load of new issues, from $1.47 billion in 1927 to $5.294 billion in 1929, with $1 billion in new corporate stocks offered in September 1929 alone.

Last-minute attempts failed to stanch the drain of credit to the call money market. New York Federal Reserve Bank Governor George L. Harrison urged a rise in the discount rate, only to confront officials in Washington who worried that rising interest rates in New York would cause an outflow of gold reserves from England and jeopardize the British pound. In March 1929, Harrison was defied by Charles E. Mitchell of National City Bank, who proclaimed "an obligation which is paramount to any Federal Reserve warning" and pledged easy credit to investors. The New York Reserve tried to jawbone the market down and in August 1929 raised the discount rate from 6 to 9 percent. The move put a temporary crimp on call loans while others—notably industrial corporations with idle cash—increased their lending. Wall Street's magnetism was the ultimate tribute to New York in the Electric Age.

Chapter 30

Public Work in the Great Depression

ON "BLACK THURSDAY," OCTOBER 24, 1929, INVESTORS traded nearly 13 million shares on the New York Stock Exchange, wiping out $10 billion in value in the first two hours. That morning Thomas W. Lamont of J. P. Morgan, Charles Mitchell of National City, and Seward J. Prosser of Bankers Trust organized a buyers' pool to stem the panic. But on October 29 the spiral renewed. Another 16 million shares were dumped, including General Electric, which lost 47 points. By November 1, the value of stocks totaled $72 billion, down from $90 billion in September. The "Great Crash" had begun.

Banks and brokerages unloaded stocks held as collateral for call loans and cut back on new lending. Trades in mortgage bonds came to a standstill at the New York Real Estate Securities Exchange; only two changed hands on February 1, 1930. Credit contraction closed the fifty-seven-branch Bank of United States, ruining scores of thousands of small depositors throughout the city. In 1932, Wall Street suffered further humiliation when congressional hearings into "bear" raids and insider trading implicated Charles Mitchell of the National City Bank and partners at J. P. Morgan. A year later corporate underwriting was just 4 percent of what it had been in 1929.

Statewide factory employment wavered until April 1930, and then plummeted. The Glens Falls Trades and Labor Assembly reported: "Building trades slow; half of plumbers idle; work for common laborers at a standstill; 75 carpenters out of work; shirt factories running low." The New York Central Railroad and other freight carriers slashed purchases of capital goods, reducing 1934 output at American Locomotive in Schenectady to forty-two engines. Buffalo joblessness reached 33 percent in November 1932, and one-third of those jobless had been seeking work for over two years. Only three thousand apartment units were built in New York City in 1933, while construction fell 91 percent in Westchester, and the housing decline bankrupted suburban tax districts across Erie County. White-collar ranks thinned, and wages for female clerks fell 40 percent in New York City. In 1933 the New York University Employment Bureau told graduates, the "$22 job is now about $15." What participants called a "slave market" opened on Simpson Street in the Bronx, where black women lined up for 20 cent-per-hour work as domestics.

Thousands of homeless tramped roads and jammed flophouses, hoping to find cheap bunks. In 1931 Syracuse and Rochester opened free municipal lodgings, and the 643,248 total registrations at the Erie County Lodging House that year was nine times the 1928 figure. During fall 1933, the town of Hornell on the Erie Railroad sheltered nearly 10,000 "floaters" at the police station. In Manhattan, shantytowns of cardboard and scrap lumber arose at 76th Street and Riverside Drive and in the mud flats of the Central Park Reservoir. The Salvation Army opened a soup kitchen on the Bowery, a form of handout copied by churches, hospitals, and even National Guard units, which distributed food at their armories. Some jobless turned to barter through organizations like the Emergency Exchange Association, which was founded in Manhattan in late 1932 and spread to New Rochelle, White Plains, and upstate. The Greenwich Village Exchange enrolled a few hundred unemployed, mainly white-collar workers, drawn to the cooperative ideal. Most schemes used scrip, like the Exchange Circle in Rochester, which paid for work in credits redeemable "in any service or commodity available."

Agriculture, long in slump, faced utter disaster. By 1931, butter sold at 25 cents per pound on the farm, eggs at 15 to 20 cents per dozen, wheat at 40 cents per bushel. Between 1928 and 1932 the prices dairymen received for fluid milk fell 61 percent, and during the bitter winter of 1931–32 prices dropped from $2.90 to $1.79 per hundred pounds in two months. By 1932, when potatoes slumped to 37 cents per bushel and corn was down to 45 cents, the farm price index had fallen three-fifths from the already-depressed level of 1928. Angry at the collapse in milk, dairymen in Jefferson, Cattaraugus, and Wyoming Counties quit the Dairymen's League in early 1933; and in Monroe County pickets attacked milk trucks on the way to market and confronted state police escorting them. A "home-made" movement spread among Wyoming County farmers embittered by the market system. They vowed to switch from tractors to horses and to give up "money" crops.

Voluntary Stabilization

Governor Franklin D. Roosevelt's first impulse was to enact regulatory laws to remove women and children from factory payrolls and to urge employers to adopt a five-day week to spread jobs. In March 1930, he named a Committee on the Stabilization of Industry for the Prevention of Unemployment, which publicized a variety of local solutions, like job sharing at John A. Manning Paper Co. of Troy and the Rochester Unemployment Benefit Plan, a fund that accumulated contributions from Eastman Kodak and other firms. Industrial Commissioner Frances Perkins got the Committee on Stabilization to counsel Roosevelt to establish a system that would build up unemployment "reserves" (based on corporate contributions) in key industrial sectors, and, in an important departure from voluntarism, Roosevelt recommended state-supported systems of unemployment insurance "on an actuarial basis." This championship of aid for the jobless gave him an early lead in the 1932 presidential sweepstakes.

Meanwhile, local communities battled hard times on their own. In January 1930, the Rochester city manager appointed a Civic Committee on Unemployment, headed by Eastman Kodak's Marion B. Folsom, to coordinate the Community Chest "Spending Bee" for part-time jobs. The Buffalo Civic Committee, chaired by Alfred H. Schoellkopf, organized the "Man-a-Block Plan," which assigned 2,200 men and women to work as snow shovelers and "household helpers." The New York City charitable effort, led by the Association for Improving the Condition of the Poor and Bankers Trust chairman Seward J. Prosser, raised $150,000 per week to employ 10,000 family heads on work projects. Men cleared garbage from lots and spruced up parks, while women served as aids in libraries, schools, and hospitals. Mayor Jimmy Walker declared a moratorium on evictions and appointed an Official Committee for the Relief of the Unemployed, which used the police to hand out slips for food and lodging.

During the winter of 1930–31, public effort began to supplement voluntarism. Niagara Falls's Man-a-Block Plan used $80,000 in municipal borrowing. When the Rochester Civic Committee asked for funds for work relief, $815,000 in public and private contributions was raised, which paid for seventy-seven winter projects. At its peak in January 1931, the Prosser Committee's Emergency Work Bureau spent $8.4 million to employ 26,000. When the bureau disbanded, social welfare advocates forced Mayor Walker to intervene. With approval from the state legislature, his commissioner of public welfare assigned men to work in parks and women to libraries and sewing rooms. By the end of the second Depression winter, most large cities, including Rochester, Schenectady, and Binghamton, had moved beyond voluntarism to municipal spending.

The efforts were hastened by fears of social unrest. In Harlem, black nationalists, including members of Marcus Garvey's old movement, and Communists agitated on street corners. Communists distributed leaflets outside factories in the South Bronx and Long Island City, and they paraded for "jobs and bread" in Rochester and Buffalo. Their demonstration at New York City's Union Square in March 1930 brought out 35,000 protesters, who battled police. Eviction protests were added flashpoints, after landlords challenged Mayor Walker's moratorium and began removing 30,000 tenants a month by summer 1932. In Greenwich Village and on the Lower East Side, Communists confronted eviction marshals, and one fracas in Bronx Park East touched off a riot. Trotskyists and other Communist factions joined the protests, as did the Young People's Socialist League, which rivaled the appeal of the Young Communist League (YCL) on college campuses. Angered by Columbia University's crackdown on campus protests, undergraduate (later newspaper editor) James A. Wechsler joined the YCL. Convinced that capitalism was dying, thousands of workers, students, and intellectuals became "Reds" to fight for a better world.

The sense that society was on the brink persuaded social welfare leaders of the need for government action. In the summer of 1931, Homer Folks of the State Charities Aid Association and William Hodson of the New York City Department of Public Welfare urged a state emergency program that would offer *direct* home relief and employment. With the slump in durable goods and the serious drain on corporate benefits, General Electric president Gerard Swope proposed the creation of federal cartels to provide "stabilization of employment." As the Community Chest drive exhausted its voluntary resources, the Rochester Family Welfare Society resolved that "public work—Federal, State, and local—be substituted in part for our present relief system."

On August 28, 1931, Governor Roosevelt told an extraordinary session of the legislature that "aid must be extended by Government . . . as a matter of social duty." He called for a temporary state commission to provide $20 million in matching grants to localities for work relief. Rejecting Republican demands that funds come from budget cuts, Roosevelt gained support from Suffolk County GOP boss W. Kingsland Macy by promising "pay-as-you-go"—a 50 percent increase in state income taxes. The Wicks Law of September 1931 created the Temporary Emergency Relief Administration (TERA). Roosevelt also pushed through farm aid with state assumption of the costs of county highways and grade crossings. The Hewitt Amendment of 1931 provided a $19 million bond issue for Forest Reserve purchases by Conservation Commissioner Henry Morgenthau, Jr., who used it as a practical program to buy out bankrupt farmers. With pay-as-you-go budgets, "temporary" agencies, and disguised forms of relief, New York backed into the welfare age.

The Depression worsened during the winter of 1931–32. In December William Hodson told Congress that "tremendous" unemployment left one-quarter million New York City families in need. Half the families in Harlem were without money for food or rent, and in Buffalo 22,000 families existed on city relief. In early 1932, Governor Roosevelt requested a $30 million TERA bond issue, which Republican leaders endorsed and voters approved by a landslide. To head the TERA, Roosevelt appointed social worker Harry L. Hopkins, a veteran of the private charity world, who approached the administration of public relief with extraordinary zeal. He hired social workers to apply the "means test" for eligibility and hoped to provide work instead of "handing a man a grocery order." By August 1932, Hopkins employed 100,000 on TERA-funded projects, mostly in state parks and on highways. TERA also organized nine thousand subsistence gardens, including one thousand 50 × 100–foot plots in Binghamton and six hundred gardens in Johnson City. In summer 1932 Hopkins claimed that he was feeding one million New Yorkers, but said, "We should be feeding at least 250,000 more."

The cost of aiding the unemployed divided communities between tax payers and relief recipients. In Utica and Binghamton, businessmen successfully campaigned for city-manager government to end "political" relief. After City Manager Stephen Story of Rochester "reluctantly" requested $1 million for winter aid, the League of Citizens for Tax Relief led a revolt that brought the election of Charles S. Owen as mayor and C. Arthur Poole as city manager, who promptly slashed welfare spending. Overcome by Roosevelt's support in the 1932 presidential election, Rochester Republicans regrouped behind conservatives, attorney T. Carl Nixon and Bausch & Lomb executive Carl Hallauer, who influenced further cuts in work relief.

In New York City, the tax revolt ended good times for Jimmy Walker. A Joint Legislative Committee, chaired by State Senator Samuel H. Hofstadter, with Judge Samuel Seabury as chief counsel, heard testimony that millions in unaccounted funds went to Mayor Walker's friends, including the New York County sheriff, who kept $387,000 in a "tin box." Summoned by Roosevelt to Albany hearings, Walker resigned in September 1932. While Tammany managed to elect Surrogate John P. O'Brien in the 1932 mayoral election, bankers refused to refinance New York City bonds, creating a fiscal crisis. An emergency loan from the U.S. Reconstruction Finance Corporation kept the city afloat until an October 1933 "Bankers' Agreement" in which it accepted a sales tax to finance relief in exchange for the banks' pledge to renew purchases of municipal bonds. Across the state, business leaders forced cities to accept regressive taxes and slashes in relief.

Despite these limits, New York's struggle against the Depression prefigured much of Franklin Roosevelt's New Deal. Industrial Commissioner Frances Perkins tried to modernize the state employment service and create a system of unemployment insurance—initiatives that U.S. Senator Robert F. Wagner injected into his federal stabilization bill of 1931. A version of Gerard Swope's plan for government cartels in manufacturing was realized in the National Recovery Administration. After Roosevelt's 1932 presidential triumph, Harry Hopkins urged the federal government to provide $1 billion in relief grants to the states. Within months, Hopkins would apply TERA precedents to the administration of federal emergency relief. In the meantime, New York City welfare leaders were strenuously lobbying for federal aid for slum clearance and low-rent public housing.

The Little New Deal

In the 1932 gubernatorial election, Lieutenant Governor Herbert H. Lehman trounced his Republican opponent, war hero William J. Donovan. A jovial, out going man, Lehman came from "Our Crowd," the Temple Emanu-El circle of Reform German Jews. He apprenticed in the textiles business, then entered the family bank, Lehman Brothers, where he helped finance garment firms, chain stores, and trucking companies. He joined a Tammany club and became chummy with Al Smith, who used him as a labor arbitrator and a Democratic fund-raiser. On his way to becoming New York's first Jewish governor, Lehman proved a dull, plodding campaigner, but one who radiated warmth and decency. In Albany, he faced a Republican Old Guard, shaken by FDR's presidential victory and lashed by W. Kingsland Macy, the blunt Suffolk County leader, into the political center. Lehman's "Little New Deal" depended on the votes of Democrats and moderate Republicans, desperate for political footing in the Age of Roosevelt.

Governor Lehman was the reluctant leader of New York's welfare revolution. Avoiding further tax increases, he financed TERA with bond issues, which voters approved after elaborate campaigns led by welfare advocates like Homer Folks. By 1934, TERA was handling two-thirds of state and local relief costs, a volume supplemented by Harry Hopkins's federal emergency grants. TERA's support of the unemployed was supplemented by the State Emergency Public Works Commission, chaired by Robert Moses, chief of the State Council on Parks, whom Governor Lehman named to coordinate project funds from Washington. The inflow of welfare monies allowed Lehman's public welfare commissioner, David C. Adie, to modernize a system that had treated recipients like shiftless paupers and to call for a state minimum income. In 1935, the legislature, advised by Lehman's Commission on Unemployment Relief, moved TERA into the State Department of Social Welfare. "Temporary" no longer qualified the state's welfare responsibility.

Governor Lehman had mixed results in his attempts to complete Al Smith's agenda. He backed efforts for a state minimum wage, spearheaded by the strenuous appeals of the Consumers' League. With the support of liberal Republicans like Assemblymen Thomas C. Desmond and Herbert Brownell, Jr., the legislature enacted the Wald-Eberhard Law of 1933, which mandated minimum wages for women and minors in laundries and garment shops. But Lehman's proposal to regulate public utilities ran headlong into upstate Republicans loyal to Niagara-Mohawk Power. Republican chairman W. Kingsland Macy sensed political disaster and accused Niagara-Mohawk's chief lobbyist, ex-Speaker H. Edmund Machold, of running an "invisible government" in Albany. The charge pried loose twenty moderate Republicans, who joined Macy in trying to nominate an amenable candidate in the 1934 gubernatorial elections. The Republican Old

Guard, however, closed ranks around the arrogant progressive Robert Moses. Macy's fears were promptly realized. The New Deal had taken hold, and Moses's intemperate campaign, during which he called Governor Lehman a Tammany "puppet" and a liar, infuriated Jewish voters. Lehman won by 808,000 votes, a landslide that gave Democrats control of the state Senate and Assembly for the first time since 1913.

Lehman pounced on the opportunity in the 1935 legislature. Working with Macy's Republicans, he reintroduced and had passed his public utility bill, which forbade use of corporate funds for political lobbying, required the Public Service Commission to set maximum rates, and allowed municipalities to construct electric plants. Lehman followed with a sweeping eighteen-point message on labor. The legislation virtually ended child labor and adopted strict regulations against work in tenements. After Industrial Commissioner Elmer F. Andrews convinced the State Federation of Labor to accept GE-style unemployment reserves based upon corporate and employee contributions, the state insurance system was enacted to cover industrial workers. Lehman's program climaxed with the Doyle-Neustein Law, the "Little Wagner Act," which declared it state policy "to encourage . . . collective bargaining" and established the State Labor Relations Board to end unfair labor practices and (Lehman's own contribution) a State Mediation Board to handle strikes.

Lehman's 1936 reelection campaign revolved around an eight-point social welfare message designed to carry out President Roosevelt's Social Security Act. While moderate Republicans pleaded with conservatives not to hand Lehman "another popular issue," upstate reactionaries continued to sputter about the "monstrosity, commonly called the New Deal." This time, moderates managed to nominate Westchester leader William F. Bleakley, a moderate Republican from Yonkers, with a platform that endorsed "public aid" to eradicate slums. But President Roosevelt headed the Democratic ticket, and the needle trades mobilized 300,000 labor votes in New York City. Lehman buried Bleakley by half a million votes.

A three-time winner, Lehman submitted to the legislature an omnibus social welfare program, including ratification of the national child labor amendment, a new minimum wage law (to replace Wald-Eberhard, declared unconstitutional by the U.S. Supreme Court), and a state welfare program of old-age pensions, aid to dependent children, and state-assisted public housing. Lawmakers rubber-stamped his measures for public welfare and old-age pensions. After the U.S. Supreme Court's 1937 reversal on the constitutionality of state minimum wage laws, Governor Lehman and Industrial Commissioner Elmer Andrews huddled with the Consumers' League to draft the Fischel-Steingut minimum wage bill, which passed overwhelmingly in the legislature. Republican Assemblyman Abbot Low Moffat sponsored a $100 million state bond issue for public housing. Another GOP liberal, State Senator Thomas C. Desmond of New-

President Franklin D. Roosevelt, Governor Herbert H. Lehman, and New York City
Mayor Fiorello H. La Guardia en route in 1940 to the ground-breaking of the Brooklyn-
Battery Tunnel, a project completed under Robert Moses' (far left) Triborough Bridge and
Tunnel authority. Franklin D. Roosevelt Library, Hyde Park, N.Y.

burgh, conceded the "responsibility of the Republican party to solve the housing problem."

The Lehman administration spent a decade trying to rescue dairy farmers.
Most agricultural experts, along with dairy leaders, believed in the cooperative
ideal; and the Joint Legislative Committee to Investigate the Milk Industry was
inclined to regulate the market, not impose production controls. When Senator
Perley A. Pitcher, a Jefferson County Republican, proposed a state board to
investigate and set wholesale prices, Governor Lehman said it would undermine the spirit of cooperative farming. But Monroe County firebrands, the
backbone of the Western New York Milk Producers Association, converged on
Albany to lobby for the Pitcher bill. Although many rural leaders had deplored a
"political" solution to milk prices, the Monroe County movement changed
their minds and Governor Lehman's as well. With overwhelming upstate support, Lehman gained passage of the Pitcher bill. It established the State Milk
Price Board to set minimum retail prices, the revenue from which the Dairymen's League and wholesalers pledged to pass on to producers. The measure

nonetheless failed to satisfy dissidents in Monroe and Oneida Counties, where 10,000 dairymen joined a "farm holiday."

The State Milk Price Board proved only a stopgap. It could not embargo interstate shipments, which left market prices unstable, and the Dairymen's League and agriculture officials remained loath to request federal controls. There were also regional divisions over policy. While the league and the Borden Milk Co. wanted a state-enforced cartel for the competitive New York City market, Monroe County dairymen, further removed from interstate competition, were wary of price-fixing by downstaters. In 1937 the Lehman administration pushed the Rogers-Allen Law to keep the Dairymen's League–Borden's marketing structure. Within a year, however, sagging prices brought renewed milk dumping and clamors for price-fixing and federal controls. The former came with federal-state orders of September 1938, which set prices and quotas for the New York milkshed. But without production quotas and limits on independents, guaranteed prices invited shipments by interlopers, and prices fluctuated badly until World War II.

By far the Little New Deal's greatest contribution came as a conduit for federal relief and construction funds. From 1933 to 1935, New York spent $727 million on relief, $386 million (53 percent) from federal sources, $125 million (17 percent) from the state, and $216 million (30 percent) from cities and counties. In 1935, the state counted 2,148,450 people on relief, more than one-sixth of the population. An increasing number were getting paychecks from work relief. During the winter of 1933–34, the New Deal's Civil Works Administration (CWA) put half a million New Yorkers on work projects. By March 1936, 364,112 or 17 percent of state relief recipients were working under the U.S. Works Progress Administration (WPA). During that election year, New York City alone received one-seventh of the nation's WPA funds. Between 1935 and 1943 (when the program ended), 700,000 city residents had been on the WPA.

Public construction refurbished much of the state. As chairman of the State Council on Parks, Robert Moses organized a network of special authorities—Niagara Frontier, Thousand Islands Bridge, New York State Bridge, and Saratoga Springs—which used federal and state funds to build bridges, parks, and parkways like the 400-foot-wide Taconic Parkway, running from Westchester County to near Albany. Civilian Conservation Corps (CCC) camps opened at Mohansic, Yorktown, Pound Ridge, and Blue Mountain in the Catskills; and a camp for war veterans was established on Route 202 in Peekskill. At Fahnestock State Park in Putnam Valley, two CCC crews dammed Canopus Creek. Between 1933 and 1937, 115,000 New Yorkers enrolled in the CCC. Federal funds also bankrolled a wave of school consolidations to build regional high schools. In the lower Hudson Valley, WPA-funded high schools included Hyde Park, Arlington (a suburb of Poughkeepsie), and Red Hook Central School District.

Courts could not overlook the election returns—or angry demands for social justice. Law was rapidly rewritten from the bottom up, from eviction disputes to labor cases, before judges who agreed with Chief Judge Cuthbert W. Pound of the Court of Appeals, a Republican in the Cardozo mold, that "constitutional law is a progressive science." In the *Nebbia* decision (1933), the Court of Appeals found the State Milk Price Board's minimum price system constitutional. In *Bourjois Sales Corp. v. Dorfman* (1937), Chief Judge Frederick E. Crane upheld the minimum sales price provisions of the Fair Trade Law of 1935, and in *W. H. H. Chamberlin, Inc. v. Andrews et al.* (1936), Crane swept aside due process objections to the state unemployment insurance law. While in *People ex rel. Tipaldo v. Morehead* (1936), Crane agreed with the employer's attorney, former governor Nathan L. Miller, that the Minimum Wage Law of 1933 impinged on congressional authority, his was a moderately conservative holding action. More typical was *Adamec v. Post* (1937) in which a unanimous court rejected due process objections to the Multiple Dwelling Law of 1929. As Judge Irving Lehman wrote: "The power of the state to place reasonable restrictions upon the use of property for the promotion of the general welfare is no longer subject to challenge."

The Municipal Revival

Across New York State, the New Deal empowered Democrats and moderate Republicans willing to work with Roosevelt. In New York City the political revolution was led by Republican Fiorello H. La Guardia. Elected mayor in 1933 as an anti-Tammany Fusionist, La Guardia ran the city with a volatile mixture of, as his biographer Thomas Kessner put it, "the Roosevelt rhetoric and the Mussolini style." He bullied subordinates, cleared the streets of Italian organ-grinders, and had the police run gambler Frank Costello out of town. He appointed Dr. Sigismund Goldwater to put the city's sprawling hospitals under a merit system and brought Emergency Works and Home Relief under Commissioner of Public Welfare William Hodson. Beholden to the bankers and Seabury reformers, La Guardia balanced his budget with payroll cuts and regressive sales taxes. But he championed the welfare state and married himself to Roosevelt's New Deal. Winning reelection in 1937 by 450,000 votes, La Guardia left Tammany in disarray and the city's ethnic politics realigned. Old-line Tammany supporters—Germans, and particularly Irish Catholics—felt that Jews were "taking everything." In fact, Jewish voters replaced Italians as La Guardia's most reliable supporters.

Welfare spending entrenched the Albany machine of Daniel Peter O'Connell, whom neither Roosevelt nor Lehman could afford to antagonize. O'Connell applied political tests to distribute WPA relief and Public Works Administration (PWA) construction contracts, which strengthened his hold on the city. As Albany writer William Kennedy remembered, "from the political hierarchy came a way of life: the job, the perpetuation of the job, the dole when there was no job, the loan when there was no dole." The New Deal helped sweep mayors into power: Democrat Thomas L. Holling, reformer and Roosevelt backer, in Buffalo in 1936, Democrat Charles Stanton in Rochester in 1934, and moderate Republican Charles W. Kress in Binghamton in 1936.

Mayor La Guardia watched with enormous pleasure as City Park Commissioner Robert Moses rebuilt the five boroughs. La Guardia's close relationship with President Roosevelt gave the city its own WPA district, and Moses capitalized on it. WPA crews labored on 1,700 projects, from Jacob Riis and Alley Pond Parks to the Central Park Zoo and Interborough Parkway, and almost every jungle gym, drinking fountain, and comfort station in between. The WPA also funded construction of the lower extension of the East River Drive, Queens General Hospital, and North Beach (renamed La Guardia) Airport, the largest single WPA project in the country. Moses captured a $44 million PWA grant for the Triborough Bridge Authority, and he strung together federal and state grants for New York State's largest public work, the $205 million West Side Improvement which extended Riverside Park over the New York Central tracks and built the Henry Hudson Parkway to connect with the Saw Mill River Parkway.

Work relief rebuilt the infrastructure and provided basic services in other cities. During brutal January weather in 1934, CWA paving crews laid miles of new streets in Buffalo. In 1937 the WPA helped Schenectady lay a half mile of sewers and improve three miles of streets. State and federal jobs programs provided for 53 percent of Syracuse's municipal maintenance and repairs, and the WPA paid for Mayor Rolland Marvin's Clinton Square improvement, which reclaimed the War Memorial and created a civic plaza. In Utica, the CWA took up the New York State Railways' trolley tracks, and the WPA laid out South Drive and the Barnes Avenue overpass, built Proctor High School and Buckley bathhouse, and equipped city parks with nine tennis courts, six pools, and four baseball fields. Rochester's routine spending went down two-thirds when relief money took the place of city outlay for operations and maintenance. In Kingston, combined TERA and CWA funds in 1934 provided for 97 percent of sewer and drain construction. With good reason, the mayor called the infusion "a life-saver," although state auditors concluded that the city "did not want to bond itself further."

Energized by state and federal funds, citizens in Syracuse, Buffalo, Lackawanna, and Yonkers identified slums and campaigned for municipal housing authorities. After Congress passed the Wagner Housing Act of 1937, the Schenectady Municipal Housing Authority embarked on a plan to remove "breeding places of crime, disease, juvenile delinquency and dependency." Utica's Municipal Housing Authority applied for federal grants to clear tenements in the Second Ward and build row houses at Avery Place and Adrean Terrace. In New York City, U.S. Reconstruction Finance Corporation mortgages launched the

State Board of Housing's "limited-dividend" projects, Knickerbocker Village on the Lower East Side and Hillside Homes in the Bronx. PWA grants enabled the New York City Housing Authority (NYCHA) to start construction of the Williamsburg Houses in Brooklyn and the Harlem River Houses in Manhattan. By 1941, Wagner Act money had helped the NYCHA to build low-rent projects for 17,000 families, nearly one-third of the national figure.

Roosevelt's programs reached the suburbs, where Republicans modernized government to spend on relief and public works. Except for Lackawanna and perhaps Cheektowaga, Erie County was "iron-bound" Republican. Nevertheless, Erie Republican Daniel J. Kenefick, a former judge and district attorney, and county leader Edwin F. Jaeckle proposed several liberal measures including county takeover of relief costs from Buffalo. In Westchester, Republican William F. Bleakley carried on the public services of his predecessor, William Ward. Bleakley sponsored the Westchester County Government Law of 1938, which created the office of county executive. Elected to the post himself in 1939, Bleakley controlled an executive budget office, planning bureau, and over 2,400 employees. J. Russel Sprague, nephew and successor of Nassau GOP boss G. Wilbur Doughty, secured legislation for the Nassau county executive in 1938, and, with PWA funds, built a county center in Mineola. As Nassau executive from 1938 to 1952, Sprague streamlined county government and broadened the GOP's political base. A classic easy boss, he spread public works jobs (largely funded by Lehman and Roosevelt) among local Republican politicians and welcomed Italians into the GOP fold.

The Labor Front

New Deal labor legislation had a half-way impact on New York manufacturers. Although the State Federation of Labor claimed 850,000 members in 1935, 80 percent of nonagricultural workers remained unorganized. But in the industrial centers, particularly New York City, breadlines and eviction protests spurred class consciousness, while TERA and WPA work relief shrank the potential number of strikebreakers among the vast numbers of unemployed. Industries like construction and garment making that were dependent on seasonal output were vulnerable to work stoppages. And pro-labor Governor Lehman much preferred to send in state mediators rather than state troopers.

The New Deal's industrial-regulatory agency, the National Recovery Administration (NRA), revived unionism in the New York City needle trades. In late summer 1933, the Amalgamated Clothing Workers, with only 7,000 paid-up members, struck the men's clothing industry and won 10 percent wage increases. In the women's garment trades, an ILGWU strike won the closed shop and solid wage gains and brought in 200,000 new members. On the Hud-

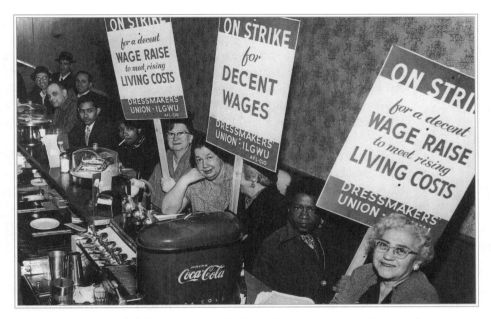

Striking International Ladies' Garment Workers' Union members take a break at an integrated lunch counter in New York City (ca. 1940s). UNITE Archives, Kheel Center, Cornell University.

son and Brooklyn waterfronts, the Seaman's Union faced a challenge from a Communist-run Rank-and-File Committee among merchant seamen, and the Longshoreman's Local was confronted by Joe Curran's Maritime Workers International Union, which vied for the support of stevedores. After two separate eighty-day stoppages in 1936, the MWIU established its hold on the docks.

Left-wing radicals brought upheaval to the services and white-collar trades. The NRA newspaper code inspired the Guild of New York Newspaper Men and Women to campaign for a forty-hour week and a $35 minimum wage. Led by the columnist Heywood Broun, the organization expanded into other cities as the American Newspaper Guild. Mayor La Guardia's intervention helped the Building Service Employees win a wage increase for 50,000 porters, doormen, and scrubwomen in 1935. Communists in the United Retail Employees struck Woolworth's chain stores, and in 1936 Trotskyists led a strike against R. H. Macy's. Communists also helped shift control of many school locals from the more moderate AFL Teachers' Guild to the more militant Teachers' Union. Local 1199 of the Retail Drug Employees organized pharmacies in chains like Whelan's and joined the Congress of Industrial Organization's Retail, Wholesale, Department Store Union (RWDSU) in 1938.

In the mid-1930s, labor had remarkable success in upstate open-shop towns. The Amalgamated Clothing Workers' strength in New York City helped its 1933 organizational campaign against Rochester men's clothing manufacturer Keller-Heumann-Thompson, and the Amalgamated's Rochester Joint Board was, in turn, a springboard for the drive among men's clothiers in Buffalo, Utica, and Syracuse. James B. Carey headed the AFL–United Electrical Workers (UE) campaign among radio workers in plants like King-Colonial in Buffalo and Wurlitzer in Tonawanda. In Schenectady, the UE overwhelmed General Electric's company union thanks to the level of political fervor during the 1936 election, when labor came out in droves for Roosevelt.

Labor's upstate march was halted by the 1937–38 recession, when management painted the CIO as a disruptive outside force. In the "Little Steel" strikes in Buffalo (1937), Bethlehem's Lackawanna plant effectively locked out the CIO's Organizing Committee. AFL and CIO unions vied for the allegiance of shoemakers at paternalist Endicott Johnson, but the company shrewdly adjusted pay grievances, and George F. Johnson walked the shops urging workers not to allow "strangers" to destroy what took "50 years to build." The effort withstood a rancorous 1937 strike and kept unionism at bay for another ten years. The most notorious corporate resistance occurred at Ilion, in 1936, when Remington Rand rejected talks with the CIO-UE and the Machinists Union and organized a "right to work" movement that broke a strike. Months later, the union-busting scenario which James H. Rand, Jr., called "Mohawk Valley Formula" was condemned as an unfair labor practice by the National Labor Relations Board.

While labor gained a toehold upstate, unionism achieved a formidable political presence in New York City. The needle trades' American Labor party became the makeweight in local politics when ALP endorsements allowed Jewish garment workers to vote for Roosevelt and Lehman without having to pull the lever for Tammany. Democratic slatemakers and La Guardia's City Fusion party were soon forced to make cross-endorsements of ALP candidates. The ALP became the vital center of radical politics after Stalinists, fearful of Hitler's threat to the Soviet Union in 1935, summoned all antifascists into a Communist-led "popular front." The move made the ALP the Communists' political lever among leftists, CIO activists, and New Dealers.

Labor's commitment to racial solidarity broadened the struggle against Jim Crow. Since 1934 Harlem's Communists and African nationalists had staged street demonstrations and "Don't Buy Where You Can't Work" boycotts against white-owned stores on 125th Street. Reverend Adam Clayton Powell, Jr., of the Abyssinian Baptist Church campaigned against the "job ceiling" at companies like Edison Electric and New York Telephone, which hired blacks for menial labor, if at all. On March 19, 1935, a scuffle at a 125th Street department store erupted into a window-smashing riot. Shocked by the violence, La Guardia appointed a Mayor's Commission on Conditions in Harlem to probe Jim Crow in jobs and housing. Two years later, Governor Lehman's Committee on the Condition of the Colored Urban Population spotlighted lily-white policies of major employers. With pickets and publicity stunts (which convinced Harlem residents to pay their electric bills in pennies), Powell's Greater New York Coordinating Committee pressed the utilities to hire blacks. Powell scored a breakthrough in 1939 when the united front with the Transport Workers Union forced the Omnibus Corporation to hire black bus drivers.

Collective bargaining also extended to broad lifestyle issues. The Amalgamated Clothing Workers, ILGWU, and Transport Workers enlarged labor's demands to include housing and consumer policies. Led by Amalgamated, which had pioneered the development of housing cooperatives for workers, unions spoke out on rent control, public housing, and city planning. They also became advocates of prepaid health insurance. In 1939, Mayor La Guardia's hospital commissioner, Sigismund Goldwater, became president of Associated Hospital Services, better known as Blue Cross. Organized by voluntary hospitals facing stiff competition from municipal hospitals, Blue Cross offered "three-cents a day" contributory hospital insurance. It appealed to employers, particularly in the public sector, as a painless item to throw onto the bargaining table. Blue Cross was also favored by CIO unions, which saw that dues check-offs could support the "three-cents" system.

The Financial Sector

The New Deal brought a sober morning-after to Wall Street, when it separated commercial deposit and investment banks, regulated stock and commodities markets, and gave greater control of open-market operations to the Federal Reserve Board in Washington. The U.S. Securities and Exchange Commission's rules, which required full disclosure for companies trading securities publicly and prohibited insider trading, ended the tendency of the New York Stock Exchange to behave as a private club. Bailing out local banks, the U.S. Reconstruction Finance Corporation invested in the Savings Bank Trust Company, the state consortium of savings banks, which, in turn, refinanced insolvent savings and loan institutions.

Ironically, New Deal restrictions strengthened New York's financial primacy. SEC enforcers came to value the New York Stock Exchange's "liquidity," its efficiency as a marketplace for stock shares (particularly during the 1937 recession, when corporations were desperate for funds). The SEC also saw the Exchange as an ally to regulate "private" traders and over-the-counter "penny" stocks. SEC regulations lent influence as well to Wall Street investment banks and law firms, which could perform the "due diligence" searches required for stock registration and handle the needs of institutional investors, notably life insurance companies. In the late 1930s, midwestern bankers complained about Wall Street's grip on "private placements," sales of securities to "qualified" institutional investors. In 1939, the top fifteen investment firms, mostly New York houses, handled 90 percent of public issues. While the SEC, in 1941, promulgated Rule U-50, which required competitive bids in public utilities offerings, most industrials were still wholesaled in traditional Wall Street fashion.

The Depression put New York corporate practice in the doldrums, but legal work expanded in the aftermath of 1929. The large law firm of Cadwalader, Wickersham & Taft specialized in bank foreclosures, developed "on an assembly-line basis." Another, Shearman & Sterling, profited from congressional investigations, litigating shareholders' claims against "bear" traders who allegedly forced down stock prices in 1932. Called upon by trade associations to deal with the National Recovery Administration, Cadwalader drafted twenty-one NRA codes of fair competition.

The New Deal bolstered IBM's earnings when federal agencies like the Social Security Administration bought IBM tabulators and helped it pass Remington Rand in sales. New York City also intervened to help air transport. The Pan American executive Juan T. Trippe, with headquarters in the Chrysler Building, outbid British interests for coveted Atlantic routes largely because he could parlay New York as the hub of trans-Atlantic service and count on air-minded Mayor La Guardia, who leased North Beach, Queens, to Pan Am flying boats. World War I ace Eddie Rickenbacker was general manager of Eastern Air Transport, owned by General Motors. When GM sold Eastern to Rickenbacker and his partner Laurence S. Rockefeller, they scheduled flights around the clock as a "shuttle" for businessmen between New York and Washington. The unlikely duo, La Guardia and Rockefeller, made New York the center of the air age.

Life in Hard Times

While the New Deal eased New York's emergency, it hardly brought a new day. Millions remained out of work and dependent. Social workers reported that family life wilted under the "constant bickering and quarreling," as idleness drooped the shoulders of ex-breadwinners. Ordinary activities like grocery shopping became shameful experiences, reminding unemployed men of their unworthiness. One husband remarked that his wife kept repeating: "F.D.R. is the head of the household since he gives me the money." The WPA means test required applicants to prove their destitution to get on the job rolls. The WPA "security wage" also meant that 80 percent of the relief labor in New York City earned under $70 per month, hardly more than home relief allowed for a family of four.

By 1935, the birth rate had dropped below the death rate in Utica and Albany. Hard times also accelerated the rural migration toward regional cities.

In Tompkins County, only 42 percent of unmarried rural men between fifteen and twenty-nine years of age worked full time in 1935. Even among young men who lived on farms, 21 percent were unemployed. Those lucky enough to find jobs took home an average of $13 per week. Women had a harder time, for one-third of Tompkins County women had no work at all. Upstate areas were sadly forlorn. Hamlets north of Malone on the Saint Lawrence struck the author Carl Carmer as New York's Appalachia: "It is a country of heart breaking poverty, of ignorance and incredible shiftlessness."

The Depression withered spectator sports. The New York Rangers, pillar of the National Hockey League, imposed salary caps of $7,500 in 1933, slashed ticket prices to 50 cents, and got by with team payrolls of $70,000. Their Manhattan rivals, the Americans, had their franchise taken over by the league in 1937 and moved to Brooklyn. The Rangers remained relatively secure; their franchise included Madison Square Garden, and they had up-and-coming stars like Bryan Hextall and Lynn Patrick. The "Amerks," on the other hand, were dubious prospects, and only the money provided by defenseman Red Dutton's father's construction business kept the club afloat.

The Depression also loosened decorum in baseball stadiums. By the early 1930s, owners needed new rules—and ballpark police—to quiet the fans. To

The popularity of both men's and women's amateur athletics grew rapidly during the Depression. These young dressmakers, members of ILGWU Local 22, were champions of their women's basketball league (ca. 1938). UNITE Archives, Kheel Center, Cornell University.

boost attendance, night games were adopted in 1930 by ten clubs in the International League (which included the Buffalo Bisons, Rochester Red Wings, and Syracuse Chiefs). The Bisons played the first professional ball game after dark—at home, against Montreal, on July 3, 1930. The New York Giants, managed by the immortal John McGraw through the 1932 season and then by "Memphis" Bill Terry (1933–41), remained strong in the fans' affections. The fate of the Brooklyn Dodgers was in the hands of Lee McPhail, who rescued the franchise from poor attendance and certain bankruptcy. The Dodgers were the first New York major league team to play night baseball, on June 15, 1938 (the Yankees did not play at night until 1941). McPhail acquired Babe Ruth to coach at first base and in 1938 started radio broadcasts with Walter Lanier ("Red") Barber. McPhail also hired a manager, Leo Durocher, whose dustups with umpires inspired the tabloid moniker "Leo the Lip."

The turbulent 1930s ruffled the world of higher education. Under President William H. Cowley, conservative Hamilton College substituted foreign languages for traditional Latin or Greek and promoted Hamilton's reputation in modern liberal arts. Oswego State Teachers College downgraded pedagogy and introduced programs in contemporary issues. The farm debacle ravaged enrollments at Cornell's State College of Agriculture, while the engineering faculty feared losing ground to midwestern schools. The mid-1930s also saw the nadir of Cornell football, when losses to powerhouse teams like Syracuse and Colgate brought a December 1936 resolve to end "degrading" subsidies to the team and to begin a closer attachment to the Ivy League.

On campuses, undergraduates flocked to join the class struggle. It was said that Vassar girls talked incessantly about the left-wing magazine the *New Masses* and that Stalinism had "fastened" onto Brooklyn College. Certainly, the radicalism of City College students was intense; you could tell who were Communists, Socialists, or Trotskyists by where they congregated in the college "alcoves." Many campuses were affected by the American Youth Congress, the "front" that Joseph Lash and James Wechsler forged among the Young Communist League and the (Socialist) Student League for Industrial Democracy. Youth movements headquartered in New York City, like the Institute of International Education, run by Edward R. Murrow (later the eminent radio and television newsman), sponsored campus forums on world issues and students to study abroad. European émigrés added another dimension to academic ranks. By 1934 the Carnegie- and Rockefeller-funded International Rescue Committee was placing political refugees, mainly German and Austrian professors, in teaching posts. The New School for Social Research created a graduate faculty of refugee scholars—the "University in Exile."

The Depression transformed voluntary hospitals into virtual public institutions, as revenues shrank for both private pavilions and charity wards. By the late 1930s, funding came from municipal welfare and prepaid insurance, which supported semiprivate wards. In 1929 Montefiore Hospital in the Bronx pioneered the "full-time" principle, replacing part-time physician volunteers with salaried house staff committed to full-time patient care and hospital routine. Montefiore's initiative was soon followed by several other Jewish hospitals (with salary expenses largely defrayed by the Federation of Jewish Philanthropies), heavily staffed by Jewish refugees from Europe.

Radical Thoughts

Hard times stimulated the York State tradition of historical and folk material reworked into literature; Walter D. Edmonds' novels and short stories were prime examples. Edmond's spare language and sharp eye for Seneca practice and class distinctions among the colonials were on view in *In the Hands of the Seneca* (1942). Carl Carmer's *Listen for a Lonesome Drum* (1936) disinterred the bizarre tale of the Cardiff Giant, depicted the "Calebrogeurs" around Geneseo, and told of Adirondack lumber camps where the intense cold "froze flame." The folklore revival found another outlet in regional theater, championed by Alexander Drummond, a Cornell professor, and Hallie Flanagan, who taught community theater at Vassar. Drummond coordinated theater activities at the 1939 New York State Fair at Syracuse, highlighted by a performance of Zona Gale's *Neighbors*. Another influence, *Harper's* book critic Bernard de Voto, scorned what he called the "literary fallacy," the narcissism that put writers' angst at the center of literature. De Voto wanted a return to bedrock American subjects, homespun stories of workers and pioneers.

Newspaper publishing, buffeted by radio competition and dwindling circulation, fell on grim times after the Crash. One notable casualty was the *New York World*, which was neither institution nor tabloid and was folded into Roy Howard's *New York Telegram* in 1931. The *World-Telegram* learned the ways of survival and refused to go along with the publishers' ban against printing radio broadcast schedules. But others, including the *Herald, Globe, Mail, American*, and *Sun*, all folded or were merged with competitors. Stabilized by Ogden Reid's money and Helen Rogers Reid's moderate politics, the *Herald-Tribune* became the country's voice for moderate Republicanism. But journalism's future in the radio era belonged to cut-rate chains. Samuel I. Newhouse, owner-publisher of the *Staten Island Advance*, acquired papers in Queens, Nassau County, and Syracuse. Stinting on expenditures, he left his editors alone—as long as they turned a profit.

Magazines underwent a slow and steady shake-up. Mushy and sentimental in the 1920s, women's periodicals needed corporate resources and new slants to survive the thirties. *McCall's* did well, stylishly packaged by editor Otis L. Weise and designer Henry Dreyfuss. But radio advertising undercut revenues of

Butterick Company magazines like the *Delineator*. The *New Yorker*, edited by Harold Ross, a playful middlebrow, let writers James Thurber and E. B. White mold its off-hand, astonished tone. More whimsical than serious, the *New Yorker* had the best style of any literary magazine. Clifton Fadiman reviewed books for it until Edmund Wilson took over in 1944, to crusade for Henry James and Russian literature. In the meantime, the *New Yorker*'s literary distinction remained the James Thurber yarn and John O'Hara short story.

In book publishing, price competition and literature for the masses stimulated the first wave of the paperback revolution. A Doubleday alumnus, Robert de Graff (backed by Simon & Schuster), launched Pocket Books in 1939 to sell 25-cent reprints to independent wholesalers and displayed them at newsstands and drugstores. Ian Ballantine guided British Penguin's invasion of America in 1939 but became publisher in his own right when the war cut off supplies of English titles.

The hard-bitten decade spawned a proletarian school of literature, driven by Communists, who declared art a weapon in the class struggle. The party launched John Reed Clubs to enroll writers and published agitprop in the *New Masses* and *Art Front*. Working-class anger produced a few gems, like Mike Gold's *Jews without Money* (1930), a raw look at Rumanians on the Lower East Side, and Pietro Di Donato's *Christ in Concrete* (1937), which described the bitter lives of Italian construction workers. Inevitably, Communists sought to influence the New York State Writers' Project, the WPA's work relief for hundreds of jobless writers. Communists and Trotskyists constantly fought over the project's political "line," while director Henry Alsberg tried to get his crew to work. Most contributed to the New York State Guide, a collection of scenic descriptions for tourists, edited by Syracuse newsman Robert West Howard. According to Jerre Mangione, a project alumnus, Howard careened along back roads with a companion who "took notes while Howard yelled out his observations and drove." New York City's project turned out the *New York City Guide*, worked on by Philip Rahv (who balked at making it into a literary history) and John Cheever, who edited final drafts.

In the late 1930s, radicals split over Stalinism, particularly after the Moscow Purge Trials revealed the brazenness of Soviet tyranny. Along with Trotskyists, who numbered about a thousand, a few influential leaders including Max Shachtman and James Burnham attacked Communist totalitarianism. In 1937, ex-Communists Philip Rahv, William Phillips, and William Barrett founded the *Partisan Review*, which published anti-Stalinist polemics that caught, wrote Barrett, "some terrifying vision of the Devil." The *PR*'s editors pursued a democratic socialism, served by art that rose above Marxist dogma. They led the first American literary movement that was separate from the dominant Protestant sensibility and contributed, wrote the critic Irving Howe, "a new voice in American literary life: a roughening of tone, a brush with demotic speech." They made patron saints of Walt Whitman and Herman Melville, worshipped the psychological probing of Dostoyevsky and Kafka, and championed new voices like the poet and short story writer Delmore Schwartz and the critic Alfred Kazin.

During the 1930s, the musical revue died out along with "big-time" vaudeville, while theatrical productions plunged to a low of one hundred in 1938–39. The theater got Depression-serious with Jack Kirkland's *Tobacco Road* (1933), whose realism included southern dirt that wafted into the front seats; and the 1935 standouts, Lillian Hellman's *Children's Hour* and Robert Sherwood's *Petrified Forest*. But Broadway's heart belonged to screwball comedy, especially as interpreted by George S. Kaufman, who teamed with Morrie Ryskind and the Gershwins to produce *Of Thee I Sing* (1931), a satiric but resolutely sweet look at politics, the first musical to win the Pulitzer Prize.

The Depression invigorated radical theater, notably productions by actors' collectives such as the Group Theatre, founded by Theatre Guild alumni Harold Clurman and Cheryl Crawford. The Group's resident playwright, Clifford Odets, wrote *Waiting for Lefty* (1935), a proletarian melodrama that climaxed when the cast chanted "Strike! Strike! Strike!" The militant tone also dominated the WPA Federal Theatre, launched when playwright Elmer Rice and Hallie Flanagan convinced Harry Hopkins to sponsor "community" performance. The New York project spawned "Living Newspaper" (performed by the Newspaper Guild's unemployed) and Harlem's Negro Theater, which gave Orson Welles the chance to direct an all-black *Macbeth* (1936). The Federal Theatre's 1936 highlight, Marc Blitzstein's folk opera, *The Cradle Will Rock*, was pure CIO propaganda, which Hopkins tried to quash, and the theater was ordered closed. Defying "censorship," Welles marched the opening night audience to another stage, where, with rehearsed spontaneity, a bare-bones version of the show triumphed.

Artists were deeply moved by the grim reality of the Depression city. William Gropper, Philip Evergood, and Jacob Lawrence painted the homeless and the unemployed on breadlines. Photographers such as Berenice Abbott and Arthur ("Weegee") Fellig documented street scenes and Broadway nightlife. At the Whitney Museum, abstractionists like Stuart Davis and American regionalists like Charles Burchfield were joined by Depression realists, notably Ben Shahn and Katherine Schmidt. The Whitney's educational effort, led by curator Lloyd Goodrich, made an icon of Edward Hopper's *Early Sunday Morning* (1930), which seemed to capture Manhattan's forlorn reality. The Whitney's engagement with social realism brought it direction of the New Deal's Public Works of Art Project (PWAP), which employed artists including Shahn and Davis to paint murals in post offices and courthouses, and established the New York art community's control of the much larger WPA Federal Arts Project.

The Whitney, nevertheless, lost ground to the Museum of Modern Art and its director Alfred H. Barr, Jr.'s steely vision of modernism. Barr assembled art, photography, architecture, and decor to demonstrate how the major European movements, cubism, surrealism, and Bauhaus, were transforming the entirety of twentieth-century culture. The museum held stunning shows of "Machine Art," which encoded Bauhaus forms on the American imagination, and "International Style Architecture," whose functional steel-and-glass boxes influenced New York architects like George Howe and William Lescaze. The museum's 1936 landmark, "Cubism and Abstract Art," exalted European modernists and what Barr said was the realism of their canvases—their "attention to . . . immediate, sensuous, physical surface."

Music of all kinds was transformed by the Depression. With anemic sales and competition from radio, New York's record companies consolidated into three Manhattan majors, Victor, Columbia, and Decca. Radio play reinforced the impact of a handful of "swing" bands, notably Artie Shaw's and Glenn Miller's, that had hefty trombone-sax-and-horn sections, celebrity bandleaders, and access to Manhattan's midtown hotels. Competition came from a few black jazz bands, like those led by Duke Ellington and Cab Calloway, whose special flare gave them regular radio time in the mid-1930s. William "Count" Basie's break came in 1938 when CBS recorded his band from a tiny club, the Famous Door, on West 52nd Street. But already a few black musicians, frustrated by big band's overly "concertized" style, were drifting to small after-hours clubs in Harlem and along 52nd Street to "jam" together for a different sound.

Classical music struggled for an audience during the Depression and found it in music that reached to America's roots. Although the New York Philharmonic-Symphony offered weekly radio concerts on the CBS network, it shared the Musicians' Union's aversion to "canned" music and the long-playing record. As a consequence, the Philharmonic Society, with a budget of barely $1 million, could employ musicians for only thirty-two weeks a year. Throwing off their classicist inclinations, composers such as Virgil Thomson, Aaron Copland, and Samuel Barber turned toward people's music. Thomson composed folksy, lyrical scores for documentary filmmaker Pare Lorentz's *Plow That Broke the Plains* (1936) and *The River* (1937). Samuel Barber's moving romantic piece *Adagio for Strings* (1936) was made an immediate part of the New York Philharmonic's repertoire by maestro Toscanini.

Composers were also moved by powerful new dance traditions. One was the work of the modern dance choreographer Martha Graham, who filled stark, bare stages with allusions to Jungian archetypes and Greek myth in works like *Primitive Mysteries* (1933). Another influence was the arts patron Lincoln Kirstein, a deep admirer of formal Russian ballet. Despising Graham's style of modernism, which he blamed on "incomplete training," Kirstein brought the Russian star Georges Balanchine to America in 1933 to help develop a new company, the New York Ballet. Kirstein also formed a dance school, and, in

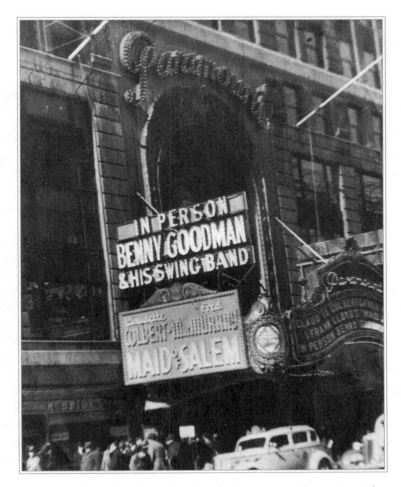

Benny Goodman's big band played at the Paramount Theater in mid-town Manhattan in March 1937. Frank Driggs Collection.

good 1930s fashion, a performing troupe, Ballet Caravan, to take dance to the people. The New York Ballet put on Virgil Thomson's *Filling Station* (1937), and in 1938 the Ballet Caravan performed Aaron Copland's *Billy the Kid*, a stunning evocation of American folk imagery. Copland was also writing incidental music for the theater. Collaborating with his cousin Harold Clurman, head of the Group Theatre, he composed a theatrical piece, *Quiet City* (1940), an elegy to New York.

While New York City lost the movies to Hollywood in the 1920s, its five radio networks, NBC's comedy and variety networks, CBS, ABC, and Mutual, strengthened the city's grip on mass culture. David Sarnoff's NBC led the pack. It was President Roosevelt's favorite, and well known overseas, where the Radio

Corporation of America (RCA) meant American wireless. But by 1935, CBS had pulled abreast of NBC in affiliates and profits; and in 1936 William S. Paley staged the first of his talent "raids," luring away NBC's "Major Bowes's Amateur Hour," a popular entertainment program. In 1936 Paley put on the "Columbia Workshop," repertory theater, including Archibald MacLeish's *Fall of the City*, starring Burgess Meredith and Orson Welles. Welles got the 9:00 P.M. Monday slot for his Mercury Theatre, whose repertory included "War of the Worlds," the depiction of a Martian attack on the earth that scared the country on Halloween night, 1938. CBS had an asset in the psychologist Frank Stanton, who, with Columbia University professor Paul F. Lazarsfeld, pioneered the measurement of audience ratings. Stanton's research helped the network garner an advertising coup—the cigarette manufacturer Liggett & Myers's entire budget for radio.

New York radio mixed crass commercialism with touching decency. When CBS began to broadcast Metropolitan Opera performances "live" in 1935, Sarnoff countered by organizing the NBC Symphony Orchestra, conducted by the indomitable antifascist Arturo Toscanini. CBS had no regular news operation, but presented talk shows, like the "American University of the Air," or occasional guest interpreters of events, like local newsman Hans von Kaltenborn. Paley and news director Paul Klauber sent Edward R. Murrow to London as CBS's coordinator of international talks. Murrow ended up hiring local print journalists, including William L. Shirer in Berlin, as on-air commentators. After Stanton's research showed that the 1938 Munich crisis generated an audience for news, Paley told Murrow to set up a receiving station for European shortwave broadcasts at Riverhead, Long Island. The "World News Roundup" was not planned as a news program so much as a chance to read late-breaking bulletins. But the anti-Hitler reporting of CBS correspondents Kaltenborn and Shirer made CBS, Paley biographer Sally Bedell Smith pointed out, "the beacon for all right-thinking citizens."

At Loggerheads

Governor Lehman's power crested during the 1937 recession, giving Republicans hope of political resurgence. Liberals had expected to preserve the Little New Deal with a constitutional convention, a move favored by Lehman, Mayor La Guardia, and interests as diverse as the American Labor party and Albany's O'Connell machine. La Guardia and the ALP wanted charter revision to include home rule for New York City and proportional representation in its city council. New Dealers like Senator Wagner envisioned a sweeping public welfare clause and constitutional authority to finance work relief and public housing. But the recession intruded, and the GOP elected a majority of moderate conservatives to the 1938 constitutional convention. They crafted reapportionment that added to upstate (Republican) assembly seats and banned proportional representation. They did, however, write the "Little Wagner Act" into the constitution and adopted language endorsing public funds and credit, which Republicans claimed, "would remove any doubts as to the power of the State" to spend for social welfare. The voters approved amendments for public housing, the labor "bill of rights," and social welfare.

By 1938, however, the Little New Deal had run its course. An unenthusiastic Lehman had to be dragged to run again by party leader Jim Farley and Albany boss Dan O'Connell. Republicans ran Thomas E. Dewey, a Michigan-born Columbia Law School graduate, who had made headlines as special prosecutor of "Murder Inc.," the Brooklyn mob that specialized in rubouts. An overnight sensation, Dewey nearly won the governorship, emboldening Republicans to reject Lehman's $415 million fiscal-1940 budget. After debate in April 1939 before a radio audience and huge crowds at the Capitol, GOP lawmakers trimmed the budget and substituted a cigarette tax for increases in taxes on business and personal income. In 1940, Republicans followed with a Joint Legislative Committee, headed by Herbert A. Rapp and Frederic R. Coudert, Jr., to investigate subversives in public schools. Designed to embarrass Lehman and La Guardia, the committee uncovered Communists in New York City high schools and at City College and wrote a loyalty oath, which the legislature imposed on public school teachers. Rapp-Coudert confirmed prejudices, particularly strong among disaffected Irish-Catholics, that New Deal Democrats coddled "Reds."

Hard times stubbornly lingered. The New York City Planning Commission declared the city's economy permanently shrunken, with chronic 15 percent unemployment. When the 1940 U.S. Census recorded statewide unemployment at 14 percent, the *Buffalo Evening News* commented: "It is inevitable that many thousands of families never again will become self-supporting." The post-1937 mood appeared in the paintings by Ben Shahn and Edward Hopper of frowsy cityscapes, the stories of Delmore Schwartz and Bernard Malamud about Jews in dreamlike states, walking in slow motion, and the mournful chords of Copland's *Quiet City*.

At the end of the decade, New York State was at a troubling crossroads. For liberal Democrats, the Little New Deal was a fragile achievement, made all the more vulnerable by the Republican comeback and President Roosevelt's uncertainties about seeking a third term. Domestic preoccupations were soon overshadowed by the European war. In April 1939, the New York World's Fair opened a steel-and-concrete "world of tomorrow." One month later, on May 20, 1939, the Pan Am *Yankee Clipper* took off and buzzed the fair on its first commercial flight to Europe. The crowds below, celebrating "Aviation Day," could scarcely imagine how global events would reshape their dreams.

31

War Brings a New Day

WORLD WAR II WAS A GLOBAL CONFLICT, FOUGHT AND managed to an extraordinary extent with the resources of the Empire State. America's strategic alliance with Great Britain made New York the anchor for the "bridge of ships" across the Atlantic. The state led all others in output of war materiel. That output depended upon mobilization of labor and capital, which, in turn, rested on New York's tradition of liberalism. The rancorous relations between companies and unions in the 1930s were eased under a moderate Republican, who could accept the Little New Deal. In 1944, Governor Thomas E. Dewey challenged President Franklin D. Roosevelt in a campaign that emphasized differences in approach rather than in goals of domestic or foreign policy.

Above all, the war marked the height of the Empire State's influence over the country's economy and culture. Americans learned of Pearl Harbor on December 7, 1941, when New York radio announcers interrupted the Sunday afternoon broadcast of the NBC Symphony Orchestra to report the Japanese attack. The war forced Washington's grudging appreciation of New York's financial power. The instinctive Anglophilia of J. P. Morgan & Co. helped erase New Deal suspicions of Wall Street financiers and welded the fortunes of Washington, New York, and London together in a common cause. When the war ended, New York's liberalized capitalism had proved triumphant and was about to be imprinted on the globe. With the establishment of the United Nations at Flushing Meadows in Queens, New York City became the center of the world's postwar political and economic system.

Gearing Up the Arsenal

The war swept away the Depression lulls in manufacturing, making New York the bedrock of the "arsenal of democracy." By 1943, factory employment reached an all-time high—nearly 2.2 million of the state's civilian workforce of 5.2 million (compared to 1940 figures of 1.5 million out of 4.3 million). Exceeding all other states in war production, New York turned out $21.5 billion worth or nearly 12 percent of national ordnance. By the end of the war, New York claimed 13.3 percent of the national income. The U.S. War Finance Corporation concentrated New York's ordnance factories in two major districts. Metropolitan New York City, including Westchester, Nassau, and Suffolk Counties, received 35 percent of the state's federally financed plant investment. Erie and Niagara Counties got another 29 percent.

The Niagara Frontier ranked fourth in U.S. war production, and Buffalo was the state's busiest ordnance center. Firms like Bell Aircraft and Curtiss-Wright, the Chevrolet division of General Motors (which subcontracted Pratt & Whitney engines), and Hewitt Rubber (which made self-sealing fuel tanks) accounted for Buffalo's output of $6.5 billion in aircraft and parts. The city's manufacturing workforce rose from 138,000 in 1940 to 256,000 by 1944. Bell and Curtiss-Wright alone employed 85,000 at peak compared to the 1939 figure of less than 2,000. Overall, jobs in Buffalo soared from 330,000 in 1940 to nearly half a million, including close to 200,000 women in defense industries. Meanwhile the city was stripped of civilian workers, like taxi drivers, laundresses, and bellhops. This constricted labor market prompted the U.S. War Manpower Commission in June 1943 to initiate the "Buffalo Plan" (a system of labor requisitions) to control the movements of 29,000 workers that summer. Washington soon applied the Buffalo system to other congested labor markets.

Sheer size made the New York City–Long Island war production district the national leader. The Port of New York buzzed with war work, as untold thousands on the East and Hudson Rivers loaded and unloaded four hundred ships a day. By summer 1944, 75,000 punched in at the New York (Brooklyn) Navy Yard, building one-third of the navy's capital ships, including nine battleships, twenty-six cruisers, and twelve *Essex*-class fleet carriers. The city contained specialized manufacturers, such as Charles Pfizer & Co., the Brooklyn pharmaceutical giant that produced half the world's supply of penicillin. New York's white-collar pool also made the city the administrative subcenter for the war. At the Federal Office Building on Varick Street, the U.S. Army Air Forces coordinated bomber attacks on German submarines in the Atlantic. Fifty-five thousand civilians worked at Brooklyn's Port of Embarkation processing 3,283,678 men and women overseas. At the other end of the pipeline, Halloran Hospital on Staten Island, the largest reception center on the continent, handled 163,000 sick and wounded soldiers on their return to the United States.

Nevertheless, New York City's small manufacturers, particularly in the garment trades, worked at less than capacity. After Pearl Harbor, curtailments of nonessential production, like cosmetics and office furniture, shut down nine

The Curtiss-Wright facility in Buffalo was the largest combat airplane plant in the United States during World War II. From Karl D. Hartzell, *The Empire State at War* (State of New York, 1949).

hundred firms and eliminated 41,000 jobs. Preemption of materials closed retail stores, and the output of some consumer goods like chocolate candy at Barricini's was limited by the shortage of sugar. By summer 1942 half the membership of the ILGWU was idle. "With the exception of a recent contract for 100,000 pairs of army pants," remarked a federal official, "there is no evidence yet that the New York City area will receive war work proportionate to the size of its market." The city became a net exporter of labor to needier production zones upstate, on Long Island, and in New Jersey.

In contrast, suburban counties became war production machines. In Westchester, the Fisher Body Plant in North Tarrytown became Eastern Aircraft, employing 10,000 to make U.S. Navy fighters. Alexander Smith Carpet Company in Yonkers produced tents and uniforms. On Long Island, Republic Aviation took over the Seversky plant at Farmingdale, while Grumman Engineering moved to Bethpage, turning out the navy fighters that won the Pacific war. Grumman's payroll, which reached 25,527 by September 1943, included machinists trained at New York University's Guggenheim School of Aeronautics at nearby Hofstra University. Grumman provided lunchtime amusements, day care, and carpools that reduced labor downtime and helped slash the cost of the Navy F6F Hellcat to $30,000 per plane.

Other New York cities made prodigious contributions to the war effort. In Utica, Savage Arms Company assembled 1,250,000 Thompson submachine guns, Utica Cutlery turned out 2 million army bayonets, and the Bossert Company machined 20 million 75 mm and 105 mm artillery shells. In Schenectady, General Electric fabricated half the steam turbines required for the wartime increase in U.S. electric capacity and turbine propulsion systems for 1,700 naval and merchant vessels, including over 200 destroyers. By September 1942, 9,000 worked for American Locomotive Company, whose wartime production included 7,211 tanks, besides a 1944 output of 1,414 locomotives.

War contracts and production brought marked social consequences. Most factories were located on "greenfield" sites outside cities, which accelerated the suburbanization of manufacturing. In Nassau County, Bulova Watch Co. took over plant space at Valley Stream Airport and Brooklyn's Sperry Gyroscope expanded into Lake Success; Grumman, Republic, and Fairchild built an aviation complex across Nassau and Suffolk Counties. In Syracuse, Mac-Law Tool & Aircraft Parts located on Erie Boulevard East, and Bristol Laboratories built a penicillin plant on Thompson Road. By early 1941, a mere 18 percent of Syracuse industrial workers had jobs within a half mile of downtown compared to 40 percent in 1913. While the war drastically cut automobile usage, it laid the economic base for postwar suburban advance.

Defense contracts were also a harbinger of New York's industrial future. The state turned out 12 percent of U.S. war production, but ranked second to California in the value of federally financed war plants. California's surging aircraft industry would dwarf New York's investment in modern manufacturing. During the war, General Electric increased manufacturing floor space by 41 percent, mostly in the Midwest and South, which made GE Schenectady increasingly a coordinator of far-flung production. The war tripled IBM's manufacturing space and revenues. With the wad of cash—and Thomas J. Watson's indulgence—IBM built the Mark I, an electro-mechanical calculating machine, at Endicott in 1943 and brought scientists to work on vacuum-tube systems. But as symbolized by the wartime shift of Manhattan Project atomic scientists from Columbia University to the University of Chicago and then to Los Alamos, New Mexico, high technologies would slip away to the Sunbelt.

Wartime Liberalism

Wartime labor shortages lowered barriers against women, first in female trades and then in other fields. In 1940, 1,453,000 females (29.2 percent) were in the state's labor force of 6 million. By April 1945, overall employment decreased to 5,848,000, but nearly 1.9 million women (34 percent) remained who constituted nearly 36 percent of the workforce in manufacturing. By mid-1942, because of the dearth of manpower, Manhattan hotels were hiring chamber maids up to sixty-five years of age and female elevator operators, front office clerks, and cashiers. The Pennsylvania Railroad "experimented" with twenty-five women as information clerks and ticket sellers at Penn Station. Across New York City, there were shortages of sales clerks, nurses' aides, and kitchen workers, buoying these low-wage occupations. Cleaning women in Manhattan offices, lucky to earn 35 to 40 cents per hour in 1939, were earning 50 to 60 cents per hour in late 1942.

Despite women's gains, male-dominant traditions died hard in war production. In Westchester, Ward Leonard Electric, Sonotone Corporation, and Anaconda Wire and Cable hired women, and four hundred enrolled in aviation training courses in local high schools. Employers usually insisted, however, on applicants between the ages of twenty-five and thirty-five, and often used them as unskilled packers or in jobs suited to their supposed manual dexterity. Companies might train high school girls for lens grinding or light machine work but refuse to replace boys for stockroom and errand jobs. The New York City Board of Education shunted girls into radio, blueprint tracing, and machine tool operation, refusing to place them in metal shop or welding—highly paid categories considered men's work.

For all the effort to enroll "Rosie the Riveter" (women war workers), wide disparities persisted in female job placements. In May 1944, nearly 100,000 women (29 percent of the war plant force) worked in the New York City–Long Island district. Nearly 29,000 women were employed in electrical machinery, 18,100 in scientific instruments, 10,400 in shipyards, and 9,850 in ordnance. The highest proportions of female employment within industrial trades occurred in electrical machinery (58 percent of the labor force), nonferrous metals (51 percent), and professional and scientific instruments (43 percent). By comparison, females made up only 8 percent of shipyard workers. In 1940 women were 20 percent of GE employees. By 1944 they reached 40 percent—mainly in low-paid, "light assembly line" work or coil winding. Rochester's mobilization set the record for female participation: women increased in manufacturing from 27.5 percent in 1940 to 42 percent in 1945, the highest regional percentage in the state.

While women advanced in the job market, Jim Crow proved a tougher barrier. At the beginning of the war, ordnance works employed only handfuls of African Americans. Washburn Wire in East Harlem and Ford Instruments in Long Island City were among the many that refused to put blacks on the payroll. Grumman Aircraft in Bethpage had no African Americans among its 5,000 employees, while Sperry Gyroscope, just after Pearl Harbor, had 11,212 employees of whom 21 were black, including 8 in service occupations. A 1940 survey of 17,447 Queens industrial workers counted 779 African Americans (4.4 percent) but only 26 in skilled jobs, including 8 in aircraft sheet metal. Racial prejudice marked entire production sectors off-limits to blacks. One manufacturer explained that because he made "a highly specialized mechanical product, we have never endeavored to employ Negroes."

To bend the color line took persistent pressure from the U.S. War Manpower Commission and fair-employment groups, notably Reverend Adam Clayton Powell's Greater New York Coordinating Committee on Employment and the New York Urban League. In 1942 Sperry hired blacks in the assembly and sand-blasting departments, despite whites' objections to wearing gloves and goggles once worn by blacks. Sperry concluded that "the best policy" was to "segregate negro workers into separate work groups." Federal officials and the Urban League sent sixty-five black applicants to Fairchild Aviation, which hired two. Nonetheless, some gains were made. In Buffalo, Curtiss-Wright had only a "handful" of black employees in 1942, and local African Americans considered Bell a strictly Jim Crow employer. By the end of the war, Curtiss-Wright had over 1,000 black employees, while over 900 black men and women worked at Bell. From negligible numbers in 1941, 21,200 blacks labored in New York City's chief ordnance plants by 1945, in

Welder Hazel Liquori was one of more than 6,000 women employed at the Brooklyn Navy Yard during World War II. Official U.S. Navy Photo. Brooklyn Collection, Brooklyn Public Library.

addition to the 6,250 at the Brooklyn Navy Yard, the city's largest employer of nonwhites.

Inquiries by federal agencies coupled with the labor shortage opened slots for African Americans in the civilian economy as well. In June 1942, a nondiscriminatory contract was signed by the employers' association and the Cafeteria Employees' Union, which broke the color line at Horn & Hardart and other New York City restaurant chains. The U.S. Employment Service (USES) noted: "Colored applicants are reported as more readily placeable in some fields" of office work, and during the war the first black women appeared in midtown typing pools. Hospitals solved labor shortages by agreeing to take black workers. The USES nudged the Long Island College Hospital in Brooklyn to mix orderlies and other staff at its graduate facility. But only Harlem's Suydenham Hospital had fully integrated staffs and allowed black patients to obtain private rooms.

Wartime dislocations forced government intervention in the private economy, amounting to a frank widening of New Deal social welfare. In December 1940, twenty-five skilled workers quit the Watervliet Arsenal because they could not find places to live. A year later, the housing shortage in Niagara Falls reduced the apartment vacancy rate to 0.1 percent. Federal and state governments weighed in to redress the balance. In spring 1942, the U.S. Office of Price Administration (OPA) declared the most congested regions—Albany, Binghamton, Buffalo, Elmira, Rochester, Schenectady, Syracuse, and Troy—"war-rental areas," with rents "frozen" at the March 1, 1942 level. The OPA considered the same measure for New York City but retreated when landlord groups brandished evidence of 78,000 vacancies. It put the city on standby notice, however, while the Metropolitan Fair Rent Association, a landlord group, pledged to act against "gouging."

In many communities, standby status meant OPA investigation of rent levels, accompanied by intense pressure from landlords and tenant groups to sway the final outcome. When the OPA recommended rent ceilings for Westchester County, local politicians listened to landlords and prevailed upon the OPA not to impose controls. But in July 1944 tenant protests forced community leaders in Yonkers, Mount Vernon, Rye, and New Rochelle to request another OPA survey. Despite assurances from the Westchester Real Estate Owners' Association that increases had been minimal, the OPA concluded that rents were "piercing the cost-of-living line" and froze them at the August 1, 1944 level. In Westchester as elsewhere, the decree required landlords to register properties and apartment rents at the local OPA office. Landlords might request a "hardship" increase, usually 15 percent, but that entailed a lengthy statement of fact, followed by a hearing before the local OPA review board, which was usually contested by vocal tenant groups. Landlords learned to detest the OPA and the radical tenants who supported it.

New York State subsidized a total of 1,381 housing units in Niagara Falls,

Tonawanda and North Tonawanda, Schenectady, Elmira, and Utica. The New York City Housing Authority rushed to complete the Wallabout and Fort Greene projects in Brooklyn for occupation by families of navy yard workers. The state also provided loans to local authorities to construct over 6,000 units of temporary housing, galvanized-steel Quonset huts, in upstate manufacturing centers like Buffalo, Lackawanna, Cheektowaga, Niagara Falls, Tonawanda, Sampson, and Sidney. In New York City, Quonset villages for 30,000 sprang up at Flushing Meadows, Queens, Manhattan Beach, Brooklyn, and other locations. Many cities organized their own voluntary campaigns. In Niagara Falls, "Rent a Room for Victory" produced 1,289 rooms, and Rome's door-to-door effort turned up 400.

Child care and after-school programs never matched the needs of parents working overtime, particularly in crowded boomtowns. The Federal Works Agency sponsored forty-seven child care projects in New York State to accommodate nearly 5,500 preschool and school-age children. By 1943, New York City ran sixty-four WPA nurseries and play centers for 3,300 children. But Buffalo's war economy had only nine units for 326 preschoolers, and five more for 226 school-age children. Niagara Falls had two day-care centers for 60 preschoolers and two more for 88 school-age children. By war's end, the State War Council, which coordinated state and federally funded efforts, had established 221 after-school centers with an enrollment of 9,000.

The war intensified the growth of black ghettos in the big cities. By 1940, 95 percent of Brooklyn's 106,000 blacks resided between DeKalb and Atlantic Avenues, with nearly one-quarter crammed between Lexington Avenue and Fulton Street in an area known as Bedford-Stuyvesant, a district of dilapidated three-story walkups, notorious for gambling and juvenile delinquency that went on in "cellar clubs." Another ghetto formed in Queens (in part settled by refugees cleared for the construction of La Guardia Airport), which had 27,000 inhabitants in 1940. Despite the 1930s protests, La Guardia's New York had few black policemen and bus drivers and no black firemen. Boycotts forced token employment in stores along 125th Street, but no black saleswomen stood behind the counters in Macy's, Gimbels, or any other downtown store. Harlem's Hotel Theresa was owned by whites, who refused to admit black guests until 1940.

In upstate cities, African Americans were an invisible minority. In 1940, only 2,082 blacks were part of Syracuse's population of 205,000. In Buffalo, where blacks were 3 percent of the population, the tiny community lived a life apart from the rest of the city. Blacks could find only the lowest-paid jobs— "bull work"—at Bethlehem Steel's Lackawanna plant. The few black students admitted to the Buffalo Technical High School were denied the course in sheet metal work because the city's aviation firms, Bell and Curtiss-Wright, simply would not hire them. Blacks suffered the indignity of Jim Crow practices in the

Capitol District, where whites refused to dine with or serve them—but flocked to watch "shadow ball," the razzle-dazzle games played by Negro League baseball clubs, notably the Schenectady Mohawk Giants and the Albany Senators.

The growing realization that the war was being fought in part for racial ideals kindled a renewed campaign against Jim Crow. The Harlem movement, spearheaded by Reverend Powell's pickets against discrimination in employment, was joined by white liberals on the City-Wide Citizens Committee on Harlem, which investigated barriers in housing and employment. The effort failed, however, to head off African American frustrations, which boiled over in the 1943 Harlem riot. On August 1, at a seedy hotel, police scuffled with a black military policeman, who was shot and hustled away. After an angry crowd gathered at the 123rd Street precinct house, Mayor La Guardia deployed five thousand police, which only drew larger crowds. Looting broke out along 125th Street, and police responded with nightsticks and riot guns. Six blacks were killed, three by police gunfire, and more than seven hundred were injured.

Shaken by the blow to New York City's wartime pride, Mayor La Guardia named a Mayor's Committee on Unity to encourage racial harmony. The OPA studied Harlem's crowded housing and froze New York City's rents at the March 1, 1943 level, making it the last major American city to have controls imposed. Liberals found a related cause when Metropolitan Life Insurance Company announced that Stuyvesant Town, the company's housing redevelopment in lower Manhattan, was planned for whites only. The City-Wide Citizens Committee joined forces with Powell's protesters to demand "open" housing, and a City-Wide Citizens member, attorney Charles Abrams, brought suit against Met Life's color barrier. Although Abrams's suit failed and Stuyvesant Town remained all white, it stirred the movement for fair housing. At the height of the war, Harlem's agony brought New York liberals to the goal of an interracial society.

War Comes to Kendaia

Modern war's demand for exotic metals and petroleum reversed the rural-to-urban migration and revived the state's extractive industries. In the North Country, hydroelectric facilities powered Alcoa's massive aluminum plant at Massena, which supplied light metal to aircraft producers in Buffalo. Demand for titanium forced the National Lead Company to reopen the McIntyre Mines at Tahawus in Essex County, which touched off a boom in employment that reached as far away as Johnsburg, Warren County. The Olean petroleum industry, kept alive by the hydrostatic process, which pumped water into aging wells, brought new flows of "rock oil" for war industry.

The construction and operation of wartime facilities overwhelmed small towns. Kendaia Corners near Seneca Lake was a hamlet of two hundred farms. But Washington chose Kendaia as the location for the Seneca Army Depot, a complex of five hundred concrete igloos for storage of 100,000 tons of ammunition. In 1942, more than eight thousand construction workers converged on the site. "Farmers placed cots in chicken coops," observers wrote. "Trailers were at a premium. . . . Tool shacks became houses." Federal officials tried without much success to enlarge a trailer camp at Geneva but instead parked one hundred trailers at the local fair grounds to rent at $6.50 per week. Faced with primitive sanitary facilities, state health officials urged farmers to chlorinate their wells.

Construction of Seneca Naval Station at Sampson brought in 17,583 workers, who swamped the Geneva area as far south as Trumansburg. No plans were made for emergency housing, and local home owners were hostile toward the interlopers. "The residents will not house Negro, Jewish or other persons of foreign extraction," the U.S. Employment Service reported in July 1942. African American construction workers were particular objects of discrimination, and, by Labor Day, some 4,000 returned to New York City. When completed, the Sampson Naval Training Station and Seneca Army Depot employed 25,000, including 7,000 African Americans. The OPA imposed rent controls on Sampson in 1942 and on Geneva in 1943.

Medium-sized cities with ordnance factories were overwhelmed by workers, who commuted for miles on trolleys and in automobiles using rationed gasoline. In Sidney, employment at the Scientific Magneto Division of Bendix Aviation soared from 1,100 in January 1940 to 8,600 by January 1943, bringing crowded housing conditions across Delaware County. The Tri-Cities area, where Link Flight Instruments operated at Hillcrest, Endicott Johnson made combat boots, and Agfa Ansco of Binghamton made optical equipment and photographic film and became the area's largest industry, was another jobs magnet. In Binghamton, Johnson City, and Endicott, one-third of war plant employees were rural residents, who jammed State Route 17 and county roads. In Elmira Heights, Bendix's Eclipse Machine Division, which mass-produced fuel-injection pumps, became Chemung County's largest employer as its workforce rose from 715 in January 1940 to nearly 8,600 by January 1943.

Wartime demand for food production halted the decline in tilled farmland, which increased from 17.5 million acres in 1940 to nearly 18 million by 1945. The northern Steuben County potato belt regions of Prattsburg and Wheeler revived with superior seed and crop dusting and could not produce potatoes fast enough. Second in output to Nassau County's, the area's potato fields utilized migrant workers, mainly African Americans and West Indians. Peach and apple orchards as well as grape yards flourished on the Niagara tableland north of Lewiston Heights. South Erie County was poultry country, with 4,500 farms. The North Collins and Brant areas claimed the biggest berry patches in Erie County and raised strawberries and black and red raspberries.

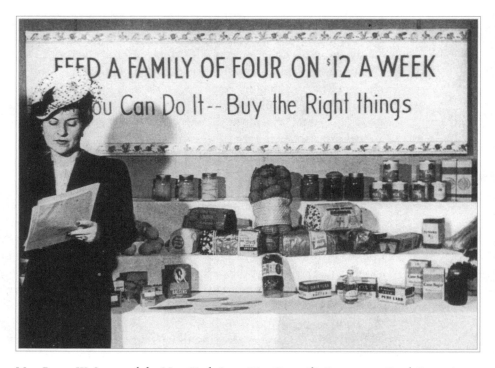

Mrs. Roger W. Straus of the New York State War Council's Emergency Food Commission demonstrates grocery shopping economy during World War II food rationing. From Karl D. Hartzell, *The Empire State at War* (State of New York, 1949).

From the maple sugar farms at Gouverneur in Saint Lawrence County to the apple orchards in the Hudson Valley, the rural economy was sorely tested by wartime labor shortages. Farmers, who required harvest help of 140,000 men and women, including 20,000 migrants, were stymied by the draft and wage competition from war industries. Pickers' piece rates for bushels of peas and beans soared from 25 or 30 cents in 1942 to 50 cents by 1945. Hourly wages rose from 35 cents for women and 40 cents for men in 1942 to 50 and 65 cents per hour by 1945.

To cope with labor shortages, state education officials extended time off from school for pupils over fourteen and experimented with Saturday schools. A Farm Cadet Victory Corps enrolled 55,000 youths in 1944, and the state branch of the Women's Land Army organized work camps like Clermont in Columbia County and Tuttle in Dutchess, where college students picked beans and tomatoes and saved the apple crop. Fruit and berry growers along Lake Ontario resorted to Italian prisoners of war, and in Geneva a growers' cooperative hired 250 German POWs (paid 60 cents per hour to work in fields and canneries). The worst off were families scattered among 154 migrant labor camps. While the State Labor Department struggled to provide basic amenities in 22 larger camps, an observer reported "hundreds of migrant families living as pariahs" in squalid cabins and out-dwellings.

Meeting the New Deal Halfway

In 1940, President Franklin Roosevelt won New York State by 225,000 votes over the challenger, Wall Street lawyer Wendell Willkie. Roosevelt's narrow victory in his home state signaled a weakening in the New Deal's hold on the electorate. While Mayor La Guardia gained a third-term victory in 1941, he won by only 132,000 votes. Tammany's candidate, William O'Dwyer, a former policeman and a municipal judge, had good government credentials and a rapport with the American Labor party that went back to his championship of the Transport Workers Union. In Bill O'Dwyer, Tammany had found the way to court the Jewish vote, and he came back a winner in 1945, when La Guardia retired from Gracie Mansion.

In early 1940 Governor Lehman's liberalism was trimmed by Republican legislators impatient with big government. Lehman asked for only a $5 million budget increase for fiscal 1941, despite a projected windfall in tax revenues, and a $9 million decrease in fiscal 1942, along with a $21 million reduction in taxes. Sensing a new vulnerability, he announced in May 1942 that he would not seek reelection. Wartime population shifts had cut into working-class voter registration, and the Republican-controlled legislature refused measures like mail-in registration that would have made voting easier, especially for soldier-absentees. Across the state, war-industry towns suffered inflated rents and inadequate housing—nasty issues for any incumbent. The falloff in Democratic votes was crucial in the 1942 state elections, but so was the political skill of the Republican challenger. Moderate Republican Thomas E. Dewey buried his Democratic opponent, Lehman's attorney general, John J. Bennett, Jr., by 647,000 votes.

Only forty-two years old, Dewey took charge of gubernatorial affairs with a remorseless precision. A perfectionist with a passion for neatness, Dewey, his staff joked, even seemed to sweat in "an orderly, efficient manner." He hated glad-handing and patronage politics and ordered the state police to review the credentials of his chief appointees. His cabinet was made up of top-drawer, businesslike Republicans. Mental Hygiene Commissioner Dr. Frederick MacCurdy took a dim view of warehousing 98,000 patients in the state's mental hospitals. Emphasizing more aggressive drug treatments, he effected the first decline in the hospitalized population in decades. Budget Director

John E. Burton applied modern accounting methods to state tax collection. Bank Superintendent Elliott V. Bell proposed incentives to mobilize private credit in real estate and housing. Dewey immediately established a disciplined gubernatorial office centered on the "pre-veto." Conferring with moderate Republicans, Senate Majority Leader Irving M. Ives and Assembly Speaker Oswald D. Heck, Dewey methodically reviewed pending bills and crossed off those he did not like. His authority was such that few of them survived the legislative process.

Dewey rebuilt the modern GOP on the back of suburban good government. He worked closely with Republican leaders like Edwin F. Jaeckle of Erie County and Clarence King and Rolland Marvin of Onondaga. He handed GOP boss J. Russel Sprague patronage to ensure his grip on Nassau County. He gave the nod to Westchester Republicans William F. Bleakley and Herbert C. Gerlach to shape the Reoux-Hampton Reapportionment Law of 1943, the first in twenty-six years. Bleakley chaired the Joint Committee on Reapportionment, which gave a windfall of legislative seats (mostly Republican) to Queens, Nassau, Westchester, and other suburban counties at the expense of upstate, rural senatorial districts.

Governor Dewey matched Democrats in the "politics of recognition," campaigning in Harlem, appointing Assemblyman Francis E. Rivers to a top judgeship, and naming a gubernatorial commission to investigate racial bias. He also added 400,000 workers to categories covered by the state minimum wage and, in a gesture toward organized labor, established the State School of Industrial and Labor Relations at Cornell University. A coalition of Dewey Republicans and liberal Democrats revived significant portions of the Little New Deal. In 1942 the legislature approved construction of a motorway—the Thruway—from New York City to Buffalo, and, in 1944, authorized state highway funds, heretofore limited to rural districts, for major routes within cities. Under Bertram D. Tollamy, the State Department of Public Works began engineering studies for "Urban Area Arterial Route Plans."

Soon after his election, Dewey's supporters were saying that the moderate Republican could take on Roosevelt in 1944. Dewey endorsed New Deal programs like social security and wages and hours legislation but condemned Roosevelt's "senseless creation of innumerable overlapping agencies" and derided the WPA as amateurish public works. Regarding the welfare state as "here to stay," Dewey promised to administer it with scientific management. He clinched the Republican presidential nomination with an April 1944 speech calling for "cohesion" with Great Britain. The idea pleased Republicans like attorney John Foster Dulles, *New York Herald Tribune* owner John Hay Whitney, and Columbia University president Nicholas Murray Butler, who despaired at the GOP's traditional isolationism. Dewey steered Republicans toward acceptance of the New Deal and global responsibilities.

Fanfares for Common Men

The war had transformed New York City, which was all tawdry power, the navy's best liberty port. Strollers on Fifth Avenue during "dim-outs" found that the Empire State Building glowed in moonlight, while Broadway's oyster bars and nightclubs burst with tireless revelers. Arthur Fellig, the runty "Weegee," who aimed his Graflex "where the people are," photographed many of them. Most New Yorkers, numbed by crowded subways and war work, never ventured inside a nightclub and were in bed by 10:30 P.M. Nevertheless, Mayor La Guardia quipped that if wartime America had a midnight curfew, New Yorkers would stay up past 1:00 A.M.

The war effort wiped away the Depression's hard edge and grimness but left many city dwellers in limbo. Transformed by defense training, public schools took on a serious intensity. By July 1942, some 16,000 students had registered for New York City Board of Education defense courses, offered in high schools open twenty-four hours a day. But the city's demand for teenage labor slackened, as commercial offices shrank operations and no longer hired errand runners. "For the first time in many months," commented U.S. Employment Service investigators, "there was no shortage of persons qualified for office boy work." Teenagers found the war a long period of uncertainty, when they could only look over the shoulders of grownups and wait for their draft notices. Social psychologists warned about unsupervised, "latchkey" children and feared a rise in juvenile delinquency.

The lively arts, blacked out in Europe, lit up New York City. Lincoln Kirstein's Ballet Theatre gathered the talents of choreographers Agnes de Mille and Antony Tudor, scenic designer Oliver Smith, and composer Aaron Copland. The Ballet Theatre triumphed with a reprise in 1942 of the de Mille-Copland folk ballet *Billy the Kid* and Jerome Robbins and Leonard Bernstein's *Fancy Free* (1944), which critics hailed as an all-American "manly" piece. De Mille left the Ballet Theatre for a rival company, the Ballet Russe de Monte Carlo, which put on Copland's *Rodeo* (1942). The city's dance companies also included Katherine Dunham's troupe, which offered ethnographic displays of African and Caribbean forms, and Martha Graham's, which debuted on Broadway in 1944 with signature ballets about mythic heroines protesting their ineluctable fate. Wartime New York molded an American style of powerful, exuberant modern dance.

With the arrival of European émigrés like Béla Bartók and Paul Hindemith, classical composition centered in New York City. After Arturo Toscanini's 1937 departure, the New York Philharmonic experienced uncertain times under conductor Artur Rodzinski, whose conservatism was reflected by his attack on boogie-woogie as "the greatest contributing factor to juvenile delinquency." The Philharmonic was overshadowed by the NBC Symphony Orchestra, which maestro Toscanini made into America's symphony of the airwaves. Conductor Leopold Stokowski contributed his flamboyance to the NBC Symphony and in 1943 also organized an upstart, the New York City Orchestra, to perform compositions by Americans. That same year the New York City Opera began offering low-priced performances at New York's City Center.

What resulted was an astonishing outpouring of Americana. In 1943 came Aaron Copland's *Fanfare for the Common Man*, a paean to wartime patriotism; and the following year saw Martha Graham's performance of Copland's masterful *Appalachian Spring*. The musical *Oklahoma!* made history on Broadway in 1943. It not only featured Richard Rodgers's lilting tunes and Oscar Hammerstein II's apple-pie lyrics but set a new standard for the musical stage by making Agnes de Mille's "dream ballet" and Oliver Smith's haunting scenic designs an integral part of the drama. Further highlights in 1944 included Leonard Bernstein's *On the Town* (1944), with book by Betty Comden and Adolph Green, and, as noted above, the Robbins choreography of Bernstein's *Fancy Free*. New York had opened the golden age of musical theater.

During the war, Broadway mounted patriotic shows like Irving Berlin's revue *This Is the Army* (1942), and sponsored the Service Canteen, which hosted visiting soldiers and sailors. Drama was largely escapist fare, notably *Life with Father*, which ran throughout the war, and *Harvey* (1945), the whimsical account of a man and his imaginary friend, a seven-foot rabbit, which beat out Tennessee Williams's brooding, sexually ambivalent *Glass Menagerie* for the Pulitzer Prize. Several Shakespearean productions marked social breakthroughs, notably the black actor Paul Robeson's lead in *Othello*, and *The Tempest*, which starred Canada Lee, another African American, as Caliban. In 1941 the Group Theatre, run by Harold Clurman and Lee Strasberg, put on Thornton Wilder's sentimental tale of humankind's progress, *The Skin of Our Teeth*, worthy of note for Elia Kazan's direction of Montgomery Clift's Broadway debut.

Publishing had come light years from the stuffiness of the 1920s. At Random House, Bennett Cerf packaged classics in economics and sociology that would shape a generation of highbrows. Publishers resorted to splashy new sales campaigns, epitomized by the June 1941 blitz by Knopf, CBS radio, and the Book-of-the-Month Club for William L. Shirer's *Berlin Diary*, which detailed his reporting experience in Hitler's Reich. New York publishers like W. W. Norton, who said that "books are weapons in the war of ideas," aimed their volumes at the average citizen. Pocket Books, a division of Simon and Schuster, blossomed during the war, publishing 25-cent copies of titles as disparate as *See Here, Private Hargrove* (1942) and the *Merriam-Webster Pocket Dictionary* (1943). The publishers also combined to print GI editions, cheap paperbacks that servicemen could shove into knapsacks. The nation hungered for books on war issues, and Simon and Schuster had a best seller with the $1 edition of Wendell Willkie's *One World* (1943).

The war shifted the focus of the contemporary art scene decisively from Paris to New York City—as reflected by Peggy Guggenheim's Art-of-this-Century Gallery, which showcased the abstractionists Hans Hofmann, William Baziotes, and Jackson Pollock. Another abstract artist, Willem de Kooning, debuted at the John Graham Gallery in 1942. A year later, Mark Rothko, Adolf Gottlieb, and others fired a salvo against the *New York Times*, which had confessed its "befuddlement" about an exhibit of abstract art. "No possible set of notes can explain our paintings," they lectured. "We wish to reassert the picture plane. We are for flat forms because they destroy illusion and reveal truth." Abstract artists were contributing the power of pure form to democracy's war.

A tougher political realism arose during the war among leftists, who warned against Stalin's "grinning lust for power." At the *Partisan Review*, ex-Communists William Barrett and Philip Rahv continued to pursue a Marxism kept pure by modern writers, who shuddered at the twentieth century's bleak, totalitarian drift. *Partisan Review* was joined by another voice, Dwight Macdonald, the irascible Trotskyist, who founded *Politics* in 1944 to polemicize for what he called "noncollective socialism." During 1943, when *Life* magazine and other mainstream media heralded the "Grand Alliance" with Soviet Russia, Trotskyists including Macdonald, City College professor Sidney Hook, and *Partisan Review* critic Alfred Kazin blasted the pro-Soviet propaganda. In 1944, Socialist anti-Stalinists, led by David Dubinsky of the International Ladies' Garment Workers' Union, stormed out of the Communist-dominated American Labor party and organized the Liberal party. New York's independent socialists launched the first salvos of the Cold War.

Wartime transformed college campuses. At City College, where radicals took the Oxford Oath against military service and the faculty ended Army ROTC in the late 1930s, military training was returned in 1942. The search for wartime causes infused Columbia College's "Contemporary Civilization" course and the pan-Europeanism of the "University in Exile" at the New School for Social Research. At Brooklyn College, President Harry D. Gideonse, objecting to the curriculum's "sloppy vocationalism," brought about a reexamination that eventually resulted in core courses in English and the social sciences. The University of Buffalo's full-time enrollment, 1,525 in 1939, increased fourfold by the end of the war, when construction of a new campus was nearly completed. In 1942, when William Tolley became chancellor, Syracuse University had 5,600 students, including just 400 graduate students, and an annual budget of $3.7 million. Tolley filled the Syracuse campus with Air Force cadets, ended the quiet quota on Jewish enrollment, and started buying real estate to expand the campus for the expected postwar crush.

Most significant, wartime idealism and worries about the prospects for returning veterans clinched the argument for a state university. The war forced

Officer candidates leaving class at the U.S. Naval Schools of Indoctrination and Training at Cornell University in 1943. From Karl D. Hartzell, *The Empire State at War* (State of New York, 1949).

recognition that New York could no longer make do with a loose network of teachers colleges, Regents scholarships, and state aid to private schools. The cause united downstate legislators, infuriated by quotas on Jews, Italians, and African Americans, medical societies concerned about postwar sources of trained physicians, and nondiscrimination lobbies like the American Jewish Committee and the Mayor's Committee on Unity. The forces came together via the Assembly leader, Democrat Irwin Steingut of Brooklyn, who called for a state university system that answered postwar needs for scientific and medical research and ability to meet the size of the estimated postwar college population. The movement eventually culminated in the establishment in 1948 of the State University of New York.

While wartime New York moved to a robust Americana and hope for a better world, it also engendered an outrageous new dissidence among those on its margins. In Harlem, "bebop" became a virtual act of resistance among jazz musicians including Charlie Parker and John B. "Dizzy" Gillespie against the white-controlled record business. In the early 1940s African American bands had retrenched, leaving some musicians to form small combos that played clubs in Harlem and on West 52nd Street. In 1943, Charlie Parker, by all accounts intense, brilliant, and self-destructive, playing his alto saxophone in after-hours jam sessions, began what many critics called "the revolution." From big band jazz that was "stuck in the same diatonic groove," Parker, in works like *Anthropology* (1943) and *Red Cross* (1944), vastly "broadened the harmonic territory available to the improvising musician." With music meant for serious listening—and not dancing—bebop had broken through a commercial divide in American pop music.

A related eddy—certainly not yet a movement—developed from the ease with which people could get by in wartime Manhattan, where anyone could find work and the black market was tempting. On the Upper West Side and in Greenwich Village, a disaffected lifestyle sprang up among Columbia University students, who found occasional jobs while waiting for the draft. College friends Jack Kerouac and Allen Ginsberg hung around campus apartments, often in the company of William S. Burroughs, a layabout and morphine user; and through Burroughs they met Herbert Huncke, a Times Square hustler, thief, and drug addict. They explored an intense underground of lowlifes and junkies, who defied wartime's commitment and causes. Huncke, arguably the first "Beat," lived the perverse idealism that a Jack Kerouac and a Charlie Parker would give to the postwar world.

Anticipations

Postwar obligations—toward returning veterans and the potentially unemployed—brought many communities to a consensus on the necessity for planning. In 1942 Governor Lehman appointed a Post-War Public Works Planning Commission, which accumulated blueprints from state agencies for public works, including a "throughway" auto road marked on official maps in October 1942. In 1944, as Governor Dewey geared up his presidential campaign, the Republican legislature embraced an ambitious program of postwar public works. It resolved that: "The modernization and construction of arterial highways, which are to pass through cities, will contribute greatly to post-war reemployment and to the stimulation of industrial recovery." The highway program would be financed by the Postwar Reconstruction Fund, accumulated from surplus wartime revenues. In addition, the legislature established the State Dormitory Authority to enlarge facilities at the state's teachers colleges.

Many communities got an early jump on postwar development. The Niagara Frontier Post-War Planning Council, which included planners, highway experts, and housing officials from Buffalo and Lackawanna, identified what they called the "present decay" of slums and obsolete commercial structures and sketched likely routes for a Niagara Throughway system of express highways. Rochester's Council of Postwar Problems, headed by Eastman Kodak's Marion B. Folsom, envisioned highway loops around the central business district and low-rent housing for veterans. In Binghamton, Republican Mayor Walter B. Lounsbery proposed a sewage treatment plant, veterans' garden apartments, and even public housing. The Syracuse planning movement brought together Chancellor William Tolley of Syracuse University, the Syracuse Housing Authority, and executives at Niagara-Mohawk Power, Carrier, and Smith-Corona, into the Syracuse-Onondaga Post-War Planning Council. The council called for a "shelf" of "flexible public works" to guard against postwar unemployment and sketched bypass highways around the city, with spokes like University-Downtown Thruway; clearance of the Adams Street slum for a university athletic field and shopping center; and "orderly rebuilding of the obsolete" central business district.

The most important effort occurred in New York City, where Robert Moses, parks commissioner, leading voice on the City Planning Commission, and chairman of the Triborough Bridge and Tunnel Authority, was appointed postwar works coordinator by Mayor La Guardia in 1942. Working closely with State Housing Commissioner Edward Weinfeld and Insurance Superintendent Louis H. Pink, Moses established tax incentives to engage savings banks and insurance companies in the reclamation of blighted areas. The result was the Redevelopment Companies Law of 1942, which authorized the establishment of quasi-public corporations to condemn blighted areas and build new housing. Under it, Metropolitan Life Insurance Company pledged in 1943 to build Stuyvesant Town, an apartment complex for 24,000 on a decayed tenement tract on the Lower East Side. In the meantime, Moses coordinated the New York City Housing Authority's "Ten-Year Program" for hundreds of acres of slum clearance and scores of future housing projects.

The La Guardia administration's efforts encouraged private institutions like hospitals and universities to carry out their own postwar blueprints. Hospitals such as Mount Sinai and Bellevue (the latter in tandem with New York University Medical School) drew plans for comprehensive medical "centers" with government-aided redevelopment. In 1944, Mayor La Guardia announced that New York City would subsidize the cost for city employees of group health insurance for comprehensive medical coverage—the origin of the Health Insurance Plan of

Greater New York (HIP). Planners anticipated a cohort of married veterans impatient to finish their education, but with the potential income to support universities and health care.

The glossy plans often cloaked practical attempts at racial resettlement. The New York City Housing Authority's Ten-Year Program envisioned slum clearance within the boundaries of such established racial ghettos as Central Harlem, Brownsville in Brooklyn, and South Jamaica in Queens, where projects were seen as catchments for the city's growing black and Hispanic population. The Utica Municipal Housing Authority planned for slum clearance on Whitesboro Street between Seneca and Hoyt Street, with a new project called Washington Court for "colored people" and Adrean Terrace for whites. The authority overstepped, however, when it tried to extend Washington Court westward into a white neighborhood after the war. The property was razed, but the ground earmarked for a black project was soon taken over for commercial renewal. Additional projects for African Americans were planned for North Utica and the Sunset Park district, but community protests delayed both. In 1943, plans by the Buffalo Municipal Housing Authority for war housing for blacks in largely Irish South Buffalo were stymied by neighborhood protests against expansion of the existing ghetto on the East Side.

Marie and Fiorello La Guardia bid a final farewell to City Hall on December 31, 1945.
La Guardia and Wagner Archives, La Guardia Community College.

When Governor Dewey lost New York State to President Roosevelt by 315,000 votes in 1944, he blamed it on his failure to outbid FDR for liberal support. His January 1945 message to the legislature resolved to end that shortcoming. He reported a $150 million surplus in his fiscal 1944 budget, but, resisting the Republican legislature's instincts to use the windfall to cut taxes, he proposed to divert it to the Post War Reconstruction Fund. He favored extending coverage of the state workmen's compensation law to domestics and restaurant workers, along with a 20 percent wage increase for low-wage state workers and institutional employees. He called for a permanent state commission against discrimination, which was realized by the Ives-Quinn Law of 1945. He wanted a permanent State Veterans' Commission to administer state additions to the federal law providing educational and housing benefits to returning servicemen, the "GI Bill of Rights." He coupled a continuation of 25 percent cuts in state income taxes with demands for vast new spending: $100 million for state building construction, $50 million in state matching funds for projects in 450 municipalities, $35 million in loans to New York City for public housing, and $800 million for highways and grade crossing projects.

In 1945, wartime New York had prosperous manufacturing cities with union members earning fat paychecks. Tensions had touched off nasty race riots at the very time that the war brought the promise of an interracial era. The global conflict brought a European cosmopolitanism to Manhattan, sharpening its energies and sense of citizens' mission. But the future remained in suspension, while New Yorkers waited out the war. They waited for the lifting of federal controls on prices and rents while they worried whether the CIO would make exorbitant wage demands and go on strike. They worried about postwar inflation and about the coming of another depression. Who knew what the postwar era would bring? The confident builder William J. Levitt had returned from the Navy Seabees filled with ideas for constructing tracts of cheap homes in the suburbs. Worrying about demand, Levitt built his first Cape Cods for rent on Long Island.

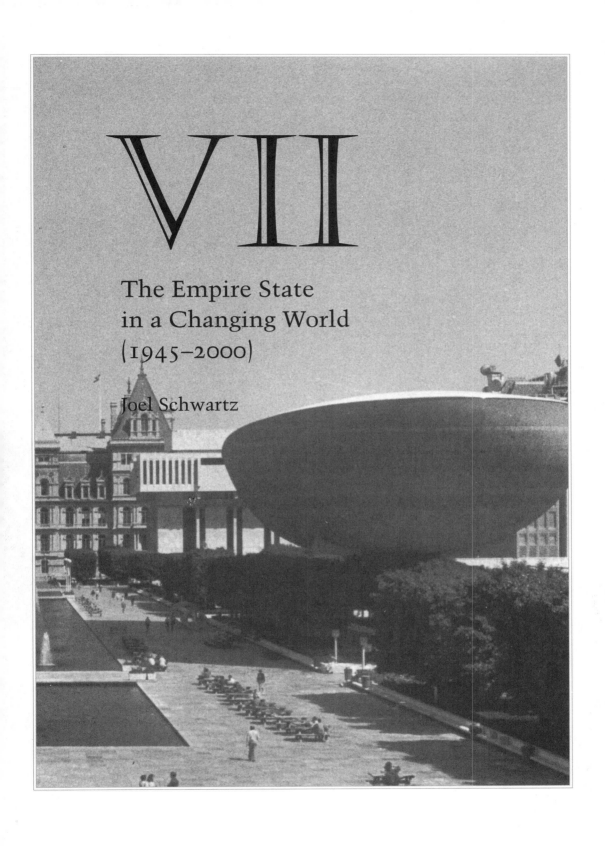

VII

The Empire State
in a Changing World
(1945–2000)

Joel Schwartz

Chapter 32

Top of the World

IN 1945 NEW YORK STATE WAS SUSPENDED BETWEEN HIS-toric eras. While total war stirred citizens for global causes, political bosses still ruled Manhattan, the Bronx, and Albany. Gotham was a worldly metropolis and a raucous liberty port, but throughout the state divorce was illegal, women had to sneak into Sanger clinics for diaphragms, and police confiscated "obscene" books. Franklin D. Roosevelt's New Deal made New York City and Buffalo bastions of blue-collar unions in the Congress of Industrial Organizations (CIO). Rochester, Syracuse, and Utica, however, remained company towns; and in Binghamton shoemakers at Endicott Johnson abided their paternalist founder, George F. Johnson, and still did things "the George F. way."

Despite World War II's upheaval, New Yorkers stayed homebodies. They labored for companies like Mohawk Carpet (Mohasco) in Amsterdam, wore their Saturday best to shop in downtown Rochester and Poughkeepsie, and swore by local brands like Buffalo's Gerhard Lang beer. Old folks spoke Sicilian on Rochester's "Mount Allegro" and bargained in Polish at Buffalo's Fillmore Street market. Teenagers knew the silhouettes of Allied planes, worshiped New York Giants manager (and home-run great) Mel Ott, and lived with their parents until they saved enough to get married. Cheektowaga was a rural hamlet beyond Buffalo's city line, and Nassau County's "Five Towns" (Hewlett, Lawrence, Woodmere, Cedarhurst, and Inwood on the border of Queens), were villages on state routes. Before the war, New York City had 55 percent of the state's population, but some 153,000 farms spread over half its area.

On the Threshold of the Postwar World

Although the war moved people across the country, throughout those years New York remained the Empire State, its 13.5 million people anchoring the Northeast. The state delegation to the U.S. House of Representatives totaled forty-five and, with two senators, provided forty-seven of the 266 electoral votes needed to elect presidents. New York City sent twenty-four congressmen to Washington, including seven from Manhattan. One of every ten Americans was a New Yorker, and one of every sixteen lived in New York City. Brooklyn's population was nearly three million, which explains in part why every Hollywood war platoon had a GI from Flatbush.

New Yorkers mass-produced the means for American victory, and the armed forces marched across the country to orders that were largely processed in New York, the war's bureaucratic subcapital. The Battle of the Atlantic was directed from federal offices in Manhattan, where commanders routed merchant convoys and the bombers that patrolled for German submarines. In late 1945 Fort Ontario in Oswego became the largest center for resettling war refugees from Europe.

The state dominated the precarious balance of genteel tradition and mass taste that was American culture. Its universities turned out 18 percent of American Ph.D.s during the war. Broadway had one-quarter of the legitimate theaters in the country, and 52nd Street was the epicenter of the big band, trombone-heavy jazz known as "swing." News media led by the *New York Herald–Tribune*, the *New York Times*, and five radio networks, all headquartered in New York City, determined what Americans read and heard, and increasingly the media were bringing a New York style to big-time sports, exploiting their business possibilities at the same time that innovations were making basketball and hockey faster games.

Wartime labor shortages had opened doors to women, increasing female participation in the state labor force from 24 to 34 percent, but did not bring decisive changes. New York City garment firms kept new hires in traditional female categories (and paid them less than men doing similar work), while Bulova and Sperry put women to work on light machines suited to supposed female patience and dexterity. While most women workers hoped to keep their jobs after the war, one-third were let go during the summer of 1945.

Wartime demand had also affected Native and African Americans. Many of the five thousand Iroquois on the Six Nation Reservation worked at plants in North Tonawanda and Niagara and sent their children to nearby district schools. The lures of assimilation, however, were countered by a religious movement, the Handsome Lake ritual, which attracted followers, particularly among the Seneca on the Southern Tier. Severe labor shortages, coupled with wartime idealism, bent the rigid Jim Crow rules that confined African Americans to low-paid dirty work. In 1944, a year after Harlem rioted against Jim Crow, the district elected Adam Clayton Powell, Jr., New York's first African American congressman. The following spring, Brooklyn scouts eyed ballplayers from the Negro leagues at the Dodgers' Bear Mountain training camp. Although segregation remained pervasive, interracialism had become a thinkable dream.

Wartime ideals had less impact on marginal groups. The state's 90,000 Puerto Ricans remained nearly invisible in Greenpoint, Brooklyn, and East Harlem, where they worked in tobacco factories and garment lofts. Exclusion Acts limited Chinese (mostly male sojourners) to perhaps 20,000 in the New York City area. One-third crowded "Chinatown," five square blocks bordered by Pell, Doyer, and Mott Streets. Despised by their bohemian neighbors, Greenwich Village homosexuals ducked into Eighth Street bars whose Mafia owners paid the police for the right to serve liquor to "queers." While wartime wages gave women independence, lesbians met in places apart from their workday lives. In Buffalo they frequented Ralph Martin's and Winter's bars, where crewcut "butches" defied the outside world.

The New Deal and the war brought political bosses toward a grudging acceptance of reform. The head of Utica's Democratic machine, Rufus P. Elefante, supported reformer Boyd E. Golder for mayor. Buffalo's reform Republicans along with rebels from an upstart People's party, elected Bernard J. Dowd in 1945, and even Albany's O'Connell machine endorsed a respectable figurehead, Mayor Erastus Corning, 2nd. No other reformer had the impact of New York City Mayor Fiorello H. La Guardia, who helped make New Deal issues more important than party loyalty and launched the insurgency of Democratic reform.

In cities where blue-collar workers lived in cold-water flats, reformers espoused the cause of urban renewal. Wartime fervor helped Chancellor William P. Tolley of Syracuse University bring the Niagara-Mohawk Power Corporation and the Onondaga County GOP into a citizens' movement for postwar planning, highways, and housing. In Rochester, Kodak executive Marion B. Folsom and Haloid's Joseph C. Wilson led the Council on Postwar Problems, urging public housing and center-city renewal. Mayor La Guardia's vision for New York City included highways like the East River (later FDR) Drive, the Marine Air Terminal (renamed La Guardia Field), and slum clearance by the New York City Housing Authority. In 1945 La Guardia appointed Robert Moses expediter of postwar projects. Already in control of the independent authorities that built the Triborough and Whitestone Bridges, Queens-Midtown and Brooklyn-Battery Tunnels, and connecting highways, the imperious Moses became the city's construction czar.

Governor Thomas E. Dewey embodied the contradictions of the Empire State. Dewey came to power in 1942 as the good government icon, who inspired Republican insurgents like Edwin F. Jaeckle of Erie County and Manhattan attorney Herbert Brownell, Jr. He also courted Republican bosses like Tom

Broderick of Monroe County and Rolland Marvin of Onondaga County. Dewey wanted efficient Republican government in the suburbs but handed Nassau County Executive J. Russel Sprague patronage for his Five Towns machine.

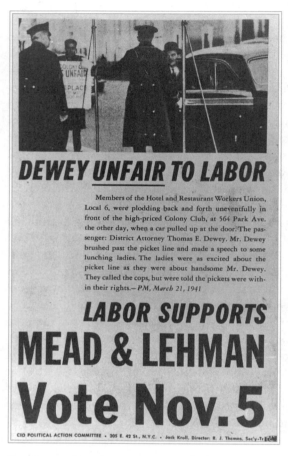

DEWEY UNFAIR TO LABOR

Members of the Hotel and Restaurant Workers Union, Local 6, were plodding back and forth uneventfully in front of the high-priced Colony Club, at 564 Park Ave. the other day, when a car pulled up at the door. The passenger: District Attorney Thomas E. Dewey. Mr. Dewey brushed past the picket line and made a speech to some lunching ladies. The ladies were as excited about the picket line as they were about handsome Mr. Dewey. They called the cops, but were told the pickets were within their rights.— *PM, March 21, 1941*

LABOR SUPPORTS
MEAD & LEHMAN
Vote Nov. 5

CIO POLITICAL ACTION COMMITTEE • 205 E. 42 St., N.Y.C. • Jack Kroll, Director; R. J. Thomas, Sec'y-Tr

Despite a contentious campaign, Thomas E. Dewey prevailed over James M. Mead in the gubernatorial election of 1946, and Irving M. Ives defeated Herbert Lehman in the race for the U.S. Senate. New York State Historical Association, Cooperstown, N.Y.

Dewey pushed the 1945 Ives-Quinn Law, which forbade bias in employment, and created a $623 million postwar reconstruction fund for bridges, highways, and public housing, which amounted to GOP-style full-employment spending. When Irving Lehman, the pro-labor chief judge of the state Court of Appeals, died in 1945, Dewey elevated Associate Judge John T. Loughran, the "stalwart liberal," who upheld the state's "Little Wagner Act" and rent controls. Although Dewey lost presidential campaigns to Roosevelt in 1944 and Harry S. Truman in 1948, his liberalism influenced Republican politics for two decades.

At the end of the war, New York State was on top of the world. Its politics, fashioned by Roosevelt and accepted by Dewey, formed America's "vital center." Demand for industrial products made Buffalo, Rochester, and Syracuse high-wage towns and kept state per-capita income number one, roughly 36 percent above the U.S. average. The liberalism that brought organized labor into the mainstream began to open doors for African Americans. The wartime blackout of London and Paris made Manhattan, with its galleries, recital halls, and book publishers, the world's art capital. While the postwar world was filled with uncertainties, in 1945 that world seemed New York's to shape.

Liberalism Ascendant

The onset of the Cold War made New York the headquarters of the liberal capitalism that molded the Free World. The Marshall Plan boosted the Port of New

York and durable goods producers from Buffalo to Long Island. International Business Machines processors made in Binghamton became the standard for office equipment in London, while Syracuse's Carrier Corporation designed air conditioners for palaces in Saudi Arabia. Government spending enlarged cities into metropolitan regions, and the state's universities, medical centers, and churches spread the gospel of American competence around the globe. Superhighways and airports linked the state to the rest of the nation and to the world, and Manhattan lawyer John Foster Dulles helped organize the United Nations. In the heady years after World War II, the ambitions of the Empire State had no limits.

Confident about large-scale, active government—and his chances for the White House in 1948—Governor Thomas E. Dewey called on the state legislature to complete the New York State Power Authority's Niagara River project, add huge acreages to the Forest Preserve, and expand government office space with the "state campus" at Albany. In 1948 he appointed a committee headed by Owen D. Young, retired chairman of General Electric, to recommend a state university, and wrested approval from the legislature for a system of community colleges, four-year campuses, and two medical centers. While the State University of New York (SUNY) was being cobbled together from normal schools, community colleges, and agricultural institutes to enroll 42,000, it galvanized local boosters, who lobbied for a share of the Postwar Reconstruction Fund. Dewey asked the legislature to fund a New York-to-Buffalo toll road, calling it the "Erie Canal of the Atomic Age." Delayed by the Korean War, construction reached full throttle under Superintendent of Public Works Bertram D. Tollamy, a believer in interregional highways. The gargantuan thruway, opened to motorists in 1955, required 52 interchanges and 264 bridges, including the three-mile Tappan Zee on the Hudson River, and accounted for one-fifth of all construction across the state.

Governor Dewey consolidated Albany's takeover of local social welfare programs which had been initiated under Alfred E. Smith. When federal rent controls lapsed, Dewey secured legislation to "freeze" apartment rents at July 1947 levels in major cities, including 1.4 million units in New York City. Influenced by State Housing Commissioner Herman T. Stichman, Dewey increased construction grants to the New York City Housing Authority, which quadrupled tenancy to more than 200,000 people. The legislature also aided suburban counties in health and pollution control, provided grants to consolidate school districts (which shrank from 6,397 in 1940 to 3,390 by 1950), and doubled the state's share of local welfare costs to 40 percent. Steadied by cross-party endorsements and the elevation of Catholics and Jews to the judiciary, the Court of Appeals reflected the political consensus. On the death of Chief Judge John T. Loughran in 1953, Dewey appointed Edmund H. Lewis, a moderate liberal known for the 1950 opinion that upheld the Feinberg Law, which author-

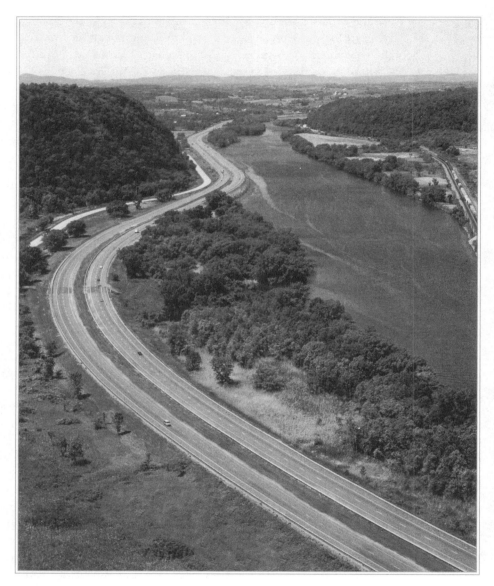

A history of New York State transportation in microcosm: the Mohawk River near Fort Plain, once a major shipping artery, joined by the New York State Thruway and State Route 5S on the left and the railroad on the right. New York State Thruway Authority.

ized school boards to fire "subversives," and for the 1951 *Jockey Club* decision, which narrowed the privileges accorded to a private club.

Advised by his legal counsel, Charles D. Breitel, and Elliott V. Bell, head of the Budget Bureau, Dewey built a strong gubernatorial office on executive budgets and "pre-veto" huddles with Assembly Speaker Oswald D. Heck and

Senate Majority Leader Irving M. Ives. Although GOP conservatives grumbled that he spent like a New Dealer, Dewey kept his budgets under $1 billion and the portion paid by the income tax to less than 23 percent. He favored "pay-as-you-go" financing, with consumption taxes on cigarettes and liquor, and users' fees like the tolls that paid for thruway bonds. His initiatives in social insurance (private-sector pension and health plans like Blue Cross–Blue Shield) were sustained by payroll deductions and state tax credits. Dewey prevailed until the 1948 presidential defeat emboldened conservatives, led by Senator Walter J. Mahoney of Buffalo, to rewrite his 1949 budget. Still, Dewey's "modern" Republicanism helped send the president of Columbia University, Dwight D. Eisenhower, to the White House in 1952 and place John Foster Dulles and Herbert Brownell in the Eisenhower cabinet.

Insurgent Democrats, armed with the issues of reform and social welfare, transformed urban politics. Union College professor Samuel S. Stratton led reformers to victory on the Schenectady City Council in 1949 and, six years later, was elected mayor on his promise to modernize the city. In Rochester, a coalition of University of Rochester professors and organized labor, led by Francis J. D'Amanda and Amalgamated Clothing Workers president Abe Chatman, ousted the local Democratic boss Roy Bush. In New York City, reformers headed by Herbert H. Lehman and Eleanor Roosevelt fought Tammany mayors William O'Dwyer and Vincent R. Impellitteri. Rallying behind issues like the Marshall Plan, urban redevelopment, and civil rights, they elected insurgents including Franklin D. Roosevelt, Jr., to Congress and forced Tammany leader Carmine De Sapio to support Robert F. Wagner, Jr., for mayor in 1953. Reform also shuffled the ethnic deck, solidifying the Democrats' appeal to Jews, African Americans, and liberal Republicans, while alienating Irish and Italians.

Behind the transformation of politics lay the arrival of racial newcomers. One-quarter of the 3.2 million blacks who left the southern cotton belt in the 1940s and 1950s came to New York State. Some 753,000 settled in New York City, spilling beyond Harlem into Morrisania in the Bronx, South Jamaica in Queens, and Bedford-Stuyvesant in Brooklyn, the state's largest African American community by 1960. Buffalo's black population tripled to 79,000, filling the East Side ghetto; migrants poured into Rochester's Baden-Ormond and Clarissa Street neighborhoods; and a small stream remade Syracuse's Fifteenth Ward. A parallel influx of Puerto Rican *jibaros* (sugar cane workers) engulfed New York City. In 1948 the city counted 200,000 Puerto Ricans, with additional arrivals entering at the rate of 45,000 per year. They overflowed *El Barrio*, East Harlem north of 96th Street, into Washington Heights and the South Bronx. By 1960 the city contained over a million African Americans and more than half a million Puerto Ricans, a total of 22 percent of the population.

On the surface the newcomers made memorable gains. In 1947 Jackie Robinson joined the Brooklyn Dodgers and broke baseball's color line. A year later Democrats elected Brooklyn's first African American assemblyman. Both

When he stepped onto Ebbets field on April 15, 1947, as a rookie with the Brooklyn Dodgers, Jackie Robinson became the first African American to play baseball in the major leagues. He won the National League's Most Valuable Player award in 1949, when he led the league with a .342 batting average and 37 stolen bases. Photograph ca. 1949. National Baseball Hall of Fame Library, Cooperstown, N.Y.

parties endorsed an African American for Manhattan borough president in the 1953 elections, making the Democrat, Hulan E. Jack, the first person of color to win the coveted post. Four years later, Buffalo Democrats nominated the first black candidate for city-wide office. New York City, Rochester, and Syracuse appointed fair housing and interracial commissions, while the Migration Office of the Commonwealth of Puerto Rico smoothed the way for Hispanics in New York City.

The influx, however, changed neighborhoods dramatically. In New York City, Jews, Italians, and Irish vacated tenements, businesses, and houses of worship in the South Bronx, East Harlem, and Brownsville, Brooklyn. Brownsville's Jews left for Queens, then Cedarhurst and Lawrence in the Five Towns, while Bushwick's Italians were drawn to Inwood, Glen Cove, and Westbury. In Syracuse the arrival of African Americans on Irving Avenue dispersed the Jewish neighborhood into suburban North Syracuse, Clay, and Fayetteville. The "turnover" was completed with the sale in 1963 of Beth Israel synagogue to Bethany Baptist, an African American congregation. The black ghetto scattered Buffalo's "Polonia" toward Kensington and suburban Cheektowaga, Alden, and Sloan. An influx of blacks into Utica in the 1950s moved the Welsh on Corn Hill into South Utica and the suburbs.

The upheaval interrupted the ethnic succession to homes and jobs. In New York City, Puerto Ricans who sought low-wage work saw cigar making and apparel manufacturing shrink with changes in the local economy. Families crowded with children (Puerto Rico's birth rate was 42.3 per 1,000 in 1945), relatives, and boarders overflowed East Harlem tenements, congested with *bodegas* (small groceries), domino players, and idle young men. Their neighborhoods, moreover, were often the target of urban redevelopment, which brought highways, upper-middle-class housing, and civic improvements. Robert Moses used federal and state funds to build the Cross-Bronx, Van Wyck, Clearview, Brooklyn-Queens, and Long Island Expressways; and Title I redevelopments which turned Bellevue Hospital into a medical center, expanded New York University on Washington Square, and fashioned Lincoln Center for the Performing Arts. By 1960 Moses had bulldozed 300,000 people, hundreds of factories, and thousands of blue-collar jobs.

Housing authorities cleared slums but avoided building new projects beyond ghetto boundaries, a policy that ravaged poor neighborhoods and increased segregation. The Lower East Side, Brownsville, and the South Bronx underwent a frenzy of slum clearance between 1947 and 1949, when the New York City Housing Authority opened "a project a month." Clearance leveled one-third of East Harlem, including 1,800 stores and a half-dozen churches for "superblocks" of twelve-to-eighteen-story buildings. Superblocks included schools, clinics, and social settlements, where trained professionals could reach families plagued by poverty, delinquency, and drugs. The basic form was observed in projects across the state. Syracuse housing administrators accepted segregated projects and "steered" applicants by race. When black families were disrupted by relocation, Syracuse called on the counseling aid of psychiatrists at the Upstate Medical Center. The Rochester Housing Authority, hesitating to move African Americans into projects planned for whites, built Hanover Houses on a superblock in Baden-Ormond with space for the Baden Settlement House.

Small cities also participated in the vogue of modernization. Binghamton and Newburgh pulled down trolley poles, replaced street lamps with fluorescents, and created parking plazas with metered slots. Under mayors Donald Kramer and John J. Burns, Binghamton broke ground for state highways on the Susquehanna riverfront, part of an $80 million redevelopment. Salamanca on the Southern Tier and Plattsburgh in the North Country established housing authorities. Plattsburgh's 150-unit project was completed with the advice of the Home Economics Department of Plattsburgh State Teachers College. Across the state, officials shared the assumption that modern housing projects, run by social welfare experts, could make model citizens of the poor.

The Suburban Trek

The suburbs boomed after World War II as New Yorkers were lured into private dwellings on the edges of cities. The GI Bill of Rights and Cold War budgets for armaments and technical research offered secure futures for young veterans. Experts like the president of Barnard College, Millicent McIntosh, told women that marriage and children came before careers. Cornell University Law School restricted female admissions to 3 percent, and an Albany Medical College dean doubted he "could ever recommend accepting a woman." In 1951, according to historian William Graebner, 99 percent of the young women at a Buffalo private school expected to marry by twenty-five. Marriage meant child bearing, and state law prohibited abortion, except as medical "therapy." The birth rate, which recorded a historic low in 1936, 13.8 per 1,000 women, climbed to 22.6 in 1947. "All my friends around me," a Long Island housewife remarked, "were busy having babies."

The nesting urge was encouraged by a host of government subsidies. Federal Housing Administration (FHA) mortgage insurance underwrote the construction of garden apartments in Queens, Ellison Park Apartments on the Rochester city line, and Loudon Arms Apartments in Albany. FHA insurance enabled small builders to construct subdivisions like Coventry Gardens and Hillaire Estates in Deer Park, Long Island. The ultimate economies in mass building were demonstrated in Levittown, Long Island, in 1947. Using nonunion crews to pour concrete-slab floors and install modular plumbing (mass-produced off-site), William J. Levitt sold FHA-insured Cape Cod homes for $7,990. "They showed us several houses," a woman remembered, "and told us for a hundred dollars down we could move into a house that had venetian blinds, a washing machine, and refrigerator." Levitt went on to build 17,447 houses on Long Island. Construction in Westchester, Nassau, and Suffolk Counties accounted for nearly 40 percent of the state's residential starts through 1951.

The subsidies included generous government spending on infrastructure. Federal dollars underwrote Hancock Field outside Syracuse, Buffalo Airport in Cheektowaga, the new focus of Erie County's aviation industry, and the Port Authority of New York and New Jersey's international field at Idlewild, Queens. Nassau, Suffolk, and Westchester Counties were opened up by Moses's Long Island Expressway, Sunrise Highway Extension, Saw Mill River Parkway, and the federally funded New England Thruway. Local governments cooperated with zoning ordinances and special districts. Binghamton politicians organized Kirkwood Industrial Park, and Buffalo realtors opened Niagara Industrial Park in the town of Wheatfield. Onondaga Republicans lobbied Superintendent Bertram Tollamy for five thruway exits at Syracuse, convenient to GE's Electronic Park at Liverpool and Syracuse Industrial Park, which attracted Carrier's two-million-square-foot plant. The suburban town of De Witt adopted industrial zoning for a factory complex which by 1960 employed 20,000 workers, one-third the manufacturing force in metropolitan Syracuse.

Highways and industrial zones helped Nassau and Suffolk Counties create the state's third-largest manufacturing complex, employing nearly 111,000 workers in 1954. Pentagon spending during the Korean War underlay most of the boom. Long Island's Big Five contractors—Republic, Grumman, Sperry,

Fairchild, and American Bosch Arma—needed huge production space (5 million square feet for Republic's F-84 fighter), not to mention the requirements of 2,200 local subcontractors. By 1960, 75,000 Nassau defense jobs had generated 125,000 others in related work and provided the livelihood for half the county's 1.3 million people.

Corporate headquarters were also drawn to suburban sites. After General Foods left midtown Manhattan for White Plains in 1954, Westchester's green pastures lured Standard-Vacuum Oil, Allstate Insurance, and regional offices of Union Carbide and General Electric. Tarrytown was favored for corporate research centers, including General Foods and Mallory Battery. The corporate environment, for instance Standard-Vacuum's, featured dining halls, recreation rooms, and "music while you work." Many, like IBM headquarters in Armonk, resembled college campuses, with landscaped gardens, reflecting pools, and parking lots. In the mid-1950s realtors found that every one hundred employees required sixty cars, whose owners drove from other suburbs. One-third were female, including suburban wives earning what the realtors condescendingly termed "secondary" incomes.

Suburban mobility required shopping facilities geared to the automobile. The earliest were uptown store "strips" with recessed parking like the Sheridan Shopping Plaza in Tonawanda and South Salina Plaza in Syracuse. Arterial highways, however, brought volumes of cars that required stores arranged around parking lots on the pattern of Thruway Plaza, which opened in Cheektowaga in 1952 with space for 2,360 cars, and Rochester's Northgate, developed by Emil Muller in 1955 for twenty-four stores, including a McCurdy's department store. Developers soon saw the advantage of self-contained, all-weather environments—shopping "malls" located near the interchanges of superhighways. In 1956 Long Island developers opened Roosevelt Field in Garden City, Green Acres in Valley Stream, and Mid-Island Plaza in Hicksville. Roosevelt Field was the island's first "mall" and, at the time, the world's largest shopping center, with 120 acres of parking and 2.2 million square feet of enclosed retail space, including Macy's largest suburban store.

Downtowns could not match suburban centers' prices, inventory, and what developer James W. Rouse called the informality of families in "shorts, jeans, open shirts and slacks." Aggressive "discounters" like Eugene Ferkauf sold appliances out of the box, profiting from volume sales. His E. J. Korvette's sprouted in White Plains, Hempstead, and Carle Place, Westbury, the banner store that opened to phenomenal crowds during Christmas 1953. Between 1954 and 1958, downtown New York City's share of regional sales slid from nearly half to 41 percent, Buffalo's from 54 to 48 percent, and Rochester's from 89 to 75 percent. In 1958 Monroe County's Northgate, Irondequoit, and giant South Town malls had 37 percent of Rochester's downtown volume, and two of Buffalo's largest centers, Thruway Plaza and L. B. Simpson Plaza, did three-quarters of downtown's business. By the mid-1960s Long Island malls, "anchored" by retailers like Abraham & Straus, Macy's, and Gimbels, were a $4 billion market, fourth largest (after New York City, Los Angeles, and Chicago) in the country.

The suburbs were a demi-paradise for nuclear families struggling on single incomes and homemakers caught in the suburban "trap." Ranches and Cape Cods were built on separate forty-foot lots on residential streets far from commercial centers, a separation that guarded the peace of family life but required a car. Kitchens faced front lawns so that mothers could mind the children, and living rooms looked on backyards through Thermopane windows. Wives complained of stress from child bearing, while men decried less frequent sex. The living room was meant for togetherness, but middle-class status required that each child have a bedroom for individual growth. Parents soon learned that suburban ranch houses made for competitive and costly consumption.

In houses that were too small for extended families and too distant from old city neighborhoods, suburban living weakened ethnic loyalties except where they reinforced a home owner's solidarity. The leader of Rochester's Ukrainian Civic Center lamented that suburban "young people" no longer took "interest in our work and ideas." Buffalo's "Polonia" scattered into suburban parishes like Saint Josaphat in Cheektowaga and Saint Andrews in Sloan, where family contact was kept by women over the phone. Irish and Italian ethnicity faded into a middle-class Catholic culture built around family rites, which drew adult males to communion. Conservative and Reform Jewish "centers" took root in North Syracuse and Clay, New Rochelle and Scarsdale in Westchester, and a host of communities on Long Island, even though few families observed dietary laws or orthodox rituals. According to sociologists, subdued ethnicity was creating a "triple melting pot": a generalized Catholicism among Irish, Italians, and Poles; growing intermarriage between Protestants and Jews; and a separate sphere for African Americans.

Racial discrimination defined the suburbs as segregated preserves. Exclusion of nonwhites was abetted by large-scale builders and realtors, often with the connivance of the FHA. According to the historian Kenneth T. Jackson, not a single African American was among Levittown's 82,000 residents in 1960; Levitt refused to sell to blacks. Zoning laws, which blanketed Westchester, Nassau, Monroe, and Erie Counties by the mid-1950s, provided a de facto restriction. Barring apartment houses and other "incompatible" uses, zoning limited African Americans to cheap rental units in old suburbs. While Westchester's nonwhite population reached 7.2 percent by 1960, 42 percent of these minorities lived in Mount Vernon and New Rochelle. The villages of Roosevelt and Wyandanch became black enclaves in Nassau County, the same way that Lackawanna gave African Americans limited access to suburban Erie County.

Homeowner demands for services transformed suburban government. A centralization trend had begun in the late 1930s when GOP bosses like Westchester's William F. Bleakley and Nassau's J. Russel Sprague took advantage of home-rule legislation to supplement boards of supervisors with urban-style county executives. Still, postwar newcomers often chafed at the primitive level of services. In the 1940s, the Taxpayers' Association of the Motor Parkway Acreage and Deer Park Non-Partisan League badgered Nassau County for fire protection, garbage removal, and mail delivery. Most voters, as in the Long Island communities of Levittown, Port Jefferson, East Meadow, and Franklin Square, chose the system of special districts, which taxed separately for water and fire service, sewerage lines, and garbage collection.

The chance that suburbs might access downtown "ratables," prime taxable property, in Rochester, Utica, Syracuse, and Buffalo clinched the argument for county responsibility. With state enabling legislation, Suffolk (in 1958), Oneida (1961), and Erie (1962) adopted county charters and elected executives. Onondaga County Republican chairman Rolland Marvin steered acceptance of the county executive form in 1962 to coordinate water pollution controls, planning, and public health in metropolitan Syracuse. With a substantial portion of the Rochester sales tax, Monroe County took over city and town public health, planning, highways, welfare aid, and park police. In 1961, Westchester County created bureaus for county parks, construction and planning, and budget, making County Executive Edwin G. Michaelian one of the country's most powerful suburban politicians.

Fifteen years of suburban growth after World War II redistributed New York State's population. In 1945 the "Big Six" cities (New York, Buffalo, Rochester, Syracuse, Albany, and Yonkers) had three-fourths of the state's population, while New York City alone had 58 percent. During the 1950s, growth in the Buffalo–Niagara Falls region shifted to residential suburbs like Cheektowaga, Williamsville, and Depew and to industrial concentrations like Tonawanda and Lockport. Along the thruway north and west of Syracuse, such towns as Clay, Salina, and Camillus boomed; and Webster, Penfield, and Henrietta in Monroe County gained a total of 100,000, while Rochester lost 16,414. Nassau County, whose phenomenal population surge after the war reached 672,765 in 1950, added nearly 600,000 more during the following decade. By 1960 New York City had slipped to 46 percent, while the Big Six plunged to 54.6 percent of the state's population, and Nassau and Suffolk Counties held 11 percent. Suburban sprawl merged New York City, Long Island, Westchester and Rockland Counties into a "megalopolis" that stretched from Boston to Washington.

Adding Value

Dewey liberalism and the suburban trend depended upon the state's economy, which led the nation in manufacturing. In the late 1940s, one-third of America's clothes were stitched by 424,000 workers in Manhattan's garment center. Buffalo contained General Mills's flour mill, the world's largest, and Bethlehem Steel's Lackawanna Works, the fourth largest. Durable goods manufacturers like International Business Machines, Carrier, and Eastman Kodak kept state factory wages 10 percent above the nation's. New York liberals boasted of the mature relationship achieved between capitalism and industrial unions, although often it was less a matter of attitude than the ability of many firms to afford that amity because of the profits of oligopolistic markets, "basing point" price protections, and positions astride the Northeast. Already, however, there were portents of change. Carrier's control of the office and department store market blinded it to the growth of suburban demand for room air conditioners. In the early 1950s Otis Elevator lost market share outside the Northeast, prompting executives to warn two thousand Yonkers employees that their union would have to accept wage cuts or the plant would close.

Market share and government contracts often determined whether companies maintained amicable relations with industrial workers. Remington Rand, which made typewriters and Kardex tabulators in Elmira and Ilion, was a union buster in the 1930s but reached a postwar contract with the United Electrical Workers (UE) of the CIO. The company led the office equipment industry during its greatest expansion, while Rand engineers tinkered with a vacuum-tube calculating device, called UNIVAC, which the U.S. Atomic Energy Commission (AEC) acquired for research on the hydrogen bomb. Eastman Kodak's dominance of postwar film and camera markets, on the other hand, sustained its penchant for a welfare capitalism of solid wages, job security, and pensions. In turn, "the Yellow Father," as Rochester workers called Kodak, regimented its 40,000 employees, particularly "coaters" who spread silver emulsion in dark, cavernous, dust-free rooms. While CIO victories at Smith-Corona and GM Products perturbed Rochester's "open-shop" regime, Kodak's retirement and medical plans fended off the United Electrical Workers.

Remington Rand's chief rival, IBM, was a $140 million corporation that Thomas J. Watson, Sr., kept profitable through the rental of typewriters, IBM punch-cards, and processors. After he turned control over to Thomas, Jr., in 1947, IBM plowed $19 million into vacuum-tube research at Poughkeepsie and Endicott and produced the 702 and 705 machines that overtook UNIVAC. IBM's real asset, the Watson managerial style, kept a disciplined sales force and nonunion assembly workers satisfied with "job enlargement" benefits. By the time a 1956 antitrust decree forced the company to sell (rather than rent) business products, the IBM Selectric had captured 18 percent of the U.S. typewriter market, IBM mainframes were in scores of corporate offices, and the company's export arm, IBM World Trade, was stirring global demand for data processors.

General Electric joined the shift toward small-batch output, services, and production outside the region. Led by Charles E. Wilson and Ralph J. Cordiner, GE built a quarter-mile-long Schenectady plant that fabricated half the country's turbine generators and a Syracuse plant that mass-produced television sets. By 1954, however, 14 percent of GE's gross income came from engineering services like management of the Syracuse Heavy Weapons Division for the U.S. Army and the Knolls Atomic Power Laboratory outside Schenectady for the AEC. The company consolidated production of television sets at Syracuse's Electronics Park, assembled refrigerators, washers, and other durables in Louisville, Kentucky, and provided jet engine services for the U.S. Air Force in Ohio. Facing down the UE during a bitter strike in 1946, GE employee-relations chief Lemuel R. Boulware handed the union take-it-or-leave-it contracts and used the federal Taft-Hartley Act of 1947 to divide the Schenectady rank and file.

Two-thirds of state factory workers made nondurable products such as leather, textiles, and apparel in aging plants that were the mainstays of small towns. Carpet manufacturers in Amsterdam and Gloversville were hit hard by competition from low-wage southern mills. Mohasco moved its carpet production from Amsterdam to Georgia and tried to diversify into home furnishings. Decreased demand for hand-crafted furniture shut down Jamestown's workshops, ending two generations of Swedish woodworking on the Southern Tier. When Utica-Rome's textile mills slashed operations, they handed Oneida and Herkimer Counties 15 percent unemployment in 1948. Binghamton's largest employer, Endicott Johnson, lost market share to manufacturers of light, suburban styles and women's footwear. Across the state, steady jobs in nondurables dropped by 104,000 between 1947 and 1957.

The largest decrease occurred in New York City, which had one-third of its workforce in manufacturing in 1950. The city made an array of nondurables like apparel, books, and foods in small plants with small capital investment. Between 1947 and 1954, as factory jobs surged in New Jersey and on Long Island, those in the city slipped by 4 percent. Losses included 40,000 workers in the garment center and a shrinkage in food processing, including Nabisco's West Side plant in 1958. During the decade, six hundred manufacturers of electrical appliances and radio parts closed or moved to Long Island. Interstate trucking forced out brewers like Ebling in Manhattan and made Brooklyn's Piel Brothers a subsidiary of a midwestern firm. Manufacturers complained of taxes, labor costs, and lack of space for modern, single-story plants. The city's decline helped erase the state's lead in factory wages to just a penny an hour above the national average by 1957.

New York's industrial prowess and market position had made politicians complacent about the fate of manufacturing. In 1944 Governor Dewey created a Department of Commerce to collect statistics and trumpet the state's natural advantages. Rochester experimented with municipal aid to researchers and inventors. Most efforts, however, were quick fixes like the Syracuse GOP's attempt to lure plants to Onondaga County or Utica boss Rufus Elefante's zoning deals to attract out-of-state companies.

Service Cities

While factory employment steadied between 1947 and 1957, service jobs grew by 618,000, a nearly 17 percent increase. During the national recession in 1958, manufacturing was overtaken by services, which employed 35 percent of the state labor force and earned nearly half the state's income. Services were both a product and an accelerant of postwar change. They concentrated office bureaucracies in central business districts, provided white-collar careers that humbled blue-collar ambitions, and lured unprecedented numbers of women into stores and offices.

Across the state, civic leaders pursued the growth potential of finance, data processing, and higher education. Led by Chancellor William P. Tolley, Syracuse University's 6,000-student campus became a "multiversity" in the late 1950s, with college and graduate enrollment of 26,000 and off-campus centers in Utica, Rome, Endicott (Harpur College), and Poughkeepsie. The university worked with the Metropolitan Development Association to promote academic and industrial research for the Syracuse economy. In Utica the chamber of commerce's development corporation attracted an extension campus of Syracuse University and state aid for the Mohawk Valley Technical Institute. Civic leaders had similar ambitions for the University of Buffalo, which, under Chancellors Samuel P. Capen and Thomas R. McConnell, added basic science facilities for its schools of medicine and dentistry, and a nuclear research program.

The critical mass of services in New York City led academics to herald the nation's "first city," which connected America to the world. In 1960 Gotham was still America's corporate capital, with headquarters for 128 *Fortune* 500 industrials, and dominated finance, law, advertising, and publishing. Offices were in curtain-walled towers designed in the international style like the Lever Brothers Building on Park Avenue, with architecture by Gordon Bunshaft of Skidmore, Owings & Merrill, marble and steel lobby by abstract sculptor Isamu Noguchi, and indoor air by Carrier. The city was also home to the United Nations, philanthropies like the Ford Foundation, growing universities, and research complexes including the Rockefeller Institute and the Memorial–Sloan Kettering Cancer Center. Banker David Rockefeller, lawyer John J. McCloy, and NYU chancellor Henry T. Heald helped Robert Moses encourage "post-industrial" growth.

Despite the shift of U.S. monetary authority to Washington, New York City remained not only America's financial capital but, with Great Britain's decline, the seat of world trade and finance. The Port of New York handled more than half of U.S. imports and 40 percent of its exports, while in 1947 La Guardia's runways received 80 percent of all inbound air cargo. The city did a quarter of the country's wholesale business, particularly in dry goods, jewelry, and home furnishings. Commodity traders on Canal and Water Streets handled one-third of U.S. copper sales and over half the trade in coffee, tea, and spices.

Wall Street, thanks to New Deal regulations that encouraged individual investors, saw 2-million-share days on the New York Stock Exchange (NYSE) become routine in the 1950s. The Big Board, along with the smaller American Stock Exchange, handled 92 percent of the country's equity trades and enforced NYSE Rule 390 barring members from trading listed stocks on regional exchanges including Chicago and San Francisco. City underwriters like Kuhn, Loeb; Goldman Sachs; Lehman Brothers; and Morgan, Stanley divided among themselves 70 percent of the national market in corporate bonds and securities. Rival commercial banks, Chase and First National City, absorbed small institutions and moved spectacularly, along with Chemical Bank and Trust Company, into branch banking and consumer loans. Their trust departments expanded with New Deal labor-management policies that induced corporations to develop pension funds. By the mid-1960s Chase Manhattan's Pension Fund Department handled Ford, General Motors, and some 1,200 other corporate plans, with total assets of $4.5 billion, and advised on an equal volume of public funds.

Other corporate services included public relations by firms like Burson-Marsteller, which became the largest in the world. The city had six of the nation's Big Eight accounting firms, including Price Waterhouse and Peat, Marwick, Mitchell. While these firms were small partnerships (Peat, Marwick grossed under $10 million in 1947) that specialized in corporate audits, they handled 90 percent of the companies listed on the NYSE. By the late 1950s New York City was home to twenty-one of the thirty-eight largest American law firms in terms of client billings. Some had begun to outgrow the "Cravath system," which groomed young "associates," mostly WASP Ivy Leaguers, for partnership, while hiring only token Irish Catholics and Jews, few women, and no blacks. Companies tapped such elite firms to advise on complicated overseas matters, while institutional investors like insurance companies and pension funds called on commercial banks and their counsel to handle private placements of public utilities and special authorities such as the Triborough Bridge and Tunnel Authority.

New York advertising flourished as oligopolistic firms guarded market share with brand loyalty and indelible images. Few Madison Avenue "shops" conjured up better imagery than Ted Bates, whose creative stars were David Ogilvy and his brother-in-law Rosser Reeves. Ogilvy made an icon of the man with an eyepatch and a Hathaway shirt, and Reeves proved successful with the televised "hard sell," particularly his thirty-second Alka-Seltzer commercial, depicting headaches as a pounding hammer. Reeves's faith in the "unique selling proposition" (i.e., slogans endlessly repeated) drove Ted Bates's billings from $16 million at the end of World War II to $130 million by 1960. A chief rival, Batten, Barton, Durstine & Osborn, expanded its media department from a staff of twelve in 1948 to 150 in the mid-1950s, while billings increased sixfold. One response to the mammoth growth was McCann-Erickson, whose market research, overseas operations, and aggressive buyouts of smaller shops produced an unwieldy management structure. In 1960 it reorganized as Interpublic, a veritable conglomerate with operating subdivisions in advertising, market research, and publicity.

New York publishing was still a genteel world where editors like Kurt Wolff of Pantheon Books and Alfred A. Knopf personally handled Nobel Prize authors and worried about the Society for the Suppression of Vice, which had Edmund Wilson's *Memoirs of Hecate County* (1946) declared obscene and banned in New York State. But the book trade, as M. Lincoln Schuster cracked, was fast becoming "Hollywoodized, networked, televisioned, merged, and high pressured." After the war, Simon & Schuster was sold to Field Enterprises, which controlled newspapers, radio stations, and Pocket Books; Texas oilman Clint Murchison bought Henry Holt; and Nelson Doubleday plunged into book clubs and mail-order advertising. The new corporate ethic had a profound impact on postwar culture. Simon & Schuster's mail order and supermarket sales made Golden Books a fixture of baby boom life. After Holt quadrupled its college sales force and came to dominate the textbook trade, rivals jumped into the university market. Few succeeded as thoroughly as Doubleday's subsidiary, Anchor Books, developed by *wunderkind* Jason Epstein, whose quality paperbacks transformed the curriculum as professors increasingly assigned cheap classics in the social sciences and humanities.

With a special flair, New York publishers made the paperback central to American mass culture. During World War II, Pocket Books issued a $1 Collector's Edition and New American Library sold 50-cent Giant editions, while Bantam Books hit pay dirt with reprints tied to movie releases. When Ian Ballantine left Bantam in 1952 to found Ballantine Books, publishing simultaneous cloth and paperback editions, his success touched off a bidding war for new authors. Ballantine moved into science fiction with works like Ray Bradbury's *Fahrenheit 451* (1953), and pleased adolescent tastes with *The Mad Reader* (1954). Competition drew publishers toward what one writer called "the Three S's"—sex, sadism, and the smoking gun. Mickey Spillane's potboilers, starting with *I, the Jury* (1947), sold 24 million copies, mostly 25-cent New American Library editions. By 1953 Bantam, New American Library, Dell, Popular, and Pocket Books dominated an industry which that year churned out 1,061 titles and 259 million copies.

The city commanded television during its "golden age." TV emerged from New York radio, which depended on vaudeville veterans, Borscht Belt humor, and political liberalism, and on corporate sponsors like Procter and Gamble, who owned programs, often in partnership with their ad agencies. In the late 1940s the city's six TV stations made up nearly one-tenth of the nation's

A clown and his dog perform in 1949 for the cameras of General Electric's pioneering television station, WRGB Schenectady. General News Bureau, General Electric Company.

broadcasters, and its "sets"—nearly half of the country's one million—were tuned to hometown favorites like Milton Berle's Saturday night comedy hour. The city contributed serious drama like the *Goodyear Television Playhouse*, which aired Paddy Chayefsky's *Marty* in 1953. Rising profits encouraged Columbia Broadcasting System owner William S. Paley and National Broadcasting Company executive Sylvester ("Pat") Weaver to assume direct production (and ownership) of programs, for which the network sold advertising "slots." Weaver perfected the approach on new shows that included *Today* and *Tonight*.

Audience growth, however, loosened Manhattan's hold on the medium. Multiple sponsors craved national audiences, measured by A. C. Nielsen ratings, and "spectaculars," costly programs that forced production to cheap locales like Television City, Paley's Hollywood studio, which opened in 1952. Shifting audiences also proved fickle toward New York material, and when the American Broadcasting Company purchased Warner Brothers telefilms, mainly westerns, in 1956, the networks stampeded to Hollywood. By then, only one major entertainment form was produced in New York: quiz shows, notably *The $64,000 Question* and *Twenty-One*. The gaudy contests were dogged by charges of fakery that were heard by a Manhattan grand jury. But for sensation nothing matched the congressional hearings in 1959, when a former contestant, Columbia University professor Charles Van Doren, admitted that he had been coached on *Twenty-One*. The bombshell ended the last made-in-New York product on network television.

Production costs kept out the city's other homegrown medium—movies—except when Hollywood needed lurid backgrounds for late 1940s film noir. The city attracted such directors as Stanley Donen, whose *On the Town* (1945) improvised location shots, and Jules Dassin, who gave *The Naked City* (1948) a documentary look. Elia Kazan's *On the Waterfront* (1953), while shot in Hoboken, New Jersey, caught the "crucifixion" of the city's working class. To early 1950s anticommunists, however, New York's grimy *verité* was suspect, along with its left-wing politics. Aside from the experimental "trance" films of Maya Deren and modest commercial ventures like Morris Engel's *Little Fugitive* (1953) and John Cassavetes's *Shadows* (1959), the movies stayed in Hollywood.

Postwar affluence, television, and the suburban trek transformed city life. They brought the demise of working-class institutions, street games like stickball, and neighborhood standbys like the *New York Mirror* and *Brooklyn Eagle*, bowling alleys and taverns. At the Long Island Bowl, Sunnyside Stadium, and other arenas, attendance dwindled for boxing, wrestling, and roller derby (which enjoyed brief exposure on local TV, then disappeared). Organized crime withered after La Guardia's attacks on "tin-horn" gamblers, prosecutions by New York District Attorney Frank S. Hogan, and the dispersal of neighborhood bookies. Fans casually bet on high school and college games, including those allegedly thrown by CCNY's champion basketball team in 1950. But that pastime, too, went out of fashion.

Urban change distanced fans from professional sports that had become large franchises. In 1954 National Basketball Association clubs, led by Syracuse owner Danny Biasone and Knicks owner Ned Irish, ended the Rochester Royals' control of the stalled dribbling game by changing the rules to impose the twenty-four-second clock and a limit on team fouls. Syracuse won the 1955 NBA championship, but in 1957 the Rochester Royals became the first NBA franchise to leave a "small market city." A similar crisis confronted New York City's three baseball clubs, when attendance at home games slumped 42 percent in the ten years after 1947. In 1957 Dodger owner Walter O'Malley quit Brooklyn for Los Angeles's parking space and media revenues and dragged Horace Stoneham's Giants to the West Coast with him. It was the cruelest change of all.

The Center Holds

New York's liberal capitalism earned guarded praise from intellectuals disillusioned with left-wing politics. Some ex-Communists saw in Stalinism the terrible will-to-power described by Christian realists like Reinhold Niebuhr of Union Theological Seminary. Others abandoned Marxist dialectics to seek truth in literature. At *Partisan Review*, the Trotskyist magazine edited by Philip Rahv, critics Mary McCarthy, Delmore Schwartz, and Lionel Trilling judged writers by how well they hewed to a standard of "moral realism" that kept freedom alive. The *PR*'s polemics against Stalin's apologists in the *New Republic*, the *Nation*, and *P.M.* changed the minds of a generation of intellectuals. Many vowed with Diana Trilling, the *Nation*'s fiction critic, never again to be gulled by Communism's pretense.

In early 1947, intellectuals and reform Democrats, spearheaded by Eleanor Roosevelt, Reinhold Niebuhr, and *New York Post* editor James Wechsler, founded the Americans for Democratic Action (ADA) to defend President Harry S. Truman's anti-Soviet foreign policy against challenger Henry Wallace, whom they branded a Communist stooge. At the 1949 Waldorf-Astoria Conference, convened by Stalinist apologists Lillian Hellman, Paul Robeson, and Leonard Bernstein, *Partisan Review* activists asked why Stalin had jailed Russian dissidents. Intellectuals who gagged on American mass culture nonetheless enlisted in the Cold War.

Grudging approval of America's material ways turned to celebrations of American "pluralism," particularly on college campuses undergoing postwar change. Ivy halls had been remarkably insular places. In 1945 Syracuse University sought freshmen with "good citizenship and responsibility," while Columbia College looked for "social adaptability, community spirit, manliness." Oswego State Normal School had compulsory chapel, forbade women from smoking, and regarded Jews and Italians as exotics from "the city." The war shook up the curriculum, as did hordes of veterans on the GI Bill. New students and perspectives forced universities to cut through disciplinary lines and hastened the trend toward "area" studies. A flood of applicants came from urban areas, particularly Jewish students, who attended college at twice the rate of non-Jews. Campus life exemplified the opportunity America gave to the children of immigrants.

Universities became complex operations tied to business and government. Cornell's enrollment rose from six thousand to ten thousand after the war. It tripled housing for married veterans, built laboratories for industrial and nuclear research, and endowed schools of business and labor relations. Cornell's engineering program took over the Curtiss-Wright Aeronautical Laboratory in Buffalo, and in the 1950s Cornell joined Associated Universities, Inc., which ran

Brookhaven National Laboratory, the nuclear facility on Long Island. Alfred University, a Seventh-Day Baptist college on the Southern Tier, underwent a $600,000 construction campaign under President M. Ellis Drake, who built new dormitories and guided its transition into a secular institution. Nearby, the New York State Agricultural and Technical Institute expanded under the leadership of President Paul B. Orvis, a Marshall Plan administrator, who envisioned scientific agriculture enriching the postwar world.

The sense of "pluralist" opportunity shifted attention from skeptics like Hannah Arendt at the New School for Social Research, who accused "mass society" of grinding individuals into aimless particles. Columbia University political scientist David B. Truman, by contrast, hailed the post–New Deal matrix of corporations, labor unions, and associations that gave individuals a sense of belonging. The Maxwell School of Citizenship and Public Affairs at Syracuse University studied decision-making and community politics in Onondaga County and found power loosely dispersed. Conservatives, who charged that the "statist" New Deal had destroyed small-scale America, were ridiculed as nostalgic carpers, blind to the benefits of complex, large-scale institutions which spread wealth and fostered opportunity. Cornell University professor Clinton Rossiter traced conservatism's pedigree to eighteenth-century New England churchmen and the Founding Fathers, research that proved, he complained, to be an unappreciated, "thankless" exercise. Anti–New Dealers protested that pluralist academics wrote them off as "compulsive Catholics," if not paranoid, which was the judgment of Columbia University historian Richard Hofstadter.

Robbed of ideological nerve and drawn to the corporate profits of the Cold War, left-wingers moved to the political center. In June 1947 the New York Newspaper Guild elected a slate of anti-Communist officers. On the New York City waterfront, Joe Curran purged Communists from the National Maritime Union. In Schenectady and Rochester, James Carey's Roman Catholic movement, the United Electrical Members for Democratic Action, used anti-Communist affidavits required by the Taft-Hartley Act of 1947 to drive out Communist officers so that the union could bargain with General Electric, Remington Rand, and General Motors. Michael Quill, the fiery president of the International Transportation Workers Union, had to moderate his views when an anticommunist faction demanded less concern for the "proletariat" and more for wage gains. In New York City, the Teachers Guild's attacks forced Communists from the ranks of the rival CIO Teachers Union. With the purge accomplished, the unions merged in 1960 as Local 2 of the United Federation of Teachers (UFT). Political fears, along with postwar inflation and suburban economic priorities, moved labor to the pragmatic center.

The middle ground was accommodated by liberal New York City, whose municipal services vastly increased the union labor force. Despite the Condon-

Wadlin Law of 1947, which forbade strikes by public employees, Jerry Wurf's District Council 37 of the Public Service Union dueled with rival Teamsters Local 237 for the hearts and minds of service workers. Wurf defied Robert Moses and organized Parks Department workers, an affront that forced Mayor Robert F. Wagner, Jr., in 1955, to issue an executive order that regularized collective bargaining. By 1965 Wurf claimed 25,000 of the city's white-collar employees in District Council 37. Steady campaigns by UFT Local 2 gained 50,000 teachers, and a 1961 victory in bargaining elections gave union president Albert Shanker national prominence.

The politics of employment turned Socialists into mainstream Democrats and Liberals. By the mid-1950s, the Liberal party had become a political machine controlled by Alex Rose of the United Hatters, Cap, and Millinery Workers Union, which traded Liberal endorsements (worth some 400,000 votes) for Democratic patronage. Rose's influence lent support to the Mitchell-Lama Law of 1955, which gave state subsidies to developers of middle-class housing, particularly the cooperative apartments sponsored by the needle-trades' United Housing Foundation. With Robert Moses's Title I help and Mitchell-Lama subsidies, the UHF built Cooperative Village on the Lower East Side, Rochedale Village in Queens, and the mammoth 25,372-unit Co-op City in the Bronx. Property ownership and retirement benefits completed the political domestication of the Jewish left.

New York's materialism turned religion toward the ruddy modernism of Harry Emerson Fosdick, pastor of Riverside Church, and the "positive thinking" of Dr. Norman Vincent Peale of Marble Collegiate Church. Judaism flourished in middle-class Conservative and Reform temples and in the Reconstructionist movement shaped by Rabbi Mordecai M. Kaplan, who downplayed divine intervention and Jewish "chosenness." Comparable growth occurred in large, middle-class African American congregations like Abyssinian Baptist and Saint Philip's Episcopal in Harlem, which looked down on storefront "holiness" churches. A confident modernism eased, if it did not chase away, grim thoughts. The Holocaust remained a personal meditation, as Jews concentrated on the challenge of founding the State of Israel. Under Francis Cardinal Spellman, the Catholic archdiocese focused on such practicalities as the struggle against Communism and the organization of suburban parishes. Only a few were drawn to Dorothy Day's Catholic Worker movement, which extended charity to the Bowery homeless.

The Established Arts

While prosperity fostered arts across the state, it entrenched the authority of Manhattan's grand stages and museums, where established culture triumphed.

The city, of course, had a diverse avant-garde. Otto Luening, a Columbia University professor, composed electronic music on RCA synthesizers, and Miles Davis and Thelonius S. Monk were turning Charlie Parker's bebop into a more spare "cool" jazz. Dissident painters held forth in Greenwich Village bars, and writers like William S. Burroughs and Frank O'Hara were subverting literary convention. For the time being, however, New York was more at home with brand-name classics.

The University of Rochester's Eastman School of Music vied with Columbia University and the Juilliard School as patrons of classical composition. Howard Hanson, head of the Eastman School of Music and director of the Eastman-Rochester Symphony, and Eastman professor Bernard Rogers penned romantic symphonies and trained a generation of conservative composers like Norman Dello Joio. Aaron Copland's pursuit of an American sound inspired Morton Gould's *Fall River Legend* (1948), Samuel Barber and Gian Carlo Menotti's opera *Vanessa* (1958), and William Schuman's symphonies, which mixed romanticism with jazz and American pop. But intellectual fashion was drawn to twelve-tone "serialism," a highly abstract system of composition. It affected Elliott Carter's chamber music, pieces written "with a minimal concern for their reception," and Copland's less accessible works like *Piano Quartet* (1950) and *Connotations* (1962). Another influence was the unabashed experimentalism of John Cage. Aided by his partner in whimsy, the modern dancer Merce Cunningham, Cage assembled sounds and Zen spells of silence into aleatory—random—taped mixes. While Cage remained a performance curiosity, his ideas attracted younger composers restless under the twelve-tone regime.

In the meantime, the music establishment thrived on spectacle. At the Metropolitan Opera, manager Rudolf Bing staged Puccini and Verdi for divas like Maria Callas, leaving the New York City Opera, the first major company conducted by an American, Julius Rudel, to debut homegrown works including Barnard professor Douglas Moore's *Ballad of Baby Doe* (1958). While modernist Martha Graham continued to draw audiences to what she called her "ancestral footsteps," dance was dominated by the New York City Ballet, founded in 1948 by Lincoln Kirstein and George Balanchine to impose classic Russian form on naive Americans. The New York Philharmonic was in the hands of Leonard Bernstein, who moved its repertory toward the work of twentieth-century Americans like Copland and Schuman, starred on CBS Television's "Young People's Concerts," and contracted with Columbia Records for the series of Philharmonic recordings, particularly of Stravinsky, that revived the classical music industry. When the U.S. State Department wanted to display American culture at the height of the Cold War, it sent Bernstein and Balanchine on festive European tours.

The late 1940s and early 1950s were golden years for Broadway theater. The success of Richard Rodgers and Oscar Hammerstein's *Oklahoma!* (1943) ushered in an era of wondrous musicals, which included Alan Jay Lerner and Frederick Loewe's beguiling fantasy, *Brigadoon* (1947); Cole Porter's *Kiss Me, Kate* (1948), a vivacious and sarcastic look at show business and Shakespeare; and Rodgers and Hammerstein's memorable and moving hits, *South Pacific* (1949) and *The King and I* (1953). Other highlights included *Wonderful Town* (1953), the satire on Greenwich Village by Leonard Bernstein and Betty Comden and Adolph Green; Frank Loesser's *Guys and Dolls* (1950), whose protagonist was Broadway itself; and Lerner and Loewe's *My Fair Lady* (1956).

Broadway's dramatic tone was shaped by the Group Theatre alumni Lee Strasberg, Elia Kazan, and Cheryl Crawford, who founded the Actors Studio in 1947. The studio's "Method," a system of breathing exercises and introspection, taught actors to draw upon latent memories to convey emotions and had a cult following in New York. Method found its match in Tennessee Williams's *Glass Menagerie* (1945) and *A Streetcar Named Desire* (1947), for which director Kazan cast Marlon Brando, who delivered an electrifying performance. In 1947, Kazan also directed Arthur Miller's debut play, *All My Sons*, which exposed a conniver to his children and foreshadowed Miller's classic of paternal shame, *Death of a Salesman* (1949). William Inge, Robert Anderson, and William Gibson completed the lineup of "serious" playwrights. Half art form, half money machine, Broadway was a network of theatrical businesses, midtown nightclubs and restaurants, and Actors Equity, the union that enforced standard wages. During the 1949–50 season, Broadway opened eighty-seven Equity-scale productions.

In the visual arts, the avant-garde was dominated by the "New York School" of abstract expressionists, which included Robert Motherwell, Lee Krasner, and, above all, Willem de Kooning and Krasner's husband, Jackson Pollock, the movement's celebrity. Pollock flicked paint on canvases stretched on the floor, an almost physical attack which critic Clement Greenberg saw as heroic struggle with form and color on the "picture plane." Alfred H. Barr, Jr., director of the Museum of Modern Art, gave abstract expression a crucial endorsement, but the Whitney Museum stayed with established realists like Edward Hopper and showcased others like Robert Gwathmey, Isabel Bishop, and Fairfield Porter. It was still possible for a primitive artist like Ralph Fasanella to paint his Lower East Side neighbors with an utter fidelity to their faces and livelihoods. Still, Pollock's pulsating canvases stirred postwar New York, influencing John Cage's random sounds, the "action writing" of poets like Frank O'Hara and John Ashbery, and filmmaker Stan Brakhage's drips and scratches on celluloid.

The modern realist novel dominated the New York literary scene after World War II. Norman Mailer's *Naked and the Dead* (1948) and Herman Wouk's *Caine Mutiny* (1951) offered grand war stories with straightforward narratives. Themes of acculturation and marginality were explored by Ralph Ellison in

Invisible Man (1952), a stunning revelation of the black experience in a hostile world, and James Baldwin in his rhetorical *Go Tell It on the Mountain* (1953). Upstate had its regionalists like Carl Carmer, Walter D. Edmonds, and Constance Robertson, and also attracted such occasional interlopers as Edmund Wilson, who wrote about the passage of time in Talcottville, Lewis County, and Mary McCarthy, who taught a year at Bard College, which inspired *The Groves of Academe* (1952) and prefigured her best-seller about Vassar alumnae, *The Group* (1963). Writers accepted what Columbia University critic Lionel Trilling said was their obligation to probe the individual's encounter with modern mass society.

Under the surface, the literary mood harbored an edginess toward conventional realism. One could sense it in the unfathomable restlessness of Holden Caulfield in J. D. Salinger's *Catcher in the Rye* (1951), the perverse Jewish daydreams in Bernard Malamud's *Assistant* (1957), and John Cheever's *New Yorker* stories, in which half-mad suburbanites woke at 3:00 A.M., "talking into the dark." Novelist Philip Roth discerned a "bouncy" style in the stories of Herbert Gold and Grace Paley, second-generation Jews raised on tabloids and movies, who used language "to jolt and surprise us." Some writers had turned to overt experimentation. William Gaddis's *Recognitions* (1955) used dense, superimposed narratives, while Russian émigré (and Cornell University professor) Vladimir Nabokov wrote novels like *Pale Fire* (1962), which featured dazzling word play. Fiction strained to keep pace with the social change of postwar New York.

Much of this avant-garde spread upstate among regionalists like Charles Burchfield, who lived near Buffalo, and patrons like Arthur B. Davies and Edward Wales Root. Root taught at Hamilton College and collected Burchfield's watercolors, some of which he donated to Utica's Munson-Williams-Proctor Institute. The sculptor David Smith, an arc-welder at the American Locomotive Works in Schenectady during the war, established his promethean presence at Bolton Landing, turning out abstract works like "Hudson River Landscape" (1951) that caught emotions before "they were befouled by words." In 1955 Gordon M. Smith, director of Buffalo's Albright Gallery (and no relation to the sculptor), persuaded the chainstore heir Seymour H. Knox II to buy de Koonings and Pollocks and endow a wing designed by architect Gordon Bunshaft for the Albright-Knox Art Gallery.

Upstate provided the inspiration and patronage for artists of national stature. Anna Mary Robertson ("Grandma") Moses of Eagle Bridge painted local scenes in a primitive style. The Shaker Museum, founded in 1955, in Old Chatham, the Fenimore House's American folk art, and the Farmers' Museum's vernacular tools, both at Cooperstown, were sources for the 1950s revival of Americana. The Corning Museum of Glass, founded in 1951, housed a remarkable collection of objects and studio art, while the nucleus of Syracuse's Everson

Museum of Art, which sponsored national tours of ceramics, was the works of Adelaide Alsop Robineau. Rochester's School of American Craftsmen became a leading center for "studio glass," pottery, and weaving. Musical performance blossomed at the Chautauqua Opera Association's summer season of opera, symphonies, and chamber music; the Yaddo Colony at Saratoga Springs, which drew composers like Samuel Barber and Gian Carlo Menotti; and nearby Saratoga Springs, which developed a summer festival. In 1956 the Caramoor Summer Festival hosted Julius Rudel's performances of Renaissance music, which helped revive interest in early music played on authentic instruments.

Although cities like Buffalo and Syracuse accommodated the arts' new status, none could match the imperial backdrop of New York. In quick succession, the Metropolitan Museum of Art expanded along Fifth Avenue, the Museum of Modern Art occupied Bauhaus-style quarters on 53rd Street, the Whitney Museum took enlarged space down the block (from which it later moved to Madison Avenue), and in 1960 the Guggenheim Museum moved into an architectural masterpiece designed by Frank Lloyd Wright. In 1955, city construction chief Robert Moses and the Rockefeller family joined to build Lincoln Center for the Performing Arts, to house the New York Philharmonic, Metropolitan Opera, New York City Ballet, and New York City Opera. When President Eisenhower laid the cornerstone for Lincoln Center in 1958, the New York Philharmonic played Copland's *Fanfare for the Common Man*. New York City gave America both celebrative occasions and resplendent public arts.

Rural Change

Postwar developments in the cities also brought far-reaching change to small towns, farm hamlets, and the North Country. Chain stores like H. L. Greene and Grant's refurbished Auburn's business blocks with enameled steel, plate glass fronts, and modern "self-service." Television closed down Saturday night band concerts in Hammondsport, forced Trumansburg store owners to end their traditional Saturday night hours, and destroyed the amateur theatricals of the Players Guild of Collinsville. Local newspapers, like the Macy family's dailies in Westchester and Rockland Counties, were acquired by such media giants as Rochester's Gannett Corporation. As minor league baseball teams went out of business, big leagues' player development contracts subsidized play in Auburn, Elmira, Niagara Falls, Newark-Wayne, and Oneonta.

The state thruway proved a particularly disruptive presence. It rammed through hamlets like Fultonville in Montgomery County while bypassing others, like Cazenovia, Auburn, and Seneca Falls on Route 20. As the truckers' main line from New York to Buffalo, it threatened the railroads, squeezed by declining revenues and the costly investment in diesel-electric locomotives.

The Metropolitan Opera House at Lincoln Center. New York State Department of Economic Development.

The Erie closed steam locomotive repair shops at Salamanca and Hornell on the Southern Tier, and the New York Central sold West Albany steam shops in 1954, idling 2,300 mechanics. The Central's consolidation of freight routes left such towns as Oneonta and Canandaigua dependent on trucking. The Delaware and Hudson ended passenger service between Albany and Binghamton, and in 1957 the New York Central shut down commuter lines on the Putnam Division. Passenger trains lost riders to intercity buses and the brash Ithaca air taxi, Mohawk Airlines, which in 1959 carried half a million passengers a year. By 1962 one-third of the state's railroad tracks had been retired before the onslaught of 4.9 million cars and 570,000 trucks.

Towns became the hubs for region-wide commuting by automobile. Corning Glass, which employed nine thousand, was the center of a commuter-shed along Routes 36 and 17 that stretched to Bath, Hornell, Dansville, and Wayland on the Southern Tier. Richard Russo's novel *The Risk Pool* (1988) recalled hard times in Gloversville, northwest of Albany, which sent men driving across the Mohawk Valley to work on road construction. Binghamton spread out across Broome County, as workers at IBM, Afga Ansco, and Link moved into Union and Vestal, which grew from hamlets to suburbs of 20,000. In 1967 local historian Tom Cawley concluded that Binghamton was less a city than "one of the several densely populated neighborhoods within the confines of Broome County."

Metropolitan growth gave farmers lucrative markets but also rising land costs, labor shortages, and new competition. The state's 17.6 million acres of cropland in 1945 shrank to 15.5 million by 1955, as suburbs, highways, and abandoned farms claimed one-quarter million acres per year. On Erie County's suburban frontier, farmers switched from oats and potatoes to snap beans and corn, increased their output of grapes eight times, and joined the Agway Pro-Fac company to can and market vegetables under the "Blue Boy" label. Long Island potato farmers invested in mechanized harvesters, and duck farms at Moriches and Riverhead introduced heated brooder houses and automatic feeders. Sullivan County poultrymen of the Inter-County Farmers' Cooperative Association shifted to "caponettes," sold under the Empire brand, used plastic-foam egg cartons, and invested in automated feed mills. Still more sold out to summer resorts. By 1953 the Borscht Belt around Monticello and Liberty had 538 hotels, nearly 2,000 bungalow colonies, and 1,000 rooming houses.

Market cooperatives and corporate investment aided vegetable and fruit growers along Lake Ontario and around the Finger Lakes. Chautauqua County's Welch Grape Juice Company was acquired in 1945 by New York City investors, who gave growers price guarantees while capitalizing on new brands of concentrates and jellies at plants in Westfield and Brocton. When investors resold Welch to the National Grape Co-operative Association in 1952, Chautauqua growers took over one of the most successful agricultural marketers. Pleasant Valley's wineries including Taylor, Urbana, and Putnam were purchased by New York City and California holding companies which kept the labels and made the wines from blended grapes shipped from across the country.

Increased competition from Wisconsin and Canada made New York's dairy farms depend on government programs, chiefly the Federal Milk Price Order of 1938, which guaranteed income for dairymen in the New York Milk Shed. Approximately 85 percent of commercial farms in the Black River and Champlain Valleys and in Chenango, Delaware, Otsego, and Schoharie Counties concentrated on dairy products. Saint Lawrence County, seventh in the nation in the number of milk cows and thirteenth in milk production, contained hamlets like Heuvelton and New Bremen that had modern, corporate-owned cheese plants. In Lewis County the Lowville Producers Dairy Cooperative sold milk to the Kraft Foods Division of the National Dairy Products Corporation, whose plants made bulk American cheese. The number of centralized plants in Saint Lawrence, Lewis, and Clinton Counties dropped from thirty-six in 1951 to eighteen by 1963.

By 1960 only 2 percent of the state's inhabitants lived on farms. Strapped rural communities voted for state takeovers of highway maintenance, school

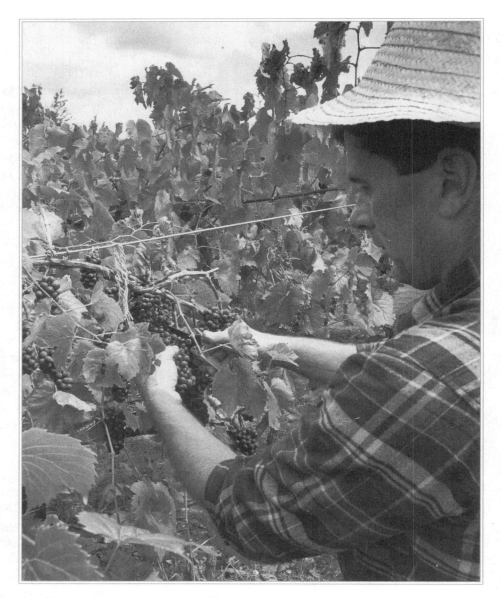

Harvesting grapes in the Hudson Valley. New York State Department of Economic Development.

busing, and vocational education. In Candor, a Tioga County hamlet southeast of Ithaca, each state tax dollar collected was returned in the form of twenty dollars in state aid, as Tioga Republicans wooed the rural vote. Tompkins County grew by 56 percent between 1940 and 1950, while the number of residents on working farms plummeted from 23 percent to 7 percent. In 1954 some 14,300

Young dairy farmers relax between events at the Farmers' Museum Junior Livestock Show. Photograph by Jerry Reese. New York State Historical Association, Cooperstown, N.Y.

farms dotted the countryside in Orleans and Wayne Counties along Lake Ontario, but one-third of the residents drove to the Buffalo and Rochester areas for their livelihoods.

The automobile and the decline in timber resources transformed the distant North Country into a place for mass recreation. With diesel trucks, scattered stands of timber could be harvested by small crews, hired on "portal-to-portal" contracts. Newsprint manufacturing virtually disappeared on the Black River. One company, St. Regis Paper's Deferiet plant, survived by consolidating operations in Canadian pulp. Watertown lost paper mills on Beebee's Island, except for Knowlton Brothers, which produced customized papers and colors. State highways, crowded with motorists, ended the exclusivity of private "camps" near Lake George. By the mid-1950s, the state Department of Conservation had built more than twenty tourist camps, including Fish Creek near Saranac Inn with 380 campsites, whose size made it seem like a veritable tent city. Elsewhere, limited employment at resorts like the Silver Bay Association and Arcady Golf Club near Ticonderoga was supplemented by opportunity at tourist sites such as Fort Ticonderoga, the Saratoga Arts Festival, and the Saratoga National Historical Park.

Government decisions to develop the North Country renewed debate on the future of the Adirondacks. After the state approved Niagara-Mohawk power

Lake Colden in the High Peaks region of the Adirondacks (1957). Division of Rare and Manuscript Collections, Cornell University Library.

dams on the Raquette River and flood control projects on the Moose River, the Adirondack Mountain Club challenged construction of the reservoir on the scenic Moose. The "Battle of Panther Valley" raged until 1953, when the legislature enacted the Ostrander Amendment which barred large water projects in Hamilton and Herkimer Counties. Development pressures were further relieved by job growth beyond the Forest Preserve's boundaries or "Blue Line." Plattsburgh boomed after the U.S. Air Force built a bomber base there in 1957. The Power Authority dam at Barnhart Island (renamed for Robert Moses) energized Alcoa's and Reynolds Metals' aluminum smelters and the town of Massena. Construction of the Saint Lawrence Seaway (1951–1959) spread thousands of jobs and promised the economic revival of Ogdensburg and Watertown.

Conservationists soon turned on the insidious intrusion posed by vacationers and would-be improvers. The "Big Blow" of November 25, 1950, a storm that flattened 250,000 acres of pine and hemlock in the preserve, prompted calls for modern "managed cutting." Supporters of a pristine wilderness were led by Harold K. Hochschild, founder of the Adirondack Museum at Blue Mountain Lake, and Lithgow Osborne of the Association for the Preservation of the

A freighter passing through the Eisenhower Lock of the St. Lawrence Seaway near Massena, New York. The United States' and Canada's completion of the Seaway in 1959 linked the Great Lakes region to global markets. The New York State Department of Economic Development.

Adirondacks, who warned against state campsites, speed boats on Lakes George and Champlain, and plans for a thruway to Plattsburgh. Postwar economic growth nonetheless brought the casual exurbanization of the Adirondacks.

The vast economic and social changes that were sweeping the Empire State would soon undermine its preeminence in the nation. New manufacturing and distribution technologies would burst apart once dense working-class neighborhoods. The demographic tide extending metropolitan areas would also shift population toward the Sunbelt and California and end New York's leadership in population, manufacturing, and national politics. The growth of suburbs, filled with mortgage payers and baby boom children, would blur ethnic identities and raise questions about the future of young people, racial justice, and civic obligation. A halcyon era was about to end.

Chapter 33

Things Fall Apart

NEW YORK STATE'S PREEMINENCE RESTED ON A TIGHT COIL of manufacturing prowess, family traditions, and confident liberalism. By the late 1950s, the suburban trek had frayed families, youth was questioning authority, and the issue of racial equality was straining party politics. In 1958 these symptoms of social change helped elect Nelson A. Rockefeller governor, and for the next ten years Rockefeller forged a political leadership that pursued the proposition that public spending could bring economic growth, educate a generation, and heal social wounds. During the turbulent 1960s, however, quarrels about race, urban justice, and the Vietnam War saddled Rockefeller liberalism with obligations that the optimistic governor never foresaw.

Loose Ends

In the mid-1950s, cities and suburbs were rattled by restless youth, at loose ends as a result of postwar change. Suburban life distanced children from the world of work and gave them money to idle at shopping malls. Middle-class youths devoured the magazines of William E. Gaines's Entertaining Comics Group: *Tales from the Crypt*, *Panic*, and *Mad*, which ridiculed adult seriousness. In city neighborhoods, parental authority ebbed with the disappearance of factory jobs. On Buffalo's Polish East Side and along the Italian streets of Corona, Queens, teens lounged outside candy stores, practicing the fine art of sidewalk spitting. When Manhattan delinquents "rumbled" with home-made "zip-guns" and African American youths fought whites at Buffalo's Crystal Beach in May 1956, tabloids screamed about a "shook-up generation."

656

Adults blamed rock 'n' roll, which Manhattan record companies introduced in 1954 with Bill Haley and the Comets' "Rock around the Clock" and the Chords' "Sh-Boom." After Allan Freed and other radio disc jockeys played "race" music on New York City's WINS and George "Hound Dog" Lorenz broadcast from Buffalo's black Ellicott neighborhood, producers like Ahmat Ertegun of Atlantic Records scrambled to put black rhythm and blues on 45-rpm records. Grownups were aghast at the craze. At Schenectady's Oneida Junior High School, the principal banned clothes worn by what he called the "black leather crowd." Buffalo schools aimed "dress right codes" at wearers of duck-tail hair and pink-and-black jackets (colors of defiant love).

Young bohemians challenged the culture of white middle-class high schools and colleges. Seniors at Forest Hills High School in Queens sported beards like that of Cuban rebel Ernesto (Che) Guevara and contributed to a dissident magazine, *The Thinker*, which attacked the "duck-and-cover drills" that were "the mass-insanity campaign for . . . nuclear war." Columbia University was stirred by resident radicals like C. Wright Mills, who wrote *The Power Elite* (1956), and by what one observer called the "great books and long perspectives" that nurtured "critical and even utopian ideas." The peace movement was quickened by Quaker protests against Cold War nuclear tests and Christian witness against southern Jim Crow. *Liberation*, founded in 1956 by pacifists David Dellinger and Bayard Rustin, preached civil rights and nonviolence. A year later, *Saturday Review* editor Norman Cousins and psychiatrist Erich Fromm founded the Committee for a Sane Nuclear Policy.

Dissident youth also had Greenwich Village, a refuge just a subway ride from the "square" 1950s. In Village bars one could brush shoulders with Willem de Kooning and hear Miles Davis and Thelonius Monk (in beret and sunglasses, the epitome of hipness) play cool jazz. The Village had the Mattachine Society, founded by homosexuals in Los Angeles in 1950; Grove Press, which published erotica and won a landmark obscenity suit; and a pioneer alternative paper, the *Village Voice*, co-founded by Norman Mailer in 1955. By then, a crowd of hipsters including Jack Kerouac and Allen Ginsberg were prowling the Village seeking the jazz and Benzedrine that seemed to inspire their experiments in spontaneous prose. Kerouac said his friends were "beat"—beatified by drugs and tilts against capitalist "neck-tied" America. They burst on the American consciousness with Ginsberg's epic poem, *Howl* (1956), and Kerouac's *On the Road* (1957). Many laughed off their bohemianism and "like, uh" ways of speech, but Norman Mailer in a 1957 *Dissent* essay, "The White Negro," compared hipsters to African Americans, who lived on society's edge, nurturing "the psychopath in oneself."

In the late 1950s New York's media "discovered" the Village's different voices. *Life* began publishing the grainy photos of realist Robert Frank and the stranger work of Diane Arbus, whose pictures lingered over "human oddities."

Network television spotlighted stand-up comedians like Woody Allen, whose sardonic one-liners drew crowds at Art D'Lugoff's Village Gate. Late-night Village hours, moreover, encouraged a round-the-clock lifestyle oriented toward youth. By summer 1960, the beat "scene" spilled over into the East Village and drew fugitives from high school. Benzedrine was eclipsed by marijuana, the choice of slumming Ivy Leaguers; and bebop lost ground to folk music, authentic ballads of social protest, sung by Pete Seeger, Odetta, and a teenager from Minnesota who called himself Bob Dylan.

Restless youth struck at the core of child-centered suburbs—and their finances. Residential taxpayers who spent millions to educate baby boomers and counter Soviet mathematics and science after the 1957 Sputnik scare now paid for quality schools to enthrall their teens. Statewide school debt increased from $100 million in 1950 to $330 million in 1959, incurred to equip modern schools like Schenectady's Linton High, where students were educated for "accelerated life in a changing world." Communities as diverse as Ossining in Westchester County and Long Beach in Nassau offered expensive programs for "gifted" students. Between 1957 and 1963, qualitative improvements raised per-pupil costs at twice the pace of enrollment, while state aid dropped from 40 to 30 percent of local budgets.

Spending hinged on taxpayer control of school district elections. In Nassau County, where school debt tripled in the 1950s, a citizens' committee used sound trucks and house-to-house canvasses to win voter approval for Sewanhaka Central High School's $15.5 million bond issue. Citizens in Greece Central District No. 1 outside Rochester, on the other hand, pored over architects' drawings, voted down plans, and demanded cheaper alternatives before they approved the school budget. While the Temporary State Commission on Educational Finances, created in 1954, proposed state aid to consolidated districts, voters preferred to join Boards of Cooperative Educational Services (BOCES) that supplied contract services to local districts. By the late 1950s, eighty-three BOCES offered reading specialists and speech therapists, enrolled retarded students, and administered central high schools on a per-pupil fee basis.

Suburban tax weariness mounted in the late 1950s. In one Westchester town, the Barnard College sociologist Mirra Komarovsky found blue-collar couples strapped for cash and ready for the wives to go to work. Many Westchester communities rezoned residential tracts for corporate headquarters to provide tax "ratables" and jobs for women. In 1955 Joseph Suozzi was elected mayor of Glen Cove, Long Island, on the promise to create commercial zones to "lift the [tax] load" off homeowners. Betty Friedan, then a Rockland County mom, returned to journalism to write an article about her college reunion that became a profile of suburban women's empty lives, entitled "Is This All?" Economic and social pressures influenced the turnaround in the state's birth rate, which peaked in 1957.

The legislature responded to the crisis by establishing the Joint Legislative Committee on Metropolitan Areas, chaired by Senator John H. Hughes, a Syracuse Republican, who pledged to give "the county its due." School budget defeats rose from fifteen in 1958 to thirty-four in 1959. Suburbs around Syracuse were one hotbed, but on Long Island, where voters rejected fifteen budgets, Nassau Republicans warned Albany of outright "revolt." In 1959 Republicans chose Joseph F. Carlino of Long Beach as Assembly speaker, the first GOP leader from downstate in one hundred years.

The Impatient First Citizen

In 1954 Governor Thomas E. Dewey wanted to retire from Albany and endorsed U.S. Senator Irving Ives as his successor. Democrats divided in their nominating convention between reformers and clubhouse regulars. Eleanor Roosevelt led the reformers behind the candidacy of her son, Congressman FDR, Jr., but was stopped by Tammany's Carmine De Sapio, who supported W. Averell Harriman, the old investment banker and New Dealer. Stammering into the TelePrompTer, Harriman managed to beat Ives and promptly named De Sapio his secretary of state.

Harriman pledged liberal programs but confronted fiscal limits that allowed only modest spending increases. He made the best of his predicament, replenishing Dewey's reconstruction fund with a bond issue and delivering stern vetoes on spending. His main reform centered on 94,000 patients in state hospitals affected by the Community Mental Health Law of 1954. In response to citizens' groups, Harriman appointed as state commissioner of mental hygiene the psychiatrist Paul H. Hoch, who favored Thorazine and psychotherapy as part of out-patient care. Hoch prepared the 1962 state master plan for mental health catchment areas served by a state psychiatric hospital, a landmark toward the goal of deinstitutionalization.

Looking forward to reelection in 1958, Governor Harriman was sabotaged by bickering Democrats and hard times. Reformers despised Secretary De Sapio, whose trademarks were dark glasses (for his iritis), camel-hair coats, and back-room deals, and focused on the issue of corruption, popularized by congressional investigations of organized crime and labor racketeers. The issue hit home in November 1957, when state police spotted Cadillacs parked in the Tioga County hamlet of Apalachin and traced license plates to crime bosses, allegedly gathered for a Mafia summit. Reformers, hinting at connections between crime bosses and Democratic politicians in 1958, supported Manhattan lawyer Thomas K. Finletter for U.S. senator, while De Sapio offered Manhattan District Attorney Frank Hogan. Mrs. Roosevelt told Harriman to "control" De Sapio, but when Hogan was nominated anyway, reformers felt betrayed. Harriman's prospects ended with the recession of 1957, which brought 10 percent unemployment to Buffalo and Utica-Rome and forced the New York Central to merge with its arch rival, the Pennsylvania Railroad.

In 1958 Harriman was challenged by Republican Nelson A. Rockefeller, the restless millionaire who took the pulse of citizen politics. Patrons of conservation, Planned Parenthood, and the Museum of Modern Art, the Rockefellers helped add quality-of-life issues to the political agenda. After service on Eisenhower's White House staff, Nelson sponsored a panel of academic experts, whose "Rockefeller Reports" urged Cold War spending for arms and schools that were vital to the nation's "survival." Settling into the family estate at Pocantico Hills, Westchester County, Rockefeller attacked the state's sluggish economy and outmoded government. During the 1958 campaign, his experts examined issues and drafted solutions that he unveiled at citizens' gatherings around the state. Rockefeller also proved to be a political natural, who could work crowds with a gravelly "Hi-ya, fella," and gorge on ethnic foods like a gastronomic balanced ticket. Attracting downstate Democrats, particularly Jews and African Americans, he defeated Harriman by 557,000 votes.

Governor Nelson A. Rockefeller. New York State Department of Commerce.

Taking charge in Albany, Rockefeller vexed Republican regulars, who learned that the party "existed, as far as the governor was concerned, to nominate him." He remained his own boss, spending his personal funds lavishly on polls and media, divorcing and remarrying (Mrs. Margaretta "Happy" Fitler Murphy in 1963) while running for president. His personal machine reached beyond his own party to compliant Democrats, labor leaders (particularly from the construction unions, which enjoyed good wages on state projects), and 40,000 state jobholders, whom Rockefeller controlled outside of the civil service. His staff, though wearied by his personal whims, remained attracted to his infectious optimism and impulsive generosity ($1.8 million in loans and gifts). Rockefeller "consumed people," his speech writer concluded, "their energies, their loyalties, occasionally their judgment."

Believing that public spending could end the "lethargy" in economic growth, Rockefeller ignored his budget bureau and turned to fiscal liberals like William J. Ronan and ad hoc study groups. Nagged by the state comptroller, Democrat Arthur J. Levitt, Rockefeller called for tax increases eight times between 1959 and 1972, which raised rates and began payroll with-holding. Rockefeller also introduced a 2 percent sales tax, later increased to 4, and went after the rich to an unprecedented degree. The estate tax rose 350 per-cent, and between 1960 and 1968 the tax rate on the highest income bracket doubled to 14 percent. Personal income tax collections skyrocketed from $569 million in 1959 to $3.065 billion in 1973, when they constituted 40 percent of state revenues. Under Rockefeller, expenditures rose an average of 13 percent annually (compared to 10.6 percent for all the states). Two-thirds of the money went for social welfare, education, and hospitals, in part to meet federal man-dates, and for aid to municipalities.

At the same time that state "full-faith-and-credit" bonds soared from $912 million to $3.4 billion under Rockefeller, additional debt was incurred by inde-pendent agencies. When voters defeated highway and slum clearance bond issues after 1958 (and Comptroller Levitt refused to commit state employment retirement funds), Rockefeller used a formula devised by Manhattan attorney John N. Mitchell for the New York State Housing Finance Agency—bonds backed by the legislature's promise to make up for any shortfalls in interest pay-ments (dubbed the state's "moral obligation"). A related device was the "lease-purchase" agreement, which allowed special authorities to pay off construction debts with "rent" from other state agencies. Directed by William J. Ronan, who sat on several boards including the Housing Finance Agency, State Dormitory Authority, State University Construction Fund, Metropolitan Transportation Authority, and Urban Development Corporation, the special authorities issued $6.7 billion in bonds by 1971. In December 1973 the total debt reached $12.1 billion.

Impatience to do good made government by authority a Rockefeller habit; he called it "taking risks for people." The Metropolitan Transportation Author-ity was created in 1959 to recapitalize and operate bankrupt commuter lines on the New York Central, New Haven Railroad, and Long Island Railroad. To speed the acquisition of nuclear reactor sites, the Atomic Space and Power Authority conferred the power of eminent domain on local utilities. The Urban Develop-ment Corporation was expected to spearhead new building types and commu-nity forms. Corporation head Edward J. Logue embarked on projects that ranged from a 375-unit housing development in Newburgh to the 93-acre reclamation of the Buffalo waterfront for 2,400 middle-income apartments. Logue also started three new towns for 60,000 people: Audubon, adjacent to the State Uni-versity of New York's Buffalo campus at Amherst; Radisson in the town of Lysander, north of Syracuse; and Roosevelt Island in New York City.

Rockefeller nurtured the State University of New York's mammoth expan-sion. He once intoned that "mean structures breed small vision," and in Henry T. Heald of the Ford Foundation he found a visionary. As chairman of a SUNY advisory commission, Heald advocated tripling enrollment in the state's public

The State University of New York system enjoyed explosive growth under Rockefeller. James V. Sturgess Hall at SUNY Geneseo. Photograph by Ron Pretzer. Office of Communications and Publications, SUNY Geneseo.

and private colleges to 1,102,000 by 1980, with public universities responsible for 60 percent of the total. In January 1961 SUNY trustees approved a ten-year, $600 million expansion to triple full-time enrollment to 145,000 students and to create university centers at Buffalo, Albany, Stony Brook, and Binghamton. SUNY contracted $1.8 billion in projects on thirty-four campuses financed by the Housing Finance Agency, State Dormitory Authority, and State University Construction Fund, while the Urban Development Corporation worked on

SUNY at Purchase and SUNY Buffalo at Amherst. Under Rockefeller, enrollments in public colleges and universities increased from 142,081 (37 percent of all students) in 1958 to 300,093 (50 percent) in 1970. The sixfold increase in SUNY spending also transformed the community colleges. In 1958 public two-year institutions enrolled 28,029, just 7 percent of college attendees. By 1970 over 111,000 were enrolled, 18 percent of all college students.

While Rockefeller commanded, his rivals spun out of control. Tammany lost ground to Democratic reform and withered away after De Sapio was disgraced by a bribery scandal in 1959. Squabbling reform clubs and Democratic organizations in the Bronx and Brooklyn, however, could never replace Tammany's influence. Among Republicans, the influx of conservative Irish and Italian Americans brought a rising tide of criticism of Rockefeller's liberal spending. In 1960 the legislature challenged Rockefeller by enacting a residency requirement for welfare recipients, which he vetoed. A year later the city of Newburgh made headlines with welfare restrictions aimed at "undesirable newcomers," and J. Daniel Mahoney and Kieran O'Doherty launched the Conservative party to challenge Rockefeller's "march to the left." In the 1962 gubernatorial elections, Rockefeller won by 518,000 votes but ran behind the GOP ticket. The Conservative candidate, Syracuse businessman David H. Jaquith, received 142,000 votes, mostly in Queens, Nassau, and Onondaga Counties.

Race and Renewal

Inspired by Robert Moses's example in New York City and fueled by federal Title I grants, urban renewal accelerated economic and racial change in metropolitan areas. An extension of postwar campaigns for efficient, modern cities, renewal swept away tenements and factories to make room for residential towers, retail centers, and parking garages for suburban shoppers. Turning cities inside out required a steely Moses in New York, an independent authority in Buffalo, and "strong-mayor" and city manager governments in Syracuse and Rochester. While the migration of newcomers kept its pace in New York City and doubled the black population in Rochester and Syracuse, redevelopers cleared slums and shunted migrants into inadequate public housing.

Moses was forced aside by controversy in 1959, but modified Title I policies were carried on by business leaders like David Rockefeller, the governor's brother, chairman of Chase National Bank, who directed investment to revive the financial district. The television, advertising, and publishing industries spurred office construction along Park and Madison Avenues and speculation in high-rise luxury apartments on the East Side. Factories were cleared below Canal Street for the World Trade Center and for government complexes in Foley Square and downtown Brooklyn. The shipping piers on the Chelsea waterfront in Manhattan and around the navy yard and Gowanus Canal in Brooklyn were abandoned by the Port Authority, which poured money into New Jersey container ports and transport facilities at John F. Kennedy International Airport. Between 1960 and 1965, developers erected 120,000 luxury and semiluxury apartment units, while 200,000 factory jobs disappeared from Manhattan and Brooklyn.

In the 1950s Buffalo's population decline was matched by a 20 percent loss in factory jobs, after Bell Aircraft moved to the Sunbelt and New York Car Wheel and Allegheny Ludlum were hit by the 1957 recession. The problem, city leaders concluded, was Ellicott, the "colored slum," a banker remarked, "just a stone's throw from our best business district." In 1965 the Reform Democratic mayor, Frank A. Sedita, with the cooperation of Governor Rockefeller, guided the construction of the Erie County office building and One M & T Plaza, a two-block shopping mall and bank tower. The Buffalo Urban Renewal Agency cleared a quarter-mile of Ellicott, affecting 2,200 families and seventy black-owned businesses, for the Frederick Douglass Towers, and the Kensington Expressway displaced African Americans into predominantly Polish Humboldt Park, causing white flight to West Seneca and Cheektowaga. Rockefeller hailed One M & T Plaza as the "catalyzing agent" for Buffalo's growth, but experts later concluded that the redevelopment program undermined the city's future.

Rochester's business leaders agreed with City Manager Robert P. Aex on a coordinated effort to remove "blight" and attract suburban shoppers. City and state aid was mobilized to build an Inner Loop expressway, parking garages, and a convention center, while retailers McCurdy and B. Forman collaborated on Midtown Plaza, the country's first downtown shopping mall. The Title I program contributed the Genesee Crossroads redevelopment, which cleared obsolete structures from much of Baden-Ormond. By the early 1960s, highways and renewal leveled 1,852 housing units near downtown. "All the streets have disappeared," Rochester-born author Jerre Mangione wrote about his Mount Allegro neighborhood; "there is not the slightest trace of them."

In the mid-1960s Syracuse leveled twenty-seven square blocks, including the location of most black-owned stores and restaurants, near the central business district, ran a superhighway through the black Fifteenth Ward, and aided Syracuse University's expansion. Removal of low-income units, combined with the influx of newcomers, squeezed African Americans into segregated public housing or marginal areas nearby. Syracuse renewal dealt less with the city's basic social needs as much as, a black official remarked, "dispersed the discontented" into other neighborhoods.

Smaller cities were transformed in proportion. Schenectady and Troy cleared downtown acres for parking and commercial plazas, and Batavia replaced business blocks with a $2 million enclosed mall. Binghamton, with Governor Rockefeller's nod, secured a new courthouse square and commercial complex linked by pedestrian arcades to parking garages. Suburban hubs also pursued redevelopment in order to keep pace with regional malls. White Plains's 130-acre Central Renewal obliterated one-tenth of the city's housing for a commercial plaza, and Mount Vernon's Midtown project revitalized the commercial core but demolished the nearby black neighborhood.

Albany's redevelopment centered on Governor Rockefeller's obsession, the South Mall—a quarter-mile-long complex comprising the Bureau of Motor Vehicle headquarters, state office towers, and an ellipsoid auditorium on a pedestal (soon dubbed "The Egg") sitting astride a half-mile plaza and a reflecting pool, all linked by an underground concourse. At one end was the late nineteenth-century state capitol; at the other, the new cultural education center, which housed the state museum, library, and archives. When the legislature balked at the cost, Rockefeller turned to Mayor Erastus Corning, 2nd, for "creative financing": a $450 million Albany County bond issue and lease-purchase, amortized by rent on the South Mall over forty years. The megaproject cleared a neighborhood of 9,000 African Americans while providing jobs for 40,000 state

The Empire State Plaza in Albany. A view from the steps of the Cultural Education Center, with the state capitol at center, state office towers on the left, and the "Egg" on the right. New York State Department of Economic Development.

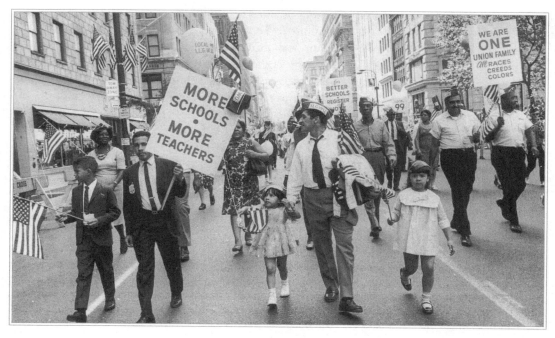

A diverse group of union members and their families march in New York City's 1960 Labor Day parade. Photograph by Jerry Soalt, ILGWU *Justice*. UNITE Archives, Kheel Center, Cornell University.

workers, many of whom commuted from the suburbs. Completed in the fall of 1973, the complex was renamed the Nelson A. Rockefeller Empire State Plaza in 1978 (though some called it the Governor's Edifice Complex).

Redevelopment's attack on urban blight had little impact on local job discrimination. In Syracuse in the early 1960s, less than 1 percent of the downtown sales force was black, and only six African Americans were on the Niagara-Mohawk Power Corporation's payroll of fifteen hundred. In Utica, four African Americans were among the New York Telephone Company's 986 employees, but none were at the local branch of Niagara-Mohawk or Sears, Roebuck. Rochester's voluntary hospitals, notably Strong Memorial and Park Avenue, were the largest employers of blacks—as orderlies and cleaning personnel. While Eastman Kodak hired a few African American chemists and engineers, production ranks at Kodak Park remained lily-white. At the same time an "ethnic lock" controlled New York City's blue-collar sector. The three-thousand-member Plumbers Local 1 of Brooklyn and Queens listed six African Americans with union cards. The building trades kept precious credentials in the family. Between 1940 and 1960 factory workers within New York City's black labor force rose from 20 to 25 percent, while foremen and skilled craftsmen inched up from 8 to 11 percent.

As factory slots dwindled, African Americans came to depend on service and government jobs. In New York City in the mid-1950s seven of the largest banks employed at least one hundred blacks, with Chase and Chemical having more than three hundred each. Only eight of the twenty largest insurance companies had any African American employees. In 1956 blacks made up 10 percent of the workforce in department stores and 5 percent in media studios. Early 1960s politics, however, widened opportunities for public employment. African Americans, who held only 150 jobs (less than 1 percent) in the New York City Police Department in 1949, had 700 (2.6 percent) of 26,171 in 1962 and 1,300 (4.6 percent) by 1966. While only 700 African Americans and 200 Puerto Ricans were among the New York City Transit Authority's 34,984 employees, a higher percentage found work at the Department of Hospitals.

The story was much the same in Syracuse, where Syracuse University, the Upstate Medical Center, and business services helped increase professional and technical employment among black males from 10.2 percent in 1960 to 15.6 percent in 1970. Otherwise, the African American male labor force was badly skewed. Between 1960 and 1970, the percentage in clerical and sales jobs rose from 12 to 20 among black males, but the portion of unskilled and laborer categories remained at 30 percent. "Menial jobs of earlier generations," concluded Syracuse experts, "have been severely reduced, but the newer types of jobs . . . were slow in coming."

Disproportionate gains in employment were made by African American women, who joined the female trek to work. In New York City between 1940 and 1960, factory jobs rose from 14 to 21 percent among black women, and sales and clerical positions soared from 3 to 17 percent. The change ended African American women's historic dependence on domestic labor, which fell from 64 percent in 1940 to 25 percent by 1960. In Syracuse the portion of black females occupying clerical and sales positions skyrocketed from 13.8 percent in 1960 to 36.2 in 1970—a gain three times that of black men. In New York City, employment gains narrowed the wage gap between blacks and whites from three-fifths in 1940 to seven-tenths by 1960. African American women closed to within 93 percent of white women's wages.

For black men in New York City, the wage gap in 1960 was 68 percent and widening, largely a result of redevelopment and the suburbanization of jobs. In 1966 Harlem unemployment was 8.1 percent, while "subemployment" (the total of unemployed, "discouraged" dropouts, and part-time workers) had reached 29 percent. More ominous was the decline in labor force participation, which among Brooklyn males sank from 79 percent in 1960 to 72.5 percent in 1970. The devastation of factory employment in Buffalo brought down black male participation to 54 percent in 1970. Faltering prospects for African American males tore at family relationships. Female-headed black families in Brooklyn rose from one-quarter in 1960 to one-third by 1970. Although experts debated the significance of traditional family structure, they agreed that female-headed families were more likely to be affected by poverty. In 1969 two-thirds of Brooklyn's poor families were headed by women.

Neighborhood schools were overwhelmed by ghetto turmoil and lack of economic opportunity. Junior High School No. 40 in the South Bronx was "turf" contested by Puerto Rican "Crowns," who claimed one side of Prospect Avenue, and black "Sportsmen," who ruled the other. "In the school," remembered the Black Panther activist Dharuba (Richard Moore), "you could get jacked up just for going into the bathroom and bumping into a Crown." In Buffalo in the mid-1950s, police cracked down on street corner lounging, and a Youth Bureau was founded to tackle the gangs. Harlem teens turned to heroin in the early 1950s, roughly when "dope" first appeared in Buffalo's Ellicott district. Kids snorted, then skin-popped, and denied they were hooked. "I'm not shooting, I'm just snorting," a Harlem teenager told his pals in 1957.

In the mid-1950s, anxieties about jobs and adolescents lay behind the demand of African American parents, with their suburban counterparts, for schools to inspire the young. After the U.S. Supreme Court decision of *Brown v. Board of Education* (1954), the demand became a call for racial integration. Under pressure from black activists like Reverend Milton A. Galamison, who led Bedford-Stuyvesant demonstrations against segregated schools in 1955, school administrators devised tentative integration plans. But in Brooklyn, Queens, Buffalo, and Rochester, angry whites forced school boards to emphasize voluntary and limited "open enrollment." To thwart integration, Buffalo permitted thousands of white students, districted for largely black East Side High, to take foreign languages in alternative all-white schools. African Americans were also "tracked" into vocational education in Buffalo, where "vo-ed" became a largely black system, and in New York City, where blacks and Hispanics were 44 percent of "vo-ed" enrollment. New York City educators knew that vocational education was a segregated, dead-end route. Manufacturing jobs were disappearing, and the apprenticeship programs of white unions were virtually shut to black graduates.

In 1962 State Education Commissioner James E. Allen, Jr., ordered school boards to devise plans to eliminate racial imbalances. When New York City dragged its feet, the Brooklyn Congress on Racial Equality (CORE) staged demonstrations and the city's first school boycott. The board tried another tack, pairing black and white intermediate schools (grades seven to nine). At Brooklyn I.S. 258 on the edge of Canarsie, white parents mobbed buses filled with black children from Bedford-Stuyvesant. The reaction was nearly the same in Rochester, where white parents at School No. 30 sued against being "compelled arbitrarily to join a different ethnic group living miles away." The suburban trek in the meantime worsened racial balance in most cities. In 1965 whites were reported leaving the New York City public system for private or suburban schools at the rate of 40,000 per year. Despite Commissioner Allen's policies and remonstrances, the number of minorities attending segregated schools in New York City, Buffalo, Rochester, and Syracuse rose from 45 percent in 1968 to 49 percent by 1971.

School failure and joblessness fed the growth of gangs and felony arrests, which clogged courts and overcrowded prisons. During what one lawyer called the "mid-century law explosion," felony arraignments in New York City's criminal courts rose from 20,646 in 1954 to 63,842 in 1969. By the late 1950s prosecutions in Harlem, Bedford-Stuyvesant, and Ellicott in Buffalo institutionalized youth violence in upstate locales like Woodbourne Correctional Facility in Sullivan County, which one teenager called a "gang-fighting haven." Six hundred African Americans and Puerto Ricans were among Woodbourne's eight hundred inmates, but whites got the best jobs in the trade shops. At Great Meadow Correctional Facility in Washington County, 1,300 black prisoners were assigned to labor gangs and the prison laundry, not to the radio and auto shops reserved for whites. In maximum-security Attica Correctional Facility in Wyoming County, inmates remembered one officer who doled out summer refreshments, "'white ice' and 'nigger ice.'"

By the early 1960s, racial anger behind bars molded inmates into fiery nationalists, particularly the Puerto Rican Young Lords and the Nation of Islam. Some Great Meadow inmates had heard Black Muslim organizer Malcolm X in Harlem denounce white devils. They agreed because, as Lumumba Shakur, a Black Panther from Jamaica, Queens, remembered, "in prison we felt and saw racism raw and buck-naked daily." After a 1962 riot at Great Meadow, prisoners went to solitary confinement in Attica, punished, they said, for preaching Islam behind bars.

The Community Revolution

In the early 1960s, concern about youth gangs, Moses-style "Negro removal," and civil rights all fed a community revolution across the state. At its core was an intellectual revulsion against the large-scale, impersonal, and bureaucratic aspects of modern metropolitan life. In Greenwich Village, urban critic Jane Jacobs led her brownstone neighbors in a war against Title I redevelopment. Students and neighbors attacked multiversities like Columbia, Buffalo, and Syracuse. At the Upstate Medical Center in Syracuse, psychiatrist Thomas Szasz denounced incarceration in "totalist" mental hospitals. New York City's Phoenix House campaigned for residential treatment of drug addicts, and Floyd Ohlin and Richard A. Cloward of the Columbia University School of Social

Work attacked welfare rules that "regulated" the poor. They were joined by religious activists and social scientists who saw poverty as a behavior pattern that might respond to spirited intervention.

Activists soon confronted bureaucracies that ran programs-as-usual. The psychologist Kenneth B. Clark found Harlem youngsters to be alienated from white teachers and bureaucrats in the public schools. Clark called for reorganized schools and "People's Boards of Education." Ohlin and Cloward proposed community storefronts to engage teenagers with the city's "opportunity tracks." Their idea for a Mobilization for Youth (MFY) reached Ford Foundation officer Paul Ylvisaker, who believed in going beyond "fixed ways of doing things." Ylvisaker funded MFY and early experiments with school decentralization.

The attack on institutional power was abetted by the state Court of Appeals, under Charles S. Desmond, the Buffalo saloon keeper's son who became chief judge in 1960. Determined to make "law conform to right," Desmond staked out advanced ground in tort law and often was ahead of the U.S. Supreme Court in recognizing the rights of the accused. Insisting on the right to counsel at every stage of a court proceeding, he led the court to declare confessions made in the absence of an attorney inadmissible; to reject, in *People v. Masseli* (1963), undue delay in jury trials; and to guide the state's acceptance in 1965 of the *Gideon* rule that gave criminal defendants, even indigents, the right to counsel. Desmond led Judges Stanley H. Fuld, Adrian P. Burke, and Charles D. Breitel toward a broad recognition of prisoners' rights under the Sixth Amendment. At the same time, Desmond's ruling in *Goldberg v. Kollsman Instrument Corp.* (1963) extended the doctrine of product liability, holding an equipment subcontractor as well as the carrier liable for the death of an airline passenger.

Fervor for community empowerment went national in 1964, when MFY inspired the neighborhood "demonstration" projects of President Lyndon B. Johnson's War on Poverty. The U.S. Office of Economic Opportunity funded community corporations like Harlem's HARYOU-Act and Bedford-Stuyvesant's Youth in Action, which pledged "maximum feasible participation" of the poor. Syracuse University ran the OEO-funded Community Development Association to train "indigenous" leaders in public housing. An interracial coalition launched Buffalo's East Side Community Organization to secure better housing and jobs. The O'Connell machine in Albany was challenged when churches and settlement houses organized a task force named Better Homes. Many activists built their movements on what the Syracuse training manual called "intense anger about continued injustice." George Wiley, the gifted Syracuse civil rights leader, founded the National Welfare Rights Organization, whose sit-ins at welfare centers aimed at "bureaucratic disruption." Lawyers from MFY's Legal Services Unit, arguing for poor people's "new property," sued in New York City,

Labor leaders speaking in support of equal opportunity employment at a Civil Rights rally in midtown Manhattan in 1960. UNITE Archives, Kheel Center, Cornell University.

Saint Lawrence County, and Newburgh to expand eligibility for welfare, rent supplements, and public housing.

The fervor spread to campuses, where undergraduates confronted the academic order. Inspired by the civil rights movement, free speech demonstrations broke out at SUNY Buffalo in 1962. Syracuse University students challenged the administrative prerogative to limit the number of days off for the Christmas 1964 vacation. Dissidents read C. Wright Mills's *Power Elite*, knottier works by the Marxist theoretician Herbert Marcuse, and the manifestos of the Students for a Democratic Society (SDS), which revealed U.S. imperialist "hegemony," the university's molding of complacent "false consciousness," and the role of liberal academics in prosecuting the war in Vietnam. In the spring of 1966, when SUNY Buffalo gave the Selective Service Qualification Test to determine draft deferments, SDS accused Chancellor Clifford C. Furnas of making the university "a propaganda arm" of the government and staged Buffalo's first sit-in.

Frustration with the pace of civil rights and antipoverty measures was also radicalizing many African Americans. Moderates who advocated integration lost face to fiery champions of Black Power like Stokely Carmichael of the Student Non-Violent Coordinating Committee (SNCC), black nationalists like Roy Innis, and the brilliant Black Muslim orator Malcolm X. Many whites found the rhetoric part and parcel of the abrasive tactics of the antipoverty crusade, and when the first ghetto riots occurred, white conservatives blamed President Johnson's War on Poverty. After a July 1964 confrontation of Harlem blacks with police that spread to Bedford-Stuyvesant, Irish and Italian Democrats called on Mayor Wagner to close down MFY. Syracuse conservatives loathed the Community Development Association's work among public housing tenants and forced Republican Mayor William F. Walsh to defund the effort. When Syracuse in January 1966 hosted the country's first Poor People's Convention, summoned by George Wiley's call for "total participation" of the poor, local conservatives dug in against reform.

Violence stunned Rochester, which considered itself immune from racial conflict. On July 24, 1964, the arrest of a teenager drew a crowd of African Americans whom the police scattered with fire hoses and dogs. Enraged by the dogs, the crowd threw bottles and looted stores along Joseph Avenue, forcing Governor Rockefeller to deploy 1,200 National Guardsmen, the first time in the 1960s that troops were used against a racial disturbance in a northern city. Counting four dead and 350 injured, Rochester blamed outside agitators. During the summer of 1967, African American youths rampaged in downtown Buffalo, Rochester, and Syracuse. Syracuse experienced several incidents, including a black gang that raided the central business district in May 1970.

For all the rhetoric, the War on Poverty had little impact on the ghetto economy. After the Rochester riot, FIGHT, a black pressure group led by Reverend Franklin D. R. Florence, demanded six hundred "Instamatic jobs" at Eastman Kodak and brought in SNCC's Stokely Carmichael, who was eager to take on "a big company." Kodak countered with the "Rochester Plan" to train 1,500 from the unemployment rolls. The Rochester Business Opportunity Corporation, headed by Kodak executive Bernard Gifford, stimulated participation by black-owned subcontractors. Senator Robert F. Kennedy secured business support for the Bedford-Stuyvesant Restoration Corporation (BSRC) and convinced IBM to locate a plant in the Brooklyn ghetto. But the IBM operation remained small, and the BSRC proved little more than a spruce-up operation. In Buffalo, efforts spawned East Side community organizations that employed several hundred but remained, according to historian Henry Louis Taylor, Jr., "dependent on politics." The War on Poverty never compensated for the flight of jobs to the suburbs.

The war's political mobilization, however, launched the careers of Percy Sutton and H. Carl McCall of Manhattan and Arthur O. Eve, the fiery antipoverty leader in Buffalo. In Bedford-Stuyvesant, community activists like Major R. Owen and Al Vann emerged as African American Democratic leaders.

Aided by the Federal Voting Rights Act of 1965, they forced the creation of a second state Assembly seat, won by Shirley Chisholm, who went on to represent Bedford-Stuyvesant in Congress in 1970—the first African American woman on Capitol Hill. During that year Charles Rangel succeeded to Adam Clayton Powell, Jr.'s Harlem seat and Bronx Borough President Herman Badillo was elected to Congress. The enlarged electorate encouraged municipal leaders including Buffalo's Sedita, Syracuse's Walsh and his successor, Democrat Lee F. Alexander, and Yonkers mayor Alfred Del Bello to head biracial coalitions for what they called "urban America."

The most famous of the new political breed, Republican Congressman John V. Lindsay, won the New York mayoralty race in 1965 with a "Fusion" of liberal Republicans, Jewish Democrats, blacks, and Hispanics. Building his own progressive organization, Lindsay shook up City Hall but alienated the municipal bureaucracy and uniformed services. When he took office on New Year's Day 1966, he faced a strike called by Michael Quill of the Transport Workers Union, and during the next eight years endured walkouts by teachers, nurses, sanitation men, and social workers, and job actions by police and firemen. Lindsay bought a sullen peace with twenty-year full-pension deals with the police and firemen (and half-pay pensions for white-collar workers of District Council 37) which set new standards for municipal generosity. In minority neighborhoods, his "little City Halls" disbursed War on Poverty money to some two hundred community organizations. While ghettos burned in Chicago, Newark, and Detroit, Harlem and Bedford-Stuyvesant remained cool, the mayor's men said, because Lindsay walked the streets on summer nights. He called his job the second toughest in America.

Whites in the outer boroughs called Lindsay a spendthrift who coddled minorities. He had responded to the welfare rights upsurge by doubling the numbers of people on welfare and opening housing authority projects to welfare families (6 percent of tenants in 1966). His expanded social welfare programs were funded by city income and commuter taxes and a huge increase in state aid, which Governor Rockefeller pried from the legislature. These intergovernmental transfers revolutionized New York City's source of money. In 1959 one-quarter of city revenues came from state and federal sources. Ten years later these revenue streams had grown to 32 percent and 14 percent, respectively. Conservatives did not know which to despise more—Lindsay liberalism or Rockefeller generosity.

Suburban Empowerment

The local control growing out of the community revolution ironically enabled suburbs to draw a "white noose" around central cities. Between 1960 and 1970, Buffalo's African American population rose from 13.3 percent to 20.4 percent but in the suburbs blacks remained a steady 1.6 percent. Rochester's black population more than doubled, to 16.8 percent, compared to 1.4 percent in the suburbs. For Syracuse and its surroundings, the figures were 10.8 and 0.5 percent. While New York City's African American population reached 21.2 percent in 1970, suburban black population increased only to 5.9 percent, mainly in contiguous towns. On Long Island, gentlemen's agreements and restrictive zoning limited affordable housing to a corridor from South Jamaica to Elmont, Roosevelt, and Wyandanch and to an isolated settlement of Puerto Ricans in Brentwood. The suburban trail in Westchester ran from Yonkers and Mount Vernon (whose black population almost doubled, to 35.6 percent) to New Rochelle and White Plains. With good reason, apartment builders in the Westchester towns of Briarcliff and Rye complained about the "zoning curtain" draped over the county.

Suburbs resisted any notions of metropolitan government that smacked of racial integration. When State Education Commissioner James Allen in 1960 proposed "federated" school districts, financed by state alternatives to the property tax, suburban legislators, fearing federation with inner-city schools, supported Assembly Speaker Carlino's "Nassau Plan" for more state aid to independent districts. The debate took a rancorous turn when Commissioner Allen in 1963 declared that schools with majority black enrollments suffered from "racial imbalance" which threatened "equality of educational opportunity" and ordered the white Malverne, Long Island, district to bus students. Black parents in Roosevelt, joined by Long Island's CORE, marched to demand busing of their students to white districts. In Westchester County, Greenburgh desegregated early and quietly, but New Rochelle required a court order.

Suburban independence soon gained new authority. One element was contributed by Syracuse Senator John Hughes, whose Joint Committee on Metropolitan Areas drew up a County Home Rule Amendment, which voters approved in 1962, and a Town Home Rule Amendment for suburbs over 5,000 in population (adopted in 1964). Both eased the transition to charter government. Far more important was the U.S. Supreme Court decision *Reynolds v. Sims* (1964), which ruled in six cases, including the New York suit, *W.M.C.A. v. Simon*, that "one person, one vote" applied to state legislatures. New York apportionment had favored rural constituencies like Schuyler, Yates, Schoharie, Lewis, and Greene Counties, which had assembly districts representing 15,000 to 31,000 people, compared to 200,000 in Westchester, Onondaga, and Suffolk. *W.M.C.A.* hung over the legislature when the November 1964 landslide for President Johnson gave Democrats control of reapportionment in the new session. Preempting that prospect, Governor Rockefeller called a special session of lame-duck Republicans, who pored over voting district maps and augmented GOP strength in Nassau, Suffolk, and Westchester Counties at the expense of rural districts and New York City.

Democrats appealed without success to the courts, then took the issue to the 1967 state constitutional convention, proposing an amendment to reapportion by a nonpartisan commission. They hoped to elicit suburban support for the idea by proposing repeal of the State Constitution's Blaine Amendment, the prohibition adopted in the late nineteenth century against direct or indirect public aid to parochial schools. The deal was emphatically rejected in the November 1967 referendum. That left the Republican gerrymander to proceed with overwhelming suburban support. In the Assembly, rural seats dropped from forty to twenty-two, New York City's rose from sixty-five to sixty-eight, and the city's four suburban counties jumped from sixteen to twenty-six. "Safe" Republican Senate and Assembly seats from Westchester, Nassau, and Suffolk rose 50 percent and in 1968 accounted for nearly one-third of the Senate. A second reapportionment after the 1970 census increased GOP Assembly strength in Onondaga, Monroe, Westchester, and Suffolk Counties, which exactly matched New York City's loss.

Statewide political battles hinged on the population characteristics of suburban towns. Jews, who voted as liberal Democrats, challenged the Republican hold on Nassau and Westchester, and even the solid GOP grip on Suffolk, Rockland, and Ulster Counties, while Republicans sought a counterbalance among conservative Irish and Italians. In 1964 the Democratic vote for President Johnson made inroads in Westchester, carried the mayoralty in Rye, and made a political star of the mayor of Yonkers, Democrat Alfred Del Bello. The Nassau GOP was swept aside by Democratic chairman John F. English and his protégé, Eugene H. Nickerson, who was elected county executive. The Democratic tide also reached Suffolk, which elected the liberal H. Lee Dennison as county executive.

Republicans fought back, emphasizing suburban services and selective social spending kept under local control, particularly where programs touched schools and race. Westchester county executive Edwin Michaelian won plaudits among taxpayers for charter revision that created the seventeen-district county legislature in 1969. In Nassau County, Republican Ralph G. Caso succeeded Nickerson as county executive, and newcomer Alfonse M. D'Amato became Hempstead town supervisor. Both were fiscal moderates who favored suburban spending kept under taxpayer control. Their emergence marked the power shift in the state Republican party from rural, Protestant upstaters to downstate Catholic suburbanites.

The transformation also unraveled the traditionally tight regime in the state legislature. The 1964 Democratic landslide unseated Republican Senate Leader Walter J. Mahoney and Assembly Speaker Carlino but also gave reform Democrats control of Manhattan and the Bronx. With the lifting of party controls, along with growing fervor about the War on Poverty and the war in Vietnam, new factions formed in both parties. Senator Percy Sutton of Manhattan,

Senator Vander L. Beatty of Brooklyn, and Assemblyman Arthur O. Eve of Buffalo spearheaded the interest group that would become the Black and Puerto Rican Legislative Caucus. When Republicans retook the Senate in 1965, their ranks included abrasive types like Edward Speno and Norman Lent from Nassau County, who challenged the authority of Majority Leader Earl W. Brydges. After Republicans regained the Assembly in 1968, Speaker Perry B. Duryea faced upstaters furious at what they called Governor Rockefeller's "ownership" of the party. Proclaiming "participatory democracy," Duryea slashed Assembly committees to a workable twenty, replaced ad hoc joint committees with standing bodies, and allocated money for professional staff. The legislature gained what Syracuse University political scientist Allan Campbell called "capacity to stand up to the governor." More often it spent its time doing rancorous grandstanding on school aid, busing, and taxes.

This stalemate between Governor Rockefeller and his own party invited intervention by a third force—U.S. District Court judges, notably Leonard B. Sand and Constance Baker Motley of the Southern District of New York, Jack B. Weinstein of the Eastern District, which covered Brooklyn, Queens, and Long Island, and John T. Curtin of the Western District, which included Buffalo. Wielding court orders under *Brown*, the Civil Rights Act of 1964, and the Voting Rights Act of 1965, they pressed school integration on Long Island, Westchester, Buffalo, and Rochester, ordered scatter-site public housing projects in Yonkers, and broke the racial gerrymander of congressional districts in Brooklyn.

The community revolution's empowerment reached far beyond the suburbs. Hudson Valley activists attacked industrial river dumping and in 1962 challenged Consolidated Edison's plan to build a pump-storage hydroelectric facility on the summit of Storm King Mountain. Three years later they blocked Robert Moses's plans for an expressway on the Hudson's Westchester shore. The Indian Rights Movement on the Tuscarora Reservation protested Moses's plan to bulldoze a park along the Niagara River at Lewiston, and the Seneca Nation tried to block the Kinzua Reservoir on the Allegheny River. Around Bolton Landing, citizens joined the Adirondack Park Association to preserve Lake George. Pressed by Westchester Democrats, Governor Rockefeller in August 1965 called for a Hudson River scenic area, with land use controls for recreation and quiet wilderness modeled on the state Forest Preserve.

Culture beyond Walls

By the late 1950s, media markets, government patronage, and the community revolution gave rise to new cultural formats and locales. Playwrights mingled actors with audiences, music blurred classic and pop, and painters moved from the "picture plane" to performance space. New York City created what critic

Harold Rosenberg called a "tradition of the new"—a constantly unfolding avant-garde, which kept New York the center of the arts during the 1960s and challenged the moral sensibilities that had been at their core.

Governor Rockefeller beat the drum for community support for the fine and performing arts. He obtained appropriations for the New York State Theater at Lincoln Center, helped create the Saratoga Performing Arts Center, and festooned the Albany Mall with abstract painting and sculpture. Claiming that government can "nurture the arts without controlling their essential nature," he convened in 1960 a Council on the Arts to raise private funds, then secured legislature approval for the New York State Council on the Arts to provide seed money and technical support for local artistic groups. Directed by Gordon M. Smith, the driving force behind Buffalo's Albright-Knox Gallery, the NYSCA stimulated architectural preservation across the state and funded seventy-one dance and theater companies. Among other activities, the council helped raise funds for performance space in the hamlet of Warsaw, Wyoming County; gave technical assistance to restorers of a church in Cambridge, near Albany; and brought, for the first time, modern dance—the Erick Hawkins Company—to Jamestown.

The expansion of audiences, particularly around SUNY campuses, produced a broad movement for regional art centers and summer festivals. Visitors flocked to the University of Rochester's Memorial Art Gallery; Utica's Munson-Williams-Proctor Institute, which added an extension designed by Philip Johnson; and Syracuse's Helen S. Everson Museum of Art, designed by I. M. Pei. Buffalo's Albright-Knox Museum held its first exhibit of African art in 1968 and spearheaded the Buffalo Festival of the Arts Today, which mixed visual and performance art. Galleries opened at SUNY Binghamton and SUNY Buffalo, although none matched the Roy R. Neuberger Museum at SUNY Purchase, which Governor Rockefeller cajoled from the department store heir. Indulging a taste for monumental sculpture, Ralph Ogden endowed the Storm King Art Center, whose collection included works by David Smith. Under director Preston Hibbitt, the Tri-Cities Opera of Binghamton debuted American works like Myron Fink's *Jeremiah* (1962) and made the city a mecca for young singers. The Buffalo Philharmonic continued under the baton of Lukas Foss, while the Rochester Symphony and Eastman School prospered as classical performance centers. The Caramoor Festival in Westchester stimulated a Mozart revival that soon spread to Lincoln Center.

In the 1960s New York City remained the world capital of dance. The New York State Theater at Lincoln Center housed the New York City Ballet, where George Balanchine and Jerome Robbins put on cool, sinuous interpretations of Stravinsky. The rival American Ballet Theatre, co-directed by Lucia Chase and Oliver Smith, featured Antony Tudor's melancholy productions and Eliot Feld's choreography, notably in *Harbinger* (1967). Modernism was carried on by the

Erick Hawkins Company and by the irrepressible Merce Cunningham–John Cage troupe. In the late 1950s, Alvin Ailey's Harlem company set a muscular modernism to gospel and jazz, and choreographers like Twyla Tharp, a Cunningham student, embraced dance that was minimal and soundless.

Music expanded the boundaries of sound and concert hall performance. One influence was the Cage-Cunningham pursuit of the spontaneous, which often divorced the music from the dancing it accompanied. Another was the electronic synthesizer championed by Charles Wuorinen of the Group for Contemporary Music and upstate inventor Robert Moog, whose refinements made the instrument cheap and portable. In New York City, Bernstein brought the Philharmonic into the community. In the early 1960s he sponsored the orchestra's informal "promenade" concerts and in 1965 took classical music to Central Park. The Philharmonic hired its first African American in 1962 and its first female in 1966 and, thanks to Bernstein, increased appearances by African American soloists. By the time of his farewell concert in May 1969, Bernstein had thrust the classics onto the city's consciousness.

In the late 1950s Broadway's energies drained away to rival attractions. The first challenge was the rise of "Off Broadway" performances, driven by a growing frustration with Equity-scale productions. Cheap rents and relaxed Equity scales allowed Circle in the Square's revival of Eugene O'Neill and Joseph Papp's Shakespeare in Central Park, which began in 1956 as anti-establishment people's theater. A second development was the growth of regional theaters, particularly repertory companies in New Haven and San Francisco, and upstarts like Buffalo's Studio Arena. By the early 1960s, Off Broadway paled before the new wave of "Off-Off" stages like Joseph Chaikin's Open Theater and Julian Beck and Judith Malina's Living Theater, which by 1965 had staged some four hundred plays. While most of Off-Off's productions were "blackout" sketches or antic moments inspired by Cage-Cunningham, its triumphs included vivid theater like Jack Gelber's *Connection* (1959) and Kenneth Brown's *Brig* (1963).

Informal "performance space" freed playwrights to explore their conviction that American life was endured in autistic silence. In plays like *The Zoo Story* (1960), Edward Albee wrote about the breakdown of common language. Asked what his *Death of Bessie Smith* (1961) meant, Albee said that he wrote words for the "echo of what comes before or after." Jean-Claude van Itallie's *America Hurrah* (1965) aimed frantic dialogue at the "sensory nerves," while Sam Shepard's plays alternated bureaucratic cant and catatonic banter. Off-Off allowed Lanford Wilson to ruminate on the homosexual experience and African American playwrights, notably, LeRoi Jones to portray racism in obscenities aimed at "dimwitted, fatbellied white guys." Black theater especially developed its voice beyond Broadway. Playwright Douglas Turner Ward co-founded, with actor-director Robert Hooks, the Negro Ensemble Company, whose repertory on the black diaspora included Lonne Elder's *Ceremonies in Dark Old Men* (1969).

That year as well, Charles Gordone's *No Place to Be Somebody*, produced by Joseph Papp, was the first play by an African American to win the Pulitzer Prize.

Rigid, expensive Broadway never survived these divergent forces. As production costs mounted and audiences moved to the suburbs, shows like Alan Jay Lerner and Frederick Loewe's *Camelot* (1960) hinged on star appeal, advance sales, and marketing of the cast album. Composers were displaced by director-choreographers like Jerome Robbins, who dominated *Fiddler on the Roof* (1964). Stephen Sondheim, with television writer Larry Gelbart, composed the riotous *A Funny Thing Happened on the Way to the Forum* (1962), then went on to more ambitious works like *Company* (1970) and *Follies* (1971). Sondheim's music, deeply textured and often dissonant, was accompanied by clever, sometimes dazzling word play, which pleased discerning critics but left audiences hungering for standard ballads. The great age of musical comedy passed away along with Broadway nightclubs and café society.

Many writers still traveled the path of modern realism. As exemplified by the short stories of Cynthia Ozick and the novels of John Updike, New York provided a rich setting for stories of power and ethnic ambition. The Italian American experience was vividly detailed by Mario Puzo and Gay Talese, and Harlem was searingly portrayed in Claude Brown's *Manchild in the Promised Land* (1965) and Piri Thomas's *Down These Mean Streets* (1967). At the end of the decade, William Kennedy began his Albany saga about the Phelan's fall from Catholic grace, which made the capital city the American equivalent of James Joyce's Dublin.

Increasingly, however, fiction was disturbed by the decade's vivid, televised mayhem, by reality too intense for words. William S. Burroughs explored heroin and sodomy in his scatological classic, *Naked Lunch* (1959), and in *Nova Express* (1964) employed "cut-up" paragraphs for an almost hallucinatory stream of consciousness. Philip Roth's short stories used discontinuous narratives and grotesque, cartoonlike characters. A growing sense that events were bureaucratic fabrications drove Joseph Heller's *Catch-22* (1961) and Kurt Vonnegut's *Slaughterhouse-Five* (1969). Facts mixed with fictional forms in the "new journalism" practiced by Tom Wolfe and in Truman Capote's *In Cold Blood* (1965), whose jump-cut reportage aimed for "the immediacy of film." Norman Mailer lurched between formats in *An American Dream* (1964), a novel that let loose a psychopathic Kennedy on nighttown, and in his very personal coverage of the 1967 anti-Vietnam demonstrations, *The Armies of the Night* (1968).

The highbrow literary establishment was challenged by a profusion of little magazines and the dissonant views of critics such as Leslie Fiedler at SUNY Buffalo, who turned away from the classic works of the modernist canon to explore—and celebrate—the trashy products of mass culture. Another goad was

Susan Sontag, a young novelist and teacher at Columbia University, whose 1964 essays, "Against Interpretation," published in the *Evergreen Review*, and "Notes on 'Camp'" in the *Partisan Review*, exalted the "sensuous immediacy" of the French cinema and her impatience with novels that "fully satisfy my passion to understand." Literature as raw experience was championed by the *New York Review of Books*, which espoused "morality . . . from the barrel of a gun" and printed on its August 24, 1967, front page blueprints for making Molotov cocktails. The *Review*'s fascination with stylish violence was a prime example of what Tom Wolfe called "radical chic."

While a new generation of painters returned to imagery, they divided between serious "figuratists" like Fairfield Porter, Jane Freilicher, and Larry Rivers, and the earliest pop artists like Robert Rauschenberg and Jasper Johns, who spoofed icons of popular culture. Other pop artists included former billboard painter James Rosenquist, known for outsized paintings of banal things, and Claes Oldenburg, who sculpted "soft objects," like vinyl typewriters. Their put-on quality contributed to the wave of "happenings," absurd occasions of paint, noise, and movement by, among others, Allan Kaprow and the Judson Dance Theater. The reigning genius of art-as-inside-joke, however, was Andy Warhol, who yawned when critics sought meaning in his silkscreens of Campbell Soup cans and made a career spoofing celebrity. Pop was soon overtaken by op, notably Frank Stella's optical experiments in color, by color field painters like Agnes Martin and Ellsworth Kelly, and later in the decade, by conceptual artists such as Joseph Kosuth, who rejected visual objects for words that were "signifiers" of social meaning. Moving far beyond Jackson Pollock, painting had become a multidimensional experience.

In New York City's East Village, a hippie counterculture flourished among dealers in Day-Glo and drug paraphernalia and antimaterialist communes like the Diggers' Free Store. Abbie Hoffman joined radicals who were trying to educate alienated youth against the repressive establishment. Jerry Rubin helped with the October 1967 "Mobe," the great Central Park mobilization against the Vietnam War. The political limits of the counterculture surfaced at the August 1969 Woodstock Festival. Drawn to the rock extravaganza, 500,000 assembled on Max Yasgur's farm in Sullivan County, looking to one witness like "a gigantic cradle full of sleeping children." When Abbie Hoffman took the microphone to rouse the crowd against the Vietnam War, he was forced off the stage by The Who's Peter Townshend, brandishing his guitar. The audience seemed too stoned to care. Backstage, the Grateful Dead groused about the acoustics and lack of Deadheads. As the Woodstock Nation dispersed on a groggy Monday morning, it "liberated" personal belongings and left behind tons of trash.

New York's empire over the arts foundered on the social divide of the 1960s. The arts, like the vibrant city itself, were supposed to have a moral and exalting influence. Quarrels over race and war and simple weariness with tilting at corporatist America gradually ended both pronouncements about artistic mission and the city's confident role. The "tradition of the new" freed individuals to pursue an inspiration that reached into people's lives yet became increasingly interior and forbidding to outsiders. Large parts of the community were no longer interested in Gotham's expressions, which they viewed as outrageous self-indulgence, much like its politics.

Chapter 34

The Long Slide

BY THE LATE 1960s, THE COMMUNITY REVOLUTION LEFT neighborhoods glowering across barricades. White "backlash" erupted in Syracuse's West Side, Buffalo's East End, Yonkers, and New York City's outer boroughs, where Irish, Polish, and Italian Catholics suspected that Jewish and Protestant liberals were allied with blacks and Hispanics to wage the War on Poverty at their expense. Civil war between Rockefeller Republicans and conservative admirers of Arizona Senator Barry M. Goldwater, Republican presidential candidate in 1964, tore at the governor's leadership. Social issues like civil rights and busing to achieve racial balance in schools became irrepressible quarrels. Party politics disintegrated at the moment that New York was hit by "stagflation," global competition, and shifts in federal spending in the post-Vietnam era. Political and economic breakdown combined to bring about the 1975 fiscal crisis, both a symptom of and a factor in New York's slide.

Political Polarization

In the late 1960s, inflammatory social issues brought politics to ruinous polarization. Liberal Jews and African Americans, infused with indignation about black inequality and the Vietnam War, drove the Democrats' agenda toward social liberation. Entrenched in New York City, they could largely ignore conservative Democrats across the rest of the state. Among Republicans, political authority remained with Nelson Rockefeller, who still proclaimed his faith in civil rights, social progress, and doing good. More than most liberal Republicans, he had the resources and steely nature to withstand conservative complaints.

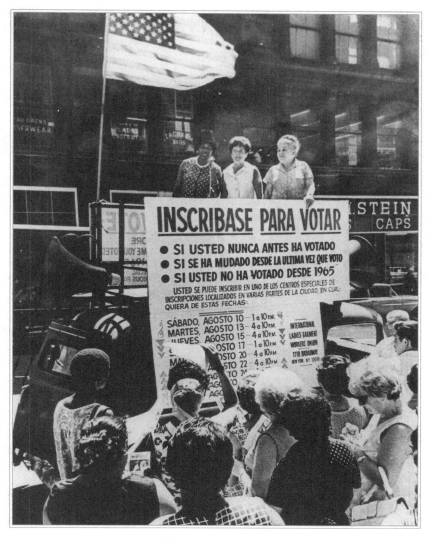

Labor Democrats sponsored this get-out-the-vote effort in Spanish-speaking
neighborhoods of New York City (ca. 1967). UNITE Archives, Kheel Center, Cornell
University.

During 1965 and 1966, white Catholic Democrats were alienated as liberals
not only championed the War on Poverty and denounced the Vietnam War, but
pressed in the state legislature a lifestyle agenda that legalized the sale of con-
traceptives, widened grounds for divorce, and abolished capital punishment.
Irish Catholic moderates like Queens County leader Matthew Troy, Erie
County's Joseph E. Crangle, and Senator Robert F. Kennedy struggled to hold

together the party's ideological wings, but civil rights, the antipoverty crusade, and school integration enlarged the breach. Governor Rockefeller's liberalism angered many conservative Republicans, but nothing stung them more than his run for the Republican presidential nomination in 1964 and his charge that Senator Goldwater's supporters were extremists. When Rockefeller ran for a third term in 1966 he was challenged by Democrat Frank O'Connor, Queens County district attorney; Franklin D. Roosevelt, Jr., Liberal party nominee; and the Conservative party candidate, college professor Paul L. Adams. Rockefeller prevailed over the splintered field, but his plurality fell under 45 percent. Adams polled 510,000 votes, ousting the Liberal party from third place (Row C) on the ballot.

Social issues continued to erode the mainstream of both parties. In 1967 Democrats took their liberal program a giant step forward by changing the state election law to replace "boss-dominated" nominating conventions with direct primaries, which gave decisive advantage to well-organized Manhattan reformers. In the 1968 presidential campaign, reform Democrats divided between support of Wisconsin Senator Eugene McCarthy and Senator Kennedy, both of whom opposed President Johnson's Vietnam policies, while some conservative Democrats were drawn to Alabama Governor George C. Wallace's third-party campaign. Wallace drew single-digit support in New York City's outer boroughs and on Long Island but his presence on the ballot gave a focus to anger over liberal policies in taxes, social justice, and school administration.

The 1968 campaign left behind an angry sense of unfinished business. In the suburbs, local politics hinged on controversies about school integration, inflamed by "single issue" candidates. Italian Republicans in Westbury and North Bellport, Long Island, harvested votes during the struggle against integration of Westbury's schools and equalized tracks for blacks and Hispanics at Bellport High. Opposition to school busing made the political careers of Nassau State Senator Norman F. Lent and Westchester Congressman Paul A. Fino. The anger surfaced in school board elections during 1968–69, when state voters defeated 20 percent of all district budgets. Reform Democrats adopted their own litmus test to ensure that candidates were simon-pure on Vietnam. Organizing to elect the antiwar South Dakota Senator George McGovern as president in 1972, they forced the state party to accept "McGovern Rules" requiring that officials, especially convention delegates, reflect the proportionate numbers of women, blacks, and Hispanics in the state population.

The women's movement added to the political splintering as women entered the workforce, beginning with the migration of suburban housewives to corporate offices and reaching a critical mass in Manhattan's publishing, media, and academic centers. During the 1970s, Manhattan feminism gave birth to new journals, notably *Working Mother*, *New Woman*, and Gloria Steinem's *Ms.* (founded in 1972). Middle-class professionals launched grassroots campaigns against pink-collar discrimination and sexual harassment. Working Women United held the first local speakout against harassment in Ithaca in 1975.

At the same time, suburban Catholicism witnessed a spiritual awakening, particularly among middle-class Irish, profoundly affected by Pope John XXIII's Second Vatican Council of 1962–65. While conservatives bemoaned reforms that substituted English for Latin in the liturgy, Catholics as a community were firmly committed to family values, female equality in the church, and parochial-school aid, and firmly against abortion. Governor Rockefeller injected another divisive issue—legalized abortion (on doctor's counsel, up to the twenty-fourth week of pregnancy), which the legislature made law in 1970. A Catholic women's discussion group in Merrick, Long Island, immediately organized the Right-to-Life party to run candidates who pledged repeal. In 1972, under pressure from the Catholic Church, the legislature voted for repeal, which Rockefeller vetoed with a lecture against imposing one "vision of morality on an entire society." Liberal New York built the climate for women's reproductive rights recognized by the U.S. Supreme Court in *Roe v. Wade* (1973). The Right-to-Life party, however, polled 130,000 votes in 1978 to oust Liberals from fourth place on the ballot.

Metropolitan Barricades

Mayor John Lindsay confronted a backlash in the outer boroughs, where his name symbolized Manhattan liberalism. In 1966 his support for a police civilian review board was rebuffed when the Patrolmen's Benevolent Association put the issue on the ballot. Lindsay also sided with the attempt by the African American community in Ocean Hill-Brownsville, Brooklyn, to implement a Ford Foundation experiment in school decentralization. When the Ocean Hill board hired black teachers in violation of city contracts, the United Federation of Teachers (UFT) struck the entire city system in September 1968. Black activists kept Ocean Hill schools open, pitting African Americans against the predominantly Jewish union. While black educators introduced Swahili, Malcolm X, and African studies into the schools, street demagogues like Sonny Carson hurled antisemitic slurs at the UFT. (After Carson's followers scuffled with Hasidim in nearby Crown Heights, Rabbi Meir Kahane organized a paramilitary patrol, the Jewish Defense League.) In 1969 the state legislature enacted a decentralization program, placing city public schools under the control of thirty-two elected neighborhood boards. At the same time Lindsay outlined his plan for "scatter-site" public housing in Corona and Forest Hills, Queens. Community protests scaled back the projects, but not before Lindsay became a curse word among Queens Italians and Jews.

Vietnam inflamed student resentments on campuses across the state. For months, Columbia University's SDS had charged that the campus presence of the Institute for Defense Analyses made the university complicit in the war. When Columbia announced plans in spring 1968 to build a campus gymnasium on the edge of Harlem, the SDS pounced on the "imperialist invasion" and called a strike of classes. On April 23, SDS members, other students, and some Harlem activists occupied college offices until administrators in the early hours of April 30 summoned police, who bloodily ended the sit-in. SUNY Buffalo, a campus simmering against Chancellor Martin E. Meyerson's plans for expansion, was also fertile ground for violence. In March 1969, Buffalo students occupied Hayes Hall to protest the war, and in March 1970 another protest had to be suppressed by city police. At Cornell University in April 1969, black students, including some armed with rifles, occupied a student union building to enforce demands for a black student center and black studies. The war even drew protests in the high schools, as on the Memorial Day 1969 "mobilization" in Hempstead, Long Island, against the war, which attracted teenagers from as far away as Amityville and Huntington.

Student leaders like Mark Rudd and Ted Gold of Columbia's SDS never got over the shock of the police on campus. Quitting college, they formed a Revolutionary Youth Movement to pursue "cadre" actions, including madcap "jail-breaks" down high school corridors. In late 1969, some two hundred adherents, including perhaps fifty in the New York City area, declared themselves Weathermen and formed underground "affinity groups" to wage terrorist war on fascist "Amerika." Fiddling with dynamite, three Weathermen, including Ted Gold, died in a blast that leveled a Greenwich Village townhouse on March 6, 1970. During the summer, Weathermen bombed New York City police headquarters and a local branch of the Bank of America. In Rochester a contingent called the Flower City Conspiracy raided a federal building, ransacking Selective Service and FBI offices.

The rage against the police was joined by the Greenwich Village homosexual community. On June 24, 1969, when the vice squad raided the Stonewall Inn, a bar on Christopher Street, crowds of homosexuals pelted the police with garbage and screamed "gay power." For the next four nights, thousands of gays descended on the Village. More astonished than deterred, the police raided another bar, the Snake Pit, three months later. Such disturbances led to a protest at the precinct house, the formation of the Gay Liberation Front, and a giant march through Manhattan from Christopher Street to Central Park.

Outer-borough contempt for Lindsay liberalism shaped the 1969 mayoral election. In the GOP primary, conservatives selected Staten Island State Senator John L. Marchi, forcing Lindsay to run on the Liberal line. Democrats chose Brooklyn's Mario A. Procaccino, the voluble conservative who represented working-class white ethnics. Lindsay tried to rouse his old coalition of Manhattan Republicans, African Americans, and Jews, and spent late October in Brooklyn and Queens, denying that he "cared too much for minorities." Marchi and Procaccino split the conservative vote, giving Lindsay a 42 percent plurality—and instant lame duck status.

Buffalo was wracked in 1968 by controversy over law-and-order measures and school integration. Demands by liberal Democrats and African Americans for a civilian review board nearly touched off a police strike. Board of education plans to advance school integration were checked by the refusal of the city council to appropriate the required money. A year later Mayor Sedita's third-term bid was challenged by black Democrats mobilized by Assemblyman Arthur O. Eve and by white, conservative Republicans headed by school board member Alfreda Slominski. Sedita fended off Eve's challenge by accepting George K. Arthur as the city council's first African American majority leader, but Slominski could not be appeased. Attacking school busing and "professional educators," she polled nearly 40 percent of the vote, largely in white working-class wards. Sedita edged by with support from affluent, normally Republican wards, the university district, and blacks.

Bitter political lines were drawn across other cities. Rochester was wracked by a police strike in May 1970 and by bomb blasts, linked to student radicals. The resulting dour mood killed off the local effort at school integration, a system of "magnet" schools to mix suburban children with inner-city blacks and Hispanics. Espousing "neighborhood schools" and "parental control," Gordon J. De Hand in 1971 ran for president of the Rochester Board of Education. Badly split between integration and Black Power candidates, FIGHT (the black protest group) mounted feeble opposition, and De Hand won easily. In Syracuse, white working-class anger at the War on Poverty, university demonstrations, and the 1970 downtown rampage by black youths, drove Italian Democrats into the Republican party. In Yonkers a backlash against housing integration poisoned city politics. After the city council rejected court-ordered integration of public housing, U.S. District Judge Leonard B. Sand virtually took over the government that refused to tax and spend.

The obstructive mood ended hopes of integrating the suburbs. Westchester officials forced the Urban Development Corporation to drop its "Nine Towns" plan for scatter-site, low-income projects. Wary of court review of exclusionary zoning, town governments adopted guidelines for "staged development," designed to limit apartment construction for minorities. Suits were filed against restrictive zoning practices in Spring Valley and New City, Rockland County, and in Oyster Bay and Glen Cove, Long Island, but the state Court of Appeals decision *Golden v. Planning Board of the Town of Ramapo* (1972) upheld the right of suburbs to control land use.

Republicans in the state legislature used the 1970 census to carry out a "bipartisan gerrymander" to strengthen their suburban ranks. They combined Syracuse's two assembly seats with suburban GOP districts, and Rochester's two seats were consolidated into one city district, with the rest added to the suburbs. The process was reviewed by President Richard M. Nixon's Justice Department, which applied the Voting Rights Act of 1965 to preserve representation in large nonwhite districts. While Democrats lost further strength in the suburbs, the Voting Rights Act increased the party's identification with the cause of African Americans and Hispanics in New York City.

Republican legislators provided support for suburban initiatives. In 1972 GOP leaders established the Joint Legislative Committee on Metropolitan and Regional Affairs to enhance the authority of local governments. Proclaiming the advent of "the urban county," the committee called for county assumption, and the administrative apparatus to support it, of a host of local functions, from welfare and solid waste disposal to police protection. They took care, however, to exempt the bulwarks of suburban life like public school administration, zoning, and subdivision planning, which remained under township control. Outlying towns soon had another source of fiscal independence. In 1973 the State Office for Local Government helped suburban and rural units apply for the first grants under President Nixon's program of federal revenue sharing.

Rockefeller's Right Turn

As Republicans dug in against liberal spending and racial integration, Governor Rockefeller resorted to "messages of necessity" in an attempt to bypass legislative committees. In 1970 he sent eighty-two such messages to the Senate and seventy-eight to the Assembly. Growing testy toward those who no longer bent to his will, he feuded with Mayor Lindsay, whom he despised as an upstart (one reason Lindsay declared himself a Democrat in 1971). Rockefeller also turned against Senator Charles Goodell, the Jamestown congressman whom he had appointed to Robert Kennedy's Senate seat in 1968. Goodell, once a reliable conservative, had turned against the Vietnam War.

Party splinters decided the 1970 elections, when Goodell sought a full term and Rockefeller wanted four more years. His estrangement from Goodell opened the way for the Conservative party to nominate businessman James L. Buckley for U.S. senator. The Democratic primary nominated the staunch liberal Arthur J. Goldberg, United Nations ambassador, for governor; Westchester Congressman Richard L. Ottinger for the Senate, and Comptroller Arthur Levitt for another term, prompting Albany boss Daniel O'Connell to mutter about "the damn most unbalanced ticket I ever heard of." Taunting Goodell and Ottinger on issues like abortion, aid to parochial schools, and school busing, Buckley asked "Isn't it time *we* had a Senator?" His harvest of Catholic votes in Utica and Syracuse, southern Queens, and Nassau and Suffolk Counties, buried Goodell and squeezed by Ottinger, 39 percent to 37 percent. Goldberg, in a lackluster campaign, was no match for Rockefeller, who supported President

Nixon's invasion of Cambodia, defied antiwar protesters on SUNY campuses, and courted blue-collar "hard hat" unions. As the state Democratic chairman concluded, "The right wing of our party—particularly the Irish, Italian, and Polish Catholics—they left the party and voted for Rocky."

The result moved Rockefeller further to the right. In March 1971, he proposed welfare reform of one-year residency and work requirements, with a welfare inspector general to catch "cheats." A year later Rockefeller turned apocalyptic on narcotics, demanding that the legislature establish new courts for drug felonies and urging life sentences for pushers. "No more of this plea bargaining, parole, and probation," he told his staff. He remained adamant, and once the "Rockefeller Plan" was passed in May 1973, even teenagers sixteen and over faced minimum sentences of fifteen years to life for the sale of two ounces of narcotics or possession of four ounces, regardless of the circumstances of the crime or the prior record of the accused.

The zeal to prosecute threatened Chief Judge Stanley H. Fuld's visions of court reform and his ambition to reclaim for the Court of Appeals its reputation as a ground-breaking tribunal. Fuld blamed the court's problems on the massive case backlog produced by the automatic right of appeal, which he wanted replaced by *certiorari*, the discretion to accept appeals enjoyed by the U.S. Supreme Court. In late 1968, Fuld presented a court-reform package to the legislature, which failed to respond. He took to the stump, urged judges to speed trials and inspect prisons, and pressured Rockefeller for funds. In April 1971 he laid down the gauntlet: judges would dismiss charges against defendants in non-homicide cases if trials had not begun within six months of arrest.

Amid the crisis in criminal justice, Governor Rockefeller confronted a revolt at the Attica Correctional Facility. Located in Wyoming County, Attica represented the state penitentiary system in microcosm. Its 2,243 inmates were 54 percent black, 9 percent Hispanic, and 37 percent white. Almost half came from New York City, with another third from Buffalo, Rochester, and Syracuse, while the guards, recruited from nearby towns, included no blacks and only one Hispanic. By the early 1970s, Attica contained a volatile population of drug felons, Muslims and Black Panthers, and radicals jailed for crimes against "the system." Resentments simmered as guards goaded Muslim convicts, then boiled over with news of the police killing of Black Panthers in California. On September 9, 1971, after a fight in the prison yard, convicts took guards hostage and barricaded cellblocks, while Sam Melville, in prison for a Weathermen's bomb conspiracy, rigged booby traps to keep the police at bay. For four days inmates bargained with the governor's representatives. While Rockefeller agreed to investigate grievances, he refused amnesty for violent acts committed during the riot and, on September 13, ordered in state troopers. Melville and forty-two others, including nine hostages, died in the melee, most of them killed by troopers' buckshot.

Attica turned Judge Fuld's reforms into a Rockefeller crusade for more

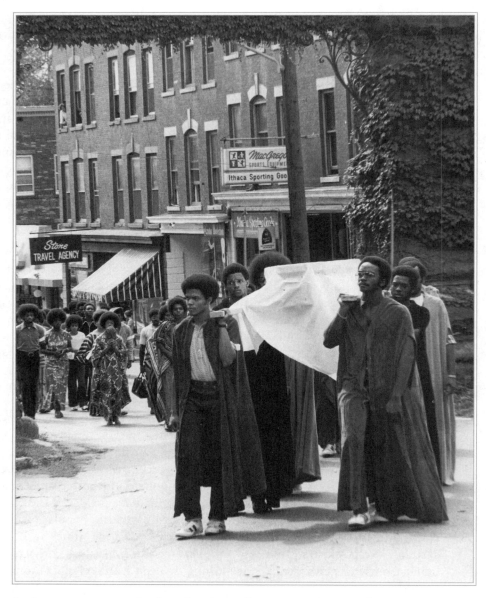

Student protesters march solemnly at Cornell University in September 1971, carrying a draped effigy of a coffin to memorialize those killed in the riot at Attica Correctional Facility. Division of Rare and Manuscript Collections, Cornell University Library.

judges, prosecutors, and prisons. His January 1972 State of the State Message proposed state takeover of local courts, including those in New York City, and a governor-appointed state court administrator. Although Assembly Democrats considered consolidation a GOP ploy to control the judiciary, the public supported Rockefeller's brand of "court reform." The legislature stalled Rockefeller's proposal for state takeover of local courts but gave him authority to appoint a host of new judges, particularly to handle the anticipated load of narcotics indictments. They also approved constitutional amendments (which would have to be approved again by the 1975 legislature before being sent to the voters) to create a court administrator and a commission of judicial conduct, which could admonish, censure, or remove wayward judges.

Economic Decline

Political disarray was accompanied by erosion in the state's economy. New York was beset by stagflation—which combined inflation, particularly in energy costs after the 1973 OPEC "oil shock," with stagnant growth after the recession of 1974. Multinational corporations brought global competition, which threatened manufacturers and even New York City's service economy. The scenic preservation movement broadened into an environmentalist challenge to manufacturing. Federal air and water enactments of the early 1970s affected North Country paper makers, Buffalo steel mills, and coal-fired utilities like Consolidated Edison.

The state curtailed economic development in wilderness areas. After a 1967 proposal by the governor's brother, Laurence S. Rockefeller, that the Forest Preserve become a national park, Governor Rockefeller appointed a commission that in 1970 recommended creation of an authority to impose land use controls, purchase private property within the park's boundaries, and protect wilderness zones from automobiles, power boats, and other intrusions. In 1971 the legislature created the Adirondack Park Agency, which promulgated land use rules, including limiting "principal buildings" to not more than fifteen per square mile. Property owners charged the state with "locking up" resources, but their suits were swept aside by the Court of Appeals. In 1979 the state Commission of Environmental Conservation declared the Hudson Highlands a scenic area, and the following year Consolidated Edison, ending a decade of quarrels with Hudson preservationists, contributed the Storm King site for a state park.

Declining economic opportunity in the Adirondacks thinned the area's population. In Essex County, abandonment and buyouts brought the farm count down to 300 by 1970 (compared to 1,757 in 1930). Successful operators specialized in birdsfoot trefoil, a silage crop superior to alfalfa, which they sold to dairymen. Republic Steel's iron mine introduced staggered layoffs in 1968, then shut down; while the J. & J. Rogers Paper Mill ran out of sufficient wood supplies and was ordered as well to stop pollution run-off into the Ausable River. Federal antipoverty funds helped the Essex County Development Corporation create tourist jobs, but an expert called them "a drop in the bucket." In 1972 Essex, Hamilton, and Franklin Counties had unemployment well over 10 percent, and it rose to 20 percent the following January.

Suburbanization continued to transform agriculture on the metropolitan fringe. Towns lost their milk or feed plants to central milk processing and large capacity tank trucks, and grew more dependent on rural cooperatives like Batavia's Agway Co-Op, which included an oil and fertilizer plant, feed mill, and egg market. Through Broome and Chemung Counties, Route 17 connected commercial "strips" and new employment centers: IBM east of Owego, A & P food products and an industrial park outside Horseheads, and Harpur College west of Binghamton. Scattered outcroppings of settlement grew in the hinterlands of Elmira-Horseheads and Binghamton–Johnson City–Endicott and alongside Routes 17 and 15 and Interstate 81, as residents purchased abandoned farmhouses and trailers and built inexpensive homes. In 1971 the state legislature reacted to the threat of rural sprawl by permitting groups of farmers to form agricultural districts to restrict development and keep land assessed at farm value. By mid-1974, 18 percent of state farmland had been placed in the preservation program.

The state shared the manufacturing decline of the Mid-Atlantic region during the late 1960s and 1970s as firms sought cheap labor and low taxes in the Sunbelt. Between 1970 and 1975, a period when the region lost one-seventh of its industrial jobs, New York State's toll was 253,000. Declines were severe in nondurables like apparel, textiles, furniture, leather, and shoes. The casualties included Endicott-Johnson, which left Broome County, and Crescant Tool Company, Jamestown's largest employer, whose assets were acquired by a Dallas firm and moved to South Carolina. Mohasco, headquartered in Amsterdam, transferred its Mohawk carpet output to Mexico and diversified into home furnishings, including Barcaloungers made in Georgia. The trend among manufacturers was to drop low-profit "commodity products" for high-profit specialty items. At General Electric the discontinued included a range of consumer items, from fans to vacuum cleaners.

Economic change interacted with national defense policy to winnow Long Island's high-tech enclaves. In 1963 the state landed $1 billion in federal research and development contracts, 9.3 percent of the national total (California captured 38.6 percent). On Long Island, American Bosch Arma and Sperry Rand slashed their payrolls, while the phaseout of Republic's F-105 fighters cut employment by three-quarters in 1965 (when Republic become a subsidiary of Fairchild-Hiller in Dallas–Fort Worth). Between 1954 and 1960, New York dropped to last place among all states in investment per worker in new plants and equipment and showed serious lags in factory output per employee. Meanwhile, California roared ahead in aircraft, electronics, and automobiles and became the top manufacturing state in 1973.

Economic woes had repercussions for the state's population, which plateaued in the late 1960s, then headed down. The change reflected the impact of family planning, which spread from affluent middle-class couples to the working class, irrespective of religion. Across the state the number of births per thousand women fell from 18.6 in 1965 to 13.0 in 1975. The five-year period, 1971–75, produced 400,000 fewer births than 1961–65. The falling rate was compounded by outmigration, which had been negligible in the 1960s but totaled 640,000 between 1970 and 1976, as residents moved to other Mid-Atlantic states, notably New Jersey, and to the Sunbelt. All the cities with populations over 50,000 lost residents in the 1970s, including Utica, which lost 17 percent, Rochester 18 percent, and Buffalo 23 percent. Between 1970 and 1976, Greater New York suffered a loss of 600,000, and metropolitan Binghamton, Elmira, Utica-Rome, and Buffalo–Niagara Falls underwent sharp declines.

These setbacks in industry and population depressed economic indicators across the board in the 1970s. Employment in transportation and public utilities slumped 15 percent in New York State while rising 12 percent nationally. Soaring energy costs and lagging freight revenues brought the Penn Central Railroad to bankruptcy and jeopardized the solvency of Consolidated Edison, which had to amortize its costly Hudson River nuclear plant, Indian Point 3. Long Island Lighting Company, which built the Shoreham nuclear plant and planned another at Lloyd Harbor in Huntington, was troubled by slackening industrial demand for power and antinuclear protests, which threatened Shoreham's chances of receiving an operating license. Statewide employment in finance, insurance, and real estate increased by only 13 percent, far behind the national 47 percent. Between 1967 and 1977 the state's share of the American tourist and lodging market dropped 42 percent, as vacationers looked to the Sunbelt, the Caribbean, and Europe.

The economic decay undermined New York's standard of living. For the first time, New York factory wages lagged behind the national average. During the 1970s, U.S. per capita income grew 36 percent compared to New York State's anemic 8 percent. By 1978 the state had 8.7 percent of the nation's personal income (compared to 11.5 percent in 1963), and 7.7 percent of employment (compared to 11.0). The state's per capita income, 22 percent above the national average as late as 1963, was barely 3 percent above it by 1978. According to Syracuse University economist Roy Bahl, New York had become "an average state."

Cities on the Edge

Economic change shook the fiscal stability of major cities. Colossal redevelopments like the South Mall failed to retain Albany's middle class, which took tax and shopping dollars to the suburbs. In 1958 nearly half the manufacturing jobs in the Albany region were within the city's limits; by 1977 the number had fallen to one in seven. The city's share of regional sales slumped from 30 percent to only 14. The economic well-being of the state capital came to depend on government—the South Mall alone employed nearly 40,000 state workers—and on college students, including 16,000 at SUNY Albany. State fiscal operations sustained local banks and contributed to the city's one bright spot, a 29 percent job increase in the central business district—largely filled by suburban commuters.

Buffalo's economic transformation accelerated racial change. The city's African American population remained static during the 1960s, but the proportion rose from 20.4 percent to 26.3 percent as white flight continued. Buffalo lost major employment sectors, including 20,000 jobs at the grain elevators on Lake Erie and nearly half that number at Bethlehem Steel's Lackawanna plant. National Gypsum, Carborundum, and Western Electric moved out, and General Motors and Ford cut back auto assemblies. The Buffalo Bills under quarterback Jack Kemp won the 1964 AFL championship, only to leave their stadium "in the heart of the ghetto" for the suburbs, where they were joined by the Buffalo Sabres of the National Hockey League. Downtown business continued to shrink. In 1967 Buffalo's 4,460 retail stores had accounted for 46 percent of Erie County's sales volume. Ten years later 3,181 stores accounted for only 29.7 percent. The weak economy detached African American men from the labor force. In 1980 fourteen census tracts had black participation rates under 50 percent, prompting local historian Henry Taylor to conclude that large numbers were "no longer . . . in the Buffalo labor force."

The sheer scale of New York City's economic slide overshadowed the rest of the state's. From 1964 to 1969, the city added an average of 47,000 jobs per year, but during the next five years it lost an average of 43,000, mostly in apparel, printing, and miscellaneous manufacturing. From 3.8 million jobs in 1969, employment slid 13 percent, a wipeout of one-half million, until bottom was reached in 1977. During the early 1970s the suburban share of regional manufacturing surpassed the city's. As garment lofts, printing plants, and bakeries closed on Seventh Avenue and Canal Street and in Long Island City, immigrants and the working poor had to depend on menial jobs in services, hospitals, hotels, bars, and restaurants.

While the city's blue-collar economy shrank, finance and corporate services experienced a new volatility. In 1970 New York City had one-third of America's office space, but high rents and living costs accelerated the exodus of corporate headquarters like Nabisco, Shell Oil, and PepsiCo. Even as the New York Stock Exchange handled a sixfold increase in volume in the 1970s, the Big Board's monopoly was attacked by mutual fund managers and institutional investors, who wanted discount commissions on "block trades," and firms like Merrill Lynch, whose president, Donald T. Regan, denounced Wall Street's "protective prices." The challenge was joined by regional exchanges in Chicago and San Francisco and by NASDAQ, the computerized stock quotation system. In the mid-1970s, the New York Stock Exchange, its president conceded, was no longer "the only game in town."

New York's banking dominance shifted as corporations raised capital on the stock exchange and invested surpluses in U.S. Treasury notes. At the same time, state and federal regulators dismantled New Deal prohibitions against large-scale financial operations and competitive practices. With "deregulation," commercial banks expanded into mortgages and consumer credit, including credit cards, which amounted to one-third of their lending by the 1970s. An array of nonfinancial institutions like credit unions, brokerage firms, and retail chains began to offer the equivalent of deposit accounts. First National City Bank, under Walter Wriston (president, 1967–70, then chairman until 1984) met the community revolution head on, opening storefront branches, pioneering the "Everything" card in the late 1960s and automatic tellers in 1978. Chase Manhattan, on the other hand, suffered from the managerial neglect of David Rockefeller, who promoted statesmanlike lending abroad but lost touch with the bank's local and small-business markets.

Law firms searched the globe for new practice areas. Cadwalader, Wickersham & Taft, for instance, moved into overseas shipping deals, including mortgage instruments, notably $1 billion for OPEC liquefied-gas transports, real estate investment trusts, and "securitization" deals with the Federal Home Loan Mortgage Corporation. By the late 1970s, Chadbourne and Parke had opened offices in the United Arab Emirates and Moscow. Skadden Arps, which had pioneered corporate takeovers, was well positioned for the takeover mania of the late 1970s.

The city's media lost stability during the 1960s as television's share of advertising overtook print, and upstart ABC pulled abreast of CBS and NBC. The community revolution and targeted markets inspired the "creative revolution" on Madison Avenue, which saw William Bernbach use street language to promote Levy's Jewish ryebread, Doyle Dane Bernbach and Benton and Bowles hire Italians and Jews, and Mary Wells, in 1966, become the first woman to found her own firm, Wells, Rich, Green. Publishing was rocked by television and by retailers eager to reach narrow "segmented" markets. General interest magazines like *Life* and *Look* gave way to specialty journals like *Travel & Leisure*, feminist venues like *New Woman* and *Ms.*, and media aimed at scattered, urbane readers like *New York* and *Los Angeles*. Venerable publishers of fiction like the *New Yorker* and *Esquire* underwent sharp editorial changes as they faced competition from *Rolling Stone* and Andy Warhol's *Interview*.

Midtown's volatility was mirrored by the upheaval in neighborhoods. During the expansive 1960s, white, college-educated professionals became concentrated in Chelsea, the Upper East Side, and the Upper West Side in Manhattan,

and Brooklyn Heights and Park Slope in Brooklyn. Turning blocks of underval-
ued brownstones into affluent neighborhoods, they "gentrified" communities,
it was said, at the expense of the poor. At the same time, New York City families earning below the poverty line increased by more than 50,000. Whole
neighborhoods collapsed when landlords walked away from 33,000 apartments
each year during the late 1960s, a total of some 200,000 by 1975. Abandonment
in the South Bronx, Harlem, and Bushwick–East New York in Brooklyn helped
shrink the city's population by 10.4 percent or 824,000 people by the end of the
1970s. Brooklyn and the Bronx suffered staggering declines—14.3 and 20.6 percent, respectively.

Along with the people went businesses, jobs, and services. In 1958 the
Bronx had 12,404 retail stores with 39,357 employees. By 1977 the borough had
lost half its businesses, and employment dropped 21 percent. Brooklyn's retail
base declined by 10,000 stores with nearly 54,000 retail employees. Neighborhoods lost doctors and pharmacists and became dependent on medical emergency rooms, like King's County Hospital in Brooklyn and Morrisania Hospital
in the Bronx. In ten Brooklyn poverty neighborhoods, the welfare population
doubled between 1965 and 1972. The number of residents on welfare in Bedford-
Stuyvesant rose from 19 percent to 36 percent, and in Brownsville from 23 percent to 38 percent. Neighborhoods were scourged by 15,000 arson fires, mostly
in abandoned buildings. Hunts Point in the South Bronx became a landscape of
bricked-up buildings roamed by junkies and wild dogs.

Social disintegration overwhelmed the education hopes of the 1960s. The
educational expert David Rogers discovered "no dramatic breakthroughs" in
reading and math scores, but soaring numbers of dropouts and absentee rates.
Another study found that the high school dropout rate in New York City rose
from 34 percent in 1970–71 to nearly 50 percent for the 1974–75 graduating
class. Aspira, a Hispanic advocacy group, reported that only 15 percent of adult
Puerto Ricans were high school graduates in 1970 compared to 53.4 percent of
whites. The future looked grim, as only 1.2 percent of Spanish-speaking high
school students received college-preparatory academic diplomas.

Experts fumbled to explain the urban disaster. Conservatives claimed that
rent control had capped landlord profits, causing many to give up on their properties, and that crime, particularly heroin addiction, ravaged honest enterprise.
Hunter College economist Peter Salins suggested that large government-
assisted projects, notably Co-op City in the Bronx, shocked the system by
siphoning off middle-class tenants from neighborhoods like the Grand Concourse south of Fordham Road. Liberals argued that growing unemployment
and poverty prevented scores of thousands of tenants from paying "market"
rents. Whatever the reasons, large portions of the inner city verged on anarchy.

Economic and social deterioration brought shifts among high-income
whites. During the economic expansion of the 1960s, the number of New York

City's upper-income families rose to 30,000, but the city's share of affluent residents in the greater New York region slipped from 66 percent in 1960 to 62 percent in 1970. During the contracting 1970s, the city's share dropped further, reaching 54 percent by 1980.

Despite the signs of underlying decay, state and local governments continued to spend. State budgets expanded 362 percent between 1963 and 1974, and per capita state spending soared from $391.81 to $1,448.20. Two-thirds of the funds went for state operations in social welfare, education, and hospitals, largely because of Great Society mandates on the state, and for state aid to municipalities. Increases in state spending were largely financed from two general sources: the state sales tax, whose collections tripled, and the state income tax.

Ravaged cities and urban services survived by the grace of the state's fiscal authority. State aid (with federal transfer payments) provided more than half the budgets of the Big Six cities by the mid-1970s. The Metropolitan Transportation Authority had taken over the operational expenses and debt for the subways, commuter railroads, and buses in New York City and its suburbs, and the Niagara Frontier Transportation Authority absorbed the cost of mass transit in the Buffalo region. Similar regional authorities kept buses running in Rochester and Monroe County, Syracuse and Onondaga County, and the Capital District, including Albany, Schenectady, and Rensselaer and Saratoga Counties. The State Power Authority relieved Consolidated Edison of the burden of supplying power to MTA's New York City subways.

Although the state's "moral obligation" debt raised eyebrows, Attorney General Louis J. Lefkowitz extended complacent approval, and Manhattan bond underwriters made millions on commissions. The Urban Development Corporation and Job Development Authority needed "hard cash" ($420 million) from the legislature in anticipation of tax revenues and bond sales. Comptroller Levitt warned that nearly two-thirds of this amount was, in effect, written off by the legislature, but otherwise kept quiet.

In December 1973, Nelson Rockefeller resigned from office to serve as President Gerald Ford's appointed vice president, leaving his longtime running mate, Lieutenant Governor Malcolm Wilson, in charge.

The Fiscal Crisis

In early 1975, Chase Manhattan, First National City, and Bankers Trust informed New York City that its short-term debt was no longer an attractive investment. This grim message set off the New York City fiscal crisis. The city's agony, however, was one among several disasters; others overtook Yonkers, Rochester, and Buffalo, the Penn Central Railroad and Consolidated

Edison, the Urban Development Corporation and Mitchell-Lama housing. More than a collapse of state and municipal institutions, the crisis signaled the break-down of belief in New Deal–Great Society policies. New York's liberalism could not correct inmates at Attica, help the retarded at Letchworth Village, cure schizophrenics at Syracuse's Richard N. Hutchings Psychiatric Center, or renew the South Bronx.

New York City was brought to the brink by built-in deficits, as tax revenues (with the shift of business and the middle class to the suburbs) lagged behind the cost of government programs. In the decade before 1975, municipal spend-ing rose at twice the rate of income. The city paid, historian Richard C. Wade observed, "the penalties of pioneering" the welfare state: relief rolls doubling from 500,000 in 1966 to 1.2 million by 1976, a municipal hospital system, and a tuition-free public university. Between 1965 and 1975 the city's long-term debt rose from $4 billion to $14.6 billion. Mayor Lindsay and City Comptroller Abra-ham D. Beame managed to avert disaster with modest layoffs, the inflation-sen-sitive sales tax, and President Nixon's revenue sharing. They also resorted to short-term, tax-anticipation notes (TANs), which were sold to banks in antici-pation of revenues. During Lindsay's second term and after Beame's succession in 1973, TAN debt rose steadily, reaching $3.4 billion by 1974, when the OPEC oil shock and the national recession made the banks reconsider their portfolios.

Political breakdown hastened the crisis. The city's fiscal woes were com-pounded by the feud between Mayor Lindsay and Governor Rockefeller, who ridiculed Lindsay's abilities. In 1971, when Rockefeller requested $1.1 billion in new taxes, GOP rebels, led by Syracuse Senator John Hughes, vowed to "cut the hell" out of the budget. Conceding that more taxes would mean economic di-saster, Rockefeller accepted a 10 percent budget cut that reduced state aid to city welfare and Medicaid programs and slashed New York City's tax authoriza-tion. More important, the crisis over school busing embittered GOP legislators over the city's liberalism. The issue had been simmering as the federal courts pressed State Education Commissioner James Allen and his 1970 successor, Ewald B. Nyquist, for integration plans. In 1974 Nyquist's integration orders were pending for the school systems of Utica, Newburgh, Mount Vernon, Lack-awanna, and Buffalo. Heated opposition to plans to bus 40,000 students between Buffalo and its suburbs had put the Buffalo Board of Education under the order of U.S. District Judge John T. Curtin. White parents threatened to mob the buses and make Buffalo "another Boston," and the city council, already staggered by the 1974 recession, refused to spend funds for integration. In the spring of 1974, Nyquist retreated from the policy of forced busing, but the polit-ical damage had been done. Perhaps Rockefeller could have crammed a desper-ate rescue through the legislature or convinced bankers, particularly his brother David, chairman of Chase, to bring the city to account, short of default; but his successor, Malcolm Wilson, had fewer options.

The first domino to fall was the Urban Development Corporation, which Edward Logue had allowed to market $1.1 billion in notes with inadequate mortgages. In early 1974 several UDC projects turned sour, cash flow ran dry, and Washington curtailed anticipated federal housing grants. Logue tried to consolidate debt, and Governor Wilson quietly reassured the banks, but in February 1974 the UDC failed to pay $135 million in interest owed to note holders. With the corporation's "moral authority" shattered, investors questioned other state debts, particularly the notes of the Housing Finance Agency, which had financed Co-op City in the Bronx, then in the throes of a rent strike, and which stood behind the Dormitory Authority and the Medical Care Facilities Finance Agency. Doubts about state finance, coupled with rising unemployment during the recession, brought about Wilson's loss in the 1974 gubernatorial election to Brooklyn Congressman Hugh L. Carey. A Democratic loner, Carey had wrested the primary nomination from the party favorite, Manhattan businessman Howard Samuels. Carey was a widower (his wife had died of cancer) with twelve children, a mordant wit, and sharp political instincts.

Carey had barely assumed office when the banks shocked New York City with their announcement. Mayor Beame asked for extensions, offered budget cuts, and approached Washington for aid. President Ford rebuffed Beame, inspiring the *New York Daily News* headline, "Ford to City: Drop Dead." Beame had no choice but to accept state receivership, which Governor Carey, working with Senate Majority Leader Warren Anderson of Binghamton, wrested from a skeptical legislature. In June 1975 the Municipal Assistance Corporation transformed $3 billion of short-term city debt into longer-term "Big MAC" bonds, secured by a state-collected city sales tax. When that failed to pacify investors, Carey gained passage of the Financial Emergency Law, which froze city salaries, forced "give backs" from city unions on pensions and benefits, and brought city expenditures under an Emergency Financial Control Board (EFCB) to balance the budget within three years. To avert state default, which loomed in September, Carey pushed through a $600 million increase in state taxes—particularly on corporations and banks. In the meantime, the governor engaged investment banker Felix G. Rohatyn to sell the U.S. Congress on federal loan guarantees and to win over the municipal labor unions. Rohatyn's persuasiveness, augmented by his friendship with labor's Victor Gotbaum, convinced unions to invest pension funds in Big MAC bonds, accept municipal layoffs of 10 percent, and agree to wage freezes. Washington then guaranteed the EFCB bond issue.

As backlash politics soured voters on taxes, Buffalo, Rochester, and Yonkers went through variations of financial near-death. While Rochester Democrats and Republicans fought over control of the city council, voters rejected tax increases and brought the city close to default. Rochester came under the fiscal supervision of State Comptroller Levitt. Deadlocked plans for housing integration stymied tax votes in Yonkers. In 1975 the state legislature created the New

York State Emergency Financial Control Board for Yonkers, headed by Levitt, whose fiscal plan guaranteed the city's debt but laid off one-fourth of city employees. Buffalo teetered on the edge of bankruptcy after voters rejected a construction bond issue, the recession sank tax revenues, and the Penn Central Railroad failed to pay property taxes. During 1975 local banks refused to buy city notes, forcing Mayor Stanley M. Makowski to slash eight hundred municipal jobs. After the draconian cuts, banks refinanced the city's short-term notes.

Other bailouts occurred across the state. When the Penn Central Railroad went under in 1970, the federal government provided $150 million in loan guarantees, folded long-distance passenger service into Amtrak, and in 1975 recapitalized freight business into the Consolidated Railroad Corporation (Conrail). The UDC's notes were refinanced by a new state authority, the Project Finance Agency. In 1974 the New York State Power Authority bought the nuclear plant Indian Point 3 and the Astoria 6 coal-fired plant (renamed Charles Poletti) for $612 million, which kept Consolidated Edison afloat.

Performing Thoughts

The decade reached its low point in the summer of 1977, when the July 13 power blackout struck the Northeast, looters pillaged stores in Manhattan and Brooklyn, and the serial killer Son of Sam stalked New York City's outer boroughs. The torture of Vietnam, which climaxed in Watergate, left visions of intrigue and lurking forces, while the blackout seemed to symbolize urban life drained of energy. The jarred, disoriented city was caught on film in director Martin Scorsese's *Mean Streets* (1973) and *Taxi Driver* (1978).

The 1960s battles against censorship and the awakening of minority voices gave culture a new coarseness. Obscene, then frankly pornographic, literature flourished under First Amendment protection. Literary realism was measured against Black Panther rage and the gang graffiti admired by Norman Mailer. Late 1950s rock 'n' roll—the "Top 40" radio play of urban doo-wap, Elvis, and rhythm and blues—had been shattered in the early 1960s by the California surfer music and the British invasion, notably the Beatles, who took pop music down disparate roads. After the Stonewall riots ended police raids, a gay subculture flourished in Greenwich Village and Chelsea, allowing artists like Robert Mapplethorpe to photograph leather boys in lewd poses. Andy Warhol held court at his Chelsea "Factory," taking Polaroids of androgynous rock stars, fashion designers, and society waifs. The East Village, remarked journalist Robert Draper, was a "scabrous underground" of rock clubs, where disco vied with glitter, and crowds heard Heavy Metal groups like the Dead Boys and the Ramones.

The avant-garde congregated south of Houston Street (SoHo) when changes in the occupancy laws in 1971 permitted artists to inhabit commercial lofts and an insurgent collective, Fluxus, put on impulsive mixtures of music, dance, and video in local upstart galleries. SoHo had cavernous space, which minimalist sculptors filled with somber marble cubes and wooden latticeworks (although the most notorious minimalist work—Richard Serra's leaning wall of steel, *Tilted Arc*—was installed at Manhattan's Federal Plaza in 1981). Conceptual artists went from words to "experiences" like Owen Morrel's *Catapult 70* (1977), which cantilevered a psychiatrist's couch and chair on a loft rooftop. SoHo reveled in the shards and scraps of a discordant urban world: Barry Le Va's "scatter art" arrangements of sand, stones, and gravel; Cindy Sherman's collections of thrown-away pop culture; and Red and Mimi Grooms's anarchic assemblages, like *Ruckus Manhattan* (1975).

The New York Philharmonic underwent lean times after Bernstein's departure frayed ties with Columbia Records and philanthropies gave less to the arts. In 1969 Philharmonic executive Amyas Ames convened the county's "Big Five" urban orchestras to solve their common crisis. Ames approached the Nixon administration, which offered grants from the National Endowment for the Arts, and Governor Rockefeller, who increased aid from the New York State Council on the Arts. Meanwhile, the influence of John Cage and zenlike openness turned composers from twelve-tone complexity to minimalist effects. In works like *Pulse Music* (1968–69), often performed as SoHo happenings, Steve Reich looped fragments of voice and piano that were gradually shifted out of sync to create "a kind of controlled chaos." Another minimalist was Philip Glass of the SoHo theater collective Mabou Mines. Glass joined offbeat opera impresario Robert Wilson and dancer Lucinda Child to create *Einstein on the Beach* (1976), a five-hour montage of endlessly repeated music and absurd prose fragments that reminded one observer of "a great phonograph with a stuck needle."

Dance was still dominated by the New York City Ballet and the rival American Ballet Theatre, which proclaimed themselves national ballet companies. Balanchine's legacy was carried on by choreographer Jerome Robbins and stars like Gelsey Kirkland and Peter Martins, although there were challenges to the classical regime. Robbins's *Watermill* (1972), for instance, was influenced by Merce Cunningham and zenlike music. Dancer-choreographer Eliot Feld stormed out of the American Ballet Theatre to found a new company at the Brooklyn Academy of Music, although the Ballet Theatre soon recruited celebrated newcomers, Russian émigrés Mikhail Baryshnikov and Natalia Makarova. The Dance Theater of Harlem, founded in 1969, featured classically trained black dancers performing works by Balanchine, Robbins, and newcomer Geoffrey Holder and proved an important stimulus for expansion of the classical repertory. Modernism was carried on by Merce Cunningham's troupe, the pulsating light and sound of Alwin Nicholais, and Alvin Ailey's American Dance Theater.

Drama and musical theater increasingly depended on Off-Broadway novelties, and Stephen Sondheim's "concept" musicals. Edward Albee, who had started out in Off Broadway, with puzzling one-act plays in Greenwich Village, burst on the Broadway scene in 1962 with *Who's Afraid of Virginia Woolf?*, an enormously successful, if enigmatic, drama. Other Off-Broadway transplants included *Hair*, the "tribal love-rock musical," which Joseph Papp's New York Shakespeare Festival moved from the Cheetah discotheque to Broadway in 1968, and Entremedia's raunchy *Oh, Calcutta!* (1970). Whether because of the pall cast by *auteur*-choreographers, the resistance of rock music to Broadway treatment, or the decline in young audiences, musical productions dropped to fewer than fifteen by 1978. Two of the most innovative, the amateur theatrical *Godspell* (1971) and Michael Bennett's *Chorus Line* (1975), came from, respectively, Café La Mama and Joseph Papp's Shakespeare Festival. Genuine Broadway was dominated by Stephen Sondheim's work, notably *A Little Night Music* (1973), a wistful, ironic musical; and *Sweeney Todd* (1979), whose macabre subject, a murderous London barber, seemed in accord with the city's mood.

Having portrayed life "within quotation marks," as critic Martin Gottfried put it, Off Off Broadway had little more to say in the 1970s. Revelations of gay life were supplemented by drag culture's scathing satire, notably Charles Ludlum's Ridiculous Theater and the all-male Ballets Trockadero de Monte Carlo. Some innovators explored what they said was theater's roots in primeval experience. Richard Schechner and Joan McIntosh's Performance Group put on *Dionysius in 69* (1968), complete with a naked death ritual, and Sam Shepard's *Tooth of Crime* (1972) about gangsters, record promoters, and hit men. The best drama came from black writers' engagement with racism, notably the Negro Ensemble Company's repertory productions of plays by August Wilson. The company, however, was forced to discontinue serious repertory for crowd-pleasers like the Fats Waller confection *Ain't Misbehavin'* (1978), aimed increasingly at white audiences.

New York's anarchic images—half SoHo, half South Bronx, and all televised—fed postmodernist literary sensibilities, which rejected "official," authorized narratives about a world gone beyond understanding. In Don DeLillo's novel *Great Jones Street* (1973), Manhattan was a picture plane of random words like "licorice and roach hairs," reversed syntax, and long meditations on "latent history." One critic called William Gaddis's *J.R.* (1975) an "acoustic collage" of broken, fragmented speech that forced the reader to come up with a coherent narrative. In *Breakfast of Champions* (1973), Kurt Vonnegut intermixed plausible murmurs about American history with meaningless schoolboy aphorisms, and freely admitted the arbitrary nature of his characters. A host of influences—William Burroughs's "cut-up" stream of consciousness, the "magical realism" of Latin American literature, the immediacy of televised events—transformed the realism that had been the soul of the New York novel.

The fragmenting of taste accelerated the movement of regional art centers beyond Gotham's influence. The New York State Council on the Arts divided grants between "primary institutions" and counties on a per capita basis. Among the former in 1979 were the Saratoga Performing Arts Center and the Lake George Opera Festival Association. The Corning Glass Works Foundation became the chief supporter of the Chemung Valley Arts Council, which sponsored Market Street crafts studios. Notable ceramic displays were shown at the Everson Museum in Syracuse and in Alfred. Utica's Sculpture Space, aided by the Kirkland Art Center in Clinton and by a state council grant, offered sculptors welding torches and lifting cranes and the chance, one remarked, to escape SoHo's "politics." In 1974 New York State's Artpark opened in Lewiston on a site that overlooked the Niagara River. Vowing to bring together "Artist and Everyman," Artpark had as its feature attraction Owen Morrel's *Omega, 1980*, a 150-foot-long space frame hung over the gorge.

Perhaps because of their portability, music and performance scattered well beyond Broadway and Lincoln Center. The Saratoga Performing Arts Center, established in 1966, offered the New York City Ballet, the Newport Jazz Festival, and the Philadelphia Orchestra. Culture, concluded critic Joseph W. Ziegler in 1978, no longer depended on the big city. Ziegler pointed to some four hundred events in the Dunkirk-Fredonia region, many of them hosted by SUNY Fredonia. In the Hudson Valley, he added, "new houses of culture are filled with people who would not think of coming into Manhattan for the arts."

The Politics of Retrenchment

The fiscal crisis soured Albany's political climate. Constrained by budget limits and what he called the "overwhelming" bureaucracy of Rockefeller holdovers, Governor Carey never warmed to the capital. He kept counsel with his chief aide Robert J. Morgado and budget expert David W. Burke, leaving Lieutenant Governor Mary Anne Krupsak (the first woman to hold that office) to explain austerity upstate. Carey's January 1976 State of the State Message declared an end to "the days of wine and roses." His $10.67 billion budget called for nearly $600 million in spending cuts, particularly in social services and Medicaid, and a slash in state payrolls of 20,000 jobs.

The hard news won over few Republicans and estranged liberal Democrats. Republicans remained combative in the Senate under Majority Leader Warren M. Anderson. In the Assembly, Democrats scattered into factions: a Democratic Study Group, founded by Manhattan reformers, to push party reform and women's issues, and the Black and Puerto Rican Legislative Caucus, which pursued increased employment in the state's labor, mental hygiene, and youth services. Asserting their partnership in the budget process, Democratic assem-

blymen pored over Carey's recommendations, which passed, said one committee chairman, "only after every legislator was familiar with every detail." The
Assembly moved to control $4.2 billion in federal funds, including block grants,
and relied on its own accounting and forecasting. After the legislature overrode
Carey's veto of a bill to require New York City to stipulate specific spending for
public schools—the first override in a hundred years—Carey derided the legislative "zoo." He might have sought the White House in 1976, but Albany strife
left him with a distaste for such ambitions.

Carey's retrenchment was complemented by the deliberate conservatism of
Republican Charles D. Breitel, Thomas E. Dewey's brilliant counselor, who was
elected to the Court of Appeals in 1967 and became chief judge in 1973. He
molded a "self-restraint" and regard for precedent on the Court of Appeals,
which, an observer claimed, "recaptured its place among the top rank of state
courts." Breitel wrote the 1972 decision which upheld the state abortion law,
but in 1975 penned the decision that rejected the right of poor people seeking
divorce to have paid public counsel. Deriding New York City's claim to financial emergency in 1976, he invalidated a moratorium on interest payments on
$1 billion in short-term notes. In the first State of the Judiciary Message, deliv-
ered to a legislative joint session, Breitel had seconded Governor Rockefeller's
call for a single state court system and gubernatorial appointment of judges. In
1976 he worked closely with Governor Carey and legislative leaders to arrive at
the constitutional amendments which vested in the governor the power to
appoint judges to the Court of Appeals and merged local courts, including the
courts of New York City, into the State Supreme Court, an original trial jurisdiction. In the meantime, Breitel used the centralized court administration to
drastically cut the backlog of criminal cases.

Breitel's regimen was soon challenged by a liberal contingent led by Judges
Jacob D. Fuchsberg, Sol Wachtler, and Lawrence H. Cooke, the last of whom
was elected chief judge after Breitel's retirement in 1977. Fuchsberg had, in fact,
gone too far, openly campaigning for his seat in the general elections. The constitutional amendment finally approved by the voters in November 1977
authorized Governor Carey to appoint to the Court of Appeals candidates recommended by a nonpartisan commission.

Carey's party never accepted the politics of retrenchment. New York City's
Democratic ideology moved to the left as Republican votes disappeared except
in the East Bronx and Staten Island, and as McGovern Rules increased representation for women, blacks, and Hispanics. In 1976 Manhattan liberals like
Assemblyman Albert Blumenthal and Congresswoman Bella Abzug organized
the New Democratic Coalition to uphold abortion and the feminist agenda and
to reverse the fiscal cutbacks. They were joined by African American leaders,
alumni of the civil rights and antipoverty movements like Brooklyn Assemblyman Albert Vann, State Senator Robert Garcia, and Buffalo Assemblyman

Arthur O. Eve. In the late 1970s the Black and Puerto Rican Legislative Caucus claimed twenty-five senators and assemblymen.

The revulsion against Republicans after Watergate, however, allowed reform Democrats one last lunge for power. Bella Abzug challenged Daniel P. Moynihan for the senatorial nomination in 1976, and in 1977 she took on Congressman Edward I. Koch in the New York City mayoral primary. Moynihan, the Irish Catholic from New York City's Hell's Kitchen, had served Presidents Johnson and Nixon with a sober liberalism that enabled him to sidestep Abzug and then thrash Senator James Buckley. A year later Koch rallied Catholics and Jews in the outer boroughs with attacks on racial quotas and school busing and overwhelmed Abzug. Democrats divided over race in the Buffalo mayoral primary, which saw Assemblyman Eve defeat incumbent James D. Griffin. But Griffin stayed in the contest as a law-and-order Conservative and drew enough Republicans and white Democrats to overcome Eve. At the end of the 1970s, New York State's most liberal cities were run by Democrats who owed their offices to racist appeals among conservative whites.

In his second term Governor Carey moved the Democratic agenda right-of-center. He named a New York State Economic Development Board and an industrial coordinator to stem the flight of jobs. He sought $2 billion in tax cuts, named John S. Dyson, a blunt free marketeer, as commerce commissioner, and welcomed outside, even offshore, capital, which prompted the resignation of Muriel Siebert, the protectionist New York banking superintendent. Carey's appraisal of the tourist industry led to the advertising campaign "I Love New York." Leading the nation in what Democrats called "industrial policy," Carey named an Economic Affairs Cabinet in 1977 and, with the support of Assembly Speaker Stanley Fink, began to explore investment in infrastructure like mass transit, tax cuts for small business, and state pension funds used as venture capital. In 1981 Carey's first economic report linked social welfare to private sector growth, particularly in "sunrise" industries like data processing and financial services. The Science and Technology Foundation, a $20 million economic development agency, funded research and development centers at universities, including Rensselaer Polytechnic Institute's Center for Industrial Innovation and SUNY Stony Brook's biotechnology center. With great misgivings, liberal New York had entered a new age.

Chapter 35

Uneven Recovery

IN THE 1980s NEW YORK STATE CLAMBERED BACK AGAINST daunting odds: lingering memories of the fiscal crisis, federal defense budgets that showered Pentagon dollars on the Sunbelt and punished the Northeast, and the two-wage-earner economy, which made the state's high income tax inhospitable alongside its neighbors. Between 1980 and 1985 the state added 225,000 people to reach a population of 17,783,000. This 3 percent increase, however, lagged behind the nation and recouped only one-third of the loss since 1970. In the same period New York reversed the outflow of jobs but failed to stop the loss in factory work. The "I Love New York" campaign helped generate a 43 percent increase in tourist spending by 1983, although travelers still preferred California. A New York governor was again heard in national forums, where listeners admired his words but doubted his presidential prospects.

The New Sobriety

New York's recovery was presided over by sober Democrats, who talked balanced budgets, advocated public-private partnerships, and, like Mayor Edward Koch, no longer believed that "government solves all the problems." They faced an intellectual conservatism espoused by erstwhile liberal journals like the *New Republic*, academic centers like Columbia University's Graduate School of Business, and private think tanks like the Manhattan Institute. They had formidable opponents among Republicans, chiefly Alfonse D'Amato, who won the U.S. Senate election in 1980 as the self-styled "fighter for the forgotten middle class," with half the blue-collar and Catholic vote. Republicans pummeled

Democrats on the topics of social welfare and taxes that coddled criminals and sent jobs to the Sunbelt.

Mario Cuomo, Carey's successor, however, was no ultra-liberal pushover. He grew up in blue-collar Brooklyn among traditional Democrats like his mother and father, Italian immigrants who "killed themselves working." He practiced law in Queens, developed a reputation as a community negotiator that was burnished when he mediated the Forest Hills housing controversy, and was Governor Carey's secretary of state. He ran for governor in 1982 against Republican businessman Lewis Lehrman, who promised tax cuts to generate 200,000 jobs and made deep inroads among working-class Democrats. Cuomo nearly lost blue-collar Erie County and polled just 51 percent of the state's vote. The first Italian American to seek the office, he drew more support from Jews than Italians and probably owed his election to an estimated 82 percent of the African American vote. Cuomo's narrow triumph reinforced a hesitant, irresolute approach to decisions, especially whether to seek the White House. Journalists, tired of his agonizing soliloquies, dubbed him the "Hamlet on the Hudson."

Cuomo's liberalism, while heartfelt and abiding, was tempered by shrewd political instincts. In early 1983 he survived his first crisis, a $1.8 billion deficit

Governor Mario Cuomo meeting in 1988 with Louis Grumet and Judith Katz, executive director and president of the New York State School Boards Association. New York State Historical Association, Cooperstown, N.Y.

in the state budget, by doling out "shared pain": a $1 billion tax increase and a cut of 8,600 state jobs. A year later, he appointed the state's first director of economic development, declared economic growth "The Priority That Supports All Other Priorities," and convened the Cuomo Commission on Trade and Competitiveness. He preferred action, however, in the public sector, choosing a massive bond issue to pay for infrastructure, mainly highways and mass transit, which he called "Rebuilding NYS 2000." When tax revenues surged with the business revival, he sought spending that increased the state budget nearly 40 percent by 1989. He cut the corporate tax rate from 10 to 9 percent and the personal income tax to 7 percent by 1990 and supported Economic Development Enterprise Zones for localities, but he never trusted private enterprise to revive New York.

Cuomo also straddled the social issues that divided mainstream politics. He debated with John Cardinal O'Connor and other Catholic leaders on the morality of abortion and established what became the bedrock defense of *Roe v. Wade* for Catholic officeholders. While personally against abortion for the anguish it brought, Cuomo cited the U.S. Constitution for an unassailable right to privacy. He took the same confounding middle on the issue of capital punishment. With passionate consistency, he vetoed the legislature's passage of the death penalty, but he called for life-without-parole and surpassed Rockefeller as a prison builder, completing thirty-two for an inmate population that reached 65,862 in 1994.

Cuomo had a soul mate in Lawrence H. Cooke, the instinctive liberal appointed chief judge of the Court of Appeals in 1979. Cooke championed the right of defendants to exclude evidence seized without a warrant and in exigent circumstances. In *People v. Gohey* (1983) he held that the state constitution provided greater protection against illegal searches and seizures than the U.S. Constitution and asserted wider due process safeguards against police misconduct. In *People v. Rogers* (1979) and in *People v. Grimaldi* (1981) he issued strict admonitions about a defendant's right to refuse interrogation in the absence of counsel. Judge Cooke was forceful on the issue of discrimination against women and minorities and wrote the opinion in *Burns v. Robert Miller Construction, Inc.* (1983) that extended death benefits to children born out of wedlock. He presided over the liberalization of family and adoption law, arguing, in dissent, for a putative father's rights to notice of an adoption hearing in *Matter of Jessica XX* (1981) and *Lehr v. Robertson* (1983) and writing the court's opinion regarding grandparents' visitation rights in *People ex rel. Sibley v. Sheppard* (1981).

In the 1980s Judge Cooke combined two profound New York strengths— Sixth Amendment liberalism and media power. He was a partisan of open trials and the right of the public to attend judicial proceedings. In an expansive reading of New York's "Shield Law," he also upheld reporters' rights to protect confidential sources. Cooke was a vigorous proponent of administrative reform, including arbitration panels and community-dispute centers. As a staunch supporter of television access to courtrooms, he gained the public's implicit support for a speed-up of the judicial process.

Cooke's successor, Republican Sol Wachtler, reined in the Court of Appeals' activism. Under Chief Judge Wachtler, the court expanded the scope of evidence admissible from rape-trauma victims. Wachtler in late 1991 confronted Governor Cuomo with a "decade of underfunding" that imperiled the basic right to trial by jury, and, taking unprecedented action, he sued the state for $961 million in full funding for the court system. (Wachtler's assertiveness raised his name as a GOP gubernatorial prospect, but his arrest in November 1992 for threats against his former mistress ended his career.)

In Albany, Governor Cuomo was buffeted by the fractured legislature. He was impatient with the minutiae of the legislative process, and never enjoyed the sort of working relationship that developed between Hugh Carey and Senate Majority Leader Warren Anderson during the fiscal crisis. Republican power, in any case, shifted to a duo of Long Island moderates: Joseph Margiotta, boss of Nassau County's formidable GOP organization, and Senator D'Amato, who took time off from Washington business to pull the strings on state politics, largely through his increasing control over local patronage. But Republicans had few tactical advantages as long as the business revival allowed Cuomo to spend without major tax increases. They trimmed his budgets, except for state aid for suburban schools, particularly on Long Island. Otherwise, they were at a loss to challenge the governor on key issues, and their candidates, Westchester County Executive Andrew P. O'Rourke in 1986 and Manhattan banker Pierre Rinfret in 1990, were no match for Cuomo's presidential aura.

Cuomo was more often vexed by liberal Democrats. Party power slipped further toward New York City, which, in the mid-1980s, cast nearly 60 percent of the Democratic primary vote but less than one-third of the general vote in statewide elections, a ratio that ensured the nomination of downstate liberals who fared poorly upstate. Assembly Speaker Stanley Fink kowtowed to the Manhattan liberals and the Black and Puerto Rican Legislative Caucus, and his successor, Mel Miller, an observer remarked, "had to give more and more." In the late 1980s, Cuomo asserted his prerogative to impound appropriated monies, which earned the legislature's rebuke that appropriation meant expenditure. The impasse between the legislature and the governor made for budget delays that were resolved, according to the Temporary State Commission on Constitutional Revision, by "artful, one-shot arrangements" that "delegitimized state government."

The Restructured Economy

The New York economy was aided by the national surge in services in the mid-1980s. Between 1979 and 1984 the state gained 378,000 jobs, a 5.3 percent increase, the fourth largest in the country. Factory work, however, continued to decline. By 1981 the state's share of U.S. manufacturing fell to 7.1 percent, and only 1.5 million New Yorkers worked in factories. Apparel dropped to 13.3 percent of the national share, printing and publishing declined to 12.3 percent, leather products slipped to 11.9 percent, and food processing amounted to only 5.7 percent. The only significant share retained was in opticals and scientific instruments (31.2 percent in 1981), which firms like Eastman Kodak dominated.

Across the state, manufacturers undertook corporate "restructuring" aimed at batch output of high-profit, high-tech durables, like CAT scanners and electron microscopes, instead of mass-produced consumer goods. Envisioning General Electric as a firm "constantly renewing itself," chairman John F. Welch sold off GE's housewares and consumer electronics divisions and paid $6.5 billion for Radio Corporation of America, including its subsidiary, NBC broadcasting, and $1.7 billion for the investment firm of Kidder Peabody and Employers' Reinsurance, a financial services company. Welch slashed a quarter of GE's workforce, some 100,000, between 1981 and 1987. GE also exploited "outsourcing," the purchase of component parts from other suppliers, often overseas, and spent $1.4 billion in 1985 for imports sold with the GE label. In the mid-1980s, Xerox outsourced 20 percent of its parts for photocopiers. Eastman Kodak abandoned camera manufacturing, which was pounded by Japanese competition, and fired one-third of its Rochester production force to buy foreign-made camera parts, video cameras, and videotapes.

Manufacturers who tried to hold the line against overseas competition underwent drastic changes in corporate culture. Carrier, which joined Otis Elevator as a subsidiary of Connecticut-based United Technologies, still had 25 percent of the country's commercial air conditioning market in the 1980s but saw itself backed against the wall by the advancing Japanese. Slashing white-collar employment by one-third, it poured money into the design of compressors, once outsourced, for production in an automated factory in Arkansas. After ceding market share in low-cost copiers to Japanese competitors in the early 1980s, Xerox restructured, adopted Japanese-style "just-in-time" deliveries to cut inventory costs, and slashed six thousand suppliers down to four hundred with product-design partnerships, long-term contracts, and quality-training seminars. Xerox helped launch Rensselaer Polytechnic Institute's Center for Quality and Applied Statistics in 1983 and High Tech of Rochester, an advisory body. Kodak strengthened its grip on suppliers, adopted flexible manufacturing techniques, and formed an R&D partnership with the University of Rochester to produce OPTICAM for advanced manufacturing of optical equipment.

IBM's roller-coaster ride during the 1980s was the restructuring story in microcosm. Satisfied with profits from mainframe computers in corporate headquarters, the company missed the implications of decentralized operations in suburban offices and the market for personal computers, which spawned Apple and Microsoft. IBM fought back with the PC, but the spread of personal computers and networked desktops eroded its mainframe business, while West Coast competitors spewed out cheap "clones," sold in discount outlets. Still, IBM's industrial resources and sales force were unmatched, and CEO John F. Akers mobilized research for a new generation of hardware, including the $500 million East Fishkill complex for semiconductor development in the late 1980s.

Behind the manufacturing crisis lay the lure and perils of global markets. U.S. exports increased fivefold during the 1970s, and a large percentage passed through the ports of New York City and Buffalo, to Canada, the country's largest trading partner. The global reach of manufacturers like IBM and GE sent 12 percent of New York State output overseas in 1980. By 1983 export-related manufacturing accounted for 388,100 jobs (second only to California's 518,000), mainly in electrical machinery, electronics, aerospace, power generation, and transportation equipment. Some 375,000 jobs in the New York City region were tied to the Port of New York Authority's container yards and airport cargo bays, along with the financial and legal services that accompanied them. Buffalo's surge was more spectacular after the U.S.-Canada Free Trade Agreement of 1988 spread Toronto's boom into Erie and Niagara Counties. In 1989 jobs in Buffalo grew 2.8 percent, outpacing the state.

Low-tech labor-intensive producers, on the other hand, faced "import exposure" from overseas manufacturers of apparel, footwear, toys, and cheap electronics, which multinational companies wholesaled to discount chains. The apparel industry withered to 180,000 jobs in New York City and Rochester. The manufacture of shoes and rugs also virtually disappeared. Mohasco, which had shifted rug and furniture work to the South in the late 1960s, left Amsterdam altogether in 1987. The manufacturing decline dragged down wages and living standards. In 1960 New York's per capita income exceeded the national average by 22.7 percent, but by 1980 it was ahead by only 8.2 percent. The state, along with much of the Northeast, grappled with a two-tiered manufacturing economy. High-tech producers like GE could compete anywhere in the world, while labor-intensive producers were undercut by cheap labor around the globe.

The Blurred Landscape

New York State's economic decline in the 1970s hastened the population shift from rural hamlets to metropolitan regions. The North Country withered in the early 1970s when mines and quarries closed, removing secondary incomes for rural workers. In 1984 Governor Cuomo referred to the "abject poor" in Essex County's Lake Placid, which was staggered when a nearby paper mill closed, taking five thousand jobs. Four upstate counties—Allegany, Cattaraugus, Franklin, and Schoharie—had per capita incomes lower than West Virginia's, and twenty distressed counties across the state had more people living below the poverty line than the national figure of 12.4 percent. The 1980 Winter Olympics briefly stimulated Lake Placid, while Saint Lawrence and Franklin Counties rebounded with the opening of another state prison, which a local official termed the area's "growth industry." The Cuomo administration had few answers, except to dole out tax relief in rural enterprise zones at Moriah–Port Henry in Essex County, Olean in Cattaraugus, and Ogdensburg in Saint Lawrence. The only real boon came when the U.S. Army activated the 11th Mountain Division at Fort Drum outside Watertown, complete with $1 billion in construction and spending by 25,000 soldiers and dependents.

During the early 1980s the state's 38,000 farmers faced hard times. Hammondsport's vintners were absorbed into the market strategies of metropolitan corporations during the 1980s. The Taylor and Pleasant Valley Wineries, the last of the independents, were bought by Coca-Cola, then Seagrams, which resold the labels to a German holding company. Interstate competition, confirmed by federal antitrust rulings like the *Farmland Dairies* case (1987), and the advent of bovine growth hormones brought down milk prices and contributed to a 16 percent loss of farms in the state between 1983 and 1986. The federal Dairy Termination Program bought out some 560 marginal farms in 1986 and 1987. Despite the steady drop in the number of dairy farms—from 18,000 in 1983 to 13,840 in 1987, and only 10,693 in 1993—New York remained in third place in dairy products behind Wisconsin and California. Scientific management, richer feeds, and improved husbandry gave an advantage to large, better capitalized farms but put small operators further on the margin. Across the dairy belt in Delaware, Chenango, and Allegany Counties, the ethnographer Janet Fitchen found an invisible poverty and hundreds of homeless families.

Farm acreage dwindled to 8.4 million in 1987 as rural property was sold to developers of ski resorts and vacation homes. Affluent city dwellers reversed the traditional farm-to-city migration. In Delaware County, three hours by thruway from New York City, nonresidents owned 40 percent of farm properties by the late 1980s. Demographers also found an increase in the populations of Columbia, Sullivan, and Greene Counties, on the fringe of the New York City metropolitan area, and in Essex County in the Adirondacks. The New York State Grange, a farm organization with only 28,000 members in 1988, began recruiting weekend cultivators, along with anyone "dedicated to preservation of rural lifestyle."

Broome, Tioga, and Orange Counties were examples of the metro-fringe growth made possible by decentralized manufacturing and government spending. Despite the near disappearance of Endicott Johnson, the Binghamton metropolitan area, which included Broome and Tioga Counties, benefited from the job boom at IBM, GE's aerospace center in Conklin, and shopping centers in Vestal. Local boosters, like Senate Majority Leader Anderson and businessman George L. Hinman, who served on the SUNY Board of Trustees, lavished money on the SUNY Binghamton campus and the network of roads, Route 17 and Interstates 81 and 88, that tied the region together. After 1980, the Census Bureau gave New York State another Standard Metropolitan Statistical Area (SMSA), Newburgh-Middletown. The Orange County agglomeration of 260,000 was a suburb of suburbs, created by radial arteries, Interstates 287 and 84, which marked the edge of New York City's region. In the late 1980s, Stewart Airport drew manufacturers and warehousers, rural Harriman tripled with single-family and condominium developments, and Sterling Forest attracted corporate subdivisions of International Paper and IBM. Residential subdivisions, corporate headquarters, and shopping centers were linked by an intricate web of lateral interstates and county roads.

Newburgh-Middletown was part of a vast "outer city" of 10.5 million people that followed the interstates across New York–northern New Jersey. By 1984, 60 percent of New York City's regional population lived beyond the city line; and by 1987, according to geographer Peter O. Muller, 58 percent of regional jobs were located there. In 1987, 71 percent of manufacturing jobs and 67 percent in wholesaling and retailing were located in the suburban ring. Suburban business services also grew from 45 to 53 percent between 1982 and 1987. While FIRE, the economists' shorthand for finance, insurance, and real estate, remained attached to downtown Manhattan, suburban FIRE employment had, in fact, reached 37 percent of the regional total.

The regional blur concentrated in business nodes that were the outer city versions of old downtowns. Journalist Joel Garreau called them "edge cities," defined by at least 5 million square feet of office space (half of Rockefeller Center) and 600,000 square feet of retail space (three hundred city stores). In the late 1980s, the New York City region had eleven edge cities, including the White Plains and Purchase-Rye centers in Westchester County, Great Neck–Lake Success on Long Island's north shore, and Route 110–Melville and Hauppauge in Suffolk County. The enclosed mass of offices, shopping galleries, multistory garages, and cineplexes anchored suburban life for millions who no longer gave the central city a thought.

Older suburbs, by contrast, underwent a difficult middle age. Many communities were saddled with the isolated single-family homes and extensive public schools that were the legacy of the postwar era. Large-lot zoning and restrictions against multiple dwellings limited the ability of communities to provide housing for a younger, cash-strapped, generation that included increasing numbers of childless and singles' households. Developers turned toward the construction of planned units and cluster houses, like Cheektowaga's Garden Village Town Houses, for economies of scale in basic upkeep. Inflation in home prices during the mid-1980s compounded the problem. "If you're earning $15,000 to $20,000," commented Suffolk County planner Lee E. Koppelman in 1987, "you're fairly well locked out of the market."

In most aging suburbs, the cost of services, particularly for environmental maintenance, impinged on the quality of life. In Westchester, health restrictions forced the county government to close the Croton dump in the mid-1980s and construct a costly garbage-to-energy plant in Peekskill, along with a giant sewage-treatment plant in Yonkers. Long Island's trash collection districts were forced to build an even more expensive incinerator in Glen Cove in 1983. The island's economic future, officials concluded, hinged on the quality of ground water, improvements in garbage recycling, and decreasing energy costs from an expected state takeover of LILCO. High-wage manufacturing jobs grew scarce on Long Island, and suburban governments were unprepared to handle social services. Suburban voters would have to shoulder municipal-type social welfare and the taxes to pay for it. Former Nassau County Executive Ralph G. Caso doubted, however, that suburbanites would accept changes in the sort of government that had "attracted them out here in the first place."

Urban Revivals

New York State's struggle for solvency gutted the Democratic liberalism that had been the soul of postwar city politics. Sharing a general pessimism about blue-collar prospects, cities turned their factory districts into office condominiums, shopping galleries, and theme parks for white suburbanites. Municipal governments answered corporate "calls to action" and explored "privatization" of public services. Liberal Democrats talked public purpose and interracial compromise while showering tax breaks on private enterprise.

Proclaiming "If it'll bring jobs to the city, I'm for it," Buffalo Mayor James D. Griffin backed the Buffalo Venture Capital Company, whose seed money lured Nanodata Computer from suburban Williamsville and Comtek from Cheektowaga. The latter was the centerpiece of a two-mile High-Tech Park stretching from Elm Street to the Roswell Park Cancer Research Center. Municipal tax breaks built downtown hotels, the $177 million Waterfront Village, and the Canal Place theme park. Congressman Henry Nowak secured $597 million in federal grants for the Niagara Frontier Transportation Authority's Gateway Metroport and the light rail system on Main Street, which became a pedestrian mall, Buffalo Place. The city's transformation affected Marine Midland Banks, the Buffalo-based group of smaller banks in Syracuse, Utica, and New York City, that was the nation's fifteenth largest. Bank president Edward Duffy sought fresh investment capital and found it in the partial takeover by a Hong Kong bank. Marine Midland became the first large American bank acquired by offshore interests.

Outside funding allowed Mayor Griffin to finance Buffalo's comeback without raising taxes on white homeowners in South Buffalo. But his trickle-down economics and abrasive stance toward African Americans brought his defeat in the 1985 Democratic mayoral primary at the hands of city council president George K. Arthur. Heading an all-white "new majority," Griffin ran on the Republican, Conservative, and Right-to-Life tickets and won a third term. The blue-collar town passed a further milestone in 1987, when Bethlehem Steel's Lackawanna plant closed, leaving the Roswell Park Cancer Research Center as the city's largest employer.

Syracuse enhanced its claim as a regional hub with a city-financed $100 million hotel-convention center and the $48.3 million Galleries, another retail and office complex. Its four-term mayor, Democrat Lee F. Alexander, energized Syracuse's growth through generous tax concessions to hotel chains and realtors. (The extent of Alexander's largesse became clear in 1988 when the ex-mayor pleaded guilty to federal charges of extorting $1.6 million in kickbacks from developers, for which he was sentenced to ten years in prison.) While the city council cut mayoral prerogatives in 1985, Alexander's successor, Thomas Young, leveraged tax concessions and Syracuse University's research facilities into a high-tech climate. His triumph was the $1 billion Oil City, an eight hundred–acre residential and commercial complex on Onondaga Lake, made possible by the Syracuse Industrial Development Agency's mortgage guarantees and $75 million in tax concessions.

Rochester halted its economic slide with corporate-style barn-raising presided over by Mayor Thomas P. Ryan, Jr., who proclaimed the city's prowess in high tech. When education officials complained of 15 percent high school dropout rates, Eastman Kodak, Bausch & Lomb, and Xerox led a campaign that brought together the Urban League and the Rochester Teachers Association, whose president, Adam Urbanski, favored school-based management and parental involvement. Monroe County officials agreed to pass-alongs of taxes, corporations "adopted" schools and mentored students, and Wegman's Supermarkets offered college scholarships. Rochester attracted private investment along the Genesee waterfront with recreational piers and "discovery centers."

In New York City, Mayor Koch courted the corporate sector with zoning permits and tax concessions which added 45 million square feet of office space (the equivalent of twenty Empire State Buildings) to midtown between 1978 and 1985. Donald Trump received $100 million for his residential tower on Fifth Avenue; developer James W. Rouse handled the South Street Seaport; and Rose Associates brought downtown Brooklyn's Metrotech to fruition. While the ardent pursuit of deals reminded one critic of the "*dependencia* known to many 'banana' republics," trickle-down policies worked. The midtown boom helped the city to add 170,000 jobs, mostly in office work, in the late 1970s and to ride out the 1981 manufacturing recession largely because factories comprised only 13 percent of city jobs. By late 1985 city payrolls had reached 3.5 million, the highest since 1973, and unemployment had dropped to 8.2 percent. During the

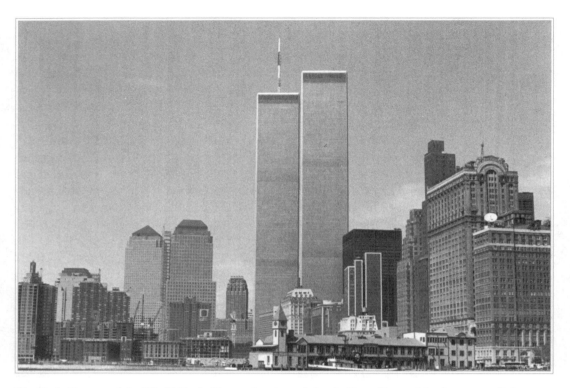

The Twin Towers of the World Trade Center dominated the skyline of lower Manhattan until the buildings were destroyed in a terrorist attack on September 11, 2001. *New York State Department of Economic Development.*

same period, the city shed one-fifth of its factory jobs, which fell below 400,000. What had been the nation's largest manufacturing city now depended on what economist Roselyn Silverman called "the movement of information."

The economy's heart was some 250,000 jobs in finance, insurance, and real estate located south of 59th Street, but never was this nexus more uncertain. Banking deregulation by the U.S. Congress in the 1980s had opened "wholesale" corporate services to competition; transformed consumer banking into a free-for-all among commercial banks, savings banks, and credit card operations; and allowed foreign banks, with strong currencies and OPEC-fueled reserves, to invade New York's home grounds. During the early 1980s, foreign banks opened (or took over) some three hundred branches across the state, creating a workforce of 38,000. Their Manhattan offices rivaled London's as the place to syndicate Eurodollar deals. Citibank pioneered the array of services that characterized the one-stop financial "supermarket" and moved into London-based Euromarket transactions and "packaged" financing of large-scale projects. But the turmoil that humbled Chase Manhattan in the 1970s caught up with Citicorp in the late

1980s, unraveling Walter Wriston's regime of high-risk deals. Citicorp underwent drastic restructuring in December 1990 under President John S. Reed.

The New York Stock Exchange was challenged by regional upstarts and Securities and Exchange Commission edicts, which ended the Rule 390 that had given the Big Board its monopoly. Deregulators hoped to make Wall Street function within a system of national securities markets, but the stock exchange proved remarkably resilient. Its sheer size enabled it to invest in computerized technology that handled 250-million-share days, and brokerages like Merrill Lynch had the resources to provide even larger wholesale services to corporate clients and to open elaborate financial supermarkets to middle-class investors. The advent of global capital markets and ventures, moreover, placed a premium on the city's experience at packaging complicated "project finance."

While New York City's share of the largest American law firms dropped from one-half in the 1950s to less than one-quarter in the late 1980s, the city still had one-third of the very largest firms, which led the aggressive drive for overseas offices, particularly in London, Frankfurt, and Hong Kong. Between 1960 and 1985 the city's largest firms grew in average size from 45 to 214 lawyers by taking on additional associates and 50 percent more paralegals. Partners welcomed Catholics and Jews, and in 1987 nearly 40 percent of new associates at the most prestigious firms were women. African Americans, however, comprised only 2.3 percent of associates at Wall Street firms in 1988.

In 1979 Manhattan investment partners Kohlberg Kravis Roberts & Co. (KKR) acquired Houdaille Industries for a $355 million sale of its corporate segments. This early "leveraged buyout" (a form of corporate takeover that swept through the business world in the 1980s) put at risk seven hundred jobs at Houdaille's Erie County subsidiaries—Houdaille Hydraulics of Buffalo and Strippit, a machine-tool manufacturer—as KKR accountants readied units for the auction block. The millions to be made from mergers, acquisitions, and LBOs attracted Wall Street law firms like Skadden, Arps, which grew enormous (712 lawyers in 1987) on hostile takeovers, as well as KKR, which made Wall Street history with the dismemberment of RJR-Nabisco in 1987. Skadden epitomized what the professional journal *American Lawyer* called the "national full-service firm" that could even merge with investment banks to offer clients a complete range of services in a world where law and high finance were components of one operation.

In the mid-1970s and 1980s, the city's biggest accounting firms, led by Peat, Marwick (which grossed close to $1 billion in 1980) and Coopers & Lybrand, had expanded from corporate audits to business services, including management consulting, nonprofit advisement, feasibility studies, and executive recruiting. Touche Ross pioneered in services by industry specialization, publishing manuals that ranged from cash management to stockholder challenges, while Price Waterhouse issued a well-known advisory series, *Doing Business in. . . .* The firms aspired to total, one-stop information services for corporate clients, including feasibility studies and productivity analyses. Twenty percent of Touche Ross revenues came from tax advice, particularly "private letter rulings" elicited from the IRS.

Publishing became further consolidated and multinationalized. Condé Nast, which was owned by Samuel I. Newhouse, Jr., repositioned old-line magazines like *House & Garden* and *Gentlemen's Quarterly* and revived *Vanity Fair* under English editor Tina Brown. Owners of the *New Yorker* hawked the literary institution around among a large number of publishers before it wound up as a Newhouse property. Anglo-Australian publisher Rupert Murdoch purchased a host of New York perennials, from the *New York Post* to the *Village Voice.* Broadcast media followed the trend toward narrow-cast, segmented markets. MTV, a New York City–based cable subsidiary of Warner Brothers, began twenty-four-hour telecasts of rock videos in August 1981.

Madison Avenue's services were in demand as corporations worried about competition from low-price, no-name clones and the whims of aging baby boomers. The more competitive environment put a damper on the "creative revolution" and brought a return to the hard sell and market research. Advertising specialists gushed about VALS ("values and lifestyles") analysis, which would enable corporate advertisers to fathom the buying motivations of target groups. Other marketeers replaced psychological profiles with "focus groups," which monitored consumers' reactions to new products. The expansion of in-house services hastened consolidation of companies like J. Walter Thompson and the Ogilvy Group, and the Omnicom Group, created by the merger of BBDO International, Doyle Dane Bernbach, and Needham Harper Worldwide.

Dual Fortunes

The erosion of manufacturing jobs combined with the boom in global finance and commerce completed New York's transformation into a city of stark contrasts. The cheap dollar in the late 1980s brought crowds of European and Japanese tourists to hotels, Broadway shows, and midtown restaurants. With strong Japanese and Euro-currencies, multinational retailers purchased Saks, Gimbels, and Macy's. The Japanese alone spent $6 billion on Manhattan real estate, including the AT&T Building, Tiffany's, and Rockefeller Center. The boom spilled over into the construction of luxury apartments and the "conversion" of dowdy rooming houses into upscale cooperatives across Manhattan and downtown Brooklyn. Developers erected expensive high-rises along Central Park West and Upper Broadway, with housing starts reaching 20,000 units in 1985.

Rising FIRE wages proved an incentive that helped bring about a 50 percent increase in the city's college graduates to some 750,000 and drew into the Manhattan job market an army of suburbanites, mostly white and female, who filled an estimated two-thirds of the city's new jobs between 1977 and 1981. The demand for labor also substantially increased employment of minority women, who replaced a generation of white females in secretarial pools. The percentage of African American females in clerical work grew from 13.6 in 1970 to 23 in 1980; for Hispanics the increase was from 7.5 to 11.8. Among midtown media giants, African American women increased their share of clerical jobs from 23 percent in 1970 to 47 percent in 1980; and among Hispanic women, employment in media mail rooms and in message delivery services increased from 38 to 52 percent.

New York City's population rebounded to 7,380,000 in 1985, largely owing to an influx of immigrants. The Immigration and Nationality Act of 1965 revived Greenpoint, Brooklyn's "little Poland," brought enough Greeks into Astoria, Queens, to Hellenize the ritual in Orthodox churches, and stimulated a rebirth of Irish folk culture in Woodside, Queens. The most important consequence of the federal law, however, was the huge influx of Hispanics and Asians. In the early 1980s, the city gained more than 400,000 Hispanics, including 146,000 Dominicans and Haitians and appreciable numbers from South America. Nearly 90 percent of all the Asian immigrants in New York State were in New York City and its suburbs, with fully one-third of the state's Asian population in Queens. The influx, coupled with the flow of one-quarter million whites to the suburbs, brought another demographic milestone: minorities—Hispanics, African Americans, and Asians—jointly made up more than half the city's population, 54 percent, in 1985.

The new arrivals energized the economy. Asians from Taiwan, Singapore, and South Korea penetrated small business. Part of their success involved the growth of the "informal" economy beyond government regulation. Skilled nonunion tradesmen from Ireland, Poland, and Guyana moved into residential construction, once the province of organized labor, while the International Ladies' Garment Workers' Union estimated that illegal sweatshops rose from two hundred in the early 1970s to three thousand by the early 1980s. City streets were crowded with 21,000 gypsy cabs, curbside auto-repair "shops," and unlicensed vendors.

Fresh immigration fed the growth of insular neighborhoods, shaped by conservative social and religious ideologies. In 1980 Manhattan's Chinatown sprawled beyond Canal Street with 60,000 residents but remained its own world, driven by a ferocious work ethic, family bonds, and child labor. The Nation of Islam spread a web of mosques, schools, and storefronts throughout Harlem and Bedford-Stuyvesant. In the South Bronx, Reverend Louis Gigante reclaimed abandoned tenements, block by block, with the iron will of a Latin *caudillo*. In Brooklyn's Borough Park, nearly 100,000 Jews, mostly Orthodox, held to austere belief in some two hundred synagogues. The Orthodox often split into rival sects, like the Lubavitchers under the seventh *rebbe*, Menachem Mendel Schneerson, and the Satmars in Williamsburg, established by Joel Teitelbaum, whose sealed-off community spread to Kiryas Joel in Monroe, Orange County. Their *eruvim*, which marked holiness boundaries around neighborhoods in Flushing, Queens, and North Woodmere, Nassau, attracted thousands of the observant.

The growth of private enclaves was part of a larger withdrawal of residents from public life. The middle class exited from areas with deteriorating parks, libraries, and particularly schools, which seemed like warehouses for minority children. Many relied on the kind of private law enforcement provided by apartment house doormen, elaborate alarm systems, and hand-printed signs on car windshields, reading "NO RADIO/NOTHING TO STEAL." The homosexual community was ravaged by the virus that produced acquired immune deficiency syndrome (AIDS). In the early 1980s the plague closed an array of post-Stonewall institutions that had flaunted casual sex and gay pride. Faced with a new source of homophobia, Greenwich Village organized a private response to the AIDS menace, the Gay Men's Health Crisis and a more radical advocacy group, ACT-UP.

The private forces that advanced part of New York City brought despair to much of the other half. The boom in the Manhattan service economy sharpened the "skills mismatch" of African American and Hispanic males. Between 1972 and 1986, New York City lost half a million jobs in industries where the average wage earner had never completed high school. Garment industry employment alone slumped from 180,000 in 1973 to 120,000 in 1983. A dire consequence was the continued drop in labor force participation by black males from 81 percent in 1965 to 67 percent in 1985. Posed against the shrinking factory sector, the 38 percent high school dropout rate, particularly among African American men, was a calamity. Officials were no longer preoccupied with racial imbalance in the schools. In the mid-1980s the beleaguered educational system was struggling to teach black males the basic skills they would need in the post-industrial economy.

The services boom enlarged the business district and spread gentrified areas at the expense of lower-class neighborhoods in Hell's Kitchen (Clinton) and the East Village in Manhattan and Park Slope in Brooklyn. Luxury apartments replaced cheap single-room-occupancy (SRO) hotels along Broadway that had sheltered the deinstitutionalized mentally ill, addicts, and other dependents. Destruction of SROs, mental health advocate Kim Hopper warned, would create a "new mendicancy" on the streets. While luxury housing boomed, public housing was choked off by the Nixon administration's phaseout of construction grants and President Ronald Reagan's outright termination of the program in 1982. The city completed only 4,000 units of public housing in 1982 compared to 33,790 in the banner year 1965. Mayor Koch, in any case, shifted emphasis to subsidized private efforts like the 5,000-unit Nehemiah Houses in Brownsville, Brooklyn, built by a consortium of African American churches. The private efforts, however, failed to keep ahead of the continued deterioration in the poorest neighborhoods like the South Bronx and Brooklyn's Bushwick–East New York.

Crack cocaine, family disintegration, and AIDS completed the ghetto agony. New York State experts reported in 1986 that more than half of black children and 45 percent of Hispanic children in New York City were born into families without married fathers present (compared to the 1966 figure of one-quarter of African American and 11 percent of Hispanic children). The social crisis hastened the decline of minority neighborhoods like Harlem, which lost one-third of its population between 1970 and 1986. By the mid-1980s, moreover, poverty and intravenous drug use shifted the AIDS epidemic to growing numbers of African Americans and Hispanics. An urban underclass emerged, seemingly dominated by drug gangs, crack dealers, and unemployed men, bereft of community attachments and involvement in the political system.

A vast gulf opened between black and Hispanic ghettos and white neighborhoods across parks and expressways. According to the sociologist Jonathan Rieder, Canarsie Italians took for granted that "lower class blacks lacked industry, lived for momentary erotic pleasure and . . . glorified the fashions of a high-stepping street life." In an atmosphere in which such stereotypes substituted for reality, confrontations were waiting to happen, and did in 1986 in Howard Beach, Queens, when white youths with baseball bats chased three African American men on to the Belt Parkway, where one was killed by a car. In polarized New York, whites imagined blacks as lurking addicts and thieves; and people of color thought that whites were racist murderers.

The arts reflected New York's surreal extremes in a wide array of styles. The city that oozed sediment and encouraged "traumatic art" was the tableau for eddying relationships in Tama Janowitz's *Slaves of New York* (1984) and the languid narrative of Jay McInerney's *Bright Lights, Big City* (1984). Midtown's predatory ethics were satirized in Tom Wolfe's *Bonfire of the Vanities* (1987), whose protagonist, Sherman McCoy, was "king of the hill," a New York investment banker. Paul Auster's *New York Trilogy* (1985–86), a series of short novels, mixed a hard-boiled detective story with postmodernist confusion of identities. Art Spiegelmann's *Maus* (1986) retold the Holocaust as a comic book, with Jewish mice persecuted by Nazi cats.

The fine arts were another kaleidoscope of styles, mostly throwbacks to the 1960s. The distracted nature of urban life spawned an interest in media and in collectibles such as Laura Simons's scattering of family snapshots and Barbie dolls and Jeff Koons's installations of floating basketballs in water tanks. Neo-geometric artists like Peter Halley and Philip Taaffe painted wildly rhythmic color patterns and optical illusions. The avant-garde also returned to imagery, notably with figuratists like Susan Rothenberg and Robert Moskowitz. Aggressive SoHo galleries made overnight wonders of Julian Schnabel and Ross Bleckner, whose moody portraits and ethereal clouds of light struck some critics as shallow spirituality.

In the 1980s, New York City music pursued what one critic called a "multiplicity of paths." Philip Glass continued to compose minimalist scores: *Satyagraha* (1980), based on Hindu texts, and *The CIVIL WarS* (1984), his collaboration with Robert Wilson. But neoromantics like George Rochberg and John Corigliano led a revival in tonal, more emotional, work. Among the best was Jacob Druckman's *Prism* (1980), which mixed scraps of traditional music and even a "bouncy Baroque line" with a near random display of dissonant notes.

The city's arts mirrored what New York had become by the 1980s. Its creative imagination depended increasingly on its role as the global crossroads and less on the indigenous currents that had inspired its culture since the turn of the century. In part this was tribute to New York's success as generator and exporter of the American avant-garde, the place that gave Cage, Burroughs, and Warhol to the world. But it also reflected the growing disconnection of the city from the art of minority neighborhoods such as Harlem or Bedford-Stuyvesant, compared to its close relationship with artistic trends in California, Europe, and Latin America. More troubling was the fact that, aside from literature, few works of post-1950s contemporary culture had entered the standard repertoire. Virtually no American composers since Copland and Barber were in the classical pantheon. Cage and Glass were performed as curiosities at singular SoHo or Brooklyn Academy of Music events. No contemporary artist could rival the reputations of Pollock, de Kooning, and Warhol, and, more often than not, it was wealthy collectors in Los Angeles and London who determined the current luminaries shown in downtown galleries. New York's inexorable avant-garde had succeeded in splintering its moral and cultural force.

Chapter *Chapter* 36

New York State at the End of the Century

THE LAST DECADE OF THE TWENTIETH CENTURY FOUND New York State with only a portion of its former primacy. In 1990, its thirty-three electoral votes ranked far behind California's fifty-four, which had more presidential influence than the Empire State had enjoyed after World War II. Leading Democrats like Senator Daniel P. Moynihan became regional spokesmen for a liberalism with little impact on the party's center of gravity in the Sunbelt. "Rockefeller Republicanism" meant nothing outside the Northeast to GOP stalwarts, who had long since opted for Goldwater and Reagan. The only New York Republicans with a national impact were former Buffalo Congressman Jack Kemp, who enjoyed acclaim as a Reagan supply-sider, and Senator Alfonse D'Amato, whose folksy barbs vexed the Clinton White House.

New York Additions

New York State had nearly 18 million people by 1990. It had grown by 25 percent, nearly 3.5 million, since World War II, but California expanded by a supercharged 335 percent to 30 million, and Texas in early 1994 surpassed New York's estimated 18,151,000 to become the nation's second largest state. New York City gained one-fourth of a million residents by 1990, but the state's other cities were gaunt companions, with the Big Six accounting for only 46 percent of the state's population. Old suburban areas like Westchester, Nassau, and Suffolk Counties continued to lose ground to the new suburban fringe spreading up the Hudson Valley. By 1992, the farm population had dropped to 32,306 on 7.5 million acres, down 14 percent and 11 percent, respectively, from 1987; and the number of dairy farms sank from 15,371 in 1982 to 10,625 in 1992. Two-fifths of New York "farmers" had to maintain second occupations in addition to farming.

Deindustrialization continued apace through the mid-1990s. Lingering recession between 1989 and 1992 cost the state an estimated 580,000 jobs. Manufacturing employment dropped 22.4 percent to 1,235,600—one out of every six members of the workforce. One casualty was IBM, which never regained markets in software and microprocessors and in 1993, under CEO Louis V. Gerstner, Jr., cut 11,000 jobs in the Binghamton area. Global markets and fluctuations in the dollar turned New York manufacturers into coordinators of multinational output. In 1994 GE Schenectady reduced turbine-generator employment to 6,000 while repositioning assembly plants in East Asia. Xerox announced a preemptive slash of 10,000 workers to stay, its CEO said, "a lean and flexible organization"; and Eastman Kodak, no longer Rochester's guarantor of steady work, followed suit. Long Island's manufacturing suffered from phaseouts in military orders and rising energy costs that were made worse by the dismantling of LILCO's Shoreham nuclear plant.

Service employment grew from 25.5 percent in 1981 to 30 percent in 1991 with the expansion of health care and business services. White-collar jobs in corporate headquarters declined, however, as leveraged buyouts and cost-cutting hit managerial ranks. Downsizing in the early 1990s slashed 85,000 employees at IBM, 83,500 at AT&T, 22,000 at New York Telephone, and 14,000 at Eastman Kodak. Across the state, wholesale and retail employment sank 10.1 percent as stores like Abraham & Straus and Macy's were absorbed by chains and multinationals. Business services shed 7.5 percent of their employees for networks of computers that promised "paperless" offices. Employment in banks and brokerages slumped 15.4 percent after the October 1987 stock market crash.

Cities prospered to the extent that they became global warehousers and niche manufacturers. Buffalo resurged with Canadian distributors who filled warehouse space in Erie and Niagara Counties. The Rochester Chamber of Commerce aggressively pursued foreign trade with computerized information networks. The trend was most apparent in New York City, where book publishers, drug manufacturers, designers of clothes, and Wall Street firms looked forward to the export opportunities of the North American Free Trade Agreement, while the International Ladies' Garment Workers' Union feared that the city's 80,000 remaining garment workers, mostly African American, Hispanic, and Asian women, would be consigned to oblivion with the rest of blue-collar New York. In 1994 the number of factory jobs in the city slipped to 286,000 and then stabilized as some manufacturers adopted rapid "custom-tailored" work geared to exports. In the early 1990s, however, the garment center fell behind the health and hospitals sector as the city's largest employer.

New York City remained the nation's corporate headquarters, although one-third of the firms operated from offices outside the center city. Downtown contained one-half of the top twenty diversified financial corporations including American Express, Salomon Brothers, and Merrill Lynch, and fifteen of the twenty largest advertising agencies. Citicorp was a global retailer, with 1,279 overseas branches, but in New York it was a cautious superregional that applied what it had learned in Asia about treating customers as clients—what was called "relationship banking." Corporations like Philip Morris and AT&T viewed their Manhattan headquarters as "profit centers" to maximize yields on assets and looked to city investment houses to plug them into "derivatives," newfangled securities instruments which provided a cash-flow "hedge" against global currency fluctuations. Madison Avenue was buffeted by nervous clients who demanded that advertising fees be tied to brand performance and, as IBM did in 1994, ended relations with their traditional agencies. Scrambling to regroup, some ad firms opened "boutique" subunits to provide specialized services, others opened overseas offices to hunt global markets, but many were absorbed by larger firms such as the British giant Saatchi & Saatchi.

The arts generated some 107,000 jobs among New York City's cultural institutions and media giants, many of which were no longer based in New York. Venerable imprints like Atheneum and Simon & Schuster were absorbed by communications conglomerates like Paramount and Viacom, which included movie, video, and cable businesses. The city's role as administrative capital of the nation's culture overshadowed its avant-garde. The Metropolitan Opera's penchant for masterworks made it, wrote historian John Dizikes, America's "National Gallery of Opera," whose conservatism, conveyed by its Opera Guild, shaped the repertoire of regional companies. Serious drama opened in London's West End and on New Haven's Long Wharf, not necessarily on Broadway, which had become "the place," a critic wrote, "where everything checks in before heading elsewhere." Painting had become a free association of styles, none, a critic remarked, "more important than any other." New York still ruled the contemporary art world, largely because the Museum of Modern Art interpreted what modern meant, namely Andy Warhol's pop art and its media references. But potent rivals existed in Los Angeles, London, and Berlin.

Immigration that barely affected upstate continued to reshape New York City. Newcomers helped increase population by 3.5 percent to 7,322,564 in 1990—the only major northern city to post a gain—and to lift the city's foreign born to 29 percent. (In 1993, the state had an estimated 490,000 illegal immigrants, of whom 80 percent lived in New York City.) Colombians flowed into Jackson Heights, Queens, while 373,000 West Indians leapfrogged beyond Bedford-Stuyvesant to Jamaica, Queens, and the North Bronx. The city passed another demographic threshold when the 1990 count found that Hispanics had displaced Italians as its second largest ethnic group. Nearly 200,000 Chinese,

Koreans, and Hindus in Queens helped make Flushing the city's third largest business hub. By the mid-1990s, Asian household income surpassed that of whites in Queens, and West Indian household income in St. Albans, Hollis, and Springfield Gardens, Queens, approached, then surpassed, that of white households in the borough.

Other neighborhoods, however, slipped further behind. In parts of the South Bronx, median income had fallen 13 percent since 1980, and one-quarter of households had incomes under $5,000. In that struggling community, more than half the residents lived below the poverty level, including two-thirds of children under eighteen. One-quarter of those between the ages of sixteen and nineteen neither were in high school nor had graduated, and were mainly jobless. The labor force participation rate in the city had sunk to 55 percent of the working age population (compared to 65 percent nationally). Wage gains made by African American women in New York City left the men further behind. In 1995 an estimated one out of three African American men aged eighteen to thirty-four was in prison, on parole, or subject to probation. AIDS had climbed to first place, ahead of homicide, as the leading cause of death among young African American males.

These forces overwhelmed New York City's liberalism. In 1989 Democrat David M. Dinkins barely defeated Republican Rudolph W. Giuliani to become the city's first African American mayor. While voters admired Dinkins's healing words after the Howard Beach incident, they grew impatient with 8 percent unemployment and continued street crime. In the 1993 election, Giuliani slipped by Dinkins. His victory marked a consensus among conservative whites against social welfare spending for blacks and Puerto Ricans. The public applauded Giuliani's "quality-of-life" policing campaign against subway beggars and street crime and generally supported his 1994 municipal budget, which decreased spending for the first time since the 1970s. Middle-class whites agreed with the judgment of the Morgan Bank that New York City could no longer afford "the extensive public sector that it had built up since the Great Depression." Blacks and Puerto Ricans, however, saw retrenchment aimed at their share of the dream. Many supported strident figures like Nation of Islam leaders and Reverend Al Sharpton, who received 70 percent of the black vote in 1992 when he ran for the U.S. Senate on the slogan "No justice, no peace."

Giuliani's advent, along with growing doubts on the economy, should have warned Democrats about political troubles ahead. The recession's impact on factory jobs had focused voter attention on Republican laments about high taxes and to what they claimed was Governor Cuomo's indifference toward the private sector. During Cuomo's watch, the Democrats lost ten county executive seats as well as mayoral offices in Yonkers, Syracuse, and New York City. Still, the party had a solid majority in the state Assembly, and they had Governor Cuomo's commanding presence—his undeniable star power and rhetorical gifts—which was enough to gain the steady cooperation on taxes and spending of the Senate leader, Republican Ralph Marino. Cuomo could feel reasonably secure in seeking a fourth term in 1994. His opponent was a relative unknown, State Senator George E. Pataki, an amiable conservative from Peekskill. Pataki had never accepted Marino's entente with Cuomo, and in 1993, when still a freshman senator, joined Senator Joseph Bruno of Troy in a challenge to Marino's rule. While the move was an abject failure, it established Pataki's reputation among Republican faithful as the man to take on Cuomo himself.

In the 1994 race, Governor Cuomo tried to rally Democrats with attacks on the "harshness" of Pataki's message, but Pataki seemed anything but harsh. Although he went around the state vowing to sign a death-penalty bill, he linked his call for a 25-percent tax cut to the need to reverse New York's loss of young people to the Sunbelt, and to his desire, he told voters, "to have our children living down the block instead of at the other end of the country." Cuomo's dispirited campaign failed to rally upstate Democrats, particularly in forlorn Erie County, and even his usual support in New York City. Blacks were unmoved by the governor's plight, choosing instead to support Manhattanite H. Carl McCall for state comptroller, the first African American to gain statewide office. The voters also kept Democratic control of the state Assembly under Speaker Sheldon Silver and reelected Senator Moynihan, although his GOP opponent, a virtual unknown, furniture heiress Bernadette Castro, managed to hold down his usual thumping landslide.

George Pataki understood the electorate's divided feelings toward government. While his inaugural address lectured that "more government means higher taxes and fewer jobs," he represented enough moderate Republicans like Senator D'Amato, who responded to the people's demand for reasonable spending at tax levels they could bear. With support from the new Senate leader, Joseph Bruno, and enough of the Assembly's "death-penalty" Democrats, Long Island and upstate conservatives, who followed their constituents' demand for tax relief as well as capital punishment, Pataki's program was passed by the legislature. It included $1.2 billion in cuts in Medicaid reimbursement, a freeze in school aid and higher SUNY tuition, and the centerpiece, a $6.8 billion tax reduction package that Pataki said would generate 350,000 jobs.

Along with his budget austerity, Pataki pushed broad changes in government that reflected his conservative values. To the delight of small businessmen, he ordered a freeze in new state regulations that covered occupational hazards, health, and the environment. Over bitter protests from the United Federation of Teachers and other advocates of public education, he pried from the legislature a modest measure to establish a pilot program for charter schools. He appointed Mary Glass a state commissioner of social services to oversee the creation of workfare, which required the able-bodied to work on public jobs for their home relief, and he gained legislative enactment of a five-year time limit on the support of families with dependent children. Besides signing the legislature's capital punishment bill, Pataki's crime package included the end of work release and the end of parole for violent offenders. He called for easing of the Rockefeller drug laws—if Assembly Democrats would agree to his demand to get rid of parole altogether. In his unpretentious way, Governor Pataki had reversed an eighty-year liberal tide.

The Long Boom

Nevertheless, Pataki's conservatism, along with most other aspects of New York life in the 1990s, was driven forward by an economic expansion of extraordinary duration. It was generated by forces as distant as Japan's nagging recession and as familiar as Manhattan's lively streets. America had become an investment haven for global capital, especially as the belief took hold that it had developed a "new economy" whose corporations profited from the unprecedented efficiencies of digital technology, such as networked PCs and the Internet. Its center was New York City, where the NASDAQ funneled speculation in high-tech companies and young professionals talked deals over cellular phones at sidewalk cafés. Manhattan's gadabout environment, the sheer freedom to enjoy streets made safe by Mayor Giuliani's war on crime, was home to America's prosperity era.

Brisk times completed New York City's transformation as a post-industrial center. Between 1995 and 2000, the city added 300,000 jobs to reach a total of 3.6 million, a figure not seen since 1988. Factory work dwindled to a mere 7 percent of the labor force, and producers of feature films, commercials, and television series rivaled the city's once vaunted garment lofts as industrial employers. On Wall Street, the rise in the Dow Jones average lofted employment at brokerage firms from 201,000 in 1990 to 270,000 by late 1997 and created demand for business services, from clerks to data-processors. Even more important was the so-called New Media, which linked providers of print and video content with the fiber-optic world of Manhattan's "Silicon Alley." Startups of computer software firms, Internet websites, and dot.coms reached a frenzy by 1999 when venture capitalists launched scores of initial stock offerings for anything connected with the Internet. Alley employment quintupled to 139,000 in mid-2000 to overtake Wall Street as the city's growth engine. By then, the city was adding private-sector jobs at a pace ahead of the country's for the first time in fifty years.

Greater numbers of New Yorkers at work jammed subways and, for the first time in decades, gave the transit authority a profit which it promptly invested in a huge capital improvement program. Midtown filled with tourists, who flocked to Broadway shows, particularly spectacles like "The Lion King," the

Disney fabrication which won the Tony Award for best musical in 1998. The West Side's Nabisco plant and Starrett-Lehigh Building, relics of the industrial economy, provided floorspace for cable TV studios and media ventures such as Martha Stewart Living Omnimedia and the Internet hopeful SmartMoney.com. Luxury apartments sprouted on the East Side, and the abandoned rail yard at West 66th Street was the site of Donald Trump's signature city of towers. Gentrifiers reclaimed lofts in the Tribeca meat market and tenements in Williamsburg and Bushwick in Brooklyn, and even Harlem saw stores and restaurants spring up along 125th Street.

Good times turned the immigrant flow into a tide that made New York City one-third foreign born by 2000. From the Asian Subcontinent came nearly a half million Indians, Pakistanis, and Bangladeshis, who flooded the engineering, health care, and software professions, and took over an array of small businesses that ranged from taxi fleets to cut-rate clothing stores. The city gained some 400,000 Hispanics in the 1990s to reach an estimated 2.2 million in 2000. In the process, the city's Puerto Rican population was eclipsed by Dominicans and by the more recent arrivals of Mexicans, whose numbers soared from 52,000 in 1990 to nearly 200,000 in 2000. In that year, Puerto Ricans made up only 37 percent of Hispanics compared to 48 percent in 1990. Although much of the decline owed to suburban migration, at least one-third of outmigrants had moved back to Puerto Rico.

In 1997, Mayor Giuliani sought reelection and crushed his Democratic challenger, Manhattan Borough President Ruth Messinger, by a nearly two-to-one majority. He had become the most powerful and controversial mayor since La Guardia. He was a no-nonsense puritan, who shut X-rated shops in Times Square and tried to close down controversial art at the Brooklyn Museum. He bullied two schools' chancellors and sought greater authority for a third until he had the right mix of policies at the board of education. He straddled the ideological divide, demanding the kind of personal responsibility that he said helped slash the city's welfare roles by half a million, while matter-of-factly supporting abortion rights for women and legal rights for gays. With bourgeoning city tax receipts he became all things to all people. His 2000 budget—a generous $36.7 billion—called for $2 billion in tax cuts, huge borrowing for new schools and court houses, and a $2 billion West Side sports and entertainment complex to host his beloved New York Yankees, Jets football, and the 2012 Olympics.

Above all there was the extraordinary reduction in crime. The number of murders fell from 2,262 in 1993 to 633 in 1998, auto thefts declined by 76 percent between 1990 and 2000, and an even steeper drop occurred in thefts of auto parts, which prompted the *New York Times* to mark the passing of those pathetic signs that pleaded "NO RADIO IN CAR." Although the economy had an undeniable impact (and other cities reported similar decreases), many credited the crime drop to Giuliani's zero tolerance for misdemeanors such as panhandling and turnstyle jumping which fostered, theorists said, a climate of criminality, and to Police Commissioner William Bratton's deployment of street units to go after drug marts and repeat felons. Admirers said that Giuliani's war on crime made midtown safe for tourists, reclaimed marginal neighborhoods like Tribeca and the Lower East Side, and showed the world that the city was once more governable and ready for business. Detractors worried about racial profiling and other selective enforcement by a police force with fewer legal and administrative restraints.

Giuliani had less success with the city's unemployment rate, which was 9.9 percent in July 1997 before drifting down to 6 percent by late 1999. One-quarter of city residents still had incomes below the poverty line, a population which included 40 percent of Puerto Rican families. A huge proportion of poor people, notably blacks and Puerto Ricans, lacked health insurance, a figure which increased with the immigrant tide that besieged hospital emergency rooms for primary care. More ominous was the mayor's failure to improve educational standards in the city's schools, as marked by faltering test scores in reading and math and a troubling jump in the high school dropout rate. While critics accused Giuliani of choking opportunity by bringing about the end to open admissions at the City University, they had few solutions to educational problems, particularly those faced by African Americans and Hispanics trying to prepare for the services economy.

In Albany, good times and the turnaround in state revenues caused even Governor Pataki's fiscal discipline to waver. Preparing for reelection in 1998, he boasted an 8 percent budget increase, which prompted his Independence party challenger, Rochester businessman Tom Golisano, to jibe that he spent like a "compulsive credit card user." The governor cited $8.7 billion in tax cuts and brushed Golisano aside, then confronted his Democratic opponent, Peter F. Vallone, the speaker of the New York City Council, and won handily. During Pataki's second term, the sheer volume of state revenues further loosened the spending breaks. For fiscal 2000, he proposed a $76.8 billion budget, one-quarter larger than the one he inherited from Mario Cuomo. He expanded the state Medicaid program with the Health Care Reform Law which extended coverage to one million uninsured, and, like Nelson Rockefeller, resorted to public debt finance for an environmental bond issue and for the Long Island Power Authority to absorb the bankrupt LILCO.

For all the economic stimulus, however, upstate remained a persistent laggard, vexed by the disappearance of factory work. Manufacturing's share of the upstate job market tumbled from 30 percent in 1970 to 16 percent by 1998. While the country recovered from the recession in the mid-1990s, employment grew by only 5.3 percent in Rochester, 3 percent in Albany, and 0.6 percent in Syracuse and contracted by 0.1 percent in Buffalo and 3.4 percent in Binghamton. The economic doldrums were accompanied by surprisingly low unemployment because, the Syracuse *Post-Standard* explained, young people were leaving "in droves." The jobless toll in Rochester, for instance, was less than 4 percent in 1997 despite downsizing at Xerox and Bausch & Lomb. Among the nation's one hundred largest metropolitan areas from 1997 to 1999, Syracuse, Rochester, and Buffalo stood near the bottom in both job and population growth. Upstate was haunted by the specter of discouraged workers seeking opportunity elsewhere.

The region saw a hesitant turnaround during 1997. By September unemployment in the Albany area had dropped to 4.1 percent, and similar gains were registered in Binghamton, Elmira, Rome, and Glens Falls. During 1998 Rochester added 6,240 jobs, a 1.2 percent increase, and there was a 2.1 percent increase in Utica, both reflecting gains in the services sector. The Ithaca area had become a hub for high tech, and another was Binghamton, where IBM entered into chip-making ventures with startup firms and Corning built a photonics plant. Still, conditions remained bleak in several areas like the Niagara Frontier where, in November 1999, Buffalo unemployment was 8.5 percent and the rate was 10.4 percent in Niagara Falls.

The boom finally reached upstate in 1999, when it joined the New York City region to give the state a rate of job growth greater than the national figure. During that banner year, the state added 200,000 jobs, which ranked it seventh behind several Sunbelt states but ahead of Texas. The growth leaders included Utica, which became a center of business services like telemarketing, and Syracuse, where the Metropolitan Development Authority helped transform the Fisher Body plant into the Salina Industrial Powerpark. Governor Pataki did his part with a Semi N.Y. Initiative to aid manufacturers of semiconductors; the state, he said, would hasten approval of environmental and other permits for "shovel ready" factory sites. While upstate joblessness slipped below 4 percent in early 2000, factory work continued to decline, particularly in Buffalo and Rochester. During that year, the state registered a loss of 19,000 manufacturing jobs, or 2.1 percent, while gaining 124,000 jobs in services, a jump of 4.4 percent.

Already the boom was pitting job developers against affluent vacationers and proponents of tourism. In the scenic Hudson Valley, industrial boosters ran headlong into environmentalists and supporters of the bed-and-breakfast economy. One battleground was near Hudson and Greenport, where the city's antique dealers bitterly opposed plans to locate a nearby cement works, and in Delmar, where protesters claimed that a gas-fired electrical generator would ruin pristine views. In the Adirondacks, the shoreline along Brant Lake and Lake George was crowded with so many boat houses and guest cottages, complained the Albany *Times Union*, that the vista resembled "suburbia more than wilderness." Nevertheless officials from communities within the Forest Preserve's Blue Line coveted that investment and complained of the Adirondack Park Agency's wilderness regulations. In Hamilton County, where unemployment was 18 percent during winter, residents demanded additional snowmobile trails and permits for outboard motors, while the Adirondack Council insisted on preserving the mountains' solitude.

The new economic climate forced Democrats to confront the issues of jobs and growth. That is how Brooklyn Congressman Charles E. Schumer defeated Al D'Amato when the Republican senator ran for reelection in 1998. Schumer cultivated a tough pro-business image while jabbing at D'Amato's ethical record and affirming support for gun control and abortion rights. But the stance could not help Mayor Giuliani when New York City was jolted by cases of police brutality against Abner Louima, a Haitian sodomized with a toilet plunger in a Brooklyn precinct in August 1997, and African immigrant Amadou Diallo, shot nineteen times by police as he stood unarmed in his Bronx doorway in February 1999. When black leaders like Reverend Al Sharpton condemned "an epidemic of police violence" and performed acts of civil disobedience at police headquarters, whites carried signs saying "GIULIANI=HITLER" and joined in defiance of the police. Mayor Giuliani defended the department's anticrime record, but many residents no longer agreed that safe streets and good times were worth stripping away the liberties of people of color.

Jobs and lifestyle issues vied for the attention of voters during the 2000 election when Senator Moynihan declined to seek a fifth term and Democrats made history by coaxing First Lady Hillary Rodham Clinton to run. The Illinois native tried to dispel her carpetbagger image with a "listening tour" among the people, while Governor Pataki cleared the GOP field for her all-but-announced opponent, Mayor Giuliani. Giuliani twitted Clinton as an outsider and big-spending liberal but she doggedly criss-crossed New York City and, more important, upstate, where she accused Republicans of shortchanging its economic future. Voters could not wait for the battle to begin when Giuliani withdrew, citing his bout with prostate cancer, although behind the decision loomed his crumbling marriage and image as the protector of thuggish cops. His place was taken by the boyish-looking congressman from Nassau County, Rick A. Lazio. Soon Clinton was questioning Lazio's experience and commitment to abortion rights, an issue much on the minds of women voters. Upstate she nursed the jobs issue while surrogates turned her outsider image to advantage by suggesting that the First Lady could bring real federal help to the region. In the end, Clinton held her New York City support, gained upstaters who remained cold toward Lazio, and won by a landslide.

For New York State, the election said more about celebrity than political power. The 2000 census recorded almost 19 million residents (although New York City officials continued to insist that there were 370,000 uncounted households among the city's immigrants and the poor). It was an increase of 5.5 percent during the 1990s, but not enough to keep abreast with Texas, which loped ahead to 20.8 million, or to deny the challenge of Florida, whose population approached 16 million. New York's modest gains, moreover, meant a loss of two more seats in the U.S. House of Representatives—down to twenty-nine compared to California's projected fifty-three. Although Jack Kemp had taken the second spot on Robert Dole's Republican presidential ticket in 1996, the state's political hopefuls, particularly Governor Pataki, were passed over entirely in 2000, then studiously ignored (with much of the Northeast) by the political campaign—and cabinet choices—of the new Republican president, George W. Bush. The country seemed set on a conservative course, while New York had two U.S. Senators identified with New York City and the Democratic party's liberal wing.

The state had become a successful example of modern conservatism at work but the country chose not to notice. To be sure it was a rather outsized conservatism. In 2001 George Pataki requested a state budget of $83.7 billion, somewhat larger than Governor Dewey's budget of nearly $1 billion which outraged the Republican Old Guard in 1949. Nevertheless, Pataki's policies had overturned many cherished Democratic causes, from parole and corrections to home relief and welfare. The mantra in Albany had become tax cuts and job creation, while the aura of state competence had given way to faith in the private sector. The state that gave Al Smith and Franklin Roosevelt their national forums and whose liberalism had shaped the nation was now taking its initiatives from tax-cutters in Michigan and Wisconsin.

There was even less consolation for liberals in New York City. Giuliani's troubles aside, all the social welfare programs since the John Lindsay era proved to have less impact on the city's disadvantaged than eight years of stock market advances and booming employment. It turned out that law-and-order could produce significant social results as well as engender a more civil society. Liberal politics had not saved the city's blue-collar economy for another generation of struggling immigrants, and it remained questionable whether the city's racial polarization would allow a second African American to follow David Dinkins into the mayoralty. While liberals dreamed of a multiracial candidacy behind Fernando Ferrer, the Puerto Rican borough president of the Bronx, the decline in the city's Puerto Rican population suggested that their political importance in New York may have come and gone.

New York City has remained the ground where dreams are made. It is still the country's idea factory, its powerhouse of content. More than ever it is the place that wires America to the world and where the world, in turn, comes to test the offer of American opportunity. As New York celebrated the millennium, the only constants in the lives of its people seemed to be the same forces that had controlled its destiny for almost four centuries. Ever since the days of Peter Stuyvesant, the durable elements in the state's history had been materialism, diversity, and change. Deal makers from Manhattan to Buffalo still looked to global markets, and their energy attracted diverse peoples and talents from around the world to the teeming society along the Hudson. New Yorkers never stood still, always changing their landscape, economy, and society in a frenetic effort to move on. For better or worse, these trends will continue to determine the character of the Empire State into the twenty-first century.

Selected Readings

Part I. Before the English (1609–1664)

Primary Sources

The Dutch left behind thousands of pages of documents in America and the Netherlands, but time has taken a heavy toll, and much of value to historians has been lost. In the Netherlands, the records suffered an ignominious fate when a portion of the West India Company archives was sold as scrap paper in 1821. By the time the pioneer in New Netherland history, John Romeyn Brodhead, arrived in Holland in 1841 with a commission from the governor of New York to acquire, transcribe, and catalog Dutch archival materials related to the early history of the state, the company archives were gone. With determination and ingenuity, Brodhead was able to transcribe a surprising amount of material that related to New Netherland. Most of the documents were formal resolutions or petitions that had somehow been preserved in other archives, such as the minutes of the States General. The information on New Netherland was often indirect and emphasized crisis resolution, since any matter that reached the States General or other national body tended to be serious and unrepresentative of the more mundane communications that must have filled the company's records.

Brodhead's tour through European archives was part of an ambitious effort to collect for publication all the important documents of the colonial period. Between 1856 and 1887 New York State published the monumental 15–volume *Documents Relative to the Colonial History of the State of New York* (Albany, 1856–87), hereafter referred to as *DCHNY*. Brodhead, who did not live to see the project to completion, along with translator and coeditor Edmund B. O'Callaghan, who also died before all the volumes had appeared, and Berthold Fernow, who took over in the last years as translator and editor, produced the single most important collection of primary documents on New York's colonial period. Volumes 1 and 2 of *DCHNY* were devoted to the Dutch period, but other documents related to New Netherland can be found in volume 14.

No one did more than Edmund B. O'Callaghan to recover the history of the Dutch in New York. A former physician, who had given up the healing arts to pursue the study of history, O'Callaghan taught himself Dutch and began the work of rendering the mountain of Dutch documents into English. In addition to his work as a translator and editor of *DCHNY*, he produced his own abridged and original collection of colonial documents, *The Documentary History of the State of New York*, 4 vols. (Albany, 1849–51), as well as several specialized translations, such as the *Laws and Ordinances of New Netherland, 1638–1674* (Albany, 1868), and *Voyages of the Slavers St. John and Arms of Amsterdam, 1659–1663; together with Additional Papers Illustrative of the Slave Trade Under the Dutch, Translated from Original Manuscripts with an Introduction and Index* (Albany, 1867), hereafter cited as *Voyages of the Slavers*. His two-volume *History of New Netherland; or, New York under the Dutch* (New York, 1845–48) was the first treatment to use Dutch-language documents. Much of his life, however, was devoted to organizing and translating the so-called colonial manuscripts.

When New Netherland surrendered in 1664, the administrative records were turned over to the English. Since it was imperative that legal continuity be maintained, the Dutch records continued to be stored at the fort on Manhattan. During the American Revolution, the records were transferred to warships in New York harbor for safekeeping. After independence the Dutch records were returned to New York and became part of the records of the office of the secretary of the state of New York in Albany. There they remained until 1881, when they were removed to the New York State Library. While the manuscripts were still in the hands of the secretary of state, Edmund B. O'Callaghan reorganized the collection by breaking up the forty-six original folio volumes (which had been indexed by an alphabetical code) into twenty numbered volumes organized largely by politics and chronology. Two volumes of land patents and deeds were left in their original state and have been published in English translation by Charles T. Gehring under the title *Land Papers, 1630–1664* (Baltimore, 1980).

Although O'Callaghan meant well, his reorganization of the documents altered forever the juxtaposition of events and actions and obscured the administrative organization that lay behind the Dutch filing system. His plan was to translate all twenty volumes and publish them. As a first step, he prepared a *Calendar of Historical Manuscripts in the Office of the Secretary of State* (Albany, 1865) that has remained the principal index to the collection.

Before his death in 1880, O'Callaghan had completed a manuscript translation of four volumes in the series. These volumes contained the Register of the Provincial Secretary for the years 1638–64 and the Council Minutes for the years 1638–49. Since the colonial secre-

tary served as the government's notary, the material in the register was largely taken up with copies of contracts, wills, inventories of estates, and promissory notes that had been registered at New Amsterdam for legal purposes. O'Callaghan's manuscript translation of the first four volumes remained unknown to all but a few specialists until the arrival of Arnold J. F. van Laer (1869–1955).

Van Laer, a Dutch immigrant, was hired by the New York State Library as assistant archivist in 1899 and promoted to state archivist five years later. He held the position until his retirement at the age of seventy. Van Laer threw himself into the task of translating and publishing all twenty-two volumes of the colonial manuscripts. His forty years of work produced over a dozen volumes. Of special importance for this study has been the four-volume collection titled *New York Historical Manuscripts: Dutch* (Baltimore, 1974). Volumes 1–3 contain the Register of the Provincial Secretary for the years 1638–60. Volume 4 contains the Council Minutes for the years 1638–49. Van Laer's work, published nineteen years after his death, was based on O'Callaghan's manuscript translation of the Register of the Provincial Secretary and the Council Minutes. Van Laer had originally planned to prepare his own translation of these documents and had nearly completed the first volume when disaster struck. On March 29, 1911, the New York Capitol suffered a terrible fire that spread to the wing containing the state library and manuscripts division. Van Laer's translation was destroyed as was the original register. Thousands of documents burned or were damaged by water, but O'Callaghan's translations of volumes 1–4 of the colonial manuscripts survived, and, with his own translation still fresh in his mind, Van Laer annotated O'Callaghan's translation from memory. Over the next ten years, he worked tirelessly to preserve and rescue over 12,000 pages of Dutch documents. He also completed the translations of volumes 2–4 before financial support for the project was terminated. Van Laer's four stacks of typescripts lay in the New York State Library until 1974, when they were finally published under the direction of the Holland Society.

The publication of Van Laer's translations of the first four volumes of the "colonial manuscripts" in 1974 renewed scholarly interest in the recovery of the remaining Dutch records. The New Netherland Project of the New York State Library is presently completing Van Laer's work of translation under the able editorship of Charles T. Gehring.

The colonial manuscripts commence with the administration of Willem Kieft, but earlier records relating to New Netherland have survived. One collection housed in the Huntington Library in San Marino, California, contains the provisional orders for the Walloon settlers of 1625 along with orders for Commander Willem Verhulst and the original instructions for the construction of the fort at New Amsterdam. These so-called Van Rappard Documents (named after the last family to possess them) were translated by A. J. F. Van Laer under the title *Documents Relating to New Netherland, 1624–26, in the Henry E. Huntington Library* (San Marino, 1924), hereafter cited as *Huntington Library Documents*. For the period before the founding of the West India Company, the activities of the numerous private fur traders of Amsterdam can be traced in Simon Hart, *The Prehistory of the New Netherland Company: Amsterdam Notarial Records of the First Dutch Voyages to the Hudson* (Amsterdam, 1959).

New Amsterdam's city government, established in 1653, kept its own records independent of the director general's council in the fort. When the city fell to the English in 1664, the municipal records were bundled up and stored with the "colonial manuscripts." These records contained the minutes of the city council and the records of the burgomasters

and schepens. The majority of the documents are legal instruments, such as powers of attorney, indentures, inventories, conveyances, acknowledgments of debts, and mortgages. The city records also contain the notarial copy books of Salomon Lachaire and Walewijn van der Veen, as well as the minutes of the orphanmasters. All the records were translated by O'Callaghan during his lifetime except for a volume titled "Original Dutch Records: Mortgages 1660–1665." O'Callaghan's translations appear in a number of publications: Berthold Fernow, ed., *The Records of New Amsterdam, 1653–1674*, 7 vols. (New York, 1897; rpt. Baltimore, 1976); Fernow, trans. and ed., *Minutes of the Orphanmasters of New Amsterdam, 1655–1663* (New York, 1902–7); Kenneth Scott and Kenn Stryker-Rodda, eds., *Minutes of the Orphanmasters of New Amsterdam, 1663–1668* (Baltimore, 1976); and Scott and Stryker-Rodda, eds., *Register of Salomon Lachaire* (Baltimore, 1978). An excellent and comprehensive collection of primary sources for New Amsterdam remains Isaac Newton Phelps Stokes, *The Iconography of Manhattan Island, 1498–1909*, 6 vols. (New York, 1915–28), hereafter cited as *Iconography*.

The upper Hudson Valley produced two independent sets of Dutch records: those of the patroonship of Rensselaerswyck and, after 1652, the records of the town of Fort Orange/Beverwyck. Of the two, Rensselaerswyck produced far more documents in its almost 250 years of existence. Van Laer edited and translated several volumes from these records including *The Van Rensselaer–Bowier Manuscripts* (Albany, 1908), *The Court Minutes of Rensselaerswyck, 1648–1652* (Albany, 1922), *The Court Minutes of Fort Orange and Beverwyck, 1652–1660*, 2 vols. (Albany, 1920–23), *The Correspondence of Jeremias van Rensselaer, 1651–1674* (Albany, 1932), *Correspondence of Maria van Rensselaer, 1669–1689* (Albany, 1935), and "Protocol of Dirck van Schelluyne, Secretary of the Colony of Rensselaerswyck, 1660–1665," *Dutch Settlers Society Yearbook* 16 (1940–41). However, most of the records remain in manuscript. A large collection known as the "Van Rensselaerswyck Manor Papers" in the New York State Library at Albany contains hundreds of boxes of manuscripts. The records span the period from the early 1630s to the mid-nineteenth century. The records of Fort Orange/Beverwyck are contained in the two-volume edition by A. J. F. Van Laer cited above and in a recent one-volume edition by Charles T. Gehring titled, *Fort Orange Court Minutes, 1652–1660* (Syracuse, 1990). Van Laer's three-volume *Minutes of the Court of Albany, Rensselaerswyck and Schenectady, 1668–1685* (Albany, 1926–31) also contains much useful information. Other related legal papers have been translated by Jonathan Pearson in *Early Records of the City and County of Albany, 1654–1679* (Albany, 1869). Van Laer revised and edited Pearson's work and completed three more volumes of translations for the series between 1916 and 1919.

The establishment of a court at Wiltwyck in 1661 generated independent records for the mid-Hudson Valley. This collection was translated by Dingman Versteeg and published as *New York Historical Manuscripts: Kingston Papers* (Baltimore, 1976). The papers include the court records from 1661 to 1675 and the secretary's register. The register contains copies of conveyances, contracts, bonds, wills, and powers of attorney for the period 1664–75.

The area called by the Dutch *de Suyt Rivier* (the South River) and the Delaware by the English produced a significant documentary record comprising several volumes in O'Callaghan's reorganized "colonial manuscripts." These have been translated by Charles T. Gehring and published as *Delaware Papers (Dutch Period), 1648–1664* (Baltimore, 1981). Unfortunately the records for the city of Amsterdam's colony Nieuwer Amstel were destroyed in the brief English siege in 1664.

Several documents survived, however, in the Municipal Archives of Amsterdam (Gemeente Archief) and were transcribed by Brodhead and appear in *DCHNY*, volumes 1 and 2.

This region also produced numerous records in Swedish. The most comprehensive collection of translations remains Amandus Johnson, trans. and ed., *The Swedish Settlements on the Delaware*, 2 vols. (New York, 1911). See also, Stellan Dahlgren and Hans Norman, *The Rise and Fall of New Sweden: Governor Johan Risingh's Journal, 1654–1655 in Its Historical Context* (Uppsala, 1988).

Finally, any serious reading in the history of New Netherland must begin with J. Franklin Jameson's excellent *Narratives of New Netherland, 1609–1664* (New York, 1909; rpt. 1990), hereafter cited as *NNN*. This comprehensive single volume of primary documents was published as part of Charles Scribner's famed Original Narratives of Early American History series and contains twenty-one documents as well as a superb introduction.

Secondary Sources

The historiography of New Netherland is extensive and rich. Beginning with Edmund B. O'Callaghan's *History of New Netherland; or, New York under the Dutch*, 2 vols. (New York, 1846, 1848), each generation has produced scholars interested in this somewhat quaint backwater of colonial history. A sense of the scope and topics that scholars of New Netherland have pursued may be seen in two historiographical essays by Joyce D. Goodfriend: "The Historiography of the Dutch in Colonial America," in Eric Nooter and Patricia U. Bonomi, eds., *Colonial Dutch Studies: An Interdisciplinary Approach* (New York, 1988), 6–32, and "Writing/Righting Dutch Colonial History," *New York History* 80 (1999): 5–28. For a more specific list of primary and secondary sources see the bibliography in my *Holland on the Hudson: An Economic and Social His-*

tory of Dutch New York (Ithaca, N.Y., 1986), 267–76.

In the present study, primary sources have been used whenever possible. However, the conclusions and structure of the narrative have been informed by a broad sampling of secondary literature in English and Dutch. Those that have had the most influence in shaping the judgments and conclusions of this work are cited below.

Native Americans before the Invasion

The field of Native American history is a rapidly expanding area of scholarship, and New York has been especially well served by scholars interested in the important Native American cultures in the region at the time of contact. Of special relevance to this chapter are Douglas T. Price and James A. Brown, eds., *Prehistoric Hunter-Gatherers: The Emergence of Cultural Complexity* (Orlando, Fla., 1985); Brian M. Fagan, *Ancient North America: The Archaeology of a Continent* (London, 1990); William C. Sturtevant, ed., *Handbook of North American Indians* (Washington, D.C., 1978–), especially vol. 15, *The Northeast*, edited by Bruce Trigger; Anthony F. C. Wallace, *The Death and Rebirth of the Seneca* (New York, 1969); and Daniel K. Richter, *The Ordeal of the Longhouse: The Peoples of the Iroquois League in the Era of European Colonization* (Chapel Hill, N.C., 1992).

The effects of contact with Europeans may be traced in Alfred W. Crosby, "Virgin Soil Epidemics as a Factor in the Aboriginal Depopulation in America," *William and Mary Quarterly* 33 (1976): 289–99. The cultural effects of market-oriented fur hunting is discussed in Calvin Martin, "The European Impact on the Culture of a Northeastern Algonquian Tribe: An Ecological Interpretation," *William and Mary Quarterly* 31 (1974): 3–26. James Axtell, *The Invasion Within: The Contest of Cultures in Colonial North America*

(New York, 1985), is a good starting point for reading in this general area. An older but standard work is William M. Beauchamp, *A History of the New York Iroquois* (New York, 1976; reprt., 1905). Also useful are Lawrence M. Hauptman and Jack Campisi, eds., *Neighbors and Intruders: an Ethnohistorical Exploration of the Indians of Hudson's River* (Ottawa, 1978), and Hauptman and Campisi, eds., *The Oneida Indian Experience: Two Perspectives* (Syracuse, 1988). The latest and most comprehensive reference work is Bruce E. Johansen and Barbara Alice Mann, eds., *Encyclopedia of the Haudenosaunee [Iroquois Confederacy]* (Westport, Conn., 2000). For an overview, see Dean R. Snow, *The Iroquois* (Cambridge, 1994).

The Dutch Stake Their Claim

Most of the documents chronicling the career of Henry Hudson have been collected in George M. Asher, *Henry Hudson the navigator. The original documents in which his career is recorded* (London, 1860). Many of the important eyewitness accounts are also available in J. Franklin Jameson, *NNN*, 1–28. A useful summary and narrative are provided in Milton W. Hamilton, *Henry Hudson and the Dutch in New York* (Albany, 1964), while the difficulties of reconstructing a seventeenth-century ship are detailed in Andrew A. Hendricks, "Construction of the 1988 Half Moon," *de Halve Maen* 66 (Fall 1993): 45. For a recent biography of Hudson see Donald S. Johnson, *Charting the Sea of Darkness: The Four Voyages of Henry Hudson* (Camden, Me., 1993). Material on the geological history of the Hudson Valley is available in Robert H. Boyle, *The Hudson River: A Natural and Unnatural History* (New York, 1969), William A. Ritchie, *Introduction to Hudson Valley Prehistory* (Albany, 1958), and the same author's *The Archaeology of New York State* (New York, 1965).

The story of the so-called *voorcompag-nieën* (precompanies, i.e., pre–West India Company) is told in several works, although all are based on the New Netherland Collection of the late Simon Hart, director of the Gemeentelijke Archief van Amsterdam, who was the first scholar to reconstruct the events on the Hudson in the years 1610–23 by piecing together dozens of notarial records. His book *The Prehistory of the New Netherland Company* contains translations of the notarial records and biographical sketches of the prominent merchants engaged in the transoceanic fur trade. The period has been interpreted differently by several scholars: see Van Cleaf Bachman, *Peltries or Plantations: The Economic Policies of the Dutch West India Company in New Netherland, 1623–1639* (Baltimore, 1969); Thomas J. Condon, *New York Beginnings: The Commercial Origins of New Netherland* (New York, 1968); and my own *Holland on the Hudson*.

Dutch colonialism is taken up in several works, among the best of which are those of the late British historian Charles R. Boxer. His book *The Dutch in Brazil, 1624–1654* (Oxford, 1957) remains the definitive study of Dutch imperialism in South America, and his classic *The Dutch Seaborne Empire: 1600–1800* (New York, 1965) still bears careful reading. Also of interest are D. W. A. Davies, *A Primer of Dutch Seventeenth-Century Trade* (The Hague, 1961) and Cornelis C. Goslinga, *The Dutch in the Caribbean and on the Wild Coast, 1580–1680* (Gainesville, Fla., 1971).

The events for the period 1623–30 are told in Van Laer, *Huntington Library Documents,* and in several contemporary Dutch accounts, including the curiously fascinating multivolume compilation of Nicolaes Janszoon van Wassenaer, whose seventeen-volume news pamphlet appeared serially in Amsterdam over a nine-year period in the 1620s. In his chatty, jingoistic, and apocryphal style van Wassenaer, the son of a prominent Amsterdam minister, thrilled his readers with tales of Dutch adventures overseas. He tried to encompass all the events transpiring in Holland's vast seaborne empire, and in the process mentioned New Netherland several times. Edmund B. O'Callaghan translated the passages that pertained to New Netherland and published them as part of his *Documentary History of the State of New York,* 3:27–48. An abridged translation is also provided in Jameson, *NNN,* 67–96. Also of importance on this subject are the works of Charles T. Gehring, "Dutch and Swedish Settlements," in Jacob E. Cooke et al., eds., *Encyclopedia of the North American Colonies,* 3 vols. (New York, 1993), 1:143, hereafter cited as *ENAC,* and the same author's "Peter Minuit's Purchase of Manhattan Island—New Evidence," *de Halve Maen* 55 (Spring 1980): 6–7, 17.

Establishing a Colony

Primary sources for this theme were drawn from my own research in archives in the Netherlands and the United States and the published collections of Van Laer, *Van Rensselaer–Bowier Manuscripts*; Stokes, *Iconography*; *DCHNY*; and Jameson, *NNN.* Useful secondary works on these topics include Goslinga, *The Dutch in the Caribbean*; Charlotte Wilcoxen, *Dutch Trade and Ceramics in America in the Seventeenth Century* (Albany, 1987); Frederick J. Thorpe, "The Fur Trade," *ENAC,* 1:639–51; S. G. Nissenson, *The Patroon's Domain* (New York, 1937); Martha Dickinson Shattuck, "A Civil Society: Court and Community in Beverwijck, New Netherland, 1652–1664" (Ph.D. diss., Boston University, 1993); Charles McKew Parr, *The Voyages of David de Vries* (New York, 1969); Violet Barbour, *Capitalism in Amsterdam in the 17th Century* (Ann Arbor, Mich., 1966); Johan Huizinga, *Dutch Civilisation in the Seventeenth Century, and Other Essays* (New York, 1969); Simon Schama, *The Embarrassment of Riches: An Interpretation of Dutch Culture in the Golden Age* (New York, 1987); Pieter Geyl,

The Revolt of the Netherlands, 1555–1609 (London, 1932); John Lothrop Motley, *The Life and Death of John of Barneveld*, 2 vols. (New York, 1874–75); and Jan den Tex, *Oldenbarnevelt*, 2 vols. (Cambridge, 1973).

The tragic story of the Indian rebellions is revealed in several primary source collections including Van Laer, *New York Historical Manuscripts: Dutch Register of the Provincial Secretary*, 3 vols. (Baltimore, 1974), and the same author's *Council Minutes, 1638–1649* (Baltimore, 1974); Jameson, *NNN*; and Johnson, *Swedish Settlements on the Delaware*. The ecological and cultural causes of the rebellion may be seen in Charles T. Gehring and William A. Starna, trans. and eds., *A Journey into Mohawk and Oneida Country, 1634–1635: The Journal of Harmen Meyndertsz van den Bogaert* (Syracuse, 1988). A broad ecological perspective is provided in Alfred W. Crosby, *Ecological Imperialism: The Biological Expansion of Europe, 900–1900* (New York, 1986), and William McNeill, *Plagues and Peoples* (New York, 1976). The military tactics of Europeans and Native Americans are examined in Neil Asher Silberman, "The Pequot Massacres," *MHQ: The Quarterly Journal of Military History* 1 (Spring 1989): 74–81, and for those who read Dutch, the motives of New Netherland's Europeans are brilliantly analyzed in J. W. Schulte-Nordholt, "Nederlanders in Nieuw Nederland, de oorlog van Kieft," *Bijdragen en Mededelingen van het Historische Genootschap* 80 (1966): 38–94. See also C. A. Weslager, *New Sweden on the Delaware: 1638–1655* (Wilmington, Del., 1988), and George L. Smith, *Religion and Trade in New Netherland: Dutch Origins and American Development* (Ithaca, N.Y., 1973).

Peter Stuyvesant and the New Immigrants

Several collections provide primary sources for this subject, including Charles T. Gehring and J. A. Schiltkamp, trans. and eds., *New Netherland Documents: Curacao Papers, 1640–1665* (Interlaken, N.Y., 1987); O'Callaghan, *Voyages of the Slavers*; Fernow, *Records of New Amsterdam*; A. P. G. Jos van der Linde, trans. and ed., *Old First Dutch Reformed Church of Brooklyn, New York. First Book of Records, 1660–1752* (Baltimore, 1983); Van Laer, trans. and ed., *Register of the Provincial Secretary, 1648–1660*, vol. 3; Kenneth Scott and Kenn Stryker-Rodda, eds., *The Register of Salomon Lachaire, Notary Public of New Amsterdam, 1661–1662*, trans. E. B. O'Callaghan (Baltimore, 1978); and Gehring, *Fort Orange Court Minutes, 1652–1660*. Much of the statistical data on European immigration is based upon my research in the notarial archives of the city of Amsterdam and has been summarized in my article "The People of New Netherland: Notes on Non-English Immigration to New York in the Seventeenth Century," *New York History* 62 (1981): 15–45.

The following secondary works have been especially helpful in conceptualizing the demographic history of New Netherland: David Cohen, "How Dutch Were the Dutch of New Netherland?" *New York History* 62 (1981): 43–60; Peter Christoph, "The Freedmen of New Amsterdam," in Nancy A. M. Zeller, ed., *A Beautiful and Fruitful Place: Selected Rensselaerswijck Seminar Papers* (Albany, 1991), 157–70; Jan Folkerts, "Van Rensselaer and Agricultural Productivity in His Domain," in ibid., 295–308; Joyce Goodfriend, "Black Families in New Netherland," *Journal of the Afro-American Historical and Genealogical Society* 5 (Fall and Winter 1984): 103–4, and the same author's "Burgers and Blacks: The Evolution of a Slave Society at New Amsterdam," *New York History* 59 (1978): 125–44; Ernst van den Boogaart and Pieter C. Emmer, "The Dutch Participation in the Atlantic Slave Trade, 1596–1650," in Henry A. Gemery and Jan S. Hogendorn, eds., *The Uncommon Market: Essays in the Economic History of the*

Atlantic Slave Trade (New York, 1979), 353–75; and Morton Wagman, "Corporate Slavery in New Netherland," *Journal of Negro History* 65 (Winter 1980): 34–42.

Life in New Netherland

This subject has been informed by Linda Biemer, "Criminal Law and Women in New Amsterdam and Early New York," in Zeller, ed., *A Beautiful and Fruitful Land*, 73–82; Thomas E. Burke, Jr., *Mohawk Frontier: The Dutch Community of Schenectady, New York, 1661–1710* (Ithaca, N.Y., 1991); David S. Cohen, *The Dutch American Farm* (New York, 1992); Firth Fabend, *A Dutch Family in the Middle Colonies, 1660–1800* (New Brunswick, N.J., 1991); Joyce Goodfriend, *Before the Melting Pot: Society and Culture in Colonial New York City, 1664–1730* (Princeton, 1992); Ronald W. Howard, "Childhood and Adolescence: Dutch," in *ENAC*, 2:753–57; and the same author's "Apprentice and Economic Education in New Netherland and Seventeenth-Century New York" in Zeller, ed., *A Beautiful and Fruitful Place*, 205–18; David E. Narrett, *Inheritance and Family Life in Colonial New York City* (Ithaca, N.Y., 1992); and Willem Frederik (Eric) Nooter, "Between Heaven and Earth: Church and Society in Pre-Revolutionary Flatbush, Long Island" (Ph.D. diss., University of Amsterdam, 1994). Also consulted were the informative works of Alice Morse Earle, *Colonial Days in Old New York* (New York, 1896; rpt. 1990); Esther Singleton, *Dutch New York* (New York, 1909; rpt. 1968); and Ellis Laurence Raesly, *Portrait of New Netherland* (New York, 1945; rpt. 1965).

The relationship between church and state can be traced in several primary source collections, including Edward T. Corwin, ed. *Ecclesiastical Records of the State of New York,* 7 vols. (Albany, 1901–16); *DCHNY*; Jameson, *NNN*; and Dingman Versteeg, *Manhattan in 1628 as Described in the Recently Discovered Autograph Letter of Jonas Michaëlius Written from the Settlement on the 18th of August of That Year, and Now First Published; with a Review of the Letter and an Historical Sketch of New Netherland to 1628* (New York, 1904). Several secondary works were also consulted, including Albert Eekhof, *De Hervormde Kerk in Noord Amerika, 1624–1664,* 2 vols. (The Hague, 1913), and the same author's English-language biography of the Reverend Michaëlius, *Jonas Michaëlius, Founder of the Church of New Netherland* (Leiden, 1926). The work of Gerald F. De Jong is indispensable for any study of the Dutch Reformed Church, especially *The Dutch Reformed Church in the American Colonies* (Grand Rapids, Mich., 1978) and his informative article "The Education and Training of Dutch Ministers," in Zeller, ed., *A Beautiful and Fruitful Place*, 191–98. See also Robert Alexander, "Religion in Rensselaerswijck," in ibid., 309–15. The best treatment of the intellectual difficulties confronting the church in New Netherland is Smith, *Religion and Trade in New Netherland.* John W. Pratt, *Religion, Politics, and Diversity: The Church-State Theme in New York History* (Ithaca, N.Y., 1967), provides a theoretical framework for church-state relations and places the Dutch period within the context of New York's religious pluralism.

New Netherland's Last Years

Primary sources have provided the bulk of the documentation for this topic. The following collections have been used: *DCHNY*; Jameson, *NNN*; Gehring, *Fort Orange Court Minutes,* and the same author's *Delaware Papers*; Johnson, *Swedish Settlements on the Delaware*; Fernow, *Records of New Amsterdam*; David Pietersz de Vries, *Korte Historiaele ende Journaels Aenteyckeninge van verscheyden voyagiens in de vier deelen des wereldts-ronde, als Europa, Africa, Asia ende*

Amerika gedaen door David Pietersz de Vries, (The Hague, 1911); and Adriaen Van Der Donck, *A Description of the New Netherlands,* ed. Thomas F. O'Donnell (Syracuse, 1968). I am also indebted to the work of scholars C. A. Weslager, *The English on the Delaware, 1610–1682* (New Brunswick, N.J., 1967), and Charles T. Gehring, "De Suyt Rivier: New Netherland's Delaware Frontier," *de Halve Maen* 65 (1992): 21–25, for the discussion of the history and conquest of New Sweden. Robert C. Ritchie, *The Duke's Province: A Study of New York Politics and Society, 1664–1691* (Chapel Hill, N.C., 1977), is especially useful for understanding the motives and personalities behind the English conquest of 1664. The role of the merchant class in New Amsterdam is treated in Dennis J. Maika, "Commerce and Community: Manhattan Merchants in the Seventeenth Century" (Ph.D. diss., New York University, 1995).

Analysis of Dutch cultural persistence has recently attracted a number of scholars to the history of New Netherland. For this study I have relied on the following works: Charles T. Gehring, "The Dutch Language in Colonial New York: An Investigation of a Language in Decline and Its Relationship to Social Change" (Ph.D. diss., Indiana University, 1973); Craig M. Carver, "Colonial English," in *ENAC,* 3:17–18; David S. Cohen, "In Search of Carolus Africanus Rex: Afro-Dutch Folklore in New York and New Jersey," *Journal of the Afro-American Historical and Genealogical Society* 5, nos. 3 and 4 (1984): 149–62; Shane White, "Afro-Dutch Syncretization in New York City and the Hudson Valley," *Journal of American Folklore* 102, no. 403 (1989): 68–75; Barbara Carroll Burhans, "Enduring Dutch Nursery Rhyme," *de Halve Maen* 65 (Winter 1992): 61–63; David E. Narrett, *Inheritance and Family Life,* and the same author's "From Mutual Will to Male Prerogative: The Dutch Family and Anglicization in Colonial New York," *de Halve Maen* 65 (Spring 1992): 1–4; Joyce D. Goodfriend, *Before the Melting Pot,* and the same author's "The Dutch Legacy: 'Not Hasty to Change Old Habits for New'," *de Halve Maen* 65 (Spring 1992): 5–9; Donna Merwick, *Possessing Albany, 1630–1710: The Dutch and English Experiences* (Cambridge, England, 1990), and her *Death of a Notary* (Ithaca, N.Y., 1999); and the dissertations of Eric Nooter and Martha Dickinson Shattuck previously cited.

Part II. The English Province (1664–1776)

General Sources

For an introduction to the historiography of early New York, see Douglas Greenberg, "The Middle Colonies in Recent American Historiography," *William and Mary Quarterly* 35 (1979): 396–427, and Wayne Bodle, "Themes and Directions in Middle Colonies Historiography, 1980–1994," *William and Mary Quarterly* 51 (1994): 355–88. The best single-volume monograph is Michael Kammen's *Colonial New York: A History* (New York, 1975). The best contemporary history is William Smith, Jr., *History of the Province of New-York,* originally appearing in 1757 and extended in 1829. It is most readily consulted in a modern edition by Michael Kammen, 2 vols. (Cambridge, Mass., 1972). The most detailed account for the seventeenth century is

John R. Brodhead, *History of the State of New York*, 2 vols. (New York, 1853–57). Another older scholarly work that is still useful is Alexander C. Flick, ed., *History of the State of New York*, 10 vols. (New York, 1933–37); vols. 2 and 3 cover the English period. The geography of early New York is explained by Donald W. Meinig, "The Colonial Period, 1609–1775," in John H. Thompson, ed., *Geography of New York State* (Syracuse, 1966).

Illuminating politics is Alan Tully, *Forming American Politics: Ideals, Interests, and Institutions in Colonial New York and Pennsylvania* (Baltimore, 1994). Also informative is Benjamin Newcomb, *Political Partisanship in the American Middle Colonies, 1700–1776* (Baton Rouge, 1995). Path-breaking works on eighteenth-century politics whose insights have yet to be fully explored are Patricia U. Bonomi, *A Factious People: Politics and Society in Colonial New York* (New York, 1971), and Milton M. Klein, *The Politics of Diversity: Essays in the History of Colonial New York* (Port Washington, N.Y., 1974). The essays in Jacob Judd and Irwin Polishook, eds., *Aspects of Early New York Society and Politics* (Tarrytown, N.Y., 1971) are also insightful.

Three excellent family studies covering much of the provincial era are Philip L. White, *The Beekmans of New York in Politics and Commerce, 1647–1877* (New York, 1956); Cynthia A. Kierner, *Traders and Gentlefolk: The Livingstons of New York, 1675–1790* (Ithaca, N.Y., 1992); and Alice P. Kenney, *The Gansevoorts of Albany: Dutch Patricians in the Upper Hudson Valley* (Syracuse, 1969).

There are a limited number of biographies of important persons for the colonial era. For the governors, see Mary Lou Lustig's excellent biography *Robert Hunter, 1666–1734, New York's Augustan Statesman* (Syracuse, 1983). Brief and inadequate is John H. Kennedy, *Thomas Dongan, Governor of New York* (Washington, D.C., 1930). A much better (unpublished) work is Lance A. Betros, "A

Glimpse of Empire: New York Governor Thomas Dongan and the Evolution of English Imperial Policy" (Ph.D. diss., University of North Carolina, 1988). Cadwallader Colden, a towering figure in New York's early history, does not have a published biography worthy of his stature. A book by Alice Keys, *Cadwallader Colden: A Representative Eighteenth Century Official* (New York, 1906), is both dated and inadequate. Colden has been the subject of several dissertations including Alfred R. Hoermann, "A Figure of the American Enlightenment: Cadwallader Colden" (Ph.D. diss., University of Toronto, 1970); Allen R. Raymond, "The Political Career of Cadwallader Colden" (Ph.D. diss., Ohio State University, 1971); Miriam Ellen Murphy, "Cadwallader Colden, President of the Council, Lieutenant Governor of New York, 1760–1775" (Ph.D. diss., Fordham University, 1957); Siegfried Rolland, "Cadwallader Colden: Colonial Politician and Imperial Statesman, 1718–1760" (Ph.D. diss., University of Wisconsin, 1952); and Stephen Steacy, "Cadwallader Colden: Statesman and Savant of Colonial New York" (Ph.D. diss., University of Kansas, 1987). Countering the negative image of one of New York's most controversial governors is Patricia U. Bonomi, *The Lord Cornbury Scandal: The Politics of Reputation in British America* (Chapel Hill, N.C., 1997).

Biographies of other important colonial New Yorkers include Lawrence W. Leder, *Robert Livingston, 1654–1728, and the Politics of Colonial New York* (Chapel Hill, N.C., 1962); Eugene R. Sheridan, *Lewis Morris, 1671–1746: A Study in Early American Politics* (Syracuse, 1981); George Dangerfield, *Chancellor Robert R. Livingston of New York, 1746–1813* (New York, 1960); Frank Monaghan, *John Jay: Defender of Liberty* (New York, 1935); Edward P. Alexander, *A Revolutionary Conservative: James Duane of New York* (New York, 1935); Milton M. Klein, *The American Whig: William Livingston of New*

York (New York, 1993); Leslie F. Upton, *The Loyal Whig: William Smith of New York and Quebec* (Toronto, 1969); James T. Flexner, *Mohawk Baronet: Sir William Johnson of New York* (New York, 1959); Milton W. Hamilton, *Sir William Johnson: Colonial American, 1715–1763* (New York, 1989); Arthur Pound, *Johnson of the Mohawks* (New York, 1930); John P. Kaminski, *George Clinton: Yeoman Politician of the New Republic* (Madison, Wis., 1993); and Michael Watson, "Judge Lewis Morris, the New York Vice-Admiralty Court and Colonial Privateering, 1739–1762," *New York History* 78 (1997): 117–46. Still readable is Dixon Ryan Fox, *Caleb Heathcote, Gentleman Colonist: The Story of a Career in the Province of New York, 1692–1721* (New York, 1926).

The most comprehensive collections of primary source materials are Edmund B. O'Callaghan, ed., *Documents Relative to the Colonial History of the State of New York*, 15 vols. (Albany, 1856–87), and *The Documentary History of the State of New York*, 4 vols. (Albany, 1849–51). Religious developments are documented by Hugh Hastings and Edward T. Corwin, comps., *Ecclesiastical Records of the State of New York*, 7 vols. (Albany, 1901–16). Isaac Newton Phelps Stokes, *The Iconography of Manhattan Island, 1498–1909*, 6 vols. (rpt., New York, 1967), is a cornucopia of maps, pictures, and pertinent quotations and information drawn from innumerable sources, many not now available, and presented chronologically. For Albany records, see Joel Munsell, ed., *The Annals of Albany*, 10 vols. (Albany, 1850–59), and *Collections on the History of Albany from its Discovery to the Present Time*, 4 vols. (Albany, 1865–71).

Among the most useful collections of private papers are *The Letters and Papers of Cadwallader Colden*, 9 vols., New-York Historical Society *Collections*, vols. 50–56, 67–68 (1918–24, 1937), and *The Colden Letterbooks*, 2 vols., New-York Historical Society *Collections*, vols. 9–10 (1877–78). Another remarkable collection is James Sullivan et al., eds., *The Papers of Sir William Johnson*, 14 vols. (Albany, 1921–65). Very useful for understanding religious and cultural life in eighteenth-century New York is Herbert and Carol Schneider, eds., *Samuel Johnson, President of King's College, His Career and Writings*, 4 vols. (New York, 1929).

Transition from Dutch Colony to English Province

The most comprehensive recent treatment is Robert C. Ritchie, *The Duke's Province: A Study of New York Politics and Society, 1664–1691* (Chapel Hill, N.C., 1977). Demonstrating the tenacity of Dutch culture in New York is Alice P. Kenney, *Stubborn for Liberty: The Dutch in New York* (Syracuse, 1975). Thomas Archdeacon, *New York City, 1664–1710* (Ithaca, N.Y., 1976), details the rise of the English and decline of the Dutch in the socio-economic structure of New York City.

Joyce D. Goodfriend, *Before the Melting Pot: Society and Culture in Colonial New York City, 1664–1730* (Princeton, 1992), documents the continuity and change among the polyglot peoples of New York City. Comparing and contrasting English and Dutch views of life, labor, and the land is Donna Merwick, *Possessing Albany, 1630–1710: The Dutch and English Experience* (Cambridge, England, 1990). Thomas E. Burke, Jr., *Mohawk Frontier: The Dutch Community of Schenectady, New York, 1661–1710* (Ithaca, N.Y., 1991), finds individualism rather than communalism shaping this frontier town. For Long Island developments, see Langdon G. Wright, "In Search of Peace and Harmony: New York Communities in the Seventeenth Century," *New York History* 61 (1980): 5–21. Dated but still useful is Albert E. McKinley, "The Transition from Dutch to English Rule in New York," *American Historical Review* 6 (1900): 693–724. For the Dutch reconquest, see Ronald D. Cohen,

"The New England Colonies and the Dutch Recapture of New York, 1673–1674," *New-York Historical Society Quarterly* 56 (1971): 54–78.

Leisler's revolt has been interpreted variously. Jerome R. Reich, *Leisler's Rebellion: A Study of Democracy in New York, 1664–1720* (Chicago, 1953), sees the upheaval largely in terms of lower classes struggling for political rights. Displaying other dimensions to Leisler's revolt are Charles H. McCormick, *Leisler's Rebellion* (New York, 1989), which sees the event as the result of the province's instability; Randall Balmer, "Traitors and Papists: The Religious Dimensions of Leisler's Rebellion," *New York History* 70 (1989): 341–72, whose focus on anti-Catholic motivation is obvious from the title; and David William Voorhees, "The 'fervent Zeale' of Jacob Leisler," *William and Mary Quarterly* 51 (1994): 447–62 and Voorhees, *"In Behalf of the True Protestant Religion": The Glorious Revolution in New York* (unpublished Ph.D. diss., New York University, 1988), which views the rebellion as a conflict between two differing groups of Calvinists. Emphasizing differing political traditions is the seminal essay by John Murrin, "English Rights as Ethnic Aggression: The English Conquest, the Charter of Liberties of 1683, and Leisler's Rebellion in New York," in William Pencak and Conrad E. Wright, eds., *Authority and Resistance in Early New York* (New York, 1988), 56–96.

For reforms that came in the wake of Leisler's Revolt, see Lawrence Leder, "Dongan's New York and Fletcher's London: Personality and Politics," *New-York Historical Society Quarterly* 55 (1971): 28–37. The involvement of New York officials with both privateering and piracy is detailed in Robert C. Ritchie, *Captain Kidd and the War against the Pirates* (Cambridge, Mass., 1986). See also John C. Rainbolt, "The Creation of a Governor and Captain General for the Northern Colonies," *New-York Historical Society Quarterly* 57

(1973): 101–20. Also useful is John D. Runcie, "The Problem of Anglo-American Politics in Bellomont's New York," *William and Mary Quarterly* 26 (1969): 191–217. See also Adrian Howe, "The Bayard Treason Trial: Dramatizing Anglo-Dutch Politics in Early Eighteenth-Century New York," *William and Mary Quarterly* 47 (1990): 57–89, and Robert Ziebarth, "The Role of New York in King George's War, 1739–1748" (Ph.D. diss., New York University, 1972).

Among the most useful primary sources for the period are Victor H. Paltsits, ed., *Minutes of the Executive Council of the Province of New York: Administration of Francis Lovelace, 1668–1673*, 2 vols. (Albany, 1910); Arnold J. F. Van Laer, trans. and ed., *Early Records of the City and County of Albany and Colony of Rensselaerswyck*, 4 vols. (Albany, 1869–1919); Van Laer, ed., *Minutes of the Court of Albany, Rensselaerswyck, and Schenectady*, 3 vols. (Albany, 1926–32); and Peter R. Christoph and Florence A. Christoph, eds., *The Andros Papers, 1674–1680: Files of the Provincial Secretary during the Administration of Governor Sir Edmund Andros, 1674–1680*, 3 vols. (Syracuse, 1989–91).

A remarkable source for both domestic and business life is Arnold J. F. Van Laer, ed., *Correspondence of Jeremias van Rensselaer, 1651–1674* (Albany, 1932), and *Correspondence of Maria van Rensselaer, 1669–1689* (Albany, 1935). Descriptions of late seventeenth-century New York are found in Daniel Denton, *A Brief Description of New York* (London, 1670; New York, 1845); Bartlett B. James, ed., *Journal of Jasper Danckaerts, 1679–1680* (New York, 1913), written by a Labadist (pietistic sect of Dutch Reformed faith) missionary; and Charles Wolley, *A Two Years' Journal in New York, 1678–1680* (London, 1701; rpt. Cleveland, 1902). Also useful are Rev. John Miller, *New York Considered and Improved, 1695* (London, 1843; rpt. Cleveland, 1902), and Wayne Andrews, ed., "A

Glance at New York in 1697: The Travel Diary of Dr. Benjamin Bullivant," *New-York Historical Society Quarterly* 40 (1956): 53–73.

Economic and Social Expansion

An overview of New York's economy is given in John McCusker and Russell Menard, *The Economy of British America, 1607–1789* (Chapel Hill, N.C., 1985), especially ch. 9. Particularly insightful for the "emerging market" is Deborah A. Rosen, *Courts and Commerce: Gender, Law, and the Market Economy in Colonial New York* (Columbus, Ohio, 1997). Dated but still helpful are Samuel McKee, "The Economic Pattern of Colonial New York," in Flick's *History of the State of New York*, 2: 247–82; Ulysses Hedrick, *A History of Agriculture in the State of New York* (New York, 1933); Ruth L. Higgins, *Expansion in New York with Especial Reference to the Eighteenth Century* (Columbus, Ohio, 1931); William S. Sachs, "Interurban Correspondents and the Development of a National Economy before the Revolution: New York as a Case Study," *New York History* 36 (1936): 320–35; and Curtis P. Nettels, "The Economic Relations of Boston, Philadelphia, and New York, 1680–1715," *Journal of Economic and Business History* 3 (1931): 185–215.

The impact of economic change on New York's two major urban centers is delineated by Bruce Wilkenfield, *The Social and Economic Structure of the City of New York, 1695–1796* (New York, 1979), and Stefan Bielinski, "A Middling Sort: Artisans and Tradesmen in Colonial Albany," *New York History* 73 (1992): 261–90. Landlord-tenant relations are treated by Sung Bok Kim, *Landlord and Tenant in Colonial New York: Manorial Society, 1664–1775* (Chapel Hill, N.C., 1978). Philip Schwarz, *The Jarring Interests: New York's Boundary Makers, 1664–1776* (Albany, 1979), examines land disputes on New York's borders. See also William Chaz-

anof, "Land Speculation in Eighteenth-Century New York," in Joseph R. Frese and Jacob Judd, eds., *Business Enterprise in Early New York* (Tarrytown, N.Y., 1979), 55–76. Significant to both economic development and demographic dispersion is George W. Roach, "Colonial Highways in the Upper Hudson Valley," *New York History* 40 (1959): 93–116.

On commerce Cathy Matson, *Merchants & Empire: Trading in Colonial New York* (Baltimore, 1998), is a wonderfully comprehensive work. Bruce M. Wilkenfeld, "The New York City Shipowning Community, 1715–1764," *American Neptune* 37 (1977): 50–65, is also important. Still vital are two older studies by Virginia Harrington: "The Colonial Merchant's Ledger," in Flick's *History of the State of New York*, 2: 331–74, and *The New York Merchant on the Eve of the Revolution* (New York, 1935). Making clear the importance of the West Indian trade is William I. Davisson and Lawrence J. Bradley, "New York Maritime Trade: Ship Voyage Patterns, 1715–1765," *New-York Historical Society Quarterly* 55 (1971): 309–17. David A. Armour, *The Merchants of Albany, New York, 1686–1760* (New York, 1986), demonstrates that Albany merchants were involved in much more than the fur trade.

Helpful in understanding how New Yorkers made up the huge imbalance of trade with Britain are James Shepherd and Gary Walton, "Estimates of 'Invisible' Earnings in the Balance of Payments of the British North American Colonies, 1768–1772," *Journal of Economic History* 29 (1969): 230–63; Shepherd and Walton, "The Coastal Trade of the British North American Colonies, 1768–1772," *Journal of Economic History* 32 (1972): 783–810; James G. Lydon, "Fish and Flour for Gold: Southern Europe and the Colonial American Balance of Payments," *Business History Review* 8 (1972): 171–83; Richard Pares, *Yankees and Creoles: The Trade between North America and the West Indies before the Ameri-*

can Revolution (Cambridge, Mass., 1956);
Geoffrey L. Rossano, "Down to the Bay: New
York Shippers and the Central America Logwood Trade, 1748–1761," New York History
70 (1989): 229–50; and Glen Gabert, "The New
York Tobacco Trade, 1716–1742," Essex Institute Historical Collections 105 (1969): 103–27.

The still significant but declining commerce in peltry is explained in Thomas Elliot
Norton, The Fur Trade in Colonial New York,
1686–1776 (Madison, Wis., 1974). Privateering,
which played a major role in New York commerce, is explored in Marcus Rediker, Between
the Devil and the Deep Blue Sea: Merchant
Seamen, Pirates, and the Anglo-American Maritime World, 1700–1750 (New York, 1987);
James G. Lydon, Pirates, Privateers, and Profits
(Upper Saddle River, N.J., 1970); Carl E. Swanson, Predators and Prizes: American Privateering and Imperial Warfare, 1739–1748 (Columbia, S.C., 1991); and James G. Lydon, "Barbary
Pirates and Colonial New Yorkers," New-York
Historical Society Quarterly 45 (1961): 281–89.
The slave trade is examined in Jacob Judd,
"Frederick Philipse and the Madagascar
Trade," New-York Historical Society Quar-
terly 55 (1971): 354–74, and in James G. Lydon,
"New York and the Slave Trade, 1700–1774,"
William and Mary Quarterly 35 (1978):
374–94. Significant changes in the law and
judicial procedures that advanced commerce
are discussed in Herbert A. Johnson, The Law
Merchant and Negotiable Instruments in Colo-
nial New York (Chicago, 1963), and Deborah
A. Rosen, "Courts and Commerce in Colonial
New York," American Journal of Legal History
36 (1992): 139–63.

Manufacturing is explored in Charles
Howell and Allan Keller, The Mill at Philips-
burg Manor Upper Mills and a Brief History of
Milling (Tarrytown, N.Y., 1977), and Irene
Neu, "The Iron Plantations of Colonial New
York," New York History 33 (1952): 3–24. For
industries see Neu, "Hudson Valley Extractive
Industries before 1815," in Frese and Judd,

eds., Business Enterprise in Early New York,
133–65. For an enterprise that failed miserably,
see Philip Otterness, "The New York Naval
Stores Project and the Transformation of the
Poor Palatines," New York History 75 (1994):
133–56.

Among the important works on craftsmen
and laborers are Samuel McKee, Jr., Labor in
Colonial New York, 1664–1776 (New York,
1935), and Rita S. Gottesman, comp., The Arts
and Crafts in New York, 1726–1776: Advertisements and News Items from New York
City Newspapers (New York, 1938). For the
life of the craftsman, see Carl Bridenbaugh,
The Colonial Craftsman (New York, 1950). For
New York in particular, see Charles F. Hum-
mel, With Hammer in Hand: The Dominy
Craftsmen of East Hampton, New York (Charlottesville, Va., 1982); Mrs. Russell Hastings,
"Peter Van Dyck of New York, Goldsmith,
1684–1750." Antiques 31 (1937): 236–39, and
302–5; and Helen B. Smith, "Nicholas Roo-
sevelt—Goldsmith (1715–1769)," New-York
Historical Society Quarterly 34 (1950): 301–14.
Insight into the life of working-class whites
can be gained from Graham Russell Hodges,
The New York City Cartmen, 1667–1850
(New York, 1986).

For the economic enterprise of individuals
and families, see Julian Gwyn, "Prize Money
and Rising Expectations: Admiral Warren's
Personal Fortune," Histoire Sociale/Social
History 8 (1971): 84–101; Gwyn, "Private
Credit in Colonial New York: The Warren
Portfolio, 1731–1795," New York History 54
(1973): 268–93; Catherine S. Crary, "The
American Dream: John Tabor Kempe's Rise
from Poverty to Riches," William and Mary
Quarterly 14 (1957): 176–95; and A. J. Wall,
"Samuel Loudon (1727–1813) (Merchant,
Printer, and Patriot) with Some of his Let-
ters," New-York Historical Society Quarterly
6 (1922): 75–92. Lawrence Leder, "Military
Victualing in Colonial New York," and
William Chazanof, "Land Speculation in Eigh-

teenth-Century New York," are both in Frese and Judd, eds., *Business Enterprise in Early New York*, 21–54, and 55–76. Of special interest is Beverly McAnear, *The Income of the Colonial Governors of British North America* (New York, 1967), which deals mainly with the chief executives of New York.

Among the useful primary sources are Julius M. Bloch et al., eds., *An Account of Her Majesty's Revenue in the Province of New York, 1701–1709* (Chapel Hill, N.C., 1960); Philip L. White, ed., *The Beekman Mercantile Papers, 1746–1799*, 3 vols. (New York, 1956); and Charles M. Hough, ed., *Reports of Cases in the Vice Admiralty Court of the Province of New York and in the Court of Admiralty of the State of New York, 1715–1788* (New Haven, Conn., 1925).

Women, the Family, and Society

Early works on women in New York focused on their domestic enterprise and business endeavors. For example, see Mrs. John King Van Rensselaer, *The Goede Vrow of Manaha-ta: At Home and In Society, 1609–1760* (New York, 1898). Social histories were largely anecdotal, such as Alice Morse Earle, *Colonial Days in Old New York* (New York, 1898), and Ellen Singleton, *Social New York under the Georges, 1714–1776* (New York, 1902). More recent work has focused on women's legal status. See Linda Biemer, *Women and Property in Colonial New York: The Transition from Dutch to English Law, 1643–1727* (Ann Arbor, Mich., 1983), and Biemer, "Criminal Law and Women in New Amsterdam and Early New York," in Nancy Anne McClure Zeller, ed., *A Beautiful and Fruitful Place: Selected Rensselaerswijck Seminar Papers* (Albany, 1991), 73–82; and David Narrett, "Dutch Customs of Inheritance, Women, and the Law in Colonial New York City," in Pencak and Wright, eds., *Authority and Resistance in Early New York*, 27–55. The changing role of women in commerce is documented in Jean P. Jordan, "Women Merchants in Colonial New York," *New York History* 58 (1977): 412–39. Carole Shammas, "English Inheritance Law: Its Transfer to the Colonies," *American Journal of Legal History* 31 (1987): 145–63, places New York within the broader British-American context.

Outdated but containing interesting anecdotal materials on domestic life is Charles Edward Ironside, *The Family in Colonial New York: A Sociological Study* (New York, 1942). A more substantial study is Paula Dorman Christenson, "The Colonial Family in New York: A Study of Middle and Upper Class Interpersonal and Institutional Relationships" (Ph.D. diss., State University of New York at Albany, 1984); see also Peter Christoph, "The Colonial Family: Kinship and Power," in Zeller, ed., *A Beautiful and Fruitful Place*, 111–18; and Brook Hindle, "A Colonial Governor's Family: The Coldens of Coldenham," *New-York Historical Society Quarterly* 45 (1961): 233–50. Especially useful are Faith H. Fabend, *A Dutch Family in the Middle Colonies, 1660–1800* (Rutgers, N.J., 1991), and David Narrett, *Inheritance and Family Life in Colonial New York City* (Ithaca, N.Y., 1992). For a prominent Jewish family, consult Leo Hershkowitz, ed., *Letters of the Franks Family (1733–1743)* (Waltham, Mass., 1968).

The growth and development of colonial New York City has received its latest—and best—treatment in the early chapters of *Gotham: A History of New York City to 1898*, by Edwin Burrows and Mike Wallace (New York, 1999). Its demographic expansion is discussed in Ira Rosenwaike, *The Population History of New York City* (Syracuse, 1972). For the seventeenth century, the best study is still Mrs. Schuyler van Rensselaer, *History of the City of New York in the Seventeenth Century*, 2 vols. (New York, 1909). For both the seventeenth and eighteenth centuries, Martha J. Lamb, *History of the City of New York*, 2 vols. (New York, 1877–80), is still very useful.

For a superb example of urban anthropology based on both archaeological excavation and literary sources, see Nan A. Rothschild, *New York City Neighborhoods: The Eighteenth Century* (New York, 1990). Affirming the continued importance of occupational status and religious affiliation in early New York is Carl Abbott, "The Neighborhoods of New York, 1760–1775," *New York History* 55 (1974): 33–54. The older institutional approach to economic and social change is surveyed by Arthur E. Peterson, *New York as an Eighteenth-Century Municipality, Prior to 1731* (New York, 1917), and George W. Edwards, *New York as an Eighteenth-Century Municipality, 1731–1776* (New York, 1917). Poverty is treated by Robert E. Cray, *Paupers and Poor Relief in New York City and Its Rural Environs, 1700–1830* (Philadelphia, 1988); Stephen J. Ross, "Objects of Charity: Poor Relief, Poverty, and the Rise of the Almshouse in Early Eighteenth Century New York," in Pencak and Wright, eds., *Authority and Resistance in Early New York*, 138–72; and Raymond A. Mohl, "Poverty in Early America, a Reappraisal: Eighteenth-Century New York City," *New York History* 50 (1969): 5–27.

Outside of New York City, community developments may be traced in Stefan Bielinski, "The People of Colonial Albany, 1650–1850: The Profile of a Community," in Pencak and Wright, eds., *Authority and Resistance in Early New York*, 1–26. For Long Island, see Jessica Kross, *The Evolution of an American Town: Newtown, New York, 1642–1775* (Philadelphia, 1983); William MacLaughlin, "Dutch Rural New York: Community, Economy, and Family in Colonial Flatbush" (Ph.D. diss., Columbia University, 1981); and Jean B. Peyer, "Jamaica, Long Island, 1656–1710" (Ph.D. diss., Cornell University, 1974).

Among primary sources, revealing accounts are Carl Bridenbaugh, ed., *Gentleman's Progress: The Itinerarium of Dr. Alexander Hamilton* (Chapel Hill, N.C., 1948); Peter Kalm, *Travels in North America*, ed. Adolph B. Benson, 2 vols. (New York, 1934); Andrew Burnaby, *Travels through the Middle Settlements of North America in the Years 1759 and 1760*, ed. Rufus Rockwell (1798; rpt. New York, 1904); and Anne Grant, *Memoirs of an American Lady*, ed. James G. Wilson, 2 vols. (rev. ed., New York, 1901). Also covering family matters are Dorothy C. Barck, ed., *The Letter Book of John Watts: Merchant and Councillor of New York* (New York, 1928); Leo Hershkowitz, *Wills of Early New York Jews (1704–1799)* (New York, 1967); and Jacob Judd, ed., *The Van Cortlandt Family Papers*, 4 vols. (Tarrytown, N.Y., 1976–81).

Ethnic and Religious Diversity

Immigration and its cultural impact are discussed in Robert K. McGregor, "Cultural Adaptation in Colonial New York: The Palatine Germans of the Mohawk Valley," *New York History* 69 (1988): 5–34, and McGregor, "Settlement Variation and Cultural Adaptation in the Immigration History of Colonial New York," *New York History* 73 (1992): 193–212. Immigration to New York is detailed in John Butler, *The Huguenots in America* (Cambridge, Mass., 1983); James G. Leyburn, *The Scotch-Irish: A Social History* (Chapel Hill, N.C., 1962); George S. Pryde, "Scottish Colonization in the Province of New York," *New York History* 16 (1935): 138–57; A. G. Roeber, "'The Origin of Whatever Is Not English Among Us': The Dutch-speaking and German-speaking Peoples of Colonial British America," in Bernard Bailyn and Philip D. Morgan, eds., *Strangers within the Realm: Cultural Margins of the First British Empire* (Chapel Hill, N.C., 1993), 220–83; Maldwyn A. Jones, "The Scotch-Irish in British America," in ibid., 284–313; R. J. Dickson, *Ulster Emigration to Colonial America, 1718–1775* (London, 1966); and Ian C. C. Graham, *Colonists from*

Scotland: Emigration to North America, 1707–1783 (Ithaca, N.Y., 1956). David de Sola Pool, An Old Faith in the New World: Portrait of Shearith Israel, 1654–1954 (New York, 1955), describes the Jewish community. See also Jacob R. Marcus, The Colonial American Jew, 3 vols. (Detroit, 1970), and Hyman B. Grinstein, The Rise of the Jewish Community of New York, 1654–1860 (Philadelphia, 1945).

Patricia U. Bonomi, Under the Cope of Heaven: Religion, Society, and Politics in Colonial America (New York, 1986) deals extensively with New York. The relationship of church and state in New York is discussed in John W. Pratt, Religion, Politics, and Diversity: The Church-State Theme in New York History (Ithaca, N.Y., 1967), and Carl Bridenbaugh, Mitre and Sceptre: Transatlantic Faiths, Ideas, Personalities, and Politics, 1689–1775 (New York, 1962). For the interaction of various Protestant groups, see Richard Pointer, Protestant Pluralism and the New York Experience: A Study of Eighteenth Century Religious Diversity (Bloomington, Ind., 1988). Detailing tensions within the Dutch Reformed faith is Randall Balmer, A Perfect Babel of Confusion: Dutch Religion and English Culture in the Middle Colonies (New York, 1989). David G. Hackett, The Rude Hand of Innovation: Religion and Social Order in Albany, New York, 1652–1836 (New York, 1991), applies modernization theory to changing religious affiliation. Yet Dutch folkways persisted, as is demonstrated by Firth Fabend in "The Synod of Dort and the Persistence of Dutchness in Nineteenth-Century New York and New Jersey," New York History 77 (1996): 273–300, and A Dutch Family in the Middle Colonies, 1660–1800 (New Brunswick, N.J., 1991). Also see Joyce D. Goodfriend, "Writing/Righting Dutch Colonial History," New York History 80 (1999): 5–28.

The fullest interpretation of Germans in early New York is found in A. G. Roeber, Palatines, Liberty, and Property: German

Lutherans in Colonial British America (Baltimore, 1991), and David J. Webber, "Berkenmeyer and Lutheran Orthodoxy in Colonial New York," Concordia Historical Institute Quarterly 60 (1987): 19–31. English Calvinism in the province is examined by Joyce D. Goodfriend in "A New Look at Presbyterianism in New York City," American Presbyterian 67 (1989): 199–207, and "The Social Dimensions of Congregational Life in Colonial New York City," William and Mary Quarterly 46 (1989): 252–78.

Among the older but still important works are Gerald F. De Jong, The Dutch Reformed Church in the American Colonies (Grand Rapids, Mich., 1978); Harry L. Kreider, Lutheranism in Colonial New York (New York, 1942); Robert Hastings Nichols, Presbyterianism in New York State: A History of the Synod and Its Predecessors (Philadelphia, 1963); and Leonard J. Trinterud, The Forming of an American Tradition: A Re-examination of Colonial Presbyterianism (Philadelphia, 1949). The most comprehensive history of Anglicanism in early New York is Jean P. Jordan, "The Anglican Establishment in Colonial New York, 1693–1783" (Ph.D. diss., Columbia University, 1971); see also Morgan Dix, A History of the Parish of Trinity Church in the City of New York, 4 vols. (New York, 1898–1906). The various efforts of the Anglican Society for the Propagation of the Gospel in Foreign Parts are discussed in Frank Klingberg, Anglican Humanitarianism in Colonial New York (Philadelphia, 1940).

For the activities of the Society of Friends, see Arthur J. Worrall, Quakers in the Colonial Northeast (Hanover, N.H., 1980), and Rufus M. Jones, The Quakers in the American Colonies (London, 1923). For the United Brethren, see Harry E. Stocker, A History of the Moravian Church in New York City (New York, 1922). Early Catholic efforts can be traced in William H. Bennett, Catholic Footsteps in Old New York: A Chronicle of

Catholicity in the City of New York from 1524 to 1808 (1909; rpt. New York, 1973), and Martin J. Becker, *History of Catholic Life in the Diocese of Albany, 1609–1864* (New York, 1975).

Relations between the various religious groups are discussed in Nelson R. Burr, "The Episcopal Church and the Dutch in Colonial New York and New Jersey, 1664–1784," *Historical Magazine of the Protestant Episcopal Church* 19 (1951): 90–111; Cynthia A. Kierner, "A Concept Rejected: New York's 'Anglican Establishment,' 1693–1715," *Essays in History* 26 (1982): 291–303; and Milton M. Klein, "Church, State, and Education: Testing the Issue in Colonial New York," *New York History* 45 (1964): 291–303.

The impact of the Great Awakening in New York is minimized in Charles H. Maxson, *The Great Awakening in the Middle Colonies* (Chicago, 1920), but given more significance by Martin E. Lodge in "The Crisis of the Churches in the Middle Colonies, 1720–1750," *Pennsylvania Magazine of History and Biography* 95 (1971): 195–220. For the Dutch Reformed Church, see Alexander Wall, "The Controversy in the Dutch Church in New York Concerning Preaching in English, 1754–1758," *New-York Historical Society Quarterly Bulletin* 12 (1928): 39–58. The lasting impact of the Awakening is detailed by Robert Cray, Jr., "More Light on a New Light: James Davenport's Religious Legacy, Eastern Long Island, 1740–1840," *New York History* 73 (1992): 5–28.

There is a vast array of primary materials on religion, apart from the *Ecclesiastical Records*, including Henry M. Muhlenberg, *The Journals of Henry Melchoir Muhlenberg*, trans. Theodore G. Tappert and John W. Doberstein, 3 vols. (Philadelphia, 1942); J. F. Van Laer, trans., *The Records in the Lutheran Church at Amsterdam, Holland, relating to Lutheranism in Colonial New York* (New York, 1942); and John P. Dern, ed., *The Albany Protocol: Wil-*

helm Christoph Berkenmeyer's *Chronicle of Lutheran Affairs in New York Colony, 1731–1750*, trans. Simon Hart and Sibrandina Geertuid Hart-Runeman (Ann Arbor, Mich., 1971). See also A. D. Gillette, ed., *Minutes of the Philadelphia Baptist Association from 1707 to 1807* (Philadelphia, 1851).

Native Americans

A general account is Gary Nash, *Red, White, and Black: The Peoples of Early North America* (New York, 1992). The experience of Amerindians finding themselves increasingly drawn into the white man's world is explained in John A. Strong, *The Algonquian People of Long Island from Earliest Times to 1700* (Interlaken, N.Y., 1997), and Christopher Densmore, "Indian Religious Beliefs on Long Island: A Quaker Account," *New York History* 73 (1992): 431–41. See also Laurence Hauptman and Jack Compisi, eds., *Neighbors and Intruders: An Ethnohistorical Exploration of the Indians of Hudson's River* (Ottawa, 1978); Paul Bailey, *The Thirteen Tribes of Long Island* (Syosset, N.Y., 1982); and T. J. C. Brasser, "The Coastal Algonkian: People of the First Frontier," in Eleanor Leacock and Nancy Oestreich Lurie, eds., *North American Indians in Historical Perspective* (New York, 1971): 64–91. See also Alan Trelease, *Indian Affairs in Colonial New York: The Seventeenth Century* (Ithaca, N.Y., 1960).

The renaissance in Amerindian studies over the past twenty years has especially illuminated the Iroquois Confederation. A major work is William N. Fenton, *The Great Law and the Longhouse: A Political History of the Iroquois Confederacy* (Norman, Okla., 1998). For a summary and extensive up-to-date bibliography, see Daniel Richter, *The Ordeal of the Longhouse: The Peoples of the Iroquois League in the Era of European Colonization* (Chapel Hill, N.C., 1992). See also Richter, "Cultural Brokers and Intercultural Politics: New York-

Iroquois Relations, 1664–1701," *Journal of American History* 75 (1989): 40–67; Richter, "War and Culture: The Iroquois Experience," *William and Mary Quarterly* 40 (1983): 528–59; and Richter and James H. Merrill, eds., *Beyond the Covenant Chain: The Iroquois and Their Neighbors in Indian North America, 1600–1800* (Syracuse, 1987). Focusing on diplomacy from the Amerindian perspective is Matthew J. Dennis, *Cultivating a Landscape of Peace: Iroquois-European Encounters in Seventeenth-Century America* (Ithaca, N.Y., 1993). A good source for Amerindian-white relations in the eighteenth century is Richard Aquila, *The Iroquois Restoration: Iroquois Diplomacy on the Colonial Frontier, 1701–1754* (Detroit, 1983).

A pioneer work that still has much to contribute is William N. Fenton, "The Iroquois in History," in Leacock and Lurie, eds., *North American Indians in Historical Perspective,* 129–68. Filled with pertinent insight while dedicated to arguing the Indians' cause is the work of Francis Jennings, whose compelling writings have enlivened the literature immensely: *The Ambiguous Iroquois Empire: The Covenant Chain Confederation of Indian Tribes with English Colonies from Its Beginnings to the Treaty of Lancaster of 1744* (New York, 1984), *Empire of Fortune: Crowns, Colonies, and Tribes in the Seven Years' War in America* (New York, 1988), and *The Invasion of America: Indians, Colonialism, and the Cant of Conquest* (Chapel Hill, N.C., 1975). For a much more cultural approach, see James Axtell, *After Columbus: Essays in the Ethnohistory of Colonial North America* (New York, 1988), and the classic by Anthony F. C. Wallace, *The Death and Rebirth of the Seneca* (New York, 1969).

Background to Iroquois participation in the American Revolution is examined in George F. G. Stanley, "The Six Nations and the American Revolution," *Ontario History* 56 (1964): 217–32. Two other important works are

Isabel T. Kelsay, *Joseph Brandt, 1743–1807: Man of Two Worlds* (Syracuse, 1984), and especially Barbara Graymont, *The Iroquois in the American Revolution* (Syracuse, 1972), the first comprehensive study of the Six Nations and the American Revolution.

A major primary source for New York Amerindians is Peter Wraxall, *An Abridgment of the Indian Affairs Contained in Four Folio Volumes, Transacted in the Colony of New York, from the Year 1678 to the year 1751,* ed. Charles H. McIlwain (Cambridge, Mass., 1915). Especially useful in conjunction with Wraxall's *Abridgment* is Lawrence H. Leder, ed., *The Livingston Indian Records* (Gettysburg, Penn., 1956).

African Americans

The standard study of slavery in the province is Edgar McManus, *A History of Negro Slavery in New York* (Syracuse, 1966). See also David Kobrin, *The Black Minority in Early New York* (Albany, 1971); Roi Ottley and William J. Weatherby, *The Negro in New York: An Informal Social History, 1626–1940* (New York, 1967); and Shane White, *Somewhat More Independent: The End of Slavery in New York City, 1770–1810* (Athens, Ga., 1991). For African Americans on Long Island, see Lynda R. Day, *Making a Way to Freedom: A History of African Americans on Long Island* (Interlaken, N.Y., 1997); Ralph R. Ireland, "Slavery on Long Island: A Study of Economic Motivation," *Journal of Long Island History* 6 (Spring 1966): 1–12; and Richard S. Moss, *Slavery on Long Island* (New York, 1993). For slavery in the Hudson Valley, see A. J. Williams-Myers, "The African Presence in the Hudson River Valley: The Defining of Relationships between the Masters and the Slaves," *Afro-Americans in New York Life and History* 12 (1988): 81–95. Slavery in the cities is discussed in Oscar R. Williams, "The Regimentation of Blacks on the Urban Frontier in Colonial

Albany, New York City, and Philadelphia," *Journal of Negro History* 63 (1978): 329–38.

The growth of the African American population in colonial New York is examined in Thomas Davis, "New York's Long Black Line: A Note on the Growing Slave Population, 1676–1790," in Wendell Tripp, ed., *Coming and Becoming: Pluralism in New York State History* (Cooperstown, N.Y., 1999), 79–97. The legal history of slavery is treated generally in William M. Wiececk, "The Statutory Law of Slavery and Race in the Thirteen Mainland Colonies of British America," *William and Mary Quarterly* 34 (1977): 258–80, and in A. Leon Higginbotham, *In the Matter of Color: Race and the American Legal Process* (New York, 1978). With respect to New York, see Edwin Olsen, "The Slave Code in Colonial New York," *Journal of Negro History* 29 (1944): 147–65, and Carl Nordstrom, "The New York Slave Code," *Afro-Americans in New York Life and History* 4 (1980): 7–26.

Also of interest are Sherrill D. Wilson, *New York City's African Slaveowners: A Social and Material Culture History* (New York, 1994); Willie F. Page, "The African Slave during the Early English Period, 1664–1700," *Journal of the Afro-American Historical and Genealogical Society* 5 (1984): 123–32; and Robert Cray, "White Welfare and Black Strategies: The Dynamics of Race and Poor Relief in Early New York, 1700–1825," *Slavery & Abolition* 7 (1986): 273–89. See also Thomas Joseph Davis, "Slavery in Colonial New York City" (Ph.D. diss., Columbia University, 1974); Vivienne I. Kruger, "Born to Run: The Slave Family in Early New York, 1626–1827" (Ph.D. diss., Columbia University, 1985); Thelma W. Foote, "Black Life in Colonial Manhattan, 1664–1786" (Ph.D. diss., Harvard University, 1991); and Graham Hodges, *Root and Branch: African Americans in New York and East Jersey, 1613–1863* (Chapel Hill, N.C., 1999).

Black celebration of the Dutch holiday of Pinkster (Pentecost) is discussed in A. J.

Williams-Meyers, "Pinkster Carnival: Africanisms in the Hudson River Valley," *Afro-Americans in New York Life and History* 9 (1985): 7–17, and Shane White, "Pinkster: Afro-Dutch Syncretization in New York City and the Hudson Valley," *Journal of American Folklore* 102 (1989): 68–74. See also Edwin Olson, "Social Aspects of the Slave in Early New York," *Journal of Negro History* 26 (1944): 147–65.

The attitude of the Dutch Reformed Church toward slavery is examined by Gerald F. De Jong, "The Dutch Reformed Church and Negro Slavery in Colonial America," *Church History* 40 (1971): 423–36. White missionary efforts among New York slaves are the subject of Sheldon S. Cohen, "Elias Neau, Instructor to New York's Slaves," *New-York Historical Society Quarterly* 55 (1971): 7–27, and John Calam, *Parsons and Pedagogues: The S. P. G. Adventure in American Education* (New York, 1971). Conflict between whites and blacks is the topic in Kenneth Scott, "Slave Insurrection in New York in 1712," *New-York State Historical Quarterly* 45 (1961): 43–74, and Don C. Skemer, "New Evidence of Black Unrest in Colonial Brooklyn," *Long Island History* 12 (1975): 46–49. The so-called slave conspiracy of 1741 is most thoroughly studied in Thomas L. Davis, *A Rumor of Revolt: The "Great Negro Plot" in Colonial New York* (New York, 1985). See also Ferenc Szasz, "The New York Slave Revolt of 1741: A Re-examination," *New York History* 48 (1967): 215–30.

Daily life of the slave and the master-slave relationship in Albany are revealed in Anne Grant, *Memoirs of an American Lady*, and the 1741 revolt is covered in the account of Attorney General Daniel Horsmanden, *The New York Conspiracy: History of the Negro Plot, 1741–1742*, ed. Thomas J. Davis (Boston, 1971). Early Anglican efforts among African Americans is described by David Humphreys, *An Account of the Endeavours Used by the Society for the Propagation of the Gospel in Foreign Parts to Instruct the Negro Slaves in*

New York (New York, 1730). See also Harry B. Yoshpe, "Record of Slave Manumission in New York During the Colonial and Early National Periods," *Journal of Negro History* 26 (1941): 78–107.

Education and Culture

A provocative essay on cultural life is Milton M. Klein, "The Cultural Tyros of Colonial New York," *South Atlantic Quarterly* 66 (1967): 218–32. Formal education in New York City is treated in Carl Kaestle, *The Evolution of an Urban School System: New York City, 1750–1850* (Cambridge, Mass., 1973). Apprenticeship, the popular pattern of informal education, is discussed in Ronald Howard, "Apprenticeship and Economic Education in New Netherland and Seventeenth-Century New York," in Zeller, ed., *A Beautiful and Fruitful Place*, 205–18, and Robert Seybolt, *Apprenticeship and Apprenticeship Education in Colonial New England and New York* (New York, 1917). Educational concerns of two upper-class families are explored in Lawrence Leder, "Robert R. Livingston's Sons: Preparation for Futurity," *New York History* 50 (1969): 234–49, and Brooke Hindle, "A Colonial Governor's Family: The Coldens of Coldenham," *New-York Historical Society Quarterly* 45 (1961): 233–50. A farm family's efforts to educate its children is discussed by Fabend, *A Dutch Family in the Middle Colonies, 1660–1800*.

Paul M. Hamlin, *Legal Education in Colonial New York* (New York, 1939), examines training in the law. Shedding light on the training of doctors is Stils D. Ezell, "Regulation and Licensing of Physicians in New York," *New York Medical Journal* 57 (1952): 347–48, 577–78. The rise of evening schooling is discussed by Robert Seybolt, "The Evening Schools of Colonial New York City," in *Fifteenth Annual Report of the [New York State] Education Department* 1 (1919): 630–52. The relationship between religion and schools is explored in William H. Kilpatrick, *The Dutch Schools of New Netherland and Colonial New York* (Washington, D.C., 1912); William Webb Kemp, *The Support of Schools in Colonial New York by the Society for the Propagation of the Gospel in Foreign Parts* (New York, 1913); and Golda G. Stander, "Jesuit Educational Institutions in the City of New York (1683–1860)," *United States Catholic Historical Record* 24 (1934): 209–75.

The emergence of the theater is recorded in Allston Brown, *A History of the New York Stage, from the First Performance in 1732 to 1901*, 3 vols. (New York, 1903). See also Mary C. Henderson, *The City and the Theater: New York Playhouses from Bowling Green to Times Square* (rev. ed., New York, 1982). For architecture, consult Harold D. Eberlein, *Manors and Historic Homes of the Hudson Valley* (Philadelphia, 1924); Helen W. Reynolds, *Dutch Houses in the Hudson Valley before 1776* (New York, 1929); and Donald M. Reynolds, *The Architecture of New York City: Histories and Views of Important Structures, Sites, and Symbols* (New York, 1984). For furniture and material culture, see Norman S. Rice, *New York Furniture before 1840* (Albany, 1962); and V. Isabelle Miller, *Furniture by New York Cabinetmakers, 1650 to 1860* (New York, 1956). Especially useful is Alice Kenney, "Neglected Heritage: Hudson River Valley Dutch Material Culture," *Winterthur Portfolio* 20 (Spring 1985): 49–70. The continued use of the Dutch language is discussed in Edgar F. Romig, "'The English and Low-Dutch School-Master' (New York: William Bradford, 1730)," *New-York Historical Society Quarterly* 43 (1959): 149–59.

The progress of portraiture in New York is explained in Mary C. Black, "Pieter Vanderlyn and Other Limners of the Upper Hudson," and Wayne Craven, "Painting in New York City, 1750–1775," both in Ian M. G. Quimby, ed., *American Painting to 1776: A Reappraisal*

(Charlottesville, Va., 1971), 217–49, and 251–97. For Dutch New Yorkers, see Ruth Piwonka, "Dutch Colonial Arts," in Eric Nooter and Patricia U. Bonomi, eds., *Colonial Dutch Studies: An Interdisciplinary Approach* (New York, 1988), 78–94; and Roderick H. Blackburn and Ruth Piwonka, *Remembrance of Patria: Dutch Art and Culture in Colonial America, 1609–1776* (Albany, 1988).

The pursuit of literary refinement is discussed in Eleanor Bryce Scott, "Early Literary Clubs in New York City," *American Literature* 5 (1933): 3–16. The development of the press is surveyed in two older but still useful works: Charles R. Hildeburn, *Sketches of Printers and Printing in Colonial New York* (New York, 1895), and Harry B. Weiss, "A Graphic Summary of the Growth of Newspapers in New York and Other States, 1704–1820," *Bulletin of the New York Public Library* 52 (1948): 182–96. The most comprehensive study of the early press is John Z. C. Thomas, "Printing in Colonial New York, 1693–1763" (Ph.D. diss., University of Tennessee, Knoxville, 1974). For libraries, see Austin B. Keep, *History of the New York Society Library* (New York, 1908), and Edwin D. Hoffman, "The Bookshops of New York, 1743–1948," *New York History* 30 (1949): 53–65. New York printers and their presses are included in the classic work by Isaiah Thomas, *The History of Printing in America* (Worcester, Mass., 1810; 2d ed., New York, 1970). Individual biographies of New York printers include Alan Dyer, *A Biography of James Parker, Colonial Printer* (Troy, N.Y., 1982); Alfred L. Lorenz, *Hugh Gaine, A Colonial Printer's Odyssey to Loyalism* (Carbondale, Ill., 1972); and Alexander J. Wall, "William Bradford, Colonial Printer: A Tercentenary Review," *Proceedings of the American Antiquarian Society* 73 (1963): 361–84. The literary culture of New York is discussed in Thomas Jefferson Wertenbaker, *The Founding of American Civilization: The Middle Colonies* (New York, 1938).

Another measure of cultural maturity in early New York is the emergence of professional and voluntary organizations. For the legal profession, consult Milton M. Klein, "The Rise of the New York Bar: The Legal Career of William Livingston," *William and Mary Quarterly* 21 (1964): 493–515, and "From Community to Status: The Development of the Legal Profession in Colonial New York," *New York History* 60 (1979): 135–56. For a discussion of medicine in early America, see Richard H. Shryock, *Medicine and Society in America, 1660–1860* (New York, 1960). The best single source for most of the more significant voluntary organizations is Jacquetta May Haley, "Voluntary Organizations in Pre-Revolutionary New York City, 1750–1776" (Ph.D. diss., State University of New York at Binghamton, 1976).

For the acknowledged intellectual leader of provincial New York, see Brooke Hindle, "Cadwallader Colden's Extension of the Newtonian Principles," *William and Mary Quarterly* 13 (1956): 459–75. Bringing together public and private efforts was the drive to establish a college in New York. The most complete study is David C. Humphrey, *From King's College to Columbia, 1746–1800* (New York, 1976). See also Donald F. Gerardi, "The King's College Controversy, 1753–1756, and the Ideological Roots of Toryism in New York," *Perspectives in American History* 11 (1972): 147–96, and Milton M. Klein, "Church, State, and Education: Testing the Issue in Colonial New York," cited earlier.

The best sources on colonial New York culture are its newspapers. Especially significant because of its criticism of culture and society is Milton M. Klein, ed., *The Independent Reflector, or Weekly Essays on Sundry Important Subjects . . . by William Livingston and Others* (Cambridge, Mass., 1964). See also Beverly McAnear, ed., "American Imprints Concerning King's College," *Papers of the Bibliographical Society of America* 44 (1950):

301–39. For the first play written in British America, see Lawrence H. Leder, ed., "Robert Hunter's *Androboros*," *Bulletin of the New York Public Library* 67 (1964): 153–90. The work of provincial New York's remarkable African American poet is presented in Oscar Wegelin, ed., *Jupiter Hammon, American Negro Poet: Selections from His Writings and a Bibliography* (1915; rpt. New York, 1970).

Elements of New York's popular culture are explored in J. A. Stevens, "Old World New York Coffee Houses," *Harper's New Monthly Magazine* 64 (1882): 481–99, and W. Harrison Bayles, *Old Taverns of New York* (New York, 1915). Of special interest is Thomas Myers Garrett, "A History of Pleasure Gardens in New York City" (Ph.D. diss., New York University, 1978).

Law, the Courts, and Politics

The rich literature on law and lawyers is led by the work of Herbert A. Johnson, many of whose writings are included in his *Essays on New York Colonial Legal History* (Westport, Conn., 1981); see also his *John Jay, Colonial Lawyer* (New York, 1989). A number of articles on the subject are included in Leo Hershkowitz and Milton M. Klein, eds., *Courts and Law in Early New York: Selected Essays* (Port Washington, N.Y., 1978). See also John R. Aiken, *Utopianism and the Emergence of the Colonial Legal Profession: New York, 1664–1710, A Test Case* (New York, 1965); and Alden Chester, *Courts and Lawyers of New York: A History, 1609–1925*, 3 vols. (New York, 1925). A useful summary is Julius W. Goebel, "The Courts and the Law in Colonial New York," in volume 3 of Flick's *History of the State of New York*, 1–43. Goebel and T. Raymond Naughton, *Law Enforcement in Colonial New York: A Study in Criminal Procedure* (New York, 1944), is a classic.

Other aspects of legal development are treated in Deborah Rosen, *Courts and Commerce, cited earlier,* and Rosen, "Migrating Inequality: Women and Justice in Colonial New York," in Larry D. Eldridge, ed., *Women and Freedom in Early America* (New York, 1997), 313–29. Law enforcement is covered in works by Douglas Greenberg: *Crime and Law Enforcement in the Colony of New York, 1691–1776* (Ithaca, N.Y., 1976); "Patterns of Criminal Prosecution in Eighteenth-Century New York," *New York History* 56 (1975): 133–53; and "The Effectiveness of Law Enforcement in Eighteenth-Century New York," *American Journal of Legal History* 19 (1975): 173–207. For the courts, see Paul M. Hamlin and Charles E. Baker, *Supreme Court of Judicature of the Province of New York, 1691–1704*, 3 vols. (New York, 1959), and Deborah Rosen, "The Supreme Court of Judicature of Colonial New York: Civil Practice in Transition, 1691–1760," *Law and History Review* 5 (1987): 213–47.

New York proved fruitful ground for the raising of significant constitutional issues. Dated but still informative is Charles W. Spencer, "Colonial Wars and Constitutional Development in New York," *Addresses and Sermons Delivered before the Society of Colonial Wars in the State of New York, and Year Book for 1914–15* (New York, 1915). The early importance of both popular rule and freedom of religion is discussed in Christopher Densmore, "The Samuel Bownas Case: Religious Toleration and the Independence of Juries in Colonial New York, 1703–1704," *Long Island Historical Journal* 2 (1990): 177–88; Kenneth B. West, "Quakers and the State: The Controversy over Oaths in the Colony of New York," *Michigan Academician* 2 (1970): 95–105; and Randall H. Balmer, "Schism on Long Island: The Dutch Reformed Church, Lord Cornbury, and the Politics of Anglicanization," in Pencak and Wright, eds., *Authority and Resistance in Early New York*, 95–117. The issue of legislative control over the establishment of courts is examined by Joseph H. Smith, "Adolph

Philipse and the Chancery Resolves of 1727," in Hershkowitz and Klein, eds., *Courts and Law in Early New York*, 30–48, and Stanley Katz, "The Politics of Law in Colonial America: Controversies over Chancery Courts and Equity Law in the Eighteenth Century," *Perspectives in American History* 5 (1971): 257–84.

The celebrated Zenger case in 1735 has elicited a rash of publications, emphasizing both its legal and its political impact. The original account of the trial, written by James Alexander, one of Zenger's lawyers, and published by Zenger himself in 1736, has been reprinted numerous times. A relatively recent imprint, with an excellent critical introduction is provided by Stanley N. Katz, *A Brief Narrative of the Case and Trial of John Peter Zenger . . . by James Alexander* (2d ed., Cambridge, Mass., 1972). Two articles that challenge the significance of the case are Ellen M. James, "Decoding the Zenger Trial: Andrew Hamilton's 'Fraudful Dexterity' with Language," and Morris D. Forkosch, "Zenger versus Croswell and the Rule of Law," both in William Pencak and Wythe W. Holt, Jr., eds., *Law in America, 1607–1861* (New York, 1989), 1–26 and 28–72.

The most serious criticism of the popular view that the Zenger trial introduced freedom of the press is the work of Leonard Levy in the following publications: "Did the Zenger Case Really Matter? Freedom of the Press in Colonial New York," *William and Mary Quarterly* 17 (1960): 35–50, and *Legacy of Suppression* (Cambridge, Mass., 1960), which was revised as *Freedom of Speech and Press in Early American History: Legacy of Suppression* (New York, 1963), and again updated in *Emergence of a Free Press* (New York, 1985). The trial is also treated in Richard B. Morris, *Fair Trial: Fourteen Who Stood Accused* (New York, 1952), 69–95, and Paul Finkelman, "The Zenger Case: Prototype of a Political Trial," in Michael R. Belknap, ed., *American Political*

Trials (Westport, Conn., 1981), 21–42. More sympathetic approaches are in Larry D. Eldridge, *A Distant Heritage: The Growth of Free Speech in Early America* (New York, 1994), and Jeffery A. Smith, *Printers and Press Freedom: The Ideology of Early American Journalism* (New York, 1988).

Rights and criminal procedure are explored in Leonard W. Levy and Lawrence H. Leder, "'Exotic Fruit': The Right against Compulsory Self-Incrimination in Colonial New York," *William and Mary Quarterly* 20 (1963): 3–31. The role of the lower house as a judicial body is examined in Christine A. Desan, "Remaking Constitutional Tradition at the Margin of the Empire: The Creation of Legislative Adjudication in Colonial New York," *Law and History Review* 16 (1998): 257–317. The extent to which fundamental constitutional issues set the stage for trouble with England in the 1760s is analyzed by Milton M. Klein, "Prelude to Revolution in New York: Jury Trials and Judicial Tenure," *William and Mary Quarterly* 17 (1960): 446–53, and Herbert A. Johnson, "George Harison's Protest: New Light on Forsey versus Cunningham," *New York History* 50 (1969): 61–83. Daniel J. Hulsebosch, "*Imperia in Imperio*: The Multiple Constitutions of Empire in New York, 1750–1777," *Law and History Review* 16 (1998): 319–79, explains that the constitutional fluidity of the concept of empire brought New Yorkers and the British government increasingly into conflict.

For the view that colonial New York politics represented a paradigm for later American political developments, see Milton M. Klein, "New York in the American Colonies: A New Look," in his *Politics of Diversity*, 183–204, and "Shaping the American Tradition: The Microcosm of Colonial New York," *New York History* 59 (1978): 173–97. Patricia U. Bonomi takes a similar view in "The Middle Colonies: Embryo of the New Political Order," in Alden T. Vaughan and George A. Billias, eds., *Per-*

spectives in Early American History: Essays in Honor of Richard B. Morris (New York, 1973), 63–92. Another important analysis by Bonomi is her work *A Factious People: Politics and Society in Colonial New York*, cited earlier. See also Bonomi, "Local Government in Colonial New York: A Basis for Republicanism," in Judd and Polishook, eds., *Aspects of Early New York Society and Politics*, 29–50.

On freemanship, see Beverly McAnear, "The Place of the Freeman in Old New York," *New York History* 21 (1940): 418–30, and Graham R. Hodges, "Legal Bonds of Attachment: The Freemanship Law of New York City, 1648–1801," in Pencak and Wright, eds., *Authority and Resistance in Early New York*, 226–44. The mechanics of politics are discussed in Nicholas Varga, "Election Procedures and Practices in Colonial New York," *New York History* 41 (1960): 249–77, and Milton M. Klein, "Democracy and Politics in Colonial New York," *New York History* 40 (1959): 221–46. The politics of the upper house are explored by Jessica Kross, "'Patronage Most Ardently Sought': The New York Council, 1665–1775," in Bruce C. Daniels, ed., *Power and Status: Officeholding in Colonial America* (Middletown, Conn., 1986), 205–31. Councillors occupy a major place in Mary Lou Lustig's *Privilege and Prerogative: New York's Provincial Elite, 1710–1776* (Madison, N.J., 1995).

The intersection of provincial and imperial politics is discussed by Edward P. Lilly, *The Colonial Agents of New York and New Jersey* (Washington, D.C., 1936); Nicholas Varga, "Robert Charles, New York Agent, 1748–1770," *William and Mary Quarterly* 18 (1961): 211–35; Ross J. S. Hoffman, *Edmund Burke: New York Agent with His Letters to the New York Assembly and Intimate Correspondence with Charles O'Hara, 1761–1776* (Philadelphia, 1956); and Stanley Katz, *Newcastle's New York: Anglo-American Politics, 1732–1753* (Cambridge, Mass., 1969).

Among the best collections of legal documents relating to early New York is Richard B. Morris, ed., *Select Cases of the Mayor's Court of New York City, 1764–1784* (Washington, D.C., 1935). Cases involving the Navigation Acts are detailed in Hough, ed., *Reports of Cases in the Vice-Admiralty of the Province of New York . . . 1715–1788*. Land cases dealing with both Indians and tenants are examined in Oscar Handlin and Irving Mark, eds., "Chief Daniel Ninham *v.* Roger Morris, Beverly Robinson, and Philip Philipse—An Indian Land Case in Colonial New York, 1765–1767," *Ethnohistory* 11 (1964): 193–246, and in Handlin and Mark, "Land Cases in Colonial New York, 1765–1767," *New York University Law Quarterly Review* 9 (1942): 165–94. The Lewis Morris appeal to London is described in Stanley Katz, ed., "A New York Mission to England: The London Letters of Lewis Morris to James Alexander, 1735 to 1736," *William and Mary Quarterly* 28 (1971): 439–84. "The Colden Letters on Smith's History," New-York Historical Society *Collections* 1 (1868): 181–235, comprises Colden's corrections of Smith's *History*. They are continued in his "History of Gov. William Cosby's Administration and of Lt. Gov. George Clarke's Administration through 1737," New-York Historical Society *Collections* 68 (1935): 283–355.

The Coming of the Revolution

For publications before 1974, the best bibliography is Milton M. Klein, comp., *New York in the American Revolution: A Bibliography* (Albany, 1974) which has an excellent introductory essay on historiography. Research and writing on the Revolution in New York continues to revolve around the thesis set forth by Carl Becker in *The History of Political Parties in the Province of New York, 1760–1776* (Madison, Wis., 1909) that the War for Independence in New York was not only a war for home rule but for who should rule at home.

For the influence of the Becker thesis on the historiography of the American Revolution, see Bernard Mason, "The Heritage of Carl Becker: The Historiography of the Revolution in New York," *New-York Historical Society Quarterly* 52 (1969): 127–47; Robert E. Brown, *Carl Becker on History and the American Revolution* (East Lansing, Mich., 1970); and Milton M. Klein, "Detachment and the Writing of American History: The Dilemma of Carl Becker," in Vaughan and Billias, eds., *Perspectives on Early American History*, 120–66.

Becker's thesis was taken up by Alexander Flick, *Loyalism in New York during the American Revolution* (New York, 1901), who believed that "a majority" of New Yorkers did not want independence. Taking issue with Flick and also with Becker is Bernard Mason, *The Road to Independence: The Revolutionary Movement in New York, 1773–1776* (Lexington, Ky., 1966). John A. Neuenschwander, *The Middle Colonies and the Coming of the American Revolution* (Port Washington, N.Y., 1974), argues that the prosperity of the mid-Atlantic region made the upper classes especially cautious in the face of revolutionary protest. Tying together political rivalry and cultural diversity is Leopold S. Launitz-Schürer, Jr., *Loyal Whigs and Revolutionaries: The Making of the Revolution in New York, 1765–1776* (New York, 1980). Edward Countryman, *A People in Revolution: The American Revolution and Political Society in New York, 1760–1790* (Baltimore, 1981), has adopted a modified Becker view of the triumph of the middling classes in revolutionary New York. Challenging Countryman's conclusion is Joseph Tiedemann, *Reluctant Revolutionaries: New York City and the Road to Independence, 1763–1776* (Ithaca, N.Y., 1997), who argues persuasively that while economic and social tensions were part of the mix, the main reason citizens of Manhattan moved cautiously toward independence was their ethnic and religious pluralism.

For the unsettling impact of the French and Indian War, see Jessica Kross, "Taxation and the Seven Years' War: A New York Test Case," *Canadian Review of American Studies* 18 (1987): 351–66, and Fred Anderson, *Crucible of War: The Seven Years' War and the Fate of Empire in British North America, 1754–1766* (New York, 2000). For the military struggle in New York, see Stanley Pargellis, *Lord Loudoun in North America* (New Haven, Conn., 1933); Edward P. Hamilton, *The French and Indian Wars: The Story of Battles and Forts in the Wilderness* (New York, 1962); and I. K. Steele, *Betrayals: Fort William Henry and the "Massacre"* (New York, 1990). The efforts at intercolonial cooperation during the war are treated in Robert C. Newbold, *The Albany Congress and Plan of Union* (New York, 1955); Timothy Shannon, *Indians and Colonists at the Crossroads of Empire: The Albany Congress of 1754* (Ithaca, N.Y., 1999); and John V. Jezierski, "The Context of Union: The Origin, Provenance, and Failure of the Albany Plan of Union of 1754" (Ph.D. diss., Indiana University, 1971). For New Yorkers promoting imperial expansion, see Milton M. Klein's essays on Archibald Kennedy and William Livingston in Lawrence Leder, ed., *The Colonial Legacy*, vol. 2: *Some Eighteenth-Century Commentators* (New York, 1971), 75–105, and 107–40.

For the provocative role Lieutenant Governor Colden played in all this, see Carole Shammas, "Cadwallader Colden and the Role of the King's Prerogative," *New-York Historical Society Quarterly* 53 (1969): 103–26, and F. L. Engleman, "Cadwallader Colden and the New York Stamp Act Riots," *William and Mary Quarterly* 10 (1953): 560–78. See also Jesse Lemisch, *Jack Tar vs. John Bull: The Role of New York's Seamen in Precipitating the Revolution* (Hamden, Conn., 1997), which argues for extensive working-class influence. Written in the same vein is Staughton Lynd, "The Mechanics in New York Politics, 1774–1778," *Labor History* 5 (1964): 225–46. Lynd makes a similar argument for the influence of class conflict among the rural proletariat in "The Tenant Rising at Livingston Manor, May 1777," in his book *Class Conflict, Slavery, and the United States Constitution* (Indianapolis, 1967), 63–77. Challenging Lynd's economic thesis is Cynthia A. Kierner, "Landlord and Tenant in Revolutionary New York: The Case of Livingston Manor," *New York History* 70 (1989): 133–52. Bernard Friedman, "The Shaping of the Radical Consciousness in Provincial New York," *Journal of American History* 56 (1970): 781–801, argues for an emerging critical attitude toward Britain that connected with but ultimately transcended class differences. A convergence of grievances real and suspected is discussed in Roger Champagne, "The Military Association of the Sons of Liberty," *New-York Historical Society Quarterly* 41 (1957): 338–50; Lee R. Boyer, "Lobster Backs, Liberty Boys, and Laborers in the Streets: New York's Golden Hill and Nassau Street Riots," *New-York Historical Society Quarterly* 57 (1973): 281–308; and Paul Gilje, *The Road to Mobocracy: Popular Disorder in New York City, 1763–1834* (Chapel Hill, N.C., 1987).

For the Sons of Liberty, see Herbert Morais, "The Sons of Liberty in New York," in Richard B. Morris, ed., *The Era of the American Revolution* (New York, 1939), 269–89; Roger Champagne, "The Sons of Liberty and the Aristocracy in New York Politics" (Ph.D. diss., University of Wisconsin, 1960); Champagne, *Alexander McDougall and the American Revolution* (Syracuse, 1975); and Robert J. Christen, *King Sears: Politician and Patriot in a Decade of Revolution* (New York, 1982). Also pertinent is Isaac Leake, *Memoir of the Life and Times of General John Lamb* (1850; rpt. New York, 1971), a fairly factual but uncritical account. See also Donald A. Grinde, Jr., "Joseph Allicocke: African-American Leader of the Sons of Liberty," *Afro-Americans in New York History and Life* 14 (1990): 61–69; Allicocke ultimately became a loyalist. Other lesser leaders have been studied; see Bernard Friedman, "Hugh Hughes, A Study in Revolutionary Idealism," *New York History* 64 (1983): 229–60.

Detailing the development of anti-British protest are Neil R. Stout, "Captain Kennedy and the Stamp Act," *New York History* 37 (1956): 233–58; Nicholas Varga, "The New York Restraining Act: Its Passage and Some Effects, 1766–1768," *New York History* 37 (1956): 233–58; Lee E. Olm, "The Mutiny Act for America: New York's Non-compliance," *New-York Historical Society Quarterly* 58 (1974): 188–214; Roger Champagne, "Family Politics versus Constitutional Principles: The New York Assembly Elections of 1768 and 1769," *William and Mary Quarterly* 20 (1963): 57–79; Bernard Friedman, "The New York Assembly Elections of 1768 and 1769: The Disruption of Family Politics," *New York History* 46 (1965): 3–24; and Patricia U. Bonomi, "Political Patterns in Colonial New York City: The General Assembly Election of 1768," *Political Science Quarterly* 81 (1966): 432–47. The interaction of local politics and events outside the province are the focus of Roger Champagne, "New York and the Intolerable Acts," *New York History* 45 (1961): 195–207, and Champagne, "New York's Radicals and the Coming of Independence," *Journal of American History* 51 (1964): 21–40.

The role of religious affiliation in revolutionary sentiment is essayed in Donald F. M. Gerardi, "The Episcopate Controversy Reconsidered: Religious Vocation and Anglican Perceptions of Authority in Mid-Eighteenth-Century America," *Perspectives in American History* 3 (1987): 81–111; James S. Olson, "The New York Assembly, the Politics of Religion, and the Origins of the American Revolution, 1768–1771," *Historical Magazine of the Protestant Episcopal Church* 43 (1974): 21–28; and Joseph S. Tiedemann, "Queens County, New York, Quakers in the American Revolution: Loyalists or Neutrals?" *Historical Maga-*

zine of the *Protestant Episcopal Church* 52 (1983): 215–28.

That many New Yorkers hoped for a reconciliation between Britain and its American provinces is discussed in Milton M. Klein, "Failure of a Mission: The Drummond Peace Proposal of 1775," *Huntington Library Quarterly* 35 (1972): 343–80, and in Joseph S. Tiedemann, "A Revolution Failed: Queens County, New York, 1775–1776," *Journal of American History* 74 (1988): 417–44. The emergence of extralegal local government is examined by Alexander C. Flick, "Rise of the Revolutionary Committee System," in Flick, ed., *The American Revolution in New York: Its Political, Social, and Economic Significance* (Albany, 1926), 27–46. The reasons why New Yorkers ultimately embraced independence are discussed by Milton M. Klein, "Why Did the British Fail to Win the Hearts and Minds of New Yorkers?" *New York History* 64 (1983): 357–76.

The most interesting, if biased, contemporary account is Thomas Jones, *History of New York during the Revolutionary War*, ed. Edwin F. DeLancey, 2 vols. (New York, 1879). Along with Jones, another good source is Jones's nemesis, William Smith, Jr., *Historical Memoirs from 16 March 1763 to 12 November 1783*, ed. William H. Sabine, 3 vols. (New York, 1956, 1958). Also very insightful is Henry Cruger Van Schaack, *Memoir of Henry Van Schaack, Embracing Selections of His Correspondence and other Writings* (Chicago, 1892), and Richard B. Morris, ed., *John Jay, the Making of a Revolutionary: Unpublished Papers, 1745–1780* (New York, 1975). A good account of the rioting against the Stamp Act in both New York City and Albany is John Montrésor, *The Montrésor Journals*, ed. G. D. Scull, New-York Historical Society *Collections* 14 (1882). Another useful source is Kenneth Scott, ed., *Rivington's New York Newspaper: Excerpts from a Loyalist Press, 1773–1778* (New York, 1973).

Part III. From Revolution to Statehood (1776–1825)

Sources on the Revolution

The scholarship on Revolutionary New York is monumental. The most famous single volume is still Carl L. Becker, *The History of Political Parties in the Province of New York: 1760–1776* (Madison, Wis., 1909), which set the terms of debate to the present day. Becker's reading of early New York history and the Revolution in terms of internal conflict is challenged in: Milton M. Klein, *The Politics of Diversity: Essays in the History of Colonial New York* (Port Washington, N.Y., 1974); Patricia U. Bonomi, *A Factious People: Politics and Society in Colonial New York* (New York, 1970); Sung Bok Kim, *Landlord and Tenant in Colonial New York: Manorial Society: 1664–1775* (Chapel Hill, N.C., 1978); Bernard Mason, *The Road to Independence: The Revolutionary Movement in New York, 1773–1777* (Lexington, Ky., 1966); Philip Ranlet, *The New York Loyalists* (Knoxville, Tenn., 1986); and Leopold S. Launitz-Schürer, Jr., *Loyal Whigs and Revolutionaries: The Making of the Revolution in New York, 1765–1776* (New York, 1980). Others have continued to write in Becker's shadow. Among these are Staughton Lynd, "Who Should Rule at Home? Dutchess County, New York, in the American Revolution," *William and Mary Quarterly* 18 (1961): 330–59; Alfred F. Young, *The Democratic*

Republicans of New York: The Origins, 1763–1787 (Chapel Hill, N.C., 1966); and Edward Countryman, A People in Revolution: The American Revolution and Political Society in New York, 1760–1790 (Baltimore, 1981). An interesting appraisal of Becker, including his interpretation of New York politics in the colonial and Revolutionary era, is contained in Milton M. Klein's essay "Detachment and the Writing of American History: The Dilemma of Carl Becker," in Alden T. Vaughan and George A. Billias, eds., Perspectives on Early American History: Essays in Honor of Richard B. Morris (New York, 1973), 120–66.

New York's Revolutionary leadership is well served with both primary sources and biographies. The George Clinton papers were edited by Hugh Hastings: Public Papers of George Clinton, First Governor of New York, 1777–1795, 1801–1804, 10 vols. (Albany, 1899–1914). E. Wilder Spaulding's study of Clinton, His Excellency George Clinton: Critic of the Constitution (New York, 1938), is now supplanted by John P. Kaminski, George Clinton: Yeoman Politician of the New Republic (Madison, Wis., 1993). Other major biographies of Revolutionary figures include George Dangerfield, Chancellor Robert R. Livingston of New York, 1746–1813 (New York, 1960); Roger J. Champagne, Alexander McDougall and the American Revolution in New York (Schenectady, 1975); Don R. Gerlach, Philip Schuyler and the American Revolution in New York, 1733–1777 (Lincoln, Nebr., 1964), and Proud Patriot: Philip Schuyler and the War of Independence, 1775–1783 (Syracuse, 1987); and Max M. Mintz, Gouverneur Morris and the American Revolution (Norman, Okla., 1970). See also Stefan Bielinski's pamphlet, Abraham Yates, Jr., and the New Political Order in Revolutionary New York (Albany, 1975). Yates deserves a full study.

John Jay is best served in Richard B. Morris et al., eds., John Jay: Unpublished Papers, 2 vols. (New York, 1975–80), which supplements H. P. Johnston, ed., The Correspondence and Public Papers of John Jay, 3 vols. (New York, 1890–91). There are several major biographies of Alexander Hamilton: a two-volume account by Broadus Mitchell, Alexander Hamilton: Youth to Maturity, 1757–1788 (New York, 1957), and Alexander Hamilton: The National Adventure, 1788–1804 (New York, 1962); and one-volume treatments by Forrest McDonald, Alexander Hamilton: A Biography (New York, 1979), Jacob E. Cooke, Alexander Hamilton (New York, 1982), John C. Miller, Alexander Hamilton: Portrait in Paradox (New York, 1959), Nathan Schachner, Alexander Hamilton (New York, 1957), and Richard Brookhiser, Alexander Hamilton, American (New York, 1999). The Papers of Alexander Hamilton appear in a modern edition edited by Harold C. Syrett and Jacob E. Cooke, 27 vols. (New York, 1961–87). Aaron Burr is covered in two volumes by Milton Lomask: Aaron Burr: The Years from Princeton to Vice President, 1756–1805 (New York, 1979), and Aaron Burr: The Conspiracy and Years of Exile, 1805–1836 (New York, 1982); in Suzanne Geissler, Jonathan Edwards to Aaron Burr, Jr.: From the Great Awakening to Democratic Politics (New York, 1981; and most recently in Roger G. Kennedy, Burr, Hamilton, and Jefferson: A Study in Character (New York, 2000). Burr's papers have been edited by Mary Jo Kline, Political Correspondence and Public Papers of Aaron Burr, 2 vols. (Princeton, 1983). The "interview" between Burr and Hamilton has been the subject of three recent studies: Joanne B. Freeman "Dueling as Politics: Reinterpreting the Burr-Hamilton Duel," William and Mary Quarterly 53 (1996): 298–318; Arnold Rogow, A Fatal Friendship: Alexander Hamilton and Aaron Burr (New York, 1998); and W. J. Rorabaugh, "The Political Duel in the Early Republic: Burr v. Hamiton," Journal of the Early Republic 15 (1995): 1–23. Still useful is Harold C. Syrett and Jean Cooke, eds., Interview in Weehawken: The Burr-Hamilton Duel as Told in the Original Documents (Middletown, Conn., 1960).

The war years in New York are covered in: Ira D. Gruber, *The Howe Brothers and the American Revolution* (New York, 1972); Bruce Bliven, *Under the Guns: New York City, 1775–1776* (New York, 1972); and Max M. Mintz, *The Generals of Saratoga: John Burgoyne and Horatio Gates* (New Haven, Conn., 1990). The civilian side is treated fully in Oscar T. Barck, *New York City during the War for Independence* (New York, 1931, rpt. 1966); Wilbur C. Abbott, *New York in the American Revolution* (New York, 1929); and Thomas J. Wertenbaker, *Father Knickerbocker Rebels: New York City during the Revolution* (New York, 1948). For a briefer account, see William A. Polf, *Garrison Town: The British Occupation of New York City, 1776–1783* (Albany, 1976). A social history of New York City during the Revolution emphasizing relations between civilians on both sides is Judith Van Buskirk, "Generous Enemies: Civility and Conflict in Revolutionary New York" (Ph.D. diss., New York University, 1997). An old but still useful work covering civilian and military developments is [Alexander C. Flick], *The American Revolution in New York: Its Political and Economic Significance* (Albany, 1926). The war years as viewed by a British general who served in both military and civilian command positions in New York are covered in Milton M. Klein and Ronald W. Howard, eds., *The Twilight of British Rule in Revolutionary America: The New York Letter Book of General James Robertson, 1780–1783* (Cooperstown, N.Y., 1983). A "Hessian" soldier's experience can be traced in Johann Bense, "A Brunswick Grenadier with Burgoyne: The Journal of Johann Bense, 1776–1783," trans. Helga B. Doblin, *New York History* 66 (1985): 420–44. For the most recent treatment of the Nathan Hale story, see F. K. Donnelly, "A Possible Source for Nathan Hale's Dying Words," *William and Mary Quarterly* 42 (1985):

394–96. A comprehensive bibliography of older works is Milton M. Klein, *New York in the American Revlution: A Bibliography* (Albany, 1974).

The New York State Constitution of 1777 is discussed in the studies by Young, Mason, and Countryman noted above and in William A. Polf, *1777: The Political Revolution and New York's First Constitution* (Albany, 1977), which includes the document's text. The records of two Revolutionary committees have been printed: J. Howard Hanson and Samuel Ludlow Frey, eds., *The Minute Book of the Committee of Safety of Tryon County* (New York, 1905), and James Sullivan, ed., *Minutes of the Albany Committee of Correspondence, 1775–1778*, 2 vols. (Albany, 1923–25). Two sets of records of the Commissioners for Detecting and Defeating Conspiracies are also published: Dorothy C. Barck, ed., *Minutes of the Committee and of the First Commission for Detecting and Defeating Conspiracies . . . , Collections* of the New-York Historical Society, vols. 57 and 58 (1924–25), and Victor H. Paltsits, ed., *Minutes of the Commissioners for Detecting and Defeating Conspiracies, Albany County Sessions*, 3 vols. (Albany, 1909–10). A great many primary sources on New York's revolution are also scattered through Peter Force, comp., *American Archives*, 9 vols. (Washington, D.C., 1837–53), Edmund B. O'Callaghan, ed., *The Documentary History of the State of New York*, 4 vols. (Albany, 1849–51), and I. N. P. Stokes, ed., *The Iconography of Manhattan Island, 1498–1909*, 6 vols. (New York, 1915–28).

Loyalism

Loyalism is explored in the volume by Ranlet noted above, and in: Michael Kammen, "The American Revolution as a *Crise de Conscience*," in Richard M. Jellison, ed., *Society, Freedom, and Conscience: The American Revolution in Virginia, Massachusetts, and New*

York (New York, 1976); Janice Potter, *The Liberty We Seek: Loyalist Ideology in Colonial New York and Massachusetts* (Cambridge, Mass., 1983); Staughton Lynd, "The Tenant Rising at Livingston Manor, May, 1777," *New-York Historical Society Quarterly* 48 (1964): 163–77; Cynthia A. Kierner, "Landlord and Tenant in Revolutionary New York: The Case of Livingston Manor," *New York History* 70 (1989): 132–52; Milton M. Klein, "Why Did the British Fail to Win the Minds and Hearts of New Yorkers?" *New York History* 64 (1983): 357–75; Leopold S. Launitz-Schürer, Jr., "Whig-Loyalists: The DeLanceys of New York," *New-York Historical Society Quarterly* 56 (1972): 178–98; in a major series of articles by Joseph S. Tiedemann: "Loyalists and Conflict Resolution in Post-Revolutionary New York: Queens County as a Test Case," *New York History* 68 (1987): 27–43; "A Revolution Foiled: Queens County, New York, 1775–1776," *Journal of American History* 75 (1988): 417–44; and "Patriots by Default: Queens County, New York, and the British Army, 1776–1783," *William and Mary Quarterly* 43 (1986): 35–63, and in Tiedemann's book *Reluctant Revolutionaries: New York City and the Road to Independence, 1763–1776* (Ithaca, N.Y., 1997); in Edward Countryman, "The Uses of Capital in Revolutionary America: The Case of the New York Loyalist Merchants," *William and Mary Quarterly* 49 (1992): 3–28; in Jonathan Clark, "The Problem of Allegiance in Revolutionary Poughkeepsie," in David D. Hall et al., eds., *Saints and Revolutionaries: Essays on Early American History* (New York, 1984), 288–317; and in Robert A. East and Jacob Judd, eds., *The Loyalist Americans: A Focus on Greater New York* (Tarrytown, N.Y., 1975). An older but still useful work is Alexander C. Flick, *Loyalism in New York during the American Revolution* (New York, 1901). The war and the political developments that it brought can be seen through one loyalist's eyes in William Smith, Jr., *Historical Memoirs from*

16 March, 1763 to 25 July, 1778, ed. William H. W. Sabine, 2 vols. in one (New York, 1969).

The fate of the loyalist estates in New York has been a disputed matter among historians. The first comprehensive treatment of the subject was Harry Yoshpe's *Disposition of Loyalist Estates in the Southern District of the State of New York* (New York, 1939; rpt. 1967). This is complemented by Catherine S. Crary, "Forfeited Loyalist Lands in the Western District of New York," *New York History* 35 (1954): 435–56, and Beatrice C. Reubens, "Preemptive Rights in the Disposition of a Confiscated Estate: Philipsburgh Manor, New York," *William and Mary Quarterly* 22 (1965): 435–56. The most recent treatment of the subject, which demonstrates conclusively that widespread diffusion of landholding occurred as a result of the confiscation process, is John T. Reilly, "The Confiscation and Sale of the Loyalist Estates and Its Effect upon the Democratization of Landholding in New York State, 1779–1800" (Ph.D. diss., Fordham University, 1974).

General Works on the Post-Revolutionary Period

The large theme of post-independence change is explored in Robert V. Wells, "While Rip Napped: Social Change in Late Eighteenth-Century New York," *New York History* 71 (1990): 4–23, and in the anthology edited by Wells, *New Opportunities in a New Nation: The Development of New York after the Revolution* (Syracuse, 1982). For general treatments see also the volumes by Young and Countryman cited above. See also Allan Kulikoff, "The Transition to Capitalism in Rural America," *William and Mary Quarterly* 46 (1989): 120–44; Countryman, "The Uses of Capital"; Pauline Maier, "The Revolutionary Origins of the American Corporation," *William and Mary Quarterly* 50 (1993): 51–84; and Alice Kenney, "The Transformation of the Albany Patricians,

1778–1860," *New York History* 68 (1987): 151–73.

Political partisanship during the 1780s and 1790s and its relation to the debate in New York on the federal Constitution are considered in different ways in: Young, *Democratic Republicans;* Countryman, *A People in Revolution;* Linda Grant DePauw, *The Eleventh Pillar: New York State and the Federal Constitution* (Ithaca, N.Y., 1966); Stephen L. Schechter, ed., *The Reluctant Pillar: New York and the Adoption of the Federal Constitution* (Troy, N.Y., 1985); John P. Kaminski's essay in Patrick T. Conley and John P. Kaminski, eds., *The Constitution and the States* (Madison, Wis., 1988); and Jackson Turner Main, *Political Parties before the Constitution* (Chapel Hill, N.C., 1973). See also Robert H. Webking, "Melancton Smith and the Letters from the Federal Farmer," *William and Mary Quarterly* 44 (1987): 510–28. A whole range of subjects dealing with New York in the era of the federal Constitution is covered in the essays in Stephen L. Schechter and Richard B. Bernstein, eds., *New York and the Union* (Albany, 1990), and in Paul Gilje and William Pencak, eds., *New York in the Age of the Constitution, 1775–1800* (Rutherford, N.J., 1992). New York and the Bill of Rights is the subject of Milton M. Klein's "Origins of the Bill of Rights in Colonial New York," *New York History* 72 (1991): 389–405, also published as "Liberty as Nature's Gift: The Colonial Origins of the Bill of Rights in New York," in Patrick T. Conley and John P. Kaminski, eds., *The Bill of Rights and the States* (Madison, Wis., 1992). The standard works on New York during the Confederation era are still E. Wilder Spaulding, *New York in the Critical Period, 1783–1789* (New York, 1932), and Thomas C. Cochran, *New York in the Confederation: An Economic Study* (Philadelphia, 1932; rpt. 1972). Major primary source collections that bear on New York and the Constitution include: Merrill Jensen, ed., *The Documentary History of the Ratification of the Constitution,* 20 vols. to date (Madison, Wis., 1976–); Herbert J. Storing, ed., *The Complete Anti-Federalist,* 7 vols. (Chicago, 1981), vol. 6; and Bernard Bailyn, ed., *The Debate on the Constitution: Federalist and Antifederalist Speeches, Articles, and Letters during the Struggle over Ratification,* 2 vols. (New York, 1993); in addition to Syrett, ed., *Papers of Hamilton,* which shows in detail his contribution to *The Federalist.*

Ethnic, Social, and Economic Groups

The specific Revolutionary and post-Revolutionary experiences of different New York social groups are explored in many studies. For African Americans see Shane White, *Somewhat More Independent: The End of Slavery in New York City, 1770–1810* (Athens, Ga., 1991), as well as White's articles "Pinkster in Albany, 1803: A Contemporary Description," *New York History* 70 (1989): 191–99, and "'We Dwell in Safety and Pursue Our Honest Callings': Free Blacks in New York City, 1783–1810," *Journal of American History* 75 (1988): 445–70. See also: Edgar McManus, *Negro Slavery in New York* (Syracuse, 1966); W. Jeffrey Bolster, "'To Feel Like a Man': Black Seamen in the Northern States, 1800–1860," *Journal of American History* 76 (1990): 1173–99; Carleton Mabee, "Researching the History of Black Education in New York State," *Afro-Americans in New York Life and History* 6 (1982): 31–39; James O. Horton, "Black Urbanites: An Interpretation of Afro-American Life in the Antebellum City," *Afro-Americans in New York Life and History* 7 (1983): 63–70; Thomas J. Davis, "Three Dark Centuries around Albany: A Survey of Black Life in New York's Capital City Area before World War I," *Afro-Americans in New York Life and History* 7 (1983): 7–23; A. J. Williams-Meyers, "Pinkster Carnival: Africanisms in the Hudson River Valley," *Afro-Americans in New York Life and History* 9 (1985): 7–17;

John R. McKivigan and Jason H. Silverman, "Monarchical Liberty and Republican Slavery: West Indies Emancipation Celebrations in Upstate New York and Canada West," *Afro-Americans in New York Life and History* 10 (1986): 7–18; Ena L. Farley, "The African-American Presence in the History of Western New York," *Afro-Americans in New York Life and History* 14 (1990): 27–89; Donald A. Grinde, Jr., "Joseph Allicocke: African-American Leader of the Sons of Liberty," *Afro-Americans in New York Life and History* 14 (1990): 61–69; Ralph Watkins, "A Survey of the African-American Presence in the History of the Downstate New York Area," *Afro-Americans in New York Life and History* 15 (1991): 53–79; Graham Russell Hodges and Alan Edward Brown, eds., *Pretends to Be Free: Runaway Slave Advertisements from Colonial and Revolutionary New York and New Jersey* (New York, 1994); and, most recently, Graham Russell Hodges, *Root and Branch: African-Americans in New York and East Jersey, 1613–1863* (Chapel Hill, N.C., 1999).

For Native Americans see three major books: Anthony F. C. Wallace, *The Death and Rebirth of the Seneca* (New York, 1970); Barbara Graymont, *The Iroquois in the American Revolution* (Syracuse, 1972); and Isabel Thompson Kelsey, *Joseph Brant, 1743–1807: Man of Two Worlds* (Syracuse, 1984). See also the collection of photographs by Fred R. Wolcott, *Onondaga: Portrait of a Native People* (Syracuse, 1986). In addition see: Laurence M. Hauptman, "Samuel George (1795–1873): A Study of Onondaga Indian Conservatism," *New York History* 70 (1989): 4–22; J. David Lehman, "The End of the Iroquois Mystique: The Oneida Land Cession Treaties of the 1780s," *William and Mary Quarterly* 47 (1990): 523–47; Jadviga DaCosta Nunes, "Red Jacket: The Man and His Portraits," *American Art Journal* 12 (1980): 4–20; James O'Donnell, "Joseph Brant," in R. David Edmunds, ed., *American Indian Leaders: Studies in Diversity* (Lincoln, Nebr., 1980), 21–40; Diane Rothenberg, "The Mothers of the Nation: Seneca Resistance to Quaker Intervention," in Mona Etienne and Eleanor Leacock, eds., *Women and Colonization: Anthropological Perspectives* (New York, 1980), 63–87; Jack Campisi, "The Iroquois and the Euro-American Concept of Tribe," *New York History* 63 (1982): 165–82; William A. Starna, "Mohawk Iroquois Populations: A Revision," *Ethnohistory* 27 (1980): 371–82; Harry Robie, "Red Jacket's Reply: Problems in the Verification of a Native American Speech Text," *New York Folklore* 12 (1986): 99–117; and Elisabeth Tooker, "On the Development of the Handsome Lake Religion," *Proceedings of the American Philosophical Society* 133 (1989): 35–50. A major microfilm documentary collection on Iroquois history has been assembled by Francis Jennings et al.: *Iroquois Indians: A Documentary History*, 50 reels (Woodbridge, Conn., 1984). For one Iroquois nation's history in detail, see Jack Campisi and Laurence M. Hauptman, eds., *The Oneida Indian Experience: Two Perspectives* (Syracuse, 1988), and Laurence M. Hauptman and L. Gordon McLester III, eds., *The Oneida Indian Journey: From New York to Wisconsin, 1784–1860* (Madison, 1999).

Women during the American Revolution have received three major recent treatments: Linda K. Kerber, *Women of the Republic: Intellect and Ideology in Revolutionary America* (Chapel Hill, N.C., 1980); Mary Beth Norton, *Liberty's Daughters: The Revolutionary Experience of American Women, 1750–1800* (Boston, 1980); and Cathy N. Davidson, *Revolution and the Word: The Rise of the Novel in America* (New York, 1986). None of these is specific to New York, but all bear on it. Studies that do deal specifically with New York include Linda Grant DePauw, *Four Traditions: Women of New York during the American Revolution* (Albany, 1974), and, for the early national period, Christine Stansell, *City of Women: Sex and Class in New York, 1789–*

1860 (New York, 1986), and Mary P. Ryan, *Cradle of the Middle Class: The Family in Oneida County, New York, 1790–1865* (New York, 1981).

Urban workingmen have been the subjects of a great deal of study. The key original texts were Staughton Lynd, "The Mechanics in New York Politics, 1774–1785," *Labor History* 5 (1964): 215–46, and Alfred F. Young, "The Mechanics and the Jeffersonians: New York, 1789–1801," *Labor History* 5 (1964): 247–76. Young expands on this work in *The Democratic Republicans of New York.* Major accounts include Sean Wilentz, *Chants Democratic: New York City and the Rise of the American Working Class, 1788–1850* (New York, 1984); Howard B. Rock, *Artisans of the New Republic: The Tradesmen of New York City in the Age of Jefferson* (New York, 1979); and Graham R. Hodges, *New York City Cartmen, 1667–1850* (New York, 1986).

The debate on New York's agricultural system and the politics that grew from it begins with the many studies of the colonial period, including the works of Irving Mark, *Agrarian Conflicts in Colonial New York, 1711–1775* (New York, 1940), as well as Kim and Bonomi cited above. For discussions that bear on the Revolutionary and post-Revolutionary eras see: Henry Christman, *Tin Horns and Calico: A Decisive Episode in the Emergence of Democracy* (New York, 1945); David Maldwyn Ellis, *Landlords and Farmers in the Hudson-Mohawk Region, 1790–1850* (Ithaca, N.Y., 1946); Staughton Lynd, *Anti-Federalism in Dutchess County, New York: A Study of Democracy and Class Conflict in the Revolutionary Era* (Chicago, 1962); Philip L. White, *Beekmantown, New York: Forest Frontier to Farm Community* (Austin, Tex., 1979); Alan Taylor, "'The Art of Hook & Snivey': Political Culture in Upstate New York during the 1790s," *Journal of American History* 79 (1993): 1371–96; and Taylor, *William Cooper's Town: Power and Persuasion on the Frontier of the*

Early American Republic (New York, 1995). The emergence of Vermont is dealt with most fully and with most sophistication in Michael A. Bellesiles, *Revolutionary Outlaws: Ethan Allen and the Struggle for Independence on the Early American Frontier* (Charlottesville, Va., 1993). Young, *Democratic Republicans,* and Ryan, *Cradle of the Middle Class,* also contain valuable information about rural life.

Political, economic, and social changes in New York City, Newtown, Albany, the Hudson River Valley, and the western frontier during the post-Revolutionary period are analyzed in the essays in Stephen L. Schechter and Wendell Tripp, eds., *World of the Founders: New York Communities in the Federal Period* (Albany, 1990).

The Erie Canal

The standard narrative account of the building of the Erie Canal is Ronald E. Shaw, *Erie Water West: A History of the Erie Canal 1792–1794* (Lexington, Ky., 1966; rpt. 1990). The financing of the canal and the impact of canal finance on the state economy are the subjects of Nathan Miller, *The Enterprise of a Free People: Aspects of Economic Development in New York State during the Canal Period, 1792–1838* (Ithaca, N.Y., 1962). The most recent treatment, which deals with the canal as a cultural artifact, is Carol Sheriff, *The Artificial River: The Erie Canal and the Paradox of Progress, 1817–1862* (New York, 1996). The canal forms a major subject in any treatment of De Witt Clinton. See Dorothie Bobbe, *De Witt Clinton* (New York, 1933); Steven E. Siry, *De Witt Clinton and the American Political Economy: Sectionalism, Politics, and Republican Ideology, 1787–1828* (New York, 1990); and Evan W. Cornog, *The Birth of Empire: DeWitt Clinton and the American Experience, 1769–1828* (New York, 1998). See also: John F. Stover, "Canals and Turnpikes: America's Early-Nineteenth-Century Transportation Network," in Joseph R. Frese and Jacob Judd, eds., *An Emerging Independent American Economy, 1815–1875* (Tarrytown, N.Y., 1980), 60–98; Patricia Cooke, "The Erie Canal: American History through Folklore," *New York Folklore* 5 (1979): 155–67; David M. Ellis, "Whitestown: From Yankee Outpost to Cradle of Reform," *New York History* 65 (1984): 32–59; Richard F. Palmer, "Oswego: Lumber Trade Capital of the U.S.," *Inland Seas* 40 (1984): 30–38, and "The Forwarding Business in Oswego, 1800–1820," *Inland Seas* 41 (1985): 100–111, 175–84; John Seelye, "'Rational Exultation': The Erie Canal Celebration," *Proceedings of the American Antiquarian Society* 94 (1984): 241–67; Roger Evan Carp, "The Erie Canal and the Liberal Challenge to Classical Republicanism, 1785–1850" (Ph.D. diss., University of North Carolina, Chapel Hill, 1986), and "The Limits of Reform: Labor and Discipline on the Erie Canal," *Journal of the Early Republic* 10 (1990): 191–219. See also Mary P. Ryan, *Cradle of the Middle Class* and Philip L. White, *Beekmantown*.

Religion and Education

Religious development along the canal corridor is discussed in Paul A. Johnson, *A Shopkeeper's Millennium: Society and Revivals in Rochester, New York, 1815–1837* (New York, 1978), and Ryan, *Cradle of the Middle Class*. See also: Richard W. Pointer, "Religious Life in New York during the Revolutionary War," *New York History* 66 (1985): 356–73; John Webb Pratt, *Religion, Politics, and Diversity: The Church-State Theme in New York History* (Ithaca, N.Y., 1967); Robert E. Cray, Jr., "Forging a Majority: The Methodist Experience on Eastern Long Island, 1789–1845," *New York History* 67 (1986): 284–303; and David G. Hackett, *The Rude Hand of Innovation: Religion and Social Order in Albany, New York, 1652–1836* (New York, 1991). All of these supplement but do not

replace Whitney R. Cross, *The Burned-Over District: The Social and Intellectual History of Enthusiastic Religion in Western New York, 1800–1850* (Ithaca, N.Y., 1950).

Education in the early state is the subject of the innovative account by Daniel Calhoun, *The Intelligence of a People* (Princeton, 1973).

The Early Nineteenth Century

The study of New York City still begins with Stokes, *Iconography of Manhattan Island*, and with Robert Greenhalgh Albion, *The Rise of New York Port (1815–1860)* (New York, 1939). Wilentz, *Chants Democratic*, Stansell, *City of Women*, Shane White, *Somewhat More Independent*, and Elizabeth Blackmar, *Manhattan for Rent, 1785–1850* (Ithaca, N.Y., 1989), are necessary modern supplements. But all other studies now stand secondary to Edwin G. Burrows and Mike Wallace, *Gotham: A History of New York City to 1898* (New York, 1999). Albany's early nineteenth-century development is traced most recently in Hackett, *The Rude Hand of Innovation*. Kingston is discussed in Stuart Blumin, *The Urban Threshold: Growth and Change in a Nineteenth-Century American Community* (Chicago, 1976). For Poughkeepsie, see Clyde Griffen and Sally Griffen, *Natives and Newcomers: The Ordering of Opportunity in Mid-Nineteenth Century Poughkeepsie* (Cambridge, Mass., 1978). For Utica, see Ryan, *Cradle of the Middle Class*, and for Rochester see Johnson, *Shopkeeper's Millennium*.

Political partisanship is the main theme of Young, *Democratic Republicans*, and of the earlier classics by Dixon Ryan Fox, *The Decline of Aristocracy in the Politics of New York* (New York, 1919), and Lee Benson, *The Concept of Jacksonian Democracy: New York as a Test Case* (Princeton, 1961). Formal political life at the state level during the nineteenth century's first quarter revolves around the figures of De Witt Clinton and Martin Van Buren. For Clinton see the studies by Dorothie Bobbe and Steven Siry noted above, and Siry's "The Sectional Politics of 'Practical Republicanism': De Witt Clinton's Presidential Bid, 1810–1812," *Journal of the Early Republic* 5 (1985): 441–62. For Van Buren see: Donald B. Cole, *Martin Van Buren and the American Political System* (Princeton, 1984); Robert V. Remini, *Martin Van Buren and the Making of the Democratic Party* (New York, 1959); John Niven, *Martin Van Buren: The Romantic Age of American Politics* (New York, 1983); James C. Curtis, "In the Shadow of Old Hickory: The Political Travail of Martin Van Buren," *Journal of the Early Republic* 1 (1981): 249–67; and Joseph C. Rayback, "Martin Van Buren: His Place in the History of New York and the United States," *New York History* 64 (1983): 121–35.

Part IV. Antebellum Society and Politics (1825–1860)

General Works

In the absence of a comprehensive synthesis of the period, the best introduction to the broad contours of antebellum New York history remains the relevant portions of the more general histories of the state. David M. Ellis, James A. Frost, and Harry J. Carman, *A Short History of New York State* (Ithaca, N.Y., 1957; rev. ed., 1967), continues to be invaluable. Ellis's briefer work, *New York: State and City* (Ithaca, N.Y., 1979), is also insightful. Among the many older surveys of New York history, Alexander C. Flick, ed., *History of the State of New York*, 10 vols. (New York, 1933–37), is the most informative. The most detailed surveys of the political history of the period are Jabez D. Hammond, *The History of Political Parties in the State of New York*, 3 vols. (Syracuse, 1852), and D. S. Alexander, *A Political History of the State of New York*, 3 vols. (Rpt. Port Washington, N.Y., 1969). Constitutional developments are best followed in Charles Z. Lincoln, *Constitutional History of New York*, 5 vols. (Rochester, 1906). A more recent, brief survey is Peter J. Galie, *Ordered Liberty: A Constitutional History of New York* (New York, 1996). J. H. Dougherty, *Constitutional History of the State of New York* (New York, 1915), should also be consulted. Alden Chester, ed., *Legal and Judicial History of New York*, 3 vols. (New York, 1911), remains the most comprehensive treatment of the bench and bar, although those interested in particular aspects of the legal history of the period should consult the many more specialized studies of the law which have appeared in recent years. A good starting point is Morton J. Horwitz, *The Transformation of American Law, 1780–1860* (Cambridge, Mass., 1977). The complicated fiscal history of the state is effectively traced in Donald C. Sowers, *The Financial History of New York State from 1789 to 1912* (New York, 1914). Charles Z. Lincoln, ed., *Messages from the Governors, Comprising Executive Communications to the Legslature and Other Papers . . . 1683–1906*, 11 vols. (Albany, 1909), is an invaluable resource for the public history of the period.

Important regional studies include David Maldwyn Ellis, *Landlords and Farmers in the Hudson-Mohawk Region, 1790–1850* (Ithaca, N.Y., 1946); Neil Adams McNall, *An Agricultural History of the Genesee Valley, 1790–1860* (Philadelphia, 1952); and Whitney R. Cross, The Burned-Over District: *The Social and Intellectual History of Enthusiastic Religion in Western New York, 1800–1850* (Ithaca, N.Y., 1950).

Histories of particular localities are too numerous to list in their entirety, but some are especially noteworthy. For New York City, Edwin G. Burrows and Mike Wallace, *Gotham: A History of New York City to 1898* (New York and Oxford, 1999) is essential reading. J. G. Wilson, ed., *Memorial History of the City of New York from Its Earliest Settlement to the Year 1892*, 4 vols. (1892–93), also remains useful. Two important collections of sources, maps, and photographs are Isaac Newton Phelps Stokes, *The Iconography of Manhattan Island, 1498–1909*, 6 vols. (New York, 1915–28), and J. A. Kouwenhoven, *The Columbia Historical Portrait of New York* (Garden City, N.Y., 1953). For a comprehensive synthesis of the city's history in the last two decades before the Civil War, see Edward K. Spann, *The New Metropolis: New York City, 1840–1857* (New York, 1981). Intellectual life in the city is surveyed magnificently in Thomas A. Bender, *New York Intellect: A History of Intellectual Life in New York City, from 1750 to the Beginnings of Our Own Time* (New York, 1987). An invaluable source for the history of Albany is Joel Munsell, comp., *The Annals of Albany*, 10 vols. (Albany, 1850–59). More modern works on the state's capital include Codman Hislop, *Albany: Dutch, English, and American* (Albany, 1936), and David G. Hackett, *The Rude Hand of Innovation: Religion and Social Order in Albany, New York, 1652–1836* (New York, 1991).

Other notable local histories for this period include Blake McKelvey, *Rochester: The Water Power City, 1812–1854* (Cambridge, Mass., 1945); Stuart Blumin, *The Urban Threshold: Growth and Change in a Nineteenth-Century American Community* (Chicago, 1976), which focuses on Kingston; Philip L. White, *Beekmantown, New York: Forest Frontier to Farm Community* (Austin, Tex., 1979); and Roberta Balstad Miller, *City and Hinterland: A Case Study of Urban and Regional Development* (Westport, Conn.,

1979), which examines the changing relationship between Syracuse and its economic hinterland.

New York Modernizes

General works that are especially helpful in understanding the relationship of New York to national economic developments in this period include George R. Taylor, *The Transportation Revolution, 1815–1860* (New York, 1951); Douglas C. North, *The Economic Growth of the United States, 1790–1860* (New York, 1966); Clarence Danhof, *Change in Agriculture: The Northern United States, 1820–1870* (Cambridge, Mass., 1969); Glenn Porter and Harold C. Livesay, *Merchants and Manufacturers: Studies in the Changing Structure of Nineteenth-Century Marketing* (Baltimore, 1971); Stuart Bruchey, *The Roots of American Economic Growth: An Essay in Social Causation* (New York, 1968); Richard D. Brown, *Modernization: The Transformation of American Life, 1600–1865* (New York, 1976); and Charles Sellers, *The Market Revolution: Jacksonian America, 1815–1846* (New York, 1991).

Demographic trends for the period can be followed in New York State, *Census, 1855*, and U.S. Bureau of the Census, *The Statistical History of the United States, from Colonial Times to the Present* (1976). David Maldwyn Ellis, "Rise of the Empire State, 1790–1820," *New York History* 56 (January 1975): 5–27, and Ellis, "The Yankee Invasion of New York, 1783–1850," *New York History* 32 (January 1951): 3–17, are succinct overviews of the state's development; also useful is Ira P. Rosenwaike, *The Population History of New York City* (Syracuse, 1972). On urbanization, see George R. Taylor, "American Urban Growth Preceding the Railway Age," *Journal of Economic History* 27 (September 1967): 309–39. The extent and impact of immigration is best traced in Robert Ernst, *Immigrant Life in New York City, 1825–1863* (Port Washington, N.Y.,

1949), and in the *Annual Reports of the Commissioners of Emigration of the State of New York . . . 1847–1860* (New York, 1861).

For general developments in transportation in this period, see Taylor, *The Transportation Revolution,* and Caroline E. MacGill et al., *History of Transportation in the United States before 1860* (Washington, D.C., 1917). The best overview of the role of turnpikes remains Joseph A. Durrenberger, *Turnpikes: A Study of the Toll Road Movement in the Middle Atlantic States and Maryland* (Rpt. Cos Cob, Conn., 1968), but Oliver Wendell Holmes, "The Turnpike Era," in Flick, ed., *History of the State of New York,* Vol. 5, *Conquering the Wilderness* is also worth consulting. The state's canal system has received extensive scholarly treatment. Noble E. Whitford's *History of the Canal System of the State of New York,* 2 vols. (Albany, 1906) remains an indispensable starting point. Other general treatments of the subject include Carter Goodrich, ed., *Canals and American Economic Development* (New York, 1961); Goodrich, *Government Promotion of Canals and Railroads, 1800–1890* (New York, 1960); and Ronald E. Shaw, *Canals for a Nation: The Canal Era in the United States, 1790–1860* (Lexington, Ky., 1990). The most comprehensive modern treatment of the Erie Canal is Ronald E. Shaw, *Erie Water West: A History of the Erie Canal, 1792–1854* (Lexington, Ky., 1966). Nathan Miller, *The Enterprise of a Free People: Aspects of Economic Development of New York during the Canal Period, 1792–1838* (Ithaca, N.Y., 1962), is an important study of the economic consequences of the canal. L. Ray Gunn, *The Decline of Authority: Public Economic Policy and Political Development in New York State, 1800–1860* (Ithaca, N.Y., 1988), considers canal policy in the context of the broader issue of political development. Carol Sheriff, *The Artificial River: The Erie Canal and the Paradox of Progress, 1817–1862* (New York, 1996), is an elegant treatment of the social and cultural impact of the canal. Peter Way, *Common Labour: Workers and the Digging of North American Canals, 1780–1860* (Cambridge, England, 1993), and Patricia Anderson, *The Course of Empire: The Erie Canal and the New York Landscape, 1825–1875* (Rochester, 1984), also provide important perspectives on the meaning of the canal. For the early history of railroads, readers should consult: MacGill, *History of Transportation in the United States*; Frank W. Stevens, *The Beginnings of the New York Central, 1826–1853* (New York, 1926); Harry H. Pierce, *Railroads of New York: A Study of Government Aid, 1826–1875* (Cambridge, Mass., 1953); and Lee Benson, *Merchants, Farmers, and Railroads: Railroad Regulation and New York Politics, 1850–1887* (Cambridge, Mass., 1955), as well as the local and regional studies mentioned above. The collection of essays on transportation and business in Joseph R. Frese and Jacob Judd, eds., *An Emerging Independent American Economy, 1815–1875* (Tarrytown, N.Y., 1980), is also useful for the topics treated in this paragraph and those below.

Two older general works provide valuable introductions to agricultural developments in the state: Percy W. Bidwell and John I. Falconer, *History of Agriculture in the Northern United States, 1620–1860* (Washington, D.C., 1925), and Ulysses Prentiss Hedrick, *A History of Agriculture in the State of New York* (1933; rpt. New York, 1966). These should be supplemented by Paul W. Gates, *The Farmers' Age: Agriculture, 1815–1860* (Armonk, N.Y., 1960); Danhof, *Change in Agriculture*; Ellis, *Landlords and Farmers*; and McNall, *An Agricultural History of the Genesee Valley.* William Chazanof, *Joseph Ellicott and the Holland Land Company: The Opening of Western New York* (Syracuse, 1970), and William Wyckoff, *The Developer's Frontier: The Making of the Western New York Landscape* (New York, 1988), should also be consulted. Early attempts to understand the antirent movement include Henry Christman, *Tin Horns and Calico: A Decisive Episode in the Emergence of Democracy* (New York, 1945), and E. P. Cheyney, "The Anti-Rent Movement and the Constitution of 1846," in Flick, ed., *History of the State of New York*, vol. 6, *The Age of Reform*. A recent account is Reeve Huston, *Land and Freedom: Rural Society, Popular Protest, and Party Politics in Antebellum New York* (New York, 2000).

The growth of manufacturing in the state can be traced in Victor S. Clark, *History of Manufactures in the United States*, 3 vols. (New York, 1929); the various federal and state censuses between 1810 and 1860; Taylor, *The Transportation Revolution*; and the histories of particular localities and regions. Harry J. Carman, "The Beginnings of the Industrial Revolution," in vol. 5 of Flick, ed., *History of the State of New York*, and Harry J. Carman and August B. Gold, "The Rise of the Factory System," in vol. 6 of the same work, are useful introductions to the subject. Richard L. Ehrlich, "The Development of Manufacturing in Selected Counties in the Erie Canal Corridor, 1815–1860" (Ph.D. diss., State University of New York at Buffalo, 1972) is also helpful. Sean Wilentz, *Chants Democratic: New York City and the Rise of the American Working Class, 1788–1850* (New York, 1984), is indispensable for an understanding of the process of metropolitan industrialization in New York City.

Robert G. Albion, *The Rise of New York Port, 1815–1860* (New York, 1939), remains the indispensable treatment of New York City's involvement in foreign trade in this period, but one should also consult such general works as North, *The Economic Growth of the United States*, Taylor, *The Transportation Revolution*, and Porter and Livesay, *Merchants and Manufacturers*. Ralph W. Hidy, *The House of Baring in American Trade and Finance, 1763–1861* (Cambridge, Mass., 1949), is a valuable study of New York's financial ties to England. J. A. Scoville, *The Old Merchants of New York*, 5 vols. (New York, 1863–66), remains a useful resource, but there are also numerous biographies of leading merchants and businessmen. See particularly: Kenneth Wiggins Porter, *John Jacob Astor: Business Man* (New York, 1966); John D. Haeger, *John Jacob Astor: Business and Finance in the Early Republic* (Detroit, 1991); and W. J. Lane, *Commodore Vanderbilt: An Epic of the Steam Age* (New York, 1942).

For the history of corporations in the state, see: Ronald E. Seavoy, *The Origins of the American Business Corporation, 1784–1855: Broadening the Concept of Public Service during Industrialization* (Westport, Conn., 1982); Joseph S. Davis, *Essays in the Earlier History of America Corporations*, 2 vols. (Cambridge, Mass., 1917); George H. Evans, Jr., *Business Incorporations in the United States, 1800–1943* (New York, 1943); and L. Ray Gunn, "Political Implications of General Incorporation Laws in New York to 1860," *Mid-America* 59 (October 1977), 171–91. The best general study of banks in this period is Bray Hammond, *Banks and Politics in America from the Revolution to the Civil War* (Princeton, 1957). Specific aspects of the New York banking system can be followed in Robert E. Chaddock, *The Safety Fund Banking System in New York, 1829–1866* (Washington, D.C., 1910), and Fritz Redlich, *The Molding of American Banking: Men and Ideas* (New York, 1947). New York City's growing dominance of the capital market is best followed in Margaret Myers, *Origins and Development of the New York Money Market* (New York, 1931).

Society, Religion, and Reform

The social history of antebellum New York has received extensive treatment in recent decades. Two older studies provide good introductions to the history of labor in this period: J. R. Commons et al., *History of Labour in the United States*, 4 vols. (New York, 1918–35), and Philip Foner, *History of the Labor Movement in the United States* (New York, 1947). Sean Wilentz's *Chants Democratic* is an exhaustive and sophisticated investigation of the impact of economic change on labor in New York City in these years. Richard B. Stott's *Workers in the Metropolis: Class, Ethnicity, and Youth in Antebellum New York City* (Ithaca, N.Y., 1990) examines the transformation of working-class culture in the city in the two decades before the Civil War. Also useful are Walter Hugins, *Jacksonian Democracy and the Working Class: A Study of the New York Workingmen's Movement, 1829–1837* (Stanford, Calif., 1960); Edward Pessen, *Most Uncommon Jacksonians: The Radical Leaders of the Early Labor Movement* (Albany, 1967); and Daniel Walkowitz, *Worker City, Company Town: Iron and Cotton Worker Protest in Troy and Cohoes, New York, 1855–1884* (Urbana, Ill., 1981).

The development of a distinctive urban middle class is the subject of Stuart Blumin, *The Emergence of the Middle Class: Social Experience in the American City, 1760–1900* (Cambridge, England, 1989). The role of religion, family, and gender in the emergence of middle-class culture can be followed in Paul E. Johnson, *A Shopkeeper's Millennium: Society and Revivals in Rochester, New York, 1815–1837* (New York, 1978), and Mary P. Ryan, *Cradle of the Middle Class: The Family in Oneida County, New York, 1790–1865* (New York, 1981). Clyde Griffen and Sally Griffen, *Natives and Newcomers: The Ordering of Opportunity in Mid-Nineteenth-Century Poughkeepsie* (Cambridge, Mass., 1978), and Edward Pessen, *Riches, Class, and Power before the Civil War* (New Brunswick, N.J., 1990), also emphasize the increasing differentiation of classes in antebellum New York.

Recreation and the changing urban landscape of New York City are the subjects of Roy Rosenzweig and Elizabeth Blackmar, *The Park and the People: A History of Central Park* (Ithaca, N.Y., 1992); Laura Roper, *FLO: A Biography of Frederick Law Olmsted* (Baltimore, 1983); and David Schuyler, *The New Urban Landscape: The Redefinition of City Form in Nineteenth-Century America* (Baltimore, 1986). Schuyler, *Apostle of Taste: Andrew Jackson Downing, 1815–1852* (Baltimore, 1996), should also be consulted for insight into landscape, rural architecture, and the development of city parks.

There is an extensive and lively literature on religious revivalism in this period. For background to the events in New York, see: Nathan O. Hatch, *The Democratization of American Christianity* (New Haven, Conn., 1989); Jon Butler, *Awash in a Sea of Faith: Christianizing the American People* (Cambridge, Mass., 1990); and William G. McLoughlin, *Revivals, Awakenings, and Reform: An Essay on Religion and Social Change in America, 1607–1977* (Chicago, 1978). Whitney Cross, *The Burned-Over District,* is indispensable for understanding revivalism and its impact in western New York, but it should be supplemented by Michael Barkun, *Crucible of the Millennium: The Burned-Over District of New York in the 1840s* (Syracuse, 1986), and David L. Rowe, *Thunder and Trumpets: Millerites and Dissenting Religion in Upstate New York, 1800–1850* (Chico, Calif., 1985). On Finney, see Keith Hardman, *Charles Grandison Finney, 1792–1875: Revivalist and Reformer* (Syracuse, 1987), and William G. McLoughlin, *Modern Revivalism: Charles Grandison Finney to Billy Sunday* (New York, 1959). For the social and cultural impact of revivalism, see Johnson, *A Shopkeeper's Millennium*, Ryan, *Cradle of the Middle Class*, and Paul E. Johnson and Sean Wilentz, *The Kingdom of Matthias: A Story of Sex and Salvation in 19th-Century America* (New York, 1994).

On the relationship between religion and

reform, see, in addition to the works cited in the previous paragraph: C. C. Cole, Jr., *The Social Ideas of the Northern Evangelists, 1826–1860* (New York, 1954); Timothy L. Smith, *Revivalism and Social Reform: American Protestantism on the Eve of the Civil War* (Baltimore, 1957); Clifford Stephen Griffin, *Their Brothers' Keepers: Moral Stewardship in the United States, 1800–1865* (New Brunswick, N.J., 1960); and Robert H. Abzug, *Cosmos Crumbling: American Reform and the Religious Imagination* (New York, 1994). Two excellent overviews of reform in this period are Alice Felt Tyler, *Freedom's Ferment: Phases of American Social History to 1860* (Freeport, N.Y., 1944), and Ronald G. Walters, *American Reformers, 1815–1860* (New York, 1978).

The history of specific reform activities in New York can be followed in the appropriate chapters of Flick, ed., *History of the State of New York*, in general studies of particular reform movements, and in the biographies of the principal reformers. W. J. Rorabaugh, *The Alcoholic Republic: An American Tradition* (New York, 1979), and James Kirby Martin and Mark Lender, *Drinking in America: A History* (New York, 1987), trace the use of alcohol in early American society, while Ian R. Tyrrell, *Sobering Up: From Temperance to Prohibition in Antebellum America, 1800–1860,* provides an excellent overview of the temperance movement. The best recent survey of the abolitionist movement is James Brewer Stewart, *Holy Warriors: The Abolitionists and American Slavery* (New York, 1976), but Gilbert H. Barnes, *The Anti-Slavery Impulse, 1830–1844* (New York, 1933), is still worth consulting. Both should be supplemented by Gerald Sorin, *The New York Abolitionists: A Case Study of Political Radicalism* (Westport, Conn., 1971). Two biographies that shed light on abolitionism in New York are Ralph Volney Harlow, *Gerrit Smith, Philanthropist and Reformer* (New York, 1939), and Bertram Wyatt-Brown,

Lewis Tappan and the Evangelical War against Slavery (Cleveland, 1969).

Particularly noteworthy studies of women in New York in this period include Ryan, *Cradle of the Middle Class*; Ryan, *Women in Public: From Banners to Ballots, 1825–1880* (Baltimore, 1990); Christine Stansell, *City of Women: Sex and Class in New York, 1789–1860* (New York, 1986); Nancy A. Hewitt, *Women's Activism and Social Change: Rochester, New York, 1822–1872* (Ithaca, N.Y., 1984); Timothy J. Gilfoyle, *City of Eros: New York City, Prostitution, and the Commercialization of Sex, 1790–1920* (New York, 1992); and Marilynn Wood Hill, *Their Sisters' Keepers: Prostitution in New York City, 1830–1870* (Berkeley, Calif., 1993). The changing legal status of women can be traced in Norma Basch, *In the Eyes of the Law: Women, Marriage, and Property in Nineteenth-Century New York* (Ithaca, N.Y., 1982). The best survey of the women's rights movement is Eleanor Flexner, *Century of Struggle: The Woman's Rights Movement in the United States* (Cambridge, Mass., 1959). See also: Ellen Carol DuBois, *Feminism and Suffrage: The Emergence of an Independent Women's Movement in America, 1848–1869* (Ithaca, N.Y., 1978); Lois W. Banner, *Elizabeth Cady Stanton: A Radical for Women's Rights* (Boston, 1980); and Elisabeth Griffith, *In Her Own Right: The Life of Elizabeth Cady Stanton* (New York, 1984).

A number of works treat the African American experience in New York. A good overview for this period is Graham R. Hodges, *Root and Branch: African Americans in New York and East Jersey, 1613–1863* (Chapel Hill, N.C., 1999). For essential background on slavery in the state, see Edgar J. McManus, *A History of Negro Slavery in New York* (Syracuse, 1966), and Shane White, *Somewhat More Independent: The End of Slavery in New York City, 1770–1810* (Athens, Ga., 1991). Two studies of the status of free blacks in the

North which contain much information on New York are Leon Litwack, *North of Slavery: The Negro in the Free States, 1790–1860* (Chicago, 1961), and Leonard P. Curry, *The Free Black in Urban America, 1800–1850: The Shadow of the Dream* (Chicago, 1981). Works focusing specifically on New York include: Roi Ottley and William J. Weatherby, eds., *The Negro in New York: An Informal Social History, 1626–1940* (New York, 1967); George E. Walker, *The Afro-American in New York City, 1827–1860* (New York, 1993); Rhonda G. Freeman, *The Free Negro in New York City in the Era before the Civil War* (New York, 1994), and Freeman, *The African American Presence in New York State History* (Albany, 1989); Phyllis Francis Field, *The Politics of Race in New York: The Struggle for Black Suffrage in the Civil War Era* (Ithaca, N.Y., 1982); Howard Coles, *The Cradle of Freedom: A History of the Negro in Rochester, Western New York, and Canada* (Rochester, 1941); Carleton Mabee, *Black Education in New York State* (Syracuse, 1979); and Carol M. Hunter, *To Set the Captives Free: Reverend Jermain Wesley Loguen and the Struggle for Freedom in Central New York, 1835–1872* (New York, 1993).

The literature on nonevangelical religious developments and communitarianism in this period is also extensive. The best starting point remains Cross, *The Burned-Over District*, which should be supplemented by Barkun, *Crucible of the Millennium*, and, for the Millerites in particular, Rowe, *Thunder and Trumpets*. Lawrence Foster's *Religion and Sexuality: The Shakers, the Mormons, and the Oneida Community* (Urbana, Ill., 1984) is a valuable treatment of the impact of religion on the family and sexual values of the groups studied. For Mormonism, consult: Jan Shipps, *Mormonism: The Story of a New Religious Tradition* (Urbana, Ill., 1985); Leonard J. Arrington and Davis Bitton, *The Mormon Experience: A History of the Latter-Day Saints* (New York, 1979); and John L. Brooke, *The*

Refiner's Fire: The Making of Mormon Cosmology, 1644–1844 (Cambridge, England, 1996). On John Humphrey Noyes and the Oneida community, see Robert David Thomas, *The Man Who Would Be Perfect: John Humphrey Noyes and the Utopian Impulse* (Philadelphia, 1977), and Maren Lockwood Carden, *Oneida: Utopian Community to Modern Corporation* (Baltimore, 1969). In addition to the general studies on the burned-over district, Ann Braude, *Radical Spirits: Spiritualism and Women's Rights in Nineteenth-Century America* (Boston, 1989), should be consulted on the subject of spiritualism.

The history of Catholicism in New York can be traced in Mark A. Noll, *A History of Christianity in the United States and Canada* (Grand Rapids, Mich., 1992); Jay P. Dolan, *The American Catholic Experience: A History from Colonial Times to the Present* (Garden City, N.Y., 1985); and Dolan, *The Immigrant Church: New York's Irish and German Catholics, 1815–1865* (Baltimore, 1975). Ray A. Billington, *The Protestant Crusade, 1800–1860* (Chicago, 1938), remains the best overview of nativism in the period, but there are a number of works which deal specifically with New York. See especially: Vincent P. Lannie, *Public Money and Parochial Education: Bishop Hughes, Governor Seward, and the New York School Controversy* (Cleveland, 1968); Louis Dow Scisco, *Political Nativism in New York State* (New York, 1901); Carl F. Siracusa, "Political Nativism in New York City, 1843–1848" (Ph.D. diss., Columbia University, 1965); Leo Hershkowitz, "The Native American Democratic Association in New York City, 1835–1836," *New-York Historical Society Quarterly* 46 (1962): 41–59; and Ira M. Leonard, "The Rise and Fall of the American Republican Party in New York City, 1843–1845," *New-York Historical Society Quarterly* 50 (1966): 151–92.

The Jewish experience in New York State in this period can be followed in Joseph Blau and Salo Baron, *The Jews in the United States, 1790–1840: A Documentary History*, 3 vols. (New York, 1963); Anita Lebeson, *Jewish Pioneers in America, 1492–1848* (New York, 1931); David de Sola Pool, *Portraits Etched in Stone: Early Jewish Settlers, 1682–1831* (New York, 1953); Hyman B. Grinstein, *The Rise of the Jewish Community of New York, 1654–1860* (Philadelphia, 1945); and Naomi W. Cohen, *Encounters with Emancipation: The German Jews in the United States, 1830–1914* (Philadelphia, 1984). Studies of specific communities include Selig Adler and Thomas E. Connolly, *From Ararat to Suburbia: The Jewish Community of Buffalo* (Philadelphia, 1960); Solomon J. Kohn, *The Jewish Community of Utica, New York, 1847–1958* (New York, 1959); Stuart E. Rosenberg, *The Jewish Community in Rochester, 1843–1925* (New York, 1954); and Bernard G. Rudolph, *From a Minyan to a Community: A History of the Jews of Syracuse* (Syracuse, 1970).

A good starting point for the institutional response to dependency and social deviancy in New York is David M. Schneider, *The History of Public Welfare in New York State, 1609–1866* (Chicago, 1938). Important general works that provide insight into the New York experience include David J. Rothman, *The Discovery of the Asylum: Social Order and Disorder in the New Republic* (Boston, 1971), and Gerald N. Grob, *Mental Institutions in America: Social Policy to 1875* (New York, 1972). W. David Lewis, *From Newgate to Dannemora: The Rise of the Penitentiary in New York, 1796–1848* (Ithaca, N.Y., 1965), should be consulted for the history of prisons in the state. On the response to poverty, see Raymond A. Mohl, *Poverty in New York, 1783–1825* (New York, 1971), and Carroll Smith Rosenberg, *Religion and the Rise of the American City: The New York City Mission Movement, 1812–1870* (Ithaca, N.Y., 1971). The *Yates Report* on poor relief can be found in New York *Senate Journal*, 47 Sess. (1824):

95–108. Joseph M. Hawes, *Children in Urban Society: Juvenile Delinquency in Nineteenth-Century America* (New York, 1971), deals with houses of refuge.

New York at the Crossroads of Culture

For New York City's centrality in the communications and information network, see Allan R. Pred, *Urban Growth and the Circulation of Information: The United States System of Cities, 1790–1840* (Cambridge, Mass., 1973), and Spann, *The New Metropolis*. The spread of newspapers and the transformation of newspaper publishing can be traced in Frank Luther Mott, *American Journalism: A History of Newspapers in the United States through 250 Years, 1690–1940* (New York, 1941); Michael Schudson, *Discovering the News: A Social History of American Newspapers* (New York, 1978); John D. Stevens, *Sensationalism and the New York Press* (New York, 1991); Allan Nevins, "The Newspapers of New York State, 1783–1900," in Flick, ed., *History of the State of New York*, vol. 9, *Mind and Spirit*, 267–305; and James L. Crouthamel, "The Newspaper Revolution in New York, 1830–1860," *New York History* 45 (April 1964): 91–113. Biographies of influential New York editors include: Charles Henry Brown, *William Cullen Bryant* (New York, 1971); James L. Crouthamel, *Bennett's New York Herald and the Rise of the Popular Press* (Syracuse, 1989); Glyndon G. Van Deusen, *Horace Greeley: Nineteenth Century Crusader* (Philadelphia, 1953); Francis Brown, *Raymond of the Times* (New York, 1951); and Glyndon G. Van Deusen, *Thurlow Weed: Wizard of the Lobby* (Boston, 1947). Information on black newspapers in the state can be obtained in Ottley and Weatherby, eds., *The Negro in New York: An Informal Social History, 1626–1940*; Walker, *The Afro-American in New York City*; and Freeman, *The Free Negro in New York City in the Era before the Civil War*. On magazines, see: Frank Luther Mott, *A*

History of American Magazines, vol. 1, *1741–1850* (New York, 1930); John William Tebbel and Mary Ellen Zuckerman, *The Magazine in America, 1741–1990* (New York, 1991); and Bender, *New York Intellect.*

Numerous works treat developments in literature in this period. A good starting point is R. E. Spiller et al., *Literary History of the United States*, 3 vols. (New York, 1948). The essays on Irving, Bryant, Cooper, Melville, and Whitman in Spiller, *The Cycle of American Literature: An Essay in Historical Criticism* (New York, 1955), are also very useful. The literary scene of the era is ably described in Perry Miller, *The Raven and the Whale: The War of Words and Wits in the Era of Poe and Melville* (New York, 1956), which should be supplemented by: James T. Callow, *Kindred Spirits; Knickerbocker Writers and American Artists, 1807–1855* (Chapel Hill, N.C., 1967); Andrew D. Meyers, ed., *The Knickerbocker Tradition: Washington Irving's New York* (Tarrytown, N.Y., 1974); Larzer Ziff, *Literary Democracy: The Declaration of Cultural Independence* (New York, 1981); and, especially, Bender, *New York Intellect.* Essential for an understanding of the relationship between major literary figures and the popular culture of this period is David S. Reynolds, *Beneath the American Renaissance: The Subversive Imagination in the Age of Emerson and Melville* (Cambridge, Mass., 1988). For specific writers, see: Brown, *William Cullen Bryant*; Lewis G. Leary, *Washington Irving* (Minneapolis, 1963); Edwin Haviland Miller, *Melville* (New York, 1975); Stephen Railton, *Fenimore Cooper: A Study of His Life and Imagination* (Princeton, 1978); Alan Taylor, *William Cooper's Town: Power and Persuasion on the Frontier of the Early American Republic* (New York, 1995); and David S. Reynolds, *Walt Whitman's America: A Cultural Biography* (New York, 1995).

Artistic developments can be followed in Neil Harris, *The Artist in American Society: The Formative Years, 1790–1860* (New York,

1966); Barbara Novak, *Nature and Culture: American Landscape and Painting, 1825–1875* (New York, 1980); Angela Miller, *The Empire of the Eye: Landscape Representation and American Cultural Politics, 1825–1875* (Ithaca, N.Y., 1993); John K. Howat, *American Paradise: The World of the Hudson River School* (New York, 1987); and William Sawitzky, "History of Art in New York State," in Flick, ed., *History of the State of New York*, 9: 347–67.

The essential starting point for an understanding of the growth of education in the pre–Civil War decades is Lawrence A. Cremin, *American Education: The National Experience, 1783–1876* (New York, 1980). Carl F. Kaestle, *The Evolution of an Urban School System: New York City, 1750–1850* (Cambridge, Mass., 1973), is a careful study of the emergence of the public school system in New York City. Older studies of education in the state which remain useful include: Samuel S. Randall, *The Common School System of the State of New York . . . .* (Troy, N.Y., 1851); Thomas E. Finegan, ed., *Free Schools: A Documentary History of the Free School Movement in New York State* (Albany, 1921); and Frank P. Graves, "History of the State Education Department," in Flick, ed., *History of the State of New York*, 9: 1–43. Two pioneering women are treated in Alma Lutz, *Emma Willard: Pioneer Educator of American Women* (Boston, 1964), and Nancy Kline, *Elizabeth Blackwell: A Doctor's Triumph* (Berkeley, Calif., 1997). Mabee, *Black Education in New York State,* is the best treatment of that subject. For a good, brief overview of the establishment of libraries and the lyceum movement in the state, see Frank L. Tolman's essay in Flick, ed., *History of the State of New York*, 9: 45–91.

General developments in higher education can be followed in Sidney Sherwood, *The University of the State of New York: A History of Higher Education in the State of New York*

(Washington, D.C., 1900), and Frank C. Abbott, *Government Policy and Higher Education: A Study of the Regents of the University of the State of New York, 1784–1949* (Ithaca, N.Y., 1958). Bender, *New York Intellect,* is quite helpful on higher education in New York City, but should be supplemented by histories of individual institutions, particularly Willis Rudy, *The College of the City of New York: A History, 1847–1947* (New York, 1949), and Theodore F. Jones, ed., *New York University, 1832–1932* (New York, 1933). Valuable studies of other New York State institutions include: Warren H. Smith, *Hobart and William Smith: The History of Two Colleges* (Geneva, N.Y., 1972); Edward J. Blankman, *The Scarlet and the Brown: A History of St. Lawrence University, 1856–1987* (Canton, N.Y., 1987); Howard D. Williams, *A History of Colgate University, 1819–1969* (New York, 1969); William Freeman Galpin, *Syracuse University,* vol. 1: *The Pioneer Days* (Syracuse, 1952); and Arthur J. May, *A History of the University of Rochester, 1850–1962* (Rochester, 1977).

New Yorkers' contributions to scientific knowledge can be traced in Robert V. Bruce, *The Launching of Modern American Science, 1846–1876* (Ithaca, N.Y., 1987); George H. Daniels, *American Science in the Age of Jackson* (New York, 1968); Carleton Mabee, *The American Leonardo: A Life of Samuel F. B. Morse* (New York, 1943); Dixon Ryan Fox, "The Rise of Scientific Interests in New York," in Flick, ed., *History of the State of New York,* 9: 93–123; J. M. Clarke, *James Hall of Albany, Geologist and Paleontologist, 1811–1898* (Albany, 1921); and Albert E. Moyer, *Joseph Henry: The Rise of an American Scientist* (Washington, D.C., 1997).

Scholars have devoted increasing attention to the emergence of a commercialized popular culture in antebellum America, and much of that literature relates directly or indirectly to the New York experience. For background, see: Karen Halttunen, *Confi-*dence *Men and Painted Women: A Study of Middle Class Culture in America, 1830–1870* (New Haven, Conn., 1982); Jane Tompkins, *Sensational Designs: The Cultural Work of American Fiction, 1790–1860* (New York, 1985); Reynolds, *Beneath the American Renaissance;* and Michael Denning, *Mechanic Accents: Dime Novels and Working-Class Culture in America* (New York, 1987). Also relevant are Elliott J. Gorn, *The Manly Art: Bare-Knuckle Prize Fighting in America* (Ithaca, N.Y., 1986); Melvin L. Adelman, *A Sporting Time: New York City and the Rise of Modern Athletics* (Urbana, Ill., 1986); Alexander P. Saxton, *The Rise and Fall of the White Republic: Class Politics and Mass Culture in Nineteenth-Century America* (New York, 1990), and the previously cited Stott, *Workers in the Metropolis.*

For the development of New York theater, see: David Grimsted, *Melodrama Unveiled; American Theater and Culture, 1800–1850* (Chicago, 1968); Thomas Allston Brown, *A History of the New York Stage* (New York, 1903); Peter G. Buckley, "To the Opera House: Culture and Society in New York City, 1820–1860" (Ph.D. diss., State University of New York at Stony Brook, 1984); Richard Moody, *The Astor Place Riot* (Bloomington, Ind., 1958); and Oral Sumner Coad, "The New York Theater," in Flick, ed., *History of the State of New York,* 9: 307–46. The early history of black theater in New York City can be found in Walker, *The Afro-American in New York City,* and Freeman, *The Free Negro in New York City in the Era before the Civil War.* On black minstrelsy, see the relevant chapters in Jean H. Baker, *Affairs of Party: The Political Culture of Northern Democrats in the Mid-Nineteenth Century* (Ithaca, N.Y., 1983), and, especially, Eric Lott, *Love & Theft: Blackface Minstrelsy and the American Working Class* (New York, 1993). P. T. Barnum is ably treated in Neil Harris, *Humbug: The Art of P. T. Barnum* (Chicago, 1981), and A. H. Saxon, *P. T.*

Barnum: The Legend and the Man (New York, 1989).

The Emergence of the Second Party System, 1825–1838

Given New York's importance in national politics, it is not surprising that the literature on the political history of the state in this period is vast and exceedingly rich. Jabez Hammond, *The History of Political Parties in the State of New York,* is a detailed and generally reliable narrative of political developments down to the early 1850s by a contemporary participant. It should, however, be supplemented by D. S. Alexander, *A Political History of the State of New York.* The intricacies of state politics in the 1820s can be followed in Dixon Ryan Fox, *The Decline of Aristocracy in the Politics of New York* (New York, 1919); Alvin Kass, *Politics in New York State, 1800–1830* (New York, 1965); and Craig Hanyan, *De Witt Clinton and the Rise of the People's Men* (Montreal, 1996). Richard Hofstadter, *The Idea of a Party System: The Rise of Legitimate Opposition in the United States, 1780–1840* (Berkeley, Calif., 1970), is invaluable for understanding New York's importance in the evolution of new concepts of party and partisanship. Constitutional developments are traced in Lincoln, *Constitutional History of New York;* the relevant section of Merrill Peterson, *Democracy, Liberty, and Property: The State Constitutional Conventions of the 1820s* (Indianapolis, 1966); and Hugh M. Flick, "The Council of Appointment in New York State: The First Attempt to Regulate Political Patronage, 1777–1822," *New York History* 15 (1934): 253–80.

Biographies provide an additional resource for understanding politics in the 1820s and 1830s. Especially notable are: Steven E. Siry, *De Witt Clinton and the American Political Economy: Sectionalism, Politics, and Republican Ideology, 1787–1828* (New York, 1990);

Evan W. Cornog, *The Birth of Empire: DeWitt Clinton and the American Experience, 1769–1828* (New York, 1998); Robert V. Remini, *Martin Van Buren and the Making of the Democratic Party* (New York, 1959); John Niven, *Martin Van Buren: The Romantic Age of American Politics* (New York, 1983); Donald B. Cole, *Martin Van Buren and the American Political System* (Princeton, 1984); Jerome Mushkat, *Martin Van Buren: Law, Politics, and the Shaping of Republican Ideology* (De-Kalb, Ill., 1997); Ivor D. Spencer, *The Victor and the Spoils: A Life of William L. Marcy* (Providence, 1959); Glyndon G. Van Deusen, *Thurlow Weed: Wizard of the Lobby;* and Van Deusen, *William H. Seward* (New York, 1968).

Several studies have detailed the emergence and significance of the Albany Regency. See particularly Robert V. Remini, "The Albany Regency," *New York History* 39 (October 1958): 341–55, and Kalman Goldstein, "The Albany Regency" (Ph.D. diss., Columbia University, 1969). Michael Wallace examines Van Buren's views on the positive benefits of parties in "Changing Concepts of Party in the United States: New York, 1815–1828," *American Historical Review* 74 (December 1968): 453–91, as does Hofstadter in *The Idea of a Party System.*

Richard P. McCormick's essay on New York in *The Second American Party System: Party Formation in the Jacksonian Era* (Chapel Hill, N.C., 1966) is a succinct treatment of the formation of the Democratic and Whig parties in the state, with an emphasis on the electoral functions of the parties. Lee Benson, *The Concept of Jacksonian Democracy: New York as a Test Case* (Princeton, 1961), challenged earlier socioeconomic interpretations of politics in this period and stressed the importance of ethnocultural divisions. Michael F. Holt, *The Rise and Fall of the American Whig Party: Jacksonian Politics and the Onset of the Civil War* (New York and Oxford, 1999) is the most comprehensive treatment of the Whig party and is invaluable for an understanding of party politics in New York. Several studies illuminate the differing ideologies or worldviews of the two major parties: Daniel Walker Howe, *The Political Culture of the American Whigs* (Chicago, 1979); Elliot R. Barkan, "The Emergence of the Whig Persuasion: Conservatism, Democratism, and the New York State Whigs," *New York History* 52 (October 1971): 367–95; Marvin Meyers, *The Jacksonian Persuasion: Politics and Belief* (Stanford, Calif., 1957); and John Ashworth, *"Agrarians" and "Aristocrats": Party Political Ideology in the United States, 1837–1846* (Cambridge, England, 1983). Also useful is Douglas T. Miller, *Jacksonian Aristocracy: Class and Democracy in New York, 1830–1860* (New York, 1967). The best recent accounts of Antimasonry are Ronald P. Formisano and Kathleen S. Kutolowski, "Antimasonry and Masonry," *American Quarterly* 29 (Summer 1977), 139–65; Michael F. Holt, "The Antimasonic and Know Nothing Parties," in Arthur M. Schlesinger, Jr., ed., *History of U.S. Political Parties*, vol. 1, *1789–1860: From Factions to Parties* (New York, 1973), 575–620; William Preston Vaughn, *The Antimasonic Party in the United States, 1826–1842* (Lexington, Ky., 1982); and Paul Goodman, *Towards a Christian Republic: Antimasonry and the Great Transition in New England, 1826–1836* (New York, 1988).

For New York City politics in this period, see: Wilentz, *Chants Democratic*; Hugins, *Jacksonian Democracy and the Working Class*; Amy Bridges, *A City in the Republic: Antebellum New York and the Origins of Machine Politics* (Cambridge, England, 1984); Carl N. Degler, "The Loco-Focos: Urban 'Agrarians,'" *Journal of Economic History* 16 (September 1956): 322–33; Jerome Mushkat, *Tammany: The Evolution of a Political Machine, 1789–1865* (Syracuse, 1971); Oliver E. Allen, *The Tiger: The Rise and Fall of Tammany Hall* (Reading, Mass., 1992); and Hendrik Hartog,

Public Property and Private Power: The Corporation of the City of New York in American Law, 1730–1870 (Chapel Hill, N.C., 1983). Paul A. Gilje, *The Road to Mobocracy: Popular Disorder in New York City, 1763–1834* (Chapel Hill, N.C., 1987), is an invaluable study of the changing character of violence in the city. On the politics of banking, see, in addition to the above, Bray Hammond, *Banks and Politics in America from the Revolution to the Civil War*, and James Roger Sharp, *The Jacksonians versus the Banks: Politics in the States after the Panic of 1837* (New York, 1970).

Politics and Policy, 1838–1848

Many of the sources cited for the previous chapter are also relevant to the history of politics after 1838, especially Jabez Hammond and D. S. Alexander. Readers wishing to understand the larger context of New York partisan politics in this period should consult Joel Silbey, *The American Political Nation, 1838–1893* (Stanford, Calif., 1991), which contains much useful information about New York. The broad contours of electoral behavior in the state are systematically examined in Lee Benson, Joel H. Silbey, and Phyllis F. Field, "Toward a Theory of Stability and Change in American Voting Patterns: New York State, 1790–1970," in Joel H. Silbey, Allan G. Bogue, and William H. Flanigan, eds., *The History of American Electoral Politics* (Princeton, 1978). Benson's *Concept of Jacksonian Democracy* is also an invaluable source for voting behavior in the 1830s and 1840s.

The relationship between economic issues, especially canal policy, and politics in this period can be followed in Shaw, *Erie Water West*, and Gunn, *The Decline of Authority*. The most detailed and reliable account of partisan maneuvering and internal factionalism is Herbert D. A. Donovan, *The Barnburners: A Study of the Internal Movements in the Political History of New York*

State and the Resulting Changes in Political Affiliations, 1830–1852 (New York, 1925). Also useful is Patricia E. McGee, "Issues and Factions: New York State Politics from the Panic of 1837 to the Election of 1848" (Ph.D. diss., St. John's University, 1970). For the antirent movement, see: Henry Christman, Tin Horns and Calico: A Decisive Episode in the Emergence of Democracy (New York, 1945); E. P. Cheyney, "The Anti-Rent Movement and the Constitution of 1846," in Flick, ed., History of the State of New York, 6: 283–321; Ellis, Landlords and Farmers, and Huston, Land and Freedom. In addition to the biographies mentioned in the previous sections, readers should consult John A. Garraty, Silas Wright (New York, 1949), and Stewart Mitchell, Horatio Seymour of New York (Cambridge, Mass., 1938).

The demands for constitutional revision and the work of the convention of 1846 are treated in Gunn, The Decline of Authority; Lincoln, Constitutional History of New York; and Dougherty, Constitutional History of the State of New York. The most reliable source for the convention debates is S. Croswell and R. Sutton, Debates and Proceedings in the New York State Convention, For the Revision of the Constitution (Albany, 1846), but serious students of the subject may also wish to consult William G. Bishop and W. H. Attree, Report of the Debates and Proceedings of the Convention of the State of New York, 1846 (Albany, 1846), which was published by the Albany Atlas, the Radical Democratic newspaper. On the issue of black suffrage, see Field, The Politics of Race in New York. The best account of the Free Soil movement and its impact on New York politics is Frederick J. Blue, The Free Soilers: Third Party Politics, 1848–54 (Urbana, Ill., 1973).

Politics Transformed, 1848–1861

There are a number of valuable accounts of the breakup of the second party system and the emergence of the Republican party in New York. Three studies that are essential for understanding New York's relationship to the national context are Michael F. Holt, The Political Crisis of the 1850s (New York, 1983), Holt, The Rise and Fall of the American Whig Party, and William E. Gienapp, The Origins of the Republican Party, 1852–1856 (New York, 1987). Mark L. Berger, The Revolution in the New York Party Systems, 1840–1860 (Port Washington, N.Y., 1970), and Hendrik Booraem, The Formation of the Republican Party in New York: Politics and Conscience in the Antebellum North (New York, 1983), focus directly on party developments in the state, but both deal primarily with party leaders. Dale Baum and Dale T. Knobel examine voter realignment in New York in the 1850s in "Anatomy of a Realignment: New York Presidential Politics, 1848–1860," New York History 65 (January 1984): 61–81. Judah B. Ginsberg, "Barnburners, Free Soilers, and the New York Republican Party," New York History 57 (October 1976): 475–500, is also useful.

The role played by temperance and prohibition in New York politics in this period can be followed in Tyrrell, Sobering Up: From Temperance to Prohibition in Antebellum America 1800–1860; John A. Krout, "The Maine-Law in New York Politics," Proceedings of the New York State Historical Association 17 (July 1936): 260–72; John A. Krout, The Origins of Prohibition (New York, 1925); and William J. Rorabaugh, "Rising Democratic Spirits: Immigrants, Temperance, and Tammany Hall, 1854–1860," Civil War History 22 (June 1976): 138–57.

Tyler Anbinder, Nativism and Slavery: The Northern Know Nothings and the Politics of the 1850s (New York, 1992), is an important study of the Know Nothing party which contains a wealth of information on New York. The best and most detailed account of the movement in the state is Thomas J. Curran,

"Know-Nothings of New York State" (Ph.D. diss., Columbia University, 1963). Readers should also consult: Curran, "Seward and the Know Nothings," *New-York Historical Society Quarterly* 51 (April 1967): 141–59; Louis Dow Scisco, *Political Nativism in New York State*; and Joel H. Silbey, "The Undisguised Connection: Know Nothings into Republicans: New York as a Test Case," in Joel H. Silbey, *The Partisan Imperative: The Dynamics of American Politics before the Civil War* (New York, 1985).

In addition to the biographies of Seward, Weed, Greeley, Seymour, Marcy, and others previously cited, readers should consult Jeter A. Isely, *Horace Greeley and the Republican Party, 1853–1861* (Princeton, 1947); Ernest P. Muller, "Preston King: A Political Biography" (Ph.D. diss., Columbia University, 1957); James A. Rawley, *Edwin D. Morgan, 1811–1883, Merchant in Politics* (New York, 1955); Robert J. Rayback, *Millard Fillmore: Biography of a President* (Buffalo, 1959); and Jerome Mushkat, *Fernando Wood: A Political Biography* (Kent, Ohio, 1990). Memoirs and autobiographies include: Harriet A. Weed, ed., *Autobiography of Thurlow Weed* (New York, 1884); Horace Greeley, *Recollections of a Busy Life* (New York, 1868); and John A. Dix, *Memoirs of John Adams Dix, Compiled by his Son*, 2 vols. (New York, 1883).

Part V. The Gilded Age (1860–1914)

General and Local Histories

General works on this period in New York State history are David M. Ellis, James A. Frost, Harold C. Syrett, and Harry J. Carman, *A History of New York State* (Ithaca, N.Y., 1967), and Alexander C. Flick, ed., *History of the State of New York*, vol. 7, *Modern Party Battles* (New York, 1935). New York City is the subject of numerous specialized works. Among general surveys, see Kenneth T. Jackson, ed., *The Encyclopedia of New York City* (1995); Edwin G. Burrows and Mike Wallace, *Gotham: A History of New York City to 1898* (1998); and George Lankevich, *American Metropolis: A History of New York* (1998). Valuable works on other cities include Blake McKelvey, *Rochester: The Quest for Quality, 1890–1925* (Cambridge, Mass., 1956), and Mark Goldman, *High Hopes: The Rise and Decline of Buffalo, New York* (Albany, 1983). Depictions of small cities also contain useful information. See for an example, Warren E. Schultz, *Ilion: The Town Remington Made* (Hicksville, N.Y., 1977). Most counties and sizable cities are the subject of celebratory histories that include biographical sketches of local notables. For example, see William Foote Seward, ed., *Binghamton and Broome County, New York: A History* (New York, 1924). A delightful study of a central New York village is Stuart Blumin, in collaboration with Deborah Adelman Blumin, with photographs by Hansi Durlach, *The Short Season of Sharon Springs: Portrait of Another New York* (Ithaca, N.Y., 1980).

Society and Culture

Population trends can be traced in the federal census and the state census (taken in the middle of decades). Analyses of population changes include Ira Rosenwaike, *Population History of New York City* (Syracuse, 1972), and the extensive Walter Laidlaw, *Population of the City of New York, 1890–1930* (New York, 1932). Informative on rural areas are three Experiment Station reports: Wilbert A. Anderson, "Population Trends in New York State, 1900–1930," Cornell University Agricultural Experiment Station, *Bulletin* 547 (Ithaca, N.Y., 1932); Bruce L. Melvin, "Rural Population of New York, 1855 to 1925," Cornell University Agricultural Experiment Station, *Memoir* 116 (Ithaca, N.Y., 1928); and E. C. Young, "The Movement of Farm Population," Cornell University Agricultural Experiment Station, *Bulletin* 426 (Ithaca, N.Y., 1924).

Immigration, of course, is a central part of New York State's population history, and also of its social and cultural history. Not surprisingly, given the size of its immigrant population, a large literature focuses on New York City. An excellent place to begin study of immigration there is Frederick M. Binder and David M. Reimers, *All the Nations under Heaven: An Ethnic and Racial History of New York City* (New York, 1995). A recent account of immigrant life is the evocative but uneven Mario Maffi, *Gateway to the Promised Land: Ethnic Cultures on New York's Lower East Side* (New York, 1995).

Most work on immigration covers a single group. Among the best of these studies on New York City are Donna R. Gabaccia, *From Sicily to Elizabeth Street: Housing and Social Change among Italian Immigrants, 1880–1930* (Albany, 1984); Robert Orsi, *The Madonna of 115th Street: Faith and Community in Italian Harlem, 1880–1950* (New Haven, Conn., 1985); the classic Irving Howe (with the assistance of Kenneth Libo), *World of our Fathers* (New York, 1976); and Moses Rischin, *The Promised City: New York Jews, 1870–1914* (Cambridge, Mass., 1962). A valuable comparison of these two groups is Thomas Kessner, *The Golden Door: Italian and Jewish Mobility in New York City, 1880–1915* (New York, 1977). Especially good on gender and work in Buffalo is Virginia Yans-McLaughlin, *Family and Community: Italian Immigrants in Buffalo* (Ithaca, N.Y., 1977). The standard account of

nativism remains John Higham, *Strangers in the Land* (New Brunswick, N.J., 1955).

Numerous studies of immigrant life—and immigrant poverty—appeared as the result of reformers' efforts to raise public awareness of the social costs of poverty and to find the data that would provide solutions. Among the most useful of these are Lillian D. Wald, *House on Henry Street* (New York, 1915); Lillian Williams Betts, *Leaven in a Great City* (New York, 1902); Mabel Louise Nassau, *Old Age Poverty in Greenwich Village, a Neighborhood Study* (New York, 1915); and *West Side Studies, Carried on under the Direction of Pauline Goldmark* (New York, 1914). Two classics that nicely illustrate ethnic stereotypes and hostility toward the "unworthy" poor are Jacob A. Riis, *How the Other Half Lives: Studies Among the Tenements* (New York, 1890), and *Out of Mulberry Street: Stories of Tenement Life in New York City* (New York, 1898). A maudlin fictional account of city life is Stephen Crane, *Maggie: A Girl of the Streets. A Story of New York* (New York, 1896).

There is no general synthesis of the experiences of African Americans in New York State. But on education, see Carleton Mabee, *Black Education in New York State* (Syracuse, 1980). On the development of an African American community in New York City, see Gilbert Osofsky, *Harlem: The Making of A Ghetto* (New York, 1966), and Seth M. Scheiner, *Negro Mecca* (New York, 1965). A useful contemporary account is Mary White Ovington, *Half a Man: The Status of the Negro in New York City* (New York, 1911). For Buffalo see Lillian S. Williams, "Afro-Americans in Buffalo, 1900–1930: A Study in Community Formation," *Afro-Americans in New York Life and History* 8 (July 1984): 7–36. African American culture is covered in Jervis Anderson, *This Was Harlem: A Cultural Portrait, 1900–1950* (New York, 1981, 1982), and Lawrence W. Levine, *Black Culture and Black Consciousness* (New York, 1977). A number of contemporary studies and memoirs do the same and also provide insight into race relations. See, for example, James Weldon Johnson, *Black Manhattan* (New York, 1930), and his *Autobiography of an Ex-Coloured Man* (Garden City, N.Y., 1927). An intriguing study of African Americans in Geneva, New York, is Kathryn Grover, *Make a Way Somehow: African-American Life in a Northern Community, 1790–1965* (Syracuse, 1994). Ann Douglas, *Terrible Honesty: Mongrel Manhattan in the 1920s* (New York, 1995), offers some information about turn-of-the-century New York City and fascinating, if overdrawn, arguments about gender, race, and culture.

There is not a substantial literature on Indians in New York State in the late nineteenth and early twentieth centuries. But see Helen M. Upton, *The Everett Report in Historical Perspective: The Indians of New York* (Albany, 1980); Christopher Vecsey and William A. Starna, *Iroquois Land Claims* (Syracuse, 1988); Laurence M. Hauptman, *Formulating American Indian Policy in New York State, 1970–1986* (Albany, 1988), and Hauptman, *The Historical Background to the Present Day Seneca Nation–Salamanca Lease Controversy: The First One Hundred Years, 1851–1951* (Albany, 1985); and New York State Assembly, Special Committee to Investigate the Indian Problem, *Report* (Albany, 1889).

The study of mass culture—which ideally combines attention to race, age, ethnicity, sexuality, class, and commerce—has received a good deal of attention in recent years. Here, too, work has focused on New York City as a place where residents pioneered new cultural forms and forged new cultural relations. See: John Kasson, *Amusing the Million: Coney Island at the Turn of the Century* (New York, 1978); Elizabeth Ewen, *Immigrant Women in the Land of Dollars: Life and Culture on the Lower East Side, 1890–1925* (New York, 1985); Kathy Peiss, *Cheap Amusements: Working Women and Leisure in Turn-of-the-Century*

New York (Philadelphia, 1986); George Chauncey, *Gay New York: Gender, Urban Culture, and the Making of the Gay Male World, 1890–1940* (New York, 1994), a pathbreaking study of gay male culture; Timothy J. Gilfoyle, *City of Eros: New York City, Prostitution, and the Commercialization of Sex, 1790–1920* (New York, 1992), which is especially good on the geography of prostitution; Lewis A. Erenberg, *Steppin' Out: New York Nightlife and the Transformation of American Culture, 1890–1930* (Chicago, 1981); David Nasaw, *Children of the City: At Work and at Play* (Garden City, N.Y., 1985); and Luc Sante, *Low-Life: Lures and Snares of Old New York* (New York, 1991). On department stores and commerce see William Leach, *Land of Desire: Merchants, Power, and the Rise of a New American Culture* (New York, 1993). Individual merchants and stores have their own biographies; the best among them is Ralph M. Hower, *History of Macy's of New York, 1858–1919: Chapters in the Evolution of the Department Store* (Cambridge, Mass., 1943).

Unlike recent scholarship, contemporary depictions of the city highlighted danger and corruption, not pleasure and the agency of ordinary people. See Edward Crapsey, *The Nether Side of New York; or, the Vice, Crime, and Poverty of the Great Metropolis* (New York, 1872); James D. McCabe, Jr., *Lights and Shadows of New York Life* (1872; rpt. New York, 1970); and Helen Campbell, Thomas W. Knox, and Thomas Byrnes, *Darkness and Daylight; Or, Lights and Shadows of New York Life* (Hartford, Conn., 1897). Investigations of vice and corruption generated some of the records that historians have relied upon to reconstruct working-class leisure, gay culture, prostitution, and changing sexual mores. See Committee of Fourteen, *Annual Reports* (New York, 1912–16); New York Society for the Suppression of Vice, *Annual Report* (New York, 1875–1907); New York State Senate, *Report and Proceedings of the Senate Committee*

Appointed to Investigate the Police Department of New York City, 5 vols. (Albany, 1895); and New York State Assembly, *Special Committee Appointed to Investigate Public Officers and Departments of the City of New York*, 5 vols. (Albany, 1900).

Laborers and Capitalists

Labor historians have usually tried to examine the working class in one of three places: working-class communities, workplaces, or institutions (especially unions). All three approaches have added to our understanding of tensions between classes, tensions within the working classes, and politics. The pioneer of the community approach was Herbert G. Gutman; his work on New York during the late nineteenth century includes "The Tompkins Square 'Riot' in New York City on January 13, 1874: A Re-Examination of Its Causes and Its Aftermath," *Labor History* 6 (Winter 1965): 44–70, and "The Failure of the Movement for Public Works by the Unemployed in 1873," *Political Science Quarterly* 80 (June 1965): 254–76. Other studies of working-class communities and ethnic tensions include Brian Greenberg, *Worker and Community: Response to Industrialization in a Nineteenth-Century City: Albany, New York, 1850–1884* (Albany, 1985), and Michael A. Gordon, *The Orange Riots: Irish Political Violence in New York City, 1870 and 1871* (Ithaca, N.Y., 1993). The exemplar of the shop-floor approach and the departure point of numerous later studies is David Montgomery, *Beyond Equality: Labor and the Radical Republicans, 1862–1872* (New York, 1967), which is densely packed with information about New York labor and labor politics. On the strikes of 1877, see Dorthee Schneider, "The New York City Cigar Makers Strike of 1877," *Labor History* 26 (Summer 1985): 325–83; the vivid descriptions of strikes in various places in Robert V. Bruce, *1877: Year of Violence* (Indianapolis, 1959); and

Jeremy Brecher, *Strike!* (Greenwich, Conn., 1972). Labor organizations and politics are covered well in Howard Lawrence Hurwitz, *Theodore Roosevelt and Labor in New York State, 1880–1900* (New York, 1943); Irwin Yellowitz, *Labor and the Progressive Movement in New York State, 1897–1916* (Ithaca, N.Y., 1965); and Melvyn Dubofsky, *When Workers Organize: New York City in the Progressive Era* (Aherst, Mass., 1968). Gerald Zahavi's *Workers, Managers, and Welfare Capitalism: The Shoemakers and Tanners of Endicott Johnson, 1890–1950* (Urbana, Ill., 1988) is an innovative study of a single firm.

In contrast to examinations of male workers and unions, studies of women workers often cover such topics as generational conflict, the family, service work, youth culture, the construction of identities, and cross-class coalitions, although the last three subjects are of increasing interest to historians of the male working class as well. On working-class youth and immigrant cultures, see: Miriam Cohen, *Workshop to Office: Two Generations of Italian Women in New York City, 1900–1950* (Ithaca, N.Y., 1992); Susan Glenn, *Daughters of the Shtetl: Life and Labor in the Immigrant Generation* (Ithaca, N.Y., 1990); Ewen, *Immigrant Women in the Land of Dollars*; and Peiss, *Cheap Amusements*. The tensions and possibilities within cross-class coalitions are covered in Nancy Schrom Dye, *As Equals and as Sisters: Feminism, Unionism, and the Women's Trade Union League of New York* (Columbia, Mo., 1980), and Meredith Tax, *The Rising of the Women: Feminist Solidarity and Class Conflict, 1880–1917* (New York, 1980). Leon Stein, ed., *Out of the Sweatshop* (New York, 1977) is a helpful source on women and strikes. National studies of domestic service refer to New York at points. See Faye E. Dudden, *Serving Women: Household Service in Nineteenth-Century America* (Middletown, Conn., 1983), and David M. Katzman, *Seven Days a Week: Women and*

Domestic Service in Industrializing America (New York, 1978).

The working conditions of both male and female workers are detailed in New York State Factory Investigating Commission, *Second Report of the Factory Investigating Commission* (Albany, 1913). Following workers from workplaces to homes were studies that attempted to determine what families needed to survive. See Louise Bolard More, *Wage Earners' Budgets: A Study of Standards and Cost of Living in New York City* (New York, 1907); and Robert Coit Chapin, *The Standard of Living among Workingmen's Families in New York City* (New York, 1914). Major reports on the labor of women and children are Mary Stevenson Callcott, *Child Labor Legislation in New York: The Historical Development and the Administrative Practices of Child Labor Laws in the State of New York, 1905–1930* (New York, 1931); Elizabeth Faulkner Baker, *Protective Labor Legislation, with Special Reference to Women in the State of New York* (New York, 1925); and Katherine Anthony, *Mothers Who Must Earn* (New York, 1914).

The study of elites has not been marked by the same analytical richness as the study of the working class. Among the best analytical treatments are Peter Dobkin Hall, *The Organization of American Culture, 1700–1900: Private Institutions, Elites, and the Origins of American Nationality* (New York, 1984); David C. Hammack, *Power and Society: Greater New York at the Turn of the Century* (New York, 1982); and Frederick C. Jaher, "Style and Status: High Society in Late Nineteenth-Century New York," in Jaher, ed., *The Rich, The Well Born, and the Powerful: Elites and Upper Classes in History* (Urbana, Ill., 1973). Now dated, but full of anecdotes and denunciations of the new rich, is Matthew Josephson, *The Robber Barons: The Great American Capitalists, 1861–1901* (New York, 1934). Otherwise, wealthy New Yorkers can be tracked through biographies. See Meade Minnigerode, *Certain Rich Men: Stephen Girard, John Jacob Astor, Jay Cooke, Daniel Drew, Cornelius Vanderbilt, John Fiske* (New York, 1927); Ellis Paxon Oberholtzer, *Jay Cooke: Financier of the Civil War* (Philadelphia, 1907); Wayne Andrews, *The Vanderbilt Legend: The Story of the Vanderbilt Family, 1794–1940* (New York, 1941); and Louis Auchincloss, *The Vanderbilt Era: Profiles of a Gilded Age* (New York, 1989). Biographies of wealthy women include William Rhinelander Stewart, *The Philanthropic Work of Josephine Shaw Lowell* (New York, 1905), and Clarice Stasz, *The Vanderbilt Women: Dynasty of Wealth, Glamour, and Tragedy* (New York, 1991).

Reform Movements

The turn to science and tough-mindedness on the part of post–Civil War elite reformers is analyzed in George M. Fredrickson, *The Inner Civil War: Northern Intellectuals and the Crisis of the Union* (New York, 1965). Lori D. Ginzberg's *Women and the Work of Benevolence: Morality, Politics, and Class in the 19th-Century United States* (New Haven, Conn., 1990) covers reformers in New York and New England and offers a similar argument about the turn away from sentiment, adding that for female reformers, that turn included a rejection of the ideal of cross-class female solidarity. On the development of social science and its part in reform thought, see Thomas L. Haskell, *The Emergence of Professional Social Science: The American Social Science Association and the Nineteenth-Century Crisis of Authority* (Urbana, Ill., 1977). An important male reform organization is traced in Henry Bellows, *Historical Sketch of the Union League Club of New York: Its Origin, Organization, and Work, 1863–1879* (New York, 1877).

Debate about reform since the 1960s has focused on the intent and meaning of reformers' actions. Did they attempt to force social control on an unruly population? Did they seek to improve an abysmal urban environment? Did they try to do both? Bypassing this debate, some scholars have examined the actions of the poor, working-class, immigrant, and young in the cities. See the works on urban leisure cited above. For an overview of public welfare policies, see David M. Schneider and Albert Deutsch, *The History of Public Welfare in New York State, 1867–1940* (Chicago, 1941). Among the vast number of works on reformers, see Carroll S. Rosenberg, "Protestants and Five Pointers: The Five Points House of Industry, 1850–1870," *New-York Historical Society Quarterly* 48 (October 1964): 327–447; Brenda K. Shelton, *Reformers in Search of Yesterday: Buffalo in the 1890s* (Albany, 1976); Phillip M. Hosay, *The Challenge of Urban Poverty: Charity Reformers in New York City, 1835–1890* (New York, 1980); and Paul T. Ringebach, *Tramps and Reformers, 1873–1916: The Discovery of Unemployment in New York* (Westport, Conn., 1973). On rural reform and the "country life movement," see Paula Baker, *The Moral Frameworks of Public Life: Gender, Politics, and the State in Rural New York, 1870–1930* (New York, 1991); William L. Bowers, *The Country Life Movement in America, 1900–1920* (Port Washington, N.Y., 1974); and, as a guide to the voluminous writings of a major figure in New York, Philip Dorf, *Liberty Hyde Bailey: An Informal Biography* (Ithaca, N.Y., 1956).

There is a large, high-quality literature on specific reform causes. See, for example: Robert H. Bremner, "The Big Flat: History of a New York Tenement House," *American Historical Review* 64 (October 1958): 54–62; Roy Lubove, *The Progressives and the Slums: Tenement House Reform in New York City, 1890–1917* (Pittsburgh, 1962); Jeremy P. Felt, *Hostages of Fortune: Child Labor Reform in New York State* (Syracuse, 1965); John Duffy, *A History of Public Health in New York City,*

1625–1866 (New York, 1968); and Charles E. Rosenberg, *The Cholera Years: The United States in 1832, 1849, and 1866* (Chicago, 1962).

On the settlement house movement, see Allen F. Davis, *Spearheads for Reform: The Social Settlements and the Progressive Movement, 1890–1914* (New York, 1967). A fine analysis of the settlement movement and race is Elisabeth Lasch-Quinn, *Black Neighbors: Race and the Limits of Reform in the American Settlement House Movement, 1890–1945* (Chapel Hill, N.C., 1993). On African American settlement houses, see Lillian S. Williams, "And I Still Rise: Black Women and Reform in Buffalo, New York, 1900–1940," *Afro-Americans in New York Life and History* 14 (July 1990): 7–33, and Floris Barnett Cash, "Radicals or Realists: African American Women and the Settlement House Spirit in New York City," *Afro-Americans in New York Life and History* 15 (January 1991): 7–17.

Agriculture and Rural Life

The literature concerning rural New York is thin in contrast to that covering urban centers. The few secondary studies should be supplemented with contemporary analyses. Solid accounts of the state's agricultural economy include Clarence Danhof, *Change in Agriculture: The Northern United States, 1820–1870* (Cambridge, Mass., 1969); Ulysses Prentice Hedrick, *A History of Agriculture in the State of New York* (Albany, 1933); Elmer O. Fippin, *Rural New York* (1921; rpt. Port Washington, N.Y., 1971); John J. Dillon, *Seven Decades of Milk: A History of New York's Dairy Industry* (New York, 1941); and Eric Brunger, "Changes in the New York State Dairying Industry, 1850–1900" (Ph.D. diss., Syracuse University, 1954). The standard references for farm prices were produced by Cornell University agricultural economists: George F. Warren, "Prices of Farm Products in New York," Cornell University Agricultural Experiment Station, *Bulletin*

423 (Ithaca, N.Y., 1923); and Samuel E. Ronk, "Prices Received by Producers in New York State, 1841–1933" (Ph.D. diss., Cornell University, 1935). Sally McMurry's *Transforming Rural Life: Dairying Families and Agricultural Change, 1820–1885* (Baltimore, 1995) is an important study of rural social life, gender, and family. Also useful are social surveys done by Cornell University rural sociologists. For example, see Lawrence M. Vaughan, "Abandoned Farm Areas in New York," Cornell University Agricultural Experiment Station, *Bulletin* 490 (Ithaca, N.Y., 1929). A fascinating analysis (focusing on New York communities) of rural economics and its impact on personality is James Mickel Williams, *The Expansion of Rural Life: The Social Psychology of Rural Development* (New York, 1926). Combining education, economics, and policy is Gould P. Coleman, *Education and Agriculture: A History of the New York State College of Agriculture at Cornell University* (Ithaca, N.Y., 1963). Also see Ruby Green Smith, *The People's Colleges: A History of the New York State Extension Service in Cornell University and the State, 1876 to 1948* (Ithaca, N.Y., 1949).

Politics and New Political Constituencies

An older style of political history focused on the upper reaches of party leadership and closely followed electoral and legislative twists and turns as explained in the press. While such work has been out of fashion for a long time, these studies contain much useful information. An overview of New York State politics in this genre is DeAlva S. Alexander, *A Political History of the State of New York*, 4 vols. (New York, 1906–23). For intraparty factionalism and a sense of the flow of political events in the Civil War years, see Sidney D. Brummer, *Political History of New York State during the Period of the Civil War* (New York, 1911). Biographies of important political figures in the 1860s and 1870s include Chester L.

Barrows, *William M. Evarts: Lawyer, Diplomat, Statesman* (Chapel Hill, N.C., 1941); Irving Katz, *August Belmont: A Political Biography* (New York, 1968); Ralph Ray Fahrney, *Horace Greeley and the Tribune in the Civil War* (New York, 1970); and three volumes by Glyndon G. Van Deusen: *Horace Greeley: Nineteenth Century Crusader* (Philadelphia, 1953); *Thurlow Weed, Wizard of the Lobby* (Boston, 1947); and *William Henry Seward* (New York, 1967).

By the late 1950s and 1960s, the "new" political history directed scholars away from the utterances of political elites and toward a systematic analysis of voting and legislative behavior. On patterns of electoral behavior, see Lee Benson, Joel H. Silbey, and Phyllis F. Field, "Toward a Theory of Stability and Change in American Voting Patterns: New York State, 1792–1970," in Joel H. Silbey, Allan G. Bogue, and William H. Flanigan, eds., *The History of American Electoral Behavior* (Princeton, 1978). Samuel T. McSeveney, *The Politics of Depression: Political Behavior in the Northeast, 1893–1896* (New York, 1972), is a fine analysis of the interplay of economic and cultural issues during the depression of the 1890s. Also see Albert C. E. Parker, "Empire Stalemate: Voting Behavior in New York State, 1860–1892" (Ph.D. diss., Washington University, 1975). On machine politics in New York City, see Martin Shefter, "The Electoral Foundations of the Political Machine: New York City, 1884–1897," in Silbey, Bogue, and Flanigan, eds., *The History of American Electoral Behavior*. Interrelationships among voting behavior, ballot laws, and party politics are analyzed in John F. Reynolds and Richard L. McCormick, "Outlawing 'Treachery': Split Tickets and Ballot Laws in New York and New Jersey, 1880–1910," *Journal of American History* 72 (March 1986): 835–58.

A number of party histories analyze changing party strategies, voting behavior, and public policy. The best of these illuminate broad political transformations through the lens of one party. On Reconstruction politics, James C. Mohr, *The Radical Republicans and Reform in New York during Reconstruction* (Ithaca, N.Y., 1973), is extremely helpful on legislative initiatives; while Jerome Mushkat, *The Reconstruction of the New York Democracy, 1861–1874* (Rutherford, N.J., 1981), traces the responses of the party out of power. An influential analysis of voting behavior, policymaking, and Republican party leadership that provides the framework for my discussion is Richard L. McCormick, *From Realignment to Reform: Political Change in New York State, 1893–1910* (Ithaca, N.Y., 1981). For the Democratic party, see Robert F. Wesser, *A Response to Progressivism: The Democratic Party and New York Politics, 1902–1918* (New York, 1986). A classic study of "boss" rule and the Republican machine is Harold F. Gosnell, *Boss Platt and His New York Machine: A Study of the Political Leadership of Thomas C. Platt, Theodore Roosevelt, and Others* (Chicago, 1924). Detailed discussions of the platforms and electoral fortunes of third parties are Charles V. Groat, "Political Greenbackism in New York State, 1876–1884" (Ph.D. diss., Syracuse University, 1963), and John Joseph Coffey, "A Political History of the Temperance Movement in New York State, 1808–1912" (Ph.D. diss., Pennsylvania State University, 1976). Antiparty movements are discussed in John G. Sproat, *"The Best Men": Liberal Reformers in the Gilded Age* (New York, 1968); Gerald W. McFarland, *Mugwumps, Morals, and Politics, 1884–1920* (Amherst, Mass., 1975); Michael McGerr, *The Decline of Popular Politics: The American North, 1865–1928* (New York, 1986); and Richard L. McCormick, "Anti-Party Thought in the Gilded Age," in McCormick, *The Party Period and Public Policy: American Politics from the Age of Jackson to the Progressive Era* (New York, 1986), 228–59.

Several biographies of important party and reform leaders also provide insight into the working of state politics. Biographies that contribute to the picture of political reform include G. Wallace Chessman, *Governor Theodore Roosevelt: The Albany Apprenticeship, 1898–1900* (Cambridge, Mass., 1965), and Robert Wesser, *Charles Evans Hughes: Politics and Reform in New York, 1905–1910* (Ithaca, N.Y., 1967). Herbert J. Bass, *"I am a Democrat": The Political Career of David Bennett Hill* (Syracuse, 1961), and David M. Jordan, *Roscoe Conkling of New York: Voice in the Senate* (Ithaca, N.Y., 1971), trace the careers of two state "bosses." Also see: Nancy Joan Weiss, *Charles Francis Murphy, 1858–1924: Respectability and Responsibility in Tammany Politics* (Northampton, Mass., 1968); Philip C. Jessup, *Elihu Root,* 2 vols. (New York, 1938); W. A. Swanberg, *Citizen Hearst: A Biography of William Randolph Hearst* (New York, 1961); Herbert Mitgang, *The Man Who Rode the Tiger: The Life and Times of Judge Samuel Seabury* (Philadelphia, 1963); and Gerald Kurland, *Seth Low: The Reformer in an Urban and Industrial Age* (New York, 1971).

On New York City politics (and social life) during the Civil War, see Ernest A. McKay, *The Civil War and New York City* (Syracuse, 1990). Mayor Fernando Wood's career in New York City Democratic factions is treated in Tyler G. Anbinder, "Fernando Wood and New York City's Secession from the Union: A Political Reappraisal," *New York History* 68 (1987): 67–92, and Jerome Mushkat, *Fernando Wood: A Political Biography* (Kent, Ohio, 1990). An appreciation of Governor Morgan is James F. Rawley, *Edwin D. Morgan, 1811–1883: Merchant in Politics* (New York, 1955). A famous New Yorker's reactions to the Civil War and New York City politics is Allan Nevins, ed., *Diary of the Civil War, 1860–1865: George Templeton Strong* (New York, 1962).

Tammany Hall has inspired its own extensive literature. Overviews include Alfred Connable and Edward Silverfarb, *Tigers of Tammany: Nine Men Who Ran New York*

(New York, 1967), and Oliver E. Allen, *The Tiger: The Rise and Fall of Tammany Hall* (Reading, Mass., 1993). The good and evil of "Boss" Tweed and his "ring" have been debated by numerous scholars. Alexander B. Callow, Jr., *The Tweed Ring* (New York, 1966), details the ring's frauds; Leo Herschkowitz, *Tweed's New York: Another Look* (New York, 1977), is a thorough revision. Worthwhile, too, are Seymour Mandelbaum, *Boss Tweed's New York* (New York, 1965), and Warren Moscow, *The Last of the Big Time Bosses* (New York, 1971). Individual men involved in the "ring" and its downfall have received biographical treatment; generally biographers highlight the virtues of their subjects. See Croswell Bowen, *The Elegant Oakey* (New York, 1956); Alexander Flick, *Samuel Jones Tilden: A Study in Political Sagacity* (Port Washington, N.Y., 1963); and, on Richard Connolly, Eric Homberger, *Scenes from the Life of a City: Corruption and Conscience in Old New York* (New Haven, Conn., 1994). Welcome relief from the tiresome emphasis on heroes and villains that has shaped the debate on Tweed in particular is provided by Steven Erie, *Rainbow's End: Irish-Americans and the Dilemmas of Urban Machine Politics, 1840–1985* (Berkeley, Calif., 1988), which analyzes the life cycle of machines; and Iver Bernstein, *The New York City Draft Riots: Their Significance for American Society and Politics in the Age of the Civil War* (New York, 1990), which emphasizes the role of elites in Tammany politics and the importance of a fiscal crisis in bringing down Tweed. On the draft riots, see Bernstein, *New York City Draft Riots*; and for a painstaking breakdown of the riots' participants, Adrian Cook, *The Armies of the Streets: The New York City Draft Riots of 1863* (Lexington, Ky., 1974). Also see Albon P. Man, Jr., "Labor Competition and the New York Draft Riots of 1863," *Journal of Negro History* 36 (October 1951): 375–405. An important article that brings together mass culture and machine poli-

tics is Daniel Czitrom, "Underworlds and Underdogs: Big Tim Sullivan and Metropolitan Politics in New York, 1889–1913," *Journal of American History* 78 (December 1993): 536–58.

The effects of ethnicity and race on New York politics are covered in studies of labor, electoral alignments, and machine politics. Among such specialized studies, see Eric Foner, "Class, Ethnicity, and Radicalism in the Gilded Age: The Land League and Irish-America," *Marxist Perspectives* 1 (1978): 6–55, and Florence E. Gibson, *The Attitudes of New York Irish toward State and National Affairs* (New York, 1951). For a later period, see Thomas M. Henderson, *Tammany Hall and the New Immigrants: The Progressive Years* (New York, 1976). On the 1860 ballot question concerning African American suffrage—and the series of attempts by blacks to achieve the right to vote—see Phyllis F. Field, *The Politics of Race in New York: The Struggle for Black Suffrage in the Civil War Era* (Ithaca, N.Y., 1982). On African Americans and urban politics, see Michael Louis Goldstein, "Race Politics in New York City, 1890–1930: Independent Political Behavior" (Ph.D. diss., Columbia University, 1973).

The impact of women and gender on politics before women gained the right to vote is a relatively new subject for historians. But see Mary P. Ryan, *Women in Public: Between Banners and Ballots, 1825–1880* (Baltimore, 1990), on gender politics, including the gendered uses of public spaces and gender conflicts in New York City as well as San Francisco and New Orleans. Paula Baker, *The Moral Frameworks of Public Life,* covers men's and women's ideas about politics and their political behavior. Mari Jo Buhle, *Women and American Socialism, 1870–1920* (Urbana, Ill., 1981), contains information about women Socialists in New York. In addition to work on the settlement house movement and reform, studies of temperance also highlight women's political activism. A number of national studies contain a good deal of information about New York. See Ruth Bordin, *Woman and Temperance: The Quest for Power and Liberty, 1873–1900* (Philadelphia, 1981), and Barbara Leslie Epstein, *The Politics of Domesticity: Women, Evangelism, and Temperance in Nineteenth-Century America* (Middletown, Conn., 1981). On the woman suffrage movement, see: Eleanor Flexner, *Century of Struggle: The Woman's Rights Movement in the United States*, rev. ed. (Cambridge, Mass., 1975); Ellen Carol DuBois, "Working Women, Class Relations, and Suffrage Militance: Harriot Stanton Blatch and the New York Woman Suffrage Movement, 1894–1909," *Journal of American History* 74 (June 1987): 34–58; Doris Daniels, "Building a Winning Coalition: The Suffrage Fight in New York State," *New York History* 60 (1979): 59–80; and Elinor Lerner, "Immigrant and Working Class Involvement in the New York City Woman Suffrage Movement, 1905–1917: A Study in Progressive Era Politics" (Ph.D. diss., University of California, Berkeley, 1981). The most thorough analysis of the "New Departure" strategy during Reconstruction is Ellen Carol DuBois, "Outgrowing the Compact of the Fathers: Equal Rights, Woman Suffrage, and the United State Constitution, 1820–1878," *Journal of American History* 74 (December 1987): 836–62.

Economics and Law

Changes in economic policy in New York are covered in many of the party histories cited above; see especially Mohr, McCormick, and Wesser. Two superb specialized studies also provide essential information and interpretive direction: Lee Benson, *Merchants, Farmers, & Railroads: Railroad Regulation and New York Politics, 1850–1887* (Cambridge, Mass., 1955), and Hammack, *Power and Society*. A useful corrective to work that describes regulation as a departure from older patterns of governance is Donald J. Pisani, "Promotion and Regulation: Constitutionalism and the American Economy," *Journal of American History* 74 (December 1987): 740–68. A useful overview of public finance as well as public policy is John Archibald Fairlie, *The Centralization of Administration in New York State* (New York, 1898). Tax policy determined what state government could do. Perhaps because of the difficult and arcane quality of the subject, however, taxation has not received much scholarly attention, but see the extremely suggestive work on taxation and party politics, Clifton K. Yearley, *The Money Machines: The Breakdown and Reform of Governmental and Party Finance in the North, 1860–1920* (Albany, 1970). Other studies include: Don C. Sowers, *The Financial History of New York State: From 1789 to 1912* (New York, 1914); Merlin Harold Hunter, *The Development of Corporate Taxation in the State of New York* (Urbana, Ill., 1917); Edward D. Durand, *The Finances of New York City* (New York, 1898); John Christopher Schwab, *History of the New York State Property Tax: An Introduction to the History of State and Local Finance in New York* (Baltimore, 1890); and Albert Luther Ellis III, "The Regressive Era: Progressive Era Tax Reform and the National Tax Association—Roots of the Modern American Tax Structure" (Ph.D. diss., Rice University, 1991).

Changes in New York's constitution are analyzed in many of the studies of state politics and public policy. A handy overview of changes to and proposed revisions of the state constitution is Finla G. Crawford, "Constitutional Developments, 1867–1915," in Flick, ed., *History of the State of New York*, 7: 199–239. A complete account of proposals for 1867–94 is found in Charles Z. Lincoln, *The Constitutional History of New York*, 5 vols. (Rochester, 1906). A briefer account appears in Peter J. Galie, *Ordered Liberty: A Constitutional History of New York* (New York, 1996). In addition, see New York State, *Proceedings and Debates of the Constitutional Convention of the State of New York, 1867–68* (Albany, 1868); *Journal of the Constitutional Commission of the State of New York, 1872–1873* (Albany, 1873); *Constitutional Convention, 1894, Record,* 6 vols. (Albany, 1894); *Constitutional Convention, 1894, Documents,* 2 vols. (Albany, 1894); and *Constitutional Convention of 1894, Proposed Constitutional Amendments,* 3 vols. (Albany, 1894).

Part VI. The Triumph of Liberalism (1914–1945)

General Sources

For statistics and general information, see *The New York Red Book: An Illustrated State Manual* (Albany, 1892); WPA Writers' Program, *New York: A Guide to the Empire State* (New York, 1940); *The WPA Guide to New York City,* American Guide Series (New York, 1939); and Kenneth T. Jackson, ed., *Encyclopedia of New York City* (New Haven, Conn., 1995). Political baedekers include *The Convention Manual of Proceedings, Forms, and Rules for the Regulation of Business in the Seventh New York State Constitutional Convention* (Albany, 1915), and Lynton K. Caldwell, *The Government and Administration of New York,* American Commonwealth Series (New York, 1954).

Progressivism

For the progressive climate, see: Richard L. McCormick, *From Realignment to Reform: Political Change in New York State, 1893–1910* (Ithaca, N.Y., 1981); Robert F. Wesser, *A Response to Progressivism: The Democratic Party and New York Politics, 1902–1918* (New York, 1986); Wesser, *Charles Evans Hughes: Politics and Reform in New York, 1905–1910* (Ithaca, N.Y., 1967); J. Joseph Huthmacher, "Charles Evans Hughes and Charles Francis Murphy: The Metamorphosis of Progressivism," *New York History* 46 (January 1965): 25–40; Irwin Yellowitz, *Labor and the Progressive Movement in New York State, 1897–1916* (Ithaca, N.Y., 1965); and Nancy Schrom Dye, *As Equals and as Sisters* (Columbia, Mo., 1980), on the Women's Trade Union League of New York.

For progressivism's regulatory impulse, see: State of New York, *Third Report of the Factory Investigating Commission, 1914, Transmitted to the Legislature, February 14, 1914* (Albany, 1914); and State of New York, Department of Labor, *New York Labor Bulletin* (1914–1919) and *Special Bulletins* (1914–1917), which reviewed legal decisions and factory investigations; Martin S. Decker, "History of the Regulation of Public Service Corporations in New York," *New York State Historical Association, Quarterly Journal 3* (July 1922): 133–46; Jared N. Day, *Urban Castles: Tenement Housing and Landlord Activism in New York City, 1890–1943* (New York, 1999); and Bruce W. Dearstyne, "Regulation in the Progressive Era: The New York Public Service Commission," *New York History* 58 (July 1977): 331–47.

For the 1915 constitutional convention, the best study is Thomas Schick, *The New York State Constitutional Convention of 1915 and the Modern State Governor* (New York, 1978). Also see *Record of the Constitutional Convention of the State of New York, 1915,* 4 vols. (Albany, 1915); and Gilbert Giddings Benjamin, "The Attempted Revision of the State

Constitution of New York," *American Political Science Review* 10 (February 1916): 20–43.

For urban progressivism, see: Edwin R. Lewinson, *John Purroy Mitchel* (New York, 1965); Augustus Cerillo, Jr., "Reform in New York City: A Study of Urban Progressivism" (Ph.D. diss., Northwestern University, 1969); Bernard Hirschhorn, *Democracy Reformed: Richard Spencer Childs and His Fight for Better Government* (Westport, Conn., 1997); Donald S. Ritchie, "The Gary Committee: Businessmen, Progressives and Unemployment in New York City, 1914–1915," *New-York Historical Society Quarterly* 57 (1973): 327–47; and Herbert Mitgang, *The Man Who Rode the Tiger* (Philadelphia, 1963), on Judge Samuel Seabury. The few accounts of urban bosses include Nancy Joan Weiss, *Charles Francis Murphy* (Northampton, Mass., 1968), and Clement G. Lanni, *George W. Aldridge* (Rochester, 1939).

On social welfare trends, see: David Schneider, *The History of Public Welfare in New York State*, 2 vols.; 2d volume with Albert Deutsch (Chicago, 1938–41); Jeremy P. Felt, *Hostages of Fortune: Child Labor Reform in New York State* (Syracuse, 1965); Jack M. Holl, *Juvenile Reform in the Progressive Era* (Ithaca, N.Y., 1971); *The Newburgh Survey: Reports of Limited Investigation of Social Conditions in Newburgh, N.Y.* (Newburgh, N.Y., June 1913), a typical "social audit"; *Sixteenth New York State Conference of Charities and Correction, Proceedings, Albany, New York, November 16–18, 1915* (Albany, 1916), a good compendium of urban relief efforts; and Walter I. Trattner, *Homer Folks: Pioneer in Social Welfare* (New York, 1968), which describes the professionalization of charities. Trattner, *From Poor Law to Welfare State: A History of Social Welfare in America* (New York, 1974), is an excellent overall account.

For higher education, see: Dwight Miner, ed., *A History of Columbia College on Morningside* (New York, 1954); Robert I. Gannon, *Up to the Present: The Story of Fordham* (Garden City, N.Y., 1967); *New York State Teachers College at Buffalo: A History, 1871–1946* (N.p., 1946); Dorothy Rogers, *Oswego: Fountainhead of Teacher Education* (New York, 1961); Sherry Gorelick, *City College and the Jewish Poor* (New Brunswick, N.J., 1981); Willis Rudy, *The College of the City of New York: A History* (New York, 1949); Thomas Evans Coulton, *A City College in Action: Struggle and Achievement at Brooklyn College, 1930–1955* (New York, 1955); Selma Berrol, *Getting Down to Business: Baruch College in the City of New York, 1847–1987* (New York, 1989); Jeffrey S. Gurock, *The Men and Women of Yeshiva* (New York, 1988); Morris Bishop, *A History of Cornell* (Ithaca, N.Y., 1962); and Constance Dimock Ellis, ed., *The Magnificent Enterprise: A Chronicle of Vassar College* (Poughkeepsie, N.Y., 1961).

World War I and Postwar Politics

For the World War I period, see: Daniel J. Sweeney, comp., *History of Buffalo and Erie County, 1914–1919*, 2d ed. (Buffalo, 1919); James L. Brewer, "Centennial History of Organized Labor in Rochester," in Edward R. Foreman, comp., *Centennial History of Rochester, New York*, vol. 4, *Jubilee* (Rochester, 1934), 399–437; John D. Lynn, "The United States Marshal's Office in the World War," Rochester Historical Society, Publication Fund Series, vol. 4 (Rochester, 1925), 133–89; and [Rome War Chest Association], *How Rome Raised War Relief* [1918?]. David M. Kennedy, *Over Here* (New York, 1980) is an excellent general account of the war's impact.

For varied aspects of postwar turbulence, see: *Report of the Reconstruction Commission to Governor Alfred E. Smith on Retrenchment and Reorganization of the State Government* (October 10, 1919); A. A. Hoehling, *The Great Epidemic* (Boston, 1961); Theodore Draper, *The Roots of American Communism* (New

York, 1957); Julian F. Jaffe, *Crusade against Radicalism: New York during the Red Scare, 1914–1924* (Port Washington, N.Y., 1972); State of New York, *Proceedings of Conference on Industrial Conditions in the State of New York . . . September 16, 1919* (Albany, 1919); and *Proceedings of the Tenth Anniversary of the Conference of Mayors and other City Officials of the State of New York, Schenectady, N.Y. on June 10, 11, and 12, 1919* (N.p., n.d.).

Despite the enormous literature on Al Smith, he remains an elusive figure. The best biography is Henry F. Pringle, *Alfred E. Smith: A Critical Study* (New York, 1927). Other biographies include Matthew Josephson and Hannah Josephson, *Al Smith: Hero of the Cities* (Boston, 1969); Norman Hapgood and Henry Moskowitz, *Up from the City Streets* (New York, 1927); Paula Eldot, *Governor Alfred E. Smith: The Politician as Reformer* (New York, 1983); and Oscar Handlin, *Al Smith and His America* (Boston, 1958). Lawrence H. Madaras, "Theodore Roosevelt, Jr. versus Al Smith: The New York Gubernatorial Election of 1924," *New York History* 47 (October 1966): 372–90, is a discerning study. *Campaign Addresses of Governor Alfred E. Smith, Democratic Candidate for President, 1928*, issued by the Democratic National Committee (Albany, 1929), captures the politician on the stump.

Specialized studies of Smith and his policies include Elisabeth Israels Perry, *Belle Moskowitz* (New York, 1987); George Martin, *Madam Secretary, Frances Perkins* (Boston, 1976); Richard W. Wallace, "The New York State System and Its Problem of Reorganization," *Annals of the American Academy of Political and Social Science* 105 (January 1923): 113–18, on the state charities; A. Blair Knapp, *Water Power in New York State* (Syracuse, 1930); and John E. Missall, *The Moreland Act* (New York, 1946). *State Service*, a monthly magazine published by the secretary of state and *State Bulletin*, published by the good-government New York State Association, provide

a glimpse of Albany's growing administrative expertise. For public works during the 1920s, see Robert Moses, *Public Works: A Dangerous Trade* (New York, 1970); and *First Annual Report of the State Council of Parks . . .* (October 1925), and subsequent annual reports.

The chieftains of the Democratic party are portrayed in: J. Joseph Huthmacher, *Senator Robert F. Wagner and the Rise of Urban Liberalism* (New York, 1968); Frances Perkins, *The Roosevelt I Knew* (New York, 1946); Julius Henry Cohen, *They Builded Better Than They Knew* (Freeport, N.Y., 1971); Allan Nevins, *Herbert H. Lehman and His Era* (New York, 1963); and William H. Harbaugh, *Lawyer's Lawyer: The Life of John W. Davis* (New York, 1973).

On the state judiciary, see: Andrew L. Kaufman, *Cardozo* (Cambridge, Mass., 1998); Richard A. Posner, *Cardozo: A Study in Reputation* (Chicago, 1990); Cuthbert W. Pound, "The Judicial Power," *Harvard Law Review* 35 (May 1922): 787–96; and Irving Lehman, "Judge Cardozo on the Court of Appeals," *Harvard Law Review* 52 (January 1939): 12–19. Cardozo's opinions are accessible in *Law Is Justice*, ed. A. L. Sainer (New York, 1938), but see also Cardozo's comments in "Commission to Investigate Defects in the Law," in New York City Bar Association, *Reports* (1925): 360–74. Other accounts of the Court of Appeals include Francis Bergan, *The History of the New York Court of Appeals, 1847–1932* (New York, 1985), and Franklin A. Smith, *Judicial Review of Legislation in New York, 1906–1938* (New York, 1952).

City, Community, and Regional Studies

Urban histories include William Kennedy, *O Albany!* (New York, 1983); Nelson Greene, ed., *History of the Valley of the Hudson*, 5 vols. (Chicago, 1931), vol. 2; Blake McKelvey, *Rochester: The Quest for Quality, 1890–1925* (Cambridge, Mass., 1956); McKelvey,

Rochester: An Emerging Metropolis, 1925–1961 (Rochester, 1961); Mark Goldman, *High Hopes: The Rise and Decline of Buffalo, New York* (Albany, 1983); Henry Wayland Hill, editor-in-chief, *Municipality of Buffalo, New York: A History, 1720–1923*, 4 vols. (New York, 1923); Walter S. Dunn, Jr., ed., *History of Erie County, 1870–1970* (Buffalo, 1972); Franklin H. Chase, *Syracuse and Its Environs: A History*, 3 vols. (New York, 1924); and William Foote Seward, editor-in-chief, *Binghamton and Broome County, New York: A History*, 3 vols. (New York, 1924).

Studies of New York City's physical development include: Clifton Hood, *722 Miles* (New York, 1993), on the subway system; Richard Plunz, *A History of Housing in New York City* (New York, 1990); Harvey A. Kantor, "Modern Urban Planning in New York City: Origins and Evolution, 1890–1935" (Ph.D. diss., New York University, 1971); Max Page, *The Creative Destruction of Manhattan, 1900–1940* (Chicago, 1999); Evelyn Gonzalez, "City Neighborhoods: Formation, Growth, and Change in the South Bronx, 1840–1940" (Ph.D. diss., Columbia University, 1993); Jeffrey Kroessler, "Building Queens: The Urbanization of New York City's Largest Borough" (Ph.D. diss., Graduate Center of the City University of New York, 1991); and Lloyd Ultan and Gary Hermalyn, *The Bronx in the Innocent Years, 1890–1925* (New York, 1985). Harold X. Connolly, "Blacks in Brooklyn from 1900 to 1960" (Ph.D. diss., New York University, 1972), is an important study of Bedford-Stuyvesant. Joel Schwartz, *The New York Approach: Robert Moses, Urban Liberals, and Redevelopment of the Inner City* (Columbus, Ohio, 1993), and David A. Johnson, *Planning the Great Metropolis: The 1929 Regional Plan of New York and Its Environs* (London, 1996), describe the major planning emphases of the 1920s and 1930s.

For accounts of smaller cities, see: Harry F. Landon, *150 Years of Watertown . . . A History* (Watertown, N.Y., 1950); Rt. Rev. P. S. Garand, *The History of the City of Ogdensburg* (Ogdensburg, N.Y., 1927); Rutherford Hayner, *Troy and Rensselaer County, New York: A History*, 3 vols. (New York, 1925); *The Upper Mohawk Valley: A Land Of Industry* (Utica, 1923), revealing of Rome, Little Falls, Dolgeville, and Sauquoit; and Glenn Joseph Socki, "The Endicott Johnson Home-Building Program: Welfare Capitalism and the Meaning of Domestic Architecture in the Early Twentieth Century Industrial Suburb" (Ph.D. diss., State University of New York at Binghamton, 1994), which details Johnson City.

Ethnic community studies include Chris McNickle, "When New York Was Irish, and After," in Ronald H. Bayor and Timothy J. Meagher, eds., *The New York Irish* (Baltimore, 1996); John A. Beadles, "The Syracuse Irish, 1912–1928: Immigration, Catholicism, Socio-Economic Status, Politics, and Irish Nationalism" (Ph.D. diss., Syracuse University, 1974); Kathryn Grover, *Make a Way Somehow: African-American Life in a Northern Community, 1790–1963* (Syracuse, 1994), on Geneva; Myra B. Young Armstead, *"Lord, Please Don't Take Me August": African Americans in Newport and Saratoga Springs, 1870–1930* (Urbana, Ill., 1999), a rare look at the color line in those resorts; Eugene E. Obidinski, *Ethnic to Status Group: A Study of Polish Americans in Buffalo* (New York, 1980); Obidinski and Helen Stankiewicz Zand, *Polish Folkways in America: Community and Family*, Polish Studies Series, vol. 1 (Latham, N.Y., 1987); Niles Carpenter with Daniel Katz, "The Cultural Adjustment of the Polish Group in the City of Buffalo," *Social Forces* 6 (September 1927): 76–85; and Paul A. Spengler, *Yankee, Swedish, and Italian Acculturation and Economic Mobility in Jamestown, New York, from 1860 to 1920* (New York, 1980).

The rich literature on Italian Americans includes Virginia Yans-McLaughlin, *Family and Community* (Ithaca, N.Y., 1977), on Buffalo Italians; John Walker Briggs, *An Italian Passage: Immigrants to Three American Cities, 1890–1930* (New Haven, Conn., 1978), on Utica and Rochester; Donna R. Gabaccia, *From Sicily to Elizabeth Street* (Albany, 1984), on the settlement in Greenwich Village; George Schiro, *Americans by Choice* (New York, 1975), on Utica; Robert A. Orsi, *The Madonna of 115th Street* (New Haven, Conn., 1985), on the East Harlem settlement; Donald Tricarico, *The Italians of Greenwich Village* (Staten Island, 1984); and Mary Jane Capozzoli, *Three Generations of Italian American Women in Nassau County, 1925–1981* (New York, 1990).

Studies on the settlement and assimilation of Jewish Americans include Moses Rischin, *The Promised City: New York's Jews, 1870–1914* (Cambridge, Mass., 1962); Irving Howe, *World of Our Fathers* (New York, 1975); Selma Berrol, *East Side/East End: East European Jews in London and New York, 1870–1920* (Westport, Conn., 1994); Michael R. Weisser, *A Brotherhood of Memory: Jewish Landsmanshaftn in the New World* (New York, 1985); Deborah Dash Moore, *At Home in America* (New York, 1989); and B. G. Rudolph, *From a Minyan to a Community* (Syracuse, 1970), on Syracuse. Thomas Kessner, *The Golden Door* (New York, 1977), is a pathbreaking study of Jewish and Italian mobility, and Ronald H. Bayor, *Neighbors in Conflict* (Baltimore, 1978), is an important study of intergroup relations.

There are few suburban studies of the era before World War II. The best place to start is Kenneth T. Jackson, *Crabgrass Frontier* (New York, 1985), an excellent overview. I have also relied upon Harry Hansen, *Scarsdale* (New York, 1954); Neil Martin, "Westchester as an Evolving Suburb," and Jane McMahon and Edmund McMahon, "Westchester from the Roaring Twenties to V-J Day," both in Marilyn E. Weigold, ed., *Westchester County: The Past Hundred Years, 1883–1983* (Valhalla, N.Y.,

1984); Henry Isham Hazelton, *The Boroughs of Brooklyn and Queens, Counties of Nassau and Suffolk, Long Island, 1609–1924*, 5 vols. (New York, 1925); and Ernest Freeland Griffin, ed., *Westchester County and Its People: A Record*, 3 vols. (New York, 1946). The evolution in suburban responsibility is revealed in New York State, Niagara Frontier Planning Board, *Annual Reports* (New York, 1925–).

For regional accounts, see: Ted Aber and Stella King, *The History of Hamilton County* (Lake Pleasant, N.Y., 1965); William H. Brown, ed., *History of Warren County, New York*, published by the Board of Supervisors of Warren County (Glens Falls, N.Y., 1963); Michael C. Donovan, *Historical Review of Cattaraugus County* (n.d.); and Arch Merrill, *Southern Tier*, 2 vols. (New York, n.d.).

Accounts of the Adirondacks include William Chapman White, *Adirondack Country* (New York, 1954), and some Adirondack classics: Frederick J. Seaver, *Historical Sketches of Franklin County and Its Several Towns with Many Short Biographies* (Albany, 1918); Alfred L. Donaldson, *A History of the Adirondacks*, 2 vols. (New York, 1921); Peter C. Welsh, *Jacks, Jobbers and Kings: Logging the Adirondacks* (Utica, N.Y., 1995); and the splendid details in Philip G. Terrie, *Contested Terrain: A New History of Nature and People in the Adirondacks* (Syracuse, 1997); and Harold K. Hochschild, *Township 34* (New York, 1952). *Rockefeller v. Lamora* 83 N.Y.S. 289 (1903), details the impact of the Private Park Law of 1892. For the Saratoga area, see: State of New York, *Sixth Annual Report of the Commissioners of the State Reservation at Saratoga Springs, 1915*, transmitted to the Legislature January 6, 1915 (Albany, 1915); George Waller, *Saratoga: Saga of an Impious Era* (Englewood Cliffs, N.J., 1966); and Marjorie Peabody Waite, *Yaddo, Yesterday and Today* (Saratoga Springs, N.Y., 1933).

Other upstate histories include Edward T. Williams, *Niagara County, New York*, 2 vols.

(Chicago, n.d.); Merton M. Milner, *Niagara Frontier: A Narrative and Documentary History*, 2 vols. (Chicago, 1931); Theodora Vinal, *Niagara Portage, from Past to Present* (Buffalo, 1949); Howard Thomas, *Black River in the North Country* (Prospect, N.Y., 1963); Nelson Greene, ed., *History of the Mohawk Valley, Gateway to the West, 1614–1925*, 4 vols. (Chicago, 1925); and Codman Hislop, *The Mohawk* (New York, 1948). On the Catskills region, see Roland Van Zandt, *The Catskill Mountain House* (New Brunswick, N.J., 1966), and Anita M. Smith, *Woodstock: History and Hearsay* (Saugerties, N.Y., 1959), which reveals the art colony's bourgeois high jinks. Irwin Richman, *Borscht Belt Bungalow: Memories of Catskill Summers* (Philadelphia, 1998) recalls that Jewish cultural moment.

Some of the best village histories include *A Chronicle of Auburn, from 1793 to 1955* (Auburn, N.Y., 1955); Walter R. Wood, *History of DeRuyter and Vicinity, from Time of Indians to 1964* (DeRuyter, N.Y., 1964); Walter R. Littell, "A History of Cooperstown, 1886–1929," in *A History of Cooperstown* (Cooperstown, N.Y., 1929); *The Story of Hartford: A History*, compiled by Isabella Brayton, in collaboration with John B. Norton (Glens Falls, N.Y., 1929); Charles B. Warner, *History of Port Henry, N.Y.* (Rutland, Vt., 1931); and Carl F. Schmidt, *History of the Town of Wheatland* (Rochester, 1953).

Agriculture, Industry, and Finance

For agriculture, see: Ulysses Prentiss Hedrick, *A History of Agriculture in the State of New York* (Albany, 1933); James Mickel Williams, *The Expansion of Rural Life* (New York, 1926); State of New York, Department of Farms and Markets, Division of Agriculture, Bulletin 133, *Agricultural Manual of New York State, Arranged by Counties* [1922]; Bruce L. Melvin, *Rural Population of New York, 1855 to 1925*, Cornell University Agricultural Exper-

iment Station, Memorandum No. 116 (Ithaca, N.Y., 1928); and Gould P. Colman, *Education & Agriculture: A History of the New York State College of Agriculture at Cornell University* (Ithaca, N.Y., 1963). See also specialized studies: W. A. Anderson, *Mobility of Rural Families*, I, Bulletin 607, Cornell University Agricultural Experiment Station, June 1934, and II, Bulletin 623, March 1935; and *Rural Youth: Activities, Interests, Problems*, I, Bulletin 649, Cornell University Agricultural Experiment Station, May 1936, and II, Bulletin 661, January 1937; and F. G. Crawford and H. W. Peck, *Motor Vehicles and the Highway in New York* (School of Citizenship and Public Affairs, Syracuse University, 1924). For the Clarence Stein-Lewis Mumford viewpoint, see *State of New York, Report of the Commission of Housing and Regional Planning to Governor Alfred E. Smith . . . May 7, 1926* (Albany, 1926); "The Regional Plan Number" in *Survey Graphic* 7 (May 1925); and the fine account in Edward K. Spann, *Designing Modern America: The Regional Planning Association of America and Its Members* (Columbus, Ohio, 1996).

Modern, critical histories of industrial sectors include James W. Cortada, *Before the Computer* (Princeton, 1993), which has excellent discussions of IBM and Remington Rand; Leonard S. Reich, *The Making of American Industrial Research: Science and Business at GE and Bell, 1876–1926* (New York, 1985); Reese Jenkins, *Images and Enterprise* (Baltimore, 1975) on Eastman Kodak; and Emerson W. Pugh, *Building IBM* (Cambridge, Mass., 1995). David Loth, *Swope of G.E.* (New York, 1976), and Josephine Young Case and Everett Needham Case, *Owen D. Young and American Enterprise* (Boston, 1982), are revealing of the industrial statesmen of the 1920s and 1930s. More traditional, celebratory business histories include: Cloud Wampler, *Dr. Willis H. Carrier: Father of Air Conditioning* (New York, 1949); Francis Brown, *Edmund Niles Huyck* (New York, 1935), on the paper industry's benevolent capitalist; "Cluett, Peabody," *Fortune,* February 1937, pp. 13ff.; William S. Frame, *History of the Schenectady Plant of the American Locomotive Company* (Schenectady, 1945); William Cahn, *Out of the Cracker Barrel: The Nabisco Story* (New York, 1969); and Henry W. Wendt and Edgar F. Wendt, "*Buffalo Forge*" *(1877–1952)* (New York, 1952). The growing anxiety of manufacturers can be seen in *Proceedings of New York State-Wide Economic Conference, held in New York City, April 15, 16 and 17, 1929* (New York, 1929).

For labor, see New York State, Factory Investigating Commission, *Reports* (1911–14), particularly *Fourth Report* (1914); Thomas J. Kerr IV, "New York Factory Investigating Commission and the Progressives" (D.S.S. diss., Syracuse University, 1965); Melvyn Dubofsky, *When Workers Organize: New York City in the Progressive Era* (Amherst, Mass., 1968); Jack Hardy, *The Clothing Workers* (New York, 1935); Matthew Josephson, *Sidney Hillman* (Garden City, N.Y., 1952), which covers the Amalgamated Clothing Workers in Rochester and New York City; New York State, Department of Labor, *Statistics of Organized Labor* (1912); New York State, Department of Labor, *Second Annual Industrial Directory of New York State, 1913,* compiled and published under the Direction of James M. Lynch, Commissioner of Labor (Albany, 1913); and State of New York, Department of Labor, *Special Bulletin: The Employment of Women in 5 and 10 Cent Stores* (No. 109, September, 1921). New York State Federation of Labor, *Proceedings [of] Annual Conventions,* details the open-shop campaign; and State of New York, Department of Labor, *Special Bulletin, No. 171, 1931; Course of Factory Employment in New York State from 1921 to 1930* provides a useful statistical profile. Gerald Zahavi, *Workers, Managers, and Welfare Capitalism: The Shoemakers and Tanners of Endicott Johnson, 1890–1950* (Champaign, Ill., 1988), is a fine study of workers in their community.

Studies of New York City's financial and legal establishment include Lester V. Chandler, *Benjamin Strong, Central Banker* (Washington, D.C., 1958); Ron Chernow, *The House of Morgan* (New York, 1990); Vincent T. Carosso, *Investment Banking in America* (Cambridge, Mass., 1970); Robert Sobel, *The Great Bull Market* (New York, 1968); Harold Van B. Cleveland and Theodore Huertas, *Citibank* (Cambridge, Mass., 1985); John Donald Wilson, *The Chase* (Boston, 1986); Arthur H. Dean, *William Nelson Cromwell* (New York, 1957); Walter K. Earle, *Mr. Shearman and Mr. Sterling and How They Grew* (New York, 1963); Deborah S. Gardner, *Cadwalader, Wickersham & Taft: A Bicentennial History* (New York, 1994); and Paul D. Cravath, "Reorganization of Corporations," in Francis Lynde Stetson, ed., *Some Legal Phases of Corporation Financing, Reorganization, and Regulation* (New York, 1917).

Culture in the 1920s

For New York City life in the 1920s, see: Gene Fowler, *Beau James: The Life & Times of Jimmy Walker* (New York, 1949); Caroline Ware, *Greenwich Village, 1920–1930* (Boston, 1935); and Roy V. Peel, *The Political Clubs of New York City* (New York, 1935). Aspects of midtown life are portrayed in William R. Taylor, *In Pursuit of Gotham* (New York, 1992); Neal Gabler, *Winchell* (New York, 1994); James W. Barrett, ed., *The End of The World* (New York, 1931); Howard Taubman, *The Making of the American Theatre* (New York, 1965); Douglas Gilbert, *American Vaudeville* (1940; rpt. New York, 1963); and Lula Rosenfeld, *Bright Star of Exile: Jacob Adler and the Yiddish Theatre* (New York, 1977).

For the relationship between highbrow and popular culture that was at the heart of Manhattan, see: William B. Scott and Peter M. Rutkoff, *New York Modern: The Arts and the City* (Baltimore, 1999); Thomas Bender, *New*

York Intellect (New York, 1987); Ann Douglas, Terrible Honesty (New York, 1995); and Michael Kammen, The Lively Arts: Gilbert Seldes and the Transformation of Cultural Criticism in the United States (New York, 1996). Other glimpses are provided by David Belasco, The Theatre through Its Stage Door, ed. Louis V. De Foe (New York, 1919); Gilbert Seldes, The 7 Lively Arts (1924; rpt. New York, 1957); and Richard Maney, Fanfare: The Confessions of a Press Agent (New York, 1957). David Ward and Olivier Zunz, eds., The Landscape of Modernity: Essays on New York City, 1900–1940 (New York, 1992) offers a stimulating glimpse at the formative elements behind Manhattan's mass society.

The Greenwich Village milieu is portrayed in Richard Whalen, Alfred Stieglitz (Boston, 1995); Rick Beard and Leslie Cohen Berlowitz, eds., Greenwich Village: Culture and Counterculture (New Brunswick, N.J., 1993); Avis Berman, Rebels on Eighth Street: Juliana Force and the Whitney Museum of American Art (New York, 1990); Paul Rosenfeld, The Port of New York (Urbana, Ill., 1961); and Malcolm Cowley, Exile's Return (New York, 1951). For aspects of the Harlem Renaissance, see: James Weldon Johnson, Black Manhattan (New York, 1930); Nathan Irving Huggins, Harlem Renaissance (New York, 1971); George Hutchinson, The Harlem Renaissance in Black and White (Cambridge, Mass., 1995); and Gilbert Osofsky, Harlem: Making of a Ghetto (New York, 1963).

For music, from classical to pop to jazz, I have relied upon: George Martin, The Damrosch Dynasty (Boston, 1983); Edward Jablonski, Gershwin (1987; rpt. Boston, 1990); Laurence Bergreen, As Thousands Cheer (New York, 1990), a probing biography of Irving Berlin; Aaron Copland and Vivian Perlis, Copland, 1900 through 1942 (New York, 1984); the LP album Sissle & Blake's Shuffle Along (New World Records, 1976); Burton W. Peretti, The Creation of Jazz (Champaign, Ill., 1992); Benny Green, The Reluctant Art (1971; rpt. New

York, 1991), classic essays in the history of jazz; and Scott DeVeaux, The Birth of Bebop (Berkeley, Calif., 1997). I have also relied on Joan Peyser, The Music of My Time (White Plains, N.Y., 1995), and the astringent comments in Gilbert Chase, America's Music (New York, 1955).

For the transformation of publishing, see: John Tebbel, A History of Book Publishing in the United States, 4 vols. (New York, 1972–81), vol. 3; Cass Canfield, Up and Down and Around (New York, 1971); Tom Dardis, Firebrand: The Life of Horace Liveright (New York, 1995); Kenneth Davis, Two-Bit Culture: The Paperbacking of America (Boston, 1984); Frank Luther Mott, A History of American Magazines (Cambridge, Mass., 1968), vol. 5; and Caroline Seebohm, The Man Who Was Vogue: The Life and Times of Condé Nast (New York, 1982).

The Crash and the Depression Years

Wall Street's collapse and its repercussions are detailed in John K. Galbraith, The Great Crash, 1929 (Boston, 1954); Charles P. Kindleberger, The World in Depression, 1929–1939 (Berkeley, Calif., 1986); Joel Seligman, Transformation of Wall Street (Boston, 1982); Susan Estabrook Kennedy, The Banking Crisis of 1933 (Lexington, Ky., 1973); and Robert Sobel, N.Y.S.E.: A History of the New York Stock Exchange, 1935–1975 (New York, 1975).

The best treatment of urban liberalism is John D. Buenker, Urban Liberalism and Progressive Reform (New York, 1973). Additional accounts include Edward J. Flynn, You're the Boss (New York, 1947); and Frank Freidel, Franklin D. Roosevelt: The Ordeal (Boston, 1954).

The FDR literature includes Geoffrey C. Ward, A First-Class Temperament (New York, 1989); Kenneth S. Davis, FDR: The Beckoning of Destiny, 1882–1928 (New York, 1972); Joseph P. Lash, Eleanor and Franklin (New

York, 1971); and Alfred B. Rollins, Jr., *Roosevelt and Howe* (New York, 1962). The most thorough treatment of FDR in the New York years can be found in Frank Freidel, *Franklin D. Roosevelt: The Triumph* (Boston, 1956). Other useful accounts of Roosevelt's gubernatorial policies are in Bernard Bellush, *Franklin D. Roosevelt as Governor of New York* (New York, 1955), and George McJimsey, *Harry Hopkins* (Cambridge, Mass., 1987).

For the Little New Deal, see Robert P. Ingalls, *Herbert H. Lehman and New York's Little New Deal* (New York, 1975). For the liberalism of La Guardia's New York, see Arthur Mann, *La Guardia Comes to Power, 1933* (Chicago, 1965); Charles Garrett, *The La Guardia Years* (New Brunswick, N.J., 1961); and Thomas Kessner, *Fiorello H. La Guardia and the Making of Modern New York* (New York, 1989). State of New York, *Preliminary Report of the Joint Legislative Committee on Unemployment*, transmitted to the Legislature February 15, 1932 (Albany, 1932), details employment stabilization schemes. The Temporary Emergency Relief Administration is described in Alexander Radomski, *Work Relief in New York State, 1931–1935* (New York, 1948); and Governor's Commission on Unemployment Relief, *Work Relief in the State of New York: A Review of Its Characteristics, Functioning, and Value*, submitted to Governor Herbert H. Lehman, August 10, 1936 (Albany, 1936).

Local relief profiles include John D. Millett, *The Works Progress Administration in New York City* (Chicago, 1938); Barbara Blumberg, *The New Deal and the Unemployed: The View from New York City* (Lewisburg, Penn., 1979); Niles Carpenter, "Trends in Relief Expenditure in Buffalo," *Statistical Survey*, The University of Buffalo Bureau of Business and Social Research, 9 (February 1934): 1–4; and Martha Collins Bayne, *County at Large* (Poughkeepsie, N.Y., 1937). For life on the dole, see Eli Ginzberg, *The Unemployed* (New York, 1943).

The emerging role played by moderate Republicans is detailed in: Judith Stein, "The Impact of the New Deal on New York Politics: Kenneth Simpson and the Republican Party," *New-York Historical Society Quarterly* 54 (January 1972): 29–53; and Stein, "The Birth of Liberal Republicanism in New York State" (Ph.D. diss., Yale University, 1968); and Alva Johnston, "Profile: The King," *New Yorker*, September 12, 1931, pp. 25–30, on W. Kingsland Macy. Curt Gerling, *Smugtown, U.S.A.* (Webster, N.Y., 1957), recalls moderate Republicanism in Rochester.

There are no good scholarly biographies of Thomas E. Dewey. The following, however, are useful: Rupert Hughes, *Attorney for the People* (Boston, 1940), which details the sudden emergence of Dewey as gangbuster; Barry K. Beyer, *Thomas E. Dewey, 1937–1947: A Study in Political Leadership* (New York, 1979); Richard Norton Smith, *Thomas E. Dewey and His Times* (New York, 1982); and Leo F. McCue, "Thomas E. Dewey and the Politics of Accommodation, 1940–1952" (Ph.D. diss., Boston University, 1979).

On labor during the 1930s, see: Herbert Harris, *American Labor* (New Haven, Conn., 1938); Joshua B. Freeman, *In Transit: The Transit Workers Union in New York City, 1933–1966* (New York, 1989); Leon Fink and Brian Greenberg, *Upheaval in the Quiet Zone: A History of Hospital Workers' Union, Local 1199* (Chicago, 1989); and Zahavi, *Workers, Manager, and Welfare Capitalism*, cited earlier.

Langdon Post, *The Challenge of Housing* (New York, 1938) and Gail Radford, *Modern Housing for America* (Chicago, 1996) describe slum clearance and public housing efforts in New York City. Ronald Lawson, ed., *The New York City Tenants Movement, 1904–1974* (New Brunswick, N.J., 1986), and Joel Schwartz, "Tenant Unions in New York City's Low-Rent Housing, 1934–1949," *Journal of Urban History* 12 (August 1986): 234–58, detail aspects of housing as a radical issue. For the

Little New Deal's impact on the state consti-
tution, see Vernon A. O'Rourke and Douglas
W. Campbell, *Constitution-Making in a
Democracy: Theory and Practice in New York
State* (Baltimore, 1943), which describes the
constitutional convention of 1938; and Peter J.
Galie, *Ordered Liberty: Constitutional History
of New York State* (New York, 1996).

On race relations, see: WPA, Federal Writ-
ers Project, *The Negro in New York* (New
York, 1967); *The Complete Report of Mayor La
Guardia's Commission on the Harlem Riot of
March 19, 1935* (New York, 1969); Mark Nai-
son, *Communists in Harlem during the
Depression* (Urbana, Ill., 1983); William
Muraskin, "The Harlem Boycott of 1934:
Black Nationalism and the Rise of Labor-
Union Consciousness," *Labor History* 12
(Summer 1972): 361–73; Larry A. Greene,
"Harlem in the Great Depression, 1928–1936"
(Ph.D. diss., Columbia University, 1979);
Charles V. Hamilton, *Adam Clayton Powell,
Jr.: The Political Biography of an American
Dilemma* (New York, 1991); Adam Clayton
Powell, *Marching Blacks* (New York, 1945);
and Cheryl Greenberg, *"Or Does it Explode?"*
(New York, 1991).

On the city's Depression intelligentsia,
see: William Barrett, *The Truants* (Garden
City, N.Y., 1982); Lionel Abel, *The Intellectual
Follies* (New York, 1984); Alfred Kazin, *Start-
ing Out in the Thirties* (Boston, 1965); Irving
Howe, *A Margin of Hope* (New York, 1982);
*Creators and Disturbers: Reminiscences by
Jewish Intellectuals of New York*, drawn from
conversations with Bernard Rosenberg and
Ernest Goldstein (New York, 1982); and Beth
S. Wenger, *New York Jews and the Great
Depression: Uncertain Promise* (New Haven,
Conn., 1996). The radicalization of young
Communists is the subject of George Charney,
Long Journey (Chicago, 1968), and James A.
Wechsler, *The Age of Suspicion* (New York,
1953).

On New York City's Depression culture,
see: Daniel Aaron, *Writers on the Left* (New
York, 1961); Jerre Mangione, *The Dream and
the Deal: The Federal Writers' Project,
1935–1943* (Boston, 1972); Alfred Kazin, *A
Walker in the City* (New York, 1951); Mordecai Gorelik, *New Theatres for Old* (New York,
1947), useful despite its Stalinism; Robert E.
Gard, *Grassroots Theater* (Madison, Wis.,
1955); Howard Teichmann, *George S. Kaufman* (New York, 1972); Barbara Leaming,
Orson Welles: A Biography (New York, 1986);
and Jane De Hart Mathews, *The Federal Theatre, 1935–1939* (Princeton, 1967). Robert W.
Merry, *Taking on the World: Joseph and Stewart Alsop—Guardians of the American Century* (New York, 1996), is a revealing look at
New York City journalism in the 1930s. Russell Flinchum, *Henry Dreyfuss, Industrial
Designer* (New York, 1997), profiles Art Deco
and 1930s streamline design. David Gelertner,
1939: The Lost World of the Fair (New York,
1995); and Victoria Newhouse, *Wallace K.
Harrison, Architect* (New York, 1989), provide
splendid looks at the 1939 New York World's
Fair.

On professional sports, see: Robert W.
Creamer, *Babe: The Legend Comes to Life*
(New York, 1974); Charles C. Alexander, *John
McGraw* (New York, 1988), on the legendary
manager of the New York Giants; Neil J. Sullivan, *The Minors* (New York, 1990); Jim Man-
delaro and Scott Pitoniak, *Silver Seasons: The
Story of the Rochester Red Wings* (Syracuse,
1997); Peter Filichia, *Professional Baseball
Franchises* (New York, 1993); Roger Kahn, *The
Era, 1947–1957* (New York, 1993), which
lingers on New York City's love affair with
baseball in the forties; and Bill Chadwick, *The
Big Whistle* (New York, 1974), a fascinating
book on scrub ice hockey. On New York City's
radio media, see: A. M. Sperber, *Murrow: His
Life and Times* (New York, 1986); Robert
Metz, *CBS: Reflections in a Bloodshot Eye*

(Chicago, 1975); and Erik Barnouw, *A History of Broadcasting in the United States*, 3 vols. (New York, 1966–70), vol. 2, *The Golden Web, 1933 to 1953*.

The World War II Period

For wartime ordnance production, see: Karl Drew Hartzwell, *The Empire State at War: World War II* (Albany, 1949); Leonard P. Adams, *Wartime Manpower Mobilization*, Cornell Studies in Industrial and Labor Relations, vol. 1 (Ithaca, N.Y., 1951), which focuses on Buffalo; John Anderson Miller, *Men and Volts at War: The Story of General Electric in World War II* (New York, 1947); "Staging Area—Brooklyn" (supplement to the *Brooklyn Eagle*, December 9, 1945); and Richard Thruelsen, *The Grumman Story* (New York, 1976).

The relationship between wartime production and discriminatory hiring is detailed in James R. Burress, Jr., "The Negro Worker in Queens" (M.A. thesis, New York School of Social Work, August 1941); Labor Market Survey Reports, United States Employment Service, Record Group 183; and Division of Field Operations, Series 41, Commission on Fair Employment Practices, Record Group 228, National Archives, which also includes material on women and ethnic minorities. Further discussions of Jim Crow include James D. Bilotta, "Reflections of an African-American on His Life in the Greater Buffalo Area, 1930's–1960's," *Afro-Americans in New York Life and History* 13 (1989): 47–55; William B. Thomas, "Schooling as a Political Instrument of Social Control: School Response to Black Migrant Youth in Buffalo, New York, 1917–1940," *Teacher's College Record* 86 (1985): 579–92; and William M. Kimok, "Black Baseball in New York State's Capital District, 1907–1950," *Afro-Americans in New York Life and History* 16 (1992): 41–74. Dominic J. Capeci, *The Harlem Riot of 1943* (Philadel-phia, 1977), and Joel Schwartz, "The Consolidated Tenants League of Harlem: Afro-American Self-Help vs. White Liberal Intervention in Ghetto Housing, 1933–1944," *Afro-Americans in New York Life and History* 10 (1986): 31–51, describe Harlem's turmoil and the birth of the interracial movement.

M. Gardner, "Boom Town, Cautious Style," *Saturday Evening Post*, December 5, 1943, pp. 16ff., portrays wartime Elmira. The upheaval in Kendaia Corners is in Oscar and Minna Mintzer, "Along the Kendaia Sector," *Social Work Today* 9 (January 1942): 8–10; while Kathryn Close, "They Harvest New York State's Crops," *Survey Graphic* 34 (January 1945): 21ff., and Mitchell C. Robinson, "Men of Peace in a World at War: Civilian Public Service in New York State, 1941–1946," *New York History* 78 (April 1997): 173–210 look at aspects of rural labor. On wartime politics, see Richard Norton Smith, *Thomas E. Dewey and His Times,* cited earlier; the cover story, "In Mid-Career," *Time*, November 1, 1943, pp. 15–18; and Forrest Davis, "Dewey's April Choice: Swimming Pool Cabinet," *Saturday Evening Post*, August 12, 1944, pp. 9ff., among the best of journalistic accounts. On higher education during the war, see William Pearson Tolley, *At the Fountain of Youth* (Syracuse, 1989), and Oliver Cromwell Carmichael, Jr., *New York State Establishes a State University* (Nashville, Tenn., 1955).

For wartime culture, see: William Barrett, *The Truants* cited earlier; Dore Ashton, *The New York School* (New York, 1973); [Arthur Fellig], *Weegee's People* (New York, 1946); John Mosedale, *The Men Who Invented Broadway* (New York, 1981); Jan Morris, *New York '45* (New York, 1987); and William Wright, *Lillian Hellman* (New York, 1986). For postwar metropolitan plans, see the series "Reports on Arterial Routes in New York State Urban Areas," published by the New York State Department of Public Works, 35 vols. (Albany,

1947–56), and New York State, Department of Public Works, *Report on Arterial Routes in the Rochester Urban Area* (mimeo, 1947). For the vogue in postwar planning see "Syracuse Tackles Its Future," *Fortune*, May 1943, pp. 120ff.; *Progress Report on the Programming of Improvements in the City of Watertown* (City Planning Commission, June 30, 1942); and *The Report of the Syracuse-Onondaga Post-War Planning Council* (December 15, 1945).

Part VII. The Empire State in a Changing World (1945–2000)

General Sources

Statistical compilations of New York State include the U.S. Department of Commerce, *County and City Data Book* (Washington, D.C., 1947–87); and annual issues of *New York State Statistical Yearbook* (Albany: Nelson A. Rockefeller Institute of Government). The physical transformation of major cities can be seen in Norval White and Elliot Willensky, eds., *AIA Guide to New York City* (New York, 1978), and Francis R. Kowsky, *Buffalo Architecture* (Cambridge, Mass., 1981). Robert J. Rayback, ed., *Richards Atlas of New York State*, 2d ed. (Phoenix, N.Y., 1968); and Kenneth T. Jackson, ed., *The Encyclopedia of New York City* (New Haven, Conn., 1995), are treasures.

The Postwar Years

For New York in the 1940s, see: *The Empire State at War*, compiled and written for the New York State War Council by Karl Drew Hartzell (Albany, 1949); Richard Thruelsen, *The Grumman Story* (New York, 1976); John Anderson Miller, *Men and Volts at War: The Story of General Electric in World War II* (New York, 1947); Jan Morris, *New York '45* (New York, 1987); Elliot Willensky, *When Brooklyn Was the World* (New York, 1986); Charles Champlin, *Back There Where the Past Was* (Syracuse, 1989), about Hammondsport;

William Kennedy, *O Albany!* (New York, 1983); and Verlyn Klinkenborg, *The Last Fine Time* (New York, 1991), on Buffalo.

Political baedekers include Warren Moscow, *Politics in the Empire State* (Westport, Conn., 1979), and Lynton K. Caldwell, *The Government and Administration of New York State* (New York, 1954). For Governor Dewey's administration, see Richard Norton Smith, *Thomas E. Dewey and His Times* (New York, 1982), and Robert P. Kerker, "The Battle for Control of the Budget," *Empire State Report* 5 (June–July 1979): 20–27. New York City liberalism is discussed in Thomas F. Kessner, *Fiorello H. La Guardia and the Making of Modern New York* (New York, 1989); Wallace S. Sayre and Herbert Kaufman, *Governing New York City* (New York, 1960); and Chris McNickle, *To Be Mayor of New York* (New York, 1993). For upstate politics, see: Roscoe C. Martin, *Decisions in Syracuse* (New York, 1968); Frank S. Robinson, *Machine Politics: A Study of Albany's O'Connells* (New Brunswick, N.J., 1977); Allan Ehrenhalt, *The United States of Ambition* (New York, 1991), describing Utica's machine; Blake McKelvey, *Rochester: An Emerging Metropolis, 1925–1961* (Rochester, 1961); and Paul Grondahl, *Mayor Erastus Corning: Albany Icon, Albany Enigma* (Albany, 1997).

The state power authority and thruway are discussed in Donald Braider, *The Niagara* (New York, 1972); Roscoe C. Martin, *Water for*

New York (Syracuse, 1960); Edmund Wilson, *Apologies to the Iroquois* (New York, 1978), which includes Joseph Mitchell's classic, "The Mohawks in High Steel"; and Section 10, "The Thruway—Highroad of Empire," in *New York Times*, June 20, 1954.

New York City's physical transformation is described in Raymond Vernon, *Anatomy of a Metropolis* (Cambridge, Mass., 1959); Richard Plunz, *A History of Housing in New York City* (New York, 1990); Robert A. Caro, *The Power Broker: Robert Moses and the Fall of New York* (New York, 1974); and Joel Schwartz, *The New York Approach: Robert Moses, Urban Liberals, and Redevelopment of the Inner City* (Columbus, Ohio, 1993). For the city's reform movement, see Edward N. Costikyan, *Behind Closed Doors* (New York, 1966), and James Q. Wilson, *The Amateur Democrat* (Chicago, 1962). Salvatore J. LaGumina, *New York at Mid-Century: The Impellitteri Years* (Westport, Conn., 1992) profiles mayoral leadership in the postwar years. Jules Tygiel, *Baseball's Greatest Experiment: Jackie Robinson and His Legacy* (New York, 1983), and Neil J. Sullivan, *The Dodgers Move West* (New York, 1987), show another consequence of the city's liberalism.

Postwar ghettos are detailed in Harold X. Connolly, *A Ghetto Grows in Brooklyn* (New York, 1977); Seymour Sacks and Ralph Andrew, *The Syracuse Black Community, 1970* (Syracuse, 1974); and Henry Louis Taylor, Jr., *African Americans and the Rise of Buffalo's Post-Industrial City* (Buffalo, 1990). For Puerto Rican settlement, see C. Wright Mills, *The Puerto Rican Journey* (New York, 1950); and Patricia Cayo Sexton, *Spanish Harlem* (New York, 1965). Black politics are detailed in Charles V. Hamilton, *Adam Clayton Powell, Jr.* (New York, 1991), and J. Raymond Jones, *The Harlem Fox* (Albany, 1989). Postwar ethnicity is framed by Oscar Handlin, *The Newcomers* (Cambridge, Mass., 1959); and Daniel P. Moynihan and Nathan Glazer, *Beyond the Melting Pot* (Cambridge, Mass., 1963). Hidden communities are discussed in Madeline Davis and Elizabeth Lapovsky Kennedy, *Boots of Leather, Slippers of Gold* (New York, 1993), on lesbian Buffalo, and essays by Eric Garber and Allan Berube in Martin Bauml Duberman, *Hidden from History; Reclaiming the Gay and Lesbian Past* (New York, 1989). Eric C. Schneider, *Vampires, Dragons, and Egyptian Kings: Youth Gangs in Postwar New York* (Princeton, N.J., 1999) describes the neighborhood impact of postwar social change.

Postwar urban histories include: Wilbur Cross, *Samuel S. Stratton* (New York, 1964), on the Schenectady insurgent; Walter S. Dunn, ed., *History of Erie County, 1870–1970* (Buffalo, 1972); Mark Goldman, *High Hopes; The Rise and Decline of Buffalo, New York* (Albany, 1983); Frank Manuele, "The Politics of Redevelopment: The Evolution of the Buffalo Urban Renewal Agency, 1949 to 1966" (Ph.D. diss., State University of New York, Buffalo, 1983); David C. Perry, "The Politics of De-industrialization in America: The Case of Buffalo, New York," in Michael Peter Smith and Joe R. Feagin, eds., *The Capitalist City* (London, 1987); Blake McKelvey, *Rochester on the Genesee* (Syracuse, 1973); Jerre Mangione, *Mount Allegro: A Memoir of Italian American Life* (New York, 1981); James D. Brutash, *A Historical Documentary of the Ukrainian Community of Rochester, New York*, trans. Anastasia Smerychyuska (Rochester, 1973); Victor Gruen, *The Heart of Our Cities* (New York, 1964), which details Midtown Plaza; essays by John R. Searles, Jr., and Louis Kriesberg in *Maxwell Review* 5 (Summer 1969) on Syracuse; Tom Cawley, "Appraisal, 1940–1967," included in *J. B. Wilkinson's Annals of Binghamton of 1840* (Binghamton, 1967); and Marjory Barnum Hinman, *Court House Square: A Social History of Binghamton, Broome County, New York* (Endicott, N.Y., 1984). George Raymond's essay in Marilyn E. Weigold, ed., *Westchester County: The Past*

Hundred Years, 1883–1983 (Valhalla, N.Y., 1984), describes the transformation of White Plains and New Rochelle.

For suburban trends, see Robert C. Wood, *1400 Governments: The Political Economy of the New York Metropolitan Region* (Cambridge, Mass., 1961), and Harold Herman, *New York State and the Metropolitan Problem* (Philadelphia, 1963). For the ethnic dimension, see Albert I. Gordon, *Jews in Suburbia* (Boston, 1959); Salvatore J. LaGumina, *From Steerage to Suburbia: Long Island Italians* (New York, 1988); and Richard Bugelski, "Assimilation through Intermarriage," *Social Forces* 40 (December 1961): 148–53, on suburban Buffalo. Essays by Geoffrey Rossano and Kenneth T. Jackson in Roger W. Lotchin, ed., *The Martial Metropolis* (New York, 1984), tell the impact of defense spending on greater New York City. Articles in *Empire State Architect*, *Architectural Record*, and *Urban Land* chart schools, shopping centers and corporate complexes.

For New York City's northern suburbs, see: Carol A. O'Connor, *A Sort of Utopia: Scarsdale* (Albany, 1983); Jeff Canning and Wally Buxton, *History of the Tarrytowns, Westchester County, New York* (Harrison, N.Y., 1975); Norman R. Baker, *The Way It Was: An Informal History of New City* (Orangeburg, N.Y., 1973); and Marilyn E. Weigold, ed., *Westchester County,* cited above. For Long Island, see Bernice Marshall, "The Rest of the Story, 1929–1961," in Jacqueline Overton, *Long Island's Story* (Port Washington, N.Y., 1961); Joann P. Krieg and Natalie Naylor, eds., *Nassau County: From Rural Hinterland to Suburban Metropolis* (Interlaken, N.Y., 2000); Verne Dyson, *Deer Park–Wyandanch History* (Brentwood, N.Y., 1957); Barbara M. Kelly, ed., *Long Island: The Suburban Experience* (Interlaken, N.Y., 1990); Joann P. Krieg, ed., *Robert Moses: Single-Minded Genius*, Long Island Studies (Interlaken, N.Y., 1989), which includes discussions on Moses's impact

on the island; and Barbara M. Kelly, *Expanding the American Dream: Building and Rebuilding Levittown* (Albany, 1993). For Buffalo, see Paul Beaudet, "The Growth of Buffalo's Suburban Zone," *Niagara Frontier* 18 (Summer 1971): 47–63.

Economics and Education

On state economic trends, see: Donald J. Bogue and Calvin L. Beale, eds., *Economic Areas of the United States* (Glencoe, Ill., 1961), and the entire issue of *New York State Commerce Review* 1 (November 1946). For postwar business, see Robert Sobel, *The Fallen Colossus* (New York, 1977) on the New York Central Railroad; Eli G. White, *The Awakening of a Company: The Story of Endicott Johnson Corporation* (New York, 1967); Robert Sobel, *I.B.M.* (New York, 1981); and "Reminiscences of Marion B. Folsom" (1965), Columbia University Oral History Collection, which details social welfare policies of Eastman Kodak.

For organized labor, see Ronald Schatz, *The Electrical Workers* (Champaign, Ill., 1983); Joshua B. Freeman, *In Transit* (New York, 1989); and Gerald Zahavi, *Workers, Managers, and Welfare Capitalism: The Shopkeepers and Tanners of Endicott Johnson* (Champaign, Ill., 1988). The organization of clerical workers and teachers is told in Joseph E. Finley, *White Collar Union* (New York, 1975); Philip Taft, *United They Teach* (Los Angeles, 1974); and Stephen Cole, *The Unionization of Teachers* (New York, 1969), on the United Federation of Teachers.

For the New York City economy, see volumes of the Metropolitan Region Survey, including Sidney M. Robbins, *Money Metropolis* (Cambridge, Mass., 1960), and Max Hall, ed., *Made in New York* (Cambridge, Mass., 1959). The city's money markets are covered in Robert Sobel, *N.Y.S.E.: A History of the New York Stock Exchange, 1935–1975* (New York, 1975); Vincent P. Carosso, *Investment*

Banking in America (Cambridge, Mass., 1970); and Harold van B. Cleveland and Thomas F. Huertas, *Citibank, 1812–1970* (Cambridge, Mass., 1985). The city's media dominance is described in Stephen R. Fox, *The Mirror Makers: A History of American Advertising and Its Creators* (New York, 1984); Erik Barnouw, *The Image Empire* (New York, 1970); John Tebbel, *A History of Book Publishing in the United States*, vol. 4 (New York, 1981); and Frank L. Schick, *The Paperbound Book in America* (New York, 1958).

On higher education, see Oliver Cromwell Carmichael, Jr., *New York State Establishes a State University* (Nashville, Tenn., 1955), which traces the impact of Dewey administration politics; Frank A. Cooper, *The Plattsburgh Idea in Education, 1889–1964* (Plattsburgh, N.Y., 1964); and S. Willis Rudy, *The College of the City of New York: A History, 1847–1947* (New York, 1949), which details changes on public-supported campuses. Accounts of the postwar transformation in private universities include: W. Freeman Galpin, *Syracuse University*, vol. 3, *The Critical Years* (Syracuse, 1984); John Robert Greene et al., *Syracuse University*, vol. 5, *The Eggers Years* (Syracuse, 1998); William Pearson Tolley, *At the Fountain of Youth: Memoirs of a College President* (Syracuse, 1989); Morris Bishop, *A History of Cornell* (Ithaca, N.Y., 1962); *The New York University Self-Study: Final Report* (New York, 1956); Thomas J. Frusciano and Marilyn H. Pettit, *New York University and the City: An Illustrated History* (New Brunswick, N.J., 1997); and Dwight C. Miner, ed., *A History of Columbia College on Morningside Heights* (New York, 1954). Walter Pilkington, *Hamilton College, 1812–1962* (Clinton, N.Y., 1962); and John B. Harcourt, *The Ithaca College Story* (Ithaca, N.Y., 1983), describe the challenges faced by small liberal arts colleges.

For the public school crisis, see Edmund H. Crane, "New York," in Jim B. Pearson and Edgar Fuller, eds., *Education in the States*

(Washington, D.C., 1969), which reviews administrative trends; the Syracuse University Maxwell School of Government series Economics and Politics of Public Education, including Stephen K. Bailey, *Schoolmen and Politics* (Syracuse, 1962), and Warner Bloomberg, Jr., *Suburban Power Structures and Public Education* (Syracuse, 1963). Diane Ravitch, *The Great School Wars: New York City, 1805–1973* (New York, 1974), and Robert A. Dentler, "Barriers to Northern School Desegregation," *Daedalus* 95 (Winter 1966): 45–63, discuss the integration struggle.

Intellectual and Artistic Life

For the postwar intelligentsia see Harold Rosenberg, *The Tradition of the New* (New York, 1965), and Allan M. Wald, *The New York Intellectuals* (Chapel Hill, N.C., 1987). Literary trends are discussed in Brendan Gill, *Here at the New Yorker* (New York, 1975); Gigi Mahon, *The Last Days of the New Yorker* (New York, 1988); Jeffrey Meyers, *Edmund Wilson* (Boston, 1995); Ted Solotaroff, *The Red-Hot Vacuum* (New York, 1970), particularly good on Philip Roth and Saul Bellow; Mary McCarthy, *Occasional Prose* (New York, 1985); David Lehman, *The Last Avant-Garde* (New York, 1998), on the New York School of poets; and Brad Gooch, *City Poet* (New York, 1993), on their most influential member, Frank O'Hara.

A discussion of Gotham's arts must begin with Leonard Wallock, ed., *New York: Culture Capital of the World, 1940–1965* (New York, 1988), and William B. Scott and Peter M. Rutkoff, *New York Modern: The Arts and the City* (Baltimore, 1999). For music, see: John Warthen Struble, *The History of American Classical Music* (New York, 1995); Joan Peyser, *The Music of My Time* (White Plains, N.Y., 1995); Paul Griffiths, *Cage* (London, 1981); Howard Shoret, *Philharmonic* (Garden City, N.Y., 1975); John Dizikes, *Opera in America*

(New Haven, Conn., 1993); Scott De Veaux, *The Birth of Bebop: A Social and Musical History* (Berkeley, Calif., 1997); and Arnold Shaw, *52nd Street: The Street of Jazz* (New York, 1977). For the lively arts, see: Foster Hirsch, *A Method to Their Madness: The History of the Actors Studio* (New York, 1984); Joseph P. Swain, *The Broadway Musical* (New York, 1990); Gerald M. Berkowitz, *New Broadways* (Totowa, N.J., 1982); and Lincoln Kirstein, *Thirty Years: Lincoln Kirstein's The New York City Ballet* (New York, 1978); and *Dance for a City: Fifty Years of the New York City Ballet*, edited by Lynn Garafola with Eric Foner (New York, 1999). Experimental film is examined in P. Adams Sitney, *Visionary Film* (New York, 1979); and David E. James, ed., *To Free the Cinema: Jonas Mekas & the New York Underground* (Princeton, 1992). On the impact of abstract expressionism, see Dore Ashton, *The New York School* (New York, 1973); Stephen Naifeh and Gregory White Smith, *Jackson Pollock* (New York, 1989); and Patricia Hills and Roberta K. Tarbell, *The Figurative Tradition and the Whitney Museum of American Art* (New York, 1980). For upstate culture, see Anita M. Smith, *Woodstock: History and Hearsay* (Saugerties, N.Y., 1959); S. Lane Faison, Jr., *Art Tours & Detours in New York State* (New York, 1964); and articles in *Art Digest, American Artist, Art in America, Craft Horizons, Antiques, Musical America*, and *Opera News*.

For the impact of rock 'n' roll in the 1950s, see William Graebner, *Coming of Age in Buffalo* (Philadelphia, 1990); Carl Belz, *The Story of Rock* (New York, 1972); and Charlie Gillett, *The Sound of the City* (New York, 1970). Beat culture is recounted in Ned Polsky, *Hustlers, Beats, and Others* (Chicago, 1967); Ted Morgan, *Literary Outlaw* (New York, 1988), on William S. Burroughs; and J. Hoberman, "The Forest and *The Trees*," in James, ed., *To Free the Cinema* (cited earlier). Ann Charters, ed., *The Portable Beat Reader* (New York, 1992), is a superb anthology. The evolution from beatniks to hippies can be traced in Paul Krassner, *Confessions of a Raving, Unconfined Nut* (New York, 1993), and Jack Curry, *Woodstock* (New York, 1989).

Upstate Towns and Transformations

Literature on the transformation of small town life includes Arthur J. Vidich and Joseph Bensman, *Small Town in Mass Society* (Princeton, 1958); Edmund Wilson, *Upstate* (New York, 1971); M. Lorimer Moe, *Saga from the Hills: A History of the Swedes of Jamestown, New York* (Jamestown, 1983); and Wendell Tripp, comp., *Coming and Becoming: Pluralism in New York State History* (Cooperstown, N.Y., 1991). Other local histories include: Carl F. Schmidt, *History of the Town of Wheatland* (Rochester, 1953); Hilda R. Watrous, *The County between the Lakes: A Public History of Seneca County, New York, 1876–1982* (Waterloo, N.Y., 1983); Arch Merrill, *Southern Tier* (New York, n.d.); Martha Elston Howe, *A History of the Town Wellsville, New York* (Wellsville, 1963); Thomas E. Byrne, ed., *Chemung County, 1890–1975* (Elmira, N.Y., [1976]); Lydia Sears, *A History of Trumansburg, New York, 1792–1967* (Trumansburg, 1968); and Carol Kammen, *The Peopling of Tompkins County* (Interlaken, N.Y., 1985).

Rural change is appraised in Donald G. Hay and Robert A. Polson, *Rural Organizations in Oneida County, New York* (Ithaca, N.Y., 1951), and Abraham D. Lavender and Clarence B. Steinberg, *Jewish Farmers in the Catskills* (Gainesville, Fla., 1995). North Country accounts include: Lloyd Graham, *Niagara Country* (New York, 1949); William Chapman White, *Adirondack Country* (New York, 1954); Charles W. Bryan, Jr., *The Raquette: River of the Forest* (Blue Mountain Lake, N.Y., 1964); William H. Brown, ed., *History of Warren County, N.Y.* (Glens Falls, N.Y., 1963); Ted Aber and Stella King, *The*

History of Hamilton County (Lake Pleasant, N.Y., 1965); and Howard Thomas, *Black River in the North Country* (Prospect, N.Y., 1963).

Other local studies and community histories include: Mary McCulley, *History of Genesee County, New York, 1890–1987* (Interlaken, N.Y., 1985); Stuart Blumin, *The Short Season of Sharon Springs* (Ithaca, N.Y., 1980); Alfred Donaldson, *A History of the Adirondacks* (Port Washington, N.Y., 1963); and Stuart D. Scott, comp., *An Archaeological Survey of Artpark and the Lower Landing, Lewiston, New York* (Lewiston, 1993). For the Adirondack Park Agency, see Frank Graham, Jr., *The Adirondack Park* (New York, 1978), and Burton Bernstein, *The Sticks: A Profile of Essex County* (New York, 1971). See also two excellent studies on the Adirondacks and their cultural impact: Paul Schneider, *A History of America's First Wilderness* (New York, 2000), and Philip G. Terrie, *Contested Terrain: A New History of Nature and People in the Adirondacks* (Syracuse, 1997).

For the decline of upstate agriculture, see Janet M. Fitchen, *Endangered Spaces, Enduring Places* (Boulder, Colo., 1991); Joseph L. Richardson and Olaf F. Larson, "Small Community Trends: A 50-Year Perspective on Social-Economic Changes in 13 New York Communities," *Rural Sociology* 41 (Spring 1976): 45–59; Frederick H. Buttel, "Farm Structure and Rural Communities in the Northeast," in Louis E. Swanson, ed., *Agriculture and Community Change in the United States* (Boulder, Colo., 1988); and Thomas A. Hirschl, "Dairy Farm Survival in a Metropolitan Area: Dutchess County, New York, 1984–1990," *Rural Sociology* 58 (Fall 1993): 461–74.

The Era of Rockefeller

The best accounts of Averell Harriman are Rudy Abramson, *Spanning the Century; The Life of W. Averell Harriman, 1891–1986* (New York, 1992), and Clark D. Ahlberg and Daniel P. Moynihan, "Changing Governors—and Policies," *Public Administration Review* 20 (Autumn 1960): 195–204. Rockefeller literature includes Robert H. Connery and Gerald Benjamin, eds., *Governing New York State*, Proceedings of the Academy of Political Science 31 (May 1974); James E. Underwood and William J. Daniels, *Governor Rockefeller in New York* (Westport, Conn., 1982); and Joseph E. Persico, *The Imperial Rockefeller* (New York, 1982). Additional accounts include: Ann Marie H. Walsh, *The Public's Business* (Cambridge, Mass., 1978), on the moral authorities; Alan G. Hevesi, *Legislative Politics in New York State* (New York, 1975); Susan Collens Wick, "Implementing a Deinstitutionalization Process for the Mentally Retarded: The Case of New York City's Retarded Citizens" (Ph.D. diss., Boston University, 1984); Victoria Newhouse, *Wallace K. Harrison, Architect* (New York, 1989), which details Albany's South Mall; and Samuel Kaplan, "Bridging the Gap from Rhetoric to Reality: The New York State Urban Development Corporation," *Architectural Forum* 131 (November 1969): 70–73. Chief Judge Charles S. Desmond is assessed in *Buffalo Law Review* 15 (Winter 1965). For the modernization of county government, see Edwin G. Michaelian's essay in Weigold, ed., *Westchester County* (cited earlier), and articles in *The American City*, *National Civic Review*, and *Metropolitan Viewpoints*.

Racial discrimination is analyzed in Eli Ginzburg, *The Negro Potential* (New York, 1956); New York State Commission Against Discrimination, *Negroes in Five New York Cities* (Albany, 1959); and Louis A. Ferman, ed., *Negroes and Jobs* (Ann Arbor, Mich., 1968). Papers of the Congress on Racial Equality, from University Microfilms, detail employment for African Americans in upstate cities. For the debate on the black family, see Oscar Lewis, *Five Families* (New York, 1959), and Louis Kriesberg, *Mothers in Poverty* (Chicago, 1970).

Community action can be traced in Kenneth Clark, *Dark Ghetto* (New York, 1965); Ellen Lurie, "Community Action in East Harlem," in Leonard J. Duhl, ed., *The Urban Condition* (New York, 1963); and Michael Lipsky, *Protest in City Politics* (Chicago, 1969). Clarence Taylor, *Knocking at Our Own Door: Milton A. Galamison and the Struggle for School Integration in New York City* (New York, 1997) is an important account of the civil rights movement in Brooklyn. For Syracuse, see Warren C. Hagstrom, "On Eliminating Poverty," in Warner Bloomberg, Jr., and Henry J. Schmandt, eds., *Power, Poverty, and Urban Policy*, Urban Affairs Annual Reviews 2 (Beverly Hills, Calif., 1968); Nick Kotz and Mary Lynn Kotz, *A Passion for Equality; George Wiley and the Movement* (New York, 1977); and the series on the First Congress of the Poor in the *Reporter*. Edward V. Sparer's article "The New Property Law" in Bernard J. Frieden and Robert Morris, eds., *Urban Planning and Social Policy* (New York, 1968), describes the legal expansion of welfare benefits.

New York City politics in the 1960s is recounted in Costikyan, *Behind Closed Doors* (cited earlier); Martin Tolchin and Susan Tolchin, *To the Victor . . .* (New York, 1971); and Oliver Pilat, *Lindsay's Campaign* (Boston, 1968). Seymour Sacks, "New York's Fiscal Environment: Taxes, Public Sector Productivity and Intergovernmental Aid," *Maxwell Review* 8 (Winter 1971–1972): 1–7, reveals state aid behind Lindsay liberalism. Reapportionment is discussed in Ruth C. Silva, "Apportionment in the New York State Legislature," *American Political Science Review* 55 (December 1961): 870–81. For the preservationist movement, see Henry W. Clune, *The Genesee* (New York, 1963), and Raymond J. O'Brien, *American Sublime: Landscape and Scenery of the Lower Hudson Valley* (New York, 1981).

For the culture of the 1960s, see Morris Dickstein, *Gates of Eden* (New York, 1977); Daniel Hoffman, ed., *The Harvard Guide to Contemporary American Writing* (Cambridge, Mass., 1979), particularly Mark Schneider's essay on Jewish writers; Richard Kostelanetz, *The End of Intelligent Writing* (New York, 1973); Philip Nobile, *Intellectual Skywriting: Literary Politics & the New York Review of Books* (New York, 1974); and Carl Rollyson and Lisa Paddock, *Susan Sontag: The Making of an Icon* (New York, 2000). On trends in 1960s art, see Hilton Kramer, *The Art of the Avant-Garde: An Art Chronicle of 1956–1972* (New York, 1973); Gregory Battcock, ed., *The New Art* (New York, 1966); Lawrence Alloway, *American Pop Art* (New York, 1974); and Patricia Bosworth, *Diane Arbus: A Biography* (New York, 1984). Theater accounts include Mel Gussow, *Edward Albee: A Singular Journey* (New York, 1999); John Lahr and Jonathan Price, eds., *The Great American Life Show* (New York, 1974); essays by C. W. E. Bigsby and Ellen Foreman in Errol Hill, ed., *The Theater of Black Americans* (Englewood Cliffs, N.J., 1980); and Richard Schechner, *Environmental Theater* (New York, 1973). Deborah Jowitt, *Time and the Dancing Image* (New York, 1988), and Elinor Rogosin, *The Dance Makers* (New York, 1980), reveal rivalries among breakaway companies. Appraisals of the New York State Council on the Arts appear in *Dance Magazine*, *Saturday Review*, and *Opera News*, which also covers the arts on SUNY campuses and regional centers.

Ghetto riots are analyzed in Fred C. Shapiro and James W. Sullivan, *Race Riots: New York 1964* (New York, 1964), which looks at Harlem and Bedford-Stuyvesant; Frank P. Besag, *Anatomy of a Riot: Buffalo '67* (Buffalo, 1967); and stunned accounts of Rochester in the *Reporter* and *New Republic* in 1964 and 1965. Campus radicalism is surveyed in Bill Ward, "Why the Students Revolt," *Nation*, January 25, 1965, 81–85, on Syracuse University; Cushing Strout and

David I. Grossvogel, *Divided We Stand* (Garden City, N.Y., 1970), on Cornell; and Richard A. Siggelkow, *Dissent and Disruption* (Buffalo, 1992), on SUNY-Buffalo. Columbia's turmoil is remembered by James Simon Kunen, *The Strawberry Statement* (New York, 1968), and Jerry L. Avorn, *Up against the Ivy Wall* (New York, 1968). Charles F. Howlett, "The Anti-Vietnam War Movement on Long Island, Part Two: The High Schools, the October 1969 Moratorium, and Kent State (1970)," *Long Island Historical Journal* 8 (Fall 1995): 56–75, is a rare look at high school protest. Events behind the New York City school strike are traced in Ravitch, *The Great School Wars* (cited earlier); David Rogers, *110 Livingston Street* (New York, 1968); and Melvin I. Urofsky, *Why Teachers Strike* (Garden City, N.Y., 1970). For the Revolutionary Action Movement, see essays by Shin'ya Ono and J. Kirk Sale in Harold Jacobs, comp., *Weatherman* (Berkeley, Calif., 1970). Gay liberation is seen in Martin Bauml Duberman, *Stonewall* (New York, 1993).

The Years of Decline and Partial Recovery

For the Carey administration, see Joseph F. Zimmerman, *The Government and Politics of New York State* (New York, 1981); Gerald Benjamin and T. Norman Hurd, eds., *Making Experience Count: Managing Modern New York in the Carey Era* (Albany, 1985); and articles in *Empire State Report* by Amy Plumer in July 1975 and by Michael McKeating in September and October 1975. Howard A. Scarrow, *Parties, Elections, and Representation in the State of New York* (New York, 1983); Richard C. Lehne, "New York Reapportionment: The City and the State," *Maxwell Review* 8 (Winter 1971/72): 27–32; David I. Wells, "Redistricting in New York State," *Empire State Report* 4 (October/November 1978): 9–13; and "The Reapportionment Game," ibid. 5 (December 1979): 8–14, trace

reapportionment's impact on the legislature. Suburban barricades are discussed in Michael N. Danielson, *The Politics of Exclusion* (New York, 1976), and James W. Hughes, "Dilemmas of Suburbanization and Growth Controls," in Louis H. Massotti, ed., *The Suburban Seventies* (November 1975). Buffalo school integration is detailed in *Arthur v. Nyquist* (U.S. Court of Appeals, 2nd Circuit, 573 F.2d 134, 1978), and *Arthur v. Nyquist* 473 F. Supp. 830 (1979).

For New York State's economic decline, see Benjamin Chinitz, ed., *The Declining Northeast* (New York, 1978); Alecia Swasy, *Changing Focus: Kodak and the Battle to Save a Great American Company* (New York, 1997); David Puryear and Roy Bahl, "Economic Problems of a Mature Economy," in F. Foltman and P. McClelland, eds., *New York State's Economic Crises* (Ithaca, N.Y., 1977); and Rona B. Stein, "The Economy of Upstate New York," *Federal Reserve Bank of New York Quarterly Review* 3 (Autumn 1978): 26–30. Deregulation is discussed in David Rogers, *The Future of American Banking* (New York, 1993), and Benjamin Friedman, "Postwar Changes in the American Financial Markets," in Martin Feldstein, ed., *The American Economy in Transition* (Chicago, 1981). New York law firms are examined in Marc Galanter and Thomas Palay, "The Large Law Firm in Transition: An Historical Analysis," in Susan S. Samuelson, ed., *Law Firm Management* (Boston, 1992), and "Fifteen Years" issue of *American Lawyer* 16 (March 1994).

Growing doubts about government programs are considered in: Ann Brader Johnson, "Unravelling of a Social Policy: The History of Deinstitutionalization of the Mentally Ill in New York State" (Ph.D. diss., New York University, 1987); *Attica; The Official Report of the New York State Special Commission on Attica* (New York, 1972); "Beyond Attica: Prison Reform in New York State, 1971–1973," *Cornell Law Review* 58 (June 1973):

924–1034; Myer Kutz, "How Could It Happen to the UDC?" *Planning* 41 (May 1975): 14–16; and devastating details of the Housing Finance Agency in the *Wall Street Journal*, April 7 and December 12, 1975. Accounts of New York City's collapse includes Peter D. Salins, *The Ecology of Housing Destruction* (New York, 1980); Jill Jonnes, *We're Still Here: The Rise, Fall, and Resurrection of the South Bronx* (Boston, 1986); Robert Jensen, ed., *Devastation/Resurrection: The South Bronx* (Bronx, 1979); Charles R. Morris, *The Cost of Good Intentions* (New York, 1980); and Fred Ferretti, *The Year the Big Apple Went Bust* (New York, 1976).

The best entrée to the drugged downtown is found in Pat Hackett, ed., *The Andy Warhol Diaries* (New York, 1989); Jack Fritcher, *Mapplethorpe: Assault with a Deadly Camera* (Mamaroneck, N.Y., 1994); Robert Draper, *Rolling Stone* (Garden City, N.Y., 1990); and Bob Harris, "Video at Anthology," in James, ed., *To Free the Cinema* (cited earlier). For regional culture, see Lenore Malen, "Artpark's Fifth Year," *Arts Magazine* 53 (December 1978): 152–53; "Sculpture at the Olympics," *Artforum* 18 (April 1980): 36–45; "New University Art Gallery at Binghamton," *Art Journal* 29 (Winter 1969–70): 204–8; and Mark Lamos, "Glimmerglass," *Opera News*, May 1991, 14–16. *New York Affairs* 4, no. 4 (1978), discusses the political economy of the arts.

For the politics and perspective of the Cuomo administration, see Peter W. Colby and John K. White, *New York State Today* (Albany, 1989); Mario M. Cuomo, *Forest Hills Diary* (New York, 1983); Ken Auletta, "Governor," *New Yorker*, April 9, 1984, 50–52+, and April 16, 1984, 53–57+; and Mary Hedglon, "Rebuilding New York State 2000," *Empire State Report* 11 (May 1985): 9–10+. The *New York Times*, November 10–11, 1994, describes George E. Pataki's triumph over Cuomo's failing liberalism. Temporary State Commission on Constitutional Revision, *The New York State Constitution*, edited by Gerald Benjamin for the Nelson A. Rockefeller Institute of Government (1994), outlines the structural challenges that beset the Pataki administration.

For the state's reckoning with the global economy, see Jeryl L. Mumpower and Warren F. Ilchman, eds., *New York State in the Year 2000* (Albany, 1988), which is good on demographic trends; Morton Schoolman and Alvin Magid, eds., *Reindustrializing New York State* (Albany, 1986), particularly Walter Goldstein's essay on "export" industries; Aaron S. Gurwitz, "New York State's Economic Turnaround: Services or Manufacturing," *Federal Reserve Bank of New York Quarterly Review* 8 (Autumn 1983): 30–34; Paul Carrol, *Big Blues: The Unmaking of IBM* (New York, 1993); and Mark Reutter, *When the Machine Stopped* (Boston, 1989), on the breakup of Houdaille. New York City's regional economy is discussed in L. A. Winokur, "Who's Working Where in New York?" *Empire State Report* 18 (October 1992): 26–28+; and Lee E. Koppelman and Pearl M. Kamer, "Anatomy of the Long Island Economy: Prospective for Development," *Long Island Historical Journal* 7 (Fall 1994).

For New York City in the Koch era, see Ken Auletta, "The Mayor," *New Yorker*, September 10, 1979, 54–56+, and September 17, 1979, 50–52+; John H. Mollenkopf, *Phoenix in the Ashes* (Princeton, 1992); David E. Chall, "New York City's 'Skills Mismatch,'" *Federal Reserve Bank of New York Quarterly Review* 10 (Spring 1985): 20–27; and John H. Mollenkopf and Manuel Castells, eds., *Dual City* (New York, 1991), which qualifies the "dual" interpretation. Accounts of the new immigration include Betty Boyd Caroli and Thomas Kessner, *Today's Immigrants* (New York, 1981); Kyeyoung Park, *The Korean Dream: Immigrants and Small Business in New York City* (Ithaca, N.Y., 1997); Hsiang-shui Chen, *Chinatown No More: Taiwan Immigrants in Contemporary New York* (Ithaca, N.Y., 1992); and Philip Kasinitz, *Caribbean New York* (Ithaca, N.Y., 1992). The passing of ethnic liberalism is the subject of Jonathan Rieder, *Canarsie: The Jews and Italians of Brooklyn against Liberalism* (Cambridge, Mass., 1985), and Jim Sleeper, *The Closest of Strangers* (New York, 1990). The AIDS crisis is related in Randy Shilts, *And the Band Played On* (New York, 1987), and Larry Kramer, "The Unwanted Messenger," in Eric Marcus, *Making History: The Struggle for Gay and Lesbian Equal Rights, 1945–1990* (New York, 1992).

Upstate metropolitan developments appear in special-interest journals like *American Demographics, National Real Estate Investor, Professional Geographer, Public Management*, and *American City and County*, and in regional journals, notably Robert J. McCarthy, "Civil War in Buffalo," *Empire State Report* 13 (September 1987): 49–56, and Terry Galway, "Mirror Images," ibid. 15 (April 1989): 12–17, which compares Buffalo Mayor Griffin with New York City Mayor Koch. For New York City's changing suburbs see Barbara M. Kelly, *Suburbia Re-Examined* (New York, 1989); and Joel Garreau, *Edge City* (New York, 1991).

For comments on the culture of the 1980s and 1990s, see: Leo Rubinfien, "New York: The State of Art," *Art in America* 66 (March 1978): 70–73; Albany Institute of History and Art, *The New Response* (Albany, 1985); Robert Hughes, "There's No Geist Like the Zeit-geist," *New York Review of Books*, October 27, 1983, 63–68; Barbara Rose, "Letter to a Young Artist," *Vanity Fair*, July 1983, 66–69; and Edward Rothstein, "The Return of Romanticism," *New Republic*, August 27, 1984, 60. Matthew Collings, *It Hurts: New York Art from Warhol to Now* (London, 1998) is a candid look at pop art's bewildering legacy.

The Long Boom's impact across the state and particularly in New York City can be traced in Federal Reserve Bank of New York, *Current Issues in Economics and Finance*; articles in *Empire State Report* and *City Journal*; and the files of the *New York Times*. For political trends in the late 1990s, see Sarah F. Liebschutz, ed., *New York Politics and Government: Competition and Compassion* (Lincoln, Nebr., 1998); George E. Pataki, with Daniel Paisner, *Pataki: An Autobiography* (New York, 1998); Godfrey Hodgson, *The Gentleman from New York: Daniel Patrick Moynihan: a Biography* (Boston, 2000); Andrew Kirtzman, *Rudy Giuliani: Emperor of the City* (New York, 2000); William Bratton, *Turnaround: How America's Top Cop Reversed the Crime Epidemic* (New York, 1998); and Michael Tomasky, *Hillary's Turn: Inside Her Improbable, Victorious Senate Campaign* (New York, 2001).

Contributors

PAULA BAKER is associate professor of history at the University of Pittsburgh, where she has been a member of the department since 1991. She received her doctoral degree at Rutgers and is the author of *The Moral Framework of Political Life in Rural New York, 1870–1930* (1991) and essays on women's and political history. Her current interest is in campaign finance from the 1840s to the 1970s.

EDWARD COUNTRYMAN is University Distinguished Professor of history at Southern Methodist University, where he has been a member of the department since 1991. He is a native New Yorker who received his undergraduate education at Manhattan College and his Ph.D. at Cornell University. He is the author of *A People in Revolution: The American Revolution and Political Society in New York* (1981), which received the Bancroft Prize, *The American Revolution* (1985), and *Americans: A Collision of Histories* (1966).

L. RAY GUNN is associate professor of history and chairman of the department at the University of Utah, where he has been since 1974. He received his doctoral degree at Rutgers. He is the author of *The Decline of Authority: Public Economic Policy and Political Development in New York, 1800–1860* (1988) and numerous articles on New York State history.

RONALD W. HOWARD is dean of the college of arts and sciences and professor of history at Mississippi College, where he has been since 1977. He received his Ph.D. at the University of Tennessee, Knoxville. He is the author of numerous articles on colonial history and co-editor of *The Twilight of British Rule in Revolutionary America: The New York Letter Book of General James Robertson, 1780–1783* (1983).

MILTON M. KLEIN is Alumni Distinguished Service Professor emeritus of history at the University of Tennessee, Knoxville. He is the author of *The Politics of Diversity: Essays in the History of Colonial New York* (1974) and *The American Whig: William Livingston of New York* (1993) and co-editor of the thirteen-volume *History of the American Colonies* (1973–1986) and of the four-volume *North America in Colonial Times* (1998).

OLIVER RINK is professor of history at California State University, Bakersfield, where he has been a member of the department since 1975 and was voted the outstanding professor in 1995–1996. He is the author of *Holland on the Hudson: An*

Economic and Social History of Dutch New York (1986), winner of the New York State Historical Association manuscript award and the New Netherland Project's Hendricks Prize, and numerous articles on the Dutch period of New York history.

JOEL SCHWARTZ is professor of history at Montclair State University. He is the author of *The New York Approach: Robert Moses, Urban Liberals, and Redevelopment of the Inner City* (1993), winner of the New York State Historical Association manuscript award, *The Development of New Jersey Society* (1997), and co-editor of *Cities of the Garden State: Essays in the Urban and Suburban History of New Jersey* (1977).

Index